T0143039

Lecture Notes in Artificial Intelligence 12897

Subseries of Lecture Notes in Computer Science

Series Editors

Randy Goebel
University of Alberta, Edmonton, Canada

Yuzuru Tanaka
Hokkaido University, Sapporo, Japan

Wolfgang Wahlster
DFKI and Saarland University, Saarbrücken, Germany

Founding Editor

Jörg Siekmann
DFKI and Saarland University, Saarbrücken, Germany

More information about this subseries at http://www.springer.com/series1244

Jiřina Vejnarová · Nic Wilson (Eds.)

Symbolic and Quantitative Approaches to Reasoning with Uncertainty

16th European Conference, ECSQARU 2021
Prague, Czech Republic, September 21–24, 2021
Proceedings

 Springer

Editors
Jiřina Vejnarová 🆔
Institute of Information Theory
and Automation
Prague, Czech Republic

Nic Wilson 🆔
Insight Centre for Data Analytics,
School of Computer Science and IT
University College Cork
Cork, Ireland

ISSN 0302-9743   ISSN 1611-3349 (electronic)
Lecture Notes in Artificial Intelligence
ISBN 978-3-030-86771-3   ISBN 978-3-030-86772-0 (eBook)
https://doi.org/10.1007/978-3-030-86772-0

LNCS Sublibrary: SL7 – Artificial Intelligence

This Springer imprint is published by the registered company Springer Nature Switzerland AG
The registered company address is: Gewerbestrasse 11, 6330 Cham, Switzerland

Preface

The biennial ECSQARU conference is a major forum for advances in the theory and practice of reasoning under uncertainty. Contributions are provided by researchers in advancing the state of the art and by practitioners using uncertainty techniques in applications. The scope of the ECSQARU conferences encompasses fundamental topics, as well as practical issues, related to representation, inference, learning, and decision making both in qualitative and numeric uncertainty paradigms. The formalisms studied in this volume include argumentation frameworks, belief functions, logics of probability, and systems for imprecise probability, possibility theory, and reasoning about inconsistency.

Previous ECSQARU events were held in Belgrade (2019), Lugano (2017), Compiegne (2015), Utrecht (2013), Belfast (2011), Verona (2009), Hammamet (2007), Barcelona (2005), Aalborg (2003), Toulouse (2001), London (1999), Bonn (1997), Fribourg (1995), Granada (1993), and Marseille (1991).

The 16th European Conference on Symbolic and Quantitative Approaches to Reasoning with Uncertainty (ECSQARU 2021) was held in Prague (Czech Republic) during 21–24 September, 2021. The 48 papers in this volume were selected from 63 submissions, after a rigorous peer-review process by the members of the Program Committee and some external reviewers. Each submission was reviewed by at least three reviewers, and almost all received four reviews. ECSQARU 2021 also included invited talks by outstanding researchers in the field: Cassio de Campos, Tomas Kroupa, and Steven Schockaert.

We would like to thank all those who submitted papers, and the members of the Program Committee and the external reviewers for their valuable reviews, and also the members of the local Organizing Committee, Jirka Vomlel, Milan Studený, and especially Václav Kratochvíl, for all their support and contributions to the success of the conference. We acknowledge gratefully both material and technical support of the Institute of Information Theory and Automation of the Czech Academy of Sciences, as well as the support of Science Foundation Ireland.

Thanks also to Springer Nature for granting a fund for the Best Student Paper Award of the conference, and for the smooth collaboration when preparing the proceedings. Moreover, EasyChair proved to be a convenient platform for handling submissions, reviews, and final papers for the proceedings of ECSQARU 2021, which was greatly appreciated.

August 2021

Jiřina Vejnarová
Nic Wilson

Organization

Program Committee Chairs

Jiřina Vejnarová   Czech Academy of Sciences, Czech Republic
Nic Wilson   Insight, University College Cork, Ireland

Program Committee

Alessandro Antonucci   IDSIA, Switzerland
Ringo Baumann   Leipzig University, Germany
Christoph Beierle   University of Hagen, Germany
Nahla Ben Amor   Institut Supérieur de Gestion de Tunis, Tunisia
Jonathan Ben-Naim   IRIT-CNRS, France
Salem Benferhat   CRIL, CNRS, Université d'Artois, France
Concha Bielza Lozoya Universidad Politécnica de Madrid, Spain
Isabelle Bloch   CNRS, LIP6, Sorbonne Université, France
Janneke Bolt   Eindhoven University of Technology, The Netherlands
Richard Booth   Cardiff University, UK
Olivier Cailloux   Université Paris-Dauphine, France
Andrés Cano   University of Granada, Spain
Federico Cerutti   University of Brescia, Italy
Andrea Cohen   CONICET-UNS, Argentina
Giulianella Coletti   University of Perugia, Italy
Inés Couso   University of Oviedo, Spain
Fabio Cozman   University of São Paulo, Brazil
Jasper De Bock   Ghent University, Belgium
Thierry Denoeux   Université de technologie de Compiègne, France
Sébastien Destercke   Université de technologie de Compiègne, France
Dragan Doder   Utrecht University, The Netherlands
F. Dupin De Saint Cyr Université de Strasbourg/ENGEES, France
Zied Elouedi   Institut Supérieur de Gestion de Tunis, Tunisia
Patricia Everaere   University of Lille, France
Alessandro Facchini   IDSIA, Switzerland
Eduardo Fermé   University of Madeira, Portugal
Tommaso Flaminio   IIIA-CSIC, Spain
Laurent Garcia   Université d'Angers, France
Laura Giordano   Università del Piemonte Orientale, Italy
Lluis Godo   IIIA-CSIC, Spain
Anthony Hunter   University College London, UK
Nebojša Ikodinović   University of Belgrade, Serbia
Ulrich Junker   Biot, France

Souhila Kaci	LIRMM, France
Gabriele Kern-Isberner	TU Dortmund, Germany
Sébastien Konieczny	CRIL, France
Václav Kratochvíl	Czech Academy of Sciences, Czech Republic
Christophe Labreuche	Thales Research and Technology, France
M. Lagasquie-Schiex	IRIT, Université de Toulouse, CNRS, France
Sylvain Lagrue	Université de technologie de Compiègne, France
Helge Langseth	NTNU, Norway
Florence Le Ber	ENGEES, France
Philippe Leray	University of Nantes, France
Weiru Liu	University of Bristol, UK
Peter Lucas	University of Twente, The Netherlands
Thomas Lukasiewicz	University of Oxford, UK
Carsten Lutz	University of Bremen, Germany
Maria Vanina Martinez	University of Buenos Aires, Argentina
Denis Maua	University of São Paulo, Brazil
Jérôme Mengin	IRIT, Université de Toulouse, France
David Mercier	Université d'Artois, France
Enrique Miranda	University of Oviedo, Spain
Serafín Moral	University of Granada, Spain
Farid Nouioua	LIS, Aix-Marseille University, France
Zoran Ognjanović	Mathematical Institute, Serbia
Odile Papini	LIS, Aix-Marseille University, France
Davide Petturiti	University of Perugia, Italy
Frédéric Pichon	Université d'Artois, France
Nico Potyka	University of Stuttgart, Germany
Marc Pouly	Lucerne University of Applied Sciences and Arts, Switzerland
Henri Prade	IRIT, CNRS, Toulouse university, France
Silja Renooij	Utrecht University, The Netherlands
Regis Riveret	CSIRO, Australia
Régis Sabbadin	Inrae, France
Steven Schockaert	Cardiff University, UK
Choh Man Teng	Florida Institute for Human & Machine Cognition, USA
Matthias Thimm	Universität Koblenz-Landau, Germany
Matthias Troffaes	Durham University, UK
Jirka Vomlel	Czech Academy of Sciences, Czech Republic
Renata Wassermann	University of São Paulo, Brazil
Emil Weydert	University of Luxembourg, Luxembourg
Marco Wilhelm	TU Dortmund, Germany
Stefan Woltran	Vienna University of Technology, Austria
Eric Würbel	LIS, Aix-Marseille University, France
Bruno Zanuttini	Université de Caen Normandie, France
Cassio P. de Campos	Eindhoven University of Technology, The Netherlands
Leon van der Torre	University of Luxembourg, Luxembourg
Linda C. van der Gaag	Eindhoven University of Technology, The Netherlands

Additional Reviewers

Matti Berthold	Leipzig University, Germany
Paola Daniela Budán	University of Santiago del Estero, Argentina
Pilar Dellunde	IIIA-CSIC, Spain
Maximilian Heinrich	Leipzig University, Germany
Johannes Marti	University of Amsterdam, The Netherlands
Anna Rapberger	TU Wien, Austria
Olivier Roy	University of Bayreuth, Germany
Milan Studený	Czech Academy of Sciences, Czech Republic
Sara Ugolini	IIIA-CSIC, Spain
Markus Ulbricht	Vienna University of Technology, Austria

Contents

Bayesian Networks and Graphical Models

Belief Functions

Imprecise Probability

Inconsistency Handling and Preferences

Possibility Theory and Fuzzy Approaches

Probability Logics

Argumentation and Analogical Reasoning

Analogies Between Sentences: Theoretical Aspects - Preliminary Experiments

Stergos Afantenos[1], Tarek Kunze[1], Suryani Lim[2], Henri Prade[1(✉)], and Gilles Richard[1]

[1] IRIT, Toulouse, France
tarek.kunze@protonmail.com,
{stergos.afantenos,henri.prade,gilles.richard}@irit.fr
[2] Federation University, Churchill, Australia
suryani.lim@federation.edu.au

Abstract. Analogical proportions hold between 4 items a, b, c, d insofar as we can consider that "a is to b as c is to d". Such proportions are supposed to obey postulates, from which one can derive Boolean or numerical models that relate vector-based representations of items making a proportion. One basic postulate is the preservation of the proportion by permuting the central elements b and c. However this postulate becomes debatable in many cases when items are words or sentences. This paper proposes a weaker set of postulates based on *internal reversal*, from which new Boolean and numerical models are derived. The new system of postulates is used to extend a finite set of examples in a machine learning perspective. By embedding a whole sentence into a real-valued vector space, we tested the potential of these weaker postulates for classifying analogical sentences into valid and non-valid proportions. It is advocated that identifying analogical proportions between sentences may be of interest especially for checking discourse coherence, question-answering, argumentation and computational creativity. The proposed theoretical setting backed with promising preliminary experimental results also suggests the possibility of crossing a real-valued embedding with an ontology-based representation of words. This hybrid approach might provide some insights to automatically extract analogical proportions in natural language corpora.

1 Introduction

Analogies play an important role in human reasoning, and are thus involved in natural language discourses. The study of analogical reasoning has a long history (see, e.g., Chap. 1 in [32]). It departs from case-based reasoning [29]. Beyond different classical works on analogical reasoning such as [13–16,35]), there has been a noticeable renewal of interest in analogical studies with a variety of approaches, ranging from reasoning [2], machine learning [5,23] to word analogies [6,11,20,27,36,37] and natural language processing [12,19,34]. These approaches have in common to deal with analogical proportions, i.e., statements of the form "a is to b as c is to d" relating 4 items a, b, c and d [30].

© Springer Nature Switzerland AG 2021
J. Vejnarová and N. Wilson (Eds.): ECSQARU 2021, LNAI 12897, pp. 3–18, 2021.
https://doi.org/10.1007/978-3-030-86772-0_1

Recently, some authors [10,39] have started to study analogical proportions between sentences, motivated by question-answering concerns or the evaluation of sentence embeddings. This paper pursues this study, but first questions the modeling of analogical proportions that is used. Indeed, it is generally assumed that, as for the numerical proportions, the permutation of the central elements b and c preserves the validity of analogical proportions. This postulate is quite debatable for natural language items. For this reason, the paper proposes a postulate weaker than the stability under central permutation. Its main contributions are:

- i) A formal setting to deal with the notion of *analogical sentences*, where only an *internal reversal* property is assumed for the pairs (a, b) and (c, d).
- ii) A rigorous way to extend a finite set of analogical sentences with both valid and non-valid examples. In a machine learning perspective, this process is also known as data augmentation.
- iii) A set of preliminary experiments showing that this notion of analogical sentences is valid and could bring interesting perspectives in terms of applications.

The paper is structured as follows. Section 2 investigates the related works. Section 3 recalls the postulates characterizing analogical proportions and proposes a weaker set of postulates avoiding central permutation. This allows the identification of a rigorous method for enlarging a set of examples and counterexamples. Section 4 presents and discusses the experimental settings as well as the way we generate datasets of analogical sentences. Section 5 reports the results for experiments based on two datasets, showing that machine learning-based techniques are quite accurate to classify diverse analogical sentences. Section 6 points out some candidate applications, before concluding.

2   Related Work

Although lexical analogies have been more thoroughly studied recently due to the advent of distributed representations ([6,11,20,27,36,37, for example], to cite but a few papers), few works have focused on *sentence* analogies.

In [39], the authors try to show how existing embedding approaches are able to capture analogies between sentences. They view analogies between pairs of sentences in very broad terms, which is reflected in the various corpora that they have constructed. For example, in order to create quadruples of analogous sentences they replace individual words with the corresponding words from the Google word analogy dataset [25]. Sentences that share more or less common semantic relations (entailment, negation, passivization, for example) or even syntactic patterns (comparisons, opposites, plurals among others) are also considered analogous. Using these datasets, analogies are evaluated using various embeddings, such as GloVe [28], word2vec [25], fastText [4,26], etc. showing that capturing syntactic analogies which were based on lexical analogies from the Google word analogies dataset is more effective with their models than recognising analogies based on more semantic information.

In [10] the authors focus on the task of identifying the correct answer to a question from a pool of candidate answers. More precisely, given a question q the goal is to select the answer $a_i \in A$ from a set A of candidate answers. In order to do so they leverage analogies between (q, a_i) and various pairs of what they call *"prototypical"* question/answer pairs, assuming that there is an analogy between (q, a_i) and the prototypical pair (q_p, a_p). The goal is to select the candidate answer $a_i^* \in A$ such that:

$$a_i^* = \arg min_i(\|(q_p - a_p) - (q - a_i)\|)$$

exploiting the properties of arithmetic proportion and analogical dissimilarities. The authors limit the question/answer pairs to $wh-$ questions from WikiQA and TrecQA. They use a Siamese bi-GRUs as their architecture in order to represent the four sentences. In this manner the authors learn embedding representations for the sentences which they compare against various baselines including random vectors, *word2vec, InferSent* and *Sent2Vec* obtaining better results with the WikiQA corpus.

Most of the tested sentence embedding models succeed in recognizing syntactic analogies based on lexical ones, but had a harder time capturing analogies between pairs of sentences based on semantics.

3   Formal Framework

Analogies are often expressed in terms of analogical proportions. An analogical proportion over a set X of items (Boolean vectors, real-valued vectors, words or even sentences in natural language) is a quaternary relation involving 4 elements, $a, b, c, d \in X$, often denoted $a : b :: c : d$ and should be read "a is to b as c is to d", obeying postulates. Depending on the postulates, *strong* and *weak* forms of analogical proportions can be distinguished, leading to different Boolean and numerical representations.

3.1   Strong Analogical Proportions

Classically, analogical proportions are supposed to obey the 3 following first-order logic postulates (e.g., [18]) $\forall a, b, c, d \in X$,[1] which are satisfied by numerical proportions:

1. $a : b :: a : b$ (*reflexivity*);
2. $a : b :: c : d \rightarrow c : d :: a : b$ (*symmetry*);
3. $a : b :: c : d \rightarrow a : c :: b : d$ (*central permutation*).

---

[1] In the following, we omit the universal quantifier for readability.

These postulates have straightforward consequences like:

- $a : a :: b : b$ (*identity*);
- $a : b :: c : d \rightarrow b : a :: d : c$ (*internal reversal*);
- $a : b :: c : d \rightarrow d : b :: c : a$ (*extreme permutation*);
- $a : b :: c : d \rightarrow d : c :: b : a$ (*complete reversal*).

Among the 24 permutations of a, b, c, d, the previous postulates lead to 3 distinct classes each containing 8 syntactically different proportions regarded as equivalent due to the postulates. Thus $a : b :: c : d$ has in its class $c : d :: a : b$, $c : a :: d : b$, $d : b :: c : a$, $d : c :: b : a$, $b : a :: d : c$, $b : d :: a : c$, and $a : c :: b : d$. But $b : a :: c : d$ and $a : d :: c : b$ are not in the class of a:b::c:d and are in fact elements of two other classes.

A typical example of an analogical proportion over $X = \mathbb{R}$ is the arithmetic proportion defined as:

$$a : b :: c : d \text{ holds if and only if } a - b = c - d$$

easily extended to a real-valued vector space $X = \mathbb{R}^n$ with the same definition. From a geometric viewpoint in $\mathbb{R}^n$, it means that (a, b, c, d) is a parallelogram [35]. In practice, it may be weakened into an approximate equality $a - b \approx c - d$ using some tolerance.

Considering now X as the Boolean set $\mathbb{B} = \{0, 1\}$, various equivalent Boolean formulas satisfy the postulates of analogical proportion over X. One of them making explicit that "a differs from b as c differs from d (and vice-versa)" [24] is:

$$a : b :: c : d =_{def} ((a \wedge \neg b) \equiv (c \wedge \neg d)) \wedge ((\neg a \wedge b) \equiv (\neg c \wedge d))$$

It is easy to check that this formula is only valid for the 6 valuations in Table 1. As shown in [31], this set of 6 valuations is the *minimal* Boolean model obeying the 3 postulates of analogy. It can be seen on this table that 1 and 0 play a symmetrical role, which makes the definition *code-independent*. This is formally expressed in $X = \mathbb{B}$ with the negation operator as: $a : b :: c : d \rightarrow \neg a : \neg b :: \neg c : \neg d$.

Table 1. Valid valuations for the strong Boolean analogical proportion

$0 : 0 :: 0 : 0$
$1 : 1 :: 1 : 1$
$0 : 1 :: 0 : 1$
$1 : 0 :: 1 : 0$
$0 : 0 :: 1 : 1$
$1 : 1 :: 0 : 0$

To deal with items represented by Boolean vectors, it is straightforward to extend this definition from $\mathbb{B}$ to $\mathbb{B}^n$ with:

$$a : b :: c : d =_{def} \forall i \in [1, n], a_i : b_i :: c_i : d_i$$

This is useful when words are represented by means of key terms appearing in their dictionary definition. For instance, using the 5 key terms *mammal, bovine, equine, adult, young*, Table 2 explains why $a : b :: c : d = cow : calf :: mare : foal$ can rigorously be considered as a valid analogy (we recognize patterns of Table 1, vertically, in Table 2). More generally, series of mutually exclusive properties such as *bovine/equine, adult/young*, as encountered in taxonomic trees, induce analogical proportions [3].

Table 2. A Boolean validation of *cow : calf :: mare : foal*

	Mammal	Bovine	Equine	Adult	Young
Cow	1	1	0	1	0
Calf	1	1	0	0	1
Mare	1	0	1	1	0
Foal	1	0	1	0	1

3.2 Weak Analogical Proportions

However, the central permutation postulate (3) is debatable for analogical proportions involving two *conceptual spaces* [2]. Indeed in the following example that involves nationalities and beverages, while "wine is to French people as beer is to English people" is acceptable, "wine is to beer as French people is to English people" sounds weird.

It is then legitimate *to abandon the central permutation postulate* and to replace it by the internal reversal property which is still a widely accepted property of analogical proportion, leading to a *weaker* definition of analogical proportion:

1 $a : b :: a : b$ (*reflexivity*);
2 $a : b :: c : d \rightarrow c : d :: a : b$ (*symmetry*);
4 $a : b :: c : d \rightarrow b : a :: d : c$ (*internal reversal*).

Complete reversal $(a : b :: c : d \rightarrow d : c :: b : a)$ is still a consequence of this weaker set of postulates. Clearly a strong analogical proportion (in the sense of (1)-(2)-(3)) is also a weak proportion. According to postulates (1)-(2)-(4) $a : b :: c : d$ can be written only under 4 equivalent forms rather than 8: $a : b :: c : d$, $c : d :: a : b$, $d : c :: b : a$, and $b : a :: d : c$. Despite one might be tempted to have $a : a :: b : b$ (*identity*), this is no longer deducible from the postulates.

From a computational linguistics viewpoint (see for instance [6,11,21]), a proportion $a : b :: c : d$ is often understood as:

for some binary relation R, $R(a, b) \wedge R(c, d)$ holds.

where R is a latent relation with a semantic or discourse connotation. This definition perfectly fits with postulates (1)-(2)-(4). As an example, consider the following pairs of sentences:

John sneezed loudly (a). Mary was startled (b).
Bob took an analgesic (c). His headache stopped (d).

where one could argue that R is a kind of causal relation. Indeed, internal reversal holds because $R^{-1}(b, a) \land R^{-1}(d, c)$ holds. In the example above R^{-1} would be an explanation relation although explicit discourse markers should be utilized:

Mary was startled (b), because John sneezed loudly (a).
Bob's headache stopped (d) because he took an analgesic (c).

In practice, the fact that $R(a, b) \land R(c, d)$ holds does not entail that there also exists a semantically meaningful S such that $S(a, c) \land S(b, d)$ holds: that is why the central permutation postulate is not relevant here. It would make no sense in the above example.

The *minimal* Boolean model of postulates (1)-(2)-(4) is constituted with the 4 first lines of Table 1, still satisfying code-independence. A Boolean expression of the weak analogical proportion $a : b :: {}_wc : d$ is given by

$$a : b :: {}_wc : d = (a \equiv c) \land (b \equiv d)$$

Note that $a \land b \equiv c \land d$ and $a \lor b \equiv c \lor d$ are simple examples of formulas satisfying (1)-(2)-(4). But their Boolean models include more than the 4 first lines of Table 1 even if they are false for the last two lines of this Table.

When working on $X = \mathbb{R}$ rather than $X = \mathbb{B}$, a weak analogical proportion can be defined by:

$$a : b :: {}_wc : d \text{ holds} \begin{cases} \text{if } a = b = c = d \\ \text{if } a - b = c - d \quad \text{when } Cond \text{ is true} \end{cases}$$

where $Cond$ stands for $(a < b \ \land \ c < d) \lor (a > b \ \land \ c > d)$ with $b \neq c$. It removes the situation where $a - b = c - d = 0$ for $b \neq c$. It satisfies (1)-(2)-(4), but not (3) (e.g., we have $.3 < .9$ and $.7 < .8$ but not $.3 < .7$ and $.9 < .8$), nor $a : a :: b : b$ or $a : b :: b : a$. It has also the advantage to keep a, b, c, d distinct, which would not be the case if $a : b :: {}_wc : d$ is defined by the straightforward option '$a = c$ and $b = d$'. Obviously in practice, $=$ could be replaced by $\approx$.

3.3   Analogical Proportions and Implication

A relation of particular interest between items such as sentences (or words) is the entailment relation: "a entails b as c entails d". So we may wonder if a simplistic modeling of "a entails b" in terms of material implication ($a \rightarrow b$) would lead to a weak proportion.

In fact, $(a \rightarrow b) \land (c \rightarrow d)$ is not satisfactory as, in the Boolean universe, it is false for valuation (1010) and true for the other patterns that a strong or weak analogical proportion fulfill (together with 4 other patterns:

$(0001), (0100), (0111), (1101))$. Obviously this formula does satisfy neither central permutation nor internal reversal.

In that respect, a better option could be to consider

$$Imp(a, b, c, d) = [(a \rightarrow b) \wedge (c \rightarrow d)] \vee [(b \rightarrow a) \wedge (d \rightarrow c)]$$

which satisfies the postulates of a weak analogical proportion. However, in the Boolean universe, this formula is false only for 2 patterns $(0110), (1001)$ (which are known as maximizing analogical dissimilarity [23,24]), and true for all the 14 remaining patterns. However, one can recover $a : b :: c : d$ as well as $a : b :: {}_wc : d$ from it. Namely,

$$a : b :: c : d = Imp(a, b, c, d) \wedge Klein(a, b, c, d)$$

where $Klein(a, b, c, d) = (a \equiv b) \equiv (c \equiv d)$ is an operator introduced by S. Klein [8], true for the 6 patterns that make true an analogical proportion, plus the two forbidden patterns $(0110), (1001)$. In the Boolean universe, weak analogical proportions are recovered as

$$a : b :: {}_wc : d = Imp(a, b, c, d) \wedge Par(a, b, c, d)$$

where $Par(a, b, c, d) = ((a \wedge b) \equiv (c \wedge d)) \wedge ((\neg a \wedge \neg b) \equiv (\neg c \wedge \neg d))$ is a Boolean operator named *paralogy* [31].

The above equalities show that one cannot have a pure implication-based view of analogical proportions. Moreover $Imp(a, b, c, d)$ is much weaker than $a : b :: {}_wc : d$ and cannot be a particular case of it.

3.4 Analogical Proportions and Sentences

We distinguish two types of analogies between sentences. The first one is a natural extension of word analogies. Starting from the fact that $a : b :: c : d$ is an analogy between lexical items a, b, c and d, then sentences s_1, s_2 are analogous if they link a, b and c, d with the same predicate R—so $R(a, b) \wedge R(c, d)$. A simple example would be: *French people drink wine (s1) English people drink beer (s2)* with *French:wine :: English:beer*. It is worth noticing that already a pair of sentences making a parallel between two situations and involving words or phrases in analogical proportions, may provide an argumentative support. For example, let us consider the two sentences *Polio vaccine protects against poliomyelitis. h1n1 vaccine protects against influenza.* Clearly the pairs $(a, b) =$ *(Polio, poliomyelitis)* and $(c, d) =$ *(h1n1 vaccine, influenza)* make an analogical proportion $a : b :: c : d$ with respect to *vaccine, disease, virus* and *bacteria*, as can be checked on first four lines of Table 3. If we also consider the sentence "BCG vaccine protects against tuberculosis" associated with the pair $(a', b') =$ *(BCG vaccine, tuberculosis)*, $a' : b' :: c : d$ does not hold with respect to *virus* and *bacteria* (see Table 3), and then (a', b') appears to be a poorer support for (c, d) than (a, b). It would be still worse if one considers the sentence "umbrellas protect against the rain" instead of (a', b')! Besides, note that in all the above

Table 3. The vaccine example

	Vaccine	Disease	Virus	Bacteria
a	1	0	0	0
b	0	1	1	0
c	1	0	0	0
d	0	1	1	0
a'	1	0	0	0
b'	0	1	0	1

sentences the same relation $R = protects\ against$ takes place, and both $R(a, b)$ and $R(c, d)$ hold. In case of synonyms used in different sentences, analogy may become a matter of degree (e.g.,[5]). When sentences have a different number of words, one may apply the approach by Miclet et al. [22] for aligning the key terms. Lastly, a parallel between 2 situations may involve 4 sentences making an analogical proportion, as in the example "some cetaceans eat phytoplankton; other cetaceans are carnivorous; some mammals eat grass; other mammals are carnivorous".

The second type of sentential analogies is not limited to a, b, c and d being extension of word analogies but instead they represent more complex sentences with R being a latent relation linking a, b and c, d. This type of sentential analogies was briefly evoked in Subsect. 3.2 wherein some examples involving causal relations were provided. Here is another example involving a relation that is more temporal in nature:

Mary was working on her new book (a), while John was washing this afternoon's dishes (b).
Bob was waiting for the bus at the bus stop (c). At the same time, workers were making loud noises on the street (d).

As we can see, in this case reflexivity, symmetry, internal reversal and complete reversal (Subsect. 3.2) also hold while we cannot say the same thing for central permutation.

The latent relation linking two pairs of sentences can take several forms. Natural candidates include entailment or various discourse relations. In Sect. 4 of this paper, we use the Penn Discourse TreeBank[2] (PDTB), but other datasets, such as the Stanford Natural Language Inference (SNLI) Corpus[3] could be used as well.

---

[2] https://www.seas.upenn.edu/~pdtb/.
[3] https://nlp.stanford.edu/projects/snli/.

4   Experimental Context - Evaluation Metrics

Let us move to an empirical validation of our approach using word embeddings, and sentence embeddings[4].

4.1   Datasets

Mixing google analogies with template sentences Given a set of words W, the notion of analogical proportion between words is not *formally* defined but we have many examples of well-accepted (cognitively valid) word analogies like *man : king :: woman : queen*. One of the most well-known datasets of word analogies, originally from Google, can be downloaded at http://download. tensorflow.org/data/questions-words.txt

Starting from Google word analogies dataset, we create our own sentences analogies dataset by separating the lexical items therein into different categories. Template sentences are then created with placeholders to be replaced by the correct category of the Google word analogy dataset. With this method sentences S_A, S_B, S_C and S_D are created so that they meet the requirement $R(S_A, S_B) \land R(S_C, S_D)$. Obviously, we expect our classifiers to be successful on this artificial dataset: at this stage, this is just a toy example to check that our initial assumption (weak analogy definition) is not defeated. Below are the categories with examples used

- **Capital Common Cities.** S_A = "She arrived yesterday in *London*" and S_B = "She just landed in *England*".
- **City in State.** S_A = "Citizens in *Chicago* are more likely to vote", S_B = "Citizens in *Illinois* are more likely to vote".
- **Currencies.** S_A = "What is the currency used in *Japan*?", S_B = "Which country uses the *yen*?".
- **Family.** The possessives "his", "her" and the nouns "he", "she", are skipped. For instance in S_A = "His *father* could not be present at the annual family gathering", S_B = "His *mother* could not be present at the annual family gathering".
- **Nationality adjectives.** S_A = "The culture in *Chile* is very rich", S_B = "The *Chilean* culture is very rich".
- **Opposites.** Sentences containing an adjective listed in the Google analogy dataset. The adjective is labelled and replaced with it's antonym thus creating a pair of sentences. S_A = "I was *aware* in which direction he was going", S_B = "I was *unaware* in which direction he was going".

Once generated, we get a total set of $52,185$ sentence quadruples. Using the extension methods depicted in Subsect. 3.2, the dataset is extended by a factor 12, with 4 valid analogies per sentence quadruple, using the *symmetry*, *internal reversal* and *complete reversal* permutations and 8 invalid analogies, using the same permutations applied to the quadruples $b : a :: c : d$ and $c : b :: a : d$. We now have a dataset of size $52,185 * 12 = 626,220$ sentences.

---

[4] All our datasets and python code used in this paper are freely available at https:// github.com/arxaqapi/analogy-classifier.

Penn Discourse TreeBank Dataset. The second dataset that we use is the Penn Discourse TreeBank (PDTB) [33].[5] Our goal was to try a preliminary series of experiments to determine whether our approach could identify pairs of sentences that are linked with the same latent relation R where R in this particular case is a discourse relation. PDTB contains more than 36,000 pairs of sentences annotated with discourse relations. Relations can be explicitly expressed via a discourse marker, or implicitly expressed in which case no such discourse marker exists and the annotators provide one that more closely describes the implicit discourse relation. Relations are organized in a taxonomy which contains 4 classes of relations (Temporal, Contingency, Expansion and Comparison) as well as several types and subtypes of relations (for example Cause, Condition, Contrast, etc.). As an example, for the Temporal relation type, we have pairs of sentences like: S_A = "The results were announced", S_B = "The stock market closed" and S_C = "That happens", S_D = "Nervous stock investors dump equities and buy treasurys".

In this series of preliminary results we used primarily the four classes of relations although we also experimented with the implicit/explicit nature of relations. In total we selected 25,000 random quadruplets for a total of 300,000 instances. Each quadruple of sentences was accompanied with a Boolean class indicating whether the quadruple constituted a valid analogy—that is pairs (a, b) and (c, d) are linked with the same relation—or not.

4.2 Embedding Techniques

A word embedding ω is an injective function from a set of words W to a real-valued vector space $\mathbb{R}^n$ (usually $n \in \{50, 100, 200, 300\}$ but there is no real limitation). There are well-known word embeddings such as word2vec [25], GloVe [28], BERT [9], fastText [26], etc. It is standard to start from a word embedding to build a sentence embedding. Sentence embedding techniques represent entire sentences and their semantic information as vectors. There are diverse sentence embedding techniques. In this paper, we focus on 2 techniques relying on an initial word embedding.

- The simplest method is to average the word embeddings of all words in a sentence. Although this method ignores both the order of the words and the structure of the sentence, it performs well in many tasks. So the final vector has the dimension of the initial word embedding.
- The other approach, suggested in [1], makes use of the Discrete Cosine Transform (DCT) as a simple and efficient way to model both word order and structure in sentences while maintaining practical efficiency. Using the inverse transformation, the original word sequence can be reconstructed. A parameter k is a small constant that needs to be set. One can choose how many features are being embedded per sentence by adjusting the value of k, but undeniably increases the final size of the sentence vector by a factor k. If the

---

[5] At this stage, we used PDTB version 2.1.

initial embedding of words is of dimension n, the final sentence dimension will be $= n * k$ (see [1] for a complete description). In this paper, we chose $k = 1$ as suggested in [39].

4.3   Classifiers

Because we do not rely on any parallelogram-like formula to check whether 4 sentences build an analogy, we move to machine learning to "learn", in some sense, the formula. In fact, we classify a quadruple of 4 sentences as a valid or non valid analogy. We tried two classical methods which have been successfully used for word analogy classification [20]: Random Forest (RF) and Convolutional Neural Networks (CNN). CNN has been popular for image classification but has also been used for text classification as it could extract and select important ngrams for classification [17]. RF is relatively accurate at classification and is fast [7]. On a 10 core CPU, CNN took about 12 CPU hours (one-hour real-time) to train but RF took only about 18 CPU minutes and real-time to train.

The parameters for RF are 100 trees, no maximum depth, and a minimum split of 2. With CNN, stacking together the 4 vectors, with n components corresponding to a quadruple a, b, c, d of sentences, we get a matrix $n \times 4$ that we are going to process as we would do for an *image*. With filters respecting the boundaries of the 2 pairs, this is the structure of the CNN:

- 1st layer (convolutional): 128 filters of size $height \times width = 1 \times 2$ with strides $(1, 2)$ and Relu activation. This means that we are working component by component (with a vertical stride of 1) and we move from pair (a, b) to pair (c, d) with horizontal stride 2.
- 2nd layer (convolutional): 64 filters of size $(2, 2)$ with strides $(2, 2)$ and Relu activation, reducing the dimension before going to the final dense layer.
- 3rd layer (dense): one output with sigmoid activation.

5   Results

Below we present experimental results for two datasets: generated sentences and PDTB.

5.1   CNN and RF Results for Generated Sentences

The results in Table 4 are obtained with 10 epochs for the CNN. The Average Accuracy is computed from the average of the 10 folds accuracy for each method. The results are already extremely good (over 98%) even with a low word embedding size for both CNN and RF. The accuracy in CNN increases if we increase the size of the word vectors as more "details" are encoded in the vector so that the CNN captures more of the semantics. For RF, increasing the size of the word vectors provides no increase in the accuracy. Given that the increase in accuracy is at most 2%, we suggest using vectors of size 50 (GloVe) or reduce the fast-Text vectors from 300 to 50 to reduce the computation in CNN. The authors in [39] also used GloVe average method for sentence embedding and the highest accuracy is 90%, regardless of which parallelogram-inspired formula were used.

Table 4. Average accuracies (10 folds) for CNN (10 epochs) and RF for generated dataset using GloVe vector size 50 to 300 (G50 to G300) and fastText (F300) for average and DCT sentence embedding.

ML Method	Word embedding size				
	G50	G100	G200	G300	F300
CNN-AVG	98.39%	99.76%	99.96%	99.97%	99.91%
RF-AVG	99.97%	99.97%	99.97%	99.97%	99.98%
CNN-DCT	68.23%	68.30%	68.31%	68.31%	68.24%
RF-DCT	67.14%	67.14%	67.14%	67.14	67.10%

Table 5. Average accuracies and $F1$ (10 folds) for CNN 10 epochs and RF for PDTB dataset using GloVe and fastText for average and DCT sentence embedding.

ML Method	Word embedding size				
	G50	G100	G200	G300	F300
CNN-AVG	66.49% (0.42)	66.64% (0.42)	66.61% (0.40)	66.36% (0.41)	66.69% (0.52)
RF-AVG	62.96% (0.02)	63.79% (0.02)	64.08% (0.02)	64.33% (0.02)	65.05% (0.01)
CNN-DCT	66.46% (0.12)	66.49% (0.10)	65.31% (0.34)	66.10% (0.15)	66.05% (0.21)
RF-DCT	58.74% (0.04)	58.91% (0.04)	58.92% (0.04)	58.85% (0.04)	61.89% (0.09)

5.2 CNN and RF Results for PDTB Dataset

The accuracies for both CNN and RF are around 60%, much lower for the PDTB dataset (see Table 5) compared to the generated sentences. This is to be expected as the PDTB sentences are much more semantic/pragmatic in nature so it is much more difficult to capture the relationship between the sentences using a simple average embedding technique. The $F1$ values of RF are very low (at most 0.09), suggesting that it has difficulty identifying positive results. CNNs on the other hand perform much better achieving 0.52 $F1$ for valid analogies using fastText, but the overall highest accuracy is only 66.69%.

Our results are an improvement with respect to [10,39], although a strict comparison is difficult because not only do we use different corpora, but also the experimental setup is different. For more semantic sentences, the work reported in [39] achieves an accuracy of 0.43 in the unconstrained scenario, while we have achieved an accuracy of 0.66. In [39], a constrained scenario selected the true answer from six sentences, while the unconstrained scenario selected the true answer from the "entire corpus".

6 Candidate Applications

Analogy-making permeates human cognition and is a mechanism that is very often used in human communication. In terms of computational linguistics the study of analogies has almost exclusively been limited to the detection of word analogies [6,11,20,27,36,37, for example]. Nonetheless analogies go beyond the lexical level and can exist between sentences as well as longer discourse units. In the following we describe some areas of computational linguistics that could benefit from analogy-making.

- **Discourse:** one of the problems that current chatbots face is that they lack discourse coherence. Disposing of a mechanism that is able to handle sentence analogies, allows us to better select following sentences in a generated text yielding better overall coherence. Consider for example that in a discourse $d = (s_1, \ldots, s_n)$ where s_i represents elementary discourse units, we need to choose the next sentence from a set of candidate sentences C that a chatbot could have generated so as to maximize coherence. In order to do so we can rely upon the formal framework presented in Sect. 3 in order to choose $s_c \in C$ such that $s_c = \arg min(\|(\pi_i - \pi_j) - (s_n - s_c)\|)$ where $\pi_i : \pi_j :: s_n : s_c$. In order to bootstrap learning we can use resources such as PDTB. Given that π_i, π_j, s_n and s_c are learnt representations we can imagine a more complicated scenario in which π_i and s_n are substituted for representations of previous discourse. Corpora such as the RST which model larger contexts could be used.

- **Question-answering:** A similar approach has already been used in the context of question answering by [39] (see Sect. 2). Better selection of answers is achieved by hypothesizing that an answer is more plausible for that question if the pair (q, a) is analogical to other "prototypical" pairs of questions and answers. Extensions of this work could include representations of larger context as well as less prototypical pairs.

- **Computational creativity:** Being able to identify and propose new analogies can be very useful in understanding and advancing computational creativity. In the context of generating more "creative" text, such as poem generation [38], relaxing to a certain degree the constraint of minimization mentioned above could yield creative analogies.

- **Argumentation:** Capturing analogies that go beyond the sentential level could be very useful for argumentation. A conversational agent trying to convince their interlocutor that, for example, using a car is not anodyne since it pollutes the environment and ultimately is a cause of death for many people, could draw the analogy between driving a car and smoking. Smoking was widely accepted but studies have shown that it is detrimental to the health of active and passive smokers. The same has been shown for car pollution, so cars should be restricted or banned altogether under certain circumstances. Achieving such a goal requires representations that are capable to handle larger chunks of text.

7   Conclusion

In this paper, we have provided the basis of a weak analogical proportion theory, removing the classical central permutation postulate. Our new postulates better reflect what is generally considered as a natural language analogical proportion between sentences. From a machine learning perspective, the new system is also used to rigorously extend a set of examples. Using standard embedding techniques for sentences, we have tested our approach to classify 4 sentences into valid and invalid proportions. Preliminary experiments using simple architectures show that we can achieve an accuracy of 0.66 (with an $F1$ of 0.52 for valid analogies) for sentential analogies based on latent semantic and pragmatic similarity using the PDTB corpus. In the future we plan to perform further experiments using transformers and BERT embeddings in order to investigate which of the aforementioned postulates (central permutation, internal reversal) transfer to natural language datasets. By crossing powerful real-valued embeddings with a more semantic ontology-based representation of words, the new formal setting paves the way to hybrid approaches where analogical inference could be done on natural language corpora.

References

1. Almarwani, N., Aldarmaki, H., Diab, M.: Efficient sentence embedding using discrete cosine transform. In: EMNLP, pp. 3663–3669 (2019)
2. Barbot, N., Miclet, L., Prade, H.: Analogy between concepts. Artif. Intell. **275**, 487–539 (2019)
3. Barbot, N., Miclet, L., Prade, H., Richard, G.: A new perspective on analogical proportions. In: Kern-Isberner, G., Ognjanović, Z. (eds.) ECSQARU 2019. LNCS (LNAI), vol. 11726, pp. 163–174. Springer, Cham (2019). https://doi.org/10.1007/978-3-030-29765-7_14
4. Bojanowski, P., Grave, E., Joulin, A., Mikolov, T.: Enriching word vectors with subword information. Trans. Assoc. Comput. Linguist. **5**, 135–146 (2017)
5. Bounhas, M., Prade, H., Richard, G.: Analogy-based classifiers for nominal or numerical data. Int. J. Approx. Reasoning **91**, 36–55 (2017)
6. Bouraoui, Z., Jameel, S., Schockaert, S.: Relation induction in word embeddings revisited. In: COLING, pp. 1627–1637. Association for Computational Linguistics (2018)
7. Breiman, L.: Random forests. Mach. Learn. **45**(1), 5–32 (2001)
8. Couceiro, M., Hug, N., Prade, H., Richard, G.: Analogy-preserving functions: a way to extend Boolean samples. In: Proceedings of the IJCAI, Melbourne, pp. 1575–1581 (2017)
9. Devlin, J., Chang, M.-W., Lee, K., Toutanova, K.: BERT: pre-training of deep bidirectional transformers for language understanding. CoRR, abs/1810.04805 (2018)
10. Diallo, A., Zopf, M., Fürnkranz, J.: Learning analogy-preserving sentence embeddings for answer selection. In: Proceedings of the 23rd Conference on Computational Natural Language Learning, pp. 910–919. Association for Computational Linguistics (2019)
11. Drozd, A., Gladkova, A., Matsuoka, S.: Word embeddings, analogies, and machine learning: beyond king - man + woman = queen. In: COLING, pp. 3519–3530 (2016)
12. Fam, R., Lepage, Y.: Tools for the production of analogical grids and a resource of n-gram analogical grids in 11 languages. In: LREC (2018)
13. French, R.M., Hofstadter, D.: Tabletop: an emergent, stochastic model of analogy-making. In: Proceedings of the 13th Annual Conference of the Cognitive Science Society, pp. 175–182. Lawrence Erlbaum (1991)
14. Gentner, D., Holyoak, K.J., Kokinov, B.N. (eds.): The Analogical Mind: Perspectives from Cognitive Science. MIT Press, Cambridge (2001)

15. Hesse, M.: Models and Analogies in Science, 1st ed. Sheed & Ward, London (1963). 2nd augmented ed. University of Notre Dame Press, 1966
16. Hofstadter, D., Mitchell, M.: The copycat project: a model of mental fluidity and analogy-making. In: Fluid Concepts and Creative Analogies: Computer Models of the Fundamental Mechanisms of Thought, pp. 205–267. Basic Books Inc (1995)
17. Jacovi, A., Shalom, O.S., Goldberg, Y.: Understanding convolutional neural networks for text classification. CoRR, abs/1809.08037 (2018)
18. Lepage, Y.: Analogy and formal languages. Electr. Notes Theor. Comput. Sci. **53**, 180–191 (2004). https://doi.org/10.1016/S1571-0661(05)82582-4
19. Lepage, Y., Denoual, E.: Purest ever example-based machine translation: detailed presentation and assessment. Mach. Transl. **19**(3–4), 251–282 (2005)
20. Lim, S., Prade, H., Richard, G.: Solving word analogies: a machine learning perspective. In: Kern-Isberner, G., Ognjanović, Z. (eds.) ECSQARU 2019. LNCS (LNAI), vol. 11726, pp. 238–250. Springer, Cham (2019). https://doi.org/10.1007/978-3-030-29765-7_20
21. Lu, H., Wu, Y., Holyoak, K.H.: Emergence of analogy from relation learning. Proc. Natl. Acad. Sci. **116**, 4176–4181 (2019)
22. Miclet, L., Barbot, N., Jeudy, B.: Analogical proportions in a lattice of sets of alignments built on the common subwords in a finite language. In: Prade, H., Richard, G. (eds.) Computational Approaches to Analogical Reasoning: Current Trends. SCI, vol. 548, pp. 245–260. Springer, Heidelberg (2014). https://doi.org/10.1007/978-3-642-54516-0_10
23. Miclet, L., Bayoudh, S., Delhay, A.: Analogical dissimilarity: definition, algorithms and two experiments in machine learning. JAIR **32**, 793–824 (2008)
24. Miclet, L., Prade, H.: Handling analogical proportions in classical logic and fuzzy logics settings. In: Sossai, C., Chemello, G. (eds.) ECSQARU 2009. LNCS (LNAI), vol. 5590, pp. 638–650. Springer, Heidelberg (2009). https://doi.org/10.1007/978-3-642-02906-6_55
25. Mikolov, T., Chen, K., Corrado, G.S., Dean, J.: Efficient estimation of word representations in vector space. CoRR, abs/1301.3781 (2013)
26. Mikolov, T., Grave, E., Bojanowski, P., Puhrsch, C., Joulin, A.: Advances in pre-training distributed word representations. In: Proceedings of LREC (2018)
27. Murena, P.-A., Al-Ghossein, M., Dessalles, J.-L., Cornuéjols, A.: Solving analogies on words based on minimal complexity transformation. In: Proceedings of the 29th International Joint Conference Artificial Intelligence, pp. 1848–1854 (2020)
28. Pennington, J., Socher, R., Manning, Ch.D.: GloVe: global vectors for word representation. In: EMNLP, pp. 1532–1543 (2014)
29. Prade, H., Richard, G.: Analogical proportions and analogical reasoning - an introduction. In: Aha, D.W., Lieber, J. (eds.) ICCBR 2017. LNCS (LNAI), vol. 10339, pp. 16–32. Springer, Cham (2017). https://doi.org/10.1007/978-3-319-61030-6_2
30. Prade, H., Richard, G.: Analogical proportions: why they are useful in AI. In: Proceedings of the 30th International Joint Conference on Artificial Intelligence (IJCAI 2021), Montreal, 21–26 August 2021
31. Prade, H., Richard, G.: Analogical proportions: from equality to inequality. Int. J. Approx. Reasoning **101**, 234–254 (2018)
32. Prade, H., Richard, G. (eds.): Computational Approaches to Analogical Reasoning: Current Trends. SCI, vol. 548. Springer, Heidelberg (2014). https://doi.org/10.1007/978-3-642-54516-0
33. Prasad, R., et al.: The Penn discourse TreeBank 2.0. In: LREC 2008, May 2008

34. Rhouma, R., Langlais, P.: Experiments in learning to solve formal analogical equations. In: Cox, M.T., Funk, P., Begum, S. (eds.) ICCBR 2018. LNCS (LNAI), vol. 11156, pp. 612–626. Springer, Cham (2018). https://doi.org/10.1007/978-3-030-01081-2_40

35. Rumelhart, D.E., Abrahamson, A.A.: A model for analogical reasoning. Cogn. Psychol. **5**, 1–28 (2005)

36. Turney, P.D.: A uniform approach to analogies, synonyms, antonyms, and associations. In: COLING, pp. 905–912 (2008)

37. Turney, P.D.: Distributional semantics beyond words: supervised learning of analogy and paraphrase. TACL **1**, 353–366 (2013)

38. Van de Cruys, T.: Automatic poetry generation from prosaic text. In: Proceedings of ACL (2020)

39. Zhu, X., de Melo, G.: Sentence analogies: linguistic regularities in sentence embeddings. In: COLING (2020)

Non-monotonic Explanation Functions

Leila Amgoud[(⊠)]

CNRS – IRIT, Toulouse, France
amgoud@irit.fr

Abstract. Explaining black-box classification models is a hot topic in AI, it has the overall goal of improving trust in decisions made by such models. Several works have been done and diverse explanation functions have been proposed. The most prominent ones, like Anchor and LIME, return abductive explanations which highlight key factors that cause predictions. Despite their popularity, the two functions may return inaccurate and sometimes incorrect explanations.

In this paper, we study abductive explanations and identify the origin of this shortcoming. We start by defining two kinds of explanations: *absolute explanations* that are generated from the whole feature space, and *plausible explanations* (like those provided by Anchors and LIME) that are constructed from a proper subset of the feature space. We show that the former are coherent in that two compatible sets of features cannot explain distinct classes while the latter may however be incoherent, leading thus to incorrect explanations. Then, we show that explanations are provided by non-monotonic functions. Indeed, an explanation may no longer be valid if new instances are received. Finally, we provide a novel function that is based on argumentation and that returns plausible explanations. We show that the function is non monotonic and its explanations are coherent.

Keywords: Classification · Explainability · Argumentation

1 Introduction

In the last few years, the discussion around artificial intelligence is gaining more and more interest. This is mainly due to noteworthy advances made in data-driven AI in general, and deep learning in particular. In this sub-field of AI, the idea is to learn a targeted objective (like the class of an object) from a vast quantity of data. However, the predictions of existing models can hardly be explained in a transparent way. This opacity is seen as a great limitation, which impedes the relevance of those models in practical applications like healthcare but also in embedded systems for mobility despite their successes. Explanations are essential for increasing societal trust, and thus acceptance of those models. They help users understand why a decision was reached.

Explaining the functionality of complex classification models and their rationale becomes a vital need. Consequently, several works have been done in the

© Springer Nature Switzerland AG 2021
J. Vejnarová and N. Wilson (Eds.): ECSQARU 2021, LNAI 12897, pp. 19–31, 2021.
https://doi.org/10.1007/978-3-030-86772-0_2

literature (see [1–3] for recent surveys on explaining machine learning models). They consider as input a classifier, and provide explanations of its predictions. Those works can be divided into two families: The first family opens somehow the classifier to provide insight into the internal decision-making process (e.g. [4,5]), its explanations describe thus the classifier's algorithm. However, the use of increasingly complex algorithms (e.g. deep neural networks) has made them more difficult to explain and the inner workings of an algorithm may be inexplicable even to the developers of those classifiers [6]. Furthermore, a predominant finding from research in philosophy of sciences and social sciences is that a full causal explanation of a prediction is undesired for humans, as they do not need to understand the algorithm followed by a model. In other words, an explanation does not necessarily hinge on the general public understanding of how algorithmic systems function. Consequently, the second family provides explanations without opening the black-box (e.g. [5,7–11]) and pays particular attention to what constitutes a *good* explanation for human users. Several notions have been defined in this second family including *abductive* explanations (e.g. [12]), *counterfactuals* (e.g. [5]), *semifactuals* [13], *contrastive* explanations (e.g. [8,9]), explanations based on *pertinent positives* and *pertinent negatives* (e.g. [9]), *adversarial examples* (e.g. [14]), examples (e.g. [15]), and *counter-examples* (e.g. [12]).

In this paper, we focus on complex classifiers whose internal processes are inexplicable, and we follow the second approach for explaining their predictions. We study the abductive explanations, which highlight key factors that cause predictions. Such explanations are provided by the two prominent explanation functions: Anchors and LIME [11,16]. Despite their popularity, the two functions may return inaccurate and sometimes incorrect explanations, and the reason behind this shortcoming remains unclear.

In this paper, we elucidate the origin of the shortcoming. For that purpose, we start by defining two explanations functions. The first function generates *absolute* explanations from the whole feature space. This approach is followed for instance in [12,17]. We show that this function is coherent, i.e., its explanations are compatible and do not justify distinct classes. However, in practice the whole feature space is not available. Consequently, functions like Anchors and LIME generate (abductive) explanations from a proper subset of the feature space. Indeed, the explanations of a given instance are constructed from some instances in its close neighbourhood.

Our second function generates thus what we call *plausible* explanations from a subset of instances, which may be the neighbourhood of instances, or a set of instances on which the classifier returns a good confidence, or simply a dataset on which it was trained. Such explanations are only plausible (compared to absolute) since they are generated from incomplete information. We show that they are non monotonic in that an explanation may no longer be valid if the subset of instances is extended with further ones. We show also that this function is incoherent, leading to incorrect explanations (as in Anchors and LIME).

To sum up, generating explanations is a non-monotonic reasoning problem, and defining a non-monotonic function that is coherent remains a challenge in the XAI literature. In this paper we provide such a function that is based on argumentation.

The paper is structured as follows: Sect. 2 presents the background on classification. Section 3 defines the two first functions of explanation and Sect. 4 investigates their properties and links. Section 5 defines the argument-based explanation function and the last section concludes.

2   Classification Problem

Throughout the paper, we assume a finite and non-empty set $\mathcal{F} = \{f_1, \ldots, f_n\}$ of *features* (called also *attributes*) that take respectively their values from *finite* domains $\mathcal{D}_1, \ldots, \mathcal{D}_n$. Let $\mathcal{D} = \{\mathcal{D}_1, \ldots, \mathcal{D}_n\}$. For every feature f and every possible value v of f, the pair (f, v) is called *literal feature*, or *literal* for short. Let $\mathcal{U}$ denote the universe of all possible literal features. The set $\mathcal{X}$ contains all possible n−tuples of literal features or sets of the form $\{(f_1, v_{1i}), \ldots, (f_n, v_{nl})\}$, i.e., $\mathcal{X}$ contains all the possible *instantiations* of the n features of $\mathcal{F}$. $\mathcal{X}$ and its elements are called respectively *feature space* and *instances*. Note that $\mathcal{X}$ is finite since $\mathcal{F}$ and the n domains in $\mathcal{D}$ are finite. Let $\mathcal{C} = \{c_1, \ldots, c_m\}$, with $m > 1$, be a finite and non-empty set of possible distinct *classes*.

Definition 1. *A theory is a tuple* $\mathcal{T} = \langle \mathcal{F}, \mathcal{D}, \mathcal{C} \rangle$.

We denote by $\mathcal{X}_{\mathcal{T}}$ the feature space of theory $\mathcal{T} = \langle \mathcal{F}, \mathcal{D}, \mathcal{C} \rangle$. When it is clear from the context, we write $\mathcal{X}$ for short.

A classification model is a function that assigns to every instance $x \in \mathcal{X}_{\mathcal{T}}$ of a theory $\mathcal{T} = \langle \mathcal{F}, \mathcal{D}, \mathcal{C} \rangle$ a single prediction, which is a class from the set $\mathcal{C}$.

Definition 2. *Let* $\mathcal{T} = \langle \mathcal{F}, \mathcal{D}, \mathcal{C} \rangle$ *be a theory. A classification model is a function* f *s.t.* $f : \mathcal{X}_{\mathcal{T}} \to \mathcal{C}$.

Let us illustrate the above notions with a simple example.

Example 1. Assume a classification problem of deciding whether to hike or not. Hence, $\mathcal{C} = \{c_0, c_1\}$ where c_0 stands for not hiking and c_1 for hiking. The decision is based on four attributes: Being in vacation (V), having a concert (C), having a meeting (M) and having an exhibition (E), thus $\mathcal{F} = \{V, C, M, E\}$. Each attribute is binary, i.e., takes two possible values from $\mathcal{D}_i = \{0, 1\}$ $(i = 1, \ldots, 4)$. Assume a classification model f that assigns classes to instances of $\mathcal{Y} \subset \mathcal{X}$ as shown in the table below.

$\mathcal{Y}$	V	C	M	E	H
x_1	0	0	1	0	c_0
x_2	1	0	0	0	c_1
x_3	0	0	1	1	c_0
x_4	1	0	0	1	c_1
x_5	0	1	1	0	c_0
x_6	0	1	1	1	c_0
x_7	1	1	0	1	c_1

A set of literal features is consistent if it does not contain two literals having the same feature but distinct values.

Definition 3. *A set $H \subseteq \mathcal{U}$ is* consistent *iff $\nexists (f,v),(f',v') \in H$ such that $f = f'$ and $v \neq v'$. Otherwise, H is said to be* inconsistent.

3   Abductive Explanation Functions

In the machine learning literature, there is a decent amount of work on explaining outcomes of classifiers. Several types of explanations have then been identified, and the most prominent one is the so-called *abductive explanation*. The latter amounts at answering the following question:

Why does an outcome hold?

In other words, why a particular class is assigned to an instance? The answer consists in highlighting factors (i.e., literal features) that caused the given class. Research in cognitive science revealed that in practice, humans provide partial explanations instead of full ones. Instead of a full account, they expect an explanation for the key factors that caused the given output instead of another. Consequently, the two popular explanation functions Anchors and LIME [11,16] as well as the one that generates the so-called *pertinent positives* [9] generate sets of literals that cause a prediction. Below are two examples of such explanations:

(E_1) *I won't hike (c_0) because I am not on vacation ($V, 0$).*
(E_2) *You were denied your loan because* your annual income was £30K.

In the first example, the decision of not hiking is due to the attribute (Vacation) which takes the value 0. The second example is on decision about credit worthiness, hence there are again two possible classes (0 and 1). The explanation E_2 means that when the feature *Salary* has the value £30K, the outcome is 0.

In what follows, we define the notion of explanation function. The latter explains the predictions of a classification model in the context of a fixed theory. In other words, it takes as input a classification model f and a theory $\mathcal{T}$, and returns for every instance $x \in \mathcal{X}_{\mathcal{T}}$, the set of reasons that cause $f(x)$. The same function is thus applicable to any model f and any theory. Generally, a function generates explanations from a subset of instances which may be the dataset on which the classifier has been trained, or the set of instances on which it returns a good confidence, or the neighbourhood of some instances, etc.

Definition 4. *An explanation function is a function* $g : \mathcal{X}_T \rightarrow 2^{2^{\mathcal{U}}}$ *that generates from* $\mathcal{Y} \subseteq \mathcal{X}_T$ *the reasons behind the predictions of a classifier* f *in theory* $T = \langle \mathcal{F}, \mathcal{D}, \mathcal{C} \rangle$. *For* $x \in \mathcal{X}_T$, $g^{\mathcal{Y}}(x)$ *denotes the set of explanations of* x, *or reasons of assigning the class* $f(x)$ *to* x.

Abductive explanations have been studied in the AI literature a long time ago (e.g. [18]). More recently, they have been used for interpreting blackbox classification models (e.g. [4,17,19]). The basic idea behind these works is to look for regular behavior of a model in the whole feature space. More precisely, an abductive explanation is defined as a minimal (for set inclusion) set of literals (or features in [4]) that is sufficient for predicting a class. It is worth mentioning that a given prediction may have several abductive explanations. In what follows, we call such explanations "absolute" since they are defined by exploring the whole feature space, thus under *complete information*, and consequently they cannot be erroneous as we will see later.

Definition 5. *Let* g_a *be an explanation function of a classification model* f *applied to theory* $T = \langle \mathcal{F}, \mathcal{D}, \mathcal{C} \rangle$ *s.t. for* $\mathcal{Y} \subseteq \mathcal{X}_T$, $x \in \mathcal{Y}$, $H \subseteq \mathcal{U}$, $H \in g_a^{\mathcal{Y}}(x)$ *iff:*

- $H \subseteq x$
- $\forall y \in \mathcal{X}_T$ *s.t.* $H \subseteq y$, $f(y) = f(x)$
- $\nexists H' \subset H$ *such that* H' *satisfies the above conditions.*

H *is called* absolute abductive explanation *of* $(x, f(x))$.

Example 2. Consider the theory $T = \langle \mathcal{F}, \mathcal{D}, \mathcal{C} \rangle$ such that $\mathcal{F} = \{f_1, f_2\}$, $\mathcal{D}_1 = \mathcal{D}_2 = \{0, 1\}$, and $\mathcal{C} = \{c_1, c_2, c_3\}$. Assume a model f that assigns classes to instances as shown in the table below.

$\mathcal{Y}$	f_1	f_2	c
x_1	0	0	c_1
x_2	0	1	c_2
x_3	1	0	c_3
x_4	1	1	c_3

The absolute explanations of x_1, x_2, x_3, x_4 are as follows:

- $g_a^{\mathcal{Y}}(x_1) = \{H_1\}$ $H_1 = \{(f_1, 0), (f_2, 0)\}$
- $g_a^{\mathcal{Y}}(x_2) = \{H_2\}$ $H_2 = \{(f_1, 0), (f_2, 1)\}$
- $g_a^{\mathcal{Y}}(x_3) = \{H_3\}$ $H_3 = \{(f_1, 1)\}$
- $g_a^{\mathcal{Y}}(x_4) = \{H_3\}$

The definition of absolute explanations requires exploring the whole feature space (see the second condition of Definition 5), which is quite difficult and maybe not feasible in practice. Consequently, functions like Anchor and LIME [11,16] generate explanations from a proper subset of the feature space. They focus on the closest instances of the instance to be explained. In what follows, we define an explanation function whose outcomes are called *plausible*. It somehow generalises and improves Anchor and LIME since it also provides abductive explanations, but those that are minimal (for set inclusion). Minimality of an explanation is important since it discards irrelevant information from being part of the explanation. This condition is violated by Anchors and LIME.

Definition 6. *Let* g_p *be an explanation function of a classification model* f *applied to theory* $\mathcal{T} = \langle \mathcal{F}, \mathcal{D}, \mathcal{C} \rangle$ *s.t. for* $\mathcal{Y} \subseteq \mathcal{X}$, *and* $x \in \mathcal{Y}$, $H \in g_p^{\mathcal{Y}}(x)$ *iff:*

- $H \subseteq x$
- $\forall y \in \mathcal{Y}$ *s.t.* $H \subseteq y$, $f(y) = f(x)$
- $\nexists H' \subset H$ *such that* H' *satisfies the above conditions.*

H *is called* plausible abductive explanation *of* x.

Note that the function g_p can be applied to different subsets of $\mathcal{X}$, and as we will see later the results may not be the same.

Example 1 (Cont.). Consider the following sets:

- $U_1 = \{(V, 0)\}$
- $U_2 = \{(M, 1)\}$
- $U_3 = \{(C, 1), (E, 0)\}$
- $U_4 = \{(V, 1)\}$
- $U_5 = \{(M, 0)\}$

It can be checked that:

- $g_p^{\mathcal{Y}}(x_1) = \{U_1, U_2\}$
- $g_p^{\mathcal{Y}}(x_5) = \{U_1, U_2, U_3\}$
- $g_p^{\mathcal{Y}}(x_2) = g_p^{\mathcal{Y}}(x_4) = g_p^{\mathcal{Y}}(x_7) = \{U_4, U_5\}$

Every (absolute, plausible) abductive explanation is consistent. Furthermore, an instance may have one or several (absolute, plausible) abductive explanations.

Proposition 1. *Let* $\mathcal{T} = \langle \mathcal{F}, \mathcal{D}, \mathcal{C} \rangle$ *be a theory,* $\mathcal{Y} \subseteq \mathcal{X}$ *and* $x \in \mathcal{Y}$.

- *Every (absolute, plausible) abductive explanation of* x *is consistent.*
- *If* $\mathcal{Y} = \mathcal{X}$, *then* $g_a^{\mathcal{Y}}(x) = g_p^{\mathcal{Y}}(x)$
- $g_a^{\mathcal{Y}}(x) \neq \emptyset$ *and* $g_p^{\mathcal{Y}}(x) \neq \emptyset$
- $g_p^{\mathcal{Y}}(x) = \{\emptyset\}$ *iff* $\forall y \in \mathcal{Y} \setminus \{x\}$, $f(y) = f(x)$.

Proof. An (absolute, plausible) explanation is a part of an instance. Every instance is consistent, then its subparts are all consistent. The second property is straightforward. Let us show the third property. Since x is consistent, then $\exists H \subseteq x$ such that H is minimal (for set inclusion) such that $\forall y \in \mathcal{Y}$ s.t. $H \subseteq y$, $f(y) = f(x)$. The last property is straightforward.

4   Properties of Explanation Functions

We discuss below two formal properties of explanation functions. Such properties are important for assessing the quality of an explanation function and for comparing pairs of functions. The first property ensures *coherence* of the set of explanations provided by a function. More precisely, it states that a set of literals cannot cause two distinct predictions. Let us illustrate the idea with Example 1.

Example 1 (Cont.). Recall that $\{(V,0)\} \in g_p^{\mathcal{Y}}(x_1)$ and $\{(M,0)\} \in g_p^{\mathcal{Y}}(x_2)$. Note that the set $\{(V,0),(M,0)\}$ is consistent, then there exists an instance $y \in \mathcal{X} \setminus \mathcal{Y}$ such that $\{(V,0),(M,0)\} \subseteq y$. By definition of an abductive explanation, $f(y) = c_0$ (due to $\{(V,0)\}$) and $f(y) = c_1$ (due to $\{(M,0)\}$) which is impossible since every instance has one class. This example shows that the function g_p is not coherent even locally, i.e. when working with $\mathcal{Y} \subset \mathcal{X}$.

Below is a formal definition of the notion of coherence of an explanation function.

Definition 7 (Coherence). *An explanation function* g *is coherent iff for any model* f, *any theory* $\mathcal{T} = \langle \mathcal{F}, \mathcal{D}, \mathcal{C} \rangle$, *any* $\mathcal{Y} \subseteq \mathcal{X}_{\mathcal{T}}$, *the following holds:*
$\forall x, x' \in \mathcal{X}_{\mathcal{T}}, \forall H \in g^{\mathcal{Y}}(x), \forall H' \in g^{\mathcal{Y}}(x')$, *if* $H \cup H'$ *is consistent, then* $f(x) = f(x')$.

We show that the absolute abductive explanation function is coherent while this property is violated by the plausible function as shown above.

Proposition 2. *The function* g_a *is coherent and* g_p *is incoherent.*

Proof. Example 1 shows a counter-example for the coherence of g_p. Let us now show that g_a is coherent. Let $x, x' \in \mathcal{X}$, $c, c' \in \mathcal{C}$ and $H \in g_a(x)$, $H' \in g_a(x')$. Assume that $H \cup H'$ is consistent. Then, $\exists z \in \mathcal{X}$ s.t. $H \cup H' \subseteq z$. By Definition 5, $f(z) = c$ (due to H) and $f(z) = c'$ (due to H'). Since (z) is unique, then $c = c'$.

Remark: As said before, Anchors and LIME explanation functions are somehow instances of g_p as they generate abductive explanations from a proper subset of the feature space. They even do not use a whole dataset but only instances that are in the neighbourhood of the instance being explained. Hence, the two functions violate coherence.

Let us now investigate another property of explanation functions, that of monotony. The idea is to check whether an instance generated from a dataset remains plausible when the dataset is expanded with new instances.

Definition 8 (Monotony). *An explanation function* g *is monotonic iff for any model* f, *any theory* $\mathcal{T} = \langle \mathcal{F}, \mathcal{D}, \mathcal{C} \rangle$, *any* $x \in \mathcal{X}_{\mathcal{T}}$, *the following property holds:*
$g^{\mathcal{Y}}(x) \subseteq g^{\mathcal{Z}}(x)$ *whenever* $\mathcal{Y} \subseteq \mathcal{Z} \subseteq \mathcal{X}_{\mathcal{T}}$. *It is non-monotonic otherwise.*

The absolute function g_a is clearly monotonic since it explores the whole feature space, thus complete information. However, the plausible function is not monotonic.

Proposition 3. *The function* $\mathbf{g}_a$ *is monotonic and* $\mathbf{g}_p$ *is non-monotonic.*

Let us illustrate the non-monotonicity of $\mathbf{g}_p$ with an example.

Example 1 (Cont.). Consider the instance x_5. Recall that $U_3 = \{(C,1),(E,0)\}$ is a plausible explanation of x_5. Assume we receive the new instance x_8 below:

$\mathcal{Y}$	V	C	M	E	H
x_8	1	1	0	0	c_1

Note that $\{(C,1),(E,0)\}$ is no longer a plausible explanation of x_5 that can generated from the set $\mathcal{Y} \cup \{x_5\}$. Indeed, the second condition of Definition 6 is not satisfied.

The above example shows that a plausible explanation of an instance is not necessarily an absolute one, while, ideally $\mathbf{g}_p$ should approximate $\mathbf{g}_a$.

Property 1. Let $\mathcal{Y} \subset \mathcal{X}_T$ and $x \in \mathcal{Y}$. $\mathbf{g}_p^{\mathcal{Y}}(x) \not\subseteq \mathbf{g}_a^{\mathcal{Y}}(x)$.

To sum up, we have shown that in practice explanations are constructed from a dataset, which is a subset of the feature space of a theory. However, due to incompleteness of information in the dataset, some explanations may be incorrect, i.e., they are not absolute. Furthermore, we have seen that the actual functions (like Anchors and LIME) that generate plausible explanations suffer from another weakness which is incoherence. The latter leads also to incorrect explanations. Thus, defining a nonmonotonic explanation function that is coherent remains a challenge in the literature. In the next section, we define such a function.

5   Argument-Based Explanation Function

Throughout this section we consider an arbitrary theory $T = \langle \mathcal{F}, \mathcal{D}, \mathcal{C} \rangle$ and a subset $\mathcal{Y} \subseteq \mathcal{X}_T$ of instances. We define a novel explanation function which is based on arguments. The latter support classes, in the sense they provide the minimal sets of literals that are causing a class. They are thus independent from instances. An advantage of not considering instances is to reduce the number of arguments that can be built. Furthermore, explanations of an instance are in explanations of its predicted class.

Definition 9. *Let* $c \in \mathcal{C}$. *An* argument in favor of c *is a pair* $\langle H, c \rangle$ *s.t.*

- $H \subseteq \mathcal{U}$
- H *is consistent*
- $\forall y \in \mathcal{Y}$ *s.t.* $H \subseteq y$, $\mathbf{f}(y) = c$
- $\nexists H' \subset H$ *that verifies the above conditions.*

H and c are called respectively support *and* conclusion *of an argument. Let* $\arg(\mathcal{Y})$ *denote the set of arguments built from* $\mathcal{Y}$.

Note that the set $\arg(\mathcal{Y})$ is finite since $\mathcal{Y}$ is finite. Furthermore, its elements are closely related to the plausible explanations of the function $\mathbf{g}_p$.

Proposition 4. *Let* $c \in \mathcal{C}$. $\langle H, c \rangle \in \arg(\mathcal{Y}) \iff \exists x \in \mathcal{Y}$ *s.t.* $H \in \mathbf{g}_p^{\mathcal{Y}}(x, c)$.

Consider the initial version of our running example, which contains seven instances.

Example 1 (Cont.). There are two classes in the theory: c_0, c_1. Their arguments are given below:

- $a_1 = \langle U_1, c_0 \rangle$ $U_1 = \{(V, 0)\}$
- $a_2 = \langle U_2, c_0 \rangle$ $U_2 = \{(M, 1)\}$
- $a_3 = \langle U_3, c_0 \rangle$ $U_3 = \{(C, 1), (E, 0)\}$
- $a_4 = \langle U_4, c_1 \rangle$ $U_4 = \{(V, 1)\}$
- $a_5 = \langle U_5, c_1 \rangle$ $U_5 = \{(M, 0)\}$

These arguments may be conflicting. This is particularly the case when they violate the coherence property, namely when their supports are consistent but their conclusions are different.

Definition 10. *Let* $\langle H, c \rangle, \langle H', c' \rangle \in \arg(\mathcal{Y})$. *We say that* $\langle H, c \rangle$ *attacks* $\langle H', c' \rangle$ *iff:*

- $H \cup H'$ *is consistent, and*
- $c \neq c'$.

Obviously, the above attack relation is symmetric.

Property 2. Let $a, b \in \arg(\mathcal{Y})$. *If* a *attacks* b, *then* b *attacks* a.

Example 1 (Cont.). The attacks between the arguments are depicted below:
Note that every argument in favor of a class attacks at least one argument in favor of the other class. This shows that the plausible explanations generated by the function $\mathbf{g}_p$ are incoherent, and cannot all be correct.

Arguments and their attack relation form an argumentation system as follows.

Definition 11. *An* argumentation system *built from* $\mathcal{Y} \subseteq \mathcal{X}$ *is a pair* $AS = \langle \arg(\mathcal{Y}), \mathcal{R} \rangle$ *where* $\mathcal{R} \subseteq \arg(\mathcal{Y}) \times \arg(\mathcal{Y})$ *such that for* $a, b \in \arg(\mathcal{Y})$, $(a, b) \in \mathcal{R}$ *iff* a *attacks* b *(in the sense of Definition 10).*

Since arguments are conflicting, they should be evaluated using a semantics. There are different types of semantics in the literature. In this paper, we consider extension-based ones that have been introduced by Dung in [20]. They compute sets of arguments that can be jointly accepted. Each set is called an extension and represents a coherent position. Since the attack relation is symmetric, then it has been shown that *stable and preferred semantics coincide with the naive,* which returns maximal (for set $\subseteq$) sets that do not contain conflicting arguments. So, we focus here on naive semantics.

Definition 12. *Let* $AS = \langle \arg(\mathcal{Y}), \mathcal{R} \rangle$ *be an argumentation system and* $\mathcal{E} \subseteq$ $\arg(\mathcal{Y})$. *The set* $\mathcal{E}$ *is a* naive extension *iff:*

- $\nexists a, b \in \mathcal{E}$ *s.t.* $(a, b) \in \mathcal{R}$, *and*
- $\nexists \mathcal{E}' \subseteq \arg(\mathcal{Y})$ *s.t.* $\mathcal{E} \subset \mathcal{E}'$ *and* $\mathcal{E}'$ *satisfies the first condition.*

Let $\sigma(AS)$ *denote the set of all naive extensions of* AS.

Example 1 (Cont.). The argumentation system has four naive extensions:

- $\mathcal{E}_1 = \{a_1, a_2, a_3\}$
- $\mathcal{E}_2 = \{a_1, a_4\}$
- $\mathcal{E}_3 = \{a_2, a_5\}$
- $\mathcal{E}_4 = \{a_4, a_5\}$

Each naive extension refers to a possible set of explanations. Note that $\mathcal{E}_1$ and E_4 promote respectively the arguments in favor of c_0 and those in favor of c_1.

We are now ready to define the new explanation function. For a given instance x, it returns the support of any argument in favour of $\mathbf{f}(x)$ that is in every naive extension and the support should be part of x. The intuition is the following: when two explanations cannot hold together (coherence being violated), both are discarded since at least one of them is incorrect. Our approach is thus very cautious.

Definition 13. *Let* $\mathbf{g}_*$ *be an explanation function of a classification model* $\mathbf{f}$ *applied to theory a* $\mathcal{T} = \langle \mathcal{F}, \mathcal{D}, \mathcal{C} \rangle$ *s.t. for* $\mathcal{Y} \subseteq \mathcal{X}_T$, *for* $x \in \mathcal{Y}$,

$$\mathbf{g}_*^{\mathcal{Y}}(x) = \{H \mid \exists \langle H, \mathbf{f}(x) \rangle \in \bigcap_{\mathcal{E}_i \in \sigma(AS)} \mathcal{E}_i \text{ and } H \subseteq x\}$$

where $AS = \langle \arg(\mathcal{Y}), \mathcal{R} \rangle$.

Example 1 (Cont.). In the example, $\bigcap_{\mathcal{E}_i \in \sigma(AS)} \mathcal{E}_i = \emptyset$. Hence, $\forall x \in \mathcal{Y}$, $\mathbf{g}_*(x, \mathbf{f}(x)) = \emptyset$.

The above example shows that this function may return an emptyset of explanations, meaning with the available information, it is not possible to generate reasonable abductive explanations. Note that generation of argument is a nonmonotonic process.

Example 2 (Cont.). Assume a set $\mathcal{Y} = \{x_1, x_2\}$. It can be checked that $\arg(\mathcal{Y}) = \{b_1, b_2\}$ where $b_1 = \{(f_2, 0)\}$ and $b_2 = \{(f_2, 1)\}$. The two arguments are not conflicting, thus $\mathcal{R} = \emptyset$ and there is a single naive extension which contains the two. Hence, $\mathbf{g}_*(x_1, c_1) = \{\{(f_2, 0)\}\}$ and $\mathbf{g}_*(x_2, c_2) = \{\{(f_2, 1)\}\}$.

We show that the new function is non-monotonic and coherent.

Proposition 5. *The function* $\mathbf{g}_*$ *is non-monotonic and coherent.*

Finally, when $\mathbf{g}_*$ is applied on the whole feature space, the attack relation of the corresponding argumentation system would be empty, and the generated explanations coincide with the absolute ones.

Proposition 6. *If* $\mathcal{Y} = \mathcal{X}$, *then* $\mathbf{g}_* = \mathbf{g}_a$.

6   Related Work

Most work on finding explanations in the ML literature is experimental, focusing on specific models, exposing their internal representations to find correlations *post hoc* between these representations and the predictions. There haven't been a lot of formal characterizations of explanations in AI, with the exception of [12], which defines abductive explanations and adversarial examples in a fragment of first order logic, and [17], who focused on semi-factuals, that they consider a specific form of counterfactuals. Both works considered binary classifiers with binary features. Furthermore, they generate explanations from the whole feature space, which in practice is not reasonable since a classification model is trained on a dataset. In our work, we focused on abductive explanations for general classifiers, and discussed two particular properties: monotony and coherence.

Unlike our work, which explains existing Black-box models, [21, 22] proposed novel classification models that are based on arguments. Their explanations are defined in dialectical way as fictitious dialogues between a proponent (supporting an output) and an opponent (attacking the output) following [20]. The authors in [23–26] followed the same approach for defining explainable multiple decision systems, recommendation systems, or scheduling systems. In the above papers an argument is simply an instance and its label while our arguments pro/con are much richer. This shows that they are proposed for different purposes.

7   Conclusion

This paper presented a preliminary investigation on functions that would explain predictions of black-box classifiers. It focused on one type of explanations, those that identify the key features that caused predictions. Such explanations are popular in the XAI literature, however there are a few formal attempts at formalizing them and investigating their properties. Existing definitions consider the whole feature space, and this is not reasonable in practice.

In this paper, we argue that generating explanations consists of reasoning under incomplete information, and reasonable functions are thus nonmonotonic. We have shown that existing (nonmonotonic) functions like Anchors and LIME may return incoherent results, which means incorrect explanations. Finally, we provided the first function that satisfies coherence while generating explanations from datasets. The function is based on a well-known nonmonotonic reasoning (NMR) approach, which is argumentation. This makes thus a connection between XAI and NMR.

This work can be extended in different ways. First, we have seen that the novel function g^* may return an emptyset for an instance. While cautious reasoning is suitable when dealing with conflicting information by NMR models, it may be a great weakness in XAI since a user would always expect an explanation for the outcome provided by a classifier. Hence, a future work consists of exploring other functions that guarantee outputs. Another line of research consists of using weighted semantics for evaluating arguments. Such semantics would then lead to weighted explanations.

Acknowledgements. Support from the ANR-3IA Artificial and Natural Intelligence Toulouse Institute is gratefully acknowledged.

References

1. Biran, O., Cotton, C.: Explanation and justification in machine learning: a survey. In: IJCAI Workshop on Explainable Artificial Intelligence (XAI), pp. 1–6 (2017)
2. Guidotti, R., Monreale, A., Ruggieri, S., Turini, F., Giannotti, F., Pedreschi, D.: A survey of methods for explaining black box models. ACM Comput. Surv. **51**(5), 93:1-93:42 (2019)
3. Miller, T.: Explanation in artificial intelligence: insights from the social sciences. Artif. Intell. **267**, 1–38 (2019)
4. Ignatiev, A., Narodytska, N., Marques-Silva, J.: Abduction-based explanations for machine learning models. In: The Thirty-Third Conference on Artificial Intelligence, pp. 1511–1519. AAAI (2019)
5. Wachter, S., Mittelstadt, B.D., Russell, C.: Counterfactual explanations without opening the black box: automated decisions and the GDPR. CoRR abs/1711.00399 (2017)
6. Eiband, M., Schneider, H., Bilandzic, M., Fazekas-Con, J., Haug, M., Hussmann, H.: Bringing transparency design into practice. In: Proceedings of the 24th International Conference on Intelligent User Interfaces IU I, pp. 211–223 (2018)
7. Biran, O., McKeown, K.R.: Human-centric justification of machine learning predictions. In: Proceedings of the Twenty-Sixth International Joint Conference on Artificial Intelligence, pp. 1461–1467. IJCAI (2017)
8. Luss, R., Chen, P., Dhurandhar, A., Sattigeri, P., Shanmugam, K., Tu, C.: Generating contrastive explanations with monotonic attribute functions. CoRR (2019)
9. Dhurandhar, A., et al.: Explanations based on the missing: towards contrastive explanations with pertinent negatives. In: Annual Conference on Neural Information Processing Systems, NeurIPS, pp. 590–601 (2018)
10. Mittelstadt, B., Russell, C., Wachter, S.: Explaining explanations in AI. In: Proceedings of the Conference on Fairness, Accountability, and Transparency, pp. 279–288 (2019)
11. Ribeiro, M.T., Singh, S., Guestrin, C.: Anchors: high-precision model-agnostic explanations. In: Proceedings of the Thirty-Second AAAI Conference on Artificial Intelligence, (AAAI 2018), pp. 1527–1535 (2018)
12. Ignatiev, A., Narodytska, N., Marques-Silva, J.: On relating explanations and adversarial examples. In: Thirty-Third Conference on Neural Information Processing Systems, NeurIPS, pp. 15857–15867 (2019)
13. Byrne, R.: Semifactual "even if" thinking. Thinking Reasoning **8**(1), 41–67 (2002)
14. Szegedy, C., et al.: Intriguing properties of neural networks. In: 2nd International Conference on Learning Representations, ICLR (2014)
15. Cai, C.J., Jongejan, J., Holbrook, J.: The effects of example-based explanations in a machine learning interface. In: Proceedings of the 24th International Conference on Intelligent User Interfaces IUI, pp. 258–262 (2019)
16. Ribeiro, M.T., Singh, S., Guestrin, C.: Why should I trust you?: explaining the predictions of any classifier. In: Proceedings of the 22nd ACM SIGKDD International Conference on Knowledge Discovery and Data Mining, pp. 1135–1144 (2016)
17. Darwiche, A., Hirth, A.: On the reasons behind decisions. In: 24th European Conference on Artificial Intelligence ECAI, vol. 325, pp. 712–720. IOS Press (2020)

18. Dimopoulos, Y., Dzeroski, S., Kakas, A.: Integrating explanatory and descriptive learning in ILP. In: Proceedings of the Fifteenth International Joint Conference on Artificial Intelligence, IJCAI, pp. 900–907 (1997)
19. Kakas, A., Riguzzi, F.: Abductive concept learning. New Gener. Comput. **18**(3), 243–294 (2000)
20. Dung, P.M.: On the acceptability of arguments and its fundamental role in nonmonotonic reasoning, logic programming and n-person games. Artif. Intell. **77**, 321–357 (1995)
21. Amgoud, L., Serrurier, M.: Agents that argue and explain classifications. Auton. Agent. Multi-Agent Syst. **16**(2), 187–209 (2008)
22. Cocarascu, O., Stylianou, A., Cyras, K., Toni, F.: Data-empowered argumentation for dialectically explainable predictions. In: 24th European Conference on Artificial Intelligence ECAI, vol. 325, pp. 2449–2456. IOS Press (2020)
23. Zhong, Q., Fan, X., Luo, X., Toni, F.: An explainable multi-attribute decision model based on argumentation. Expert Syst. Appl. **117**, 42–61 (2019)
24. Cyras, K., et al.: Explanations by arbitrated argumentative dispute. Expert Syst. Appl. **127**, 141–156 (2019)
25. Cyras, K., Letsios, D., Misener, R., Toni, F.: Argumentation for explainable scheduling. In: The Thirty-Third Conference on Artificial Intelligence, pp. 2752–2759. AAAI (2019)
26. Rago, A., Cocarascu, O., Toni, F.: Argumentation-based recommendations: fantastic explanations and how to find them. In: Proceedings of the Twenty-Seventh International Joint Conference on Artificial Intelligence, IJCAI, pp. 1949–1955 (2018)

Similarity Measures Based on Compiled Arguments

Leila Amgoud[1] and Victor David[2(✉)]

[1] CNRS – IRIT, Toulouse, France
leila.amgoud@irit.fr
[2] Paul Sabatier University – IRIT, Toulouse, France
victor.david@irit.fr

Abstract. Argumentation is a prominent approach for reasoning with inconsistent information. It is based on the justification of formulas by arguments generated from propositional knowledge bases. It has recently been shown that similarity between arguments should be taken into account when evaluating arguments. Consequently, different similarity measures have been proposed in the literature. Although these measures satisfy desirable properties, they suffer from the side effects of being syntax-dependent. Indeed, they may miss redundant information, leading to undervalued similarity. This paper overcomes this shortcoming by compiling arguments, which amounts to transforming their formulas into clauses, and using the latter for extending existing measures and principles. We show that the new measures deal properly with the critical cases.

1 Introduction

Argumentation is a reasoning process based on the justification of claims by *arguments*, i.e., reasons for accepting claims. It has been extensively developed in Artificial Intelligence. Indeed, it was used for different purposes including decision making (e.g. [1,2]), defeasible reasoning (e.g. [3,4]), and negotiation [5,6].

Argumentation is also used as an alternative approach for handling inconsistency in knowledge bases [7–9]. Starting from a knowledge base encoded in propositional logic, arguments are built using the consequence operator of the logic. An argument is a pair made of a set of formulas (called support) and a single formula (called conclusion). The conclusion follows logically from the support. Examples of arguments are $A = \langle \{p \wedge q \wedge r\}, p \wedge q \rangle$, $B = \langle \{p \wedge q\}, p \wedge q \rangle$ and $C = \langle \{p, q\}, p \wedge q \rangle$. Once arguments are defined, attacks between them are identified and a semantics is used for evaluating the arguments, finally formulas supported by strong arguments are inferred from the base.

Some semantics, like h-Categorizer [7], satisfy the Counting (or Strict Monotony) principle defined in [10]. This principle states that each attacker of an argument contributes to weakening the argument. For instance, if the

© Springer Nature Switzerland AG 2021
J. Vejnarová and N. Wilson (Eds.): ECSQARU 2021, LNAI 12897, pp. 32–44, 2021.
https://doi.org/10.1007/978-3-030-86772-0_3

argument $D = \langle\{\neg p \vee \neg q\}, \neg p \vee \neg q\rangle$ is attacked by A, B, C, then each of the three arguments will decrease the strength of D. However, the three attackers are somehow similar, thus D will lose more than necessary. Consequently, the authors in [11] have motivated the need for investigating the notion of similarity between pairs of such logical arguments. They introduced a set of principles that a reasonable similarity measure should satisfy, and provided several measures that satisfy them. In [12–14] several extensions of h-Categorizer that take into account similarities between arguments have been proposed.

While the measures from [11] return reasonable results in most cases, it was shown in [15], that they may lead to inaccurate assessments if arguments are not *concise*. An arguments is concise if its support contains only information that is useful for inferring its conclusion. For instance, the argument A is not concise since its support $\{p \wedge q \wedge r\}$ contains r, which is useless for the conclusion $p \wedge q$. The similarity measures from [11] declare the two arguments A and B as not fully similar while they support the same conclusion on the same grounds ($p \wedge q$). Consequently, both A and B will have an impact on D using h-Categorizer. In [15], such arguments are cleaned up from any useless information by generating the concise versions of each argument, the measures from [11] are applied on concise arguments. However, these works fail to detect the full similarity between the two concise arguments B and C. In this paper, we solve the above issue by compiling arguments. The idea is to transform every formula in an argument's support into clauses. We extend the Jaccard-based similarity measures from [11] and show that new versions improve accuracy of similarity.

The article is organised as follows: Sect. 2 recalls the notions of logical argument and similarity measure. Section 3 introduces compilation of arguments. Section 4 extends some measures of similarity. Section 5 extends and propose new principles for similarity measures, and the last Sect. 6 concludes.

2   Background

2.1   Logical Concepts

Throughout the paper, we consider classical propositional logic $(\mathcal{L}, \vdash)$, where $\mathcal{L}$ is a propositional language built up from a *finite* set $\mathcal{P}$ of variables, the two Boolean constants $\top$ (true) and $\bot$ (false), and the usual connectives ($\neg$, $\vee$, $\wedge$, $\rightarrow$, $\leftrightarrow$), and $\vdash$ is the consequence relation of the logic. A literal is either a variable or the negation of a variable of $\mathcal{P}$, the set of all literals is denoted $\mathcal{P}^{\pm}$. Two formulas $\phi, \psi \in \mathcal{L}$ are *logically equivalent*, denoted by $\phi \equiv \psi$, iff $\phi \vdash \psi$ and $\psi \vdash \phi$.

A formula ϕ is in negation normal form (NNF) if and only if it does not contain implication or equivalence symbols, and every negation symbol occurs directly in front of an atom. Following [16], we slightly abuse words and denote by $\text{NNF}(\phi)$ the formula in NNF obtained from ϕ by "pushing down" every occurrence of $\neg$ (using De Morgan's law) and eliminating double negations. For instance, $\text{NNF}(\neg((p \rightarrow q) \vee \neg t)) = p \wedge \neg q \wedge t$.

Let $\phi \in \mathcal{L}$, ϕ is in a conjunctive normal form (CNF) if is a conjunction of clauses $\bigwedge_i c_i$ where each clause c_i is a disjunction of literals $\bigvee_j l_j$. For instance $p \wedge (q \vee t)$ is in a CNF while $(p \wedge q) \vee t$ is not.

We denote by $\mathtt{Lit}(\phi)$ the set of literals occurring in $\mathtt{NNF}(\phi)$, hence $\mathtt{Lit}(\neg((p \to q) \vee \neg t)) = \{p, \neg q, t\}$. The function $\mathtt{Var}(\phi)$ returns all the variables occurring in the formula ϕ (e.g., $\mathtt{Var}(p \wedge \neg q \wedge t) = \{p, q, t\}$).

A finite subset Φ of $\mathcal{L}$, denoted by $\Phi \subseteq_f \mathcal{L}$, is *consistent* iff $\Phi \nvdash \bot$, it is *inconsistent* otherwise. Let us now define when two finite sets Φ and Ψ of formulas are equivalent. A natural definition is when the two sets have the same logical consequences, i.e., $\{\phi \in \mathcal{L} \,|\, \Phi \vdash \phi\} = \{\psi \in \mathcal{L} \,|\, \Psi \vdash \psi\}$. Thus, the three sets $\{p, q\}$, $\{p \wedge p, \neg\neg q\}$, and $\{p \wedge q\}$ are pairwise equivalent. This definition is strong since it considers any inconsistent sets as equivalent. For instance, $\{p, \neg p\}$ and $\{q, \neg q\}$ are equivalent even if the *contents* (i.e. meaning of variables and formulas) of the two sets are unrelated (assume that p and q stand respectively for "bird" and "fly"). Furthermore, it considers the two sets $\{p, p \to q\}$ and $\{q, q \to p\}$ as equivalent while their contents are different as well. Clearly, the two rules "birds fly" and "everything that flies is a bird" express different information. Thus, the two sets $\{p, p \to q\}$ and $\{q, q \to p\}$ should be considered as different. Thus, in what follows we consider the following definition borrowed from [17]. It compares formulas contained in sets instead of logical consequences of the sets.

Definition 1 (Equivalent Sets of Formulas). *Two sets of formulas* $\Phi, \Psi \subseteq_f \mathcal{L}$ *are* equivalent, *denoted by* $\Phi \cong \Psi$, *iff there is a bijection* $f : \Phi \to \Psi$ *s.t.* $\forall \phi \in \Phi$, $\phi \equiv f(\phi)$.

Example 1. $\{p, p \to q\} \ncong \{q, q \to p\}$, $\{p, \neg p\} \ncong \{q, \neg q\}$, $\{p, q\} \ncong \{p \wedge q\}$ while $\{p, q\} \cong \{p \wedge p, \neg\neg q\}$.

Let us define the notion of *argument* as in [7].

Definition 2 (Argument). *An* argument *built under the logic* $(\mathcal{L}, \vdash)$ *is a pair* $\langle \Phi, \phi \rangle$, *where* $\Phi \subseteq_f \mathcal{L}$ *and* $\phi \in \mathcal{L}$, *such that:*

- Φ *is consistent,*   (Consistency)
- $\Phi \vdash \phi$,   (Validity)
- $\nexists \Phi' \subset \Phi$ *such that* $\Phi' \vdash \phi$.   (Minimality)

An argument $\langle \Phi, \phi \rangle$ *is* trivial *iff* $\Phi = \emptyset$ *and* $\phi \equiv \top$.

Example 2. The three pairs $A = \langle \{p \wedge q \wedge r\}, p \wedge q \rangle$, $B = \langle \{p \wedge q\}, p \wedge q \rangle$ and $C = \langle \{p, q\}, p \wedge q \rangle$ are arguments.

Notations: $\mathtt{Arg}(\mathcal{L})$ denotes the set of all arguments that can be built in $(\mathcal{L}, \vdash)$. For any $A = \langle \Phi, \phi \rangle \in \mathtt{Arg}(\mathcal{L})$, the functions $\mathtt{Supp}$ and $\mathtt{Conc}$ return respectively the *support* ($\mathtt{Supp}(A) = \Phi$) and the *conclusion* ($\mathtt{Conc}(A) = \phi$) of A.

Note that the argument A in the above example is not concise since r is irrelevant for the argument's conclusion. In [15], the concise versions of arguments are computed using the following technique of *refinement*.

Definition 3 (Refinement). *Let $A, B \in \mathtt{Arg}(\mathcal{L})$ s.t. $A = \langle\{\phi_1, \ldots, \phi_n\}, \phi\rangle$, $B = \langle\{\phi'_1, \ldots, \phi'_n\}, \phi'\rangle$. B is a refinement of A iff:*

1. $\phi = \phi'$,
2. There exists a permutation ρ of the set $\{1, \ldots, n\}$ such that $\forall k \in \{1, \ldots, n\}$, $\phi_k \vdash \phi'_{\rho(k)}$ and $\mathtt{Lit}(\phi'_{\rho(k)}) \subseteq \mathtt{Lit}(\phi_k)$.

Let $\mathtt{Ref}$ *be a function that returns the set of all refinements of a given argument.*

Compared to the definition in [15], we extended the second constraint so that literals of $\phi'_{\rho(k)}$ are also literals of ϕ_k. The reason is that we would like the arguments $\langle\{p \wedge (p \vee q)\}, p \vee q\rangle$ and $\langle\{(p \vee \neg q) \wedge (p \vee q)\}, p \vee q\rangle$ can be refined into $\langle\{p \vee q\}, p \vee q\rangle$ while this was not possible in the original definition.

It is worth mentioning that an argument may have several refinements as shown in the following example.

Example 2 (Continued). The following sets are subset of refinement of these arguments.

- $\{\langle\{p \wedge q \wedge r\}, p \wedge q\rangle, \langle\{p \wedge q \wedge (p \vee q)\}, p \wedge q\rangle, \langle\{p \wedge q\}, p \wedge q\rangle\} \subseteq \mathtt{Ref}(A)$
- $\{\langle\{p \wedge q\}, p \wedge q\rangle, \langle\{p \wedge \neg\neg q\}, p \wedge q\rangle\} \subseteq \mathtt{Ref}(B)$
- $\{\langle\{p, q\}, p \wedge q\rangle, \langle\{(p \vee p) \wedge q\}, p \wedge q\rangle\} \subseteq \mathtt{Ref}(C)$

Every argument is a refinement of itself.

Proposition 1. *For any argument $A \in \mathtt{Arg}(\mathcal{L})$, $A \in \mathtt{Ref}(A)$.*

2.2 Similarity Measures

In [11], various measures have been proposed for assessing similarity between pairs of logical arguments. They extended existing measures which compare sets of objects including Jaccard measure [18]. Due to space limitation, in this paper we will focus only on the latter.

Definition 4 (Jaccard Measure). *Let X, Y be arbitrary sets of objects. If $X \neq \emptyset$ or $Y \neq \emptyset$, then*[1]

$$s_{\mathtt{jac}}(X, Y) = \frac{|X \cap Y|}{|X \cup Y|}$$

If $X = Y = \emptyset$, then $s_{\mathtt{jac}}(X, Y) = 1$.

We recall below how the above measure is used in [11] for logical arguments.

Definition 5 (Jaccard Similarity Measure). *Let $0 < \sigma < 1$. We define* $\mathtt{sim}^{\sigma}_{\mathtt{jac}}$ *as a function assigning to any pair $(A, B) \in \mathtt{Arg}(\mathcal{L}) \times \mathtt{Arg}(\mathcal{L})$ a value* $\mathtt{sim}^{\sigma}_{\mathtt{jac}}(A, B) =$

$$\sigma.s_{\mathtt{jac}}(\mathtt{Supp}(A), \mathtt{Supp}(B)) + (1 - \sigma)s_{\mathtt{jac}}(\{\mathtt{Conc}(A)\}, \{\mathtt{Conc}(B)\}).$$

Example 2 (Continued). $\mathtt{sim}^{0.5}_{\mathtt{jac}}(A, B) = \mathtt{sim}^{0.5}_{\mathtt{jac}}(A, C) = \mathtt{sim}^{0.5}_{\mathtt{jac}}(B, C) = 0.5 \cdot 0 + 0.5 \cdot 1 = 0.5$.

---

[1] $^3\|$ stands for the cardinality of a set.

3   Compilation of Arguments

Recall that $\{p, q\} \not\equiv \{p \wedge q\}$ while the two sets contain the same information. For getting them equivalent, we transform every formula into a CNF, then we split it into a set containing its clauses. Note that it is well known (e.g. [19]) that any formula can be transformed into equivalent CNFs using the same literals. In our approach, we consider one CNF per formula. For that purpose, we will use a finite sub-language $\mathcal{F}$ that contains one formula per equivalent class and the formula should be in a CNF.

Definition 6 (Finite CNF language $\mathcal{F}$). *Let $\mathcal{F} \subset_f \mathcal{L}$ such that $\forall \phi \in \mathcal{L}$, there exists a unique $\psi \in \mathcal{F}$ such that:*

- *$\phi \equiv \psi$,*
- *$\mathtt{Lit}(\phi) = \mathtt{Lit}(\psi)$,*
- *ψ is in a CNF.*

Let $\mathtt{CNF}(\phi) = \psi$.

While we do not specify the elements of $\mathcal{F}$, we use concrete formulas in the examples, and they are assumed to belong to $\mathcal{F}$.

Notation: For $\Phi \subseteq_f \mathcal{L}$, $\mathtt{UC}(\Phi) = \bigcup_{\phi \in \mathtt{CNF}(\Phi)} \bigcup_{\delta \text{ clause } \in \phi} \delta$.

Let us now introduce the notion of compiled argument.

Definition 7 (Compiled Argument).   *The compilation of $A \in \mathtt{Arg}(\mathcal{L})$ is $A^* = \langle \mathtt{UC}(\mathtt{Supp}(A)), \mathtt{Conc}(A) \rangle$.*

Example 2 (Continued). The compilations of the three arguments A, B, C are:

- $A^* = \langle \{p, q, r\}, p \wedge q \rangle$,
- $B^* = \langle \{p, q\}, p \wedge q \rangle$,
- $C^* = \langle \{p, q\}, p \wedge q \rangle$.

Note that the compilation of an argument is not necessarily an element of $\mathtt{Arg}(\mathcal{L})$ as it may violate the minimality condition. For instance, we can see that $A^* \notin \mathtt{Arg}(\mathcal{L})$ since the set $\{p, q, r\}$ is not minimal.

To solve this problem of non-minimal compiled arguments, we will extend the notion of concise argument (from [15]) while fixing the syntax-dependency issue. To define what a concise argument is, we first need to introduce what equivalent arguments are.

Thanks to the use of the language $\mathcal{F}$ in the compiled arguments, any equivalent formulas using the same literals have an identical syntax. Using this feature, we define that arguments are equivalent when they have identical compiled supports and conclusions.

Definition 8 (Equivalent Arguments). *Two arguments $A, B \in \text{Arg}(\mathcal{L})$ are equivalent, denoted by $A \approx B$, iff*

$$\text{UC}(\text{Supp}(A)) = \text{UC}(\text{Supp}(B)) \ and \ \text{UC}(\{\text{Conc}(A)\}) = \text{UC}(\{\text{Conc}(B)\}).$$

We denote by $A \not\approx B$ when A and B are not equivalent.

Example 2 (Continued). $B \approx C$ while $A \not\approx B$ and $A \not\approx C$.

Note that arguments having the same compilation of their supports may not be equivalent. This is for instance the case of the two arguments D and E such that $D = \langle \{(p \vee q) \wedge (p \vee \neg q)\}, (p \vee q) \wedge (p \vee \neg q) \rangle$ and $E = \langle \{(p \vee q) \wedge (p \vee \neg q)\}, p \rangle$. Clearly, $D \not\approx E$.

We show that trivial arguments are not equivalent. For instance $\langle \emptyset, p \vee \neg p \rangle \not\approx \langle \emptyset, q \vee \neg q \rangle$ because $\{p \vee \neg p\} \neq \{q \vee \neg q\}$.

Proposition 2. *Trivial arguments are pairwise non equivalent.*

The objective of the notion of concise arguments is to produce the set of compiled arguments that satisfy the Definition 2. To do this, we observed that any non-equivalent refined argument A', of a compiled argument $A^* \in \text{Arg}(\mathcal{L})$, produces a new clause by inference between several clauses of the same formula.

Proposition 3. *Let $A \in \text{Arg}(\mathcal{L})$. If $A' \in \text{Ref}(A)$, $A' \not\approx A$ and $A^* \in \text{Arg}(\mathcal{L})$ then $\exists \delta' \in \text{UC}(\text{Supp}(A'))$ such that $\forall \delta \in \text{UC}(\text{Supp}(A))$, $\delta \neq \delta'$.*

Let us define a concise argument.

Definition 9 (Conciseness). *An argument $A \in \text{Arg}(\mathcal{L})$ is* concise *iff for all $B \in \text{Ref}(A)$ such that:*

- *$B^* \in \text{Arg}(\mathcal{L})$ and,*
- *$\forall \delta \in \text{UC}(B)$, $\exists \delta' \in \text{UC}(A)$ s.t. $\delta = \delta'$,*

we have $A \approx B$.

Let $\text{CR}(A)$ denote the set of all A' concise refinements of A such that $\text{UC}(\text{Supp}(A')) \subseteq \text{UC}(\text{Supp}(A))$.

The first constraint ensures that argument A does not have unnecessary information (clause) to infer its conclusion. The second constraint prevents argument A from being compared with arguments that have created new information (clause) in their support.

Example 2 (Continued). The following sets are subset of concise refinements of the arguments A, B, C:

- $\{\langle \{p \wedge q\}, p \wedge q \rangle, \langle \{p \wedge p \wedge q\}, p \wedge q \rangle\} \subset \text{CR}(A)$
- $\{\langle \{p \wedge q\}, p \wedge q \rangle, \langle \{p \wedge q \wedge q\}, p \wedge q \rangle\} \subset \text{CR}(B)$
- $\{\langle \{p, q\}, p \wedge q \rangle, \langle \{p \wedge p, q \wedge q\}, p \wedge q \rangle\} \subset \text{CR}(C)$

The non trivial argument have an infinite set of concise refinements.

Proposition 4. *Let $A \in \text{Arg}(\mathcal{L})$, if A is not trivial then $|\text{CR}(A)| = \infty$.*

A trivial argument have only one concise refinement, itself.

Proposition 5. *Let a trivial argument $A \in \text{Arg}(\mathcal{L})$, $\text{CR}(A) = \{A\}$.*

We show in the following theorem that the notion of a concise argument is equivalent to that of a compiled argument satisfying the conditions of the Definition 2.

Theorem 1. *For any $A \in \text{Arg}(\mathcal{L})$, A is concise iff $A^* \in \text{Arg}(\mathcal{L})$.*

When two arguments are equivalent they have equivalent concise refinements. In the same way that we define a set of equivalent formulae (Definition 1), we may define a set of equivalent arguments.

Definition 10 (Equivalent sets of Arguments). *Two sets of arguments $\Omega_A, \Omega_B \subseteq_f \text{Arg}(\mathcal{L})$, are equivalent, denoted by $\Omega_A \cong_{arg} \Omega_B$, iff there is a bijection $f : \Omega_A \rightarrow \Omega_B$ s.t. $\forall A' \in \Omega_A$, $A' \approx f(A')$. Otherwise Ω_A and Ω_B are not equivalent, denoted by $\Omega_A \ncong_{arg} \Omega_B$.*

Equivalent arguments have equivalent concise refinements.

Proposition 6. *Let $A, B \in \text{Arg}(\mathcal{L})$, if $A \approx B$ then $\text{CR}(A) \cong_{arg} \text{CR}(B)$.*

Example 2 (Continued). $B \approx C$ and $\text{CR}(B) \cong_{arg} \text{CR}(C)$.
We can also see in this example that there are non-equivalent arguments with equivalent concise refinements: $A \napprox B$ and $\text{CR}(A) \cong_{arg} \text{CR}(B)$. This is because the equivalent arguments take into account irrelevant information.

Finally, note that when a compiled argument is not minimal, this may be due to the presence of unnecessary literals in the support which will be removed in the concise arguments; or because the argument is complex, i.e. it has different reasonings to conclude, which will produce different concise arguments.

Example 2 (Continued). Let $A = \langle \{p \wedge q \wedge r\}, p \wedge q \rangle, F = \langle \{p \wedge q, (p \rightarrow r) \wedge (q \rightarrow r)\}, r \rangle \in \text{Arg}(\mathcal{L})$.
The compiled argument of A and F are:

- $A^* = \langle \{p, q, r\}, p \wedge q \rangle$, and
- $F^* = \langle \{p, q, p \rightarrow r, q \rightarrow r\}, r \rangle$.

Clearly, r is irrelevant in A^* and F^* may infer r according to p or q. We may see in the concise versions of the arguments A and F that unnecessary information is removed and complex information is separated to have minimal arguments:

- $\{\langle \{p \wedge q\}, p \wedge q \rangle\} \subset \text{CR}(A)$, and
- $\{\langle \{p, p \rightarrow r\}, r \rangle, \langle \{q, q \rightarrow r\}, r \rangle\} \subset \text{CR}(F)$.

4   Extended Similarity Measures

We are ready now to introduce the new extended similarity measures.

First, we propose to apply similarity measure between set of objects on compiled supports and conclusions.

Definition 11 (Extended Jaccard Similarity Measure). *Let $0 < \sigma < 1$. We define* $\mathtt{sim}^{\sigma}_{\mathtt{jac*}}$ *as a function assigning to any pair* $(A, B) \in \mathtt{Arg}(\mathcal{L}) \times \mathtt{Arg}(\mathcal{L})$ *a value* $\mathtt{sim}^{\sigma}_{\mathtt{jac*}}(A, B) =$

$$\sigma.s_{\mathtt{jac}}(\mathtt{UC}(\mathtt{Supp}(A)), \mathtt{UC}(\mathtt{Supp}(B))) + (1 - \sigma)s_{\mathtt{jac}}(\mathtt{UC}(\mathtt{Conc}(A)), \mathtt{UC}(\mathtt{Conc}(B))).$$

Example 2 (Continued).

- $\mathtt{sim}^{0.5}_{\mathtt{jac*}}(A, B) = \mathtt{sim}^{0.5}_{\mathtt{jac*}}(A, C) = 0.5 \cdot \frac{2}{3} + 0.5 \cdot 1 = \frac{5}{6} = 0.833$.
- $\mathtt{sim}^{0.5}_{\mathtt{jac*}}(B, C) = 0.5 \cdot 1 + 0.5 \cdot 1 = 1$.

As we can see, working only with the compilation of arguments is not sufficient to assess degrees of similarity. It is also necessary to eliminate irrelevant information. In the following we propose to extend the two family from [15] dealing with concise refinements of an argument.

Definition 12 (Finite Conciseness). *Let $A \in \mathtt{Arg}(\mathcal{L})$. We define the set*

$$\overline{\mathtt{CR}}(A) = \{B \in \mathtt{CR}(A) \mid \mathtt{Supp}(B) \subset \mathcal{F}\}.$$

In this way, we obtain a finite set of non-equivalent concise refinements.

Proposition 7. *For every $A \in \mathtt{Arg}(\mathcal{L})$, the set $\overline{\mathtt{CR}}(A)$ is finite.*

We may now extend the two families of similarity measures (from [15]), to add a syntax independent treatment.

Definition 13 (A-CR Jaccard Similarity Measure). *Let $A, B \in \mathtt{Arg}(\mathcal{L})$, and let* $\mathtt{sim}^{\sigma}_{\mathtt{jac*}}$ *and* $\sigma \in]0, 1[$. *We define* A-CR *Jaccard Similarity Measure*[2] *by* $\mathtt{sim}^{A}_{\mathtt{CR}}(A, B, \mathtt{sim}^{\sigma}_{\mathtt{jac*}}) =$

$$\frac{\displaystyle\sum_{A_i \in \overline{\mathtt{CR}}(A)} \mathtt{Max}(A_i, \overline{\mathtt{CR}}(B), \mathtt{sim}^{\sigma}_{\mathtt{jac*}}) + \sum_{B_j \in \overline{\mathtt{CR}}(B)} \mathtt{Max}(B_j, \overline{\mathtt{CR}}(A), \mathtt{sim}^{\sigma)}_{\mathtt{jac*}}}{|\overline{\mathtt{CR}}(A)| + |\overline{\mathtt{CR}}(B)|}.$$

The value of A-CR Jaccard Similarity Measure always belongs to the unit interval.

Proposition 8. *Let $A, B \in \mathtt{Arg}(\mathcal{L})$, $\mathtt{sim}^{\sigma}_{\mathtt{jac*}}$ and $\sigma \in]0, 1[$. Then $\mathtt{sim}^{A}_{\mathtt{CR}}(A, B, \mathtt{sim}^{\sigma}_{\mathtt{jac*}}) \in [0, 1]$.*

---

[2] The letter A in A-CR stands for "average".

Now we define our second family of similarity measures, which is based on comparison of sets obtained by merging supports of concise refinements of arguments. For an argument $A \in \text{Arg}(\mathcal{L})$, we denote that set by

$$\text{US}(A) = \bigcup_{A' \in \overline{\text{CR}}(A)} \text{UC}(\text{Supp}(A')).$$

Definition 14 (U-CR Jaccard Similarity Measure). *Let* $A, B \in \text{Arg}(\mathcal{L})$, $0 < \sigma < 1$, *and* s_{jac}. *We define* U-CR *Jaccard Similarity Measure*[3] *by* $\text{sim}^{\text{U}}_{\text{CR}}(A, B, s_{\text{jac}}, \sigma) =$

$$\sigma \cdot s_{\text{jac}}(\text{US}(A), \text{US}(B)) + (1 - \sigma) \cdot s_{\text{jac}}(\text{UC}(\text{Conc}(A)), \text{UC}(\text{Conc}(B))).$$

More generally, using the compilations allows to be more accurate even in the supports. Given that each clause are a formula the similarity degree can increase or decrease.

Example 3. Let $A = \langle \{p \wedge q, t\}, p \wedge q \wedge t \rangle$, $B = \langle \{p \wedge q, r\}, p \wedge q \wedge r \rangle$, $C = \langle \{p \wedge q, r\}, p \wedge q \wedge r \rangle$, $D = \langle \{s \wedge t \wedge u \wedge v, r\}, s \wedge t \wedge u \wedge v \wedge r \rangle \in \text{Arg}(\mathcal{L})$ and $\sigma = 0.5$.

- $\text{sim}^{0.5}_{\text{jac}}(A, B) = 0.5 \cdot \frac{1}{3} + 0.5 \cdot 0 = \frac{1}{6} = 0.167$.
- $\text{sim}^{0.5}_{\text{jac*}}(A, B) = 0.5 \cdot \frac{2}{4} + 0.5 \cdot \frac{2}{4} = \frac{1}{2} = 0.5$.
- $\text{sim}^{0.5}_{\text{jac}}(C, D) = 0.5 \cdot \frac{1}{3} + 0.5 \cdot 0 = \frac{1}{6} = 0.167$.
- $\text{sim}^{0.5}_{\text{jac*}}(C, D) = 0.5 \cdot \frac{1}{7} + 0.5 \cdot \frac{1}{7} = \frac{1}{7} = 0.143$.

Therefore $\text{sim}^{0.5}_{\text{jac}}(A, B) \leq \text{sim}^{0.5}_{\text{jac*}}(A, B)$ and $\text{sim}^{0.5}_{\text{jac}}(C, D) \geq \text{sim}^{0.5}_{\text{jac*}}(C, D)$.

Returning to our running example (from the introduction), we see that the three arguments A, B, C are now identified as being completely similar. That is, we have dealt with both the irrelevant information problem and the syntax-dependency problem.

Example 2 (Continued). For any $\sigma \in \,]0, 1[$:

- $\text{sim}^{\text{A}}_{\text{CR}}(A, B, \text{sim}^{\sigma}_{\text{jac*}}) = \text{sim}^{\text{A}}_{\text{CR}}(A, C, \text{sim}^{\sigma}_{\text{jac*}}) = \text{sim}^{\text{A}}_{\text{CR}}(B, C, \text{sim}^{\sigma}_{\text{jac*}}) = 1$.
- $\text{sim}^{\text{U}}_{\text{CR}}(A, B, s_{\text{jac}}, \sigma) = \text{sim}^{\text{U}}_{\text{CR}}(A, C, s_{\text{jac}}, \sigma) = \text{sim}^{\text{U}}_{\text{CR}}(B, C, s_{\text{jac}}, \sigma) = 1$.

The next Theorem ensure that the two family of similarity measures (A-CR and U-CR) give the maximal degree of similarity between arguments only on arguments having equivalent concise refinements.

Theorem 2. *Let* $A, B \in \text{Arg}(\mathcal{L})$, *for any* $\sigma \in \,]0, 1[$, $\text{sim}^{\text{A}}_{\text{CR}}(A, B, \text{sim}^{\sigma}_{\text{jac*}}) = \text{sim}^{\text{U}}_{\text{CR}}(A, B, s_{\text{jac}}, \sigma) = 1$ *iff* $\text{CR}(A) \cong_{arg} \text{CR}(B)$.

From Proposition 6, we know that if $A \approx B$ then $\text{CR}(A) \cong_{arg} \text{CR}(B)$, then we can deduce the following corollary.

Corollary 1. *Let* $A, B \in \text{Arg}(\mathcal{L})$, *for any* $\sigma \in \,]0, 1[$, *if* $A \approx B$ *then* $\text{sim}^{\text{A}}_{\text{CR}}(A, B, \text{sim}^{\sigma}_{\text{jac*}}) = \text{sim}^{\text{U}}_{\text{CR}}(A, B, s_{\text{jac}}, \sigma) = 1$.

---

[3] U in U-CR stands for "union".

5   Extended Principles

The issue of syntax-dependence also exists in some principles. We propose here new principles for similarity measure between pairs of logical arguments and we extend some principles from [11].

The first new principle, called Minimality, ensures that similarity depends on the *content* of arguments. It states that if two arguments do not share any variables, then they are completely different. An example of such arguments are $\langle \{p\}, p \vee q \rangle$ and $\langle \{t\}, t \rangle$.

Principle 1 (Minimality). *A similarity measure* sim *satisfies* Minimality *iff for all* $A, B \in \text{Arg}(\mathcal{L})$, *if*

- $\displaystyle \bigcup_{\phi_i \in \text{Supp}(A)} \text{Var}(\phi_i) \cap \bigcup_{\phi_j \in \text{Supp}(B)} \text{Var}(\phi_j) = \emptyset$ *and*
- $\text{Var}(\text{Conc}(A)) \cap \text{Var}(\text{Conc}(B)) = \emptyset$,

then $\text{sim}(A, B) = 0$.

Example 4. Let $A = \langle \{p, q\}, p \wedge q \rangle, B = \langle \{r\}, r \rangle \in \text{Arg}(\mathcal{L})$. A similarity measure sim satisfying Minimality ensure that $\text{sim}(A, B) = 0$.

The second new principle consider that when two concise arguments have common information in their supports or conclusions hence they own some similarity between them.

Principle 2 (Non-Zero). *A similarity measure* sim *satisfies* Non-Zero *iff for all* $A, B, A^*, B^* \in \text{Arg}(\mathcal{L})$, *if*

- $\text{UC}(\text{Supp}(A)) \cap \text{UC}(\text{Supp}(B)) \neq \emptyset$, *or*
- $\text{UC}(\text{Conc}(A)) \cap \text{UC}(\text{Conc}(B)) \neq \emptyset$,

then $\text{sim}(A, B) > 0$.

Example 5. Let $A = \langle \{p, q\}, p \wedge q \rangle, B = \langle \{p\}, p \rangle \in \text{Arg}(\mathcal{L})$. A similarity measure sim satisfying Non-Zero ensure that $\text{sim}(A, B) > 0$.

The Maximality, Symmetry, Substitution, Syntax Independence principles defined in [11] do not need to be extend while (Strict) Monotony and (Strict) Dominance have to because they are dependent of the content.

Monotony states that similarity between two arguments is all the greater when the supports of the arguments share more formulas.

Principle 3 (Monotony – Strict Monotony). *A similarity measure* sim *satisfies* Monotony *iff for all* $A, B, C, A^*, B^*, C^* \in \text{Arg}(\mathcal{L})$, *if*

1. $\text{UC}(\text{Conc}(A)) = \text{UC}(\text{Conc}(B))$ *or* $\text{Var}(\text{UC}(\text{Conc}(A))) \cap \text{Var}(\text{UC}(\text{Conc}(C))) = \emptyset$,
2. $\text{UC}(\text{Supp}(A)) \cap \text{UC}(\text{Supp}(C)) \subseteq \text{UC}(\text{Supp}(A)) \cap \text{UC}(\text{Supp}(B))$,
3. $\text{UC}(\text{Supp}(B)) \setminus \text{UC}(\text{Supp}(A)) \subseteq \text{UC}(\text{Supp}(C)) \setminus \text{UC}(\text{Supp}(A))$,

then the following hold:

- $\text{sim}(A, B) \geq \text{sim}(A, C)$ *(Monotony)*
- *If the inclusion in condition 2 is strict or,* $\text{UC}(\text{Supp}(A)) \cap \text{UC}(\text{Supp}(C)) \neq \emptyset$ *and condition 3 is strict, then* $\text{sim}(A, B) > \text{sim}(A, C)$. *(Strict Monotony)*

This extended monotony principle works only on concise arguments (i.e. using only relevant clauses). Indeed, when an argument has irrelevant information (e.g. $\langle \{p \wedge q \wedge r\}, p \wedge q \rangle$, r is irrelevant), this distorts the measurement.

In addition, constraints 2 and 3 are more precise than the original one. By making this compilation of supports we can go deeper into the formulas for a better evaluation.

Example 6. Let $A = \langle \{p \wedge q, r\}, p \wedge q \wedge r \rangle$, $B = \langle \{p, q, s\}, p \wedge q \wedge s \rangle$, $C = \langle \{p, s, (p \wedge s) \rightarrow t\}, t \rangle \in \text{Arg}(\mathcal{L})$. Their compiled arguments are:

- $A^* = \langle \{p, q, r\}, p \wedge q \wedge r \rangle$,
- $B^* = \langle \{p, q, s\}, p \wedge q \wedge s \rangle$, and
- $C^* = \langle \{p, s, \neg p \vee \neg s \vee t\}, t \rangle$.

Thanks to the compilation of arguments, a similarity measure sim which satisfies the new principle of Strict Monotony, ensures that $\text{sim}(A, B) > \text{sim}(A, C)$.

Let us present the last principle dealing with the conclusions.

Principle 4 *[Dominance – Strict Dominance]. A similarity measure* sim *satisfies* Dominance *iff for all* $A, B, C, A^*, B^*, C^* \in \text{Arg}(\mathcal{L})$, *if*

1. $\text{UC}(\text{Supp}(B)) = \text{UC}(\text{Supp}(C))$,
2. $\text{UC}(\text{Conc}(A)) \cap \text{UC}(\text{Conc}(C)) \subseteq \text{UC}(\text{Conc}(A)) \cap \text{UC}(\text{Conc}(B))$,
3. $\text{UC}(\text{Conc}(B)) \setminus \text{UC}(\text{Conc}(A)) \subseteq \text{UC}(\text{Conc}(C)) \setminus \text{UC}(\text{Conc}(A))$,

then the following hold:

- $\text{sim}(A, B) \geq \text{sim}(A, C)$.   *(Dominance)*
- *If the inclusion in condition 2 is strict or,* $\text{UC}(\text{Conc}(A)) \cap \text{UC}(\text{Conc}(C)) \neq \emptyset$ *and condition 3 is strict, then* $\text{sim}(A, B) > \text{sim}(A, C)$. *(Strict Dominance)*

Example 7. Let $A = \langle \{p \wedge q, r\}, p \wedge q \wedge r \rangle$, $B = \langle \{p, p \rightarrow q\}, p \wedge q \rangle$, $C = \langle \{p \wedge p \rightarrow q\}, q \rangle \in \text{Arg}(\mathcal{L})$. Their compiled arguments are:

- $A^* = \langle \{p, q, r\}, p \wedge q \wedge r \rangle$,
- $B^* = \langle \{p, \neg p \vee q\}, p \wedge q \rangle$, and
- $C^* = \langle \{p, \neg p \vee q\}, q \rangle$.

Thanks to the compilation of arguments, a similarity measure sim which satisfies the new principle of Strict Dominance, ensures that $\text{sim}(A, B) > \text{sim}(A, C)$.

Theorem 3. *The three novel extended jaccard similarity measures satisfy all the principles.*

Table 1. Satisfaction of the principles of similarity measures

	$\text{sim}_{\text{jac}}^{\sigma}$	$\text{sim}_{\text{jac}*}^{\sigma}$	$\text{sim}_{\text{CR}}^{\text{A}}$	$\text{sim}_{\text{CR}}^{\text{U}}$
Minimality	•	•	•	•
Non-Zero	○	•	•	•
Monotony	○	•	•	•
Strict Monotony	○	•	•	•
Dominance	○	•	•	•
Strict Dominance	○	•	•	•

The symbol • (resp. ○) means the measure satisfies (resp. violates) the principle.

Note that the use of compilation in conclusions provides more accurate syntactic measures than in [11], as seen with the satisfaction of Strict Dominance (Table 1).

Clearly, the original Jaccard measure is syntax-dependent and violates all the principles except Minimality (because without common literals, the syntax of the content does not matter).

Finally, we may also remark that the measure (Finally, we may also remark that the measure ($\text{sim}_{\text{j}*}^{\sigma}$) not taking into account concise arguments satisfies all the principles. This is due to the fact that the compiled arguments belong to the universe of possible arguments. We made this choice because a principle is a mandatory property. Thanks to this condition we keep the application of the principles general, by basing them on $\text{sim}_{\text{j}*}^{\sigma}$) not taking into account concise arguments satisfies all the principles. This is due to the fact that the compiled arguments belong to the universe of possible arguments. We made this choice because a principle is a mandatory property. Thanks to this condition we keep the application of the principles general, by basing them on simple cases.

6   Conclusion

The paper further investigates the similarity between logical arguments. Based on the observation that existing similarity measures are syntax-dependent, they may provide inaccurate evaluations. We propose to compile the arguments in order to make the existing principles and similarity measures syntax-independent.

This work may be extended in several ways. The first is to identify a principle, or formal property, for distinguishing families of measures on concise arguments. The second is to use the new measures to refine argumentation systems that deal with inconsistent information. The third is to study the notion of similarity for other types of arguments, such as analogical arguments. The fourth is to study the usefulness of compiled arguments to produce simple and accurate explanations. Finally, we plan to study the notion of compiled arguments between other types of argument relations such as attacks and supports.

References

1. Amgoud, L., Prade, H.: Using arguments for making and explaining decisions. Artif. Intell. **173**, 413–436 (2009)
2. Zhong, Q., Fan, X., Luo, X., Toni, F.: An explainable multi-attribute decision model based on argumentation. Expert Syst. Appl. **117**, 42–61 (2019)
3. Governatori, G., Maher, M., Antoniou, G., Billington, D.: Argumentation semantics for defeasible logic. J. Log. Comput. **14**(5), 675–702 (2004)
4. García, A., Simari, G.: Defeasible logic programming: an argumentative approach. Theory Pract. Logic Program. **4**(1–2), 95–138 (2004)
5. Sycara, K.: Persuasive argumentation in negotiation. Theor. Decis. **28**, 203–242 (1990)
6. Hadidi, N., Dimopoulos, Y., Moraitis, P.: Argumentative alternating offers. In: Proceedings of the International Conference on Autonomous Agents and Multi-agent Systems (AAMAS 2010), pp. 441–448 (2010)
7. Besnard, P., Hunter, A.: A logic-based theory of deductive arguments. Artif. Intell. **128**(1–2), 203–235 (2001)
8. Amgoud, L., Besnard, P.: Logical limits of abstract argumentation frameworks. J. Appl. Non-Classical Logics **23**(3), 229–267 (2013)
9. Vesic, S.: Identifying the class of maxi-consistent operators in argumentation. J. Artif. Intell. Res. **47**, 71–93 (2013)
10. Amgoud, L., Ben-Naim, J.: Axiomatic foundations of acceptability semantics. In: Proceedings of the Fifteenth International Conference on Principles of Knowledge Representation and Reasoning KR, pp. 2–11 (2016)
11. Amgoud, L., David, V.: Measuring similarity between logical arguments. In: Proceedings of the Sixteenth International Conference on Principles of Knowledge Representation and Reasoning KR, pp. 98–107 (2018)
12. Amgoud, L., Bonzon, E., Delobelle, J., Doder, D., Konieczny, S., Maudet, N.: Gradual semantics accounting for similarity between arguments. In: Proceedings of the Sixteenth International Conference on Principles of Knowledge Representation and Reasoning KR, pp. 88–97 (2018)
13. Amgoud, L., David, V.: An adjustment function for dealing with similarities. In Prakken, H., Bistarelli, S., Santini, F., Taticchi, C., (eds.) Computational Models of Argument - Proceedings of COMMA 2020, Perugia, Italy, 4–11 September 2020. Volume 326 of Frontiers in Artificial Intelligence and Applications, pp. 79–90. IOS Press (2020)
14. Amgoud, L., David, V.: A general setting for gradual semantics dealing with similarity. In: 35th AAAI Conference en Artificial Intelligence (AAAI 2021), Virtual Conference, United States, AAAI: Association for the Advancement of Artificial Intelligence. AAAI Press, February 2021
15. Amgoud, L., David, V., Doder, D.: Similarity measures between arguments revisited. In: Kern-Isberner, G., Ognjanović, Z. (eds.) ECSQARU 2019. LNCS (LNAI), vol. 11726, pp. 3–13. Springer, Cham (2019). https://doi.org/10.1007/978-3-030-29765-7_1
16. Lang, J., Liberatore, P., Marquis, P.: Propositional independence-formula-variable independence and forgetting. J. Artif. Intell. Res. **18**, 391–443 (2003)
17. Amgoud, L., Besnard, P., Vesic, S.: Equivalence in logic-based argumentation. J. Appl. Non-Classical Logics **24**(3), 181–208 (2014)
18. Jaccard, P.: Nouvelles recherches sur la distributions florale. Bulletin de la Société Vaudoise des Sciences Naturelles **37**, 223–270 (1901)
19. Russell, S., Norvig, P.: Artificial Intelligence: A Modern Approach (1995)

Necessary and Sufficient Explanations for Argumentation-Based Conclusions

AnneMarie Borg[1]([✉]) [iD] and Floris Bex[1,2] [iD]

[1] Department of Information and Computing Sciences, Utrecht University,
Utrecht, The Netherlands
{a.borg,f.j.bex}@uu.nl
[2] Tilburg Institute for Law, Technology, and Society, Tilburg University,
Tilburg, The Netherlands

Abstract. In this paper, we discuss *necessary* and *sufficient* explanations – the question whether and why a certain argument or claim can be accepted (or not) – for abstract and structured argumentation. Given a framework with which explanations for argumentation-based conclusions can be derived, we study necessity and sufficiency: what (sets of) arguments are necessary or sufficient for the (non-)acceptance of an argument or claim? We will show that necessary and sufficient explanations can be strictly smaller than minimal explanations, while still providing all the reasons for a conclusion and we discuss their usefulness in a real-life application.

Keywords: Computational argumentation · Structured argumentation · Explainable artificial intelligence

1 Introduction

In recent years, *explainable AI* (XAI) has received much attention, mostly directed at new techniques for explaining decisions of (subsymbolic) machine learning algorithms [18]. However, explanations traditionally also play an important role in (symbolic) knowledge-based systems [10]. Computational argumentation is one research area in symbolic AI that is frequently mentioned in relation to XAI. For example, arguments can be used to provide reasons for or against decisions [1,10,15]. The focus can also be on the argumentation itself, where it is explained whether and why a certain argument or claim can be accepted under certain semantics for computational argumentation [7–9,19]. It is the latter type of explanations that is the subject of this paper.

Two central concepts in computational argumentation are *abstract argumentation frameworks* [6] – sets of arguments and the attack relations between them – and *structured argumentation frameworks* [3] – where arguments are constructed from a knowledge base and a set of rules and the attack relation is based

---

This research has been partly funded by the Dutch Ministry of Justice and the Dutch National Police.

J. Vejnarová and N. Wilson (Eds.): ECSQARU 2021, LNAI 12897, pp. 45–58, 2021.
https://doi.org/10.1007/978-3-030-86772-0_4

on the individual elements in the arguments. The explanations framework that is introduced in [5] is designed to provide explanations for the (non-)acceptance of arguments and the claim of an argument in case of a structured setting. However, like the other existing works on explanations for argumentation-based conclusions, the framework does not account for findings from the social sciences on human explanations [15].

One of the important characteristics of explanations provided by humans is that they select *the* explanation from a possible infinite set of explanations [15]. In this paper we look at how to select minimal,[1] necessary and sufficient explanations for the (non-)acceptance of an argument. To this end we will introduce variations to the basic framework from [5] that will provide necessary or sufficient explanations for both abstract and structured argumentation (i.e., ASPIC$^+$[17]). Intuitively, a necessary explanation contains the arguments that one has to accept in order to accept the considered argument and a sufficient explanation contains the arguments that, when accepted, guarantee the acceptance of the considered argument. We will show that such explanations exist in most cases and how these relate to the basic explanations from [5] as well as to minimal explanations as introduced in [7]. Moreover, we will discuss a real-life application from the Dutch National Police, where the necessary and sufficient explanations will reduce the size of the provided explanations in a meaningful way.

The paper is structured as follows. We start with a short overview of related work and present the preliminaries on abstract and structured argumentation and the basic explanations from [5]. Then, in Sect. 4 we introduce necessary and sufficient explanations and study how these relate to the better known minimal explanations. In Sect. 5 we show how a real-life application benefits from these explanations and we conclude in Sect. 6.

2   Related Work

We are interested in local explanations for computational argumentation: explanations for a specific argument or claim. We work here with the framework from [5] for several reasons. Often, explanations are only defined for a specific semantics [7,8] and can usually only be applied to abstract argumentation [8,11,19],[2] while the framework from [5] can be applied on top of any argumentation setting (structured or abstract) that results in a Dung-style argumentation framework. Furthermore, when this setting is a structured one based on a knowledge base and set of rules (like ASPIC$^+$ or logic-based argumentation [3]), the explanations can be further adjusted (something which is not considered at all in the literature). To the best of our knowledge, this is the first approach to explanations for formal argumentation in which necessary and sufficient explanations are considered and integrated into a real-life application.

---

[1] Interpreting [15]'s simplicity as minimality.

[2] These explanations do not account for the sub-argument relation in structured argumentation. For example, in structured argumentation one cannot remove specific arguments or attacks without influencing other arguments/attacks.

3   Preliminaries

An *abstract argumentation framework* (AF) [6] is a pair $\mathcal{AF} = \langle \mathsf{Args}, \mathsf{Att} \rangle$, where Args is a set of *arguments* and Att $\subseteq$ Args $\times$ Args is an *attack relation* on these arguments. An AF can be viewed as a directed graph, in which the nodes represent arguments and the arrows represent attacks between arguments.

Fig. 1. Graphical representation of the AF $\mathcal{AF}_1$.

Example 1. Figure 1 represents $\mathcal{AF}_1 = \langle \mathsf{Args}_1, \mathsf{Att}_1 \rangle$ where $\mathsf{Args}_1 = \{A, B, C, D, E, F\}$ and $\mathsf{Att}_1 = \{(B, A), (C, B), (C, D), (D, C), (E, B), (E, F), (F, E)\}$.

Given an AF, Dung-style semantics [6] can be applied to it, to determine what combinations of arguments (called *extensions*) can collectively be accepted.

Definition 1. *Let* $\mathcal{AF} = \langle \mathit{Args}, \mathit{Att} \rangle$ *be an argumentation framework,* S $\subseteq$ *Args a set of arguments and let* $A \in \mathit{Args}$*. Then:* S *attacks* A *if there is an* $A' \in$ S *such that* $(A', A) \in \mathit{Att}$*, let* S^+ *denote the set of arguments attacked by* S*;* S *defends* A *if* S *attacks every attacker of* A*;* S *is* conflict-free *if there are no* $A_1, A_2 \in$ S *such that* $(A_1, A_2) \in \mathit{Att}$*; and* S *is an* admissible extension *(Adm) if it is conflict-free and it defends all of its elements.*

An admissible extension that contains all the arguments that it defends is a complete extension *(Cmp). The* grounded extension *(Grd) is the minimal (w.r.t.* $\subseteq$*) complete extension; A* preferred extension *(Prf) is a maximal (w.r.t.* $\subseteq$*) complete extension; and A* semi-stable extension *(Sstb) is a complete extension for which* S $\cup$ S^+ *is* $\subseteq$*-maximal.* Sem$(\mathcal{AF})$ *denotes the set of all the extensions of* $\mathcal{AF}$ *under the semantics* Sem $\in \{\mathsf{Adm}, \mathsf{Cmp}, \mathsf{Grd}, \mathsf{Prf}, \mathsf{Sstb}\}$*.*

In what follows we will consider an argument accepted if it is part of at least one extension and non-accepted if it is not part of at least one extension.[3]

Definition 2. *Where* $\mathcal{AF} = \langle \mathit{Args}, \mathit{Att} \rangle$ *is an AF,* Sem *a semantics such that* Sem$(\mathcal{AF}) \neq \emptyset$*, it is said that* $A \in \mathit{Args}$ *is:*

- accepted *if* $A \in \bigcup \mathsf{Sem}(\mathcal{AF})$*: there is some* Sem*-extension that contains* A*;*
- non-accepted *if* $A \notin \bigcap \mathsf{Sem}(\mathcal{AF})$*:* A *is not part of at least one* Sem*-extension.*

Example 2. For $\mathcal{AF}_1$ we have that $\mathsf{Grd}(\mathcal{AF}_1) = \{\emptyset\}$ and there are four preferred and semi-stable extensions: $\{A, C, E\}$, $\{A, C, F\}$, $\{A, D, E\}$ and $\{B, D, F\}$. Therefore, all arguments from Args_1 are accepted and non-accepted for Sem $\in$ $\{\mathsf{Prf}, \mathsf{Sstb}\}$.

---

[3] In [5], four acceptance strategies are considered, the other two are not relevant for our study on necessity and sufficiency and are therefore not introduced here.

3.1   ASPIC$^+$

For our discussion on explanations for structured settings we take ASPIC$^+$ [17] which allows for two types of premises – *axioms* that cannot be questioned and *ordinary premises* that can be questioned – and two types of rules – *strict* rules that cannot be questioned and *defeasible* ones. We choose ASPIC$^+$ since it allows to vary the form of the explanations in many ways (see Sect. 3.2 and [5]).

An ASPIC$^+$ setting starts from an *argumentation system* (AS $= \langle \mathcal{L}, \mathcal{R}, n \rangle$), which contains a logical language $\mathcal{L}$ closed under negation ($\neg$), a set of rules $\mathcal{R} = \mathcal{R}_s \cup \mathcal{R}_d$ consisting of strict ($\mathcal{R}_s$) and defeasible ($\mathcal{R}_d$) rules and a naming convention n for defeasible rules. Arguments are constructed in an argumentation setting from a knowledge base $\mathcal{K} \subseteq \mathcal{L}$ which consists of two disjoint subsets $\mathcal{K} = \mathcal{K}_p \cup \mathcal{K}_n$: the set of axioms ($\mathcal{K}_n$) and the set of ordinary premises ($\mathcal{K}_p$).

Definition 3. *An argument A on the basis of a knowledge base $\mathcal{K}$ in an argumentation system $\langle \mathcal{L}, \mathcal{R}, n \rangle$ is:*

1. *ϕ if $\phi \in \mathcal{K}$, where $\mathsf{Prem}(A) = \mathsf{Sub}(A) = \{\phi\}$, $\mathsf{Conc}(A) = \phi$, $\mathsf{Rules}(A) = \emptyset$ and $\mathsf{TopRule}(A) = undefined;$*
2. *$A_1, \ldots, A_n \rightsquigarrow \psi$, where $\rightsquigarrow \in \{\rightarrow, \Rightarrow\}$, if $A_1, \ldots, A_n$ are arguments such that there exists a rule $\mathsf{Conc}(A_1), \ldots, \mathsf{Conc}(A_n) \rightsquigarrow \psi$ in $\mathcal{R}_s$ if $\rightsquigarrow = \rightarrow$ and in $\mathcal{R}_d$ if $\rightsquigarrow = \Rightarrow$.*
   $\mathsf{Prem}(A) = \mathsf{Prem}(A_1) \cup \ldots \cup \mathsf{Prem}(A_n)$; $\mathsf{Conc}(A) = \psi$; $\mathsf{Sub}(A) = \mathsf{Sub}(A_1) \cup \ldots \cup \mathsf{Sub}(A_n) \cup \{A\}$; $\mathsf{Rules}(A) = \mathsf{Rules}(A_1) \cup \ldots \cup \mathsf{Rules}(A_n) \cup \{\mathsf{Conc}(A_1), \ldots, \mathsf{Conc}(A_n) \rightsquigarrow \psi\}$; $\mathsf{DefRules}(A) = \{r \in \mathcal{R}_d \mid r \in \mathsf{Rules}(A)\}$; and $\mathsf{TopRule}(A) = \mathsf{Conc}(A_1), \ldots, \mathsf{Conc}(A_n) \rightsquigarrow \psi$.

The above notation can be generalized to sets. For example, where S is a set of arguments $\mathsf{Prem}(\mathsf{S}) = \bigcup \{\mathsf{Prem}(A) \mid A \in \mathsf{S}\}$ and $\mathsf{Conc}(\mathsf{S}) = \{\mathsf{Conc}(A) \mid A \in \mathsf{S}\}$.

Attacks on an argument are based on the rules and premises applied in the construction of that argument.

Definition 4. *Let A and B be two arguments, we denote $\psi = -\phi$ if $\psi = \neg\phi$ or $\phi = \neg\psi$. A attacks an argument B iff A undercuts, rebuts or undermines B:*

- *A undercuts B (on B') iff $\mathsf{Conc}(A) = -n(r)$ for some $B' \in \mathsf{Sub}(B)$ such that B''s top rule r is defeasible, it denies a rule;*
- *A rebuts B (on B') iff $\mathsf{Conc}(A) = -\phi$ for some $B' \in \mathsf{Sub}(B)$ of the form $B''_1, \ldots, B''_n \Rightarrow \phi$, it denies a conclusion;*
- *A undermines B (on ϕ) iff $\mathsf{Conc}(A) = -\phi$ for some $\phi \in \mathsf{Prem}(B) \setminus \mathcal{K}_n$, it denies a premise.*

Argumentation theories and their corresponding Dung-style argumentation frameworks can now be defined.

Definition 5. *An argumentation theory is a pair $AT = \langle AS, \mathcal{K} \rangle$, where AS is an argumentation system and $\mathcal{K}$ is a knowledge base.*

From an argumentation theory AT the corresponding AF can be derived such that $\mathcal{AF}(AT) = \langle \mathsf{Args}, \mathsf{Att} \rangle$, where Args is the set of arguments constructed from AT and $(A, B) \in \mathsf{Att}$ iff $A, B \in \mathsf{Args}$ and A attacks B as defined in Definition 4.

Example 3. Let $AS_1 = \langle \mathcal{L}_1, \mathcal{R}_1, n \rangle$ where the rules in $\mathcal{R}_1$ are such that, with $\mathcal{K}_1 = \mathcal{K}_n^1 = \{r, s, t, v\}$ the following arguments can be derived:[4]

$$A : s, t \overset{d_1}{\Rightarrow} u \qquad\qquad B : p, \neg q \overset{d_2}{\Rightarrow} \neg n(d_1) \qquad\qquad C : r, s \overset{d_3}{\Rightarrow} q$$

$$D : v \overset{d_4}{\Rightarrow} \neg q \qquad\qquad E : r, t \overset{d_5}{\Rightarrow} \neg p \qquad\qquad F : v \overset{d_6}{\Rightarrow} p.$$

The graphical representation of the corresponding argumentation framework $\mathcal{AF}(AT_1)$ with $AT_1 = \langle AS_1, \mathcal{K}_1 \rangle$ is the graph from Fig. 1.

Dung-style semantics (Definition 1) can be applied in the same way as they are applied to abstract argumentation frameworks (recall Example 2). In addition to (non-)acceptance of arguments, in a structured setting we can also consider (non-)acceptance of formulas:

Definition 6. *Let $\mathcal{AF}(AT) = \langle \textsf{Args}, \textsf{Att} \rangle$ be an AF, based on AT, let Sem be a semantics such that $\textsf{Sem}(\mathcal{AF}) \neq \emptyset$ and let $\phi \in \mathcal{L}$. Then ϕ is:*

- *accepted: if $\phi \in \bigcup \textsf{Concs}(\textsf{Sem}(\mathcal{AF}(AT)))$, that is: there is some argument with conclusion ϕ that is accepted;*
- *non-accepted: if $\phi \notin \bigcap \textsf{Concs}(\textsf{Sem}(\mathcal{AF}(AT)))$, that is: there is some Sem-extension without an argument with conclusion ϕ.*

Example 4. As was the case for arguments (recall Example 2), all formulas in $\{p, \neg p, q, \neg q, r, s, t, u, v\}$ are accepted and $\{p, \neg p, q, \neg q, u\}$ are also non-accepted.

3.2 Basic Explanations

In [5] four types of explanations for abstract and structured argumentation were introduced. These explanations are defined in terms of two functions: $\mathbb{D}$, which determines the arguments that are in the explanation and $\mathbb{F}$, which determines what elements of these arguments the explanation presents. For the basic explanations in this paper, we instantiate $\mathbb{D}$ with the following functions, let $A \in \textsf{Args}$ and $\mathcal{E} \in \textsf{Prf}(\mathcal{AF})$ for some AF $\mathcal{AF} = \langle \textsf{Args}, \textsf{Att} \rangle$:[5]

- Defending$(A) = \{B \in \textsf{Args} \mid B \text{ defends } A\}$ denotes the set of arguments that defend A and Defending$(A, \mathcal{E}) = \textsf{Defending}(A) \cap \mathcal{E}$ denotes the set of arguments that defend A in $\mathcal{E}$.
- NoDefAgainst$(A, \mathcal{E}) = \{B \in \textsf{Args} \mid B \text{ attacks } A \text{ and } \mathcal{E} \text{ does not defend } A \text{ against } B\}$ denotes the set of all attackers of A that are not defended by $\mathcal{E}$.

The explanations are defined for arguments and formulas.

---

[4] We ignore the arguments based on the elements from $\mathcal{K}_1$, since these neither attack nor are attacked by any argument.

[5] We write that $B \in \textsf{Args}$ defends $A \in \textsf{Args}$ if it attacks an attacker of A or it defends an argument that defends A.

Definition 7. *Let $\mathcal{AF} = \langle Args, Att \rangle$ be an AF and suppose that $A \in Args$ [resp. $\phi \in \mathcal{L}$] is accepted w.r.t. Sem. Then:*

$$\mathsf{SemAcc}(A) = \{\mathsf{Defending}(A, \mathcal{E}) \mid \mathcal{E} \in \mathsf{Sem}(\mathcal{AF}) \text{ and } A \in \mathcal{E}\}.$$
$$\mathsf{SemAcc}(\phi) = \{\mathbb{F}(\mathsf{Defending}(A, \mathcal{E})) \mid \mathcal{E} \in \mathsf{Sem}(\mathcal{AF}) \text{ such that } A \in \mathcal{E} \text{ and}$$
$$\mathsf{Conc}(A) = \phi\}.$$

An acceptance explanation, for an argument or formula, contains all the arguments that defend the argument (for that formula) in an extension. If it is an explanation for a formula, the function $\mathbb{F}$ can be applied to it.

Definition 8. *Let $\mathcal{AF} = \langle Args, Att \rangle$ be an AF and suppose that $A \in Args$ [resp. $\phi \in \mathcal{L}$] is non-accepted w.r.t. Sem. Then:*

$$\mathsf{SemNotAcc}(A) = \bigcup_{\mathcal{E} \in \mathsf{Sem}(\mathcal{AF}) \text{ and } A \notin \mathcal{E}} \mathsf{NoDefAgainst}(A, \mathcal{E}).$$

$$\mathsf{SemNotAcc}(\phi) = \bigcup_{A \in Args \text{ and } \mathsf{Conc}(A) = \phi} \bigcup_{\mathcal{E} \in \mathsf{Sem}(\mathcal{AF}) \text{ and } A \notin \mathcal{E}} \mathbb{F}(\mathsf{NoDefAgainst}(A, \mathcal{E})).$$

A non-acceptance explanation contains all the arguments that attack the argument [resp. an argument for the formula] and to which no defense exists in some Sem-extension. For a formula $\mathbb{F}$ can be applied again.

The function $\mathbb{F}$ can be instantiated in different ways. We recall here some of the variations introduced in [5].

- $\mathbb{F} = \mathsf{id}$, where $\mathsf{id}(\mathsf{S}) = \mathsf{S}$. Then explanations are sets of arguments.
- $\mathbb{F} = \mathsf{Prem}$. Then explanations only contain the premises of arguments (i.e., knowledge base elements).
- $\mathbb{F} = \mathsf{AntTop}$, where $\mathsf{AntTop}(A) = \langle \mathsf{TopRule}(A), \mathsf{Ant}(\mathsf{TopRule}(A)) \rangle$. Then explanations contain the last applied rule and its antecedents.
- $\mathbb{F} = \mathsf{SubConc}$, where $\mathsf{SubConc}(A) = \{\mathsf{Conc}(B) \mid B \in \mathsf{Sub}(A), \mathsf{Conc}(B) \notin \mathcal{K} \cup \{\mathsf{Conc}(A)\}\}$. Then the explanation contains the sub-conclusions that were derived in the construction of the argument.

Example 5. Consider the AF $\mathcal{AF}(\mathrm{AT}_1)$ from Examples 1 and 3. We have that:

- $\mathsf{PrfAcc}(A) \in \{\{C\}, \{E\}, \{C, E\}\}$ and $\mathsf{PrfAcc}(B) = \{D, F\}$;
- $\mathsf{PrfNotAcc}(A) = \{B, D, F\}$ and $\mathsf{PrfNotAcc}(B) = \{C, E\}$.

If we take $\mathbb{F} = \mathsf{Prem}$, then: $\mathsf{PrfAcc}(u) \in \{\{r, s\}, \{r, t\}, \{r, s, t\}\}$, $\mathsf{PrfAcc}(\neg n(d_1)) = \mathsf{PrfNotAcc}(u) = \{v\}$ and $\mathsf{PrfNotAcc}(\neg n(d_1)) = \{r, s, t\}$.

A conclusion derived from an argumentation system can have many causes and therefore many explanations. When humans derive the same conclusion and are asked to explain that conclusion they are able to select *the* explanation from all the possible explanations. In the social sciences a large amount of possible selection criteria that humans might apply have been investigated, see [15] for an overview. In this paper we focus on necessity and sufficiency.

4   Necessity and Sufficiency

Necessity and sufficiency in the context of philosophy and cognitive science are discussed in, for example, [13,14,20]. Intuitively, an event Γ is sufficient for Δ, if no other causes are required for Δ to happen, while Γ is necessary for Δ, if in order for Δ to happen, Γ has to happen as well. In the context of logical implication (denoted by $\rightarrow$), one could model sufficiency by $\Gamma \rightarrow \Delta$ and necessity by $\Delta \rightarrow \Gamma$ [12].

In the next sections we formulate these logical notions in our argumentation setting. We will assume that the arguments on which the explanation for an argument A is based are relevant for A: $B \in$ Args [resp. S $\subseteq$ Args] is *relevant* for A if B (in)directly attacks or defends A (i.e., there is a path from B to A) and does not attack itself [resp. for each $C \in$ S, C is relevant for A].

4.1   Necessity and Sufficiency for Acceptance

In the context of argumentation, a set of accepted arguments is sufficient if it guarantees, independent of the status of other arguments, that the considered argument is accepted, while an accepted argument is necessary if it is impossible to accept the considered argument without it.

Definition 9. *Let* $\mathcal{AF} = \langle$Args, Att$\rangle$ *be an AF and let* $A \in$ *Args be accepted (w.r.t. some* Sem*). Then:*

- S $\subseteq$ *Args is* sufficient *for the acceptance of* A *if* S *is relevant for* A, S *is conflict-free and* S *defends* A *against all its attackers;*
- $B \in$ *Args is* necessary *for the acceptance of* A *if* B *is relevant for* A *and if* $B \notin \mathcal{E}$ *for some* $\mathcal{E} \in$ Adm$(\mathcal{AF})$, *then* $A \notin \mathcal{E}$.

We denote by Suff$(A) = \{$S $\subseteq$ *Args* | S *is sufficient for the acceptance of* $A\}$ *the set of all sufficient sets of arguments for the acceptance of* A *and by* Nec$(A) = \{B \in$ *Args* | B *is necessary for the acceptance of* $A\}$ *the set of all necessary arguments for the acceptance of* A.

Example 6. In $\mathcal{AF}_1$ *both* $\{C\}$ *and* $\{E\}$ *are sufficient for the acceptance of* A *but neither is necessary, while for* B, $\{D, F\}$ *is sufficient and* D *and* F *are necessary.*

Necessary and sufficient explanations are now defined by replacing Defending in the basic explanations from Sect. 3.2 with Nec resp. Suff.

Definition 10. *Let* $\mathcal{AF} = \langle$Args, Att$\rangle$ *be an AF and let* $A \in$ *Args [resp.* $\phi \in \mathcal{L}$*] be accepted. Then sufficient explanations are defined by:*

- Acc$(A) \in$ Suff(A);
- Acc$(\phi) \in \bigcup\{\mathbb{F}($Suff$(A)) \mid A \in$ *Args and* Conc$(A) = \phi\}$.

Necessary explanations are defined by:

- Acc$(A) =$ Nec(A);

– $\mathsf{Acc}(\phi) = \bigcap\{\mathbb{F}(\mathsf{Suff}(A)) \mid A \in \textit{Args and } \mathsf{Conc}(A) = \phi\}$.

Example 7. For $\mathcal{AF}(\mathrm{AT}_1)$ we have that sufficient explanations are $\mathsf{Acc}(A) \in \{\{C\}, \{E\}, \{C, E\}, \{C, F\}, \{D, E\}\}$, $\mathsf{Acc}(B) = \{D, F\}$, $\mathsf{Acc}(u) \in \{\{r, s\}, \{r, t\}, \{r, s, t\}\}$ and $\mathsf{Acc}(\neg n(d_1)) = \{v\}$. Moreover, necessary explanations are $\mathsf{Acc}(A) = \emptyset$, $\mathsf{Acc}(B) = \{D, F\}$, $\mathsf{Acc}(u) = \{r\}$ and $\mathsf{Acc}(\neg n(d_1)) = \{v\}$.

Next we show that the sets in $\mathsf{Suff}(A)$ are admissible and contain all the needed arguments. Additionally, we look at conditions under which Suff and Nec are empty, as well as the relation between Suff and Nec. These last results provide the motivation for the necessary formula acceptance explanation.[6]

Proposition 1. *Let $\mathcal{AF} = \langle \textit{Args}, \textit{Att}\rangle$ be an AF and let $A \in \textit{Args}$ be accepted w.r.t. some* $\mathsf{Sem} \in \{\mathsf{Adm}, \mathsf{Cmp}, \mathsf{Grd}, \mathsf{Prf}, \mathsf{Sstb}\}$. *Then:*

1. *For all $\mathsf{S} \in \mathsf{Suff}(A)$, $\{\mathsf{S}, \mathsf{S} \cup \{A\}\} \subseteq \mathsf{Adm}(\mathcal{AF})$;*
2. *$\mathsf{Suff}(A) = \emptyset$ iff there is no $B \in \textit{Args}$ such that $(B, A) \in \textit{Att}$.*
3. *$\mathsf{Nec}(A) = \emptyset$ iff there is no $B \in \textit{Args}$ such that $(B, A) \in \textit{Att}$ or $\bigcap \mathsf{Suff}(A) = \emptyset$.*
4. *$\mathsf{Nec}(A) \subseteq \bigcap \mathsf{Suff}(A)$.*

The next proposition relates the introduced notions of necessity and sufficiency with Defending and therefore with the basic explanations from Sect. 3.2.

Proposition 2. *Let $\mathcal{AF} = \langle \textit{Args}, \textit{Att}\rangle$ be an AF and let $A \in \textit{Args}$ be accepted w.r.t.* $\mathsf{Sem} \in \{\mathsf{Adm}, \mathsf{Cmp}, \mathsf{Grd}, \mathsf{Prf}, \mathsf{Stb}\}$. *Then:*

– *for all $\mathcal{E} \in \mathsf{Sem}(\mathcal{AF})$ such that $A \in \mathcal{E}$, $\mathsf{Defending}(A, \mathcal{E}) \in \mathsf{Suff}(A)$;*
– $\bigcap_{\mathcal{E} \in \mathsf{Sem}(\mathcal{AF}) \textit{ and } A \in \mathcal{E}} \mathsf{Defending}(A, \mathcal{E}) = \mathsf{Nec}(A)$.

4.2   Necessity and Sufficiency for Non-acceptance

When looking at the non-acceptance of an argument A, the acceptance of any of its direct attackers is a sufficient explanation. However, other arguments (e.g., some of the indirect attackers) might be sufficient as well. An argument is necessary for the non-acceptance of A, when it is relevant and A is accepted in the argumentation framework without it. In what follows we will assume that $(A, A) \notin \mathsf{Att}$, since otherwise A itself is the reason for its non-acceptance.

We need the following definition for our notion of sufficiency.

Definition 11. *Let $\mathcal{AF} = \langle \textit{Args}, \textit{Att}\rangle$ be an AF and let $A, B \in \textit{Args}$ such that A indirectly attacks B, via $C_1, \ldots, C_n \in \textit{Args}$, i.e., $(A, C_1), (C_1, C_2), \ldots, (C_n, B) \in \textit{Att}$. It is said that the attack from A on B is uncontested if there is no $D \in \textit{Args}$ such that $(D, C_{2i}) \in \textit{Att}$ for $i \in \{1, \ldots, \frac{n}{2}\}$. It is contested otherwise, in which case it is said that the attack from A is contested in C_{2i}.*

The need for the above definition is illustrated in the next example:

---

[6] Full proofs of our results can be found in the online technical appendix at: https://nationaal-politielab.sites.uu.nl/necessary-sufficient-explanations-proofs/.

Example 8. In $\mathcal{AF}_1$, the indirect attacks from D and F on A are contested: the attack from D is contested in B, since $(E, B) \in$ Att and the attack from F is also contested in B since $(C, B) \in$ Att. It is therefore possible that A and D or F are part of the same extension (recall Example 2).

For the definition of necessity for non-acceptance we define subframeworks, which are needed because an argument might be non-accepted since it is attacked by an accepted or by another non-accepted argument.[7]

Definition 12. *Let $\mathcal{AF} = \langle Args, Att \rangle$ be an AF and let $A \in Args$. Then $\mathcal{AF}_{\downarrow A} = \langle Args \setminus \{A\}, Att \cap (Args \setminus \{A\} \times Args \setminus \{A\}) \rangle$ denotes the AF based on $\mathcal{AF}$ but without A.*

Since indirect attacks might be sufficient for not accepting an argument, but they also might be contested, the definition of sufficiency for non-acceptance is defined inductively.

Definition 13. *Let $\mathcal{AF} = \langle Args, Att \rangle$ be an AF and let $A \in Args$ be non-accepted (w.r.t. Sem). Then:*

- *$S \subseteq Args$ is sufficient for the non-acceptance of A if S is relevant for A and there is a $B \in S$ such that:*
  - *$(B, A) \in$ Att; or*
  - *B indirectly attacks A and that attack is uncontested; or*
  - *B indirectly attacks A and for every argument C in which the attack from B on A is contested and every $D \in Args$ such that $(D, C) \in$ Att, there is an $S' \subseteq S$ that is sufficient for the non-acceptance of D.*
- *$B \in Args$ is necessary for the non-acceptance of A if B is relevant for A and A is accepted w.r.t. Sem in $\mathcal{AF}_{\downarrow B}$.*

We denote by $\mathsf{SuffNot}(A) = \{S \subseteq Args \mid S$ is sufficient for the non-acceptance of $A\}$ the set of all sufficient sets of arguments for the non-acceptance of A and by $\mathsf{NecNot}(A) = \{B \in Args \mid B$ is necessary for the non-acceptance of $A\}$ the set of all necessary arguments for the non-acceptance of A.

Example 9. For $\mathcal{AF}_1$ from Example 1 we have that B is both necessary and sufficient for the non-acceptance of A. Moreover, while D and F are neither sufficient for the non-acceptance of A, $\{D, F\}$ is. For the non-acceptance of B we have that C and E are sufficient, but neither is necessary.

Definition 14. *Let $\mathcal{AF} = \langle Args, Att \rangle$ be an AF and let $A \in Args$ [resp. $\phi \in \mathcal{L}$] be non-accepted. Then sufficient explanations are defined by:*

- *$\mathsf{NotAcc}(A) \in \mathsf{SuffNot}(A)$;*
- *$\mathsf{NotAcc}(\phi) \in \bigcup \{\mathbb{F}(\mathsf{SuffNot}(A)) \mid A \in Args$ and $\mathsf{Conc}(A) = \phi\}$.*

---

[7] In terms of labeling semantics (see e.g., [2]) an argument is non-accepted if it is **out** (i.e., attacked by an **in** argument) or **undecided**.

Necessary explanations are defined by:

- $\mathsf{NotAcc}(A) = \mathsf{NecNot}(A)$;
- $\mathsf{NotAcc}(\phi) = \bigcap \{\mathbb{F}(\mathsf{SuffNot}(A)) \mid A \in Args \text{ and } \mathsf{Conc}(A) = \phi\}$.

Example 10. For $\mathcal{AF}_1$ we have, for sufficiency $\mathsf{NotAcc}(A) \in \{\{B\}, \{D, F\}, \{B, D, F\}\}$, $\mathsf{NotAcc}(B) \in \{\{C\}, \{E\}, \{C, E\}\}$, $\mathsf{NotAcc}(u) = \{v\}$ and $\mathsf{NotAcc}(\neg n(d_1)) \in \{\{r, s\}, \{r, t\}, \{r, s, t\}\}$ and for necessity $\mathsf{NotAcc}(B) = \emptyset$ and $\mathsf{NotAcc}(u) = \{v\}$.

The next propositions are the non-acceptance counterparts of Propositions 1 and 2. First some basic properties of sufficiency and necessity for non-acceptance.

Proposition 3. *Let* $\mathcal{AF} = \langle Args, Att \rangle$ *be an AF and let* $A \in Args$ *be non-accepted w.r.t.* $\mathsf{Sem} \in \{\mathsf{Adm}, \mathsf{Cmp}, \mathsf{Grd}, \mathsf{Prf}, \mathsf{Sstb}\}$. *Then:* $\mathsf{SuffNot}(A) \neq \emptyset$; *and* $\mathsf{NecNot}(A) = \emptyset$ *implies that there are at least two direct attackers of* A.

Now we show how $\mathsf{NoDefAgainst}$ (and hence the basic explanations from Sect. 3.2) is related to our notions of sufficiency and necessity for non-acceptance.

Proposition 4. *Let* $\mathcal{AF} = \langle Args, Att \rangle$ *be an AF and let* $A \in Args$ *be an argument that is not accepted w.r.t.* $\mathsf{Sem} \in \{\mathsf{Cmp}, \mathsf{Grd}, \mathsf{Prf}, \mathsf{Sstb}\}$. *Then:*

- *for all* $\mathcal{E} \in \mathsf{Sem}(\mathcal{AF})$ *such that* $A \notin \mathcal{E}$, $\mathsf{NoDefAgainst}(A, \mathcal{E}) \in \mathsf{SuffNot}(A)$;
- $\mathsf{NecNot}(A) \subseteq \bigcap_{\mathcal{E} \in \mathsf{Sem}(\mathcal{AF}) \text{ and } A \notin \mathcal{E}} \mathsf{NoDefAgainst}(A, \mathcal{E})$.

4.3   Necessity, Sufficiency and Minimality

In this paper we have introduced necessity and sufficiency to reduce the size of an explanation. More common in the literature is to place a minimality condition on the explanation [7,8]. In this section we show that our notions of necessity and sufficiency result in explanations that do not contain more arguments than the minimal explanations from [7]. To this end we introduce, for $\preceq \in \{\subseteq, \leq\}$:

- $\mathsf{MinDefending}^{\preceq}(A, \mathcal{E}) = \{S \in \mathsf{Defending}(A, \mathcal{E}) \mid \nexists S' \in \mathsf{Defending}(A, \mathcal{E}) \text{ such that } S' \preceq S\}$ denotes the $\preceq$-minimal $\mathsf{Defending}(A, \mathcal{E})$ sets.[8]
- $\mathsf{MinNotDefAgainst}^{\preceq}(A, \mathcal{E}) = \{S \in \mathsf{NoDefAgainst}(A, \mathcal{E}) \mid \text{ there is no } S' \in \mathsf{NoDefAgainst}(A, \mathcal{E}) \text{ such that } S' \preceq S\}$, denotes the set with all $\preceq$-minimal $\mathsf{NoDefAgainst}(A, \mathcal{E})$ sets.
- $\mathsf{MinSuff}^{\preceq}(A) = \{S \in \mathsf{Suff}(A) \mid \nexists S' \in \mathsf{Suff}(A) \text{ such that } S' \preceq S\}$, denotes the set of all $\preceq$-minimally sufficient sets for the acceptance of A.
- $\mathsf{MinSuffNot}^{\preceq}(A) = \{S \in \mathsf{SuffNot}(A) \mid \nexists S' \in \mathsf{SuffNot}(A) \text{ such that } S' \preceq S\}$, denotes the set of all $\preceq$-minimally $\mathsf{SuffNot}$ sets for the non-acceptance of A.

The next example shows that sufficient explanations can be smaller than minimal basic explanations.

---

[8] In view of the result in [5], these sets correspond to the minimal ($\preceq = \leq$ and where $S \leq S'$ denotes $|S| \leq |S'|$) and compact ($\preceq = \subseteq$) explanations from [7].

Example 11. Let $\mathcal{AF}_2 = \langle \mathsf{Args}_2, \mathsf{Att}_2 \rangle$, shown in Fig. 2. Here we have that $\mathsf{Prf}(\mathcal{AF}_2) = \{\{A,B\},\{C,D\}\}$ and that $\mathsf{PrfAcc}(B) = \{A,B\}$, $\mathsf{PrfAcc}(D) = \{C, D\}$, $\mathsf{PrfNotAcc}(B) = \{C,D\}$ and $\mathsf{PrfNotAcc}(D) = \{A,B\}$. These are the explanations for B and D, whether as defined in Sect. 3.2 or with Defending [resp. NoDefAgainst] replaced by MinDefending [resp. MinNotDefAgainst].

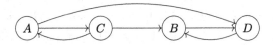

Fig. 2. Graphical representation of $\mathcal{AF}_2$.

When looking at minimally sufficient sets instead, we have that $\mathsf{Acc}(B) = \{A\}$ and $\mathsf{NotAcc}(D) \in \{\{A\},\{B\}\}$. To see that these explanations are still meaningful, note that A defends B against all of its attackers and as soon as A is accepted under complete semantics, B will be accepted as well. Thus, the minimally sufficient explanations for B and D are $\leq$- and $\subseteq$-smaller than the minimal basic explanations for B and D, but still meaningful.

That minimally sufficient explanations can be smaller than minimal explanations is formalized in the next propositions.

Proposition 5. *Let $\mathcal{AF} = \langle \mathsf{Args}, \mathsf{Att} \rangle$ be an AF, let $A \in \mathsf{Args}$ be accepted w.r.t. Sem $\in \{\mathsf{Adm}, \mathsf{Cmp}, \mathsf{Grd}, \mathsf{Prf}, \mathsf{Sstb}\}$ and let $\preceq \in \{\subseteq, \leq\}$. Then:*

- *for all $\mathcal{E} \in \mathsf{Sem}(\mathcal{AF})$ and all $\mathsf{S} \in \mathsf{MinDefending}^{\preceq}(A,\mathcal{E})$ there is some $\mathsf{S}' \in \mathsf{MinSuff}^{\preceq}(A)$ such that $\mathsf{S}' \preceq \mathsf{S}$;*
- *for all $\mathcal{E} \in \mathsf{Adm}(\mathcal{AF})$ and all $\mathsf{S} \in \mathsf{MinSuff}^{\preceq}(A)$ also $\mathsf{S} \in \mathsf{MinDefending}^{\preceq}(A,\mathcal{E})$;*
- *for all $\mathcal{E} \in \mathsf{Sem}(\mathcal{AF})$ and all $\mathsf{S} \in \mathsf{MinDefending}^{\preceq}(A,\mathcal{E})$, $\mathsf{Nec}(A) \subseteq \mathsf{S}$.*

Proposition 6. *Let $\mathcal{AF} = \langle \mathsf{Args}, \mathsf{Att} \rangle$ be an AF and let $A \in \mathsf{Args}$ be not accepted w.r.t. Sem $\in \{\mathsf{Cmp}, \mathsf{Grd}, \mathsf{Prf}, \mathsf{Sstb}\}$. Then:*

- *for all $\mathcal{E} \in \mathsf{Sem}(\mathcal{AF})$ and all $\mathsf{S} \in \mathsf{MinNotDefAgainst}^{\preceq}(A,\mathcal{E})$, there is some $\mathsf{S}' \in \mathsf{MinSuffNot}^{\preceq}(A)$ such that $\mathsf{S}' \preceq \mathsf{S}$;*
- *for all $\mathcal{E} \in \mathsf{Sem}(\mathcal{AF})$ and all $\mathsf{S} \in \mathsf{MinNotDefAgainst}^{\preceq}(A,\mathcal{E})$, $\mathsf{NecNot}(A) \subseteq \mathsf{S}$.*

5 Applying Necessity and Sufficiency

At the Dutch National Police several argumentation-based applications have been implemented [4]. These applications are aimed at assisting the police at working through high volume tasks, leaving more time for tasks that require human attention. In this section we illustrate how necessity and sufficiency can be applied in the online trade fraud application from [16].

Consider the following language $\mathcal{L}_3$: the complainant delivered (*cd*), the counterparty delivered (*cpd*); the received product seems fake (*fake*); a package is expected (pex); the complainant waited before filing the complaint ($wait$); the received packages is indeed fake ($recfake$); the delivery may still arrive ($deco$); it is a case of fraud (f); and their negations. Based on Dutch Criminal Law (i.e., Article 326) we can derive the following arguments:

$$A_1 : cpd \quad A_2 : \neg cpd \quad A_3 : fake \quad A_4 : \neg fake \quad A_5 : pex \quad A_6 : \neg pex$$

$$A_7 : wait \quad A_8 : \neg wait \quad A_9 : cd \quad A_{10} : \neg cd \quad B_1 : A_1, A_3 \Rightarrow recfake$$

$$B_2 : A_2, A_6 \Rightarrow \neg deco \quad B_3 : A_2, A_5, A_7 \Rightarrow \neg deco \quad B_4 : A_5, A_8 \Rightarrow deco$$

$$C_1 : A_9, B_1 \Rightarrow f \quad C_2 : A_2, A_9, B_2 \Rightarrow f \quad C_3 : A_2, A_9, B_3 \Rightarrow f$$

$$C_4 : A_9, B_4 \Rightarrow \neg f \quad C_5 : A_4, A_9 \Rightarrow \neg f \quad C_6 : A_{10} \Rightarrow \neg f.$$

The above arguments are only a small subset of the possible arguments in the actual application, yet this framework already results in 30 preferred and semi-stable extensions. We can therefore not provide a detailed formal analysis. However, we can already show the usefulness of necessary and sufficient explanations.

The necessary explanation for the acceptance of f is cd, while for the acceptance of $\neg f$ the necessary explanation is empty. The reason for this is that, by Article 326, the complainant must have delivered (e.g., sent the goods or money) before it is a case of fraud but $\neg f$ can be accepted for a variety of reasons. In the basic explanations it is not possible to derive this explanation, yet it can be the sole reason for not accepting f. Moreover, minimal sufficient explanations for the acceptance of $\neg f$ when cd and $\mathbb{F} = \mathsf{Prem}$ are $\{cd, pex, \neg wait\}$ and $\{cd, \neg fake\}$, these are both $\subset$ and $<$-smaller than any basic explanation for the acceptance of $\neg f$, while still providing the main reasons for the acceptance of $\neg f$.

Therefore, with necessary and sufficient explanations, we can provide compact explanations that only contain the core reasons for a conclusion, something which is not possible with the (minimal) explanations from the basic framework.

6 Conclusion

We have discussed how the explanations from the basic framework introduced in [5] can be adjusted to account for findings from the social sciences on necessary and sufficient explanations [13,14,20]. To this end we have introduced necessary and sufficient sets of arguments for the (non-)acceptance of an argument and formula and integrated these into the explanations definition. The result is a meaningful reduction in the size of an explanation, which almost always exists. Moreover, we have shown that our necessary and sufficient explanations can be smaller than the minimal explanations from [7] and reduce the explanations to the core reasons of (not) accepting a conclusion in a real-life application.

To the best of our knowledge this is the first investigation into necessary and sufficient sets for (non-)acceptance of arguments, especially in the context of integrating findings from the social sciences (e.g., [12]) into (explanations for) argumentation-based conclusions and into a real-life application. In future work we plan to investigate how to integrate further findings, such as contrastiveness and other selection mechanisms.

References

1. Atkinson, K., et al.: Towards artificial argumentation. AI Mag. **38**(3), 25–36 (2017)
2. Baroni, P., Caminada, M., Giacomin, M.: Abstract argumentation frameworks and their semantics. In: Baroni, P., Gabay, D., Giacomin, M., van der Torre, L. (eds.) Handbook of Formal Argumentation, pp. 159–236. College Publications (2018)
3. Besnard, P., et al.: Introduction to structured argumentation. Argum. Comput. **5**(1), 1–4 (2014)
4. Bex, F., Testerink, B., Peters, J.: AI for online criminal complaints: from natural dialogues to structured scenarios. In: Workshop Proceedings of Artificial Intelligence for Justice at ECAI 2016, pp. 22–29 (2016)
5. Borg, A., Bex, F.: A basic framework for explanations in argumentation. IEEE Intell. Syst. **36**(2), 25–35 (2021)
6. Dung, P.M.: On the acceptability of arguments and its fundamental role in non-monotonic reasoning, logic programming and n-person games. Artif. Intell. **77**(2), 321–357 (1995)
7. Fan, X., Toni, F.: On computing explanations in argumentation. In: Bonet, B., Koenig, S. (eds.) Proceedings of the 29th AAAI Conference on Artificial Intelligence (AAAI 2015), pp. 1496–1502. AAAI Press (2015)
8. Fan, X., Toni, F.: On explanations for non-acceptable arguments. In: Black, E., Modgil, S., Oren, N. (eds.) TAFA 2015. LNCS (LNAI), vol. 9524, pp. 112–127. Springer, Cham (2015). https://doi.org/10.1007/978-3-319-28460-6_7
9. García, A., Chesñevar, C., Rotstein, N., Simari, G.: Formalizing dialectical explanation support for argument-based reasoning in knowledge-based systems. Expert Syst. Appl. **40**(8), 3233–3247 (2013)
10. Lacave, C., Diez, F.J.: A review of explanation methods for heuristic expert systems. Knowl. Eng. Rev. **19**(2), 133–146 (2004)
11. Liao, B., van der Torre, L.: Explanation semantics for abstract argumentation. In: Prakken, H., Bistarelli, S., Santini, F., Taticchi, C. (eds.) Proceedings of the 8th International Conference on Computational Models of Argument (COMMA 2020). Frontiers in Artificial Intelligence and Applications, vol. 326, pp. 271–282. IOS Press (2020)
12. Lin, F.: On strongest necessary and weakest sufficient conditions. Artif. Intell. **128**(1), 143–159 (2001)
13. Lipton, P.: Contrastive explanation. R. Inst. Philos. Suppl. **27**, 247–266 (1990)
14. Lombrozo, T.: Causal-explanatory pluralism: how intentions, functions, and mechanisms influence causal ascriptions. Cogn. Psychol. **61**(4), 303–332 (2010)
15. Miller, T.: Explanation in artificial intelligence: insights from the social sciences. Artif. Intell. **267**, 1–38 (2019)
16. Odekerken, D., Borg, A., Bex, F.: Estimating stability for efficient argument-based inquiry. In: Prakken, H., Bistarelli, S., Santini, F., Taticchi, C. (eds.) Proceedings of the 8th International Conference on Computational Models of Argument (COMMA 2020). Frontiers in Artificial Intelligence and Applications, vol. 326, pp. 307–318. IOS Press (2020)
17. Prakken, H.: An abstract framework for argumentation with structured arguments. Argum. Comput. **1**(2), 93–124 (2010)
18. Samek, W., Wiegand, T., Müller, K.R.: Explainable artificial intelligence: understanding, visualizing and interpreting deep learning models. arXiv preprint arXiv:1708.08296 (2017)

19. Saribatur, Z., Wallner, J., Woltran, S.: Explaining non-acceptability in abstract argumentation. In: Proceedings of the 24th European Conference on Artificial Intelligence (ECAI 2020). Frontiers in Artificial Intelligence and Applications, vol. 325, pp. 881–888. IOS Press (2020)
20. Woodward, J.: Sensitive and insensitive causation. Philos. Rev. **115**(1), 1–50 (2006)

Addressing Popular Concerns Regarding COVID-19 Vaccination with Natural Language Argumentation Dialogues

Lisa Chalaguine[(⊠)] and Anthony Hunter[(⊠)]

Department of Computer Science, University College London, London, UK
ucablc3@ucl.ac.uk, anthony.hunter@ucl.ac.uk

Abstract. Chatbots have the potential of being used as dialogical argumentation systems for behaviour change applications. They thereby offer a cost-effective and scalable alternative to in-person consultations with health professionals that users could engage in from the comfort of their own home. During events like the global COVID-19 pandemic, it is even more important than usual that people are well informed and make conscious decisions that benefit themselves. Getting a COVID-19 vaccine is a prime example of a behaviour that benefits the individual, as well as society as a whole. In this paper, we present a chatbot that engages in dialogues with users who do not want to get vaccinated, with the goal to persuade them to change their stance and get a vaccine. The chatbot is equipped with a small repository of arguments that it uses to counter user arguments on why the user is reluctant to get a vaccine. We evaluate our chatbot in a study with participants.

Keywords: Chatbots · Argumentative persuasion systems · Computational persuasion · Natural language argumentation · Knowledge base construction

1 Introduction

During events like the global COVID-19 pandemic, it is even more important than usual that people are well informed and make conscious decisions that benefit themselves and society. One such example is the willingness to get a vaccine. Vaccines have historically proven to be highly successful and cost-effective public health tools for disease prevention [19]. But the effectiveness of a vaccine in controlling the spread of COVID-19 depends on the willingness to get vaccinated in the general population. A sufficiently high vaccine coverage may generate herd immunity, which will protect everyone, including those particularly susceptible to the virus [11]. However, a barrier to reaching herd immunity is the prevalence of people who refuse or are hesitant to take vaccines [14,20]. For example, the most recent numbers from YouGov surveys on vaccine hesitancy from late March 2021 show that whereas the numbers in the UK are quite high (around

© Springer Nature Switzerland AG 2021
J. Vejnarová and N. Wilson (Eds.): ECSQARU 2021, LNAI 12897, pp. 59–73, 2021.
https://doi.org/10.1007/978-3-030-86772-0_5

86%), the numbers in, for example, neighbouring France are much lower, at only 49%. In the USA they are a bit higher, at around 59% [1]. Interviewing all those people who refuse to vaccinate in person and trying to convince them to get the vaccine, would be an impossible task.

This problem can be tackled as an argumentation problem: Arguments can be used to provide information and overturn misconceptions [13]. They are an essential part of sensible discussions on controversial and problematic topics. However, despite an increasing body of literature on computational models of argument, there is still a lack of practical applications. Conversational agents, also known as chatbots, have the potential of being used as dialogical argumentation systems for behaviour change applications by applying computational models of argument. A chatbot could engage in an argumentative dialogue with people over the internet from the comfort and safety of their own home, trying to persuade them to get a COVID-19 vaccine. Chatbots could thereby offer a cost-effective and scalable alternative to in-person consultations with health professionals. In order to represent arguments and concerns in the chatbot's knowledge base, we introduce a variant of an argument graph called a *concern-argument graph*.

The problem with controversial topics like the COVID-19 vaccine is that people block out information they disagree with: through creating social media echo chambers, reading partisan news, or only surrounding themselves with like-minded people. A recent paper [16] found that people select more belief-consistent information and perceive belief-confirming information as more credible, useful, and convincing when searching for online health information, also known as *confirmation bias*. Therefore, a dialogue with someone (or something - like a chatbot) could expose people to new information and potentially have a positive effect on their decision-making process.

However, different people worry about different things and hence arguments for not getting a COVID-19 vaccine will vary in a population. One person might be worried about the potential side effects of a newly developed vaccine, whereas someone else might think that he or she does not need a vaccine because they are young and healthy. A chatbot could address those different concerns by providing counterarguments tailored to the different user arguments and during the course of an argumentative dialogue, try to persuade the user to change their stance about getting vaccinated.

Whilst this seems like an obvious idea, there is a lack of a general framework for using concerns in making strategic choices of move in dialogical argumentation systems. A concern is not the same as a value in value-based argumentation frameworks [4,5], since values are used for ignoring attacks by counterarguments where the value of the attacking argument is lower ranked than the attacked one [12]. In our case, however, the chatbot's counterargument addresses the *same* concern as the user's argument, instead of presenting an argument that raises an *opposing* value.

In this paper, we present a chatbot that engages in persuasive dialogues with users who are reluctant to get a COVID-19 vaccine. We show that given a novel domain, like the COVID-19 pandemic and the associated vaccine development, it requires a relatively small repository of counterarguments to address the majority of possible arguments people might have for not getting the vaccine.

The rest of the paper is structured as follows: Sect. 2 gives some background theory on concerns and the use of argument graphs to construct a chatbot knowledge base; Sect. 3 gives the aim of the paper and the hypotheses; Sect. 4 describes the chatbot architecture that was used for the experiments; Sect. 5 describes the experiments that were conducted with the chatbot, Sect. 6 presents the results, and in Sect. 7 we discuss and conclude our findings.

2   Conceptualising Argumentation

2.1   Using Arguments and Concerns for a Persuasive Chatbot

In order for the chatbot to be able to engage in persuasive dialogues, it needs to be equipped with arguments from both perspectives. It needs arguments for (not) engaging in a certain behaviour, that could potentially be given by the user, and arguments that attack the user's arguments (counterarguments). Furthermore, the chatbot should also be able to identify the *concerns* of the user, a concern being a matter of interest or importance to the user. We have shown in a previous study unrelated to healthcare [8], that arguments and counterarguments can be crowdsourced, represented as a graph, and used as the chatbot's knowledge base. Further, we have shown that the chatbot can automatically identify the concerns of the user that she raises in her arguments during the chat, in order for the chatbot to present counterarguments that address the user's concerns.

Taking the user's concerns into account when presenting an argument is important. The chatbot might present a perfectly valid argument that the user might not even disagree with. However, the chatbot's argument may have no impact on her stance, if the argument does not address her concerns. Whereas, if the chatbot presents a counterargument that addresses her concern, the user is more likely to be convinced. In order to choose a suitable counterargument in a given dialogue, our chatbot tries to identify the concern of the user argument and counter with an argument that addresses the user's concern.

To illustrate how concerns arise in argumentation, and how they can be harnessed to improve persuasion, consider a person who is reluctant to the idea of getting a COVID-19 vaccine due to the short time it took to be developed compared to other vaccines. The chatbot (that argues for getting a COVID-19 vaccine) could choose one of the following arguments:

- Option 1: *A vaccine is the only safe way to create herd immunity which is necessary to stop the virus from spreading. This will protect us all from getting the virus, as well as those who, for some reason, cannot get the vaccine.*
- Option 2: *Yes, the vaccine was developed fast. That's because a lot of funding and research priority is currently directed at developing COVID-19 vaccines around the world. As a result, the process is being sped up, allowing for more clinical trials to take place in a shorter period of time.*

Both arguments are perfectly reasonable. However, option 2 addresses the concern regarding the short time frame by acknowledging it and providing an argument on why the user should not worry about it, whereas option 1 does not, even though it provides a valid argument for getting a COVID-19 vaccine.

2.2   Using an Argument Graph as Chatbot Knowledge Base

Argument graphs as proposed by Dung [10] are directed graphs where each node denotes an argument and each arc denotes one argument attacking another. Such graphs provide a useful representation to study attack and support relationships of a given set of arguments.

In our previous studies we have used chatbots to persuade people to cycle more, instead of driving or using public transport [12]; to reduce meat consumption [9], and to change their stance on UK university fees [8]. The arguments were either compiled and edited by hand by the researchers [12] or crowdsourced [8,9] and stored as directed graphs in the chatbot's knowledge base. In [7] we described a method for automatically acquiring a large argument graph via crowdsourcing.

In this study, we used a hybrid approach where we crowdsourced the arguments that people have for not taking a COVID-19 vaccine and hand-crafted the counterarguments for the chatbot ourselves to avoid including invalid or emotionally-loaded arguments in the argument graph. Crowdsourcing arguments provides insight into the reasons for people's behaviour, and an indication of what sort of free natural language input the chatbot needs to handle.

We refrained from crowdsourcing counterarguments because COVID-19 is a serious health issue with global impacts. It is a new domain and research on this disease contains many uncertainties, and scientists still do not know many crucial aspects regarding the virus and its transmission characteristics. Moreover, it is the first time that humans are being injected with vaccines based on mRNA technology. All these form a highly uncertain information landscape and we believe that a carefully curated knowledge base is better than a crowdsourced one in such a critical communication framework.

3   Hypotheses

In this paper, we present a chatbot that utilises a set of arguments for taking a COVID-19 vaccine as a knowledge base. The chatbot uses concerns to make strategic choices of moves in order to engage in argumentative dialogues with users to persuade them to get the vaccine.

Given this setting, we want to address the following three questions: Firstly, whether a small and shallow argument graph is enough to counter the majority of arguments people might have for not getting the vaccine and thereby create persuasive dialogues. Secondly, whether it is possible by only identifying the concern of a user argument to give a suitable counterargument. And finally, whether an interactive chatbot is more persuasive than a static web page that presents arguments for getting the vaccine. We summarise these points in the following three hypotheses:

H1 Given a novel domain (i.e. a domain which is relatively new to the user of the chatbot and for which their knowledge and opinions might be limited), a small set of arguments (between 30–50 arguments) can be used to represent most of the possible arguments that a set of normal users would know and appropriate counterarguments, and can be utilised by a chatbot to create persuasive dialogues, meaning that the stance of the user changes after the chat.

H2 Given a novel domain, the arguments that address the same concern are sufficiently similar to allow for the provision of suitable counterarguments just by identifying the concern of the arguments.

H3 An argumentative dialogue with an interactive chatbot has a higher persuasive effect than presenting the same arguments on a static web page for people to read.

Further, we were also interested in whether during the chats new concerns could be identified which were not raised in the crowdsourced arguments that were used to construct the chatbot's knowledge base.

We would like to note that the authors of this paper are neither psychologists, nor health professionals and that in this work we are (1) not taking any personality traits of the user attributes into account in order to evaluate what sort of argument might be more effective for this particular person, (2) do not compare the persuasiveness of the chatbot's arguments to other potential arguments, and (3) do not incorporate any other methods of persuasion apart from argumentation. Our aim is to present a prototype chatbot that can be used to convince people to get a COVID-19 vaccine using argumentation, and leave the aforementioned issues for future work.

In the remainder of this paper, we describe the design of our chatbot that was used for the argumentative dialogues and explain the experiments conducted with the chatbot in order to test our hypotheses.

4 Chatbot Design

In this section, we describe the acquisition of arguments used to construct the chatbot's knowledge base, and the concern classifier, used by the chatbot to identify the concerns of the incoming user arguments.

4.1 Knowledge Base Construction

To construct the chatbot's knowledge base which consists of a concern-argument graph, which we define below, we recruited 100 participants via Prolific[1], which is an online recruiting platform for scientific research studies, and asked them to provide three arguments against getting a COVID-19 vaccine. We identified 7 concerns that were raised by the majority of the 300 crowdsourced arguments by inspecting the most common, meaningful words, namely: **short-term side**

---

[1] https://prolific.co.

effects of the vaccine, **long-term side effects** of the vaccine, its **fast development**, the **mutation** of the virus, the **safety** of the vaccine, comparison of COVID-19 to the **flu** and downplaying its danger, and **young** people believing they do not need a vaccine.

The arguments given by users for each of the identified concerns were quite similar as the following example demonstrates:

- *I will not get a COVID-19 vaccine because of its potential side effects.*
- *It's a new vaccine, so we don't yet know what the side effects are.*
- *The vaccine may have a lot of side effects that could be more dangerous than COVID-19 itself.*

The arguments regarding side effects are very similar, and could all be countered with the same argument, for example, that there is high scrutiny over the research on those particular vaccines and nobody would allow giving it to the public if it was unsafe. Whereas, drafting individual counterarguments would make the graph unnecessarily big and might result in the inclusion of many similar counterarguments. We, therefore, structured the knowledge base as a *concern-argument graph* which we define as follows:

Definition 1. *A* **concern-argument graph** *is an acyclic graph (N, E, L) where N is a set of nodes, E is a set of edges, and L is a labelling function such that*

- *N can be partitioned into a set of arguments A and a set of concerns C (i.e. $N = A \cup C$ and $A \cap C = \emptyset$);*
- *the root of the tree, denoted ρ, is an argument in A;*
- *for each argument $\alpha \in A \setminus \{\rho\}$, the labelling function assigns a set of concerns to α (i.e. $L(\alpha) \subseteq C$);*
- *E is the smallest set satisfying the following conditions:*
  - *for each concern $\sigma \in C$, there is an edge $(\sigma, \rho) \in E$*
  - *for each argument $\alpha \in A \setminus \{\rho\}$, if $\sigma \in L(\alpha)$, there is an edge (α, σ)*

So a concern-argument graph can be regarded as a compacted version of a three-level acyclic argument graph (i.e. an argument graph with an argument at the root, counterarguments to the root argument, and counter-counterarguments to the counterarguments). Furthermore, in the concern-argument graph, instead of counterarguments, we use concerns as place-holders for a set of similar arguments raising that concern. This information about concerns we will use in the dialogue strategy.

The resulting graph is, therefore, much smaller and shallower than the traditional argument graph that includes both arguments and counterarguments. Figure 1 shows an example of such a graph, where the goal argument is being attacked by two concerns and each concern is being attacked by one counterargument. One could, of course, extend the concern-argument graph and include more concerns that attack specific counterarguments in level 4, and counterarguments that attack these in level 5. But we aimed to investigate whether a simple 3-layer model would be sufficient in this particular domain where people are more likely to present a new argument, instead of countering the chatbot's counterargument.

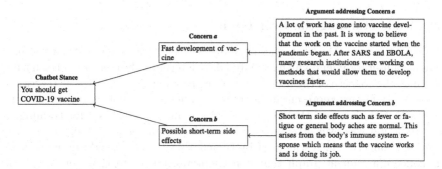

Fig. 1. Part of the chatbot's knowledge base with concerns a and b representing clusters of arguments in level 1 (concerned about insufficient testing of the vaccine and possible side effects respectively) attacking the chatbot's goal argument, and arguments in level 2 addressing the concerns.

The counterarguments for level 3 in the concern-argument graph were carefully researched using reliable sources. Some arguments included links to the NHS website that lists potential short-term side effects from the vaccine[2], or videos that explain how the vaccine was developed so quickly without compromising its safety[3]. As already stated above, we did not individually evaluate the persuasiveness of the arguments, as this is out of the scope of this study.

The chatbot also needed *default arguments* for getting a COVID-19 vaccine that it could use in case the concern of the user argument could not be identified. These arguments are therefore not counterarguments in the traditional sense as they do not directly counter the user argument but instead "change topic" and present a new, important issue in the debate. We also added phrases like *"Ok but"*, *"Have you considered that"* and *"Nevertheless"* to the beginning of the default arguments to indicate that a deviation from the topic occurs. This way the dialogue would resemble argumentation as it would happen between two people: if two human agents engage in an argumentative dialogue, just because one presents an argument the other cannot counter, the dialogue does not necessarily end at that point. The other agent might switch topics and present a new argument he or she believes in, without referencing and directly countering the previous argument. Two out of the three default arguments stated the importance of the vaccine in order to reach *herd immunity*.

---

[2] https://www.nhs.uk/conditions/coronavirus-covid-19/coronavirus-vaccination/ coronavirus-vaccine/.

[3] All arguments were fact-checked by a medical doctor trainee and a machine learning consultant who works in the pharmaceutical industry.

Our initial concern-argument graph consisted of 7 concerns each with 2–4 counterarguments, with 19 leaves in total in the concern-argument graph. Additionally, the chatbot was equipped with three default arguments it could use in case no concern could be identified.

4.2 Understanding the User Input

The initial move is the root argument presented by the chatbot, then the user gives a counterargument which is analysed to determine the concern. The chatbot identified the concern of the user argument using a multinomial logistic regression and a binary feature representation of the arguments (one-hot encoded vectors)[4]. For the initial classifier, the crowdsourced arguments were used for training. If the prediction was over 40% in confidence, the argument was labelled with the identified concern which was used by the chatbot to pick a leaf argument from the concern-argument graph that is a counterargument to that concern. If no concern cannot be identified, or all the leaves of the identified concern had been used, a default argument was presented to the user.

5 Experiments

The purpose of the chatbot was to test all three of our hypotheses. Prior to recruiting participants for the study, we ran a survey where we asked people to choose from a scale of 1–5 whether they would get a COVID-19 vaccine. The options were *very unlikely, somewhat unlikely, neither likely nor unlikely, somewhat likely* and *very likely*. We recruited 300 participants from those that chose *very unlikely, somewhat unlikely* and *neither likely nor unlikely*, i.e. those that had a negative or neutral stance. 240 participants chatted with the chatbot and 60 participants were presented a static web page.

Before the chat, the users were directed to a Microsoft Form and asked again how likely they would get a COVID-19 vaccine. After submitting their answer they were redirected to a web page where they could begin the chat. The chatbot was composed of a front-end we coded in Javascript and a Python back-end using the Flask web server library. The chatbot started the chat by instructing the user that they could end the chat anytime by sending the word *"quit"* and then asking why the user would not get a COVID-19 vaccine, once it became available to him/her. The user then presented his/her first argument. The chatbot replied with either a counterargument from the concern-argument graph or a default argument, depending on whether it could identify the concern of the user argument. The counterarguments were stored in a Python dictionary with the concerns as the keys and the list of counterarguments that addressed that concern as the values. If the concern could be identified, the chatbot replied

---

[4] Due to the small amount of data and the use of one-hot encoded vectors, there was no considerable difference when evaluating different classifiers. More sophisticated methods, like pre-trained language models, could not be used due to the lack of data that could be used for pretraining on the given topic.

with the first counterargument in the list. If the message of the user was less than 7 words in length and contained a negation, the chatbot queried *Why?* or *Why not?* to force the user to expand. This process was repeated with each subsequent argument given by the user. The chatbot would end the chat as soon as all default arguments were used up and no concern could be identified, or all counterarguments that addressed the concern were also used up. At the end of the chat the chatbot presented the user with a link that redirected them to another Microsoft Form where they were asked a series of questions:

1. Did you feel understood by the chatbot? (Yes/No/Sometimes)
2. Did you feel that the chatbot's arguments were relevant? (Yes/No/Some of them)
3. Do you feel like all your concerns were addressed? (The majority of them/None of them/Some of them)
4. How likely would you get a COVID-19 vaccine, once one becomes available to you? (Very unlikely - very likely)

Questions 1–3 were used to test our second hypothesis and judge the relevance, length and quality of the chats, and question 4 was to test our first and third hypotheses and compare the stances of the participants before and after the chat with the chatbot in order to judge persuasiveness. In order to test our third hypothesis, 60 out of the 300[5] participants did not chat with the chatbot but instead were presented the chatbot's 10 most commonly used counterarguments in *persuasive* chats on a static web page.

Table 1. Breakdown of the 240 participants' stance for getting a COVID-19 vaccine before and after chatting with the chatbot.

	Very unlikely	Somewhat unlikely	Neither likely nor unlikely	Somewhat likely	Very likely
Before	30%	42%	28%	0%	0%
After	22.5%	37.5%	29%	9.5%	1.5%

In order to test whether new concerns can be identified during the chats that were not identified in the crowdsourced arguments, we analysed the chats after every batch of 60 participants (we also recruited participants in batches of 60). By inspecting common, meaningful words we could identify new concerns after each batch of 60 participants and re-train the classifier with enough examples of the new concern, and add suitable counterarguments to the concern-argument graph. We only added a new concern to the chatbot's concern-argument graph if we could automatically identify at least 10 arguments that addressed that concern. The training set was also updated with more training examples to an

---

[5] Due to limited funding we did not want to split the participants in half but rather collect more data in form of chatlogs, since a web page does not provide data for further research.

already existing concern. For example, in the crowdsourced arguments, many people used the word *mutation* whereas in the chats the word *strain* was prevalent.

This way 8 additional concerns could be identified: **death**, that the vaccine does not prevent you from **getting** and **spreading** COVID-19, people claiming they already **had** COVID-19, that COVID-19 has a too high of a **survival rate** to be worried about it, that the vaccine may impact **fertility**, that the vaccine might not be **effective**, that the **ingredients** of the vaccine are unknown, and that herd immunity can be created **naturally** by catching the virus and hence no vaccine is needed.

6   Evaluation of the Chatbot

Table 2. Percentage of the 240 participants who changed their stance after chatting with the chatbot.

Negative to neutral	Neutral to positive	Negative to positive	Total
9%	7.5%	3.5%	20%

Table 1 shows the stance of the 240 participants who chatted with the chatbot, before and after chatting with the chatbot. We divided the change in stance into 3 categories: a change from negative to neutral (from *very unlikely/ somewhat unlikely* to *neither likely nor unlikely*); a change from neutral to positive (from *neither likely nor unlikely* to *somewhat likely/very likely*); and a change from negative to positive (from *very unlikely/somewhat unlikely* to *somewhat likely/very likely*). We do not consider a change from *very unlikely* to *somewhat unlikely*. Table 2 shows the percentage of the 240 participants who changed their stance by engaging in an argumentative dialogue with the chatbot. 20% of the participants (48 out of 240) had a positive change in stance. This verifies our first hypothesis - that a small, shallow concern-argument graph can be utilised by a chatbot to create persuasive dialogues.

Given that the chatbot did not use natural language generation and was not able to address novel arguments or expand on existing ones by giving more information, and solely relied on correct concern classification, the given results are promising. The length of the chats were on average 12 alternating turns. This means that the chatbot, on average, gave 6 arguments, 3 of which were default arguments and 3 from the graph. Table 3 shows the results for the first three questions. 35% of the participants felt understood by the chatbot and further 41% felt sometimes understood. 32% perceived the chatbot's arguments as relevant and further 55% perceived them as sometimes relevant. 23% felt that the majority of their concerns were addressed and further 54% felt that some of their concerns were addressed. This supports our second hypothesis that only by identifying the concern of an argument, suitable counterarguments can be presented and that the resulting argumentation dialogues are of satisfactory length and quality. An example of a chat can be seen in Fig. 2. All chatlogs, the data for the concern-argument graph, the concerns and their descriptions, and the code for the chatbot can be found on github [2].

As mentioned in the previous section, we recruited the participants in batches of 60. To evaluate our third hypothesis, the chatbot's persuasive effect compared to a static web page, we compared the results of the 60 participants who were presented with the static web page with a batch of 60 participants who chatted with the chatbot with similar starting distributions of their stance. The fourth (and last) batch of participants had a similar distribution as the batch that was recruited to read the arguments on a static web page. The starting distributions are shown in Table 4 and the change of stance for both groups are shown in Table 5.

We used a Chi-Square test to compare the number of participants who changed their stance after chatting with the chatbot with the number of participants who changed their stance after reading the 10 most common arguments used by the chatbot (this means that the participants who only saw the static web page, on average saw 4 more arguments than those who chatted with the chatbot). The results were statistically significant with a p-value of .023 at p < .05. The results, therefore, support our hypothesis that an interactive chatbot is more persuasive than a static web page.

Table 3. Answers to the first three questions by the 240 participants who chatted with the chatbot.

Felt understood			Relevance			Concern addressed		
Yes	Sometimes	No	Yes	Some	No	Majority	Some	None
35%	41%	24%	32%	55%	13%	23%	54%	23%

Table 4. Breakdown of stance for getting a COVID-19 vaccine of the group of 60 participants before chatting with the chatbot, and the group of 60 participants who was presented with a static web page.

	Very unlikely	Somewhat unlikely	Neither likely nor unlikely
Chatbot	60%	33%	7%
Web page	52%	28%	20%

Table 5. Change of stance for the group of 60 participants who chatted with the chatbot, and the group of 60 participants who was presented with a static web page.

	Negative to neutral	Neutral to positive	Negative to positive	Total (no of participants)
Chatbot	12%	5%	2%	18% (11)
Web Page	5%	0%	0%	5% (3)

The newly identified concerns mentioned in the previous section were also raised by some arguments that were collected during the initial argument collection described in Sect. 4.1. So claiming that new concerns could be identified during the chats would be incorrect. Given a large enough sample of crowdsourced arguments, more concerns could have been identified and included (together with appropriate counterarguments). in the concern-argument graph that was used as the chatbot's knowledge base.

Side effects (short and long term) are by far the most popular concern, with 45% of user arguments given during the chats (where a concern could be identified) raising it. This is coherent with previous studies which analysed vaccine hesitancy in France [21], the US [15] and the EU [17]. The second most prevalent concern was about the safety of the vaccine in general (28%), and in the third place, the vaccines fast development and young people believing they do not need one (both 10%).

7   Discussion and Conclusion

The aim of this paper was to present a prototype chatbot that can engage in persuasive dialogues with people who are opposed to the COVID-19 vaccine using computational models of argument. Our contribution in this paper is threefold. Firstly, we have shown that for a new domain, where there exists a lot of uncertainty, a small argument graph can be used to represent most of the possible arguments in this domain. This argument graph can be utilised by a chatbot to create persuasive dialogues, and we presented a method how to acquire and structure such a graph in form of a concern-argument graph. In our previous work [8] the chatbot's knowledge base consisted of an argument graph that included both arguments and counterarguments. The chatbot matched the incoming user argument with a similar argument in the graph (target argument) using cosine similarity of the vector representations of the two arguments (the vectors were created using GloVe word embeddings [18]). The graph was therefore much bigger (containing over 1200 arguments) than the one presented in this paper.

Secondly, we have demonstrated that no sophisticated natural language understanding of the user arguments is needed in order to provide suitable counterarguments that address the majority of the concerns of the users. And thirdly, we have shown that an interactive chatbot has a higher persuasive effect than a static web page.

Further, we have shown that in this domain a concern-argument graph (a three-level acyclic graph) where after the initial move, the chatbot only picks a leaf at every turn or uses a default argument, is enough to generate persuasive dialogues. Using a modest concern-argument graph, as described in this paper, and to not constrain the chatbot to use a larger argument graph that may involve long paths, has two main benefits: firstly, the graph can be constructed with less data than for a larger argument graph; secondly, this allows the chatbot to counter user arguments that are not direct counterarguments to the previously given chatbot argument. This is important, as during the chats people often

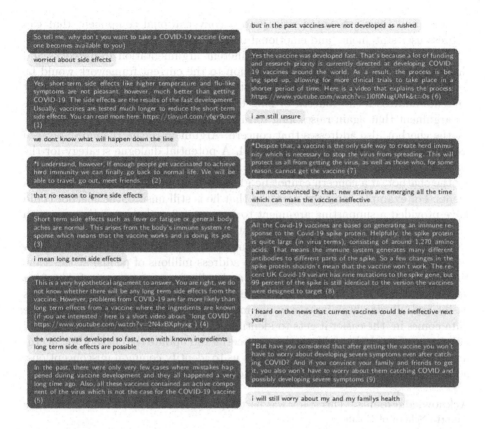

Fig. 2. Example chat between a participant from the fourth batch. Chatbot arguments are in the dark boxes and user arguments in the light boxes. Default arguments are indicated with an *. The chat begins in the left column and continues in the right one. The participant indicated that he or she was *somewhat unlikely* to get vaccinated before the chat, but changes his/her stance to *neither likely nor unlikely* after the chat.

ignored the chatbot's counterargument but instead gave a new argument on why not to take the vaccine.

It would, of course, be desirable to use more sophisticated natural language processing methods to process the user's input. For that, however, much more data is needed which currently is not available. The chatbot, hence, can only reply to well-phrased arguments that raise common concerns that it can identify. These sort of replies contributed to only 50% of the users' replies. Other types of responses included novel arguments, statements like *"I don't care* or *"I will take my chances"*, emotional accusations (about the government not caring or the chatbot being stupid) and questions about the vaccine. In future work, argumentation will, therefore, only be one component of the chatbot, paired with the ability to answer questions and provide information about COVID-19 vaccines and their associated risks, and a conversational component that can address user statements and emotional responses.

We also want to experiment with different argumentation frameworks and dialogue strategies. A reasonable extension to the current framework would be *bipolar argumentation* [3,6]. In Fig. 2, the fourth argument that the chatbot presents addresses the concern of long term side effects. The user replies with an argument that again raises long term side effects. Hence, the fifth argument by the chatbot also addresses that concern. Argument 5 can, therefore, be seen as a supporting argument to argument 4. A potential dialogue strategy for the chatbot could be to use arguments that support the previously given argument by the chatbot, if a concern cannot be identified, instead of giving default arguments. For example, after the user said that he is still unsure, the chatbot could have provided a supporting argument to argument 6 and present the user with another argument that addresses the fast development of the vaccine.

To conclude this paper, we want to emphasise the advantage of using a chatbot for such a task: a chatbot is able to address millions of people at the same time in the comfort of their own home and collect a vast amount of data in a very short time. Our method of analysing the incoming user arguments scales easily and allows obtaining many arguments from different people. The more data comes in, the easier it gets to identify patterns, discover new concerns, and acquire arguments that address these concerns and update the chatbot's concern-argument graph accordingly. This allows us to identify common misconceptions, address the lack of information, and potentially even fake news.

Acknowledgements. This study was partially supported by Noah Castelo from the Alberta School of Business.

References

1. https://yougov.co.uk/topics/international/articles-reports/2021/01/12/covid-19-willingness-be-vaccinated
2. https://github.com/lisanka93/covid-19_vacc_bot
3. Amgoud, L., Cayrol, C., Lagasquie-Schiex, M.C., Livet, P.: On bipolarity in argumentation frameworks. Int. J. Intell. Syst. **23**(10), 1062–1093 (2008)
4. Bench-Capon, T., Atkinson, K.: Abstract argumentation and values. In: Simari, G., Rahwan, I. (eds.) Argumentation in Artificial Intelligence, pp. 45–64. Springer, Boston (2009). https://doi.org/10.1007/978-0-387-98197-0_3
5. Bench-Capon, T.J.: Persuasion in practical argument using value-based argumentation frameworks. J. Log. Comput. **13**(3), 429–448 (2003)
6. Cayrol, C., Lagasquie-Schiex, M.C.: On the acceptability of arguments in bipolar argumentation frameworks. In: Godo, L. (ed.) ECSQARU 2005. LNCS (LNAI), vol. 3571, pp. 378–389. Springer, Heidelberg (2005). https://doi.org/10.1007/11518655_33
7. Chalaguine, L.A., Hunter, A.: Knowledge acquisition and corpus for argumentation-based chatbots. In: Proceedings of the 3rd Workshop on Advances in Argumentation in Artificial Intelligence, pp. 1–14. CEUR (2019)

8. Chalaguine, L.A., Hunter, A.: A persuasive chatbot using a crowd-sourced argument graph and concerns. In: Proceedings of Computational Models of Argument (COMMA), pp. 9–20. IOS Press (2020)
9. Chalaguine, L.A., Hunter, A., Hamilton, F.L., Potts, H.W.W.: Impact of argument type and concerns in argumentation with a chatbot. In: Proceedings of the 31st International Conference on Tools with Artificial Intelligence, pp. 1557–1562. IEEE (2019)
10. Dung, P.: On the acceptability of arguments and its fundamental role in nonmonotonic reasoning, logic programming and n-person games. Artif. Intell. **77**(2), 321–357 (1995)
11. Fines, P., Eames, K., Heymann, D.: "Herd immunity": a rough guide. Clin. Infect. Dis. **52**(7), 911–916 (2011)
12. Hadoux, E., Hunter, A.: Comfort or safety? Gathering and using the concerns of a participant for better persuasion. Argument Comput. **10**(2), 113–147 (2019)
13. Hunter, A.: Towards a framework for computational persuasion with applications in behaviour change. Argument Comput. **1**, 15–40 (2018)
14. MacDonald, N.: Vaccine hesitancy: definition, scope and determinants. Vaccine **33**(34), 4161–4164 (2015)
15. Marco-Franco, J.E., Guadalajara-Olmeda, N., de Julián, S.G., Vivas-Consuelo, D.: Covid-19 healthcare planning: predicting mortality and the role of the herd immunity barrier in the general population. Sustainability **12**(13), 5228 (2020)
16. Meppelink, C.S., Smit, E.G., Fransen, M.L., Diviani, N.: "I was right about vaccination": confirmation bias and health literacy in online health information seeking. J. Health Commun. **24**(2), 129–140 (2019)
17. Neumann-Böhme, S., et al.: Once we have it, will we use it? A European survey on willingness to be vaccinated against COVID-19. Eur. J. Health Econ. **21**(7), 977–982 (2020). https://doi.org/10.1007/s10198-020-01208-6
18. Pennington, J., Socher, R., Manning, C.D.: GloVe: global vectors for word representation. In: Empirical Methods in Natural Language Processing (EMNLP), pp. 1532–1543. ACL (2014)
19. Rémy, V., Largeron, N., Quilici, S., Carroll, S.: The economic value of vaccination: why prevention is wealth. J. Market Access Health Policy **3**(1), 29284 (2015)
20. Sherman, S.M., et al.: COVID-19 vaccination intention in the UK: Results from the COVID-19 vaccination acceptability study (CoVAccs), a nationally representative cross-sectional survey. medRxiv (2020)
21. Ward, J.K., Alleaume, C., Peretti-Watel, P.: The French public's attitudes to a future Covid-19 vaccine: the politicization of a public health issue (2020). https://doi.org/10.31235/osf.io/xphe9

Argument Strength in Probabilistic Argumentation Using Confirmation Theory

Anthony Hunter[(✉)] [iD]

Department of Computer Science, University College London, London, UK
anthony.hunter@ucl.ac.uk

Abstract. It is common for people to remark that a particular argument is a strong (or weak) argument. Having a handle on the relative strengths of arguments can help in deciding on which arguments to consider, and on which to present to others in a discussion. In computational models of argument, there is a need for a deeper understanding of argument strength. Our approach in this paper is to draw on confirmation theory for quantifying argument strength, and harness this in a framework based on probabilistic argumentation. We show how we can calculate strength based on the structure of the argument involving defeasible rules. The insights appear transferable to a variety of other structured argumentation systems.

Keywords: Argument strength · Probabilistic argumentation · Deductive argumentation · Defeasible logic

1 Introduction

In real-world argumentation, it is common for arguments to be considered in terms of their strength. Yet in computational models of argument, we lack formalisms that adequately measure strength in arguments. Some variants of abstract argumentation touch on the notion of strength such as rankings (e.g. [1,2,4,6,21]), and probabilities (e.g. [11,15,18,20,30,34]). However, these do not capture a notion of argument strength in terms of the quality of the contents of the premises and/or claim, rather they either assume that some kind of strength value is given for each argument and/or they calculate strength in terms of attacking and supporting arguments.

Using logical (i.e. structured) arguments allows the quality of the contents of the premises and claim to be directly considered. Some proposals assume strength is an input to the system (e.g. [8]). Others assess the strength of an argument in terms of the belief in it, often in terms of belief in the premises and claim (e.g. [14,15,29]), and in terms of the conditional probability of the claim given the premises of the argument (e.g. [16,28,36]). So these draw on uncertainty in argumentation to quantify the strength. But as we shall see, these only give us an incomplete picture of the strength of an argument.

© Springer Nature Switzerland AG 2021
J. Vejnarová and N. Wilson (Eds.): ECSQARU 2021, LNAI 12897, pp. 74–88, 2021.
https://doi.org/10.1007/978-3-030-86772-0_6

The use of defeasible logic is well-established in argumentation (see for example [13, 27, 33]), and key approaches to structured argumentation incorporate various kinds of defeasible rules [3]. There are also some proposals for probabilistic quantification of uncertainty in argumentation systems based on defeasible logic (e.g. [11, 31, 32]), but quantifying notions of strength have not been systematically considered in these formalisms.

To formalize argument strength for defeasible logic, we draw on measures from confirmation theory. These were originally proposed to determine the degree to which scientific evidence supports a hypothesis. They can capture how uncertainty associated with premises can impact a claim. To use these, we adapt the epistemic approach to probabilistic argumentation [15, 18, 34].

The proposal in this paper could be used in various ways. However, to illustrate and motivate, we focus on the following **audience scenario**: Someone presents us with an argument graph and the knowledgebase from which it has been constructed. The knowledge represents patterns that normally hold in the world (e.g., *if it is bird, then it is capable of flying*). As the audience, we are at liberty to identify a probability distribution over the possible worlds (in the following sections we make this precise) that represent our beliefs about the propositions in the language, and then we can use this probability distribution to analyze the strength of the arguments presented to us.

2 Defeasible Logic

We assume a finite **set of atoms** $\mathcal{A}$. We form a **set of literals** $\mathcal{L}(\mathcal{A}) = \mathcal{A} \cup \{\neg\phi \mid \phi \in \mathcal{A}\}$. A **defeasible rule** is of the form $\psi_1 \wedge \ldots \wedge \psi_n \to \phi$ where $\psi_1, \ldots, \psi_n, \phi \in \mathcal{L}(\mathcal{A})$. For a rule ρ of the form $\psi_1 \wedge \ldots \wedge \psi_n \to \phi$, let $\mathsf{Tail}(\rho) = \{\psi_1, \ldots, \psi_n\}$ and $\mathsf{Head}(\rho) = \phi$. The **set of rules** is $\mathcal{R}(\mathcal{A})$ and the **set of formulae** is $\mathcal{F}(\mathcal{A}) = \mathcal{L}(\mathcal{A}) \cup \mathcal{R}(\mathcal{A})$. A **knowledgebase** is a subset of $\mathcal{F}(\mathcal{A})$.

Example 1. Consider b for *bird*, p for *penguin*, and f for *capable of flying*. Then $\Delta = \{\mathsf{b}, \mathsf{p}, \mathsf{b} \to \mathsf{f}, \mathsf{p} \to \neg\mathsf{f}\} \subseteq \mathcal{F}(\mathcal{A})$ is a knowledgebase.

Next, we present a variant of defeasible logic, incorporating *ex falso quodlibet*, to build arguments, and a semantics to analyze arguments.

Definition 1. *Let* Δ *be a knowledgebase and* $\phi, \psi \in \mathcal{L}(\mathcal{A})$. *The* **consequence relation**, *denoted* $\vdash$, *is defined as follows: (1)* $\Delta \vdash \phi$ *if* $\phi \in \Delta$; *(2)* $\Delta \vdash \phi$ *if there is a* $\psi_1 \wedge \ldots \wedge \psi_n \to \phi \in \Delta$ *and* $\Delta \vdash \psi_1$ *and* ... *and* $\Delta \vdash \psi_n$; *and (3)* $\Delta \vdash \phi$ *if* $\Delta \vdash \psi$ *and* $\Delta \vdash \neg\psi$. *Let* $\mathsf{Closure}(\Delta) = \{\phi \in \mathcal{A} \mid \Delta \vdash \phi\}$.

Example 2. For $\Delta = \{\mathsf{b}, \mathsf{b} \to \mathsf{f}\}$, $\mathsf{Closure}(\Delta) = \{\mathsf{b}, \mathsf{f}\}$.

The Tarskian properties (widely regarded as requirements for a logic) are satisfied (though for reflexivity, it is restricted to literals): (Reflexivity) $(\Delta \cap \mathcal{L}(\mathcal{A})) \subseteq \mathsf{Closure}(\Delta)$; (Monotonicity) $\mathsf{Closure}(\Delta) \subseteq \mathsf{Closure}(\Delta')$ if $\Delta \subseteq \Delta'$; and (Idempotency) $\mathsf{Closure}(\Delta) \subseteq \mathsf{Closure}(\mathsf{Closure}(\Delta))$.

A **model** is an assignment of true or false to the literals of the language. We represent each model by a subset of $\mathcal{A}$. The set of models of the language, denoted $\mathcal{M}(\mathcal{A})$, is the power set of $\mathcal{A}$. For $m \in \mathcal{M}(\mathcal{A})$, $\phi \in \mathcal{A}$, the **satisfaction relation**, denoted $\models$, is: (1) $m \models \phi$ iff $\phi \in m$; And (2) $m \models \neg\phi$ iff $\phi \notin m$. We define the models for a set of formulae using the following fixpoint function.

Definition 2. *For $\Delta \subseteq \mathcal{F}(\mathcal{A})$, and $i \in \mathbb{N}$, the **inference operators**, denoted Inf^i, are defined as: $\mathsf{Inf}^1(\Delta) = \Delta \cap \mathcal{L}(\mathcal{A})$ and $\mathsf{Inf}^{i+1}(\Delta) = \mathsf{Inf}^i(\Delta) \cup \{\mathsf{Head}(\rho) \mid \rho \in \Delta \cap \mathcal{R}(\mathcal{A})$ and for all $\psi \in \mathsf{Tail}(\rho), \psi \in \mathsf{Inf}^i(\Delta)\}$. Let $\mathsf{Infer}(\Delta) = \mathsf{Inf}^k(\Delta)$ where k is the smallest value s.t. $\mathsf{Inf}^k(\Delta) = \mathsf{Inf}^{k+1}(\Delta)$.*

Definition 3. *The **satisfying models** for $\Delta \subseteq \mathcal{F}(\mathcal{A})$, is $\mathsf{Models}(\Delta) = \{m \in \mathcal{M}(\mathcal{A}) \mid m \models \phi$ for all $\phi \in \mathsf{Infer}(\Delta)\}$.*

Example 3. For $\Delta = \{\mathsf{b}, \neg\mathsf{o}, \mathsf{b} \to \mathsf{f}, \mathsf{p} \to \neg\mathsf{f}\}$, where $\mathcal{A} = \{\mathsf{b}, \mathsf{p}, \mathsf{f}, \mathsf{o}\}$, $\mathsf{Infer}(\Delta) = \{\mathsf{b}, \neg\mathsf{o}, \mathsf{f}\}$, and $\mathsf{Models}(\Delta) = \{\{\mathsf{b}, \mathsf{f}\}, \{\mathsf{b}, \mathsf{p}, \mathsf{f}\}\}$.

Definition 4. *For $\Delta \subseteq \mathcal{F}(\mathcal{A})$, $\phi \in \mathcal{L}(\mathcal{A})$, the **entailment relation** holds, denoted $\Delta \models \phi$, iff $\mathsf{Models}(\Delta) \subseteq \mathsf{Models}(\phi)$.*

Example 4. For knowledgebase $\Delta = \{\mathsf{b}, \mathsf{p}, \mathsf{b} \to \mathsf{f}\}$, $\Delta \models \mathsf{f}$.

A knowledgebase is consistent iff it does not imply an atom and its negation. So Example 1 (respectively Example 4) is inconsistent (respectively consistent). Obviously, Δ is consistent iff $\mathsf{Models}(\Delta) \neq \emptyset$.

Proposition 1. *For $\Delta \subseteq \mathcal{F}(\mathcal{A})$, $\phi \in \mathcal{L}(\mathcal{A})$, $\Delta \vdash \phi$ iff $\Delta \models \phi$.*

When Δ is consistent, this correctness result can be shown via the notion of a proof tree where ϕ is at the root, each leaf is a literal in Δ, and each non-leaf node ϕ' is such that there is a rule $\psi_1 \wedge \ldots \wedge \psi_n \to \phi' \in \Delta$ and each $\psi_i \in \{\psi_1, \ldots, \psi_n\}$ is a child of ϕ'. So $\Delta \vdash \phi$ holds iff there is such a tree where each branch is finite. We can use the same tree to consider entailment. So $\Delta \models \phi$ holds iff the leaves and inferences are satisfied by all the models of Δ, and hence all these models satisfy ϕ. When Δ is inconsistent, the consequence relation entails any literal (Proof rule 3), and similarly the entailment relation for defeasible logic is trivializable in the sense that any literal is entailed by inconsistency. This is because when Δ is inconsistent, $\mathsf{Models}(\Delta) = \emptyset$, and therefore for any $\beta \in \mathcal{L}$, $\mathsf{Models}(\Delta) \subseteq \mathsf{Models}(\beta)$.

3   Probabilistic Argumentation

In this section, we adapt the epistemic approach to probabilistic argumentation for use with defeasible logic. To present models, we use a **signature**, denoted $\mathcal{S}$, which is the atoms of the language $\mathcal{L}$ given in a sequence $\langle a_1, \ldots, a_n \rangle$, and then each model $m \in \mathcal{M}(\mathcal{A})$ is a binary number $b_1 \ldots b_n$ where for each digit b_i, if b_i is 1, then a_i is true in m, and if b_i is 0, then a_i is false in m. For example, for $\mathcal{S} = \langle \mathsf{a}, \mathsf{b}, \mathsf{c} \rangle$, $\mathcal{M}(\mathcal{A})$ is $\{111, 110, 101, 100, 011, 010, 001, 000\}$. So for $m = 101$, a is true, b is false, and c is true.

Definition 5. *A* **probability distribution** P *over* $\mathcal{M}(\mathcal{A})$ *is a function* P : $\mathcal{M}(\mathcal{A}) \to [0,1]$ *s.t.* $\sum_{m \in \mathcal{M}(\mathcal{A})} P(m) = 1$.

Definition 6. *The* **probability of literal** $\phi \in \mathcal{L}(\mathcal{A})$ *w.r.t. probability distribution* P *is* $P(\phi) = \sum_{m \in \mathcal{M}(\mathcal{A})} s.t. \ m \models \phi \ P(m)$.

Next, for an argument: (1) the premises imply the claim; (2) the premises are consistent; and (3) the premises are minimal for entailing the claim.

Definition 7. *For* $\Phi \subseteq \mathcal{F}(\mathcal{A})$, *and* $\alpha \in \mathcal{L}(\mathcal{A})$, $\langle \Phi, \alpha \rangle$ *is an* **argument** *iff (1)* $\Phi \vdash \alpha$; *(2)* Φ *is consistent; and (3) there is no* $\Phi' \subset \Phi$ *such that* $\Phi' \vdash \alpha$.

Example 5. For $\Delta = \{b, p, b \to f, p \to \neg f\}$, the arguments are $\langle \{b, b \to f\}, f \rangle$, $\langle \{p, p \to \neg f\}, \neg f \rangle$, $\langle \{b\}, b \rangle$, and $\langle \{p\}, p \rangle$.

A **reflexive** argument is of the form $A = \langle \{\alpha\}, \alpha \rangle$. For argument $A = \langle \Phi, \alpha \rangle$, Support($A$) returns Φ, Claim(A) returns α, Facts(A) returns the literals in Φ, Rules(A) returns the rules in Φ, and Frame(A) returns Facts(A) $\cup$ {Claim(A)}.

The probability of an argument being acceptable is based on the facts in the premises and the claim of the argument. So returning to the audience scenario, if the audience has been presented with an argument graph, they can use their probability distribution to calculate the probability of each argument.

Definition 8. *The* **probability of argument** A *being acceptable is denoted* $P(A)$, *where* $P(A) = \sum_{m \in \mathsf{Models}(\mathsf{Frame}(A))} P(m)$.

Example 6. Continuing Example 1, with probability distribution P below, and signature $\mathcal{S} = \langle b, p, f \rangle$, $P(\langle \{b, b \to f\}, f \rangle) = 0.95$ and $P(\langle \{p, p \to \neg f\}, \neg f \rangle) = 0.01$.

$\langle b, p, f \rangle$	110	101	100
P	0.01	0.95	0.04

Definition 9. *For* $\phi, \phi' \in \mathcal{L}(\mathcal{A})$, *let* $\phi \equiv \phi'$ *denote* $\mathsf{Models}(\phi) = \mathsf{Models}(\phi')$ *and let* $\neg\neg\phi = \phi$. *For arguments* A *and* B, A *is a* **direct undercut** *of* B *if there is* $\phi \in$ Support(B) *s.t.* Claim(A) $\equiv \neg\phi$. A *is a* **rebuttal** *of* B *if* Claim(A) $\equiv$ $\neg$Claim(B). A **attacks** B *iff* A *is a direct undercut or* A *is a rebuttal of* B.

The following coherence property holds because the sum of belief in complementary literals is less than or equal to 1.

Proposition 2. *For probability distribution* P, *if* B *attacks* A, *then* $P(A) + P(B) \leq 1$.

We use the usual notion of an argument graph, where each node is an argument, and each arc denotes an attack by one argument on another [10]. For a knowledgebase, a **complete argument graph** contains all arguments and attacks (e.g. Fig. 1). However, we are not using the argument graph to determine which arguments are acceptable. Rather, we use a probability distribution to determine the acceptable arguments as explained below. So the role of the argument graph is to provide a presentation of the arguments.

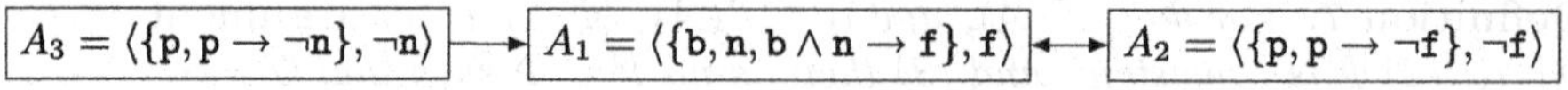

$$\boxed{A_3 = \langle\{p, p \to \neg n\}, \neg n\rangle} \longrightarrow \boxed{A_1 = \langle\{b, n, b \land n \to f\}, f\rangle} \longleftrightarrow \boxed{A_2 = \langle\{p, p \to \neg f\}, \neg f\rangle}$$

Fig. 1. The following is a complete argument graph (excluding reflexive arguments) from $\Delta = \{b, p, b \land n \to f, p \to \neg f, p \to \neg n\}$ where b is *bird*, p is *penguin*, f is *capable of flying*, and n is a normality atom. Argument A_3 has the claim that negates n, and so represents an attack on the use of the rule with n as condition in A_1.

When $P(A) > 0.5$, then the argument is believed to be acceptable, whereas when $P(A) \leq 0.5$, then it is not believed to be acceptable. The epistemic extension for a graph G, denoted $\mathsf{Extension}(P, G)$, is the set of arguments that are believed to be acceptable (i.e. $A \in \mathsf{Extension}(P, G)$ iff A is in G and $P(A) > 0.5$). For example, for graph G in Fig. 1, with $P(A_1) = 0.95$, and $P(A_2) = P(A_3) = 0.15$, $\mathsf{Extension}(P, G) = \{A_1\}$. As shown in [15], for any probability distribution P and graph G, $\mathsf{Extension}(P, G)$ is conflict-free.

The epistemic approach provides a finer-grained assessment of an argument graph than given by the definitions for Dung's extensions. By adopting constraints on the distribution, the epistemic approach subsumes Dung's definitions [18,26,34]. The epistemic approach also provides alternatives to Dung's approach. For instance, we may wish to represent disbelief in arguments even when they are unattacked [25].

4   Modelling Normality

Defeasible rules are normally correct, but sometimes are incorrect, and so we need to attack them. To address this, we use normality atoms as illustrated in Fig. 1. We assume the set of atoms $\mathcal{A}$ is partitioned into **normality atoms**, denoted $\mathcal{N}$, and **ordinary atoms**, denoted $\mathcal{Q}$. So $\mathcal{A} = \mathcal{Q} \cup \mathcal{N}$ and $\mathcal{Q} \cap \mathcal{N} = \emptyset$. We read the normality atom in the condition as saying that the context for applying the rule is normal. If there are reasons to believe that it is not a normal context, then a counterargument attacks this assumption of normality.

We will use the following **normality modelling convention**: Each rule has at most one normality atom as a condition, and if a normality atom appears as condition in a rule, it is unique to that rule. No other rule in the knowledgebase has the same normality atom as a condition. However, multiple rules in the knowledgebase can have the same negated normality atom as head. This convention helps us to specify an appropriate probability distribution over a set of atoms that includes normality atoms. We quantify the probability of a normality atom in terms of the unique rule that contains it as an antecedent: For a defeasible rule $\beta_1 \wedge \ldots \wedge \beta_n \wedge \gamma \rightarrow \alpha$ with normality atom γ, the probability of γ is $P(\beta_1 \wedge \ldots \wedge \beta_n \wedge \alpha)$.

Example 7. Consider probability distribution P, with the rules in Δ being $\mathsf{b} \wedge \mathsf{n_1} \rightarrow \mathsf{f}$ and $\mathsf{p} \wedge \mathsf{n_2} \rightarrow \neg\mathsf{f}$. So P satisfies our constraints that $P(\mathsf{n_1}) = P(\mathsf{b} \wedge \mathsf{f})$ and $P(\mathsf{n_2}) = P(\mathsf{p} \wedge \neg\mathsf{f})$.

$\langle \mathsf{b}, \mathsf{p}, \mathsf{f}, \mathsf{n_1}, \mathsf{n_2} \rangle$	11001	10110	10000
P	0.01	0.95	0.04

The use of normality propositions to disable rules is analogous to the use of abnormality predicates in formalisms such as circumscription [22]. Furthermore, we can use normality atoms to capture the specificity principle where a more specific rule is preferred over a less specific rule.

5 Argument Strength

Given an argument A and probability distribution P, we let $S_P(A)$ be an assignment in the $[-1, 1]$ interval to denote the strength of A. If $S_P(A) \leq 0$, then the support of the argument does not provide a good reason for the claim. As $S_P(A)$ rises above zero, then the support of the argument gives an increasingly good reason for the claim.

In the rest of this paper, we will focus on arguments that involve relationships between observations. We will assume that all the atoms, apart from the normality atoms, are observations. These are atoms that can ultimately be verified as true or false, though at any specific time, there may be uncertainty about which observations are true or false. Examples of observations include $\mathsf{b} = bird$, $\mathsf{d} = duck$, $\mathsf{p} = penguin$, $\mathsf{e} = eagle$, and $\mathsf{f} = fly\text{-}thing$. Given an argument A, the **evidence** in A, denoted $\mathsf{Ev}(A)$, is the set of observations in the support of A that are not normality atoms. (i.e. $\mathsf{Ev}(A) = \mathsf{Facts}(A) \cap \mathcal{L}(\mathcal{Q})$). So when we investigate strength, we want to quantify some aspect of how believing the evidence in the premises supports the claim.

There are various ways of defining S_P. To clarify some of the issues consider the simple situation of an argument A of the form $\langle \{\mathsf{b}, \mathsf{b} \rightarrow \mathsf{a}\}, \mathsf{a} \rangle$. For this, consider the four models for signature $\langle \mathsf{a}, \mathsf{b} \rangle$. Mass on 11 indicates positive correlation between a and b, and mass on 10 and 01 indicates negative correlation. On this basis, the conditional probabilities $P(\mathsf{a}|\mathsf{b})$ and $P(\mathsf{b}|\mathsf{a})$ indicate positive correlation, and the conditional probabilities $P(\mathsf{a}|\neg\mathsf{b})$, $P(\neg\mathsf{a}|\mathsf{b})$, $P(\mathsf{b}|\neg\mathsf{a})$, and $P(\neg\mathsf{b}|\mathsf{a})$, indicate negative correlation.

So there are multiple dimensions to connecting the evidence and claim. We will draw some of these out in the following seven properties that capture desirable, though not mandatory, features of argument strength. For a set of literals Γ, $\wedge\Gamma$ is the conjunction of the literals. We extend the definition for the probability of a literal so that if λ is a Boolean combination of literals in $\mathcal{L}(\mathcal{A})$, then $P(\lambda)$ is the sum of the probability of the models that classically satisfy λ. Also $P(\lambda|\lambda')$ is $P(\lambda \wedge \lambda')/P(\lambda')$, and if $P(\lambda) = 0$, then we let $P(\lambda|\lambda') = 0$.

$(X1)$ If $\mathsf{Claim}(A) \equiv \wedge\mathsf{Ev}(A)$ and $P(\mathsf{Claim}(A)) > 0$, then $S(A) < 1$
$(X2)$ If $\wedge\mathsf{Ev}(A) \equiv \wedge\mathsf{Ev}(B)$ and $\mathsf{Claim}(A) = \mathsf{Claim}(B)$, then $S(A) = S(B)$
$(X3)$ If $S(A) > 0$, then $P(\mathsf{Claim}(A)| \wedge\mathsf{Ev}(A)) > 0$
$(X4)$ If $P(\mathsf{Claim}(A)| \wedge\mathsf{Ev}(A)) = P(\mathsf{Claim}(A))$, then $S(A) = 0$
$(X5)$ If $P(\wedge\mathsf{Ev}(A)|\mathsf{Claim}(A)) = P(\wedge\mathsf{Ev}(A)|\neg\mathsf{Claim}(A))$, then $S(A) = 0$
$(X6)$ If P is a uniform probability distribution, then $S(A) = 0$
$(X7)$ If $P(\mathsf{Claim}(A)| \wedge\mathsf{Ev}(A)) = P(\mathsf{Claim}(A)|\neg \wedge\mathsf{Ev}(A))$, then $S(A) = 0$

We explain these properties as follows: (X1) If the evidence and claim are logically equivalent, and there is non-zero belief in the claim, then the argument is not providing a good reason for the claim because the reason is just the claim reiterated, and hence the strength is below 1; (X2) If two arguments are logically equivalent with respect to support and claim, then they provide equivalent reasons for equivalent claims, and so they are equally strong; (X3) Positive strength requires the probability of the claim conditional on the evidence to be non-zero; (X4) If the probability of the claim conditional on the evidence equals the probability of the claim, then the argument has zero strength as the premises are not giving a useful reason for the claim; (X5) If the probability of the evidence conditional on the claim equals the probability of the evidence conditional on the negation of the claim, then the argument has zero strength; (X6) If there is a uniform distribution, there is no material relationship between the evidence and claim and so the argument has zero strength; And (X7) If the probability of the claim conditional on the evidence equals the probability of the claim conditional on the negation of the evidence, then the argument has zero strength.

The first strength function we consider is the plausibility strength function which is the probability of the claim conditional on the evidence.

Definition 10. *The* **plausibility** *of an argument A w.r.t. probability distribution P, denoted S_P^p, is $P(\mathsf{Claim}(A)| \wedge\mathsf{Ev}(A))$.*

Example 8. Continuing Example 7, the plausibility of argument $A = \langle\{\mathsf{b}, \mathsf{b} \wedge \mathsf{n}_1 \rightarrow \mathsf{f}\}, \mathsf{f}\rangle$ is $S_P^p(A) = 0.95$.

Proposition 3. *The plausibility measure S_P^p satisfies $X2$ and $X3$, but it does not satisfy $X1$, $X4$, $X5$, $X6$, or $X7$.*

Proof. For counterexamples for X4, X5 and X7, consider the signature $\langle \mathsf{a}, \mathsf{b}\rangle$ with argument $\langle\{\mathsf{b}, \mathsf{b} \rightarrow \mathsf{a}\}, \mathsf{a}\rangle$. (X1) Assume $\mathsf{Claim}(A) \equiv \wedge\mathsf{Ev}(A)$ and $P(\mathsf{Claim}(A)) > 0$. So $P(\mathsf{Claim}(A) \wedge \mathsf{Ev}(A))/P(\mathsf{Claim}(A)) = 1$. So $S_P^p(A) \not< 1$. (X2 and X3)

Direct from definition. (X4) Let $P(11) = 0.2$, $P(10) = 0.3$, $P(01) = 0.2$, and $P(00) = 0.3$. (X5) Let $P(11) = 0.2$, $P(10) = 0.2$, $P(01) = 0.3$, and $P(00) = 0.3$. (X6) If P is uniform, then $P(\mathsf{Claim}(A) \wedge \mathsf{Ev}(A))|P(\wedge\mathsf{Ev}(A)) \neq 0$. So $S_P^p(A) \neq 0$. (X7) Let $P(11) = 0.2$, $P(10) = 0.3$, $P(01) = 0.2$, and $P(00) = 0.3$.

The failure of the $X1$, $X4$, $X5$, $X6$, and $X7$ properties suggests that there may be useful alternatives to the plausibility for measuring the strength of an argument. We are not suggesting that there is a single measure that tells us everything we need to know about the strength of a probabilistic argument based on defeasible rules, but we do expect that different measures can tell us different useful things about the strength of arguments.

6 Confirmation Theory

For an alternative perspective on the strength of an argument, we turn to confirmation measures. Originally, confirmation measures were developed in the philosophy of science to investigate the development of scientific hypotheses [9]. The aim of a confirmation measure $C(E, H)$ is to capture the degree to which evidence E supports hypothesis H. Confirmation measures have been proposed as a measure of argument strength in [24] but only in the restricted context of an argument that is a conditional probability statement. For our purposes, we assume that the evidence is a set of literals Δ and the hypothesis is a literal ϕ. We review some well-known confirmation measures next.

Definition 11. *For $\Delta \subseteq \mathcal{L}(\mathcal{A})$, $\phi \in \mathcal{L}(\mathcal{A})$, and probability distribution P, the C_P^d [5], C_P^s [7], and C_P^k [19] confirmation measures are defined as follows.*

- $C_P^d(\Delta, \phi) = P(\phi | \wedge \Delta) - P(\phi)$
- $C_P^s(\Delta, \phi) = P(\phi | \wedge \Delta) - P(\phi | \neg(\wedge \Delta))$
- $C_P^k(\Delta, \phi) = \frac{P(\wedge\Delta|\phi) - P(\wedge\Delta|\neg\phi)}{P(\wedge\Delta|\phi) + P(\wedge\Delta|\neg\phi)}$ *when $P(\wedge\Delta|\phi) + P(\wedge\Delta|\neg\phi) > 0$ and 0 otherwise.*

We explain these measures as follows: (C_P^d) the increase in belief in the claim that can be attributed to believing the evidence to be true, i.e. for it to be positive, $P(\phi) < P(\phi | \wedge\Delta)$ holds; (C_P^s) the difference in belief in the claim conditioned on the evidence being true and belief in the claim conditioned on the evidence being untrue, i.e. for it to be positive, $P(\phi | \neg(\wedge\Delta)) < P(\phi | \wedge\Delta)$ holds; and (C_P^k) the difference in belief in the evidence conditioned on the claim being true and belief in the evidence conditioned on the claim being untrue, normalized by the maximum range for the value, i.e. for it to be positive, $P(\wedge\Delta | \neg\phi) < P(\wedge\Delta | \phi)$ holds.

Example 9. Consider $S = \langle \mathsf{a}, \mathsf{b} \rangle$ with the following the distribution (left) and strength measures (right) for $\Delta = \{\mathsf{b}\}$ and $\phi = \mathsf{a}$. Here, the conditional probability gives a quite high score, whereas the confirmation measures give lower scores, reflecting the mass assigned to the models 10 and 01.

$\langle \mathsf{a}, \mathsf{b} \rangle$	11	10	01	00
P	0.5	0.1	0.2	0.2

	$P(.)$	S_P^p	S_P^d	S_P^s	S_P^k
A	0.5	0.71	0.11	0.38	0.25

We can harness confirmation theory for argumentation (where arguments concern relationships between observations) as below, where the greater the value, the stronger the argument. In order to focus on the evidence, we consider the ordinary facts (i.e. observations) in the support of the argument.

Definition 12. *The* **confirmation strength** *of argument A w.r.t. probability distribution P and confirmation measure C_P^x, for $x \in \{d, s, k\}$, denoted $S_P^x(A)$, is $S_P^x(A) = C_P^x(\mathsf{Ev}(A), \mathsf{Claim}(A))$.*

Example 10. Consider the following probability distribution (left), with signature $\langle d, p, f \rangle$, for an insectarium, where d is *dragonfly*, p is *pollinator*, and f is *flying insect*.

$\langle d, p, f \rangle$	101	011
P	0.2	0.8

	$P(.)$	S_P^p	S_P^d	S_P^s	S_P^k
A_1	0.00	0.00	−0.80	−1.00	−1.00
A_2	0.20	1.00	0.80	1.00	1.00

For arguments $A_1 = \langle \{d, d \rightarrow p\}, p \rangle$ and $A_2 = \langle \{d, d \rightarrow \neg p\}, \neg p \rangle$, the values for argument strength are given in the table on the right above where $P(.)$ is the probability of the argument being acceptable. Since dragonflies are not pollinators (as shown by the probability distribution), A_1 has low scores, and A_2 has high scores, for confirmation strength.

Example 11. Consider the probability distribution P, with signature $\langle b, p, f, n \rangle$, where b is *bird*, p is *penguin*, f is *capable of flying*, and $\mathcal{N} = \{n\}$, for a zoo with a large aviary.

$\langle b, p, f, n \rangle$	1100	1011	1000	0000
P	0.01	0.75	0.04	0.2

	$P(.)$	S_P^p	S_P^d	S_P^s	S_P^k
A_1	0.75	0.94	0.19	0.94	0.67
A_2	0.01	1.00	0.75	0.76	1.00
A_3	0.01	1.00	0.75	0.76	1.00

For the arguments $A_1 = \langle b, b \wedge n \rightarrow f\}, f \rangle$, $A_2 = \langle p, p \rightarrow \neg f\}, \neg f \rangle$, and $A_3 = \langle \{p, p \rightarrow \neg n\}, \neg n \rangle$, the strengths are given in the table on the above right. So A_1 has a high probability of acceptability, and some good scores for confirmation strength, and A_2 and A_3 have a low probability of acceptability but are quite strong arguments.

Proposition 4. *The table captures satisfaction ✓, or non-satisfaction ×, of the X1 to X7 properties.*

	X1	X2	X3	X4	X5	X6	X7
S_P^d	✓	✓	✓	✓	✓	✓	✓
S_P^s	×	✓	✓	×	✓	✓	✓
S_P^k	×	✓	✓	×	✓	✓	✓

Proof. For counterexamples, consider the signature $\langle \mathsf{a}, \mathsf{b} \rangle$ with $\langle \{\mathsf{a}, \mathsf{a} \to \mathsf{a}\}, \mathsf{a} \rangle$ for X1, and $\langle \{\mathsf{b}, \mathsf{b} \to \mathsf{a}\}, \mathsf{a} \rangle$ for X4 and X7. (S_P^d) (X1) Assume $\wedge \mathsf{Cn}(\mathsf{Ev}(A)) = \wedge \mathsf{Cn}(\mathsf{Claim}(A)) = \phi$. So $S(A) = P(\phi|\phi) - P(\phi) = 1 - P(\phi)$. So if $P(\phi) > 0$, then $S(A) < 1$. (X2) Direct from definition. (X3) If $S_P^d(A) > 0$, then $P(\mathsf{Claim}(A)| \wedge \mathsf{Ev}(A)) - P(\mathsf{Claim}(A)) > 0$. So $P(\mathsf{Claim}(A)| \wedge \mathsf{Ev}(A)) > 0$. (X4) Direct from definition. (X5) From the assumption $P(\wedge \mathsf{Ev}(A)|\mathsf{Claim}(A)) = P(\wedge \mathsf{Ev}(A)|\neg\mathsf{Claim}(A))$, we can show $P(\mathsf{Claim}(A)| \wedge \mathsf{Ev}(A)) = P(\mathsf{Claim}(A))$. (X6) If P is uniform, then $P(\mathsf{Claim}(A)| \wedge \mathsf{Ev}(A)) = 0.5$ and $P(\mathsf{Claim}(A)) = 0.5$. So $S_P^d(A) = 0$. (X7) From the assumption $P(\mathsf{Claim}(A)| \wedge \mathsf{Ev}(A)) = P(\mathsf{Claim}(A)|\neg \wedge \mathsf{Ev}(A))$ we can show $P(\mathsf{Claim}(A)| \wedge \mathsf{Ev}(A)) = P(\mathsf{Claim}(A))$. (S_P^s) (X1) Let $P(11) = 0.5$ and $P(00) = 0.5$. (X2) Direct from definition. (X3) If $S_P^s(A) > 0$, then $P(\mathsf{Claim}(A)| \wedge \mathsf{Ev}(A)) - P(\mathsf{Claim}(A)|\neg \wedge \mathsf{Ev}(A)) > 0$. So $P(\mathsf{Claim}(A)| \wedge \mathsf{Ev}(A)) > 0$. (X4) Let $P(11) = 1$. (X5) Follows from the fact that $P(\mathsf{Claim}(A)| \wedge \mathsf{Ev}(A)) = P(\mathsf{Claim}(A)|\neg \wedge \mathsf{Ev}(A))$ holds iff $P(\wedge \mathsf{Ev}(A)|\mathsf{Claim}(A)) = P(\wedge \mathsf{Ev}(A)|\neg\mathsf{Claim}(A))$ holds. (X6) If P is uniform, then $P(\mathsf{Claim}(A)| \wedge \mathsf{Ev}(A)) = 0.5$ and $P(\mathsf{Claim}(A)|\neg \wedge \mathsf{Ev}(A)) = 0.5$. So $S_P^s(A) = 0$. (X7) Direct from definition. (S_P^k) (X1) Let $P(11) = 0.5$ and $P(00) = 0.5$. (X2) Direct from defn. (X3) If $S_P^p(A) > 0$, then $P(\mathsf{Claim}(A)|\wedge\mathsf{Ev}(A)) > 0$. So $P(\mathsf{Ev}(A)|\mathsf{Claim}(A)) > 0$. (X4) Let $P(11) = 1$. (X5) Direct from definition. (X6) If P is uniform, then $P(\wedge\mathsf{Ev}(A) \wedge \mathsf{Claim}(A)) = P(\wedge\mathsf{Ev}(A))/2$ and $P(\wedge\mathsf{Ev}(A) \wedge \neg\mathsf{Claim}(A)) = P(\wedge\mathsf{Ev}(A))/2$. Hence $P(\wedge\mathsf{Ev}(A)|\mathsf{Claim}(A)) = ((P(\wedge\mathsf{Ev}(A))/2)/0.5 = P(\wedge\mathsf{Ev}(A))$ and $P(\wedge\mathsf{Ev}(A)|\neg\mathsf{Claim}(A)) = ((P(\wedge\mathsf{Ev}(A))/2)/0.5 = P(\wedge\mathsf{Ev}(A))$. So $\frac{P(\wedge\mathsf{Ev}(A)|\mathsf{Claim}(A)) - P(\wedge\mathsf{Ev}(A)|\neg\mathsf{Claim}(A)}{P(\wedge\mathsf{Ev}(A)|\mathsf{Claim}(A)) + P(\wedge\mathsf{Ev}(A)|\neg\mathsf{Claim}(A)} = \frac{P(\wedge\mathsf{Ev}(A)) - P(\wedge\mathsf{Ev}(A))}{P(\wedge\mathsf{Ev}(A)) + P(\wedge\mathsf{Ev}(A))} = 0$ (X7) Same as for S_P^s X5.

Recall that the plausibility measure S_P^p only satisfies $X2$ and $X3$. So S_P^d, S_P^s and S_P^k offer potentially valuable alternatives to S_P^p as they satisfy most/all of the properties. Note, four of these properties concern what zero strength means, and so in future work, we will consider further properties to explore what positive and negative strength mean, and to differentiate the measures.

7 Multiple Defeasible Rules

We now consider the question of the strength of an argument with multiple defeasible rules in the premises. To illustrate some of our concerns, consider the following arguments where b denotes *bird*, w denotes *has wings*, y denotes *yellow*, f denotes *capable of flying*.

- $A_1 = \langle \{\mathsf{b}, \mathsf{b} \to \mathsf{f}\}, \mathsf{f} \rangle$
- $A_2 = \langle \{\mathsf{b}, \mathsf{b} \to \mathsf{w}, \mathsf{w} \to \mathsf{f}\}, \mathsf{f} \rangle$
- $A_3 = \langle \{\mathsf{b}, \mathsf{b} \to \mathsf{y}, \mathsf{y} \to \mathsf{f}\}, \mathsf{f} \rangle$

Intuitively, A_1 is a reasonably strong argument since most birds have the capability to fly. But does A_2 have the same strength as A_1 since it starts from the same fact (i.e. bird) or is it stronger because it makes the intermediate point concerning having wings? And does A_3 have the same strength as A_1 or is it weaker because it makes the intermediate point (i.e. being yellow) that is irrelevant (and unlikely to be correct)? Assuming the probability distribution over the atoms b and f is the same for each argument, then the strength of each argument is the same since it is based on b and f. However, taking the rules into account, we might expect the following: (A_2) A strong confirmation by *birds* for *has wings*, and by *has wings* for *capable of flying*; and (A_3) A weak confirmation by *birds* for *yellow*, and a weak confirmation by *yellow* for *capable of flying*. To capture this, we consider how the assessment of the strength of an argument can depend on its intermediate steps.

Definition 13. *Argument B is an* **intermediate** *of argument A iff* Rules$(B) \subseteq$ Rules(A). *Let* Intermediates$(A) = \{B \mid B$ *is an intermediate of* $A\}$.

Example 12. For $A_1 = \langle\{b, b \rightarrow w, w \rightarrow f\}, f\rangle$, the intermediates are A_1, $B_1 = \langle\{b, b \rightarrow w\}, w\rangle$, and $B_2 = \langle\{w, w \rightarrow f\}, f\rangle$,

If B is a strict intermediate of A (i.e. Rules$(B) \subset$ Rules(A)), and Claim$(B) \neq$ Claim(A), then there is defeasible rule $\beta_1 \wedge \ldots \wedge \beta_n \rightarrow \phi \in$ Support(A) where Claim$(B) \in \{\beta_1, \ldots, \beta_n\}$ (e.g. B_1 in Example 12). This is because arguments are minimal, and so if the claim of the intermediate differs from that of the argument, then it is also a condition in a defeasible rule. Also, if B is a strict intermediate of A, it is not necessarily the case that Support$(B) \subset$ Support(A) (e.g. B_2 in Example 12). In order to consider the intermediates in the derivation of a claim from its premises, we use the following definition that judges not just the argument but also the intermediates.

Definition 14. *An argument A is* **compositionally strong** *with respect to strength measure S_P and threshold $\tau \in [-1, 1]$ iff for all $B \in$ Intermediates(A), $S_P(B) \geq \tau$.*

We now return to the arguments A_2 and A_3 from the introduction of this section, and analyze them in the following two examples.

Example 13. For $A_2 = \langle\{b, b \rightarrow w, w \rightarrow f\}, f\rangle$, with the following probability distribution for a zoo, where $\mathcal{S} = \langle b, w, f\rangle$, then A_2 and its strict intermediates have high strength.

$\langle b, w, f \rangle$	111	110	001	000
P	0.09	0.01	0.02	0.88

	S_P^p	S_P^d	S_P^s	S_P^k
$\langle\{b, b \rightarrow w, w \rightarrow f\}, f\rangle$	0.90	0.79	0.88	0.97
$\langle\{b, b \rightarrow w\}, w\rangle$	1.00	0.90	1.00	1.00
$\langle\{w, w \rightarrow f\}, f\rangle$	0.90	0.79	0.88	0.97

Example 14. For $A_3 = \langle\{b, b \rightarrow y, y \rightarrow f\}, f\rangle$, with the following probability distribution for a zoo, where $\mathcal{S} = \langle b, y, f\rangle$, then A_3 has the same high strength as A_2 in the previous example (because the marginals involving b and f are the same) but low strength for the strict intermediates.

$\langle b, y, f \rangle$	111	101	100	010	001	000
P	0.01	0.08	0.01	0.02	0.02	0.86

	S_P^p	S_P^d	S_P^s	S_P^k
$\langle\{b, b \rightarrow y, y \rightarrow f\}, f\rangle$	0.90	0.79	0.88	0.97
$\langle\{b, b \rightarrow y\}, y\rangle$	0.10	0.07	0.08	0.56
$\langle\{y, y \rightarrow f\}, f\rangle$	0.33	0.22	0.23	0.60

In the same way that we consider the strength of an argument, we can consider the strength of a defeasible rule.

Definition 15. *The* **strength** *of rule* $\psi_1 \wedge \ldots \wedge \psi_n \to \phi$ *is* $S_P^x(A)$ *where* $A = \langle \{\psi_1, \ldots, \psi_n, \psi_1 \wedge \ldots \wedge \psi_n \to \phi\}, \phi \rangle$ *and* P *is a probability distribution and* $x \in \{p, d, s, k\}$.

The following result says that if we want compositionally strong arguments, then we only need to consider strong defeasible rules.

Proposition 5. *If argument* A *is compositionally strong w.r.t. strength measure* S_P^x *and threshold* τ, *then the strength of any rule* $\rho \in \mathsf{Support}(A)$ *is greater than or equal to* τ.

Proof. An argument A is compositionally strong with respect to strength measure S_P^x and threshold $\tau \in [-1, 1]$ iff for all $B \in \mathsf{Intermediates}(A)$, $S_P^x(B) \geq \tau$. So for all $B \in \mathsf{Intermediates}(A)$ of the form $B = \langle \{\psi_1, \ldots, \psi_n, \psi_1 \wedge \ldots \wedge \psi_n \to \phi\}, \phi \rangle$, $S_P^x(B) \geq \tau$. So for all rules $\rho = \psi_1 \wedge \ldots \wedge \psi_n \to \phi \in \mathsf{Support}(A)$, the strength of ρ is greater than or equal to τ.

The above result means that if we do select strong defeasible rules for our knowledgebase, then we do not risk missing strong arguments. In other words, by rejecting weak defeasible rules, rules that are not going to lead to strong arguments are eliminated from the knowledgebase.

8   Discussion

Returning to the **audience scenario** given in the introduction, the confirmation measures give us different ways to judge the arguments, and decide which we regard as strong arguments. For those arguments that we identify as weak, we may argue with the person who provided the arguments in order to question those arguments. Possibly, they may provide supporting arguments to back-up the arguments under question, and if we are convinced by those supporting arguments, we have the option to then update our probability distribution. The protocol for this, the criteria for being convinced by the supporting arguments, and the method for updating the probability distribution, are beyond the scope of this paper, but this expanded scenario indicates how being able to analyze the strength of the arguments presented by others is potentially useful as part of an argumentation process.

Another application is in a **persuasion scenario** (for a review of persuasion see [17]). Assume we have a knowledgebase from which we can construct arguments. In a dialogue with another agent, we may want to select the best arguments to present in order to maximize the likelihood that they will be persuaded. For this, we can construct a probability distribution that reflects what we think the other agent believes about the world. Then using that probability distribution, we could select the stronger arguments to present.

A third example of an application is an **analytical scenario**. If we have acquired knowledge (perhaps from multiple sources), we may want to analyze the quality of the arguments generated from that knowledge. We can construct multiple probability distributions in order to investigate the arguments. Each probability distribution could reflect a possible modelling of the world, and so the change in strength for specific arguments could be investigated. Robustness could be investigated by identifying how extreme the modelling would be for arguments to be substantially weakened or strengthened. We leave the framework for undertaking robustness analysis to future work.

So there are potential applications for measuring argument strength, but it is an insufficiently understood notion in the literature on computational models of arguments. To address this, we consider a very simple defeasible logic with a clear semantics. This is so that we can get a clear understanding of the key concepts. We could have used an existing proposal for argumentation, but then the underlying issues we wanted to explore would be less clear in a more complex framework (e.g. defeasible logic programming [12]). Nonetheless, we believe this paper provides insights relevant for other argumentation systems, and so in future work, we will adapt existing proposals for structured argumentation systems (e.g. [12, 23, 35]) to quantify strength in a probabilistic context.

References

1. Amgoud, L., Ben-Naim, J.: Axiomatic foundations of acceptability semantics. In: Proceedings of KR 2016, pp. 2–11. AAAI Press (2016)
2. Baroni, P., Rago, A., Toni, F.: From fine-grained properties to broad principles for gradual argumentation: a principled spectrum. Int. J. Approximate Reasoning **105**, 252–286 (2019)
3. Hunter, A., et al.: Introduction to structured argumentation. Argument Comput. **5**(1), 1–4 (2014)
4. Bonzon, E., Delobelle, J., Konieczny, S., Maudet, N.: A comparative study of ranking-based semantics for abstract argumentation. In: Proceedings of AAAI 2016 (2016)
5. Carnap, R.: Logical Foundations of Probability, 2nd edn. University of Chicago Press (1962)
6. Cayrol, C., Lagasquie-Schiex, M.: Graduality in argumentation. J. Artif. Intell. Res. **23**, 245–297 (2005)
7. Christensen, D.: Measuring confirmation. J. Philos. **96**, 437–461 (1999)
8. Cohen, A., Gottifredi, S., Tamargo, L., García, A., Simari, G.: An informant-based approach to argument strength in defeasible logic programming. Argument Comput. **12**(1), 115–147 (2021)
9. Crupi, V.: Confirmation, Spring 2020 edn. In: The Stanford Encyclopedia of Philosophy. Metaphysics Research Lab, Stanford University (2020)
10. Dung, P.: On the acceptability of arguments and its fundamental role in non-monotonic reasoning, logic programming and n-person games. Artif. Intell. **77**(2), 321–358 (1995)
11. Dung, P., Thang, P.: Towards (probabilistic) argumentation for jury-based dispute resolution. In: Proceedings of COMMA 2010, pp. 171–182. IOS Press (2010)

12. Garcia, A., Simari, G.R.: Defeasible logic programming: an argumentative approach. Theor. Pract. Logic Program. **4**(1–2), 95–138 (2004)
13. Governatori, G., Maher, M., Antoniou, G., Billington, D.: Argumentation semantics for defeasible logic. J. Logic Comput. **14**(5), 675–702 (2004)
14. Haenni, R.: Modeling uncertainty with propositional assumption-based systems. In: Hunter, A., Parsons, S. (eds.) Applications of Uncertainty Formalisms. LNCS (LNAI), vol. 1455, pp. 446–470. Springer, Heidelberg (1998). https://doi.org/10.1007/3-540-49426-X_21
15. Hunter, A.: A probabilistic approach to modelling uncertain logical arguments. Int. J. Approximate Reasoning **54**(1), 47–81 (2013)
16. Hunter, A.: Generating instantiated argument graphs from probabilistic information. In: Proceedings of ECAI 2020. IOS Press (2020)
17. Hunter, A., Chalaguine, L., Czernuszenko, T., Hadoux, E., Polberg, S.: Towards computational persuasion via natural language argumentation dialogues. In: Benzmüller, C., Stuckenschmidt, H. (eds.) KI 2019. LNCS (LNAI), vol. 11793, pp. 18–33. Springer, Cham (2019). https://doi.org/10.1007/978-3-030-30179-8_2
18. Hunter, A., Thimm, M.: Probabilistic reasoning with abstract argumentation frameworks. J. Artif. Intell. Res. **59**, 565–611 (2017)
19. Kemeny, J., Oppenheim, P.: Degrees of factual support. Philos. Sci. **19**, 307–324 (1952)
20. Li, H., Oren, N., Norman, T.J.: Probabilistic argumentation frameworks. In: Modgil, S., Oren, N., Toni, F. (eds.) TAFA 2011. LNCS (LNAI), vol. 7132, pp. 1–16. Springer, Heidelberg (2012). https://doi.org/10.1007/978-3-642-29184-5_1
21. Matt, P.-A., Toni, F.: A game-theoretic measure of argument strength for abstract argumentation. In: Hölldobler, S., Lutz, C., Wansing, H. (eds.) JELIA 2008. LNCS (LNAI), vol. 5293, pp. 285–297. Springer, Heidelberg (2008). https://doi.org/10.1007/978-3-540-87803-2_24
22. McCarthy, J.: Circumscription: a form of non-monotonic reasoning. Artif. Intell. **28**(1), 89–116 (1980)
23. Modgil, S., Prakken, H.: The ASPIC+ framework for structured argumentation: a tutorial. Argument Comput. **5**, 31–62 (2014)
24. Pfeifer, N.: On Argument strength. In: Zenker, F. (eds.) Bayesian Argumentation. Synthese Library. Studies in Epistemology, Logic, Methodology, and Philosophy of Science, vol 362. Springer, Dordrecht (2013). https://doi.org/10.1007/978-94-007-5357-0_10
25. Polberg, S., Hunter, A.: Empirical evaluation of abstract argumentation: supporting the need for bipolar and probabilistic approaches. Int. J. Approx. Reason. **93**, 487–543 (2018)
26. Polberg, S., Hunter, A., Thimm, M.: Belief in attacks in epistemic probabilistic argumentation. In: Moral, S., Pivert, O., Sánchez, D., Marín, N. (eds.) SUM 2017. LNCS (LNAI), vol. 10564, pp. 223–236. Springer, Cham (2017). https://doi.org/10.1007/978-3-319-67582-4_16
27. Pollock, J.: Defeasible reasoning. Cogn. Sci. **11**(4), 481–518 (1987)
28. Pollock, J.: Cognitve Carpentry. MIT Press (1995)
29. Prakken, H.: Probabilistic strength of arguments with structure. In: Proceedings of KR 2018, pp. 158–167. AAAI Press (2018)
30. Riveret, R., Governatori, G.: On learning attacks in probabilistic abstract argumentation. In: Proceedings of the AAMAS 2016, pp. 653–661 (2016)
31. Riveret, R., Rotolo, A., Sartor, G., Prakken, H., Roth, B.: Success chances in argument games: a probabilistic approach to legal disputes. In: Proceedings of JURIX 2007, pp. 99–108. IOS Press (2007)

32. Shakarian, P., et al.: Belief revision in structured probabilistic argumentation - model and application to cyber security. Ann. Math. Artif. Intell. **78**(3–4), 259–301 (2016)
33. Simari, G., Loui, R.: A mathematical treatment of defeasible reasoning and its implementation. Artif. Intell. **53**(2–3), 125–157 (1992)
34. Thimm, M.: A probabilistic semantics for abstract argumentation. In: Proceedings of ECAI 2012 (2012)
35. Toni, F.: A tutorial on assumption-based argumentation. Argument Comput. **5**(1), 89–117 (2014)
36. Verheij, B.: Arguments and their strength: revisiting Pollock's anti-probabilistic starting points. In: Proceedings of COMMA 2014. IOS Press (2014)

The Degrees of Monotony-Dilemma in Abstract Argumentation

Timotheus Kampik[1]([⊠]) and Dov Gabbay[2,3,4]

[1] Umeå University, Umeå, Sweden
tkampik@cs.umu.se
[2] University of Luxembourg, Esch-sur-Alzette, Luxembourg
dov.gabbay@kcl.ac.uk
[3] King's College London, London, UK
[4] Bar Ilan University, Ramat Gan, Israel

Abstract. In this paper, we introduce the notion of the degree of monotony to abstract argumentation, a well-established method for drawing inferences in face of conflicts in non-monotonic reasoning. Roughly speaking, the degree of monotony allows us, given an abstract argumentation semantics and an abstract argumentation framework to be *as monotonic as possible*, when iteratively drawing inferences and expanding the argumentation framework. However, we also show that when expanding an argumentation framework several times using so-called normal expansions, an agent may, at any given step, select a conclusion that has the highest degree of monotony w.r.t. the previous conclusion (considering the constraints of the semantics), but end up with a conclusion that has a suboptimal degree of monotony w.r.t. one or several conclusions that precede the previous conclusion. We formalize this observation as the *degrees of monotony*-dilemma.

Keywords: Abstract argumentation · Non-monotonic reasoning · Argumentation dynamics

1 Introduction

When reasoning in dynamic environments, we expect that an intelligent agent can draw inferences in a *non-monotonic* manner, *i.e.* that the agent is able to reject previously inferred statements on the basis of newly acquired beliefs. In research on formal methods of reasoning, the design and analysis of inference approaches that systematically relax monotony of entailment has been an active field of research since several decades, in particular since the emergence of relaxed monotony principles like restricted [11] and rational monotony [13,15]. More recently, similar principles [4,7,12] have been introduced to formal argumentation approaches, which constitute a particularly vibrant research area related to the study of knowledge representation and reasoning [2]. In this paper, we provide a new perspective on relaxed monotony in the context of formal argumentation that we base on a *measure* of monotony, instead of on Boolean conditions.

© Springer Nature Switzerland AG 2021
J. Vejnarová and N. Wilson (Eds.): ECSQARU 2021, LNAI 12897, pp. 89–102, 2021.
https://doi.org/10.1007/978-3-030-86772-0_7

Assuming that we have an agent that iteratively infers possible conclusions (sets of atoms) from a belief base, selects a conclusion, and then expands the belief base to again infer possible conclusions (and so on), the agent measures the *degree of monotony* of the conclusions she can infer w.r.t. a previous conclusion she selected, and then commits to an inference result that implies a maximal degree of monotony, *i.e.* to a conclusion that rejects as few of the previously inferred statements as possible. This can, however, lead to a dilemma: if the belief base is expanded several times, and the agent draws inferences after all expansions, selecting a conclusion that is as monotonic as possible w.r.t. *one* of the previously inferred conclusions may lead to the selection of a "suboptimally" monotonic conclusion w.r.t. *another* previous inference result, even if our agent always selects the conclusion that is maximally monotonic (considering constraints imposed by the inference function) w.r.t. the immediately preceding inference result. Indeed, this paper shows that this dilemma occurs in the context of several argumentation semantics that Dung defines in his seminal paper on abstract argumentation [10].

Let us introduce the following informal example to further motivate the research this paper presents.

Example 1. We have an agent $\mathcal{A}_1$ that draws inferences from a belief base BB. Over time, the agent acquires new beliefs and adds them to the belief base, *i.e.* in our example, we have the belief bases BB_1, $BB_2 = BB_1 \cup BB'_1$, and $BB_3 = BB_2 \cup BB'_2$. Any newly added belief may conflict with any other belief; our agent's inference function *concls* resolves conflicts at run-time and draws new inferences every time the agent updates the belief base. In addition, we have two agents $\mathcal{A}_2$ and $\mathcal{A}_3$ that observe the inferences that agent $\mathcal{A}_1$ draws at different steps.

- $\mathcal{A}_2$ observes $\mathcal{A}_1$'s inferences from BB_1 and BB_3.
- $\mathcal{A}_3$ observes $\mathcal{A}_1$'s inferences from BB_2 and BB_3.

At any point, $\mathcal{A}_1$'s belief base may contain conflicting beliefs and hence allows for a range of alternative conclusions (sets of atoms), *e.g.*:

1. $concls(B_1) = \{C_{1,1}\} = \{\{a, b\}\}$;
2. $concls(B_2) = \{C_{2,1}, C_{2,2}\} = \{\{a, b, c, d, e\}, \{c, d, e, f\}\}$;
3. $concls(B_3) = \{C_{3,1}, C_{3,2}\} = \{\{a, b, g\}, \{c, d, e, f\}\}$.

$\mathcal{A}_1$'s inference function is non-monotonic: a belief that has been inferred as true may be rejected by a future inference after a belief update. Still, to ensure some degree of consistency in her decision process, $\mathcal{A}_1$ attempts to be *as monotonic as possible*, using a measure that determines the *degree of monotony* of a newly inferred conclusion C' w.r.t. a previously inferred conclusion C. We denote the degree of monotony of C' w.r.t. C by $deg_{mon}(C', C)$, and define $deg_{mon}(C', C) = \frac{|C \cap C'|}{|C|}$ if $|C| \neq 0$; 1, otherwise. With this, $\mathcal{A}_1$ proceeds as follows:

- $deg_{mon}(C_{2,1}, C_{1,1}) = 1$ and $deg_{mon}(C_{2,2}, C_{1,1}) = 0$: after having inferred $C_{1,1}$ and having expanded the belief base from BB_1 to BB_2, $\mathcal{A}_1$ chooses to infer

$C_{2,1}$ from BB_2, because it ensures a higher degree of monotony w.r.t. $C_{1,1}$ than inferring $C_{2,2}$.

- $deg_{mon}(C_{3,1}, C_{2,1}) = \frac{2}{5}$ and $deg_{mon}(C_{3,2}, C_{2,1}) = \frac{3}{5}$; according to these measures, $\mathcal{A}_1$ should choose to infer $C_{3,2}$, which means $\mathcal{A}_3$ observes that $\mathcal{A}_1$'s inference is *as monotonic as possible*.

- However, $deg_{mon}(C_{3,1}, C_{1,1}) = 1$ and $deg_{mon}(C_{3,2}, C_{1,1}) = 0$; according to these measures, $\mathcal{A}_1$ should choose to infer $C_{3,1}$, which means $\mathcal{A}_2$ observes that $\mathcal{A}_1$'s inference is as monotonic as possible. We say that $\mathcal{A}_1$ is in a *degrees of monotony*-dilemma, because she can maximize the degree of monotony merely w.r.t. *either $C_{2,1}$ or $C_{1,1}$*.

The reader may consider this scenario a (simplified) model of the following example use-case. Our agents represent different IT systems in a complex enterprise system landscape[1]. $\mathcal{A}_1$ is the so-called *leading system*, and provides business insights to $\mathcal{A}_2$ and $\mathcal{A}_3$, which these two systems then use to update their own configurations. From a practical perspective, we can realistically claim that $\mathcal{A}_2$ and $\mathcal{A}_3$ may observe $\mathcal{A}_1$'s inferences with different frequencies; for example, $\mathcal{A}_2$ could be a legacy system, whose synchronization with $\mathcal{A}_1$ runs as an overnight batch job, whereas $\mathcal{A}_3$ is a modern system that *listens* to updates from $\mathcal{A}_1$, approximately in real-time. Every time $\mathcal{A}_2$ or $\mathcal{A}_3$ observe that $\mathcal{A}_1$ has reversed a previously inferred statement, this implies invasive changes to the systems' configurations and operations. For example, active cases might need to get re-routed or even require manual (human) intervention. Hence, for both $\mathcal{A}_2$ and $\mathcal{A}_3$, the inferences the systems observe should be *as monotonic as possible*. However, because of the differences in observation frequencies, an inference that is *maximally monotonic* w.r.t. the last update that $\mathcal{A}_2$ has observed may not be maximally monotonic w.r.t. the last update that $\mathcal{A}_3$ has observed.

We formalize the notion of a degree of monotony for abstract argumentation [10], an approach for drawing inferences from conflicting beliefs (or: arguments) that has gained tremendous attention in the symbolic artificial intelligence community. Then, we show that for most[2] of Dung's original argumentation semantics (inference functions), the *degrees of monotony*-dilemma in fact occurs as a problem and present an initial mitigation approach.

The rest of this paper is organized as follows. Section 2 provides the theoretical preliminaries of abstract argumentation. Then, Sect. 3 introduces the notion of the degree of monotony to abstract argumentation, based on which Sect. 4 formally defines and analyzes the *degrees of monotony*-dilemma, and also outlines a mitigation approach. Subsequently, Sect. 5 discusses the findings in the light of related and potential future research, before Sect. 6 concludes the paper.

---

[1] For an introduction to academic literature on the topic, see Lankhorst [14] or Dumas *et al.* [9], for example.

[2] Precisely, the problem occurs for three of the four semantics. The exception is grounded semantics, which always infers exactly one extension and is typically regarded as "too skeptical" for many use-cases.

2   Theoretical Preliminaries

The central model of this paper is an (abstract) argumentation framework, as introduced by Dung [10].

Definition 1 (Argumentation Framework [10]). *An argumentation framework AF is a tuple (AR, AT), such that AR is a set of elements (called arguments) and $AT \subseteq AR \times AR$ (called attacks).*

We assume that the set of arguments in an argumentation framework is finite. Given an argumentation framework $AF = (AR, AT)$, and $a, b \in AR$, we say that "a attacks b" iff $(a, b) \in AT$. For $S \subseteq AR$, we say that "S attacks a" iff $\exists(c, a) \in AT$, such that $c \in S$. We say that "S defends a" iff $\forall d \in AR$, such that d attacks a, it holds true that S attacks d. To model dynamics in abstract argumentation, Baumann and Brewka introduce the notion of argumentation framework *expansions* [4].

Definition 2 (Argumentation Framework Expansions [4]). *Let $AF = (AR, AT)$ and $AF' = (AR', AT')$ be argumentation frameworks.*

- *AF' is an* expansion *of AF (denoted by $AF \preceq AF'$) iff $AR \subseteq AR'$ and $AT \subseteq AT'$.*
- *AF' is a* normal expansion *of AF (denoted by $AF \preceq_N AF'$) iff $AF \preceq AF'$ and $(AR \times AR) \cap (AT' \setminus AT) = \{\}$.*
- *AF' is a* weak expansion *of AF (denoted by $AF \preceq_W AF'$) iff $AF \preceq_N AF'$ and $\forall a \in AR$, $AR' \setminus AR$ does not attack a.*

In words, an expansion of an argumentation framework AF adds new arguments and attacks to AF, without removing "old" arguments or attacks, a normal expansion of AF is an expansion of AF that only adds attacks involving at least one new argument, and a weak expansion of AF is a normal expansion of AF in which no new argument attacks an "old" argument. Let us provide an example that illustrates the notions of expansions and normal expansions.

Example 2. Consider the following argumentation frameworks: *i)* $AF = (AR, AT) = (\{a, b\}, \{(a, b)\})$; *ii)* $AF' = (AR', AT') = (\{a, b, c\}, \{(a, b), (b, c), (c, a)\})$; *iii)* $AF'' = (AR'', AT'') = (\{a, b, c\}, \{(a, b), (b, c), (c, a), (b, a)\})$. AF' is a normal expansion of AF ($AF \preceq_N AF'$): $AR \subseteq AR'$, $AT \subseteq AT'$, and

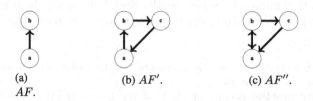

(a)
AF.

(b) AF'.

(c) AF''.

Fig. 1. $AF \preceq_N AF'$ and $AF' \preceq AF''$, but $AF \npreceq_N AF''$ and $AF' \npreceq_N AF''$.

$(AR \times AR) \cap (AT' \setminus AT) = \{\}$. This implies that AF' is an expansion of AF $(AF \preceq AF')$. In contrast, $AF' \preceq AF''$, but $AF' \npreceq_N AF''$: $AR' \subseteq AR''$ and $AT' \subseteq AT''$, but $(AR' \times AR') \cap (AT'' \setminus AT') \neq \{\}$. Also, $AF \preceq AF''$, but $AF \npreceq_N AF'''$. In this example, we do not have any weak expansions. Counterfactually, if AF' (which is a normal expansion of AF) did not feature the attack (c, a), it would be a weak expansion of AF. Figure 1 depicts the example's argumentation frameworks.

Let us now define the notions of *conflict-free* and *admissible* sets of arguments, which play a crucial role in abstract argumentation.

Definition 3 (Conflict-Free and Admissible Sets [10]**).** *Let* $AF = (AR, AT)$ *be an argumentation framework. A set* $S \subseteq AR$:

- *is* conflict-free *iff* $\nexists a, b \in S$ *such that a attacks b;*
- *is* admissible *iff S is conflict-free and* $\forall a \in S$, *S defends a.*

In his seminal paper that introduces abstract argumentation, Dung defines four *argumentation semantics*, functions that take an argumentation framework and return a set of *extensions*, where each extension is a set of arguments. We say that an argumentation semantics is universally defined iff it yields at least one extension for every argumentation framework.

Definition 4 (Stable, Complete, Preferred, and Grounded Semantics and Extensions [10]**).** *Let* $AF = (AR, AT)$ *be an argumentation framework. A set* $S \subseteq AR$ *is a:*

- stable extension *of AF iff S is admissible and S attacks each argument that does not belong to S. Stable semantics* $\sigma_{stable}(AF)$ *denotes all stable extensions of AF;*
- complete extension *of AF iff S is admissible and each argument that is defended by S belongs to S. Complete semantics* $\sigma_{complete}(AF)$ *denotes all complete extensions of AF;*
- preferred extension *of AF iff S is a maximal (w.r.t. set inclusion) admissible subset of AR. Preferred semantics* $\sigma_{preferred}(AF)$ *denotes all preferred extensions of AF;*
- grounded extension *of AF iff S is the minimal (w.r.t. set inclusion) complete extension of AF. Grounded semantics* $\sigma_{grounded}(AF)$ *denotes all grounded extensions of AF.*

Note that *i)* for some argumentation frameworks there does not exist a stable extension (consider the argumentation framework $AF = (\{a, b\}, \{(a, a)\})$; *ii)* each preferred extension is also a complete extension [1]; *iii)* for every argumentation framework, there exists exactly one grounded extension [3]. Because this work deals with the selection of extensions from the set of extensions a semantics returns, we focus our analysis on complete and preferred semantics, *i.e.* the two original Dung-semantics that are universally defined [3] but may return more than one extension. Let us note that the four semantics all rely on the notion of

admissibility. Over the past decades, additional abstract argumentation semantics families have been designed that are not admissible set-based, most notably
naive set-based semantics [17] and weak admissible set-based semantics [5]. However, for the sake of conciseness, we do not consider these semantics families in
our analysis. Finally, let us provide the definition of the *weak cautious monotony*
argumentation principle, which describes argumentation semantics that satisfy
a notion of relaxed monotony.

**Definition 5 (Weak Cautious Monotony in Abstract Argumenta-
tion [12]).** *Let σ be an argumentation semantics. σ satisfies weak cautious
monotony iff for every two argumentation frameworks $AF = (AR, AT)$ and
$AF' = (AR', AT')$, such that $AF \preceq_N AF'$, and $\forall E \in \sigma(AF)$, it holds true that
if $\{(a, b) \mid (a, b) \in AT', a \in AR' \setminus AR, b \in E\} = \{\}$ then $\exists E' \in \sigma(AF')$ such that
$E \subseteq E'$.*

3   Degrees of Monotony

This section formalizes the notion of the degree of monotony in the context of
abstract argumentation and provides a brief theoretical analysis on how normally
expanding an argumentation framework may affect the degree of monotony of
an extension inferred from the argumentation framework expansion w.r.t. an
extension inferred from the original argumentation framework.

Definition 6 (Degree of Monotony). *Let E and E' be two finite sets
of arguments. We define the degree of monotony of E' w.r.t. E, denoted by
$deg_{mon}(E', E)$, as follows:*

$$deg_{mon}(E', E) = \begin{cases} 1 & if |E| = 0; \\ \frac{|E' \cap E|}{|E|} & otherwise. \end{cases}$$

The degree of monotony tells us to what extent we violate monotony/are
non-monotonic in a dynamic inference scenario, in which we draw conclusions
from a changing knowledge base. Having such a measure can be useful because
in practice, knowledge bases typically change with time, and the "more non-
monotonic" (colloquially speaking) we are, the more careful we need to be when
assessing the consequences of the changed inference, for example when updating documents and IT system configurations to accommodate the change. The
normalization (division by $|E|$) can have practical advantages as it facilitates
benchmarking. Let us highlight that potentially, argumentation variants that
extend abstract argumentation could assign a weight to each argument in an
argumentation framework, and this weight could then inform the *costs* of violating monotony, roughly speaking. However, for the sake of conciseness, we abstain
from introducing such a formal argumentation framework variant here. Let us
prove the infimum and supremum of the degree of monotony.

Proposition 1. *Given two finite sets of arguments E and E', the infimum of
$deg_{mon}(E', E)$ is 0 and the supremum of $deg_{mon}(E', E)$ is 1.*

Proof. Let us first prove the infimum. By definition of the degree of monotony (Definition 6), $deg_{mon}(E', E)$ is minimal iff $|E' \cap E| = 0$ and $|E| > 0$. Given E and E', such that $|E| > 0$ and $|E' \cap E| = 0$, it holds that $deg_{mon}(E', E) = 0$.

Let us now prove the supremum. By definition of the degree of monotony (Definition 6), $deg_{mon}(E', E)$ is maximal iff $E' \cap E = E$. Given E and E', such that $E' \cap E = E$, it holds that $deg_{mon}(E', E) = 1$. □

We define a notion that allows us to select the *monotony-maximizing extensions* w.r.t. a previously inferred set of arguments E from the extensions an argumentation semantics infers from an argumentation framework.

Definition 7 (Monotony-Maximizing Extensions). *Let* $AF = (AR, AT)$ *be an argumentation framework. Let* σ *be a universally defined argumentation semantics, and let* S *be a finite set of arguments. We define the monotony-maximizing* σ*-extensions of* AF *w.r.t.* S*, denoted by* $Exts_{mon}(S, AF, \sigma)$*, as* $\{E | E \in \sigma(AF), \nexists E' \in \sigma(AF), \text{ such that } deg_{mon}(E, S) < deg_{mon}(E', S)\}$.

Let us introduce an example to illustrate the notions of the *degree of monotony* and *monotony maximizing extensions* in the context of an argumentation framework and one of its normal expansions.

Example 3. Let us consider the following argumentation frameworks (AF and AF', such that $AF \preceq_N AF'$):

- $AF = (AR, AT) = (\{a, b, c, d\}, \{(a, b), (b, a), (b, c), (d, c)\})$.
- $AF' = (AR', AT') = (\{a, b, c, d, e\}, \{(a, b), (b, a), (b, c), (d, c), (a, e), (e, d)\})$.

Let us consider complete, preferred, and grounded semantics[3].

- Complete semantics: $\sigma_{\text{complete}}(AF) = \{\{d\}, \{a, d\}, \{b, d\}\}$ and $\sigma_{\text{complete}}(AF') = \{\{\}, \{a, d\}, \{b, e\}\}$. Given $E_c = \{d\}, E_c \in \sigma_{\text{complete}}(AF)$, we have $Exts_{mon}(E_c, AF', \sigma_{\text{complete}}) = \{\{a, d\}\}$ and $deg_{mon}(\{a, d\}, E_c) = 1$.
- Preferred semantics: $\sigma_{\text{preferred}}(AF) = \{\{a, d\}, \{b, d\}\}$ and $\sigma_{\text{preferred}}(AF') = \{\{a, d\}, \{b, e\}\}$. Given $E_p = \{b, d\}, E_p \in \sigma_{\text{preferred}}(AF)$, we have $Exts_{mon}(E_p, AF', \sigma_{\text{preferred}}) = \{\{a, d\}, \{b, e\}\}$ and $deg_{mon}(\{a, d\}, E_p) = deg_{mon}(\{b, e\}, E_p) = \frac{1}{2}$.
- Grounded semantics: $\sigma_{\text{grounded}}(AF) = \{\{d\}\}$ and $\sigma_{\text{grounded}}(AF') = \{\{\}\}$. Given $E_g = \{d\}, E_g \in \sigma_{\text{grounded}}(AF)$, we have $Exts_{mon}(E_g, AF', \sigma_{\text{grounded}}) = \{\{\}\}$ and $deg_{mon}(\{\}, E_g) = 0$.

---

[3] We do not consider stable semantics for the sake of conciseness, and because stable semantics is not universally defined.

Figure 2 depicts the example's argumentation frameworks.

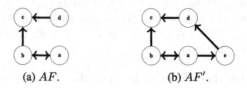

(a) *AF*.   (b) *AF'*.

Fig. 2. Example argumentation frameworks to illustrate degrees of monotony.

Intuitively (and roughly speaking), the maximal degree of monotony may be 0 even in case of a small expansion of a large initial argumentation framework from which we infer a large set of arguments.

Proposition 2. *Let σ_x be an argumentation semantics, such that $x \in \{stable, complete, preferred, grounded\}$, and let $n \in \mathbb{N}, n > 1$. There exist two argumentation frameworks $AF = (AR, AT)$, $AF' = (AR', AT')$, such that $|AR| = n + 1$, $AF \preceq_N AF'$, $|AR' \setminus AR| = 1$, $|AT' \setminus AT| = 1$, and $\exists E \in \sigma(AF)$, such that $|E| = n$ and $\forall E' \in Exts_{mon}(E, AF', \sigma_x)$, $deg_{mon}(E', E) = 0$.*

Proof. Let us consider the following argumentation framework constructions:

- $AF = (AR, AT)$, such that $AR = \{a_1, \ldots, a_n, a_{n+1}\}$ and $AT = \{(a_{n+1}, a_i) | 1 \leq i < n\} \cup \{(a_n, a_{n+1})\}$;
- $AF' = (AR', AT')$, such that $AR' = AR \cup \{b\}, b \notin AR$ and $AT' = AT \cup \{(b, a_n)\}$.

Note that $AF \preceq_N AF'$ and $|AR' \setminus AR| = 1$, $|AT' \setminus AT| = 1$. We observe that $\sigma_x(AF) = \{E\}$, such that $E = \{a_1, \ldots, a_n\}, |E| = n$ and $\sigma_x(AF') = \{\{b, a_{n+1}\}\}$. Hence, $\forall E$ such that $E \in \sigma_x(AF), \forall E' \in Exts_{mon}(E, AF', \sigma_x), deg_{mon}(E', E) = 0$. This proves the proposition[4]. $\square$

In contrast, if a normal expansion of an argumentation framework does not add any attacks to a specific extension E that has been inferred from the original argumentation framework, using complete, preferred, or grounded semantics, then we can infer an extension E' from the expansion such that the degree of monotony of E' w.r.t. E is 1. To prove this, let us first introduce the notion of (normal) E-weak expansions. Note that this definition draws upon the theoretical preliminaries provided by Definitions 2 and 5.

Definition 8 ((Normal) E-Weak Expansions). *Let $AF = (AR, AT)$ and $AF' = (AR', AT')$ be argumentation frameworks and let $E \subseteq AR$.*

---

[4] Note that the fact that stable semantics is not universally defined is not relevant for this proof, as we prove the *existence* of a phenomenon, roughly speaking.

- AF' is an E-weak *expansion of* AF *(denoted by* $AF \preceq_{W(E)} AF'$*) iff* $AF \preceq$ AF' *and* $\{(a,b) \mid (a,b) \in AT', a \in AR' \setminus AR, b \in E\} = \{\}$.
- AF' is an E-weak *normal expansion of* AF *(denoted by* $AF \preceq_{NW(E)} AF'$*)* *iff* $AF \preceq_N AF'$ *and* $\{(a,b) \mid (a,b) \in AT', a \in AR' \setminus AR, b \in E\} = \{\}$.

Note that colloquially speaking, we can say that cautious monotony (Definition 5) is monotony in the face of normal E-weak expansions.

Now, we can introduce and prove the proposition.

Proposition 3. *Let* σ_x *be an argumentation semantics, such that* $x \in$ $\{complete, preferred, grounded\}$. *For every argumentation framework* $AF =$ (AR, AT), $\forall E \in \sigma_x(AF)$ *and for every argumentation* $AF' = (AR', AT')$, *such that* $AF \preceq_{NW(E)} AF'$, $\exists E' \in \sigma_x(AF')$ *such that* $deg_{mon}(E', E) = 1$.

Proof. Let us provide a proof by contradiction. Let us assume that $\exists E \in \sigma_x(AF)$, such that $\nexists E' \in \sigma_x(AF')$ and $deg_{mon}(E', E) = 1$.

1. By definition of the degree of monotony (Definition 6), the following statement holds true:

$$\forall E \in \sigma(AF),$$
$$\text{if } \nexists E' \in \sigma(AF'), \text{ such that } deg_{mon}(E', E) = 1$$
$$\text{then } \nexists E' \in \sigma(AF'), \text{ such that } E \subseteq E'$$

2. Because $AF \preceq_N AF'$, by definition of σ_x (Definition 4, σ_x is universally defined and each σ_x-extension contains all arguments it defends; consider that each preferred/grounded extension also is a complete extension), the following statement holds true:

$$\forall E \in \sigma(AF),$$
$$\text{if } \nexists E' \in \sigma(AF'), \text{ such that } E \subseteq E'$$
$$\text{then } \exists a \in E, \text{ such that } a \text{ is attacked by } AR' \setminus AR$$

3. From 1. and 2., it follows that the following statement holds true:

$$\forall E \in \sigma(AF),$$
$$\text{if } \nexists E' \in \sigma(AF'), \text{ such that } deg_{mon}(E', E) = 1$$
$$\text{then } \exists a \in E, \text{ such that } a \text{ is attacked by } AR' \setminus AR$$

4. From 3. it follows that $\forall E \in \sigma_x(AF)$ if $\nexists E' \in \sigma(AF')$ such that $deg_{mon}(E', E) \neq 1$ then $AF \npreceq_{NW(E)} AF'$. Contradiction! This proves the proposition.

$\square$

Let us claim this proof entails the proof that complete, grounded, and preferred semantics satisfy cautious monotony and note that there exist argumentation semantics for which an analogous proposition does not hold true, consider *e.g.*, stable semantics and the argumentation frameworks $AF =$ $(\{a\}, \{\}), AF' = (\{a, b\}, \{(b, b)\})$. This claim can be extended to other semantics like stage semantics [17], by considering the argumentation frameworks $AF =$ $(\{a, b, c\}, \{(a, b), (b, c), (c, a)\}), AF' = (\{a, b, c, d\}, \{(a, b), (b, c), (c, a), (d, a)\})$.

4   The "Degrees of Monotony"-Dilemma

This section formally introduces the notion of the degrees of monotony-dilemma and defines a possible mitigation approach.

Definition 9 (The Degrees of Monotony-Dilemma). *Let σ be an argumentation semantics. σ is affected by the degrees of monotony-dilemma iff there exist argumentation frameworks $AF = (AR, AT)$, $AF' = (AR', AT')$, and $AF'' = (AR'', AT'')$, such that $AF \preceq_N AF'$, $AF' \preceq_N AF''$ and the following statement does not hold true:*

$$\forall E \in \sigma(AF), \forall E' \in \sigma(AF'), \text{ such that } E' \in Exts_{mon}(E, AF', \sigma),$$
$$\exists E'' \in \sigma(AF''), \text{ such that } E'' \in Exts_{mon}(E', AF'', \sigma)$$
$$\text{and } E'' \in Exts_{mon}(E, AF'', \sigma)$$

Let us note that we constrain the definition to normal expansions because arguments can be *defeated* instead of removed to keep track of history and the addition of new attacks between existing arguments can be emulated by adding new arguments as well (for an analogy, think of immutable variables in some programming languages). Moreover, the constraint allows us to show that the degrees of monotony-dilemma occurs even under these somewhat strict conditions. Complete and preferred semantics (the two universally defined Dung-semantics that may return more than one extension for a given argumentation framework) are affected by the degrees of monotony-dilemma.

Proposition 4 (Complete and Preferred Semantics are Affected by the Degrees of Monotony-Dilemma). *Let σ_x be an argumentation semantics, such that $x \in \{complete, preferred\}$. σ_x is affected by the degrees of monotony-dilemma.*

Proof. We provide a proof by counter-example. Let us consider the following argumentation frameworks: *i)* $AF = (AR, AT) = (\{a, b, c\}, \{(a, b), (b, a), (b, c)\})$; *ii)* $AF' = (AR', AT') = (\{a, b, c, d, e, f\}, \{(a, b), (b, a), (b, c)\})$; *iii)* $AF'' = (AR'', AT'') = (\{a, b, c, d, e, f, g\}, \{(a, b), (b, a), (b, c), (b, g), (g, d), (g, e), (g, f)\})$. Let us observe that $AF \preceq_N AF'$ and $AF' \preceq_N AF''$ and that: *i)* $\sigma_{preferred}(AF) = \{\{b\}, \{a, c\}\}$ and $\sigma_{complete}(AF) = \sigma_{preferred}(AF) \cup \{\{\}\}$; *ii)* $\sigma_{preferred}(AF') = \{\{b, d, e, f\}, \{a, c, d, e, f\}\}$ and $\sigma_{complete}(AF') = \sigma_{preferred}(AF') \cup \{\{d, e, f\}\}$; *iii)* $\sigma_{preferred}(AF'') = \{\{b, d, e, f\}, \{a, c, g\}\}$ and $\sigma_{complete}(AF'') = \sigma_{preferred}(AF'') \cup \{\{\}\}$.

Let us consider $E = \{a, c\}$, $E \in \sigma_x(AF)$. $Exts_{mon}(E, AF', \sigma_x) = \{\{a, c, d, e, f\}\}$. Given $E' = \{a, c, d, e, f\}$, $E' \in Exts_{mon}(E, AF', \sigma_x)$, we have $Exts_{mon}(E', AF'', \sigma_x) = \{\{b, d, e, f\}\}$. However, $Exts_{mon}(E, AF'', \sigma_x) = \{\{a, c, g\}\}$. Hence, we can conclude that given $E = \{a, c\}$, the following statement does not hold true:

$$\forall E' \in \sigma_x(AF'), \text{ such that } E' \in Exts_{mon}(E, AF', \sigma_x), \exists E'' \in \sigma_x(AF''),$$
$$\text{such that } E'' \in Exts_{mon}(E', AF'', \sigma_x) \text{ and } E'' \in Exts_{mon}(E, AF'', \sigma_x)$$

By definition of the degrees of monotony-dilemma (Definition 9), this proves the proposition.   □

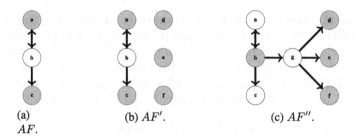

(a)   (b) AF'.   (c) AF''.
AF.

Fig. 3. Complete and preferred semantics are affected by the degrees of monotony-dilemma.

Figure 3 illustrates the argumentation frameworks that are used in the proof of Proposition 4. The proposition highlights that the degrees of monotony-dilemma that we have colloquially described in the introduction does indeed occur in the context of abstract argumentation. Let us observe that grounded semantics is not affected by the degrees of monotony-dilemma, as it is universally uniquely defined [3][5]. In contrast, given an argumentation framework and its normal expansion, stable semantics may yield an extension for the original framework, but return no extension for the expansion (consider $AF = (\{a\}, \{\}), AF' = (\{a, b\}, \{(b, b)\})$); i.e., even the more basic problem of maximally monotonic extension selection cannot be guaranteed for stable semantics.

To mitigate the degrees of monotony-dilemma, we can, for instance, compute a weighted average of several degrees of monotony, considering the results of past inferences. Let us first define the notion of the *weighted average degree of monotony*.

Definition 10 (Weighted Average Degree of Monotony). *Let E' be a finite set of arguments and let $ES = \langle E_0, \ldots, E_n \rangle$ be a finite sequence of finite sets of arguments. We define the weighted average degree of monotony (denoted by $deg_{\gamma,wmon}(E', ES)$) as follows:*

$$deg_{\gamma,wmon}(E', ES) = \frac{\sum_{i=0}^{n} \gamma^{(n-i)} deg_{mon}(E', E_i)}{|n+1|},$$

where $0 < \gamma \leq 1$.

---

[5] However, grounded semantics is typically considered a simplistic approach to abstract argumentation, roughly speaking because it is too skeptical.

Note that in the definition, γ can be considered the *discount factor*, and a smaller γ gives a higher importance to recent inferences (relative to less recent inferences), roughly speaking.

Now, we can define the mitigation approach.

Definition 11 (Weighted Average Monotony-Maximizing Extensions). *Let $AF = (AR, AT)$ be an argumentation framework, let σ be an argumentation semantics, and let $ES = \langle E_0, \ldots, E_n \rangle$ be a finite sequence of finite sets of arguments. We define the weighted average monotony-maximizing σ-extensions of AF w.r.t. ES, denoted by $Exts_{\gamma,wmon}(ES, AF, \sigma)$ as $\{E | E \in \sigma(AF), \nexists E' \in \sigma(AF), \text{ such that } deg_{\gamma,wmon}(E, ES) < deg_{\gamma,wmon}(E', ES)\}$, where $0 < \gamma \leq 1$.*

Let us illustrate this approach using an example.

Example 4. We consider preferred semantics and the argumentation frameworks depicted by Fig. 3. We start by "selecting" $E_0 = \{a, b\}, E_0 \in \sigma_{\text{preferred}}(AF)$. Then, we have $Exts_{mon}(E, AF', \sigma_{\text{preferred}}) = Exts_{\gamma,wmon}(\langle E \rangle, AF', \sigma_{\text{preferred}}) = \{E_1\}$, such that $E_1 = \{a, c, d, e, f\}$. We assume $\gamma = 0.9$. Now, we want to select an extension from $\sigma_{\text{preferred}}(AF'')$, considering E_0 and E_1. $\sigma_{\text{preferred}}(AF'') = \{\{a, c, g\}, \{b, d, e, f\}\}$. We have $deg_{\gamma,wmon}(\{a, c, g\}, \langle E_0, E_1 \rangle)\} = \frac{13}{20}$ and $deg_{\gamma,wmon}(\{b, d, e, f\}, \langle E_0, E_1 \rangle)\} = \frac{3}{10}$. Hence, we select $\{a, c, g\}$.

5   Discussion

This paper contributes to the continuation of a long line of research on systematically relaxing monotony, see for example the works by Gabbay [11] and Makinson [15] that introduce the restricted monotony and rational monotony principles. In the context of formal argumentation research, this paper adds to the body of research on *dynamics* in formal argumentation (see [8] for a survey), and in particular relies on work by Baumman and Brewka that presents monotony results in abstract argumentation [4]. Let us highlight that the work presented in this paper is different from (but has a similar motivation to) our recent results that show how to ensure consistent preferences over powersets of arguments in the context of normal expansions and naive set-based semantics [12], taking principles of economic rationality as a starting point (Dung's admissible set-based semantics violate the corresponding argumentation principle). The results this paper provides raise the following questions.

1. Can we specify more bounds to the degree of monotony when expanding a belief base (argumentation framework), given some constraints to the nature of the expansion and the inference function (argumentation semantics)?
2. What additional approaches can mitigate the *degrees of monotony*-dilemma and according to which criteria can these approaches be formally analyzed?
3. What roles can degrees of monotony play in formal argumentation variants that extend abstract argumentation, such as value-based argumentation [6]?

Future research can set out to answer these questions for abstract argumentation, other formal argumentation variants, and indeed for any method of non-monotonic reasoning in the face of uncertainty. In the context of abstract argumentation, the analysis provided in this paper can, for example, be extended to other argumentation semantics (see [1] for an overview, and also see the weak admissible set-based semantics family as recently introduced by Baumann *et al.* [5]), and consider additional constraints, *e.g.* other notions of expansions [4], constraints to the structure of an argumentation framework, or formal argumentation principles [16] that constrain semantics behavior.

6 Conclusion

In this paper, we have defined the notion of the degree of monotony to abstract argumentation and then introduced the *degrees of monotony*-dilemma, which can occur when repeatedly first determining the extensions of an argumentation framework and then normally expanding the argumentation framework. The *degrees of monotony*-dilemma highlights that selecting extensions from every argumentation framework that maximize the degree of monotony w.r.t. an extension that has been inferred by the immediate predecessor may lead to a suboptimal degree of monotony of any extension inferred from an argumentation framework and any "indirect" predecessor. With this, the findings shed new light on the challenge of drawing "consistent" inferences from an expanding base of conflicting beliefs, and provide an increment to the point of departure for work on relaxed notions of monotony in formal argumentation and beyond.

Acknowledgments. We thank the anonymous reviewers for their thoughtful and useful feedback. This work was partially supported by the Wallenberg AI, Autonomous Systems and Software Program (WASP) funded by the Knut and Alice Wallenberg Foundation.

References

1. Baroni, P., Caminada, M., Giacomin, M.: Abstract argumentation frameworks and their semantics, chap. 4. In: Baroni, P., Gabbay, D., Massimiliano, G., van der Torre, L. (eds.) Handbook of Formal Argumentation. College Publications, pp. 159–236. College Publications (2018)
2. Baroni, P., Gabbay, D.M., Giacomin, M., van der Torre, L.: Handbook of Formal Argumentation. College Publications (2018)
3. Baumann, R.: On the nature of argumentation semantics: Existence and uniqueness, expressibility, and replaceability. J. Appl. Logics 4(8), 2779–2886 (2017)
4. Baumann, R., Brewka, G.: Expanding argumentation frameworks: enforcing and monotonicity results. COMMA 10, 75–86 (2010)
5. Baumann, R., Brewka, G., Ulbricht, M.: Revisiting the foundations of abstract argumentation-semantics based on weak admissibility and weak defense. In: AAAI, pp. 2742–2749 (2020)
6. Bench-Capon, T.J.: Persuasion in practical argument using value-based argumentation frameworks. J. Log. Comput. 13(3), 429–448 (2003)

7. Čyras, K., Toni, F.: Non-monotonic inference properties for assumption-based argumentation. In: Black, E., Modgil, S., Oren, N. (eds.) TAFA 2015. LNCS (LNAI), vol. 9524, pp. 92–111. Springer, Cham (2015). https://doi.org/10.1007/978-3-319-28460-6_6

8. Doutre, S., Mailly, J.G.: Constraints and changes: a survey of abstract argumentation dynamics. Argument Comput. **9**, 223–248 (2018). https://doi.org/10.3233/AAC-180425

9. Dumas, M., Rosa, M.L., Mendling, J., Reijers, H.: Fundamentals of Business Process Management (2018)

10. Dung, P.M.: On the acceptability of arguments and its fundamental role in nonmonotonic reasoning, logic programming and n-person games. Artif. Intell. **77**(2), 321–357 (1995)

11. Gabbay, D.M.: Theoretical foundations for non-monotonic reasoning in expert systems. In: Apt, K.R. (ed.) Logics and Models of Concurrent Systems. NATO ASI Series, pp. 439–457. Springer, Heidelberg (1985). https://doi.org/10.1007/978-3-642-82453-1_15

12. Kampik, T., Nieves, J.C.: Abstract argumentation and the rational man. J. Logic Comput. **31**(2), 654–699 (2021). https://doi.org/10.1093/logcom/exab003

13. Kraus, S., Lehmann, D., Magidor, M.: Nonmonotonic reasoning, preferential models and cumulative logics. Artif. Intell. **44**(1), 167–207 (1990). https://doi.org/10.1016/0004-3702(90)90101-5, https://www.sciencedirect.com/science/article/pii/0004370290901015

14. Lankhorst, M.: Enterprise Architecture at Work: Modelling, Communication and Analysis. The Enterprise Engineering Series, Springer, Heidelberg (2017). https://doi.org/10.1007/978-3-662-53933-0

15. Makinson, D.: General theory of cumulative inference. In: Reinfrank, M., de Kleer, J., Ginsberg, M.L., Sandewall, E. (eds.) NMR 1988. LNCS, vol. 346, pp. 1–18. Springer, Heidelberg (1989). https://doi.org/10.1007/3-540-50701-9_16

16. van der Torre, L., Vesic, S.: The principle-based approach to abstract argumentation semantics. IfCoLog J. Logics Appl. **4**(8), 1–44 (2017)

17. Verheij, B.: Two approaches to dialectical argumentation: admissible sets and argumentation stages. Proc. NAIC **96**, 357–368 (1996)

Constrained Incomplete Argumentation Frameworks

Jean-Guy Mailly[(✉)] [iD]

LIPADE, University of Paris, Paris, France
jean-guy.mailly@u-paris.fr

Abstract. Operations like belief change or merging have been adapted to the context of abstract argumentation. However, these operations may require to express some uncertainty or some disjunction in the result, which is not representable in classical AFs. For this reason, some of these works require a set of AFs or a set of extensions as the outcome of the operation, somehow to represent a disjunction of AFs or extensions. In parallel, the notion of Incomplete AFs (IAFs) has been developed recently. It corresponds to AFs where the existence of some arguments or attacks may be uncertain. Each IAF can be associated with a set of classical AFs called completions, that correspond to different ways of "resolving the uncertainty". While these IAFs could be good candidates for a compact representation of a "disjunction" of AFs, we prove that this model is not expressive enough. Then we introduce Constrained IAFs, that include a propositional formula allowing to select the set of completions used for reasoning. We prove that this model is expressive enough for representing any set of AFs, or any set of extensions. Moreover, we show that the complexity of credulous and skeptical reasoning is the same as in the case of IAFs. Finally, we show that CIAFs can be used to model a new form of extension enforcement.

Keywords: Abstract argumentation · Uncertainty · Extension enforcement

1 Introduction

Representing uncertainty and reasoning with uncertain information is of utmost importance in artificial intelligence. Indeed, there are many reasons that may lead an intelligent agent to face uncertainty or impossibility to choose between alternatives. For instance, she can receive information from different sources, which can have different degrees of reliability. This information can be incompatible with her previous knowledge, or with information provided by other sources. This kind of problem can be formalized as belief change operations ("How to incorporate a new piece of information to my knowledge if it is not logically consistent?") [1,21,22] or belief merging ("How to give a coherent representation of several agent's knowledge even if they are globally inconsistent?") [23]. In this kind of application, a simple way to deal with the uncertainty of the result is

© Springer Nature Switzerland AG 2021
J. Vejnarová and N. Wilson (Eds.): ECSQARU 2021, LNAI 12897, pp. 103–116, 2021.
https://doi.org/10.1007/978-3-030-86772-0_8

the logical disjunction: if the result of revising an agent's knowledge is "I am not sure whether a is true or b is true.", then it can be expressed with $a \vee b$. However, there are formalisms where this kind of simple representation of undecidedness cannot be done. For instance, in abstract argumentation frameworks (AFs) [18], either there is certainly an attack between two arguments, or there is certainly no attack between them. But an agent cannot express something like "I am not sure whether a attacks b or not." AFs have been extended in this direction: Partial AFs (PAFs) [9] allow to represent uncertain attacks. Later, Incomplete AFs (IAFs) [5,6] have been proposed, as a generalization of PAFs where also arguments can be uncertain. Reasoning with a PAF or an IAF is possible thanks to a set of *completions*, that are classical AFs that correspond to the different possible worlds encoded in the uncertain information. While this framework allows to express uncertainty in abstract argumentation in a rich way, there are still situations that cannot be modeled. Consider, *e.g.*, that an agent faces the information "Either a attacks b, or b attacks a, but I am not sure which one is true.". There is no way to represent this information with an IAF. However, this may be necessary in some situations. For instance, several adaptations of belief change [11,13] or merging [9,15] to abstract argumentation lead to results that can contain such an uncertainty over the result, impossible to be represented by a single AF. So, these works propose to represent the "disjunction" in the result as a set of AFs, or even as a set of extensions (and it is also known that not every set of extensions can be represented by a single AF [19]).

In this paper, we define a generalization of IAFs, that adds a constraint to it. The constraint in a Constrained IAF (CIAF) is a propositional formula that allows to specify which subset of the completions of the IAF should be used for reasoning. We show that this framework is more expressive than IAFs, in the sense that any set of AFs can be the set of completions of a CIAF. Also, any set of extensions can be obtained from (the completions of) a CIAF. We prove that, despite being more expressive than IAFs, the complexity of credulous and skeptical reasoning does not increase compared to IAFs, under various classical semantics. Interestingly, we also identify a relation between our CIAFs and extension enforcement [3]. This operation consists in modifying an AF s.t. a given set of arguments becomes part of an extension. Classical enforcement operators are based on expansions, *i.e.* addition of arguments and attacks s.t. the attack relation between former arguments remain unchanged. Theoretical results show under which conditions enforcement is possible under expansions. However, these results may suppose the possibility to perform unnatural expansions, like adding a new argument that attacks all the undesired arguments. In a real dialogue, such an "ultimate attacker", that defeats every unwanted argument, is not likely to exist. We show that completions of a CIAF can be used to model the set of expansions that are available to an agent, and then enforcement is possible iff the desired set of arguments is credulously accepted w.r.t. the CIAF.

The paper is organized as follows. Section 2 describes background notions of abstract argumentation. Our first contributions are presented in Sect. 3: the definition of CIAFs, the properties of the framework regarding its expressivity, and finally the computational complexity of credulous and skeptical acceptance. Then in Sect. 4, we show how CIAFs can be used to model scenarios of extension enforcement. We discuss related work in Sect. 5, and finally Sect. 6 concludes the paper and highlights some topics of interest for future research.[1]

2   Background

2.1   Dung's Abstract Argumentation

Abstract argumentation was introduced in [18], where arguments are abstract entities whose origin or internal structure are ignored. The acceptance of arguments is purely defined from the relations between them.

Definition 1 (Abstract AF). *An* abstract argumentation framework *(AF) is a directed graph* $\mathcal{F} = \langle A, R \rangle$*, where A is a set of arguments, and $R \subseteq A \times A$ is an* attack relation.

We say that a *attacks* b when $(a, b) \in R$. If $(b, c) \in R$ also holds, then a *defends* c against b. Attack and defense can be adapted to sets of arguments: $S \subseteq A$ attacks (respectively defends) an argument $b \in A$ if $\exists a \in S$ that attacks (respectively defends) b.

Example 1. Let $\mathcal{F} = \langle A, R \rangle$ be the AF depicted in Fig. 1, with $A = \{a, b, c, d, e\}$ and $R = \{(b, a), (c, a), (c, d), (d, b), (d, c), (e, a)\}$. Each arrow represents an attack. d defends a against both b and c, since these are attackers of a that are, in turn, both attacked by d.

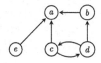

Fig. 1. The AF $\mathcal{F}$

Different semantics have been introduced to evaluate the acceptability of arguments [18], relying on two basic concepts: *conflict-freeness* and *admissibility*.

Definition 2 (Conflict-Freeness and Admissibility). *Given $\mathcal{F} = \langle A, R \rangle$, a set of arguments $S \subseteq A$ is:*

- *conflict-free iff $\forall a, b \in S$, $(a, b) \notin R$;*
- *admissible iff it is conflict-free, and defends each $a \in S$ against its attackers.*

---

[1] Proofs are omitted for space reasons.

We use cf($\mathcal{F}$) and ad($\mathcal{F}$) for denoting the sets of conflict-free and admissible sets of an argumentation framework $\mathcal{F}$. The intuition behind these principles is that a set of arguments may be accepted only if it is internally consistent (conflict-freeness) and able to defend itself against potential threats (admissibility). The semantics proposed by [18] can be defined as follows.

Definition 3 (Extension Semantics). *Given* $\mathcal{F} = \langle A, R \rangle$, *an admissible set* $S \subseteq A$ *is:*

- *a complete extension iff it contains every argument that it defends;*
- *a preferred extension iff it is a* $\subseteq$-*maximal complete extension;*
- *the unique grounded extension iff it is the* $\subseteq$-*minimal complete extension;*
- *a stable extension iff it attacks every argument in* $A \setminus S$.

The sets of extensions of an AF $\mathcal{F}$, for these semantics, are denoted (respectively) co($\mathcal{F}$), pr($\mathcal{F}$), gr($\mathcal{F}$) and st($\mathcal{F}$). Based on these semantics, we can define the status of any (set of) argument(s), namely *skeptically accepted* (belonging to each σ-extension), *credulously accepted* (belonging to some σ-extension) and *rejected* (belonging to no σ-extension). Given an AF $\mathcal{F}$ and a semantics σ, we use (respectively) $\mathrm{sk}_\sigma(\mathcal{F})$, $\mathrm{cr}_\sigma(\mathcal{F})$ and $\mathrm{rej}_\sigma(\mathcal{F})$ to denote these sets of arguments.

Example 2. We consider again $\mathcal{F}$ given in Fig. 1. Its extensions for the different semantics, as well as the sets of accepted arguments, are given in Table 1.

Table 1. Extensions and accepted arguments of $\mathcal{F}$ for $\sigma \in \{\mathrm{co, pr, gr, st}\}$

σ	$\sigma(\mathcal{F})$	$\mathrm{cr}_\sigma(\mathcal{F})$	$\mathrm{sk}_\sigma(\mathcal{F})$	$\mathrm{rej}_\sigma(\mathcal{F})$
co	$\{e\}, \{d, e\}, \{b, c, e\}$	$\{b, c, d, e\}$	$\{e\}$	$\{a\}$
pr	$\{d, e\}, \{b, c, e\}$	$\{b, c, d, e\}$	$\{e\}$	$\{a\}$
gr	$\{e\}$	$\{e\}$	$\{e\}$	$\{a, b, c, d\}$
st	$\{d, e\}, \{b, c, e\}$	$\{b, c, d, e\}$	$\{e\}$	$\{a\}$

For more details about argumentation semantics, we refer the interested reader to [2, 18].

2.2   Incomplete AFs

Now, we describe Incomplete Argumentation Frameworks [5, 6, 9].

Definition 4 (Incomplete AF). *An* Incomplete Argumentation Framework *(IAF) is a tuple* $\mathcal{I} = \langle A, A^?, R, R^? \rangle$, *where* A *and* $A^?$ *are disjoint sets of arguments, and* $R, R^? \subseteq (A \cup A^?) \times (A \cup A^?)$ *are disjoint sets of attacks.*

Elements from A and R are certain arguments and attacks, *i.e.* the agent is sure that they appear in the framework. On the opposite, $A^?$ and $R^?$ represent uncertain arguments and attacks. For each of them, there is a doubt about their actual existence.

Example 3. Let us consider $\mathcal{I} = \langle A, A^?, R, R^? \rangle$ given in Fig. 2. We use plain nodes and arrows to represent certain arguments and attacks, *i.e.* $A = \{a, b, c, d, e\}$ and $R = \{(b, a), (c, a), (d, b), (d, c)\}$. Uncertain arguments are represented as dashed square nodes (*i.e.* $A^? = \{f\}$) and uncertain attacks are represented as dotted arrows (*i.e.* $R^? = \{(e, a), (f, d)\}$).

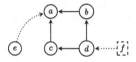

Fig. 2. The IAF $\mathcal{I}$

The notion of completion in abstract argumentation was first defined in [9] for Partial AFs (*i.e.* IAFs with $A^? = \emptyset$), and then adapted to IAFs. Intuitively, a completion is a classical AF which describes a situation of the world coherent with the uncertain information encoded in the IAF.

Definition 5 (Completion of an IAF). *Given* $\mathcal{I} = \langle A, A^?, R, R^? \rangle$, *a completion of* $\mathcal{I}$ *is* $\mathcal{F} = \langle A', R' \rangle$, *s.t.* $A \subseteq A' \subseteq A \cup A^?$ *and* $R_{|A'} \subseteq R' \subseteq R_{|A'} \cup R^?_{|A'}$, *where* $R_{|A'} = R \cap (A' \times A')$ *(and similarly for* $R^?_{|A'}$).

The set of completions of an IAF $\mathcal{I}$ is denoted $comp(\mathcal{I})$.

Example 4. We consider again the IAF from Fig. 2. Its set of completions is described at Fig. 3.

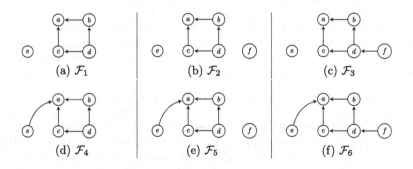

Fig. 3. The completions of $\mathcal{I}$

Concerning the question of compact representation of a set of AFs by means of an incomplete AF, the following example proves that some sets of AFs (even simple ones) cannot be represented by an IAF.

Example 5. Suppose that the result of revising an AF [11] is the set $\mathfrak{F} = \{\mathcal{F}_1 = \langle\{a, b\}, \{(b, a)\}\rangle, \mathcal{F}_2 = \langle\{a, c\}, \{(c, a)\}\rangle\}$. The question is to determine whether this set can be compactly represented by a single IAF. Towards a contradiction, suppose that there is an IAF $\mathcal{I} = \langle A, A^?, R, R^?\rangle$ s.t. $comp(\mathcal{I}) = \mathfrak{F}$. Since a belongs to both $\mathcal{F}_1$ and $\mathcal{F}_2$, it must belong to the certain arguments A. On the contrary, the uncertain arguments are $A^? = \{b, c\}$, each of them belongs to some (but not all) completions. $A = \{a\}$ and $A^? = \{b, c\}$ imply the existence of some completions that only contain a, and some completions that contain the three arguments a, b, c. This is not the case. So $\mathcal{I}$ does not exist.

3   Constrained IAFs

Now we introduce the Constrained Incomplete Argumentation Frameworks, that generalize IAFs by adding a constraint on the set of possible completions.

3.1   Constraints on Completions

Intuitively, for a given $\mathcal{I}$, a constrained version of it is a pair $\langle\mathcal{I}, C\rangle$ where $C \subseteq comp(\mathcal{I})$. Then, reasoning on $\langle\mathcal{I}, C\rangle$ requires to use only C instead of the full set of completions of $\mathcal{I}$. For instance, let us consider applications where the uncertainty about the world is encoded as a set of AFs or a set of extensions (for instance, revision [11,13] or merging of argumentation frameworks [9,15]). This set of AFs or extensions may not be encodable in a single IAF, while being representable with a single Constrained IAF. But rather than defining the constraint with a set of completions, we define a logical language to express information on the structure of an AF, *i.e.* a propositional language s.t. the models of a formula correspond to AFs, inspired by [10] for selecting extensions. This is a more compact representation of the constraint.

Definition 6 (Constraint). *Given A a set of arguments, we define the set of propositional atoms $Prop_A = Arg_A \cup Att_A$ where $Arg_A = \{arg_a \mid a \in A\}$ and $Att_A = \{att_{a,b} \mid (a, b) \in A \times A\}$. Then, $\mathcal{L}_A$ is the propositional language built from $Prop_A$ with classical connectives $\{\neg, \vee, \wedge\}$.*

The satisfaction of a constraint by an AF is defined as follows.

Definition 7 (Constraint Satisfaction). *Given A a set of arguments, and $\phi \in \mathcal{L}_A$ a formula, the set of models of ϕ is denoted $mod(\phi)$. An AF $\mathcal{F} = \langle A', R\rangle$ with $A' \subseteq A$ and $R \subseteq A' \times A'$ satisfies ϕ iff there is a model $\omega \in mod(\phi)$ s.t. $A' = \{a \in A \mid \omega(arg_a) = \top\}$, and $R = \{(a, b) \in A \times A \mid \omega(att_{a,b}) = \top\}$.*

3.2 Definition and Expressivity of CIAFs

Definition 8 (Constrained IAF). *A* Constrained Incomplete Argumentation Framework *(CIAF) is a tuple* $\mathcal{C} = \langle A, A^?, R, R^?, \phi \rangle$, *where* $\langle A, A^?, R, R^? \rangle$ *is an IAF, and* $\phi \in \mathcal{L}_{A \cup A^?}$ *is a constraint.*

The constraint ϕ is used to select a subset of the completions of the IAF $\mathcal{I}_\mathcal{C} = \langle A, A^?, R, R^? \rangle$. The completions of a CIAF are then defined as follows.

Definition 9 (Completions of a CIAF). *Given* $\mathcal{C} = \langle A, A^?, R, R^?, \phi \rangle$ *a CIAF, we define its set of completions by* $comp(\mathcal{C}) = \{c \in comp(\mathcal{I}_\mathcal{C}) \mid c$ *satisfies* $\phi\}$ *where* $\mathcal{I}_\mathcal{C} = \langle A, A^?, R, R^? \rangle$.

Example 6. Let $\mathcal{C} = \langle A, A^?, R, R^?, \phi \rangle$ be a CIAF s.t. $\mathcal{I}_\mathcal{C} = \langle A, A^?, R, R^? \rangle$ is the IAF from Fig. 2, and $\phi = att_{e,a} \wedge arg_f$. Recall that the completions of $\mathcal{I}_\mathcal{C}$ are given in Fig. 3. Only two of them satisfy ϕ, namely $\mathcal{F}_5$ (Fig. 3e) and $\mathcal{F}_6$ (Fig. 3f). So $comp(\mathcal{C}) = \{\mathcal{F}_5, \mathcal{F}_6\}$.

Let us mention that, in order to be meaningful, the constraint ϕ must satisfy some conditions. Indeed, there must be at least one model of ϕ s.t. arg_a is true for each $a \in A$, $att_{a,b}$ is true for each $(a, b) \in R$, and $att_{a,b}$ is false for each $(a, b) \in ((A \cup A') \times (A \cup A')) \setminus (R \cup R^?)$. Otherwise, $comp(\mathcal{C})$ is trivially empty. More generally, a CIAF $\mathcal{C}$ is *over-constrained* when $comp(\mathcal{C}) = \emptyset$.

Now, we focus on the expressivity of CIAFs, *i.e.* given a set of AFs (or a set of extensions), is there a CIAF s.t. its completions (or the extensions of its completions) correspond to the given set? We show that, in both cases, the answer is yes.

Representing a Set of AFs First, we define a particular formula, that is only satisfied by one given AF.

Definition 10. *Given A a set of arguments, and $\mathcal{F} = \langle A', R \rangle$ with $A' \subseteq A$, and $R \subseteq A' \times A'$, we define $\psi_\mathcal{F} \in \mathcal{L}_A$ as*

$$\psi_\mathcal{F} = \left(\bigwedge_{a \in A'} arg_a \right) \wedge \left(\bigwedge_{a \in A \setminus A'} \neg arg_a \right) \wedge \left(\bigwedge_{(a,b) \in R} att_{a,b} \right) \wedge \left(\bigwedge_{(a,b) \in (A \times A) \setminus R} \neg att_{a,b} \right)$$

Proposition 1. *Let $\mathfrak{F} = \{\mathcal{F}_1 = \langle A_1, R_1 \rangle, \ldots, \mathcal{F}_n = \langle A_n, R_n \rangle\}$ be a set of AFs. There is a CIAF $\mathcal{C} = \langle A, A^?, R, R^?, \phi \rangle$ s.t. $comp(\mathcal{C}) = \mathfrak{F}$.*

Intuitively, a simple CIAF that does the job consists of all the arguments and attacks from $\mathfrak{F}$ defined as uncertain, and then ϕ is the disjunction of the $\psi_\mathcal{F}$ formulas, for $\mathcal{F} \in \mathfrak{F}$. Let us exemplify this result.

Let us exemplify this result.

Example 7. We continue Example 5. For $\mathfrak{F} = \{\mathcal{F}_1 = \langle \{a, b\}, \{(b, a)\} \rangle, \mathcal{F}_2 = \langle \{a, c\}, \{(c, a)\} \rangle\}$, we define $\mathcal{C} = \langle A, A^?, R, R^?, \phi, \rangle$, with $A = \emptyset$, $A^? = \{a, b, c\}$, $R = \emptyset$, $R^? = \{(b, a), (c, a)\}$, $\phi = \psi_{\mathcal{F}_1} \vee \psi_{\mathcal{F}_2}$, where

$$\psi_{\mathcal{F}_1} = arg_a \wedge arg_b \wedge \neg arg_c \wedge att_{b,a} \wedge \left(\bigwedge_{(x,y) \in (\{a,b,c\} \times \{a,b,c\}) \setminus \{(b,a)\}} \neg att_{x,y} \right)$$

and

$$\psi_{\mathcal{F}_2} = arg_a \wedge \neg arg_b \wedge arg_c \wedge att_{c,a} \wedge (\bigwedge_{(x,y)\in(\{a,b,c\}\times\{a,b,c\})\setminus\{(c,a)\}} \neg att_{x,y})$$

We have $comp(\mathcal{C}) = \mathfrak{F}$.

Representing a Set of Extensions Now, we focus on the expressibility of a set of extensions with a CIAF.

Proposition 2. *Let* $\mathfrak{E} = \{E_1, \ldots, E_n\}$ *be a set of extensions, and* $\sigma \in \{co, pr, st, gr\}$. *There is a CIAF* $\mathcal{C} = \langle A, A^?, R, R^?, \phi \rangle$ *s.t.* $\bigcup_{c \in comp(\mathcal{C})} \sigma(c) = \mathfrak{E}$.

Of course, the construction described in Example 7 only shows the existence of a CIAF that satisfies the expected property. This does not mean that this given CIAF is the best way to represent the set of AFs (or extensions). A first possible simplification consists in choosing $A = \bigcap_{i=1}^{n} A_i$ and $A^? = \bigcup_{i=1}^{n} A_i \setminus A$. This natural simplification means that an argument that appears in every AF must be considered as certain. A similar reasoning can be made with the attacks, and the constraint can also be simplified. In a context of belief revision [11,13] or belief merging [9,15], it is important to ensure that the resulting CIAF is as close as possible to the initial AF(s). This question is out of the scope of this paper, and is kept for future research.

3.3 Complexity Issues

Observation 1. *Verifying whether an AF (or a completion) satisfies a constraint* ϕ *is a polynomial task: the correspondence between an AF and an interpretation* ω *described in Definition 7 can be done polynomially, as well as checking whether* ω *satisfies* ϕ.

This means that, given a CIAF $\mathcal{C} = \langle A, A^?, R, R^?, \phi \rangle$, guessing a completion of $\mathcal{C}$ is equivalent to guessing a set of arguments $A \subseteq A' \subseteq A^?$, a set of attacks $R_{|A'} \subseteq A' \subseteq R^?_{|A'}$, and verifying (in polynomial time) whether $\langle A', R' \rangle$ satisfies ϕ. This will be useful in the proofs of complexity results.

Now we study the complexity of credulous and skeptical reasoning. More specifically, given $\mathcal{C} = \langle A, A^?, R, R^?, \phi \rangle$ a CIAF, $a \in A$, and σ a semantics,

Cred-σ is $a \in \bigcup_{\mathcal{F} \in comp(\mathcal{C})} \bigcup_{S \in \sigma(\mathcal{F})} S$?
Skep-σ is $a \in \bigcap_{\mathcal{F} \in comp(\mathcal{C})} \bigcap_{S \in \sigma(\mathcal{F})} S$?

These problems correspond to *possible credulous acceptance* (PCA) and *necessary skeptical acceptance* (NSA) for IAFs [5]. We prove that complexity does not increase from IAFs to CIAFs.

Proposition 3. *The following hold:*

1. For $\sigma \in \{ad, st, co, gr, pr\}$, *Cred-*$\sigma$ *is* NP-*complete.*

2. *For $\sigma \in \{st, co, gr\}$, Skep-$\sigma$ is coNP-complete.*
3. *Skep-pr is Π_2^P-complete.*

Concerning skeptical reasoning, the problem is trivial under $\sigma = ad$, as usual, since $\emptyset$ is admissible in any AF, there is no skeptically accepted argument in any completion.

Finally, let us mention that credulous and skeptical acceptance can be generalized to sets of arguments. These versions consists, respectively, in determining whether a given set of arguments S satisfies $S \subseteq \bigcup_{\mathcal{F} \in comp(\mathcal{C})} \bigcup_{S \in \sigma(\mathcal{F})} S$, or $S \subseteq \bigcap_{\mathcal{F} \in comp(\mathcal{C})} \bigcap_{S \in \sigma(\mathcal{F})} S$. The generalized versions keep the same complexity.

4   CIAFs and Extension Enforcement

4.1   Expansion-Based Enforcement

Now we introduce the notions of AF expansion and extension enforcement [3].

Definition 11. *Let $\mathcal{F} = \langle A, R \rangle$ be an AF. An* expansion *of $\mathcal{F}$ is an AF $\mathcal{F}' = \langle A \cup A', R \cup R' \rangle$ s.t. $A' \neq \emptyset$ and $A \cap A' = \emptyset$. An expansion is called* normal *if $\forall (a, b) \in R'$, $a \in A'$ or $b \in A'$. Moreover, a normal expansion is* strong *(resp. weak) if $\forall (a, b) \in R'$, $a \notin A$ (resp. $b \notin A$).*

In words, an expansion adds some arguments, and possibly attacks. In the case of a normal expansion, the only added attacks concern at least one new arguments, *i.e.* the attacks between the former arguments are not modified. Finally, a normal expansion is strong (resp. weak) if it adds only strong (resp. weak) arguments, *i.e.* arguments that are not attacked by (resp. do not attack) the former arguments. The fact that $\mathcal{F}'$ is an expansion of $\mathcal{F}$ is denoted $\mathcal{F} \preceq_E \mathcal{F}'$ (and normal, strong, weak expansions are denoted by $\preceq_N, \preceq_S, \preceq_W$).

Definition 12. *Given $\mathcal{F} = \langle A, R \rangle$, a set of arguments $S \subseteq A$, and a semantics σ, the AF $\mathcal{F}'$ is a normal (resp. strong, weak) σ-enforcement of S in $\mathcal{F}$ iff $\mathcal{F}'$ is a normal (resp. strong, weak) expansion of $\mathcal{F}$, and $\exists E \in \sigma(\mathcal{F}')$ s.t. $S \subseteq E$.*

Definition 12 only considers "non-strict" enforcement, *i.e.* the desired set of arguments must be included in an extension of the new AF. Strict enforcement is defined in a similar manner, but the desired set of arguments must exactly correspond to an extension.

Some (im)possibility results for these operations have been presented in [3]. However, some results rely on examples that are not representative of realistic argument-based dialogues. The following example is inspired by [3, Theorem 4].

Example 8. Let $\mathcal{F} = \langle A, R \rangle$ be the AF given in Fig. 1. Recall that its stable extensions are $st(\mathcal{F}) = \{\{d, e\}, \{b, c, e\}\}$. Now let $S = \{a, d\}$ be the set of arguments to be enforced. We can define the (strong) expansion $\mathcal{F}' = \langle A \cup \{x\}, R \cup R' \rangle$ where x is a fresh argument, and $R' = \{(x, y) \mid y \in A \setminus S\}$. $\mathcal{F}'$ is shown at Fig. 4. $st(\mathcal{F}') = \{\{x, a, d\}\}$, thus it is a strong enforcement of S in $\mathcal{F}$.

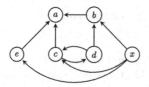

Fig. 4. The expansion $\mathcal{F}'$ enforces $S = \{a, d\}$

Example 8 illustrates the (theoretical) possibility to enforce any (conflict-free) set of arguments if strong (or normal) expansions are permitted. However, in an application context like dialogue (*e.g.* argument-based negotiation [17] or persuasion [7]), the existence of an "ultimate" attacker like x, that defeats all the undesired arguments, is unlikely.

4.2   Enforcement as Credulous Acceptability in CIAFs

To handle the problem highlighted by Example 8, we propose to take into account the set of arguments and attacks that an agent has at her disposal for participating to the debate. This means that we parameterize the expansion operation by the set of possible expanded AFs resulting of using some of the available arguments and attacks.

Definition 13. *Given $\mathcal{F} = \langle A, R \rangle$ an AF, $\mathcal{A}$ a set of available arguments s.t. $A \cap \mathcal{A} = \emptyset$, and $\mathcal{R} \subseteq ((A \cup \mathcal{A}) \times (A \cup \mathcal{A})) \setminus (A \times A)$, we say that $\mathcal{F}' = \langle A', R' \rangle$ is an $\mathcal{A}$-$\mathcal{R}$-parameterized expansion of $\mathcal{F}$ (denoted by $\mathcal{F} \preceq^{A, \mathcal{R}} \mathcal{F}'$) iff $\mathcal{F} \preceq_E \mathcal{F}'$, $A \subseteq A' \subseteq A \cup \mathcal{A}$ and $R' = (R \cup \mathcal{R}) \cap (A' \times A')$.*

We use $\preceq_N^{A, \mathcal{R}}$ (resp. $\preceq_S^{A, \mathcal{R}}$, $\preceq_W^{A, \mathcal{R}}$) to denote $\mathcal{A}$-$\mathcal{R}$-parameterized normal (resp. strong, weak) expansions, *i.e.* $\mathcal{A}$-$\mathcal{R}$-parameterized expansions where $\mathcal{F}'$ is (additionally) normal (resp. strong, weak). This definition allows to take into account the arguments and attacks that are actually known by an agent that participates in a debate. We can show that a set of arguments that can be enforced with an arbitrary (strong) expansion (like in Example 8) may not be enforceable with parameterized expansions.

Example 9. We continue Example 8. Suppose that the available arguments and attacks are $\mathcal{A} = \{f, g\}$ and $\mathcal{R} = \{(f, c), (g, b)\}$. Figure 5 depicts the agent's possible actions: say nothing (*i.e.* keep the initial AF, Fig. 5a), say "f attacks c" (Fig. 5b), say "g attacks b" (Fig. 5c), or both (Fig. 5d). In all the possible cases, $S = \{a, d\}$ is not enforced, since a is never defended against e.

What we call here the "possible actions" of the agent can actually be seen as the set of completions of a CIAF, and the possibility of enforcing a set of arguments corresponds to the credulous acceptance of this set w.r.t. the CIAF.

Definition 14. *Given $\mathcal{F}$ an AF, $\mathcal{A}$ a set of arguments, $\mathcal{R}$ a set of attacks, and $X \in \{E, N, S, W\}$ denoting the type of expansion, we define $\mathfrak{F} = \{\mathcal{F}\} \cup \{\mathcal{F}' \mid \mathcal{F} \preceq_X^{A, \mathcal{R}} \mathcal{F}'\}$. Then, $\mathcal{C}_{\mathcal{F}, X}^{A, \mathcal{R}}$ is a CIAF s.t. $comp(\mathcal{C}_{\mathcal{F}, X}^{A, \mathcal{R}}) = \mathfrak{F}$.*

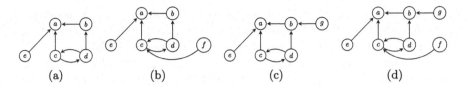

Fig. 5. The agent's possible actions

The existence of $\mathcal{C}_{\mathcal{F},X}^{\mathcal{A},\mathcal{R}}$ is guaranteed by Proposition 1. The construction illustrated by Example 7 provides a suitable $\mathcal{C}_{\mathcal{F},X}^{\mathcal{A},\mathcal{R}}$. However, other CIAFs can be defined, for instance all the arguments and attacks from the initial $\mathcal{F}$ can be defined as certain elements. The following proposition states that CIAFs can be used as a computational tool for determining the possibility of enforcement.

Proposition 4. *Given an AF $\mathcal{F} = \langle A, R \rangle$, a set of arguments $S \subseteq A$, $X \in \{E, N, S, W\}$, $\mathcal{A}$ a set of arguments and $\mathcal{R}$ a set of attacks, and a semantics σ, S can be σ-enforced in $\mathcal{F}$ by means of a $\mathcal{A}$-$\mathcal{R}$-parameterized X-expansion iff S is credulously accepted in $\mathcal{C}_{\mathcal{F},X}^{\mathcal{A},\mathcal{R}}$ w.r.t. σ.*

Observe that this result holds for non-strict enforcement, as given in Definition 12. Strict enforcement requires, instead, the notion of extension verification [20] for CIAFs, *i.e.* we must check that the set of arguments S is actually an extension of one of the completions.

5   Related Work

We have described the main existing work on IAFs. Let us also mention [20], which defines an alternative notion of extension (compared to the one from [6]). This does not have an impact on the work presented here, since we focus on argument acceptance; our definitions are consistent with the ones in [5]. However, as mentioned previously, this will be useful for characterizing strict extension enforcement with CIAF-based reasoning.

Besides IAFs, our contribution is related to other previous works. Using propositional formulas as constraints in an argumentation framework has been originally proposed in [10], which defines Constrained Argumentation Frameworks. In this setting, the propositional formula is a constraint on arguments that is used for selecting the best extensions. Intuitively, we use here the constraint in CIAFs in a similar way, but for selecting completions of a IAF instead of selecting the extensions of a (classical) AF.

We have shown how to represent any set of extensions with a single CIAF. The question of representing sets of extensions has already arisen in classical AFs. This corresponds to the notion of realizability in the literature [4,19], *i.e.* given a set of extensions E and a semantics σ, is there an AF $\mathcal{F}$ s.t. $\sigma(\mathcal{F}) = E$. Existing results show that it is not possible in general for most classical semantics. The non-realizability of some sets of extensions is the reason why some operations (like belief revision or merging) cannot be easily adapted to AFs, as mentioned in the introduction. With Proposition 2, we continue this line of research, by proving the realizability of any set of extensions by means of CIAFs.

Regarding extension enforcement, it has been proven that (non-strict) enforcement is NP-complete [28] for another type of authorized change: argument-fixed enforcement [12], where the set of arguments cannot be modified, but all the attacks (or non-attacks) can be questioned. Although this is out of the scope of this paper, we believe that this kind of enforcement can also be captured by the CIAF setting, which will allow to define a parameterized version of argument-fixed enforcement. The parameters $\mathcal{A}$ and $\mathcal{R}$ are also reminiscent of the "control part" of Control AFs [16,24,25], that allows to enforce a set of arguments in presence of uncertainty.

Constraints that express dependencies between arguments of an ADF [8] in a dynamic context have been studied in [27]. While there is some similarity between these constraints and the ones defined here, both studies have different purposes. Indeed, [27] does not focus on uncertain environment as we do here, but only on dynamic scenarios. Connections with enforcement based on $\mathcal{A}$-$\mathcal{R}$-parameterized expansions will be studied.

6   Conclusion

We have defined Constrained Incomplete Argumentation Frameworks (or CIAFs, for short) that generalize IAFs by adding a constraint over the set of completions. This new framework increases the expressivity of IAFs without a gap in complexity, and paves the way for the definition of revision or merging operators for AFs that return a CIAF, $i.e.$ a more compact result than a (potentially exponentially large) set of AFs or extensions. However, the CIAF that we have exhibited here to prove the representability of any set of AFs or extensions may not be a suitable solution in scenarios like belief revision or belief merging, where the notion of minimal change is important. We will study how to generate a CIAF that is optimal in such contexts. Knowledge compilation [14] is an interesting way for providing a succinct equivalent propositional constraint such that relevant reasoning tasks are polynomially doable. Other interesting research tracks are the study of complexity for other decision problems ($e.g.$ extension verification, or possible skeptical and necessary credulous acceptance), and the implementation of efficient algorithms ($e.g.$ based on Boolean encoding, in the line of [26]). We will also study how to encode other extension enforcement operators as CIAF-based reasoning.

Acknowledgements. The author warmly thanks Antonio Yuste-Ginel for the interesting discussion that lead to this work, as well as the reviewers that provided valuable feedback.

References

1. Alchourrón, C.E., Gärdenfors, P., Makinson, D.: On the logic of theory change: partial meet contraction and revision functions. J. Symb. Log. **50**(2), 510–530 (1985)
2. Baroni, P., Caminada, M., Giacomin, M.: Abstract argumentation frameworks and their semantics. In: Baroni, P., Gabbay, D., Giacomin, M., van der Torre, L. (eds.) Handbook of Formal Argumentation, pp. 159–236. College Publications (2018)
3. Baumann, R., Brewka, G.: Expanding argumentation frameworks: enforcing and monotonicity results. In: Proceedings of the COMMA 2010, vol. 216, pp. 75–86 (2010)
4. Baumann, R., Dvořák, W., Linsbichler, T., Strass, H., Woltran, S.: Compact argumentation frameworks. In: Proceedings of the ECAI 2014, vol. 263, pp. 69–74 (2014)
5. Baumeister, D., Neugebauer, D., Rothe, J.: Credulous and skeptical acceptance in incomplete argumentation frameworks. In: Proceedings of the COMMA 2018, pp. 181–192 (2018)
6. Baumeister, D., Neugebauer, D., Rothe, J., Schadrack, H.: Verification in incomplete argumentation frameworks. Artif. Intell. **264**, 1–26 (2018)
7. Bonzon, E., Delobelle, J., Konieczny, S., Maudet, N.: A parametrized ranking-based semantics for persuasion. In: Proceedings of the SUM 2017, pp. 237–251 (2017)
8. Brewka, G., Strass, H., Ellmauthaler, S., Wallner, J.P., Woltran, S.: Abstract dialectical frameworks revisited. In: Rossi, F. (ed.) Proceedings of the IJCAI 2013, pp. 803–809 (2013)
9. Coste-Marquis, S., Devred, C., Konieczny, S., Lagasquie-Schiex, M., Marquis, P.: On the merging of dung's argumentation systems. Artif. Intell. **171**(10–15), 730–753 (2007)
10. Coste-Marquis, S., Devred, C., Marquis, P.: Constrained argumentation frameworks. In: Proceedings of the KR 2006, pp. 112–122 (2006)
11. Coste-Marquis, S., Konieczny, S., Mailly, J.G., Marquis, P.: On the revision of argumentation systems: minimal change of arguments statuses. In: Proceedings of the KR 2014 (2014)
12. Coste-Marquis, S., Konieczny, S., Mailly, J.G., Marquis, P.: Extension enforcement in abstract argumentation as an optimization problem. In: Proceedings of the IJCAI 2015, pp. 2876–2882 (2015)
13. Coste-Marquis, S., Konieczny, S., Mailly, J.G., Marquis, P.: A translation-based approach for revision of argumentation frameworks. In: Proceedings of the JELIA 2014, pp. 77–85 (2014)
14. Darwiche, A., Marquis, P.: A knowledge compilation map. J. Artif. Intell. Res. **17**, 229–264 (2002)
15. Delobelle, J., Haret, A., Konieczny, S., Mailly, J.G., Rossit, J., Woltran, S.: Merging of abstract argumentation frameworks. In: Proceedings of the KR 2016, pp. 33–42 (2016)
16. Dimopoulos, Y., Mailly, J.G., Moraitis, P.: Control argumentation frameworks. In: Proceedings of the AAAI 2018, pp. 4678–4685 (2018)
17. Dimopoulos, Y., Mailly, J.G., Moraitis, P.: Argumentation-based negotiation with incomplete opponent profiles. In: Proceedings of the AAMAS 2019, pp. 1252–1260 (2019)

18. Dung, P.M.: On the acceptability of arguments and its fundamental role in non-monotonic reasoning, logic programming and n-person games. Artif. Intell. **77**, 321–357 (1995)
19. Dunne, P.E., Dvořák, W., Linsbichler, T., Woltran, S.: Characteristics of multiple viewpoints in abstract argumentation. Artif. Intell. **228**, 153–178 (2015)
20. Fazzinga, B., Flesca, S., Furfaro, F.: Revisiting the notion of extension over incomplete abstract argumentation frameworks. In: Proceedings of the IJCAI 2020, pp. 1712–1718 (2020)
21. Katsuno, H., Mendelzon, A.O.: On the difference between updating a knowledge base and revising it. In: Proceedings of the KR 1991, pp. 387–394 (1991)
22. Katsuno, H., Mendelzon, A.O.: Propositional knowledge base revision and minimal change. Artif. Intell. **52**(3), 263–294 (1992)
23. Konieczny, S., Pérez, R.P.: Merging information under constraints: a logical framework. J. Log. Comput. **12**(5), 773–808 (2002)
24. Mailly, J.G.: Possible controllability of control argumentation frameworks. In: Proceedings of COMMA 2020, vol. 326, pp. 283–294 (2020)
25. Niskanen, A., Neugebauer, D., Järvisalo, M.: Controllability of control argumentation frameworks. In: Proceedings of the IJCAI 2020, pp. 1855–1861 (2020)
26. Niskanen, A., Neugebauer, D., Järvisalo, M., Rothe, J.: Deciding acceptance in incomplete argumentation frameworks. In: Proceedings of the AAAI 2020, pp. 2942–2949 (2020)
27. Wallner, J.P.: Structural constraints for dynamic operators in abstract argumentation. Argument Comput. **11**(1–2), 151–190 (2020)
28. Wallner, J.P., Niskanen, A., Järvisalo, M.: Complexity results and algorithms for extension enforcement in abstract argumentation. J. Artif. Intell. Res. **60**, 1–40 (2017)

Complexity of Nonemptiness in Control Argumentation Frameworks

Daniel Neugebauer[1], Jörg Rothe[1] , and Kenneth Skiba[2]([✉])

[1] Institut für Informatik, Heinrich-Heine-Universität, Düsseldorf, Germany
[2] Institute for Web Science and Technologies, University of Koblenz-Landau, Koblenz, Germany
Kennethskiba@uni-koblenz.de

Abstract. Control argumentation frameworks (CAFs) [4] extend the standard model of argumentation framework (AF) due to Dung [6] in a way that takes unquantified uncertainty regarding arguments and attacks into account. Complementing recent work by Skiba et al. [21] for incomplete argumentation frameworks, we study the (nonempty) existence problem for CAFs and fully analyze its computational complexity for the most common semantics.

1 Introduction

Argumentation theory is a key research field within artificial intelligence. In his seminal early work, Dung [6] introduced the central model of *abstract argumentation framework*, where— neglecting the actual contents of arguments—a discussion is represented as a directed graph (AF) whose vertices are the arguments and whose directed edges represent the attacks among arguments.

Later work established various extensions of this basic model so as to overcome its shortcomings, especially regarding its inability to handle structural uncertainty and incomplete information about the existence of arguments or attacks. One such model— which is central to this paper—proposes *control argumentation frameworks (CAF)* [4], which feature uncertain arguments and attacks and are intended specifically to model strategic scenarios from the point of view of an agent. The model divides the uncertain elements of an argumentation into a *control* part and an *uncertain* part, where the existence of elements in the control part is controlled by the agent, and the existence of elements in the uncertain part is not. This distinguishes CAFs from the related *incomplete* argumentation frameworks [2], which also feature uncertain arguments and attacks, but which do not specify such a sub-division.

Acceptability of arguments in AFs can be determined using one of several different *semantics*, where a set of arguments that satisfies a semantics is called an *extension*. To model various central reasoning tasks in argumentation frameworks formally, a number of decision problems have been introduced and studied. The *verification* problem asks whether a given set of arguments is an extension; the *credulous acceptance* and *skeptical acceptance* problems ask whether a given argument is contained in at least one extension or in all extensions, respectively; and the even more fundamental problem of *existence* asks whether an extension exists in the first place.

© Springer Nature Switzerland AG 2021
J. Vejnarová and N. Wilson (Eds.): ECSQARU 2021, LNAI 12897, pp. 117–129, 2021.
https://doi.org/10.1007/978-3-030-86772-0_9

In control argumentation frameworks, the problem of *controllability* generalizes the credulous and skeptical acceptance problems and asks whether there exists a selection of arguments in the control part (i.e., a *control configuration*) such that for all selections of elements in the uncertain part (i.e., all *completions*), a given target set of arguments is a subset of an extension (or of all extensions). This problem was analyzed by Dimopoulos et al. [4] and Niskanen et al. [17].

Extending their work, we tackle natural generalizations of the *(nonempty) existence* problem for CAFs, which—even though being very fundamental—can be a very hard problem for some semantics. Recall that all other reasoning problems, such as the verification, acceptability, or controllability problems, are based on the existence of extensions. Therefore, it is decisive to know the computational complexity of the (nonempty) existence problem first of all. This enables us to conclude whether the hardness of a variant of verification, acceptability, or controllability comes from the problem itself or is simply an artifact of the underlying (nonempty) existence problem. Thus an analysis of (nonempty) existence problems for control argumentation frameworks is sorely missing and crucially needed.

The existence problem can be trivially solved whenever a semantics guarantees existence of at least one extension, and this is the case for all semantics that allow the empty set to be an extension. This gives rise to consider the *nonempty existence* (or, *nonemptiness*, for short) problem, which only accepts nonempty extensions. The existence and nonemptiness problems coincide for semantics that do not allow empty extensions, so we henceforth will focus on the nonemptiness problem only. For CAFs, we define (nonempty) existence problems analogously to the controllability problem studied by Dimopoulos et al. [4] and Niskanen et al. [17]: Does there exist a control configuration such that for all completions, there exists a nonempty set of arguments satisfying a given semantics?

We provide a full analysis of the computational complexity of these generalized nonempty existence problems with respect to the most common Dung semantics. The relationship between the controllability and the nonempty existence problem is the following: A "yes"-instance for controllability is also a "yes"-instance of the nonempty existence problem, and a "no"-instance for nonempty existence is also a "no"-instance of the controllability problem. Table 1 on page 11 in the conclusions gives an overview of our complexity results for this problem regarding the considered semantics, and compares them with those of Skiba et al. [21] for the analogous problems in the related *incomplete argumentation frameworks* and of Chvátal [3], Modgil and Caminada [16], and Dimopoulos and Torres [5] in standard argumentation frameworks.

This paper is structured as follows. In Sect. 2, we describe the formal models of abstract AFs and its extension to CAFs, and we present a formal definition of the nonemptiness problem in this setting. This is followed by a full analysis of the computational complexity of nonemptiness for CAFs in Sect. 3. In Sect. 4, we summarize our results and point out some related work in this field.

2   Preliminaries

First, we briefly present the model of (abstract) argumentation framework that is due to Dung [6]. We then describe the extension of this model to *control* argumentation frameworks, as introduced by Dimopoulos et al. [4].

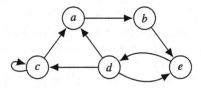

Fig. 1. Argumentation framework for Example 1

2.1   Abstract Argumentation Frameworks

For a finite set $\mathcal{A}$ of arguments and a set $\mathcal{R}$ of attacks between them, we call the pair $\langle \mathcal{A}, \mathcal{R} \rangle$ with $\mathcal{R} \subseteq \mathcal{A} \times \mathcal{A}$ an *argumentation framework (AF)*. Whenever $(a,b) \in \mathcal{R}$, argument a *attacks* argument b. An argument a is said to be *acceptable with respect to a set* $S \subseteq \mathcal{A}$ if for all arguments $b \in \mathcal{A}$ attacking a, there is an argument $c \in S$ attacking b; in this case, a is *defended by c against its attacker b*.

An argumentation framework $\langle \mathcal{A}, \mathcal{R} \rangle$ can be depicted by a directed graph with vertex set $\mathcal{A}$ and edge set $\mathcal{R}$.

Example 1. Figure 1 shows the graph representing $AF = \langle \mathcal{A}, \mathcal{R} \rangle$ with $\mathcal{A} = \{a,b,c,d,e\}$ and $\mathcal{R} = \{(a,b),(b,e),(c,a),(c,c),(d,a),(d,c),(d,e),(e,d)\}$.

For argumentation frameworks, Dung [6] also introduced the notion of *semantics*. A set of arguments satisfying the properties of a given semantics is called an *extension*. We will use the following semantics.

Definition 1. *Let $AF = \langle \mathcal{A}, \mathcal{R} \rangle$ be an argumentation framework. A set $S \subseteq \mathcal{A}$ is said to be* conflict-free (CF) *if no arguments in S attack each other. Further, a conflict-free set S is* admissible (AD) *if all arguments in S are acceptable with respect to S;* complete (CP) *if S is closed under defense (i.e., S contains all arguments that are acceptable with respect to S);* grounded (GR) *if S is the least complete set with respect to set inclusion;* preferred (PR) *if it is a set-maximal admissible set; and* stable (ST) *if every $b \in \mathcal{A} \setminus S$ is attacked by at least one argument $a \in S$.*

Every stable extension is preferred, every preferred extension is complete, and every complete extension is admissible. There always is a conflict-free, admissible, preferred, complete, and grounded extension in every argumentation framework (it is possible that this is just the empty set, though). For the stable semantics, by contrast, existence cannot be taken for granted.

Example 2. Continuing Example 1, the conflict-free sets in our argumentation framework are $\{a,e\}$, $\{b,d\}$, and all their subsets. The only two nonempty admissible sets are $\{d\}$ (since d defends itself against e's attack) and $\{b,d\}$ (as a's attack on b is defended by d, and e's attack on d is defended by b and d). However, no other nonempty, conflict-free set can defend all its arguments: No member of $\{a\}$ or $\{a,e\}$ defends a against c's attack; $\{e\}$ lacks a defending attack against b's attack; and $\{b\}$ cannot be defended against a's attack. Among $\{d\}$ and $\{b,d\}$, only the latter is complete, since d defends b against a's attack. Further, the empty set is complete, since there are no unattacked arguments—i.e., there are no arguments that are defended by the empty set. Since $\emptyset$ is complete, it is also the (unique) grounded extension. On the other hand, the complete extension $\{b,d\}$ is the only preferred (i.e., maximal admissible) extension. Since d attacks each of a, c, and e, the preferred extension $\{b,d\}$ is also a stable extension (and since there are no other preferred extensions, it is the only stable extension).

We are interested in the *existence* problem restricted to *nonempty* extensions (the *nonemptiness* problem, for short) for the above semantics in control argumentation frameworks. In standard argumentation frameworks, the existence problem was first studied by Dimopoulos and Torres [5] and later on by Dunne and Wooldridge [8]. For each semantics $s \in \{CF, AD, CP, GR, PR, ST\}$, define the following problem:

---

s-NONEMPTINESS (s-NE)

Given: An argumentation framework $\langle \mathcal{A}, \mathcal{R} \rangle$.

Question: Does there exist a nonempty set $S \subseteq \mathcal{A}$ satisfying the conditions specified by semantics s?

2.2 Control Argumentation Frameworks

Next, we formally define control argumentation frameworks due to Dimopoulos et al. [4], while adapting some notation from Niskanen et al. [17].

Definition 2. *A control argumentation framework (CAF) is a triple $(\mathcal{F}, C, \mathcal{U})$ consisting of a fixed part $\mathcal{F}$ of elements known to exist, a control part C of elements that may or may not exist (and whose existence is controlled by the agent), and an uncertain part $\mathcal{U}$ of elements that may or may not exist (and whose existence is not controlled by the agent):*

$$\mathcal{F} = \langle \mathcal{A}_F, \mathcal{R}_F \rangle \text{ with } \mathcal{R}_F \subseteq (\mathcal{A}_F \cup \mathcal{A}_U) \times (\mathcal{A}_F \cup \mathcal{A}_U),$$
$$C = \langle \mathcal{A}_C, \mathcal{R}_C \rangle \text{ with } \mathcal{R}_C \subseteq (\mathcal{A}_C \times (\mathcal{A}_F \cup \mathcal{A}_C \cup \mathcal{A}_U)) \cup ((\mathcal{A}_F \cup \mathcal{A}_C \cup \mathcal{A}_U) \times \mathcal{A}_C),$$
$$\mathcal{U} = \langle \mathcal{A}_U, \mathcal{R}_U \cup \mathcal{R}_U^{\leftrightarrow} \rangle \text{ with } \mathcal{R}_U, \mathcal{R}_U^{\leftrightarrow} \subseteq (\mathcal{A}_F \cup \mathcal{A}_U) \times (\mathcal{A}_F \cup \mathcal{A}_U),$$

where $\mathcal{A}_F$, $\mathcal{A}_C$, and $\mathcal{A}_U$ are pairwise disjoint sets of arguments, and $\mathcal{R}_F$, $\mathcal{R}_C$, $\mathcal{R}_U$, and $\mathcal{R}_U^{\leftrightarrow}$ are pairwise disjoint sets of attacks. While the existence of attacks in $\mathcal{R}_U$ is not known at all, attacks in $\mathcal{R}_U^{\leftrightarrow}$ are known to exist, but their direction is unknown.

For elements in the control part, we always look for only (at least) one configuration to achieve the given goal, while for elements in the uncertain part, we always require all their completions to achieve that goal. Also, the control part always "moves first," i.e., a configuration of the control part must be chosen before knowing how the uncertain part will be completed.

Example 3. Consider a control argumentation framework with the argument sets $A_F = \{a,c,d\}, A_C = \{b\}, A_U = \{e\}$ and the attack relations $R_F = \{(c,a),(d,a),(d,c)\}$, $R_C = \{(a,b),(b,e)\}, R_U = \{(c,c)\}$, and $R_U^{\leftrightarrow} = \{(d,e),(e,d)\}$. Its graph representation is given in Fig. 2, where we follow the style of display introduced in the original work on CAFs by Dimopoulos et al. [4].

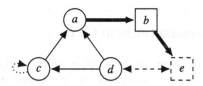

Fig. 2. Control argumentation framework for Example 3, where control arguments are drawn as solid rectangles, uncertain arguments as dashed rectangles, attacks from R_C are drawn as bold-faced arrows, uncertain attacks from R_U are drawn as dotted arrows, and uncertain attacks from $R_U^{\leftrightarrow}$ are drawn as doubleheaded dashed arrows.

Configurations of the control part are formally captured by the notion of *control configurations*, which are used to represent a move of the controlling agent. Here, the arguments from A_C that the agent wants to use are included in the *control configuration*, and the arguments that the agent does not want to include are discarded.

Definition 3. *A subset $A_{conf} \subseteq A_C$ is called a* control configuration. A_{conf} *induces a CAF $(F, \langle A_{conf}, R_{conf} \rangle, U)$ with $R_{conf} = R_C|_{(A_F \cup A_U \cup A_{conf})}$, where the corresponding control move has been made (we define $R|_A = R \cap (A \times A)$). When the CAF is known from context, we may sometimes use the control configuration A_{conf} to represent its induced CAF.*

Now, assuming that a control configuration has been chosen, the remaining uncertainty of the uncertain part is resolved via a *completion*.

Definition 4. *A completion of a CAF $(F, \langle A_{conf}, R_{conf} \rangle, U)$ is an argumentation framework $AF^* = (A^*, R^*)$ with*

$$A_F \cup A_{conf} \subseteq A^* \subseteq A_F \cup A_{conf} \cup A_U,$$

$$(R_F \cup R_{conf})|_{A^*} \subseteq R^* \subseteq (R_F \cup R_{conf} \cup R_U \cup R_U^{\leftrightarrow})|_{A^*},$$

and it is required that $(a,b) \in R^*$ or $(b,a) \in R^*$ (or both) for all $(a,b) \in R_U^{\leftrightarrow}$.

Example 4. We continue Example 3. Using the control configuration $\{b\}$ and the completion that includes the uncertain argument e and all uncertain attacks $(c,c), (d,e)$, and (e,d) produces the AF of Example 1, with the properties mentioned in Example 2.

2.3 Some Background on Complexity Theory

We will study the computational complexity of the nonemptiness problem for CAFs to be defined in the next section. We assume that the reader is familiar with the needed background on complexity theory, such as the complexity classes of the polynomial hierarchy [15,22], the zeroth level of which is P, the first level of which consists of NP and coNP, the second level of which consists of $\Sigma_2^p = \mathrm{NP}^{\mathrm{NP}}$ and $\Pi_2^p = \mathrm{coNP}^{\mathrm{NP}}$, and the third level of which consists of $\Sigma_3^p = \mathrm{NP}^{\mathrm{NP}^{\mathrm{NP}}}$ and $\Pi_2^p = \mathrm{coNP}^{\mathrm{NP}^{\mathrm{NP}}}$. We also assume familiarity with the concepts of hardness and completeness based on polynomial-time many-one reducibility. For more background on computational complexity, we refer the reader to, e.g., the textbooks by Papadimitriou [18] and Rothe [20].

3 Complexity of Nonemptiness in CAFs

For CAFs, we generalize the nonemptiness problem following the pattern of the controllability problem [17]. The generalized problem s-CONTROL-NONEMPTINESS wraps the s-NE problem for standard argumentation frameworks with an outer existential quantifier over control configurations followed by an inner universal quantifier over completions. Using the notation from Definitions 2 and 3, we define this problem as follows for any semantics s.

---

s-CONTROL-NONEMPTINESS (s-CONNE)

Given: A control argumentation framework $(\mathcal{F}, C, \mathcal{U})$.

Question: Does there exist a control configuration $\mathcal{A}_{conf} \subseteq \mathcal{A}_C$ such that every completion $AF^* = (\mathcal{A}^*, \mathcal{R}^*)$ of $(\mathcal{F}, \langle \mathcal{A}_{conf}, \mathcal{R}_{conf} \rangle, \mathcal{U})$ has a nonempty s extension?

We now determine the computational complexity of s-CONNE for each semantics $s \in \{\mathrm{CF}, \mathrm{GR}, \mathrm{AD}, \mathrm{CP}, \mathrm{ST}, \mathrm{PR}\}$. First, we extend a result of Skiba et al. [21] for incomplete argumentation frameworks to CAFs and show that CF-CONNE can be solved in polynomial time.

Proposition 1. CF-CONNE *is in* P.

Proof. Let $CAF = (\mathcal{F}, C, \mathcal{U})$ be a given control argumentation framework. Consider the control configuration $\mathcal{A}_{conf}^{\max} = \mathcal{A}_C$ of CAF that includes every control argument in C. If the CAF induced by $\mathcal{A}_{conf}^{\max}$ has an argument a for which the self-attack (a,a) does not exist in any of the attack relations, then clearly $\{a\}$ is a nonempty conflict-free set in every completion, so $CAF \in$ CF-CONNE. On the other hand, if the CAF induced by $\mathcal{A}_{conf}^{\max}$ has no such argument without a self-attack, then there cannot be a nonempty conflict-free set in any of its completions. Further, no control configuration other than $\mathcal{A}_{conf}^{\max}$ can change this fact, since these cannot provide the existence of such an argument. Therefore, it holds that $CAF \notin$ CF-CONNE.

The control configuration $\mathcal{A}_{conf}^{\max}$ and its induced CAF can be created in polynomial time, and checking whether there exists an argument without a self-attack in any of the attack relations can be done in polynomial time, too.   □

Next, we provide a result analogous to that of Skiba et al. [21] for incomplete argumentation frameworks (IAFs) by showing that GR-CONNE can also be solved in polynomial time.

Proposition 2. GR-CONNE *is in* P.

Proof. For a GR-CONNE instance $(\mathcal{F}, C, \mathcal{U})$ with $C = \langle \mathcal{A}_C, \mathcal{R}_C \rangle$, consider the control configurations $\mathcal{A}^0_{conf} = \emptyset$ and $\mathcal{A}^a_{conf} = \{a\}$ for each $a \in \mathcal{A}_C$. For each of these $|\mathcal{A}_C| + 1$ control configurations, GR-CONNE can be solved by the following algorithm. Recall that a nonempty grounded extension exists in a completion if and only if the completion has an unattacked argument.

Consider a sequence AF_i of completions for control configuration $\mathcal{A}^x_{conf}$ that is constructed as follows. AF_0 is the maximal completion that includes all uncertain elements $\mathcal{U}$ and all selected control elements C^x_{conf}:

$$AF_0 = \langle \mathcal{A}_F \cup \mathcal{A}^x_{conf} \cup \mathcal{A}_U, \mathcal{R}_F \cup \mathcal{R}^x_{conf} \cup \mathcal{R}_U \cup \{(a,b),(b,a) \mid (a,b) \in \mathcal{R}^{\leftrightarrow}_U\} \rangle.$$

Initially, let $i = 1$. Define AF_i to be AF_{i-1} but with all arguments removed that originally were in $\mathcal{A}_U$ and are unattacked in AF_{i-1}, and with all attacks incident to these arguments removed as well. Repeat this step (incrementing i) until $AF_i = AF_{i-1}$ for some i. Then $AF^* = AF_i$ is our so-called critical completion.

If AF^* has no unattacked arguments, it also has no nonempty grounded extension. If, on the other hand, AF^* has an unattacked argument y, then every completion must have an unattacked argument y: In every completion, either y itself is unattacked, or else the completion must include some arguments $u \subseteq \mathcal{A}_U$ attacking y. The only candidates are removed by the algorithm. These uncertain arguments can only be attacked by other uncertain arguments. Also, at least one of the uncertain arguments needs to be not attacked by any other argument (definite or uncertain); otherwise, the algorithm would not delete such an argument in the first iteration. Hence, one argument must be unattacked in any given completion. Note that excluding any additional uncertain attacks from completions can only make it more likely for unattacked arguments to exist in the completion, so we do not need to consider this separately in the algorithm. Note further that if AF^* has a nonempty grounded extension then it is allowed to answer "yes" for the given GR-CONNE instance.

Clearly, when we get a "yes" answer for at least one of the control configurations, this allows a "yes" answer for the given instance of the GR-CONNE problem, since we have found a control configuration such that for all completions, a nonempty grounded extension exists. On the other hand, if for all control configurations $\mathcal{A}^0_{conf}$ and $\mathcal{A}^a_{conf}$ with $a \in \mathcal{A}_C$, the answer is "no," we can deduce a "no" answer for the given instance of GR-CONNE, so we know that none of the control configurations $\mathcal{A}^0_{conf}$ or $\mathcal{A}^a_{conf}$ can ensure the existence of an unattacked argument for all its completions. The only other control configuration left to be considered are those where multiple control arguments are added simultaneously, and it is clear that these cannot create any new unattacked arguments, since no new arguments are introduced, but only new attacks are possibly included.

It is easy to see that this algorithm runs in polynomial time.   □

Finally, in order to show hardness of the remaining cases of s-CONNE, we provide in Definition 5 a translation from $\Sigma_3\text{SAT}$ instances to instances of s-CONNE, where $\Sigma_3\text{SAT}$ is the canonical problem for the complexity class Σ_3^p in the polynomial hierarchy which asks, for a 3-CNF formula φ over a set $X \uplus Y \uplus Z$ of propositional variables,[1] whether $(\exists \tau_X)(\forall \tau_Y)(\exists \tau_Z)[\varphi[\tau_X, \tau_Y, \tau_Z] = \texttt{true}]$, where τ_χ denotes a truth assignment over variables in a set χ, and $\varphi[\tau_\chi]$ is the truth value that φ evaluates to under τ_χ.

Definition 5. *Given a $\Sigma_3\text{SAT}$ instance (φ, X, Y, Z) with $\varphi = \bigwedge_i c_i$ and $c_i = \bigvee_j \alpha_{i,j}$ for each clause c_i, where $\alpha_{i,j}$ are the literals in clause c_i, a control argumentation framework $CAF = (\mathcal{F}, C, \mathcal{U})$ representing (φ, X, Y, Z) is defined by its fixed part $\mathcal{F}$:*

$$\mathcal{A}_F = \{\bar{x}_j \mid x_j \in X\} \cup \{\bar{y}_k \mid y_k \in Y\} \cup \{z_\ell, \bar{z}_\ell \mid z_\ell \in Z\} \cup \{c_i \mid c_i \text{ in } \varphi\} \cup \{\varphi, d\},$$

$$\begin{aligned}
\mathcal{R}_F = {}& \{(y_k, \bar{y}_k) \mid y_k \in Y\} \cup \{(\bar{z}_\ell, z_\ell), (z_\ell, \bar{z}_\ell) \mid z_\ell \in Z\} \cup \{(\bar{x}_j, c_i) \mid \neg x_j \text{ in } c_i\} \\
& \cup \{(y_k, c_i) \mid y_k \text{ in } c_i\} \cup \{(\bar{y}_k, c_i) \mid \neg y_k \text{ in } c_i\} \\
& \cup \{(z_\ell, c_i) \mid z_\ell \text{ in } c_i\} \cup \{(\bar{z}_\ell, c_i) \mid \neg z_\ell \text{ in } c_i\} \\
& \cup \{(c_i, \varphi) \mid c_i \in \varphi\} \cup \{(d, a) \mid a \in \{\bar{x}_j, y_k, \bar{y}_k, z_\ell, \bar{z}_\ell, c_l\}\} \cup \{(\varphi, d), (d, d)\};
\end{aligned}$$

its control part C:

$$\mathcal{A}_C = \{x_j \mid x_j \in X\},$$

$$\mathcal{R}_C = \{(x_j, \bar{x}_j), (d, x_j) \mid x_j \in X\} \cup \{(x_j, c_i) \mid x_j \text{ in } c_i\};$$

and its uncertain part $\mathcal{U}$:

$$\mathcal{A}_U = \{y_k \mid y_k \in Y\},$$

$$\mathcal{R}_U = \mathcal{R}_U^{\leftrightarrow} = \emptyset.$$

We call arguments c_i *clause arguments* and arguments representing literals $\alpha_{i,j}$ *literal arguments*. A clause argument c_i can be interpreted as "clause c_i is unsatisfied."

Every assignment τ_X on X corresponds to a control configuration $\mathcal{A}_{conf}^{\tau_X}$ for CAF that includes a control argument x_j if and only if $\tau_X(x_j) = \texttt{true}$. Further, given an assignment τ_X on X and the CAF induced by the control configuration $\mathcal{A}_{conf}^{\tau_X}$, every assignment τ_Y on Y corresponds to a completion AF^{τ_X, τ_Y} of the CAF induced by the control configuration, where an uncertain argument y_k is included in the completion if and only if $\tau_Y(y_k) = \texttt{true}$. For full assignments τ_X, τ_Y, and τ_Z, we denote by $A^{\tau_X, \tau_Y}[\tau_X, \tau_Y, \tau_Z]$ the corresponding set of arguments in the completion AF^{τ_X, τ_Y}:

$$\begin{aligned}
A^{\tau_X, \tau_Y}[\tau_X, \tau_Y, \tau_Z] = {}& \{x_j \mid \tau_X(x_j) = \texttt{true}\} \cup \{\bar{x}_j \mid \tau_X(x_j) = \texttt{false}\} \cup \\
& \{y_k \mid \tau_Y(y_k) = \texttt{true}\} \cup \{\bar{y}_k \mid \tau_Y(y_k) = \texttt{false}\} \cup \\
& \{z_\ell \mid \tau_Z(z_\ell) = \texttt{true}\} \cup \{\bar{z}_\ell \mid \tau_Z(z_\ell) = \texttt{false}\}.
\end{aligned}$$

Example 5. Consider the $\Sigma_3\text{SAT}$ instance $\varphi = c_1 \wedge c_2 = (x_1 \vee \neg y_1) \wedge (y_1 \vee \neg z_1)$, with $X = \{x_1\}, Y = \{y_1\}$, and $Z = \{z_1\}$. It is a "yes"-instance of $\Sigma_3\text{SAT}$, since $\varphi[\tau_X, \tau_Y, \tau_Z] = $

---

[1] $\uplus$ denotes the disjoint union of sets.

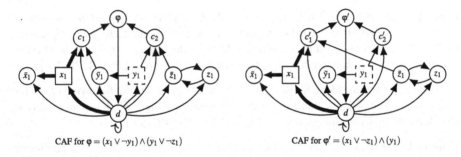

CAF for $\varphi = (x_1 \vee \neg y_1) \wedge (y_1 \vee \neg z_1)$ CAF for $\varphi' = (x_1 \vee \neg z_1) \wedge (y_1)$

Fig. 3. CAFs created for the Σ_3SAT instances from Example 5 using the translation from Definition 5. The left CAF uses $\varphi = c_1 \wedge c_2 = (x_1 \vee \neg y_1) \wedge (y_1 \vee \neg z_1)$ and is a "yes"-instance of s-CONNE for all $s \in \{AD, ST, CP, PR\}$, whereas the right CAF uses $\varphi' = c_1' \wedge c_2' = (x_1 \vee \neg z_1) \wedge (y_1)$ and is a "no"-instance of s-CONNE for all $s \in \{AD, ST, CP, PR\}$.

true for the assignment τ_X on X with $\tau_X(x_1) = \texttt{true}$, for any assignment τ_Y on Y, and for the assignment τ_Z on Z with $\tau_Z(z_1) = \texttt{false}$. The translation from Definition 5 produces the CAF representation visualized in Fig. 3 (left), where we display control arguments as rectangles, uncertain arguments as dashed rectangles, and elements of $\mathcal{R}_C$ as boldfaced arrows. This CAF is a "yes"-instance of s-CONNE for all $s \in \{AD, ST, CP, PR\}$, since for the control configuration $\{x_1\}$ and for every one of its completions, the set $\{x_1, \hat{y}_1, \bar{z}_1, \varphi\}$ is nonempty and stable (and thus also admissible, complete, and preferred), where $\hat{y}_1 = y_1$ if $\tau_Y(y_1) = \texttt{true}$ and $\hat{y}_1 = \bar{y}_1$ if $\tau_Y(y_1) = \texttt{false}$.

Now consider a modified Σ_3SAT instance $\varphi' = c_1' \wedge c_2' = (x_1 \vee \neg z_1) \wedge (y_1)$, where $\neg y_1$ in the first clause is replaced by $\neg z_1$ and "$\vee \neg z_1$" is removed from the second clause. This instance is a "no"-instance of Σ_3SAT, since for each assignment τ_X on X, the assignment τ_Y on Y with $\tau_Y(y_1) = \texttt{false}$, and for each assignment τ_Z on Z, the second clause is unsatisfied and thus $\varphi'[\tau_X, \tau_Y, \tau_Z] = \texttt{false}$. The corresponding CAF is displayed in Fig. 3 (right). Irrespective of the control configuration used, the completion that excludes argument y_1 has no literal argument that can defend φ' against the clause argument c_2', so this CAF is a "no"-instance of s-CONNE for all $s \in \{AD, ST, CP, PR\}$.

Next, we observe that the properties shown by Skiba et al. [21] (see their Lemmas 12 and 13) to hold for completions of IAFs created via their Definition 19 do hold for completions of CAFs created via Definition 5 as well. This result follows directly from [21, Lemma 12]: Given a Σ_3SAT instance (φ, X, Y, Z) and letting $X' = X \cup Y$ and $Y' = Z$, (φ, X', Y') is a Π_2SAT instance that has an IAF representation IAF via [21, Definition 19]. The completion AF^{τ_X, τ_Y} considered in the current lemma is the same argumentation framework as the completion $AF^{\tau_{X'}}$ of IAF, and the result of [21, Lemma 12] for $AF^{\tau_{X'}}$ applies here.

The first lemma states that the argument φ has to be in any nonempty extension satisfying the semantics $s \in \{AD, CP, GR, PR, ST\}$. Otherwise, the argument d is not attacked and has to be in every potential admissible set, which is impossible as this would conflict with the conflict-freeness of every set, as d attacks itself, so d cannot be part of any conflict-free set.

Lemma 1. *Given a Σ_3SAT instance (φ, X, Y, Z), let CAF be the control argumentation framework created for it according to Definition 5. Let τ_X and τ_Y be full assignments on X and Y, respectively. In the completion AF^{τ_X, τ_Y}, the argument φ has to be in every nonempty extension that satisfies any of the semantics $s \in \{\text{AD}, \text{CP}, \text{GR}, \text{PR}, \text{ST}\}$.*

Similarly, Lemma 13 by Skiba et al. [21] directly provides the following result for CAFs, which states that if there is a truth assignment for the Σ_3SAT instance, there is an extension satisfying the semantics $s \in \{\text{AD}, \text{CP}, \text{GR}, \text{PR}, \text{ST}\}$.

Lemma 2. *Let (φ, X, Y, Z) be a Σ_3SAT instance and let τ_X, τ_Y, and τ_Z be assignments on X, Y, and Z, respectively. Let CAF be the control argumentation framework created by Definition 5 for (φ, X, Y, Z). Let AF^{τ_X, τ_Y} be its completion corresponding to τ_X and τ_Y and let $\mathcal{A}^{\tau_X, \tau_Y}[\tau_X, \tau_Y, \tau_Z]$ be the set of literal arguments corresponding to the total assignment. If $\varphi[\tau_X, \tau_Y, \tau_Z] = \text{true}$, then AF^{τ_X, τ_Y} has an extension $\mathcal{A}^{\tau_X, \tau_Y}[\tau_X, \tau_Y, \tau_Z] \cup \{\varphi\}$ that is admissible, complete, preferred, and stable.*

We are now ready to show Σ_3^p-completeness of s-CONNE for the remaining semantics $s \in \{\text{AD}, \text{CP}, \text{ST}, \text{PR}\}$.

Theorem 1. *s-CONNE is Σ_3^p-complete for each $s \in \{\text{AD}, \text{CP}, \text{ST}, \text{PR}\}$.*

Proof. To show membership of the problems s-CONNE in Σ_3^p, we look at their quantifier representation. For each semantics $s \in \{\text{AD}, \text{CP}, \text{ST}, \text{PR}\}$, the problem can be written as the set of all *CAF* (using the notation from Definitions 2 and 3) such that $(\exists \mathcal{A}_{conf} \subseteq \mathcal{A}_C)(\forall \text{ completion } AF^*)[AF^* \in s\text{-NE}]$, and since s-NE is NP-complete for these semantics s [3,5], this provides a Σ_3^p upper bound of s-CONNE. Note that all quantifiers in this representation are polynomially length-bounded in the size of the encoding of the given *CAF*.

To prove Σ_3^p-hardness, let (φ, X, Y, Z) be a Σ_3SAT instance. Let $CAF = (\mathcal{F}, C, \mathcal{U})$ be the control argumentation framework created for (φ, X, Y, Z) via Definition 5. We will show that for any $s \in \{\text{AD}, \text{CP}, \text{PR}, \text{ST}\}$, $(\varphi, X, Y, Z) \in \Sigma_3$SAT if and only if $CAF \in s$-CONNE.

From left to right, assume that $(\varphi, X, Y, Z) \in \Sigma_3$SAT, i.e., there exists an assignment τ_X on X such that for every assignment τ_Y on Y, there exists an assignment τ_Z on Z such that $\varphi[\tau_X, \tau_Y, \tau_Z]$ is true. We then know from Lemma 2 that, in the completion AF^{τ_X, τ_Y} of *CAF*, the set $\mathcal{A}^{\tau_X, \tau_Y}[\tau_X, \tau_Y, \tau_Z] \cup \{\varphi\}$ is a nonempty extension that is admissible, complete, stable, and preferred. Therefore, $CAF \in s$-CONNE for $s \in \{\text{AD}, \text{CP}, \text{PR}, \text{ST}\}$.

From right to left, assume that, for any $s \in \{\text{AD}, \text{CP}, \text{PR}, \text{ST}\}$, $CAF \in s$-CONNE holds, i.e., there exists a control configuration such that in all completions, there exists a nonempty s extension $\mathcal{E}$. Every nonempty s extension has to contain φ; otherwise, d would not be attacked and thus has to be in every potentially admissible set, as it attacks every other argument. However, d also attacks itself, so every extension containing d would not be conflict-free and therefore not admissible. Therefore, no s extension $\mathcal{E}$ can contain any clause argument c_i; otherwise, we would create a set that is not conflict-free. Since we have a control configuration all completions of which have a nonempty s extension, these extensions contain a literal argument $v \in X \cup Y \cup Z$ that attacks c_i, for each c_i. It is obvious that $\mathcal{E}$ can only contain v or $\bar{v}$ and not both. Hence, the extension contains φ and several literal arguments, which together are attacking every clause

Table 1. Summary of complexity results for s-CONNE for various semantics s, in comparison with the known complexity results for s-NE, s-POSNE, and s-NECNE. C-c denotes "C-complete" for a complexity class C. New results for s-CONNE are marked by the corresponding theorem or proposition, and results due to previous work are displayed in grey. Results for s-NE in standard argumentation frameworks are marked by the respective reference (where the result marked by * is straightforward and not formally proven).

s	s-NE	s-POSNE	s-NECNE	s-CONNE
CF	in P *	in P [21]	in P [21]	in P (Proposition 1)
GR	in P [16]	in P [21]	in P [21]	in P (Proposition 2)
AD	NP-c [5]	NP-c [21]	Π_2^p-c [21]	Σ_3^p-c (Theorem 1)
CP	NP-c [5]	NP-c [21]	Π_2^p-c [21]	Σ_3^p-c (Theorem 1)
PR	NP-c [5]	NP-c [21]	Π_2^p-c [21]	Σ_3^p-c (Theorem 1)
ST	NP-c [3]	NP-c [21]	Π_2^p-c [21]	Σ_3^p-c (Theorem 1)

argument. This extension is already seen to be admissible, complete, and preferred, but regarding stability we may have some literals $v_j \in X \cup Y \cup Z$ for which neither argument v_j nor $\bar{v}_j$ is in $\mathcal{E}$. Therefore, either v_j or $\bar{v}_j$ has to be in $\mathcal{E}$. Consequently, we can define a total assignment based on the s extension depending on whether the literal arguments are in or out of $\mathcal{E}$: If a literal argument is in $\mathcal{E}$, we set the corresponding literal to true; otherwise we set its negation to true. This assignment must be a satisfying assignment, since every clause argument is attacked by $\mathcal{E}$ and, accordingly, every clause is satisfied by the assignment.   □

Finally, let us consider a few special cases of control nonemptiness. The literature on control argumentation frameworks also considers *simplified CAFs*, which are CAFs where the sets of uncertain elements $\mathcal{A}_U$, $\mathcal{R}_U$, and $\mathcal{R}_U^{\leftrightarrow}$ are empty. Clearly, the problem s-CONNE for simplified CAFs is equivalent to s-POSNE for argument-incomplete argumentation frameworks as defined by Skiba et al. [21], so their complexity results for s-POSNE carry over.

Recently, Mailly [14] introduced the idea of *possible controllability*, related to the concept of *possible* problem variants for incomplete argumentation frameworks. A corresponding problem *possible control nonemptiness* can be defined, which asks, for a given CAF, whether there exists a control configuration such that there is a completion in which a nonempty extension exists. This problem is clearly in NP via the three collapsing existential quantifiers, and NP hardness is directly inherited from s-NE for $s \in \{AD, CP, PR, ST\}$. For $s \in \{CF, GR\}$, the complexity of this variant of nonemptiness remains an open problem.

4   Conclusion

The contribution of this work is the definition of variants of the nonemptiness problem for control argumentation frameworks and a characterization of their computational complexity. Table 1 summarizes our complexity results, also providing a comparison with the corresponding complexity results of Chvátal [3], Modgil and Caminada [16], and Dimopoulos and Torres [5] for the analogous problems in standard argumentation frameworks and of Skiba et al. [21] in incomplete argumentation frameworks.

Comparing the complexity of "necessary nonemptiness" in incomplete argumentation frameworks with that of nonemptiness in control argumentation frameworks, there is a complexity jump from Π_2^p-hardness to Σ_3^p-hardness, indicating a significant difference between the two formalisms. Interestingly, the Σ_3^p-completeness that we determined for s-CONNE is the same as the complexity of credulous controllability for the same four semantics $s \in \{AD, CP, PR, ST\}$ [17]. Credulous controllability is the problem of deciding whether there is a control configuration, such that for all completions, a given target set of arguments is a subset of at least one s extension. This is a refinement of s-CONNE, since s-CONNE only requires the existence of at least one nonempty s extension. The coinciding complexities indicate that the hardness of credulous controllability in control argumentation frameworks lies predominantly in making sure that an s extension exists in the first place, while the additional requirement of enforcing that the given target set of arguments is contained in that extension does not add to the asymptotical complexity. In contrast, for the grounded semantics, credulous controllability is Σ_2^p-hard [17], while GR-CONNE is in P.

In future work, it would be interesting to extend the complexity analysis of nonemptiness in CAFs to further semantics. Control argumentation frameworks model argumentation by agents strategically. Relatedly, Maher [12] (see also [13]) introduced a model of strategic argumentation by simulating a game. However, his model does not allow any uncertainty regarding the attacks between arguments. Further, CAFs have some similarities to AF expansion due to Baumann and Brewka [1], where new arguments and new attacks incident to at least one new argument may be added. Opposed to CAFs, the set of new arguments and attacks is not fixed, and new attacks among existing arguments are not allowed. One might also modify the model of control argumentation frameworks by adding weights to the uncertain elements or by following a probabilistic approach (see, e.g., the work of Dunne et al. [7], Li et al. [11], Fazzinga et al. [9], and Gaignier et al. [10]). Such refinements of the model of CAFs may lead to new challenges in future work. One could also consider the approach of Riveret et al. [19] who combine probabilistic argumentation with reinforcement learning techniques.

Acknowledgments. This work was supported by Deutsche Forschungsgemeinschaft under grants KE 1413/11-1, RO 1202/14-2, and RO 1202/21-1 and by the NRW project "Online Participation."

References

1. Baumann, R., Brewka, G.: Expanding argumentation frameworks: enforcing and monotonicity results. In: Proceedings of the 3rd International Conference on Computational Models of Argument, pp. 75–86. IOS Press (September 2010)
2. Baumeister, D., Neugebauer, D., Rothe, J., Schadrack, H.: Verification in incomplete argumentation frameworks. Artif. Intell. **264**, 1–26 (2018)
3. Chvátal, V.: On the computational complexity of finding a kernel. Technical report CRM-300, Centre de Recherches Mathématiques, Université de Montréal (1973)

4. Dimopoulos, Y., Mailly, J., Moraitis, P.: Control argumentation frameworks. In: Proceedings of the 32nd AAAI Conference on Artificial Intelligence, pp. 4678–4685. AAAI Press (February 2018)
5. Dimopoulos, Y., Torres, A.: Graph theoretical structures in logic programs and default theories. Theoret. Comput. Sci. **170**(1), 209–244 (1996)
6. Dung, P.: On the acceptability of arguments and its fundamental role in nonmonotonic reasoning, logic programming and n-person games. Artif. Intell. **77**(2), 321–357 (1995)
7. Dunne, P., Hunter, A., McBurney, P., Parsons, S., Wooldridge, M.: Weighted argument systems: Basic definitions, algorithms, and complexity results. Artif. Intell. **175**(2), 457–486 (2011)
8. Dunne, P., Wooldridge, M.: Complexity of abstract argumentation, chap. 5. In: Rahwan, I., Simari, G. (eds.) Argumentation in Artificial Intelligence, pp. 85–104. Springer, Boston (2009). https://doi.org/10.1007/978-0-387-98197-0_5
9. Fazzinga, B., Flesca, S., Parisi, F.: On the complexity of probabilistic abstract argumentation. In: Proceedings of the 23rd International Joint Conference on Artificial Intelligence, pp. 898–904. AAAI Press/IJCAI (August 2013)
10. Gaignier, F., Dimopoulos, Y., Mailly, J.G., Moraitis, P.: Probabilistic control argumentation frameworks. In: Proceedings of the 19th International Conference on Autonomous Agents and Multiagent Systems, pp. 519–527. IFAAMAS (2021)
11. Li, H., Oren, N., Norman, T.J.: Probabilistic argumentation frameworks. In: Modgil, S., Oren, N., Toni, F. (eds.) TAFA 2011. LNCS (LNAI), vol. 7132, pp. 1–16. Springer, Heidelberg (2012). https://doi.org/10.1007/978-3-642-29184-5_1
12. Maher, M.: Resistance to corruption of strategic argumentation. In: Proceedings of the 30th AAAI Conference on Artificial Intelligence, pp. 1030–1036. AAAI Press (February 2016)
13. Maher, M.J.: Resistance to corruption of general strategic argumentation. In: Baldoni, M., Chopra, A.K., Son, T.C., Hirayama, K., Torroni, P. (eds.) PRIMA 2016. LNCS (LNAI), vol. 9862, pp. 61–75. Springer, Cham (2016). https://doi.org/10.1007/978-3-319-44832-9_4
14. Mailly, J.G.: Possible controllability of control argumentation frameworks. In: Proceedings of the 8th International Conference on Computational Models of Argument, vol. 326, pp. 283–294 (2020)
15. Meyer, A., Stockmeyer, L.: The equivalence problem for regular expressions with squaring requires exponential space. In: Proceedings of the 13th IEEE Symposium on Switching and Automata Theory, pp. 125–129. IEEE Computer Society Press (1972)
16. Modgil, S., Caminada, M.: Proof theories and algorithms for abstract argumentation frameworks, chap. 6. In: Rahwan, I., Simari, G. (eds.) Argumentation in Artificial Intelligence, pp. 105–129. Springer, Boston (2009). https://doi.org/10.1007/978-0-387-98197-0_6
17. Niskanen, A., Neugebauer, D., Järvisalo, M.: Controllability of control argumentation frameworks. In: Proceedings of the 29th International Joint Conference on Artificial Intelligence, pp. 1855–1861. ijcai.org (July 2020)
18. Papadimitriou, C.: Computational Complexity, 2nd edn. Addison-Wesley (1995)
19. Riveret, R., Gao, Y., Governatori, G., Rotolo, A., Pitt, J., Sartor, G.: A probabilistic argumentation framework for reinforcement learning agents - towards a mentalistic approach to agent profiles. J. Autonomous Agents Multi-agent Syst. **33**(1–2), 216–274 (2019)
20. Rothe, J.: Complexity Theory and Cryptology. An Introduction to Cryptocomplexity. EATCS Texts in Theoretical Computer Science. Springer, Heidelberg (2005). https://doi.org/10.1007/3-540-28520-2
21. Skiba, K., Neugebauer, D., Rothe, J.: Complexity of possible and necessary existence problems in abstract argumentation. In: Proceedings of the 24th European Conference on Artificial Intelligence. Frontiers in Artificial Intelligence and Applications, vol. 325, pp. 897–904. IOS Press (August/September 2020)
22. Stockmeyer, L.: The polynomial-time hierarchy. Theoret. Comput. Sci. **3**(1), 1–22 (1976)

Generalizing Complete Semantics to Bipolar Argumentation Frameworks

Nico Potyka[(⊠)] [ID]

University of Stuttgart, Stuttgart, Germany
nico.potyka@ipvs.uni-stuttgart.de
https://www.ipvs.uni-stuttgart.de/de/institut/team/Potyka-00001/

Abstract. Computational models of argumentation are an interesting tool to represent decision processes. Bipolar abstract argumentation studies the question of which arguments a rational agent can accept given attack and support relationships between them. We present a generalization of the fundamental complete semantics from attack-only graphs to bipolar graphs. As opposed to previous semantics, the new bi-complete semantics treats attacks and supports symmetrically and directly leads to natural generalizations of grounded, preferred, semi-stable and stable semantics. We show, in particular, that bipolar graphs are strictly more expressive than attack-only graphs under bi-complete semantics. That is, the meaning of support edges cannot be encoded by attack edges like in deductive support frameworks.

Keywords: Abstract argumentation · Bipolar argumentation · Argumentation semantics

1 Introduction

Computational argumentation provides models for reasoning based on pro and contra arguments. Given a set of arguments that may mutually attack or support each other, argumentation answers the question of which arguments can reasonably be accepted. Abstract argumentation [12] abstracts from the content of the arguments and focuses merely on their relationships. While this abstraction goes too far for some domains, abstract argumentation frameworks have been applied successfully in diverse areas like computational persuasion [6,14,15], recommender systems [25] or review aggregation [11]. Even though such applications often profit from a quantitative interpretation based on numerical degrees of acceptance, classical models remain interesting in their own right and as a basis for non-classical models. For example, [16] recently proposed probability distributions over classical argumentation graphs to learn user models from data. Classical argumentation frameworks can also often be turned into Markov networks that allow for uncertain reasoning over arguments [22].

Our focus here is on classical bipolar argumentation frameworks that consider abstract arguments and attack and support relations between them [3,7,10,18].

© Springer Nature Switzerland AG 2021
J. Vejnarová and N. Wilson (Eds.): ECSQARU 2021, LNAI 12897, pp. 130–143, 2021.
https://doi.org/10.1007/978-3-030-86772-0_10

It is interesting to note that supports are often not considered as direct counterparts of attacks, but rather as meta-relations with a special meaning. For
example, bipolar argumentation with *deductive support* uses support relations
only to derive indirect attacks between arguments [10]. In this way, the evaluation
of bipolar graphs can be reduced to the better studied evaluation of attack-only
graphs. However, this approach favors attack relationships as we will discuss
later. Another example is bipolar argumentation with *evidential support* [18].
Here, nothing can be accepted unless directly or indirectly supported by special
prima-facie arguments. Furthermore, attacks can only be successful if they are
supported. In this approach, support can be seen as the dominating relationship.

Our focus here is on bipolar argumentation frameworks that attempt to treat
attacks and supports equally. Recently, some novel bipolar semantics have been
introduced in [22,23] that are inspired by the idea of deductive supports from
[10], but try to balance the power of attacks and supports. The s-deductive and
m-deductive semantics from [23] generalize stable semantics from attack-only
graphs to bipolar graphs. However, while they cannot label arguments undecided
in attack-only graphs like stable semantics, they can label arguments undecided
in bipolar graphs. Furthermore, since the stable semantics is a refinement of
the more fundamental complete semantics, one may wonder, is there a natural generalization of complete semantics to bipolar graphs? We present such a
generalization in Sect. 3 that we call bi-complete semantics. It is strictly more
expressive than the deductive support framework from [10] in the sense that the
meaning of bipolar graphs under bi-complete semantics cannot be encoded in an
attack-only graph under most reasonable semantics. The bi-complete semantics
can be refined in different ways analogous to refinements of complete semantics.

2 Background

We begin with an overview of the relevant background. A Dung-style *(finite)*
abstract argumentation framework (AAF) is a tuple $(\mathcal{A}, \text{Att})$, where $\mathcal{A}$ is a finite
set of (abstract) arguments and $\text{Att} \subseteq \mathcal{A} \times \mathcal{A}$ is the *attack relation* [12]. For
our purposes, an argument is simply an entity that can be accepted or rejected.
If $(A, B) \in \text{Att}$, we say that A attacks B. With a slight abuse of notation, we
let $\text{Att}(A) = \{B \mid (B, A) \in \text{Att}\}$ denote the set of attackers of A. Semantics of
argumentation frameworks can be defined in terms of extensions or labellings
in an equivalent way [9]. We will use labellings here. A labelling is a function
$L : \mathcal{A} \to \{\text{in}, \text{out}, \text{und}\}$ that assigns to each argument a label. We say that an
argument A is accepted if $L(A) = \text{in}$ and that A is rejected if $L(A) = \text{out}$.
Following [9], we call a labelling.

Complete: if L satisfies
   1. $L(A) = \text{in}$ if and only if $L(B) = \text{out}$ for all $B \in \text{Att}(A)$.
   2. $L(A) = \text{out}$ if and only if $L(B) = \text{in}$ for some $B \in \text{Att}(A)$.

For a labelling L and a label $lab \in \{\text{in}, \text{out}, \text{und}\}$, we let $lab(L) = \{A \in \mathcal{A} \mid L(A) = lab\}$ denote those arguments that receive the label *lab*. We say that a
complete labelling is

Fig. 1. BAF $(\mathcal{A}, \text{Att}, \text{Sup})$ with $\mathcal{A} = \{A, B, C\}$, $\text{Att} = \{(B, A)\}$, $\text{Sup} = \{(C, A)\}$.

Grounded: if in(L) is minimal with respect to $\subseteq$.
Preferred: if in(L) is maximal with respect to $\subseteq$.
Semi-stable: if und(L) is minimal with respect to $\subseteq$.
Stable: if und(L) = $\emptyset$.

In many applications it is useful to consider not only attack relations, but also support relations. A *bipolar argumentation framework (BAF)* is a tuple $(\mathcal{A}, \text{Att}, \text{Sup})$, where $\mathcal{A}$ is a finite set of arguments, $\text{Att} \subseteq \mathcal{A} \times \mathcal{A}$ is the *attack relation* as before and $\text{Sup} \subseteq \mathcal{A} \times \mathcal{A}$ is the support relation [10]. We also assume that $\text{Att} \cap \text{Sup} = \emptyset$. We let again $\text{Sup}(A) = \{B \mid (B, A) \in \text{Sup}\}$ denote the set of supporters of A. Graphically, we denote attack relations by solid edges and support relations by dashed edges. Figure 1 shows an example BAF with one attack and one support. For example, in the context of a recommender system, the arguments could be associated with the following meaning:

A: Movie m should be recommended because the user generally likes movies from this genre.
B: M should not be recommended because the user generally does not like movies with actor a.
C: M should be recommended because the user generally likes movies written by writer w.

Different semantics have been considered for bipolar graphs. The idea of *deductive* and *necessary support* is to reduce the semantics of BAFs to AAF semantics. The intuitive idea of *deductive support* [7,10] is that if an argument is accepted, every argument that it supports must be accepted as well. The dual idea, if an argument is accepted, all its supporters must be accepted as well, is referred to as *necessary support* [10]. Since deductive support relations can be translated to necessary support relations by just reversing their direction, we will just look at the former here. A deeper discussion of both and other notions of support can be found in [10]. The deductive support frameworks gives formal meaning to support relations by translating the given BAF to an AAF with new attacks [10]. These new attacks correspond to indirect attacks that result from the interplay between attack and support relations. The following indirect attacks have been considered for this purpose in [10]:

Supported Attack from A to B: there is a sequence of arguments $A_1, \ldots, A_n$ such that $A_1 = A$, $A_n = B$, $(A_i, A_{i+1}) \in \text{Sup}$ for $1 \leq i \leq n - 2$ and $(A_{n-1}, A_n) \in \text{Att}$.
Mediated Attack from A to B: there is a sequence of arguments $A_1, \ldots, A_n$ such that $A_1 = B$, $A_n = A$, $(A_i, A_{i+1}) \in \text{Sup}$ for $1 \leq i \leq n - 2$ and $(A_n, A_{n-1}) \in \text{Att}$.

Intuitively, there is a supported attack from A to B iff A directly or indirectly supports an attacker of B. There is a mediated attack from A to B iff A attacks an argument that is directly or indirectly supported by B. The *Dung framework associated with* $(\mathcal{A}, \text{Att}, \text{Sup})$ is then defined as the Dung framework $(\mathcal{A}, \text{Att} \cup \text{Att}^s \cup \text{Att}^m)$, where Att^s and Att^m contain additional attacks that correspond to supported and mediated attacks in $(\mathcal{A}, \text{Att}, \text{Sup})$ [10]. While this is an elegant way to extend AAF semantics to BAFs, the resulting semantics does not treat attack and support equally. For example, in Fig. 1, it seems that A could as well be accepted as rejected. However, the translation takes only account of the mediated attack from B to C and ignores the fact that A has a supporter. Hence, the only complete labelling of the associated Dung framework labels B in and both A and C out. The disparity between attack and support becomes more prevalent when we keep our attacker B, but add n supporters C_i of A. Then B will still be accepted and A and all of its supporters C_i will be rejected even when A is supported by thousands of undisputed arguments. In the context of a recommender system, this would mean that an item cannot be recommended anymore if there is a single negative aspect about the item.

In order to overcome this limitation, some alternatives have been presented recently that focus on equal treatment of attack and support. *Deductive labellings* are defined by first weakening the conditions of complete labellings, and then adding a symmetrical support condition for every attack condition [22]. While the resulting semantics treats attacks and supports equally and respects supported and mediated attacks, it can be very indecisive. *S-deductive and m-deductive labellings* overcome the problem by introducing a slight asymmetry by favoring labelling arguments in, but still treat attacks and supports equally [23]. The m-deductive labellings also take the number of attackers and supporters into account to decide the state of an argument based on the state of its attackers and supporters. In this way, they can be more decisive than s-deductive labellings [23]. Both s-deductive and m-deductive labellings generalize stable labellings for AAFs to BAFs in the following sense: in a BAF $(\mathcal{A}, \text{Att}, \text{Sup})$ with empty support relation $\text{Sup} = \emptyset$, the s-deductive and m-deductive labellings are exactly the stable labellings of the corresponding AAF $(\mathcal{A}, \text{Att})$ and vice versa. This is a nice property to have since it shows consistency with a well-established AAF semantics. However, s-deductive labellings are perhaps not the most natural generalization of stable labellings since they allow labelling arguments undecided in bipolar graphs. Furthermore, since stable labellings are derived from complete labellings in AAFs, it is natural to ask, is there a generalization from complete labellings to BAFs? Such a generalized semantics could then be extended to grounded, preferred, semi-stable and stable variants like in the AAF setting.

3   Bi-Complete Semantics

Motivated by the previous discussion, we now present a generalization of complete semantics from AAFs to BAFs. Given a labelling L, we say that the

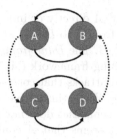

Table 1. Bi-complete labellings for the BAF in Fig. 2.

Labelling	A	B	C	D
L_1	und	und	und	und
L_2	in	out	in	out
L_3	out	in	out	in

Fig. 2. Supporting attack cycles.

attackers of an argument *dominate* its supporters if $|\{B \in \text{Att}(A) \mid L(B) = \text{in}\}| > |\{B \in \text{Sup}(A) \mid L(B) \neq \text{out}\}|$. That is, for every supporter that is not out, there is an attacker that is in and there is at least one additional attacker that is in. Intuitively, every non-rejected pro-argument is balanced out by an accepted counterargument and there is an additional counterargument that breaks a potential tie. Symmetrically, the supporters of an argument *dominate* its attackers if $|\{B \in \text{Sup}(A) \mid L(B) = \text{in}\}| > |\{B \in \text{Att}(A) \mid L(B) \neq \text{out}\}|$. Given a BAF $(\mathcal{A}, \text{Att}, \text{Sup})$, we call a labelling $L : \mathcal{A} \rightarrow \{\text{in}, \text{out}, \text{und}\}$

Bi-complete: if L satisfies
1. $L(A) = \text{in}$ if and only if $L(B) = \text{out}$ for all $B \in \text{Att}(A)$ or A's supporters dominate its attackers.
2. $L(A) = \text{out}$ if and only if A's attackers dominate its supporters.

In line with complete semantics, if all attackers of A are labelled out, A must be labelled in. However, A can also be labelled in when an attacker is in provided that the supporters dominate the attackers. In fact, A must be labelled in whenever the supporters dominate the attackers. Similarly, A can and must be labelled out when its attackers dominate its supporters. The reader may notice that a bi-complete labelling is not *conflict-free* in the AAF sense. That is, both an argument and one of its attackers can be accepted under bi-complete semantics in the bipolar setting. However, as we will show later in Proposition 1, bi-complete labellings correspond to complete labellings when there are no support edges. Therefore, they do respect conflict-freeness in the AAF setting. I would argue that conflict-freeness is not necessarily desirable in the bipolar setting. This is because people tend to consider both pro and contra arguments and not only contra and contra-contra arguments. Therefore, a pro argument should be able to compensate for a contra argument in my opinion. Let us illustrate the behaviour of the bi-complete semantics with some examples.

Example 1. Let us compute the bi-complete labellings for the BAF in Fig. 2. Since B and C have no attackers, they must be labelled in. Since there is no domination between attackers and supporters, A must be labelled undecided. Hence, there is only a single bi-complete labelling.

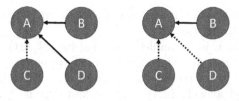

Fig. 3. Dominating attackers (left) and supporters (right).

Example 2. In the previous example, we had only one bi-complete labelling. The BAF in Fig. 2 shows an example with multiple bi-complete labellings. To begin with, all arguments can be labelled undecided. Another labelling labels A and C in and B and D out. The out-state of B and D is now justified by the in-state of A and C and their in-state is justified by the fact that B and D are out. Symmetrically, another labelling labels A and C out and B and D in. Table 1 summarizes all bi-complete labellings.

Example 3. The BAF in Fig. 3 shows two BAFs with dominating attackers and supporters. In both BAFs, B, C and D must be labelled in since they are unattacked. For the BAF on the left, A must be labelled out because the attackers dominate the supporters. Symmetrically, A must be labelled in for the BAF on the right. For both BAFs, there is only a single bi-complete labelling.

3.1   Expressiveness

We now look at the expressiveness of bipolar frameworks under bi-complete labellings. To begin with, we note that the bi-complete semantics generalizes the complete semantics in the sense of the following definition.

Definition 1. *Let S be a labelling-semantics for AAFs and let S' be a labelling-semantics for BAFs. We say that S' generalizes S to BAFs if*

1. *for every BAF $(\mathcal{A}, \mathrm{Att}, \mathrm{Sup})$ with empty support relation $\mathrm{Sup} = \emptyset$, every S'-labelling is a S-labelling for the AAF $(\mathcal{A}, \mathrm{Att})$ and*
2. *for every AAF $(\mathcal{A}, \mathrm{Att})$, every S-labelling is a S'-labelling for the BAF $(\mathcal{A}, \mathrm{Att}, \emptyset)$.*

Intuitively, if a BAF semantics generalizes an AAF semantics, bipolar frameworks under the BAF semantics are at least as expressive as AAFs under the AAF semantics.

Proposition 1. *The bi-complete semantics generalizes the complete semantics to bipolar graphs.*

Proof. First assume that L is a bi-complete labelling for $(\mathcal{A}, \mathrm{Att}, \emptyset)$. Since there are no supporters, we have $\mathrm{L}(A) = $ in if and only if all attackers are out. We have $\mathrm{L}(A) = $ out if and only if the attackers dominate the supporters. Since there are no supporters this is the case if and only if at least one attacker is in. Hence, L is a complete labelling for $(\mathcal{A}, \mathrm{Att})$.

Now assume that L is a complete labelling for $(\mathcal{A}, \mathrm{Att})$. $L(A) = $ in if and only if all attackers are out. Since there are no supporters, the case that the supporters dominate the attackers cannot occur and condition 1 of bi-complete labellings is satisfied as well. $L(A) = $ out if and only if at least one attacker is in, which is the case if and only if the attackers dominate the supporters as explained above. Hence, L is also a bi-complete labelling for $(\mathcal{A}, \mathrm{Att}, \emptyset)$.   □

Obviously BAFs with deductive supports as defined in [10] generalize diverse AAF semantics since they just translate a given BAF to the associated AAF. However, one may argue that the deductive support BAFs do not add any expressiveness to Dung frameworks. Since every BAF is translated into an AAF, it cannot capture anything that an AAF could not capture already. Of course, it may provide a more natural model, but conceptually, the support edges are just syntactic sugar without any additional expressive power. A natural question is therefore, do BAFs with bi-complete semantics provide more expressiveness? In order to answer this question, we first define more precisely what we mean by being more expressive.

Definition 2. *A BAF labelling semantics S is more expressive than an AAF labelling semantics S' if there is a BAF $(\mathcal{A}, \mathrm{Att}, \mathrm{Sup})$ such that there is no AAF $(\mathcal{A}, \mathrm{Att}')$ such that the S-labellings for $(\mathcal{A}, \mathrm{Att}, \mathrm{Sup})$ are exactly the S'-labellings for $(\mathcal{A}, \mathrm{Att}')$.*

Hence, we say that a BAF semantics is more expressive than an AAF semantics if it is not possible to find for every BAF a corresponding AAF with the same set of arguments, but potentially different attacks, such that the labellings for the BAF are exactly the labellings for the AAF. Intuitively, this just means that the meaning of the support edges cannot be encoded by attack relations already. To put it another way, we could say that a BAF semantics is not more expressive than an AAF semantics if there was a general translation function that maps every BAF to an AAF with the same labellings. If the BAF semantics S is more expressive than the AAF labelling semantics S', it is impossible to define such a translation. The deductive support framework from [10] is clearly not more expressive than AAFs because for every BAF, the associated Dung framework is an AAF with the exact same labellings. In contrast, bi-complete semantics are more expressive than most reasonable AAF semantics as we explain in the following proposition.

Proposition 2. *Let S be an AAF semantics that satisfies*

Isolated Acceptance: $L(A) = $ in *whenever* $\mathrm{Att}(A) = \emptyset$.
Hard Attack: $L(A) = $ out *whenever* $L(B) = $ in *for some* $B \in \mathrm{Att}(A)$.

Then the bi-complete semantics is more expressive than S.

Proof. Note that the condition in Definition 2 is an existential statement. Therefore, it suffices to give an example to prove the claim. We use the BAF in Fig. 4

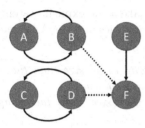

Fig. 4. BAF under bi-complete semantics that cannot be expressed as an AAF under AAF semantics that respect *Isolated Acceptance* and *Hard Attack*.

Table 2. Bi-complete labellings for the BAF in Fig. 4.

Labelling	A	B	C	D	E	F
L_1	und	und	und	und	in	und
L_2	und	und	in	out	in	und
L_3	und	und	out	in	in	und
L_4	in	out	und	und	in	und
L_5	in	out	in	out	in	out
L_6	in	out	out	in	in	und
L_7	out	in	und	und	in	und
L_8	out	in	in	out	in	und
L_9	out	in	out	in	in	in

as an example. We have to show that there is no AAF $(\{A, B, C, D, E, F\}, \text{Att})$ such that the $\mathcal{S}$-labellings are the ones shown in Table 2. To do so, let us think about candidates for the attack relations Att. Since L_9 labels F in together with B, D and E, none of them can be an attacker of F because of the *Hard Attack* property. For the same reason, F cannot be self-attacking. Hence, the only possible attackers of F are A and C. However, A cannot attack F because L_4 labels A in and F undecided and C cannot attack F because L_2 labels C in and F undecided.

Hence, we must have $\text{Att}(F) = \emptyset$. But then *Isolated Acceptance* implies that F must be accepted by every $\mathcal{S}$-labelling.

Hence, there can be no attack relation Att such that the $\mathcal{S}$-labellings of $(\{A, B, C, D, E, F\}, \text{Att})$ correspond to the bi-complete labellings of the BAF in Fig. 4. ☐

We make two assumptions about the AAF semantics. The assumptions are very weak and are, in particular, satisfied by complete semantics and its refinements. *Isolated Acceptance* demands that all isolated arguments are accepted. This is a special case of the sufficient in-condition of complete semantics (if there are no attackers, all attackers are trivially out). *Hard Attack* corresponds to the sufficient out-condition of complete semantics. Note, in particular, that every semantics that satisfies *Hard Attack* also satisfies conflict-freeness. To talk about the relationships between different semantics, we introduce some additional terminology.

Definition 3. *A BAF labelling semantics $\mathcal{S}$ is strictly more expressive than an AAF labelling semantics $\mathcal{S}'$ if*

1. $\mathcal{S}$ generalizes $\mathcal{S}'$ to BAFs and
2. $\mathcal{S}$ is more expressive than $\mathcal{S}'$.

The following corollary uses this terminology to make some explicit statements about the relationships between the bi-complete semantics and the AAF semantics that we discussed previously.

Corollary 1. *1. The bi-complete semantics is more expressive than the complete, grounded, preferred, semi-stable and stable semantics.*

2. The bi-complete semantics is strictly more expressive than the complete semantics.

Proof. 1) follows from Proposition 2 by observing that all five semantics satisfy *Isolated Acceptance* and *Hard Attack*. 2) follows from Proposition 1 and 2.   □

3.2 Refinements

We now look at refinements of bi-complete labellings that are defined analogously to refinements of complete labellings for AAFs. We say that a bi-complete labelling is

Bi-Grounded: if in(L) is minimal with respect to $\subseteq$.
Bi-Preferred: if in(L) is maximal with respect to $\subseteq$.
Bi-Semi-stable: if und(L) is minimal with respect to $\subseteq$.
Bi-Stable: if und(L) = $\emptyset$.

We first note that these labellings generalize the corresponding AAF-labellings to BAFs in the sense of Definition 1.

Corollary 2. *1. The bi-grounded semantics generalizes the grounded semantics to BAFs.*

2. The bi-preferred semantics generalizes the preferred semantics to BAFs.

3. The bi-semi-stable semantics generalizes the semi-stable semantics to BAFs.

4. The bi-stable semantics generalizes the stable semantics to BAFs.

Proof. We know from Proposition 1 that the complete labellings in AAFs correspond to the bi-complete labellings in BAFs. Hence, the complete labellings that minimize/maximize/exclude a particular label in an AAF are exactly the bi-complete labellings that minimize/maximize/exclude this label in a BAF.   □

Stable labellings for AAFs typically do not exist in graphs with odd cycles. The BAF in Fig. 2 demonstrates that, in the bipolar setting, bi-stable labellings do not necessarily exist even in tree-structured bipolar graphs. In this example, the bi-grounded, bi-prefered and bi-semi-stable labellings coincide with the unique bi-complete labelling, of course.

The BAF in Fig. 2 is a more interesting example. Its bi-complete labellings are shown in Table 1. L_1 is the bi-grounded, while L_2 and L_3 are the bi-preferred, bi-semi-stable and bi-stable labellings.

The bi-complete labellings of the BAF in Fig. 4 are shown in Table 2. L_1 is the bi-grounded labelling and L_9 is the bi-preferred labelling. L_5 and L_9 are the bi-semi-stable and bi-stable labellings.

The refinements of bi-complete semantics may potentially loose expressiveness. It seems not even obvious that they are still more expressive than their direct counterparts in AAFs. However, as we show in the following proposition, bi-semi-stable and bi-stable semantics still provide a similar expressiveness as bi-complete semantics.

Proposition 3. *Let S be an AAF semantics that satisfies*

Isolated Acceptance: $L(A) = $ in *whenever* $\text{Att}(A) = \emptyset$.
Hard Attack: $L(A) = $ out *whenever* $L(B) = $ in *for some* $B \in \text{Att}(A)$.

Then the bi-semi-stable and bi-stable semantics are more expressive than S.

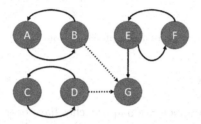

Fig. 5. BAF under bi-semi-stable/bi-stable semantics that cannot be expressed as an AAF under AAF semantics that respect *Isolated Acceptance* and *Hard Attack*.

Table 3. Bi-semi-stable/bi-stable labellings for the BAF in Fig. 5.

Labelling	A	B	C	D	E	F	G
L_1	in	out	in	out	out	in	in
L_2	out	in	in	out	out	in	in
L_3	in	out	out	in	out	in	in
L_4	out	in	out	in	out	in	in
L_5	out	in	out	in	in	out	in
L_6	in	out	in	out	in	out	out

Proof. Consider the BAF in Fig. 5. The bi-semi-stable/bi-stable labellings are shown in Table 3. We show that there is no AAF $(\{A, B, C, D, E, F, G\}, \text{Att})$ such that the S-labellings coincide with the bi-semi-stable/bi-stable labellings of the BAF. To do so, we first show that G must be isolated. Since G is in together with A, C and F in L_1, they cannot be attackers for otherwise the *Hard Attack* property would be violated. Similarly, L_4 shows that B and D cannot be attackers and L_5 that E cannot be an attacker. Since G is in in several labellings, there can be no self-attack either. Hence, G must be isolated. But then G must be labelled in because of the *Isolated Acceptance* property. Therefore, L_6 is not an S-labelling. $\qquad\square$

Together with Corollary 2, we get, in particular, the following result.

Corollary 3. *1. The bi-semi-stable semantics is strictly more expressive than the semi-stable semantics.*
2. The bi-stable semantics is strictly more expressive than the stable semantics.

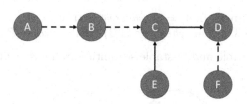

Fig. 6. Example BAF from [3].

4   Related Work

Several other bipolar argumentation approaches have been discussed in the past. We gave a brief overview of *deductive support* [10] and *evidential support* [18] in the introduction. A more elaborate discussion of both approaches can be found in [10]. Several chapters in the handbook of formal argumentation deal with other design ideas for bipolar semantics [4]. A more recent discussion and analysis of bipolar approaches can be found in [24,27]. The authors in [13] recently considered the idea of monotonic support. That is, adding a supporter should never downgrade the acceptance status of an argument and should potentially allow to upgrade it. Intuitively, bi-complete semantics should satisfy this notion of monotonicity as well, but I have not checked the formal definition. It may be interesting to consider a symmetric notion of monotonicity for attack and check if these notions are satisfied by bipolar frameworks with balanced attacks and supports.

Here, we built up on the ideas in [22] and [23] and focussed on bipolar argumentation with balanced attacks and supports. As opposed to these works, we designed our new semantics by refining complete semantics for bipolar graphs. In this way, we obtain natural generalizations of grounded, preferred, semi-stable and stable semantics. Our bi-stable semantics here differ, in particular, from the s-deductive and m-deductive semantics in [23] that generalize stable semantics as well. The bi-stable semantics remains closer to the original stable semantics in that it does not allow labelling arguments undecided even in bipolar graphs.

Instead of defining new bipolar semantics by extending AAF labellings, one may try to extend AAF extensions. This idea has indeed been studied in [3]. The authors consider a refinement of admissible sets that demands that the set is conflict-free, defends all its elements and is closed under the support relation. Figure 6 shows an example from [3]. The only admissible set is $\{D, E, F\}$ [3]. To see this, note that C cannot be defended against the attack by E. Therefore, it cannot be accepted. Since accepting A or B would entail accepting C, they cannot be accepted either. As this example shows, attack relations are again stronger than support relations under this semantics because C is necessarily rejected even though it is both attacked and supported.

Bipolar argumentation also plays a prominent role in gradual argumentation frameworks as discussed in [1–3,5,20,26]. Roughly speaking, gradual argumentation frameworks compute a numerical strength value for every argument iteratively. This is done based on an initial base score and the current strength of attackers and supporters. If this procedure converges, a well-defined degree of acceptance can be assigned to every argument. Since arguments are evaluated numerically and the solution is uniquely defined as the outcome of the iterative procedure, the idea of balanced attacks and supports is easier to formalize. Roughly speaking, an attack's negative effect on the base score should equal a support's positive effect, see [21] Definition 5.1 and Proposition 5.2 for a more precise definition. A discussion of the relevance of bipolar argumentation in the context of probabilistic argumentation can be found in [19].

While pure AAFs can be sufficient for interesting applications, support edges are vital for many recent applications of argumentation frameworks. For example, in review aggregation [11], it is important that both positive and negative aspects of a review are taken into account. In fake news detection [17], claims in an article can be contradicted or supported by other sources. In product recommendation [25], there can be features that make the product more (support) or less (attack) interesting for a user. For these reasons, recent work on modeling users' beliefs using probability distributions over classical AAFs [16] could perhaps be improved by replacing AAFs with BAFs. As we saw, the BAF semantics considered here are indeed strictly more expressive than their AAF counterparts.

Even though we generalized AAF semantics to BAFs, our goal is not to design a most general framework or to compete with such generalizations. For example, Abstract Dialectical Frameworks (ADFs) [8] generalize AAFs by abstracting away from the nature of edges between arguments and concrete semantics. This is done by considering abstract acceptance conditions that define when an argument can be accepted given the state of its parents. It may be possible to capture our semantics by appropriately defined acceptance conditions in ADFs as well.

5   Discussion

Motivated by the observation that the s-deductive and m-deductive semantics from [23] generalize stable semantics from attack-only graphs to bipolar graphs, we proposed a more elementary generalization of complete semantics called the bi-complete semantics. It yields natural generalizations of refinements of complete semantics like preferred and stable semantics. In particular, bi-stable semantics generalize stable semantics in a stricter sense than the semantics from [23] because they do not allow labelling arguments undecided in bipolar graphs. As opposed to deductive support frameworks [10], BAFs under bi-complete, bi-semi-stable and bi-stable semantics cannot be encoded by AAFs under most reasonable AAF semantics. That is, support edges add expressive power over attack-only frameworks under these semantics. In particular, attacks and supports have approximately the same power and can cancel their effects in a symmetrical manner.

Acknowledgements. This work was supported by the DFG through the projects EVOWIPE (STA572/15-1) and COFFEE (STA572/15-2).

References

1. Amgoud, L., Ben-Naim, J.: Evaluation of arguments in weighted bipolar graphs. In: Antonucci, A., Cholvy, L., Papini, O. (eds.) ECSQARU 2017. LNCS (LNAI), vol. 10369, pp. 25–35. Springer, Cham (2017). https://doi.org/10.1007/978-3-319-61581-3_3
2. Amgoud, L., Ben-Naim, J., Doder, D., Vesic, S.: Acceptability semantics for weighted argumentation frameworks. In: International Joint Conference on Artificial Intelligence (IJCAI) (2017)
3. Amgoud, L., Cayrol, C., Lagasquie-Schiex, M.C., Livet, P.: On bipolarity in argumentation frameworks. Int. J. Intell. Syst. **23**(10), 1062–1093 (2008)
4. Baroni, P., Gabbay, D.M., Giacomin, M., van der Torre, L.: Handbook of Formal Argumentation. College Publications, London (2018)
5. Baroni, P., Romano, M., Toni, F., Aurisicchio, M., Bertanza, G.: Automatic evaluation of design alternatives with quantitative argumentation. Argum. Comput. **6**(1), 24–49 (2015)
6. Black, E., Coles, A., Hampson, C.: Optimal simple strategies for persuasion. In: European Conference on Artificial Intelligence (ECAI), pp. 1736–1737 (2016)
7. Boella, G., Gabbay, D.M., van der Torre, L., Villata, S.: Support in abstract argumentation. In: International Conference on Computational Models of Argument (COMMA), pp. 40–51. Frontiers in Artificial Intelligence and Applications, IOS Press (2010)
8. Brewka, G., Woltran, S.: Abstract dialectical frameworks. In: International Conference on Principles of Knowledge Representation and Reasoning (KR), pp. 102–111 (2010)
9. Caminada, M.W., Gabbay, D.M.: A logical account of formal argumentation. Studia Logica **93**(2–3), 109 (2009)
10. Cayrol, C., Lagasquie-Schiex, M.C.: Bipolarity in argumentation graphs: towards a better understanding. Int. J. Approx. Reason. **54**(7), 876–899 (2013)
11. Cocarascu, O., Rago, A., Toni, F.: Extracting dialogical explanations for review aggregations with argumentative dialogical agents. In: International Conference on Autonomous Agents and MultiAgent Systems (AAMAS), pp. 1261–1269 (2019)
12. Dung, P.M.: On the acceptability of arguments and its fundamental role in non-monotonic reasoning, logic programming and n-person games. Artif. Intell. **77**(2), 321–357 (1995)
13. Gargouri, A., Konieczny, S., Marquis, P., Vesic, S.: On a notion of monotonic support for bipolar argumentation frameworks. In: International Conference on Autonomous Agents and MultiAgent Systems (AAMAS) (2020)
14. Hadoux, E., Hunter, A.: Learning and updating user models for subpopulations in persuasive argumentation using beta distribution. In: International Conference on Autonomous Agents and MultiAgent Systems (AAMAS), vol. 17, pp. 1141–1149. Association for Computing Machinery (ACM) (2018)

15. Hunter, A.: Modelling the persuadee in asymmetric argumentation dialogues for persuasion. In: International Joint Conference on Artificial Intelligence (IJCAI), pp. 3055–3061 (2015)
16. Hunter, A., Noor, K.: Aggregation of perspectives using the constellations approach to probabilistic argumentation. In: AAAI Conference on Artificial Intelligence (AAAI), pp. 2846–2853 (2020)
17. Kotonya, N., Toni, F.: Gradual argumentation evaluation for stance aggregation in automated fake news detection. In: Proceedings of the 6th Workshop on Argument Mining, pp. 156–166 (2019)
18. Oren, N., Norman, T.J.: Semantics for evidence-based argumentation. In: International Conference on Computational Models of Argument (COMMA), pp. 276–284. IOS Press (2008)
19. Polberg, S., Hunter, A.: Empirical evaluation of abstract argumentation: supporting the need for bipolar and probabilistic approaches. Int. J. Approx. Reason. **93**, 487–543 (2018)
20. Potyka, N.: Continuous dynamical systems for weighted bipolar argumentation. In: International Conference on Principles of Knowledge Representation and Reasoning (KR), pp. 148–157 (2018)
21. Potyka, N.: Extending modular semantics for bipolar weighted argumentation. In: International Conference on Autonomous Agents and MultiAgent Systems (AAMAS), pp. 1722–1730 (2019)
22. Potyka, N.: Abstract argumentation with markov networks. In: European Conference on Artificial Intelligence (ECAI), pp. 865–872 (2020)
23. Potyka, N.: Bipolar abstract argumentation with dual attacks and supports. In: International Conference on Principles of Knowledge Representation and Reasoning (KR), pp. 677–686 (2020)
24. Prakken, H.: On validating theories of abstract argumentation frameworks: The case of bipolar argumentation frameworks. In: International Conference on Computational Models of Argument (COMMA), pp. 21–30 (2020)
25. Rago, A., Cocarascu, O., Toni, F.: Argumentation-based recommendations: Fantastic explanations and how to find them. In: International Joint Conference on Artificial Intelligence (IJCAI), pp. 1949–1955 (2018)
26. Rago, A., Toni, F., Aurisicchio, M., Baroni, P.: Discontinuity-free decision support with quantitative argumentation debates. In: International Conference on Principles of Knowledge Representation and Reasoning (KR), pp. 63–73 (2016)
27. Yu, L., Markovich, R., van der Torre, L.: Interpretations of support among arguments. In: Legal Knowledge and Information Systems - JURIX 2020. Frontiers in Artificial Intelligence and Applications, vol. 334, pp. 194–203. IOS Press (2020)

Philosophical Reflections on Argument Strength and Gradual Acceptability

Henry Prakken[1,2]([envelope]) [ORCID]

[1] Department of Information and Computing Sciences, Utrecht University,
Utrecht, The Netherlands
h.prakken@uu.nl
[2] Faculty of Law, University of Groningen, Groningen, The Netherlands

Abstract. This paper proposes a classification of three aspects of argument strength based on philosophical insights, in particular Aristotle's distinction between logic, dialectic and rhetoric. It is then argued that when developing or evaluating gradual accounts of argument strength it is essential to be explicit about which aspect of argument strength is modelled and about the adopted interpretation of the arguments and their relations in abstract or bipolar argumentation frameworks. The underlying aim is to encourage a principled development and evaluation of (principles for) gradual argumentation semantics.

Keywords: Computational argument · Argument strength · Graduality

1 Introduction

A recent trend in the formal study of argumentation is the development of gradual notions of argument acceptability. These notions are proposed as alternatives to extension-based notions that are defined on top of the theory of abstract [16] or bipolar [13] argumentation frameworks. The gradual notions are often motivated by a discontent with the fact that extension-based notions of acceptability only allow for rather coarse distinctions between degrees of acceptability. The current developments arguably go back to [12] and really took off with publications like [29] and [1] (although largely ignored is that Pollock [35] already proposed a formalisation of gradual acceptability). In this body of work, the gradual nature of argumentation can have various sources: different base strengths of arguments, different sets or numbers of attackers and/or supporters, and attack or support relations that hold to varying degrees.

Although the new developments are very interesting and the formal achievements have been impressive, there are also reasons to take a step back. To start with, there is a need to reflect on which notions or aspects of argument acceptability, or argument strength, are modelled, and why proposed semantics or proposed sets of principles for those semantics are good. What is needed is a conceptual or philosophical underpinning of the formal ideas and constructs. Furthermore, almost all work builds on abstract or bipolar argumentation frameworks and

© Springer Nature Switzerland AG 2021
J. Vejnarová and N. Wilson (Eds.): ECSQARU 2021, LNAI 12897, pp. 144–158, 2021.
https://doi.org/10.1007/978-3-030-86772-0_11

thus does not give explicit formal accounts of the nature of arguments and their relations, while yet this may be relevant when evaluating the formal proposals. Moreover, the arguments in abstract and bipolar frameworks are increasingly not seen as genuine arguments in the sense of inferential structures (as in Dung's seminal paper and much initial follow-up work) but as statements that can be true or false. In this paper I will argue that some proposed (principles for) gradual semantics, while making sense when arguments are interpreted as statements, make less sense when arguments are regarded as inferential structures and hence cannot be regarded as general accounts of argumentation semantics.

More generally, in this paper I aim to make two contributions. First, I will propose a classification of three aspects of argument strength based on philosophical insights, in particular Aristotle's distinction between logic, dialectic and rhetoric. I then argue that when developing or evaluating gradual accounts of argument strength it is essential to be explicit about which aspect of argument strength is modelled and about the adopted interpretation of the arguments and their relations. The underlying hope is that this paper will encourage a principled and focused development and evaluation of (principles for) gradual argumentation semantics. The discussion will largely proceed in terms of examples of principles and semantics, since given the fast growing literature a comprehensive discussion and analysis is outside the scope of this paper.

The paper is organised as follows. First in Sect. 2 I informally sketch the assumed formal background, and then in Sect. 3 I present the three aspects of logical, dialectical and rhetorical strength. In Sect. 4 I discuss why it is important to be explicit about which of these aspects is modelled and about the nature of arguments and their relations. Finally, in Sect. 5 I conclude.

2   Background

In this section I informally summarise the formal background assumed in this paper. The aim of my paper is not to carry out formal investigations but to offer a conceptual framework that can guide the development and evaluation of specific formal proposals. I will therefore use as little formal notation as possible and assume that the reader is familiar with the basics of formal argumentation, in particular of the theory of abstract [5] and bipolar [13] argumentation frameworks and of the main structured accounts of argumentation [27].

2.1   Arguments as Statement or as Inferential Structures

In this subsection I explain in more detail the recent trend to view arguments as statements and how this is relevant for the evaluation of gradual argumentation semantics. Abstract argumentation frameworks as introduced by Dung [16] consist of a set of arguments with a binary relation of attack. Nothing is assumed about the structure of the arguments and the nature of the attack relations. Bipolar frameworks add to abstract argumentation frameworks a binary support relation between arguments, sometimes but not always assumed to be disjoint from the attack relation. Various semantics have been proposed for evaluating the arguments in an abstract or bipolar argumentation framework. For present purposes their details do not matter.

As noted in the introduction, the arguments in abstract or bipolar frameworks are in applications increasingly not seen as genuine arguments in the sense of inferential structures but as statements that can be true or false. For evaluating (principles for) gradual argumentation semantics it is crucial how the nodes in an argument graph are interpreted, so the adopted interpretation should be made explicit. Sometimes this is indeed done, e.g. by Baroni et al. [7] and Rago et al. [39], who present their model as a formalisation of the IBIS model [28]. Then the formalism can be evaluated on its adequacy for what it was explicitly meant for. However, often the 'statement' interpretation of the nodes in argumentation frameworks is not made explicit but has to be inferred from the informal text and from the examples that are given. For instance, in [42] an example is discussed with the following (and some other) arguments:

S_1:   *We should buy an SUV; it's the right choice for us*
C: *SUVs are very safe, safety is very important to us*

where C supports S_1. This support relation in fact expresses an argument with premises *SUVs are safe* and *Safety is important to us* and the conclusion *We should buy an SUV*, which readers familiar with the theory of argument schemes will recognise as an instance of the argument scheme from good consequences. In a formalisation where arguments are inferential structures this argument would appear as a single node in the argument graph, while here it is spread out over a subgraph of a bipolar argumentation framework with nodes C and S_1.

The difference between the inferential and statement interpretations of the nodes in an abstract or bipolar argumentation framework is important for the design and choice of abstract formalisms. While bipolar argumentation frameworks model support as a relation *between* arguments, when support expresses some kind of inference, it can also be modelled *inside* arguments, at least if arguments are interpreted as inferential structures. Then this can be done by using abstract argumentation frameworks in combination with a theory of the structure of arguments and the nature of attack. There are quite a few such theories, dating back to the seminal work of Pollock [34]. All these theories allow for support relations that are not *between* but *inside* arguments, namely as inferential relations between (sets of) *statements* in some logical language. Examples are assumption-based argumentation [44], Defeasible Logic Programming [19] and $ASPIC^+$ [37]. While this approach is possible when arguments are interpreted as inferential structures, this is different when they are interpreted as statements; then support relations *between* arguments (viewed as statements) are needed, as in bipolar argumentation frameworks. Relations between arguments then become what philosophers call *reasons* [24,34]. In this approach, arguments-as-inferential-structures are not nodes in but subgraphs of the argument graph, as illustrated by the above example. Moreover, since in general statements are supported by sets of statements, we need support relations from *sets* of arguments to arguments, which in 'standard' bipolar frameworks cannot be expressed. So how the arguments in abstract and bipolar frameworks are interpreted greatly matters for what abstract formalism is needed.

2.2 Basic Concepts of Argument Structure and Relations

I next informally sketch what I mean in this paper by arguments and their relations, trying to remain as close as possible to the formal (e.g. [27]) and informal (e.g. [18]) literature on argument structure. Basic arguments have a set of *premises* and a *conclusion* (statements that can be true or false) and an *inference* from the premises to the conclusion licensed by an *inference rule*. Basic arguments can be combined into complex arguments by letting their conclusion be among the premises of another argument. Arguments can be informally represented as directed acyclic hypergraphs, in a way similar to the usual visualisation methods in argumentation theory [40], with the nodes corresponding to premises or intermediate or final conclusions and the links from sets of nodes to nodes corresponding to inferences (see e.g. Figs. 1 and 2 below).

Both premises and inference rules can be *attackable* or *non-attackable*, so arguments can also be *attackable* or *non-attackable*. I will call attackable and non-attackable inference rules *defeasible*, respectively, *deductive*. An attackable argument can be *attacked* in three ways: it can be *undermined* by an argument of which the conclusion is incompatible with one of its premises, it can be *rebutted* by an argument of which the conclusion is incompatible with an intermediate or its conclusion, and it can be *undercut* by an argument of which the conclusion says that some inference rule applied in the attacked argument does not apply. Attacks can be *allowed* or *not allowed* depending on further constraints on these informal definitions. Finally, allowed attacks can succeed or not succeed as *defeats*. Henceforth, when I say that argument A *attacks* argument B I assume that the attack from A on B is allowed, while when I say that argument A *defeats* argument B I assume that the attack from A on B succeeds as defeat.

This informal sketch could be regarded as an abstraction of the $ASPIC^+$ framework. Depending on the precise formal definitions of arguments, of incompatibility of statements and of the constraints on allowed attacks and defeats, one variant or another of this framework can be obtained, or a variant of some related approach like assumption-based argumentation or defeasible logic programming. For present purposes the precise design choices and the differences between these formal frameworks do not matter.

3 Logical, Dialectical and Rhetorical Argument Strength

In classifying aspects of argument strength it is natural to take Aristotle's famous distinction between logic, dialectic and rhetoric as starting point. Very briefly, *logic* concerns the validity of arguments given their form, *dialectic* is the art of testing ideas through critical discussion and *rhetoric* deals with the principles of effective persuasion [17, Section 1.4]. Accordingly, I distinguish between logical, dialectical and rhetorical argument strength.

Logical argument strength divides into two aspects: inferential and contextual argument strength.

Inferential argument strength is about how well the premises support the conclusion if we only look at the arguments premises, inferences and conclusion(s). Example criteria for argument strength are that arguments with only deductive inferences are stronger than arguments with defeasible inferences, or that arguments with only non-attackable premises are stronger than arguments with attackable premises. Such criteria can be refined by combining them (for example, first looking at the type of inference and then for arguments with equally strong inferences looking at the types of premises), by defining preference relations on inference rules and/or premises, or by defining notions of strength (for example, probabilities) on inference rules and/or premises.

Contextual argument strength is about how well the conclusion of an argument is supported if we look at the context of all relevant arguments. Formal frameworks like Dung's theory of abstract argumentation frameworks, assumption-based argumentation, *ASPIC*$^+$ and defeasible logic programming formalise this kind of argument strength. The reader might wonder why this is not called dialectical strength, since after all, determining an argument's contextual strength as defined here involves the comparison of argument and counterargument. Yet this is not truly dialectical, since the just-mentioned formalisms do not model principles of critical discussion but just define mathematical consequence notions on the basis of a given body of information; likewise [20, 30]. This even holds for the argument games proposed as proof theories for extension-based semantics [32]: these apply to a given framework of arguments and their relations, while principles of discussion allow for introduction of new arguments during a dispute.

Dialectical argument strength looks at how well defended an argument is in the context of an ongoing or terminated critical discussion. This context can be regulated by formal or informal principles of fair and effective disputes. Informal examples are legal procedures or rules of order for meetings. Formal examples are the many dialogue systems for argumentation proposed in philosophy and AI, e.g. [4, 20, 31, 36, 46]. Dialectical strength has both static and dynamic aspects. A static aspect is given by the outcome of a critical discussion: has the argument been successfully defended in the discussion? Dynamic aspects concern how well-defended or challengeable an argument is in a given state of the discussion. In [49] the latter is formulated as "a function of the (un)availability of permissible move sequences originating at the present dialogue stage, and ending in a discussant?s role-specified goal being achieved".

To illustrate the idea of dialectical strength, I next suggest some possible criteria for determining dialectical argument strength, without claiming to be exhaustive. First, one might regard an argument as dialectically weaker the more attacks on it are allowed in the current state. Among other things, this may imply that arguments are dialectically weaker the more attackable premises or inference rules they have. This idea is motivated by an underlying principle that many decision makers are aware of, namely, to justify one's decisions as sparsely as possible, in order to minimize the chance of successful appeal.

One might also look at how many attacks an argument has survived in a given state. For instance, if arguments are generated by argument schemes [47], one might regard an argument as dialectically stronger the more critical questions have been asked and successfully answered.

Yet another aspect of dialectical strength is to what extent it is possible to change the current contextual strength of the argument by moving to a new state. This aspect is arguably formalised by formal work on the dynamics of argumentation, in particular on so-called preservation, realisability and enforcement properties [8,15]. Preservation is about the extent to which the current contextual status of arguments is preserved under change, while realisability and enforcement concern the extent to which particular outcomes can or will be obtained by changing the current state.

Rhetorical argument strength looks at how capable an argument is to persuade other participants in a discussion or an audience. Persuasiveness essentially is a psychological notion; although principles of persuasion may be formalised, their validation as principles of successful persuasion is ultimately psychological (as acknowledged in [26] and done in e.g. [23]). One way to formulate criteria for persuasiveness is in terms of agreement with shared background information or with information in a model of the other discussants or the audience (cf. [25]), possibly refined with probability distributions on what can be in these models. Such opponent models could also be used in game-theoretic investigations of optimal debate strategies [41]. Another way is to formulate heuristics about what is generally known or expected to be persuasive, such as the argumentation techniques of Perelman [33] or the argument schemes of Walton [45], or a technique such as *procatalepsis*, modelled by Bonzon et al. [11], which is the attempt of a speaker to strengthen their argument by dealing with possible counter-arguments before their audience can raise them.

Argument strength is multi-faceted. The classification proposed in this section shows that argument strength is a multi-faceted notion. Not only can we distinguish between logical, dialectical and rhetorical argument strength but each of these aspects of strength involves multiple criteria, which sometimes reinforce but sometimes oppose each other, and which have to be combined to provide an overall assessment of an argument's logical, dialectical or rhetorical strength. In fact, defining such overall notions seems a daunting task, and it may be better to focus on just one criterion or a small set of criteria for aspects of argument strength. This also holds for combining logical, dialectical and rhetorical strength into one overall notion for argument strength. Since the three aspects of argument strength serve different purposes, it may not be good to combine them into an overall notion. Another reason for this is that dialectical strength may *presuppose* contextual strength, since one aspect of dialectical strength is the extent to which an argument's logical strength may be changed in the course of a dispute. In any case, even if logical, dialectical and rhetorical strength are combined into an overall notion of strength, they should first be separately defined, in order to make their combination a principled one.

4   Evaluating Semantics and Principles

In this section I discuss how the above classification into three aspects of argument strength, together with the interpretation of the nodes and links in abstract or bipolar argumentation frameworks, is relevant for developing and evaluating gradual accounts of argument strength. A complication here is that several recent accounts rely on the distinction between the base and overall score of an argument, but it is not obvious whether notions of argument strength can always be suitably defined in this format. For example, such accounts presuppose that the base and overall scores are of the same sort and can therefore be compared but this does not have to be the case. Consider, for example, gradual definitions of contextual strength in terms of extension-based [10] or labelling-based [48] semantics. A very simple definition of overall strength would be that (given a grounded labelling) being *in* is better than being *undecided*, which is better than being *out*. It is not obvious what the base score of arguments would be in such an approach. For these reasons I will below mainly discuss accounts with no distinction between base and overall scores.

4.1   Be Explicit About Which Aspects of Argument Strength Are Modelled

It is important to be explicit about which aspects of argument strength are modelled (as in [11], who explicitly model two aspects of persuasiveness). The aspects serve different purposes, so principles or definitions that are good for one aspect may not be good for another aspect. Consider, for example, two arguments A and B where A defeasibly infers q from p while B first defeasibly infers r from p and then defeasibly infers q from r. Consider a definition of dialectical strength capturing that having fewer attackable elements is dialectically better and a definition of rhetorical strength that captures that a larger overlap of an argument's elements with the audience's beliefs is rhetorically better. Even without formalising these notions it is obvious that argument A is dialectically stronger than argument B, since A has one attackable element less than B. However, if the audience accepts that p defeasibly implies r and that r defeasibly implies q but not that p defeasibly implies q, then B is rhetorically stronger than A since it shares some elements with the background theory while A does not. This illustrates that while sparsely justifying one's claims or decisions may be dialectically good, it may at the same time make an argument less persuasive.

Another example is the phenomenon of procatalepsis, modelled in [11], which is the attempt to strengthen an argument by dealing with possible counter-arguments before the audience can raise them. As modelled by Bonzon et al., procatalepsis makes an argument rhetorically stronger when combined with an attacker and an attacker of that attacker than when presented alone. Bonzon et al. prove that procatalepsis is inconsistent with the principle of 'void precedence' [1], according to which an argument that has no attackers is more acceptable than an argument that has attackers, even if these attackers are counterattacked, and which is a key element of many current gradual argumentation semantics [9]. It is implied by Basic Idea 7 of [6] that a strictly larger set of attackers determine a lower strength. One interpretation of the void precedence principle is as an aspect of dialectical strength, in particular, as capturing that having fewer ways to attack an argument makes it dialectically less challengeable. On this interpretation, examples of procatalepsis are other cases where an argument can be rhetorically stronger but dialectically weaker than another argument.

Being explicit about which aspects of argument strength are modelled is not only important when formulating theories of argument strength but also when evaluating applications of computational argumentation. For instance, according to [43] the Debater system was evaluated by twenty human annotators who had to indicate to what extent they agreed with the statement 'The first speaker is exemplifying a decent performance in this debate'. It is unclear which aspects the annotators had in mind when answering this question or even whether all annotators looked at the same aspects and applied the same criteria.

4.2   Be Explicit About the Interpretation of Arguments and Their Relations

It is important to be explicit about whether the arguments in an abstract or bipolar framework are regarded as statements or as inferential structures. One reason is that trade-offs between attacks and supports, or even to regard supporters as strengthening the supported argument, may make sense in the statement interpretation but may not make sense in the inferential-structure interpretation. When the arguments are regarded as statements, then attack and support relations between arguments can hardly be interpreted as anything else but expressing reasons for or against the statement. For example, in a decision-making application [7,39] attack and support relations are reasons to adopt or not adopt a given decision option. Then it makes sense to consider trade-offs between supporting and attacking arguments, as, for example, captured in the (Strict) Franklin, Weakening and Strengthening principles proposed in [3]. The same holds for Basic Idea 8 of [6], according to which (everything else being equal) a strictly larger set of supporters determines a higher strength. In the statement interpretation of arguments it makes sense to say that (in the absence of attackers) a statement for which there are reasons to believe or accept it is more acceptable than a statement for which there are no such reasons.

However, when arguments are regarded as inferential structures, then multiple interpretations of the support relation are possible and their differences matter. In the context of the $ASPIC^+$ framework, Cohen et al. [14] define four kinds of support (visualised in Fig. 1). Subargument support corresponds to

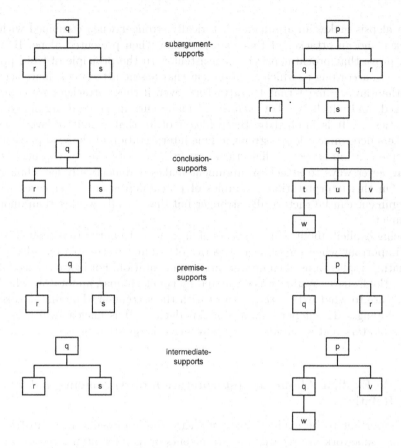

Fig. 1. Cohen et al.'s (2018) four kinds of support in $ASPIC^+$.

the $ASPIC^+$ proper-subargument relation. Informally, every argument B corresponding to subgraph of an argument A (viewed as a hypergraph) that is also an argument (so takes all its premises from the premises of A) is a subargument of A. A subargument of an argument A is not separate from A but is contained in A as part of it, as visualised in the top row of Fig. 1. Clearly, when support corresponds to (proper) subargument support, it makes no sense to consider trade-offs between attacks and support or to regard supporters as strengthening the supported argument. Logically, the number of supports of an argument is then just a measure of its inferential complexity while dialectically, having more supporters may make an argument more vulnerable to attack and thus weaker.

For conclusion support (argument A supports B whenever they have the same conclusion) these ideas may make more sense but for premise support they are again questionable. An argument A premise-supports an argument B iff the final conclusion of A is equal to a premise of B (intermediate support is a variant of premise support in which not a premise but an intermediate conclusion is supported; I will therefore not discuss it separately). Premise support may be useful in debate contexts, where there usually is no global knowledge base from which the debaters construct their arguments. Then if one debate participant presents an argument for a premise of another participant's argument, it may be less natural to say that the supporting argument is part of the supported argument as captured in the subargument relation. Instead, the arguments may be said to remain separate, as depicted in the third row of Fig. 1.

Consider an example from [38], in which John argues "Nixon was a pacifist since he was a Quaker and Quakers are usually pacifists" (argument A). Now suppose Mary supports John's argument by saying "Nixon regularly attended service in a Quaker church, people who are regularly seen in a Quaker church usually are a Quaker, so Nixon was a Quaker" (argument B). Consider contextual strength. Can we say that Mary's supporting argument makes John's argument contextually stronger? If so, then a successful attack on Mary's argument should intuitively also weaken John's argument. Suppose that Bob attacks Mary's argument by arguing that Nixon only attended service in a Quaker church to please his wife, who was a Quaker (argument C). It can be argued that this does not knock down John's argument, since why should John be blamed for Mary's flawed attempt to support his argument? However, it is still unsatisfactory that there is no logical relation at all between attacking a supporter and the status of a supported argument. If support means anything at all, then surely attacking a supporter should have some effect on the status of an argument supported by it (note that for subargument support this is automatic). The solution adopted in [38] is that whether C's attack on B also weakens A is conditional on what the audience accepts as given. If the audience accepts that Nixon was a quaker without further support, then argument C has no effect on the acceptability of A, while if the audience wants further support for this premise, then argument C reduces A's acceptability. This approach implies that whether trade-offs between premise-supporters and attackers should be considered, or whether a premise-supporter can strengthen the supported argument at all, cannot be determined in general but depends on the context, in particular on the audience's beliefs.

While this is one approach, there may also be reasons to always consider trade-offs between premise-supporters and attackers and to regard a premise-supporter as, everything else being equal, strengthening the supported argument. However, even then the nature of the arguments and their relations matters. Consider Fig. 2, with two bipolar frameworks in the top row and two instantiations of these frameworks in the bottom row (in BAF1 and BAF2 the dashed arguments depict support relations between arguments). According to the principle that, everything else being equal, having more supporters is better (e.g. the Cardinality Preference axiom of [2]), argument C on the top right is better supported than argument A on the top left since C has two premise-supporters while A has just one. However, as shown in the bottom row, all of A's premises (namely, q) are supported while only one of C's two premises is supported, so dialectically and perhaps also rhetorically A might just as well be regarded as better supported than C. Or imagine that D does not premise-support C on u but on v: then both A and C have all their premises supported, so there seems

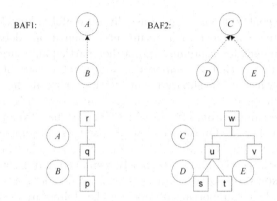

Fig. 2. Is having more supporters better?

no reason to prefer C over A. Consider next Basic Idea 8 of [6], which says that a strictly larger set of supporters (w.r.t. to set inclusion) determines a higher strength, and suppose that argument A has no premise supporters while argument C only has supporters for premise u. Since any set includes the empty set, Basic Idea 8 implies that C is stronger than A. It is not obvious why this should be, given that they both have the same number of unsupported premises. This becomes even less obvious if C is changed to have more than two premises, of which only one is supported. Concluding, even in applications in which it makes sense to regard premise-supporters as, everything else being equal, strengthening the supported argument, it is important to take the structure of arguments and the nature of their relations into account.

So far I have illustrated the importance of being explicit about whether arguments are statements or inferential structures, and in the latter case of being explicit about the structure of arguments and the nature of the support relation. I next illustrate the importance of being explicit about whether an argument is attackable or not (a distinction made in some of the main structured approaches to argumentation, such as assumption-based argumentation, defeasible logic programming and $ASPIC^+$). Consider the Cardinality Precedence principle that having fewer attackers makes an argument stronger [1,9] and consider AF1 with A being attacked by B and AF2 with C being attacked by D and E (Fig. 3; in the AFs in Figures 3 and 4 the solid arrows depict attack relations). According to Cardinality Precedence argument A is stronger than argument C. However, if B is not attackable while D and E are attackable, then it is not obvious why this should be the case. For example, from the point of view of dialectical strength C is arguably dialectically stronger than A since C can still be made in by adding new arguments and attacks while for A this cannot happen.

Another example of why the distinction between attackable and non-attackable arguments matters concerns the principle that having more defenders makes an argument stronger. Consider the AFs displayed in Fig. 4. According to the gradual semantics of [21,22], A_2 is justified to a higher degree than

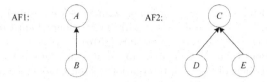

Fig. 3. Is having fewer attackers better?

Fig. 4. Is having more defenders better?

A_1, since A_2 has two defenders (C_2 and D_2) while A_1 has only one defender (C_1). However, if C_1 is unattackable while C_2 and D_2 are attackable then it is not obvious why this has to be so, whatever aspect of argument strength is modelled.

5   Conclusion

In this paper I proposed a classification of three aspects of argument strength, namely, logical, dialectical and rhetorical strength. I then showed with several examples that when developing or evaluating gradual accounts of argument strength it is essential to be explicit about which aspect of argument strength is modelled, since some principles or semantics maybe suitable for one aspect but not for another. Likewise, I showed that it is important to be explicit about the adopted interpretation of the arguments and their relations in abstract or bipolar argumentation frameworks. For example, it matters whether the arguments are interpreted as statements or as inferential structures, how support is defined, and how the structure of arguments is defined.

The underlying aim of this paper was to encourage a principled development and evaluation of (principles for) gradual argumentation semantics. As such, this was just an initial attempt. More comprehensive formal investigations should yield more systematic insights into the purposes for which (principles for) gradual semantics are suitable and into the assumptions on which they depend. This paper has aimed to lay the conceptual foundations for such investigations.

References

1. Amgoud, L., Ben-Naim, J.: Ranking-based semantics for argumentation frameworks. In: Liu, W., Subrahmanian, V.S., Wijsen, J. (eds.) SUM 2013. LNCS (LNAI), vol. 8078, pp. 134–147. Springer, Heidelberg (2013). https://doi.org/10.1007/978-3-642-40381-1_11

2. Amgoud, L., Ben-Naim, J.: Evaluation of arguments from support relations: axioms and semantics. In: Proceedings of the 25th International Joint Conference on Artificial Intelligence (IJCAI-16), pp. 900–906 (2016)
3. Amgoud, L., Ben-Naim, J.: Weighted bipolar argument graphs: axioms and semantics. In: Proceedings of the 27th International Joint Conference on Artificial Intelligence (IJCAI-18), pp. 5194–5198 (2018)
4. Atkinson, K., Bench-Capon, T., McBurney, P.: A dialogue game protocol for multi-agent argument over proposals for action. J. Auton. Agents Multi-Agent Syst. **11**, 153–171 (2005)
5. Baroni, P., Caminada, M., Giacomin, M.: An introduction to argumentation semantics. Knowl. Eng. Rev. **26**, 365–410 (2011)
6. Baroni, P., Rago, A., Toni, F.: How many properties do we need for gradual argumentation? In: Proceedings of the 32nd AAAI Conference on Artificial Intelligence (AAAI 2018), pp. 1736–1743 (2018)
7. Baroni, P., Romano, M., Toni, F., Aurisicchio, M., Bertanza, G.: Automatic evaluation of design alternatives with quantitative argumentation. Argum. Comput. **6**, 24–49 (2015)
8. Baumann, R.: What does it take to enforce an argument? Minimal change in abstract argumentation. In: Proceedings of the 20th European Conference on Artificial Intelligence, pp. 127–132 (2012)
9. Bonzon, E., Delobelle, J., Konieczny, S., Maudet, N.: A comparative study of ranking-based semantics for abstract argumentation. In: Proceedings of the 30st AAAI Conference on Artificial Intelligence (AAAI 2016), pp. 914–920 (2016)
10. Bonzon, E., Delobelle, J., Konieczny, S., Maudet, N.: Combining extension-based semantics and ranking-based semantics for abstract argumentation. In: Principles of Knowledge Representation and Reasoning: Proceedings of the Sixteenth International Conference, pp. 118–127. AAAI Press (2018)
11. Bonzon, E., Delobelle, J., Konieczny, S., Maudet, N.: A parametrized ranking-based semantics compatible with persuasion principles. Argum. Comput. **12**, 49–85 (2021)
12. Cayrol, C., Lagasquie-Schiex, M.C.: Graduality in argumentation. J. Artif. Intell. Res. **23**, 245–297 (2005)
13. Cayrol, C., Lagasquie-Schiex, M.C.: Bipolar abstract argumentation systems. In: Rahwan, I., Simari, G. (eds.) Argumentation in Artificial Intelligence, pp. 65–84. Springer, Berlin (2009). https://doi.org/10.1007/978-0-387-98197-0_4
14. Cohen, A., Parsons, S., Sklar, E., McBurney, P.: A characterization of types of support between structured arguments and their relationship with support in abstract argumentation. Int. J. Approx. Reason. **94**, 76–104 (2018)
15. Doutre, S., Mailly, J.G.: Constraints and changes: a survey of abstract argumentation dynamics. Argum. Comput. **9**, 223–248 (2018)
16. Dung, P.: On the acceptability of arguments and its fundamental role in nonmonotonic reasoning, logic programming, and n-person games. Artif. Intell. **77**, 321–357 (1995)
17. van Eemeren, F.H., Garssen, B., Krabbe, E.C.W., Snoeck Henkemans, A.F., Verheij, B., Wagemans, J.H.M.: Handbook of Argumentation Theory. Springer, Dordrecht (2014). https://doi.org/10.1007/978-90-481-9473-5
18. Freeman, J.: Dialectics and the Macrostructure of Arguments. A Theory of Argument Structure. Fors/de Gruyter, Berlin-New York (1991)
19. Garcia, A., Simari, G.: Defeasible logic programming: an argumentative approach. Theory Pract. Logic Program. **4**, 95–138 (2004)

20. Gordon, T.: The pleadings game: an exercise in computational dialectics. Artif. Intell. Law **2**, 239–292 (1994)
21. Grossi, D., Modgil, S.: On the graded acceptability of arguments. In: Proceedings of the 24th International Joint Conference on Artificial Intelligence, pp. 868–874 (2015)
22. Grossi, D., Modgil, S.: On the graded acceptability of arguments in abstract and instantiated argumentation. Artif. Intell. **275**, 138–173 (2019)
23. Hadoux, E., Hunter, A.: Comfort or safety? Gathering and using the concerns of a participant for better persuasion. Argum. Comput. **10**, 113–147 (2019)
24. Horty, J.: Reasons as Defaults. Oxford University Press, Oxford (2012)
25. Hunter, A.: Making arguments more believable. In: Proceedings of the 19th National Conference on Artificial Intelligence, pp. 6269–274 (2004)
26. Hunter, A.: Towards a framework for computational persuasion with applications in behaviour change. Argum. Comput. **9**, 15–40 (2018)
27. Hunter, A. (ed.): Argument and Computation, vol. 5 (2014). Special issue with Tutorials on Structured Argumentation
28. Kunz, W., Rittel, H.: Issues as elements of information systems. Working Paper No. 131, Institute of Urban and Regional Development, University of California, Berkeley, California (1970)
29. Leite, J., Martins: Social abstract argumentation. In: Proceedings of the 22nd International Joint Conference on Artificial Intelligence (IJCAI-11), pp. 2287–2292 (2011)
30. Loui, R.: Process and policy: resource-bounded non-demonstrative reasoning. Comput. Intell. **14**, 1–38 (1998)
31. Mackenzie, J.: Question-begging in non-cumulative systems. J. Philos. Logic **8**, 117–133 (1979)
32. Modgil, S., Caminada, M.: Proof theories and algorithms for abstract argumentation frameworks. In: Rahwan, I., Simari, G. (eds.) Argumentation in Artificial Intelligence, pp. 105–129. Springer, Berlin (2009). https://doi.org/10.1007/978-0-387-98197-0_6
33. Perelman, C., Olbrechts-Tyteca, L.: The New Rhetoric. A Treatise on Argumentation. University of Notre Dame Press, Notre Dame (1969)
34. Pollock, J.: Defeasible reasoning. Cogn. Sci. **11**, 481–518 (1987)
35. Pollock, J.: Defeasible reasoning with variable degrees of justification. Artif. Intell. **133**, 233–282 (2002)
36. Prakken, H.: Coherence and flexibility in dialogue games for argumentation. J. Logic Comput. **15**, 1009–1040 (2005)
37. Prakken, H.: An abstract framework for argumentation with structured arguments. Argum. Comput. **1**, 93–124 (2010)
38. Prakken, H.: Modelling support relations between arguments in debates. In: Chesñevar, C., Falappa, M.A., et al. (eds.) Argumentation-based Proofs of Endearment. Essays in Honor of Guillermo R. Simari on the Occasion of his 70th Birthday, pp. 349–365. College Publications, London (2018)
39. Rago, A., Toni, F., Aurisicchio, M., Baroni, P.: Discontinuity-free decision support with quantitative argumentation debates. In: Principles of Knowledge Representation and Reasoning: Proceedings of the Fifteenth International Conference, pp. 63–72. AAAI Press (2016)
40. Reed, C., Walton, D., Macagno, F.: Argument diagramming in logic, law and artificial intelligence. Knowl. Eng. Rev. **22**, 87–109 (2007)

41. Riveret, R., Prakken, H., Rotolo, A., Sartor, G.: Heuristics in argumentation: a game-theoretical investigation. In: Besnard, P., Doutre, S., Hunter, A. (eds.) Computational Models of Argument. Proceedings of COMMA 2008, pp. 324–335. IOS Press, Amsterdam etc (2008)
42. Rosenfeld, A., Kraus, S.: Providing arguments in discussions based on the prediction of human argumentative behavior. In: Proceedings of the 29th AAAI Conference on Artificial Intelligence (AAAI 2015), pp. 1320–1327 (2015)
43. Slonim, N., Bilu, Y., Alzate, C.: An autonomous debating system. Nature **591**, 397–384 (2021)
44. Toni, F.: A tutorial on assumption-based argumentation. Argum. Comput. **5**, 89–117 (2014)
45. Walton, D.: Argumentation Schemes for Presumptive Reasoning. Lawrence Erlbaum Associates, Mahwah (1996)
46. Walton, D., Krabbe, E.: Commitment in Dialogue. Basic Concepts of Interpersonal Reasoning. State University of New York Press, Albany (1995)
47. Walton, D., Reed, C., Macagno, F.: Argumentation Schemes. Cambridge University Press, Cambridge (2008)
48. Wu, Y., Caminada, M.: A labelling-based justification status of arguments. Stud. Logic **3**, 12–29 (2010)
49. Zenker, F., Debowska-Kozlowska, K., Godden, D., Selinger, M., Wells, S.: Five approaches to argument strength: probabilistic, dialectical, structural, empirical, and computational. In: Proceedings of the 3rd European Conference on Argumentation, pp. 653–674. College Publications, London (2020)

An Abstract Argumentation and Logic Programming Comparison Based on 5-Valued Labellings

Samy Sá$^{(\boxtimes)}$ ⓘ and João Alcântara ⓘ

Universidade Federal do Ceará, Fortaleza, Brazil
samy@ufc.br, jnando@lia.ufc.br

Abstract. Abstract argumentation and logic programming are two formalisms of non-monotonic reasoning that share many similarities. Previous studies contemplating connections between the two formalisms provided back and forth translations from one to the other and found they correspond in multiple different semantics, but not all. In this work, we propose a new set of five argument labels to revisit the semantic correspondences between abstract argumentation and logic programming. By doing so, we shed light on why the two formalisms are not absolutely equivalent. Our investigation lead to the specification of the novel least-stable semantics for abstract argumentation which corresponds to the L-stable semantics of logic programming.

Keywords: Abstract argumentation · Logic programming · Argument labellings

1 Introduction

Logic Programming (LP) and Abstract Argumentation Frameworks are two different formalisms widely used for the representation of knowledge and reasoning. Abstract Argumentation (AA) was itself inspired by logic programming in its origins, which naturally led to several studies concerning connections between them [5,6,8,11,14,16]. One of the main approaches to observe those connections is based on the comparison of the different semantics proposed for each formalism. To that end, the first questions were raised and answered in [6], the work that originally introduced abstract argumentation: a translation from a logic program into an abstract argumentation framework was proposed and used to prove that the stable models (resp. the well-founded model) of a logic program correspond to the stable extensions (resp. the grounded extension) of its corresponding abstract argumentation framework. Other advances were made when [16] observed the equivalence between the complete semantics for abstract argumentation and the p-stable semantics for logic programs. Those particular semantics generalise many others in their respective formalisms, wielding a plethora of results gathered in [5] and recently expanded in [4]. One particular equivalence formerly expected to hold, however, could not be achieved, namely the correspondence between the semi-stable semantics from abstract argumentation [3] and the L-stable semantics from logic

© Springer Nature Switzerland AG 2021
J. Vejnarová and N. Wilson (Eds.): ECSQARU 2021, LNAI 12897, pp. 159–172, 2021.
https://doi.org/10.1007/978-3-030-86772-0_12

programming [9]. The work we are about to present is largely motivated by that non-correspondence result.

In our efforts to understand why the semi-stable and L-stable semantics do not correspond to one another, we detected the fault is always related to some arguments whose attackees coincide; in their redundancy, one or more of those arguments would be irrelevant to the evaluation of those arguments they mutually attack. We were also able to identify that sink[1] arguments play a special role in pinpointing the culprits. To achieve our goals for this work, we follow the presentation of [5] while revising some key definitions: (i) the instantiation of abstract argumentation frameworks from logic programs is revised to include special arguments we call *default arguments* (which are always sinks) and (ii) we revise the definition of complete argument labellings [2] to use a different set of labels. Our revision of complete labellings follows [1,10] to contemplate partial labellings and different categories of undecidedness. The resulting labellings, here on called 5-valued labellings, can isolate any arguments causing semi-stable and L-stable semantics to differ and are shown to preserve the main results in [5].

Based on those results, we introduce a novel semantics for abstract argumentation called the *least-stable* (or L-stable) semantics, which we show is equivalent to the L-stable LP semantics. The new AA semantics closes the previous gap preventing the claim that AA is actually equivalent to LP. Our results add further to the literature concerning semantics of non-monotonic reasoning formalisms, potentially allowing us to import proof procedures and implementations from formal argumentation to logic programming and vice-versa. Among other implications of our work, we set precedence to the proposal of new argumentation semantics based on partial labellings. We also establish that sink arguments have a role in the semantic evaluation of abstract argumentation frameworks, which may also help us identify new interesting AA semantics. Moreover, we show that if we restrict our attention to sink arguments, the standard 3-valued labellings are enough to capture the logic programming L-stable semantics.

2 Preliminaries

2.1 Abstract Argumentation

Abstract argumentation was introduced in [7] and most of the definitions in this section are based on that work. Concerning new definitions, we will compute the set of sink arguments of an abstract argumentation framework and use them to propose argumentation semantics in the form of 5-valued labellings, a core trait of our approach.

Definition 1. *An* abstract argumentation framework *is a pair* (Ar, att) *where* Ar *is a finite set of arguments and* $att \subseteq Ar \times Ar$.

We may refer to AA frameworks simply as argumentation frameworks or AF's.

Definition 2. *Given an argumentation framework* $\mathtt{AF} = (Ar, att)$, *the set of its* sink arguments *is given by* $\mathtt{SINKS_{AF}} = \{A \in Ar \mid \forall B, (A, B) \notin att\}$.

---

[1] In graph theory, a sink node is one from which no edges emerge.

The traditional approach of [7] to semantics involves the identification of sets of arguments (called extensions) based on the concept of admissibility (see [7]). An alternative formalization of AA semantics was introduced in [2] where argument labellings are used instead of extensions. The argument labellings of [2] are functions attributing to each argument a single label from $\{\text{in}, \text{out}, \text{undec}\}$. In this work, we specialise the labels out, undec into two different labels each based on the sink arguments they attack. Our labelling concept follows the lead of [1], where the authors explore alternative sets of labels and special cases of undecidedness in argumentation semantics. We borrow some of the labels discussed in their work, namely the "*I don't care*" (idc) label (originally proposed in [10]) and the "*I don't know*" (idk) label ([1]) and we introduce a new label of our own, here dubbed "*It doesn't matter if it's out*" (ido). Hence, in our work, given an argumentation framework $\text{AF} = (Ar, att)$, an *argument labelling* Al will be a function $Al : Ar \rightarrow \{\text{in}, \text{out}, \text{ido}, \text{idk}, \text{idc}\}$. We will start defining complete labellings, since the other relevant semantics are special cases of them.

Definition 3. *An argument labelling is called a* complete argument labelling *iff for each* $A \in Ar$ *it holds that*

- $Al(A) = \text{in}$ *iff all B that attacks A has* $Al(B) \in \{\text{out}, \text{ido}\}$.
- $Al(A) = \text{out}$ *iff at least one B that attacks A has* $Al(B) = \text{in}$ *and A attacks no sink C with* $Al(C) = \text{idk}$.
- $Al(A) = \text{ido}$ *iff at least one B that attacks A has* $Al(B) = \text{in}$ *and A attacks at least one sink C with* $Al(C) = \text{idk}$
- $Al(A) = \text{idk}$ *iff at least one B that attacks A has* $Al(B) \in \{\text{out}, \text{ido}\}$, *no B that attacks A has* $Al(B) = \text{in}$, *and every sink C attacked by A has* $Al(C) = \text{idk}$.
- $Al(A) = \text{idc}$ *iff at least one B that attacks A has* $Al(B) \in \{\text{out}, \text{ido}\}$, *no B that attacks A has* $Al(B) = \text{in}$, *and at least one sink C attacked by A has* $Al(C) \neq \text{idk}$.

As one can observe, the sink arguments influence the evaluation of arguments in our definition. For instance, the only difference between labelling an argument as out or ido is whether that argument attacks any idk-labelled sinks. As such, out and ido are merely specialisations of the out label from the standard 3-valued labellings of [2]. The same holds for idk and idc, as specialisations of undec from [2]. Intuitively, idk replaces undec in most cases; idc (resp. ido) is used when the status of a classically undec (resp. out) argument is irrelevant to the status of its attackee. In a way, the labels ido, idc allow us to sometimes evaluate one extra argument (using ido) or one less argument (using idc) as undecided. This is enough to ensure that our 5-valued complete labellings from Definition 3 are one to one related to the 3-valued complete labellings of [2] and preserve the complete semantics for abstract argumentation frameworks. The same holds for the grounded, preferred, stable and semi-stable semantics, as they are all particular cases of the complete semantics. Another straightforward result is

Proposition 1. *Let (Ar, att) be an AF and Al be one of its complete argument labellings. For every sink argument $C \in \text{SINKS}_{\text{AF}}$, it holds $Al(C) \in \{\text{in}, \text{out}, \text{idk}\}$.*

Given an argument labelling Al, we write $\text{v}(Al) = \{A \mid Al(A) = \text{v}\}$ for $\text{v} \in \{\text{in}, \text{out}, \text{ido}, \text{idk}, \text{idc}\}$. An argument labelling provides a partition of Ar, so we might as well present Al as a tuple $(\text{in}(Al), \text{out}(Al), \text{ido}(Al), \text{idk}(Al), \text{idc}(Al))$.

The next definition adapts from well-known results concerning the 3-valued argument labellings of [2,5]. Our adaptation maps the 3-valued label undec to idk ∪ idc, the specialised labels we created from the standard undec.

Definition 4. *Let AL be the set of all complete argument labellings of* AF. *Then*

- *$Al \in AL$ is grounded if $\nexists Al' \in AL$ such that* in$(Al') \subsetneq$ in(Al).
- *$Al \in AL$ is preferred if $\nexists Al' \in AL$ such that* in$(Al') \supsetneq$ in(Al).
- *$Al \in AL$ is stable if* idk$(Al) \cup$ idc$(Al) = \emptyset$.
- *$Al \in AL$ is semi-stable if $\nexists Al' \in AL$ such that* idk$(Al') \cup$ idc$(Al') \subsetneq$ idk$(Al) \cup$ idc(Al).

The following example should help the reader to further understand these concepts.

Example 1. The argumentation framework AF below has complete labellings $Al_1 = (\{\,\},\{\,\},\{\,\},Ar,\{\,\})$, $Al_2 = (\{A_2,A_8\},\{A_3,A_7\},\{A_4\},\{A_1,A_5,A_6,A_9\},\{\,\})$, $Al_3 = (\{A_3,A_7,A_9\},\{A_2,A_5,A_8\},\{\,\},\{A_1,A_4,A_6\},\{\,\})$. The grounded labelling of AF is Al_1 and its preferred labellings are Al_2, Al_3. AF has no stable labellings, but has two semi-stable labellings, namely Al_2, Al_3. For contrast, the corresponding argument labellings in Caminada's 3-valued approach are $Al_1' = (\{\,\},\{\,\},Ar)$, $Al_2' = (\{A_2,A_8\},\{A_3,A_7,A_4\},\{A_1,A_5,A_6,A_9\})$, $Al_3' = (\{A_3,A_7,A_9\},\{A_2,A_5,A_8\},\{A_1,A_4,A_6\})$. We highlight the difference between Al_2 and Al_2' due to ido$(Al_2) \neq \emptyset$.

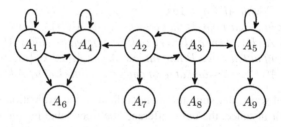

It should be noticed that sink arguments were only attributed labels in, out, idk, as previously stated in Proposition 1.

2.2 Logic Programs and Semantics

In the current paper, we account for propositional normal logic programs[2], which we call logic programs or simply programs from now on. We will follow the presentation of logic programs and their semantics as done in [5], which, in turn, is based on [13].

Definition 5. *A rule r is an expression*

$$r : c \leftarrow a_1, \ldots, a_n, \text{not } b_1, \ldots, \text{not } b_m$$

$(m, n \geq 0)$ where c, each a_i $(1 \leq i \leq n)$ and each b_j $(1 \leq j \leq m)$ are atoms and not *represents negation as failure. A literal is either an atom a (positive literal) or a*

---

[2] These are logic programs whose rules may contain weak but not strong negation and where the head of each rule is a single atom.

negated atom not *a (negative literal). Given a rule r as above, c is called the* head *of r, which we denote head(r), and* $a_1, \ldots, a_n,$ not $b_1, \ldots,$ not b_m *is called the* body *of r, denoted body(r). Further, we divide body(r) in two sets* $body^+(r) = \{a_1, \ldots, a_n\}$ *and* $body^-(r) = \{$not $b_1, \ldots,$ not $b_m\}$. *A* logic program *(or simply a* program *or LP) P is then defined as a finite set of rules. If every* $r \in P$ *has* $body^-(r) = \emptyset$, *then P is* positive. *The* Herbrand Base *of P is the set* HB_P *of all atoms appearing in the program.*

Definition 6. *A 3-valued Herbrand Interpretation I of a logic program P is a pair* $\langle T, F \rangle$ *with* $T, F \subseteq HB_P$ *and* $T \cap F = \emptyset$. *The atoms in T are said to be* true, *the atoms in F are said to be* false *and the atoms in* $HB_P \setminus (T \cup F)$ *are said to be* undefined.

Definition 7. *A 3-valued Herbrand interpretation I of a logic program P is called a* model *if* $I(head(r)) \geq \min(\{I(l) \mid l \in body(r)\})$ *for each* $r \in P$, *according to the order true > undefined > false.*

Let I be a 3-valued Herbrand Interpretation of P, the reduct of P with respect to I (written P/I) can be obtained replacing each occurrence of a naf-literal not c in P "true" if $c \in F$, by "false" if $c \in T$, or by "undefined" otherwise. In this context, "true", "false" and "undefined" are special atoms not occurring in P which are necessarily evaluated according to their naming conventions. This procedure ensures P/I has no instances of negative literals. As consequence, P/I has a unique least 3-valued model [13] hereby denoted $\Psi_P(I) = \langle T_\Psi, F_\Psi \rangle^3$ with minimal T_Ψ and maximal F_Ψ (w.r.t. set inclusion) such that, for every $a \in HB_P$:

- $a \in T_\Psi$ if there is a rule $r' \in P/I$ with $head(r') = a$ and $body^+(r') \subseteq T_\Psi$;
- $a \in F_\Psi$ if every rule $r' \in P/I$ with $head(r') = a$ has $body^+(r') \cap F_\Psi \neq \emptyset$;

Definition 8. *Let* $I = \langle T, F \rangle$ *be a 3-valued Herbrand Interpretation of program P.*

- *I is a* partial stable *(or P-stable)* model *of P iff* $\Psi_P(I) = I$.
- *T is a* well-founded model *of P iff I is a P-stable model of P where T is minimal (w.r.t. set inclusion) among all P-stable models of P.*
- *T is a* regular model *of P iff I is a P-stable model of P where T is maximal (w.r.t. set inclusion) among all P-stable models of P.*
- *T is a* stable model *of P iff I is a P-stable model of P where* $T \cup F = HB_P$.
- *T is an* L-stable model *of P iff I is a P-stable model of P where* $T \cup F$ *is maximal (w.r.t. set inclusion) among all P-stable models of P.*

While some of the above definitions are not standard in logic programming literature, their equivalence is proved in [5]. This approach is favored in our work due to the structural similarities to Definition 4, simplifying the proof of some results.

The following example should help the reader to understand the above concepts.

Example 2. Consider the following logic program P:

$$r_1 : c \leftarrow \text{not } c \quad r_4 : c \leftarrow \text{not } c, \text{not } a$$
$$r_2 : a \leftarrow \text{not } b \quad r_5 : g \leftarrow \text{not } g, \text{not } b$$
$$r_3 : b \leftarrow \text{not } a$$

---

[3] The above definition consists of a least fix-point of the immediate consequence operator Ψ defined in [13], which is guaranteed to exist and be unique for positive programs.

This program has three P-stable models: $I_1 = \langle\{\ \},\{\ \}\rangle$, $I_2 = \langle\{a\},\{b\}\rangle$, $I_3 = \langle\{b\},\{a,g\}\rangle$. P has $\{\ \}$ for its well-founded model (always unique), $\{a\}$, $\{b\}$ for its regular models, no stable models and only $\{b\}$ as an L-stable model.

3   From Logic Programs to Argumentation Frameworks

In this section, we review the procedure used to instantiate argumentation frameworks based on logic programs from [5] with slight updates to each step. Our updates are required to include special arguments we call *default arguments*, which are necessarily sinks, in the result. By design, they will be the only sinks in the output of our procedure.

3.1   Step 1: AF Instantiation

Given a normal logic program P, we recursively instantiate the following *arguments*:

Definition 9. *Let P be a logic program.*

- *If $r : c \leftarrow \text{not } b_1, \dots, \text{not } b_m$ is a rule in P then r is also an argument (say A) with* $\text{Conc}(A) = c$, $\text{Rules}(A) = \{r\}$, $\text{Vul}(A) = \{b_1, \dots, b_m\}$ *and* $\text{Sub}(A) = \{A\}$.
- *If $r : c \leftarrow a_1, \dots, a_n, \text{not } b_1, \dots, \text{not } b_m$ is a rule in P and for each $a_i \in body^+(r)$ there is an argument A_i with $\text{Conc}(A_i) = a_i$ and $r \notin \text{Rules}(A_i)$ then*

$$c \leftarrow (A_1), \dots, (A_n), \text{not } b_1, \dots, \text{not } b_m$$

is an argument (say A) with $\text{Conc}(A) = c$, $\text{Rules}(A) = \bigcup \text{Rules}(A_i) \cup \{r\}$, $\text{Vul}(A) = \bigcup \text{Vul}(A_i) \cup \{b_1, \dots, b_m\}$ and $\text{Sub}(A) = \bigcup \text{Sub}(A_i) \cup \{A\}$.
- *For each different $head(r)$ where $r \in P$, there is a default argument (say not A) such that $\text{Conc}(\text{not } A) = \text{not } head(r)$, $\text{Rules}(\text{not } A) = \emptyset$, $\text{Vul}(\text{not } A) = \{head(r)\}$ and $\text{Sub}(\text{not } A) = \{\text{not } A\}$.*

Above, $\text{Conc}(A)$, $\text{Rules}(A)$, $\text{Vul}(A)$ and $\text{Sub}(A)$ respectively refer to what we call the conclusion, rules, vulnerabilities and subarguments of A. Our definition is very similar to the one in [5], which consists of only the first two bullet points above. The difference is the third bullet point, which is required to instantiate the default arguments.

Example 3. Based on the logic program P from Example 2 we can instantiate: $A_i = r_i$, $1 \leq i \leq 5$, based on the first bullet point of Definition 9; $A_6 = \text{not } c$, $A_7 = \text{not } a$, $A_8 = \text{not } b$, $A_9 = \text{not } g$, based on the third bullet point of Definition 9. No arguments are instantiated following the second bullet point because all $r \in P$ have $body^+(r) = \emptyset$. To exemplify the components of some of those arguments, A_1 has $\text{Conc}(A_1) = c$, $\text{Rules}(A_1) = \{r_1\}$, $\text{Vul}(A_1) = \{c\}$ and $\text{Sub}(A_1) = \{A_1\}$. A_6 has $\text{Conc}(A_6) = \text{not } c$, $\text{Rules}(A_6) = \emptyset$, $\text{Vul}(A_6) = \{c\}$ and $\text{Sub}(A_6) = \{A_6\}$.

The next step is to determine the attack relation of the argumentation framework: an argument attacks another iff its conclusion is a vulnerability of the latter.

Definition 10. *Let A and B be arguments[4]. We say A attacks B iff $\text{Conc}(A) \in \text{Vul}(B)$.*

---

[4] According to Definition 9.

Example 4. The argument A_1 from Example 3 consists of $r : c \leftarrow not\ c$ and has $\text{Conc}(A_1) = c$ and $\text{Vul}(A_1) = \{c\}$; since $\text{Conc}(A_1) \in \text{Vul}(A_1)$, A_1 attacks itself. A_6, in comparison, attacks no arguments, but is also attacked by A_1.

Definition 11. *The argumentation framework* AF_P *associated with a program P is* $\text{AF}_P = (Ar_P, att_P)$, *where* Ar_P *is the set of all arguments from P (Definition 9) and* $att_P = \{(A, B) \in Ar \times Ar \mid \text{Conc}(A) \in \text{Vul}(B)\}$ *(Definition 10).*

Given AF_P, the computation of $\text{SINKS}_{\text{AF}_P}$ retrieves its set of default arguments.

Example 5. Following the names of arguments used in Example 3, the AF_P corresponding to P from Example 2 is precisely the framework depicted in Example 1.

3.2 Step 2: Applying Argumentation Semantics

Once we have AF_P, we will be interested in its semantics from the standpoint of abstract argumentation, which are given by Definition 3.

3.3 Step 3: Computing Conclusion Labellings

The goal of this step is to translate the 5-valued argument labellings obtained in the previous step to sets of conclusions comparable to the models of the original program, which are in turn 3-valued. For this reason, conclusions will be labeled exclusively within the elements of $\{\text{in}, \text{out}, \text{undec}\}$. In what follows, we will refer to the necessary sets of labels as $V_5 = \{\text{in}, \text{out}, \text{ido}, \text{idk}, \text{idc}\}$ and $V_3 = \{\text{in}, \text{out}, \text{undec}\}$.

Definition 12. *Let P be a program. A conclusion labelling is a map* $Cl : HB_P \rightarrow V_3$.

As in [5], we follow the approach of [15]: for each conclusion, we map the labels of arguments that yield it (taken from V_5) to a label in V_3. The label attributed to each $a \in HB_P$ is then the best one[5] according to the total order $\text{in} > \text{undec} > \text{out}$.

Definition 13. *The mapping* $\sigma : V_5 \rightarrow V_3$ *is such that* $\sigma(\text{in}) = \text{in}$, $\sigma(\text{out}) = \sigma(\text{ido}) = \text{out}$, $\sigma(\text{idk}) = \sigma(\text{idc}) = \text{undec}$.

Definition 14. *Let* $\text{AF}_P = (Ar_P, att_P)$ *be the AF associated with a program P and Al be an argument labelling of* AF_P. *We say that Cl is the* associated conclusion labelling *of Al iff Cl is a conclusion labelling such that for each* $c \in HB_P$ *it holds that* $Cl(c) = max(\{\sigma(Al(A)) \mid \text{Conc}(A) = c\} \cup \{\text{out}\})$ *where* $\text{in} > \text{undec} > \text{out}$.

Given a conclusion labelling Cl, we write $\text{in}(Cl)$ to denote $\{c \mid Cl(c) = \text{in}\}$, $\text{out}(Cl)$ for $\{c \mid Cl(c) = \text{out}\}$ and $\text{undec}(Cl)$ for $\{c \mid Cl(c) = \text{undec}\}$. Because a conclusion labelling defines a partition of HB_P into sets of in/out/undec-labelled conclusions, we may sometimes write Cl as the triple $(\text{in}(Cl), \text{out}(Cl), \text{undec}(Cl))$.

---

[5] In case there is no argument for a particular conclusion, it will be simply labelled out.

Example 6. Recall the complete argument labellings of AF in Example 1 are: $Al_1 = (\{\,\},\{\,\},\{\,\}, Ar, \{\,\})$, $Al_2 = (\{A_2, A_8\}, \{A_3, A_7\}, \{A_4\}, \{A_1, A_5, A_6, A_9\}, \{\,\})$, $Al_3 = (\{A_3, A_7, A_9\}, \{A_2, A_5, A_8\}, \{\,\}, \{A_1, A_4, A_6\}, \{\,\})$. Furthermore, remember $\text{Conc}(A_1) = \text{Conc}(A_4) = c$ (Example 3). Observe that $Al_2(A_4) = \text{ido}$ and $Al_2(A_1) = \text{idk}$. Given that $\sigma(\text{ido}) = \text{out}$ and $\sigma(\text{idk}) = \text{undec}$, we will find $Cl_2(c) = \text{undec}$ in the corresponding conclusion labelling Cl_2. Following Definition 14, we produce the conclusion labellings $Cl_1 = (\{\}, \{\}, \{a, b, c, g\})$, $Cl_2 = (\{a\}, \{b\}, \{c, g\})$, and $Cl_3 = (\{b\}, \{a, g\}, \{c\})$ respectively associated to Al_1, Al_2, Al_3. Please observe that $\langle \text{in}(Cl_i), \text{out}(Cl_i) \rangle$ $(1 \leq i \leq 3)$ are precisely the p-stable models of P (Example 2).

4 Semantic Correspondences

In this section, we overview results concerning semantic relations between abstract argumentation and logic programming. We show that our approach based on 5-valued labellings preserves the original results and provides us a new correspondence.

First, we must formally define functions to map argument labellings to conclusion labellings and vice-versa. Our intention is to later prove they are each other's inverse. The function AL2CL below simply follows Definition 14, while CL2AL is introduced anew. In the latter, we will find that an argument is out or ido in the resulting argument labelling if some of its vulnerabilities are in in the original conclusion labelling. Deciding if that argument is out or ido will depend solely on whether it attacks an undec-labelled sink. The case for idk and idc arguments is similarly based on undec and the status of the sink arguments they attack.

Definition 15. *Let P be a program and AF_P be its associated argumentation framework. Let $\mathcal{AL}$ be the set of all argument labellings of AF_P and let $\mathcal{CL}$ be the set of all conclusion labellings of AF_P.*

- *We define a function* AL2CL: $\mathcal{AL} \to \mathcal{CL}$ *such that for each* $Al \in \mathcal{AL}$, AL2CL(Al) *is the associated conclusion labelling of Al (Definition 14).*
- *We define a function* CL2AL : $\mathcal{CL} \to \mathcal{AL}$ *such that for each* $Cl \in \mathcal{CL}$ *and each* $A \in Ar_P$ *it holds that:*
  - CL2AL$(Cl)(A) = \text{in}$ *iff* $\text{Vul}(A) \subseteq \text{out}(Cl)$
  - CL2AL$(Cl)(A) = \text{out}$ *iff* $\text{Vul}(A) \cap \text{in}(Cl) \neq \emptyset$ *and*
    $\{\text{Conc}(B) \mid B \in \text{SINKS}_{\text{AF}_P} \text{ and } (A, B) \in att\} \cap \text{undec}(Cl) = \emptyset$
  - CL2AL$(Cl)(A) = \text{ido}$ *iff* $\text{Vul}(A) \cap \text{in}(Cl) \neq \emptyset$ *and*
    $\{\text{Conc}(B) \mid B \in \text{SINKS}_{\text{AF}_P} \text{ and } (A, B) \in att\} \cap \text{undec}(Cl) \neq \emptyset$
  - CL2AL$(Cl)(A) = \text{idk}$ *iff* $\text{Vul}(A) \cap \text{in}(Cl) = \emptyset$, *while* $\text{Vul}(A) \setminus \text{out}(Cl) \neq \emptyset$
    and $\text{Conc}(B) \mid B \in \text{SINKS}_{\text{AF}_P} \text{ and } (A, B) \in att \subseteq \text{undec}(Cl)$
  - CL2AL$(Cl)(A) = \text{idc}$ *iff* $\text{Vul}(A) \cap \text{in}(Cl) = \emptyset$, *while* $\text{Vul}(A) \setminus \text{out}(Cl) \neq \emptyset$
    and $\{\text{Conc}(B) \mid B \in \text{SINKS}_{\text{AF}_P} \text{ and } (A, B) \in att\} \setminus \text{undec}(Cl) \neq \emptyset$

Theorem 1. *When restricted to complete argument labellings and complete conclusion labellings, the functions* AL2CL *and* CL2AL *are bijections and each other's inverse.*

We are now ready to present some key results of our work. In what follows, let P be a logic program and AF_P be its associated argumentation framework. Further, assume $Cl = (\text{in}(Cl), \text{out}(Cl), \text{undec}(Cl))$ is an arbitrary conclusion labelling of AF_P. The results below are based on our σ-mapping from 5-valued labellings to the standard in/out/undec-labellings from [2] and theorems from [5] connecting the standard labellings to logic programming models. In summary, the following theorems assure our 5-valued labellings preserve all the results from [5].

Theorem 2. *Let Al be a complete argument labelling of* AF_P. *Then* $\text{AL2CL}(Al) = Cl$ *iff* $\langle\text{in}(Cl), \text{out}(Cl)\rangle$ *is a p-stable model of P.*

As our definition of complete argument labelling corresponds to the definition of [2] and the characterization of in is equivalent in both settings, we can borrow the following result from [5]:

Lemma 1. *Let P be a program and $\text{AF}_P = (Ar, att)$ be its associated argumentation framework. Let Al_1 and Al_2 be complete argument labellings of AF_P, and $Cl_1 = \text{AL2CL}(Al_1)$ and $Cl_2 = \text{AL2CL}(Al_2)$. It holds that*

1. $\text{in}(Al_1) \subseteq \text{in}(Al_2)$ *iff* $\text{in}(Cl_1) \subseteq \text{in}(Cl_2)$,
2. $\text{in}(Al_1) = \text{in}(Al_2)$ *iff* $\text{in}(Cl_1) = \text{in}(Cl_2)$, *and*
3. $\text{in}(Al_1) \subsetneq \text{in}(Al_2)$ *iff* $\text{in}(Cl_1) \subsetneq \text{in}(Cl_2)$.

From Theorem 2 and Lemma 1, we obtain:

Theorem 3. *Let Al be the grounded argument labelling of* AF_P. *Then* $\text{AL2CL}(Al) = Cl$ *iff* $\text{in}(Cl)$ *is the well-founded model of P.*

Theorem 4. *Let Al be a preferred argument labelling of* AF_P. *Then* $\text{AL2CL}(Al) = Cl$ *iff* $\text{in}(Cl)$ *is a regular model of P.*

In addition, we know $\text{idk}, \text{idc} = \emptyset$ in a complete argument labelling Al iff $\text{undec} = \emptyset$ in $\text{AL2CL}(Al) = Cl$ (Definition 14). Thus,

Theorem 5. *Let Al be a stable argument labelling of* AF_P. *Then* $\text{AL2CL}(Al) = Cl$ *iff* $\text{in}(Cl)$ *is a stable model of P.*

Following the queue of the theorems above, we can as well consider the conclusion labellings where $\text{in}(Cl)$ is an L-stable model of P. The natural candidate argument labellings to correspond to those conclusion labellings would be the semi-stable argument labellings, since both semi-stable and L-stable semantics respectively minimize undecided arguments and undecided atoms. Unfortunately, in the same way as in [5], we find there are cases where the semi-stable semantics does not exactly correspond to the L-stable semantics. Our running example is enough to show that: as one can observe from the computed labellings in Example 6, the framework from Example 1 has two semi-stable argument labellings (hence two semi-stable conclusion labellings), namely Al_2, Al_3, but Cl_3 is the sole complete conclusion labelling for which $\text{in}(Cl)$ is an L-stable model of P. In other words, P has a single L-stable model, but AF_P has two semi-stable argument labellings. Differently from previous works, however, our labellings isolated a possible culprit to that difference in Example 6, for we have $Al_2(A_4) = \text{ido}$. But why may it be a culprit? Because if A_4 was instead labelled idk in Al_2, only Al_3 would be semi-stable, fixing the expected correspondence.

5   The L-Stable Semantics for Abstract Argumentation Frameworks

The discussion about the semi-stable and L-stable semantics by the end of Sect. 4 led us to the suggestion that changing the labels of some particular arguments could lead those semantics to coincide. Unfortunately, such changes are far from trivial, as changing the label of an argument is likely to affect the labels of others. Fortunatelly, there are other parts of the three-step procedure from Sect. 3 that can be easily adapted to achieve a similar result: the conception of a new abstract argumentation semantics that corresponds perfectly to the L-stable semantics from logic programming.

Definition 16. *Let $\mathcal{AL}$ be the set of all complete argument labellings of* AF. *Then Al is a least-stable (or L-stable) argument labelling of* AF *if $Al \in \mathcal{AL}$ and $\nexists Al' \in \mathcal{AL}$ such that* $\mathrm{idk}(Al') \cup \mathrm{ido}(Al') \subsetneq \mathrm{idk}(Al) \cup \mathrm{ido}(Al)$.

Lemma 2. *Let Al be a complete labelling of an argumentation framework and $Cl = \mathrm{AL2CL}(Al)$. Then $\exists A \in \mathrm{idk}(Al) \cup \mathrm{ido}(Al)$ with $\mathrm{Conc}(A) = c$ iff $Cl(c) = \mathrm{undec}$.*

Theorem 6. *Let Al be a least-stable argument labelling of* AF_P. *Then $\mathrm{AL2CL}(Al) = Cl$ iff $\mathrm{in}(Cl)$ is an L-stable model of P.*

This correspondence ensures the L-stable semantic for argumentation frameworks has similar properties to the semi-stable semantics.

Corollary 1. *Every AF has at least one L-stable labelling.*

Corollary 2. *If Al is a stable labelling of* AF_P, *then Al is an L-stable labelling of* AF_P.

Corollary 3. *If* AF_P *has at least one stable labelling, then Al is an L-stable labelling of* AF_P *iff Al is a semi-stable labelling of* AF_P *iff Al is a stable labelling of* AF_P.

However, differently than semi-stable, the L-stable AA semantic captures the L-stable semantics for LP.

6   On the Role of Sink Arguments

We have affirmed sink arguments together with 5-valued labellings are able to isolate the possible culprits for the difference between the semi-stable and L-stable semantics. Now we resume this discussion to provide a more detailed account on the role played by sink arguments in argumentation semantics. In particular, we will emphasize the following two points:

- When considering only the sink arguments obtained in our translation (Definition 9), 3-valued labellings suffice to capture the equivalence between logic programming semantics and abstract argumentation semantics (including L-stable).
- The sink arguments together with the 5-valued labellings offer a more fine-grained view of the notion of undecidedness when compared with 3-valued labellings.

The sink arguments can be employed to obtain the conclusion labellings associated with complete argument labellings:

Theorem 7. *Let P be a logic program, $\mathrm{AF}_P = (Ar_P, att_P)$ be its associated argumentation framework and Al be a complete 5-valued argument labelling of AF_P. We define $Cl : HB_P \to V_3$:*

$$Cl(c) = \begin{cases} \overline{\sigma(Al(A))} & \text{if } \exists A \in Ar_P \text{ such that } \mathrm{Conc}(A) = \text{not } c \\ \text{out} & \text{otherwise} \end{cases}$$

in which $\overline{\text{in}} = $ out, $\overline{\text{out}} = $ in and $\overline{\text{undec}} = $ undec. Then $\mathrm{AL2CL}(Al) = Cl$ and $\langle \mathrm{in}(Cl), \mathrm{out}(Cl) \rangle$ is a p-stable model of P.

From Definition 9, there is at most one argument A in AF_P such that $\mathrm{Conc}(A) = $ not c for each $c \in HB_P$. Therefore, the function Cl above is well-defined.

Theorem 8. *Let P be a program, $\mathrm{AF}_P = (Ar_P, att_P)$ be its associated argumentation framework, Al be a 5-valued argument labelling of AF_P and $\mathrm{AL3}(Al) : \mathrm{SINKS}_{\mathrm{AF}_P} \to \{\text{in}, \text{out}, \text{undec}\}$, in which for every $A \in \mathrm{SINKS}_{\mathrm{AF}_P}$, we have $\mathrm{AL3}(Al)(A) = \sigma(Al(A))$. Let also $\mathcal{AL}$ be the set of all complete argument labellings of AF_P. Then*

- *Al is the grounded argument labelling of AF_P iff $Al \in \mathcal{AL}$ and $\nexists Al' \in \mathcal{AL}$ such that $\mathrm{out}(\mathrm{AL3}(Al')) \subsetneq \mathrm{out}(\mathrm{AL3}(Al))$.*
- *Al is a preferred argument labelling of AF_P iff $Al \in \mathcal{AL}$ and $\nexists Al' \in \mathcal{AL}$ such that $\mathrm{out}(\mathrm{AL3}(Al')) \supsetneq \mathrm{out}(\mathrm{AL3}(Al))$.*
- *Al is a stable argument labelling of AF_P iff $Al \in \mathcal{AL}$ and $\mathrm{undec}(\mathrm{AL3}(Al)) = \emptyset$.*
- *Al is an L-stable argument labelling of AF_P iff $Al \in \mathcal{AL}$ and $\nexists Al' \in \mathcal{AL}$ such that $\mathrm{undec}(\mathrm{AL3}(Al')) \subsetneq \mathrm{undec}(\mathrm{AL3}(Al))$.*

Theorem 8 highlights a distinction between the semi-stable and L-stable semantics over an argumentation framework AF_P obtained from a logic program P: the semi-stable argument labellings of AF_P are those complete argument labellings with minimal set of undec-labelled arguments, whereas the L-stable argument labellings of AF_P are those complete argument labellings with minimal set of undec-labelled sinks. Therefore, the labels assigned to the sink arguments of AF_P suffice to know if a labelling is grounded, preferred, stable and L-stable, but they may not suffice to know if it is semi-stable. Revisiting Example 6, we have both Al_2 and Al_3 are complete labellings with minimal undec arguments (semi-stable, see Example 1); in contrast, Al_3 is the only complete labelling with minimal undec sinks (L-stable, see Example 2).

One may then wonder it the 5-valued labelling semantics we introduced in this paper are of some interest on their own. First, observe that the 5 labels are a necessary condition to define the L-stable argumentation semantics (complete labellings with minimal (ido ∪ idk)-valued arguments). Further, although one can mimic the L-stable logic programming semantics with 3-valued labellings, it will work as expected just for argumentation frameworks obtained from logic programs through Definition 11; in an arbitrary argumentation framework (one that does not account for default arguments), unlike our definition of L-stable semantics based on 5 labels, this adaptation of the 3-valued approach to capture L-stable will not produce meaningful results.

Besides, we emphasize the role played by sink arguments in our 5-valued labellings: in an argumentation framework AF without sink arguments, its complete 3-valued labellings coincide precisely with its 5-valued counterpart by simply replacing undec for idk in the respective labellings. This means that the semi-stable and L-stable argumentation semantics collapse into each other for those frameworks! What is more, owing to the 5-valued labellings, we can define new semantics with interesting properties: for instance, consider a new argumentation semantics (let us call it "I-stable") defined by the complete labellings with minimal idk arguments. In an argumentation framework without sink arguments, it will coincide with both semi-stable and L-stable argumentation semantics and yet it will possibly produce distinct results for some argumentation frameworks. As such, these semantics offer three different views of undecidedness in which the difference between them is positively determined by the sink arguments.

7 Conclusion

This work was largely motivated by the curious result of [5] stating the semi-stable semantics from abstract argumentation is not equivalent to the L-stable semantics from logic programming. Both semantics are based on the minimization of undecided arguments and atoms in their respective domains, share very similar properties, and yet are different. Our efforts to understand the differences between the semantics led us to consider the instantiation of special arguments in logic programming we called default arguments and the specialization of the standard 3-valued argument labellings from [2] into more expressive 5-valued partial labellings (as previously considered in [1]). To accomplish our goals, we considered the labels in, out, ido, idk, idc and introduced a corresponding definition of complete labellings revising the meanings of out, idk, idc and introducing the new label ido, here dubbed "It doesn't matter if it's out". Following the revised concepts, we showed our approach preserves well-known results in the semantic comparison of abstract argumentation and logic programming. While we did not try to resolve the semi-stable-L-stable equivalence problem, we shed light into it, as our 5-valued labellings can isolate the possible culprit arguments causing the differences based on the labels ido, idc. Instead, we introduced a new semantics for abstract argumentation frameworks: the least-stable (or L-stable) semantics. What is more, we proved our newly established semantics to be equivalent to the logic programming L-stable semantics for normal programs and their corresponding instantiated argumentation frameworks. The non-equivalence result proved in [5] was based on a particular procedure for the instantiation of argumentation frameworks from logic programs. The 5-valued labellings, the sink arguments and our revision of their procedure are the key changes to obtain an argumentation-based semantics corresponding to L-stable. Indeed, we show that if we restrict our attention to sink arguments, the standard 3-valued labelling is enough to characterize the logic programming semantics, including L-stable.

It is worth noticing that partial labellings were also employed by [12] in an algorithm for enumerating preferred extensions of an argumentation framework. As we do, they also consider five labels, namely in, out, undec, blank, and must-out labels. In their algorithm, all arguments of the framework are initially `blank` and `must-out` is used at run time to flag arguments that are candidate to be labelled `out`.

Natural ramifications of this work include an in-depth investigation of properties of the least-stable argumentation semantics. Our newly defined 5-valued complete labellings may also lead to the proposal of other interesting semantics as we try to maximize or minimize different combinations of the labels at our disposal. We also intend to investigate whether sink arguments play other relevant roles in the characterization or computation of argumentation semantics.

References

1. Baroni, P., Giacomin, M., Liao, B.: I don't care, i don't know ... i know too much! on incompleteness and undecidedness in abstract argumentation. In: Eiter, T., Strass, H., Truszczyński, M., Woltran, S. (eds.) Advances in Knowledge Representation, Logic Programming, and Abstract Argumentation. LNCS (LNAI), vol. 9060, pp. 265–280. Springer, Cham (2015). https://doi.org/10.1007/978-3-319-14726-0_18

2. Caminada, M.: On the issue of reinstatement in argumentation. In: Fisher, M., van der Hoek, W., Konev, B., Lisitsa, A. (eds.) JELIA 2006. LNCS (LNAI), vol. 4160, pp. 111–123. Springer, Heidelberg (2006). https://doi.org/10.1007/11853886_11

3. Caminada, M.: Semi-stable semantics. In: Dunne, P.E., Bench-Capon, T.J.M. (eds.) Computational Models of Argument: Proceedings of COMMA 2006, September 11–12, 2006, Liverpool, UK. Frontiers in Artificial Intelligence and Applications, vol. 144, pp. 121–130. IOS Press (2006). http://www.booksonline.iospress.nl/Content/View.aspx?piid=1932

4. Caminada, M., Harikrishnan, S., Sá, S.: Comparing logic programming and formal argumentation; the case of ideal and eager semantics. In: Argument and Computation Pre-press, pp. 1–28 (2021). https://doi.org/10.3233/AAC-200528

5. Caminada, M., Sá, S., Alcântara, J., Dvořák, W.: On the equivalence between logic programming semantics and argumentation semantics. Int. J. Approx. Reason. **58**, 87–111 (2015)

6. Dung, P.: An argumentation procedure for disjunctive logic programs. J. Logic Program. **24**, 151–177 (1995)

7. Dung, P.: On the acceptability of arguments and its fundamental role in nonmonotonic reasoning, logic programming and n-person games. Artif. Intell. **77**, 321–357 (1995)

8. Dvořák, W., Gaggl, S.A., Wallner, J.P., Woltran, S.: Making use of advances in answer-set programming for abstract argumentation systems. In: Tompits, H., Abreu, S., Oetsch, J., Pührer, J., Seipel, D., Umeda, M., Wolf, A. (eds.) INAP/WLP -2011. LNCS (LNAI), vol. 7773, pp. 114–133. Springer, Heidelberg (2013). https://doi.org/10.1007/978-3-642-41524-1_7

9. Eiter, T., Leone, N., Saccá, D.: On the partial semantics for disjunctive deductive databases. Ann. Math. Artif. Intell. **19**(1–2), 59–96 (1997)

10. Jakobovits, H., Vermeir, D.: Robust semantics for argumentation frameworks. J. Logic Comput. **9**(2), 215–261 (1999)

11. Nieves, J.C., Cortés, U., Osorio, M.: Preferred extensions as stable models. Theory Pract. Logic Program. **8**(4), 527–543 (2008)

12. Nofal, S., Atkinson, K., Dunne, P.E.: Algorithms for decision problems in argument systems under preferred semantics. Artif. Intell. **207**, 23–51 (2014)

13. Przymusinski, T.: The well-founded semantics coincides with the three-valued stable semantics. Fundamenta Informaticae **13**(4), 445–463 (1990)

14. Toni, F., Sergot, M.: Argumentation and answer set programming. In: Balduccini, M., Son, T.C. (eds.) Logic Programming, Knowledge Representation, and Nonmonotonic Reasoning. LNCS (LNAI), vol. 6565, pp. 164–180. Springer, Heidelberg (2011). https://doi.org/10.1007/978-3-642-20832-4_11
15. Wu, Y., Caminada, M.: A labelling-based justification status of arguments. Stud. Logic **3**(4), 12–29 (2010)
16. Wu, Y., Caminada, M., Gabbay, D.M.: Complete extensions in argumentation coincide with 3-valued stable models in logic programming. Studia Logica **93**(1–2), 383–403 (2009)

Assumption-Based Argumentation
Is Logic Programming with Projection

Samy Sá$^{(\boxtimes)}$ and João Alcântara

Universidade Federal do Ceará, Fortaleza, Brazil
samy@ufc.br , jnando@lia.ufc.br

Abstract. We revisit the semantic relations between Assumption-Based Argumentation (ABA) and Logic Programming (LP) based on the recent development of model-based semantics for ABA frameworks. This effort is motivated by the close resemblance between the computation of complete ABA models and the computation of Przymuzinski's partial stable models for logic programs. As we show these concepts coincide *ipsis litteris*, multiple results about the different ABA semantics (preferred, grounded, stable, semi-stable, ideal, eager) and corresponding LP semantics (regular, well-founded, stable, L-stable, ideal, eager) follow. Our approach also introduces a new translation from ABA frameworks to logic programs that has better properties than the one available in the literatue, including lower computational complexity. The combination of our new translation and model-based ABA semantics is the key to all of our results. It is also known that the more traditional assumption extension and labelling-based semantics for ABA can be obtained from ABA models using an operation called tuple projection, so it follows from our results that ABA is LP with projection.

Keywords: Logic Programming · Assumption-Based Argumentation · Argumentation semantics

1 Introduction

In this work, we provide new perspective on the semantic relations between Assumption-Based Argumentation (ABA) [2,8,15] and Logic Programming (LP) [10]. Both are rule-based formalisms of nonmonotonic reasoning sharing very similar syntax and whose semantics may be understood through the application of 3-valued interpretations. Previous research [2,6,14] provided ways for mapping logic programs into ABA frameworks and vice-versa and found that ABA and LP are pairwise equivalent under almost every semantics, with a notable exception concerning their respective semantics minimizing undecidedness [6]: the L-stable semantics for logic programs [9] and the semi-stable semantics for ABA frameworks [4]. Here, we follow this trend of recent works on expressive power of argumentation and nonmonotonic reasoning formalisms [1,4–6,13,16], bringing some new mechanics and intuitions to this type of comparative research.

© Springer Nature Switzerland AG 2021
J. Vejnarová and N. Wilson (Eds.): ECSQARU 2021, LNAI 12897, pp. 173–186, 2021.
https://doi.org/10.1007/978-3-030-86772-0_13

For starters, we propose that the difference between ABA and LP is that given a theory in any desired logics, once adapted to each case,

- LP semantics evaluates what sentences are true in the models of the theory; while
- ABA semantics evaluates what sentences are false in the models of the theory.

This idea is largely motivated by the available translations between ABA and LP in the literature [2,6] and can be illustrated by an example even without formally introducing the relevant concepts. Towards that end, consider the logic program P^1 with four rules below[2]:

$$P: \begin{array}{ll} a \leftarrow \text{not } b & c \leftarrow \text{not } c \\ b \leftarrow \text{not } a & d \leftarrow b, c \end{array}$$

The language of P comprises four sentences, namely a, b, c, d. The semantics of LP are based on models, each one proposing which sentences from the program's language may be simultaneously true. In each case, the evaluation of the derived sentences $\text{not } a, \text{not } b, \text{not } c, \text{not } d$ will be obtained as a byproduct of those models. In particular, we highlight that (traditionally) only a, b, c, d will appear in the models of P.

Following [2], P would be translated into the ABA framework $ABA(P) = \mathcal{F}^3$ below.

$$\mathcal{F}: \begin{array}{llll} a \leftarrow \beta & c \leftarrow \gamma & \overline{\alpha} = a & \overline{\beta} = b \\ b \leftarrow \alpha & d \leftarrow b, c & \overline{\gamma} = c & \overline{\delta} = d \end{array}$$

Notice how the rules in $\mathcal{F}$ (depicted in the first two columns) mirror the rules of P, while the operator $^-$ captures the semantics of not .

The language of $\mathcal{F}$ is a bit different from the language of P, but not by much. It consists of eight sentences, namely $a, b, c, d, \alpha, \beta, \gamma, \delta$, where $\alpha, \beta, \gamma, \delta$ respectively model $\text{not } a, \text{not } b, \text{not } c, \text{not } d$ as native elements in $\mathcal{F}$'s language. Among the sentences in the language of $\mathcal{F}$, the ones we can assume to be true by default ($\alpha, \beta, \gamma, \delta$ in our example) are called *assumptions*. In this format, each assumption χ must have a unique contrary (obtained via the operator $^-$) which consists of a non-assumption capable of denying χ. In our example, a is the contrary of α (which corresponds to $\text{not } a$), b is the contrary of β (which corresponds to $\text{not } b$), and so on. The semantics of ABA are based on assumption extensions, which are sets of assumptions consistent with the set of rules. That is, in the semantics of $\mathcal{F}$ (traditionally), only $\alpha, \beta, \gamma, \delta$ will appear. Then, since the assumptions of $ABA(P)$ correspond to the negative literals in P, we can retrieve from the assumption extensions what sentences are false in the models of P.

One could expect these perspectives to be equivalent, but evidence [4–6,13] suggests this may not always be the case. More specifically, in the case of ABA

---

[1] This program is extracted from [6].

[2] not denotes negation as failure [7].

[3] At this time, to avoid the necessity of formal concepts, only the core syntactic elements of $\mathcal{F}$ are shown.

and LP, these concepts can only be guaranteed to coincide if there is bijection between defeasible sentences in the input knowledge base and their contraries [6]. While this property necessarily holds for logic programs, it does not necessarily hold for ABA frameworks. This interferes with the ability for some LP semantics to capture some ABA semantics, despite of their similarities. This suggests that ABA is somehow more expressive than LP, but the results so far may be limited by a missing property in the translation from ABA frameworks into logic programs in which they are based, which is not injective. For instance, if one follows [6] to translate $\mathcal{F}$ into a logic program, the result would be P. However, this would also be the result if the input if $\mathcal{F}'$ below, which is basically $\mathcal{F}$, but removing the assumption δ from its language.

$$\mathcal{F}' : \begin{array}{llll} a \leftarrow \beta & c \leftarrow \gamma & \overline{\alpha} = a & \overline{\beta} = b \\ b \leftarrow \alpha & d \leftarrow b, c & \overline{\gamma} = c \end{array}$$

While the difference may seem small, $\mathcal{F}, \mathcal{F}'$ have significantly different semantics. The difference is enough so that the semi-stable assumption extensions of $\mathcal{F}'$ do not correspond to the L-stable models of P, while the semi-stable assumption extensions of $\mathcal{F}$ do, and yet, $\mathcal{F}, \mathcal{F}'$ are both translated to P. Then perhaps, this undesirable behavior of the translation from [6] is what causes ABA to seem more expressive than LP. Be it or not, whether ABA and LP are equivalent is still an open problem heavily related to the concept of undecidability.

In this work, we will contribute in several ways to show how LP captures ABA and what causes the differences observed in previous works. First, we propose a new translation from ABA frameworks to logic programs satisfying some desirable properties that the one by [6] does not. For instance, their translation only works for ABA frameworks under strict syntactic assumptions, such as that (i) each assumption has a unique contrary that may not be an assumption and (ii) assumptions may not occur in the conclusions of rules. Our translation is introduced under the same syntactic assumptions to facilitate proofs and comparison, but here they are not strict: ours may be easily adapted for backwards compatibility to the original work on ABA [2], where, amongst other possibilities, assumptions may have multiple contraries (including other assumptions) and sentences may be contraries to multiple assumptions. In fact, we can even accommodate ABA frameworks where assumptions may be in the conclusions of rules. All of this is possible because we map assumptions from the ABA framework to a proper subset of positive literals in the corresponding program, instead of mapping them to negative literals (with **not**). As we do that, our translation ensures that the language (assumptions + non-assumptions) of an ABA framework matches the language of its corresponding logic program, which is a stronger relation than an arbitrary one-to-one correspondence between sentences. Another consequence of this strategy is that the contrary operator $^-$ in the input ABA framework can be modeled using **not** in a straightforward way. This means that ABA frameworks such as $\mathcal{F}, \mathcal{F}'$ in our discussion above will necessarily have different results in our translation. In fact, any changes to an ABA framework will find corresponding changes in the resulting logic program. Our approach is further motivated by the recent proposal of model-based semantics for ABA [13], where all sentences (instead of just assumptions) in the language of an ABA framework are evaluated. Using our translation, we find that the models of an ABA framework are not only in one-to-one correspondence with the models of the resulting logic program, but they coincide precisely for all particular cases of the complete ABA semantics, including semi-stable. Therefore our result are stronger than the previous ones. It confirms that ABA frameworks are inherently logic programs with somewhat different syntax and a simple twist on its semantics. That slight twist is characterized by an operation called tuple projection[4], where only a subset of sentences in the language of the input are extracted from pre-computed models. Fundamentally, it consists of a restriction to the language of the models. Our translation also benefits of lower computational complexity and is necessarily optimal: intuitively it consists of just reading the ABA framework input once. Immediately, our results allow the computation of semantics for any ABA frameworks by means of logic programming interpreters using a simple parser to perform the tuple projection.

The rest of the paper develops as follows. In Sect. 2, we will introduce the concepts of model-based ABA semantics and LP semantics, focusing on the computation and properties of the complete (resp. p-stable) models for ABA (resp. LP). In Sect. 3, we will introduce our novel translation from ABA frameworks to logic programs and explore some properties. The inverse translation is introduced in Sect. 4 and is used to characterize the class of ABA programs, which is semantically equivalent to ABA frameworks. In Sect. 5 we gather the conclusions of previous sections and organize those ideas to motivate our main results. Sect. 6 concludes the paper with a summary of our contributions, ramifications of our results and future works.

2   Formal Preliminaries

We define a set of truth values $\mathcal{V} = \{\mathbf{t}, \mathbf{u}, \mathbf{f}\}$ whose elements stand respectively for true, undecided, and false. We establish a total preorder $>$ over $\mathcal{V}$ such that $\mathbf{t} > \mathbf{u} > \mathbf{f}$ regarding how much truth is semantically attributed to each value. We also define that $-\mathbf{t} = \mathbf{f}$, $-\mathbf{f} = \mathbf{t}$, and $-\mathbf{u} = \mathbf{u}$.

Based on $\mathcal{V}$ and given a set S of propositional symbols, we say that $I = \langle T, F, U \rangle$ is an interpretation of S iff $\{T, F, U\}$ is a partition of S in sets of (respectively) *true*, *false* and *undecided* propositions. Just alike, I can be understood as the function $I : S \to \mathcal{V}$ such that (i) $I(a) = \mathbf{t}$ iff $a \in T$; (ii) $I(a) = \mathbf{f}$ iff $a \in F$; and (iii) $I(a) = \mathbf{u}$ iff $a \in U$. Given two interpretations $I = \langle T, F, U \rangle, J = \langle T', F', U' \rangle$, we say $I \preceq J$[5] if $T \subseteq T'$ and $F' \subseteq F$. An interpretation I of S is a least interpretation of S iff I is $\preceq$-least.

---

[4] In relational algebra, this is equivalent to selection, but the common name for this operation in logic programming literature is projection.

[5] The interpretation order $\preceq$ is based on $>$.

2.1   Normal Logic Programs

In the current paper, we account for propositional normal logic programs[6], which we call logic programs or simply programs from now on.

Definition 1. *A rule r is an expression $r : c \leftarrow a_1, \ldots, a_n, \text{not } b_1, \ldots, \text{not } b_m$ $(n \geq 0, m \geq 0)$ where c, each a_i $(1 \leq i \leq n)$ and each b_j $(1 \leq j \leq m)$ are atoms and not represents negation as failure. Let r be a rule, we write $hd(r)$ to denote its head (the atom c), $bd^+(r)$ to denote the set $\{a_1, \ldots, a_n\}$ and $bd^-(r)$ to denote the set $\{\text{not } b_1, \ldots, \text{not } b_m\}$. We refer to the body of r as $bd(r) = bd^+(r) \cup bd^-(r)$. A logic program P is then defined as a finite set of rules. If every $r \in P$ has $bd^-(r) = \emptyset$, we say that P is a positive program. The Herbrand Base of a program P is the set HB_P of all atoms occurring in P.*

Given a program P, we say interchangeably that an interpretation I of HB_P is an interpretation of P. In that case, we refer to the correlate function $\hat{I}$ [11,12] as the interpretation of $HB_P \cup \{\text{not } a \mid a \in HB_P\}$ where $\hat{I}(a) = I(a)$ and $\hat{I}(\text{not } a) = -\hat{I}(a)$ for every $a \in HB_P$. Below, whenever implicit, assume a generic program P.

Definition 2. *An interpretation $I = \langle T, F, U \rangle$ of a program HB_P is a 3-valued model (or simply a model) of P iff for every rule $r \in P$, $\hat{I}(hd(r)) \geq min\{\ \hat{I}(l) \mid l \in bd(r)\ \}$.*

The 3-valued stable models [12] of a program P can be obtained by a process called program division. The first step of this process eliminates rules that do not have their bodies satisfied by I; the second step eliminates from the bodies of the remaining rules all those negative literals that are necessarily true in I; the last step gets rid of the remaining negative literals, replacing them by a new literal $\mathbf{u}$.

Definition 3. *Let I be an interpretation of the program P. The reduct P/I is the program $\mathbf{D3}(P, I)$ computed as:*

1. $\mathbf{D1}(P, I) = P \setminus \{r \mid \text{not } b_i \in bd^-(r) \text{ for some } b_i \in T\}$
2. $\mathbf{D2}(P, I) = \{hd(r) \leftarrow bd(r) \setminus \{\text{not } b_i \mid b_i \in F\} \mid r \in \mathbf{D1}(P, I)\}$
3. $\mathbf{D3}(P, I) = \{r \in \mathbf{D2}(P, I) \mid bd^-(r) = \emptyset\} \cup \{hd(r) \leftarrow bd^+(r) \cup \{\mathbf{u}\} \mid r \in \mathbf{D2}(P, I) \text{ and } bd^-(r) \neq \emptyset\}$.

In the above procedure, $\mathbf{u}$ is an atom not in HB_P which is undecided in all interpretations of P (a constant). It should be noticed that P/I will always be positive [11], which ensures that P/I has a unique least model denoted $\Psi_P(I) = \langle T_\Psi, F_\Psi, U_\Psi \rangle$[7] with minimal T_Ψ and maximal F_Ψ (w.r.t. set inclusion) such that, for every $a \in HB_P$, (i) $a \in T_\Psi$ if there is a rule $r' \in P/I$ with $hd(r') = a$ and $bd^+(r') \subseteq T_\Psi$; and (ii) $a \in F_\Psi$ if every rule $r' \in P/I$ with $hd(r') = a$ has $bd^+(r') \cap F_\Psi \neq \emptyset$.

---

[6] Logic programs whose rules may contain weak but not strong negation, and the head of each rule is an atom [10].

[7] $\Psi_P(I)$ is a least fix-point of the immediate consequences operator Ψ of [11], which is guaranteed to exist and be unique for positive programs.

Definition 4. *An interpretation I of the program P is a 3-valued stable (alt. p-stable) model of P iff $\Psi_P(I) = I$.*

2.2   Assumption-Based Argumentation

For our convenience, we will introduce ABA frameworks from the perspective of model-based semantics [13]. This approach exploits the identical structure shared by inference rules (ABA) and program rules (LP), allowing the computation of the complete semantics for ABA by a process that mimics the computation of p-stable models from [11].

Definition 5. *An ABA framework is a tuple $\langle \mathcal{L}, \mathcal{R}, \mathcal{A}, ^- \rangle$ where $(\mathcal{L}, \mathcal{R})$ is a deductive system[8], with language $\mathcal{L}$ and set of inference rules $\mathcal{R}$, $\mathcal{A} \subseteq \mathcal{L}$[9] whose elements are referred as assumptions, and $^-$ is a total mapping from $\mathcal{A}$ into $\mathcal{L} \setminus \mathcal{A}$[10], where $\bar{\alpha}$ is called the contrary of α.*

Given an ABA framework $\mathcal{F}$, we say interchangeably that an interpretation I of $\mathcal{L}$ is an interpretation of $\mathcal{F}$. For every inference rule $C \leftarrow L_1, \ldots, L_n$ in $\mathcal{R}$, we define $hd(r) = C$ and $bd(r) = \{L_1, \ldots, L_n\}$, so r can be written as $hd(r) \leftarrow bd(r)$. For our current purposes, we will restrict our attention to flat ABA-frameworks, which means the heads of inference rules cannot be assumptions [8]. In what follows, whenever implicit, assume a generic flat ABA framework $\mathcal{F} = \langle \mathcal{L}, \mathcal{R}, \mathcal{A}, ^- \rangle$.

Definition 6. *An interpretation I of $\mathcal{L}$ is (3-valued) model of $\mathcal{F}$ iff (i) $\forall r \in \mathcal{R}$, $I(hd(r)) \geq min\{\ I(l) \mid l \in bd(r)\ \}$ and (ii) $\forall a \in \mathcal{A}$, $I(a) = -I(\bar{a})$.*

The concept of *framework reduction* [13] mimics the program division of [11].

Definition 7. *Let I be an interpretation of $\mathcal{F}$. The reduct $\mathcal{F}/I$ is the ABA framework $\mathbf{R3}(\mathcal{F}, I)$ where each $1 \leq i \leq 3$, $\mathbf{Ri}(\mathcal{F}, I) = \langle \mathcal{L}^i, \mathcal{R}^i, \mathcal{A}^i, ^{-i} \rangle$ s.t. that:*

1. $\mathcal{R}^1 = \mathcal{R} \setminus \{r \mid \exists a \in \mathcal{A} \cap bd(r) \text{ s.t. } \bar{a} \in T\}$, $\mathcal{A}^1 = \mathcal{A} \setminus F$, $\mathcal{L}^1 = \mathcal{L} \setminus (\mathcal{A} \cap F)$;
2. $\mathcal{R}^2 = \left(\mathcal{R}^1 \cup \{hd(r) \leftarrow bd(r) \setminus \{a \in \mathcal{A} \mid \bar{a} \in F\} \mid r \in \mathcal{R}^1\}\right) \setminus \{r \in \mathcal{R}^1 \mid \exists a \in \mathcal{A} \cap bd(r) \text{ s.t. } \bar{a} \in F\}$, $\mathcal{A}^2 = \mathcal{A}^1 \setminus T$, $\mathcal{L}^2 = \mathcal{L}^1 \setminus (\mathcal{A}^1 \cap T)$;
3. $\mathcal{R}^3 = \{r \in \mathcal{R}^2 \mid bd(r) \cap \mathcal{A} = \emptyset\} \cup \{hd(r) \leftarrow (bd(r) \setminus \mathcal{A}) \cup \{\mathbf{u}\} \mid r \in \mathcal{R}^2 \text{ and } bd(r) \cap \mathcal{A} \neq \emptyset\}$, $\mathcal{A}^3 = \mathcal{A}^2 \setminus U = \emptyset$, $\mathcal{L}^3 = (\mathcal{L}^2 \setminus (\mathcal{A} \cap U)) \cup \{\mathbf{u}\} = (\mathcal{L} \setminus \mathcal{A}) \cup \{\mathbf{u}\}$;
4. $\bar{a}^i : \mathcal{A}^i \rightarrow \mathcal{L}^i$ is such that $\bar{a}^i = \bar{a}$ for each $a \in \mathcal{A}^i$.

---

[8] The concept of deductive systems used in ABA is fully detailed in [2].

[9] Traditionally, $\mathcal{A}$ is required to be non-empty. We opt to relax that condition to favor a simpler presentation of our later concepts.

[10] In most ABA works, the codomain of $^-$ is $\mathcal{L}$, but the contraries of assumptions are implicitly assumed to be non-assumptions.

In the above, $\mathbf{u}$ is an atom not in $\mathcal{L}$ which is undecided in all interpretations of $\mathcal{L}$ (a constant).

Notice the reduct $\mathcal{F}/I$ has no assumptions, allowing us to disregard the contrariness relation in operations over $\mathcal{F}/I$, which ensures that $\mathcal{F}/I = \langle (\mathcal{L} \setminus \mathcal{A}) \cup \{\mathbf{u}\}, \mathcal{R}^3, \emptyset, \emptyset \rangle$ has a unique least model $\Psi_{\mathcal{F}}(I) = \langle T_\Psi, F_\Psi, U_\Psi \rangle$ with minimal T_Ψ and maximal F_Ψ (w.r.t. set inclusion) such that, for all $l \in \mathcal{L} \setminus \mathcal{A}$, (i) $l \in T_\Psi$ iff there is $r \in \mathcal{R}^3$ with $hd(r) = l$ and $bd(r) \subseteq T_\Psi$; and (ii) $l \in F_\Psi$ iff every $r \in \mathcal{R}^3$ with $hd(r) = l$ has $bd(r) \cap F_\Psi \neq \emptyset$ [13]. From $\Psi_{\mathcal{F}}(I)$, we can obtain a corresponding least model of $\mathcal{F}$ denoted $\mathcal{M}(\mathcal{F}/I)$ such that (iii) $\mathcal{M}(\mathcal{F}/I)(l) = \Psi_{\mathcal{F}}(I)(l)$ for all $l \in \mathcal{L} \setminus \mathcal{A}$ and (iv) $\mathcal{M}(\mathcal{F}/I)(l) = -\mathcal{M}(\mathcal{F}/I)(\bar{l})$ for all $l \in \mathcal{A}$ [13].

Definition 8. *An interpretation I of $\mathcal{L}$ is a* complete model *of $\mathcal{F}$ iff $\mathcal{M}(\mathcal{F}/I) = I$.*

Example 1. Let $\mathcal{F} = \langle \mathcal{L}, \mathcal{R}, \mathcal{A}, \bar{} \rangle$, s.t. $\mathcal{L} = \{a, b, c, \alpha, \beta, \gamma\}$, $\mathcal{R} = \{a \leftarrow \beta,\ b \leftarrow \alpha,\ b \leftarrow \gamma,\ c \leftarrow \beta,\ c \leftarrow \gamma\}$, $\mathcal{A} = \{\alpha, \beta, \gamma\}$, and $\bar{\alpha} = a, \bar{\beta} = b, \bar{\gamma} = c$. The complete models of $\mathcal{F}$ are $I_1 = \langle \{\ \}, \{\ \}, \{a, b, c, \alpha, \beta, \gamma\}\rangle$, $I_2 = \langle \{a, c, \beta\}, \{b, \alpha, \gamma\}, \{\ \}\rangle$, and $I_3 = \langle \{b, \alpha\}, \{a, \beta\}, \{c, \gamma\}\rangle$.

3   From ABA to LP

In this section, we will present a translation from any given ABA framework $\mathcal{F}$ to a corresponding logic program preserving the semantics of $\mathcal{F}$.

Definition 9. *The program corresponding to an ABA framework $\mathcal{F}$ is* $\texttt{ABAf2LP}(\mathcal{F}) = \mathcal{R} \cup \{a \leftarrow \texttt{not } \bar{a} \mid a \in \mathcal{A}\}$.

Example 2. Recall $\mathcal{F}$ from Example 1. The program associated to $\mathcal{F}$ is $\texttt{ABAf2LP}(\mathcal{F}) = \{a \leftarrow \beta,\ b \leftarrow \alpha,\ b \leftarrow \gamma,\ c \leftarrow \beta,\ c \leftarrow \gamma,\ \alpha \leftarrow \texttt{not } a,\ \beta \leftarrow \texttt{not } b,\ \gamma \leftarrow \texttt{not } c\}$. Below, we show $\mathcal{R}$ to the left and $\texttt{ABAf2LP}(\mathcal{F}) = P$ for comparison and make use of superscripts $^{\mathcal{F},P}$ for contrast. Recall that $\mathcal{F}$ has three complete models we named I_1, I_2, and I_3 (Example 1). Just alike, I_1, I_2, I_3 are the p-stable models of $\texttt{ABAf2LP}(\mathcal{F})$.

$$
\begin{array}{l|ll}
r_1^{\mathcal{F}} : a \leftarrow \beta & r_1^P : a \leftarrow \beta & r_6^P : \alpha \leftarrow \texttt{not } a \\
r_2^{\mathcal{F}} : b \leftarrow \alpha & r_2^P : b \leftarrow \alpha & r_7^P : \beta \leftarrow \texttt{not } b \\
r_3^{\mathcal{F}} : b \leftarrow \gamma & r_3^P : b \leftarrow \gamma & r_8^P : \gamma \leftarrow \texttt{not } c \\
r_4^{\mathcal{F}} : c \leftarrow \beta & r_4^P : c \leftarrow \beta & \\
r_5^{\mathcal{F}} : c \leftarrow \gamma & r_5^P : c \leftarrow \gamma &
\end{array}
$$

From the above, any $\texttt{ABAf2LP}(\mathcal{F})$ will be clearly divided in two distinguishing sets of rules. The first set is obtained by importing $\mathcal{R}$ from $\mathcal{F}$ and (therefore) has no negative literals. The second set is produced based on the contrariness relation of $\mathcal{F}$ and each of its rules has an empty positive body. This second set concentrates all the occurrences of negative literals in $\texttt{ABAf2LP}(\mathcal{F})$. This is not by chance. In fact, this rather convenient effect stems from the similarities of ABA and LP and is merely captured by our definition. Furthermore, provided that $\mathcal{F}$ is flat, the literals of $\texttt{ABAf2LP}(\mathcal{F})$ that map what originally were assumptions in $\mathcal{F}$ can only appear in the heads of rules in the second set, never the first.

Lemma 1. *Let $\mathcal{F}$ be an ABA framework, then I is an interpretation of $\mathcal{F}$ iff I is an interpretation of* ABAf2LP$(\mathcal{F})$.

Lemma 2. *If I is a model of $\mathcal{F}$, then I is a model of* ABAf2LP$(\mathcal{F})$.

The converse of Lemma 2 does not hold for every LP model because, as an example, ABAf2LP$(\mathcal{F})$ from Example 2 admits models such as I where $I(a) = \mathbf{t}$, but $I(\alpha) \neq \mathbf{f}$, while every model I' of $\mathcal{F}$ must enforce that $I'(\alpha) = -I'(a)$. Observe that for those $r \in$ ABAf2LP$(\mathcal{F}) \cap \mathcal{R}$, ABA models have the same requirement as with logic programming models, i.e., we need that $I(hd(r)) \geq min\{\ I(l) \mid l \in bd(r)\ \}$. Then any LP models where $\hat{I}(hd(r)) \not\geq min\{\ \hat{I}(l) \mid l \in bd(r)\ \}$ for each $r \in$ ABAf2LP$(\mathcal{F}) \setminus \mathcal{R}$ are also ABA models.

Lemma 3. *If I is a model of* ABAf2LP$(\mathcal{F})$ *such that $\hat{I}(a) = \hat{I}(\mathbf{not}\ \bar{a})$ for all $r : a \leftarrow \mathbf{not}\ \bar{a} \in$ ABAf2LP$(\mathcal{F}) \setminus \mathcal{R}$, then I is an ABA model of $\mathcal{F}$.*

Even though a program ABAf2LP$(\mathcal{F})$ corresponding to $\mathcal{F}$ admits some models that $\mathcal{F}$ does not, that does not prevent the complete models of $\mathcal{F}$ to coincide with the p-stable models of ABAf2LP$(\mathcal{F})$. This is one of our main original results.

Theorem 1. *Let $\mathcal{F}$ be an ABA framework, then I is a complete model of $\mathcal{F}$ iff I is a p-stable model of* ABAf2LP$(\mathcal{F})$.

Proof. Let I be an interpretation of $\mathcal{F}$, then, by Lemma 1, I is an interpretation of ABAf2LP$(\mathcal{F}) = P_{\mathcal{F}}$ (for short). We follow by comparing $\mathcal{F}/I$ and $P_{\mathcal{F}}/I$ step by step. Let $\mathcal{M}(\mathcal{F}/I) = \langle T_{\mathcal{M}}, F_{\mathcal{M}}, U_{\mathcal{M}} \rangle$ be the least model of $\mathcal{F}$ retrieved from $\mathcal{F}/I$ and $\Psi_{P_{\mathcal{F}}}(I) = \langle T_{\Psi}, F_{\Psi}, U_{\Psi} \rangle$ be the least model of $P_{\mathcal{F}}/I$. We will refer to the intermediate reducts produced in the division procedures proposed for logic programs (Definition 3) and ABA frameworks (Definition 7).

First, we will first show that if I is a model of $\mathcal{F}$, then $\Psi_P(I) = \mathcal{M}(\mathcal{F}/I)$. We can assume that I is a model of $\mathcal{F}, P_{\mathcal{F}}$, because either hypothesis that I is a complete model of $\mathcal{F}$ or that I is a p-stable model of $P_{\mathcal{F}}$ ensure as much.

Let $r \in P_{\mathcal{F}}$, we have two possibilities: $r \in P_{\mathcal{F}} \cap \mathcal{R}$ or $r \in P_{\mathcal{F}} \setminus \mathcal{R}$. Recall from Definition 9, that (a) $hd(r) \in \mathcal{L} \setminus \mathcal{A}$ and $bd^-(r) = \emptyset$ for all $r \in P_{\mathcal{F}} \cap \mathcal{R}$ while (b) $hd(r) \in \mathcal{A}$ and $bd(r) = \{\mathbf{not}\ \overline{hd(r)}\}$ for all $r \in P_{\mathcal{F}} \setminus \mathcal{R}$, which means $bd^+(r) = \emptyset$ and $|bd^-(r)| = 1$ for $r \in P_{\mathcal{F}} \setminus \mathcal{R}$. Further, take note that the program division (Definition 3) can only remove or change those $r \in P_{\mathcal{F}}$ where $bd^-(r) \neq \emptyset$, so $\mathcal{R} \subseteq P_{\mathcal{F}}/I$. For that reason, we will consider the evaluation of $bd(r)$ for $r \in \mathcal{R}$. We have four possibilities:

(1) Suppose $bd(r) \cap \mathcal{A} = \emptyset$. From that, we obtain that $r \in \mathcal{F}/I$, which means that $\mathcal{M}(\mathcal{F}/I)(hd(r)) \geq min\{\ \mathcal{M}(\mathcal{F}/I)(l) \mid l \in bd(r)\ \}$. Further, we obtain that $r \in P/I$ and $\Psi_P(I)(hd(r)) \geq min\{\ \widehat{\Psi_P(I)}(l) \mid l \in bd(r)\ \}$.

(2) Suppose $bd(r) \cap \mathcal{A} \cap F \neq \emptyset \Leftrightarrow \exists a \in bd(r) \cap \mathcal{A}$ s.t. $a \in F \Leftrightarrow \exists a \in bd(r) \cap \mathcal{A}$ s.t. $\bar{a} \in T \Leftrightarrow r \notin \mathcal{R}^1$ and $a \leftarrow \mathbf{not}\ \bar{a} \notin \mathbf{D1}(P_{\mathcal{F}}, I)$ and $\{r \in \mathcal{R} \mid a \in bd(r)\} \cap \mathcal{R}^1 = \emptyset$. Since $r \notin \mathcal{R}^3$, we can only state that $\mathcal{M}(\mathcal{F}/I)(hd(r)) \geq \mathbf{f}$.

Because $r \in P_{\mathcal{F}} \cap \mathcal{R}$, we know $r \in P_{\mathcal{F}}/I$. However, since $a \leftarrow \mathbf{not}\ \bar{a}$ is the only $r' \in P_{\mathcal{F}}$ s.t. $hd(r') = a$, we have $\{r' \in P_{\mathcal{F}}/I \mid hd(r') = a\} = \emptyset$. Then

$a \in F_\Psi$, which means $\widehat{\Psi_P(I)}(a) = \mathbf{f}$ and $min\{\ \widehat{\Psi_P(I)}(l) \mid l \in bd(r)\ \} = \mathbf{f}$. Then $\Psi_P(I)(hd(r)) \geq \mathbf{f}$.

Then, for all $r \in \mathcal{R}$ s.t. $bd(r) \cap \mathcal{A} \cap F \neq \emptyset$, we will have $\mathcal{M}(\mathcal{F}/I)(hd(r)) \geq \mathbf{f}$ and $\Psi_P(I)(hd(r)) \geq \mathbf{f}$

Cases (3) and (4) account implicitly for the possibilities concerning $bd(r) \cap \mathcal{A} \cap T$, as the second step of framework reduction and program division will only remove those $l \in bd(r) \cap \mathcal{A} \cap T$ from each r in $\mathcal{F}$ and $P_\mathcal{F}$.

(3) Suppose $bd(r) \cap \mathcal{A} \cap F = \emptyset$ and $bd(r) \cap \mathcal{A} \cap U = \emptyset$. Let $r_\mathcal{A}^T = \{a \in bd(r) \mid a \in \mathcal{A} \cap T\}$, then r will be replaced by $r' : hd(r) \leftarrow bd(r) \setminus r_\mathcal{A}^T$ in $\mathcal{R}^2$. Then $\mathcal{M}(\mathcal{F}/I)(hd(r)) \geq min\{\ \mathcal{M}(\mathcal{F}/I)(l) \mid l \in bd(r) \setminus r_\mathcal{A}^T\ \}$.

Given that $\bar{a} \in F$ for each $a \in r_\mathcal{A}^T$, each $a \leftarrow$ not $\bar{a} \in P_\mathcal{F}$ where $a \in r_\mathcal{A}^T$ will be replaced by $a \leftarrow$ in $\mathbf{D2}(P_\mathcal{F}, I)$. Recall that for each $a \in r_\mathcal{A}^T$, $a \leftarrow$ not $\bar{a}$ is the only $r' \in P_\mathcal{F}$ with $hd(r') = a$. Then the only $r' \in \mathbf{D2}(P_\mathcal{F}, I)$ s.t. $hd(r') = a$ is $a \leftarrow$. Because $body^-(r') = \emptyset$, we have $r' \in P_\mathcal{F}/I$, which means $\widehat{\Psi_P(I)}(a) = \mathbf{t}$ for every $a \in r_\mathcal{A}^T$. Then $\Psi_P(I)(hd(r)) \geq min\{\ \widehat{\Psi_P(I)}(l) \mid l \in bd(r) \setminus r_\mathcal{A}^T\ \}$.

Therefore, for all $r \in \mathcal{R}$ s.t. $bd(r) \cap \mathcal{A} \cap F = \emptyset$ and $bd(r) \cap \mathcal{A} \cap U = \emptyset$, we will have $\mathcal{M}(\mathcal{F}/I)(hd(r)) \geq min\{\ \mathcal{M}(\mathcal{F}/I)(l) \mid l \in bd(r) \setminus r_\mathcal{A}^T\ \}$ and $\Psi_P(I)(hd(r)) \geq min\{\ \widehat{\Psi_P(I)}(l) \mid l \in bd(r) \setminus r_\mathcal{A}^T\ \}$.

(4) The last case, where $bd(r) \cap \mathcal{A} \cap F = \emptyset$, but $bd(r) \cap \mathcal{A} \cap U \neq \emptyset$, has a proof analogous to that of (3).

From (1)–(4), $\Psi_P(I)$ and $\mathcal{M}(\mathcal{F}/I)$ impose the same constraints for the evaluation of the heads of each $r \in \mathcal{R}$. Given that $\Psi_P(I)$ and $\mathcal{M}(\mathcal{F}/I)$ are least models, we find that $\Psi_P(I)(hd(r)) = \mathcal{M}(\mathcal{F}/I)(hd(r))$ for all $r \in \mathcal{R}$. Then $\Psi_P(I)(a) = \mathcal{M}(\mathcal{F}/I)(a)$ for all $a \in \mathcal{L} \setminus \mathcal{A}$.

Now we need to prove that $\Psi_P(I)(a) = \mathcal{M}(\mathcal{F}/I)(a)$ for all $a \in \mathcal{A}$. Given that $a \leftarrow$ not $\bar{a}$ is the only rule in $P_\mathcal{F}$ with $hd(r) = a$, we have, for all $a \in \mathcal{A}$, $\Psi_P(I)(a) = \widehat{\Psi_P(I)}(a) = \widehat{\Psi_P(I)}(\text{not } \bar{a}) = -\widehat{\Psi_P(I)}(\bar{a}) = -\mathcal{M}(\mathcal{F}/I)(\bar{a}) = -\mathcal{M}(\mathcal{F}/I)(\bar{a}) = \mathcal{M}(\mathcal{F}/I)(a)$, i.e., $\Psi_P(I)(a) = \mathcal{M}(\mathcal{F}/I)(a)$. Then $\Psi_P(I)(l) = \mathcal{M}(\mathcal{F}/I)(l)$ for all $l \in \mathcal{L}$.

Finally, I is a complete ABA model of $\mathcal{F} \Leftrightarrow \mathcal{M}(\mathcal{F}/I) = I \Leftrightarrow \Psi_P(I) = I \Leftrightarrow I$ is a p-stable model of $P_\mathcal{F}$. $\qquad\square$

An intuition for the proof of this theorem can be obtained by comparing the division procedures for ABA and LP based on the same interpretation. This result ensures that every flat ABA framework has a corresponding LP whose p-stable models are precisely the same as the ABA framework's complete models. At this point, we can state:

Corollary 1. *Flat-ABA under model-based semantics is a fragment of NLP.*

We will complement these results with theorems in the next couple of sections to conclude that flat-ABA is actually equivalent to NLP equipped with an operation called tuple projection.

4   From LP to ABA

Previously, we showed that every ABA framework has a corresponding logic program that fully preserves its original semantics. In this section, we explore a translation from logic programs to ABA frameworks in an attempt to reverse Definition 9. The new proposed translation can only operate on some programs which we identify as *ABA programs*. Later on, we will expand the results of this section.

Ideally, we would like for every program P to have a corresponding ABA framework $\mathcal{F}_P$ such that $\texttt{ABAf2LP}(\mathcal{F}_P) = P$. If possible, we would like that mapping to be the inverse of $\texttt{ABAf2LP}$. We will start by ensuring that is the case for those programs akin to the results produced by $\texttt{ABAf2LP}$, which we denominate as ABA-programs.

Definition 10. *Given a normal logic program P, we say P is an ABA program iff (i) for all $r \in P$, if $bd^-(r) \neq \emptyset$, then $|bd(r)| = 1$; and (ii) for all $r, r' \in P$, if $bd^-(r) \neq \emptyset$ and $bd^-(r') \neq \emptyset$, then $hd(r) \neq hd(r')$.*

Definition 11. *The ABA framework corresponding to an ABA program P is $\texttt{LP2ABAf}(P) = \langle HB_P, \mathcal{R}_P, \mathcal{A}_P, ^{-P} \rangle$ such that*

- $\mathcal{R}_P = \{r \in P \mid bd^-(r) = \emptyset\}$,
- $\mathcal{A}_P = \{hd(r) \mid r \in P \text{ and } bd^-(r) \neq \emptyset\}$, *and*
- $^{-P}$ *is such that $\bar{a}^P = l$ for each $a \in \mathcal{A}_P$, where $a \leftarrow \textbf{not } l$ is the only $r \in P$ with $hd(r) = a$.*

Example 3. From Example 2, retrieve $\mathcal{F}$ and $\texttt{ABAf2LP}(\mathcal{F}) = P$. One can verify that P is an ABA program and that $\texttt{LP2ABAf}(P) = \mathcal{F}$.

We can state the following.

Lemma 4. *Given an ABA framework $\mathcal{F}$, it holds that $\texttt{LP2ABAf}(\texttt{ABAf2LP}(\mathcal{F})) = \mathcal{F}$.*

Lemma 5. *Given an ABA-program P, it holds that $\texttt{ABAf2LP}(\texttt{LP2ABAf}(P)) = P$.*

Theorem 2. *When restricted to the set of all flat ABA frameworks and the set of all ABA-programs, $\texttt{ABAf2LP}$ and $\texttt{LP2ABAf}$ are both bijective and each other's inverse.*

Proof. Let S be the set of all flat ABA frameworks and T be the set of all ABA-programs. It follows from Definition 11 that $\texttt{LP2ABAf} : S \to T$ is injective. Then, $|S| \leq |T|$ (via Lemma 4) and $|S| \geq |T|$ (via Lemma 5). Therefore, $|S| = |T|$ and $\texttt{LP2ABAf}$ is bijective. Then $\texttt{ABAf2LP} : T \to S$ is bijective and $\texttt{LP2ABAf}^{-1} = \texttt{ABAf2LP}$. ∎

Example 4. Take $\mathcal{F}, \mathcal{F}'$ from Sect. 1. The program corresponding to $\mathcal{F}$ is $\texttt{ABAf2LP}(\mathcal{F})$:

$$a \leftarrow \beta \quad c \leftarrow \gamma \quad \alpha \leftarrow \textbf{not } a \quad \gamma \leftarrow \textbf{not } c$$
$$b \leftarrow \alpha \quad d \leftarrow b, c \quad \beta \leftarrow \textbf{not } b \quad \delta \leftarrow \textbf{not } d$$

Just like the difference between $\mathcal{F}, \mathcal{F}'$ is that δ is not in the language of $\mathcal{F}'$, the program $\texttt{ABAf2LP}(\mathcal{F}')$ corresponding $\mathcal{F}'$ is $\texttt{ABAf2LP}(\mathcal{F}) \setminus \{\delta \leftarrow \textbf{not } d\}$.

Theorem 2 ensures the p-stable models of an ABA program coincide with the complete models of its corresponding ABA framework (and vice-versa).

Corollary 2. *Let P be an ABA program, then I is a p-stable model of P iff I is a complete model of* LP2ABAf(P).

The result of Corollary 2 is automatically extended to other core semantics of ABA and LP due to their isomorphic hierarchies. For instance, the well-founded model of a program P is the p-stable model of P where T is minimal w.r.t. set inclusion, whereas the grounded model of an ABA framework $\mathcal{F}$ is the complete model of $\mathcal{F}$ where T is minimal w.r.t. set inclusion. Given the mirrored conditions on those definitions, I is the well-founded model of P iff I is the grounded model of LP2ABAf(P). Similarly, the regular (resp. stable, L-stable, ideal) models of a program P are the p-stable models of P where T is maximal (resp. where $U = \emptyset$, U is minimal, T is maximally contained in each regular model of P), whereas the preferred (resp. stable, semi-stable, ideal) models of an ABA program $\mathcal{F}$ are the complete models of $\mathcal{F}$ where T is maximal (resp. $U = \emptyset$, U is minimal, T is maximally contained in each preferred model of $\mathcal{F}$), which means that I is a regular (resp. stable, L-stable, ideal) model of P iff I is the preferred (resp. stable, semi-stable, ideal) model of LP2ABAf(P). While further adaptations are required, a similar result can be obtained for the eager semantics, which was proposed for ABA frameworks in [4] via assumption extensions and more recently for LP in [3].

5 Summary and Main Result

The results we introduced up to this point have some interesting ramifications about flat-ABA, normal LP, ABA programs, and their variations using parameterized projection. For instance, we are now equipped to conclude and contextualize that

Proposition 1. *Flat-ABA under model-based semantics is equivalent to ABA Programs.*

Proof. Follows from Theorem 1 + Theorem 2.   □

This result is rather surprising: while the results of previous works [2,6] suggested flat-ABA could be more expressive than normal LP, we found that a fragment of normal LP suffices to capture flat-ABA to the point where

1. there is a bijection between all flat-ABA frameworks and all ABA programs (Theorem 2) such that
2. their semantics *coincide* precisely (Theorem 1, Corollary 2).

Again, we highlight that the *coincidence* of semantics is a lot stronger than the usual correspondences obtained using translations between ABA assumption labellings and LP models. Our approach finds the exact same semantic results given a corresponding logic program and ABA framework. It should be noticed there is a difference of perspective, since our results are based on the model semantics of ABA instead of assumption labellings. Fortunately, given an ABA framework $\mathcal{F}$, the assumption labellings of $\mathcal{F}$ in each semantics can be retrieved from the models of $\mathcal{F}$ for the same semantics using a tuple projection[11] parameterized by $\mathcal{A}$ [13]. Therefore,

Proposition 2. *Flat-ABA under assumption labelling semantics is equivalent to ABA programs with the projection $\sigma_{\mathcal{A}}$.*

Proof. Follows from Proposition 1 combined with Theorem 5 from [13].   □

This is the main conclusion of our work: while it reinforces that flat-ABA is not equivalent to normal LP, it clearly shows their difference may be characterized by the rather simple operation of tuple projection. The result is relatively straightforward from Proposition 1, for it ensures that applying the same tuple projection over the models of corresponding ABA frameworks and logic programs in any given semantics will render identical results.

6   Conclusion

In this work, we revisited the semantic connection between Assumption-Based Argumentation and Logic Programming in the light of model-based semantics for ABA [13]. Different from previous works on ABA semantics, model-based semantics explicitly evaluates sentences that are not assumptions. Based on the presentation and results of [13], we established a pair of translations ABAf2LP and LP2ABAf that are bijective and each others inverse from the set of all ABA frameworks to a class of logic programs we called ABA-programs. These translations were motivated by the original specification of ABA frameworks in [2], where assumptions may have multiple contraries (including other assumptions) and sentences may be contraries to multiple assumptions. This means that mapping the assumptions of an ABA framework to negative literals in a corresponding program is not trivial as done in the translation of [6]. For instance, their translation does not capture the semantics of ABA frameworks having an assumption as the contrary of another assumption, at least not directly. Instead, it is necessary to convert the ABA framework into another where the contrary of each assumption is necessarily a non-assumption, then apply their translation. We recognize there is a similar condition on our translation from logic programs to ABA frameworks, which requires an ABA-program to work, but this is not a drawback, since our focus is the translation from ABA frameworks into logic programs. Comparatively, our approach has an advantage compared to [6]: our translations ensure that $\texttt{ABAf2LP}(\texttt{LP2ABAf}(P)) = P$ and $\texttt{LP2ABAf}(\texttt{ABAf2LP}(\mathcal{F})) = \mathcal{F}$, while their translations only satisfy the first.

---

[11] Let S be a set and $T = \langle S_1, S_2, \ldots, S_k \rangle$ be a tuple of sets. The projection of elements of S from T is $\sigma_S(T) = \langle S_1 \cap S, S_2 \cap S, \ldots, S_k \cap S \rangle$.

The semantic coincidences we identified concerning ABA models and LP models (Theorem 2) extend also for the particular cases of the complete ABA semantics and the p-stable LP semantics. This holds trivially as a corollary for each semantics, since the complete ABA models of a framework match precisely the p-stable models of its corresponding program. In particular, the semi-stable models of a framework $\mathcal{F}$ coincide with the L-stable models of $\texttt{ABAf2LP}(\mathcal{F})$, but in some cases, as in [6], it is possible that the semi-stable labellings (that only evaluate the assumptions in $\mathcal{F}$) do not correspondence to the L-stable models of $\texttt{ABAf2LP}(\mathcal{F})$. This difference was also found when mapping semi-stable models of an ABA framework to its semi-stable assumption labellings in [13], which means that both the semi-stable and L-stable semantics are sensitive to tuple projection. When comparing the ABA semi-stable and LP L-stable semantics, we conjecture that their difference concerns whether we minimize undecidedness before or after performing the projection $\sigma_{\mathcal{A}}$. To motivate this idea, observe that $\mathcal{F}'$ (from Sect. 1) has three complete models: $I_1 = \langle \{ \ \}, \{ \ \}, \{a, b, c, d, \alpha, \beta, \gamma\}\rangle$, $I_2 = \langle \{a, \beta\}, \{b, \alpha\}, \{c, d, \gamma\}\rangle$, and $I_3 = \langle \{b, \alpha\}, \{a, d, \beta\}, \{c, \gamma\}\rangle$. Amongst them[12], only I_3 has a minimal set of undecided sentences. However, if we compute the assumption labellings corresponding to I_1, I_2, I_3 using $\sigma_{\{\alpha,\beta,\gamma\}}$ and compare again, we will have $\sigma_{\{\alpha,\beta,\gamma\}}(I_1) = \langle \{ \ \}, \{ \ \}, \{\alpha, \beta, \gamma\}\rangle$, $\sigma_{\{\alpha,\beta,\gamma\}}(I_2) = \langle \{\beta\}, \{\alpha\}, \{\gamma\}\rangle$, and $\sigma_{\{\alpha,\beta,\gamma\}}(I_3) = \langle \{\alpha\}, \{\beta\}, \{\gamma\}\rangle$. Now, both $\sigma_{\{\alpha,\beta,\gamma\}}(I_2)$ and $\sigma_{\{\alpha,\beta,\gamma\}}(I_3)$ have minimal sets of undecided sentences. To find the semi-stable ABA model semantics (which coincide to the L-stable LP model semantics) we minimized the sets of undecided sentences before applying projection. To find the semi-stable assumption labellings of $\mathcal{F}$, on the other hand, we applied projection and only then we selected those models with minimal sets of undecided sentences. Interestingly, only those semantics minimizing undecidedness seem to be sensitive to this operation. Our results suggest that, despite its simplicity, the tuple projection operator σ is instrumental to relate instances of non-monotonic formalisms, given the example concerning ABA and LP.

In future works, we intend to study the projection operation in context to find whether its properties could motivate the proposal of new ABA and LP semantics. Another potentially fruitful line of investigation regards checking whether the projection operation may capture semantic differences between other formalisms.

References

1. Alcântara, J.F.L., Sá, S., Guadarrama, J.C.A.: On the equivalence between abstract dialectical frameworks and logic programs. Theory Pract. Log. Program. **19**(5–6), 941–956 (2019)
2. Bondarenko, A., Dung, P., Kowalski, R., Toni, F.: An abstract, argumentation-theoretic approach to default reasoning. AI **93**, 63–101 (1997)

---

[12] Given some $\mathcal{F}$ (resp. P), a complete (resp. p-stable) model $I = \langle T, F, U\rangle$ of $\mathcal{F}$ is a semi-stable (resp. L-stable) model of $\mathcal{F}$ (resp. P) iff I has minimal $\{l \in \mathcal{L} \mid I(l) = \mathbf{u}\}$ amongst all complete (resp. p-stable) models of $\mathcal{F}$ (resp. P).

3. Caminada, M., Harikrishnan, S., Sá, S.: Comparing logic programming and formal argumentation; the case of ideal and eager semantics. Argum. Comput. (Preprint), 1–28 (2020)
4. Caminada, M., Sá, S., Alcântara, J., Dvorák, W.: On the difference between assumption-based argumentation and abstract argumentation. IfCoLog J. Logics Appl. **2**, 15–34 (2015). http://www.collegepublications.co.uk/journals/ifcolog/? 00003
5. Caminada, M., Sá, S., Alcântara, J., Dvorák, W.: On the equivalence between logic programming semantics and argumentation semantics. Int. J. Approx. Reason. **58**, 87–111 (2015)
6. Caminada, M., Schulz, C.: On the equivalence between assumption-based argumentation and logic programming. J. Artif. Intell. Res. **60**, 779–825 (2017)
7. Clark, K.L.: Negation as failure. In: Logic and Data Bases, pp. 293–322. Springer, Heidelberg (1978). https://doi.org/10.1007/978-1-4684-3384-5_11
8. Dung, P., Kowalski, R., Toni, F.: Assumption-based argumentation. In: Simari, G., Rahwan, I. (eds.) Argumentation in Artificial Intelligence, pp. 199–218. Springer, US (2009). https://doi.org/10.1007/978-0-387-98197-0_10
9. Eiter, T., Leone, N., Sacca, D.: On the partial semantics for disjunctive deductive databases. Ann. Math. Artif. Intell. **19**(1–2), 59–96 (1997)
10. Lloyd, J.W.: Foundations of Logic Programming; (2nd extended ed.). Springer-Verlag, New York Inc., New York (1987). https://doi.org/10.1007/978-3-642-83189-8
11. Przymusinski, T.: The well-founded semantics coincides with the three-valued stable semantics. Fundamenta Informaticae **13**(4), 445–463 (1990)
12. Przymusinski, T.C.: Stable semantics for disjunctive programs. New Gener. Comput. **9**, 401–424 (1991)
13. Sá, S., Alcântara, J.: Interpretations and models for assumption-based argumentation. In: Proceedings of the 34rd Annual ACM Symposium on Applied Computing. SAC '19, ACM, New York, NY, USA (2019). https://doi.org/10.1145/3297280.329739
14. Schulz, C., Toni, F.: Complete assumption labellings. In: Computational Models of Argument - Proceedings of COMMA 2014, Atholl Palace Hotel, Scottish Highlands, UK, 9–12 September 2014, pp. 405–412 (2014). https://doi.org/10.3233/978-1-61499-436-7-405
15. Toni, F.: A tutorial on assumption-based argumentation. Argum. Comput. **5**(1), 89–117 (2014)
16. Wu, Y., Caminada, M., Gabbay, D.: Complete extensions in argumentation coincide with 3-valued stable models in logic programming. Studia Logica **93**(1–2), 383–403 (2009). Special issue: new ideas in argumentation theory

A Paraconsistent Approach to Deal with Epistemic Inconsistencies in Argumentation

Rafael Silva$^{(\boxtimes)}$ (ID) and João Alcântara (ID)

Department of Computer Science, Federal University of Ceará, Fortaleza, Brazil
{`rafaels,jnando`}`@lia.ufc.br`

Abstract. We introduce in $ASPIC^+$ languages an interrogation mark ? as a plausibility operator to enhance any defeasible conclusion do not have the same status as an irrefutable one. The resulting framework, dubbed $ASPIC^?$, is tailored to make a distinction between strong inconsistencies and weak inconsistencies. The aim is to avoid the former and to tolerate the latter. This means the extensions obtained from the $ASPIC^?$ framework are free of strong conflicts, but tolerant to weak conflicts. As a collateral effect, the application of the *Ex Falso* principle can be prevented in $ASPIC^?$ when the last rule employed in the construction of those arguments with symmetric conflicting conclusions is defeasible. We then show $ASPIC^?$ preserves current results on the satisfaction of consistency and logical closure properties.

Keywords: Argumentation · Paraconsistency · Conflict-tolerance

1 Introduction

As noticed in [1], contradictions can be considered under the mantle of many points of views: as a consequence of the only correct description of a contradictory world, as a temporary state of our knowledge, as the outcome of a particular language which we have chosen to describe the world, as the result of conflicting observational criteria, as the superposition of world-views, or as the result from the best theories available at a given moment. Indeed, in [2], it is argued that inconsistency is a natural companion to defeasible methods of reasoning and that paraconsistency (the property of a logic admitting non-trivial inconsistent theories) should play a role in the formalisation of these methods.

Given that much current work on structured argumentation [3–5] combines strict and defeasible inference rules, unexpected results can arise when two arguments based on defeasible rules have contradictory conclusions. This is particularly critical (see [6]) if the strict inference rules include the *Ex Falso* principle (that an inconsistent set implies anything), because for any formula ϕ,

---

This research was partly financed by FUNCAP.

J. Vejnarová and N. Wilson (Eds.): ECSQARU 2021, LNAI 12897, pp. 187–200, 2021.
https://doi.org/10.1007/978-3-030-86772-0_14

an argument concluding $\neg\phi$ can be constructed from these two arguments. As consequence, any other argument is potentially under threat!

In order to solve this problem for $ASPIC^+$, Wu [7] requires that for each argument the set of conclusions of all its sub-arguments are classically consistent. She shows that this solution works for a restricted version of $ASPIC^+$ without preferences, but gives counterexamples to the consistency postulates for the case with preferences. Another approach was taken in [6] by Grooters and Prakken, in which they replace classical logic as the source for strict rules by the (weaker) paraconsistent logic presented in [8] to invalidate the *Ex Falso* principle as a valid strict inference rule. Then, they also showed under which conditions, this version of $ASPIC^+$ satisfies the consistency and closure postulates of [9].

In this paper, we exploit how to avoid the application of the *Ex Falso* principle in $ASPIC^+$ [4] when those arguments with inconsistent conclusions are based on defeasible rules. In the *Inconsistent Default Logic* [2], they introduced an interrogation mark ? as a plausibility operator to enhance any defeasible conclusion do not have the same status as an irrefutable one, obtained from deduction. Inspired by these ideas, we will impose any defeasible rule will be of the form $\phi_1, \ldots, \phi_n \Rightarrow \phi?$. Our intention is the conclusion of $\phi?$ will not necessarily prevent the conclusion of $\neg\phi?$; it is required an argument with conclusion $\neg\phi$, which can only be constructed from a strict rule, to attack the conclusion $\neg\phi?$ of an argument. Thus, to produce a (let us call) strong conflict between the conclusions of the arguments, at least in one of them, the conclusion should be a ?-free formula obtained via a strict rule.

In our argumentation framework, dubbed $ASPIC^?$, we distinguish between strong inconsistencies as in $\{\phi, \neg\phi\}$ (or $\{\phi?, \neg\phi\}$) from weak inconsistencies as in $\{\phi?, \neg\phi?\}$: the first should be avoided; the second can be tolerated. This means the (weak) conflict between $\phi?$ and $\neg\phi?$ can be accommodated in the same extension. Hence, the extensions in $ASPIC^?$ will be free of strong conflicts, but tolerant to weak conflicts. In addition, as we isolate strong conflicts from the weak ones, we can easily adapt the proofs in [9] to show the rationality postulates described there hold also for $ASPIC^?$.

One could argue why we need to change $ASPIC^+$: can the same objectives be achieved by changing the logical language used in $ASPIC^+$ in a suitable way? Roughly speaking, $ASPIC^?$ is $ASPIC^+$ with the requisite the conclusion of any defeasible rule should be an ?-suffixed formula and the base logic tolerant to weak inconsistencies. Thus a mere change in the base logic is not enough to impose defeasible and irrefutable conclusions should have different epistemic status.

The rest of the paper is organised as follows: in Sect. 2, $ASPIC^?$ framework is presented. Then, we introduce the corresponding argumentation framework with two kinds of attacks (strong and weak) and its semantics. Section 3 is focused on proving the satisfaction of the rationality postulates described in [9]. In the next section, we resort to examples to discuss the role played by ? operator and how it can be employed to avoid unexpected extensions. Finally, we summarise our contributions and themes for future developments.

2   The $ASPIC^?$ Framework

An *Abstract Argumentation Framework AF* [10] is a pair $(\mathcal{A}, \mathcal{D})$ in which $\mathcal{A}$ is a set of arguments and $\mathcal{D} \subseteq \mathcal{A} \times \mathcal{A}$ is a relation of *defeat*. An argument A defeats $\mathcal{B}$ if $(A, B) \in \mathcal{D}$. The $ASPIC^+$ framework [4,11] gives structure to the arguments and defeat relation in an *AF*. In this section, we introduce in $ASPIC^+$ languages an interrogation mark ? as a plausibility operator to enhance defeasible conclusions do not have the same status as those irrefutable. The resulting framework, $ASPIC^?$, is tailored to distinguish strong inconsistencies from weak inconsistencies. The aim is to avoid the former and to tolerate the latter. We start by defining the argumentation systems specified by $ASPIC^?$:

Definition 1 (Argumentation System). *An argumentation system is a tuple* $AS = (\mathcal{L}, ^-, \mathcal{R}, n)$, *in which*

- $\mathcal{L} = \mathcal{L}^* \cup \mathcal{L}^?$ *is a logical language with a unary negation symbol $\neg$ and a unary plausibility symbol ? such that*
  - $\mathcal{L}^*$ *is a ?-free logical language with a unary negation symbol.*
  - $\mathcal{L}^? = \{\phi? \mid \phi \in \mathcal{L}^*\}$.
- $^-$ *is a function from $\mathcal{L}$ to $2^{\mathcal{L}}$, such that*
  - φ *is a contrary of ψ if $\varphi \in \overline{\psi}$, $\psi \notin \overline{\varphi}$;*
  - φ *is a contradictory of ψ (denoted by $\varphi = -\psi$), if $\varphi \in \overline{\psi}$, $\psi \in \overline{\varphi}$;*
- $\mathcal{R} = \mathcal{R}_s \cup \mathcal{R}_d$ *is a set of strict ($\mathcal{R}_s$) and defeasible ($\mathcal{R}_d$) inference rules of the form $\phi_1, \ldots, \phi_n \rightarrow \phi$ and $\phi_1, \ldots, \phi_n \Rightarrow \psi?$ respectively (in which $\phi_1, \ldots, \phi_n, \phi$ are meta-variables ranging over wff in $\mathcal{L}$ and ψ is a meta-variable ranging over wff in $\mathcal{L}^*$), and $\mathcal{R}_s \cap \mathcal{R}_d = \emptyset$.*
- n *is a partial function such that $n : \mathcal{R}_d \longrightarrow \mathcal{L}$.*

For any formula $\phi \in \mathcal{L}^*$, we say $\psi \in -\phi$ if $\psi = \neg\phi$ or $\psi = \neg\phi?$ or $\phi = \neg\psi$ or $(\phi = \neg\gamma$ and $\psi = \gamma?)$; we say $\psi \in -\phi?$ if $\psi = \neg\phi$ or $\phi = \neg\psi$.

Note for any $\phi \in \mathcal{L}^*$, ϕ and $\phi?$ are contradictories of $\neg\phi$; whilst, only ϕ is a contradictory of $\neg\phi?$. This means $\phi?$ is not a contradictory of $\neg\phi?$. A set as $\{\phi, -\phi\}$ (or $\{\phi?, -\phi?\}$) is intended to represent a *strong inconsistency*, and $\{\phi?, \neg\phi?\}$ is intended to represent a weak inconsistency. We will refer to these two kinds of inconsistencies (strong and weak) as epistemic inconsistencies or simply inconsistencies.

It is also required a knowledge base to provide premises for the arguments.

Definition 2 (Knowledge Base). *A knowledge base in an argumentation system $AS = (\mathcal{L}, ^-, \mathcal{R}, n)$ is a set $\mathcal{K} \subseteq \mathcal{L}$ consisting of two disjoint subsets $\mathcal{K}_n$ (the axioms) and $\mathcal{K}_p$ (the ordinary premises).*

Axioms are certain knowledge and cannot be attacked, whilst, ordinary premises are uncertain and can be attacked. Now we can define an argumentation theory:

Definition 3. *An argumentation theory* $(AS, \mathcal{K})$ *is a pair in which* AS *is an argumentation system and* $\mathcal{K}$ *is a knowledge base in* AS.

In $ASPIC^?$, arguments are are constructed recursively from an argumentation theory by the successive application of construction rules:

Definition 4 (Argument). *An argument* A *on the basis of an argumentation theory* $(AS, \mathcal{K})$ *and an argumentation system* $(\mathcal{L},^-, \mathcal{R}, n)$ *is*

1. ϕ *if* $\phi \in \mathcal{K}$ *with* $\mathtt{Prem}(A) = \{\phi\}$, $\mathtt{Conc}(A) = \phi$, $\mathtt{Sub}(A) = \{\phi\}$, $\mathtt{DefR}(A) = \emptyset$, $\mathtt{Rules}(A) = \emptyset$, $\mathtt{TopRule}(A) = undefined$.
2. $A_1, \ldots, A_n \to \psi$ *if* $A_1, \ldots, A_n$ *are arguments s. t. there is a strict rule* $\mathtt{Conc}(A_1), \ldots, \mathtt{Conc}(A_n) \to \psi \in \mathcal{R}_s$; $\mathtt{Prem}(A) = \mathtt{Prem}(A_1) \cup \cdots \cup \mathtt{Prem}(A_n)$; $\mathtt{Conc}(A) = \psi$; $\mathtt{Sub}(A) = \mathtt{Sub}(A_1) \cup \cdots \cup \mathtt{Sub}(A_n) \cup \{A\}$; $\mathtt{Rules}(A) = \mathtt{Rules}(A_1) \cup \cdots \cup \mathtt{Rules}(A_n) \cup \{\mathtt{Conc}(A_1), \ldots, \mathtt{Conc}(A_n) \to \psi\}$; $\mathtt{TopRule}(A) = \mathtt{Conc}(A_1), \ldots, \mathtt{Conc}(A_n) \to \psi$.
3. $A_1, \ldots, A_n \Rightarrow \psi$? *if* $A_1, \ldots, A_n$ *are arguments such that there exists a defeasible rule* $\mathtt{Conc}(A_1), \ldots, \mathtt{Conc}(A_n) \Rightarrow \psi$? $\in \mathcal{R}_d$; $\mathtt{Prem}(A) = \mathtt{Prem}(A_1) \cup \cdots \cup \mathtt{Prem}(A_n)$; $\mathtt{Conc}(A) = \psi$?; $\mathtt{Sub}(A) = \mathtt{Sub}(A_1) \cup \cdots \cup \mathtt{Sub}(A_n) \cup \{A\}$; $\mathtt{Rules}(A) = \mathtt{Rules}(A_1) \cup \cdots \cup \mathtt{Rules}(A_n) \cup \{\mathtt{Conc}(A_1), \ldots, \mathtt{Conc}(A_n) \Rightarrow \psi?\}$; $\mathtt{TopRule}(A) = \mathtt{Conc}(A_1), \ldots, \mathtt{Conc}(A_n) \Rightarrow \psi$.

For any argument A *we define* $\mathtt{Prem}_n(A) = \mathtt{Prem}(A) \cap \mathcal{K}_n$; $\mathtt{Prem}_p(A) = \mathtt{Prem}(A) \cap \mathcal{K}_p$; $\mathtt{DefR}(A) = \{r \in \mathcal{R}_d \mid r \in \mathtt{Rules}(A)\}$ *and* $\mathtt{StR}(A) = \{r \in \mathcal{R}_s \mid r \in \mathtt{Rules}(A)\}$.

Example 1. Consider the argumentation system $AS = (\mathcal{L},^-, \mathcal{R}, n)$, in which

- $\mathcal{L} = \mathcal{L}^* \cup \mathcal{L}^?$ with $\mathcal{L}^* = \{a, b, f, w, \neg a, \neg b, \neg f, \neg w, \sim a, \sim b, \sim f, \sim w, \sim \neg a, \sim \neg b, \sim \neg f, \sim \neg w\}$. The symbols $\neg$ and $\sim$ respectively denote strong and weak negation.
- For any $\phi \in \mathcal{L}^*$ and any $\psi \in \mathcal{L}$, (1) $\phi \in \overline{\psi}$ iff (a) $\psi = \neg\phi$ or $\psi = \neg\phi$? or $\phi = \neg\psi$ or ($\phi = \neg\gamma$ and $\psi = \gamma$?); or (b) $\psi = \sim \phi$ or ($\psi = \sim \phi$?. (2) ϕ? $\in \overline{\psi}$ iff (a) $\psi = \neg\phi$ or $\phi = \neg\psi$; or (b) $\psi = \sim \phi$.
- $\mathcal{R}_s = \{\neg f \to \neg w; b \to a\}$ and $\mathcal{R}_d = \{a \Rightarrow \neg f?; b, \sim \neg w \Rightarrow w?; \neg f? \Rightarrow \neg w?\}$.

Let $\mathcal{K}$ be the knowledge base such that $\mathcal{K}_n = \emptyset$ and $\mathcal{K}_p = \{b, \sim \neg w\}$. The arguments defined on the basis of $\mathcal{K}$ and AS are $A_1 = [b]$, $A_2 = [\sim \neg w]$, $A_3 = [A_1 \to a]$, $A_4 = [A_3 \Rightarrow \neg f?]$, $A_5 = [A_1, A_2 \Rightarrow w?]$ and $A_6 = [A_4 \Rightarrow \neg w?]$.

An argument A is *for* ϕ if $\mathtt{Conc}(A) = \phi$; it is *strict* if $\mathtt{DefR}(A) = \emptyset$; *defeasible* if $\mathtt{DefR}(A) \neq \emptyset$; *firm* if $\mathtt{Prem}(A) \subseteq \mathcal{K}_n$; *plausible* if $\mathtt{Prem}(A) \cap \mathcal{K}_p \neq \emptyset$. An argument is *fallible* if it is defeasible or plausible and *infallible* otherwise. We write $S \vdash \phi$ if there is a strict argument for ϕ with all premises taken from S, and $S \mathrel{\vdash\!\!\!\sim} \phi$ if there is a defeasible argument for ϕ with all premises taken from S.

In the sequel, we introduce the c-consistent (contradictory consistent) sets:

Definition 5 (c-consistency). *A set $S \subseteq \mathcal{L}$ is c-consistent if for no ϕ it is the case that $S \vdash \phi$ and $S \vdash -\phi$. Otherwise S is c-inconsistent. We say $S \subseteq \mathcal{L}$ is minimally c-inconsistent iff S is c-inconsistent and $\forall S' \subset S$, S' is c-consistent. An argument A is c-consistent iff $\mathsf{Prem}(A)$ is c-consistent.*

The notion of c-inconsistency is what we mean by strong inconsistency.

2.1 Attacks and Defeats

In *ASPIC?* arguments are related to each other by attacks (as in *ASPIC*$^+$) and by weak attacks:

Definition 6 (Attacks). *Consider the arguments A and B. We say A attacks B iff A undercuts, undermines and rebuts B, in which*

- *A undercuts B (on B') iff $\mathsf{Conc}(A) \in \overline{n(r)}$ for some $B' \in \mathsf{Sub}(B)$ such that B''s top rule r is defeasible.*
- *A undermines B (on ϕ) iff $\mathsf{Conc}(A) \in \overline{\phi}$ and $\phi \in \mathsf{Prem}_p(B)$. In such a case, A contrary-undermines B iff $\mathsf{Conc}(A)$ is a contrary of ϕ.*
- *A rebuts B (on B') iff $\mathsf{Conc}(A) \in \overline{\phi?}$ for some $B' \in \mathsf{Sub}(B)$ of the form $B''_1, \ldots, B''_n \Rightarrow \phi?$. In such a case, A contrary-rebuts B iff $\mathsf{Conc}(A)$ is a contrary of $\phi?$.*

We say A weakly attacks B iff A weakly undermines or weakly rebuts B, in which

- *A weakly undermines B (on $\phi?$ (resp. $\neg\phi?$)) iff $\mathsf{Conc}(A) = \neg\phi?$ (resp. $\mathsf{Conc}(A) = \phi?$) for an ordinary premise $\phi?$ (resp. $\neg\phi?$) of B.*
- *A weakly rebuts B (on B') iff $\mathsf{Conc}(A) = \neg\phi?$ (resp. $\mathsf{Conc}(A) = \phi?$) for some $B' \in \mathsf{Sub}(B)$ of the form $B''_1, \ldots, B''_n \Rightarrow \phi?$ (resp. $B''_1, \ldots, B''_n \Rightarrow \neg\phi?$).*

Example 2. Recalling Example 1, we have A_5 weakly rebuts A_6 and A_6 weakly rebuts A_5. Besides, A_6 contrary-undermines A_2 and A_5 on $\sim \neg w$. If in addition, one had the argument $A_7 = [A_4 \rightarrow \neg w?]$, then A_7 (like A_6) would weakly rebut A_5 on A_5; however, A_7 (unlike A_6) would not be weakly rebutted by A_5.

Definition 7. *A (c-)structured argumentation framework ((c-)SAF) defined by an argumentation theory AT is a tuple $\langle \mathcal{A}, \mathcal{C}, \mathcal{C}', \preceq \rangle$, in which*

- *In a SAF (resp. c-SAF), $\mathcal{A}$ is the set of all arguments (resp. c-consistent arguments) constructed from $\mathcal{K}$ in ASPIC$^+$ satisfying Definition 4;*
- *$(X, Y) \in \mathcal{C}$ iff X attacks Y and $(X, Y) \in \mathcal{C}'$ iff X weakly attacks Y;*
- *$\preceq$ is a preference ordering on $\mathcal{A}$.*

It is clear a *c-SAF* is a *SAF* in which all arguments are required to have a c-consistent set of premises. Next, we define the corresponding defeat relation:

Definition 8 (Defeat). *Let $A, B \in \mathcal{A}$ and A attacks B. If A undercut, contrary-rebut or contrary-undermine attacks B on B' then A is said to preference-independent attack B on B'; otherwise A is said to preference-dependent attack B on B'. A defeats B iff for some B' either A preference-independent attacks B on B' or A preference-dependent attacks B on B' and $A \not\prec B'$.*

2.2   Abstract Argumentation Frameworks with Two Kinds of Defeats

As $(c\text{-})SAF$s have two kinds of attacks, the associated abstract argumentation frameworks have to couple not only with attacks, but also with weak attacks.

Definition 9 (Argumentation frameworks with two kinds of attacks). *An abstract argumentation framework with two kinds of attacks (AF_2) corresponding to a c-SAF $= \langle \mathcal{A}, \mathcal{C}, \mathcal{C}', \preceq \rangle$ is a tuple $(\mathcal{A}, \mathcal{D}, \mathcal{D}')$ such that $\mathcal{D} = \{(X, Y) \in \mathcal{C} \mid X \text{ defeats } Y\}$ and $\mathcal{D}' = \{(X, Y) \in \mathcal{C}' \mid X \not\prec Y\}$.*

Example 3 (Example 2 continued). Let $\preceq = \{(A_6, A_2)\}$ (i.e., $A_6 \prec A_2$) be a preference ordering on $\mathcal{A} = \{A_1, A_2, A_3, A_4, A_5, A_6\}$. In the c-SAF $(\mathcal{A}, \mathcal{C}, \mathcal{C}', \preceq)$ defined by AT, we have $\mathcal{C} = \{(A_6, A_2)\}$ and $\mathcal{C}' = \{(A_5, A_6), (A_6, A_5)\}$. As (A_6, A_2) is a preference independent attack, we obtain $\mathcal{D} = \mathcal{C}$ and $\mathcal{D}' = \mathcal{C}'$.

Traditional approaches to argumentation semantics ensure conflicting are not tolerated in the same set, which is said to be conflict free. In $ASPIC^?$, the aim is to avoid strong conflicts, which are carried over by the defeat relation $\mathcal{D}$, and to tolerate weak conflicts, which are carried over by the relation $\mathcal{D}'$.

Definition 10 (Compatible sets). *Let $(\mathcal{A}, \mathcal{D}, \mathcal{D}')$ be an AF_2 and $S \subseteq \mathcal{A}$. A set S is compatible if $\forall A \in S$, there is no $B \in S$ such that $(B, A) \in \mathcal{D}$.*

Compatible sets do not contain the arguments A and B if A attacks B (or vice versa); however they can accommodate weak attacks between their members. This means in Example 3, the set $\{A_5, A_6\}$ is compatible, but $\{A_2, A_6\}$ is not. Now we are entitled to do extend AF semantics to deal with compatible sets:

Definition 11 (Semantics). *Let $(\mathcal{A}, \mathcal{D}, \mathcal{D}')$ be an AF_2 and $S \subseteq \mathcal{A}$ be a compatible set of arguments. Then $X \in \mathcal{A}$ is acceptable with respect to S iff*

- *$\forall Y \in \mathcal{A}$ such that $(Y, X) \in \mathcal{D} : \exists Z \in S$ such that $(Z, Y) \in \mathcal{D}$ and*
- *$\forall Y \in \mathcal{A}$ such that $(Y, X) \in \mathcal{D}' : \exists Z \in S$ such that $(Z, Y) \in \mathcal{D} \cup \mathcal{D}'$.*

1) S is an admissible set iff S is compatible and $X \in S$ implies X is acceptable w.r.t. S; 2) S is a complete extension iff S is admissible and if $X \in \mathcal{A}$ is acceptable w.r.t. S then $X \in S$; 3) S is a preferred extension iff it is a set inclusion maximal complete extension; 4) S is the grounded extension iff it is the set inclusion minimal complete extension; 5) S is a stable extension iff S is complete extension and $\forall Y \notin S$, $\exists X \in S$ s.t. $(X, Y) \in \mathcal{D} \cup \mathcal{D}'$. 6) S is a semi-stable extension iff it is a complete extension such that there is no complete extension S_1 such that $S \cup S^+ \subset S_1 \cup S_1^+$.

Notice for an argument X to be acceptable w.r.t. S, if $(Y, X) \in \mathcal{D}$, there should exist an argument $Z \in S$ such that $(Z, Y) \in \mathcal{D}$, i.e., a weak defeat as $(Z, Y) \in \mathcal{D}'$ is not robust enough to defend a defeat as $(Y, X) \in \mathcal{D}$. Otherwise, X defends a weak defeat $(Y, X) \in \mathcal{D}'$ if $\exists Z \in S$ such that Z (weak) defeats Y.

Example 4 (Example 3 continued).
Regarding the AF_2 constructed in Example 3, we obtain the following results:

- Complete Extensions: $\{A_1, A_3, A_4\}$, $\{A_1, A_3, A_4, A_5\}$, $\{A_1, A_3, A_4, A_6\}$, $\{A_1, A_3, A_4, A_5, A_6\}$;
- Grounded Extension: $\{A_1, A_3, A_4\}$;
- Preferred Extension: $\{A_1, A_3, A_4, A_5, A_6\}$
- Stable/Semi-stable Extensions: $\{A_1, A_3, A_4, A_6\}$, $\{A_1, A_3, A_4, A_5, A_6\}$

3   Rationality Postulates

Caminada and Amgoud [9] proposed four postulates to constraint on any extension of an argumentation framework corresponding to an argumentation theory. It is shown in [4,11] under which conditions these postulates hold in $ASPIC^+$. In the sequel, we show $ASPIC^?$ under the same conditions also satisfies all of them in Theorems 1,2, 3 and 4. Before let us characterise some notions:

Definition 12. *Consider the argumention system* $(\mathcal{L}, ^-, \mathcal{R}, n)$. *For any* $S \subseteq \mathcal{L}$, *let the closure of* S *under strict rules, denoted* $Cl_{R_s}(S)$, *be the smallest set containing* S *and the consequent of any strict rule in* $\mathcal{R}_s$ *whose antecedents are in* $Cl_{R_s}(S)$. *Then, 1) a set* $S \subseteq \mathcal{L}$ *is directly consistent iff* $\nexists \psi, \varphi \in S$ *such that* $\psi \in \overline{\varphi}$; *2) indirectly consistent iff* $Cl_{R_s}(S)$ *is directly consistent.*

We proceed by constraining our attention to well defined $(c$-$)SAF$s:

Definition 13 (Well defined c-SAF). *Let* $AT = (AS, \mathcal{K})$ *be an argumentation theory, where* $AS = (\mathcal{L}, ^-, \mathcal{R}, n)$. *We say that* AT *is*

- *closed under contraposition iff for all* $S \subseteq \mathcal{L}$, $s \in S$ *and* ϕ, *if* $S \vdash \phi$, *then* $S \backslash \{s\} \cup \{-\phi\} \vdash -s$.
- *closed under transposition iff if* $\phi_1, \ldots, \phi_n \rightarrow \psi \in \mathcal{R}_s$, *then for* $i = 1 \ldots n$, $\phi_1, \ldots, \phi_{i-1}, -\psi, \phi_{i+1}, \ldots, \phi_n \rightarrow -\phi_i \in \mathcal{R}_s$;
- *axiom consistent iff* $Cl_{R_s}(\mathcal{K}_n)$ *is consistent.*
- *c-classical iff for any minimal c-inconsistent* $S \subseteq \mathcal{L}$ *and for any* $\varphi \in S$, *it holds that* $S \backslash \{\varphi\} \vdash -\varphi$ *(i.e., amongst all arguments defined there exists a strict argument with conclusion* $-\varphi$ *with all premises taken from* $S \backslash \{\varphi\}$).
- *well formed if whenever* φ *is a contrary of* ψ *then* $\psi \notin \mathcal{K}_n$ *and* ψ *is not the consequent of a strict rule.*

A c-SAF is well defined if it is defined by an AT that is c-classical, axiom consistent, well formed and closed under contraposition or closed under transposition. A SAF is well defined if it is defined by an AT that is axiom consistent, well formed and closed under contraposition or closed under transposition.

To prove our results, we resort to the maximal fallible sub-arguments of B:

Definition 14. *The set* $M(B)$ *of the maximal fallible sub-arguments of* B *is defined such that for any* $B' \in \mathbf{Sub}(B)$, $B' \in M(B)$ *iff:*

1. B''s top rule is defeasible or B' is an ordinary premise, and;
2. there is no $B'' \in Sub(B)$ s.t. $B'' \neq B$ and $B' \in Sub(B'')$, and B'' satisfies 1.

The maximal fallible sub-arguments of B are those with the 'last' defeasible inferences in B or else (if B is strict) they are B's ordinary premises. We also refer to an argument as a strict continuation of a set S of arguments if it is obtainable by extending S only with strict rules:

Definition 15 (Strict continuations of arguments). *For any set of arguments $S = \{A_1, \ldots, A_n\}$, the argument A is a strict continuation of S iff*

- $\text{Prem}_p(A) = \bigcup_{i=1}^n \text{Prem}_p(A_i)$;
- $\text{DefR}(A) = \bigcup_{i=1}^n \text{DefR}(A_i)$;
- $\text{StR}(A) \supseteq \bigcup_{i=1}^n \text{StR}(A_i)$ *and* $\text{Prem}_n(A) \supseteq \bigcup_{i=1}^n \text{Prem}_n(A_i)$.

In addition, $\preceq$ should satisfy properties that one might expect to hold of orderings over arguments composed from fallible and infallible elements.

Definition 16 (Reasonable Argument Ordering). *An argument ordering $\preceq$ is reasonable iff*

1. (a) $\forall A, B$, if A is strict and firm and B is plausible or defeasible, then $B \prec A$;
   (b) $\forall A, B$, if B is strict and firm then $B \not\prec A$;
   (c) $\forall A, A', B$ such that A' is a strict continuation of $\{A\}$, if $A \not\prec B$ then $A' \not\prec B$, and if $B \not\prec A$ then $B \not\prec A'$.
2. Let $\{C_1, \ldots, C_n\}$ be a finite subset of $\mathcal{A}$, and for $i = 1 \ldots n$, let $C^{+\backslash i}$ be some strict continuation of $\{C_1, \ldots, C_{i-1}, C_{i+1}, \ldots, C_n\}$. Then it is not the case that: $\forall i, C^{+\backslash i} \prec C_i$.

From now on we will assume any $(c\text{-})SAF$ $(\mathcal{A}, \mathcal{C}, \mathcal{C}', \preceq)$ is well defined and $\preceq$ is reasonable to prove $ASPIC^?$ satisfies the postulates of [9]. For space restrictions, the simplest proofs of some intermediary results have been omitted.

Proposition 1. *Let $(\mathcal{A}, \mathcal{C}, \mathcal{C}', \preceq)$ be a $(c\text{-})SAF$ and $(\mathcal{A}, \mathcal{D}, \mathcal{D}')$ be the corresponding AF_2, A and B are in $\mathcal{A}$ such that A and B have contradictory conclusions, B is plausible or defeasible with a strict top rule, and assume $\text{Prem}(A) \cup \text{Prem}(B)$ is c-consistent if A and B are defined as in Definition 5. Then*

1. For all $B' \in M(B)$, there exists a strict continuation $A_{B'}^+$ of $(M(B) \backslash \{B'\}) \cup M(A)$ such that $A_{B'}^+$ rebuts or undermines B on B'.
2. If $B \prec A$, and $\preceq$ is reasonable, then for some $B' \in M(B)$, $(A_{B'}^+, B) \in \mathcal{D}$.

The following lemma provide us with some intermediary results required to show that our approach satisfies the rationality postulates of [9]:

Lemma 1. *Let $(\mathcal{A}, \mathcal{D}, \mathcal{D}')$ be a AF_2 and $A \in \mathcal{A}$.*

1. If A is acceptable w.r.t. $S \subseteq \mathcal{A}$ then A is acceptable w.r.t. any superset of S.

2. If $(A, B) \in \mathcal{D}$, then $(A, B') \in \mathcal{D}$ for some $B' \in \text{Sub}(B)$, and if $(A, B') \in \mathcal{D}$, $B' \in \text{Sub}(B)$, then $(A, B) \in \mathcal{D}$.

3. If $(A, B) \in \mathcal{D}'$, then $(A, B') \in \mathcal{D}'$ for some $B' \in \text{Sub}(B)$, and if $(A, B') \in \mathcal{D}'$, $B' \in \text{Sub}(B)$, then $(A, B) \in \mathcal{D}'$.

4. If A is acceptable w.r.t. $S \subseteq \mathcal{A}$, $A' \in \text{Sub}(A)$, then A' is acceptable w.r.t. S.

The next result comes from the fact that if B defeats a strict continuation A of $\{A_1, \ldots, A_n\}$, then B defeats A on some $A_i \in \{A_1, \ldots, A_n\}$. This lemma is employed to prove Theorem 2 and Lemma 4.

Lemma 2. *Let $(\mathcal{A}, \mathcal{D}, \mathcal{D}')$ be a AF_2 corresponding to a $(c\text{-})SAF$ $(\mathcal{A}, \mathcal{C}, \mathcal{C}', \preceq)$. Let $A \in \mathcal{A}$ be a strict continuation of $\{A_1, \ldots, A_n\} \subseteq \mathcal{A}$, and for $i = 1 \ldots n$, A_i is acceptable w.r.t. $E \subseteq \mathcal{A}$. Then A is acceptable w.r.t. E.*

The next lemma is employed to prove Proposition 3.

Lemma 3. *Let A be acceptable w.r.t. an admissible extension $S \subseteq \mathcal{A}$ of an AF_2 $(\mathcal{A}, \mathcal{D}, \mathcal{D}')$ corresponding to a $(c\text{-})SAF$ $(\mathcal{A}, \mathcal{C}, \mathcal{C}', \preceq)$. Then $\forall B \in S \cup \{A\}$, neither $(A, B) \in \mathcal{D}$ nor $(B, A) \in \mathcal{D}$.*

For the following proposition, recall that by assumption, any $c\text{-}SAF$ is well defined and so satisfies c-classicality (Definition 13).

Proposition 2. *Let $\mathfrak{C} = (\mathcal{A}, \mathcal{C}, \mathcal{C}', \preceq)$ be a $c\text{-}SAF$. If $A_1, \ldots, A_n$ are acceptable w.r.t. some compatible $E \subseteq \mathcal{A}$, then $\bigcup_{i=1}^n \text{Prem}(A_i)$ is c-consistent.*

The next proposition shows that if an argument A is acceptable w.r.t. to an set S of arguments, then $S \cup \{A\}$ is compatible.

Proposition 3. *Let $A \in \mathcal{A}$ be acceptable w.r.t. an admissible extension S of an AF_2 $(\mathcal{A}, \mathcal{D}, \mathcal{D}')$ corresponding to a well defined $(c\text{-})SAF$ $(\mathcal{A}, \mathcal{C}, \mathcal{C}', \preceq)$. Then, $S' = S \cup \{A\}$ is compatible.*

Theorems 1, 2, 3, and 4 show $ASPIC^?$ satisfies the postulates of [9]:

Theorem 1 (Sub-argument closure). *Let $\triangle = (\mathcal{A}, \mathcal{C}, \mathcal{C}, \preceq)$ be a $(c\text{-})SAF$ and E a complete extension of $\triangle$. Then $\forall A \in E$: if $A' \in \text{Sub}(A)$ then $A' \in E$.*

Proof. According to Lemma 1 (item 3), A' is acceptable w.r.t. E, and $E \cup \{A'\}$ is compatible (Proposition 3). As E is a complete extension, $A' \in E$.

Theorem 2 (Closure under strict rules). *Let $\triangle = (\mathcal{A}, \mathcal{C}, \mathcal{C}', \preceq)$ be a $(c\text{-})SAF$ and E a complete extension of $\triangle$. Then $\{\text{Conc}(A) \mid A \in E\} = Cl_{\mathcal{R}_s}(\{\text{Conc}(A) \mid A \in E\})$.*

Proof. We will show for any strict continuation X of $\{A \mid A \in E\}$, $X \in E$. Any such X is acceptable with relation to E (Lemma 2), and $E \cup \{X\}$ is compatible (Proposition 3). Then $X \in E$ as E is a complete extension. If $\triangle$ is a $c\text{-}SAF$, Proposition 2 guarantees $\text{Prem}(X)$ is c-consistent.

The following lemma is employed to prove Theorem 3.

Lemma 4. *Let* $\triangle = (\mathcal{A}, \mathcal{C}, \mathcal{C}', \preceq)$ *be a* (c-)*SAF*, E *an admissible extension of* $\triangle$, *and* $\exists Y \in E$ *such that* Y *is defeasible or plausible and has a strict top rule. Then* $\forall X \in E$, *it holds* $\texttt{Conc}(X) \notin \overline{\texttt{Conc}(Y)}$.

Proof. By absurd, suppose $\exists X \in E$ s.t. $\texttt{Conc}(X) \in \overline{\texttt{Conc}(Y)}$. Given Y is defeasible or plausible and has a strict top rule, by the *well-formed* assumption $\texttt{Conc}(X)$ and $\texttt{Conc}(Y)$ must be contradictory. If $\triangle$ is a *c-SAF*, and $X, Y \in E$, X, Y are acceptable w.r.t. E, and so $\texttt{Prem}(A) \cup \texttt{Prem}(B)$ is c-consistent (Proposition 2). Now, we consider two cases: 1) If $Y \not\prec X$, then $(Y, X) \in \mathcal{D}$: an absurd as E is compatible. 2) If $Y \prec X$, then from Proposition 1 (item 1) for all $Y' \in M(Y)$, there is a strict continuation $X_{Y'}^+$ of $M(Y) \backslash \{Y'\} \cup M(X)$ s.t. $(X_{Y'}^+, Y) \in \mathcal{C}$, and from Proposition 1 (item 2) $(X_{Y'}^+, Y) \in \mathcal{D}$. By Lemma 2 $X_{Y'}^+$ is acceptable w.r.t. E, and by Proposition 3, $E \cup \{X_{Y'}^+\}$ is compatible, contradicting $(X_{Y'}^+, Y) \in \mathcal{D}$.

Theorem 3 (Direct consistency). *Let* $\triangle = (\mathcal{A}, \mathcal{C}, \mathcal{C}', \preceq)$ *be a* (c-)*SAF and* E *an admissible extension of* $\triangle$. *Then* $\{\texttt{Conc}(A) \mid A \in E\}$ *is consistent.*

Proof. Suppose by absurd $A, B \in E$, and $\texttt{Conc}(A) \in \overline{\texttt{Conc}(B)}$ (i.e., E is inconsistent (Definition 12)).

- If A is firm and strict, and 1) B is strict and firm. It is an absurd as it contradicts the assumption of axiom consistency (Definition 13). 2) B is plausible or defeasible, and B is an ordinary premise or has a defeasible top rule. We have $(A, B) \in \mathcal{D}$, which is an absurd since E is compatible. Note B cannot have a strict top rule according to Lemma 4.
- A is plausible or defeasible, and
  - B is strict and firm. Under the well-formed assumption (Definition 13) $\texttt{Conc}(A)$ cannot be a contrary of $\texttt{Conc}(B)$. Thus, $\texttt{Conc}(A)$ and $\texttt{Conc}(B)$ are a contradictory of each other, and A is an ordinary premise or has a defeasible top rule; in both cases $(B, A) \in \mathcal{D}$, contradicting E is compatible. By Lemma 4, A cannot have a strict top rule.
  - if B is plausible or defeasible and B is an ordinary premise or has a defeasible top rule. Then $(A, B) \in \mathcal{D}$ if $\texttt{Conc}(A)$ is the contrary of $\texttt{Conc}(B)$; otherwise, $\texttt{Conc}(A)$ and $\texttt{Conc}(B)$ are contradictory and as consequence, $(A, B) \in \mathcal{D}$ or $(B, A) \in \mathcal{D}$. In both cases, it is an absurd as E is compatible. Again by Lemma 4, B cannot have a strict top rule.

Theorem 4 (Indirect consistency). *Let* $\triangle = (\mathcal{A}, \mathcal{C}, \preceq)$ *be a* (c-)*SAF and* E *an complete extension of* $\triangle$. *Then* $Cl_{R_S}(\{\texttt{Conc}(A) \mid A \in E\})$ *is consistent.*

Proof. It follows from Theorems 2 and 3.

4 Related Work and Discussion

Over the years, diverse proposals have been presented to handle paraconsistent argumentation or conflict-tolerant semantics [6,12–19]. In [12,13], Arieli extended both the extension-based labelling-based approaches to admit conflict-tolerant semantics. In particular, he resorted to a four-valued labelling: in, out, both, and none. As usual, an argument is labelled in/out if it is acceptable/unacceptable. An argument A is labelled both when there exists both supportive and opposing evidence A, and A is labelled none when there is not enough evidence supporting or against A. In [14–16], Arieli proposed the sequent based argumentation framework to accommodate different types of languages, including paraconsistent logics. In [17,18], Ben-Nain and Amgoud defended ranking semantics for paraconsistent argumentation, in which arguments are ranked from the most to the less acceptable according to the number of attacks to them.

In this paper, we contribute to the debate by showing that not all conflicts have the same nature. In $ASPIC^?$, we introduced the plausibility operator ? to distinguish strong inconsistencies from those weak. Whereas the resulting extensions are free of strong conflicts, they are tolerant to weak conflicts. We illustrate the rationale behind it in the example below:

Example 5. The following example is adapted from [20]: let AS be the argumentation system of Example 1, in which $a = $ "*it is an animal*", $b = $ "*it is a bird*", $f = $ "*it flies*" and $w = $ "*it has wings*". The rules of $\mathcal{R}_d$ are "if it is an animal and assuming that it is not winged, then it normally cannot fly"; and "if it is a bird, then it normally has wings" ($\mathcal{R}_d = \{a, \sim f?, \sim w \Rightarrow \neg f?; b, \sim \neg w? \Rightarrow w?\}$). Recall $\mathcal{R}_s$ is constituted by the rules "if it is a bird, then it is an animal" and "if it does not fly, then it has not wings", i.e., $\mathcal{R}_s = \{b \rightarrow a; \neg f \rightarrow \neg w\}$.

The knowledge base $\mathcal{K}$ is given by $\mathcal{K}_n = \emptyset$ and $\mathcal{K}_p = \{b, \sim f?, \sim w, \sim \neg w?\}$. The resulting arguments are $A_1 = [b]$, $A_2 = [\sim f?]$, $A_3 = [\sim w]$, $A_4 = [\sim \neg w?]$, $A_5 = [A_1 \rightarrow a]$, $A_6 = [A_5, A_2, A_3 \Rightarrow \neg f?]$ and $A_7 = [A_1, A_4 \Rightarrow w?]$. We know A_7 preference-independent attacks both A_6 and A_3, and they are the only available attacks. Thus in the corresponding $AF_2 = (\{A_1, \ldots, A_7\}, \mathcal{D}, \mathcal{D}')$, we have $\mathcal{D} = \{(A_7, A_6), (A_7, A_3)\}$ and $\mathcal{D}' = \emptyset$. Its unique complete extension is $\{A_1, A_2, A_4, A_5, A_7\}$, and from A_7, we conclude it is plausible it has wings.

In the defeasible rule $a, \sim f?, \sim w \Rightarrow \neg f?$, note the idea of *normal/usual* is enhanced by $\sim f?$. This means an argument whose conclusion is f is demanded to attack it. By its turn, the exception of this rule is expressed by $\sim w$. Thus an argument with a less demanding attack (one with a plausible conclusion $w?$) suffices. In contradistinction, owing to the defeasible rule $b, \sim \neg w? \Rightarrow w?$, in order to preference-independent attack an argument for $w?$ (A_7), we have to construct an argument for $\neg w$. This is not possible here, because an argument for $\neg f?$ (A_6) is not robust enough to construct an argument for $\neg w$.

Motivated by [20], one can argue any complete extension in which it is an animal, but a wingless bird and unable to fly is anomalous. Furthermore, if the defeasible rules were as in $ASPIC^+$ [4] ($\mathcal{R}_d = \{a, \sim f, \sim w \Rightarrow \neg f; b, \sim \neg w \Rightarrow w\}$) and $\mathcal{K}_p = \{b, \sim f, \sim w, \sim \neg w\}$; instead of A_2, A_4, A_6 and A_7, we would have respectively $A_2' = [\sim f]$, $A_4' = [\sim \neg w]$, $A_6' = [A_5, A_2', A_3 \Rightarrow \neg f]$ and $A_7' = [A_1, A_4' \Rightarrow w]$. We would also have $A_8' = [A_6' \rightarrow \neg w]$ and $AF = (\{A_1, A_2', A_3, A_4', A_5, A_6', A_7', A_8'\}, \mathcal{D})$ with $\mathcal{D} = \{(A_7', A_8'), (A_7', A_6'), (A_7', A_3), (A_8', A_7'), (A_8', A_4')\}$. Its complete extensions are $\{A_1, A_2', A_5\}$, $\{A_1, A_2', A_4', A_5, A_7'\}$ and the anomalous $\{A_1, A_2', A_3, A_5, A_6', A_8'\}$, in which it is an animal (A_5), but a wingless bird (A_8') and unable to fly (A_6'). Note one can remove extraneous elements from the example and include a preference relation over the arguments to avoid this unintended extension. Our point here, however, is our proposal is more informative and flexible to deal with these subtleties inherent to knowledge representation.

In [6,19], Grooters and Prakken approached the trivialisation problem in $ASPIC^+$ in the presence of inconsistent conclusions. We illustrate this problem with the following example in $ASPIC^+$:

Example 6 [6]. Let $\mathcal{R}_d = \{p \Rightarrow q; r \Rightarrow \neg q; t \Rightarrow s\}$, $\mathcal{K}_p = \emptyset$ and $\mathcal{K}_n = \{p, r, t\}$, while $\mathcal{R}_s$ consists of all propositionally valid inferences. The corresponding AF includes the arguments $A_1 = [p]$, $A_2 = [A_1 \Rightarrow q]$, $B_1 = [r]$, $B_2 = [B_1 \Rightarrow \neg q]$, $C = [A_2, B_2 \rightarrow \neg s]$, $D_1 = [t]$ and $D_2 = [D_1 \Rightarrow s]$. We have C defeats D_2 if $C \not\preceq D_2$. This is problematic as s can be any formula. Hence, any defeasible argument unrelated to A_2 or B_2 can, depending on $\preceq$, be defeated by C owing to the explosiveness of classical logic as the source for $\mathcal{R}_s$. In [6,19], to solve such a problem, classical logic was replaced by the paraconsistent logic W [8].

In $ASPIC^?$, we circumvent this problem by preventing the defeasible rules of producing strong inconsistencies as their conclusions are all ?-suffixed. Thus, $\mathcal{R}_d$ above would be $\{p \Rightarrow q?; r \Rightarrow \neg q?; t \Rightarrow s?\}$ in $ASPIC^?$. Let $\mathcal{R}_s$ be the set of all propositionally valid inferences of a monotonic paraconsistent logic as LEI [2], which do not have an explosive behaviour for weak inconsistencies. Then, the problematic argument C is no more obtained and D_2 is no more defeated.

5   Conclusion and Future Works

Inconsistency may be present in knowledge bases for many reasons, some of which are evolving information, and merging information from multiple sources. In the literature, argumentation is frequently referred to as a natural approach to dealing with inconsistency. In this work, we presented $ASPIC^?$ by introducing in $ASPIC^+$ [4] languages an interrogation mark ? as an operator to enhance any defeasible conclusion do not have the same status than an irrefutable one.

As in [2], we make a distinction between the strong contradiction as in $\{\phi, \neg\phi\}$ (or $\{\phi?, \neg\phi\}$) and the weak contradiction as in $\{\phi?, \neg\phi?\}$. We avoid the former and tolerate the latter. This means the extensions generated from the $ASPIC^?$ framework will be strong conflict-free, but weak conflict-tolerant. In the sequel, we also showed the rationality postulates described in [9] hold also for $ASPIC^?$.

Future developments encompass to investigate which monotonic paraconsistent logics can be employed as source of strict rules to prevent trivialisation in $ASPIC^?$ when two defeasible arguments with inconsistent conclusions are available while preserving the rationality postulates of [9]. Another venture is to explore how $ASPIC^?$ improves computational models of arguments to distinguish strong inconsistencies from those weak, and in which applications $ASPIC^?$ may enable some improvements when compared to other approaches such as $ASPIC^+$. We also intend to study the relation between $ASPIC^?$ and the works presented in [21–23].

References

1. Carnielli, W., Marcos, J.: A taxonomy of c-systems. In: Paraconsistency, pp. 24–117. CRC Press, Boca Raton (2002)
2. Pequeno, T., Buchsbaum, A.: The logic of epistemic inconsistency. In: Proceedings of the Second International Conference on Principles of Knowledge Representation and Reasoning, pp. 453–460 (1991)
3. Gorogiannis, N., Hunter, A.: Instantiating abstract argumentation with classical logic arguments: postulates and properties. Artif. Intell. **175**(9–10), 1479–1497 (2011)
4. Modgil, S., Prakken, H.: A general account of argumentation with preferences. Artif. Intell. **195**, 361–397 (2013)
5. Caminada, M., Modgil, S., Oren, N.: Preferences and unrestricted rebut. Computational Models of Argument (2014)
6. Grooters, D., Prakken, H.: Combining paraconsistent logic with argumentation. In COMMA, pp. 301–312 (2014)
7. Wu, Y.: Between argument and conclusion-argument-based approaches to discussion, inference and uncertainty. PhD thesis, University of Luxembourg (2012)
8. Rescher, N., Manor, R.: On inference from inconsistent premisses. Theory Decis. **1**(2), 179–217 (1970)
9. Caminada, M., Amgoud, L.: On the evaluation of argumentation formalisms. Artif. Intell. **171**(5–6), 286–310 (2007)
10. Dung, P.: On the acceptability of arguments and its fundamental role in nonmonotonic reasoning, logic programming and n-person games. Artif. Intell. **77**(2), 321–357 (1995)
11. Prakken, H.: An abstract framework for argumentation with structured arguments. Argum. Comput. **1**(2), 93–124 (2010)
12. Arieli, O.: Conflict-tolerant semantics for argumentation frameworks. In: del Cerro, L.F., Herzig, A., Mengin, J. (eds.) JELIA 2012. LNCS (LNAI), vol. 7519, pp. 28–40. Springer, Heidelberg (2012). https://doi.org/10.1007/978-3-642-33353-8_3
13. Arieli, O.: Conflict-free and conflict-tolerant semantics for constrained argumentation frameworks. J. Appl. Logic **13**(4), 582–604 (2015)
14. Arieli, O., Straßer, C.: Sequent-based logical argumentation. Argum. Comput. **6**(1), 73–99 (2015)
15. Arieli, O., Straßer, C.: Logical argumentation by dynamic proof systems. Theor. Comput. Sci. **781**, 63–91 (2019)
16. Borg, A., Straßer, C., Arieli, O.: A generalized proof-theoretic approach to logical argumentation based on hypersequents. Studia Logica **109**(1), 167–238 (2021)
17. Amgoud, L., Ben-Naim, J.: Ranking-based semantics for argumentation frameworks. In: Liu, W., Subrahmanian, V.S., Wijsen, J. (eds.) SUM 2013. LNCS (LNAI), vol. 8078, pp. 134–147. Springer, Heidelberg (2013). https://doi.org/10.1007/978-3-642-40381-1_11

18. Ben-Naim, J.: Argumentation-based paraconsistent logics. In: Hernandez, N., Jäschke, R., Croitoru, M. (eds.) ICCS 2014. LNCS (LNAI), vol. 8577, pp. 19–24. Springer, Cham (2014). https://doi.org/10.1007/978-3-319-08389-6_2
19. Grooters, D., Prakken, H.: Two aspects of relevance in structured argumentation: minimality and paraconsistency. J. Artif. Intell. Res. **56**, 197–245 (2016)
20. Morris, P.H.: The anomalous extension problem in default reasoning. Artif. Intell. **35**(3), 383–399 (1988)
21. Dung, P., Thang, P., Son, T.C.: On structured argumentation with conditional preferences. In: Proceedings of the AAAI Conference on Artificial Intelligence, vol. 33, pp. 2792–2800 (2019)
22. Dung, P., Thang, P.: Fundamental properties of attack relations in structured argumentation with priorities. Artif. Intell. **255**, 1–42 (2018)
23. Dung, P.: An axiomatic analysis of structured argumentation with priorities. Artif. Intell. **231**, 107–150 (2016)

Gradual Semantics for Weighted Bipolar SETAFs

Bruno Yun[1] and Srdjan Vesic[2(✉)]

[1] University of Aberdeen, Aberdeen, Scotland
bruno.yun@abdn.ac.uk
[2] CNRS, Univ. Artois, CRIL – Centre de Recherche en Informatique de Lens,
62300 Lens, France
vesic@cril.fr

Abstract. Gradual semantics are now well-studied in the computational argumentation literature. In this paper, we argue that gradual semantics that can handle both bipolarity (e.g. attacks and supports) and sets of attacking arguments (i.e. several arguments together attacking an argument) might be useful in some contexts. We define the formal framework and properties for such semantics. We proceed by adapting, studying and implementing three well-known semantics from the bipolar gradual literature to this new framework.

Keywords: Argumentation · Gradual semantics

1 Introduction

Recently, gradual argumentation semantics have drawn the attention of many scholars [1,2,6,8,11,14,16,17]. Some of the existing approaches for gradual semantics allow for *intrinsic weights* of arguments [2], some for *intrinsic weights* of attacks [4], some for *sets of attacking arguments* [22], and some for *bipolarity*, i.e. two types of interactions between argument are allowed: attacks and supports [1,3,7,17]. One might need all of those features (weights on arguments and attacks, bipolarity and sets of attacking/supporting arguments) to model some situations in an intuitive manner, as illustrated by Fig. 1, which is inspired from the example by Prakken [18]. We do not claim that our example cannot be modelled by simpler frameworks, but we believe that our framework allows to represent it in a natural way.

First, the intrinsic weights of the arguments might represent the confidence level of the source or the plausibility of the argument. For instance, the argument "hot" might have a greater intrinsic weight if the outside temperature is 40° Celsius than if the outside temperature is 30°.

Srdjan Vesic was supported by "Responsible AI" ANR Chair in Artificial Intelligence, https://ia-responsable.eu/.

J. Vejnarová and N. Wilson (Eds.): ECSQARU 2021, LNAI 12897, pp. 201–214, 2021.
https://doi.org/10.1007/978-3-030-86772-0_15

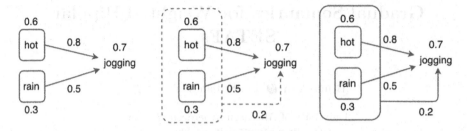

Fig. 1. Representation of the jogging example. The solid red lines represent sets of attacking arguments whereas the dashed lines represent sets of supporting arguments. (Color figure online)

Second, the intrinsic weights on attacks represent how much arguments attack another argument. For instance, hot weather may be a good reason for cancelling a jogging whereas the rain might be less important. In Fig. 1, this is represented by having a greater intrinsic weight on the attack coming from the argument "hot" (0.8) than "rain" (0.5).

Lastly, an agent might have different inclinations toward how the weather affects their jogging routine. For the sake of the example, let us model three possibilities. The simplest case is the one where both the hot weather and the rain are arguments against going for a jogging but there is no interaction between them (left part of Fig. 1). The second case is the one where both the hot weather and the rain are still arguments against going for a jogging but the combination of the hot weather and the rain is a desirable reason to go for a jogging (center part of Fig. 1). The third case is the one where the two factors (the hot weather and the rain) may interact together and represent a further reason against going for a jogging (right part of Fig. 1).

This latter case is modelled using an argumentation framework, known in the literature, under the name of set of attacking arguments framework (SETAF). Please note that to model all three possibilities, we also need supports (in addition to attacks) to model positive and negative effects of temperature and precipitation on jogging. The reader is invited to observe the intricate link with the idea of argument accrual, which is well studied in the literature [5,9,10,12,18,19,21]. Note however, that arguments accrual was not studied for gradual semantics nor was adapted to sets of attacking argument frameworks.

The contributions of this paper are: (1) a new argumentation framework with sets of attacking/supporting arguments with intrinsic weights on relations, (2) the definition of properties for this framework and (3) the definition and characterisation of bipolar gradual semantics tailored for this framework.

The paper is structured as follows. We start by presenting the background notions and a list of desirable properties that a gradual semantics for weighted bipolar SETAFs should satisfy. We then show some links between those properties (e.g. some properties imply others). We continue by adapting three semantics from the literature (namely, Euler-based, DF-Quad and Sigmoid damped max-based semantics) to our framework and execute a formal study of their properties. We also provide a JAVA implementation for several semantics and extend the existing ASPARTIX format to the case of weighted bipolar SETAFs.

2 Formal Setting

We first extend the argumentation framework proposed by [15] with sets of supporting arguments which allow arguments to jointly support an argument.

Definition 1. *A weighted bipolar SETAF (WBSETAF) is* $AS = \langle A, P, w \rangle$, *where* A *is a finite set of arguments,* $P \subseteq (2^A \setminus \emptyset) \times A \times \{att, supp\}$ *is a set of collective interactions (each interaction being either an attack or a support), and* w *is a function from* $A \cup P$ *to* $[0, 1]$.

The set of all WBSETAFs is denoted by $\mathcal{X}_{setaf}$. The set of non-maximal WBSETAFs is defined as $\mathcal{X}_{setaf}^{<1} = \{\langle A, P, w \rangle \in \mathcal{X}_{setaf} \mid$ for every $b \in A, w(b) < 1\}$ and the set of non-minimal WBSETAFs is defined as $\mathcal{X}_{setaf}^{>0} = \{\langle A, P, w \rangle \in \mathcal{X}_{setaf} \mid$ for every $b \in A, w(b) > 0\}$. $(X, j, att) \in P$ means that there is an attack from $X \in (2^A \setminus \emptyset)$ to $j \in A$ whereas $(X, j, supp) \in P$ means that there is a support from X to j. Please note that in our formal setting, we can have both an attack and a support from the same set of arguments toward an argument but all the properties in this paper still hold in the restricted case, where there is only one type of interaction (support or attack) between a set of arguments and an argument. If $a \in A$, we denote by $w(a)$ the intrinsic weight of argument a representing its trustworthiness or the certainty degree of the argument's premises. For $p \in P$, we denote by $w(p)$ the intrinsic weight of the attack/support p. The set of attackers of $a \in A$ is $Att(a) = \{X \in 2^A \mid (X, a, att) \in P\}$. Likewise, the set of supports of $a \in A$ is $Supp(a) = \{X \in 2^A \mid (X, a, supp) \in P\}$. The union of two WBSETAFs $AS = \langle A, P, w \rangle$ and $AS' = \langle A', P', w' \rangle$ s.t. $A \cap A' = \emptyset$ is $AS \oplus AS' = \langle A \cup A', P \cup P', w'' \rangle$, where $\forall a \in A \cup A' \cup P \cup P', w''(a) = w(a)$, if $a \in A \cup P$ and $w''(a) = w'(a)$, if $a \in A' \cup P'$.

A path is a sequence of sets of arguments that are linked with either sets of attacking or supporting arguments.

Definition 2 (Path). *A sequence* $\langle X_0, X_1, \ldots, X_n \rangle$ *is called a path in* $AS = \langle A, P, w \rangle$ *iff* $\forall i \in \{0, \ldots, n-1\}, \exists x \in X_{i+1}$ *s.t.* $(X_i, x, l) \in P$, *where* $l \in \{att, supp\}$.

A path is significant w.r.t. a WBSETAF $AS = \langle A, P, w \rangle$ if it is, roughly speaking, composed of attacks/supports having strictly positive weights.

Definition 3 (Significant path). *A path* $\langle X_0, X_1, \ldots, X_n \rangle$ *in* $AS = \langle A, P, w \rangle$ *is significant if and only if* $\forall i \in \{0, \ldots, n-1\}, \exists x \in X_{i+1}$ *s.t.* $(X_i, x, l) \in P$ *and* $w((X_i, x, l)) > 0$, *where* $l \in \{att, supp\}$.

We can now define the notion of cycle.

Definition 4 (Cycle). *A path* $\langle X_0, X_1, \ldots, X_n \rangle$ *is called a cycle in* $AS = \langle A, P, w \rangle$ *iff* $\exists x \in X_0$ *s.t.* $(X_n, x, l) \in P$, *where* $l \in \{att, supp\}$.

A semantics is a function assigning an overall strength from $[0,1]$ to each argument of the WBSETAF.

Definition 5 (Semantics). *Let $\mathcal{AS} = \langle \mathcal{A}, \mathcal{P}, w \rangle$ be a weighed bipolar SETAF. A semantics is a function σ transforming any $\mathcal{AS} \in \mathcal{X}_{setaf}$ into a function $\sigma_{\mathcal{AS}} : \mathcal{A} \to [0,1]$.*

When $\mathcal{AS}$ is clear from the context, we simply write $\sigma(a)$ instead of $\sigma_{\mathcal{AS}}(a)$.

Definition 6 (Isomorphism). *Let $\mathcal{AS} = \langle \mathcal{A}, \mathcal{P}, w \rangle$ and $\mathcal{AS}' = \langle \mathcal{A}', \mathcal{P}', w' \rangle$ be two WBSETAFs. We say that f is an isomorphism from $\mathcal{A}$ to $\mathcal{A}'$ w.r.t. $\mathcal{AS}$ and $\mathcal{AS}'$ iff all the following conditions are satisfied: (1) $\forall X \subseteq \mathcal{A}, a \in \mathcal{A}$, $z \in \{att, supp\}$, $(X, a, z) \in \mathcal{P}$ iff $(f(X), f(a), z) \in \mathcal{P}'$, (2) $\forall X \subseteq \mathcal{A}, a \in \mathcal{A}$ and $z \in \{att, supp\}$ s.t. $(X, a, z) \in \mathcal{P}$, $w((X, a, z)) = w'((f(X), f(a), z))$ and (3) $\forall a \in \mathcal{A}, w(a) = w'(f(a))$*

3   Desirable Properties

We now extend the desirable properties that a semantics should satisfy [1] for the more general case of WBSETAFs. In each set of attacking (resp. supporting) arguments, all the components are necessary. Thus, we follow an important intuition from the literature [22] (reflected in our new properties) which is that the strength of a set of arguments should be equal to the strength of the weakest argument. Of course, this is not the only intuition and other aggregation functions can be used without loss of generality.

The first property states that the overall strength returned by the semantics should only be computed based on the structural elements.

Property 1 (Anonymity). A semantics σ satisfies anonymity iff for any two WBSETAFs $\mathcal{AS} = \langle \mathcal{A}, \mathcal{P}, w \rangle$ and $\mathcal{AS}' = \langle \mathcal{A}', \mathcal{P}', w' \rangle$, for any isomorphism f from $\mathcal{A}$ to $\mathcal{A}'$ w.r.t. $\mathcal{AS}$ and $\mathcal{AS}'$, it holds that $\forall a \in \mathcal{A}, \sigma_{\mathcal{AS}}(a) = \sigma_{\mathcal{AS}'}(f(a))$.

The *independence* property states that overall strength of an argument should not be affected by any other arguments that are not connected to it.

Property 2 (Independence). A semantics σ satisfies independence iff for any two WBSETAFs $\mathcal{AS} = \langle \mathcal{A}, \mathcal{P}, w \rangle$ and $\mathcal{AS}' = \langle \mathcal{A}', \mathcal{P}', w' \rangle$ s.t. $\mathcal{A} \cap \mathcal{A}' = \emptyset$, it holds that $\forall a \in \mathcal{A}, \sigma_{\mathcal{AS}}(a) = \sigma_{\mathcal{AS} \oplus \mathcal{AS}'}(a)$.

The *directionality* property states that the overall strength of an argument should depend only on the significant paths directed to it.

Property 3 (Directionality). A semantics σ satisfies directionality iff for any two WBSETAFs $\mathcal{AS} = \langle \mathcal{A}, \mathcal{P}, w \rangle$ and $\mathcal{AS}' = \langle \mathcal{A}, \mathcal{P}', w' \rangle$ s.t. all the following conditions are satisfied:

- $\forall y \in \mathcal{A} \cup \mathcal{P}, w(y) = w'(y)$,

- $\forall x, b \in \mathcal{A}, \forall X \subseteq \mathcal{A}$, if $\mathcal{P}' = \mathcal{P} \cup \{(X, b, z)\}$, where $z \in \{att, supp\}$ and there is no $X' \subseteq \mathcal{A}$ s.t. $b \in X'$ and there is a significant path from X' to x,

then $\sigma_{AS}(x) = \sigma_{AS'}(x)$.

The *equivalence* property states that the overall strength of an argument depends only on the overall strength of its direct attackers and supporters and the weight of the corresponding relations.

Property 4 (Equivalence). A semantics σ satisfies equivalence iff for every WBSETAF $AS = \langle \mathcal{A}, \mathcal{P}, w \rangle$ and $\forall a, b \in \mathcal{A}$, if all the following conditions are satisfied:

- $w(a) = w(b)$,
- there exists a bijection f between $Att(a)$ and $Att(b)$ s.t. $\forall X \in Att(a)$, $\min_{x \in X} \sigma_{AS}(x) = \min_{x' \in f(X)} \sigma_{AS}(x')$ and $w((X, a, att)) = w((f(X), b, att))$,
- there exists a bijection f between $Supp(a)$ and $Supp(b)$ s.t. $\forall X \in Supp(a)$, $\min_{x \in X} \sigma_{AS}(x) = \min_{x' \in f(X)} \sigma_{AS}(x')$ and $w((X, a, supp)) = w((f(X), b, supp))$,

then $\sigma_{AS}(a) = \sigma_{AS}(b)$.

The *reinforcement* property states that an argument becomes stronger if the quality of its attackers is reduced or the quality of its supporters is increased.

Property 5 (Reinforcement). A semantics σ satisfies reinforcement iff for every WBSETAF $AS = \langle \mathcal{A}, \mathcal{P}, w \rangle$, $\forall C, C' \subseteq 2^{\mathcal{A}}$, $\forall a, b \in \mathcal{A}$ and $\forall X_1, X_2, Y_1, Y_2 \subseteq \mathcal{A}$ s.t. $X_i, Y_i \notin C \cup C'$, if all the following conditions are satisfied:

- $w(a) = w(b)$, $Att(a) = C \cup \{X_1\}$ and $Att(b) = C \cup \{Y_1\}$,
- $Supp(a) = C' \cup \{X_2\}$ and $Supp(b) = C' \cup \{Y_2\}$,
- $\min_{x_1 \in X_1} \sigma_{AS}(x_1) \leq \min_{y_1 \in Y_1} \sigma_{AS}(y_1)$,
- $w((X_1, a, att)) \leq w((Y_1, a, att))$,
- $\min_{x_2 \in X_2} \sigma_{AS}(x_2) \geq \min_{y_2 \in Y_2} \sigma_{AS}(y_2)$,
- $w((X_2, a, supp)) \geq w((Y_2, a, supp))$,

then $\sigma_{AS}(a) \geq \sigma_{AS}(b)$.

The *stability* property states that if an argument is neither attacked nor supported, then its overall strength should be equal to its intrinsic weight.

Property 6 (Stability). A semantics σ satisfies stability iff, for every WBSETAF $AS = \langle \mathcal{A}, \mathcal{P}, w \rangle$, for every argument $a \in \mathcal{A}$, if $Att(a) = Supp(a) = \emptyset$, then $\sigma_{AS}(a) = w(a)$.

In the original work of [1], it is assumed that the neutral overall strength is the minimum possible value, which is zero. The intuition is that the "worthless" arguments, i.e. those with the strength zero, do not contain any valuable information and thus should not impact the other arguments. In their initial work, [13] generalised the existing approaches by allowing for the neutral overall strength to be any value. In the later paper [14], the authors changed the neutral overall strength to be zero but left the overall strength value to be any interval. In our paper, we choose the overall strength of all semantics to be in $[0, 1]$ to align with the literature standards. As a result, the neutral overall strength is chosen in the aforementioned interval.

The *neutrality* property states that the overall strength of an argument should not be affected by sets of attacking/supporting arguments containing arguments with an overall strength equal to the neutral overall strength.

Property 7 (Neutrality). A semantics σ satisfies neutrality iff, there exists a unique $\alpha \in [0, 1]$ s.t. both of the following conditions are satisfied:

- there exists a WBSETAF $\mathcal{AS} = \langle \mathcal{A}, \mathcal{P}, w \rangle$ and $a \in \mathcal{A}$ s.t. $\sigma_{\mathcal{AS}}(a) = \alpha$,
- for every WBSETAF $\mathcal{AS} = \langle \mathcal{A}, \mathcal{P}, w \rangle$, for every argument $a, b \in \mathcal{A}$ s.t. $w(a) = w(b)$, $X \subseteq \mathcal{A}$ s.t. $Att(a) \subseteq Att(b)$, $Supp(a) \subseteq Supp(b)$ and $Att(a) \cup Supp(a) \cup \{X\} = Att(b) \cup Supp(b)$, if $\min_{x \in X} \sigma_{\mathcal{AS}}(x) = \alpha$ or $w((X, b, z)) = 0$, where $z \in \{att, supp\}$,

then $\sigma_{\mathcal{AS}}(a) = \sigma_{\mathcal{AS}}(b)$.

The first item of the neutrality property is necessary because if the semantics σ never assigns an overall strength $\beta \in [0, 1]$ to an argument then neutrality is trivially satisfied by putting $\alpha = \beta$ (under the condition that whenever the intrinsic weight of an attack/support is equal to zero, it does not affect the overall strength of its target). If σ satisfies the neutrality property, α is called the neutral overall strength.

The *monotonicity* property states that if two arguments a and b have the same intrinsic weight and a is "less attacked" and "more supported" than b, then a should have a higher overall strength than b.

Property 8 (Monotonicity). A semantics σ satisfies monotonicity iff, for every WBSETAF $\mathcal{AS} = \langle \mathcal{A}, \mathcal{P}, w \rangle$, $\forall a, b \in \mathcal{A}$ s.t. $w(a) = w(b)$, $Att(a) \subseteq Att(b)$ and $\forall X \in Att(a), w((X, a, att)) \leq w((X, b, att))$, $Supp(b) \subseteq Supp(a)$ and $\forall X \in Supp(b), w((X, b, supp)) \leq w((X, a, supp))$, then $\sigma_{\mathcal{AS}}(a) \geq \sigma_{\mathcal{AS}}(b)$.

The *resilience* property states that if the intrinsic weight of an argument is not 0 nor 1 then its overall strength cannot be 0 nor 1.

Property 9 (Resilience). A semantics σ satisfies resilience iff, for every WBSETAF $\mathcal{AS} = \langle \mathcal{A}, \mathcal{P}, w \rangle$, $\forall a \in \mathcal{A}$, if $0 < w(a) < 1$ then $0 < \sigma_{\mathcal{AS}}(a) < 1$.

Franklin states that an attacker and a supporter of equal strength should counter-balance each other. Thus, the overall strength should remain unchanged.

Property 10 (Franklin). A semantics σ satisfies Franklin iff, for every WBSETAF $\mathcal{AS} = \langle \mathcal{A}, \mathcal{P}, w \rangle$, $\forall a, b \in \mathcal{A}$ and $X, Y \subseteq \mathcal{A}$, if all of the following conditions are satisfied:

- $w(a) = w(b)$, $w((X, a, att)) = w((Y, a, supp))$,
- $Att(a) = Att(b) \cup \{X\}$, $Supp(a) = Supp(b) \cup \{Y\}$,
- $\min\limits_{x \in X} \sigma_{AS}(x) = \min\limits_{y \in Y} \sigma_{AS}(y)$,

then $\sigma_{AS}(a) = \sigma_{AS}(b)$.

The *strengthening* property states that if an argument receives more supports than attacks, then its overall strength should increase. Roughly speaking, there are three cases: (1) there are more supporters than attackers, (2) the weakest strength of a set attack is strictly weaker than the weakest strength of the corresponding supporter, (3) the intrinsic weight of one attack is strictly weaker than the corresponding support.

Property 11 (Strengthening). A semantics σ satisfies strengthening iff, for every WBSETAF $AS = \langle A, P, w \rangle$, $\forall a \in A$, if $w(a) < 1$ and there exists an injective function f from $Att(a)$ to $Supp(a)$ s.t. $\forall X \in Att(a), \min\limits_{x \in X} \sigma_{AS}(x) \leq \min\limits_{x' \in f(X)} \sigma_{AS}(x')$, $\forall X \in Att(a), w((X, a, att)) \leq w((f(X), a, supp))$ and at least one of the following conditions is satisfied:

- there exists $X' \in Supp(a) \setminus \{f(X) \mid X \in Att(a)\}$ such that $w((X', a, supp)) > 0$ and $\min\limits_{x' \in X'} \sigma_{AS}(x') > 0$,
- there exists $X \in Att(a)$ such that $\min\limits_{x \in X} \sigma_{AS}(x) < \min\limits_{x' \in f(X)} \sigma_{AS}(x')$ and $w((f(X), a, supp)) > 0$, or
- there exists $X \in Att(a)$ such that $w((X, a, att)) < w((f(X), a, supp))$ and $\min\limits_{x' \in f(X)} \sigma_{AS}(x') > 0$,

then $\sigma_{AS}(a) > w(a)$.

Similarly, the *weakening* property states that if an argument receives less supports than attacks, then its overall strength should decrease.

Property 12 (Weakening). A semantics σ satisfies weakening iff, for every WBSETAF $AS = \langle A, P, w \rangle$, $\forall a \in A$, if $0 < w(a)$ and there exists an injective function f from $Supp(a)$ to $Att(a)$ s.t. $\forall X \in Supp(a), \min\limits_{x \in X} \sigma_{AS}(x) \leq \min\limits_{x' \in f(X)} \sigma_{AS}(x')$, $\forall X \in Supp(a), w((X, a, supp)) \leq w((f(X), a, att))$ and at least one of the following conditions is satisfied:

- there exists $X' \in Att(a) \setminus \{f(X) \mid X \in Supp(a)\}$ such that $w((X', a, att)) > 0$ and $\min\limits_{x' \in X'} \sigma_{AS}(x') > 0$,
- there exists $X \in Supp(a)$ such that $\min\limits_{x \in X} \sigma_{AS}(x) < \min\limits_{x' \in f(X)} \sigma_{AS}(x')$ and $w((f(X), a, att)) > 0$, or
- there exists $X \in Supp(a)$ such that $w((X, a, supp)) < w((f(X), a, att))$ and $\min\limits_{x' \in f(X)} \sigma_{AS}(x') > 0$,

then $\sigma_{AS}(a) < w(a)$.

The next property states that adding an attack to an argument should decrease its overall strength whereas adding a support should increase it. The idea of accumulation is similar to that of monotonicity except that monotonicity is defined on two arguments of the same graph whereas accumulation is defined on the "same" argument in the "copy" of the graph. Note that in the next section, we identify the conditions under which monotonicity and accumulation are equivalent (Corollary 1).

Property 13 (Accumulation). A semantics σ satisfies accumulation iff, for every two WBSETAFs $\mathcal{AS} = \langle \mathcal{A}, \mathcal{P}, w \rangle$ and $\mathcal{AS}' = \langle \mathcal{A}, \mathcal{P}', w' \rangle$, $\forall a \in \mathcal{A}$, $\forall X \in 2^{\mathcal{A}}$, if $\forall p \in \mathcal{A} \cup \mathcal{P}$, we have $w(p) = w'(p)$, and $\mathcal{P}' = \mathcal{P} \cup \{(X, a, z)\}$ then (1) $\sigma_{\mathcal{AS}'}(a) \leq \sigma_{\mathcal{AS}}(a)$ if $z = att$ and (2) $\sigma_{\mathcal{AS}'}(a) \geq \sigma_{\mathcal{AS}}(a)$ if $z = supp$.

4   Links Between Properties

We now study the link between the properties that we previously defined.

Proposition 1. *Let σ be a semantics that satisfies independence, directionality, stability, accumulation. Then, σ satisfies monotonicity.*

Proof. Let $\mathcal{AS} = \langle \mathcal{A}, \mathcal{P}, w \rangle$ and $a, b \in \mathcal{A}$ s.t. the conditions of monotonicity are satisfied. The intuition of the next construction is the following. We will define a "copy" $\mathcal{AS}'$ of $\mathcal{AS}$. For each argument x, we create its copy x'. Furthermore, we keep only the attacks from the direct attackers of a and b and only the supports from the direct supporters of a and b. All the other attacks and supports are forgotten. This is done to allow for the application of directionality when comparing $\mathcal{AS}'$ and $\mathcal{AS}^1$ (which will be defined later in the proof).

Let us define $\mathcal{AS}' = \langle \mathcal{A}', \mathcal{P}', w' \rangle$ s.t. there exists a bijection $f : Att(b) \cup Supp(a) \cup \{a, b\} \to \mathcal{A}'$ defined as $\forall x$, $f(x) = x'$ and:

- $\mathcal{A}' = \{a', b'\} \cup \{x_i' \mid x_i \in X \text{ and } X \in Att(b)\} \cup \{y_i' \mid y_i \in Y \text{ and } Y \in Supp(a)\}$.
- $\mathcal{P}' = \{(f(X), f(a), att) \text{ such that } (X, a, att) \in \mathcal{P}\} \cup \{(f(X), f(b), att) \text{ such that } (X, b, att) \in \mathcal{P}\} \cup \{(f(Y), f(a), supp) \text{ such that } (Y, a, supp) \in \mathcal{P}\} \cup \{(f(Y), f(b), supp) \text{ such that } (Y, b, supp) \in \mathcal{P}\}$.
- Let us define w' as follows: $w'(f(a)) = w(a), w'(f(b)) = w(b)$, $\forall x \in \mathcal{A}' \setminus \{a', b'\}$, $w'(x) = \sigma_{\mathcal{AS}}(x)$ and $\forall (T, t, z) \in Att(b) \cup Supp(a)$, let $w'((f(T), f(t), z)) = w((T, t, z))$.

From stability, we know that $\forall t' \in \mathcal{A}' \setminus \{a', b'\}$, we have $\sigma_{\mathcal{AS}'}(t') = w'(t') = \sigma_{\mathcal{AS}}(t)$. By using the independence and equivalence properties, we have that $\sigma_{\mathcal{AS}}(a) = \sigma_{\mathcal{AS}'}(a')$ and $\sigma_{\mathcal{AS}}(b) = \sigma_{\mathcal{AS}'}(b')$. Let us use the notation $Att(a') = \{X_1', \ldots, X_n'\}$, $Att(b') = Att(a') \cup \{X_{n+1}', \ldots, X_m'\}$, $Supp(b') = \{Y_1', \ldots, Y_k'\}$ and $Supp(a') = Supp(b') \cup \{Y_{k+1}', \ldots, Y_l'\}$.

Let us now remove attacks from $Att(b') \setminus Att(a')$ to b' and supports from $Supp(a') \setminus Supp(b')$ to a' using the following procedures.

- Let $\mathcal{AS}^1 = \langle \mathcal{A}', \mathcal{P}^1, w^1 \rangle$ with $\mathcal{P}^1 = \mathcal{P}' \setminus \{(X'_m, b', att)\}$ and $\forall p \in \mathcal{A}' \cup \mathcal{P}^1, w^1(p) = w'(p)$. By accumulation, we have that $\sigma_{\mathcal{AS}^1}(b') \geq \sigma_{\mathcal{AS}'}(b')$. Moreover, by directionality, $\forall t \in \mathcal{A}', \sigma_{\mathcal{AS}^1}(t) = \sigma_{\mathcal{AS}'}(t)$. We repeat this procedure $m - n$ times to remove all the attacks from $Att(b') \setminus Att(a')$ to b'. Let us call the resulting graph $\mathcal{AS}^{m-n}$.
- Let us define $\mathcal{AS}^{m-n+1} = \langle \mathcal{A}', \mathcal{P}^{m-n+1}, w^{m-n+1} \rangle$ with $\mathcal{P}^{m-n+1} = \mathcal{P}^{m-n} \setminus \{(Y'_l, a', supp)\}$ and $\forall p \in \mathcal{A}' \cup \mathcal{P}^{m-n+1}, w^{m-n+1}(p) = w'(p)$. By accumulation, we have that $\sigma_{\mathcal{AS}^{m-n+1}}(a') \leq \sigma_{\mathcal{AS}^{m-n}}(a')$. Moreover, by directionality, $\forall t \in \mathcal{A}', \sigma_{\mathcal{AS}^{m-n}}(t) = \sigma_{\mathcal{AS}^{m-n+1}}(t)$. We repeat this procedure $l - k$ times to remove all the supports from $Supp(a') \setminus Supp(b')$ to a'. Let us call the resulting graph $\mathcal{AS}^*$.

By equivalence, we have that $\sigma_{\mathcal{AS}^*}(a) = \sigma_{\mathcal{AS}^*}(b)$. Thus:

$$\sigma_{\mathcal{AS}'}(b') \leq \sigma_{\mathcal{AS}^1}(b') \leq \cdots \leq \sigma_{\mathcal{AS}^*}(b') =$$
$$\sigma_{\mathcal{AS}^*}(a') \leq \cdots \leq \sigma_{\mathcal{AS}^1}(a') \leq \sigma_{\mathcal{AS}'}(a')$$

Finally, since we have that $\sigma_{\mathcal{AS}}(b) = \sigma_{\mathcal{AS}'}(b')$ and $\sigma_{\mathcal{AS}}(a) = \sigma_{\mathcal{AS}'}(a')$, we conclude that $\sigma_{\mathcal{AS}}(a) \geq \sigma_{\mathcal{AS}}(b)$.

Regarding the previous result, the proposition holds for an arbitrary semantics; note also that if σ is a semantics that is defined only on acyclic graphs, we can show that σ satisfies monotonocity (on the class of acyclic graphs).

Proposition 2. *Let σ be a semantics that satisfies anonymity, independence, directionality, equivalence and monotonicity on the class of acyclic graphs. Then, σ satisfies accumulation on the class of acyclic graphs.*

Proposition 1 also holds for a semantics σ defined on acyclic graphs only. Hence, from that fact and Proposition 2, we conclude that accumulation and monotonicity are equivalent given anonymity, independence, directionality, stability and equivalence. We formally state this in the next corollary.

Corollary 1. *Let σ be a semantics that satisfies anonymity, independence, directionality, stability and equivalence on the class of acyclic graphs. Then σ satisfies accumulation on the class of acyclic graphs iff it satisfies monotonicity on the class of acyclic graphs.*

5   Gradual Semantics

As mentioned before, in each set of attacking (resp. supporting) arguments, all the components are necessary. Thus, removing one argument from the set would make the attack (resp. support) void. In this section, we generalise the semantics from the literature by considering the force of the set of attacking (resp. supporting) arguments to be the force of the weakest argument of the set. For simplicity, we also incorporate the intrinsic weight of attacks by means of the multiplication operator but the whole approach can be generalised with other aggregating methods. Moreover, the first two semantics (Euler-based and DF-Quad) do not always converge in the class of cyclic WBSETAFs. For this reason, as usual in the literature [1,20], we consider that the class of all acyclic WBSETAFs is still expressive enough to deserve attention. In the next definitions, we generalise the existing Euler-based [1] and DF-Quad semantics [20] for the new framework.

Definition 7 (Euler-based semantics). *Let* $AS = \langle A, P, w \rangle \in \mathcal{X}_{setaf}$ *be an acyclic WBSETAF.* $\forall a \in A$, *we have:*

$$\sigma_{AS}^{EB}(a) = 1 - \frac{1 - w(a)^2}{1 + w(a)e^{E(a)}}$$

where $E(a) = Y - Z$ *with* $Y = \sum\limits_{X \in Supp(a)} \min\limits_{x \in X} \sigma_{AS}^{EB}(x) \cdot w((X, a, supp))$ *and* $Z = \sum\limits_{X \in Att(a)} \min\limits_{x \in X} \sigma_{AS}^{EB}(x) \cdot w((X, a, att))$.

Table 1. Satisfaction of the properties by the gradual semantics on acyclic graphs

	$\mathcal{X}_{setaf}$			$\mathcal{X}_{setaf}^{>0}$			$\mathcal{X}_{setaf}^{<1}$		
	σ^{EB}	σ^{DF}	σ^{SD}	σ^{EB}	σ^{DF}	σ^{SD}	σ^{EB}	σ^{DF}	σ^{SD}
Anonymity	✓	✓	✓	✓	✓	✓	✓	✓	✓
Independence	✓	✓	✓	✓	✓	✓	✓	✓	✓
Directionality	✓	✓	✓	✓	✓	✓	✓	✓	✓
Equivalence	✓	✓	✓	✓	✓	✓	✓	✓	✓
Reinforcement	✓	✓	✓	✓	✓	✓	✓	✓	✓
Stability	✓	✓	✓	✓	✓	✓	✓	✓	✓
Neutrality	✓	✓	✗	✗	✓	✗	✓	✓	✗
Monotonicity	✓	✓	✗	✓	✓	✗	✓	✓	✗
Resilience	✓	✗	✓	✓	✗	✓	✓	✓	✓
Franklin	✓	✗	✗	✓	✗	✗	✓	✗	✗
Strengthening	✗	✗	✗	✓	✗	✗	✗	✓	✗
Weakening	✗	✗	✗	✗	✗	✗	✓	✓	✗
Accumulation	✓	✓	✗	✓	✓	✗	✓	✓	✗

Definition 8 (DF-Quad semantics). *Let* $AS = \langle A, P, w \rangle \in \mathcal{X}_{setaf}$ *be an acyclic WBSETAF.* $\forall a \in A$, *we have: if* $v_s(a) = v_a(a)$, $\sigma_{AS}^{DF}(a) = w(a)$; *else* $\sigma_{AS}^{DF}(a) = w(a) + (0.5 + \frac{v_s(a) - v_a(a)}{2 \cdot |v_s(a) - v_a(a)|} - w(a)) \cdot |v_s(a) - v_a(a)|$,

where $v_a(a) = 1 - \prod\limits_{X \in Att(a)} \left(1 - \min\limits_{x \in X} \sigma_{AS}^{DF}(x) \cdot w((X, a, att)) \right)$ *and* $v_s(a) =$

$1 - \prod\limits_{X \in Supp(a)} \left(1 - \min\limits_{x \in X} \sigma_{AS}^{DF}(x) \cdot w((X, a, supp)) \right)$. *Please note that if* $Att(a) = \emptyset$ *then* $v_a = 0$. *Similarly,* $v_s = 0$ *if* $Supp(a) = \emptyset$.

We also generalise the Sigmoid damped max-based gradual semantics [14] for this framework. For presentation purposes, we changed the original definition to match the other semantics by translating the range of the semantics from $[-1, 1]$ to $[0, 1]$. We also changed the "top" operator from the original semantics to "max" because we wanted to take all the arguments into account for determining the overall strength. Note that the sets of attacking (resp. supporting) arguments with a minimum element having a score strictly inferior to 0.5 will increase (resp. decrease) the score of the attacked (resp. supported) argument. This effect is an intrinsic aspect of the original Sigmoid damped max-based semantics, which was not introduced by the generalisation we propose.

Definition 9 (Sigmoid damped max-based semantics). *Given the WBSETAF $\mathcal{AS} = \langle \mathcal{A}, \mathcal{P}, w \rangle \in \mathcal{X}_{setaf}$ and $\delta > 2$. $\forall a \in \mathcal{A}$, we have $\sigma^{SD}_{\mathcal{AS}}(a) = f\left(\frac{Y(a)}{\delta} + f^{-1}(w(a))\right)$, where*

$$Y(a) = \max_{X \in Supp(a)} \left(\min_{x \in X} f^{-1}(\sigma^{SD}_{\mathcal{AS}}(x)) \cdot w((X, a, supp)) \right)$$

$$- \max_{X \in Att(a)} \left(\min_{x \in X} f^{-1}(\sigma^{SD}_{\mathcal{AS}}(x)) \cdot w((X, a, att)) \right) \text{ and } f(x) = \frac{\tanh(x) + 1}{2}.$$

In Table 1, we show the satisfaction of the properties by the aforementioned gradual semantics on the three classes $\mathcal{X}_{setaf}, \mathcal{X}^{<1}_{setaf}$ and $\mathcal{X}^{>0}_{setaf}$. Due to space limitations, we do not show all the proofs in the paper although all the combinations were diligently proved. We now provide a brief overview of the property satisfaction on the general class $\mathcal{X}_{setaf}$.

The Euler-based semantics satisfies the greatest number of properties. The only two non-satisfied properties are strengthening and weakening. Note that the only case when an argument cannot be weakened (resp. strengthened) is the case of an argument that has the maximal (resp. minimal) intrinsic weight. It seems to us that in several reasonable application contexts, this behaviour of the Euler-based semantics can be seen as rational.

The DF-Quad semantics violates strengthening and weakening as well as Franklin and resilience. Again, this is not necessarily a fatal problem, since in some contexts it might not be a good idea to be able to cancel one positive argument with one negative argument of the same strength.

Finally, the Sigmoid damped max-based semantics violates even more properties, which is (we believe) linked to its simple idea to take into account only the strongest attacker and the strongest supporter and to ignore the others. Note that Sigmoid damped max-based semantics does not satisfy neutrality, even if we use the generalised version of the proposition that allows for any number to be the neutral overall strength. Similar to the original version by Mossakowski and Neuhaus [13], we could restrict our version of Sigmoid damped max-based semantics to arguments with intrinsic strengths above 0.5 only, which would lead to satisfying neutrality. Notice that every property is satisfied by Sigmoid damped max-based semantics on the class $\mathcal{X}_{setaf}$ iff it is satisfied on $\mathcal{X}^{>0}_{setaf}$ and on $\mathcal{X}^{<1}_{setaf}$. The reason is that the Sigmoid damped max-based semantics is only defined in the interval $(0, 1)$.

Interestingly, we also showed that the new DF-Quad semantics does not satisfy Franklin (see Example 1) and that the Euler-based semantics does not satisfy strengthening on the class of non-maximal graphs even in the acyclic case (see Example 2). Since neither of our examples uses set attacks, we conclude that the original versions of those two semantics do not satisfy the aforementioned properties, contrary to what was suggested by Amgoud and Ben-Naim [1].

Example 1. Let $\mathcal{AS} = \langle \mathcal{A}, \mathcal{P}, w \rangle$ s.t. $\mathcal{A} = \{a, b, x_1, y_1, z\}$, $\mathcal{P} = \{(\{z\}, b, att), (\{z\}, a, att), (\{y_1\}, a, supp), (\{x_1\}, a, att)\}$, $w(a) = w(b) = 0.5$, $w(x_1) = w(y_1) = 0.7$, $w(z) = 0.6$ and $w((\{x_1\}, a, att)) = w((\{z\}, b, att)) = w((\{z\}, a, att)) = w((\{y_1\}, a, supp)) = 1$, represented in Fig. 1. We have that $v_s(a) = 1 - (1 - 0.7) = 0.7$, $v_a(a) = 1 - 0.3 \cdot 0.4 = 0.88$, $v_s(b) = 0$ and $v_a(b) = 1 - (1 - 0.6) = 0.6$. As a result, $\sigma_{\mathcal{AS}}^{DF}(a) = 1 + (-0.5) \cdot 0.18 = 0.91$ whereas $\sigma_{\mathcal{AS}}^{DF}(b) = 1 + (-0.5) \cdot 0.6 = 0.7$ (Fig. 2)

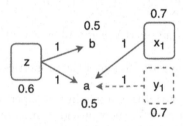

Fig. 2. Counter-example of the satisfaction of Franklin by DF-Quad.

Example 2. Let $\mathcal{AS} = \langle \mathcal{A}, \mathcal{P}, w \rangle$ s.t. $\mathcal{A} = \{a, b\}$, $\mathcal{P} = \{(\{b\}, a, supp)\}$, $w(a) = 0$, $w(b) = 0.5$ and $w((\{b\}, a, supp)) = 1$. Then, $\sigma_{\mathcal{AS}}^{EB}(a) = w(a) = 0$.

6   Discussion

In this paper, we studied gradual semantics for WBSETAFs. This is the first study of the properties that a gradual semantics should satisfy in the framework that allows for bipolar interactions (i.e. both attacks and supports), weights (on both arguments and attacks) and SETAFs (the possibility for several arguments to jointly attack or support an argument). We generalised twelve properties from the literature [1,14] and introduced a new one called "accumulation". We proved some links between the properties, and generalised three semantics from the literature to be applicable with WBSETAFs. We conducted a formal evaluation of those semantics against the properties on three classes of argumentation graphs.

We also provided an implementation of the three new semantics available at https://github.com/AnonymousConfsSubmissions/WBSETAFs. Please note that this implementation is based on an extension of the ASPARTIX format for WBSETAFs.

References

1. Amgoud, L., Ben-Naim, J.: Weighted bipolar argumentation graphs: axioms and semantics. In: Proceedings of the Twenty-Seventh International Joint Conference on Artificial Intelligence, IJCAI 2018 (2018)
2. Amgoud, L., Ben-Naim, J., Doder, D., Vesic, S.: Acceptability semantics for weighted argumentation frameworks. In: Proceedings of the Twenty-Sixth International Joint Conference on Artificial Intelligence, IJCAI 2017, pp. 56–62 (2017)
3. Amgoud, L., Cayrol, C., Lagasquie-Schiex, M.-C., Livet, P.: On bipolarity in argumentation frameworks. Int. J. Intell. Syst. **23**(10), 1062–1093 (2008)
4. Amgoud, L., Doder, D.: Gradual semantics accounting for varied-strength attacks. In: Proceedings of the 18th International Conference on Autonomous Agents and MultiAgent Systems, AAMAS 2019, pp. 1270–1278 (2019)
5. Bench-Capon, T.J.M., Prakken, H.: Justifying actions by accruing arguments. Comput. Models Argument Proc. COMMA **2006**, 247–258 (2006)
6. Bonzon, E., Delobelle, J., Konieczny, S., Maudet, N.: A comparative study of ranking-based semantics for abstract argumentation. In: Proceedings of the Thirtieth AAAI Conference on Artificial Intelligence, pp. 914–920 (2016)
7. Cayrol, C., Lagasquie-Schiex, M.-C.: On the acceptability of arguments in bipolar argumentation frameworks. In: Symbolic and Quantitative Approaches to Reasoning with Uncertainty, 8th European Conference, ECSQARU 2005, Proceedings, pp. 378–389 (2005)
8. Leite, J., Martins, J.: Social abstract argumentation. In: IJCAI 2011, Proceedings of the 22nd International Joint Conference on Artificial Intelligence, pp. 2287–2292 (2011)
9. Lucero, M.J.G., Chesñevar, C.I., Simari, G.R.: Modelling argument accrual in possibilistic defeasible logic programming. In: Symbolic and Quantitative Approaches to Reasoning with Uncertainty, 10th European Conference, ECSQARU 2009, pp. 131–143 (2009)
10. Lucero, M.J.G., Chesñevar, C.I., Simari, G.R.: On the accrual of arguments in defeasible logic programming. In: Proceedings of the 21st International Joint Conference on Artificial Intelligence, IJCAI 2009, pp. 804–809 (2009)
11. Matt, P.-A., Toni, F.: A game-theoretic measure of argument strength for abstract argumentation. In: Logics in Artificial Intelligence, 11th European Conference, JELIA 2008, Proceedings, pp. 285–297 (2008)
12. Modgil, S., Bench-Capon, T.J.M.: Integrating dialectical and accrual modes of argumentation. In: Computational Models of Argument: Proceedings of COMMA 2010, 8–10 September, 2010, pp. 335–346 (2010)
13. Mossakowski, T., Neuhaus, F.: Bipolar Weighted Argumentation Graphs. CoRR, abs/1611.08572 (2016)
14. Mossakowski, T., Neuhaus, F.: Modular Semantics and Characteristics for Bipolar Weighted Argumentation Graphs. CoRR, abs/1807.06685 (2018)
15. Nielsen, Søren Holbech., Parsons, Simon: A generalization of dung's abstract framework for argumentation: arguing with sets of attacking arguments. In: Maudet, Nicolas, Parsons, Simon, Rahwan, Iyad (eds.) ArgMAS 2006. LNCS (LNAI), vol. 4766, pp. 54–73. Springer, Heidelberg (2007). https://doi.org/10.1007/978-3-540-75526-5_4
16. C. d. C. Pereira, A. Tettamanzi, and S. Villata. Changing One's Mind: Erase or Rewind? In Proceedings of the 22nd International Joint Conference on Artificial Intelligence, IJCAI 2011, pages 164–171, 2011

17. Potyka, N.: Continuous dynamical systems for weighted bipolar argumentation. In: Principles of Knowledge Representation and Reasoning: Proceedings of the Sixteenth International Conference, KR 2018, pp. 148–157 (2018)
18. Prakken, H.: A study of accrual of arguments, with applications to evidential reasoning. Proceedings of the Tenth International Conference on Artificial Intelligence and Law, ICAIL **2005**, 85–94 (2005)
19. Prakken, H.: Modelling accrual of arguments in ASPIC+. In: Proceedings of the Seventeenth International Conference on Artificial Intelligence and Law, ICAIL 2019, pp. 103–112 (2019)
20. Rago, A., Toni, F., Aurisicchio, M., Baroni, P.: Discontinuity-free decision support with quantitative argumentation debates. In: Principles of Knowledge Representation and Reasoning: Proceedings of the Fifteenth International Conference, KR 2016, pp. 63–73 (2016)
21. Verheij, B.: Accrual of arguments in defeasible argumentation, pp. 217–224. In Dutch/German Workshop on Nonmonotonic Reasoning. Proceedings of the Second Workshop, Delft University of Technology, Universiteit Utrecht (1995)
22. Yun, B., Vesic, S., Croitoru, M.: Ranking-based semantics for sets of attacking arguments. In: The Thirty-Fourth AAAI Conference on Artificial Intelligence, AAAI 2020, pp. 3033–3040 (2020)

Bayesian Networks and Graphical Models

Multi-task Transfer Learning for Bayesian Network Structures

Sarah Benikhlef[1(✉)], Philippe Leray[1], Guillaume Raschia[1],
Montassar Ben Messaoud[2], and Fayrouz Sakly[2]

[1] LS2N, UMR CNRS 6004, University of Nantes, Nantes, France
{sarah.benikhlef,philippe.leray,guillaume.raschia}@ls2n.fr
[2] LARODEC, ISG Sousse, Sousse, Tunisia

Abstract. We consider the interest of leveraging information between related tasks for learning Bayesian network structures. We propose a new algorithm called Multi-Task Max-Min Hill Climbing (MT-MMHC) that combines ideas from transfer learning, multi-task learning, constraint-based and search-and-score techniques. This approach consists in two main phases. The first one identifies the most similar tasks and uses their similarity to learn their corresponding undirected graphs. The second one directs the edges with a Greedy Search combined with a Branch-and-Bound algorithm. Empirical evaluation shows that MT-MMHC can yield better results than learning the structures individually or than the state-of-the-Art MT-GS algorithm in terms of structure learning accuracy and computational time.

Keywords: Bayesian networks · Structure learning · Multi-task learning · Transfer learning

1 Introduction

Learning reliable models from small datasets is difficult, therefore transfer learning (also known as domain adaptation [21]) can enhance the robustness of the discovered models by leveraging data from related tasks [12]. Transfer learning is a well-studied area. It has been successfully employed in a variety of machine learning fields, focusing mainly on neural networks [13,21].

Multi-Task (MT) learning, also referred to as parallel transfer learning, is a learning paradigm that aims to leverage useful information contained in related tasks to help improve the generalization of all the tasks [20]. In order to considerably increase learning tasks performance, MT learning can be combined with other learning mechanisms [20].

Inductive transfer and MT learning are closely related. They both intend to leverage knowledge among similar problems [10]. The distinction between these two approaches lies in the transfer technique. In Transfer Learning (TL), the information is transferred from the source to the target task. Ultimately, the goal is to improve the performance of the target task with the support of source

J. Vejnarová and N. Wilson (Eds.): ECSQARU 2021, LNAI 12897, pp. 217–228, 2021.
https://doi.org/10.1007/978-3-030-86772-0_16

tasks by affording additional information. We note here that the target task has a more significant role than source tasks. On the contrary, the tasks in MT learning are considered equally [17].

Bayesian Networks (BNs) have proven to be an efficient tool to capture conditional dependencies and independencies between random variables. They give an effective way to represent the structure of real-world applications and determine the effect of many observations on an outcome. They are frequently employed in decision support systems and machine learning applications, where it is generally assumed to have sufficient data from which a reliable model can be learned. However, in some fields, as manufacturing or medicine [7], data can be rare and usually gathered from different but closely related problems. In this situation, existing solutions have been proposed for transfer and multi-task learning of Bayesian networks [8,10,11]. These approaches are mainly adaptations of basic constraint-based or score-based BN structure learning algorithms.

In this paper, we propose an extension to multi-task learning of an efficient BN structure discovery algorithm called Max-Min Hill-Climbing (MMHC) [18] that takes advantage of both constraint based and score-based algorithms.

Our three main contributions are: (1) MT-MMHC, a hybrid transfer learning algorithm that can learn multiple BN structures simultaneously by inducing information between similar tasks to improve the performance of the constructed networks; (2) one procedure to generate MT benchmarks from any reference model, by controlling the similarity between tasks; and (3) one experimental validation of MT-MMHC by using such benchmarks compared to Single Task (ST) structure learning, but also to MT-GS reference algorithm (Multi Task Greedy Search).

Section 2 introduces background information and relevant related work about BN structure learning. Section 3 describes our MT-MMHC approach. Section 4 is dedicated to the generation of MT benchmarks and to the empirical evaluation of our proposition. Finally, Sect. 5 gives a general conclusion and several research perspectives.

2   Bayesian Network Multi-task Structure Learning

A Bayesian Network (BN) $\mathcal{B} =< G, \Theta >$ represents the joint probability distribution of a set of n random variables $\{X_1, X_2, \ldots, X_n\}$ [4]. It is characterized by a Directed Acyclic Graph (DAG) G and a set Θ of Conditional Probability Tables (CPTs), also called parameters. The graph or structure G is given by a pair (V, E) where V is the set of nodes in the graph and E the set of edges between them. Each node corresponds to a random variable and each edge represents a direct dependency between the two variables that it connects. A strong property of BNs is that this representation is easy to interpret and can help in visualizing dependencies between variables.

BN Single-Task (ST) learning aims at discovering the structure of the network G and estimating the parameters Θ of the model from one dataset D.

In Multi-Task (MT) learning, we consider k tasks corresponding to k datasets $\mathcal{D} = \{D_1, D_2, \ldots, D_k\}$ from which we learn k corresponding BN graphs $\mathcal{G} =$

$\{G_1, G_2, ..., G_k\}$ and the associated parameters. The objective is to learn all the models simultaneously as a multi-task problem while leveraging information between the tasks. It is worth to notice here that Azzimonti et al. [1] propose an alternative BN learning approach where one common BN structure is learned from related data sets.

MT parameter learning, when $\mathcal{G}$ is known, have been processed in the literature [4,8]. For instance, Luis et al. [8] present a method of inductive transfer to determine the CPTs using aggregation functions from several sources.

In this paper, we are mainly interested in Bayesian network MT structure learning. In a single task context, discovering the structure of a Bayesian network can be seen as a problem of selecting a probabilistic model that fits and explains a given dataset [4]. Three main approaches are generally adopted [4] : (1) search and score based methods exploring the space of structures; (2) constraint-based methods using conditional independencies; and (3) hybrid methods combining the two previous ones.

Search and Score Approaches. One of the most widely known methods of learning Bayesian network structures is the use of search and score techniques [4]. These approaches perform an exact or a heuristic search within the space of network structures and evaluate the best candidate structure to fit the data using a given scoring metric. Generally speaking, these algorithms require: (i) a search space of allowable states of the problem, each state represents a Bayesian network structure; (ii) a scoring function to evaluate a state and see how well it matches the data; (iii) a mechanism to explore this space in an exact way when the dimension of the search space is limited, or in a heuristic way.

Greedy Search (GS) [14], for example, is a ST structure learning algorithm that starts from some initial structure and explores the DAG space by selecting at each iteration the neighbor graph with the highest score. The search stops when the current structure has a better score than all its neighbors, and may be repeated several times starting from different initial states to avoid local maxima. A neighborhood of a structure G is commonly defined as all the DAGs obtained by removing or reversing an existing edge in G, or by adding a new one. For states evaluation, several scores have been settled in the literature such as AIC, BIC or BDeu [3] or more recent ones such as qNML [15].

In [10], Niculescu-Mizil and Caruana extend this score-based search in a MT context. Let us denote this algorithm MT-GS. They consider a configuration of k structures $\{G_1, G_2, \ldots, G_k\}$ and then follow a greedy search procedure in the space of DAGs to find the k graphs that fit the best the k respective datasets. The neighborhood of a configuration is defined as the set of all configurations obtained by considering all possible subsets of the graphs and applying an add, remove or reverse operation to the same edge in each graph of each subset. The score to maximise is the posterior probability of a configuration given the data defined in Eq. 1.

$$P(\mathcal{G}|\mathcal{D}) = P(G_1,\ldots,G_k|D_1,\ldots,D_k) \propto P(\mathcal{G}) \prod_{a=1}^{k} P(D_a|G_a) \tag{1}$$

They propose two different priors (i) an edit prior which considers the minimum number of updates needed to make an edge similar in every structure and (ii) a paired prior that considers the differences among each pair of structures as defined in Eq. 2.

$$P(\mathcal{G}) = Z_{\delta,k} \prod_{1\leq a\leq k} P(G_a)^{\frac{1}{1+(k-1)\delta}} \prod_{1\leq a<b\leq k} (1-\delta)^{\frac{d(G_a,G_b)}{k-1}} \tag{2}$$

where $\delta \in [0,1]$ is a parameter that penalizes every difference between the models' structure when calculating the prior, $Z_{\delta,k}$ is a normalization constant and $d(G_a,G_b)$ is the number of edges in the symmetric difference between G_a and G_b. Thus, the scoring function takes into account data from all the tasks and leverages information between them.

As the search space can get large for large k and n (the number of variables in datasets), they provide a computational optimization based on a Branch-and-Bound strategy to find at each step the best configuration in the neighborhood of the current one. To this end, they define a partial configuration of order ℓ, $\mathcal{C}_\ell = (G_1,\ldots,G_\ell)$, as a configuration where only the first ℓ structures are specified and the other $k - \ell$ structures are not. This exploration goes through a search tree of depth k to reach the best scoring configuration. At each level $\ell < k$, only the score of the partial configuration $\mathcal{C}_\ell = (G_1,\ldots,G_\ell)$ is computed and compared to the current best score. The score of a partial configuration is defined as an upper bound to the scores of all complete configurations C that match it. By this way, each sub-tree rooted at a partial configuration whose score is lower than the current best score can be pruned.

Constraint-Based Approaches. Algorithms following this approach test conditional independencies between variables in the data, and progressively identify the graph that describes these dependencies and independencies discovered in the data [4].

In a transfer learning context, Jia et al. [5] address the problem of constraint-based learning with inductive transfer. Luis et al. [8] propose a constraint-based structure learning for BNs in a MT setting. The general outline of the algorithm is inspired from the (single task) PC algorithm [16]. It starts with a fully connected undirected graph, and measures the association between variables to decide if an edge should be removed from the graph or not. The major difference is the way the independence tests are evaluated. It is replaced by a linear combination of independence measures from the target task with the closest auxiliary task, where closeness is determined by the combination of two metrics: a global similarity Sg defined in Eq. 3 and a local similarity Sl defined in Eq. 4.

The global similarity measure Sg_{ab} computes the number of common dependencies and independencies between every possible pair of variables (X,Y) in task a and task b (i.e. in their corresponding datasets D_a and D_b)[8].

$$Sg_{ab} = \sum_{X<Y} \mathbb{1}(I_a(X,Y) - I_b(X,Y)) \tag{3}$$

where $I_a(X,Y)$ and $I_b(X,Y)$ are respectively the result of an independence test between variables X and Y performed on datasets D_a and D_b.

The local similarity measure $Sl_{ab}(X,Y|S)$ compares independencies between two variables X and Y given a subset of variables S [8].

$$Sl_{ab}(X,Y|S) = \begin{cases} 1, & \text{if } I_a(X,Y|S) = I_b(X,Y|S). \\ 0.5, & \text{otherwise.} \end{cases} \tag{4}$$

where $I_a(X,Y|S)$ and $I_b(X,Y|S)$ are respectively the result of the conditional independence test between variables X and Y given S performed on datasets D_a and D_b. Based on the two previous metrics, Luis et al. [8] define the combined similarity measure $Sc_{ab}(X,Y|S)$ as:

$$Sc_{ab}(X,Y|S) = Sg_{ab} \times Sl_{ab}(X,Y|S) \tag{5}$$

For a given task a, the confidence measure α_a estimates the confidence of the independence test between X and Y given the conditioning set S and is defined as:

$$\alpha_a(X,Y|S) = 1 - \frac{\log N_a}{2N_a} \times T \tag{6}$$

where $T = |X| \times |Y| \times |S|$, with $|x|$ is the cardinality of x, and where N_a is the size of the dataset D_a.

Finally, the combined independence function I_a, that computes the independence test between X and Y given S in task a with inductive transfer learning, is a linear weighted combination of the independence measures in a and in its most similar task b^* (with respect to the combined similarity Sc) :

$$\begin{aligned} Ic_a(X,Y|S) = {} & \alpha_a(X,Y|S) \times sgn(I_a(X,Y|S)) \\ & + \alpha_{b^*}(X,Y|S) \times Sc_{ab^*}(X,Y|S) \times sgn(I_{b^*}(X,Y|S)) \end{aligned} \tag{7}$$

where $sgn(I)$ is $+1$ if X and Y are independent given S and -1 otherwise.

Hybrid Approaches. These approaches combine the features of the constraint-based and the score-based algorithms. To our knowledge, they are only proposed so far for single task learning. Generally, these algorithms start by implementing a constraint-based strategy to reduce the space of candidate DAGs, then they perform a score-based strategy to find an optimal DAG in the restricted space. In this context, we can cite the Max-Min Hill-Climbing (MMHC) algorithm proposed in [18]. MMHC is a hybrid approach for single task Bayesian structure learning that first identifies the skeleton of the graph with a constraint-based method (named MMPC for Max-Min Parent Children) then it selects and directs the interesting edges using a search-and-score procedure.

The MMPC algorithm uses an association metric $A(X, Y|S)$ such as Mutual information or χ^2 to estimate the strength of the dependency between X and Y given S and it performs a conditional independence test $I(X, Y|S)$ from this metric. The algorithm progressively identifies for each variable X a set of candidate parents and children $CPC(X)$ (without distinction between parent or child).

Throughout the edge direction assignment step, a greedy search is performed to determine the DAG that best fits the data. The important difference from standard greedy search is that the search space is constrained by the fact that candidate edges must be consistent with the $CPCs$ discovered by MMPC.

3   The MT-MMHC Algorithm

The BN structure learning algorithms mentioned in Sect. 2 mainly perform transfer learning in single task (ST) scenario with constraint based approaches [8] or multi-task consideration with search-and-score methods [10]. In our contribution, we propose a hybrid approach for multi-task problems that we call MT-MMHC. The purpose is to learn k BN structures from k similar problems simultaneously, combining benefits from constraint-based algorithms, score-and-search based algorithms, TL and MT learning techniques.

3.1   Overall Process of MT-MMHC

The main idea is to extend the MMHC algorithm to the MT scenario, as shown in Fig. 1. As its ST counterpart, the procedure starts with a constraint-based phase to identify the CPC sets associated to each task. It performs a local search technique ensured by the MMPC algorithm (refer to the grey boxes in Fig. 1). For transfer learning adaptation, we propose in Sect. 3.2 a combined association metric. In the second phase, for edge orientation, we apply the MT greedy search algorithm proposed in [10] adapted to our context by constraining it to the discovered CPCs as described in Sect. 3.3.

3.2   The Combined Association Measure

The first phase of the MT-MMHC algorithm that we denote MT-MMPC, consists in k parallel MMPC with a new combined association measure, to identify the upper bound CPC of the skeleton of each model (refer to the grey boxes in Fig. 1).

Inspired by the work in [8], we propose in Eq. 8 this new association metric taking into account the MT setting.

$$Ac_a(X, Y|S) = \frac{\alpha_a(X, Y|S)A_a(X, Y|S) + \alpha_{b*}(X, Y|S)Sc_{ab*}(X, Y|S)A_{b*}(X, Y|S)}{\alpha_a(X, Y|S) + \alpha_{b*}(X, Y|S)Sc_{ab*}(X, Y|S)}$$

$$(8)$$

where $A_a(X, Y|S)$ is the usual association measure between two variables X and Y given a subset S from the dataset D_a and $A_{b*}(X, Y|S)$ expresses the

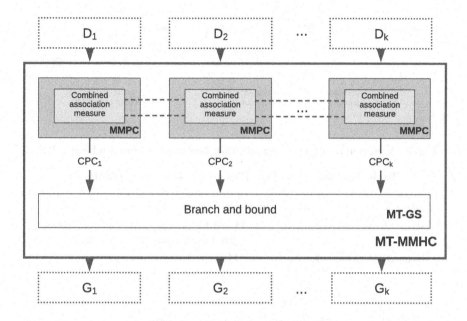

Fig. 1. Overall process of MT-MMHC.

association measure between the two same variables X and Y given the subset S from dataset D_{b*} of the closest task $b*$ determined by the combined similarity measure Sc.

This combined association measure allows us to transfer information between similar tasks while computing independence tests. We propose using Ac_a instead of the combined independence function I_a defined in Eq. 7 for the following reason: as a convex combination of two association measurements, this value can also be interpreted as an association measurement. I_a is the non convex linear combination of two signs of independence tests which is only used for its sign whereas the MMPC algorithm requires also the information provided by the strength of the association between variables.

3.3 MT Greedy Search with CPC Constraints

MT-MMPC, the constraint-based phase of MT-MMHC, outputs a CPC set $\{CPC_1, CPC_2, \ldots, CPC_k\}$ for each task.

In the second phase of MT-MMHC, as inspired by the single task MMHC, we propose to apply the MT-GS algorithm (cf. Fig. 1) described in Sect. 2. The main difference lies in the input of the algorithm and how we accordingly bound the search space by using the information provided by the $CPCs$.

The neighborhood of a configuration $\{G_1, G_2, \ldots, G_k\}$ is generated by applying for each pair of nodes in each possible subset of graphs an edit operation (add, remove, reverse or leave unchanged an edge). We adapt the generation of

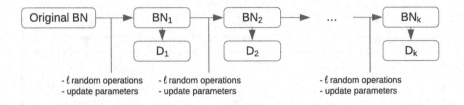

Fig. 2. A procedure to generate multi-task benchmarks from a reference BN.

Table 1. Description of the BNs used in our experimentation.

Name	Nodes	Arcs	Max in-degree	Description
Asia	8	8	2	Used for patient chest clinic diagnosis given symptoms and risk factors
Alarm	37	46	4	Medical diagnosis for monitoring intensive care patients

this neighborhood by allowing the addition of the edge $X \to Y$ in a graph G_a only if $X \in CPC_a(Y)$.

By using this definition of a neighborhood, we can perform a MT greedy search procedure while keeping all the properties of the greedy search in the context of MT with the constraints provided by the result of MT-MMPC. Hence, we can reduce the search space and decrease the computational cost of the greedy search. As the neighborhood size of a configuration $\{G_1, G_2, ..., G_k\}$ can get large for large k and n, MT-MMHC could then be more scalable than MT-GS.

4   Experiments

In this section, we present an empirical evaluation of MT-MMHC as a comparative study with state-of-the-art single task BNs structure learning algorithms GS and MMHC, and also with the MT-GS algorithm.

4.1   Experimental Protocol

Benchmark and Data Generation. When benchmarks for BN structure learning in single task context are quite popular with reference models such as ASIA [6] or ALARM [2] (see Table 1), there are no benchmarks for evaluating MT algorithms. We propose here one simple procedure that takes as an input one of the reference models used for ST learning, and generates a set of k MT reference models by controlling the similarity between each model.

As a first version of this procedure, we generate k similar networks by applying one random walk between each model (by applying randomly ℓ usual operators: add, remove or reverse edge) and recomputing randomly the parameters (see Fig. 2).

We can then generate one dataset for each model by applying the usual forward sampling algorithm, with a potentially different number of observations that we call data size N_a for each task a.

In our work, we generated three series of experiments, with small datasets size ($N_a \in [500, 1000[$), medium size ($N_a \in [1000, 5000[$) and large size ($N_a \in [5000, 10000[$) for $k = 5$ different tasks generated with $\ell = 1$.

Algorithms. We have implemented several algorithms in PILGRIM[1], our C++ library dedicated to probabilistic graphical models. We propose to compare MT-MMHC (described in Sect. 3), MT-GS (cf. Sect. 2) and the independent running of k single task structure learning algorithms kST-GS and kST-MMHC. In our experiments, we used mutual information as a measure of association, with $\alpha = 5\%$ for the independence tests, and BIC as an approximation of each marginal likelihood $P(D_a|G_a)$ in Eq. 1 and $\delta = 1e - 7$ as a penalty in Eq. 2.

Evaluation Metrics. We measure performances in terms of run time and Structural Hamming Distance (SHD) between the true structures (from which we generated sampling data) and the learned ones, and more exactly the distance between the essential graphs as proposed in [18]. For each experiment, we propose the mean and standard deviation of SHD over 10 runs x 5 tasks, and the mean and standard deviation of the execution time over the 10 runs.

4.2   Empirical Results

MT-MMHC Versus kST-GS and kST-MMHC. Figure 3 (top) presents performances in terms of SHD (the lower the better) for the three approaches MT-MMHC, kST-GS and kST-MMHC with respect to three categories of data size, and MT benchmarks generated from ASIA and ALARM networks.

The trends in the performances are as expected: learned networks are more accurate with larger datasets, and kST-MMHC performs better than kST-GS except for small datasets. It is worth to note that MT-MMHC is able to find better networks than the single task approaches.

Figure 3 (bottom) shows the average execution time to learn five tasks BNs. Single task MMHC is the fastest approach in all experiments, but we can notice that MT-MMHC is much faster than ST greedy search in a medium network like Alarm thanks to the space reduction strategy. For the small network Asia, MT-MMHC is the slowest but still runs in quite reasonable time (from 2.5 to 17.5 s on average). For instance, in the case of the largest data slice from ASIA, MT-MMHC is 17% slower but 40% more accurate than kST-GS.

MT-MMHC Versus MT-GS. Figure 4 presents performances in terms of SHD and execution time for MT-MMHC and MT-GS with respect to the sizes of datasets, for MT benchmarks generated from the ALARM network.

---

[1] https://pilgrim.univ-nantes.fr/.

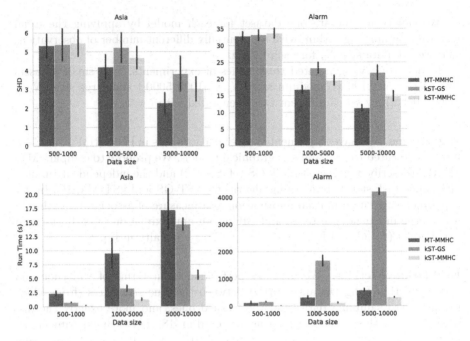

Fig. 3. SHD (top) and run time (bottom) with respect to data size for MT-MMHC, kST-GS and kST-MMHC (MT benchmarks are generated respectively from the ASIA and ALARM networks).

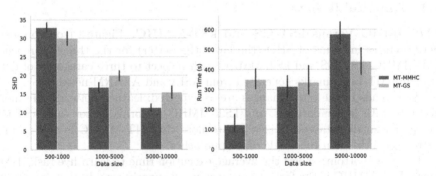

Fig. 4. SHD (left) and run time (right) with respect to datasets size for MT-MMHC and MT-GS for MT benchmarks generated from the ALARM network

For small datasets, MT-GS is slightly better than MT-MMHC with a much higher execution time. For medium and larger datasets MT-MMHC performs better in terms of quality of the learned model and runs with an affordable time cost.

5 Conclusion

In this paper, we propose an extension of an efficient BN structure discovery algorithm MMHC to a multi-task context. Our algorithm MT-MMHC is the first hybrid transfer learning algorithm. MT-MMHC can learn multiple BN structures simultaneously by inducing information between similar tasks with the help of a new combined association measure.

In order to validate our approach, we have also proposed one procedure to generate MT benchmarks from any reference model, by controlling the similarity between tasks.

The results of our experiments show that it is more beneficial to learn related tasks simultaneously than considering them individually and, both our combined association measure and the use of the CPC discovered by MT-MMPC help in finding accurate models with an affordable time cost. In these experiments, MT-MMHC was able to learn better models than kST-GS, kST-MMHC and MT-GS in medium to large MT benchmarks.

This work is the first step of our research, with several perspectives. In a very short term, we intend to perform larger experiments with other datasets to consolidate the interest of our proposition. We are also planning to work on additional procedures to generate MT benchmarks, for instance by using "longer" random walks, or by creating tasks that don't necessarily have all variables in common.

Finally, our objective is to combine such MT structure learning algorithms with differential privacy techniques (already used for BN ST learning in [19] for instance) in order to propose one general framework to Federated Learning of Bayesian networks, i.e. collaborative Structure and Parameter Learning with privacy considerations and no shared training data. Our interest is also to perform this BN federated learning for the development of BN-based medical assistants such as Medical Companion [9].

Acknowledgment. This work was supported by ANR AIby4 (Artificial Intelligence by Humans, for Humans) PhD program (ANR-20-THIA-0011) and Atlanstic2020 regional program.

References

1. Azzimonti, L., Corani, G., Scutari, M.: Structure learning from related data sets with a hierarchical bayesian score. In: Jaeger, M., Nielsen, T.D. (eds.) Proceedings of the 10th International Conference on Probabilistic Graphical Models. Proceedings of Machine Learning Research, vol. 138, pp. 5–16. PMLR (2020)
2. Beinlich, I.A., Suermondt, H.J., Chavez, R.M., Cooper, G.F.: The ALARM monitoring system: A case study with two probabilistic inference techniques for belief networks. In: Hunter, J., Cookson, J., Wyatt, J. (eds.) AIME 89, Second European Conference on Artificial Intelligence in Medicine. Lecture Notes in Medical Informatics, vol. 38, pp. 247–256. Springer (1989)
3. Carvalho, A.M.: Scoring functions for learning Bayesian networks. Technical report 54/2009 Apr 2009, INESC-ID (2009)

4. Daly, R., Shen, Q., Aitken, S.: Learning Bayesian networks: approaches and issues. Knowl. Eng. Rev. **26**(2), 99–157 (2011)
5. Jia, H., Wu, Z., Chen, J., Chen, B., Yao, S.: Causal discovery with bayesian networks inductive transfer. In: Liu, W., Giunchiglia, F., Yang, B. (eds.) KSEM 2018. LNCS (LNAI), vol. 11061, pp. 351–361. Springer, Cham (2018). https://doi.org/10.1007/978-3-319-99365-2_31
6. Lauritzen, S.L., Spiegelhalter, D.J.: Local computations with probabilities on graphical structures and their application to expert systems. J. Roy. Stat. Soc. Series B (Methodological) **50**(2), 157–224 (1988)
7. López-Cruz, P.L., Larrañaga, P., DeFelipe, J., Bielza, C.: Bayesian network modeling of the consensus between experts: An application to neuron classification. Int. J. Approximate Reasoning **55**(1), 3–22 (2014)
8. Luis, R., Sucar, L.E., Morales, E.F.: Inductive transfer for learning Bayesian networks. Mach. Learn. **79**(1), 227–255 (2010)
9. Mouchabac, S., Leray, P., Adrien, V., Gollier-Briant, F., Bonnot, O.: Beyond big data in behavioral psychiatry, the place of Bayesian network. example from a preclinical trial of an innovative smartphone application to prevent suicide relapse. J. Med. Internet Res. 16/03/2021:24560, (in press) (2021)
10. Niculescu-Mizil, A., Caruana, R.: Inductive transfer for Bayesian network structure learning. In: Meila, M., Shen, X. (eds.) Proceedings of the Eleventh International Conference on Artificial Intelligence and Statistics. Proceedings of Machine Learning Research, vol. 2, pp. 339–346. PMLR, San Juan, Puerto Rico (21–24 Mar 2007)
11. Oyen, D., Lane, T.: Leveraging domain knowledge in multitask Bayesian network structure learning. In: Proceedings of the AAAI Conference on AI 26(1) (2012)
12. Oyen, D., Lane, T.: Bayesian discovery of multiple Bayesian networks via transfer learning. In: IEEE International Conference on Data Mining (2013)
13. Salaken, S.M., Khosravi, A., Nguyen, T., Nahavandi, S.: Extreme learning machine based transfer learning algorithms. Neurocomput. **267**(C), 516–524 (2017)
14. Scutari, M., Vitolo, C., Tucker, A.: Learning Bayesian networks from big data with greedy search: computational complexity and efficient implementation. Stat. Comput. **29**(5), 1095–1108 (2019)
15. Silander, T., Leppä-Aho, J., Jääsaari, E., Roos, T.: Quotient normalized maximum likelihood criterion for learning Bayesian network structures. In: International Conference on Artificial Intelligence and Statistics, pp. 948–957. PMLR (2018)
16. Spirtes, P., Glymour, C., Scheines, R.: Causation, Prediction, and Search, 2nd edn. MIT press (2000)
17. Thung, K.H., Wee, C.Y.: A brief review on multi-task learning. Multimed. Tools Appl. **77**(22), 29705–29725 (2018)
18. Tsamardinos, I., Brown, L.E., Aliferis, C.F.: The max-min hill-climbing bayesian network structure learning algorithm. Mach. Learn. **65**(1), 31–78 (2006)
19. Zhang, J., Cormode, G., Procopiuc, C.M., Srivastava, D., Xiao, X.: PrivBayes: Private data release via Bayesian networks. ACM Trans. Database Syst. 42(4) (2017)
20. Zhang, Y., Yang, Q.: A survey on multi-task learning. IEEE Transactions on Knowledge and Data Engineering, pp. 1–20 (2021)
21. Zhou, Y., Hospedales, T.M., Fenton, N.: When and where to transfer for Bayesian network parameter learning. Expert Syst. Appl. **55**, 361–373 (2016)

Persuasive Contrastive Explanations
for Bayesian Networks

Tara Koopman and Silja Renooij[✉][iD]

Department of Information and Computing Sciences, Utrecht University,
Utrecht, The Netherlands
s.renooij@uu.nl

Abstract. Explanation in Artificial Intelligence is often focused on providing reasons for why a model under consideration and its outcome are
correct. Recently, research in explainable machine learning has initiated
a shift in focus on including so-called counterfactual explanations. In this
paper we propose to combine both types of explanation in the context
of explaining Bayesian networks. To this end we introduce *persuasive
contrastive explanations* that aim to provide an answer to the question
Why outcome t instead of t'? posed by a user. In addition, we propose an
algorithm for computing persuasive contrastive explanations. Both our
definition of persuasive contrastive explanation and the proposed algorithm can be employed beyond the current scope of Bayesian networks.

Keywords: Explainable AI · Counterfactuals · Bayesian networks

1 Introduction

Explanation of Bayesian networks has been a topic of interest ever since their
introduction [15,19]. Four categories of explanation method are distinguished,
depending on the focus of explanation: 1) explanation of evidence; 2) explanation
of reasoning; 3) explanation of the model itself, and 4) explanation of decisions [5,
11]. The last category is a recent addition to cover methods that address the
question of whether or not the user can make an informed enough decision.

In the explanation of reasoning category, methods typically aim to provide
justification for the obtained outcomes and the underlying inference process [11].
Approaches include those that extract reasoning chains from the Bayesian network, measure the impact of evidence, or identify supporting and conflicting
evidence [10–12,20,22,25]. Explanation of reasoning could also address the explanation of outcomes *not* obtained [11]. In fact, upon encountering an unexpected
event, people tend to request *contrastive* explanations that answer the question *Why outcome t instead of t'?* [14]. Such contrastive explanations were
recently adopted to explain black-box machine learning (ML) models with high-
dimensional feature spaces [23] by using counterfactuals that capture the change
in input required to change the outcome from t to t'. The use of counterfactuals

---

The original version of this chapter was revised: The errors in Algorithm 1 (page 235)
were corrected to include intentionally blank lines in the algorithm. The correction to
this chapter is available at https://doi.org/10.1007/978-3-030-86772-0_49

J. Vejnarová and N. Wilson (Eds.): ECSQARU 2021, LNAI 12897, pp. 229–242, 2021.
https://doi.org/10.1007/978-3-030-86772-0_17

for the purpose of explanation is popular in ML research, although the definition of what a counterfactual explanation entails varies greatly [21].

A recently identified challenge for ML research is that of unifying counterfactual explanations with more "traditional explainable AI" that focuses on justifying the original outcome [21]. This, however, is not a challenge specific to ML models only. In this paper we propose the *persuasive contrastive explanation* in the context of Bayesian networks. This explanation provides an answer to the question *Why t instead of t'?* posed by a user, where t is the outcome predicted as most likely by the Bayesian network and t' is the output expected (or desired) by the user. We will provide a contrastive explanation based upon an interpretation of counterfactuals by Wachter et al. [24]. Counterfactuals, however, do not serve to justify outcome t. To provide a more complete answer to the *Why... ?* question, we will try to persuade the user into believing that in fact t is the correct outcome. To this end, we propose to include the evidence that suffices to conclude t in the explanation as well. After presenting some properties of our explanations, we propose an algorithm for their computation.

This paper is organised as follows. In Sect. 2 we introduce our new type of explanation and some of its properties. In Sect. 3 we present a search structure for explanations that is exploited by the algorithm detailed in Sect. 4. We review more related work in Sect. 5 and conclude the paper in Sect. 6.

2 Persuasive Contrastive Explanations

In this section we propose our new type of explanation in the context of Bayesian networks. A Bayesian network (BN) represents a joint probability distribution Pr over a set of discrete random variables [8]. We denote such variables V by capital letters and use $\Omega(V)$ to represent their domain. We write v as shorthand for a value assignment $V = v$, $v \in \Omega(V)$. (Sub)sets of variables are denoted by bold-face capital letters $\mathbf{V}$ and their joint value combinations, or configurations, by bold-face small letters $\mathbf{v}$; $\Omega(\mathbf{V})$ is taken to represent the domain of all configurations of $\mathbf{V}$. We write $\mathbf{v}' \subseteq \mathbf{v}$ to denote that $\mathbf{v}'$ is a configuration of $\mathbf{V}' \subseteq \mathbf{V}$ that is consistent with $\mathbf{v}$; we call $\mathbf{v}'$ a sub-configuration of $\mathbf{v}$. Moreover, for a given configuration $\mathbf{v}$, we write $\overline{\mathbf{v}}$ to indicate a configuration for $\mathbf{V}$ in which *every* $V_i \in \mathbf{V}$ takes on a value from $\Omega(V_i)$ that is different from its value in $\mathbf{v}$. Note that $\overline{\mathbf{v}}$ is unique only if all variables in $\mathbf{V}$ are binary-valued.

We are interested in the probabilities $\Pr(T \mid \mathbf{e})$ that can be computed from the Bayesian network for a target variable $T \in \mathbf{V}$ and evidence $\mathbf{e}$ for a set of variables $\mathbf{E} \subseteq \mathbf{V} \setminus \{T\}$. We assume that the most likely value of T given $\mathbf{e}$, i.e. $\arg\max_{t^* \in \Omega(T)}\{\Pr(t^* \mid \mathbf{e})\} = \arg\max_{t^* \in \Omega(T)}\{\Pr(t^*\mathbf{e})\}$, is conveyed to the user as the network's output. We refer to this as the *mode* of T given $\mathbf{e}$, written $\top(T \mid \mathbf{e})$. We now define the explanation context used throughout the paper.

Definition 1. *An explanation context is a tuple $\langle \mathbf{e}, t, t' \rangle$ where $t = \top(T \mid \mathbf{e})$ and $t \neq t' \in \Omega(T)$.*[1]

---

[1] In case $\top(T \mid \mathbf{e})$ is not unique, we assume all modes are output to the user and that t' is not among these.

The explanation context describes the context for answering the question *Why t instead of t'?*. We will answer this question with a contrastive explanation that combines a sufficient explanation for t with a counterfactual explanation for t'.

Definition 2. *Consider explanation context* $\langle \mathbf{e}, t, t' \rangle$. *A persuasive contrastive explanation is any pair* $[\mathbf{s}, \mathbf{c}]$ *where* $\mathbf{s} \in \Omega(\mathbf{S})$, $\mathbf{c} \in \Omega(\mathbf{C})$, $\mathbf{S}, \mathbf{C} \subseteq \mathbf{E}$, *and*

- $\mathbf{s} \subseteq \mathbf{e}$ *is a* sufficient explanation *for* t, *i.e.* $\top(T \,|\, \mathbf{s}\tilde{\mathbf{e}}') = t$ *for all* $\tilde{\mathbf{e}}' \in \Omega(\mathbf{E}')$, $\mathbf{E}' = \mathbf{E} \setminus \mathbf{S}$, *and there is no* $\mathbf{s}' \subset \mathbf{s}$ *for which this property holds; and*
- $\mathbf{c} \subseteq \bar{\mathbf{e}}$ *is a* counterfactual explanation *for* t', *i.e.* $\top(T \,|\, \mathbf{e}'\mathbf{c}) = t'$ *for* $\mathbf{e}' \subseteq \mathbf{e}$, $\mathbf{e}' \in \Omega(\mathbf{E}')$, $\mathbf{E}' = \mathbf{E} \setminus \mathbf{C}$, *and there is no* $\mathbf{c}' \subset \mathbf{c}$ *for which this property holds.*

Since $\mathbf{e}$ is taken to represent observations in the real world, it is common practice to assume that $\Pr(\mathbf{e}) > 0$. For computing the modes in the above definition it is required that $\Pr(\mathbf{s}\tilde{\mathbf{e}}') > 0$ and $\Pr(\mathbf{e}'\mathbf{c}) > 0$. As it does not make sense for explanations to include impossible combinations of observations, any zero-probability configuration for $\mathbf{E}$ can be disregarded.

The sufficient explanation explains how the evidence relates to the outcome of the network by giving the user a sub-configuration of the evidence that results in the same outcome, regardless of which values are observed for the remaining evidence variables. The sufficient explanation generalizes the *PI-explanation* that was introduced for explaining naive Bayesian classifiers with binary-valued target variables [16], and more recently referred to as *sufficient reason* when used in explaining Bayesian network classifiers (BNCs) with both binary-valued target and evidence variables [4]. The word 'counterfactual' has various interpretations; in our case, a counterfactual explanation details how the evidence should be different to result in the outcome expected by the user. Our definition is a formalisation of the one by Wachter et al. [24], tailored to our specific context.

We will call a set $\mathbf{S}$ with which a sufficient explanation is associated a *sufficient set*; a *counterfactual set* is defined analogously. Sufficient sets and counterfactual sets have a number of properties that we will exploit to enable their computation. All properties assume an explanation context $\langle \mathbf{e}, t, t' \rangle$. The first property addresses the extent to which sufficient explanations are unique and follows directly from Definition 2.

Proposition 1. *A set* $\mathbf{S} \subseteq \mathbf{E}$ *has at most one associated sufficient explanation* $\mathbf{s}$. *Sets* $\mathbf{S}, \mathbf{S}' \subset \mathbf{E}$ *for which neither* $\mathbf{S} \subset \mathbf{S}'$ *nor* $\mathbf{S}' \subset \mathbf{S}$ *can both be sufficient sets.*

The next property addresses the relation between the type of evidence variables (binary or non-binary) and counterfactual explanations.

Proposition 2. *A counterfactual set* $\mathbf{C} \subseteq \mathbf{E}$ *can have multiple associated counterfactual explanations* $\mathbf{c}$, *unless all variables in* $\mathbf{C}$ *are binary-valued. Sets* $\mathbf{C}, \mathbf{C}' \subset \mathbf{E}$ *with* $\mathbf{C} \subset \mathbf{C}'$ *can both be counterfactual sets, unless all variables in* $\mathbf{C}$ *are binary-valued.*

Proof. If all variables in $\mathbf{C}$ are binary-valued then $\mathbf{c} \subseteq \bar{\mathbf{e}}$ is unique; in this case, by Definition 2, no subset of $\mathbf{C}$ can be a counterfactual set. Otherwise,

$\bar{\mathbf{e}}$ is not unique and there exist multiple configurations $\mathbf{c} \subseteq \bar{\mathbf{e}}$ for $\mathbf{C}$. Consider two such configurations $\mathbf{c}_1 \neq \mathbf{c}_2$. Then both can adhere to Definition 2 and be counterfactual explanations, but this is not necessary. Assume that $\mathbf{c}_1$ is a counterfactual explanation and that $\mathbf{c}_2$ is not, and consider a configuration $\mathbf{c}' \supset \mathbf{c}_2$ for a set $\mathbf{C}' \supset \mathbf{C}$. Then $\mathbf{c}' \not\supset \mathbf{c}_1$ so $\mathbf{c}'$ could be a counterfactual explanation, in which case both $\mathbf{C}$ and $\mathbf{C}'$ would be counterfactual sets.   □

We conclude that a given explanation context can be associated with multiple persuasive contrastive explanations. Finally we establish a relation between sufficient sets and counterfactual sets.

Proposition 3. *Consider a set* $\mathbf{S} \subseteq \mathbf{E}$, *and let* $\mathbf{C} = \mathbf{E} \setminus \mathbf{S}$. *If* $\mathbf{S}$ *is a sufficient set, or is a superset of a sufficient set, then* $\mathbf{C}$ *cannot be a counterfactual set.*

Proof. If $\mathbf{S}$ is a sufficient set with sufficient explanation $\mathbf{s} \subseteq \mathbf{e}$ then by Definition 3, $\top(T \,|\, \mathbf{sc}) = t$ for all $\mathbf{c} \in \Omega(\mathbf{C})$. Since $t' \neq t$, no $\mathbf{c}$ can be a counterfactual explanation and hence $\mathbf{C}$ is not a counterfactual set. Now let $\mathbf{S}' \subset \mathbf{S}$ be a sufficient set with sufficient explanation $\mathbf{s}'$ and consider configuration $\mathbf{s} = \mathbf{s}'\mathbf{d} \subseteq \mathbf{e}$ for $\mathbf{d} \in \mathbf{S} \setminus \mathbf{S}'$. Then $\mathbf{dc} \in \Omega(\mathbf{C}')$, where $\mathbf{C}' = \mathbf{E} \setminus \mathbf{S}'$ and $\mathbf{c} \in \Omega(\mathbf{C})$. Since $\mathbf{S}'$ is a sufficient set, $\top(T \,|\, \mathbf{s}'\mathbf{c}') = t$ for all $\mathbf{c}' \in \Omega(\mathbf{C}')$. As a result, $\top(T \,|\, \mathbf{s}'\mathbf{dc}) = \top(T \,|\, \mathbf{sc}) = t$ for all $\mathbf{c} \in \Omega(\mathbf{C})$. Hence, $\mathbf{C}$ is not a counterfactual set.   □

3   Explanation Lattice

To find all sufficient and counterfactual explanations for a given explanation context $\langle \mathbf{e}, t, t' \rangle$, we can typically do better than naively looping through all possible configurations $\widetilde{\mathbf{e}}$ for $\mathbf{E}$ and computing all distributions $\Pr(T \,|\, \widetilde{\mathbf{e}})$. In order to exploit the properties from Propositions 1–3 in our search for explanations, we propose to organise the search space using an annotated lattice.

Definition 3. *Consider context* $\langle \mathbf{e}, t, t' \rangle$ *and lattice* $\mathcal{L} = (\mathcal{P}(\mathbf{E}), \subseteq)$, *for powerset* $\mathcal{P}(\mathbf{E})$ *of* $\mathbf{E}$. *An* explanation lattice *for this context is the lattice* $\mathcal{L}$ *in which each lattice element* $\mathbf{S} \subseteq \mathbf{E}$ *is annotated with the tuple* $(\mathbf{s}, \mathcal{M}_{\mathbf{S}}, l_{\mathbf{S}})$ *such that*

- $\mathbf{s} \subseteq \mathbf{e}$ *is the configuration of* $\mathbf{S}$ *consistent with* $\mathbf{e}$;
- *if* $\mathbf{S} = \mathbf{E}$ *then* $\mathcal{M}_{\mathbf{S}} = \{(\emptyset, t)\}$; *otherwise,* $\mathcal{M}_{\mathbf{S}} = \{(\mathbf{c}, t^*) \mid t^* = \top(T \,|\, \mathbf{sc})$, *with* $\mathbf{c} \in \Omega(\mathbf{C}), \mathbf{C} = \mathbf{E} \setminus \mathbf{S}$ *and* $\mathbf{c} \subseteq \bar{\mathbf{e}}\}$;
- $l_{\mathbf{S}} \in \{\mathsf{true}, \mathsf{exp}, \mathsf{oth}\}$, *where* $l_{\mathbf{S}} = \mathsf{true}$ *if* $t^* = t$ *for all* $(\mathbf{c}, t^*) \in \mathcal{M}_{\mathbf{S}}$, $l_{\mathbf{S}} = \mathsf{exp}$ *if* $t^* = t'$ *for all* $(\mathbf{c}, t^*) \in \mathcal{M}_{\mathbf{S}}$, *and* $l_{\mathbf{S}} = \mathsf{oth}$, *otherwise.*

The elements of lattice $\mathcal{L}$ are all subsets of $\mathbf{E}$ and hence represent *potential* sufficient sets $\mathbf{S}$ with associated sufficient explanation $\mathbf{s}$. For each lattice element $\mathbf{S}$, the set $\mathbf{C} = \mathbf{E} \setminus \mathbf{S}$ is a *potential* counterfactual set. To determine if $\mathbf{c}$ is a counterfactual explanation, we need to know the corresponding outcome; these pairs are stored in $\mathcal{M}$. Label l summarises whether or not all $\mathbf{sc}$ configurations associated with a lattice element result in the same outcome, with true indicating that this is always the originally predicted outcome t and exp indicating that this

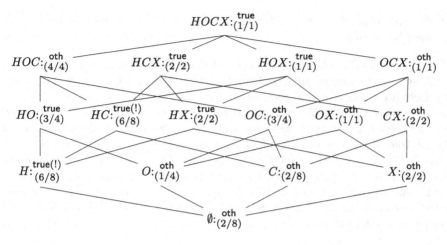

Fig. 1. A partially annotated explanation lattice for the evidence in the CHILD network: elements $\mathbf{S} \subseteq \mathbf{E} = \{H, O, C, X\}$ are annotated with label $l_{\mathbf{S}}$. Numbers between brackets indicate the fraction of modes actually computed. See Example 1 for further details.

is always the expected output t'. Note that if all variables in $\mathbf{E}$ are binary-valued then each $\mathcal{M}_{\mathbf{S}}$ contains a *single* pair $(\mathbf{c}, t^*)$. If the target variable T is binary-valued, then $l_{\mathbf{S}} = \mathsf{oth}$ can only occur with non-binary evidence variables. Figure 1 shows a partially annotated lattice, which is further explained in Sect. 4.3.

For a lattice element $\mathbf{S}$ we will use the term *ancestors* to refer to all supersets of $\mathbf{S}$ in the lattice, and *parents* to refer to the supersets of size $|\mathbf{S}| + 1$; the parent set will be denoted $\mathbf{S}_{\Uparrow}$. Similarly, the term *descendants* is used to refer to all subsets of $\mathbf{S}$ in the lattice, and a *child* is a subset of size $|\mathbf{S}| - 1$; the set of all children will be denoted $\mathbf{S}_{\Downarrow}$. The lattice now provides all information necessary for determining whether or not a lattice element represents a sufficient set.

Lemma 1. *Consider context $\langle \mathbf{e}, t, t' \rangle$ and explanation lattice $\mathcal{L}$ with lattice element $\mathbf{S} \subseteq \mathbf{E}$. Then for any possible configuration $\tilde{\mathbf{e}}' \in \Omega(\mathbf{E}')$ for $\mathbf{E}' = \mathbf{E} \setminus \mathbf{S}$, output $\top(T \mid \mathbf{s}\tilde{\mathbf{e}}')$ is available from the annotation of $\mathbf{S}$ or one of its ancestors.*

Proof. From Definition 3 we have that $\mathcal{M}_{\mathbf{S}}$ contains $\top(T \mid \mathbf{s}\mathbf{e}')$ for all $\mathbf{e}' \in \Omega(\mathbf{E}')$ with $\mathbf{e}' \subseteq \bar{\mathbf{e}}$. Now consider a configuration $\mathbf{de}^+ \in \Omega(\mathbf{E}')$ where $\mathbf{d} \subseteq \mathbf{e}$ and $\mathbf{e}^+ \subseteq \bar{\mathbf{e}}$ for some set $\mathbf{E}^+$. Then $\mathbf{S}^+ = \mathbf{E} \setminus \mathbf{E}^+$ is a superset of $\mathbf{S}$, annotated with $\mathbf{s}^+ = \mathbf{sd}$ and outcome $\top(T \mid \mathbf{sde}^+)$. We conclude that the outcomes for all remaining $\tilde{\mathbf{e}}' \in \Omega(\mathbf{E}')$ are found in the annotations of all supersets $\mathbf{S}^+$ of $\mathbf{S}$, which are exactly the ancestors of $\mathbf{S}$. □

The exact way to establish a sufficient set from the lattice is given by the following proposition.

Proposition 4. *Consider context $\langle \mathbf{e}, t, t' \rangle$ and lattice element $\mathbf{S} \subseteq \mathbf{E}$ in explanation lattice $\mathcal{L}$. Set $\mathbf{S}$ is a sufficient set iff all of the following hold:*

1. $\mathbf{S}$ and each of its ancestors $\mathbf{S}^+$ is annotated with label $l_{\mathbf{S}} = l_{\mathbf{S}+} = \mathsf{true}$, and

2. *for each child* $\mathbf{S}^- \in \mathbf{S}_{\Downarrow}$, *either* $l_{\mathbf{S}^-} \neq$ true, *or* $\mathbf{S}^-$ *has an ancestor* $\mathbf{S}^+$ *with label* $l_{\mathbf{S}^+} \neq$ true.

Proof. From Definition 3 and Lemma 1 we have that the first property holds iff $\top(T \mid \mathbf{s}\widetilde{\mathbf{e}}') = t$ for any possible configuration $\widetilde{\mathbf{e}}' \in \Omega(\mathbf{E}')$ for $\mathbf{E}' = \mathbf{E} \setminus \mathbf{S}$. Therefore, by Definition 2 $\mathbf{S}$ is a sufficient set, unless there exists a subset $\mathbf{S}^- \subset \mathbf{S}$, i.e. a lattice descendant, that adheres to the first property. This case is covered by the second property. Consider a child $\mathbf{S}^- \in \mathbf{S}_{\Downarrow}$ of $\mathbf{S}$ in the lattice. Then $l_{\mathbf{S}^-} \neq$ true iff there exists a configuration $\mathbf{e}^+ \in \Omega(\mathbf{E}^+)$ for $\mathbf{E}^+ = \mathbf{E} \setminus \mathbf{S}^-$ such that $\top(T \mid \mathbf{s}^-\mathbf{e}^+) \neq t$. Hence neither $\mathbf{S}^-$, nor any of its descendants, can represent a sufficient set. Now suppose that $l_{\mathbf{S}^-} =$ true then $\mathbf{S}^-$ can only be sufficient if all its ancestors $\mathbf{S}^+$ have $l_{\mathbf{S}^+} =$ true. If there exists an ancestor with $l_{\mathbf{S}^+} \neq$ true, then none of the descendants of $\mathbf{S}^+$, which include $\mathbf{S}^-$ and its descendants, can represent a sufficient set.   □

The next proposition provides the means for determining counterfactual explanations from the lattice.

Proposition 5. *Consider context* $\langle \mathbf{e}, t, t' \rangle$ *and lattice element* $\mathbf{S} \subseteq \mathbf{E}$ *in explanation lattice* $\mathcal{L}$. *Configuration* $\mathbf{c}$ *for set* $\mathbf{C} = \mathbf{E} \setminus \mathbf{S}$ *is a counterfactual explanation for* t' *iff* $(\mathbf{c}, t') \in \mathcal{M}_{\mathbf{S}}$ *and for none of the ancestors* $\mathbf{S}^+$ *of* $\mathbf{S}$ *there exists a* $\mathbf{c}' \subset \mathbf{c}$ *with* $(\mathbf{c}', t') \in \mathcal{M}_{\mathbf{S}^+}$.

Proof. From Definition 3 we have that $(\mathbf{c}, t') \in \mathcal{M}_{\mathbf{S}}$ iff $\top(T \mid \mathbf{sc}) = t'$. Therefore, by Definition 2, $\mathbf{c}$ is a counterfactual explanation for t', unless there exists a $\mathbf{c}' \subset \mathbf{c}$ that also results in outcome t'. Such a $\mathbf{c}'$ can only be found for a set $\mathbf{C}' = \mathbf{E} \setminus \mathbf{S}^+$ where $\mathbf{S}^+$ is a superset of $\mathbf{S}$ and hence a lattice ancestor.   □

4   Computing Sufficient and Counterfactual Explanations

We will use a breadth first search on the explanation lattice to return the sufficient and counterfactual explanations. During the search, the lattice is annotated *dynamically* in order to minimize the number of mode computations, since not all lattice elements need necessarily be visited. As a result, $l_{\mathbf{S}} = \emptyset$ as long as a lattice element has not been processed during search, and the modes in $\mathcal{M}_{\mathbf{S}}$ are unknown (unkn) until actually computed. We will first present two algorithms for separately computing the two types of explanation. We will then illustrate the combined search and discuss further optimisations.

4.1   Searching the Lattice for Sufficient Explanations

The breadth-first search for sufficient explanations (BFS-SFX) is described in pseudo code in Algorithm 1. Since sufficient explanations are set-minimal, it may seem most optimal to start the search at the bottom of the explanation lattice. However, to decide whether a lattice element represents a sufficient set, we require the labels of its lattice ancestors (see Proposition 4). Hence we start

---

Algorithm 1: BFS-SFX for computing sufficient explanations.

Input : BN $\mathcal{B}$, context $\langle \mathbf{e}, t, t' \rangle$ and explanation lattice $\mathcal{L}$
Output: Set $\mathcal{S}$ with all sufficient explanations

1   SQ $\leftarrow$ **E**; PotS $\leftarrow \emptyset$
2   **while** SQ not empty **do**
3 | **S** $\leftarrow$ Dequeue(SQ);
4 | **if** $l_\mathbf{S} = \emptyset$ and $\forall \mathbf{S}^+ \in \mathbf{S}_\Uparrow : l_{\mathbf{S}^+} = $ true **then**
5 | | ComputeModesAndLabel($\mathcal{L}$, **S**);
6 | | **if** $l_\mathbf{S} = $ true **then**
7 | | | PotS $\leftarrow$ PotS $\cup \{\mathbf{S}\}$;
8 | | | **for all** $\mathbf{S}^- \in \mathbf{S}_\Downarrow$ **do** Enqueue(SQ, $\mathbf{S}^-$);
9 | |
10 | **end**
11 | **end**
12   **end**
13   $\mathcal{S} \leftarrow \{\mathbf{s} \subseteq \mathbf{e} \mid \mathbf{S} \in \text{PotS}, \mathbf{s} \in \Omega(\mathbf{S}), \forall \mathbf{S}^- \in \mathbf{S}_\Downarrow : l_{\mathbf{S}^-} \neq \text{true}\}$;
14
15   **return** $\mathcal{S}$

---

the search at the top of the explanation lattice. We add an unvisited set **S** to the set PotS of potential sufficient sets if all its lattice parents (if any) are in PotS and $\top(T \mid \mathbf{sc}) = t$ for all configurations **c** for $\mathbf{C} = \mathbf{E} \setminus \mathbf{S}$ with $\mathbf{c} \subseteq \overline{\mathbf{e}}$. Line 5 of the algorithm (ComputeModesAndLabel) serves for computing modes from the Bayesian network and for recording them, together with the summarising label, in the explanation lattice. For a given explanation context, the algorithm returns sufficient explanations for all sufficient sets that adhere to the properties stated in Proposition 4.

Proposition 6. *Consider context $\langle \mathbf{e}, t, t' \rangle$ and explanation lattice $\mathcal{L}$. Algorithm 1 returns all sufficient explanations for t.*

Proof. Queue SQ is initially filled with the top lattice element $\mathbf{S} = \mathbf{E}$, which is subsequently processed since it wasn't visited and does not have any parents. ComputeModesAndLabel gives $\mathcal{M}_\mathbf{E} = \{(\emptyset, t)\}$ and $l_\mathbf{E} = $ true. Since all modes associated with this lattice element equal t, it is added to the set PotS of potential sufficient sets and its lattice children are enqueued in SQ. Subsequently, labels are only computed for lattice elements **S** for which all parents are potential sufficient sets, and only if $l_\mathbf{S} = $ true will its children be enqueued in SQ. As a result, a lattice element is in PotS iff it adheres to the first property in Proposition 4. The algorithm now returns (line 14) only explanations for the sets in PotS for which the children $\mathbf{S}^-$ in the lattice are labelled $l_{\mathbf{S}^-} = $ exp or $l_{\mathbf{S}^-} = $ oth, or for which $l_{\mathbf{S}^-} = \emptyset$. The former two cases clearly adhere to the second property from Proposition 4. If $l_{\mathbf{S}^-} = \emptyset$, we have not computed the modes and label for $\mathbf{S}^-$, so we could still have that in fact $l_{\mathbf{S}^-}$ should be true. However, during search the label for a set $\mathbf{S}^-$ remains undetermined if it has a parent that is not in PotS; in that case it has an ancestor $\mathbf{S}^+$ with label $l_{\mathbf{S}^+} = $ exp or $l_{\mathbf{S}^+} = $ oth. So with

---

Algorithm 2: BFS-CFX for computing counterfactual explanations.

Input : BN $\mathcal{B}$, context $\langle e, t, t' \rangle$, explanation lattice $\mathcal{L}$
Output: Set $\mathcal{C}$ with all counterfactual explanations

1 CQ $\leftarrow$ **E**; $\mathcal{C} \leftarrow \emptyset$
2 **while** CQ not empty **do**
3 $\quad$ **S** $\leftarrow$ Dequeue(CQ);
4 $\quad$ **if** $l_{\mathbf{S}} = \emptyset$ and $\forall \mathbf{S}^+ \in \mathbf{S}_{\Uparrow}: l_{\mathbf{S}+} \neq$ exp **then**
5 $\quad\quad$ potc $\leftarrow \{\mathbf{c} \mid (\mathbf{c}, \text{unkn}) \in \mathcal{M}_{\mathbf{S}}, \neg\exists \mathbf{c}' \in \mathcal{C} : \mathbf{c}' \subset \mathbf{c}\}$;
6 $\quad\quad$ **if** potc $\neq \emptyset$ **then**
7 $\quad\quad\quad$ ComputeModesAndLabel($\mathcal{L}$, **S**, potc);
8 $\quad\quad\quad$ **if** $l_{\mathbf{S}} \neq$ true **then**
9 $\quad\quad\quad\quad$ $\mathcal{C} \leftarrow \mathcal{C} \cup \{\mathbf{c} \in \text{potc} \mid (\mathbf{c}, t') \in \mathcal{M}_{\mathbf{S}}\}$;
10 $\quad\quad\quad$ **end**
11 $\quad\quad\quad$ **if** $l_{\mathbf{S}} \neq$ exp **then**
12 $\quad\quad\quad\quad$ **for all** $\mathbf{S}^- \in \mathbf{S}_{\Downarrow}$ **do** Enqueue(CQ, $\mathbf{S}^-$);
13 $\quad\quad\quad$ **end**
14 $\quad\quad$ **end**
15 $\quad$ **end**
16 **end**
17 **return** $\mathcal{C}$

$l_{\mathbf{S}-} = \emptyset$, $\mathbf{S}^-$ also adheres to property 2 of Proposition 4. Hence set $\mathcal{S}$ contains all sufficient explanations for t. $\qquad\square$

4.2 Searching the Lattice for Counterfactual Explanations

The breadth-first search for counterfactual explanations (BFS-CFX) is described in pseudo code in Algorithm 2. The search again starts at the top of the explanation lattice, processing an unvisited set **S** if it can potentially have counterfactual explanations associated with it. Whereas the extent of the search for sufficient explanations is independent of variable type (binary vs non-binary), the search for counterfactual explanations can become quite more extensive for non-binary variables. For a given explanation context, Algorithm 2 returns all counterfactual explanations that adhere to the properties stated in Proposition 5.

Proposition 7. *Consider context* $\langle e, t, t' \rangle$ *and explanation lattice* $\mathcal{L}$. *Algorithm 2 returns all counterfactual explanations for* t'.

Proof. First note that if a set $\mathbf{S} \subseteq \mathbf{E}$ is a potential sufficient set (PotS) according to Algorithm 1, then set $\mathbf{C} = \mathbf{E} \setminus \mathbf{S}$ cannot be a counterfactual set (see Proposition 3). Therefore, only if we encounter a set $\mathbf{S}$ with $l_{\mathbf{S}} \neq$ true can $\mathbf{C}$ possibly be a counterfactual set. Since the search starts at the top of the lattice, any potential counterfactual set is encountered earlier in the search than any of its supersets. Therefore, the first $\mathbf{c}$ with $(\mathbf{c}, t') \in \mathcal{M}_{\mathbf{S}}$ found is in fact a counterfactual explanation and added to the set $\mathcal{C}$ of counterfactual explanations. As result, no $\mathbf{c}' \supset \mathbf{c}$ can be a counterfactual explanation (see Proposition 5) and set potc prevents such $\mathbf{c}'$ from being added to $\mathcal{C}$ (line 5). If potc is empty then all configurations $\mathbf{c}$ associated with the current lattice element $\mathbf{S}$ are already covered by $\mathcal{C}$ so neither $\mathbf{S}$ nor its descendants can have an associated true counterfactual set $\mathbf{C}$. If potc is non-empty, then the computation of modes and the resulting label can be restricted to configurations in potc (see ComputeModesAndLabel's optional argument). Now any $\mathbf{c} \in$ potc with $(\mathbf{c}, t') \in \mathcal{M}_\mathbf{S}$ is a counterfactual explanation. If there also exists a $\mathbf{c} \in$ potc with $(\mathbf{c}, t^*) \in \mathcal{M}_\mathbf{S}$ such that $t^* \neq t'$, then this $\mathbf{c}$ could be part of a counterfactual explanation associated with a superset of $\mathbf{C}$ in one of the descendants of $\mathbf{S}$. Hence the children of $\mathbf{S}$ are enqueued in CQ. If such a child has a parent $\mathbf{S}^+$ for which $l_{\mathbf{S}+} = $ exp then all possible configurations for $\mathbf{C}^- = \mathbf{E} \setminus \mathbf{S}^+$ are counterfactual explanations or are covered by counterfactual explanations in ancestors; hence, the child is not processed further. We conclude that once queue CQ is empty, set $\mathcal{C}$ contains all counterfactual explanations. □

4.3   Combining the Search for Explanations

Both algorithms BFS-SFX and BFS-CFX do a breadth first search through the explanation lattice and can easily be combined to compute both types of explanation in a single search. Recall that Algorithm 1 goes through the lattice until it encounters lattice elements that cannot be sufficient sets. It is not until this point that the search for counterfactual explanations needs to start (Proposition 3). Rather than starting BFS-CFX at the top of the lattice, we could therefore have Algorithm 1 initialize set $\mathcal{C}$ and queue CQ. The following additions to Algorithm 1 serve for checking for counterfactual explanations upon encountering an element $\mathbf{S}$ that cannot be sufficient, adding those to $\mathcal{C}$ and, if necessary, enqueueing the children of $\mathbf{S}$ in queue CQ:

▷ line 1, add: $CQ \leftarrow \emptyset; \mathcal{C} \leftarrow \emptyset$
▷ for $l_\mathbf{S} \neq$ true, fill in blank line 9 with:

    9   else $\mathcal{C} \leftarrow \mathcal{C} \cup \{\mathbf{c} \mid (\mathbf{c}, t') \in \mathcal{M}_\mathbf{S}\};$
    9a | if $l_\mathbf{S} \neq$ exp then
    9b | | for all $\mathbf{S}^- \in \mathbf{S}_\Downarrow$ do Enqueue(CQ, $\mathbf{S}^-$);
    9c | end

If all variables are binary-valued then any lattice element $\mathbf{S}$ has only a single associated $(\mathbf{c}, t^*) \in \mathcal{M}_\mathbf{S}$; if $t^* = t'$ and this $\mathbf{c}$ is added to $\mathcal{C}$, then none of the descendants of $\mathbf{S}$ can contain counterfactual explanations. In this case, therefore, the above adaptation leaves queue CQ empty. As a result, once all sufficient sets are found, set $\mathcal{C}$ contains all counterfactual explanations and we are done. An example of computing sufficient and counterfactual explanations from the well-known ASIA network[2] with only binary-valued variables is given in the first author's MSc. thesis [9]. In case the target variable and/or the evidence variables are non-binary, queue CQ will probably be non-empty and the search can now fully focus on finding any remaining counterfactual explanations by continuing

---

[2] All mentioned networks are available from https://www.bnlearn.com/bnrepository/.

the search with the already partially filled queue CQ and set $\mathcal{C}$. That is, we add the following to Algorithm 1:

> ▷ fill in blank line 14 with: GetRemainingCounterfactuals($\mathcal{L}, \mathcal{C}$,CQ), which executes lines 2–16 of BFS-CFX;
> ▷ line 15, add $\mathcal{C}$.

We will use BFS-SFX-CFX to refer to Algorithm 1 with the four above changes to include the computation of both types of explanation. We now illustrate their computation with an example.

Example 1. We consider the CHILD Bayesian network [18] with 6-valued target variable Disease(D) and four of its evidence variables: LVH Report (H) with 2 values, Lower Body O2 (O) with 3 values, CO2 Report (C) with 2 values and X-ray Report (X) with 5 values. We enter the evidence $\mathbf{e} \equiv$ 'H = yes $\wedge$ O = 5-12 $\wedge$ C = <7.5 $\wedge$ X = Oligaemic'. We find $\top(D\,|\,\mathbf{e})$ = PAIVS, whereas the user instead expected outcome TGA $\in \Omega(D)$. Figure 1 now shows the elements $\mathbf{S} \subseteq \mathbf{E}$ in the explanation lattice for context $\langle\mathbf{e}, \text{PAIVS}, \text{TGA}\,\rangle$. In addition, the figure shows the labels $l_\mathbf{S}$ computed for each element and, between brackets, the number of computed modes versus the total number of associated configurations.

Starting at the top of the lattice, BFS-SFX-CFX first searches for potential sufficient sets. After computing modes for $HOCX$, HOC, HCX, HOX, OCX, and HX (in total: 11), the algorithm has found all sufficient sets, resulting in a single sufficient explanation: $\mathcal{S}$ = {'H = yes $\wedge$ X = Oligaemic'}. In the process, set $\mathcal{C}$ is initialised to $\mathcal{C}$ = {'X =*Plethoric*'}; had all variables been binary-valued then we would have been done. Instead, queue CQ is initialised with CQ= $[HO, HC, OC, OX, CX]$ so the search for counterfactuals continues, finally resulting in four counterfactual explanations: $\mathcal{C}$ = {'X = Plethoric', 'X = Normal $\wedge$ H = no', 'X = Grd_Glass $\wedge$ H = no', 'H = no $\wedge$ O = <5 $\wedge$ X = Asy/Patchy'}. The persuasive contrastive explanations for PAIVS are now given by all four pairs $[\mathbf{s}, \mathbf{c}]$ such that $\mathbf{s} \in \mathcal{S}$ and $\mathbf{c} \in \mathcal{C}$. □

We note that in the example we ultimately computed modes for 39 out of the 60 represented evidence configurations. The search for counterfactual explanations continued all the way to the bottom of the lattice: since the target variable has a large state-space, the majority of elements is labelled with oth, indicating that possibly another counterfactual explanation is to be found. Two of the labels in Fig. 1 have an exclamation mark (for HC and H). Here the computed labels are in fact different from what they should be according to Definition 3. These labels should be oth, since both modes PAIVS and TGA are found. However, the configurations that would result in mode TGA in both cases are excluded from potc due to 'X = Plethoric' $\in \mathcal{C}$, leaving their modes unkn. As a result, the computed labels are based only on configurations that result in mode PAIVS. Note that this does not affect the outcome or correctness of the algorithm.

4.4   Complexity and Further Optimisations

The search for sufficient and counterfactual explanations is aborted as soon as all explanations are guaranteed to be found. In worst case, however, BFS-SFX-

CFX will visit and process all of the $2^{|\mathbf{E}|}$ lattice elements. In processing a lattice element $\mathbf{S}$, at most $\prod_{C_i \in \mathbf{E} \backslash \mathbf{S}}(|\Omega(C_i)| - 1)$ modes are computed. For Bayesian networks, these computations can be time-consuming, since in general probabilistic inference in Bayesian networks is NP-hard [3], even if we prune computationally irrelevant variables from the network [2]. The overall computational burden can be reduced in at least two ways:

- We can do Bayesian network inference using so-called saturated junction trees: a $\mathbf{C}$-saturated junction tree will allow for computing all probabilities $\Pr(T\mathbf{C}s)$ through efficient local operations only [8].
- We can further reduce the number of mode computations by exploiting monotonicity properties in the domain, such as monotonicity in distribution or in mode [6]; this effectively serves for pruning the explanation lattice.

Assuming an ordering on the values of each variable, inducing a partial order on configurations, the Bayesian network is for example monotonic in mode if higher values of $\mathbf{e}$ result in a higher mode. In such a case, if we have observed the highest value $\hat{e}$ for some individual evidence variable E_i, then lower values for E_i will never result in a higher mode. If $t' > t$, then we can disregard the values of E_i in our search for counterfactuals. Exploiting such properties can greatly reduce the number of configurations BFS-SFX-CFX needs to consider. Further details on how monotonicity can be exploited to this end, including example computations on an adapted version of the INSURANCE network, can again be found in [9].

5 Related Work

As discussed in Sect. 2, our notion of sufficient explanation is similar to the concept of PI-explanation introduced for explaining Bayesian network classifiers. In the related research the Bayesian networks are assumed to be restricted in topology (naive vs general) [13,16] and/or restricted in variable type (binary vs non-binary) [4,16]. The algorithms used for computing the PI-explanations all assume that the Bayesian network is used purely as a classifier and rely on transforming the classifier into a tractable model, such as an Ordered (Binary) Decision Diagram (O(B)DD) [4,16], an Extended Linear Classifier (ELC) [13], or a representation in First Order Logic [7]. Some transformations either apply only to naive Bayesian networks [13] or require NP-hard compilations [16].

In the past year, several papers have introduced a concept of counterfactual explanation for Bayesian network classifiers, all using different definitions. A common denominator in these definitions is that they determine counterfactual explanations from PI-explanations or vice-versa. Examples include taking the evidence that is common to all PI-explanations (critical influences) together with taking the combined non-critical evidence from the PI-explanations (potential influences) [1], or using PI-explanations to explain for which changes in evidence the current mode will be left unchanged ('even-if-because') [4]. Ignatiev et al. [7] prove a formal relationship between PI-explanations and counterfactual explanations for ML models. Their definition of counterfactual explanation is also based on Wachter et al. [24], but assumes binary-valued evidence variables. In contrast, our counterfactual explanation is defined for discrete variables in general and different counterfactual explanations can include the same evidence variables with different counterfactual values. Moreover, PI-explanations do not provide any information about our counterfactual explanations other than excluding some configurations as possible counterfactuals.

6   Conclusions and Further Research

In this paper we introduced persuasive contrastive explanations for Bayesian networks, detailed an algorithm for their computation and proved its correctness. The new type of explanation combines a sufficient explanation for the current most likely outcome of the network with a counterfactual explanation that explains the changes in evidence that would result in the outcome expected by the user. Sufficient explanations were introduced before as PI-explanations and efficient algorithms for their computation exist for special cases. Counterfactual explanations such as we define have, to the best of our knowledge, not been used in this context before. We have demonstrated that for special cases the counterfactual explanations are available as soon as the search for sufficient explanations finishes; in general the search for counterfactuals then starts.

Our definitions and basic algorithm are in essence model-agnostic, albeit that the required modes are computed from the Bayesian network. The modes, however, could represent the output predicted by other types of model over the same variables, since we do not exploit properties specific to the Bayesian network. We can therefore employ the same concepts and algorithm for other types of underlying model, as long as the number of different configurations for a typical set of evidence variables is limited enough to process.

Since Bayesian network classifiers of arbitrary topology allowing non-binary evidence and target variables can now be compiled into a tractable ODD [17], it is worth investigating the suitability of ODDs for more efficiently computing persuasive contrastive explanations in Bayesian network classifiers. When many different explanations are found, it is necessary to make a selection to be presented to the user. Such a selection can for example be based on the cardinality of the explanation. A benefit of directly using Bayesian networks rather than compiled structures such as ODDs is that the computed probabilities can also be exploited for selecting explanations to present to the user. In future we aim to further study the use of probabilistic information for explanation selection. In addition, we aim to further exploit the direct use of a Bayesian network by introducing intermediate variables into the explanation.

Acknowledgements. This research was partially funded by the Hybrid Intelligence Center, a 10-year programme funded by the Dutch Ministry of Education, Culture and Science through the Netherlands Organisation for Scientific Research, https://hybrid-intelligence-centre.nl. We would like to thank the anonymous reviewers for their useful and inspiring comments.

References

1. Albini, E., Rago, A., Baroni, P., Toni, F.: Relation-based counterfactual explanations for Bayesian network classifiers. In: Bessiere, C. (ed.) Proceedings of the 29th International Joint Conference on Artificial Intelligence, pp. 451–457 (2020)
2. Baker, M., Boult, T.E.: Pruning Bayesian networks for efficient computation. In: Bonissone, P., Henrion, M., Kanal, L., Lemmer, J. (eds.) Uncertainty in Artificial Intelligence 6. Elsevier Science, Amsterdam (1991)
3. Cooper, G.F.: The computational complexity of probabilistic inference using Bayesian belief networks. Artif. Intell. **42**, 393–405 (1990)
4. Darwiche, A., Hirth, A.: On the reasons behind decisions. In: De Giacomo, G., Catala, A., Dilkina, B., Milano, M., Barro, S., Bugarín, A., Lang, J. (eds.) Proceedings of 24th European Conference on Artificial Intelligence, pp. 712–720. IOS Press (2020)
5. Derks, I.P., de Waal, A.: A taxonomy of explainable Bayesian networks. In: Gerber, A. (ed.) Artificial Intelligence Research, pp. 220–235. Springer, Cham (2020)
6. van der Gaag, L.C., Bodlaender, H.L., Feelders, A.: Monotonicity in Bayesian networks. In: Chickering, M., Halpern, J. (eds.) Proceedings of the 20th Conference on Uncertainty in Artificial Intelligence, pp. 569–576 (2004)
7. Ignatiev, A., Narodytska, N., Asher, N., Marques-Silva, J.: From contrastive to abductive explanations and back again. In: Baldoni, M., Bandini, S. (eds.) AIxIA 2020. LNCS (LNAI), vol. 12414, pp. 335–355. Springer, Cham (2021). https://doi.org/10.1007/978-3-030-77091-4_21
8. Jensen, F.V., Nielsen, T.D.: Bayesian networks and decision graphs. Springer Science & Business Media, 2 edn. (2007)
9. Koopman, T.: Computing Contrastive, Counterfactual Explanations for Bayesian Networks. Master's thesis, Universiteit Utrecht, The Netherlands (2020). https://dspace.library.uu.nl/handle/1874/398728
10. Kyrimi, E., Marsh, W.: A progressive explanation of inference in 'hybrid' Bayesian networks for supporting clinical decision making. In: Antonucci, A., Corani, G., de Campos, C.P. (eds.) Proceedings of the 8th Conference on Probabilistic Graphical Models, pp. 275–286 (2016)
11. Lacave, C., Díez, F.J.: A review of explanation methods for Bayesian networks. Knowl. Eng. Rev. **17**(2), 107–127 (2002)
12. van Leersum, J.: Explaining the reasoning of Bayesian networks with intermediate nodes and clusters. Master's thesis, Utrecht University (2015). http://dspace.library.uu.nl/handle/1874/313520
13. Marques-Silva, J., Gerspacher, T., Cooper, M., Ignatiev, A., Narodytska, N.: Explaining naive Bayes and other linear classifiers with polynomial time and delay. In: Larochelle, H., Ranzato, M., Hadsell, R., Balcan, M.F., Lin, H. (eds.) Advances in Neural Information Processing Systems, vol. 33, pp. 20590–20600. Curran Associates, Inc. (2020)
14. Miller, T.: Explanation in artificial intelligence: insights from the social sciences. Artif. Intell. **267**, 1–38 (2019)
15. Pearl, J.: Probabilistic Reasoning in Intelligent Systems: Networks of Plausible Inference. Morgan Kaufmann Publishers (1988)
16. Shih, A., Choi, A., Darwiche, A.: A symbolic approach to explaining Bayesian network classifiers. In: Proceedings of the 27th International Joint Conference on Artificial Intelligence, pp. 5103–5111 (2018)

17. Shih, A., Choi, A., Darwiche, A.: Compiling Bayesian network classifiers into decision graphs. In: Proceedings of the 33rd AAAI Conference on Artificial Intelligence, pp. 7966–7974 (2019)
18. Spiegelhalter, D.J., Dawid, A.P., Lauritzen, S.L., G.Cowell, R.: Bayesian analysis in expert systems. Stat. Sci. **8**(3), 219–247 (1993)
19. Suermondt, H.J.: Explanation in Bayesian belief networks. Ph.D. thesis, Stanford University (1992)
20. Timmer, S.T., Meyer, J.-J.C., Prakken, H., Renooij, S., Verheij, B.: Explaining Bayesian networks using argumentation. In: Destercke, S., Denoeux, T. (eds.) ECSQARU 2015. LNCS (LNAI), vol. 9161, pp. 83–92. Springer, Cham (2015). https://doi.org/10.1007/978-3-319-20807-7_8
21. Verma, S., Dickerson, J.P., Hines, K.E.: Counterfactual explanations for machine learning: A review. ArXiv abs/2010.10596 (2020)
22. Vlek, C., Prakken, H., Renooij, S., Verheij, B.: A method for explaining Bayesian networks for legal evidence with scenarios. Artif. Intell. Law **24**(3), 285–324 (2016)
23. van der Waa, J., Robeer, M., van Diggelen, J., Brinkhuis, M., Neerincx, M.: Contrastive explanations with local foil trees. In: Proceedings of the Workshop on Human Interpretability in Machine Learning, pp. 41–47 (2018)
24. Wachter, S., Mittelstadt, B., Russell, C.: Counterfactual explanations without opening the black box: automated decisions and the GPDR. Harvard J. Law Technol. **31**, 841 (2017)
25. Yap, G.E., Tan, A.H., Pang, H.H.: Explaining inferences in Bayesian networks. Appl. Intell. **29**(3), 263–278 (2008)

Explainable AI Using MAP-Independence

Johan Kwisthout[(✉)] [iD]

Donders Institute for Brain, Cognition, and Behaviour, Radboud University,
Nijmegen, The Netherlands
j.kwisthout@donders.ru.nl
http://www.socsci.ru.nl/johank/

Abstract. In decision support systems the motivation and justification of the system's diagnosis or classification is crucial for the acceptance of the system by the human user. In Bayesian networks a diagnosis or classification is typically formalized as the computation of the most probable joint value assignment to the hypothesis variables, given the observed values of the evidence variables (generally known as the MAP problem). While solving the MAP problem gives the most probable explanation of the evidence, the computation is a black box as far as the human user is concerned and it does not give additional insights that allow the user to appreciate and accept the decision. For example, a user might want to know to what extent a variable was relevant for the explanation. In this paper we introduce a new concept, MAP-independence, which tries to formally capture this notion of relevance, and explore its role towards a justification of an inference to the best explanation.

Keywords: Bayesian networks · Most probable explanations · Relevance · Explainable AI · Computational complexity

1 Introduction

With the availability of petabytes of data and the emergence of 'deep' learning as an AI technique to find statistical regularities in these large quantities of data, artificial intelligence in general and machine learning in particular has arguably entered a new phase since its emergence in the 1950s. Deep learning aims to build hierarchical models representing the data, with every new layer in the hierarchy representing ever more abstract information; for example, from individual pixels to lines and curves, to geometric patterns, to features, to categories. Superficially this might be related to how the human visual cortex interprets visual stimuli and seeks to classify a picture to be that of a cat, rather than of a dog.

When describing in what sense a cat is different from a dog, humans may use features and categories that we agreed upon to be defining features of cats and dogs, such as whiskers, location and form of the ears, the nose, etc. The deep learning method, however, does not adhere to features we humans find to be good descriptors; it bases its decisions where and how to 'carve nature's joints' solely on basis of the statistics of the data. Hence, it might very well

© Springer Nature Switzerland AG 2021
J. Vejnarová and N. Wilson (Eds.): ECSQARU 2021, LNAI 12897, pp. 243–254, 2021.
https://doi.org/10.1007/978-3-030-86772-0_18

be that the curvature of the spine (or some other apparently 'random') feature happens to be *the* statistically most important factor to distinguish cats from dogs. This imposes huge challenges when the machine learning algorithm is asked to *motivate* its classification to a human user. The sub-field of *explainable AI* has recently emerged to study how to align statistical machine learning with informative user-based motivations or explanations. Explainable AI, however, is not limited to deep neural network applications. Any AI application where trustworthiness is important benefits from justification and transparency of its internal process [6], and this includes decision support systems that are based on Bayesian networks, which is the focus of this paper. In these systems typically one is interested in the hypothesis that best explains the available evidence; for example in a medical case, the infection that is most probable given a set of health complaints and test findings.

Note that 'explainability' in explainable AI is in principle a triadic relationship between what needs to be explained, the explanation, and the *user who seeks the explanation* [15]. An explanation will be more satisfying ('lovelier', in Peter Lipton's [11] terms) if it allows the user to gain more understanding about the phenomenon to be explained. In this paper we specifically try to improve the user's understanding of a specific decision by *explicating the relevant information* that contributed to said decision. In some way, in deciding what the best explanation is for a set of observations, the process of marginalizing out the variables that are neither observed nor hypothesis variables, makes the process more opaque: some of these variables have a bigger impact (i.e., are more relevant) on the eventual decision than others, and this information is lost in the process. For example, the absence of a specific test result (i.e., a variable we marginalize out in the MAP computation) may lead to a different explanation of the available evidence compared to when a negative (or positive) test result *were* present. In this situation, this variable is more relevant to the eventual explanation than if the best explanation would be the same, irrelevant of whether the test result was positive, negative, or missing. Our approach in this paper is to motivate a decision by showing which of these variables were relevant in this sense towards arriving at this decision.

This perspective has roots in Pearl's early work on conditional independence [14]. Pearl suggests that human reasoning is in principle based on *conditional independence*: The organizational structure of human memory is such that it allows for easily retrieving context-dependent relevant information. For example (from [14, p.3]): The color of my friend's car is normally not related to the color of my neighbour's car. However, when my friend tells me she almost mistook my neighbour's car for her own, this information suddenly becomes relevant for me to understand, and for her to explain, this mistake. That is, the color of both cars is independent but becomes conditionally dependent on the evidence[1].

---

[1] Graphically one can see this as a so-called common-effect structure, where C_1 and C_2 are variables that represent my car's, respectively my neighbour's car's, color; both variables have a directed edge towards the variable M that indicates whether my friend misidentified the cars or not. When M is unobserved, C_1 and C_2 are independent, but they become conditionally dependent on observation of M.

In this paper we will argue that Pearl's proposal to model context-dependent (ir)relevance as conditional (in)dependence is in fact too strict. It generally leads to too many variables that are considered to be relevant: for some it is likely the case that, while they may not be conditionally independent on the hypothesized explanation given the evidence, they do not contribute to understanding *why* some explanation *h* is better than the alternatives. That means, for explanatory purposes their role is limited. In the remainder of this paper we will build on Pearl's work, yet provide a stronger notion of context-dependent relevance and irrelevance of variables relative to explanations of observations. Our goal is to advance explainable AI in the context of Bayesian networks by formalizing the problem of *justification* of an explanation (i.e., given an AI-generated explanation, advance the user's understanding why this explanation is preferred over others) into a computational problem that captures some aspects of this justification; in particular, by opening up the 'marginalization black box' and show which variables contributed to this decision. We show that this problem is intractable in the general case, but also give fixed-parameter tractability results that show what constraints are needed to render it tractable.

To summarize, we are interested in the potential applicability of this new concept for motivation and justification of MAP explanations, with a focus on its theoretical properties. The remainder of this paper is structured as follows. In the next section we offer some preliminary background on Bayesian networks and computational complexity and share our conventions with respect to notation with the reader. In Sect. 3 we introduce so-called MAP-independence as an alternative to conditional independence and elaborate on the potential of these computational problems for justifying explanations in Bayesian networks. In Sect. 4 we introduce a formal computational problem based on this notion, and give complexity proofs and fixed-parameter tractability results for this problem. We conclude in Sect. 5.

2   Preliminaries and Notation

In this section we give some preliminaries and introduce the notational conventions we use throughout this paper. The reader is referred to textbooks like [2] for more background.

A Bayesian network $\mathcal{B} = (\mathbf{G}_\mathcal{B}, \mathrm{Pr})$ is a probabilistic graphical model that succinctly represents a joint probability distribution $\mathrm{Pr}(\mathbf{V}) = \prod_{i=1}^n \mathrm{Pr}(V_i \mid \pi(V_i))$ over a set of discrete random variables $\mathbf{V}$. $\mathcal{B}$ is defined by a directed acyclic graph $\mathbf{G}_\mathcal{B} = (\mathbf{V}, \mathbf{A})$, where $\mathbf{V}$ represents the stochastic variables and $\mathbf{A}$ models the conditional (in)dependencies between them, and a set of parameter probabilities Pr in the form of conditional probability tables (CPTs). In our notation $\pi(V_i)$ denotes the set of parents of a node V_i in $\mathbf{G}_\mathcal{B}$. We use upper case to indicate variables, lower case to indicate a specific value of a variable, and boldface to indicate sets of variables respectively joint value assignments to such a set. $\Omega(V_i)$ denotes the set of value assignments to V_i, with $\Omega(\mathbf{V_a})$ denoting the set of joint value assignment to the set $\mathbf{V_a}$.

One of the key computational problems in Bayesian networks is the problem to find the most probable explanation for a set of observations, i.e., a joint value assignment to a designated set of variables (the explanation set) that has maximum posterior probability given the observed variables (the joint value assignment to the evidence set) in the network. If the network includes variables that are neither observed nor to be explained (referred to as intermediate variables) this problem is typically referred to as MAP. We use the following formal definition:

MAP
Instance: A Bayesian network $\mathcal{B} = (\mathbf{G}_\mathcal{B}, \text{Pr})$, where $\mathbf{V}(\mathbf{G}_\mathcal{B})$ is partitioned into a set of evidence nodes $\mathbf{E}$ with a joint value assignment $\mathbf{e}$, a set of intermediate nodes $\mathbf{I}$, and an explanation set $\mathbf{H}$.
Output: A joint value assignment $\mathbf{h}^*$ to $\mathbf{H}$ such that for all joint value assignments $\mathbf{h}'$ to $\mathbf{H}$, $\text{Pr}(\mathbf{h}^* \mid \mathbf{e}) \geq \text{Pr}(\mathbf{h}' \mid \mathbf{e})$.

We assume that the reader is familiar with standard notions in computational complexity theory, notably the classes P and NP, NP-hardness, and polynomial time (many-one) reductions. The class PP is the class of decision problems that can be decided by a probabilistic Turing machine in polynomial time; that is, where *yes*-instances are accepted with probability strictly larger than $1/2$ and *no*-instances are accepted with probability no more than $1/2$. A problem in PP might be accepted with probability $1/2 + \epsilon$ where ϵ may depend exponentially on the input size n. Hence, it may take exponential time to increase the probability of acceptance (by repetition of the computation and taking a majority decision) close to 1. PP is a powerful class; we know for example that NP $\subseteq$ PP and the inclusion is assumed to be strict. The canonical PP-complete decision problem is MAJSAT: given a Boolean formula ϕ, does the majority of truth assignments to its variables satisfy ϕ?

In computational complexity theory, so-called *oracles* are theoretical constructs that increase the power of a specific Turing machine. An oracle (e.g., an oracle for PP-complete problems) can be seen as a 'magic sub-routine' that answers class membership queries (e.g., in PP) in a single time step. In this paper we are specifically interested in classes defined by non-deterministic Turing machines with access to a PP-oracle. Such a machine is very powerful, and likewise problems that are complete for the corresponding complexity classes NP^{PP} (such as MAP) and co-NP^{PP} (such as MONOTONICITY) are highly intractable [4,13].

Finally we wish to introduce the concept of *fixed-parameter tractability* to the reader. Oftentimes, NP-hard computational problems can be rendered tractable when the set of instances is constrained to instances where the value of some (set of) problem parameter(s) is bounded. Formally a parameterized problem $k - \Pi$ is called fixed-parameter tractable for a parameter k if an instance i of Π can be decided in time $\mathcal{O}(p(|i|)f(k))$ for a polynomial p and an arbitrary function f.

3   MAP-Independence

The topic of *relevance* in Bayesian networks has been studied from several angles: while [19] aimed to reduce the number of variables in the explanation set to the relevant ones, and [12] studied the relevance of evidence variables for sensitivity analysis, in [10] the approach was to reduce the number of intermediate variables that affect an inference to the best explanation. In the current paper we take a similar approach, but here we focus on the application of this notion of relevance in explainable AI, rather than to construct a heuristic approach towards the computationally expensive MAP problem. Here the problem of interest is not so much to *find* the most probable explanation (viz., the joint value assignment to a set of hypothesis variables given observations in the network), but rather to *motivate* what information did or did not contribute to a given explanation.

That is, rather than providing the 'trivial' explanation "$\mathbf{h}^*$ is the best[2] explanation for $\mathbf{e}$, since $\mathrm{argmax}_\mathbf{h}\Pr(\mathbf{H} = \mathbf{h} \mid \mathbf{e}) = \mathrm{argmax}_\mathbf{h}\sum_{\mathbf{i}\in\Omega(\mathbf{I})}\Pr(\mathbf{H} = \mathbf{h}, \mathbf{i} \mid \mathbf{e}) = \mathbf{h}^*$" our goal is to partition the set $\mathbf{I}$ into variables I^+ that are *relevant* to establishing the best explanation and variables I^- that are *irrelevant*. One straightforward approach, motivated by [14], would be to include variables in I^+ if they are conditionally dependent on $\mathbf{H}$ given $\mathbf{e}$, and in I^- when they are conditionally independent from $\mathbf{H}$ given $\mathbf{e}$ and to *motivate* the sets I^+ and I^- in terms of a set of independence relations. This is particularly useful when inclusion in I^+ is *triggered* by the presence of an observation, such as in Pearl's example where 'color of my friend's car' and 'color of my neighbour's car' become dependent on each other once we learn that my friend confused both cars.

We argue that this way of partitioning intermediate variables into relevant and irrelevant ones, however useful, might not be the full story with respect to explanation. There is a sense in which a variable has an explanatory role in motivating a conclusion that goes beyond conditional (in)dependence. Take for example the small binary network in Fig. 1. Assume that we want to motivate the best explanation for A given the evidence $C = c$, i.e., we want to motivate the outcome of $\mathrm{argmax}_a\Pr(A = a \mid C = c) = \mathrm{argmax}_a\sum_{B,D}\Pr(A = a, B, D \mid C = c)$ in terms of variables that contribute to this explanation. Now, obviously D is *not* relevant, as it is d-separated from A given C. But the roles of B is less obvious. This node is obviously not conditionally independent from A given C.

Whether B plays an explanatory role in general in the outcome of the MAP query is dependent on whether $\mathrm{argmax}_a\sum_D\Pr(A = a, B = b, D \mid C = c) = \mathrm{argmax}_a\sum_D\Pr(A = a, B = \bar{b}, D \mid C = c)$. If both are equal ($B$'s value, were it observed, would have been irrelevant to the MAP query) than B arguably has no explanatory role. If both are unequal than the fact that B is unobserved may in fact be crucial for the explanation. For example, if B represents a variable that

---

encodes a 'default' versus 'fault' condition (with $\Pr(b) > \Pr(\bar{b})$) the *absence* of a fault (i.e., B is unobserved) can lead to a different MAP explanation than the *observation* that B takes its default value; e.g., if $\Pr(b) = 0.6$, $\Pr(a \mid c, b) = 0.6$, and $\Pr(a \mid c, \bar{b}) = 0.3$ we have that $\Pr(a \mid c) = 0.48$ yet $\Pr(a \mid c, b) = 0.6$ so the MAP explanation changes from $\bar{a}$ to a on the observation of the *default* value b. This information is lost in the marginalization step but it helps motivate *why* $\bar{a}$ is the best explanation of c.

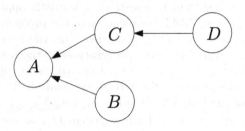

Fig. 1. An example small network. Note that the explanatory role of B in motivating the best explanation of A given an observation for C is context-dependent and may be different for different observations for C, as well as for different conditional probability distributions; hence it cannot be read off the graph alone.

Thus, the relevance of B for the explanation of A may need a *different* (and broader) notion of independence, as also suggested by [10]. Indeed, in this example, variable D is irrelevant for explaining A as D is conditionally independent from A given C; yet, we could also argue that B is irrelevant for explaining A *if its value, were it observed, could not influence the explanation for A*. We introduce the term *MAP-independence* for this (uni-directional) relationship; we say that A is MAP-independent from B given $C = c$ when $\forall_{b \in \Omega(B)} \mathrm{argmax}_{a^*} \Pr(A = a^*, B = b \mid C = c) = a$ for a specific value assignment $a \in \Omega(A)$.

3.1 MAP-independence for Justification and Decision Support

AI-based clinical decision support systems for diagnosis and treatment have been proposed since the 1970s, with MYCIN [16] as the canonical example. Whereas original systems were largely an effort to demonstrate the promise of AI techniques (i.e., isolated, difficult to maintain or generalize, of mostly academic interest, etc.), current systems have developed into systems that are integrated with the medical workflow, in particular aligned with electronic health records [17]. However, several challenges that were already identified with MYCIN still remain present in decision support systems: they are difficult to maintain and adapt to new insights, the justification of the system's advice does not match typical reasoning patterns of the user, and there is little justification of the soundness (or acknowledgement of uncertainty and ignorance) of the advice.

The concept of MAP-independence in Bayesian networks may help overcome some of these shortcomings, particularly the justification of an inference to the most probable explanation. For an unobserved variable I we have that the MAP explanation $\mathbf{h}^*$ is MAP-independent of I given the evidence if the explanation would not have been different had I be observed to some value, and MAP-dependent if this is not the case. An explication of how I may impact or fail to impact the most probable explanation of the evidence will both help motivate the system's advice as well as offer guidance in further decisions (e.g., to gather additional evidence [3,5] to make the MAP explanation more robust).

4   Formal Problem Definition and Results

The computational problem of interest is to decide upon the set I^+, the relevant variables that contribute to establishing the best explanation $\mathbf{h}^*$ given the evidence $\mathbf{e}$. In order to establish I^+ we need to decide the following sub-problem: given $\mathbf{R} \subseteq \mathbf{I}$: is $\mathbf{h}^*$ MAP-independent from $\mathbf{R}$ given $\mathbf{e}$? We formalize this problem as below.

MAP-INDEPENDENCE

Instance: A Bayesian network $\mathcal{B} = (\mathbf{G}_{\mathcal{B}}, \mathrm{Pr})$, where $\mathbf{V}(\mathbf{G})$ is partitioned into a set of evidence nodes $\mathbf{E}$ with a joint value assignment $\mathbf{e}$, a non-empty explanation set $\mathbf{H}$ with a joint value assignment $\mathbf{h}^*$, a non-empty set of nodes $\mathbf{R}$ for which we want to decide MAP-independence relative to $\mathbf{H}$, and a set of intermediate nodes $\mathbf{I}$.
Question: Is $\forall_{\mathbf{r} \in \Omega(\mathbf{R})} \mathrm{argmax}_{\mathbf{H}} \mathrm{Pr}(\mathbf{H}, \mathbf{R} = \mathbf{r} \mid \mathbf{e}) = \mathbf{h}^*$?

Observe that the complement problem MAP-DEPENDENCE is defined similarly with *yes-* and *no-*answers reversed.

4.1   Computational Complexity

We will show in this sub-section that an appropriate decision variant of MAP-INDEPENDENCE is co-NP^{PP}-complete and thus resides in the same complexity class as the MONOTONICITY problem [4]. Note that the definition of MAP-INDEPENDENCE in the previous sub-section had an explanation given in the input and assumed that $\mathbf{R}$ is nonempty. The reason therefore is that if we would allow $\mathbf{R} = \varnothing$ and leave out the explanation, the problem has MAP as a degenerate special case. As this somewhat obfuscates the computational complexity of the core of the problem (i.e., determining the relevance of the set $\mathbf{R}$ for the actual explanation) we force $\mathbf{R}$ to be non-empty and $\mathbf{h}^*$ to be provided in the input. Note that we did not explicitly require that $\mathbf{h}^* = \mathrm{argmax}_{\mathbf{h}} \mathrm{Pr}(\mathbf{H} = \mathbf{h}, \mathbf{e})$; this is neither necessary (for the hardness proof) nor desired (as it would effectively make MAP-INDEPENDENCE a so-called promise problem).

Another complication is that, while MAP-INDEPENDENCE is already defined as a decision problem, part of the problem definition requires comparing MAP explanations, and while the MAP problem has a decision variant that is $\mathsf{NP}^{\mathsf{PP}}$-complete, the functional variant is $\mathsf{FP}^{\mathsf{NP}^{\mathsf{PP}}}$-complete [7]. We therefore introduce the following decision variant[3,4] which is in the line with the traditional decision variant of PARTIAL MAP:

MAP-INDEPENDENCE-D
Instance: A Bayesian network $\mathcal{B} = (\mathbf{G}_{\mathcal{B}}, \mathrm{Pr})$, where $\mathbf{V}(\mathbf{G})$ is partitioned into a set of evidence nodes $\mathbf{E}$ with a joint value assignment $\mathbf{e}$, a non-empty explanation set $\mathbf{H}$ with a joint value assignment $\mathbf{h}^*$, a non-empty set of nodes $\mathbf{R}$ for which we want to decide MAP-independence relative to $\mathbf{H}$, and a set of intermediate nodes $\mathbf{I}$; rational number s.
Question: Is, for each joint value assignment $\mathbf{r}$ to $\mathbf{R}$, $\mathrm{Pr}(\mathbf{h}^*, \mathbf{r}, \mathbf{e}) > s$?

For the hardness proof we reduce from the canonical satisfiability co-$\mathsf{NP}^{\mathsf{PP}}$-complete variant A-MAJSAT [18] defined as follows:

A-MAJSAT
Instance: A Boolean formula ϕ with n variables $\{x_1, x_n\}$, partitioned into the sets $\mathbf{A} = \{x_1, x_k\}$ and $\mathbf{M} = \{x_{k+1}, x_n\}$ for some $k \leq n$.
Question: Does, for every truth instantiation $\mathbf{x_a}$ to $\mathbf{A}$, the majority of truth instantiations $\mathbf{x_m}$ to $\mathbf{M}$ satisfy ϕ?

As a running example for our reduction we use the formula $\phi_{ex} = \neg(x_1 \wedge x_2) \vee (x_3 \vee x4)$, with $\mathbf{A} = \{x_1, x_2\}$ and $\mathbf{M} = \{x_3, x_4\}$. This is a *yes*-instance of A-MAJSAT: for each truth assignment to $\mathbf{A}$, at least three out of four truth assignments to $\mathbf{M}$ satisfy ϕ.

We construct a Bayesian network $\mathcal{B}_\phi$ from a given Boolean formula ϕ with n variables. For each propositional variable x_i in ϕ, a binary stochastic variable

---

[3] Note that as a decision variant of MAP-INDEPENDENCE there is still a slight caveat, as the probability of $\mathrm{Pr}(\mathbf{h}^*, \mathbf{r}, \mathbf{e})$ can be different for each joint value assignment $\mathbf{r}$, implying that the 'generic' threshold s can either be too strict ($\mathbf{h}$ is still the MAP explanation although the test fails) or too loose (there is another explanation $\mathbf{h}'$ which is the MAP explanation although the test passes). As the number of joint value assignments $|\Omega(\mathbf{R})|$ can be exponential in the size of the network (and thus we cannot include individual thresholds s_i in the input of the decision problem without blowing up the input size), this nonetheless appears to be the closest decision problem variant that still captures the crucial aspects of MAP-INDEPENDENCE.

[4] One of the reviewers asked whether a 'suitable' (neither too loose nor too strict) threshold s can (or is guaranteed) to exist. A trivial example with two unconnected binary nodes H (the MAP variable, with $\mathrm{Pr}(H = h) = 0.51$) and uniformly distributed R, and a threshold $s = 0.5$ suffices to show that indeed there exists networks where a suitable s exists. On the other hand it is also easy to construct a small network where no suitable s exists; take a ternary node H instead and define $\mathrm{Pr}(H = h_1 \mid r) = 0.55$, $\mathrm{Pr}(H = h_2 \mid r) = 0.45$, $\mathrm{Pr}(H = h_3 \mid r) = 0$, $\mathrm{Pr}(H = h_1 \mid \bar{r}) = 0.45$, $\mathrm{Pr}(H = h_2 \mid \bar{r}) = 0.4$, and $\mathrm{Pr}(H = h_3 \mid r) = 0.15$. While h_1 is the MAP for each value of R, a threshold of 0.44 is too loose while a threshold of 0.45 is too strict.

X_i is added to $\mathcal{B}_\phi$, with possible values T and F and a uniform probability distribution. For each logical operator in ϕ, an additional binary variable in $\mathcal{B}_\phi$ is introduced, whose parents are the variables that correspond to the input of the operator, and whose conditional probability table is equal to the truth table of that operator. For example, the value T of a stochastic variable mimicking the *and*-operator would have a conditional probability of 1 if and only if both its parents have the value T, and 0 otherwise. The top-level operator in ϕ is denoted as V_ϕ. In Fig. 2 the network $\mathcal{B}_\phi$ is shown for the formula $\neg(x_1 \wedge x_2) \vee (x_3 \vee x_4)$.

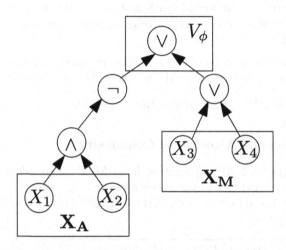

Fig. 2. The network $\mathcal{B}_\phi$ created from the A-MAJSAT instance $(\phi, \{x_1, x_2\}, \{x_3, x_4\})$ per the description above.

Theorem 1. MAP-INDEPENDENCE *is* co-NP^{PP}*-complete.*

Proof. To prove membership in co-NP^{PP}, we give a falsification algorithm for *no*-answers to MAP-INDEPENDENCE-D instances, given access to an oracle for the PP-complete [1] INFERENCE problem. Let $(\mathcal{B}, \mathbf{E}, \mathbf{e}, \mathbf{H}, \mathbf{h}^*, \mathbf{R}, \mathbf{I}, s)$ be an instance of MAP-INDEPENDENCE-D. We non-deterministically guess a joint value assignment $\bar{\mathbf{r}}$, and use the INFERENCE oracle to verify that $\Pr(\mathbf{h}^*, \bar{\mathbf{r}}, \mathbf{e}) \leq s$, which by definition implies that $\mathbf{H}$ is not MAP-independent from $\mathbf{R}$ given $\mathbf{E} = \mathbf{e}$.

To prove hardness, we reduce from A-MAJSAT. Let $(\phi, \mathbf{X_A}, \mathbf{X_M})$ be an instance of A-MAJSAT and let $\mathcal{B}_\phi$ be the Bayesian network created from ϕ as per the procedure described above. We set $\mathbf{R} = \mathbf{X_A}$, $\mathbf{H} = \{V_\phi\}$, $\mathbf{E} = \varnothing$, $\mathbf{I} = \mathbf{V}(\mathbf{G}_\mathcal{B}) \setminus \mathbf{R} \cup \{V_\phi\}$, $\mathbf{h}^* = \{T\}$, and $s = 2^{-|\mathbf{R}|-1}$.

$\implies$ Assume that $(\phi, \mathbf{X_A}, \mathbf{X_M})$ is a *yes*-instance of A-MAJSAT, i.e., for every truth assignment to $\mathbf{X_A}$, the majority of truth assignments to $\mathbf{X_M}$ satisfies ϕ. Then, by the construction of $\mathcal{B}_\phi$, we have $\sum_\mathbf{r} \Pr(V_\phi = T, \mathbf{r}) > 1/2$ and so, as the variables in $\mathbf{R}$ are all uniformly distributed, $\Pr(V_\phi = T, \mathbf{r}) > 2^{-|\mathbf{R}|-1}$ for every joint value assignment $\mathbf{r}$ to $\mathbf{R}$, and so this is a *yes*-instance of MAP-INDEPENDENCE-D.

$\impliedby$ Assume that $(\mathcal{B}, \varnothing, \varnothing, V_\phi, T, \mathbf{R}, \mathbf{I}, 2^{-|\mathbf{R}|-1})$ is a *yes*-instance of MAP-INDEPENDENCE-D. Given the construction this implies that for all joint value assignments $\mathbf{r}$ it holds that $\Pr(V_\phi = T, \mathbf{r}) > 2^{-|\mathbf{R}|-1}$. But this implies that for all truth assignments to $\mathbf{X_A}$, the majority of truth assignments to $\mathbf{X_M}$ satisfies ϕ, hence, this is a *yes*-instance of A-MAJSAT.

Observe that the construction of $\mathcal{B}_\phi$ takes time, polynomial in the size of ϕ, which concludes our proof. Furthermore, the result holds in the absence of evidence.

Corollary 1. MAP-DEPENDENCE *is* $\mathsf{NP}^{\mathsf{PP}}$*-complete.*

4.2 Algorithm and Algorithmic Complexity

To decide whether a MAP explanation $\mathbf{h}^*$ is MAP-independent from a set of variables $\mathbf{R}$ given evidence $\mathbf{e}$, the straightforward algorithm below shows that the run-time of this algorithm is $\mathcal{O}(\Omega(\mathbf{R})) = \mathcal{O}(2^{|\mathbf{R}|})$ times the time needed for each MAP computation.

Algorithm 1: Straightforward MAP-INDEPENDENCE algorithm

Input: Bayesian network partitioned in $\mathbf{E} = \mathbf{e}$, $\mathbf{H} = \mathbf{h}^*$, $\mathbf{R}$, and $\mathbf{I}$.
Output: *yes* if $\mathbf{H}$ is MAP-independent from $\mathbf{R}$ given $\mathbf{e}$, *no* if otherwise.
foreach $\mathbf{r} \in \Omega(\mathbf{R})$ **do**
    if $\mathrm{argmax}_\mathbf{H} \Pr(\mathbf{H}, \mathbf{R} = \mathbf{r} \mid \mathbf{e}) \neq \mathbf{h}^*$ **then**
        return *no*;
    end
end
return *yes*;

This implies that, given known results on fixed-parameter tractability [8] and efficient approximation [10,13] of MAP, the size of the set against which we want to establish MAP independence is the crucial source of complexity if MAP can be computed or approximated feasibly. The following fixed-parameter tractability results can be derived:

Corollary 2. *Let* $c = \max_{W \in V(G)} \Omega(W)$, $q = Pr(\mathbf{h}^*)$, *and let* tw *be the tree-width of* $\mathcal{B}$. *Then* p-MAP-INDEPENDENCE *is fixed-parameter tractable for* $p = \{|\mathbf{H}|, |\mathbf{R}|, \mathrm{tw}, c\}$, $p = \{|\mathbf{H}|, |\mathbf{R}|, |\mathbf{I}|, c\}$, $p = \{q, |\mathbf{R}|, \mathrm{tw}, c\}$, *and* $p = \{q, |\mathbf{R}|, |\mathbf{I}|, c\}$.

5 Conclusion and Future Work

In this paper we introduced MAP-independence as a formal notion, relevant for decision support and justification of decisions. In a sense, MAP-independence is a relaxation of conditional independence, suggested by Pearl [14] to be a scaffold for human context-dependent reasoning. We suggest that MAP-independence may be a useful notion to further explicate the variables that are *relevant* for the establishment of a particular MAP explanation. Establishing whether the MAP explanation is MAP-independent from a set of variables given the evidence (and so, whether these variables are relevant for justifying the MAP explanation) is a computationally intractable problem; however, for a *specific* variable of interest I (or a small set of these variables together) the problem is tractable whenever MAP can be computed tractably; in practice, this may suffice for usability in typical decision support systems.

There are many related problems of interest that one can identify, but which will be delegated to future work. For example, if the set of relevant variables is large, one might be interested in deciding whether observing one variable can bring down this set (by more than one, obviously). Another related problem would be to decide upon the observations that are relevant for the MAP explanation (i.e., had we not observed $E \in \mathbf{E}$ or had we observed a different value, would that change the MAP explanation?). This would extend previous work [12] where the relevance of E for computing a posterior probability (conditioned on $\mathbf{E}$) was established. Finally, in order to test its practical usage, the formal concept introduced in this paper should be put to the empirical test in an actual decision support system to establish whether the justifications supported by the notion of MAP-independence actually help understand and appreciate the system's advise.

Acknowledgments. The author is grateful for the valuable feedback received from Nils Donselaar on an earlier version of this paper, and acknowledges the highly constructive and thorough comments from the anonymous reviewers that helped improve this paper.

References

1. Cooper, G.F.: The computational complexity of probabilistic inference using bayesian belief networks. Artif. Intell. **42**(2–3), 393–405 (1990)
2. Darwiche, A.: Modeling and Reasoning with Bayesian Networks. Cambridge University Press (2009)
3. van der Gaag, L., Bodlaender, H.: On stopping evidence gathering for diagnostic Bayesian networks. In: European Conference on Symbolic and Quantitative Approaches to Reasoning and Uncertainty, pp. 170–181 (2011)
4. van der Gaag, L., Bodlaender, H., Feelders, A.: Monotonicity in Bayesian networks. In: Chickering, M., Halpern, J. (eds.) Proceedings of the Twentieth Conference on Uncertainty in Artificial Intelligence, pp. 569–576. AUAI press, Arlington (2004)
5. van der Gaag, L., Wessels, M.: Selective evidence gathering for diagnostic belief networks. AISB Q. **86**, 23–34 (1993)

6. Gunning, D., Stefik, M., Choi, J., Miller, T., Stumpf, S., Yang, G.: XAI–explainable artificial intelligence. Science Robotics 4(37) (2019)
7. Kwisthout, J.: Complexity results for enumerating MPE and partial MAP. In: Jaeger, M., Nielsen, T. (eds.) Proceedings of the Fourth European Workshop on Probabilistic Graphical Models, pp. 161–168 (2008)
8. Kwisthout, J.: Most probable explanations in bayesian networks: complexity and tractability. Int. J. Approximate Reasoning **52**(9), 1452–1469 (2011)
9. Kwisthout, J.: Most inforbable explanations: finding explanations in bayesian networks that are both probable *and* informative. In: van der Gaag, L.C. (ed.) ECSQARU 2013. LNCS (LNAI), vol. 7958, pp. 328–339. Springer, Heidelberg (2013). https://doi.org/10.1007/978-3-642-39091-3_28
10. Kwisthout, J.: Tree-width and the computational complexity of MAP approximations in Bayesian networks. J. Artif. Intell. Res. **53**, 699–720 (2015)
11. Lipton, P.: Inference to the Best Explanation. Routledge, London (1991)
12. Meekes, M., Renooij, S., van der Gaag, L.C.: Relevance of evidence in bayesian networks. In: Destercke, S., Denoeux, T. (eds.) ECSQARU 2015. LNCS (LNAI), vol. 9161, pp. 366–375. Springer, Cham (2015). https://doi.org/10.1007/978-3-319-20807-7_33
13. Park, J.D., Darwiche, A.: Complexity results and approximation settings for MAP explanations. J. Artif. Intell. Res. **21**, 101–133 (2004)
14. Pearl, J., Paz, A.: GRAPHOIDS: a graph-based logic for reasoning about relevance relations. Technical report R-53-L, UCLA Computer Science Department (1987)
15. Ras, G., van Gerven, M., Haselager, P.: Explanation methods in deep learning: users, values, concerns and challenges. In: Escalante, H.J., et al. (eds.) Explainable and Interpretable Models in Computer Vision and Machine Learning. TSSCML, pp. 19–36. Springer, Cham (2018). https://doi.org/10.1007/978-3-319-98131-4_2
16. Shortliffe, E., Buchanan, B.: A model of inexact reasoning in medicine. Math. Biosci. **379**, 233–262 (1975)
17. Sutton, R., Pincock, D., Baumgart, D., Sadowski, D., Fedorak, R., Kroeker, K.: An overview of clinical decision support systems: benefits, risks, and strategies for success. NPJ Digital Med. **3**(1), 1–10 (2020)
18. Wagner, K.W.: The complexity of combinatorial problems with succinct input representation. Acta Informatica **23**(3), 325–356 (1986)
19. Yuan, C., Lim, H., Lu, T.: Most relevant explanation in Bayesian networks. J. Artif. Intell. Res. **42**(1), 309–352 (2011)

Bayesian Networks for the Test Score Prediction: A Case Study on a Math Graduation Exam

Martin Plajner[1] and Jiří Vomlel[1,2(✉)]

[1] Institute of Information Theory and Automation, Czech Academy of Sciences,
Pod Vodárenskou věží 4, Prague 8, Czechia
`vomlel@utia.cas.cz`
[2] Faculty of Management, University of Economics, Prague, Jarošovská 1117/II,
377 01 Jindřichův Hradec, Czechia

Abstract. In this paper we study the problem of student knowledge level estimation. We use probabilistic models learned from collected data to model the tested students. We propose and compare experimentally several different Bayesian network models for the score prediction of student's knowledge. The proposed scoring algorithm provides not only the expected value of the total score but the whole probability distribution of the total score. This means that confidence intervals of predicted total score can be provided along the expected value. The key that enabled efficient computations with the studied models is a newly proposed inference algorithm based on the CP tensor decomposition, which is used for the computation of the score distribution. The proposed algorithm is two orders of magnitude faster than a state of the art method. We report results of experimental comparisons on a large dataset from the Czech National Graduation Exam in Mathematics. In this evaluation the best performing model is an IRT model with one continuous normally distributed skill variable related to all items by the graded response models. The second best is a multidimensional IRT model with an expert structure of items-skills relations and a covariance matrix for the skills. This model has a higher improvement with larger training sets and seems to be the model of choice if a sufficiently large training dataset is available.

Keywords: Bayesian networks · Educational testing · Score prediction · Efficient probabilistic inference · Multidimensional IRT · CP tensor decomposition

1 Introduction

In this paper we study the problem of student knowledge level estimation. For this problem we use probabilistic models learned from collected data. When a model is applied to testing a particular student the model is updated by items answered by the tested student so far and the updated model is used to select the

ⓒ Springer Nature Switzerland AG 2021
J. Vejnarová and N. Wilson (Eds.): ECSQARU 2021, LNAI 12897, pp. 255–267, 2021.
https://doi.org/10.1007/978-3-030-86772-0_19

next item to be answered by the tested student. This concept is often referred as computerized adaptive testing (CAT), see, e.g. [11,20].

In their seminal work [2] Almond and Mislevy pointed out that the students can be modelled well using Bayesian networks [9,10,14]. This idea was further elaborated in [1,19]. All probabilistic models studied in this paper can be considered Bayesian networks (BNs) in a broader sense.

The paper is organized as follows. In Sect. 2 we describe probabilistic models that can be used to model student knowledge. In Sect. 3 we explain how the probabilistic inference with these models can be performed. Section 4 represents the main theoretical contribution of the paper, which is an efficient method for the score computation based on the CP tensor decomposition. In Sect. 5, which presents the main experimental contribution of the paper, we report results of experimental comparisons using a large dataset from the Czech National Graduation Exam in Mathematics. The results are summarized in Sect. 6.

2   Models

We will model the problem using models sharing four groups of variables:

- *Skills* (in some models called Factors), denoted $S_1, \ldots, S_m$ are unobserved (hidden) variables used to specify student abilities (skills). They will be either binary variables, discrete ordinal variables, or continuous variables depending on the model used.
- *Items* (also called Questions or Tasks), denoted $X_1, \ldots, X_n$ will be discrete ordinal variables whose states correspond to the number of points received for the answer. We will assume the states (points) are from a set of integers $\{0, 1, \ldots, z - 1\}$. When testing a particular student we will estimate their probability distributions using the collected evidence.
- *Answered items* are a subset of copies of items $X_1, \ldots, X_n$. An answered item is observed for the currently tested student. Answered item corresponding to an item $X_i, i \in \{1, \ldots, n\}$ is denoted X_i'. Conditional probability of each X_i' given the skills is by definition the same as for their corresponding item X_i. The answered items are used to propagate collected evidence to the model[1].
- *The total score node*, denoted Y, which represents the total sum of scores from all questions[2]. The values of Y are all possible total sums of items' values of $X_1, \ldots, X_n$. For example, if all items are binary (taking values 0 and 1) then Y has $n + 1$ values $(0, 1, \ldots, n)$.

---

[1] For each answered item X_i' its corresponding item X_i is generally still uncertain. Items X_i represent certain type of a question or a task that can be repeated and the result need not to be the same for the same student, i.e., we estimate student's skills and admit mistakes even if he/she has required skills and vice versa.

[2] The score we estimate is not the score the tested student gets at the end of the current test but in another test of the same type. Of course, the model can also provide the estimate of the test score in the current test – in this case, another score node, say Y', would have nodes X_i' as its parents instead. In this case all methods would necessarily have the zero score prediction error at the end of the test.

The general structure of all models will be similar albeit they will differ by the number of skill variables, by the type of skill variables, and by a possible direct dependence among skills represented in the model. In Fig. 1 and Fig. 2 we give examples of two types of considered models.

The BN model in Fig. 1 has three independent skills. These skills influence scores of items. It is assumed that for each item a domain expert decided which skills are relevant. In the model of Fig. 1 skill S_1 influences item X_1, skill S_2 influences both X_2 and X_3 items, and skill S_3 also influences both items X_2 and X_3 but also item X_4. The items X_1, X_2, X_3, and X_4 are never observed while items X_1', X_2', X_3', and X_4' represent observed items and are included in the model only if they are observed. If they are not observed then they are omitted from the model since they represent barren variables.

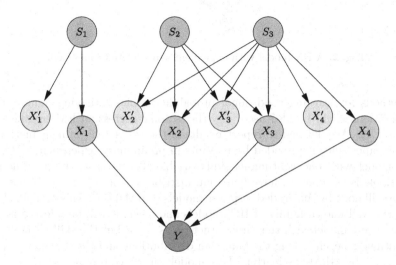

Fig. 1. An expert BN model with independent skills

Another BN model is presented in Fig. 2. This differs from the BN model in Fig. 1 in two aspects. First, in this models all items are related to all skills. Second, the skills are dependent. Typically, this model would be learned from collected data without using expert knowledge.

The models discussed above can be combined. For example, expert knowledge of relations of items to skills from the BN model of Fig. 1 can be used to reduce the number of edges in the BN model of Fig. 2.

In this paper we will compare following models:

– An expert model with independent skills (Fig. 1 type). Skills are represented by ordinal variables with three states. Items are related to their parent skills by general conditional probability tables restricted by monotonicity conditions [5]. The model parameters will be learned using restricted gradient method [15]. This model will be referred as *rgrad*. We should note that other

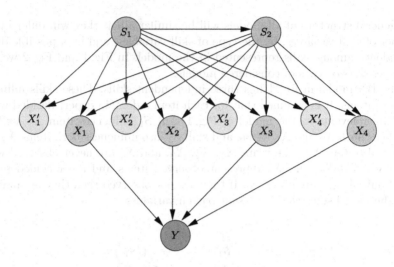

Fig. 2. A BN model with dependent skills related to all items

methods for learning conditional probability tables satisfying monotonicity conditions could be also used, e.g. the isotonic regression EM by Masegosa et al. [12]. We decided to report results of the restricted gradient method in this paper since it provided best results in preliminary experiments [16].

- A model with one continuous skill variable related to all items. The skill variable is assumed to have Gaussian distributions and items are related to the skill node by the graded response models (GRMs) [17]. This model belongs to the well-known family of IRT models and, thus, it will be referred as *irt*.
- An expert model with the same structure as *rgrad* but the skill variables are continuous, each having the Gaussian distributions and the items are related to skills by GRMs as in IRT. This model can be considered as an example of a multidimensional IRT [8] with the zero covariance among skills (often called factors in IRT). Therefore it will be referred as *mirt-cov0*.
- An expert model with the same structure as *rgrad* with continous skill variables which differs from *mirt-cov0* only by including relation between skills represented by multidimensional Gaussian distribution with a covariance matrix allowing nonzero non-diagonal elements. This model will be referred as *mirt-cov1*.
- The last group of models has the structure of model from Fig. 2, i.e., all items are related to all skills and the skills are dependent. It is a straightforward generalization of *irt* to more skills (factors). Skills are assumed to have multidimensional Gaussian distribution with the covariance matrix allowing nonzero non-diagonal elements. Depending on the number of factors these models will be referred as *mirt-2F*, *mirt-3F*, and *mirt-4F*, respectively.

The model parameters of the IRT and the multidimensional IRT models will be learned using algorithms implemented in the R mirt package [4].

The joint probability distribution of these models is defined by their structure represented by directed acyclic graph and their conditional probability distributions of each node given its parents as:

$$P(Y|X_1,\ldots,X_n) \cdot \prod_{i=1}^{n} P(X_i|pa(X_i)) \cdot \prod_{i=1}^{n} P(X_i'|pa(X_i')) \cdot \prod_{j=1}^{m} P(S_j|pa(S_j)) \ .$$

3 Probabilistic Inference

Models introduced in Sect. 2 will be used to estimate the probability distribution of the total score given the items answered so far. We will use symbol I to denote the set of indexes of already answered items X_i'. To simplify notation we will use symbol e to denote the evidence collected so far, i.e., $e = \{X_i' = x_i'\}_{i \in I}$.

The probability distribution of the total score given evidence e is (in case of discrete skill nodes) computed as:

$$P(Y|e) = \sum_{X_1,\ldots,X_n} \sum_{S_1,\ldots,S_m} P(Y, X_1,\ldots,X_n, S_1,\ldots,S_m|e) \ .$$

For the continuous skill nodes the integrals are used instead of the summation.

Using the general structure of the model this can be rewritten as:

$$P(Y|e) = \sum_{X_1,\ldots,X_n} \sum_{S_1,\ldots,S_m} P(Y|X_1,\ldots,X_n) \cdot Q(X_1,\ldots,X_n, S_1,\ldots,S_m|e)$$

where

$$Q(X_1,\ldots,X_n, S_1,\ldots,S_m|e) = \prod_{i=1}^{n} P(X_i|pa(X_i)) \cdot R(S_1,\ldots,S_m|e)$$

$$R(S_1,\ldots,S_m|e) \propto \prod_{i \in I} P(X_i' = x_i'|pa(X_i')) \cdot \prod_{j=1}^{m} P(S_j|pa(S_j))$$

and the conditional probability distribution

$$P(Y = y|X_1 = x_1,\ldots,X_n = x_n) = \begin{cases} 1 & \text{if } y = \sum_{i=1}^{n} x_i \\ 0 & \text{otherwise} \end{cases}$$

is deterministic and represents the distribution of the total sum of items' values.

In all considered models the values of items are dependent through the skills. Therefore we cannot sum out the skills for each item independently and then compute the probability distribution of the total sum. On the other hand, if a skill configuration is fixed, say it is a vector $s = (s_1,\ldots,s_m)$, then items become independent. This means that for each configuration of skills we can write

$$Q(X_1,\ldots,X_n, S_1 = s_1,\ldots,S_m = s_m|e) = \prod_{i=1}^{n} P(X_i|s) \cdot R(s|e) \ .$$

Using the above formula and denoting by x the vector $(x_1, \ldots, x_n)$, by $\mathcal{X} = \times_{i=1}^{n} \mathcal{X}_i$ the set of all configurations of x, and by $\mathcal{S}$ the set of all configurations of all skills we get:

$$P(Y|e) = \sum_{s \in \mathcal{S}} \left(\sum_{x \in \mathcal{X}} P(Y|X_1 = x_1, \ldots, X_n = x_n) \cdot \prod_{i=1}^{n} P(X_i = x_i|s) \right) \cdot R(s|e) \ .$$

In case of continuous skill nodes we will approximate the integrals over skills by a sufficiently large finite set of skill configurations $s = (s_1, \ldots, s_m)$ chosen so that they cover well the space of skill values. For this purpose, we will use Halton sequences [6] in m dimensions to generate points in the Cartesian product $\mathcal{S}$ of skills' state spaces[3]. Although these sequences are deterministic, they are of low discrepancy, i.e. they cover well the space $\mathcal{S}$. Thus, we can write:

$$P(Y|e) = \sum_{s \in \mathcal{S}} P(Y|s) \cdot R(s|e) \ , \text{ where} \tag{1}$$

$$P(Y|s) = \sum_{x \in \mathcal{X}} P(Y|X_1 = x_1, \ldots, X_n = x_n) \cdot \prod_{i=1}^{n} P(X_i = x_i|s) \ . \tag{2}$$

Now, the only remaining obstacle for efficient inference is the conditional distribution $P(Y|X_1 = x_1, \ldots, X_n = x_n)$, which can be very large since, typically, the models contain tens to hundreds of items. An efficient transformation of this distribution will be the topic of the next section.

4 Efficient Inference Method for the Score Computation

In this section we present a computationally efficient method that will be used to compute the probability distribution of the total score. It is based on the CP tensor decomposition [3,7] and can be also viewed as an application of Discrete Fourier Transformation (DFT). As we will show latter it is several orders of magnitude faster than a standard probabilistic inference approach based on, so called, parent divorcing [13]. The proposed method is especially useful for discrete random variables that have a large number of parents. This is the case of our case study since the total score variable has 37 discrete valued parents.

We assume each of n items takes values (points) from the set $\{0, 1, \ldots, z-1\}$. Therefore the maximum possible total score is $n(z-1)$ and the total number of states of Y is[4] $k = 1 + n(z-1)$. In the derivation of our algorithm we will exploit Theorem 3 and its proof given in [18]. From this result it follows that for all $y, x_1, \ldots, x_n$ we can write[5]:

---

[3] In order to use the same formula for both discrete and continuous skills we will use $\mathcal{S}$ to denote the set of skill configurations also in the continuous case.

[4] Please, note we include also the state 0.

[5] Please, note that the upper index m of $\alpha_j^m, j = 1, \ldots, k$. represents the power of α_j.

$$P(Y = y | X_1 = x_1, \ldots, X_n = x_n)$$

$$= \sum_{b=1}^{k} \alpha_b^{x_1} \cdot \ldots \cdot \alpha_b^{x_n} \cdot \beta_{b,y} \quad = \quad \sum_{b=1}^{k} \alpha_b^{x_1 + \ldots + x_n} \cdot \beta_{b,y} \ , \tag{3}$$

where $\alpha_1, \ldots, \alpha_k$ are pairwise distinct real or complex numbers and values of $\beta_{b,y}$ are solutions of the system of linear equations

$$Y = AX \ , \tag{4}$$

where Y is the $k \times k$ identity matrix, A is the $k \times k$ Vandermonde matrix defined by a vector $\alpha = (\alpha_1, \ldots, \alpha_k)$ as

$$A = \left\{ \alpha_i^j \right\}_{i=1, j=0}^{k, k-1} = \begin{pmatrix} \alpha_1^0 & \alpha_2^0 & \cdots & \alpha_k^0 \\ \alpha_1^1 & \alpha_2^1 & \cdots & \alpha_k^1 \\ \cdots & & & \\ \alpha_1^{(k-1)} & \alpha_2^{(k-1)} & \cdots & \alpha_k^{(k-1)} \end{pmatrix},$$

and X is the matrix defined as

$$X = \{ \beta_{b,y} \}_{b=1, y=0}^{k, k-1} = \begin{pmatrix} \beta_{1,0} & \beta_{1,1} & \cdots & \beta_{1,k-1} \\ \beta_{2,0} & \beta_{2,1} & \cdots & \beta_{1,k-1} \\ \cdots & & & \\ \beta_{k,0} & \beta_{k,1} & \cdots & \beta_{k,k-1} \end{pmatrix}.$$

Using the standard notation for probability tables we can write the Eq. (3) in a compact form as

$$P(Y | X_1, \ldots, X_n) = \sum_{B} P(Y, B) \cdot \prod_{i=1}^{n} P(X_i, B) \ , \tag{5}$$

where for all values b, x_i, y of variables B, X_i, Y, respectively, it holds:

$$P(Y = y, B = b) = \beta_{b,y} \quad \text{and} \quad P(X_i = x_i, B = b) = \alpha_b^{x_i} \ .$$

To achieve a good numerical stability for large dimensional problems (i.e., with high values of n) it is wise to use complex valued coefficients $\alpha_1, \ldots, \alpha_k$. We define them as the complex numbers from the unit circle (roots of unity) in the space of complex numbers, i.e., for $j = 1, \ldots, k$:

$$\alpha_j = \exp \left(j \cdot \frac{2\pi i}{k} \right) , \tag{6}$$

where i is the imaginary unit, satisfying the equation $i^2 = -1$. This brings also a very nice benefit since, in this case, the solution of the system of linear Eq. (4) is well-known:

$$X = \frac{1}{k} \cdot \overline{A^T} \ ,$$

where A^T denotes the transpose of A and $\overline{A^T}$ denotes the matrix with complex conjugated entries of A^T.

Remark 1. Vandermonde matrix A with entries specified by Eq. (6) is actually the Discrete Fourier Transformation (DFT) matrix.

Now we are ready to specify the final step of the probabilistic inference discussed in Sect. 3. In formula (2) we replace the conditional probability distribution of Y by the expression specified by formula (5)

$$P(Y|s) = \sum_{x \in \mathcal{X}} \sum_{b \in \{1,...,k\}} P(Y, B = b) \cdot \prod_{i=1}^{n} P(X_i = x_i, B = b) \cdot \prod_{i=1}^{n} P(X_i = x_i | s)$$

$$= \sum_{b \in \{1,...,k\}} P(Y, B = b) \cdot \prod_{i=1}^{n} \sum_{x_i \in \mathcal{X}_i} P(X_i = x_i, B = b) \cdot P(X_i = x_i | s)$$

$$= \sum_{b \in \{1,...,k\}} \beta_{b,y} \cdot \prod_{i=1}^{n} \sum_{x_i \in \mathcal{X}_i} \alpha_b^{x_i} \cdot P(X_i = x_i | s) \ .$$

```
score ← function(P)
{
  z ← nrow(P)
  n ← ncol(P)
  k ← 1+n*(z−1)
  alpha ← complex(modulus=1,argument=(1:k)*2*pi/k)
  A ← outer(alpha,seq(0,k−1),'^')
  X ← (1/k) * t(Conj(A))
  v ← rep(1,k)
  for (i in 1:n){
    v ← v * crossprod(t(A[,1:z]),P[,i])
  }
  y ← drop(Re(crossprod(t(X),v)))
  return(y)
}
```

Fig. 3. Scoring algorithm for a given skill configuration

In Fig. 3 we present[6] the algorithm for the total score computation for a given skill configuration s. The algorithm input is specified in $z \times n$ matrix[7] P defined by distributions $P(X_i|s)$ so that the element of jth row and i^{th} column of matrix P corresponds to the value $P(X_i = j|s)$ of distribution $P(X_i|s)$. The output y of the algorithm is $P(Y|s)$ – the probability distribution of the total score for the given s.

---

[6] We we use the notation of R, in which we implemented the algorithm and which we believe is self-explanatory.

[7] The number of rows z is the maximum item value computed over all items plus one. If a value is impossible then the corresponding matrix entry is set to zero.

Proposition 1. *The algorithm presented in Fig. 3 computes the probability distribution of the total score $P(Y|s)$ in $O(nz)$ time.*

Proof. The proof follows from the discussion above.

To estimate the total score of a particular student the scoring algorithm given a skill configuration s is repeated for each configuration s of student's skills, which can be thousands or more. Therefore, the complexity of the scoring algorithm represents an important issue. The complexity of the presented algorithm is linear with respect to the number of possible total scores.

In Fig. 4 we compare the computational CPU time of the presented scoring algorithm based on the CP tensor decomposition with the state of the art method – the parent divorcing method [13]. In the figure the horizontal axis corresponds to the number of items that are parents of the score node. The items corresponds to items from the model of the Czech National Graduation Exam in Mathematics described in Sect. 5. They are added one by one in the ascending order. Most items have two states only, but some of them have more than two states (the maximum is four). The vertical axis corresponds to the total CPU time of one thousand of actual computations of the score for the given number of items[8]. We can see that the scoring algorithm based on the CP tensor decomposition is two orders of magnitude faster than the parent divorcing method.

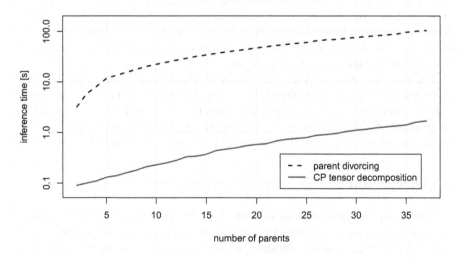

Fig. 4. Comparisons of the computational time of the scoring algorithms

5 Experimental Model Comparisons

In this section we report results of experimental comparisons performed using a large dataset from the Czech National Graduation Exam in Mathematics. This

---

[8] Please, note the vertical axis has a logarithmic scale.

dataset contains answers from more than 20,000 students who took this test in the year 2015. We randomly selected training subsets of different sizes and a testing subset consisting of answers of 100 students[9]. The test contains 37 items, most of them scored with either 0 or 1 point, the highest number of points for one item is 3. The expert model contains 8 skill nodes and is described in [15].

Model comparisons are presented in Fig. 5. We evaluate the score prediction quality during adaptive tests performed for each of 100 students from the testing set. The criteria used for evaluation was the average absolute difference of the expected score computed by each model and the true score. The items were selected for each student using an adaptive criteria. To get comparable results we used the same sequence of items for all models. The sequence was established using the *rgrad* model with the expected information gain criteria[10].

From the plots we can clearly see that the best performing algorithm is *irt* for both sizes of the training dataset[11]. The second best performing algorithm was *mirt-COV1*. This is the algorithm that uses the expert structure for items-skills relations and includes relations between skills. It is important to note that the improvement with larger training set is larger for *mirt-COV1* than for *irt*. Generally, more complex models seem to require more training data than *irt* to achieve better performance. Also, expert models that do not represent dependence between skills (*mirt-COV0* and *rgrad*) have worse performance than the corresponding expert model representing this dependence (*mirt-COV1*). This indicates that the current expert model *rgrad* could be probably improved by including such dependencies explicitly in the model. Finally, from models with more than one skill those that have the expert structure for items-skills relations perform better than those that have not.

Since the scoring algorithm provides not only the expected value of the total score but the whole probability distribution of the total score it can be used to provide confidence intervals of predicted total score as well. In Fig. 6 we present an example of 95% confidence interval for one student from the testing set using the *irt* model learned from 160 students' records from training data.

6   Discussion

In this paper we presented an experimental comparison of different Bayesian network models for score prediction during an adaptive test of student's knowledge. The key that enabled efficient computation was a new inference algorithm used for computation of the score distribution. We are not aware of any other

---

[9] Of course, the selection process ensured that the datasets were disjoint.

[10] Albeit the item sequences might slightly differ for different models we do not expect this has a significant impact on models' performance. The score prediction is independent of the order of items in the sequence if the items are the same.

[11] All claims about algorithms' performance were verified using the Wilcoxon rank test with significance level 0.01. Actually, the probability of the alternative hypothesis was always lower than 10^{-15}.

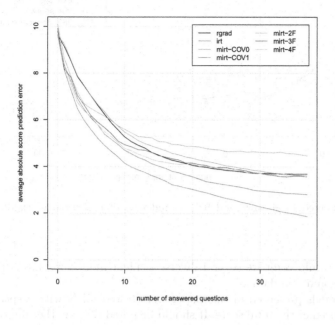

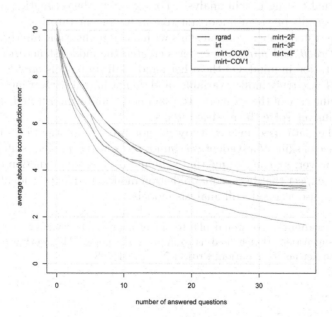

Fig. 5. Model comparisons for the training set consisting of 160 and 640 students, respectively.

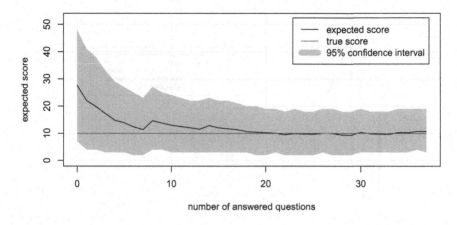

Fig. 6. Expected total score and 95% confidence interval for one student from the testing set.

work that would compare several diverse student models as those discussed in this paper on a real data.

The models presented in this paper were tested solely with respect to their ability to predict the total score. It should be noted that another important task in educational testing is skill analysis. For example, the estimation of the level of student's skills plays an important role in intelligent tutoring systems. Only some of the tested models contain skills with a comprehensible interpretation. In *rgrad*, *mirt-cov0*, and *mirt-cov1* experts created the model structures with such an interpretation in mind. On the other hand, skills in models *mirt-2F*, *mirt-3F*, and *mirt-4F* are truly hidden variables and do not have any clear interpretation. In the specific case of the *irt* model the skill node can be interpreted as a general ability to answer/solve the modeled items.

Since the data used in our study do not provide information about presence/absence of skills of a student we cannot test directly models' skill prediction quality. However, we can assume that skill and total score prediction quality are related. We expect that best score prediction models with expert-identified skills can be used also as good skill analysis models.

Acknowledgements. We would like to thank anonymous reviewers for their comments and suggestions that helped us to improve the paper. This work was supported by the Czech Science Foundation, Project No. 19-04579S.

References

1. Almond, R.G., Mislevy, R.J., Steinberg, L.S., Yan, D., Williamson, D.M.: The future of Bayesian networks in educational assessment. In: Bayesian Networks in Educational Assessment. SSBS, pp. 583–599. Springer, New York (2015). https://doi.org/10.1007/978-1-4939-2125-6_16

2. Almond, R.G., Mislevy, R.J.: Graphical models and computerized adaptive testing. Appl. Psychol. Meas. **23**(3), 223–237 (1999)
3. Carroll, J.D., Chang, J.J.: Analysis of individual differences in multidimensional scaling via an n-way generalization of Eckart-Young decomposition. Psychometrika **35**, 283–319 (1970)
4. Chalmers, R.P.: mirt: a multidimensional item response theory package for the R environment. J. Statist. Softw. **48**(6), 1–29 (2012). https://doi.org/10.18637/jss. v048.i06
5. van der Gaag, L.C., Bodlaender, H.L., Feelders, A.J.: Monotonicity in Bayesian networks. In: Proceedings of the Twentieth Conference on Uncertainty in Artificial Intelligence, pp. 569–576. AUAI Press (2004)
6. Halton, J.H.: Algorithm 247: radical-inverse quasi-random point sequence. Commun. ACM **7**(12), 701–702 (1964). https://doi.org/10.1145/355588.365104
7. Harshman, R.A.: Foundations of the PARAFAC procedure: models and conditions for an "explanatory" multi-mode factor analysis. UCLA Working Pap. Phonetics **16**, 1–84 (1970)
8. Hartig, J., Höhler, J.: Multidimensional IRT models for the assessment of competencies. Stud. Educ. Eval. **35**(2), 57–63 (2009). https://doi.org/10.1016/j.stueduc. 2009.10.002
9. Jensen, F.V.: Bayesian Networks and Decision Graphs. Springer, New York (2001). https://doi.org/10.1007/978-1-4757-3502-4
10. Lauritzen, S.L., Spiegelhalter, D.J.: Local computations with probabilities on graphical structures and their application to expert systems (with discussion). J. Roy. Stat. Soc. B **50**, 157–224 (1988)
11. Jeevan, M., Dhingra, A., Hanmandlu, M., Panigrahi, B.K.: Robust speaker verification using GFCC based i-vectors. In: Lobiyal, D.K., Mohapatra, D.P., Nagar, A., Sahoo, M.N. (eds.) Proceedings of the International Conference on Signal, Networks, Computing, and Systems. LNEE, vol. 395, pp. 85–91. Springer, New Delhi (2017). https://doi.org/10.1007/978-81-322-3592-7_9
12. Masegosa, A.R., Feelders, A.J., van der Gaag, L.C.: Learning from incomplete data in Bayesian networks with qualitative influences. Int. J. Approximate Reasoning **69**, 18–34 (2016). https://doi.org/10.1016/j.ijar.2015.11.004
13. Olesen, K.G., et al.: A Munin network for the median nerve - a case study on loops. Appl. Artif. Intell. **3**(2–3), 385–403 (1989). https://doi.org/10.1080/08839518908949933
14. Pearl, J.: Probabilistic reasoning in intelligent systems: networks of plausible inference. Morgan Kaufmann Publishers Inc., San Francisco (1988)
15. Plajner, M., Vomlel, J.: Learning bipartite Bayesian networks under monotonicity restrictions. Int. J. Gen. Syst. **49**(1), 88–111 (2020). https://doi.org/10.1080/03081079.2019.1692004
16. Plajner, M., Vomlel, J.: Monotonicity in practice of adaptive testing (2020). https://arxiv.org/abs/2009.06981
17. Samejima, F.: Estimation of latent ability using a response pattern of graded scores. Psychometrika **34**, 1–97 (1969). https://doi.org/10.1007/BF03372160
18. Savicky, P., Vomlel, J.: Exploiting tensor rank-one decomposition in probabilistic inference. Kybernetika **43**(5), 747–764 (2007)
19. Vomlel, J.: Bayesian networks in educational testing. Int. J. Uncertainty Fuzziness Knowl.-Based Syst. **12**(supp01), 83–100 (2004)
20. Wainer, H., Dorans, N.J.: Computerized Adaptive Testing: A Primer. Routledge (1990)

Fine-Tuning the Odds in Bayesian Networks

Bahare Salmani$^{(\boxtimes)}$ (iD) and Joost-Pieter Katoen$^{(\boxtimes)}$ (iD)

RWTH Aachen University, Aachen, Germany
{salmani,katoen}@cs.rwth-aachen.de

Abstract. This paper proposes new analysis techniques for Bayes networks in which conditional probability tables (CPTs) may contain symbolic variables. The key idea is to exploit scalable and powerful techniques for synthesis problems in parametric Markov chains. Our techniques are applicable to arbitrarily many, possibly dependent, parameters that may occur in multiple CPTs. This lifts the severe restrictions on parameters, e.g., by restricting the number of parametrized CPTs to one or two, or by avoiding parameter dependencies between several CPTs, in existing works for parametric Bayes networks (pBNs). We describe how our techniques can be used for various pBN synthesis problems studied in the literature such as computing sensitivity functions (and values), simple and difference parameter tuning, ratio parameter tuning, and minimal change tuning. Experiments on several benchmarks show that our prototypical tool built on top of the probabilistic model checker Storm can handle several hundreds of parameters.

1 Introduction

Parametric Bayesian Networks. We consider Bayesian networks (BNs) whose conditional probability tables (CPTs) contain symbolic parameters such as x_1, $2 \cdot x_1^2$, and $x_1 + x_2$ with $0 < x_1, x_2 < 1$. Parametric probabilistic graphical models received a lot of attention, see e.g., [7,9–11,13,14,17–19,26,34,37,40,42]. Sensitivity analysis determines the effect of the parameter values in the CPTs on the decisions drawn from the parametric BN (pBN), e.g., whether $\Pr(H=h \mid E=e) > q$ for a given $q \in \mathbb{Q} \cap [0,1]$. It amounts to establishing a function expressing an output probability in terms of the x_i parameters under study. Parameter synthesis on pBNs deals with instantiating or altering the parameters such that the resulting BN satisfies some constraint of interest. For pBNs, synthesis mostly amounts to parameter tuning: find the minimal change on the parameters such that some constraint, e.g., $\Pr(H=h \mid E=e) > q$ holds [15,40]. As sensitivity analysis and parameter synthesis are computationally hard in general [37,38,40], many techniques restrict the number of parameters per CPT (n-way for small n [13,17,29]), permit parameter dependencies in several CPTs (single CPT [14]), or consider specific structures such as join trees [37] and require all parameters to occur in the same clique of the junction tree.

This work is funded by the ERC AdG Project FRAPPANT (Grant Nr. 787914).

J. Vejnarová and N. Wilson (Eds.): ECSQARU 2021, LNAI 12897, pp. 268–283, 2021.
https://doi.org/10.1007/978-3-030-86772-0_20

Parametric Markov Chains. Quite independently, analysis techniques for Markov chains (MCs) have been developed in the formal verification community in the last two decades [21,23,24,27,30,31,39,41]; for a recent overview see [35]. Parametric MCs (pMCs) are MCs in which transitions are labelled with multivariate polynomials over a fixed set of parameters. Substitution of these variables by concrete values induces a probability distribution over the state space of the MC. Whereas early works focused on computing a rational function over the parameters expressing the reachability probability of a given target state, in the last years significant progress has been made to check whether there exists a parameter valuation inducing a MC that satisfies a given objective, or to partition the parameter space—the space of all possible parameter values—into "good" and "bad" w.r.t. a given objective, e.g., is the probability to reach some states below (or above) a given threshold q? The complexity of various pMC synthesis problems is studied in [1,36].

This paper aims to extend the spectrum of parameter synthesis techniques for parametric BNs, i.e., BNs in which arbitrary many CPTs may contain symbolic probabilities, with state-of-the-art and recently developed techniques for parametric MCs. Consider the BN adapted from [22] depicted below. The probability of a cow being pregnant given both tests are negative is about 0.45. Assume the farmer wants to replace both tests such that this false-positive error is below 0.2. Figure 1 (left) indicates the corresponding pBN while (right) shows the synthesized values of the parameters p and q (the false-negative probabilities for the new urine and blood tests) using pMC techniques [41] such that the farmer's constraint is satisfied (green) or not (red).

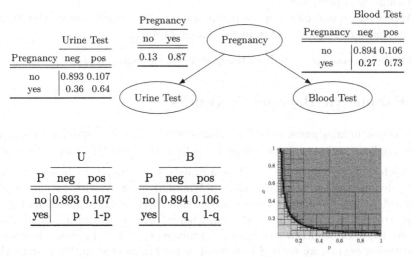

Fig. 1. (left) Parametric CPTs and (right) the parameter space split into safe and unsafe regions for the constraint $\Pr(\text{P} = \text{yes} \mid \text{U} = \text{neg and B} = \text{neg}) \leq 0.2$. (Color figure online)

Let us highlight a few issues: we can treat parameter space partitionings that go beyond rectangular shapes, and we support multiple, possibly dependent, parameters (not illustrated in our example). Thanks to approximate techniques such as parameter lifting [41], the entire parameter space can be split into safe, unsafe, and—by some approximation factor—unknown regions. This provides useful information: if it is not possible to find urine and blood tests of a certain quality, are alternatives fine too? Parameter tuning [13] for pBNs finds parameter values that are at a minimal distance to the original values in the BN. For our example, the BN sensitivity tool SamIam suggests changing the false-negative probability of the urine test (p) from 0.36 to 0.110456; or changing the false-negative probability of the blood test (q) from 0.27 to 0.082842.[1] Interestingly, if the parameters occur in multiple CPTs, the constraint can be satisfied with a smaller deviation from the original parameter values. Other recent work [5] focuses on obtaining symbolic functions for pBN-related problems such as sensitivity analysis. Note that pBNs are similar to constrained BNs [6] that focus on logical semantics rather than synthesis algorithms and tools as we do.

We treat the theoretical foundations of exploiting pMC techniques for various synthesis questions on pBNs, present a prototypical tool that is built on top of the probabilistic model checker Storm [25] and the pMC analysis tool Prophesy [24], and provide experimental results that reveal:

- pMC techniques are competitive to most common functions with the pBN tools SamIam and Bayesserver[2].
- pMC techniques are well-applicable to general pBNs, in particular by allowing parameter dependencies.
- Approximate parameter space partitioning is effective for parameter tuning e.g., ratio, difference, and minimal change problems.

Further proofs and details of this paper can be found in [44].

2   Parametric Bayesian Networks

This section defines *parametric* Bayesian networks (BNs)[3] and defines the sensitivity analysis and parameter tuning tasks from the literature that we consider.

Parameters. Let $X = \{x_1, \ldots, x_n\}$ be a finite set of real-valued *parameters* and $\mathbb{Q}(X)$ denote the set of multivariate polynomials over X with rational coefficients. A *parameter instantiation* is a function $u \colon X \to \mathbb{R}$. A polynomial f can be interpreted as a function $f \colon \mathbb{R}^n \to \mathbb{R}$ where $f(u)$ is obtained by substitution, i.e., in $f(u)$ each occurrence of x_i in f is replaced by $u(x_i)$. To make clear where substitution occurs, we write $f[u]$ instead of $f(u)$ from now on. We assume that

---

[1] When it comes to *multiple parameter suggestions*, SamIam suggests $p = 0.120097$ or $q = 0.089892$.

[2] We do not consider tools such as [48] for sensitivity analysis of Credal networks.

[3] Our notion of parametric BN should not be confused with existing parametric notions that consider variations of the structure, i.e., the topology of the BN.

all parameters are bounded, i.e., $lb_i \leq u(x_i) \leq ub_i$ for each parameter x_i. The *parameter space* of X is the set of all possible parameter values, the hyper-rectangle spanned by the intervals $[lb_i, ub_i]$. A subset R of the parameter space is called a *region*.

Parametric Bayes Networks. A parametric BN is a BN in which entries in the conditional probability tables (CPTs) are polynomials over the parameters in X.

Definition 1. *A parametric BN (pBN) $\mathcal{B}$ is a tuple (V, E, X, Θ) with:*

- $V = \{v_1, \ldots, v_m\}$ *is a set of discrete random variables with $dom(v_i) = D_{v_i}$*
- $G = (V, E)$ *with $E \subseteq V \times V$ is a directed acyclic graph on V*
- $X = \{x_1, \ldots, x_n\}$ *is a finite set of real-valued parameters*
- Θ *is a set of parametric conditional probability tables $\Theta = \{\, \Theta_{v_i} \mid v_i \in V \,\}$*

$$\Theta_{v_i} : \left(\prod_{p \in parents(v_i)} D_p \right) \to \mathbb{Q}(X)^{|D_{v_i}|}.$$

Let $\mathcal{B}[u]$ be obtained by replacing every parameter x_i in $\mathcal{B}$ by its value $u(x_i)$. A parameter instantiation u is *well-formed* for the pBN $\mathcal{B}$ if $\mathcal{B}[u]$ is a BN, i.e., for every $v_i \in V$ and parent evaluation $\overline{par}$, $\Theta_{v_i}(\overline{par})[u]$ yields a probability distribution over D_{v_i}. In the sequel, we assume u to be well-formed. A pBN defines a *parametric* joint probability distribution over V.

pBN Subclasses. We define some sub-classes of pBNs that are used in existing sensitivity analysis techniques and tools. They constrain the number of parameters, the number of CPTs (and the number of rows in a CPT) containing parameters. Let $\mathcal{B} = (V, E, X, \Theta)$ be a pBN, $c(x_i)$ the number of CPTs in $\mathcal{B}$ in which x_i occurs and $r(x_i)$ the number of CPT rows in which x_i occurs.

- $\mathcal{B} \in p_1c_1r_1$ iff $\mathcal{B}$ contains one parameter x_1 and x_1 only occurs in a single row of a single CPT, i.e., $X = \{x_1\}$, $c(x_1) = r(x_1) = 1$.
- $\mathcal{B} \in p_2c_{\leq 2}r_1$ iff $\mathcal{B}$ involves two parameters occurring only in two rows of two (or one) CPTs, i.e., $X = \{x_1, x_2\}$, $c(x_i) \in \{1, 2\}$, $r(x_i) = 1$ for $i = 1, 2$.
- $\mathcal{B} \in p_*c_1r_1$ iff $\mathcal{B}$ allows multiple distinct parameters, provided each parameter occurs in a single row of a single CPT, i.e., $r(x_i) = 1$, $c(x_i) = 1$ for each x_i and all the parameters occur in the same CPT.

The class $p_1c_1r_1$ is used in one-way, $p_2c_{\leq 2}r_1$ in two-way sensitivity analysis [13,17,29] and $p_*c_1r_1$ in single CPT [14].

Parameter Synthesis Problems in pBN. We define some synthesis problems for pBNs by their corresponding decision problems [38]. Let Pr denote the parametric joint distribution function induced by pBN $\mathcal{B} = (V, E, X, \Theta)$ and Pr$[u]$ the joint probability distribution of $\mathcal{B}[u]$ at well-formed instantiation u. Let $E \subseteq V$ be the evidence, $H \subseteq V$ the hypothesis and $q \in \mathbb{Q} \cap [0, 1]$ a threshold.

Parameter Tuning. Find an instantiation u s.t. Pr$[u](H = h \mid E = e) \geq q$.

Hypothesis Ratio Parameter Tuning. Find an instantiation u s.t.

$$\frac{\Pr[u](H = h' \mid E = e)}{\Pr[u](H = h \mid E = e)} \geq q \quad \text{i.e.,} \quad \frac{\Pr[u](H = h', E = e)}{\Pr[u](H = h, E = e)} \geq q,$$

where h and h' are joint variable evaluations for the hypothesis H.

Hypothesis Difference Parameter Tuning. Find an instantiation u s.t.

$$\Pr[u](H = h \mid E = e) - \Pr[u](H = h' \mid E = e) \geq q,$$

where h and h' are joint variable evaluations for the hypothesis H.

Minimal Change Parameter Tuning. For a given parameter instantiation u_0 and $\epsilon \in \mathbb{Q}_{>0}$, find an instantiation u s.t.

$$d(\Pr[u], \Pr[u_0]) \leq \epsilon,$$

where d is a distance notion on probability distributions, see [15].

Computing Sensitivity Function and Sensitivity Value. For the evidence $E = e$ and the hypothesis $H = h$, compute the sensitivity function:

$$f_{\Pr(H=h \mid E=e)} = \Pr(H = h \mid E = e).$$

This is a rational function over X, i.e., a fraction g/h with $g, h \in \mathbb{Q}(X)$.

The difference and ratio problems can analogously be defined for evidences. The evidence tuning problems are defined for values e and e' for E, given a fixed value h for H.

3   Parametric Markov Chains

A parametric Markov chain is a Markov chain in which the transitions are labelled with polynomials over the set X of parameters. These polynomials are intended to describe a parametric probability distribution over the pMC states.

Definition 2. *A parametric Markov chain (pMC) $\mathcal{M}$ is a tuple (Σ, σ_I, X, P) where Σ is a finite set of states with initial state $\sigma_I \in \Sigma$, X is as before, and $P : \Sigma \times \Sigma \to \mathbb{Q}(X)$ is the transition probability function.*

For pMC $\mathcal{M} = (\Sigma, \sigma_I, X, P)$ and well-formed parameter instantiation u on X, $\mathcal{M}[u]$ is the discrete-time Markov chain $(\Sigma, \sigma_I, X, P[u])$ where $P[u]$ is a probability distribution over Σ. We only consider well-formed parameter instantiations. *Reachability Probabilities.* Let $\mathcal{D}$ be an MC. Let $Paths(\sigma)$ denote the set of all infinite paths in $\mathcal{D}$ starting from σ, i.e., infinite sequences of the form $\sigma_1 \sigma_2 \sigma_3 \ldots$ with $\sigma_1 = \sigma$ and $P(\sigma_i, \sigma_{i+1}) > 0$. A probability measure $\Pr_{\mathcal{D}}$ is defined on measurable sets of infinite paths using a standard cylinder construction; for details, see, e.g., [2, Ch. 10]. For $T \subseteq \Sigma$ and $\sigma \in \Sigma$, let

$$\Pr_{\mathcal{D}}(\Diamond T) = \Pr_{\mathcal{D}}\{ \sigma_1 \sigma_2 \sigma_3 \ldots \in Paths(\sigma) \mid \exists i. \, \sigma_i \in T \} \tag{1}$$

denote the probability to eventually reach some state in T from σ. For pMC $\mathcal{M}$, $\mathrm{Pr}_{\mathcal{M}}(\lozenge T)$ is a function with $\mathrm{Pr}_{\mathcal{M}}(\lozenge T)[u] = \mathrm{Pr}_{\mathcal{D}}(\lozenge T)$ where $\mathcal{D} = \mathcal{M}[u]$, see [23]. *Parameter Synthesis Problems on pMCs.* We consider the following synthesis problems on pMCs. Let $\mathcal{M} = (\Sigma, \sigma_I, X, P)$ be a pMC and $\lambda \in \mathbb{Q} \cap [0, 1]$ a threshold, $\sim$ a binary comparison operator, e.g., $<$ or $\geq$, and $T \subseteq \Sigma$.

Feasibility Problem. Find a parameter instantiation u s.t. $\mathrm{Pr}_{\mathcal{M}[u]}(\lozenge T) \sim \lambda$.

Synthesis Problem. Partition a region R into R_a and R_r s.t.

$$\Pr_{\mathcal{M}[u]}(\lozenge T) \sim \lambda \text{ for all } u \in R_a \quad \text{and} \quad \Pr_{\mathcal{M}[u]}(\lozenge T) \not\sim \lambda \text{ for all } u \in R_r.$$

R_a is called an accepting region and R_r a rejecting region.

Approximate Synthesis Problem. Partition a region R into an accepting region R_a, rejecting region R_r, and unknown region R_u, such that $R_a \cup R_r$ covers at least $c\%$ of R. Additionally, R_a, R_r, and R_u should be finite unions of rectangular regions.

Verification Problem. Check whether region R is accepting, rejecting, or inconsistent, i.e., neither accepting nor rejecting.

Computing Reachability Functions. Compute the rational function $\mathrm{Pr}_{\mathcal{M}}(\lozenge T)$.

Algorithms for pMC Synthesis Problems. Several approaches have been developed to *compute the reachability function* $\mathrm{Pr}_{\mathcal{M}}(\lozenge T)$. This includes state elimination [23], fraction-free Gaussian elimination [1] and decomposition [28,33]. The reachability function can grow exponentially in the number of parameters, even for acyclic pMCs [1]. *Feasibility* is a computationally hard problem: finding parameter values for a pMC that satisfy a reachability objective is ETR-complete[4] [36]. Feasibility has been tackled using sampling search methods such as PSO[5] and Markov Chain Monte Carlo [16] and solving a non-linear optimization problem [4]. State-of-the-art approaches [20,21] iteratively simplify the NLP[6] encoding around a point to guide the search. The *approximate synthesis problem* checking is best tackled with parameter lifting [41]. The parameter lifting algorithm (PLA) first drops all dependencies between parameters in a pMC. It then transforms the pMC into a Markov decision process to get upper and lower bounds for the given objective.

4   Analysing Parametric BNs Using pMC Techniques

The key of our approach to tackle various synthesis problems on pBNs is to exploit pMC techniques. To that end, we transform a pBN into a pMC. We first present a recipe that is applicable to all inference queries on pBNs, and then detail a transformation that is tailored to the evidence in an inference query.

---

[4] Existential Theory of the Reals. ETR problems are between NP and PSPACE, and ETR-hard problems are as hard as finding the roots of a multi-variate polynomial.

[5] Particle swarm optimization.

[6] Nonlinear programming.

A pBN2pMC Transformation. This is inspired by our mapping of BNs onto tree-shaped MCs [43]. Here, we propose an alternative transformation that yields more succinct (p)MCs, as it only keeps track of a subset of (p)BN variables at each "level" of the (p)MC. These are the so-called *open variables* whose valuations are necessary to determine the subsequent transitions. Intuitively, the variable v_i is open if it has already been processed and at least one of its children has not. Below, we use $*$ if the value of variable $v \in V$ is *don't care*, i.e., either not yet determined or not needed any more.

Definition 3. *Let $G = (V, E)$ be a DAG with topological order $\varrho = (v_1, \ldots, v_m)$ on V. Let $v_i \in V$ be open at level[7] j iff $i <_\varrho j$ and $\exists v_k \in children(v_i). k >_\varrho j$. Let $open_\varrho(j)$ denote the set of open variables at level j under ϱ.*

Definition 4. *For pBN $\mathcal{B} = (V, E, X, \Theta)$ with topological order $\varrho = (v_1, \ldots, v_m)$ on V and $dom(v_i) = D_{v_i}$, let the pMC $\mathcal{M}_\mathcal{B}^\varrho = (\Sigma, \sigma_I, X, P)$ where:*

$-\ \Sigma = \bigcup_{j=1}^m \prod_{i=1}^m \{v_i\} \times T_j(D_{v_i})$ *with* $T_j(D_{v_i}) = \begin{cases} D_{v_i} & \text{if } i = j \text{ or } v_i \in open_\varrho(j), \\ \{*\} & \text{otherwise} \end{cases}$

$-\ \sigma_I = V \times \{*\}$ *is the initial state, and*

$-\ P$ *is the transition probability function defined for $f \in \mathbb{Q}(X)$ and function*

$$t_j(d_i) = \begin{cases} d_i & \text{if } v_i \in open_\varrho(j) \\ * & \text{otherwise} \end{cases}$$

by the following inference rules:

$$\frac{\Theta_{v_1}(d_1) = f}{\sigma_I \xrightarrow{f} ((v_1, d_1), (v_2, *), \ldots, (v_m, *))} \tag{2}$$

$$\frac{\sigma = ((v_1, t_{i-1}(d_1)), \ldots, (v_{i-2}, t_{i-1}(d_{i-2})), (v_{i-1}, d_{i-1}), (v_i, *), \ldots, (v_m, *)),}{\sigma \models parents(v_i), \quad \Theta_{v_i}(parents(v_i))(d_i) = f} \tag{3}$$
$$\sigma \xrightarrow{f} \sigma' = ((v_1, t_i(d_1)), \ldots, (v_{i-1}, t_i(d_{i-1})), (v_i, d_i), (v_{i+1}, *), \ldots, (v_m, *))$$

$$\sigma_F = ((v_1, *), \ldots, (v_{m-1}, *), (v_m, d_m)) \xrightarrow{1} \sigma_F \tag{4}$$

The states in pMC $\mathcal{M}_\mathcal{B}^\varrho$ are tuples of pairs (v_i, d_i) where v_i is a random variable in $\mathcal{B}$ and $d_i \in dom(v_i) \cup \{*\}$ is the current value of v_i. Note that (v_i, d_i) encodes $v_i = d_i$. In the initial state all variables are *don't care*. The (parametric) function P specifies the probability of evolving between pMC states, which is determined by *parametric* CPT entries of the pBN $\mathcal{B}$. Rule (2) defines the outgoing transitions of the initial state σ_I. Let $d_1 \in D_{v_1}$ and $f = \Theta_{v_1}(d_1)$ be v_1's CPT entry for d_1. σ_I evolves—with the parametric probability function f—to a state in which all variables are $*$ except that $v_1 = d_1$. Let $\sigma_F = ((v_1, *), \cdots, (v_m, d_m))$

---

[7] Levels are definable on $\mathcal{M}_\mathcal{B}^\varrho$ as Definition 4 does not impose any backward transition.

be the final state of $\mathcal{M}_{\mathcal{B}}^{\varrho}$. Since v_m has no children, $open_{\varrho}(m)=\emptyset$. It also holds that $open_{\varrho}(m-1)-\{v_m\}=\emptyset$ as v_{m-1} can not have any other unprocessed children than v_m. Thus all variables, except for v_m, have been reset to $*$ in σ_F, see rule (4). Rule (3) specifies the transitions from the states that are neither initial nor final. Let σ be the state in which $v_1, \cdots, v_{i-1}$ have been already processed, i.e., have been assigned a value in the path from σ_I to σ; some may have been reset to $*$ afterwards. Functions $t_j(d_i)$ ensures that only variables with no unprocessed children are reset. Let $parents(v_i)$ be a joint variable evaluation for v_i's parents. The second premise in rule (3) confirms that σ is consistent with $parents(v_i)$. Let $f=\Theta(parents(v_i))(d_i)$ be v_i's CPT entry for $parents(v_i)$ and $v_i=d_i$. Function f accordingly determines the (parametric) transition probability from σ to σ', i.e. a state with $v_i=d_i$ and the other variables determined by $t_i(d_j)$. Intuitively, for $j < i$, σ' forgets v_j if v_i has been v_j's only unprocessed child.

Example. Figure 2 (left) indicates the pMC for the pregnancy test pBN and the topological ordering (P, U, B) by definition 4. The node names are abbreviated by the first letter and the "don't care" evaluations are omitted.

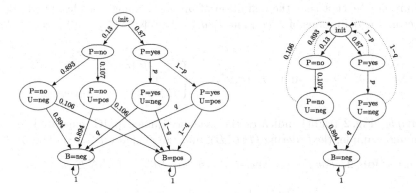

Fig. 2. The generated pMCs for the pregnancy test example based on (left) pBN2pMC and (right) evidence-guided pBN2pMC transformation.

The following result relates (conditional) inference in pBNs to (conditional) reachability objectives in pMCs.

Proposition 1. *Let $\mathcal{B}$ be a pBN. Let $E, H \subseteq V$ and ϱ be a topological ordering on V. Then, for the pMC $\mathcal{M}_{\mathcal{B}}^{\varrho}$ we have:*

$$\Pr_{\mathcal{B}}(E) = 1 - \Pr_{\mathcal{M}_{\mathcal{B}}^{\varrho}}(\Diamond \neg E) \quad and \quad \Pr_{\mathcal{B}}(H \mid E) = \frac{1 - \Pr_{\mathcal{M}_{\mathcal{B}}^{\varrho}}(\Diamond (\neg H \vee \neg E))}{1 - \Pr_{\mathcal{M}_{\mathcal{B}}^{\varrho}}(\Diamond \neg E)},$$

where the latter equality requires $\Pr_{\mathcal{B}}(\neg E) < 1$.

This result directly enables to use techniques for *feasibility checking* on pMCs to pBNs, and the use of techniques to compute reachability functions on pMCs to *computing sensitivity functions* on pBNs.

An Evidence-Tailored pBN2pMC Transformation. The above transformation is agnostic from the inference query. We now construct a pMC $\mathcal{M}_{\mathcal{B},E}^{\varrho}$ tailored to a given evidence $E \subseteq V$. This transformation is inspired by a transformation on MCs [3] for computing conditional reachability probabilities. Let $\mathcal{B} = (V, E, X, \Theta)$ be a pBN and ϱ be a topological order on V. Let evidence $E = (v_1 = d_1) \wedge \cdots \wedge (v_k = d_k)$, such that $v_1 <_\varrho \ldots <_\varrho v_k$. We construct pMC $\mathcal{M}_{\mathcal{B},E}^{\varrho}$ by the following two amendments on the pMC $\mathcal{M}_{\mathcal{B}}^{\varrho}$ as defined in Definition 4:

1. Let $\Sigma_{\neg E} = \{\sigma \in E \mid \exists i. \sigma \models (v_i = \neg d_i)\}$ be the set of states violating E. We redirect all incoming transitions of $\sigma \in \Sigma_{\neg E}$ to the initial state σ_I.
2. For $v_j \notin E$ with $v_j <_\varrho v_k$, we propagate the values of v_j until the level k. In other words, we pretend v_{k+1} is the child of v_j, so we keep v_j open.

Let us formalize this. Let Σ' and P' be defined analogously to Σ and P in Definition 4, except that the definition of *open set* changes as described above, affecting the definitions of $T_j(v_i)$ and $t_j(d_i)$. Then, let $\mathcal{M}_{\mathcal{B},E}^{\varrho} = (\Sigma_E, \sigma_I, X, P_E)$, where

$$\Sigma_E = \Sigma' \setminus \Sigma_{\neg E} \quad \text{and} \quad P_E(\sigma, \sigma') = \begin{cases} \sum_{\sigma' \not\models E} P'(\sigma, \sigma') & \text{if } \sigma' \in \Sigma_{\neg E} \\ P'(\sigma, \sigma') & \text{otherwise.} \end{cases}$$

Example. Fig. 2 (right) indicates the evidence-guided pMC generated for our running example, the ordering (P, U, B), and the evidence $U{=}neg \wedge B{=}neg$.

Proposition 2. *For the evidence-tailored MC $\mathcal{M}_{\mathcal{B},E}^{\varrho}$ of pBN $\mathcal{B}$, we have:*

$$\Pr_{\mathcal{B}}(H \mid E) = 1 - \Pr_{\mathcal{M}_{\mathcal{B},E}^{\varrho}}(\Diamond \neg H). \tag{5}$$

This result facilitates using pMC techniques for pBN *parameter tuning*.

Ratio and Difference Parameter Tuning by Parameter Lifting. The ratio problem on pBN $\mathcal{B}$ corresponds to finding an instantiation u in the pMC $\mathcal{M}_{\mathcal{B},E}^{\varrho}$ s.t.

$$\Pr_{\mathcal{M}_{\mathcal{B},E}^{\varrho}}[u](\Diamond T) \geq q \cdot \Pr_{\mathcal{M}_{\mathcal{B},E}^{\varrho}}[u](\Diamond G), \tag{6}$$

where $\Pr(\Diamond T)$ stands for $1 - \Pr_{\mathcal{M}_{\mathcal{B},E}^{\varrho}}[u](\Diamond(H = \neg h' \vee E = \neg e))$ and $\Pr(\Diamond G)$ abbreviates $1 - \Pr_{\mathcal{M}_{\mathcal{B},E}^{\varrho}}[u](\Diamond(H = \neg h \vee E = \neg e))$. This problem can be solved by using PLA: let region $R \subseteq \mathbb{R}_{\geq 0}^n$. We perform PLA for reaching G and reaching T on $\mathcal{M}_{\mathcal{B}}$, respectively. This gives upper (UB_T, UB_G) and lower bounds (LB_T, LB_G) for the probabilities on the left- and the right-hand side of (6). Then:

- If $LB_T \geq q \cdot UB_G$, the region R is accepting for the ratio property.

- If $LB_T \leq q \cdot UB_G$, the region R is rejecting for the ratio property.
- Otherwise, refine the region R.

For difference parameter tuning, we adopt the above recipe by replacing (6) by:

$$\Pr_{\mathcal{M}_{\mathcal{B},E}^{\varrho}} [u](\Diamond T) \; \geq \; q + \Pr_{\mathcal{M}_{\mathcal{B},E}^{\varrho}} [u](\Diamond G). \tag{7}$$

5   Experiments

Our pBN Analysis Tool. We developed a prototypical tool on top of the tools Storm [25] and Prophesy [24], see Fig. 3. Storm is a probabilistic model checker that dominated the last (and only) two model-checking competitions, see https://qcomp.org/; Prophesy is an efficient tool for pMC synthesis. Our tool deploys pMC parameter synthesis techniques to analyze pBNs. It includes both pBN2pMC transformations where pBNs are provided in an extended bif format. The pMCs are either encoded in Jani [8] or in the explicit drn format. It is also possible to transform non-parametric BNs into MCs and parameterize the MC. Storm is used to compute the sensitivity function and for parameter tuning using PLA. Prophesy is exploited for feasibility checking: find a parameter instance satisfying an inference query. Our tool-chain supports $p_* c_* r_*$, the general pBNs class. As baseline we used two synthesis tools for parametric BNs: SamIam and Bayesserver.

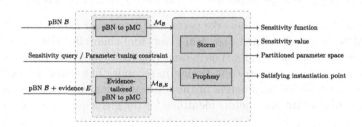

Fig. 3. Our prototypical tool-chain for synthesis problems on pBNs

SamIam. SamIam[8] is a commonly used tool for the sensitivity analysis for pBNs, developed at Darwiche's group at UCLA. It allows the specification of conditional, hypothesis ratio, and hypothesis difference constraints on pBNs. SamIam then attempts to identify minimal parameter changes that are necessary to satisfy these constraints. It supports the pBN classes $p_1 c_1 r_1$ and $p_* c_1 r_1$.

Bayesserver. Bayesserver[9] is a commercial tool that offers sensitivity analysis and parameter tuning of pBNs. For sensitivity analysis, it computes the sensitivity

---

[8] http://reasoning.cs.ucla.edu/samiam.
[9] https://www.bayesserver.com.

function and sensitivity value. It also performs minimal-change parameter tuning for conditional, hypothesis ratio, and hypothesis difference constraints. It supports the classes $p_1c_1r_1$ and $p_2c_{\leq 2}r_1$ for sensitivity analysis and the class $p_1c_1r_1$ for parameter tuning. Table 1 lists the functionalities of all tools.

Table 1. Overview of the capabilities of the pBN synthesis tools considered.

	SamIam	Bayesserver	Storm-prophesy
Computing sensitivity function	✗	$p_{\leq 2}c_{\leq 2}r_1$	$p_*c_*r_*$
Computing sensitivity value	✗	$p_{\leq 2}c_{\leq 2}r_1$	$p_1c_*r_*$
Simple parameter tuning	$p_*c_1r_1$	$p_1c_1r_1$	$p_*c_*r_*$
Difference parameter tuning	$p_*c_1r_1$	$p_1c_1r_1$	$p_*c_*r_*$
Ratio parameter tuning	$p_*c_1r_1$	$p_1c_1r_1$	$p_*c_*r_*$
Minimal change tuning	$p_*c_1r_1$	$p_1c_1r_1$	$p_*c_*r_*$

Experimental Set-up. We took benchmarks from [45] and conducted all our experiments on a 2.3 GHz Intel Core i5 processor with 16 GB of RAM. We focused on questions such as:

1. What is the scalability for computing sensitivity functions on pBNs?
2. What is the practical scalability for feasibility checking?
3. To what extent is PLA applicable to parameter tuning for pBNs?

Computing Sensitivity Function. We performed a series of experiments for computing pBN sensitivity functions using our tool-chain for the $p_*c_*r_1$ class. Figure 4 summarizes the results. The x−axis (log scale) indicates the pBN benchmarks and the y−axis denotes the timing in seconds. The numbers on the bars indicate the number of parameters in the solution functions, which is related to the number of relevant parameters identified for the given query. We observe that

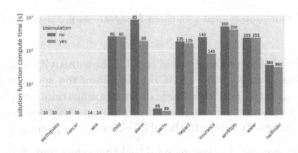

Fig. 4. Storm's performance for calculating prior sensitivity functions of pBNs. (Unfortunately, a comparison with the other tools was not possible, as SamIam does not explicitly offers sensitivity function computation and Bayesserver sensitivity analysis is limited to 1 or 2 parameters, see Table 1.)

Storm scales up to 380 parameters for very large networks such as `hailfinder`. The blue bars represent regular computations, while the orange bars indicate the impact of bisimulation minimization, a built-in reduction technique in Storm.

Feasibility Checking. Our tool exploits Prophesy to find a parameter instantiation u of pBN $\mathcal{B}$ such that the BN $\mathcal{B}[u]$ satisfies the given inference query. We have performed a set of experiments for the class $p_*c_*r_1$. Figure 5 (log-log scale) illustrates the results; the x-axis indicates the number of parameters in the pBN and the y-axis the time for feasibility checking (in seconds). Each line corresponds to a pBN and the points on the lines represent single experiments. We inserted the parameters in the predecessors of the query nodes (i.e., in H) to maximize their relevance. We also imposed queries over multiple nodes at once to push the boundaries. We used convex optimization (QCQP[10]) (left plot) and PSO (right plot). Prophesy was able to handle up to 853 parameters.

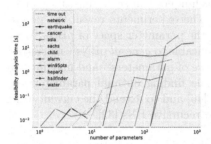 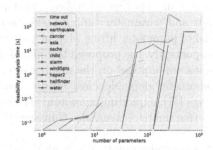

Fig. 5. Feasibility checking on pBN benchmarks by (left) QCQP and (right) PSO.

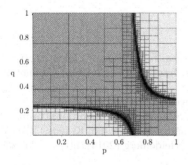 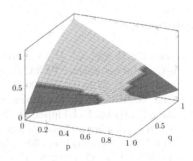

Fig. 6. PLA results on the `alarm` pBN ($p_2c_3r_{26}$) for the constraint $\Pr(venttube = 0 \mid ventlung = 0) > 0.6$ with a 99% parameter space coverage. (Color figure online)

Approximate Parameter Synthesis on pBNs: Tuning the Parameters and More. Experiments on the pBN benchmarks using PLA aimed at (a) the classes $p_1c_1r_1$

---

[10] Quadratically-constrained quadratic programming.

and $p_*c_1r_1$ to validate them against SamIam and Bayesserver, and (b) the class $p_*c_*r_*$ to investigate the potential of PLA for general pBNs. Figure 6 visualizes the results for the `alarm` pBN with 2 parameters occurring in 26 rows of 3 CPTs, i.e., a pBN with parameter dependencies. The parameter x was used in the CPT entries $e_1, \cdots, e_k$ only when the probability values of those entries coincided in the original BN. As seen in the figure, PLA can partition the entire n-way parameter space. The minimal-change parameter values can be extracted from the PLA results, where the precision depends on the PLA approximation factor.

6   Conclusion

This paper exploited tools and techniques for parameter synthesis on Markov chains to synthesis problems on parametric Bayesian networks. Prototypical tool support for pBN analysis on top of existing pMC synthesis tools has been realized. Our experiments indicate that pMC techniques can scale sensitivity analysis and parameter tuning tasks on pBNs. The experiments reveal the potential of parameter lifting [41] for partitioning the parameter space of pBNs. Most importantly, the proposed techniques are applicable to *general* pBNs—no restrictions are imposed on the number or occurrence of parameters—and may involve parameter dependencies. Future work include finding optimal parameter settings [47], exploiting monotonicity checking [46] and to extend the current work to (parametric) dynamic, Gaussian [12], and recursive BNs [32].

Acknowledgement. We thank Robin Drahovsky for his contributions on transforming pMCs into pBNs, Caroline Jabs for her implementation efforts, and Sebastian Junges, Tim Quatmann, and Matthias Volk for discussions. We also thank Arthur Choi for his support.

References

1. Baier, C., Hensel, C., Hutschenreiter, L., Junges, S., Katoen, J., Klein, J.: Parametric Markov chains: PCTL complexity and fraction-free Gaussian elimination. Inf. Comput. **272**, 104504 (2020)
2. Baier, C., Katoen, J.: Principles of Model Checking. MIT Press (2008)
3. Baier, C., Klein, J., Klüppelholz, S., Märcker, S.: Computing conditional probabilities in Markovian models efficiently. In: Ábrahám, E., Havelund, K. (eds.) TACAS 2014. LNCS, vol. 8413, pp. 515–530. Springer, Heidelberg (2014). https://doi.org/10.1007/978-3-642-54862-8_43
4. Bartocci, E., Grosu, R., Katsaros, P., Ramakrishnan, C.R., Smolka, S.A.: Model repair for probabilistic systems. In: Abdulla, P.A., Leino, K.R.M. (eds.) TACAS 2011. LNCS, vol. 6605, pp. 326–340. Springer, Heidelberg (2011). https://doi.org/10.1007/978-3-642-19835-9_30
5. Bartocci, E., Kovács, L., Stankovič, M.: Analysis of Bayesian networks via probsolvable loops. In: Pun, V.K.I., Stolz, V., Simao, A. (eds.) ICTAC 2020. LNCS, vol. 12545, pp. 221–241. Springer, Cham (2020). https://doi.org/10.1007/978-3-030-64276-1_12

6. Beaumont, P., Huth, M.: Constrained Bayesian Networks: Theory, Optimization, and Applications. CoRR https://arxiv.org/abs/1705.05326 (2017)
7. Bolt, J.H., van der Gaag, L.C.: Balanced tuning of multi-dimensional Bayesian network classifiers. In: Destercke, S., Denoeux, T. (eds.) ECSQARU 2015. LNCS (LNAI), vol. 9161, pp. 210–220. Springer, Cham (2015). https://doi.org/10.1007/978-3-319-20807-7_19
8. Budde, C.E., Dehnert, C., Hahn, E.M., Hartmanns, A., Junges, S., Turrini, A.: JANI: quantitative model and tool interaction. In: Legay, A., Margaria, T. (eds.) TACAS 2017. LNCS, vol. 10206, pp. 151–168. Springer, Heidelberg (2017). https://doi.org/10.1007/978-3-662-54580-5_9
9. Castillo, E., Gutiérrez, J.M., Hadi, A.S.: Parametric structure of probabilities in Bayesian networks. In: Froidevaux, C., Kohlas, J. (eds.) ECSQARU 1995. LNCS, vol. 946, pp. 89–98. Springer, Heidelberg (1995). https://doi.org/10.1007/3-540-60112-0_11
10. Castillo, E.F., Gutiérrez, J.M., Hadi, A.S.: Goal oriented symbolic propagation in Bayesian networks. In: AAAI/IAAI, vol. 2. pp. 1263–1268. AAAI Press/The MIT Press (1996)
11. Castillo, E.F., Gutiérrez, J.M., Hadi, A.S.: Sensitivity analysis in discrete Bayesian networks. IEEE Trans. Syst. Man Cybern. Part A 27(4), 412–423 (1997)
12. Castillo, E.F., Gutiérrez, J.M., Hadi, A.S., Solares, C.: Symbolic propagation and sensitivity analysis in Gaussian Bayesian networks with application to damage assessment. Artif. Intell. Eng. 11(2), 173–181 (1997)
13. Chan, H., Darwiche, A.: When do numbers really matter? J. Artif. Intell. Res. 17, 265–287 (2002)
14. Chan, H., Darwiche, A.: Sensitivity analysis in Bayesian networks: from single to multiple parameters. In: UAI, pp. 67–75. AUAI Press (2004)
15. Chan, H., Darwiche, A.: A distance measure for bounding probabilistic belief change. Int. J. Approx. Reason. 38(2), 149–174 (2005)
16. Chen, T., Hahn, E.M., Han, T., Kwiatkowska, M.Z., Qu, H., Zhang, L.: Model repair for Markov decision processes. In: TASE. IEEE (2013)
17. Coupé, V.M.H., van der Gaag, L.C.: Properties of sensitivity analysis of Bayesian belief networks. Ann. Math. Artif. Intell. 36(4), 323–356 (2002)
18. Coupe, V.M., van der Gaag, L.C.: Practicable sensitivity analysis of Bayesian belief networks, vol. 1998. Utrecht University, Information and Computing Sciences (1998)
19. Coupé, V.M., van der Gaag, L.C., Habbema, J.D.F.: Sensitivity analysis: an aid for belief-network quantification. Knowl. Eng. Rev. 15(3), 215–232 (2000)
20. Cubuktepe, M., et al.: Sequential convex programming for the efficient verification of parametric MDPs. In: Legay, A., Margaria, T. (eds.) TACAS 2017. LNCS, vol. 10206, pp. 133–150. Springer, Heidelberg (2017). https://doi.org/10.1007/978-3-662-54580-5_8
21. Cubuktepe, M., Jansen, N., Junges, S., Katoen, J.-P., Topcu, U.: Synthesis in pMDPs: a tale of 1001 parameters. In: Lahiri, S.K., Wang, C. (eds.) ATVA 2018. LNCS, vol. 11138, pp. 160–176. Springer, Cham (2018). https://doi.org/10.1007/978-3-030-01090-4_10
22. Darwiche, A.: Modeling and Reasoning with Bayesian Networks. Cambridge University Press (2009)
23. Daws, C.: Symbolic and parametric model checking of discrete-time markov chains. In: Liu, Z., Araki, K. (eds.) ICTAC 2004. LNCS, vol. 3407, pp. 280–294. Springer, Heidelberg (2005). https://doi.org/10.1007/978-3-540-31862-0_21

24. Dehnert, C., et al.: PROPhESY: a probabilistic parameter synthesis tool. In: Kroening, D., Păsăreanu, C.S. (eds.) CAV 2015. LNCS, vol. 9206, pp. 214–231. Springer, Cham (2015). https://doi.org/10.1007/978-3-319-21690-4_13

25. Dehnert, C., Junges, S., Katoen, J.-P., Volk, M.: A storm is coming: a modern probabilistic model checker. In: Majumdar, R., Kunčak, V. (eds.) CAV 2017. LNCS, vol. 10427, pp. 592–600. Springer, Cham (2017). https://doi.org/10.1007/978-3-319-63390-9_31

26. Druzdzel, M.J., van der Gaag, L.C.: Building probabilistic networks: "where do the numbers come from?". IEEE Trans. Knowl. Data Eng. **12**(4), 481–486 (2000)

27. Fang, X., Calinescu, R., Gerasimou, S., Alhwikem, F.: Fast parametric model checking through model fragmentation. In: ICSE, pp. 835–846. IEEE (2021)

28. Fang, X., Calinescu, R., Gerasimou, S., Alhwikem, F.: Fast parametric model checking through model fragmentation. CoRR https://arxiv.org/abs/2102.01490 (2021)

29. van der Gaag, L.C., Renooij, S., Coupé, V.M.H.: Sensitivity analysis of probabilistic networks. In: Lucas, P., Gámez, J.A., Salmerón, A. (eds.) Advances in Probabilistic Graphical Models. SFSC, vol. 213, pp. 103–124. Springer, Heidelberg (2007). https://doi.org/10.1007/978-3-540-68996-6_5

30. Gainer, P., Hahn, E.M., Schewe, S.: Accelerated model checking of parametric markov chains. In: Lahiri, S.K., Wang, C. (eds.) ATVA 2018. LNCS, vol. 11138, pp. 300–316. Springer, Cham (2018). https://doi.org/10.1007/978-3-030-01090-4_18

31. Hahn, E.M., Hermanns, H., Zhang, L.: Probabilistic reachability for parametric Markov models. Int. J. Softw. Tools Technol. Transf. **13**(1), 3–19 (2011)

32. Jaeger, M.: Complex probabilistic modeling with recursive relational Bayesian networks. Ann. Math. Artif. Intell. **32**(1–4), 179–220 (2001)

33. Jansen, N., et al.: Accelerating parametric probabilistic verification. In: Norman, G., Sanders, W. (eds.) QEST 2014. LNCS, vol. 8657, pp. 404–420. Springer, Cham (2014). https://doi.org/10.1007/978-3-319-10696-0_31

34. Jensen, F.V.: Gradient descent training of Bayesian networks. In: Hunter, A., Parsons, S. (eds.) ECSQARU 1999. LNCS (LNAI), vol. 1638, pp. 190–200. Springer, Heidelberg (1999). https://doi.org/10.1007/3-540-48747-6_18

35. Junges, S., et al.: Parameter synthesis for Markov models. CoRR https://arxiv.org/abs/1903.07993 (2019)

36. Junges, S., Katoen, J.P., Pérez, G.A., Winkler, T.: The complexity of reachability in parametric Markov decision processes. J. Comput. Syst. Sci. **119**, 183–210 (2021)

37. Kjærulff, U., van der Gaag, L.C.: Making sensitivity analysis computationally efficient. In: UAI, pp. 317–325. Morgan Kaufmann (2000)

38. Kwisthout, J., van der Gaag, L.C.: The computational complexity of sensitivity analysis and parameter tuning. In: UAI, pp. 349–356. AUAI Press (2008)

39. Lanotte, R., Maggiolo-Schettini, A., Troina, A.: Parametric probabilistic transition systems for system design and analysis. Formal Aspects Comput. **19**(1), 93–109 (2007)

40. Laskey, K.B.: Sensitivity analysis for probability assessments in Bayesian networks. IEEE Trans. Syst. Man Cybern. **25**(6), 901–909 (1995)

41. Quatmann, T., Dehnert, C., Jansen, N., Junges, S., Katoen, J.-P.: Parameter synthesis for Markov models: faster than ever. In: Artho, C., Legay, A., Peled, D. (eds.) ATVA 2016. LNCS, vol. 9938, pp. 50–67. Springer, Cham (2016). https://doi.org/10.1007/978-3-319-46520-3_4

42. Renooij, S.: Co-variation for sensitivity analysis in Bayesian networks: properties, consequences and alternatives. Int. J. Approx. Reason. **55**(4), 1022–1042 (2014)

43. Salmani, B., Katoen, J.-P.: Bayesian inference by symbolic model checking. In: Gribaudo, M., Jansen, D.N., Remke, A. (eds.) QEST 2020. LNCS, vol. 12289, pp. 115–133. Springer, Cham (2020). https://doi.org/10.1007/978-3-030-59854-9_9
44. Salmani, B., Katoen, J.: Fine-tuning the odds in Bayesian networks. CoRR https://arxiv.org/abs/2105.14371 (2021)
45. Scutari, M.: Bayesian network repository. https://www.bnlearn.com. Accessed 2019
46. Spel, J., Junges, S., Katoen, J.-P.: Are parametric Markov chains monotonic? In: Chen, Y.-F., Cheng, C.-H., Esparza, J. (eds.) ATVA 2019. LNCS, vol. 11781, pp. 479–496. Springer, Cham (2019). https://doi.org/10.1007/978-3-030-31784-3_28
47. Spel, J., Junges, S., Katoen, J.-P.: Finding provably optimal Markov chains. In: TACAS 2021. LNCS, vol. 12651, pp. 173–190. Springer, Cham (2021). https://doi.org/10.1007/978-3-030-72016-2_10
48. Tolo, S., Patelli, E., Beer, M.: An open toolbox for the reduction, inference computation and sensitivity analysis of Credal networks. Adv. Eng. Softw. **115**, 126–148 (2018)

Cautious Classification with Data Missing Not at Random Using Generative Random Forests

Julissa Villanueva Llerena[1]($\boxtimes$) ⓘ, Denis Deratani Mauá[1] ⓘ,
and Alessandro Antonucci[2] ⓘ

[1] Institute of Mathematics and Statistics, Universidade de São Paulo,
São Paulo, Brazil
{jgville,ddm}@ime.usp.br
[2] Dalle Molle Institute for Artificial Intelligence, Lugano, Switzerland
alessandro@idsia.ch

Abstract. Missing data present a challenge for most machine learning approaches. When a generative probabilistic model of the data is available, an effective approach is to marginalize missing values out. Probabilistic circuits are expressive generative models that allow for efficient exact inference. However, data is often missing not at random, and marginalization can lead to overconfident and wrong conclusions. In this work, we develop an efficient algorithm for assessing the robustness of classifications made by probabilistic circuits to imputations of the non-ignorable portion of missing data at prediction time. We show that our algorithm is exact when the model satisfies certain constraints, which is the case for the recent proposed Generative Random Forests, that equip Random Forest Classifiers with a full probabilistic model of the data. We also show how to extend our approach to handle non-ignorable missing data at training time.

Keywords: Probabilistic circuits · Generative random forests · Missing data · Conservative inference rule

1 Introduction

This work presents a new tractable algorithm for analyzing the effect of all potential imputations of non-ignorable missing values to a probabilistic classifier's response.

Missing data present a challenge in many machine learning tasks. The standard approach to inference with such data is to either impute or marginalize out the missing values [3,7]. The latter option requires a complete statistical model of features and target variables, and efficient inference routines. Recently, Correia, Peharz and de Campos [5] proposed Generative Random Forest (GeFs),

Supported by CAPES Finance 001, CNPQ grant #304012/2019-0.

J. Vejnarová and N. Wilson (Eds.): ECSQARU 2021, LNAI 12897, pp. 284–298, 2021.
https://doi.org/10.1007/978-3-030-86772-0_21

which extend standard random forest classifiers into complete statistical models with tractable marginalization of missing values. GeFs have shown superior performance to imputation approaches and other ad hoc heuristics used for random forests in classification tasks under missing data [5].

GeFs are actually part of a larger class of tractable probabilistic models, called Probabilistic Circuits, that allow for linear time marginalization [4,11]. Sum-Product Networks [21], Probabilistic Sentential Decision Diagrams [9] and Cutset Networks [22] are other notable examples of Probabilistic Circuits. These models have obtained impressive results in several machine learning tasks due to their ability to efficiently represent and manipulate intricate multidimensional distributions [20,21,24–26,31].

Imputation and marginalization are either theoretically supported by a *missing at random* assumption (MAR), that roughly considers that the probability of the missing values does not depend on the variables with missing values themselves [23]. This is not always a sensible choice [13]. For instance, in personalized recommendation, users have a strong bias towards rating items which they either strongly like or strongly dislike [14]. Automatically constructed knowledge-based systems offer another example, as they are most often populated exclusively with "positive" facts involving only a small fraction of the true facts [27]. In such cases, called *non-ignorable missing data* or MNAR (i.e., missing not at random), imputing or averaging over completions can lead to biased and inconsistent estimates and ultimately hurt performance. Importantly, it is not possible to statistically test whether or not the MAR assumption is satisfied, nor to learn from data the incompleteness process responsible for the missing values [17,23].

In the presence of MNAR data, marginalization can still be used as a heuristic, at the risk of inducing excessive bias. To analyze such potential bias, we follow [30] and propose to quantify the effect in a probabilistic classifier's decision to all possible imputations of the MNAR data. The challenge that we overcome here is doing so in a computationally tractable way, making use of the machinery of Probabilistic Circuits. Such an analysis has been previously applied to traditional probabilistic models such as Bayesian networks [1], where it suffers from intractability of inference. In fact, one can show that for Bayesian networks the task is equivalent to performing marginal inference in credal networks [2], a task whose theoretical and practical complexity far exceeds that of marginal inference in Bayesian networks [15].

In this work, we devise a polynomial-time procedure to quantify the effect of different imputations of the missing values of features in the classification of a target discrete variable *at prediction time*. This is important because while training data can often be curated and missingness mechanisms investigated, the same is generally not true for missing data at prediction time. We assume the classifier is represented as a Probabilistic Circuit, and focus on the case of GeFs (although the algorithm we present is slightly more general). The procedure can be used to determine the set of maximal values for the target variable given an observation with data (assumed) MNAR, that is, to decide which values are the most probable classification under some imputation. We also discuss how to enable conservative inferences with non-ignorable data at learning time. Experiments show that our algorithm obtains reliable conclusions often more accurate than criteria that ignores or marginalizes missing variables.

2   Probabilistic Circuits and Generative Random Forests

We start by establishing some notation and terminology. We denote random variables by upper-case letters (e.g., X_i, X), and their values by lower case (e.g., x_i, x). Sets of random variables are written in boldface (e.g., $\mathbf{X}$), as well as their realization (e.g., $\mathbf{x}$). In this work we assume that random variables take on a finite number of values, denoted as $val(X)$ for random variable X. We associate every discrete random variable X with a set of indicator functions $\{[\![X = x]\!] : x \in val(X)\}$, where the notation $[\![X = x]\!]$ describes the function that returns 1 if X takes value x and 0 otherwise.

A Probabilistic Circuit (PC) M over a set of categorical random variables $\mathbf{X}$ is a rooted weighted acyclic directed graph whose leaves are associated with indicator functions $[\![X_i = x_i]\!]$ of variables in $\mathbf{X}$, and the internal nodes are associated to either sum or product operations. The arcs $i \to j$ leaving sum node i are associated with non-negative weights w_{ij}. We write $\mathtt{M}_i$ to denote the sub-PC rooted at node i . The *scope* of a PC is the set of random variables associated with the indicator variables at the leaves, and the scope of a node is the scope of the respective sub-PC. A PC represents a joint distribution of $\mathbf{X}$ by $P_{\mathtt{M}}(\mathbf{x}) = \mathtt{M}(\mathbf{x})/(\sum_{\mathbf{x}'} \mathtt{M}(\mathbf{x}'))$. The value $\mathtt{M}(\mathbf{x})$, called the evaluation of the circuit at $\mathbf{x}$, is defined inductively in the size of the circuit as: $\mathtt{M}(\mathbf{x}) = [\![X_i = x_i]\!](\mathbf{x}_i)$ if M is a leaf node $[\![X_i = x_i]\!]$; $\mathtt{M}(\mathbf{x}) = \sum_j w_{ij}\mathtt{M}_j(\mathbf{x})$ if M is a circuit rooted at a sum node i with children j; and $\mathtt{M}(\mathbf{x}) = \prod_j \mathtt{M}_j(\mathbf{x})$ if M is a circuit rooted at a product node with children j. For example, the evaluation of the PC on the right-hand side of Fig. 1 at $X = 4$, $Y = 1$ and $Z = 1$ is $\mathtt{M}(\mathbf{x}) = 0.6 \times 0.7 \times 0.6 = 0.252$.

To ensure that marginal inference is computed in linear time in the size of the circuit, it suffices that the circuit satisfies the properties of smoothness and decomposability [9,21]. Smoothness states that the scopes of any two children of a sum node are identical.[1] Decomposability states that the scopes of any two children of a product node are disjoint. For the rest of this paper, *we assume that PCs are smooth and decomposable*. The tractability of more complex probabilistic queries rely on additional properties. One such property is determinism: each sum node has at most one child that evaluates to non-zero at any (complete) realization of its scope.[2] Determinism ensures that maximum likelihood estimates for the weights can be obtained in closed-form under complete data; it also enables finding the most probable realization in linear time [18], a NP-hard task in non-deterministic PCs. The property is also necessary (but not sufficient) for advanced operations such as encoding constraints, computing entropy or KL-divergence, and producing expected predictions with respect to a compatible regressor [7–9].

---

[1] Smoothness is also called completeness in the context of Sum-Product Networks.
[2] Determinism is also called selectivity in the context of Sum-Product Networks.

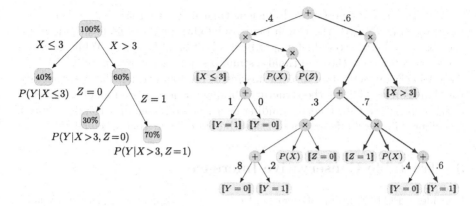

Fig. 1. A Decision Tree for classifying Y based on the values of X and Z (left) and its Generative Decision Tree extension (right).

Consider a Decision Tree mapping features $\mathbf{X}$ to a target variable Y. Generative Decision Trees (GeDT) are deterministic, decomposable and smooth PCs built from such a Decision Tree and data by converting each decision node into a sum node and each leaf into a sub-PC whose support is the partition induced by the corresponding path of the Decision Tree. The sub-PCs at the leaves can be learned with any structure learning algorithm for PCs or take simple forms such as fully factorized distributions. A particularly convenient form for the sub-PCs is to encode a distribution that factorizes as $P(\mathbf{X}|\gamma)P(Y|\gamma)$, where γ denotes the corresponding partition of the feature space. Such *class-factorized* GeDTs produce the same classifications under complete data as the original Decision Tree [5]. As that property will be crucial to ensure exactness of the procedure we develop later, we generalize it to arbitrary PCs as follows. We say that a PC is class-factorized with respect to a target variable Y if for any leaf whose scope is $\{Y\}$, its parents also have scope $\{Y\}$. Intuitively, in a class-factorized PC the leaves with indicators for variable Y cannot be used to select between different sub-PCs as in the Proof of Theorem 1 we show later.

The structure of a GeDT can be modified by "pulling the indicators up" to speed up computations, that is, by adding product nodes and indicator leaves that encode the partitions of the decision tree nodes. While this procedure violates decomposability, it renders a PC whose evaluations produce identical result (and marginal inference is therefore still linear). Hereafter, we will refer to GeDT as the PC obtained from a Decision Tree after such an operation. Figure 1 shows a decision tree (on the left) and a class-factorized GeDT extension (on the right) obtained by pulling up indicators. The numbers inside each node in the decision tree indicate the percentage of the training data instances that fall in the corresponding partition out of those instances that are in the partition defined by the parent node. Those values (transformed in probabilities) are used to define the weight of the respective outgoing arc in the GeDT.

GeDTs allow for proper and efficient treatment of missing at random data by computing $P(Y|\mathbf{o})$, the conditional probability of the target variable given the observed features $\mathbf{o}$ (which might be a subset of all features). While Decision Trees are consistent (Bayes optimal) estimators only when used in fully observed data, GeDTs are consistent also for missing at random features [5]. A Generative Random Forest (GeF) is the structure obtained as a mixture model where each component is the GeDT corresponding to a Decision Tree in a Random Forest Classifier. Marginal inference also takes therefore linear time in GeFs.

3   Tractable Conservative Inference

Consider a PC $\mathtt{M}(\mathbf{X})$, possibly learned from some (complete or MAR incomplete) dataset of realizations of variables $\mathbf{X}$. Suppose we are interested in using our model to predict the value of a target variable Y given a configuration $\mathbf{x}$ of the variables such that some of its values are missing. Let $\mathbf{o}$ denote the observed part of $\mathbf{x}$ and $\mathbf{u}$ denote a possible completion for the unobserved values. Under the missing at random hypothesis, this is best performed by computing

$$\arg\max_y P(y|\mathbf{o}) = \arg\max_y \mathtt{M}(y,\mathbf{o})/\mathtt{M}(\mathbf{o})\,, \qquad (1)$$

where $\mathtt{M}(y,\mathbf{o}) = \sum_{\mathbf{u}} \mathtt{M}(y,\mathbf{o},\mathbf{u})$ is the marginal value of the circuit at y and $\mathbf{o}$, which can be obtained in linear time as discussed, and $\mathtt{M}(\mathbf{o}) = \sum_y \mathtt{M}(y,\mathbf{o})$.

When the missingness process is non-ignorable, the inference in (1) can lead to erroneous and unreliable conclusions. As an example, consider a Boolean target Y and Boolean features O and U. Say we observe $O = o$, and assume that the value of U guides the prediction being $P(Y=1|o,u_1) = 0.7$ and $P(Y=1|o,u_2) = 0.4$, and that $P(U)$ is uniform. Also, the observation of U is missing due to the following MNAR process: when U is missing, value u_1 is nine times less likely than u_2. The Bayes-optimal classification is thus $Y = 0$ as $P(Y=1|o,U=\star) = 0.7 \times 0.1 + 0.4 \times 0.9 = 0.43 < 0.5$, yet the marginal classification is $Y = 1$ as $P(Y=1|o) = 0.55 > 0.5$.

Unlike the example above, we rarely have access to the missingness process. We can instead estimate the robustness of a classification $Y = y'$ under non-ignorable missing data with respect to an alternative classification $Y = y''$ by

$$\delta_{\mathtt{M},\mathbf{o}}(y',y'') = \min_{\mathbf{u}}[\mathtt{M}(y',\mathbf{o},\mathbf{u}) - \mathtt{M}(y'',\mathbf{o},\mathbf{u})]\,. \qquad (2)$$

A decision analyst might want to suspend the classification on the basis of the value in (2), thus producing more conservative conclusions. For example, if $\delta_{\mathtt{M},\mathbf{o}}(y',y'') > 0$, then any imputation of the values of $\mathbf{u}$ still leads to a classification y' that is more probable (as far as the model estimates) than y''; we thus say that y' dominates y''. Note that δ can be a function of $P(y|\mathbf{o})$ and $P(\mathbf{o})$, that is, it can be instance specific and account for other sources of information.

The *conservative inference rule* (CIR) prescribes that the only conclusion supported by non-ignorable missing data is to return the set of non-dominated values [30]:

$$\left\{ y : \max_{y'} \delta_{\mathtt{M},\mathbf{o}}(y', y) \leq 0 \right\}. \tag{3}$$

This is akin to classification with a rejection option, but possibly more informative (and arguably more principled).

Even though evaluation takes linear time in PCs, a brute-force approach to computing (2) requires evaluating $\mathtt{M}(y, \mathbf{o}, \mathbf{u})$ for each $\mathbf{u}$. This is unfeasible when the number of possible completions is high. The next result shows that computing such a value is coNP-hard even in deterministic PCs, ruling out the existence of an efficient exact procedure (under common assumptions of complexity theory).

Theorem 1. *Given a smooth, decomposable and deterministic PC* $\mathtt{M}$ *over random variables* Y, $\mathbf{O}$ *and* $\mathbf{U}$, *target values* y' *and* y'', *a partial observation* $\mathbf{o}$, *and a (rational) threshold* ρ, *deciding if* $\delta_{\mathtt{M},\mathbf{o}}(y', y'') > \rho$ *is coNP-complete.*

The proof is in the appendix.

We now provide a linear-time algorithm for computing $\delta_{\mathtt{M},\mathbf{o}}(y', y'')$ in tree-shaped deterministic PCs that satisfy class-factorization, which include class-factorized GeDTs. For the sake of readability, we drop the dependence on $\mathbf{o}$ in the following. The algorithm can be described straightforwardly by a collection of recursive equations depending on the type of node at which it operates. The recursive formulation also provides a proof of its correctness under the above assumptions.

Sum Nodes. If $\mathtt{M}$ is rooted at a sum node with children $\mathtt{M}_1, \ldots, \mathtt{M}_n$ and weights $w_1, \ldots, w_n$, then the algorithm computes:

$$\delta_{\mathtt{M}}(y', y'') = \min_{i=1}^{n} w_i \min_{\mathbf{u}}[\mathtt{M}_i(y', \mathbf{o}, \mathbf{u}) - \mathtt{M}_i(y'', \mathbf{o}, \mathbf{u})] = \min_{i=1}^{n} w_i \delta_{\mathtt{M}_i}(y', y''). \tag{4}$$

The correctness of the operation follows from the determinism of the circuit and the class-factorization property. The former ensures that for any realization $(y, \mathbf{x})$ at most one sub-PC $\mathtt{M}_i$ evaluates to a nonnegative value $\mathtt{M}_i(y, \mathbf{x}) > 0$. The latter ensures that either $\mathtt{M}$ encodes a distribution over Y (i.e., its scope is the singleton $\{Y\}$) or the nonnegative child for $\mathtt{M}_i(y', \mathbf{x})$ and $\mathtt{M}_i(y'', \mathbf{x})$ is the same.

Product Nodes. If instead $\mathtt{M}$ is a product node with children $\mathtt{M}_1, \ldots, \mathtt{M}_n$ such that Y is in the scope of $\mathtt{M}_1$ (and no other), then the algorithm computes:

$$\delta_{\mathtt{M}}(y', y'') = \underbrace{\min_{\mathbf{u}_1}[\mathtt{M}_1(y', \mathbf{o}_1, \mathbf{u}_1) - \mathtt{M}_1(y'', \mathbf{o}_1, \mathbf{u}_1)]}_{=\delta_{\mathtt{M}_1}(y', y'')} \prod_{i=2}^{n} \mathrm{opt}_{\mathbf{u}_i} \mathtt{M}_i(\mathbf{o}_i, \mathbf{u}_i), \tag{5}$$

where $\mathbf{o}_i$ (resp., $\mathbf{u}_i$) denotes the projection of $\mathbf{o}$ (resp., $\mathbf{u}$) into the scope of $\mathtt{M}_i$, and

$$\mathrm{opt} = \begin{cases} \max & \text{if } \delta_{\mathtt{M}_1}(y', y'') > 0, \\ \min & \text{if } \delta_{\mathtt{M}_1}(y', y'') \leq 0. \end{cases}$$

The first term denotes the recursive computation on the sub-PC M_1. The remaining terms $\text{opt}_{u_i} M_i(o_i, u_i)$ define an optimization of the configurations u_i for the sub-PC M_i; this can be performed in linear time in deterministic PCs by bottom-up traversal, replacing sums with maximizations/minimizations [18,19].

Leaves. Finally, if M is a leaf node representing an indicator variable then the algorithm computes:

$$\delta_M(y', y'') = \begin{cases} 1 & \text{if M is } [\![Y = y']\!], \\ -1 & \text{if M is } [\![Y = y'']\!], \\ 1 & \text{if M is consistent with } o \text{ or } u, \\ 0 & \text{otherwise.} \end{cases} \tag{6}$$

We thus obtain the following result.

Theorem 2. *The algorithm obtained by Eqs.* (4), (5) *and* (6) *computes* $\delta_{M,o}(y', y'')$ *in class-factorized tree-shaped deterministic PCs in linear time.*

For non-deterministic networks, the equation for sum nodes is no longer valid, as in such circuits

$$\min_u \sum_{i=1}^n w_i[M_i(y', o, u) - M_i(y'', o, u)] \neq \min_u w_i \min_{i=1}^n [M_i(y', o, u) - M_i(y'', o, u)].$$

The equations for products and leaves remain valid for non-deterministic circuits. Thus, we can use our algorithm as an effective heuristic for non-deterministic PCs or that violate class-factorization. This is the case for instance when we have a *partially ignorable missingness process* and we marginalize part of the missing variables by judging their missingness to satisfy MAR. Then, even for deterministic PCs, the algorithm described is not guaranteed to provide the correct outcome if some variables are marginalized. Yet our experiments show that it provides an effective heuristic, supporting the reasoning above.

4   Non-ignorable Training Data

In the previous section we considered PCs learned from complete (or MAR incomplete) datasets, while restricting the presence of MNAR data to prediction time. Yet, we might also have non-ignorable missingness in the training dataset and, following the ideas outlined by [28], apply the same conservative treatment to the learning of the PC. As a first step, in this work we consider that the structure of the circuit (i.e., its directed graph) is either specified in a data-free fashion (e.g., using region graphs or random structures), or learned by standard algorithms using only the complete portion of the data set [20,21]. The latter is a sensible choice when the missing values do not significantly alter the (context-specific) independences in the data, but can affect the quantification of the weights in a significant form.

Say that a PC structure is uniformly deterministic, if any quantification assigning positive weights leads to a deterministic PC. Thus assume that we have a fixed uniformly deterministic PC structure that we need to quantify using incomplete data. For complete data, the maximum likelihood estimates of the weights associated to a sum node can be obtained as

$$w_{ij} = \frac{N_{ij} + \alpha}{\sum_j N_{ij} + \alpha},$$

where N_{ij} counts the number of instances of the dataset for which the sub-PC M_j contributed to the PC value and α is a smoothing factor to counter the effect of small sample sizes.[3] Clearly, each possible completion of the non-ignorable missing values induces a different quantification of the weights using the formula above. This leads to the specification of a *credal* PC, whose weights are not specified by sharp numerical values, but only required to satisfy a finite number of linear constraints [16]. Standard inference in such models is therefore intended as the computation of the lower and upper bounds of the query with respect to all the possible specifications of the weights consistent with the constraints. A simple strategy is to obtain interval-valued weights:

$$0 \le \underline{w}_{ij} \le w_{ij} \le \overline{w}_{ij} \le 1, \quad \sum_{i \to j} w_{ij} = 1. \tag{7}$$

For deterministic PCs, the lower bound $\underline{w}_{ij}$ can be approximated as the count N_{ij} over instances which have no missing values for the scope of the corresponding node, and the upper bound $\overline{w}_{ij}$ is obtained by assuming that all completions will satisfy $M_j > 0$ and hence contribute to the corresponding count N_{ij}. Note that those bounds are loose as they ignore the dependencies among different parameters. An alternative technique to learn non-deterministic credal PCs in the presence of incomplete data was recently proposed by [10]. We could also resort to their approach for a CIR-based training of credal PCs. We leave as future work adapting their results to learning deterministic credal PCs.

Assessing the robustness with interval-valued credal PCs amounts to computing:

$$\delta_M(y', y'') = \min_{\mathbf{w}} \min_{\mathbf{u}} [M_{\mathbf{w}}(y', \mathbf{o}, \mathbf{u}) - M_{\mathbf{w}}(y'', \mathbf{o}, \mathbf{u})], \tag{8}$$

where the notation $M_{\mathbf{w}}$ denotes a PC quantified by weights $\mathbf{w}$.

The algorithm for deciding dominance can be easily adapted for handling class-factorized deterministic tree-shaped credal PCs. If M is rooted at a sum node with children $M_1, \ldots, M_n$ and weights $w_1, \ldots, w_n$, then the algorithm computes

$$\delta_M(y', y'') = \min_{i=1}^{n} w_i \min_{\mathbf{w}, \mathbf{u}} [M_i(y', \mathbf{o}, \mathbf{u}) - M_i(y'', \mathbf{o}, \mathbf{u})], \tag{9}$$

---

[3] By *contributing* to the PC value, we mean that there is path from the root to M_j where each node evaluates to a positive value for the given instance.

where $w_i = \underline{w}_i$ if the inner minimization is positive, and $w_i = \overline{w}_i$ if the inner minimization is negative. Similarly, if M is a product node with children $M_1, \ldots, M_n$ such that Y is in the scope of M_1 (and no other), then the algorithm computes:

$$\delta_M(y', y'') = \underbrace{\min_{\mathbf{w}_1, \mathbf{u}_1} [M_1(y', \mathbf{o}_1, \mathbf{u}_1) - M_1(y'', \mathbf{o}_1, \mathbf{u}_1)]}_{= \delta_{M_1}(y', y'')} \prod_{i=2}^{n} \mathrm{opt}_i M_i(\mathbf{o}_i, \mathbf{u}_i), \qquad (10)$$

where

$$\mathrm{opt}_i = \begin{cases} \max_{\mathbf{w}_i, \mathbf{u}_i} & \text{if } \delta_{M_1}(y', y'') > 0, \\ \min_{\mathbf{w}_i, \mathbf{u}_i} & \text{if } \delta_{M_1}(y', y'') \leq 0. \end{cases}$$

The sub-problems $\mathrm{opt}_i M_i(\mathbf{o}_i, \mathbf{u}_i)$ can be computed in linear time by the algorithm described in [12]. The equations for the leaves remain unchanged. We have that:

Theorem 3. *The algorithm obtained by Eqs.*(9), (10) *and* (6) *computes* $\delta_{M,\mathbf{o}}(y', y'')$ *in class-factorized tree-shaped deterministic credal PCs in linear time.*

5   Experiments

We empirically evaluate the ability of our proposed methods in assessing the robustness of classifications to non-ignorable missing feature values, by means of the index δ. To this end, we learn class-factorized GeFs from six well-known complete binary datasets for density estimation [6], using the algorithm in [5]. The characteristics of the datasets are in Table 1. Missing test values are simulated using a mix of MAR, MCAR and MNAR mechanisms. The average number of (MAR, MCAR and MNAR) missing values per instance is denoted as AvM, and the average number of MNAR values per instance is denoted as AvMNAR.

Table 1. Datasets characteristics.

Dataset	Variables	# Test Instances	AvM	AvMNAR	# Train Instances	Model Size
Audio	100	3,000	4.1	1.9	15,000	3,858
Dna	180	1,186	5.5	2.2	1,600	1,038
Msnbc	17	5,624	1.6	0.5	291,326	2,816
Mushrooms	112	5,624	7.7	3.4	2,000	1,764
Netflix	100	3,000	6.7	3.0	15,000	3,524
Nltcs	16	3,236	1.4	0.4	16,181	568

In Table 2 we report relevant performance metrics of our CIR predictions. The last column (*Acc*) shows the accuracy of classifications made by marginalizing all missing test values. Columns *RAcc* and $\neg RAcc$ report the classification accuracy on the portions of instances that are robust and non-robust, respectively. A test instance is robust if the CIR inference (Eq. 3) returns only one non-dominated class value. For the rows tagged "marg", we marginalize MAR variables and optimize over the MNAR variables. For the other rows, we optimize over all missing values. Column $\%R$ shows the percentage of robust instances. By comparing $RAcc$, Acc and $\neg RAcc$, we observe the ability of CIR in discriminating between the easy-to-classify instances, corresponding to the robust ones, and the harder ones (non-robust instances), for which a set of classes is returned. Similar conclusions can be reached by inspecting the $SAcc$ (Set Accuracy) column, which measures the percentage of (set-valued) classifications that contain the true class. Finally, the informative character of marginal classifications are captured by the discounted accuracy ($DAcc$), which penalizes "imprecise" classifications by weighting correct set-valued classifications by the reciprocal of their size (see [29] for more details and motivation about the metric). A $DAcc$ value higher than the corresponding Acc denotes that the classifier issues predictions that are on average more accurate than random classifications, hence being informative despite the false MAR assumption.

Table 2. Set accuracy ($SAcc$), Discounted accuracy ($DAcc$), percentage of robust instances ($\%R$), and classification accuracy on robust ($RAcc$), non-robust ($\neg RAcc$) and overall (Acc) instances when marginalizing missing values at prediction time.

Dataset	CIR			Marginalization		
	$SAcc$	$DAcc$	$\%R$	$RAcc$	$\neg RAcc$	Acc
Audio	0.879	0.707	65.6	0.807	0.679	0.763
Audio (marg)	0.863	0.708	69.1	0.798	0.686	0.763
Dna	0.899	0.799	80.0	0.880	0.511	0.806
Dna (marg)	0.858	0.801	88.6	0.846	0.496	0.806
Msnbc	0.978	0.956	95.5	0.978	0.925	0.976
Msnbc (marg)	0.979	0.932	90.6	0.978	0.956	0.976
Mushrooms	1.000	0.991	98.2	1.000	1.000	1.000
Mushrooms (marg)	1.000	0.991	98.2	1.000	1.000	1.000
Netflix	0.894	0.662	53.6	0.771	0.652	0.716
Netflix (marg)	0.873	0.665	58.3	0.760	0.655	0.716
Nltcs	0.980	0.912	86.4	0.977	0.856	0.961
Nltcs (marg)	0.975	0.906	86.2	0.972	0.888	0.961

To analyze the approach on a more realistic missingness scenario, we learn GeFs from a binarized version of the complete version of the Jester dataset.[4] This is an complete dataset of user ratings on 10 items (variables), divided into

---

[4] http://eigentaste.berkeley.edu/dataset.

17,467 training instances (users) and 7,486 test instances. We build a binary classification task by predicting, for each user/instance, the rating of a distinguished item given the other items ratings. We fabricate MNAR values in both training and test sets by independently omitting a positive rating with either low probability ($p = 0.05$) or high probability ($p = 0.5$). This simulates observed behaviour of users providing ratings in such systems [14]. Table 3 shows that learning an imprecise model relay better accuracy than the precise version that ignore missing values. Note that when learning a credal PC, we might produce set-valued classifications even when we marginalize (MAR) the missing test values. Figure 2 shows that for both missingness levels the measure in (2) can be used to detect easy-to-classify instances for the precise classifier that assumes MAR. Similar patterns are achieved in terms of (modified) discounted accuracy in Fig. 3, where this approach is combined with a rejection option.

Table 3. Performance of models learned from Jester with two different missingness proportions p in the training and test set. Imprecise models are obtained as in Sect. 4, precise models are obtained after removal of instances with missing values.

Model	Inference	p	Model + Inference			Precise + MAR		
			$SAcc$	$DAcc$	$\%R$	$RAcc$	$\neg RAcc$	Acc
Imprecise	MAR	0.05	0.689	0.664	95.1	0.596	0.540	0.593
Imprecise	CIR	0.05	0.716	0.661	88.9	0.600	0.540	0.593
Precise	CIR	0.05	0.644	0.602	91.5	0.598	0.536	0.593
Imprecise	MAR	0.5	0.753	0.597	68.7	0.639	0.435	0.575
Imprecise	CIR	0.5	0.847	0.597	50.0	0.693	0.457	0.575
Precise	CIR	0.5	0.827	0.578	50.3	0.657	0.493	0.575

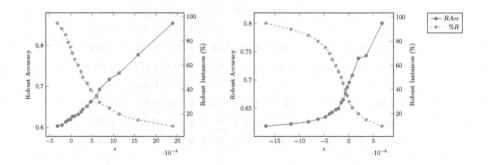

Fig. 2. Robust accuracy ($RAcc$) of the precise classifier (MAR) for the Jester dataset with low ($p = 0.05$, left) and high ($p = 0.5$, right) missingness levels. Condition $\delta_{M,o}(y, \neg y) > \epsilon$, where $\delta_{M,o}$ is defined as in Eq. (2) and y is the class returned by the classifier, is used to decide robustness. We also display $\%R$ by threshold ϵ.

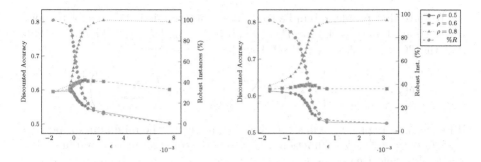

Fig. 3. Modified discounted accuracy of the (imprecise) classifier for the Jester dataset with low ($p = 0.05$, left) and high ($p = 0.5$, right) missingness levels. Robustness is decided as in Fig. 2 for different values of the threshold ϵ. A value ρ is used instead of 0.5 to score imprecise classifications, which regulates preference for model uncertainty against aleatory uncertainty (see [29]).

6   Conclusion

We developed an exact polynomial-time method for the conservative treatment of non-ignorable missing data using probabilistic circuits. Experiments with realistic data demonstrated that the approach is effective in discriminating instances which are sensitive to the missingness process from those that are not. Our approach to handling missing data at training time led us to consider *credal* circuits, which extend standard probabilistic circuits by locally associating sets of probabilities to sum nodes. Such extensions retain many of the tractable properties of probabilistic circuits, offering an interesting and more cautious alternative to marginal inference. We left as future work the treatment of other types of missing data (e.g., coarse and unreliable observations).

Proof of Theorem 1

Membership in coNP is trivial: given a configuration $\mathbf{u}$ we can compute $M(y', \mathbf{o}, \mathbf{u})$ and $M(y'', \mathbf{o}, \mathbf{u})$ in linear time and decide the sign of its difference in constant time. Hence we have a polynomial certificate that the problem is *not* in the language.

We show hardness by reduction from the *subset sum problem*: Given positive integers $z_1, \ldots, z_n$, decide

$$\exists u \in \{0,1\}^n : \sum_{i \in [n]} v_i u_i = 1, \quad \text{where } v_i = \frac{2z_i}{\sum_{i \in [n]} z_i}. \tag{11}$$

To solve that problem, build a tree-shaped deterministic PC as shown above, where U_i are binary variables, $P_1(u) = \prod_i e^{-2v_i u_i}$ and $P_2(u) = \prod_i e^{-v_i u_i}$. Note that the PC is not class-factorized. Use the PC to compute:

$$\delta(y', y'') = \min_u \left[a \exp\left(-2 \sum_i v_i u_i \right) - b \exp\left(-\sum_i v_i u_i \right) \right].$$

If we call $x := \exp(-\sum_i v_i u_i)$, the above expression is the minimum for positive x of $f(x) := ax^2 - bx$. Function f is a strictly convex function minimized at $x = b/(2a)$. Selecting a and b such that $b/(2a) = e^{-1}$ makes the minimum occur at $\sum_i v_i u_i = 1$. Thus, there is a solution to (11) if and only if $\delta(y', y'') \leq -ae^{-2}$. This proof is not quite valid because the distributions $P_1(u)$ and $P_2(u)$ use non-rational numbers. However, we can use the same strategy as used to prove Theorem 5 in [16] and exploit the rational gap between yes and no instances of the original problem to encode a rational approximation of P_1 and P_2 of polynomial size. $\square$

References

1. Antonucci, A., Piatti, A.: Modeling unreliable observations in Bayesian networks by credal networks. In: Proceedings of the Third International Conference on Scalable Uncertainty Management (SUM), pp. 28–39 (2009)
2. Antonucci, A., Zaffalon, M.: Decision-theoretic specification of credal networks: a unified language for uncertain modeling with sets of Bayesian networks. Int. J. Approximate Reasoning **49**(2), 345–361 (2008)
3. Azur, M.J., Stuart, E.A., Frangakis, C., Leaf, P.J.: Multiple imputation by chained equations: what is it and how does it work? Int. J. Methods Psychiatr. Res. **20**, 40–49 (2011)
4. Choi, Y., Vergari, A., Van den Broeck, G.: Probabilistic circuits: a unifying framework for tractable probabilistic models (2020)
5. Correia, A.H.C., Peharz, R., de Campos, C.P.: Joints in random forests. In: Advances in Neural Information Processing Systems 33 (NeurIPS) (2020)
6. Davis, J., Domingos, P.: Bottom-up learning of Markov network structure. In: Proceedings of the 27th International Conference on Machine Learning (ICML), pp. 271–280 (2010)
7. Khosravi, P., Choi, Y., Liang, Y., Vergari, A., Van den Broeck, G.: On tractable computation of expected predictions. In: Advances in Neural Information Processing Systems 32 (NeurIPS) (2019)
8. Khosravi, P., Liang, Y., Choi, Y., Van den Broeck, G.: What to expect of classifiers? Reasoning about logistic regression with missing features. In: Proceedings of the 28th International Joint Conference on Artificial Intelligence (IJCAI) (2019)
9. Kisa, D., Van den Broeck, G., Choi, A., Darwiche, A.: Probabilistic sentential decision diagrams. In: Proceedings of the 14th International Conference on Principles of Knowledge Representation and Reasoning (PKDD), pp. 1–10 (2014)
10. Levray, A., Belle, V.: Learning credal sum-product networks. In: Proceedings of the 2nd Conference on Automated Knowledge Base Construction (2020)
11. Liang, Y., Van den Broeck, G.: Learning logistic circuits. In: Proceedings of the 33rd Conference on Artificial Intelligence (AAAI) (2019)

12. Llerena, J.V., Mauá, D.D.: Efficient algorithms for robustness analysis of maximum a posteriori inference in selective sum-product networks. Int. J. Approximate Reasoning **126**, 158–180 (2020)
13. Manski, C.F.: Partial identification with missing data: concepts and findings. Int. J. Approximate Reasoning **39**(2–3), 151–165 (2005)
14. Marlin, B.M., Zemel, R.S., Roweis, S.T., Slaney, M.: Recommender systems: missing data and statistical model estimation. In: Proceedings of the 22nd International Joint Conference in Artificial Intelligence (IJCAI) (2011)
15. Mauá, D.D., De Campos, C.P., Benavoli, A., Antonucci, A.: Probabilistic inference in credal networks: new complexity results. J. Artif. Intell. Res. **50**, 603–637 (2014)
16. Mauá, D.D., Conaty, D., Cozman, F.G., Poppenhaeger, K., de Campos, C.P.: Robustifying sum-product networks. Int. J. Approximate Reasoning **101**, 163–180 (2018)
17. Mohan, K., Pearl, J., Tian, J.: Graphical models for inference with missing data. In: Proceedings of Advances in Neural Information Processing Systems (NeurIPS), pp. 1277–1285 (2013)
18. Peharz, R., Gens, R., Domingos, P.: Learning selective sum-product networks. In: Proceedings of the Workshop on Learning Tractable Probabilistic Models (2014)
19. Peharz, R., Gens, R., Pernkopf, F., Domingos, P.: On the latent variable interpretation in sum-product networks. IEEE Trans. Pattern Anal. Mach. Intell. **39**(10), 2030–2044 (2017)
20. Peharz, R., et al.: Random sum-product networks: a simple and effective approach to probabilistic deep learning. In: Proceedings of The 35th Uncertainty in Artificial Intelligence Conference (UAI) (2020)
21. Poon, H., Domingos, P.: Sum-product networks: a new deep architecture. In: Proceedings of the 27th Conference on Uncertainty in Artificial Intelligence (UAI), pp. 337–346 (2011)
22. Rahman, T., Kothalkar, P., Gogate, V.: Cutset networks: a simple, tractable, and scalable approach for improving the accuracy of Chow-Liu trees. In: Calders, T., Esposito, F., Hüllermeier, E., Meo, R. (eds.) Proceedings of the Joint European Conference on Machine Learning and Knowledge Discovery in Databases (ECML-PKDD), pp. 630–645 (2014)
23. Rubin, D.B.: Inference and missing data. Biometrika **63**(3), 581–592 (1976)
24. Shao, X., Alejandro Molina, A.V., Stelzner, K., Peharz, R., Liebig, T., Kersting, K.: Conditional sum-product networks: imposing structure on deep probabilistic architectures. In: Proceedings of the 10th International Conference on Probabilistic Graphical Models (PGM) (2020)
25. Shen, Y., Choi, A., Darwiche, A.: A tractable probabilistic model for subset selection. In: Proceedings of the 33rd Conference on Uncertainty in Artificial Intelligence (UAI) (2017)
26. Shen, Y., Goyanka, A., Darwiche, A., Choi, A.: Structured Bayesian networks: from inference to learning with routes. In: Proceedings of the Thirty-Third AAAI Conference on Artificial Intelligence (AAAI) (2019)
27. Shin, J., Wu, S., Wang, F., Sa, C.D., Zhang, C., Ré, C.: Incremental knowledge base construction using deepdive. In: Proceedings of the VLDB Endowment (2015)
28. Zaffalon, M.: Conservative rules for predictive inference with incomplete data. In: Proceedings of the 4th International Symposium on Imprecise Probabilities and Their Applications (ISIPTA), pp. 406–415 (2005)
29. Zaffalon, M., Corani, G., Mauá, D.: Evaluating credal classifiers by utility-discounted predictive accuracy. Int. J. Approximate Reasoning **53**(8), 1282–1301 (2012)

30. Zaffalon, M., Miranda, E.: Conservative inference rule for uncertain reasoning under incompleteness. J. Artif. Intell. Res. **34**, 757–821 (2009)
31. Zheng, K., Pronobis, A., Rao, R.P.N.: Learning graph-structured sum-product networks for probabilistic semantic maps. In: Proceedings of the 32nd AAAI Conference on Artificial Intelligence (AAAI) (2018)

Belief Functions

Scoring Rules for Belief Functions and Imprecise Probabilities: A Comparison

Esther Anna Corsi[1]([⊠]) [iD], Tommaso Flaminio[2] [iD], and Hykel Hosni[1] [iD]

[1] Department of Philosophy, University of Milan,
Via Festa del Perdono 7, 20122 Milano, Italy
{esther.corsi,hykel.hosni}@unimi.it
[2] Artificial Intelligence Research Institute (IIIA – CSIC),
Campus UAB, 08193 Bellaterra, Spain
tommaso@iiia.csic.es

Abstract. This paper investigates de Finetti's *coherence* as an operational foundation for a wide range of non-additive uncertainty measures and focuses, in particular, on Belief functions and Lower probabilities. In a companion paper we identify a number of non-limiting circumstances under which Dutch Book criteria for Belief functions and Lower probability are undistinguishable, which is surprising given that Lower probabilities are known to exist which do no satisfy the axioms of Belief functions. The main contribution of this paper consists in putting forward a comparison between a criterion based on the Brier scoring rule for Belief Functions and the scoring rule introduced in 2012 by Seidenfeld, Schervish and Kadane for Imprecise probabilities. Through this comparison we show that scoring rules allow us to distinguish coherence-wise between Belief functions and Imprecise probabilities.

Keywords: Scoring rules · Belief functions · Lower probabilities · Imprecise probabilities · Coherence

1 Introduction

In a companion paper [4], we observe that in any finite boolean algebra with at least three atoms there exist books defined over rich-enough sets of events that do not distinguish assignments extendible to Belief functions from those extendible to Lower probabilities. Given that all Belief functions are Lower probabilities, but the converse does not hold, our previous finding is somewhat puzzling. In this work we extend the comparison between those two well-known non-additive measures of uncertainty to the alternative, but logically equivalent (in probability), criterion of coherence based on the Brier scoring rule.

To do so, we introduce a new scoring rule in Definition 6 and (i) show that it characterises assignments that are extendible to Belief functions and (ii) compare it to the scoring rule for imprecise probabilities introduced by Seidenfeld et al. in [20]. This latter allows us to make a distinction between coherent Belief functions on the one hand, and coherent Lower probabilities on the other hand.

© Springer Nature Switzerland AG 2021
J. Vejnarová and N. Wilson (Eds.): ECSQARU 2021, LNAI 12897, pp. 301–313, 2021.
https://doi.org/10.1007/978-3-030-86772-0_22

The paper is organised as follows. In Sect. 2, we recall the Dutch Book and the proper scoring rule coherence criteria for probability functions. Early generalisations of probabilistic coherence have been proposed by [15, 22]. In Sect. 3, we give the required background on uncertainty measures, a geometric view on coherence and extendibility, and a brief outline of the key results obtained in [4]. In Sect. 4, we introduce a scoring rule that characterises assignments extendible to Belief functions. In Sect. 5, we relate our work to [20], draw some conclusions and outline the research questions opened up by the present investigation.

2   Dutch Books and Proper Scoring Rules

Bruno de Finetti proves in Chap. 3 of [7] two criteria for the coherent assessment of uncertainty. The first is based on the no-existence of a Dutch book and it is defined in terms of a two-player zero-sum game. Suppose that $\psi_1, \ldots, \psi_n$ are elements of the set of sentences built recursively from a finite set of propositional variables as usual, which are interpreted (see, e.g. [17]) as the events of interest to a bookmaker $\mathbf{B}$. Suppose further that this interest materialises with the publication of a *book* $\beta \colon \psi_1 \mapsto \beta_1, \ldots, \psi_n \mapsto \beta_n$ where for $i = 1, \ldots, n$, $\beta_i \in [0, 1]$. A gambler $\mathbf{G}$ then chooses real-valued stakes $\sigma_1, \ldots, \sigma_n$ and for $i = 1, \ldots, n$, pays $\sigma_i \beta_i$ to $\mathbf{B}$. $\mathbf{G}$ will then receive back $\sigma_i v(\psi_i)$, where $v(\psi_i) = 1$, if ψ_i is true, and $v(\psi_i) = 0$ otherwise. Thus, $\mathbf{G}$'s payoff is $\sum_{i=1}^{n} \sigma_i(v(\psi_i) - \beta_i)$ and $\mathbf{B}$'s payoff is $\sum_{i=1}^{n} \sigma_i(\beta_i - v(\psi_i))$. The book published by $\mathbf{B}$ is *coherent* if there is no choice of (possibly negative) stakes which $\mathbf{G}$ can make, exposing $\mathbf{B}$ to a sure loss. More precisely, for every $\sigma_1, \ldots, \sigma_n \in \mathbb{R}$ there is a valuation v such that,

$$\sum_{i=1}^{n} \sigma_i(\beta_i - v(\psi_i)) \geq 0. \tag{1}$$

The second criterion is framed in terms of the individual decision of a forecaster $\mathbf{F}$, who is asked to assess a value β_i to each event ψ_i (a forecast). $\mathbf{F}$ knows that they will suffer a penalty L_i (L stands for *loss*) proportional to the square of the euclidean distance between the realized value of ψ_i and the chosen value β_i. It is assumed that the forecaster's objective is to minimize their loss. A notable example of a loss function just introduced is the Brier scoring rule

$$L_i(\psi_i, \beta_i) = (\|v(\psi_i) - \beta_i\|_2)^2. \tag{2}$$

De Finetti shows that minimising the expectation of loss under the brier rule is equivalent to avoiding sure loss in the Dutch Book setting. However he argues that it is preferable as it neutralises some potential shortcomings arising from the strategic aspects of the betting game. Even if they are formally defined in the same way, in the context of the Dutch Book, any assignment on a set of events is referred to in what follows as a *book*, while in the framework of scoring rules, it is referred to as a *forecast*.

Definition 1 (Proper Scoring Rule Criterion). *Let $\Psi = \{\psi_1, \ldots, \psi_n\}$ be a set of events and, for $i = 1, \ldots, n$, let $\beta_i \in [0,1]$ be the value the forecaster $\mathbf{F}$ assigns to each ψ_i. The forecast $\beta \colon \psi_1 \mapsto \beta_1, \ldots, \psi_n \mapsto \beta_n$ is coherent if there is no distinct forecast β' whose Brier score uniformly dominates β, i.e. if $L(\Psi, \beta) = \sum_i (\|v(\psi_i) - \beta_i\|_2)^2$, that is to say there is no β' s.t. $L(\Psi, \beta') < L(\Psi, \beta)$ for every valuation v.*

De Finetti in ([7], Sects. 3.3–3.4) shows the equivalence between the Dutch Book and the Proper Scoring Rule criteria for defining (probabilistic) coherence. Therefore the following proposition holds.

Proposition 1. *Let $\Psi = \{\psi_1, \ldots, \psi_n\}$ be a set of events and let $\beta \colon \psi_i \mapsto \beta_i$ for $i = 1, \ldots, n$ a forecast over Ψ. The forecast β is coherent iff it extends to a probability measure over the algebra of events.*

Example 1. Let us consider the set of events $\Psi = \{\alpha, \neg\alpha\}$ and the relative forecast $\beta \colon \alpha \mapsto 0.8, \neg\alpha \mapsto 0.6$. The penalty that $\mathbf{F}$ will suffer depends on the realizations of the events. If $v(\alpha) = 1$ (and $v(\neg\alpha) = 0$), then $L(\Psi, \beta) = (1 - 0.8)^2 + (0 - 0.6)^2 = 0.4$. If $v(\alpha) = 0$ (and $v(\neg\alpha) = 1$), then $L(\Psi, \beta) = (0 - 0.8)^2 + (1 - 0.6)^2 = 0.8$. In the geometric interpretation of Fig. 1, the penalty relative to the first realization of the event α is the square of the euclidean distance between $(1, 0)$ and the point $\beta = (0.8, 0.6)$, while the penalty relative to the second one is the square of the euclidean distance between β and $(0, 1)$. Let us consider the projection of β onto the simplex of probabilities. This projection (also referred to as *de Finetti's projection*) identifies the point $\beta' = (0.6, 0.4)$. Since β' is closer to each endpoint of the simplex of probabilities, its Brier scoring rule is smaller than the Brier scoring rule relative to β, i.e. β' dominates β and β is *incoherent*.

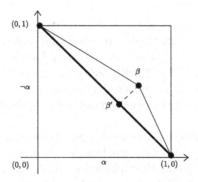

Fig. 1. Example of an incoherent forecast.

In geometrical terms, β is coherent if and only if it cannot be moved in such a way to reduce the distance from the set of all possible points. This is a characterization of a convex hull. Note that this is not to say that any point inside a convex hull shares the same distance from all its vertices, but that no matter how we move the point, it will necessarily get closer to some points of the convex hull and farther from some others. In particular, this happens if we consider the vertices of the convex hull. Instead, if we consider a point lying outside the convex hull, then we can always move it in such a way as to reduce its distance from all the point of the convex hull.

Through Definition 1, we are not minimizing the sum of the squared euclidean distance between β and the vertices of the convex hull of probabilities (property hold by the *centroid*), but we minimize every single distance between β and all the points of the convex hull. As stated in [7], (footnote 18), if we move the point β to another position β^*, its distance from a generic point P increases or decreases depending on whether P is on the same side as β or β^* with respect to the hyperplane that bisects the segment $\beta\beta^*$ orthogonally. Two cases must be considered then:

1. If β is not in the convex hull $\mathscr{P}_\Psi$ (the convex hull of the probabilities over Ψ), there exists a hyperplane separating it from $\mathscr{P}_\Psi$. Moving β to β^*, its orthogonal projection into such hyperplane, diminishes its distance from all points $P \in \mathscr{P}_\Psi$.
2. If β belongs to the convex hull $\mathscr{P}_\Psi$, then to whatever point β^* we move β, it always follows that for some point $P \in \mathscr{P}_\Psi$, the distance increases. If we construct the bisecting orthogonal hyperplane relative to $\beta\beta^*$ and P is on the same side as β^*, the point β would be distinguished from the convex hull of $\mathscr{P}_\Psi$, but this is contrary to the hypothesis.

3   Background on Uncertainty Measures and Their Geometric Interpretation

We shall assume the reader to be familiar with basic notions and results of (finitely additive) probability theory. In particular, since we will only consider measures on finite boolean algebras, we shall often identify a probability measure P on an algebra **A** with the distribution p obtained by restricting P on the atoms of **A**. As for the other uncertainty measures we will deal with in the following sections, it is convenient to recall some basic definitions and results from [1,9,14,16].

We only consider finite, and hence atomic, boolean algebras as the domain for uncertainty measures. Boolean algebras are understood as described in the signature $\{\wedge, \vee, \neg, \bot, \top\}$ and their elements are denoted by lower-case Greek letters with possible subscripts. In particular, the atoms of an algebra will be indicated as $\alpha_1, \alpha_2, \ldots$.

Definition 2 (Belief function). *A Belief function B on an algebra **A** is a $[0,1]$-valued map satisfying:*

(B1) $B(\top) = 1$, $B(\bot) = 0$;

(B2) $B\left(\bigvee_{i=1}^{n} \psi_i\right) \geq \sum_{i=1}^{n} \sum_{\{J \subseteq \{1,\ldots,n\}: |J|=i\}} (-1)^{i+1} B\left(\bigwedge_{j \in J} \psi_j\right)$

for $n = 1, 2, 3, \ldots$.

Belief functions on boolean algebras can be characterised in terms of *mass functions* as follows. Let $\mathbf{A}$ be any finite boolean algebra with atoms $\alpha_1, \ldots, \alpha_t$. A mass function is a map m that assigns to each subset X of atoms, a real number such that $m(\emptyset) = 0$ and $\sum_X m(X) = 1$. Given a mass function m, the map

$$B(\psi) = \sum_{X \subseteq \{\alpha_i | \alpha_i \leq \psi\}} m(X)$$

is a Belief function and every Belief function on $\mathbf{A}$ can be defined in this way.

Definition 3 (Lower probability). *A Lower probability $\underline{P}$ on an algebra $\mathbf{A}$ is a monotone $[0,1]$-valued map satisfying:*

(L1) $\underline{P}(\top) = 1$, $\underline{P}(\bot) = 0$;

(L2) For all natural numbers n, m, k and all $\psi_1, \ldots, \psi_n$, if $\{\{\psi_1, \ldots, \psi_n\}\}$ is an (m, k)-cover of $(\varphi, \top)^1$, then $k + m\underline{P}(\varphi) \geq \sum_{i=1}^{n} \underline{P}(\psi_i)$.

Although the definition above does not make clear why those measures are called *Lower* probabilities, [1, Theorem 1] characterises them as follows: Let $\underline{P} \colon \mathbf{A} \to [0,1]$ be a Lower probability and denote with $\mathcal{M}(\underline{P})$ the following set:

$$\mathcal{M}(\underline{P}) = \{P \colon \mathbf{A} \to [0,1] \mid P \text{ is a probability function and } \forall \psi \in A, \ \underline{P}(\psi) \leq P(\psi)\}.$$

Then, for all $\psi \in A$,

$$\underline{P}(\psi) = \min\{P(\psi) \mid P \in \mathcal{M}(\underline{P})\}.$$

Lower probabilities are more general than Belief functions. The following result characterises the Lower probabilities that are Belief functions.

Remark 1. A Lower probability $\underline{P}$ on an algebra $\mathbf{A}$ is a Belief function iff $\underline{P}$ satisfies (B2), namely

$$\underline{P}\left(\bigvee_{i=1}^{n} \psi_i\right) \geq \sum_{i=1}^{n} \sum_{\{J \subseteq \{1,\ldots,n\}: |J|=i\}} (-1)^{i+1} \underline{P}\left(\bigwedge_{j \in J} \psi_j\right) \tag{3}$$

for all $n = 1, 2, \ldots$.

---

[1] An element φ of a boolean algebra $\mathbf{A}$ is said to be covered m times by a multiset $\{\{\psi_1, \ldots, \psi_n\}\}$ of elements of A if every homomorphisms of $\mathbf{A}$ to $\{0,1\}$ that maps φ to 1, also maps to 1 at least m propositions from $\psi_1, \ldots, \psi_n$ as well. An (m, k)-cover of $(\varphi, \top)$ is a multiset $\{\{\psi_1, \ldots, \psi_n\}\}$ that covers $\top$ k times and covers φ $n+k$ times.

The geometric approach we consider is similar to Paris's [17] and is related to [5,6].

Let $\Psi = \{\psi_1, \ldots, \psi_n\}$ be a finite set of events (i.e., elements of a finite boolean algebra $\mathbf{A}$). Let us denote by $\mathbb{V} = \{v_1, \ldots, v_t\}$ the finite set of all possible homomorphisms of $\mathbf{A}$ to the boolean chain on the two-element set $\{0,1\}$. For every $j = 1, \ldots, t$, call $\mathbf{e}_j$ the binary vector

$$\mathbf{e}_j = (v_j(\psi_1), \ldots, v_j(\psi_n)) \in \{0,1\}^n. \tag{4}$$

Given this basic construction, we can characterise in geometric terms the extendability problem for assignments on Ψ to finitely additive probability measures and Belief functions. The additional notions we need are the euclidean convex hull $\overline{\mathrm{co}}(X)$ of a subset $X \subseteq \mathbb{R}^t$ (which reduces to $\mathrm{co}(X)$ in case X is finite) and the less common *tropical* convex hull $\mathrm{co}_{\wedge,+}(X)$ of X (see [8]).

Definition 4 (Tropical Hull). *Let* $\mathbf{x}_1, \ldots, \mathbf{x}_t \in [0,1]^n$. *The tropical hull of the* $\mathbf{x}_j$'s *is the subset* $\mathrm{co}_{\wedge,+}(\mathbf{x}_1, \ldots, \mathbf{x}_t)$ *of all points* $\mathbf{y}$ *of* $[0,1]^n$ *for which there exist parameters* $\lambda_1, \ldots, \lambda_t \in [0,1]$ *such that* $\bigwedge_{j=1}^t \lambda_j = 0$ *and*

$$\mathbf{y} = \bigwedge_{j=1}^t \lambda_j + \mathbf{x}_j.$$

The symbol $\wedge$ *stands for the minimum and* $+$ *for the ordinary addition in the tropical semiring* $(\mathbb{R}, \wedge, +)$. *Given* $\lambda \in [0,1]$ *and* $\mathbf{x} \in [0,1]^n$, $\lambda + \mathbf{x} = (\lambda + x_1, \ldots, \lambda + x_n)$ *and the* $\bigwedge$ *operator is defined component-wise.*

For $\mathbf{e}_1, \ldots, \mathbf{e}_t$ being defined as above from the formulas ψ_i's in Ψ, let us consider the following sets:

1. $\mathscr{P}_\Psi = \mathrm{co}(\mathbf{e}_1, \ldots, \mathbf{e}_t)$;
2. $\mathscr{B}_\Psi = \overline{\mathrm{co}}(\mathrm{co}_{\wedge,+}(\mathbf{e}_1, \ldots, \mathbf{e}_t))$, where, in this case, being $\mathrm{co}_{\wedge,+}(\mathbf{e}_1, \ldots, \mathbf{e}_t)$ usually uncountable, $\overline{\mathrm{co}}$ denotes the topological closure of the Euclidean convex hull co.

Theorem 1 ([7, 10, 12]). *Let* $\Psi = \{\psi_1, \ldots, \psi_n\}$ *be a finite set of events and let* $\beta : \Psi \to [0,1]$ *be a assignment. Then,*

1. β *extends to a probability measure iff* $(\beta(\psi_1), \ldots, \beta(\psi_n)) \in \mathscr{P}_\Psi$;
2. β *extends to a Belief function iff* $(\beta(\psi_1), \ldots, \beta(\psi_n)) \in \mathscr{B}_\Psi$.

In general, $\mathscr{P}_\Psi$ is strictly included in $\mathscr{B}_\Psi$ (i.e., $\mathscr{P}_\Psi \subset \mathscr{B}_\Psi$) and this is expected because Belief functions are strictly more general than probabilities measures. In [4], we ask whether avoiding sure loss is sufficient to distinguish Lower probabilities from Belief functions. In other words, we ask whether the above strict inclusion is matched by a detectable difference in coherence, and find that the answer is negative.

We denote with $\mathscr{L}_\Psi$ the set of all assignments β on Ψ that extend to a Lower probability $\underline{P}$. The sets of events that do not distinguish Belief functions from Lower probabilities are referred to as *adequate*. The main result of our previous work reads as follows.

Theorem 2. *For every algebra* **A** *with at least three atoms there exists an adequate subset* Ψ *of A, i.e.,* Ψ *is such that* $\mathscr{B}_\Psi = \mathscr{L}_\Psi$.

We now introduce a scoring rule that characterises assignments extendible to Belief functions. In addition, we investigate *adequate* sets of events from the perspective of this rule.

4   Coherence for Belief Functions

Let us begin by recalling Jaffray's extension of de Finetti's Dutch Book to Belief functions [15]. The key idea of his framework is that if an event ψ occurs, then every non-contradictory event which logically follows from ψ, also occurs.

Let $\Psi = \{\psi_1, \ldots, \psi_n\}$ be a set of events and $\beta \colon \psi_1 \mapsto \beta_1, \ldots, \psi_n \mapsto \beta_n$ a book published by the bookmaker **B**. If the gambler **G** places real stakes $\sigma_1, \ldots, \sigma_n$ on $\psi_1, \ldots, \psi_n$ at the betting odds written in β, then **G** pays **B** for each ψ_i the amount $\sigma_i \beta_i$ and gains the amount $\sigma_i C_\psi(\psi_i)$. The function $C_\psi(\psi_i)$ is defined as follows, where $\models_{cl}$ denotes the consequence relation of classical propositional logic.

$$C_\psi(\psi_i) = \begin{cases} 1 & \text{if } \models_{cl} \psi \to \psi_i, \\ 0 & \text{otherwise.} \end{cases}$$

The total balance for **B** is

$$\sum_{i=1}^{n} \sigma_i(\beta_i - C_\psi(\psi_i)).$$

Definition 5 (Coherence Under Partially Resolved Uncertainty). *Let* $\Psi = \{\psi_1, \ldots, \psi_n\}$ *be a set of events* β *a book over* Ψ. *The book* β *is* coherent under partially resolved uncertainty *if there is no choice of stakes which* **G** *can make, exposing* **B** *to a sure loss, i.e. it is not the case that, for every fixed non-contradictory event* ψ, $\sum_{i=1}^{n} \sigma_i(\beta_i - C_\psi(\psi_i)) < 0$.

This notion of coherence characterises Dempster-Shafer Belief functions [21] in the sense that a book β on Ψ is coherent under partially resolved uncertainty if and only if it extends to a Belief function on the algebra of events, [19].

A criterion based on a Brier-like scoring rule can be put forward for Belief functions as follows. From Definition 1 above it follows that a forecast β is *dominated* by another forecast β' if the squared euclidean distance between β and the vertices of $\mathscr{P}_\Psi$ is greater than the squared euclidean distance between β' and the same points. Thus, we can move β to reduce the distance from all points of $\mathscr{P}_\Psi$, vertices included. Hence, we can extend the definition of *dominating forecast* to Belief functions. To do this we consider the vertices of the polytope $\mathscr{B}_\Psi$, rather than those of $\mathscr{P}_\Psi$. This distance can be recovered from the C_ψ function used by Jeffray recalled above:

$$L(\psi_i, \beta_i) = (\|C_\psi(\psi_i) - \beta_i\|_2)^2. \tag{5}$$

Remark 2. As pointed out by two anonymous referees, the forthcoming [18] provides a characterisation of scoring rules for Belief functions yielding a result which is essentially equivalent to Theorem 3 below. Whilst we take this as welcome news to the effect that scoring-rule based coherence is of interest beyond the well-known probabilistic case, the present work differs substantially in its motivating question from [18]. In particular, whilst this latter reviews several candidate notions for 'coherent' Belief functions, our present concern lies in comparing Belief functions and Lower probabilities against the natural formulation provided by Definition 6. Indeed, as we point out in Subsect. 5.2, the notion captured by this Definition allows us to tell *coherence-wise* Belief functions from Lower probability, a distinction not permitted by Dutch-Book coherence [4].

Definition 6 (Scoring Rule for Belief functions). *Let* $\Psi = \{\psi_1, \ldots, \psi_n\}$ *be a set of events and, for* $i = 1, \ldots, n$, *let* $\beta_i \in [0, 1]$ *be the value the forecaster* $\boldsymbol{F}$ *assigns to each* ψ_i. *The forecast* $\beta \colon \psi_1 \mapsto \beta_1, \ldots, \psi_n \mapsto \beta_n$ *is coherent if there is no distinct forecast* β' *whose Brier score uniformly dominates* β, *i.e. if* $L(\Psi, \beta) = \sum_i (\|C_\psi(\psi_i) - \beta_i\|_2)^2$, *then there is no* β' *s.t.* $L(\Psi, \beta') < L(\Psi, \beta)$ *for every non-contradictory event* ψ *and every possible value of* $C_\psi(\psi_i)$.

As shown in the following Proposition, $\mathscr{B}_\Psi$ can be characterised by using the C_ψ function. We denote by $C_\psi(\Psi)$ the vector $(C_\psi(\psi_1), \ldots, C_\psi(\psi_n))$.

Proposition 2. *Let* $\mathbf{A}$ *be a boolean algebra,* $\Psi = \{\psi_1, \ldots, \psi_n\}$ *be a finite set of events over* $\mathbf{A}$ *and* $\beta \colon \Psi \to [0, 1]$ *be an assignment over* Ψ. *Then*

$$\mathscr{B}_\Psi = \mathrm{co}(C_\psi(\Psi) \mid \psi \text{ is a non-contradictory event in } \mathbf{A}).$$

Proof. Since both $\mathscr{B}_\Psi$ and $\mathrm{co}(C_\psi(\Psi) \mid \psi$ is a non-contradictory event in $\mathbf{A})$ are convex hulls, to show that they coincide, it is sufficient to show that they share the same vertices. In particular, recall that the vectors $\mathbf{e}_j$ are defined as $\mathbf{e}_j = (v_j(\psi_1), \ldots, v_j(\psi_n))$ where v_j is an homomorphisms of $\mathbf{A}$ to the boolean chain on the two-element set $\{0, 1\}$. Thus, $\mathbf{e}_j$ identifies in $\mathbb{R}^n$ the same point of $C_{\alpha_j}(\Psi) = (C_{\alpha_j}(\psi_1), \ldots, C_{\alpha_j}(\psi_n))$ where α_j is an atom of $\mathbf{A}$. The other vertices of $\mathscr{B}_\Psi$ are recovered from the $\mathbf{e}_j$ with $j = 1, \ldots, t$ by taking the point-wise minimum of every subset of $\mathbf{e}_j$'s. Since the entailment relation to which C_ψ refers to is the consequence relation of classical propositional logic, for any propositional formula ψ_i and ψ_j we have $\models_{cl} (\psi_i \vee \psi_j) \to \psi_i$ iff $\models_{cl} \psi_i \to \psi_i$ and $\models_{cl} \psi_j \to \psi_i$. Thus, $C_{\alpha_i \vee \alpha_j}(\psi_i) = 1$ iff $C_{\alpha_i}(\psi_i) = 1$ and $C_{\alpha_j}(\psi_i) = 1$, i.e. $\min\{C_{\alpha_i}(\psi_i), C_{\alpha_j}(\psi_i)\} = 1$. Therefore, the vertices of $\mathscr{B}_\Psi$ obtained as $\mathbf{e}_i \wedge \mathbf{e}_j$ with $i, j \in \{1, \ldots, t\}$ identify the same point of $C_{\alpha_i \vee \alpha_j}(\Psi)$ and, in general,

$$\bigwedge_{j \in J \subseteq \{1, \ldots, t\}} \mathbf{e}_j = C_{\psi_J}(\Psi),$$

where, for all $J \subseteq \{1, \ldots, t\}$, $\psi_J = \bigvee_{j \in J \subseteq \{1, \ldots, t\}} \alpha_j$.

Theorem 3. *Let* $\mathbf{A}$ *be a boolean algebra, and let* $\Psi = \{\psi_1, \ldots, \psi_n\}$ *be a finite set of elements of* $\mathbf{A}$. *A forecast* β *defined over* Ψ *is coherent if and only if it can be extended to a Belief function on* $\mathbf{A}$.

Proof. ($\Rightarrow$) If the forecast β is coherent, then there is no rival forecast β' defined over the same set of events s.t. $L(\Psi, \beta') < L(\Psi, \beta)$ for every non-contradictory event ψ and every possible value of $C_\psi(\psi_i)$. By Proposition 2, the vertices of $\mathscr{B}_\Psi$ coincide with all possible values of C_Ψ. Thus, $\beta \in \mathscr{B}_\Psi$ and by Theorem 1 it can be extended to a Belief function over **A**.

($\Leftarrow$) If the forecast β can be extended to a Belief function over **A**, then by Theorem 1, $\beta \in \mathscr{B}_\Psi$ and by Proposition 2, $\beta \in \mathrm{co}(C_\psi(\psi_i)|\ \psi$ is a non-contradictory event and $i = 1, \ldots, n)$. Therefore, no β' reduces the (euclidean) distance from all possible point of that convex hull (vertices included), which implies that there is no β' s.t. $L(\Psi, \beta') < L(\Psi, \beta)$ for any possible value of C_ψ.

Example 2. Let **A** be the boolean algebra of 8 elements and 3 atoms $\{\alpha_1, \alpha_2, \alpha_3\}$ and consider the non-trivial set of events $\Psi = \{\psi_1, \psi_2, \psi_3\} \subset A$ where $\psi_1 = \alpha_1 \vee \alpha_2$, $\psi_2 = \alpha_2 \vee \alpha_3$ and $\psi_3 = \alpha_1 \vee \alpha_3$. In Table 1 we compute the $C_\psi(\psi_i)$ function for every non-contradictory event ψ.

Table 1. Values of $C_\psi(\psi_i)$ over the boolean algebra **A** and the set of events Ψ

ψ	$C_\psi(\psi_1)$	$C_\psi(\psi_2)$	$C_\psi(\psi_3)$
α_1	1	0	1
α_2	1	1	0
α_3	0	1	1
$\alpha_1 \vee \alpha_2$	1	0	0
$\alpha_2 \vee \alpha_3$	0	1	0
$\alpha_1 \vee \alpha_3$	0	0	1
$\alpha_1 \vee \alpha_2 \vee \alpha_3$	0	0	0

Let us consider the forecasts $\beta_1 \colon \psi_1 \mapsto 3/8, \psi_2 \mapsto 3/8, \psi_3 \mapsto 3/8$ and $\beta_2 \colon \psi_1 \mapsto 7/8, \psi_2 \mapsto 7/8, \psi_3 \mapsto 7/8$. If we compute the convex hull considering the points identified by $C_\psi(\Psi_i)$, we can verify that β_1 belongs to it while β_2 does not. Since the convex hull generated by C_ψ coincides with $\mathscr{B}_\Psi$, β_1 extends to a Belief function and β_2 does not.

5   Comparing Scoring Rules for Belief Functions and Imprecise Probabilities

5.1   Scoring Rule for Imprecise Probabilities

Seidenfeld et al. introduce in [20] the following scoring rule for imprecise probabilities. Let us consider the event ψ and a Lower and Upper probability forecast (p, q) for the event ψ, that is to say, let us assume that $p, q \in [0, 1]$ are values assigned to ψ by a Lower probability and its dual Upper probability, respectively. The Brier-style IP scoring rule is hence defined as follows.

$$L(\psi, (p, q)) = \begin{cases} (1 - q)^2 & \text{if } v(\psi) = 1, \\ p^2 & \text{if } v(\psi) = 0. \end{cases}$$

Extending the concept of *dominance* between forecasts from the definitions on probabilities and Belief functions, we say that a forecast $\mathcal{F} = \{(p_i, q_i) \mid i = 1, \ldots, n\}$ over the events $\Psi = \{\psi_1, \ldots, \psi_n\}$ strictly dominates another forecast $\mathcal{F}' = \{(p_i', q_i') \mid i = 1, \ldots, n\}$ if $L(\Psi, \mathcal{F}) < L(\Psi, \mathcal{F}')$. The penalty for a set of forecasts is the sum of the individual penalty scores.

Since the forecast $\mathcal{F}_0 = \{(p_i = 0, q_i = 1) \mid i = 1, \ldots, n\}$ dominates any other forecast, coherence for imprecise probabilities based on scoring rule risks to trivialise if we do not further elaborate it. For this reason, we need to consider an additional restriction on the class of rival forecasts and an index of relative imprecision between forecasts.

This is the reason why, for each forecast $\mathcal{F} = \{(p_i, q_i) \mid i = 1, \ldots, n\}$, Seidenfeld et al., construct a *scoring set* $\mathcal{S}_\mathcal{F}$ defined as follows:

$$\mathcal{S}_\mathcal{F} = \{(q_1, p_2, \ldots, p_n), (p_1, q_2, \ldots, p_n) \ldots (p_1, \ldots, p_{n-1}, q_n)\}.$$

Thus, a forecast $\mathcal{F}$ is *at least as determinate as* a forecast $\mathcal{F}'$ if $\text{co}(\mathcal{S}_\mathcal{F})$ is isomorphic under rigid movements of a subset of $\text{co}(\mathcal{S}_{\mathcal{F}'})$.

Finally, the class $\mathcal{M}$ of *rival forecasts* considered is the ε-*contamination class*.[2] The scoring criterion for imprecise probabilities is then defined as follows.

Definition 7 (Scoring Rule for Imprecise probabilities). *Let* **A** *be a boolean algebra and let* $\mathcal{F}$ *be a forecast over the atoms of the algebra.* $\mathcal{F}$ *is IP-coherent with respect to* $\mathcal{M}$ *if there is no dominating forecast* $\mathcal{F}'$ *from* $\mathcal{M}$ *such that* $\mathcal{S}_\mathcal{F}'$ *is at least as determinate as* $\mathcal{S}_\mathcal{F}$.

The following theorem characterises coherent forecasts.

Theorem 4. *Let* **A** *be a boolean algebra and let* $\mathcal{F}$ *be a forecast over the atoms* $\Psi = \{\alpha_1, \ldots, \alpha_t\}$ *of the algebra* **A**. *Then,* $\mathcal{S}_\mathcal{F}$ *lies entirely within the probability simplex* $\mathscr{P}_\Psi$ *iff* $\mathcal{F}$ *matches an* ε-*contamination model and it is IP-coherent with respect to* $\mathcal{M}$.

It is now worth to point out that, for what concerns the *extendability problem*, an immediate consequence of the theorem above is that a forecast $\mathcal{F} = \{(p_i, q_i) \mid i = 1, \ldots, t\}$ on the atoms $\alpha_1, \ldots, \alpha_t$ is IP-coherent with respect to $\mathcal{M}$ if and only if for all $i = 1, \ldots, t$, $p_i = \min\{P(\alpha_i) \mid P \in \text{co}(\mathcal{S}_\mathcal{F})\}$ and $q_i = \max\{P(\alpha_i) \mid P \in \text{co}(\mathcal{S}_\mathcal{F})\}$ where $\Psi = \{\alpha_1, \ldots, \alpha_t\}$. In addition, as we will see in the following Section, it can be that a forecast $\mathcal{F}$ is not coherent as for Definition 7 and still being extendable to an Upper and Lower probability.

---

[2] For what concerns the present paper, we do not need to elaborate more on the previously given notions and definitions, and we invite the interested reader to consult [20] for the relative literature on this class of forecasts.

5.2 Distinguishing Belief Functions and Imprecise Probabilities Through Scoring Rules

As illustrated in [4], given a finite boolean algebra $\mathbf{A}$ with at least three atoms we can identify an *adequate* set of events and assignments β_i that do not satisfy equation (3) and still cannot distinguish Belief functions from Lower probabilities. In particular, the main result of [4] is based on the following.

Remark 3. [4, Example 2] Let us consider an algebra $\mathbf{A}$ with atoms $\alpha_1, \ldots, \alpha_t$ $(t \geq 3)$ and probability distributions $p_1(\alpha_1) = q$, $p_1(\alpha_2) = 1 - q$, $p_1(\alpha_i) = 0$ for all $i \neq 1, 2$; $p_2(\alpha_2) = q$, $p_2(\alpha_3) = 1 - q$, $p_2(\alpha_i) = 0$ for all $i \neq 2, 3$; $p_3(\alpha_1) = 1 - q$, $p_3(\alpha_3) = q$, $p_3(\alpha_i) = 0$ for all $i \neq 1, 3$ where q is any value $1/3 < q \leq 1/2$. Let us consider, as events, the co-atoms of $\mathbf{A}$: $\psi_1 = \alpha_1 \vee \alpha_2$, $\psi_2 = \alpha_2 \vee \alpha_3$, $\psi_3 = \alpha_1 \vee \alpha_3$ and the assignment $\beta : \psi_i \mapsto q$ for every $i = 1, 2, 3$. The Lower probability $\underline{P}$ derived by the probability distributions p_j extends β. Furthermore, it not difficult to show that $\underline{P}$ is not a Belief function as it fails to prove (3) of Remark 1. However, the same assignment β is coherent in the sense of Definition 5 and in fact there is a Belief function of $\mathbf{A}$ that extends it. Thus, for that set of events, it is impossible to distinguish assignments that are coherent in the sense of Belief functions, from those that are coherent in the sense of Lower probabilities.

Now, let us move to analyse what happens if we take into account coherence through proper scoring rules. First, it is easy to see that the assignment displayed in Remark 3 is coherent according to Definition 6. However, if we consider the forecast $\mathcal{F} = \{(0, 1 - q), (0, 1 - q), (0, 1 - q)\}$ relative to the same probability distribution over the atoms of $\mathbf{A}$ and construct the scoring set $\mathcal{S}_{\mathcal{F}} = \{(1 - q, 0, 0), (0, 1 - q, 0), (0, 0, 1 - q)\}$, then it does not lie in $\mathscr{P}_{\Psi'}$ where Ψ' is the set of the three atoms considered. In fact, since $1/3 < q \leq 1/2$, then $1/2 \leq 1 - q < 2/3$ and $\mathrm{co}(\mathcal{S}_{\mathcal{F}}) \not\subseteq \mathscr{P}_{\Psi'} = \mathrm{co}((1, 0, 0), (0, 1, 0), (0, 0, 1))$. Thus, by Theorem 4, the forecast $\mathcal{F}$ is not IP-coherent with respect to the ε-contamination model class even though the assignments $\beta_{\underline{P}} : \alpha_1 \mapsto 0, \alpha_2 \mapsto 0, \alpha_3 \mapsto 0$ and $\beta_{\overline{P}} : \alpha_1 \mapsto 1 - q, \alpha_2 \mapsto 1 - q, \alpha_3 \mapsto 1 - q$ can be extended to Lower and Upper probabilities, respectively.

Let us conclude with a brief discussion on why scoring rule-based coherence seems to be stronger (in the sense that allows to distinguish more) than avoiding sure loss. Indeed, although this argument needs further and deeper insights that will be addressed in our future work, it seems clear that such an asymmetry might be caused by the information that these criteria encode in their formalization. In particular, although scoring rule-based criterion for Belief functions (Definition 6) relies on the sole information carried by the events $\psi_1, \ldots, \psi_n$ on which (coherent) forecasts are defined, the same criterion for imprecise probabilities (Definition 7) needs a forecast $\mathcal{F}$ to be defined on the atoms *and on the co-atoms* of $\mathbf{A}$. In this setting, in fact, a forecast assigns values of Lower and Upper probability to each atoms and hence, in algebraic terms, it needs both atoms and co-atoms of $\mathbf{A}$ to be defined: if $q_i = \overline{P}(\alpha_i) = 1 - \underline{P}(\neg\alpha_i)$ being $\neg\alpha = \bigvee_{j \neq i} \alpha_j$ a co-atom of $\mathbf{A}$. We believe that the observed asymmetry between the Dutch Book and scoring rule-based criteria, especially for imprecise probabilities, lies in this additional information that the latter requires.

6 Conclusion

We investigated particular sets of events that do not distinguish Belief functions from Lower probabilities from the point of view of Dutch Books, but which are distinguishable through scoring rules. We introduced a loss function through which we characterise assignments defined over a generic subset of events and that can be extended to a Belief function. Considering an already existing scoring rule defined for imprecise probabilities, we observed that the same assignments from which we can recover adequate sets of events, through coherence, can distinguish Lower probabilities from Belief functions. As pointed out at the end of the previous section, this result opens up new lines of research. In particular, given the tight connection between the scoring rule criterion and the geometric interpretation of the extendibility criterion, we could first characterise geometrically the sets $\mathscr{L}_\Psi$ and $\mathscr{U}_\Psi$ of the assignments defined over Ψ and that can be extended to Lower and Upper probabilities. Then, following the same process used in Sect. 4 for the Belief functions, define additional scoring rules through which it is possible to characterise assignments defined over generic sets of events and that can be extended to Upper or Lower probabilities. We could also investigate how to define a scoring rule that characterises assignments extendible to necessity measures.

The comparison reported in this paper are limited to the unconditional case. A general logical framework to investigate conditional probability functions has recently been introduced in [11]. Combining this with the conditional approach to Duch Book coherence put forward in [2,3] on the one hand, and the approach based on scoring rules of [13] on the other hand, we aim to extend our comparison to conditional, non-additive measures of uncertainty. With regards to Belief functions the very recent [18] obtains related results from a distinct angle, as briefly noted in Remark 2 above. Further work will elucidate potential mutual relations between the two independent approaches.

Acknowledgments. We are grateful to the anonymous referees for their thorough comments on the draft and to the ECSQARU Programme Committee for their very competent handling of the paper. Corsi and Hosni acknowledge funding by the Department of Philosophy "Piero Martinetti" of the University of Milan under the Project "Departments of Excellence 2018–2022" awarded by the Ministry of Education, University and Research (MIUR). Flaminio acknowledges partial support by the Spanish project PID2019-111544GB-C21 and by the Spanish Ramón y Cajal research program RYC-2016-19799. Hosni also acknowledges funding from the Deutsche Forschungsgemeinschaft (DFG, grant LA 4093/3-1).

References

1. Anger, B., Lembcke, J.: Infinitely subadditive capacities as upper envelopes of measures. Zeitschrift für Wahrscheinlichkeitstheorie und verwandte Gebiete **68**(3), 403–414 (1985)

2. Coletti, G., Petturiti, D., Vantaggi, B.: A Dutch Book coherence condition for conditional completely alternating choquet expectations. Bollettino dell'Unione Matematica Italiana **13**(4), 585–593 (2020)
3. Coletti, G., Scozzafava, R.: Probabilistic logic in a coherent setting, vol. 15. Springer (2002). https://doi.org/10.1007/978-94-010-0474-9
4. Corsi, E.A., Flaminio, T., Hosni, H.: When belief functions and lower probabilities are indistinguishable. In: ISIPTA 2021 - Proceedings of Machine Learning Research (147), pp. 83–89 (2021)
5. Cuzzolin, F.: The geometry of consonant belief functions: simplicial complexes of necessity measures. Fuzzy Sets Syst. **161**(10), 1459–1479 (2012)
6. Cuzzolin, F.: The geometry of uncertainty. Springer (2017). https://doi.org/10.1007/978-3-030-63153-6
7. De Finetti, B.: Theory of probability, vol. 1. John Wiley & Sons (1974)
8. Develin, M., Sturmfels, B.: Tropical convexity. arXiv preprint math/0308254 (2003)
9. Dubois, D., Prade, H.: Possibility Theory: Approach to Computerized Processing of Uncertainty. Plenum Press, New York (1988)
10. Flaminio, T., Godo, L.: A note on the convex structure of uncertainty measures on MV-algebras. In: Synergies of Soft Computing and Statistics for Intelligent Data Analysis, pp. 73–81. Springer (2013). https://doi.org/10.1007/978-3-642-33042-1_9
11. Flaminio, T., Godo, L., Hosni, H.: Boolean algebras of conditionals, probability and logic. Artif. Intelli. **286**, 103347 (2020)
12. Flaminio, T., Godo, L., Marchioni, E.: Geometrical aspects of possibility measures on finite domain MV-clans. Soft Comput. **16**(11), 1863–1873 (2012)
13. Gilio, A., Sanfilippo, G.: Coherent conditional probabilities and proper scoring rules. In: Proceedings of ISIPTA, vol. 11, pp. 189–198. Citeseer (2011)
14. Halpern, J.Y.: Reasoning about uncertainty. MIT press (2017)
15. Jaffray, J.Y.: Coherent bets under partially resolving uncertainty and belief functions. Theor. Decis. **26**(2), 99–105 (1989)
16. Miranda, E.: A survey of the theory of coherent lower previsions. Int. J. Approximate Reasoning **48**(2), 628–658 (2008)
17. Paris, J.B.: A note on the Dutch book method. ISIPTA. **1**, 301–306 (2001)
18. Petturiti, D., Vantaggi, B.: How to assess coherent beliefs: a comparison of different notions of coherence in Dempster-Shafer theory of evidence. arXiv preprint arXiv:2105.10546 (2021)
19. Regoli, G.: Rational comparisons and numerical representations. Decision Theory and Decision Analysis: Trends and Challenges, pp. 113–126 (1994)
20. Seidenfeld, T., Schervish, M.J., Kadane, J.B.: Forecasting with imprecise probabilities. Int. J. Approximate Reasoning **53**(8), 1248–1261 (2012)
21. Shafer, G.: A mathematical theory of evidence, vol. 42. Princeton University Press (1976)
22. Walley, P.: Statistical reasoning with imprecise probabilities. Chapman & Hall (1991)

Comparison of Shades and Hiddenness of Conflict

Milan Daniel[1] and Václav Kratochvíl[2(✉)]

[1] Institute of Computer Sciences, Czech Academy of Sciences, Prague, Czechia
milan.daniel@cs.cas.cz
[2] Institute of Information Theory and Automation, Czech Academy of Sciences,
Prague, Czechia
velorex@utia.cas.cz

Abstract. Conflict, dissonance, inconsistency, entropy. There are many notions related to one phenomenon. When working with uncertainty, there can be different sources of information, and often they are in some level of mutual disagreement. When working with belief functions, one of the approaches how to measure conflict is closely connected with a belief mass assigned by the non-normalized conjunctive rule to the empty set. Recently, we have observed and presented cases where a conflict of belief functions is hidden (there is a zero mass assigned to the empty set by the non-normalized conjunctive rule). Above that, we distinguish several degrees of such a hiddenness. In parallel, Pichon et al. introduced a new family of conflict measures of different strengths, the so-called shades of conflict. In this paper, we compare both approaches not only from the theoretical point of view but also by examples.

Keywords: Belief function · Conflict · Hidden conflict ·
N-consistency · Shades of conflict · Auto-conflict

1 Introduction

When combining belief functions (BFs) by the conjunctive rules of combination, some conflicts often appear (they are assigned either to $\emptyset$ by the non-normalized conjunctive rule $\bigcirc\!\!\!\!\ast$ or distributed among other belief masses by normalization in Dempster's rule of combination $\oplus$). A combination of conflicting BFs may be complicated and interpretation of their conflicts is often questionable in real applications.

The sum of all multiples of conflicting belief masses (denoted by $m_{\bigcirc\!\!\!\!\ast}(\emptyset)$) was interpreted as a conflict between BFs in the classical Shafer's approach [14]. Nevertheless, examples of mutually non-conflicting BFs with high $m_{\bigcirc\!\!\!\!\ast}(\emptyset)$ were observed as early as in the 1990s [1]. Different approaches to understand and

This work was supported by the institutional support RVO: 67985807 (first author) and grant GA ČR 19-04579S (second author).

© Springer Nature Switzerland AG 2021
J. Vejnarová and N. Wilson (Eds.): ECSQARU 2021, LNAI 12897, pp. 314–327, 2021.
https://doi.org/10.1007/978-3-030-86772-0_23

cover the nature of conflicts of BFs resulted in numerous papers; for references see, e.g., [9,11,13].

The value $m_\ominus(\emptyset)$ is frequently higher than an expected value of conflict even for partially conflicting BFs, This is explained in [3] where two quantitatively different parts of conflicts are distinguished: an internal conflict of an individual BF (due to its internal inconsistency), and an actual conflict between two different BFs (due to a conflict of represented evidence).

On the other hand, even though zero-sum of all multiples of conflicting belief masses $m_\ominus(\emptyset)$ is usually considered as non-conflictness of BFs. When analysing properties of conflict between belief functions based on their non-conflicting parts [4,5], a positive value of a conflict was observed even in a situation when $m_\ominus(\emptyset)$ equals zero.

We have investigated and presented this in [8,9] where different degrees of hidden conflicts were introduced when $m_\ominus(\emptyset) = 0$. The phenomenon may appear even inside individual BFs as a hidden internal conflict (hidden auto-conflict) [6,9]. Related different degrees of non-conflictness have been presented in [7].

In parallel to our research, Pichon et al. [13] introduced an entire family of measures of conflict based on a consistency of results of conjunctive combination of BFs in question. There are different degrees/shades of consistency and of related conflicts.

Both of the approaches come from different directions, see [9] and [13], thus they present different, nevertheless analogous results of different strength. Let us sketch the approaches in Sects. 3 and 4 and then compare them both on examples in Sect. 5.1 and also theoretically in Sect. 5.2.

2 Basic Notions

In this section, we will recall some basic notations needed in this paper.

Assume a finite frame of discernment Ω. In the case of $|\Omega| = n$, we will highlight this fact using a subscript as Ω_n and we assume $\Omega_n = \{\omega_1, \omega_2, \ldots, \omega_n\}$. $\mathcal{P}(\Omega) = \{X | X \subseteq \Omega\}$ is a *power-set* of Ω. $\mathcal{P}(\Omega)$ is often denoted also by 2^Ω, e.g., in [13].

A *basic belief assignment (bba)* is a mapping $m : \mathcal{P}(\Omega) \longrightarrow [0,1]$ such that

$$\sum_{A \subseteq \Omega} m(A) = 1;$$

the values of the bba are called *basic belief masses (bbm)*. $m(\emptyset) = 0$ is usually assumed. We sometimes speak about m as of a mass function.

There are other equivalent representations of m: A *belief function (BF)* is a mapping $Bel : \mathcal{P}(\Omega) \longrightarrow [0,1]$, $Bel(A) = \sum_{\emptyset \neq X \subseteq A} m(X)$. A *plausibility function* $Pl : \mathcal{P}(\Omega) \longrightarrow [0,1]$, $Pl(A) = \sum_{\emptyset \neq A \cap X, X \subseteq \Omega} m(X)$. Because there is a unique correspondence among m and corresponding Bel and Pl, we often speak about m as of a belief function.

Let $X \subseteq \Omega$ and Bel be a belief function defined on Ω by bba m. If $m(X) > 0$ for $X \subseteq \Omega$, we say X is a *focal element* of Bel. The set of focal elements is denoted by $\mathcal{F}$. We say that a focal element $X \in \mathcal{F}$ is proper if $X \neq \Omega$. If all focal elements are *singletons* ($|X| = 1$, $X \in \mathcal{F}$), then we speak about a *Bayesian belief function* (BBF); in fact, it is a probability distribution on Ω. If there are only focal elements such that $|X| = 1$ or $|X| = n$ we speak about a *quasi-Bayesian BF (qBBF)*. In the case of $m(\Omega) = 1$ we speak about the *vacuous BF* (VBF) and about a *non-vacuous BF* otherwise. If all focal elements have a non-empty intersection, we speak about a *consistent BF*.

Dempster's (normalized conjunctive) rule of combination $\oplus$:

$$(m_1 \oplus m_2)(A) = \sum_{X \cap Y = A; X, Y \subseteq \Omega} K m_1(X) m_2(Y)$$

for $A \neq \emptyset$, where $K = \frac{1}{1-\kappa}$,

$$\kappa = \sum_{X \cap Y = \emptyset; X, Y \subseteq \Omega} m_1(X) m_2(Y), \tag{1}$$

and $(m_1 \oplus m_2)(\emptyset) = 0$, see [14]. Putting $K = 1$ and $(m_1 \copyright m_2)(\emptyset) = \kappa$ we obtain the *non-normalized conjunctive rule of combination* $\copyright$, see e.g. [15]:

$$(m_1 \copyright m_2)(A) = \sum_{X \cap Y = A; X, Y \subseteq \Omega} m_1(X) m_2(Y)$$

for any $A \subseteq \Omega$. $\kappa > 0$ is usually considered to represent a conflict of respective belief functions. Following the notation from [13], focal elements of $m_1 \copyright m_2$ are denoted as $\mathcal{F}_{12}$. To simplify formulas, we often use $\copyright_1^3 m = m \copyright m \copyright m$, and also $\copyright_1^k (m_1 \copyright m_2) = (m_1 \copyright m_2) \copyright \ldots \copyright (m_1 \copyright m_2)$, where $(m_1 \copyright m_2)$ is repeated k-times.

3   Hidden Conflict

The notion of a hidden conflict was introduced in [8,9] based on an interesting observation during the analysis of the conflicting measure based on non-conflicting parts (for definitions[1] see [4,5,9]). Specifically, a positive value of this measure has been observed while the classical measure of conflict indicated nothing (i.e. mass assigned to the empty set by the conjunctive rule was zero). Above that, several degrees of *hiddeness* can be distinguished. The definition follows:

---

[1] In this comparison, we present just the notions necessary for understanding of both the compared approaches, for more detail including motivations see [9] and [13]. For irrelevance of dependence/independence of belief sources for conflicts see also [9].

Definition 1. *Assume two BFs Bel^i, Bel^{ii} defined by m^i and m^{ii} such that for some $k > 0$ $(\bigcirc_1^k(m^i \odot m^{ii}))(\emptyset) = 0$. If there further holds $(\bigcirc_1^{k+1}(m^i \odot m^{ii}))(\emptyset) > 0$ we say that there is a conflict of BFs m^i and m^{ii} hidden in the k-th degree (hidden conflict of k-th degree). If there is already $(\bigcirc_1^{k+1}(m^i \odot m^{ii}))(\emptyset) = (m^i \odot m^{ii})(\emptyset) > 0$ for $k = 0$ then there is a conflict of respective BFs which is not hidden or we can say that it is conflict hidden in degree zero.*

Note that the existence of conflict does not correspond to any particular assignment of mass values to focal elements, but the structure of focal elements of individual belief functions. That is also why we specify just the structure of focal elements in the following examples, usually using a figure. For illustration, see Fig. 1.

In the following examples, we would like to illustrate how the hidden conflict is revealed. Note that because of the commutativity of $\odot$, we can rewrite $(\bigcirc_1^3(m^i \odot m^{ii}))$ into $(\bigcirc_1^3(m^i) \odot \bigcirc_1^3(m^{ii}))$, etc. Once a positive mass is assigned to the empty set, it cannot be removed by $\odot$. To simplify the following examples, let us highlight the first occurrence of a positive mass on an empty set by dropping some BFs from respective formulas according to Definition 1.

Introductory Example. Let us assume Bel', Bel'' on Ω_3 where $\mathcal{F}' = \{\{\omega_1, \omega_2\}, \{\omega_1, \omega_3\}\}$ and $\mathcal{F}'' = \{\{\omega_2, \omega_3\}\}$ (see Fig. 1). Then $(m' \odot m'')(\emptyset) = 0$. But $(m' \odot m' \odot m'')(\emptyset) > 0$ (as highlighted in Fig. 1 where conflicting focal elements are drawn in red), which implies $(\bigcirc_1^2(m' \odot m''))(\emptyset) > 0$ as well. Thus, there is a conflict hidden in the 1-st degree. For detail including numeric belief masses see [9].

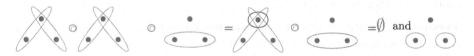

Fig. 1. Arising of a hidden conflict: focal elements of m', m', m''; $m' \odot m'$, m''; and of $m' \odot m' \odot m''$. (Color figure online)

For a conflict hidden in a higher degree, see the following Little Angel example.

Little Angel Example. Let us have two BFs Bel^i and Bel^{ii} on Ω_5: $\mathcal{F}^i = \{\{\omega_1, \omega_2, \omega_5\}, \{\omega_1, \omega_2, \omega_3, \omega_4\}, \{\omega_1, \omega_3, \omega_4, \omega_5\}\}$, $\mathcal{F}^{ii} = \{\{\omega_2, \omega_3, \omega_4, \omega_5\}\}$, i.e., $|\mathcal{F}^i| = 3$ while $|\mathcal{F}^{ii}| = 1$. Respective structures can be seen in Fig. 2 where sets of focal elements of individual BFs m^i (3×) and m^{ii} (1×) are depicted in its first row (ω_1 is on the top with ω_is clock-wise enumerated). Again, there is $(m^i \odot m^{ii})(\emptyset) = 0$ (there is no empty intersection of any $X \in \mathcal{F}^i$ with $Y \in \mathcal{F}^{ii}$). Moreover, $(\bigcirc_1^2(m^i \odot m^{ii}))(\emptyset) = 0$ in this example. Finally,

$(\bigcirc_1^3(m^i \textcircled{\odot} m^{ii}))(\emptyset) > 0$. Following the second line of Fig. 2, the empty set emerges as the intersection of focal elements drawn by red color, i.e., it appears already in $m^i \textcircled{\odot} m^i \textcircled{\odot} m^i \textcircled{\odot} m^{ii}$.

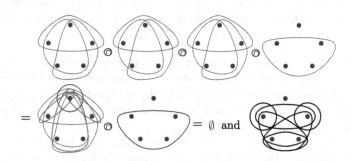

Fig. 2. Little Angel example: focal elements of m^i, m^i, m^i, m^{ii}; $\bigcirc_1^3 m^i, m^{ii}$; $(\bigcirc_1^3 m^i) \textcircled{\odot} m^{ii}$ (Color figure online)

Let us note that we can assume independent beliefs m^i and m^{ii} as originally in [8] and for low k also couples or k-tuples of same valued (identical) BFs from independent sources. Nevertheless, we are not interested in $\bigcirc_1^k m$ in general for any $k > 1$ here. We are interested only in whether its value for the empty set is zero or positive. This is needed for recognition whether the original pair of BFs has some hidden conflict or for proof that respective BFs are non-conflicting. Therefore no source independence assumption is needed in this case. For more details see [9].

Two major theorems specify an upper bound on the maximal degree of hidden conflict. For their proofs, see [9].

Theorem 1. *Hidden conflict of non-vacuous BFs on $\Omega_n, n > 1$ is always of a degree less or equal to $n - 2$; i.e., the condition*

$$(\bigcirc_1^{n-1}(m^i \textcircled{\odot} m^{ii}))(\emptyset) = 0 \tag{2}$$

always means full non-conflictness of respective BFs and there is no hidden conflict.

Theorem 2. *(i) Assume two non-vacuous BFs Bel^i, Bel^{ii} given by m^i, m^{ii} on Ω_n. Then*

$$(\bigcirc_1^c(m^i \textcircled{\odot} m^{ii}))(\emptyset) = 0$$

means full non-conflictness of respective BFs for $c = min(c^i, c^{ii}) + sgn(|c^i - c^{ii}|)$, where c^i, c^{ii} are the maximal cardinalities of proper focal elements of m^i, m^{ii}.
(ii) For any two non-vacuous quasi-Bayesian BFs m^i, m^{ii} on any frame of discernment Ω_n the condition $(m^i \textcircled{\odot} m^{ii})(\emptyset) = 0$ always means full non-conflictness of the BFs.
(iii) For any BF m^i and any quasi-Bayesian BF m^{ii} the condition $(\bigcirc_1^2(m^i \textcircled{\odot} m^{ii}))(\emptyset) = 0$ always means full non-conflictness of the BFs.

4   Shades of Conflict

There is a large family of shades of conflicts recently defined by Pichon et al. in [13] which is based on dual family of consistency measures. Let us start with unique *total inconsistency* of the *empty mass function* $m_\emptyset$, defined by the expression $m(\emptyset) = 1$ and on the other hand by definition of a family of (total) N-consistencies of belief functions. To do this we need several technical notions from [13].

Let us suppose a belief function Bel given by mass function (bba) m. Let us denote its set of focal elements (focal sets) by $\mathcal{F}$ where $|\mathcal{F}|$ is its cardinality (originally denoted by $\mathfrak{F}$ by [13]). Pichon et al. [13] similarly to Destercke and Burger [11] denote a union of all focal elements by $\mathcal{D}^2$. I.e., $\mathcal{D} = \bigcup_{X \in \mathcal{F}} X$. $\mathcal{M}$ simply denotes the set of all mass functions (bbas).

Definition 2. *(N-consistency).   A mass function m is said to be consistent of order N (N-consistent for short), with $1 \leq N \leq |\mathcal{F}|$, iff its focal sets are N-wise consistent, i.e., $\forall \mathcal{F}' \subseteq \mathcal{F}$ s.t. $|\mathcal{F}'| = N$, we have $\bigcap_{A \in \mathcal{F}'} A \neq \emptyset$.*

In addition, let Φ_N denote the measure from $\mathcal{M}$ to $[0,1]$ such that, for $1 \leq N \leq |\mathcal{F}|$, and all $m \in \mathcal{M}$, $\Phi_N(m) := 1 - (\bigcirc_1^N m)(\emptyset)$.

Note that Pichon et al. [13] use notation m^N for $(\bigcirc_1^N m) = m \bigcirc m \bigcirc \ldots \bigcirc m$ (N copies of m are combined). Similarly, Martin et al. [12] call the belief mass assigned by this combination to the empty set as the *auto-conflict* of m: $a_N(m) = (\bigcirc_1^N m)(\emptyset)$.[3] Let us further note that the auto-conflict does not work with the whole $\bigcirc_1^N m$, but with its value for the empty set only. Thus, any assumption of independence (in the sense of belief sources) is not necessary. In general, Pichon et al. [13] consider belief functions from independent sources for their conflict measures.

The family of N-consistencies represents different strengths of consistency from the weakest 1-consistency to the strongest $|\mathcal{F}|$-consistency. And as it is referred to, in [13], it covers three previously defined notions of consistency:

We can easily see that a mass function is 1-consistent iff intersections $\bigcap_{A \in \mathcal{F}'} A$ are nonempty for all sets $\mathcal{F}'$ of focal elements of cardinality $1 = |\mathcal{F}'|$, thus simply iff all focal elements are nonempty. This weakest consistency is satisfied by all normalized BFs $(m(\emptyset) = 0)$, thus by all BFs in classical Shafer's approach; this is called *probabilistic consistency* by Destercke and Burger in [11]. For $N = |\mathcal{F}'| = 2$ we obtain $\forall_{X,Y \in \mathcal{F}} X \cap Y \neq \emptyset$, i.e., Yager's *pairwise consistency* [17]. And finally, for $N = |\mathcal{F}|$ we obtain the strongest consistency $\bigcap_{A \in \mathcal{F}} A \neq \emptyset$ which corresponds to *logical consistency* from [10,11]. It also coincides with the consistency notion from Sect. 2. As $|\mathcal{F}| \leq |\mathcal{P}(\Omega)| = 2^n - 1$ there are up to $2^n - 1$

---

[2] Note, that this union is called a core of a belief function and denoted by $\mathcal{C}$ by Shafer in [14] ; on the other hand Cuzzolin uses a completely different (conjunctive) core defined as $\mathcal{C} = \bigcap_{A \in \mathcal{F}} A$ in [2].

[3] More precisely, Martin et al.do not use $\bigcirc$, but $\oplus$ sign, which we use as Shafer in his normalized approach [14] for Dempster's rule, where always $m(\emptyset) = 0$, $(m_i \oplus m_j)(\emptyset) = 0$ and $(\bigoplus_1^k m)(\emptyset) = 0$.

consistencies of different strength. These grades of consistency are referred to as *shades of consistency* in [13].

In accordance with unique total inconsistency and shades of consistency, Pichon et al. [13] consider unique *total conflict* of mass functions from [11]: m_1 and m_2 are *totally conflicting* when $\mathcal{D}_1 \cap \mathcal{D}_2 = \emptyset$, and they define a family of grades/shades of non-conflictness as N-consistency of mass function $m_{12} = m_1 \textcircled{\tiny C} m_2$ with the set of focal elements $\mathcal{F}_{12}$. And further, they define a related family of measures of conflict.

Definition 3. *(Order of Non-conflictness)* m_1 *and* m_2 *are said to be* non-conflicting of order N *(N-non-conflicting for short), with* $1 \leq N \leq |\mathcal{F}_{12}|$, *iff* $\forall A_i \in \mathcal{F}_{12}, i = 1, \ldots, N$, *we have* $\bigcap_{i=1}^{N} A_i \neq \emptyset$.

Analogously to N-consistency, also N-non-conflict subsumes several previous definitions: m_1 and m_2 are 1-non-conflicting iff all $A \in \mathcal{F}_{12}$ are nonempty, i.e. iff $X \cap Y \neq \emptyset$ for any $X \in \mathcal{F}_1, Y \in \mathcal{F}_2$, thus iff $\sum_{X \cap Y = \emptyset} m_1(X) m_2(Y) = 0$, i.e., non-conflict by Destercke & Burger [11] as well as by Shafer [14]. 2-non-conflict (of order 2) corresponds to Yager's definition of pair-wise consistency and $|\mathcal{F}_{12}|$-non-conflict is *strong non-conflict* : $\bigcap_{A \in \mathcal{F}_1 \cup \mathcal{F}_2} A \neq \emptyset$ from [11].

Definition 4. *(Measures of conflict κ_N)* *Measure of conflict* κ_N *of belief masses* m_1 *and* m_2 *is the measure* $\kappa_N(m_1, m_2) : \mathcal{M} \times \mathcal{M} \longrightarrow [0,1]$ *defined by* $\kappa_N(m_1, m_2) = 1 - \Phi_N(m_1 \textcircled{\tiny C} m_2)$, *for* $1 \leq N \leq |\mathcal{F}_{12}|$.

The above definition subsumes previous measure of conflict κ_m: $\kappa_1(m_1, m_2) = 1 - \Phi_1(m_1 \textcircled{\tiny C} m_2) = 1 - (1 - m_{12}(\emptyset)) = m_{12}(\emptyset)) = \kappa_m(m_1, m_2)$ [11,13]. It is the classical measure conflict as it is used in Smets' TBM [15,16] and its logarithm, more precisely $log(\frac{1}{1-\kappa_m})$, defines the weight of conflict in Shafer's [14]. The definition does not subsume $\kappa_\pi = 1 - \Phi_\pi$ as corresponding measures Φ_π and $\Phi_{|\mathcal{F}_{12}|}$ are not equal, see Remark 1 in [13], where Φ_π is max contour (see Φ_{pl} in [11]).

Similarly, shades of consistency are defined up to $2^n - 1$ shades where $\kappa_{|\mathcal{F}_{12}|}$ is the strongest and κ_1 is the weakest one from the family. Above that, it always holds $\kappa_{N-1}(m_1, m_2) \leq \kappa_N(m_1, m_2)$.

5   Comparison of both Approaches

In the previous sections, we have presented two different approaches to conflict. Despite that the conjunctive combination of a belief function with itself appears in both of them, there are different motivations for it. In the hidden conflict, it has been just a simple idea that a combination of two non-conflicting BFs should remain non-conflicting with any of the input belief functions, and the idea was repeated resulting in a repetitive combination of the respective belief functions.

The second approach—the so-called shades of conflict—is based on the idea of k combinations of m_{12} (i.e. of $m_\textcircled{\tiny C}$) into $\textcircled{\tiny C}_1^k m_{12}$, (i.e., based on auto-conflict of the k-th degree), to make all the intersections of k focal elements for $0 < k \leq |\mathcal{F}_{12}|$. Because N-consistency of m_{12} should be checked.

Let us compare these approaches now. We can immediately note, that the number of degrees of hidden conflict is limited by $|\Omega_n| = n$ in general and further by the cardinality of the biggest proper focal elements. On the other hand, there is no specified upper bound for shades so far. Thus, there are shades up to $2^n - 1$ (up to the maximal theoretical number of focal elements on Ω_n).

5.1 Comparison by Examples

Let us take a look at both approaches by several examples. We will start with the examples from Sect. 3.

Introductory and Little Angel Examples. There is a hidden conflict of the first degree in the Introductory example. There are two focal elements of $m_1 \odot m_2$, see Fig. 3 (i). Theoretically, two shades of conflict are defined. m' and m'' are 1-non-conflicting, but they have positive 2-conflict $\kappa_2(m', m'') > 0$. Similarly, there is a hidden conflict of the second degree in Little Angel example. There are three focal elements of $m_\odot = m^i \odot m^{ii}$, see Fig. 4 (i), thus there are three shades of conflict—three measures of conflict $\kappa_1, \kappa_2, \kappa_3$: $\kappa_1(m^i, m^{ii}) = m_\odot(\emptyset) = 0 = (\odot_1^2 m_\odot)(\emptyset) = \kappa_2(m^i, m^{ii})$ while $\kappa_3(m^i, m^{ii}) = (\odot_1^3 m_\odot)(\emptyset) > 0$. In both the examples, degree of hidden conflict corresponds with the number of shades. Nevertheless in general a number of shades can be greater. To illustrate that, see the following modification of the above mentioned examples.

Extension of the Introductory Example. Let us modify the Introductory example by adding Ω_3 as a focal element[4] to m''. Then we obtain $m' \odot m^{++}$ with four focal elements (as depicted in Fig. 3 (ii)). Note that it has four shades of conflict and four measures of conflict. Going further we can analogously add focal element of cardinality 3 to m' to obtain $m^+ \odot m^{++}$ with six focal elements – i.e. with six shades of conflict and six measures of conflict. See Fig. 3 (iii). Continuing further, we can add the singleton $\{\omega_1\}$ to m^{++}, then we obtain $m^+ \odot m^{**}$ with seven focal elements, thus with seven shades of conflict and seven measures of conflict (Fig. 3 (iv)). There are seven conflict measures[5] $\kappa_1, \kappa_2, ...\kappa_7$:
$$\kappa_1(m^+, m^{**}) = m_\odot(\emptyset) = (m^+ \odot m^{**})(\emptyset) = 0 < \kappa_2(m^+, m^{**}) = (\odot_1^2 m_\odot)(\emptyset) <$$
$$... < \kappa_7(m^+, m^{**}) = (\odot_1^7 m_\odot)(\emptyset) = m_\odot^7(\emptyset).$$
Focal elements of BFs are enough for checking N-non-conflictness and zero/positive values of conflict measures. Analogously, it is enough to check degrees of hidden conflicts. Note that there is just a hidden conflict of the first degree in all these extensions of the Introductory example from Figs. 3 (ii)-(iv).

---

[4] There are focal elements m', m'' substituted by some of m^+, m^{++}, m^*, m^{**} in the following extensions; analogously focal elements m^i, m^{ii} are substituted by m^{xi} and/or m^{xii} later in extensions of the Little Angel example.

[5] Note, that $m_\odot$ denotes here always the result of non-normalized conjunctive combination $\odot$ of a couple of bbas corresponding to the example extension in question, thus it varies and we can see its precise definition from the context.

We have reached seven measures of conflict, i.e., the maximum number $2^3 - 1$ for belief functions on Ω_3 according to definitions from the previous section. We already cannot increase the number of conflict measures, but we can increase a difference between degree of hidden conflict and number of shades by decreasing the degree of hidden conflict, e.g., as it follows. Les us add singleton $\{\omega_1\}$ also to m^+, hence we obtain un-hidden conflict of m^* and m^{**}, i.e., hidden in degree zero, see Fig. 3(v). In this case we have seven measures $0 < \kappa_1(m^*, m^{**}) < \kappa_2(m^*, m^{**}) < ... < \kappa_7(m^*, m^{**})$. As the auto-conflict $a_k(m^* \odot m^{**})$ is positive and increases already from its first degree $a_1(m^* \odot m^{**})$.

Concerning Fig. 3 and all the subsequent ones, focal elements appearing already in the previous row are drawn in gray.

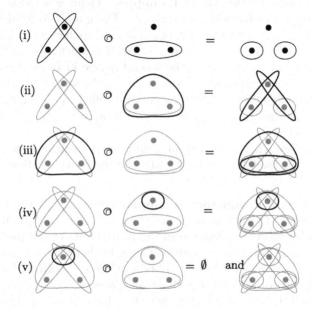

Fig. 3. Focal elements of couple of BFs on Ω_3 and their $\odot$ combination. (i) m', m'' and $m' \odot m''$, $N \leq 2$, (ii) $m' \odot m^{++}$, $N \leq 4$, (iii) $m^+ \odot m^{++}$, $N \leq 6$, (iv) $m^+ \odot m^*$, $N \leq 7$, (v) $m^* \odot m^*$, $N \leq 7$; N shades, hidden conflict of the first degree in (i)–(iv), unhidden conflict in (v).

Extension of the Little Angel Example. Let us, similarly to the previous case, add focal element of cardinality 5 to m^{ii}, see Fig. 4 (ii). Then we obtain six focal elements of $m^i \odot m^{xii}$, thus six conflict measures κ_N. Adding the same focal element also to m^i, see Fig. 4 (iii), we obtain even 8 focal element, thus eight measures of conflict, where $\kappa_1(m^{xi}, m^{xii}) = m_\odot(\emptyset) = (m^{xi} \odot m^{xii})(\emptyset) = 0 = (\odot_1^2 m_\odot)(\emptyset) = \kappa_2(m^{xi}, m^{xii}) < \kappa_3(m^{xi}, m^{xii}) = (\odot_1^3 m_\odot)(\emptyset) < ... <$

$\kappa_8(m^{xi}, m^{xii}) = (\bigcirc_1^8 m_\bigcirc)(\emptyset)$.[6] The degree of hidden conflict is kept 2 in both of these extensions.

There are many other such extensions of the example with different size up to 8 of family of conflict measures. Analogously to the Introductory Example there are also extensions decreasing the hiddeness of conflict and further increasing number[7] of conflict measures.

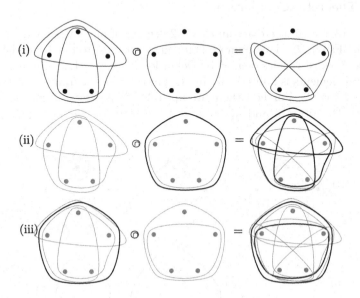

Fig. 4. Focal elements of couple of BFs on Ω_5 and their $\bigcirc$ combination. (i) m^i, m^{ii} and $m^i \bigcirc m^{ii}$, $N \leq 3$, (ii) $m^i \bigcirc m^{xii}$, $N \leq 6$, (iii) $m^{xi} \bigcirc m^{xii}$, $N \leq 8$; N shades, always hidden conflict of the second degree.

Non-conflicting Example. We have observed that the size of family of measures κ_N oversizes the degree of hiddeness of conflict in numerous examples. Let us look also at some non-conflicting cases now. Let us take Little Angel example but instead of m^{ii} consider bba m^{iii} with four focal elements $\{\omega_1, \omega_2, \omega_5\}$, $\{\omega_1, \omega_3, \omega_4\}$, $\{\omega_1, \omega_2, \omega_3\}$, $\{\omega_1, \omega_4, \omega_5\}$ as depicted in Fig. 5.

Combining non-conflicting m^i and m^{iii} we obtain $m^i \bigcirc m^{iii}$ with nine focal elements, see Fig. 5 (i), thus nine conflict measures $\kappa_1, ..., \kappa_9$. Adding Ω_5 as focal

---

[6] Let us notice, that the example from Fig. 4 (iii) is, in fact, discounting of that from 4 (i), hence conflict decreasing while the number of defined shades of conflict is increased from 3 to 8; and analogously 3 (iii) is discounting of 3 (i) with four more shades.

[7] There are interesting open issues: what is max number of shades of conflict related to a hidden conflict for this example; in general on Ω_5, and in full generality on Ω_n? And analogously, a number of shades related to a hidden conflict of the 2-nd degree and k-th degree?.

element to m^{iii} we obtain $m^i \odot m^{xiii}$ with 11 f.e., both four-elements from m^i are added, see Fig. 5 (ii); and adding Ω_5 also to m^i we obtain $m^{xi} \odot m^{xiii}$ with 12 f.e., where Ω_5 is newly added, see Fig. 5 (iii). Hence we obtain dozen conflict measures $\kappa_N(m^{xi}, m^{xiii}) = (\odot_1^N (m^{xi} \odot m^{xiii}))(\emptyset) = (\odot_1^N m_\odot)(\emptyset)$, such that $\kappa_1(m^{xi}, m^{xiii}) = 0 = \kappa_2(m^{xi}, m^{xiii}) = ... = \kappa_{12}(m^{xi}, m^{xiii})$.

5.2   A Theoretic Comparison

According to Sect. 3, there are up to $n - 2$ degrees of hiddenness conflicts for any couple of BFs on Ω_n. This number is further decreased to $c - 1$ by Theorem 2. There are N-consistencies defined by Definition 2 for $N = 1, ..., |\mathcal{F}|$, where number of focal elements is limited only by the power set of the frame of discernment thus $2^n - 1$ for Ω_n. Further, there are up to $2^n - 1$ degrees of non-conflictness defined by Definition 3 and up to $2^n - 1$ measures of conflict κ_N in general.

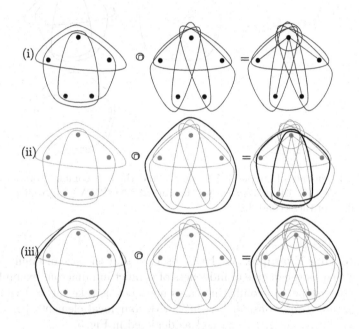

Fig. 5. Focal elements of couple of non-conflicting BFs on Ω_5 and their $\odot$ combination. (i) m^i, m^{iii} and $m^i \odot m^{iii}$, $N \leq 9$, (ii) $m^i \odot m^{xiii}$, $N \leq 11$, (iii) $m^{xi} \odot m^{xiii}$, $N \leq 12$; N shades, no conflict of any degree.

This number is decreased for a given pair of BFs m_1, m_2 by $|\mathcal{F}_{12}|$, i.e., number of focal elements of $m_{12} = m_1 \odot m_2$.[8]

As it has been illustrated by above examples, even the decreased number of κ_N is often greater than the degree of hidden conflict of particular BFs.

Observation 1. *The degree of hidden conflict of m_1 and m_2 is equal to number of zero κ_N values for the pair of BFs, i.e., it is equal to max degree of N-consistency of $m_1 \odot m_2$ and max degree of N-non-conflictness of the couple m_1 and m_2. For unhidden conflict, thus 0 degree of hidden conflict there is no N-consistency, for non-conflicting BFs there is $|\mathcal{F}_{12}|$-consistency and all κ_N equal to zero.*

The results on non-conflictness are stronger in the hidden conflict approach. Using the above comparison of the approaches we can strengthen the results on N-conflictness:

Theorem 3. $n - 1$-*non-conflicting BFs m_1 and m_2 on any Ω_n are $|\mathcal{F}_{12}|$-non-conflicting, i.e., strongly non-conflicting.*

Proof. For maximal $n-2$ degree of hidden conflict (Theorem 1) there is $n-2$-non-conflictness, hence N-non-conflictness for $N > n - 2$ already means no hidden conflict thus strong non-conflictness.

Theorem 4. *c-non-conflicting BFs m_1 and m_2 on any Ω_n such that $c = min(c^i, c^{ii}) + sgn(|c^i - c^{ii}|)$, where c^i, c^{ii} are the maximal cardinalities of proper focal elements of m_1, m_2 are $|\mathcal{F}_{12}|$-non-conflicting, i.e., strongly non-conflicting.*

Proof. Analogously, $c - 1$ is max degree of hidden conflict (Theorem 2), there is $c - 1$-non-conflictness, hence N-non-conflictness for $N > c - 1$ already means no hidden conflict thus strong non-conflictness.

On the other side, there are some cases for large frames of discernment and big minimal focal elements, where number of focal elements of $m_1 \odot m_2$ may be less than c from Theorem 2. Thus Pichon el al.'s results [13] are stronger in such cases and we can strengthen results on hidden conflicts for such cases as it follows:

Theorem 5. *A hidden conflict of any non-vacuous BFs m_1 and m_2 on any Ω_n has always a degree less than or equal to $|\mathcal{F}_{12}| - 1$.*

Proof. The assertion follows the fact that $(\odot_1^{|\mathcal{F}_{12}|}(m_1 \odot m_2))(\emptyset) = 0$ already means full/strong non-conflictness.

---

[8] More correctly, there are $2^n - 1$ measures κ_N for BFs on Ω_n, where only $|\mathcal{F}_{12}|$ values are defined as N-conflict of corresponding BFs m_1 and m_2 by Pichon et al. [13]. Nevertheless, on the other hand, a degree of auto-conflict is not limited, thus there exist values of $\kappa_N(m_1, m_2)$ for all $N \leq 2^n - 1$ regardless the definitions from Sect. 4, originally from [13] : $\kappa_N(m_1, m_2) = 1 - \Phi_N(m_1 \odot m_2) = 1 - (1 - (m_1 \odot m_2)^N(\emptyset)) = (\odot_1^N(m_1 \odot m_2))(\emptyset) = a_N(m_1 \odot m_2)$; in fact there exist values for any finite N and limit is either 0 for totally non-conflicting BFs or 1 if there is any kind of conflict.

Having the above presented strengthening of previous results, there arises a new question: whether there is some upper bound of degrees of hidden conflicts and shades of conflict following some condition about small focal elements?

6   Conclusion

We compared two approaches to different degrees of conflictness of belief functions. Starting points and motivations of these approaches are quite different, nevertheless both approaches use conjunctive combination to combine beliefs in question, and they compute belief mass assigned to empty set by repeated combination of resulting BF with itself, called auto-conflict by Martin et al. Both these approaches are compared not only from the theoretical point of view but also using both conflicting and non-conflicting examples.

Our comparison has even fruitfully improved both approaches. New theorems introducing bounds of the number of different N-non-conflictness have been presented altogether with maximum degree theorem. Above that some cases where one can create lower bound degree of hidden conflict has been observed.

From the application point of view, the presented results can improve decision making whether belief functions in question are really non-conflicting or whether some level of conflict between them is hidden there.

Besides, there are several open issues for further research and development of the topic like e.g., description of classes of non-conflicting BFs or investigation of further practical usefulness of hidden conflicts and their degrees.

References

1. Almond, R.G.: Graphical belief modeling, 1st edn. CRC Press Inc, Boca Raton (1995). https://www.routledge.com/Graphical-Belief-Modeling/Almond/p/book/9780412066610
2. Cuzzolin, F.: On consistent approximations of belief functions in the mass space. In: Liu, W. (ed.) ECSQARU 2011. LNCS (LNAI), vol. 6717, pp. 287–298. Springer, Heidelberg (2011). https://doi.org/10.1007/978-3-642-22152-1_25
3. Daniel, M.: Conflicts within and between belief functions. In: Hüllermeier, E., Kruse, R., Hoffmann, F. (eds.) IPMU 2010. LNCS (LNAI), vol. 6178, pp. 696–705. Springer, Heidelberg (2010). https://doi.org/10.1007/978-3-642-14049-5_71
4. Daniel, M.: Non-conflicting and conflicting parts of belief functions. In: 7th International Symposium on Imprecise Probability: Theories and Applications (ISIPTA 2011), pp. 149–158. SIPTA, Innsbruck (2011). https://www.sipta.org/isipta11/proceedings/041.html
5. Daniel, M.: Conflict between belief functions: a new measure based on their non-conflicting parts. In: Cuzzolin, F. (ed.) BELIEF 2014. LNCS (LNAI), vol. 8764, pp. 321–330. Springer, Cham (2014). https://doi.org/10.1007/978-3-319-11191-9_35
6. Daniel, M., Kratochvíl, V.: Hidden auto-conflict in the theory of belief functions. In: Proceedings of the 20th Czech-Japan Seminar on Data Analysis and Decision Making under Uncertainty (CJS 2017), pp. 34–45 (2017). http://hdl.handle.net/11104/0276743

7. Daniel, M., Kratochvíl, V.: Belief functions and degrees of non-conflictness. In: Kern-Isberner, G., Ognjanović, Z. (eds.) ECSQARU 2019. LNCS (LNAI), vol. 11726, pp. 125–136. Springer, Cham (2019). https://doi.org/10.1007/978-3-030-29765-7_11

8. Daniel, M., Kratochvíl, V.: On hidden conflicts of belief functions. In: 11th Conference of the European Society for Fuzzy Logic and Technology (EUSFLAT 2019). Atlantis Press (2019). https://doi.org/10.2991/eusflat-19.2019.70

9. Daniel, M., Kratochvíl, V.: Hidden conflicts of belief functions. Int. J. Comput. Intell. Syst. **14**, 438–452 (2020). https://doi.org/10.2991/ijcis.d.201008.001

10. Destercke, S., Dubois, D.: Idempotent conjunctive combination of belief functions: extending the minimum rule of possibility theory. Inf. Sci. **181**(18), 3925–3945 (2011). https://doi.org/10.1016/j.ins.2011.05.007

11. Destercke, S., Burger, T.: Toward an axiomatic definition of conflict between belief functions. IEEE Trans. Cybern. **43**(2), 585–596 (2013). https://doi.org/10.1109/TSMCB.2012.2212703

12. Martin, A., Jousselme, A.L., Osswald, C.: Conflict measure for the discounting operation on belief functions. In: 11th International Conference on Information Fusion. IEEE (2008). https://ieeexplore.ieee.org/document/4632320

13. Pichon, F., Jousselme, A.L., Abdallah, N.B.: Several shades of conflict. Fuzzy Sets Syst. **366**, 63–84 (2019). https://doi.org/10.1016/j.fss.2019.01.014

14. Shafer, G.: A mathematical theory of evidence. Princeton University Press Princeton (1976). https://press.princeton.edu/books/paperback/9780691100425/a-mathematical-theory-of-evidence

15. Smets, P.: Decision making in the TBM: the necessity of the pignistic transformation. Int. J. Approximate Reasoning **38**(2), 133–147 (2005). https://doi.org/10.1016/j.ijar.2004.05.003

16. Smets, P., Kennes, R.: The transferable belief model. Artif. Intell. **66**(2), 191–234 (1994). https://doi.org/10.1016/0004-3702(94)90026-4

17. Yager, R.R.: On considerations of credibility of evidence. Int. J. Approximate Reasoning **7**, 45–72 (1992). https://doi.org/10.1016/0888-613X(92)90024-T

Games of Incomplete Information:
A Framework Based on Belief Functions

Hélène Fargier[1], Érik Martin-Dorel[2], and Pierre Pomeret-Coquot[2(✉)]

[1] CNRS, IRIT, Toulouse, France
helene.fargier@irit.fr
[2] University Paul Sabatier, IRIT, University of Toulouse, Toulouse, France
{erik.martin-dorel,pierre.pomeret}@irit.fr

Abstract. This paper proposes a model for incomplete games where the knowledge of the players is represented by a Dempster-Shafer belief function. Beyond an extension of the classical definitions, it shows such a game can be transformed into an equivalent hypergraphical complete game (without uncertainty), thus generalizing Howson and Rosenthal's theorem to the framework of belief functions and to any number of players. The complexity of this transformation is finally studied and shown to be polynomial in the degree of k-additivity of the mass function.

Keywords: Game theory · Incomplete games · Belief functions

1 Introduction

Game theory [21, 25] proposes a powerful framework to capture decision problems involving several agents. In non-cooperative games of complete information, the players do not coordinate their actions but each of them knows everything about the game: the players, their available actions and all their utilities. This assumption of complete knowledge cannot always be satisfied. In the real world indeed, players are not so well informed and have only limited knowledge about the game. This is why Bayesian games of incomplete information have been proposed [16]. Nevertheless, the Bayesian hypothesis is strong, and requires a good knowledge of the environment. For instance, in case of ignorance, the Bayesian way is to suppose equiprobability, but this can lead to a model that does not fit with the agents' behavior (e.g. see Ellsberg's paradox [9]).

In the present paper, we propose a new kind of game of incomplete information, which we call *credal game*. Agents have a partial knowledge, represented by a Dempster-Shafer belief function [5, 30], and cardinal utilities, but do not necessarily make the equiprobability assumption. The underlying decision rule is the Choquet integral based on the *Bel* measure [4], in order to capture the agents' aversion for ambiguity [12, 13, 22]. We then follow the line defined by Howson and Rosenthal [17] who have shown that any 2-player Bayesian game can be

Pierre Pomeret-Coquot and Helene Fargier have benefited from the AI Interdisciplinary Institute ANITI. ANITI is funded by the French "Investing for the Future – PIA3" program under the Grant agreement n°ANR-19-PI3A-0004.

© Springer Nature Switzerland AG 2021
J. Vejnarová and N. Wilson (Eds.): ECSQARU 2021, LNAI 12897, pp. 328–341, 2021.
https://doi.org/10.1007/978-3-030-86772-0_24

transformed into a complete knowledge *polymatrix game* [33]. In this paper, we show that such a transformation is possible for credal games, and for any number of agents, producing a *hypergraphical game* [26]. An important consequence of this result is that the algorithmics developed for hypergraphical games [3,32] can be reused for the search of Nash equilibria in credal games.

2   Background and Motivations

To illustrate and motivate our work, we will use the following example inspired by the *murder of Mr. Jones* [31], where the suspects are *Peter, Paul and Mary*.

Example 1 (Peter, Quentin and Rose).   Two agents, named Agent 1 and Agent 2, are independently looking for a business association, with either Peter (P), Quentin (Q), or Rose (R). The point is that a crime has been committed, for which these three people are suspected. Several testimonies, not very reliable, allowed to estimate that there is 50% of chance that the culprit is a man (P or Q), and 50% of chance that it is a woman (R).

   As to the interest of the associations, making the deal with an innocent leads to a payoff of $6k (to be shared between the people making the deal), while associating with a guilty person produces no payoff ($0k). Moreover, Agent 1 is investigating about P and will knows whether he is guilty or not. Similarly, Agent 2 will knows whether R is guilty before making the decision.

   The Bayesian approach is not relevant here. Indeed, if Agent 1 learns that P is innocent, the probability of guilt should become $1/2$ for Q and $1/2$ for R. However, in a purely Bayesian view, equiprobability would be applied and the prior probability of guilt would be $1/4$ for P and $1/4$ for Q. Then, after conditioning, Agent 1 would get a probability of $1/3$ for Q and $2/3$ for R.

2.1   Dempster-Shafer's Theory of Evidence

Let us first look at the epistemic aspect of the problem. The prior knowlege is simply that $P(\{P, Q\}) = P(\{M\}) = \frac{1}{2}$, and nothing more. The kind of knowledge at work here is well captured in Dempster-Shafer's theory of evidence, that does not restrict probability assignments to elements of the frame of discernment:

Definition 1 (Mass function). *A mass function for a frame of discernment Ω (or "bpa" for basic probability assignment) is a function $m : 2^\Omega \to [0, 1]$ such that $m(\emptyset) = 0$ and $\sum_{A \subseteq \Omega} m(A) = 1$.*

   A set with a nonzero mass is called a *focal element* and the set of focal elements is denoted $\mathcal{S}_m$. Two dual measures on 2^Ω derive from m:

$$Bel(A) = \sum_{B \in \mathcal{S}_m, B \subseteq A} m(B) \quad \text{and} \quad Pl(A) = \sum_{B \in \mathcal{S}_m, B \cap A \neq \emptyset} m(B).$$

$Bel(A)$ (resp. $Pl(A)$) estimates to what extent A is implied by (resp. is compatible with) the knowledge captured by m.

Probabilities are belief functions where the focal elements are then singletons – where m is "1-additive". k-additivity is more generally defined as follows:

Definition 2 (k-additivity). *A mass function is k-additive if all its focal elements are at most of size k, i.e., $\forall B \in \mathcal{S}_m, |B| \leq k$.*

Even if the agents share the same prior knowledge, as in our example, they may acquire different pieces of information and thus have a different posterior knowledge. In the example, Agent 1 eventually learns whether P is guilty or not while Agent 2 will acquire information about R. Each agent thus revises his/her knowledge on the basis on the information C she learns (e.g. R for Agent 2). States where C is false are considered as impossible by the agent, so she modifies the initial belief function in such a way that $Pl(\bar{C}) = 0$: the conditioning at work here is Dempster's rule [5] (see also [1,7] for more details about the conditioning).

Definition 3 (Dempster conditioning). *For any nonempty $A, C \subseteq \Omega$,*

$$m_{|C}(A) := K_C \cdot \sum_{B \in \mathcal{S}_m, C \cap B = A} m(B),$$

where $K_C = 1/\sum_{B \in \mathcal{S}_m, B \cap C \neq \emptyset} m(B)$ is a normalization factor.

2.2   Decision Making with Belief Functions

Let us now consider belief functions in a (single-agent) decision making context. Following Savage's modelling of decision making under uncertainty [28], a decision (or "action") is a function $a : \Omega \rightarrow X$ where Ω is the set of possible states, as previously, and X is the set of possible outcomes. The preferences of an agent are represented by an utility function $u : X \rightarrow \mathbb{R}$. When the knowledge about Ω is captured by a belief function, the discrete Choquet integral [4] based on the *Bel* measure is classically advocated because of its ability to capture the agents' aversion for ambiguity [12, 13, 22]:

Definition 4 (Discrete Choquet integral). *Let $\Lambda(a) = \{\lambda_1 \leq \cdots \leq \lambda_{|\Lambda(a)|}\}$ be the set of utility values reached by an action a, labelled by increasing order, and $E_{\lambda_i}(a) = \{\omega \mid u(a(\omega)) \geq \lambda_i\}$ denote the set of worlds for which the utility of action a is at least λ_i. The discrete Choquet utility value (or CEU) of a is :*

$$CEU(a) = \lambda_1 + \sum_{i=2}^{|\Lambda(a)|} (\lambda_i - \lambda_{i-1}) \times Bel(E_{\lambda_i}(a)).$$

The *CEU* has a simple expression based on the mass function:

$$CEU(a) = \sum_{B \in \mathcal{S}_m} m(B) \times \min_{\omega \in B} u(a(\omega)).$$

2.3   Game Theory

A simultaneous game of complete information models a situation where several agents make a decision (the term "action" is rather used in game theory) without coordination with the other agents – the final utility of each agent depending on the actions chosen by all agents.

Definition 5 (Complete game). *A simultaneous game of complete information (also called* complete game*) is a tuple* $G = \left(N, (A_i)_{i \in N}, (u_i)_{i \in N}\right)$ *where:*

- $N = \{1, \ldots, n\}$ *is a finite set of agents (or "players"),*
- A_i *is the set of actions of Agent i; $A := \prod_{i \in N} A_i$ contains all the possible combinations of actions or "profiles",*
- $u_i : A \to \mathbb{R}$ *is the utility function of Agent i.*

A mixed strategy for player i is a probability distribution on A_i. The strategy is said to be pure *when only one action receives a non-zero probability.*
A pure *(resp.* mixed*) joint strategy (or* strategy profile*) is a vector $p = (p_1, \ldots, p_n)$ which specifies a pure (resp. mixed) strategy for each player.*

A mixed strategy is classically interpreted as distributions the players use to randomly choose among available actions in order to avoid being predictable – this is especially useful in repeated games. An alternative view is to consider that each p_i represents the knowledge that the other agents have about i's decision.

In the following, we will use the following notations: for any vector $v = (v_1, \ldots, v_n)$ in some product domain $V = \prod_{i \in N} V_i$ and for any $e \subseteq N$, v_e is the restriction of v to e and $V_e = \prod_{i \in e} V_i$. By abuse of notation, we write v_i for $v_{\{i\}}$. For any i, $-i$ denotes the set $N \setminus \{i\}$, i.e. $v_{-i} = (v_1, \ldots, v_{i-1}, v_{i+1}, \ldots, v_n) \in V_{-i} = \prod_{j \neq i} V_j$. Thus, v_{-i} is the restriction of v to all players but i. Finally, "." denotes the concatenation, e.g., $v_i'.v_{-i} = (v_1, \ldots, v_{i-1}, v_i', v_{i+1}, \ldots, v_n)$. Hence $a = a_i.a_{-i}$ belongs to A and given two profiles $a, a' \in A$, $a_i'.a_{-i}$ denotes the profile a where a_i is replaced with a_i'.

Because the strategies can be randomized, the global utility for a player of a joint mixed strategy p is defined as the expected utility of u_i according to the probability distribution it induces over A (Obviously, when the strategy is pure, EU_i is equal to the utility value given by u_i):

Definition 6 (Utility of a strategy). *Given a joint strategy p in a complete game $\left(N, (A_i)_{i \in N}, (u_i)_{i \in N}\right)$, the expected utility of player i is defined by:*

$$EU_i(p) = \sum_{a \in A} \left(\prod_{i \in N} p_i(a_i) \right) \times u_i(a).$$

Among the profiles of interest, Nash equilibria are emphasized, i.e., profiles in which no player can increase his/her utility by changing his/her own strategy.

Definition 7 (Nash equilibrium [25]). *A strategy profile p is a* Nash equilibrium *iff for all $i \in N$, there exists no p_i' such that $u_i(p_i'.p_{-i}) > u_i(p)$.*
A pure strategy profile p is a Nash equilibrium *iff for all $i \in N$, there exists no pure strategy p_i' such that $u_i(p_i'.p_{-i}) > u_i(p)$.*

When the utility functions are described explicitly, G is said to be in standard normal form (SNF). SNF representations become spatially costly when the number of players increases ($O(n\alpha^n)$ for a game with n players and α actions per player). More succinct forms have been proposed, that suit cases where utility functions can be decomposed as a sum of smaller utility functions – namely hypergraphical games [26] and polymatrix games [33].

Definition 8 (Hypergraphical game). *A hypergraphical game is a tuple $G = (N, E, (A_i)_{i \in N}, (u_i^e)_{e \in E, i \in e})$ where N is a set of players, $E = \{e_1, \dots e_m\}$ is a multiset of subsets of N ((N, E) is an hypergraph) and for each $e \in E$, $(e, (A_i)_{i \in e}, (u_i^e)_{i \in e})$ is a classical standard normal form game. The global utility of Agent i is the sum of i's local utilities: $u_i(a) = \sum_{e \in E} u_i^e(a_e)$.*
Polymatrix games are hypergraphical games with 2-player local games.

This framework assumes that each player knows everything about the game: the players, the actions available to each player, all their utilities for each combination of actions, etc. The assumption of complete knowledge cannot always be satisfied. In the real world indeed, players have only a limited knowledge about the outcomes of their strategies – the final outcomes may depend on an ill-known event (in our example, the payoff for making the deal with one of P, Q, or R depends on whether they are guilty or innocent).

Harsanyi [16] proposed games of incomplete information as a way to capture such situations (see also [24], for more details). A game of incomplete information can be first understood as a set of possible classical games (of complete information) – one for each possible world $\omega \in \Omega$. Players don't know exactly which world is the real one, but may have some knowledge about it. Just before playing, each player i will receive some information $\tau_i(\omega^*)$ about the real world ω^*. τ_i maps any world to an element θ_i of a set Θ_i called the set of "types" of Agent i. After having observed $\tau_i(\omega^*)$, Agent i knows more about the real game, but several games may still be plausible. The player then conditions his/her knowledge on $\tau_i(\omega^*)$ and decides which action to play. Notice that the different agents may receive different pieces of information and thus have a different posterior knowledge. The question is then, for each player, to determine a strategy (either an action, or a probabilistic strategy) for each of his/her possible types.

Harsanyi has shown that such games can be described on the space of types $\Theta = \Theta_1 \times \cdots \times \Theta_n$ (the underlying worlds are omitted). The idea of Harsanyi when defining types is that this concept can encapsulate every piece of information agents may have access to. It includes the agent-observable world status, but also their beliefs on other agents and their introspective mental states.

3   Credal Games

Bayesian games are games of incomplete information where prior knowledge is captured by a probability measure. To capture problems where the Bayesian assumption is not obeyed (as in our motivating example), we propose in this paper the framework of credal games:

Definition 9 (Credal game). *A credal game G is defined as a tuple composed of $\left(N, (A_i)_{i \in N}, (\Theta_i)_{i \in N}, (u_i)_{i \in N}, m\right)$ where:*

- $N = \{1, \ldots, n\}$ *is a finite set of players,*
- A_i *is the set of actions of player i; $A = \prod_{i \in N} A_i$ denotes the set of all action profiles,*
- Θ_i *is the set of types of player i; let $\Theta = \prod_{i \in N} \theta_i$,*
- $m : 2^\Theta \to [0,1]$ *is the mass function describing the common prior knowledge,*
- $u_i : A \times \Theta \to \mathbb{R}$ *is the utility function of Agent i.*

G is said to be in standard normal form iff the utility functions u_i and the mass function m are given in extenso.

Following Harsyani's approach of incomplete games, we consider the "ex interim" setting where each player plans a strategy for each of the types he/she can receive, ideally a strategy which is a best response to that of the other players. We thus adopt the definition of strategy proposed by Harsyani's in the general context of incomplete games:

Definition 10 (Pure and mixed strategies [16]). *A pure (resp. mixed) strategy for player i in a credal game is a function ρ_i which maps each "type" $\theta_i \in \Theta_i$ to an action of (resp. a probability over) A_i.*

A pure (resp. mixed) joint strategy is a vector $p = (p_1, \ldots, p_n)$ which specifies a pure (resp. mixed) strategy for each player.

$\rho(\theta) = \left(\rho_1(\theta_1), \ldots, \rho_n(\theta_n)\right)$ denotes the profile which will be played if the configuration of types is θ.

Let us first consider pure strategies. In the *ex interim* approach of incomplete games, Agent i may consider the strategy ρ_{-i} planned by the other players for each of their types. When receiving her type θ_i, he/she revises his/her knowledge – in a credal game, his/her posterior knowledge over the joint type configuration is $m_{|\theta_i}$. According to the definition of the Choquet expected utility, the utility of a pure strategy profile for Agent i of type θ_i, shall thus be defined as:

Definition 11 (Choquet Expected Utility of a pure strategy profile). *The utility of a pure strategy profile $\rho = (\rho_1, \ldots, \rho_n)$, for Agent i of type θ_i, is:*
$$CEU_{(i,\theta_i)}(\rho) = \sum_{B \in S_{m_{|\theta_i}}} m_{|\theta_i}(B) \times \min_{\theta' \in B} u_i(\rho(\theta'), \theta').$$

Let us now consider mixed strategies. For each configuration θ, $\rho(\theta)$ defines a probability distribution over A: the probability that a is played when agents have types θ is equal to $\prod_{i \in N} \rho_i(\theta_i)(a_i)$. If we now consider all the θ's, we get a bpa m^ρ over $A \times \Theta$. To any focal element $B \in S_m$ and any pure strategy profile $\sigma : \Theta \to A$ corresponds an element $\sigma.B := \{(\sigma(\theta), \theta) \mid \theta \in B\}$ of mass $m^\rho(\sigma.B) = m(B) \times \prod_{\theta \in B} \prod_{i \in N} \rho_i(\theta_i)(\sigma_i(\theta_i)) - \sigma.B$ is focal iff B is focal and σ is possible according to ρ. Finally, Agent i recieving type θ_i conditions his/her knowledge which becomes $m^\rho_{|\theta_i}$. Hence the following definition of the utility of a mixed strategy profile:

Definition 12 (Choquet Expected Utility of a mixed strategy profile).
The utility of a mixed strategy profile $\rho = (\rho_1, \ldots, \rho_n)$, *for player i of type θ_i, is:*

$$CEU_{(i,\theta_i)}(\rho) = \sum_{\sigma. B \in \mathcal{S}_{m^\rho_{|\theta_i}}} \left(m_{|\theta_i}(B) \times \prod_{\theta' \in B} \prod_{j \in N} \rho_j(\theta'_j)(\sigma_j(\theta'_j)) \right) \times \min_{\theta' \in B} u_i(\sigma(\theta'), \theta')$$

Obviously, Definition 12 leads to Definition 11 when ρ is a pure strategy profile. Now, recall that a strategy profile is a Nash equilibrium if no player can improve unilaterally his/her utility. This concept straightforwardly extends to credal games:

Definition 13 (Nash equilibrium). *A mixed (resp. pure) strategy profile ρ is a Nash equilibrium for CEU iff, whatever i, there exists no mixed (resp. pure) strategy ρ'_i such that for any θ_i, $CEU_{(i,\theta_i)}(\rho'_i.\rho_{-i}) > CEU_{(i,\theta_i)}(\rho)$.*

Example. Our running example (see Example 1) is captured by the credal game $G = \big(N, (A_i)_{i \in N}(\Theta_i)_{i \in N}, (u_i)_{i \in N}, m\big)$ where:

- $N = \{1, 2\}$;
- $A_1 = \{P_1, Q_1, R_1\}$, $A_2 = \{P_2, Q_2, R_2\}$ (each agent chooses an associate).
- $\Theta_1 = \{P, \bar{P}\}$, $\Theta_2 = \{R, \bar{R}\}$ (Agent 1 investigates on Peter, Agent 2 investigates on Rose).
- $m : 2^\Theta \to [0, 1]$ has two focal elements: $m(\{(\bar{P}, R)\}) = 1/2$ (the murderer is a woman, thus necessarily Rose – in this case Agent 1 will learn $\bar{P}$ and Agent 2 will learn R) and $m(\{(P, \bar{R}), (\bar{P}, \bar{R})\}) = 1/2$ (the murderer is a man: Agent 2 necessarily learns $\bar{R}$ but Agent 1 can learn either $\bar{P}$ – which happens when Quentin is the murderer – or P – Peter is the murderer).
- Making a deal with a murderer has a utility value of 0, making a deal with an innocent leads to a utility of $\frac{6}{2} = 3$, unless the other agent approaches the same associate, in which case each agent receives $\frac{6}{3} = 2$. The utility functions are summarized below (Table 1). Null values (in gray) are given for the case where $\theta = (P, R)$ (both R and P are guilty) which is not a possible world.

Let ρ be the pure strategy where Agent 1 makes the deal with R when learning that P is guilty and with P otherwise, and Agent 2 joins Q when learning that R is guilty and R otherwise: $\rho_1(P) = R_1$, $\rho_1(\bar{P}) = P_1$, $\rho_2(R) = Q_2$ and $\rho_2(\bar{R}) = R_2$.

- Consider Agent 1 receiving type P: the conditioned bpa, $m_{|P}$, has only one focal element $\{(P, \bar{R})\}$, $K_P = 1/\frac{1}{2}$ and $m_{|P}(\{(P, \bar{R})\}) = 1$. In short, Agent 1 knows that P is guilty and R is not. In the only possible configuration, $(P, \bar{R})$, ρ prescribes $\rho_1(P) = R_1$ for Agent 1 and $\rho_2(\bar{R}) = R_2$ for Agent 2. Then $CEU_{(1,P)}(\rho) = m_{|P}(\{(P, \bar{R})\}) \times u_1\big((R_1, R_2), (P, \bar{R})\big) = 1 \times 2 = 2$.
- Consider now Agent 1 receiving $\bar{P}$: his/her revised knowledge, $m_{|\bar{P}}$, has two focal elements, $\{(\bar{P}, R)\}$ and $\{(\bar{P}.\bar{R})\}$ (each with probability $\frac{1}{2}$, thus $K_{\bar{P}} = 1$). The strategy prescribes $\rho(\bar{P}) = P_1$ for Agent 1, who doesn't know whether Agent 2 learns R (and plays $\rho(R) = Q_2$) or $\bar{R}$ (and plays $\rho(\bar{R}) = R_2$). Hence $CEU_{(1,\bar{P})}(\rho) = \frac{1}{2} \times u_1\big((P_1, R_2), (\bar{P}, \bar{R})\big) + \frac{1}{2} \times u_1\big((P_1, Q_2), (\bar{P}, R)\big) = 3$.

Table 1. Example 1: Utility matrices for each configuration of the types

		$\theta_2 = \bar{\text{R}}$				$\theta_2 = \text{R}$		
		P_2	Q_2	R_2		P_2	Q_2	R_2
	P_1	$(0,0)$	$(0,3)$	$(0,3)$	P_1	$(0,0)$	$(0,0)$	$(0,0)$
$\theta_1 = \text{P}$	Q_1	$(3,0)$	$(2,2)$	$(3,3)$	Q_1	$(0,0)$	$(0,0)$	$(0,0)$
	R_1	$(3,0)$	$(3,3)$	$(2,2)$	R_1	$(0,0)$	$(0,0)$	$(0,0)$
		P_2	Q_2	R_2		P_2	Q_2	R_2
	P_1	$(2,2)$	$(3,0)$	$(3,3)$	P_1	$(2,2)$	$(3,3)$	$(3,0)$
$\theta_1 = \bar{\text{P}}$	Q_1	$(0,3)$	$(0,0)$	$(0,3)$	Q_1	$(3,3)$	$(2,2)$	$(3,0)$
	R_1	$(3,3)$	$(3,0)$	$(2,2)$	R_1	$(0,3)$	$(0,3)$	$(0,0)$

- Similarly, the bpa of Agent 2 receiving R, $m_{|\text{R}}$, has only one focal element, $\{(\bar{\text{P}},\text{R})\}$ (thus $K_\text{R} = 1/\frac{1}{2}$) in which ρ prescribes P_1 for Agent 1 and Q_2 for Agent 2. Then $CEU_{(2,\text{R})}(\rho) = 1 \times u_2((P_1,Q_2),(\bar{\text{P}},\text{R})) = 1 \times 3 = 3$.
- Finally, the bpa of Agent 2 receiving $\bar{\text{R}}$, $m_{|\bar{\text{R}}}$, has one focal element, $\{(\bar{\text{P}}.\bar{\text{R}}),(\text{P}.\bar{\text{R}})\}$ and $K_{\bar{\text{R}}} = 1/\frac{1}{2}$. Agent 2 does not know whether Agent 1 receives $\bar{\text{P}}$ or P. Since ρ prescribes Agent 1 to play P_1 in the first case, R_1 in the second one, and prescribes Agent 2 to play R_2 in both cases, $CEU_{(2,\bar{\text{R}})}(\rho) = 1 \times \min\left[u_2((P_1,R_2),(\bar{\text{P}},\bar{\text{R}})),u_2((R_1,R_2),(\text{P},\bar{\text{R}}))\right] = 1 \times \min(3,2) = 2$.

In this strategy, Agent 1 does not give the best possible response to Agent 2's strategy: when learning that P is guilty, he/she plays R_1 while knowing that in this case Agent 2 learns $\bar{\text{R}}$ and thus plays R_2. Let Agent 1 modify his/her strategy and play Q_1 when learning P – hence the strategy ρ':
$\rho'_1(\text{P}) = Q_1, \rho'_1(\bar{\text{P}}) = P_1, \rho'_2(\text{R}) = Q_2, \rho'_2(\bar{\text{R}}) = R_2$.

- $CEU_{(1,\text{P})}(\rho') = K_\text{P} \times u_1((Q_1,R_1),(\text{P},\bar{\text{R}})) = 1 \times 3 = 3$,
- $CEU_{(1,\bar{\text{P}})}(\rho') = K_{\bar{\text{P}}} \times u_1((P_1,R_2),(\bar{\text{P}},\bar{\text{R}})) + K_{\bar{\text{P}}} \times u_1((P_1,Q_2),(\bar{\text{P}},\text{R})) = 3$,
- $CEU_{(2,\text{R})}(\rho') = K_\text{R} \times u_2((P_1,R_2),(\bar{\text{P}},\text{R})) = 1 \times 3 = 3$,
- $CEU_{(2,\bar{\text{R}})}(\rho') = K_{\bar{\text{R}}} \times \min\left(u_2((P_1,R_2),(\bar{\text{P}},\bar{\text{R}})),u_2((Q_1,R_2),(\text{P},\bar{\text{R}}))\right) = 3$.

It can be checked in ρ' each player has his/her maximal possible utility ($\$3k$) – no player has an incentive to change: ρ' is a pure Nash equilibrium.

4   From Credal Games to Complete Games

One of the most prominent results about Bayesian games is Howson's and Rosenthal's theorem [17]: any 2-player Bayesian game can be transformed into a (complete information) polymatrix game equivalent to the original one. This result is important from the computational point of view since it provides 2-player Bayesian games with practical resolution tools: to solve a 2-player Bayesian games, it is enough to use this theorem and to solve the resulting polymatrix game by one of algorithms proposed for such games [3,32]. In the sequel, we generalize this theorem to credal games and extend it to any number of players.

4.1   The Direct Transform

A first idea is to define from a credal game G, an hypergraphical game $\tilde{G}$, the vertices (players) of which are pairs (i, θ_i) with action set A_i – to each pure strategy ρ of G corresponds a unique pure strategy $\tilde{\rho}$ of $\tilde{G}$ and conversely – we call $\tilde{\rho}$ the Selten transform of ρ:[1],[2]

Definition 14 (Selten transform of a pure strategy). *For any pure strategy ρ of G, the Selten transform of ρ is the vector $\tilde{\rho}$ defined by $\tilde{\rho}_{(i,\theta_i)} = \rho_i(\theta_i)$.*

The local games correspond to the focal elements of m. Roughly, (i, θ_i) plays in the local game corresponding to the focal element B if the type θ_i is plausible for B – technically, if there exists $\theta' \in B$ such that $\theta'_i = \theta_i$. In this local game, (i, θ_i) obtains a local utility $K_{|\theta_i} \cdot m(B) \cdot \min_{\theta' \in B, \theta'_i = \theta_i} u_i(\rho(\theta'), \theta')$.

Given a profile of actions $\tilde{\rho}$, and a player (i, θ_i), the hypergraphical game sums these local utilities over all the focal elements for which θ_i is plausible. Hence the global utility for (i, θ_i) is equal to the CEU of the joint ρ.

One may note that two pairs (i, θ_i) and (i, θ'_i) may play in the same local game – this happens when θ and θ' belong to the same focal set. In this case, the utility of (i, θ'_i) does not depend on the action played by (i, θ_i) and conversely.

For any focal element B of m, let $Players(B) := \{(i, \theta_i) \mid \theta \in B, i \in N\}$ – $Players(B)$ denotes the future players involved in the local game corresponding to B. Let $\tilde{E}$ be the multiset $\tilde{E} := [Players(B) \mid B \in S_m]$. The elements e of $\tilde{E}$ and the focal elements in S_m are in bijection and we denote B_e the focal element of m which leads to e. These notations allow us to propose a first, direct generalization to credal games of the Howson's and Rosenthal's transform:

Definition 15 (Direct transform of a credal game). *The direct transform of a credal game $G = \big(N, (A_i, \Theta_i, u_i)_{i \in N}, m\big)$ is the hypergraphical game $\tilde{G} = \big(\tilde{N}, \tilde{E}, (\tilde{A}_{(i,\theta_i)})_{(i,\theta_i) \in \tilde{N}}, (\tilde{u}^e_{(i,\theta_i)})_{e \in \tilde{E}, (i,\theta_i) \in e}\big)$ where:*

- $\tilde{N} = \{(i, \theta_i) \mid i \in N, \theta_i \in \Theta_i\}$,
- *For each $i \in N$, $\theta_i \in \Theta_i$, $\tilde{A}_{(i,\theta_i)} = A_i$,*
  $\tilde{A} = \prod_{i \in N, \theta_i \in \Theta_i} \tilde{A}_{(i,\theta_i)}$ *denotes the set of all the pure strategy profiles in $\tilde{G}$.*
- $\tilde{E} = [Players(B) \mid B \in S_m]$,
- *For each $e \in \tilde{E}$, $(i, \theta_i) \in e$ and $\tilde{\rho} \in \tilde{A}$,*
  $\tilde{u}^e_{(i,\theta_i)}(\tilde{\rho}_e) = K_{|\theta_i} \cdot m(B_e) \cdot \min_{\theta' \in B_e, \theta'_i = \theta_i} u_i\big(\rho(\theta'), \theta'\big).$

It is easy to show that the CEU value of a pure strategy ρ in G and the global utility of $\tilde{\rho}$ in $\tilde{G}$ are equal, whatever is the couple (i, θ_i) considered.

Proposition 1. [3] *Let G be a credal game and $\tilde{G}$ its direct transform. For any pure strategy ρ of G, it holds that $CEU_{(i,\theta_i)}(\rho) = \tilde{u}_{(i,\theta)}(\tilde{\rho})$.*

---

[1] Named after Selten, who proposed a similar definition for Bayesian games [16].

[2] We could use the notation ρ for both, but the pure strategy profiles of the credal game are vectors of functions $\rho_i : \Theta_i \mapsto A_i$ while the pure strategy profiles of $\tilde{G}$ are vectors in $\prod_{i \in N, \theta_i \in \Theta_i} A_i$. So, we keep the two notations $\tilde{\rho}$ and ρ.

[3] The proofs are omitted for the sake of brevity and can be found at [11].

Let us extend the Selten transform to mixed strategy profiles ρ of G: each $\tilde{\rho}_{(i,\theta_i)} = \rho_i(\theta_i)$ is then a probability distribution over A_i, and $\tilde{\rho}$ is then a vector of such distributions.

Corollary 1. *Let G be a credal game and $\tilde{G}$ its direct transform. For any mixed strategy profile ρ of G, it holds that $CEU_{(i,\theta_i)}(\rho) = \tilde{u}_{(i,\theta)}(\tilde{\rho})$.*

When m is a probability distribution and G is a 2-player game, we get at most $|\Theta|$ local games, each involving two players (i, θ_i) and (j, θ_j): $\tilde{G}$ is a polymatrix game, and Howson and Rosenthal's Theorem is recovered. More generally, we get:

Theorem 1 (Generalized Howson-Rosenthal Theorem). *For any credal game G, there exists an hypergraphical game $\tilde{G}$ such that ρ is a pure (resp. mixed) Nash equilibrium of G iff $\tilde{\rho}$ is a pure (resp. mixed) Nash equilibrium of $\tilde{G}$.*

Example 2. Let us define the direct transform of the credal game G corresponding to our running example. The set of players is: $\tilde{N} = \{(1,P), (1,\bar{P}), (2,R), (2,\bar{R})\}$. The set of actions are $\tilde{A}_{(i,\theta_i)} = \{P_i, Q_i, R_i\}$.

Because m has two focal elements $B_1 = \{(\bar{P}, R)\}$ and $B_2 = \{(P, \bar{R}), (\bar{P}, \bar{R})\}$ each with probability $\frac{1}{2}$, $\tilde{G}$ involves two local games. The set of players involved are respectively $e_1 = \{(1,\bar{P}), (2,R)\}$ and $e_2 = \{(1,\bar{P}), (1,P), (2,\bar{R})\}$. $\tilde{G}$'s hypergraph is drawn on Fig. 1.

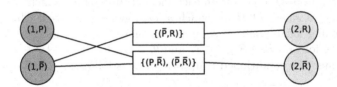

Fig. 1. G's direct transform. Gray circles denote vertices (players; one shade per agent), white boxes denote hyperedges (local games; linked to the players involved).

Player $(2,\bar{R})$ plays only in e_2, we have for instance:

$$\tilde{u}^{e_2}_{(2,\bar{R})}(R_1, P_1, R_2) = K_{\bar{R}} \cdot m(B_2) \times \min \left[u_2\big((R_1, R_2), (P, \bar{R})\big),\ u_2\big((P_1, R_2), (\bar{P}, \bar{R})\big) \right] = 2.$$

For player $(1,\bar{P})$, which plays in both local games, we have for instance:

$$\tilde{u}^{e_1}_{(1,\bar{P})}(P_1, P_2) = K_{\bar{P}} \cdot m(B_1) \times u_1\big((P_1, P_2), (\bar{P}, R)\big) = 0.5 \times 2 = 1$$

$$\tilde{u}^{e_2}_{(1,\bar{P})}(\_, P_1, Q_2) = K_{\bar{P}} \cdot m(B_2) \times u_1\big((P_1, Q_2), (\bar{P}, \bar{R})\big) = 0.5 \times 3 = 1.5.$$

The Selten transform of the Nash equilibrium ρ' described in the previous section is $\tilde{\rho}'((1,\bar{P})) = P_1$, $\tilde{\rho}'((1,P)) = Q_1$, $\tilde{\rho}'((2,\bar{R})) = R_1$, $\tilde{\rho}'((2,R)) = Q_2$. It is easy to check that: $\tilde{u}_{(1,\bar{P})}(\tilde{\rho}') = \tilde{u}^{e_1}_{(1,\bar{P})}\big((P_1, Q_2)\big) + \tilde{u}^{e_2}_{(1,\bar{P})}\big((Q_1, P_1, R_2)\big) = CEU_{(1,\bar{P})}(\rho')$. Notice that in the sum, one part of the utility of $(1,\bar{P})$ comes from the local game e_1 (i.e., from B_1) and the other part comes from e_2 (i.e., from B_2).

As to the complexity of the transform, let α (resp. β) be the maximum number of actions (resp. types) per player in G and k the degree of additivity of m. G contains n utility tables of size $(\alpha\beta)^n$ and the size of the description of m is bounded by $k \cdot n \cdot |S_m|$. So, $Size(G)$ is in $O\big(n(\alpha\beta)^n + kn \cdot |S_m|\big)$.

$\tilde{G}$ contains $|S_m|$ local games. Each of them involves at most kn players (i, θ_i) – the size of their SNF representation is thus at most $kn\alpha^{kn}$ – hence a spatial cost for the representation of $\tilde{G}$ in $O(|S_m| \cdot kn\alpha^{kn})$. Notice now that since m is k-additive, $|S_m| < \beta^{kn}$. So, $Size(\tilde{G})$ is bounded by $kn(\alpha\beta)^{kn}$. In short, we get:

Proposition 2. *The direct transform of a credal game G has a temporal complexity in $O\big(|S_m| \cdot kn^2\alpha^{kn}\beta\big)$, also bounded by $k^2 \cdot Size(G)^{k+1}$ and a spatial complexity in $O\big(|S_m| \cdot kn\alpha^{kn}\big)$, also bounded by $k \cdot Size(G)^k$.*

So, the degree of additivity of the bpa is the main factor of complexity. Hopefully, low degrees of additivity can be assumed – it has indeed been shown [15,19] that such low values (typically, $k \leq 3$) allow the description of many cases of interest. In such situations, the transform is quadratic or, at worst, cubic.

4.2 The Conditioned Transform

Now, when for each focal element B and each θ_i, only a few types are compatible for the other players, one shall use a more sophisticated transform. In the following, we propose to condition each focal element B for which θ_i is plausible – we thus get a *subset* of B for which a local game is created. This transform leads to smaller local games as soon as this subset involves less players than B.

Formally, for any $B \in S_m$, $i \in N$ and $\theta_i \in \Theta_i$, let $B_{|\theta_i} = \{\theta' \in B \mid \theta'_i = \theta_i\}$. We thus define the conditioned transform of G as follows:

Definition 16 (The conditioned transform of a credal game). *The conditioned transform of a credal game $\big(N, (A_i)_{i\in N}, (\Theta_i)_{i\in N}, (u_i)_{i\in N}, m\big)$ is the hypergraphical game $\tilde{G} = \big(\tilde{N}, \tilde{E}, (\tilde{A}_{(i,\theta_i)})_{(i,\theta_i)\in\tilde{N}}, (\tilde{u}^e_{(i,\theta_i)})_{e\in\tilde{E},(i,\theta_i)\in e}\big)$ where:*

- $\tilde{N} = \{(i, \theta_i) \mid i \in N, \theta_i \in \Theta_i\}$.
- *For each $i \in N, \theta_i \in \Theta_i$, $\tilde{A}_{(i,\theta_i)} = A_i$.*
- $\tilde{A} = \prod_{i\in N, \theta_i\in\Theta_i} \tilde{A}_{(i,\theta_i)}$ *denotes the set of all the pure strategy profiles in $\tilde{G}$.*
- $\tilde{E} = [Players(B_{|\theta_i}) \mid B \in S_m, i \in N, \theta_i \in \Theta_i]$.
- *For each $e \in \tilde{E}$, $(i, \theta_i) \in e$, $\tilde{\rho}_e \in \tilde{A}_e$, $\tilde{u}^e_{(i,\theta_i)}(\tilde{\rho}_e) = m_{|\theta_i}(B_e) \cdot \min_{\theta'\in B_e} u_i(\rho_e(\theta), \theta)$.*

The hypergraph of the conditioned transform our running example is drawn on Fig. 2. And finally, we can show that:

Proposition 3. *Let G be a credal game and $\tilde{G}$ its conditioned transform. For any pure or mixed strategy ρ of G, it holds that (i) $CEU_{(i,\theta_i)}(\rho) = \tilde{u}_{(i,\theta)}(\tilde{\rho})$ and (ii) ρ is a Nash equilibrium of G iff $\tilde{\rho}$ is a Nash equilibrium of $\tilde{G}$.*

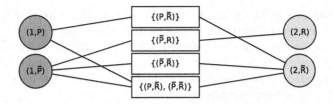

Fig. 2. G's conditioned transform. Gray circles are vertices (players; one color per agent), white boxes are hyperedges (local games; linked to the involved players).

Proposition 4. *The conditioned transform of a credal game G has a temporal complexity in $O\big(|\mathcal{S}_m| \cdot kn^2\alpha^{kn}\beta\big)$ which is bounded by $O\big(k^2 \cdot Size(G)^{k+1}\big)$ and a spatial complexity in $O\big(|\bigcup \mathcal{S}_{m_{|\theta_i}}| \cdot kn\alpha^{kn}\big)$ which is bounded by $O\big(k \cdot Size(G)^k\big)$.*

So, the conditioned transform has the same worst case spatial complexity than the direct one. In practice, the size of the transform depends on the structure of the mass function. Typically, if a focal element B involves only one θ_i for Agent i, both transforms contain the same local game $Players(B)$ (as $B = B_{|\theta_i}$), but the conditioned one may produce many more local games. If on the contrary many types are compatible with a focal B for any agent, the local game produced by the direct transform is needlessly large. For instance, from a 2-player credal game where both agents have types $a, b, \ldots$ and considering the focal element $\{(a,a), (b,b), \ldots\}$, the conditioned transform produces several 2-player games while the direct one has one single local game linked to *all* vertices (i, θ_i).

5   Conclusion

This article provides two main contributions. On the one hand, we define a model for games of incomplete information based of belief functions. On the other hand, we introduce two transformations that make it possible to build an hypergraphical game (of complete information) equivalent to the initial credal game, generalizing Howson–Rosenthal's theorem. As a result, the algorithmic tools developed for hypergraphical games [3,32] can be used to solve credal games.

This work opens several research directions. First, we shall let the model use other decision rules, e.g. Jaffray's [6,18], which generalize Hurwicz's approach to belief functions, or Gilboa and Schmeider's multiple prior expected utility [14, 29][4]. Beyond belief functions, we aim at extending the model to other Choquet capacities and encompass other decision principles, based e.g. on rank-dependent utility [27], probability intervals [2] or on some neighborhood models such as the PPM model [20]. Finally, we shall also study how belief function based extensions

---

[4] Notice that in the latter approach, the belief function is understood as the lower bound of an imprecise probability – under this interpretation, the conditioning at work must rather be Fagin-Halpern's [10].

of mixed strategies [8,23] extend to credal games. In this extended framework, the power of representation belief functions will be used not only to capture the uncertainty about the game, but also as a way to describe the agents' knowledge about the others' strategies. Finally, we like to formalize those results with the COQ proof assistant in order to build, with other in-progress results, a modular formal library on incomplete games and decision theory.

References

1. Augustin, T., Schollmeyer, G.: Comment: on focusing, soft and strong revision of choquet capacities and their role in statistics. Stat. Sci. **36**(2), 205–209 (2021)
2. Campos, L.M.D., Huete, J.F., Moral, S.: Probability intervals: a tool for uncertain reasoning. Int. J. Uncertain. Fuzziness Knowl. Based Syst. **2**(2), 167–196 (1994)
3. Chapman, A., Farinelli, A., de Cote, E.M., Rogers, A., Jennings, N.: A distributed algorithm for optimising over pure strategy nash equilibria. In: Proceedings AAAI (2010)
4. Choquet, G.: Theory of capacities. Ann. de l'institut Four. **5**, 131–295 (1954)
5. Dempster, A.P.: Upper and lower probabilities induced by a multivalued mapping. Ann. Math. Stat. **38**, 325–339 (1967)
6. Denoeux, T., Shenoy, P.P.: An interval-valued utility theory for decision making with dempster-shafer belief functions. Int. J. Approx. Reason. **124**, 194–216 (2020)
7. Dubois, D., Denoeux, T.: Conditioning in dempster-shafer theory: prediction vs. revision. In: Proceedings BELIEF, vol. 164, pp. 385–392. Springer, Heidelberg (2012). https://doi.org/10.1007/978-3-642-29461-7_45
8. Eichberger, J., Kelsey, D.: Non-Additive Beliefs and Game Theory. Tilburg University, Center for Economic Research, Technical report (1994)
9. Ellsberg, D.: Risk, ambiguity, and the savage axioms. Q. J. Econ. **75**, 643–669 (1961)
10. Fagin, R., Halpern, J.Y.: A new approach to updating beliefs. In: Proceedings UAI, pp. 347–374 (1990)
11. Fargier, H., Martin-Dorel, E., Pomeret-Coquot, P.: Games of Incomplete Information: a Framework Based on Belief Functions – version with proofs. https://www.irit.fr/~Erik.Martin-Dorel/ecrits/2021_credal-games_ecsqaru_extended.pdf or in HAL
12. Ghirardato, P., Le Breton, M.: Choquet rationality. J. Econ. Theory **90**(2), 277–285 (2000)
13. Gilboa, I.: Expected utility with purely subjective non-additive probabilities. J. Math. Econ. **16**(1), 65–88 (1987)
14. Gilboa, I., Schmeidler, D.: Maxmin expected utility with non-unique prior. J. Math. Econ. **18**(2), 141–153 (1989)
15. Grabisch, M.: Upper approximation of non-additive measures by k-additive measures-the case of belief functions. In: ISIPTA, pp. 158–164 (1999)
16. Harsanyi, J.C.: Games with incomplete information played by "bayesian" players, I-III part I. The basic model. Manag. Sci. **14**(3), 159–182 (1967)
17. Howson, J.T., Jr., Rosenthal, R.W.: Bayesian equilibria of finite two-person games with incomplete information. Manag. Sci. **21**(3), 313–315 (1974)
18. Jaffray, J.Y.: Linear utility theory for belief functions. Oper. Res. Lett. **8**(2), 107–112 (1989)

19. Miranda, P., Grabisch, M., Gil, P.: Dominance of capacities by k-additive belief functions. Eur. J. Oper. Res. **175**(2), 912–930 (2006)
20. Montes, I., Miranda, E., Destercke, S.: Unifying neighbourhood and distortion models: Part II - new models and synthesis. Int. J. Gen. Syst. **49**(6), 636–674 (2020)
21. Morgenstern, O., Von Neumann, J.: Theory of Games and Economic Behavior. Princeton University Press (1953)
22. Mukerji, S.: Understanding the nonadditive probability decision model. Econ. Theory **9**(1), 23–46 (1997)
23. Mukerji, S., Shin, H.S.: Equilibrium departures from common knowledge in games with non-additive expected utility. Adv. Theor. Econ. **2**(1), 1011 (2002)
24. Myerson, R.B.: Game Theory. Harvard University Press, Cambridge (2013)
25. Nash, J.: Non-cooperative games. Ann. Math., 286–295 (1951)
26. Papadimitriou, C.H., Roughgarden, T.: Computing correlated equilibria in multiplayer games. J. ACM **55**(3), 1–29 (2008)
27. Quiggin, J.: A Theory of Anticipated Utility. J. Econ. Behav. Organ. **3**(4), 323–343 (1982)
28. Savage, L.J.: The Foundations of Statistics. Wiley, Hoboken (1954)
29. Schmeidler, D.: Integral representation without additivity. Proc. Am. Math. Soc. **97**(2), 255–261 (1986)
30. Shafer, G.: A Mathematical Theory of Evidence. Princeton University Press, Princeton (1976)
31. Smets, P., Kennes, R.: The transferable belief model. Artif. Intell. **66**(2), 191–234 (1994)
32. Wahbi, M., Brown, K.N.: A distributed asynchronous solver for nash equilibria in hypergraphical games. Front. Artif. Intell. Appl. **285**, 1291–1299 (2016)
33. Yanovskaya, E.: Equilibrium points in polymatrix games. Lithuanian Math. J. **8**, 381–384 (1968)

Uncertainty-Aware Resampling Method for Imbalanced Classification Using Evidence Theory

Fares Grina[1,2]([✉]), Zied Elouedi[1], and Eric Lefèvre[2]

[1] Institut Supérieur de Gestion de Tunis, LARODEC,
Université de Tunis, Tunis, Tunisia
fares.grina@isg.u-tunis.tn, zied.elouedi@gmx.fr
[2] Univ. Artois, UR 3926, Laboratoire de Génie Informatique et d'Automatique de
l'Artois (LGI2A), 62400 Béthune, France
eric.lefevre@univ-artois.fr

Abstract. Class imbalance is a common issue in many real world classification problems. It refers to situations where the number of observations in the training dataset significantly differs for each class. Ignoring this issue will make it more challenging for classifiers to properly learn data characteristics, which results in poor performance. Many strategies have been proposed to deal with this issue. The most common one is tackling the imbalance at the preprocessing level, by re-sampling the training set. However, imbalanced classification can be affected by other data factors, such as uncertainty, i.e., ambiguous samples and noise. In this paper, we propose an uncertainty-aware hybrid re-sampling technique based on the theory of evidence to tackle imbalanced binary datasets in the presence of aleatoric uncertainty. A soft evidential structure is assigned to each object in the training set, which is later used to clean the dataset out of overlapping and noisy majority samples, and then selectively generate synthetic minority objects using a modified SMOTE algorithm. Experimental results on benchmark imbalanced datasets have shown significant improvement over popular re-sampling techniques.

Keywords: Resampling · Imbalanced datasets · Evidence theory · Data uncertainty

1 Introduction

Imbalanced classification is an active research topic in machine learning and data mining. It is a scenario in which class sizes are not equal making the class distribution imbalanced. Data imbalance exist in many real-life domains such as fraudulent credit card detection [25], medical diagnosis [5], drug discovery [18], etc. For instance, in imbalanced binary datasets, the class with the highest number of instances is referred to as the *majority* class, while the *minority* class is defined as the one with the fewest examples. In most cases, the minority

© Springer Nature Switzerland AG 2021
J. Vejnarová and N. Wilson (Eds.): ECSQARU 2021, LNAI 12897, pp. 342–353, 2021.
https://doi.org/10.1007/978-3-030-86772-0_25

class is more relevant than the majority one [7]. As an example, failing to detect intrusions in a company's network may result in huge financial losses. A variety of variables may cause the class imbalance, such as the domain's nature (e.g. rare disease) or data collection factors (e.g. storage). Additionally, most classifier algorithms (such as decision trees, k-nearest neighbors, neural networks, etc.) were designed with the presumption that training datasets have an even distribution, which reduces greatly their efficiency [13].

Many methods have been proposed over the years to cope with imbalanced datasets. Data resampling is one of the most efficient strategies for dealing with class imbalance [10]. This approach aims at fixing the uneven class distribution at the preprocessing level by re-balancing the training dataset. Being algorithm-independent, resampling is versatile and could be applied with any selected classifier.

In addition, recent findings show that class imbalance is not an issue in and of itself, but rather gets amplified by other data difficulties. Data uncertainty (can also be referred to as aleatoric uncertainty) refers to the imperfections present in the data. This type of uncertainty can include class overlapping and noise, which were proven to worsen the class imbalance issue [13].

To improve performance on imbalanced and uncertain binary datasets, we suggest an Uncertainty-Aware Hybrid reSampling (UAHS) method based on Evidence Theory, which was recently used for imbalanced classification [11,12]. After creating soft evidential labels for each object, our method efficiently selects the majority instances to remove in an undersampling phase first, and the minority objects to focus on in the oversampling procedure lastly. The considered evidential label is appropriate for our goal, since it includes membership values towards single classes, in addition to a belief mass assigned to meta-classes (ambiguous region). This versatility allows us to create precise rules for the process of selecting undesirable samples in the undersampling phase, and intelligently select minority instances to generate new synthetic objects. It is important to note that our proposal is a hybrid resampling method, meaning that it performs both undersampling and oversampling, unlike [11] and [12] which are respectively pure oversampling and undersampling approaches.

The remainder of this paper will be divided as follows. First, related work for resampling methods is presented in Sect. 2. Evidence Theory is recalled in Sect. 3. Section 4 details each step of our idea. Experimental evaluation is discussed in Sect. 5. Our paper ends with a conclusion and an outlook on future work in Sect. 6.

2   Related Work

Data resampling is one of the most common approaches for dealing with imbalanced classification [13]. In fact, data resampling deals with class imbalance at the preprocessing level by changing the class distribution of the training set. As a result, it alleviates the effects of distribution skewness of the learning process. These methods can be further categorized into three groups, namely:

- **Oversampling**: These techniques introduce new minority synthetic samples to re-balance the dataset. The most straightforward method is random over-sampling (ROS), which consists of selecting minority observations in the original data set and simply replicating them. Although it appears to be tech-nically effective since the class balance is adjusted, it can lead to overfitting [16]. To cope with overfitting, the Synthetic Minority Oversampling Technique (SMOTE) was suggested in [6]. Unlike ROS, SMOTE generates new synthetic samples by interpolating among several minority objects that are close to each other. However, many studies [9,30] have shown SMOTE's drawbacks which involve potential amplification of noise, overlap already present in the data. SMOTE's improvement include Borderline-SMOTE [14], which identi-fies borderline minority class examples to generate new samples. Clustering-based oversampling techniques were also proposed [9,23] to smartly select the regions where to generate new points.
- **Undersampling**: These approaches create a subset of the original dataset by removing some majority class instances. Like random oversampling, the naive undersampling technique is to randomly remove majority objects, which may potentially remove meaningful information from the dataset. Therefore, other techniques have been suggested to smartly remove unwanted majority class instances. Commonly, traditional filtering techniques have been used to perform undersampling. For example, Neighborhood Cleaning Rule (NCL) discards majority class instances using the Edited Nearest Neighbors (ENN) introduced in [37]. Similarly, Tomek Links (TL) [15] is occasionally used as an undersampling method. Clustering has also been used for undersampling in a number of occasions [26,34], to optimize the selection process of majority instances to eliminate.
- **Hybrid**: This strategy combines both oversampling and undersampling in order to re-balance the dataset. Typically, SMOTE is paired with an under-sampling procedure to fix its drawbacks. For instance, SMOTE-ENN and SMOTE-TL were suggested in [3] to combine SMOTE with ENN and TL respectively. SMOTE-RSB* [29] is a method which combines SMOTE for oversampling with the Rough Set Theory [27] as a cleaning technique. In SMOTE-IPF [17], SMOTE is firstly executed, and then the Iterative-Partitioning Filter (IPF) [17] is performed to remove noisy original examples, and those introduced by SMOTE. Authors in [20] suggested a combination of a SMOTE-like algorithm with a cleaning procedure to reduce the effects of overlapping. Similarly, the class overlap issue is touched upon in [35] com-bining a soft clustering method with Borderline-SMOTE.

3   Theory of Evidence

The theory of evidence [8,31,33], also referred to as Dempster-Shafer theory (DST) or belief function theory, is a flexible and well-founded framework for the representation and combination of uncertain knowledge. The frame of discern-ment defines a finite set of M exclusive possible events, e.g., possible labels for an object to classify, and is denoted as follows:

$$\Omega = \{\omega_1, \omega_2, ..., \omega_M\} \tag{1}$$

A basic belief assignment (*bba*) denotes the amount of belief stated by a source of evidence, committed to 2^Ω, i.e., all subsets of the frame including the whole frame itself. Precisely, a *bba* is represented by a mapping function $m : 2^\Omega \to [0, 1]$ such that:

$$\sum_{A \in 2^\Omega} m(A) = 1 \tag{2}$$

$$m(\emptyset) = 0 \tag{3}$$

Each mass $m(A)$ quantifies the amount of belief allocated to an event A of Ω. A *bba* is unnormalized when $m(\emptyset) > 0$, and must be normalized under a closed-world assumption [32]. A focal element is a subset $A \subseteq \Omega$ where $m(A) \neq 0$.

The *Plausibility* function is another representation of knowledge defined by *Shafer* [31] as follows:

$$Pl(A) = \sum_{B \cap A \neq \emptyset} m(B), \quad \forall \ A \in 2^\Omega \tag{4}$$

$Pl(A)$ represents the total possible support for A and its subsets.

4 Uncertainty-Aware Hybrid Re-Sampling Method (UAHS)

To tackle binary imbalanced datasets, we propose an Uncertainty-Aware Hybrid re-sampling method (UAHS). Observations are firstly assigned soft evidential labels (*bbas*) using the credal classification rule (CCR) introduced in [22].

CCR uses the centers of each class and meta-class as pieces of evidence for each example's membership, instead of using nearest neighbors as it has been employed in [11]. Unlike [11], our case deals with the soft labeling of both majority and minority classes. Thus, an evidential nearest neighbor-based approach might produce biased memberships towards the majority class, since the latter usually have a much higher density than the minority one.

The computed *bba* is later used for cleaning unwanted majority objects and selectively generating synthetic minority instances.

Each step is detailed in the following subsections.

4.1 Creating Soft Labels

UAHS proceeds by determining the centers of each class and meta-class (the overlapping region), then creating a *bba* based on the distance between the majority sample and each class center.

The class centers are simply computed by the mean value of the training set in the corresponding class. For the meta-class U, representing the overlapping region, the center is defined by the barycenter of the involved class centers as follows:

$$C_U = \frac{1}{|U|} \sum_{\omega_i \in U} C_i \qquad (5)$$

where ω_i are the classes involved in U, C_i is the corresponding center and U represents the meta-class.

Once the centers are created, the evidential soft label of each example is represented by a *bba* over the frame of discernment $\Omega = \{\omega_0, \omega_1, \omega_2\}$ where ω_1 and ω_2 represent respectively the majority and the minority class. The proposition ω_0 is included in the frame of discernment explicitly to represent the outlier class.

Let x_s be a sample belonging to the training set. Each class center represents a piece of evidence to the evidential membership of the sample. The mass values in regard to the class memberships of x_s should depend on $d(x_s, C)$, i.e., the distance between x_s and the respective class center. The greater the distance, the lower the mass value. Consequently, the closer x_s is to a specific class center, the more likely it belongs to the corresponding class. Hence, the initial unnormalized masses should be represented by decreasing distance based functions. We use the Mahalanobis distance [24], in this work, as recommended by [22] in order to deal with anisotropic datasets.

The unnormalized masses are calculated accordingly:

$$\hat{m}(\{\omega_i\}) = e^{-d(x_s, C_i)}, \quad i \in \{1, 2\} \qquad (6)$$

$$\hat{m}(U) = e^{-\gamma \, \lambda \, d(x_s, C_U)}, \quad U = \{\omega_1, \omega_2\} \qquad (7)$$

$$\hat{m}(\{\omega_0\}) = e^t \qquad (8)$$

where $\lambda = \beta \, 2^\alpha$. A value of $\alpha = 1$ is fixed as recommended to obtain good results on average, and β is a parameter such that $0 < \beta < 1$. It is used to tune the number of objects committed to the overlapping region. The value of γ is equal to the ratio between the maximum distance of x_s to the centers in U and the minimum distance. It is used to measure the degree of distinguishability among the majority and minority classes. The smaller γ indicates a poor distinguishability degree between the classes of U for x_s. The outlier class ω_0 is taken into account in order to deal with objects far from both classes, and its mass value is calculated according to an outlier threshold t.

As performed in [22], the unnormalized belief masses are finally normalized as follows:

$$m(A) = \frac{\hat{m}(A)}{\sum_{B \subseteq \Omega} \hat{m}(B)} \qquad (9)$$

As a result, a *bba* is created to formally represent each object's soft label.

4.2 Cleaning the Majority Class

As a result of bba creation, each majority object will have masses in 4 focal elements namely: $m(\{\omega_1\})$ for the majority class, $m(\{\omega_2\})$ for the minority class,

$m(U)$ for the overlapping region U, and $m(\{\omega_0\})$ for the outlier class. These masses are used to remove problematic samples from the majority class. There are different types of unwanted samples which could be removed namely:

– **Overlapping:** Ambiguous samples are usually located in regions where there is strong overlap between classes as seen in Fig. 1a. This situation could correspond to what is called "conflict" in Evidence Theory. In our framework, this type of examples will have a high mass value in $m(U)$. Thus, majority instances whose *bba* has the maximum mass committed to $m(U)$ are considered as part of an overlapping region, and are automatically discarded. To avoid excessive elimination and allow tuning, it is also possible to tune the parameter β. The higher value of β will result in fewer objects committed to the overlapping region. As for majority instances whose highest mass is not committed to $m(U)$ (i.e. not in overlapping regions), the observation is necessarily committed to one of the singletons in Ω ($\{\omega_1\}$, $\{\omega_2\}$, or $\{\omega_0\}$). In this situation, we make use of the *plausibility* function defined in Eq. (4) to make a decision of acceptance or rejection. Each majority instance x_s is affected to the class with the maximum plausibility $Pl_{max} = max_{\omega \in \Omega} Pl(\{\omega\})$.

– **Label noise:** Normally, majority observations should have the maximum plausibility committed to $m(\{\omega_1\})$ which measures the membership value towards the majority class. By contrast, having Pl_{max} committed to $m(\{\omega_2\})$ signify that they are located in a minority location, as illustrated in Fig. 1c. Consequently, these objects are eliminated from the dataset.

– **Outlier:** The final scenario occurs when the sample in question is located in a region far from both classes, as shown in Fig. 1b. In our framework, this is characterized by the state of ignorance and could be discarded in the undersampling procedure. Hence, majority objects whose maximum plausibility Pl_{max} committed to $m(\{\omega_0\})$ are considered as outliers and removed from the dataset.

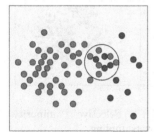 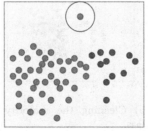 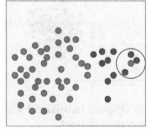

(a) Ambiguous samples in an overlapping area.

(b) An outlier far from both classes.

(c) A sample that could be characterized as label noise.

Fig. 1. Illustrations describing the different data difficulty factors that could worsen class imbalance. Green and red colors respectively represent the majority class and the minority one. (Color figure online)

4.3   Applying Selective Minority Oversampling

Once the cleaning procedure (undersampling) is performed, we execute the oversampling phase. The created *bbas* at the first step are further exploited in this stage, to intelligently create new synthetic minority samples.

Similarly to the cleaning step, the minority objects are categorized into three possible difficulties: overlapping, label noise, or outlier. The object is considered as "safe" if it does not belong to any of the three types. Thus, it does not need to participate in the oversampling phase. The same goes for both label noise and outlier, since using these types to create synthetic data could result in overgeneralization, which is a major drawback for oversampling [14]. Although, samples belonging to overlapping signify that they are located at the borders of the minority class. Hence, those are the samples that we are most uncertain about, and should focus on in the oversampling phase. Much like other popular oversampling methods such as BorderlineSMOTE [14], our goal is to emphasize the borders of the minority class in order to further improve its visibility.

More formally, let P denote the set of minority examples whose highest mass is committed to $m(U)$ (the set of ambiguous minority objects). We firstly compute the k minority nearest neighbors for each object in P. In this step, we generate $|P| * s$ synthetic minority points, where s is a value between 1 and k. In other words, for each minority instance in P, we randomly select s samples from its k minority nearest neighbors. Finally, s new synthetic points are generated anywhere on the lines joining the samples in P and its s randomly selected neighbors:

$$\overrightarrow{new} = \overrightarrow{a} + w * (\overrightarrow{b} - \overrightarrow{a}) \tag{10}$$

where $\overrightarrow{a}$ is the sample in P, $\overrightarrow{b}$ is a selected minority neighbor, and w represents a random value between 0 and 1. This procedure is repeated for each sample in P, similarly to the SMOTE algorithm (more details in [6]).

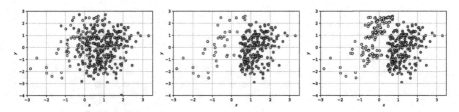

(a) Original imbalanced and uncertain dataset.

(b) Cleaning the majority class.

(c) Selective minority oversampling.

Fig. 2. An imbalanced binary example showing the behavior of our proposed algorithm at each step.

Furthermore, we tested our resampling method on a two-dimensional imbalanced dataset in order to showcase the behavior of the algorithm at each step (see Fig. 2).

5   Experimental Study

In this section, we will describe firstly the setup of the conducted experiments in Subsect. 5.1. Lastly, we will present the results and discuss them in Subsect. 5.2.

5.1   Setup

Datasets. For the purpose of this evaluation, we selected binary imbalanced datasets from the keel repository [1]. The datasets are further detailed in Table 1. The imbalance ratio was calculated as $IR = \frac{\#majority}{\#minority}$. The variations of the different parameters (IR, features, and size) allowed for experimenting in different real world settings.

Table 1. Description of the imbalanced datasets selected from the KEEL repository.

Datasets	Imbalance ratios (IR)	Features	Samples
wisconsin	1.860	9.000	683.000
glass0	2.060	9.000	214.000
vehicle3	2.990	18.000	846.000
ecoli1	3.360	7.000	336.000
yeast3	8.100	8.000	1484.000
page-blocks0	8.790	10.000	5472.000
ecoli-0-6-7 vs 3-5	9.090	7.000	222.000
yeast-0-3-5-9 vs 7-8	9.120	8.000	506.000
ecoli-0-2-6-7 vs 3-5	9.180	7.000	224.000
ecoli-0-1-4-7 vs 2-3-5-6	10.590	7.000	336.000
glass4	15.460	9.000	214.000
yeast-2 vs 8	23.100	8.000	482.000
yeast5	32.730	8.000	1484.000
kr-vs-k-zero vs eight	53.070	6.000	1460.000
abalone-20 vs 8-9-10	72.690	8.000	1916.000

Baseline Classifier. As baseline, we use the decision tree classifier, more specifically CART [4]. The implementation provided in the scikit-learn machine learning python library [28] was used, with the default parameters.

Metrics and Evaluation Strategy. To appropriately assess the methods in imbalanced scenarios, we use the G-Mean (GM) [2]. The GM is a popular measure for evaluating classifiers in imbalanced settings. It is calculated as the geometric mean of sensitivity and specificity:

$$\text{G-Mean} = \sqrt{sensitivity \times specificity} \qquad (11)$$

In order to ensure the fairness of the observed results, we adopt a 10-fold strat-ified cross validation to eliminate inconsistencies. The dataset is split into 10 parts taking into account the class distribution, 90% of which is the training set, the rest is the test set, and the average of G-mean is taken as the final result. It is worth noting that at each fold, resampling was performed only on the training set.

To better evaluate the significance of the results, statistical analysis was run using the Wilcoxon's signed rank tests [36] for the significance level of $\alpha = 0.05$.

Reference Methods and Parameters. We compared our proposed method (UAHS) against 4 well known re-sampling methods, in addition to Baseline (BL). The compared methods are SMOTE [6], SMOTE-IPF [30], SMOTE-ENN [3], and SMOTE-TL [3]. The SMOTE-IPF implementation in Smote-variants [19] was used. For the rest of the methods, the implementations provided by the python toolbox imbalanced-learn [21] were applied.

The following parameters were considered for our proposed method UAHS: α was set to 1 as recommended in [22], the tuning parameter t for $m(\{\omega_0\})$ was fixed to 2 to obtain good results in average, and we tested three different values for β in $\{0.3, 0.5, 0.7\}$ and selected the most performing one for each dataset, since the amount of class overlap differs in each case. For the other reference methods, we used the recommended parameters in their respective original papers.

5.2   Results Discussion

Results on 15 binary imbalanced datasets are shown in Table 2. The best G-Mean value is marked in bold. Our proposed method UAHS achieved the top performances across 10 out of 15 datasets. It showed clear improvement over the compared resampling methods and baseline across complex datasets, espe-cially with high imbalance degree and class overlapping. Furthermore, UAHS performed significantly better in cases where there is a high number of bor-derline instance. This confirms that our proposal succeeded at emphasizing on the visibility of the minority class, and improving its borders by cleaning the uncertain samples present in the overlapping and noisy regions of the majority class.

The results for Wilcoxon's pairwise test are shown in Table 3. $R+$ represents the sum of ranks in favor of UAHS, $R-$, the sum of ranks in favor of the reference methods, and exact p-values are calculated for each comparison. All comparisons can be considered as statistically significant under a level of 5% since all p-values are lower than the threshold 0.05. This reveals statistically significant improvements by our method against SMOTE, SMOTE-IPF, SMOTE-ENN, SMOTE-TL, and baseline.

Table 2. G-Mean results for KEEL datasets using CART.

Datasets	BL	SMOTE	SMOTE-IPF	SMOTE-ENN	SMOTE-TL	UAHS
wisconsin	0.934	0.928	0.924	0.950	0.932	**0.964**
glass0	0.737	**0.789**	0.772	0.763	0.782	0.786
vehicle3	0.689	0.660	0.682	**0.727**	0.679	0.673
ecoli1	0.816	0.849	0.856	0.871	0.836	**0.883**
yeast3	0.791	0.834	0.854	0.878	0.849	**0.921**
page-blocks0	0.904	0.928	0.920	0.930	0.923	**0.958**
ecoli-0-6-7 vs 3-5	0.764	0.721	0.769	0.772	0.782	**0.790**
yeast-0-3-5-9 vs 7-8	0.532	0.620	0.606	**0.677**	0.582	0.613
ecoli-0-2-6-7 vs 3-5	0.762	**0.783**	0.781	0.751	0.780	0.761
ecoli-0-1-4-7 vs 2-3-5-6	0.735	0.797	**0.878**	0.857	0.861	0.835
glass4	0.735	0.637	0.706	0.658	0.706	**0.838**
yeast-2 vs 8	0.547	0.666	0.664	0.722	0.734	**0.737**
yeast5	0.840	0.830	0.812	0.912	0.855	**0.932**
kr-vs-k-zero vs eight	0.976	**1.000**	**1.000**	0.999	**1.000**	**1.000**
abalone-20 vs 8-9-10	0.477	0.695	0.602	0.679	0.587	**0.743**

Table 3. Wilcoxon's signed ranks test results comparing the G-Mean scores for CART.

Comparisons	$R+$	$R-$	p-value
UAHS vs BL	117.0	3.0	0.000153
UAHS vs SMOTE	98.0	22.0	0.002364
UAHS vs SMOTE-IPF	95.0	25.0	0.004187
UAHS vs SMOTE-ENN	94.0	26.0	0.027679
UAHS vs SMOTE-TL	83.5	36.5	0.004377

6   Conclusion

Solutions for imbalanced datasets are increasingly being applied to critical real world domains. In order to deal with such scenarios, the proposed methods should also handle the uncertainty in the data. In this work, we propose an Uncertainty-Aware Hybrid resampling which combines undersampling and oversampling phases to efficiently re-balance binary datasets. We use an evidential structure to represent soft labels for each sample in the dataset. These representations are later used to remove majority samples which are ambiguous and noisy, and to select minority observations at the borders to generate new minority points.

For future work, we plan to further optimize our method using heuristic methods in order to approximate the amount of instances which should be cleaned, and the number of instances to generate.

References

1. Alcala-Fdez, J., et al.: Keel data-mining software tool: data set repository, integration of algorithms and experimental analysis framework. J. Multiple-Valued Logic Soft Comput. **17**, 255–287 (2010)
2. Barandela, R., Valdovinos, R.M., Sánchez, J.S.: New applications of ensembles of classifiers. Pattern Anal. Appl. **6**(3), 245–256 (2003)
3. Batista, G., Prati, R., Monard, M.C.: A study of the behavior of several methods for balancing machine learning training data. SIGKDD Explor. **6**, 20–29 (2004)
4. Breiman, L., Friedman, J., Stone, C.J., Olshen, R.A.: Classification and Regression Trees. CRC Press, Boca Raton (1984)
5. Bridge, J., et al.: Introducing the gev activation function for highly unbalanced data to develop covid-19 diagnostic models. IEEE J. Biomed. Health Inf. **24**(10), 2776–2786 (2020)
6. Chawla, N.V., Bowyer, K.W., Hall, L.O., Kegelmeyer, W.P.: Smote: synthetic minority over-sampling technique. J. Artif. Intell. Res. **16**, 321–357 (2002)
7. Chawla, N.V., Japkowicz, N., Drive, P.: Editorial: special issue on learning from imbalanced data sets. ACM SIGKDD Explor. Newsl. **6**(1), 1–6 (2004)
8. Dempster, A.P.: A generalization of bayesian inference. J. Roy. Stat. Soc. Ser. B (Methodol.) **30**(2), 205–232 (1968)
9. Douzas, G., Bacao, F., Last, F.: Improving imbalanced learning through a heuristic oversampling method based on k-means and SMOTE. Inf. Sci. **465**, 1–20 (2018)
10. Feng, Y., Zhou, M., Tong, X.: Imbalanced classification: an objective-oriented review. arXiv preprint arXiv:2002.04592 (2020)
11. Grina, F., Elouedi, Z., Lefevre, E.: A preprocessing approach for class-imbalanced data using SMOTE and belief function theory. In: Analide, C., Novais, P., Camacho, D., Yin, H. (eds.) IDEAL 2020. LNCS, vol. 12490, pp. 3–11. Springer, Cham (2020). https://doi.org/10.1007/978-3-030-62365-4_1
12. Grina, F., Elouedi, Z., Lefevre, E.: Evidential undersampling approach for imbalanced datasets with class-overlapping and noise. In: The 18th International Conference on Modeling Decisions for Artificial Intelligence. Springer, Heidelberg (2021)
13. Haixiang, G., Yijing, L., Shang, J., Mingyun, G., Yuanyue, H., Bing, G.: Learning from class-imbalanced data: review of methods and applications. Expert Syst. Appl. **73**, 220–239 (2017)
14. Han, H., Wang, W.-Y., Mao, B.-H.: Borderline-SMOTE: a new over-sampling method in imbalanced data sets learning. In: Huang, D.-S., Zhang, X.-P., Huang, G.-B. (eds.) ICIC 2005. LNCS, vol. 3644, pp. 878–887. Springer, Heidelberg (2005). https://doi.org/10.1007/11538059_91
15. Ivan, T.: Two modifications of CNN. IEEE Trans. Syst. Man Commun. SMC **6**, 769–772 (1976)
16. Japkowicz, N.: Class imbalances: are we focusing on the right issue. In: Workshop on Learning from Imbalanced Data Sets II, vol. 1723, p. 63 (2003)
17. Khoshgoftaar, T.M., Rebours, P.: Improving software quality prediction by noise filtering techniques. J. Comput. Sci. Technol. **22**(3), 387–396 (2007)
18. Korkmaz, S.: Deep learning-based imbalanced data classification for drug discovery. J. Chem. Inf. Model. **60**(9), 4180–4190 (2020)
19. Kovács, G.: Smote-variants: a python implementation of 85 minority oversampling techniques. Neurocomputing **366**, 352–354 (2019)
20. Koziarski, M., Woźniak, M., Krawczyk, B.: Combined cleaning and resampling algorithm for multi-class imbalanced data with label noise. Knowl.-Based Syst. **204**, 106223 (2020)

21. Lemaître, G., Nogueira, F., Aridas, C.K.: Imbalanced-learn: a python toolbox to tackle the curse of imbalanced datasets in machine learning. J. Mach. Learn. Res. **18**(1), 559–563 (2017)
22. Liu, Z.G., Pan, Q., Dezert, J., Mercier, G.: Credal classification rule for uncertain data based on belief functions. Pattern Recogn. **47**(7), 2532–2541 (2014)
23. Ma, L., Fan, S.: CURE-SMOTE algorithm and hybrid algorithm for feature selection and parameter optimization based on random forests. BMC Bioinf **18**(1), 1–18 (2017)
24. Mahalanobis, P.C.: On the generalized distance in statistics, vol. 2, pp. 49–55. National Institute of Science of India (1936)
25. Makki, S., Assaghir, Z., Taher, Y., Haque, R., Hacid, M.S., Zeineddine, H.: An experimental study with imbalanced classification approaches for credit card fraud detection. IEEE Access **7**, 93010–93022 (2019)
26. Ofek, N., Rokach, L., Stern, R., Shabtai, A.: Fast-CBUS: a fast clustering-based undersampling method for addressing the class imbalance problem. Neurocomputing **243**, 88–102 (2017)
27. Pawlak, Z.: Rough sets. Int. J. Comput. Inf. Sci. **11**(5), 341–356 (1982)
28. Pedregosa, F., et al.: Scikit-learn: machine learning in python. J. Mach. Learn. Res. **12**, 2825–2830 (2011)
29. Ramentol, E., Caballero, Y., Bello, R., Herrera, F.: SMOTE-RSB *: a hybrid preprocessing approach based on oversampling and undersampling for high imbalanced data-sets using SMOTE and rough sets theory. Knowl. Inf. Syst. **33**(2), 245–265 (2012)
30. Sáez, J.A., Luengo, J., Stefanowski, J., Herrera, F.: SMOTE-IPF: addressing the noisy and borderline examples problem in imbalanced classification by a re-sampling method with filtering. Inf. Sci. **291**(C), 184–203 (2015)
31. Shafer, G.: A Mathematical Theory of Evidence, vol. 42. Princeton University Press, Princeton (1976)
32. Smets, P.: The nature of the unnormalized beliefs encountered in the transferable belief model. In: Uncertainty in Artificial Intelligence, pp. 292–297. Elsevier (1992)
33. Smets, P.: The transferable belief model for quantified belief representation. In: Smets, P. (ed.) Quantified Representation of Uncertainty and Imprecision. HDRUMS, vol. 1, pp. 267–301. Springer, Dordrecht (1998). https://doi.org/10.1007/978-94-017-1735-9_9
34. Tsai, C.F., Lin, W.C., Hu, Y.H., Yao, G.T.: Under-sampling class imbalanced datasets by combining clustering analysis and instance selection. Inf. Sci. **477**, 47–54 (2019)
35. Vuttipittayamongkol, P., Elyan, E.: Improved overlap-based undersampling for imbalanced dataset classification with application to epilepsy and parkinson's disease. Int. J. Neural Syst. **30**(08), 2050043 (2020)
36. Wilcoxon, F.: Individual comparisons by ranking methods. In: Breakthroughs in Statistics, pp. 196–202. Springer, Heidelberg (1992). https://doi.org/10.1007/978-1-4612-4380-9_16
37. Wilson, D.L.: Asymptotic properties of nearest neighbor rules using edited data. IEEE Trans. Syst. Man Cybern. **3**, 408–421 (1972)

Approximations of Belief Functions Using Compositional Models

Radim Jiroušek[1,2] and Václav Kratochvíl[1,2]($\boxtimes$)

[1] The Czech Academy of Sciences, Institute of Information Theory and Automation, Prague, Czech Republic
{radim,velorex}@utia.cas.cz
[2] Faculty of Management, Prague University of Economics and Business, Jindřichův Hradec, Czech Republic

Abstract. For applications to practical problems, the paper proposes to use the approximations of belief functions, which simplify their dependence structure. Using an analogy with probability distributions, we represent these approximations in the form of compositional models. As no theoretical apparatus similar to probabilistic information theory exists for belief functions, the problems arise not only in connection with the design of algorithms seeking the optimal approximations but even in connection with a criterion comparing two different approximations. With this respect, the application of the analogy with probability theory fails. Therefore, the paper suggests the employment of simple heuristics easily applicable to real-life problems.

Keywords: Compositional models · Entropy of belief functions · Decomposable entropy · Heuristics · Optimality criterion

1 Motivation

Consider a large set of discrete random variables $\mathcal{W}$ with a joint probability distribution π. For an arbitrary partition $\{\mathcal{U}_1, \mathcal{U}_2, \ldots, \mathcal{U}_k\}$ of $\mathcal{W}$, one can decompose the joint distribution π using the chain rule as follow:

$$\pi = \pi(\mathcal{U}_1)\pi(\mathcal{U}_2|\mathcal{U}_1)\ldots\pi(\mathcal{U}_k|(\mathcal{U}_1 \cup \ldots \cup \mathcal{U}_{k-1}))$$
$$= \prod_{i=1}^{k} \pi(\mathcal{U}_i|(\mathcal{U}_1 \cup \ldots \cup \mathcal{U}_{i-1})). \tag{1}$$

Notice that in the product formula of Eq. (1) (which will be often used throughout this paper), for $i = 1$, $\pi(\mathcal{U}_i|(\mathcal{U}_1 \cup \ldots \cup \mathcal{U}_{i-1}))$ is just the marginal $\pi(\mathcal{U}_1)$. For $i = 2$, $\pi(\mathcal{U}_2|\mathcal{U}_1)$ is the conditional probability table for $\mathcal{U}_2$ given $\mathcal{U}_1$, etc. In large models ($|\mathcal{W}|$ is large), it is rarely the case that the conditional marginal of $\mathcal{U}_i$ depends on all variables in $\mathcal{U}_1 \cup \ldots \cup \mathcal{U}_{i-1}$. This fact was exploited by Perez

Supported by the Czech Science Foundation – Grant No. 19-06569S.

J. Vejnarová and N. Wilson (Eds.): ECSQARU 2021, LNAI 12897, pp. 354–366, 2021.
https://doi.org/10.1007/978-3-030-86772-0_26

[10], who suggested using an *ε-admissible approximation by simplification of the dependence structure*[1] to overcome the computational-complexity problems accompanying the application of multidimensional probability distributions. His basic idea is as follows. Substitute each set $(\mathcal{U}_1 \cup \ldots \cup \mathcal{U}_{i-1})$ in Eq. (1) by its smaller subset $\mathcal{T}_i$ such that the conditional probability distribution $\pi(\mathcal{U}_i|\mathcal{T}_i)$ is almost the same as $\pi(\mathcal{U}_i|(\mathcal{U}_1 \cup \ldots \cup \mathcal{U}_{i-1}))$. The non-similarity of probability distributions π and κ defined on Ω can be measured using Kullback-Leibler (KL) divergence [9] defined as follows[2]

$$KL(\pi\|\kappa) = \sum_{x \in \Omega : \kappa(x) > 0} \pi(x) \log\left(\frac{\pi(x)}{\kappa(x)}\right). \qquad (2)$$

Let $\kappa = \prod_{i=1}^{k} \pi(\mathcal{U}_i|\mathcal{T}_i)$. If $KL(\pi\|\kappa) \leqslant \varepsilon$, then κ is called an *ε-admissible approximation of* π.

Now, consider a different problem. Let $\{\mathcal{V}_1, \mathcal{V}_2, \ldots, \mathcal{V}_k\}$ be a set of subsets of $\mathcal{W}$ (generally not disjoint) such that $\bigcup_{i=1}^{k} \mathcal{V}_i = \mathcal{W}$. Given a set of low-dimensional distributions $\{\kappa_i(\mathcal{V}_i)\}_{i=1,\ldots,k}$, a question is whether there exists a multidimensional distribution for $\mathcal{W}$ such that all κ_i's are its marginals. If there exists a distribution π such that all κ_i are its marginals, Perez [10] found an answer to a related question: What is the best *ε-admissible* approximation of π (in the sense of the smallest ε) that can be assembled from $\{\kappa_i(\mathcal{V}_i)\}_{i=1,\ldots,k}$? Thus, Perez was looking for a permutation $(j_1, j_2, \ldots, j_k)$ of indices $(1, 2, \ldots, k)$, which minimizes $KL\left(\pi\| \prod_{i=1}^{k} \kappa_{j_i}(\mathcal{V}_{j_i} \setminus \mathcal{T}_{j_i}|\mathcal{T}_{j_i})\right)$, where $\mathcal{T}_{j_i} = \mathcal{V}_{j_i} \cap (\mathcal{V}_{j_1} \cup \ldots \cup \mathcal{V}_{j_{i-1}})$. For this, he showed [10] that (H denotes the Shannon entropy [12])

$$KL\left(\pi\| \prod_{i=1}^{k} \kappa_{j_i}(\mathcal{V}_{j_i} \setminus \mathcal{T}_{j_i}|\mathcal{T}_{j_i})\right) = -H(\pi) + \sum_{i=1}^{k}\left(H(\kappa_{j_i}(\mathcal{V}_{j_i})) - H(\kappa_{j_i}(\mathcal{T}_{j_i}))\right), \quad (3)$$

which equals $H(\prod_{i=1}^{k} \kappa_{j_i}(\mathcal{V}_{j_i} \setminus \mathcal{T}_{j_i}|\mathcal{T}_{j_i})) - H(\pi)$ in case that all κ_i are marginals of both π and $\prod_{i=1}^{k} \kappa_{j_i}(\mathcal{V}_{j_i} \setminus \mathcal{T}_{j_i}|\mathcal{T}_{j_i})$. Thus, regardless of whether distribution π is known or not, he proved that its best approximation (that simplifies the dependence structure), which can be set up from $\{\kappa_i(\mathcal{V}_i)\}_{i=1,\ldots,k}$, is that which minimizes $\sum_{i=1}^{k}\left(H(\kappa_{j_i}(\mathcal{V}_{j_i})) - H(\kappa_{j_i}(\mathcal{T}_{j_i}))\right)$. If one considers only the approximations $\prod_{i=1}^{k} \kappa_{j_i}(\mathcal{V}_{j_i} \setminus \mathcal{T}_{j_i}|\mathcal{T}_{j_i})$ having all κ_i for its marginals, then the best approximation minimizes its Shannon entropy $H(\prod_{i=1}^{k} \kappa_{j_i}(\mathcal{V}_{j_i} \setminus \mathcal{T}_{j_i}|\mathcal{T}_{j_i}))$ (which corresponds with the intuition that it maximizes its information content).

---

[1] The notion reflects the fact that the considered approximation extends the set of conditional independence relations holding for the probability distribution in question [15].

[2] Eq. (2) defines the KL divergence if κ dominates π, i.e., if for all $x \in \Omega$, for which $\kappa(x) = 0$, $\pi(x)$ is also 0. Otherwise, the KL divergence is defined to be $+\infty$.

2   Belief Functions

As in Sect. 1, let W denote a set of variables with finite number of states. For $X \in W$, Let Ω_X denote the set of states of variable X. A *basic assignment* for variables $\mathcal{U} \subseteq W$ (or equivalently basic assignment on the Cartesian product $\Omega_{\mathcal{U}} = \times_{X \in \mathcal{U}} \Omega_X$) is a mapping $m_{\mathcal{U}} : 2^{\Omega_{\mathcal{U}}} \to [0, 1]$, such that $\sum_{\mathbf{a} \subseteq \Omega_{\mathcal{U}}} m_{\mathcal{U}}(\mathbf{a}) = 1$ and $m_{\mathcal{U}}(\emptyset) = 0$.

Consider a basic assignment $m_{\mathcal{U}}$. If the set of the corresponding variables is clear from the context, we omit the subscript $\mathcal{U}$. Thus, we say that $\mathbf{a}$ is a *focal element* of m if $m(\mathbf{a}) > 0$.

For basic assignment $m_{\mathcal{V}}$, we often consider its *marginal* basic assignment $m_{\mathcal{V}}^{\downarrow \mathcal{U}}$ for $\mathcal{U} \subseteq \mathcal{V}$. A similar notation is used also for *projections*: for $a \in \Omega_{\mathcal{V}}$, symbol $a^{\downarrow \mathcal{U}}$ denotes the element of $\Omega_{\mathcal{U}}$, which is obtained from a by omitting the values of variables in $\mathcal{V} \setminus \mathcal{U}$. For $\mathbf{a} \subseteq \Omega_{\mathcal{V}}$,

$$\mathbf{a}^{\downarrow \mathcal{U}} = \{a^{\downarrow \mathcal{U}} : a \in \mathbf{a}\}.$$

Thus, the marginal $m_{\mathcal{V}}^{\downarrow \mathcal{U}}$ of basic assignment $m_{\mathcal{V}}$ for $\mathcal{U}$ is defined as follows:

$$m_{\mathcal{V}}^{\downarrow \mathcal{U}}(\mathbf{b}) = \sum_{\mathbf{a} \subseteq \Omega_{\mathcal{V}} : \, \mathbf{a}^{\downarrow \mathcal{U}} = \mathbf{b}} m_{\mathcal{V}}(\mathbf{a}).$$

for all $\mathbf{b} \subseteq \Omega_{\mathcal{U}}$.

The projection of sets enables us to define a *join* of two sets. Consider two arbitrary sets $\mathcal{U}$ and $\mathcal{V}$ of variables (they may be disjoint or overlapping, or one may be a subset of the other). Consider two sets $\mathbf{a} \subseteq \Omega_{\mathcal{U}}$ and $\mathbf{b} \subseteq \Omega_{\mathcal{V}}$. Their join is defined as

$$\mathbf{a} \bowtie \mathbf{b} = \{c \in \Omega_{\mathcal{U} \cup \mathcal{V}} : c^{\downarrow \mathcal{U}} \in \mathbf{a} \ \& \ c^{\downarrow \mathcal{V}} \in \mathbf{b}\}.$$

Notice that if $\mathcal{U}$ and $\mathcal{V}$ are disjoint, then $\mathbf{a} \bowtie \mathbf{b} = \mathbf{a} \times \mathbf{b}$, if $\mathcal{U} = \mathcal{V}$, then $\mathbf{a} \bowtie \mathbf{b} = \mathbf{a} \cap \mathbf{b}$, and, in general, for $\mathbf{c} \subseteq \Omega_{\mathcal{U} \cup \mathcal{V}}$, $\mathbf{c}$ is a subset of $\mathbf{c}^{\downarrow \mathcal{U}} \bowtie \mathbf{c}^{\downarrow \mathcal{V}}$, which may be a proper subset.

A basic assignment m can equivalently be defined by the corresponding *belief function*, or by *plausibility function*, or by *commonality function* [11] as follows:

$$Bel_m(\mathbf{a}) = \sum_{\mathbf{b} \subseteq \Omega : \, \mathbf{b} \subseteq \mathbf{a}} m(\mathbf{b}),$$

$$Pl_m(\mathbf{a}) = \sum_{\mathbf{b} \subseteq \Omega : \, \mathbf{b} \cap \mathbf{a} \neq \emptyset} m(\mathbf{b}),$$

$$Q_m(\mathbf{a}) = \sum_{\mathbf{b} \subseteq \Omega : \, \mathbf{b} \supseteq \mathbf{a}} m(\mathbf{b}).$$

These representations are equivalent in the sense that when one of these functions is given, it is always possible to compute the others uniquely. For example:

$$Pl_m(\mathbf{a}) = 1 - Bel_m(\Omega \setminus \mathbf{a}),$$

$$m(\mathbf{a}) = \sum_{\mathbf{b} \subseteq \mathbf{a}} (-1)^{|\mathbf{a} \setminus \mathbf{b}|} Bel_m(\mathbf{b}),$$

$$m(\mathbf{a}) = \sum_{\mathbf{b} \in 2^{\Omega}: \, \mathbf{b} \supseteq \mathbf{a}} (-1)^{|\mathbf{b} \setminus \mathbf{a}|} Q_m(\mathbf{b}). \tag{4}$$

After normalizing the plausibility function for singleton subsets, one gets for each $\mathbf{a} \subseteq \Omega$

$$\lambda_m(\mathbf{a}) = \frac{\sum_{b \in \mathbf{a}} Pl_m(\{b\})}{\sum_{b \in \Omega} Pl_m(\{b\})} \tag{5}$$

a probability function on Ω. λ_m is called a *plausibility transform* of basic assignment m [1]. There is a number of other probabilistic transforms of a mass assignment m described in literature (e.g., [2]) but in this text we need only the so-called *pignistic transform* [13,14] defined as follows:

$$\pi_m(\mathbf{a}) = \sum_{a \in \mathbf{a}} \sum_{\mathbf{b} \subseteq \Omega: a \in \mathbf{b}} \frac{m(\mathbf{b})}{|\mathbf{b}|}. \tag{6}$$

To construct multidimensional models from low-dimensional building blocks, we need some operators connecting two low-dimensional basic assignments into one more-dimensional. One possibility is the classical Dempster's combination rule, which is used to combine distinct belief functions. Consider two basic assignments $m_{\mathcal{U}}$ and $m_{\mathcal{V}}$ for arbitrary sets of variables $\mathcal{U}$ and $\mathcal{V}$. Dempster's combination rule is defined for each $\mathbf{c} \subseteq \Omega_{\mathcal{U} \cup \mathcal{V}}$ as follows:

$$(m_{\mathcal{U}} \oplus m_{\mathcal{V}})(\mathbf{c}) = \frac{1}{1-K} \sum_{\mathbf{a} \subseteq \Omega_{\mathcal{U}}, \mathbf{b} \subseteq \Omega_{\mathcal{V}}: \mathbf{a} \bowtie \mathbf{b} = \mathbf{c}} m_{\mathcal{U}}(\mathbf{a}) \cdot m_{\mathcal{V}}(\mathbf{b}), \tag{7}$$

where

$$K = \sum_{\mathbf{a} \subseteq \Omega_{\mathcal{U}}, \mathbf{b} \subseteq \Omega_{\mathcal{V}}: \mathbf{a} \bowtie \mathbf{b} = \varnothing} m_{\mathcal{U}}(\mathbf{a}) \cdot m_{\mathcal{V}}(\mathbf{b}), \tag{8}$$

which can be interpreted as the amount of conflict between $m_{\mathcal{U}}$ and $m_{\mathcal{V}}$. If $K = 1$, then we say that the basic assignments $m_{\mathcal{U}}$ and $m_{\mathcal{V}}$ are in total conflict and their Dempster's combination is undefined.

3   Compositional Models

Dempster's rule of combination may be equivalently expressed using the corresponding commonality functions $Q_{m_{\mathcal{U}}}$ and $Q_{m_{\mathcal{V}}}$ [11]

$$Q_{m_{\mathcal{U}} \oplus m_{\mathcal{V}}}(\mathbf{c}) = \left(\frac{1}{1-K}\right) Q_{m_{\mathcal{U}}}(\mathbf{c}^{\downarrow \mathcal{U}}) \cdot Q_{m_{\mathcal{V}}}(\mathbf{c}^{\downarrow \mathcal{V}}),$$

where K is the same as defined in Eq. (8). Let us stress that it was designed to combine independent sources of information. When combining the sources of uncertain information, which may not be distinct, we have to ensure that no information is double-counted. For this, an operator of composition was designed.

Definition 1. *Consider two arbitrary basic assignments* $m_\mathcal{U}$, $m_\mathcal{V}$, *and their commonality functions* $Q_{m_\mathcal{U}}$ *and* $Q_{m_\mathcal{V}}$. *Their composition is a basic assignment* $m_\mathcal{U} \triangleright m_\mathcal{V}$, *the corresponding commonality function of which is given by the composition of their commonality functions defined for each* $\mathbf{c} \subseteq \Omega_{\mathcal{U} \cup \mathcal{V}}$ *by the following expression:*

$$(Q_{m_\mathcal{U}} \triangleright Q_{m_\mathcal{V}})(\mathbf{c}) = \begin{cases} \frac{1}{L} \frac{Q_{m_\mathcal{U}}(\mathbf{c}^{\downarrow \mathcal{U}}) \cdot Q_{m_\mathcal{V}}(\mathbf{c}^{\downarrow \mathcal{V}})}{Q_{m_\mathcal{V}}^{\downarrow \mathcal{U} \cap \mathcal{V}}(\mathbf{c}^{\downarrow \mathcal{U} \cap \mathcal{V}})} & \text{if } Q_{m_\mathcal{V}}^{\downarrow \mathcal{U} \cap \mathcal{V}}(\mathbf{c}^{\downarrow \mathcal{U} \cap \mathcal{V}}) > 0, \\ 0 & \text{otherwise,} \end{cases} \qquad (9)$$

where the normalization constant

$$L = \sum_{\mathbf{d} \subseteq \Omega_{\mathcal{U} \cup \mathcal{V}} : Q_{m_\mathcal{V}}^{\downarrow \mathcal{U} \cap \mathcal{V}}(\mathbf{c}^{\downarrow \mathcal{U} \cap \mathcal{V}}) > 0} (-1)^{|\mathbf{d}|+1} \frac{Q_{m_\mathcal{U}}(\mathbf{c}^{\downarrow \mathcal{U}}) \cdot Q_{m_\mathcal{V}}(\mathbf{c}^{\downarrow \mathcal{V}})}{Q_{m_\mathcal{V}}^{\downarrow \mathcal{U} \cap \mathcal{V}}(\mathbf{c}^{\downarrow \mathcal{U} \cap \mathcal{V}})}.$$

If $L = 0$ *then* $m_\mathcal{U}$ *and* $m_\mathcal{V}$ *are in total conflict and the composition is undefined.*

Remark. Definition 1 is taken from [4], where the reader can find the motivation not repeated in this paper. Unfortunately, there is no explicit formula for computing the composition of two basic assignments. However, there is a way to avoid the necessity to transform the first argument into its commonality representation. When computing the composition of two basic assignments we transform the second argument $m_\mathcal{V}$ into $Q_{m_\mathcal{V}}$, and compute the corresponding *conditional commonality function* $Q_{m_{\mathcal{V} \setminus \mathcal{U} | \mathcal{V} \cap \mathcal{U}}} = Q_{m_\mathcal{V}} / Q_{m_\mathcal{V}}^{\downarrow \mathcal{U} \cap \mathcal{V}}$. Then, using Eq. (4), we compute the corresponding *conditional basic assignment* $m_{\mathcal{V} \setminus \mathcal{U} | \mathcal{V} \cap \mathcal{U}}$. Eventually

$$m_\mathcal{U} \triangleright m_\mathcal{V} = m_\mathcal{U} \oplus m_{\mathcal{V} \setminus \mathcal{U} | \mathcal{V} \cap \mathcal{U}}.$$

Thus, the computations of composition are limited by the dimensionality of the second argument because, as a rule, the representation of the corresponding commonality function requires the space for $2^{(2^{|\mathcal{V}|})}$ values regardless of the number of focal elements of $m_\mathcal{V}$.

In the following assertion, we briefly describe the main properties of the composition operator. These properties are proved for Shenoy's valuation-based systems (VBS) in [4], from which it follows that all of them hold for belief functions also. Notice that Properties 2 and 3 of the following assertion prove the fact that the introduced operator of composition avoids double-counting the information about the variables $\mathcal{U} \cap \mathcal{V}$. Namely, we can see that the operator disregards the information about these variables that is contained in the second argument.

Proposition 1. *For arbitrary basic assignments* $m_{\mathcal{U}_1}, m_{\mathcal{U}_2}, m_{\mathcal{U}_3}$ *the following statements hold, if the respective expressions are defined.*

1. (Domain): $m_{\mathcal{U}_1} \triangleright m_{\mathcal{U}_2}$ *is a basic assignment for variables* $\mathcal{U}_1 \cup \mathcal{U}_2$.
2. (Composition preserves first marginal): $(m_{\mathcal{U}_1} \triangleright m_{\mathcal{U}_2})^{\downarrow \mathcal{U}_1} = m_{\mathcal{U}_1}$.
3. (Reduction:) *If* $\mathcal{U}_2 \subseteq \mathcal{U}_1$ *then,* $m_{\mathcal{U}_1} \triangleright m_{\mathcal{U}_2} = m_{\mathcal{U}_1}$.

4. (Non-commutativity): *In general,* $m_{\mathcal{U}_1} \rhd m_{\mathcal{U}_2} \neq m_{\mathcal{U}_2} \rhd m_{\mathcal{U}_1}$.

5. (Commutativity under consistency): *If* $m_{\mathcal{U}_1}$ *and* $m_{\mathcal{U}_2}$ *are consistent, i.e.,* $m_{\mathcal{U}_1}^{\downarrow \mathcal{U}_1 \cap \mathcal{U}_2} = m_{\mathcal{U}_2}^{\downarrow \mathcal{U}_1 \cap \mathcal{U}_2}$, *then* $m_{\mathcal{U}_1} \rhd m_{\mathcal{U}_2} = m_{\mathcal{U}_2} \rhd m_{\mathcal{U}_1}$.

6. (Non-associativity): *In general,* $(m_{\mathcal{U}_1} \rhd m_{\mathcal{U}_2}) \rhd m_{\mathcal{U}_3} \neq m_{\mathcal{U}_1} \rhd (m_{\mathcal{U}_2} \rhd m_{\mathcal{U}_3})$.

7. (Associativity under RIP): *If* $\mathcal{U}_1 \supset (\mathcal{U}_2 \cap \mathcal{U}_3)$, *or,* $\mathcal{U}_2 \supset (\mathcal{U}_1 \cap \mathcal{U}_3)$ *then,* $(m_{\mathcal{U}_1} \rhd m_{\mathcal{U}_2}) \rhd m_{\mathcal{U}_3} = m_{\mathcal{U}_1} \rhd (m_{\mathcal{U}_2} \rhd m_{\mathcal{U}_3})$.

By a *belief function compositional model* we understand a basic assignment $m_1 \rhd \cdots \rhd m_n$ obtained by a multiple application of the composition operator. Let us emphasize that if not specified otherwise by parentheses, the operators are always performed from left to right, i.e.,

$$m_1 \rhd m_2 \rhd m_3 \rhd \ldots \rhd m_n = (\ldots ((m_1 \rhd m_2) \rhd m_3) \rhd \ldots \rhd m_{n-1}) \rhd m_n.$$

Consider a (finite) system $\mathbb{W}$ of small subsets of the considered variables $\mathcal{W}$. The vague assumption that $\mathcal{U} \in \mathbb{W}$ is small is accepted to avoid the computational problems connected with computations with the corresponding basic assignments. Thus, we assume that for each $\mathcal{U} \in \mathbb{W}$ we have (or we can easily get) a basic assignment $m_{\mathcal{U}}$. Moreover, we assume that these basic assignments, as well as the corresponding commonality functions $Q_{m_{\mathcal{U}}}$, can effectively be represented in computer memory.

Using an analogy with Perez' approximations of probability distributions, we are looking for the best approximation simplifying the dependence structure of some basic assignment m, the marginals of which for sets from $\mathbb{W}$ are at our disposal. In other words, we are looking for a sequence of sets $(\mathcal{U}_i)_{i=1,\ldots,n}$ from $\mathbb{W}$ such that the model $m_{\mathcal{U}_1} \rhd m_{\mathcal{U}_2} \rhd \cdots \rhd m_{\mathcal{U}_n}$ approximates the unknown basic assignment m best. To simplify notation, we denote $m_i = m_{\mathcal{U}_i}$. Therefore we will speak about a model $m_1 \rhd m_2 \rhd \ldots \rhd m_n$, in which basic assignment m_i is defined for variables $\mathcal{U}_i$, and the corresponding commonality function is Q_i.

The considered compositional model is a $|\mathcal{U}_1 \cup \ldots \cup \mathcal{U}_n|$-dimensional basic assignment. It is said to be *perfect* if all m_i are marginals of $m_1 \rhd m_2 \rhd \ldots \rhd m_n$. Thus, perfect models reflect all the information represented by the low-dimensional basic assignments from which they are composed. So, it is not surprising that the optimal approximation simplifying the dependence structure will be, as a rule, a perfect model.

If a model is not perfect, it can always be *perfectized* using the following assertion (proved in [4]).

Proposition 2 (perfectization procedure). *For any compositional model* $m_1 \rhd m_2 \rhd \ldots \rhd m_n$, *the model* $\bar{m}_1 \rhd \bar{m}_2 \rhd \ldots \rhd \bar{m}_n$ *defined*

$$\bar{m}_1 = m_1,$$
$$\bar{m}_2 = \bar{m}_1^{\downarrow \mathcal{U}_2 \cap \mathcal{U}_1} \rhd m_2,$$
$$\vdots$$
$$\bar{m}_n = \bar{m}_n^{\downarrow \mathcal{U}_n \cap (\mathcal{U}_1 \cup \ldots \cup \mathcal{U}_{n-1})} \rhd m_n,$$

is perfect, and $m_1 \rhd m_2 \rhd \ldots \rhd m_n = \bar{m}_1 \rhd \bar{m}_2 \rhd \ldots \rhd \bar{m}_n$.

The procedure applies to any compositional model, nevertheless, its computational efficiency is guaranteed only for decomposable models introduced below. As a rule, a perfect model can equivalently be represented by several permutations of low-dimensional basic assignments. In [4], the following two important assertions are proved.

Proposition 3 (on perfect models). *Consider a perfect model* $m_1 \triangleright \ldots \triangleright m_n$, *and a permutation of its indices* $i_1, i_2, \ldots, i_n$ *such that* $m_{i_1} \triangleright m_{i_2} \triangleright \ldots \triangleright m_{i_n}$ *is also perfect. Then,*

$$m_1 \triangleright m_2 \triangleright \ldots \triangleright m_n = m_{i_1} \triangleright m_{i_2} \triangleright \ldots \triangleright m_{i_n}.$$

Compositional model $m_1 \triangleright m_2 \triangleright \ldots \triangleright m_n$ is said to be *decomposable* if the sequence $\mathcal{U}_1, \mathcal{U}_2, \ldots, \mathcal{U}_n$ of the corresponding basic assignments meets the so called *running intersection property* (RIP): $\forall i = 2, \ldots, n \ \exists j \ (1 \leqslant j < i)$: $\mathcal{U}_i \cap (\mathcal{U}_1 \cup \ldots \cup \mathcal{U}_{i-1}) \subseteq \mathcal{U}_j$.

Proposition 4 (on consistent decomposable models). *Consider a decomposable model* $m_1 \triangleright m_2 \triangleright \ldots \triangleright m_n$. *The model is perfect if and only if basic assignments* $m_1, m_2, \ldots, m_n$ *are pairwise consistent, i.e.,* $\forall \{i, j\} \subset \{1, 2, \ldots, n\}, m_i^{\downarrow \mathcal{U}_i \cap \mathcal{U}_j} = m_j^{\downarrow \mathcal{U}_i \cap \mathcal{U}_j}$.

4 Entropy

In this paper, we primarily consider Shenoy's entropy introduced in [6]. It is defined

$$H_S(m_\mathcal{V}) = \sum_{\mathbf{a} \subseteq \Omega_\mathcal{V}} (-1)^{|\mathbf{a}|} Q_{m_\mathcal{V}}(\mathbf{a}) \log(Q_{m_\mathcal{V}}(\mathbf{a})) \tag{10}$$

using the commonality function of basic assignment $m_\mathcal{V}$ (no formula based on a basic assignment is known). This function is not always non-negative. However, its merit is that it is the only definition of belief function entropy that satisfies an additivity property in the sense that $H_S(m_X \oplus m_{Y|X}) = H_S(m_X) + H_S(m_{Y|X})$ (here, m_X is a basic assignment for X, and $m_{Y|X}$ is a conditional basic assignment for Y given X such that its marginal for X is vacuous). This additivity, which is one of the fundamental properties in probabilistic information theory, makes the computation of the entropy for perfect compositional models of very high dimensions possible. Namely, the conditional entropy should be computed according to the following formula ($\mathcal{U}$ and $\mathcal{T}$ are disjoint sets of variables):

$$H_S(m_{\mathcal{U}|\mathcal{T}}) = \sum_{\mathbf{a} \subseteq \Omega_{\mathcal{U} \cup \mathcal{T}}} (-1)^{|\mathbf{a}|} Q_{m_{(\mathcal{U} \cup \mathcal{T})}}(\mathbf{a}) \log(Q_{m_{\mathcal{U}|\mathcal{T}}}(\mathbf{a})), \tag{11}$$

where $Q_{m_{\mathcal{U}|\mathcal{T}}}(\mathbf{a}) = Q_{m_{(\mathcal{U} \cup \mathcal{T})}}(\mathbf{a}) / Q_{m_{(\mathcal{U} \cup \mathcal{T})}^{\downarrow \mathcal{T}}}(\mathbf{a}^{\downarrow \mathcal{T}})$ for all $\mathbf{a} \subseteq \Omega_{\mathcal{U} \cup \mathcal{T}}$. Note that for $\mathcal{T} = \varnothing$, $H_S(m_{\mathcal{U}|\mathcal{T}}) = H_S(m_\mathcal{U})$, and that the definition of conditional entropy in Eq. (11) is analogous to Shannon's definition of conditional entropy of probabilistic conditionals [12].

Thus, for arbitrary $\mathcal{U}$ and $\mathcal{V}$, entropy H_S of a composition of two consistent $m_{\mathcal{U}}$ and $m_{\mathcal{V}}$ (i.e., $m_{\mathcal{U}}^{\downarrow \mathcal{U} \cap \mathcal{V}} = m_{\mathcal{V}}^{\downarrow \mathcal{U} \cap \mathcal{V}}$) can be computed as a sum of $H_S(m_{\mathcal{U}})$ and the respective conditional entropy computed from $m_{\mathcal{V}}$

$$H_S(m_{\mathcal{U}} \rhd m_{\mathcal{V}}) = H_S(m_{\mathcal{U}}) + H_S(m_{\mathcal{V} \setminus \mathcal{U} | \mathcal{V} \cap \mathcal{U}}). \tag{12}$$

5 Example

In this example, we consider an 8-dimensional basic assignment m for binary variables S, T, U, V, W, X, Y, Z. Let us start studying the approximations of m assembled from its marginals. We consider the approximations that are analogous to Perez' probabilistic approximations simplifying the dependence structure. For this purpose, consider the five marginals described in Table 1.

Table 1. Five low-dimensional basic assignments

Basic assignments	Number of focal elements	H_S
$m_{\{S,T,U\}}$	9	0.1951790
$m_{\{T,U,V\}}$	9	0.1644314
$m_{\{V,W,X\}}$	10	0.1562828
$m_{\{W,Y\}}$	5	0.0702895
$m_{\{X,Z\}}$	5	0.1385793

Checking the validity of RIP, one can easily verify that compositional model $m_{\{S,T,U\}} \rhd m_{\{T,U,V\}} \rhd m_{\{V,W,X\}} \rhd m_{\{W,Y\}} \rhd m_{\{X,Z\}}$ is decomposable. Due to Proposition 4, it means that this model is perfect, and therefore it contains all the information from all the given low-dimensional basic assignments. Therefore, we are sure that this compositional model is optimal among those approximations that can be assembled from the marginals from Table 1.

In addition to this optimal one, let us consider four other approximations defined by the permutations not satisfying RIP. Thus, in this example, we compare the following five compositional models:

$$\mathfrak{M}_1 : m_{\{S,T,U\}} \rhd m_{\{T,U,V\}} \rhd m_{\{V,W,X\}} \rhd m_{\{W,Y\}} \rhd m_{\{X,Z\}},$$
$$\mathfrak{M}_2 : m_{\{S,T,U\}} \rhd m_{\{V,W,X\}} \rhd m_{\{W,Y\}} \rhd m_{\{X,Z\}} \rhd m_{\{T,U,V\}},$$
$$\mathfrak{M}_3 : m_{\{S,T,U\}} \rhd m_{\{W,Y\}} \rhd m_{\{X,Z\}} \rhd m_{\{T,U,V\}} \rhd m_{\{V,W,X\}},$$
$$\mathfrak{M}_4 : m_{\{W,Y\}} \rhd m_{\{X,Z\}} \rhd m_{\{V,W,X\}} \rhd m_{\{T,U,V\}} \rhd m_{\{S,T,U\}},$$
$$\mathfrak{M}_5 : m_{\{W,Y\}} \rhd m_{\{S,T,U\}} \rhd m_{\{X,Z\}} \rhd m_{\{V,W,X\}} \rhd m_{\{T,U,V\}}.$$

To efficiently compute their entropy H_S, we modify the expressions defining the considered models using the properties from Proposition 1 receiving

$$\mathfrak{M}_2 : m_{\{S,T,U\}} \rhd m_{\{V,W,X\}} \rhd m_{\{W,Y\}} \rhd m_{\{X,Z\}},$$
$$\mathfrak{M}_3 : m_{\{S,T,U\}} \rhd m_{\{W,Y\}} \rhd m_{\{X,Z\}} \rhd m_{\{T,U,V\}},$$
$$\mathfrak{M}_4 : \left(m_{\{W,Y\}} \rhd m_{\{X,Z\}}\right) \rhd m_{\{V,W,X\}} \rhd m_{\{T,U,V\}} \rhd m_{\{S,T,U\}},$$
$$\mathfrak{M}_5 : \left(m_{\{W,Y\}} \rhd m_{\{X,Z\}}\right) \rhd m_{\{V,W,X\}} \rhd m_{\{S,T,U\}}.$$

Notice, these models are decomposable (for this we have to consider that models $\mathfrak{M}_4$ and $\mathfrak{M}_5$ start with a four-dimensional basic assignment in parentheses), and therefore they can easily be perfectized using Proposition 2. Therefore, the values of H_S presented in the first row of Table 2 can be computed by a successive application of Formula (12). Using the analogy with the probabilistic paradigm (introduced in Sect. 1) we expect that the lower the entropy, the better the model. Thus, the values of H_S from Table 2 suggest the following preferences of models:

$$\mathfrak{M}_2 \approx \mathfrak{M}_5 \succ \mathfrak{M}_1 \approx \mathfrak{M}_4 \succ \mathfrak{M}_3,$$

which is not what we would like to see because we are sure that model $\mathfrak{M}_1$ is the best one. Thus, entropy H_S cannot be recommended as an ultimate criterion determining, which of the compared approximations is better. In general, it is not an easy task to say, which of two compositional models approximates better a given basic assignment, and finding a corresponding criterion function remains an open problem. In the next section, we consider three functions and study whether they can heuristically be used for this purpose.

Table 2. Comparison of compositional models $\mathfrak{M}_i$ based on H_S, H_A, H_P

	$\mathfrak{M}_1$	$\mathfrak{M}_2$	$\mathfrak{M}_3$	$\mathfrak{M}_4$	$\mathfrak{M}_5$
H_S	0.5346689	0.5324691	0.537525	0.5346689	0.5324691
H_A	11.21685	11.13043	11.27071	11.23775	11.14948
H_P	10.23799	10.33313	10.28555	10.24451	10.3397

Let us repeat that we can recognize the optimal solution only in very special situations. Namely, when the considered approximation is a perfect compositional model constructed from all the considered basic assignments $\{m_U\}_{U \in W}$. Then, the approximation reflects all the information from the system of the considered low-dimensional basic assignments, and therefore it is optimal.

This fact was already employed in [3], in which we compared simple heuristic ("hill-climbing") algorithms that were controlled by H_S and other two functions proposed as entropy for belief functions. In short, in addition to H_S, we considered the entropy suggested in [5].

$$H_A(m_V) = \sum_{\mathbf{a} \subseteq \Omega_V} m(\mathbf{a}) \log(|\mathbf{a}|) + H(\lambda_m) = \sum_{\mathbf{a} \subseteq \Omega_V} m(\mathbf{a}) \log(|\mathbf{a}|) - \sum_{a \in \Omega_V} \lambda(a) \log(\lambda(a)),$$

and its modification (inspired by [7])

$$H_P(m_\mathcal{V}) = \sum_{\mathbf{a} \subseteq \Omega_\mathcal{V}} m(\mathbf{a}) \log(|\mathbf{a}|) + H(\pi_m) = \sum_{\mathbf{a} \subseteq \Omega_\mathcal{V}} m(\mathbf{a}) \log(|\mathbf{a}|) - \sum_{a \in \Omega_\mathcal{V}} \pi(a) \log(\pi(a))$$

(recall that H denotes Shannon entropy, and λ_m and π_m are the respective plausibility and pignistic transforms defined by Formulas (5) and (6), respectively). The values of H_A and H_P for models $\mathfrak{M}_1 - \mathfrak{M}_5$ are in Table 2. Looking at their values, one can see that H_P detects the optimal model suggesting the preferences

$$\mathfrak{M}_1 \succ \mathfrak{M}_4 \succ \mathfrak{M}_3 \succ \mathfrak{M}_2 \succ \mathfrak{M}_5.$$

Note that this observation is also in agreement with results published in [3]. Nevertheless, in contrast to H_S, neither H_A nor H_P is additive, and therefore one cannot compute their values for compositional models of practical size. This is why in the next section, we propose and test heuristics applicable to real size problems.

6   Comparison of Heuristics on Random Models

In the example in Sect. 5, we mentioned three functions H_S, H_A and H_P proposed to serve as entropy for belief functions. The great advantage of H_S is its additivity expressed in Formula (12), which is the property holding also for Shannon entropy. It enables us to compute H_S for perfect models of very high dimensions as a sum

$$H_S(m_1 \rhd \ldots \rhd m_n) = \sum_{i=1}^{n} H_S(m_{\mathcal{U}_i \setminus \hat{\mathcal{U}}_i | \mathcal{U}_i \cap \hat{\mathcal{U}}_i}), \tag{13}$$

where $\hat{\mathcal{U}}_i = \mathcal{U}_1 \cup \mathcal{U}_2 \cup \ldots \cup \mathcal{U}_{i-1}$, and $m_{\mathcal{U}_i \setminus \hat{\mathcal{U}}_i | \mathcal{U}_i \cap \hat{\mathcal{U}}_i}$ is computed from m_i. No analogous formulas for the computations of the other two entropies H_A and H_P exist. Not being able to compute their values for models of higher dimensions, we performed computational experiments with a derived heuristic function $\overline{H_A}$ (and analogously also $\overline{H_P}$)

$$\overline{H_A}(m_1 \rhd \ldots \rhd m_n) = \sum_{i=1}^{n} \left(H_A(m_i^{\downarrow \mathcal{U}_i}) - H_A(m_i^{\downarrow \mathcal{U}_i \cap \hat{\mathcal{U}}_i}) \right).$$

Using the codes developed in R-studio, we randomly generated 110 perfect decomposable compositional models for 26 variables[3]. Realizing random simple swaps on the order of the basic assignments defining the decomposable models, we damaged the running intersection property. In this way, likewise in the

---

[3] To generate a decomposable model, first, we generate a sequence of sets of variables satisfying running intersection property. Then we generated random basic assignments for given sets of variables and run the perfectization procedure as described in Proposition 2.

example presented in the previous section, we got for each randomly generated decomposable model 19 non-decomposable models. For each model from such a 20-tuple, we computed three values: $\overline{H_S}$, and $\overline{H_A}$, $\overline{H_P}$. By $\overline{H_S}$ we denote the value computed according to Formula (13). Notice that $\overline{H_S} = H_S$ only for perfect models. Repeat that this equality is guaranteed, due to the pairwise consistency of randomly generated low-dimensional basic assignments, only for the decomposable model from each of the considered 20-tuple of compositional models.

Table 3. Results from random experiments

	$\overline{H_S}$	$\overline{H_A}$	$\overline{H_P}$
Minimum achieved for the decomposable model	13	110	110
Minimum achieved **only** for the decomposable model	12	107	107

In Table 3, we depict how many times the respective heuristic functions achieved their minimum for the decomposable models. From this, one can see that both $\overline{H_A}$ and $\overline{H_P}$ detected all the decomposable models as optimal. Only for 3 out of all 110 of these experiments, a non-decomposable model was found, for which the value of $\overline{H_A}$ (and also $\overline{H_P}$) was the same as that for the decomposable model.

Realize, that in total we generated 2,200 compositional models. In Fig. 1, the reader can see how the values of the considered heuristics for non-decomposable models differ from those for the respective decomposable model. The histograms (a), (b) and (c) describe the behavior of values of heuristics $\overline{H_A}$, $\overline{H_P}$ and $\overline{H_S}$ for all $19 \times 110 = 2,090$ non-decomposable models. Notice that while from histograms (a) and (b) we see that all the differences were non-negative, histogram (c) shows that values of $\overline{H_S}$ for non-decomposable models were both higher and lower than the corresponding values for the respective decomposable models.

Though the results achieved with $\overline{H_A}$ and $\overline{H_P}$ are rather promising, neither of these heuristics guarantees the detection of the optimal model with certainty. Have a look at Table 4 containing values of $\overline{H_A}$ and $\overline{H_P}$ for models from Sect. 5. From this, one can see that not only entropy H_A (as shown in Table 2), but also the heuristic $\overline{H_A}$ does not achieve its minimum for the optimal model.

Table 4. Comparison of compositional models $\mathfrak{M}_i$ based on $\overline{H_A}, \overline{H_P}$

	$\mathfrak{M}_1$	$\mathfrak{M}_2$	$\mathfrak{M}_3$	$\mathfrak{M}_4$	$\mathfrak{M}_5$
$\overline{H_A}$	11.20454	11.12313	11.26799	11.22912	11.14770
$\overline{H_P}$	10.25123	10.33647	10.29524	10.26100	10.34624

Let us finish this section by mentioning that these results fully correspond with the results presented in [3] describing the experiments with heuristic model learning procedures.

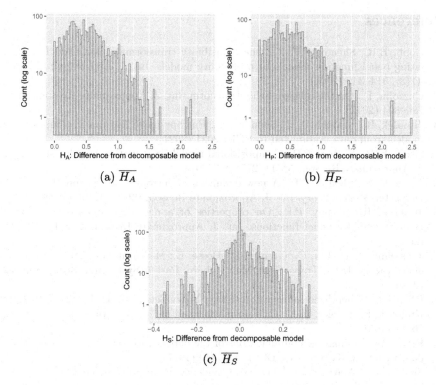

(a) $\overline{H_A}$ (b) $\overline{H_P}$

(c) $\overline{H_S}$

Fig. 1. .

7   Conclusions

Because of their high computational complexity, one cannot make an inference with multidimensional belief functions. Therefore, we suggest using their approximations. In this paper, we studied the approximations called approximations simplifying the dependence structure. As illustrated with an example, the open problem is not only to find an optimal approximation but even the problem of recognizing, which of two approximations is better. Inspired by an analogy with probability theory, we studied the possibility of using information-theoretic characteristics[4] to evaluate the quality of an approximation. Based on the results from random experiments, we suggest heuristic functions denoted by $\overline{H_A}$ and $\overline{H_P}$, for this purpose.

Acknowledgment. The authors wish to acknowledge that the final version of the paper reflects long discussions with Prakash P. Shenoy.

---

[4] Most of the characteristics suggested in [8] cannot be used because of their high computational complexity. As said above, only H_S can be computed for high-dimensional models due to its additivity.

References

1. Cobb, B.R., Shenoy, P.P.: On the plausibility transformation method for translating belief function models to probability models. Int. J. Approximate Reason. **41**(3), 314–340 (2006)
2. Cuzzolin, F.: On the relative belief transform. Int. J. Approximate Reason. **53**(5), 786–804 (2012)
3. Jiroušek, R., Kratochvíl, V., Shenoy, P.P.: Entropy-based learning of compositional models from data. Submitted to Belief 2021 (2021)
4. Jiroušek, R., Shenoy, P.P.: Compositional models in valuation-based systems. Int. J. Approximate Reason. **55**(1), 277–293 (2014)
5. Jiroušek, R., Shenoy, P.P.: A new definition of entropy of belief functions in the Dempster-Shafer theory. Int. J. Approximate Reason. **92**(1), 49–65 (2018)
6. Jiroušek, R., Shenoy, P.P.: On properties of a new decomposable entropy of Dempster-Shafer belief functions. Int. J. Approximate Reason. **119**(4), 260–279 (2020)
7. Jousselme, A.-L., Liu, C., Grenier, D., Bossé, É.: Measuring ambiguity in the evidence theory. IEEE Trans. Syst. Man Cybern. Part A Syst. Hum. **36**(5), 890–903 (2006)
8. Klir, G.J.: Generalized information theory. Fuzzy Sets Syst. **40**(1), 127–142 (1991)
9. Kullback, S., Leibler, R.A.: On information and sufficiency. Ann. Math. Stat. **22**, 76–86 (1951)
10. Perez, A.: ε-admissible simplifications of the dependence structure of a set of random variables. Kybernetika **13**(6), 439–449 (1977)
11. Shafer, G.: A Mathematical Theory of Evidence. Princeton University Press (1976)
12. Shannon, C.E.: A mathematical theory of communication. Bell Syst. Tech. J. **27**(379–423), 623–656 (1948)
13. Smets, P.: Constructing the pignistic probability function in a context of uncertainty. In: Henrion, M., Shachter, R., Kanal, L.N., Lemmer, J.F. (eds.) Uncertainty in Artificial Intelligence, vol. 5, pp. 29–40. Elsevier (1990)
14. Smets, P., Kennes, R.: The transferable belief model. Artif. Intell. **66**(2), 191–234 (1994)
15. Studený, M.: Formal properties of conditional independence in different calculi of AI. In: Clarke, M., Kruse, R., Moral, S. (eds.) ECSQARU 1993. LNCS, vol. 747, pp. 341–348. Springer, Heidelberg (1993). https://doi.org/10.1007/BFb0028219

Dempster-Shafer Approximations and Probabilistic Bounds in Statistical Matching

Davide Petturiti[1](✉) ⓘ and Barbara Vantaggi[2] ⓘ

[1] Dip. Economia, University of Perugia, Perugia, Italy
davide.petturiti@unipg.it
[2] Dip. MEMOTEF, "La Sapienza" University of Rome, Rome, Italy
barbara.vantaggi@uniroma1.it

Abstract. Many economic applications require to integrate information coming from different data sources. In this work we consider a specific integration problem called statistical matching, referring to probabilistic distributions of $Y|X$, $Z|X$ and X, where X, Y, Z are categorical (possibly multi-dimensional) random variables. Here, we restrict to the case of no logical relations among random variables X, Y, Z. The non-uniqueness of the conditional distribution of $(Y, Z)|X$ suggests to deal with sets of probabilities. For that we consider different strategies to get a conditional belief function for $(Y, Z)|X$ that approximates the initial assessment in a reasonable way. In turn, such conditional belief function, together with the marginal probability distribution of X, gives rise to a joint belief function for the distribution of $V = (X, Y, Z)$.

Keywords: Statistical matching · Belief functions · Inference

1 Introduction

In the era of big data the integration of knowledge coming from several separate data bases is a problem of primary interest. Many economic applications provide situations in which the data sets have some variables in common as well as some variables recorded only in one data base. Some distinguished examples are marketing research [13] and microsimulation modeling [19–21, 26, 31]. In particular, in this work we deal with the so called *statistical matching* problem for categorical variables, where there are two or more different sources with some overlapping variables while some variables are collected only in one source. Thus, data are missing by design since they have been already collected separately, and the gathering of joint data on variables collected separately would be expensive and time-consuming.

This problem has been studied in a coherent probability setting in [27] by showing that when no logical constraints among the variables are present, then the assignment is coherent, but there is more than one probability compatible with the given assignment.

© Springer Nature Switzerland AG 2021
J. Vejnarová and N. Wilson (Eds.): ECSQARU 2021, LNAI 12897, pp. 367–380, 2021.
https://doi.org/10.1007/978-3-030-86772-0_27

Traditionally, to cope with this problem by avoiding to manage a class of distributions, assumptions that are strong enough to assure a unique compatible distribution are used. For instance, the available data are assumed to satisfy conditional independence among the variables collected separately given the common variables. Nevertheless, it turns out that, it is too restrictive to consider just one of the compatible distributions (as already noted for the statistical matching problem in [7,9,12,22,27] and for the missing data problem in [3,15,24]).

As suggested in [6,27] we could consider the envelopes of the compatible probabilities. In [6] it has been proved that the lower envelope is not 2-monotone and the upper envelope is not 2-alternating, therefore the computation of probability bounds on new conditional events must be solved through linear programming.

Here, we consider just two data sources, namely A and B, each characterized by (possibly multi-dimensional) categorical random variables (X, Y) and (X, Z). We assume to know the probabilistic distributions of $Y|X$, $Z|X$ and X and restrict to the case of no logical relations among random variables X, Y, Z. The non-uniqueness of the conditional distribution of $(Y, Z)|X$ suggests to deal with sets of probabilities. A first aim of the paper is to approximate the probabilistic bounds for $(Y, Z)|X$ arising from statistical matching in order to provide an approximation of the lower envelope of the joint distribution of $V = (X, Y, Z)$ by means of a belief function. This problem can be faced by looking to inner and outer approximations. The main peculiarity of inner approximation resides on the fact that we determine a subset of the core of the lower envelope given by the bounds estimated from data only, by taking a subset of compatible probabilities. However, we prove here that the belief functions that are inner approximations reduce to probability measures, so this approach reduces to the choice of any probability distribution built from copulas, as shown in Subsection 4.1.

Then, we face the problem by looking for an outer approximation of the probabilistic bounds for the distribution of $(Y, Z)|X$. The main peculiarity of outer approximation resides on the fact that we complete the core of the lower envelope by adding further probability distributions. Obviously there are different outer approximations as already mentioned for other problems in [16–18], and the choice of the outer approximation depends on the distance used for this aim. In analogy with [17], we provide a method to get the outer approximations based on linear programming for the L^1 and L^∞ distance and based on quadratic programming for the L^2 distance.

Then, we study ϵ-contaminated models that are obtained from the ϵ-contamination [11] of a probability measure in the core of $(Y, Z)|X$ for a fixed x. In particular we show that such models are neither inner nor outer approximations.

Finally, we show that the global assessment arising from the approximation procedure is a coherent lower conditional probability in the sense of Williams [30]. Further, relying on results given in [1], we show that the least committal coherent lower conditional probability extension of the approximated assessment can be computed, in many cases, just through a generalized Bayesian conditioning rule [1,29].

2   Preliminaries

Let $\mathcal{A}$ be a finite Boolean algebra of events, where $\emptyset$ and Ω stand for the impossible and sure events. Further, $\vee$, $\wedge$, $(\cdot)^c$ denote the disjunction, conjunction, and contrary operations, while $\subseteq$, $=$ stand for implication and double implication. Moreover, $\mathcal{A}^0$ stands for $\mathcal{A}^0 = \mathcal{A} \setminus \{\emptyset\}$.

A function $\varphi : \mathcal{A} \to [0,1]$ such that $\varphi(\emptyset) = 0$ and $\varphi(\Omega) = 1$ is said to be a:

probability measure: if $\varphi(A \vee B) = \varphi(A) + \varphi(B)$, for all $A, B \in \mathcal{A}$ with $A \wedge B = \emptyset$;
belief function: if, for every $k \geq 2$ and every $E_1, \ldots, E_k \in \mathcal{A}$,

$$\varphi\left(\bigvee_{i=1}^{k} E_i\right) \geq \sum_{\emptyset \neq I \subseteq \{1,\ldots,k\}} (-1)^{|I|+1} \varphi\left(\bigwedge_{i \in I} E_i\right);$$

2-monotone capacity: if $\varphi(A \vee B) \geq \varphi(A) + \varphi(B) - \varphi(A \wedge B)$, for all $A, B \in \mathcal{A}$;
(coherent) lower probability: if there exists a closed (in the product topology) set $\mathcal{P}$ of probability measures on $\mathcal{A}$ such that, for all $A \in \mathcal{A}$,

$$\varphi(A) = \min_{P \in \mathcal{P}} P(A).$$

In particular, a lower probability [28,29] is normally denoted as $\underline{P}$ and $\mathcal{P}$ is taken equal to the set

$$\mathcal{P} = \{P : P \text{ is a probability measure on } \mathcal{A}, P \geq \underline{P}\},$$

said *core* [10] or *credal set* [14]. It turns out that 2-monotone capacities are particular lower probabilities, belief functions are particular 2-monotone capacities, and probability measures are particular belief functions. Further, every function φ has an associated *dual* function ψ defined, for every $A \in \mathcal{A}$, as $\psi(A) = 1 - \varphi(A^c)$.

In the rest of the paper we will be mainly concerned with belief functions, whose theory has been essentially developed by Dempster and Shafer in [4,25]. A belief function is usually denoted as Bel and its dual, said *plausibility function*, as Pl. Every belief function is completely characterized by its *Möbius inverse* $m : \mathcal{A} \to [0,1]$, also said *basic probability assignment*, which is a non-negative function with $m(\emptyset) = 0$ and summing up to 1 such that, for all $A \in \mathcal{A}$, $Bel(A) = \sum_{\substack{B \subseteq A \\ B \in \mathcal{A}}} m(B)$.

In the rest of the paper, we refer to the notion of conditional probability due to Dubins [8]. A function $P : \mathcal{A} \times \mathcal{A}^0 \to [0,1]$ is a *full conditional probability on* $\mathcal{A}$ if it satisfies:

(i) $P(E|H) = P(E \wedge H|H)$, for every $E \in \mathcal{A}$ and $H \in \mathcal{A}^0$;
(ii) $P(\cdot|H)$ is a probability measure on $\mathcal{A}$, for every $H \in \mathcal{A}^0$;
(iii) $P(E \wedge F|H) = P(E|H) \cdot P(F|E \wedge H)$, for every $H, E \wedge H \in \mathcal{A}^0$ and $E, F \in \mathcal{A}$.

More generally, given a non-empty $\mathcal{G} \subseteq \mathcal{A} \times \mathcal{A}^0$, a function $P : \mathcal{G} \rightarrow [0,1]$ is a *coherent conditional probability* (see [2]) if there exists a full conditional probability Q on $\mathcal{A}$ such that $P(E|H) = Q(E|H)$, for all $E|H \in \mathcal{G}$.

This allows to introduce the notion of *coherent lower conditional probability* due to Williams [30] as a function $\underline{P} : \mathcal{G} \rightarrow [0,1]$ such that there exists a closed (in the product topology) set $\mathcal{P}$ of full conditional probabilities on $\mathcal{A}$ such that $\underline{P}(E|H) = \min_{Q \in \mathcal{P}} Q(E|H)$, for all $E|H \in \mathcal{G}$.

All notions introduced so far adapt in a straightforward way if we take a field of sets in place of $\mathcal{A}$.

3   Statistical Matching

Consider two or more different sources with some overlapping variables and some variables collected only in one source. For example let A and B be two sources and let X represent the common variables, Y denotes the variables collected only in A, and Z those only in B. Thus, the data consist of two samples, one on (X, Y) and the other one on (X, Z). In this context data are missing by design since they have been already collected separately.

Traditionally, to cope with these problems, the available data are combined with assumptions, as conditional independence between Y and Z given X, strong enough to assure a unique compatible distribution. Actually, since there are many distributions on (X, Y, Z) compatible with the available partial information on (X, Y) and (X, Z), it is too restrictive to consider just one of the compatible distributions (as already noted in [6,7,12,22,27]).

The available information allows to estimate probability distributions $P_{Y|X}$ from A and $P_{Z|X}$ from B and the marginal probability P_X from both sources. For instance, assuming that units in A and B are i.i.d. observations from probability distributions $P_{(X,Y)}$ and $P_{(X,Z)}$, respectively, and assuming that (X, Y) has range $\mathcal{X} \times \mathcal{Y}$ and (X, Z) has range $\mathcal{X} \times \mathcal{Z}$, the ML estimates of $P_{Y|X}, P_{Z|X}, P_X$ can be obtained from the corresponding observed frequencies. In detail, we set

$$\hat{P}_{Y|X}(y|x) = \frac{n_{xy}^A}{n_x^A}, \quad \hat{P}_{Z|X}(z|x) = \frac{n_{xz}^B}{n_x^B}, \quad \hat{P}_X(x) = \frac{n_x^A + n_x^B}{n^A + n^B},$$

where n_{xy}^A is the number of units in A with categories (x, y), n_{xz}^B is the number of units in B with categories (x, z), n_x^A and n_x^A are the number of units with category x in A and B, respectively, and n^A and n^B are the total number of units in A and B.

Let X, Y, Z be categorical random variables, ranging in the finite sets $\mathcal{X}, \mathcal{Y}, \mathcal{Z}$. Such random variables determine the Boolean algebras $\mathcal{B}(X), \mathcal{B}(Y), \mathcal{B}(Z)$ generated by the partitions of the sure event

$$\{(X = x) : x \in \mathcal{X}\}, \quad \{(Y = y) : y \in \mathcal{Y}\}, \quad \text{and} \quad \{(Z = z) : z \in \mathcal{Z}\}.$$

Let $V = (X, Y, Z)$ and assume no logical relations are present between the random variables X, Y, Z, that is $\mathcal{B}(V) = \mathcal{B}(X) \otimes \mathcal{B}(Y) \otimes \mathcal{B}(Z)$ having

$\mathcal{B}(X), \mathcal{B}(Y), \mathcal{B}(Z)$ as Boolean sub-algebras. This implies that the vector V has range $\mathcal{V} = \mathcal{X} \times \mathcal{Y} \times \mathcal{Z}$ and a probability measure $P : \mathcal{B}(V) \to [0,1]$ induces a probability distribution $P_V : 2^{\mathcal{V}} \to [0,1]$ for V by setting, for every $A \in 2^{\mathcal{V}}$,

$$P_V(A) = P(V \in A).$$

Notice that $\mathcal{B}(V)$ is a Boolean algebra isomorphic to $2^{\mathcal{V}}$, thus P can be actually identified with P_V.

Consider the assessment

$$\{P_{Y|X}(y|x), P_{Z|X}(z|x), P_X(x) : x \in \mathcal{X}, y \in \mathcal{Y}, z \in \mathcal{Z}\}. \tag{1}$$

The *statistical matching* problem in this case amounts to finding a probability distribution P_V for V consistent with (1), and this reduces to a problem of coherence of the given assessment.

The coherence of assessment (1) is assured (see [27]) whenever there is no logical constraint between the variables X, Y, Z.

Theorem 1. *Let X, Y, Z be three finite random variables such that $\mathcal{B}(V) = \mathcal{B}(X) \otimes \mathcal{B}(Y) \otimes \mathcal{B}(Z)$, then the assessment (1) is coherent.*

Remark 1. In other terms, Theorem 1 states that there exists a full conditional probability Q on $\mathcal{B}(V)$ such that, for all $x \in \mathcal{X}, y \in \mathcal{Y}, z \in \mathcal{Z}$, it holds that $Q(Y = y|X = x) = P_{Y|X}(y|x)$, $Q(Z = z|X = x) = P_{Z|X}(z|x)$, and $Q(X = x) = P_X(x)$, where $Q(\cdot|\Omega)$ is identified with $Q(\cdot)$, as usual.

The assessment (1) gives rise to a closed and convex set of probability distributions $\mathcal{P}_V$ for V defined on $2^{\mathcal{V}}$. The lower and upper envelopes $\underline{P}_V = \min \mathcal{P}_V$ and $\overline{P}_V = \max \mathcal{P}_V$, where minima and maxima are pointwise on $2^{\mathcal{V}}$, have been characterized in [6].

In analogy, for every $x \in \mathcal{X}$, the sub-assessment

$$\{P_{Y|X}(y|x), P_{Z|X}(z|x) : y \in \mathcal{Y}, z \in \mathcal{Z}\} \tag{2}$$

determines a closed and convex set of probability distributions $\mathcal{P}_{(Y,Z)|(X=x)}$ for $(Y,Z)|(X = x)$ defined on $2^{\mathcal{Y} \times \mathcal{Z}}$. The set $\mathcal{P}_{(Y,Z)|(X=x)}$ induces the lower and upper envelopes

$$\underline{P}_{(Y,Z)|(X=x)} = \min \mathcal{P}_{(Y,Z)|(X=x)} \quad \text{and} \quad \overline{P}_{(Y,Z)|(X=x)} = \max \mathcal{P}_{(Y,Z)|(X=x)},$$

where minima and maxima are pointwise on $2^{\mathcal{Y} \times \mathcal{Z}}$.

Actually, for all $A \in 2^{\mathcal{Y}}$ and $B \in 2^{\mathcal{Z}}$, since $\mathcal{B}(V) = \mathcal{B}(X) \otimes \mathcal{B}(Y) \otimes \mathcal{B}(Z)$, and, so, $\mathcal{B}(Y, Z) = \mathcal{B}(Y) \otimes \mathcal{B}(Z)$ is isomorphic to $2^{\mathcal{Y} \times \mathcal{Z}}$, from the Frechét-Hoeffding inequality, the lower bound on $(A \times \mathcal{Z}) \cap (\mathcal{Y} \times B) = A \times B$ is

$$\underline{P}_{(Y,Z)|(X=x)}(A \times B) = \max\{0, P_{Y|X}(A|x) + P_{Z|X}(B|x) - 1\},$$

where $P_{Y|X}(A|x) = \sum_{y \in A} P_{Y|X}(y|x)$ and $P_{Z|X}(B|x) = \sum_{z \in B} P_{Z|X}(z|x)$. Moreover, from Theorem 1 in [23], for all $H \in 2^{\mathcal{Y} \times \mathcal{Z}}$, it follows that

$$\underline{P}_{(Y,Z)|(X=x)}(H) = \max_{\substack{A \times B \subseteq H \\ A \in 2^{\mathcal{Y}}, B \in 2^{\mathcal{Z}}}} \max\{0, P_{Y|X}(A|x) + P_{Z|X}(B|x) - 1\}. \tag{3}$$

It turns out that $\underline{P}_V$ and $\underline{P}_{(Y,Z)|(X=x)}$ are generally not 2-monotone capacities (see [6]). Actually, in Proposition 2 in the aforementioned paper it has been proved that $\underline{P}_V$ is 2-monotone only in the case that at least a distribution between $P_{Y|X}$ and $P_{Z|X}$ is degenerate, for all $x \in \mathcal{X}$ with $P_X(x) > 0$.

For completeness we provide the following example that will be developed in the rest of the paper.

Example 1. Let X, Y, Z be dichotomic random variables ranging in $\mathcal{X} = \mathcal{Y} = \mathcal{Z} = \{0, 1\}$ and consider the conditional distributions,

$$P_{Y|X}(y|0) = \begin{cases} \frac{1}{3} & \text{if } y = 0, \\ \frac{2}{3} & \text{if } y = 1, \end{cases} \quad \text{and} \quad P_{Z|X}(z|0) = \begin{cases} \frac{1}{2} & \text{if } z = 0, \\ \frac{1}{2} & \text{if } z = 1. \end{cases}$$

Denote

$$\mathcal{Y} \times \mathcal{Z} = \{\underbrace{(0,0)}_{=a_1}, \underbrace{(0,1)}_{=a_2}, \underbrace{(1,0)}_{=a_3}, \underbrace{(1,1)}_{=a_4}\}$$

and let $A_i = \{a_i\}$, $A_{ij} = \{a_i, a_j\}$, $A_{ijk} = \{a_i, a_j, a_k\}$ and $A_{1234} = \mathcal{Y} \times \mathcal{Z}$.

We have that $\mathcal{P}_{(Y,Z)|(X=0)} = \{\alpha P_1 + (1 - \alpha)P_2 : \alpha \in [0,1]\}$, where the probability distributions P_1, P_2 and the lower envelope $\underline{P}_{(Y,Z)|(X=0)}$ are

$2^{\mathcal{Y} \times \mathcal{Z}}$	∅	A_1	A_2	A_3	A_4	A_{12}	A_{13}	A_{14}	A_{23}	A_{24}	A_{34}	A_{123}	A_{124}	A_{134}	A_{234}	A_{1234}
P_1	0	0	$\frac{2}{6}$	$\frac{3}{6}$	$\frac{1}{6}$	$\frac{2}{6}$	$\frac{3}{6}$	$\frac{1}{6}$	$\frac{5}{6}$	$\frac{3}{6}$	$\frac{4}{6}$	$\frac{5}{6}$	$\frac{3}{6}$	$\frac{4}{6}$	1	1
P_2	0	$\frac{2}{6}$	0	$\frac{1}{6}$	$\frac{3}{6}$	$\frac{2}{6}$	$\frac{3}{6}$	$\frac{5}{6}$	$\frac{1}{6}$	$\frac{3}{6}$	$\frac{4}{6}$	$\frac{3}{6}$	$\frac{5}{6}$	1	$\frac{4}{6}$	1
$\underline{P}_{(Y,Z)|(X=0)}$	0	0	0	$\frac{1}{6}$	$\frac{1}{6}$	$\frac{2}{6}$	$\frac{3}{6}$	$\frac{1}{6}$	$\frac{1}{6}$	$\frac{3}{6}$	$\frac{4}{6}$	$\frac{3}{6}$	$\frac{3}{6}$	$\frac{4}{6}$	$\frac{4}{6}$	1

It is easy to see that $\underline{P}_{(Y,Z)|(X=0)}$ is not 2-monotone since

$$\underline{P}_{(Y,Z)|(X=0)}(A_{123}) = \frac{3}{6} < \frac{5}{6} = \underline{P}_{(Y,Z)|(X=0)}(A_{12}) + \underline{P}_{(Y,Z)|(X=0)}(A_{13})$$
$$- \underline{P}_{(Y,Z)|(X=0)}(A_1).$$

◆

4   Dempster-Shafer Inner and Outer Approximations

Our aim is to obtain a belief function $Bel_{(Y,Z)|(X=x)}$ approximating in some reasonable sense $\underline{P}_{(Y,Z)|(X=x)}$. This allows to define

$$Bel_{(Y,Z)|X}(A|x) = Bel_{(Y,Z)|(X=x)}(A), \tag{4}$$
$$Pl_{(Y,Z)|X}(A|x) = Pl_{(Y,Z)|(X=x)}(A), \tag{5}$$

for every $A \in 2^{\mathcal{Y} \times \mathcal{Z}}$ and $x \in \mathcal{X}$, with $Pl_{(Y,Z)|(X=x)}(A) = 1 - Bel_{(Y,Z)|(X=x)}(A^c)$, where the complement is intended in $\mathcal{Y} \times \mathcal{Z}$.

For every $B \in 2^{\mathcal{V}}$ and $x \in \mathcal{X}$ let

$$[B]_x = \{(y, z) \in \mathcal{Y} \times \mathcal{Z} : (x, y, z) \in B\}, \tag{6}$$

where possibly $[B]_x = \emptyset$. It is easily seen that, every $B \in 2^{\mathcal{V}}$ can be expressed as

$$B = \bigcup_{x \in \mathcal{X}} (\{x\} \times [B]_x)$$

in which a Cartesian product is set to $\emptyset$ if one of the factors is equal to $\emptyset$.

Then we define, for every $B \in 2^{\mathcal{V}}$

$$Bel_V(B) = \sum_{x \in \mathcal{X}} Bel_{(Y,Z)|X}([B]_x|x) P_X(x), \tag{7}$$

$$Pl_V(B) = \sum_{x \in \mathcal{X}} Pl_{(Y,Z)|X}([B]_x|x) P_X(x). \tag{8}$$

Proposition 1. Bel_V and Pl_V defined as in (7) and (8) are dual belief and plausibility functions on $2^{\mathcal{V}}$. Moreover, for every $A \in 2^{\mathcal{Y} \times \mathcal{Z}}$ and $x \in \mathcal{X}$ it holds that

(a) $Bel_V(\{x\} \times \mathcal{Y} \times \mathcal{Z}) = Pl_V(\{x\} \times \mathcal{Y} \times \mathcal{Z}) = P_X(x)$,
(b) $Bel_{(Y,Z)|X}(A|x) = \frac{Bel_V(\{x\} \times A)}{P_X(x)}$ and $Pl_{(Y,Z)|X}(A|x) = \frac{Pl_V(\{x\} \times A)}{P_X(x)}$, provided that $P_X(x) > 0$.

Proof. It is sufficient to prove that Bel_V is a belief function on $2^{\mathcal{V}}$ and that Pl_V is the dual capacity of Bel_V.

Since $[\emptyset]_x = \emptyset$ and $[\mathcal{V}]_x = \mathcal{Y} \times \mathcal{Z}$, we have that

$$Bel_V(\emptyset) = \sum_{x \in \mathcal{X}} Bel_{(Y,Z)|X}(\emptyset|x) P_X(x) = 0,$$

$$Bel_V(\mathcal{V}) = \sum_{x \in \mathcal{X}} Bel_{(Y,Z)|X}(\mathcal{Y} \times \mathcal{Z}|x) P_X(x) = 1.$$

For every $A, B \in 2^{\mathcal{V}}$ with $A \subseteq B$, we have that $[A]_x \subseteq [B]_x$ for every $x \in \mathcal{X}$, and this implies $Bel_{(Y,Z)|X}([A]_x|x) \leq Bel_{(Y,Z)|X}([B]_x|x)$. Hence, by the monotonicity of the expectation operator with respect to P_X, it follows that $Bel_V(A) \leq Bel_V(B)$. This implies that Bel_V is a normalized capacity on $2^{\mathcal{V}}$.

For every $k \geq 2$, every $E_1, \ldots, E_k \in 2^{\mathcal{V}}$, and every $\emptyset \neq I \subseteq \{1, \ldots, k\}$, since for every $x \in \mathcal{X}$ it holds that

$$\left[\bigcup_{i \in I} E_i\right]_x = \bigcup_{i \in I} [E_i]_x \quad \text{and} \quad \left[\bigcap_{i \in I} E_i\right]_x = \bigcap_{i \in I} [E_i]_x$$

we have that

$$Bel_{(Y,Z)|X}\left(\bigcup_{i=1}^{k} [E_i]_x \,\Big|\, x\right) \geq \sum_{\emptyset \neq I \subseteq \{1,\ldots,k\}} (-1)^{|I|+1} Bel_{(Y,Z)|X}\left(\bigcap_{i \in I} [E_i]_x \,\Big|\, x\right).$$

Hence, by the monotonicity and the linearity of the expectation operator with respect to P_X, it follows that

$$Bel_V\left(\bigcup_{i=1}^{k} E_i\right) \geq \sum_{\emptyset \neq I \subseteq \{1,\ldots,k\}} (-1)^{|I|+1} Bel_V\left(\bigcap_{i \in I} E_i\right).$$

Further, for every $B \in 2^{\mathcal{V}}$, since $([B]_x)^c = [B^c]_x$, where the complement in the first member is taken with respect to $\mathcal{Y} \times \mathcal{Z}$, while the complement in the second member is taken with respect to $\mathcal{V}$, we have that

$$
\begin{aligned}
Bel_V(B) &= \sum_{x \in \mathcal{X}} Bel_{(Y,Z)|X}([B]_x|x) P_X(x) \\
&= \sum_{x \in \mathcal{X}} \left[1 - Pl_{(Y,Z)|X}([B]_x^c|x) \right] P_X(x) \\
&= 1 - \sum_{x \in \mathcal{X}} Pl_{(Y,Z)|X}([B]_x^c|x) P_X(x) \\
&= 1 - \sum_{x \in \mathcal{X}} Pl_{(Y,Z)|X}([B^c]_x|x) P_X(x) \\
&= 1 - Pl_V(B^c).
\end{aligned}
$$

Statements *(a)* and *(b)* follow since, for every $x, x' \in X$ and $A \in 2^{\mathcal{Y} \times \mathcal{Z}}$, $[\{x\} \times A]_{x'}$ is equal to A if $x = x'$ and to $\emptyset$ otherwise.   □

Below we explore some strategies to arrive to a $Bel_{(Y,Z)|X}$. We stress that $Bel_{(Y,Z)|X}$ is a collection of conditional belief functions on $2^{\mathcal{Y} \times \mathcal{Z}}$ for $x \in \mathcal{X}$. Their combination through Dempster's rule (see [4,25]) does not seem suitable both from a semantic point of view and since it would result in a belief function on $2^{\mathcal{Y} \times \mathcal{Z}}$ disregarding P_X.

4.1   Inner Approximating Conditional Belief Functions

For all $x \in \mathcal{X}$, the most intuitive way for defining $Bel_{(Y,Z)|(X=x)}$ is to require that $Bel_{(Y,Z)|(X=x)} \geq \underline{P}_{(Y,Z)|(X=x)}$, pointwise on $2^{\mathcal{Y} \times \mathcal{Z}}$. In such a way we get an *inner approximating conditional belief function*.

The following theorem shows that, for all $x \in \mathcal{X}$, every inner approximating conditional belief function is actually additive and belongs to $\mathcal{P}_{(Y,Z)|(X=x)}$.

Theorem 2. *For all $x \in \mathcal{X}$, every belief function $Bel_{(Y,Z)|(X=x)}$ on $2^{\mathcal{Y} \times \mathcal{Z}}$ satisfying*

- *$Bel_{(Y,Z)|(X=x)}(\{y\} \times \mathcal{Z}) \geq P_{Y|X}(y|x)$, for all $y \in \mathcal{Y}$,*
- *$Bel_{(Y,Z)|(X=x)}(\mathcal{Y} \times \{z\}) \geq P_{Z|X}(z|x)$, for all $z \in \mathcal{Z}$,*

is additive and belongs to $\mathcal{P}_{(Y,Z)|(X=x)}$.

Proof. Since every $Bel_{(Y,Z)|(X=x)}$ is completely characterized by its Möbius inverse $m : 2^{\mathcal{Y} \times \mathcal{Z}} \to [0,1]$, we need to find an m solving the system

$$
\begin{cases}
\displaystyle\sum_{B \subseteq \{y\} \times \mathcal{Z}} m(B) \geq P_{Y|X}(y|x), & \text{for all } y \in \mathcal{Y}, \\
\displaystyle\sum_{B \subseteq \mathcal{Y} \times \{z\}} m(B) \geq P_{Z|X}(z|x), & \text{for all } z \in \mathcal{Z}, \\
\displaystyle\sum_{B \subseteq \mathcal{Y} \times \mathcal{Z}} m(B) = 1, & \\
m(B) \geq 0, & \text{for all } B \subseteq \mathcal{Y} \times \mathcal{Z}, \\
m(\emptyset) = 0.
\end{cases}
$$

Summing memberwise the inequalities related to $y \in \mathcal{Y}$ and those related to $z \in \mathcal{Z}$, we get

$$\sum_{y \in \mathcal{Y}} \sum_{B \subseteq \{y\} \times \mathcal{Z}} m(B) \geq 1 \quad \text{and} \quad \sum_{z \in \mathcal{Z}} \sum_{B \subseteq \mathcal{Y} \times \{z\}} m(B) \geq 1.$$

The two inequalities above, together with $\sum_{B \subseteq \mathcal{Y} \times \mathcal{Z}} m(B) = 1$ imply that m can be positive only on singletons, therefore $Bel_{(Y,Z)|(X=x)}$ is additive (see [25]). Further, since $\underline{P}_{(Y,Z)|(X=x)}(\{y\} \times \mathcal{Z}) = P_{Y|X}(y|x)$ and $\underline{P}_{(Y,Z)|(X=x)}(\mathcal{Y} \times \{z\}) = P_{Z|X}(z|x)$, it follows that $Bel_{(Y,Z)|(X=x)} \in \mathcal{P}_{(Y,Z)|(X=x)}$. $\qquad \square$

The previous theorem also implies that the only belief functions having a core contained in $\mathcal{P}_{(Y,Z)|(X=x)}$ are actually additive and coincide with the elements of $\mathcal{P}_{(Y,Z)|(X=x)}$.

4.2   Outer Approximating Conditional Belief Functions

Since only trivial inner approximations are possible, another possibility for defining $Bel_{(Y,Z)|(X=x)}$ is to require that $\underline{P}_{(Y,Z)|(X=x)} \geq Bel_{(Y,Z)|(X=x)}$, pointwise on $2^{\mathcal{Y} \times \mathcal{Z}}$. In such a way we get an *outer approximating conditional belief function*.

The problem of finding an outer approximation of a lower probability through a belief function has been investigated by a series of papers [16–18]. In the cited papers, the outer approximation is found by minimizing a suitable distance defined, in our context, over the set of lower probabilities on $2^{\mathcal{Y} \times \mathcal{Z}}$. In detail, the three most investigated distances are defined, for every $\underline{P}, \underline{Q}$ as:

- $d_1(\underline{P}, \underline{Q}) = \sum_{A \subseteq \mathcal{Y} \times \mathcal{Z}} |\underline{P}(A) - \underline{Q}(A)|,$
- $d_2(\underline{P}, \underline{Q}) = \sum_{A \subseteq \mathcal{Y} \times \mathcal{Z}} (\underline{P}(A) - \underline{Q}(A))^2,$
- $d_\infty(\underline{P}, \underline{Q}) = \max_{A \subseteq \mathcal{Y} \times \mathcal{Z}} |\underline{P}(A) - \underline{Q}(A)|.$

Notice that d_1, d_2, and d_∞ can be seen as restrictions of distances induced by the L^1, L^2, and L^∞ norms on the space $[0,1]^{2^{\mathcal{Y} \times \mathcal{X}}}$.

In our context, for a chosen distance d, the problem is to find a Möbius inverse $m : 2^{\mathcal{Y} \times \mathcal{Z}} \to [0,1]$ for the belief function $Bel_{(Y,Z)|(X=x)}$, solving the optimization problem

$$\text{minimize } d(\underline{P}_{(Y,Z)|(X=x)}, Bel_{(Y,Z)|(X=x)})$$

subject to:

$$
\begin{cases}
\sum_{B \subseteq A} m(B) \leq \underline{P}_{(Y,Z)|(X=x)}(A), \text{ for all } A \subseteq \mathcal{Y} \times \mathcal{Z}, \\[2mm]
\sum_{B \subseteq \mathcal{Y} \times \mathcal{Z}} m(B) = 1, \\[2mm]
m(B) \geq 0, \qquad\qquad\qquad \text{ for all } B \subseteq \mathcal{Y} \times \mathcal{Z}, \\[2mm]
m(\emptyset) = 0.
\end{cases}
\tag{9}
$$

In particular, due to the outer approximation constraint between $\underline{P}_{(Y,Z)|(X=x)}$ and $Bel_{(Y,Z)|(X=x)}$, we can remove the absolute value in d_1 and d_∞. Therefore, using d_1 problem (9) reduces to a linear programming problem, while using d_2 problem (9) reduces to a quadratic programming problem. Finally, using d_∞ problem (9) reduces to the optimization of a convex piecewise linear (affine) function with linear constraints that, in turn, can be transformed to a linear programming problem, by adding an extra scalar variable.

As highlighted in [17], the main disadvantage connected to distance d_1 is the non-uniqueness of the found solution, while d_2 always leads to a unique solution. Further, both d_1 and d_2 guarantee that the found solution is *undominated*, i.e., there is no other belief function pointwise comprised between $\underline{P}_{(Y,Z)|(X=x)}$ and the found solution (see [17]). On the other hand, using d_∞ we generally lose both uniqueness and undomination.

Example 2. Take X, Y, Z, and $P_{Y|X}(y|0)$ and $P_{Z|X}(z|0)$ as in Example 1. Solving problem (9) using d_1 we get infinitely many undominated solutions, two of which are

$2^{\mathcal{Y}\times\mathcal{Z}}$	$\emptyset$	A_1	A_2	A_3	A_4	A_{12}	A_{13}	A_{14}	A_{23}	A_{24}	A_{34}	A_{123}	A_{124}	A_{134}	A_{234}	A_{1234}
$\underline{P}_{(Y,Z)|(X=0)}$	0	0	0	$\frac{1}{6}$	$\frac{1}{6}$	$\frac{2}{6}$	$\frac{3}{6}$	$\frac{1}{6}$	$\frac{1}{6}$	$\frac{3}{6}$	$\frac{4}{6}$	$\frac{3}{6}$	$\frac{3}{6}$	$\frac{4}{6}$	$\frac{4}{6}$	1
m^1	0	0	0	$\frac{1}{6}$	$\frac{1}{6}$	0	$\frac{2}{6}$	0	0	$\frac{2}{6}$	0	0	0	0	0	0
$Bel^1_{(Y,Z)|(X=0)}$	0	0	0	$\frac{1}{6}$	$\frac{1}{6}$	0	$\frac{3}{6}$	$\frac{1}{6}$	$\frac{1}{6}$	$\frac{3}{6}$	$\frac{2}{6}$	$\frac{1}{6}$	$\frac{3}{6}$	$\frac{4}{6}$	$\frac{4}{6}$	1
m^2	0	0	0	$\frac{1}{6}$	$\frac{1}{6}$	$\frac{1}{6}$	$\frac{1}{6}$	0	0	$\frac{1}{6}$	$\frac{1}{6}$	0	0	0	0	0
$Bel^2_{(Y,Z)|(X=0)}$	0	0	0	$\frac{1}{6}$	$\frac{1}{6}$	$\frac{1}{6}$	$\frac{2}{6}$	$\frac{1}{6}$	$\frac{1}{6}$	$\frac{2}{6}$	$\frac{3}{6}$	$\frac{3}{6}$	$\frac{3}{6}$	$\frac{4}{6}$	$\frac{4}{6}$	1

whose d_1 distance from $\underline{P}_{(Y,Z)|(X=0)}$ is equal to $\frac{4}{6}$.

Using d_2 we get a unique undominated solution that coincides with the belief function $Bel^2_{(Y,Z)|(X=0)}$ also minimizing d_1, whose d_2 distance from $\underline{P}_{(Y,Z)|(X=0)}$ is equal to $\frac{1}{9}$.

Finally, we have that $Bel^2_{(Y,Z)|(X=0)}$ turns out to minimize also d_∞, and its d_∞ distance from $\underline{P}_{(Y,Z)|(X=0)}$ is equal to $\frac{1}{6}$. In this case it holds that $Bel^2_{(Y,Z)|(X=0)}$ is the unique solution minimizing d_∞ and is also undominated. ◆

Besides minimizing a distance, other approaches are available, like minimizing a measure of nonspecificity (or imprecision) as done in [5]. Independently of the objective function, problem (9) has an exponential number of constraints and unknowns thus it is a computationally hard problem in general. However, the number of unknowns can be reduced limiting to *k-additive belief functions* [10].

4.3 ϵ-Contamination Models

Previous subsections showed that to avoid triviality, only outer approximations of $\underline{P}_{(Y,Z)|(X=x)}$ make sense, as no non-additive belief function inner approximating $\underline{P}_{(Y,Z)|(X=x)}$ exists.

Another method to get a belief function connected to $\mathcal{P}_{(Y,Z)|(X=x)}$ is to choose a reference $P^* \in \mathcal{P}_{(Y,Z)|(X=x)}$, as that determined by the independence copula between $P_{Y|X}(\cdot|x)$ and $P_{Z|X}(\cdot|x)$, and then build an ϵ-*contamination model* [11]. This amounts to choose an $\epsilon \in (0,1)$ and build the class of probability distributions on $2^{\mathcal{Y} \times \mathcal{Z}}$ defined as

$$\mathcal{P}^{P^*,\epsilon}_{(Y,Z)|(X=x)} = \{Q = (1-\epsilon)P^* + \epsilon P \ : \ P \text{ is a probability on } 2^{\mathcal{Y} \times \mathcal{Z}}\}.$$

The lower envelope of $\mathcal{P}^{P^*,\epsilon}_{(Y,Z)|(X=x)}$ is the belief function $Bel^{P^*,\epsilon}_{(Y,Z)|(X=x)}$ defined, for every $A \in 2^{\mathcal{Y} \times \mathcal{Z}}$ as

$$Bel^{P^*,\epsilon}_{(Y,Z)|(X=x)}(A) = \begin{cases} (1-\epsilon)P^*(A) & \text{if } A \neq \mathcal{Y} \times \mathcal{Z}, \\ 1 & \text{otherwise.} \end{cases} \tag{10}$$

For $0 < \epsilon < \epsilon' < 1$, we have $Bel^{P^*,\epsilon'}_{(Y,Z)|(X=x)} \leq Bel^{P^*,\epsilon}_{(Y,Z)|(X=x)}$ pointwise on $2^{\mathcal{Y} \times \mathcal{Z}}$. Since $Bel^{P^*,\epsilon}_{(Y,Z)|(X=x)}$ is non-additive for all $\epsilon \in (0,1)$, we automatically get from Theorem 2 that $Bel^{P^*,\epsilon}_{(Y,Z)|(X=x)}$ cannot be an inner approximation of $\underline{P}_{(Y,Z)|(X=x)}$.

The following example shows that, in general, $Bel^{P^*,\epsilon}_{(Y,Z)|(X=x)}$ is neither an outer approximation of $\underline{P}_{(Y,Z)|(X=x)}$.

Example 3. Take X, Y, Z, and $P_{Y|X}(y|0)$ and $P_{Z|X}(z|0)$ as in Example 1. Let P^* be the element of $\mathcal{P}_{(Y,Z)|(X=0)}$ determined by the independence copula between $P_{Y|X}(\cdot|0)$ and $P_{Z|X}(\cdot|0)$. For $A_1 = \{(0,0)\}$, since $P^*(A_1) = \frac{1}{6}$ and $\underline{P}_{(Y,Z)|(X=0)}(A_1) = 0$, there is no $\epsilon \in (0,1)$ such that $Bel^{P^*,\epsilon}_{(Y,Z)|(X=0)}(A_1) \leq \underline{P}_{(Y,Z)|(X=0)}(A_1)$. Actually, it is possible to show that for all $P^* \in \mathcal{P}_{(Y,Z)|(X=0)}$ and all $\epsilon \in (0,1)$, the resulting $Bel^{P^*,\epsilon}_{(Y,Z)|(X=0)}$ is not an outer approximation of $\underline{P}_{(Y,Z)|(X=0)}$. ◆

5   Dempster-Shafer Approximation and Inference

The main advantage in approximating the probabilistic assessment (2) with the conditional belief assessment $Bel_{(Y,Z)|X}$ is that the global Dempster-Shafer assessment $\{Bel_V, Bel_{(Y,Z)|X}\}$ can be viewed as a lower conditional probability assessment on the set of conditional events

$$\mathcal{G} = \{(V \in B)|\Omega \ : \ B \in 2^{\mathcal{V}}\} \cup \{((Y,Z) \in A)|(X = x) \ : \ A \in 2^{\mathcal{Y} \times \mathcal{Z}}, x \in \mathcal{X}\}.$$

In particular, the resulting assessment on $\mathcal{G}$ turns out to be *coherent* in the sense of Williams [30] since there exists a closed set $\mathcal{Q}$ of full conditional probabilities on $\mathcal{B}(V)$ whose lower envelope $\underline{Q} = \min \mathcal{Q}$, where minima are pointwise on $\mathcal{B}(V) \times \mathcal{B}(V)^0$, is such that, for all $B \in 2^{\mathcal{V}}$, $A \in 2^{\mathcal{Y} \times \mathcal{Z}}$, and $x \in \mathcal{X}$, it holds that

$$\underline{Q}(V \in B) = Bel_V(B) \quad \text{and} \quad \underline{Q}((Y,Z) \in A|X = x) = Bel_{(Y,Z)|X}(A|x),$$

where we identify $Q(\cdot|\Omega)$ with $Q(\cdot)$, as usual. This claim is an immediate consequence of Proposition 1.

In turn, the assessment on $\mathcal{G}$ can be extended on the entire $\mathcal{B}(V) \times \mathcal{B}(V)^0$ searching for the least committal coherent lower conditional probability. This amounts to taking $\mathcal{Q}$ equal to the set of all full conditional probabilities on $\mathcal{B}(V)$ compatible with $\{Bel_V, Bel_{(Y,Z)|X}\}$.

By results in [1], we have that, in many cases, the computation of the least committal Q can be simply reduced to a generalized version of the Bayesian conditioning rule [28]. In particular, for all $E|H \in \mathcal{B}(V) \times \mathcal{B}(V)^0$, we have that

$$Q(E|H) = \frac{Q(E \wedge H)}{Q(E \wedge H) + \overline{Q}(E^c \wedge H)}, \tag{11}$$

provided that $Q(E \wedge H) + \overline{Q}(E^c \wedge H) > 0$, where $\overline{Q}$ is the upper envelope of $\mathcal{Q}$.

For instance, for all $A \in 2^{\mathcal{X}}$ and non-empty $B \in 2^{\mathcal{Y} \times \mathcal{Z}}$, we can compute

$$Q(X \in A|(Y,Z) \in B) = \frac{Q((X \in A) \wedge ((Y,Z) \in B))}{Q((X \in A) \wedge ((Y,Z) \in B)) + \overline{Q}((X \in A^c) \wedge ((Y,Z) \in B))}$$

$$= \frac{Bel_V((A \times \mathcal{Y} \times \mathcal{Z}) \cap (\mathcal{X} \times B))}{Bel_V((A \times \mathcal{Y} \times \mathcal{Z}) \cap (\mathcal{X} \times B)) + Pl_V((A^c \times \mathcal{Y} \times \mathcal{Z}) \cap (\mathcal{X} \times B))}, \tag{12}$$

provided that $Bel_V((A \times \mathcal{Y} \times \mathcal{Z}) \cap (\mathcal{X} \times B)) + Pl_V((A^c \times \mathcal{Y} \times \mathcal{Z}) \cap (\mathcal{X} \times B)) > 0$.

Example 4. Take X, Y, Z, and $P_{Y|X}(y|0)$ and $P_{Z|X}(z|0)$ as in Example 1. Consider the outer approximation $Bel^2_{(Y,X)|(X=0)}$ computed in Example 2 by minimizing distance d_2, which is also optimal according to d_1 and d_∞. Suppose $P_{Y|X}(y|1) = P_{Y|X}(y|0)$ and $P_{Z|X}(z|1) = P_{Z|X}(z|0)$, therefore we can take $Bel^2_{(Y,X)|(X=1)} = Bel^2_{(Y,X)|(X=0)}$, obtaining $Bel_{(Y,Z)|X}$. Let $P_X(0) = P_X(1) = \frac{1}{2}$. Simple computations show that

$$Q(X = 1|Y = 1, Z = 1) = \frac{Bel_V(\{(1,1,1)\})}{Bel_V(\{(1,1,1)\}) + Pl_V(\{(0,1,1)\})} = \frac{\frac{1}{12}}{\frac{1}{12} + \frac{3}{12}} = \frac{1}{4}.$$

♦

6   Conclusions and Future Works

In this paper we have addressed the statistical matching problem for two data sources, assuming no logical relations between the variables X, Y, Z. Due to the relevance of avoiding assumptions imposing a unique probability measure, we proposed strategies in order to approximate the initial assessment inside Dempster-Shafer theory. We showed that one of the advantages of such approximation with respect to dealing with the original coherent lower conditional probability is an easier way to compute the least committal extension on new events, in many cases. The aim of future research is threefold: *(i)* to generalize the problem to the case of logical relations among the random variables X, Y, Z; *(ii)* to consider more than two data sources; *(iii)* to carry out an experimental analysis.

References

1. Coletti, G., Petturiti, D., Vantaggi, B.: Conditional belief functions as lower envelopes of conditional probabilities in a finite setting. Inf. Sci. **339**, 64–84 (2016)
2. Coletti, G., Scozzafava, R.: Probabilistic Logic in a Coherent Setting, Trends in Logic, vol. 15. Kluwer Academic Publisher, Dordrecht/Boston/London (2002)
3. de Cooman, G., Zaffalon, M.: Updating beliefs with incomplete observations. Artif. Intell. **159**, 75–125 (2004)
4. Dempster, A.: Upper and lower probabilities induced by a multivalued mapping. Ann. Math. Stat. **38**(2), 325–339 (1967)
5. Denœux, T.: Constructing belief functions from sample data using multinomial confidence regions. Int. J. Approximate Reasoning **42**(3), 228–252 (2006)
6. Di Zio, M., Vantaggi, B.: Partial identification in statistical matching with misclassification. Int. J. Approximate Reasoning **82**, 227–241 (2017)
7. D'Orazio, M., Di Zio, M., Scanu, M.: Statistical Matching: Theory and Practice. Wiley (2006)
8. Dubins, L.: Finitely additive conditional probabilities, conglomerability and disintegrations. Ann. Probab. **3**(1), 89–99 (1975)
9. Endres, E., Fink, P., Augustin, T.: Imprecise imputation: a nonparametric micro approach reflecting the natural uncertainty of statistical matching with categorical data. J. Official Stat. **35**(3), 599–624 (2019)
10. Grabisch, M.: Set Functions, Games and Capacities in Decision Making. Theory and Decision Library C. Springer International Publishing (2016)
11. Huber, P.J.: Robust Statistics. Wiley, New York (1981)
12. Kadane, J.B.: Some statistical problems in merging data files. J. Official Stat. **17**, 423–433 (2001)
13. Kamakura, W.A., Wedel, M.: Statistical data fusion for cross-tabulation. J. Mark. Res. **34**, 485–498 (1997)
14. Levi, I.: The Enterprise of Knowledge. MIT Press, Cambridge (1980)
15. Manski, C.: Identification Problems in the Social Sciences. Harvard University Press, Cambridge (1995)
16. Miranda, E., Montes, I., Vicig, P.: On the selection of an optimal outer approximation of a coherent lower probability. Fuzzy Sets and Systems (2021)
17. Montes, I., Miranda, E., Vicig, P.: 2-monotone outer approximations of coherent lower probabilities. Int. J. Approximate Reasoning **101**, 181–205 (2018)
18. Montes, I., Miranda, E., Vicig, P.: Outer approximating coherent lower probabilities with belief functions. Int. J. Approximate Reasoning **110**, 1–30 (2019)
19. Okner, B.: Constructing a new microdata base from existing microdata sets: The 1966 merge file. Ann. Econ. Soc. Meas. **1**, 325–362 (1972)
20. Okner, B.: Data matching and merging: an overview. Ann. Econ. Soc. Meas. **3**, 347–352 (1974)
21. Paass, G.: Statistical match: evaluation of existing procedures and improvements by using additional information. In: Orcutt, G., Quinke, H. (eds.) Microanalytic Simulation Models to Support Social and Financial Policy, vol. 1, pp. 401–422. Elsevier Science (1986)
22. Rubin, D.: Statistical matching using file concatenation with adjusted weights and multiple imputations. J. Bus. Econ. Stat. **2**, 87–94 (1986)
23. Rüschendorf, L.: Fréchet-Bounds and Their Applications, Mathematics and Its Applications, vol. 67, pp. 151–187. Springer, Netherlands (1991)
24. Schafer, J.: Analysis of incomplete multivariate data. Chapman & Hall (1997)

25. Shafer, G.: A Mathematical Theory of Evidence. Princeton University Press, Princeton (1976)
26. Szivós, P., Rudas, T., Tóth, I.: A tax-benefit microsimulation model for hungary. In: Workshop on Microsimulation in the New Millennium: Challenges and Innovations (1998)
27. Vantaggi, B.: Statistical matching of multiple sources: a look through coherence. Int. J. Approximate Reasoning **49**, 701–711 (2008)
28. Walley, P.: Coherent lower (and upper) probabilities. Department of Statistics, University of Warwick, Technical report (1981)
29. Walley, P.: Statistical Reasoning with Imprecise Probabilities. Chapman and Hall, London (1991)
30. Williams, P.M.: Note on conditional previsions (1975), unpublished report of School of Mathematical and Physical Science, University of Sussex (Published in International Journal of Approximate Reasoning, 44, 366–383 (2007))
31. Wolfson, M., Gribble, S., Bordt, M., Murphy, B., Rowe, G.: The social policy simulation database and model: an example of survey and administrative data integration. Surv. Curr. Bus. **69**, 36–41 (1989)

The Vehicle Routing Problem with Time Windows and Evidential Service and Travel Times: A Recourse Model

Tekwa Tedjini[(✉)], Sohaib Afifi, Frédéric Pichon, and Eric Lefèvre

Univ. Artois, UR 3926, Laboratoire de Genie Informatique et d'Automatique de l'Artois (LGI2A), 62400 Béthune, France
{tekwa.tedjini,sohaib.afifi,frederic.pichon,eric.lefevre}@univ-artois.fr

Abstract. This paper addresses a variant of the vehicle routing problem with time windows where service and travel times are modeled within the framework of belief function theory. This theory is general as it offers to model several facets of information imperfection, including uncertainty and imprecision. An extension of stochastic programming with recourse is used to tackle the problem. This approach aims to regain the feasibility of the routes that missed one or more of the customer time windows due to the uncertain nature of the problem. A memetic algorithm is devised to solve the problem on an adaptation of literature instances.

Keywords: Vehicle routing · Time windows · Recourse · Belief function · Memetic algorithm

1 Introduction

The Vehicle Routing Problem with Time Windows (VRPTW) [9] is one of the most studied variants of vehicle routing problems (VRP). VRPTW routes are subject to time and capacity restrictions. Customers must be served within their time windows, vehicles have to return to the depot before its closure and their capacity must be respected. The main objective is to optimize the operating costs including the cost of vehicles and the overall traversed distances. The VRPTW is NP-hard. Indeed, even finding a feasible solution for the problem is itself NP-complete in the strong sense [15].

Usually, external factors like weather condition or unexpected road accidents affect one or more of the input parameters such as service and travel times, thus, the planned routes must account for the possible variations of those parameters. Accordingly, most of the research papers handled this issue using probability theory giving rise to the Stochastic VRPTW (SVRPTW) [11,18]. SVRPTW models are either tackled in a Chance-Constrained Programming (CCP) fashion [3,4,11], where the probabilities (chances) of time windows violations are below a given threshold, or in a Stochastic Programming with Recourse (SPR) one [5,11,20]. In SPR models, routes are first planned, then, when actual service and travel times are

© Springer Nature Switzerland AG 2021
J. Vejnarová and N. Wilson (Eds.): ECSQARU 2021, LNAI 12897, pp. 381–395, 2021.
https://doi.org/10.1007/978-3-030-86772-0_28

revealed, corrections (so-called recourse actions) are performed on routes that are subject to time windows violations in order to regain their feasibility. For instance, when a vehicle arrives late at a customer's location, the service is dropped and a new visit will be rescheduled to serve him. Each correction induces a penalty cost that must be added to the routing costs. Both of the CCP and SPR approaches have their advantages and drawbacks, they can either be combined as in [6], or applied separately depending on the needs of the decision maker.

Set theory has also been used to handle the uncertainty in time parameters, yielding the Robust VRPTW (RVRPTW) [1,8,12]. This model assumes that uncertain parameters belong to a predefined set, i.e., parameters are known imprecisely, and provides solutions that are immunized against imprecision. This is commonly done by optimizing the routing costs considering extreme scenarios for service and travel times. Nevertheless, solutions tend to be overly conservative.

Recently, more general uncertainty reasoning frameworks have emerged in the VRP's literature to serve as complementary tools to the existent set/probabilistic approaches, among others the theory of belief function also known as evidence theory [16]. Beyond imprecision or (probabilistic) uncertainty, this theory offers to represent problem parameters that are affected by more subtle forms of information imperfection arising from partial lack of knowledge. In the context of VRPs, belief function theory was used, for the first time, to model the uncertainty on customers demands in the Capacitated VRP (CVRP) variant [7]. Extensions of the CCP and the SPR approaches were proposed yielding the Belief-Constrained Programming and the Belief Programming with Recourse approaches. In this paper, we follow this line of work by tackling the VRPTW with uncertain service and travel times represented within the belief function framework. A Belief-Constrained Programming version for the same problem was already proposed in [19]. Herein, a belief programming with recourse approach is devised. We assume that time windows are hard, i.e., no early or late services are allowed. The recourse policy is based on skipping service at the failures locations to regain routes feasibility. This problem is very challenging from a computational perspective, to our knowledge, even in the case of stochastic programming, few papers handled the SPR version of VRPTW with stochastic service and/or travel times and hard time windows [5,6,20]. Most of the works focused either on total or partial soft time windows due to the difficulty of the problem. We also design a memetic algorithm [13] to solve an adaptation of literature instances.

The paper is organized as follows. Section 2 defines the VRPTW and recalls the fundamentals of belief function theory. In Sect. 3 we describe the proposed recourse approach as well as some particular cases of the model. Section 4 is dedicated to the experimental results. Section 5 concludes the paper.

2   Definitions and Notations

This section provides a brief background on the necessary tools required for our developments.

2.1   Problem Formulation

Given a fleet of K vehicles of the same capacity Q and cost M (M is a large value), the VRPTW is defined on a graph $G = (V, E)$, where $V = \{0, 1, \ldots, n\}$ is the node set and $E = \{(i, j) : i \neq j, i, j \in V\}$ is the arc set. The depot is denoted by 0 and $V_c = \{1, \ldots, n\}$ is the set of customers. Each node i has a demand $q_i \leq Q$, a service time s_i and a time interval (window) $[e_i, l_i]$ in which service can start, $q_0 = s_0 = 0$ and $[e_0, l_0] = [0, l_0]$ is the time horizon for the depot. Time windows are considered to be hard, that is if a vehicle k arrives at node j earlier than e_j, the service is postponed until the opening of the time window, and arrivals after l_j are forbidden. A non negative distance d_{ij} and travel time t_{ij} are associated with every arc $(i, j) \in E$. We assume that distances satisfy the triangle inequalities. A solution of VRPTW is composed of multiple routes, each one must respect the following constraints: 1) Each customer is only served once; 2) A vehicle k leaves each visited customer and travels toward the next one on the route and each route starts and ends at the depot; 3) The total demand on any route does not exceed Q; 4) Finally, the service at each customer must start within his time window and vehicles must return to the depot before l_0. A formal description of those constraints can be found in [9]. The objective (1) minimizes the overall operating costs:

$$\min \left[M. \sum_{k \in K} \sum_{j \in V_c} x_{0jk} + \sum_{k \in K} \sum_{(i,j) \in E} d_{ij} x_{ijk} \right] \tag{1}$$

where x_{ijk} is the decision variable. It is equal to 1 if vehicle k traverses arc (i, j) and 0 otherwise. In (1), due to M being large, the cost of vehicles is first minimized then the overall traversed distance is reduced. This means that a solution with fewer routes but higher distance is preferred over another one with more routes but lower distance.

2.2   Belief Function Theory

Belief function theory was first introduced by Shafer [16]. In this theory, the available knowledge about a variable x defined on a finite set $\mathcal{X}$, known as the frame of discernment, is represented by a *mass function* $m^{\mathcal{X}} : 2^{\mathcal{X}} \mapsto [0, 1]$ s.t. $\sum_{A \subseteq \mathcal{X}} m^{\mathcal{X}}(A) = 1$ and $m^{\mathcal{X}}(\emptyset) = 0$. $m^{\mathcal{X}}(A)$ quantifies the part of our belief that $x \in A$ without providing any further information about $x \in A' \subset A$. Each subset $A \subseteq \mathcal{X}$ such that $m^{\mathcal{X}}(A) > 0$ is called focal element of $m^{\mathcal{X}}$. If all the focal elements $A \subseteq \mathcal{X}$ of $m^{\mathcal{X}}$ are singletons ($|A| = 1$) then $m^{\mathcal{X}}$ is called Bayesian and it is equivalent to a probability measure. If $m^{\mathcal{X}}$ has a unique focal element $A \subseteq \mathcal{X}$, i.e., $m^{\mathcal{X}}(A) = 1$, $m^{\mathcal{X}}$ is said to be categorical and it corresponds to a set. In the remainder of this paper, a variable x whose true value is known in the form of a mass function will be referred to as *evidential variable*. The notion of expected value, in probability theory, of a function $f : \mathcal{X} \mapsto \mathbb{R}$ related to a probability mass function $p^{\mathcal{X}}$ is extended, in belief function theory, to the notions of lower ($\underline{E}(f, m^{\mathcal{X}})$) and upper ($\overline{E}(f, m^{\mathcal{X}})$) expected values of f related to a mass function $m^{\mathcal{X}}$ as follows [2]:

$$\underline{E}(f, m^{\mathcal{X}}) = \sum_{A \subseteq \mathcal{X}} m^{\mathcal{X}}(A) \min_{x \in A} f(x), \qquad (2)$$

$$\overline{E}(f, m^{\mathcal{X}}) = \sum_{A \subseteq \mathcal{X}} m^{\mathcal{X}}(A) \max_{x \in A} f(x). \qquad (3)$$

3 A Recourse Model for the VRPTW with Evidential Times

In this section, we present the VRPTW with evidential service and travel times under the recourse programming approach. Our model is inspired from the work in [7] and adapted to account for uncertainty in both service and travel times, the time windows requirements as well as a different recourse policy. We will start by formalizing the problem and by showing how to incorporate and compute the expected cost of recourse actions. Then, we will present an efficient method to compute these costs in presence of particular evidential information about service and travel times. Finally, we will discuss some special cases of the problem.

3.1 Formalization

Consider a solution to the VRPTW where time windows constraints are relaxed. Let $R = \{1, \ldots, i, \ldots, n, n+1 = 0\}$ be a route from this solution. For the sake of simplicity we suppose, without loss of generality, that the ith visit on R corresponds to customer i of the problem. To account for the time windows constraints, one must check the feasibility of R at each of its visits: If the time needed for a vehicle to arrive at visit i (customer or depot) meets its corresponding time window $[e_i, l_i]$ then the time window constraint is verified for i. In case where the vehicle arrives later than l_i, a failure occurs and i can not be served, so the vehicle skips the service of i and travels directly toward visit $i + 1$ the immediate successor of i on R. An exclusive visit will be rescheduled later to serve i. We adopt this policy since the actual values of service and travel times are only revealed once the vehicle arrives at the visit's location, thus failures can not be predicted. This is equivalent to the strategy used in [6] for the stochastic case. Formally, let f_i be a binary variable describing the failure situation at visit i. f_i equals 1 if the vehicle arrives later than l_i otherwise it is equal to 0. Arrival times are computed recursively by cumulating service and travel times up to visit i with possible truncations induced by waiting times. Formally, let $a_i, i = 1, \ldots, n + 1$ be the arrival time at visit i. a_i is a function of the set $\mathcal{T}_{01} \times \mathcal{S}_1 \times \ldots \times \mathcal{S}_{i-1} \times \mathcal{T}_{i-1i}$ of all service and travel times up to i, where $\mathcal{S}_i$ (resp. $\mathcal{T}_{i-1i}$) is the set on which the service time s_i (resp. travel time t_{i-1i}) is defined:

$$a_i = \begin{cases} v_{i-1} + t_{i-1i} & \text{if } i \in \{2, \ldots, n+1\}, \\ t_{01} & \text{if } i = 1. \end{cases} \qquad (4)$$

where v_i is the departure time from visit i which is expressed by:

$$v_i = \begin{cases} \max\{e_i, a_i\} + s_i & \text{if } a_i \le l_i, \\ a_i & \text{if } a_i > l_i. \end{cases} \tag{5}$$

The failure situation along R is represented by a unique vector $f = (f_1, \ldots, f_{n+1}) \in \mathcal{F} = \{0,1\}^{n+1}$ in presence of a certain and precise (deterministic) knowledge about service and travel times. This vector is a function of all service and travel times on R:

$$\begin{aligned} g : \mathcal{T}_{01} \times \mathcal{S}_1 \times \ldots \times \mathcal{S}_n \times \mathcal{T}_{nn+1} &\mapsto \mathcal{F} \\ (t_{01}, s_1, \ldots, s_n, t_{nn+1}) &\mapsto f = (f_1, \ldots, f_{n+1}). \end{aligned} \tag{6}$$

Each rescheduled visit induces a penalty that must be added to the routing cost of R. A penalty is an extra cost that measures, for instance, customers dissatisfaction or simply the cost of dedicating exclusive vehicles to serve them. Note that it is possible to define more complex recourse policies, nonetheless, we chose this simple policy to somehow manage the tractability of the problem given the complexity of belief functions. Let $f = (f_1, \ldots, f_{n+1}) \in \mathcal{F}$ be a failure vector and let p be the function defined from $\mathcal{F}$ to $\mathbb{R}^+$, representing the penalty induced by f. This penalty is composed of the cost of using an extra vehicle to serve visit i, whose service has been skipped, plus the total distance of a round trip from i to the depot:

$$p(f) = \sum_{i=1}^{n+1} f_i \times (M + 2d_{0i}). \tag{7}$$

The cost $\overline{C}(R)$ of a route R in presence of a deterministic failure vector f is composed of the routing cost $C(R)$ plus the penalty $p(f)$ induced by f:

$$\begin{aligned} \overline{C}(R) &= C(R) + p(f) \\ &= M + \sum_{(i,j) \in E(R)} d_{ij} + \sum_{i=1}^{n+1} f_i \times (M + 2d_{0i}). \end{aligned} \tag{8}$$

When service and travel times are evidential, i.e., knowledge about these variables is represented by mass functions, the failure situation is no longer deterministic but evidential and it is represented by a mass function $m^{\mathcal{F}}$ as will be detailed in Sect. 3.2. In this case, the cost $\overline{C}(R)$ of a route R consists of the routing cost part $C(R)$ to which is added the (lower or upper) expected value of p related to $m^{\mathcal{F}}$ as recalled in Sect. 2.2. In this work, we assume a pessimistic attitude toward the possible failures that may occur on route R, and therefore choose to use the upper expectation (3). We denote this upper expected value by $\overline{E}(p, m^{\mathcal{F}})$:

$$\overline{E}(p, m^{\mathcal{F}}) = \sum_{F \subseteq \mathcal{F}} m^{\mathcal{F}}(F) \times \max_{f \in F} p(f). \tag{9}$$

The cost $\overline{C}(R)$ of a route R is then expressed as:

$$\overline{C}(R) = C(R) + \overline{E}(p, m^{\mathcal{F}})$$
$$= M + \sum_{(i,j) \in E(R)} d_{ij} + \overline{E}(p, m^{\mathcal{F}}). \tag{10}$$

Consequently, the overall cost $\overline{C}(S)$ of a solution $S = \{R_1, \dots, R_K\}$ of the VRPTW with evidential service and travel times under the recourse approach, is nothing but the sum of all the expected costs of its K routes.

$$\overline{C}(S) = \sum_{k \in K} \overline{C}(R_k). \tag{11}$$

3.2 Evidential Failures

In this section, we start by describing how evidential knowledge about service and travel times induces evidential failures that are represented by a mass function. Then, we present an efficient method to compute this mass function under some particular assumptions.

Let us first consider the route R defined in Sect. 3.1 and suppose that service s_i and travel t_{ij} times are evidential and represented, respectively, by mass functions $m_{\mathcal{S}_i}^{\mathcal{S}_i}$ and $m_{t_{ij}}^{\mathcal{T}_{ij}}$ defined on the sets $\mathcal{S}_i$ and $\mathcal{T}_{ij}$, such that $|\mathcal{S}_i| \leq S \in \mathbb{N}_+^*$ and $|\mathcal{T}_{ij}| \leq T \in \mathbb{N}_+^*$. Assume that service and travel time variables are independent (this assumption is not required but only stated here to simplify the explanation of our method), hence, the joint mass function $m^{\mathcal{T}_{01} \times \mathcal{S}_1 \times \dots \times \mathcal{S}_n \times \mathcal{T}_{nn+1}}$ of service and travel times on R is equal to the product of independent mass functions $m_{s_i}^{\mathcal{S}_i}$ and $m_{t_{ij}}^{\mathcal{T}_{ij}}$, for all $i \in V_c(R)$ and $(i,j) \in E(R)$. When $m^{\mathcal{T}_{01} \times \mathcal{S}_1 \times \dots \times \mathcal{S}_n \times \mathcal{T}_{nn+1}}$ has a unique focal set $T \subseteq \mathcal{T}_{01} \times \mathcal{S}_1 \times \dots \times \mathcal{S}_n \times \mathcal{T}_{nn+1}$ such that $m^{\mathcal{T}_{01} \times \mathcal{S}_1 \times \dots \times \mathcal{S}_n \times \mathcal{T}_{nn+1}}(T) = 1$, knowledge about the failure situation is imprecise, i.e., all we know is that it belongs to a set of possible failures denoted by F, which is the image of the set T by function g defined in (6). F can be described as:

$$F = g(T) = \bigcup_{(t_{01}, s_1, \dots, s_n, t_{nn+1}) \in T} g(t_{01}, s_1, \dots, s_n, t_{nn+1}). \tag{12}$$

In general, when $m^{\mathcal{T}_{01} \times \mathcal{S}_1 \times \dots \times \mathcal{S}_n \times \mathcal{T}_{nn+1}}$ has at most $c \in \mathbb{N}_+^*$ focal sets, knowledge about the failure situation is both imprecise and uncertain, and can be represented by the mass function $m^{\mathcal{F}}$ defined as:

$$m^{\mathcal{F}}(F) = \sum_{g(T)=F} m^{\mathcal{T}_{01} \times \mathcal{S}_1 \times \dots \times \mathcal{S}_n \times \mathcal{T}_{nn+1}}(T), \forall F \in \mathcal{F}. \tag{13}$$

To compute $m^{\mathcal{F}}$ defined in (13), $g(T)$ is evaluated for each focal set $T \subseteq \mathcal{T}_{01} \times \mathcal{S}_1 \times \dots \times \mathcal{S}_n \times \mathcal{T}_{nn+1}$ of the mass function $m^{\mathcal{T}_{01} \times \mathcal{S}_1 \times \dots \times \mathcal{S}_n \times \mathcal{T}_{nn+1}}$. In the worst case, T can have up to $\mathcal{S}^n \times \mathcal{T}^{n+1}$ element ($|T| = |\mathcal{S}_i|^{|V(R)|} \times |\mathcal{T}_{ij}|^{|E(R)|}$

$\leq \mathcal{S}^{|V(R)|} \times \mathcal{T}^{|E(R)|} \leq \mathcal{S}^n \times \mathcal{T}^{n+1}$), thus evaluating (13) requires a worst case time complexity of $\mathcal{O}([\mathcal{S}^n \times \mathcal{T}^{n+1}] \times c)$ which is intractable. However, following a similar tree-based approach to that of [7, Section 3.2.3] described in the next paragraph, if service and travel time variables are modeled by intervals, i.e., $s_i \in [\![\sigma_i]\!] = [\underline{\sigma}_i, \overline{\sigma}_i] \subseteq \mathcal{S}_i$ and $t_{ij} \in [\![\theta_{ij}]\!] = [\underline{\theta}_{ij}, \overline{\theta}_{ij}] \subseteq \mathcal{T}_{ij}$ and $T = [\![\theta_{01}]\!] \times [\![\sigma_1]\!] \dots \times [\![\sigma_n]\!] \times [\![\theta_{nn+1}]\!]$ is the Cartesian product of interval service and travel times along R, one can demonstrate that only the bounds of the intervals $[\![\sigma_i]\!], i \in V(R)$ and $[\![\theta_{ij}]\!], (i, j) \in E(R)$ has to be evaluated rather than each element of $\mathcal{S}_i$ and $\mathcal{T}_{ij}$. Subsequently, the complexity of evaluating (13) drops to $\mathcal{O}(2^{2n+1} \times c)$. Furthermore, this complexity can also be decreased to $\mathcal{O}(2^n \times c)$ if travel times t_{ij} are considered as singletons rather than intervals, that is the marginalization of $m^{\mathcal{T}_{01} \times \mathcal{S}_1 \times \dots \times \mathcal{S}_n \times \mathcal{T}_{nn+1}}$ onto $\mathcal{T}_{ij}$, for any travel time variable t_{ij} is a Bayesian mass function where $[\![\theta_{ij}]\!] = \{\tilde{\theta}_{ij}\}$. As a consequence $T = \{\tilde{\theta}_{01}\} \times [\![\sigma_1]\!] \dots \times [\![\sigma_n]\!] \times \{\tilde{\theta}_{nn+1}\}$. A similar result holds when service times are singletons, that is $[\![\sigma_i]\!] = \{\tilde{\sigma}_i\}$ and $T = [\![\theta_{01}]\!] \times \{\tilde{\sigma}_1\} \dots \times \{\tilde{\sigma}_n\} \times [\![\theta_{nn+1}]\!]$, in which case the overall complexity becomes $\mathcal{O}(2^{n+1} \times c)$.

Consider, in the following, a categorical mass function $m^{\mathcal{T}_{01} \times \mathcal{S}_1 \times \dots \times \mathcal{S}_n \times \mathcal{T}_{nn+1}}$ having a unique focal set $T = [\![\theta_{01}]\!] \times [\![\sigma_1]\!] \dots \times [\![\sigma_n]\!] \times [\![\theta_{nn+1}]\!]$, that is, $s_i \in [\![\sigma_i]\!], \forall i \in V_c$ and $t_{ij} \in [\![\theta_{ij}]\!], \forall (i, j) \in E$. Note that arrival times (resp. departure times) are imprecise in this case: $a_i \in [\![\alpha_i]\!] = [\underline{\alpha}_i, \overline{\alpha}_i]$ (resp. $v_i \in [\![v_i]\!] = [\underline{v}_i, \overline{v}_i]$), where bounds $\underline{\alpha}_i$ and $\overline{\alpha}_i$ (resp. $\underline{v}_i$ and $\overline{v}_i$) are obtained by applying the recursive reasoning described below. As mentioned before, in this case, the failure situation that can be encountered by a vehicle is described by a set F defined by (12). In the following, we adapt the evaluation procedure in [7, Section 3.2.3] to our problem in order to efficiently compute F. Suppose that the vehicle operating on R travels from visit $i - 1$ to visit i. The arrival time a_i at visit i induces the following three cases:

1. If $\overline{\alpha}_i \leq l_i$: there will be no failure at visit i, hence $f_i = 0$ and $v_i \in [\max\{e_i, \underline{\alpha}_i\} + \underline{\sigma}_i, \max\{e_i, \overline{\alpha}_i\} + \overline{\sigma}_i]$.
2. If $\underline{\alpha}_i > l_i$: the failure situation is *"precise"* and service at visit i is skipped i.e., $f_i = 1$ and $v_i \in [\underline{\alpha}_i, \overline{\alpha}_i]$.
3. if $\underline{\alpha}_i \leq l_i < \overline{\alpha}_i$: the failure situation at visit i is *"imprecise"*, so we account for both possibilities:
   (a) When the true arrival time belongs to $[\underline{\alpha}_i, l_i]$, there will be no failure at visit i, i.e., $f_i = 0$ and $v_i \in [\max\{e_i, \underline{\alpha}_i\} + \underline{\sigma}_i, l_i + \overline{\sigma}_i]$.
   (b) When the true arrival time belongs to $]l_i, \overline{\alpha}_i]$, service at visit i is skipped, i.e., $f_i = 1$ and $v_i \in]l_i, \overline{\alpha}_i]$.

This reasoning is applied for all the visits of R, starting from the first customer up to the depot, to get all the failure situations related to the focal set T. This latter procedure is sketched in Algorithm 1 and its execution induces a tree of $n + 1$ levels. Each level i represents the potential failure situations that a vehicle encounters when reaching visit i. Each node of a level i contains information about the failure component f_i as well as the arrival and departure time intervals. The evaluation is extended from a level to another one, and stops after evaluating level $n + 1$ which corresponds to the depot. To guarantee the feasibility of single customer routes, we assume that there is no particular reason for a vehicle to arrive late at the first visit of any route R, thus $f_1 = 0$. Consider a branch from the tree induced by Algorithm 1. The concatenation of the binary failure variables f_i from the root up to level $n + 1$ induces a failure vector $f = (f_1, \ldots, f_{n+1})$ describing one possible failure situation on R. The set of all the vectors f obtained from all the branches of the recourse tree, denoted by F, expresses all the failures that can occur on R. Using a similar proof to that of [7, Proposition 6], we can show that the set F verifies $F = g([\![\theta_{01}]\!] \times [\![\sigma_1]\!] \times \ldots \times [\![\sigma_n]\!] \times [\![\theta_{nn+1}]\!])$. Note that in case $m^{\mathcal{T}_{01} \times \mathcal{S}_1 \times \ldots \times \mathcal{S}_n \times \mathcal{T}_{nn+1}}$ has multiple focal sets, then given (13) the previous reasoning is applied for each one of them as demonstrated in the following example:

Algorithm 1. Failures tree-based Evaluation (FE)

Require: Visit $i \in \{1, \ldots, n + 1\}$, service time $[\underline{\sigma}_i, \overline{\sigma}_i]$, travel time $[\underline{\theta}_{ij}, \overline{\theta}_{ij}]$.
Ensure: A tree describing all failures on R.

1: $i = 1$;
2: $[\underline{\alpha}_1, \overline{\alpha}_1] = [\underline{\theta}_{01}, \overline{\theta}_{01}]$;
3: $f_1 = 0$;
4: $[\underline{v}_1, \overline{v}_1] = [\max\{e_1, \underline{\alpha}_1\} + \underline{\sigma}_1, \max\{e_1, \overline{\alpha}_1\} + \overline{\sigma}_1]$;
5: Create the root node of T $([\underline{\alpha}_1, \overline{\alpha}_1], [\underline{v}_1, \overline{v}_1], f_1)$; $i ++$;
6: **while** $(i > 1$ and $i \leq n + 1)$ **do**
7: $\quad [\underline{\alpha}_i, \overline{\alpha}_i] = [\underline{v}_{i-1} + \underline{\theta}_{i-1i}, \overline{v}_{i-1} + \overline{\theta}_{i-1i}]$;
8: $\quad$ **if** $\overline{\alpha}_i \leq l_i$ **then**
9: $\quad\quad f_i^{\text{left}} = 0$;
10: $\quad\quad [\underline{v}_i^{\text{left}}, \overline{v}_i^{\text{left}}] = [\max\{e_i, \underline{\alpha}_i\} + \underline{\sigma}_i, \max\{e_i, \overline{\alpha}_i\} + \overline{\sigma}_i]$;
11: $\quad\quad T^{\text{left}} = FE([\underline{\alpha}_i, \overline{\alpha}_i], [\underline{v}_i^{\text{left}}, \overline{v}_i^{\text{left}}], f_i^{\text{left}}, i ++)$;
12: $\quad\quad$ Attach T^{left} as a left branch of T;
13: $\quad$ **else if** $\underline{\alpha}_i > l_i$ **then**
14: $\quad\quad f_i^{\text{right}} = 1$;
15: $\quad\quad [\underline{v}_i^{\text{right}}, \overline{v}_i^{\text{right}}] = [\underline{\alpha}_i, \overline{\alpha}_i]$;
16: $\quad\quad T^{\text{right}} = FE([\underline{\alpha}_i, \overline{\alpha}_i], [\underline{v}_i^{\text{right}}, \overline{v}_i^{\text{right}}], f_i^{\text{right}}, i ++)$;
17: $\quad\quad$ Attach T^{right} as a right branch of T;
18: $\quad$ **else**
19: $\quad\quad [\underline{\alpha}_i, \overline{\alpha}_i] = [\underline{v}_{i-1} + \underline{\theta}_{i-1i}, l_i]$;
20: $\quad\quad f_i^{\text{left}} = 0$;
21: $\quad\quad [\underline{v}_i^{\text{left}}, \overline{v}_i^{\text{left}}] = [\max\{e_i, \underline{\alpha}_i\} + \underline{\sigma}_i, l_i + \overline{\sigma}_i]$;
22: $\quad\quad T^{\text{left}} = FE([\underline{\alpha}_i, \overline{\alpha}_i], [\underline{v}_i^{\text{left}}, \overline{v}_i^{\text{left}}], f_i^{\text{left}}, i ++)$;
23: $\quad\quad$ Attach T^{left} as a left branch of T;
24: $\quad\quad [\underline{\alpha}_i, \overline{\alpha}_i] =]l_i, \overline{v}_{i-1} + \overline{\theta}_{i-1i}]$;
25: $\quad\quad f_i^{\text{right}} = 1$;
26: $\quad\quad [\underline{v}_i^{\text{right}}, \overline{v}_i^{\text{right}}] =]l_i, \overline{\alpha}_i]$;
27: $\quad\quad T^{\text{right}} = FE([\underline{\alpha}_i, \overline{\alpha}_i], [\underline{v}_i^{\text{right}}, \overline{v}_i^{\text{right}}], f_i^{\text{right}}, i ++)$;
28: $\quad\quad$ Attach T^{right} as a right branch of T;
29: $\quad$ **end if**
30: **end while**

Example 1. Let us illustrate Algorithm 1 by considering a route $R = \{1, 2, 3, 0\}$, where time windows are $[e_0, l_0] = [0, 200], [e_1, l_1] = [5, 30], [e_2, l_2] = [40, 95], [e_3, l_3] = [80, 120]$. The available information about service and travel times is represented by the joint mass function: $m^{T_{01} \times S_1 \times T_{12} \times S_2 \times T_{23} \times S_3 \times T_{30}}$ denoted by m for simplification:

$$m([15, 20] \times [20, 25] \times [40, 50] \times [30, 35] \times [10, 20] \times [15, 20] \times [10, 15]) = 0.6,$$
$$m([15, 20] \times [20, 25] \times [25, 30] \times [20, 30] \times [10, 15] \times [15, 20] \times [10, 15]) = 0.4.$$
$$(14)$$

$\mathcal{F} = \{(0, 0, 0, 0), (0, 1, 0, 0), (0, 0, 1, 0), (0, 0, 0, 1), (0, 1, 1, 0), (0, 1, 0, 1), (0, 0, 1, 1), (0, 1, 1, 1)\}$ is the set of all possible failure situations on R, such that $f_1 = 0$.

The first focal set induces the tree illustrated in Fig. 1 and the second one induces the tree depicted in Fig. 2. Take for instance the tree in Fig. 1, it has two branches representing two possible failure situations on R when information about service and travel times is given by the first focal set of m. The concatenation of the binary variables f_i from the root to the leaves starting from the left branch yields the subset $F_1 = \{(f_1, f_2, f_3^1, f_0^1), (f_1, f_2, f_3^2, f_0^2)\} = \{(0, 0, 0, 0), (0, 0, 1, 0)\}$, which means that either all the customers of R will be successfully served or that a failure will occur at customer 3 and the latter can not be served. Similarly, the tree in Fig. 2 yields the subset $F_2 = \{(f_1, f_2, f_3, f_0)\} = \{(0, 0, 0, 0)\}$ with respect to the second focal set of m, which means that no failure will occur on R. Formally, using equation (13) with g being the function given in (12) and $m^{T_{01} \times S_1 \times \ldots \times S_n \times T_{nn+1}}$ defined such as in (14), our knowledge about the entire failure situation on R can be expressed via the mass function $m^{\mathcal{F}}$ defined by:

$$m^{\mathcal{F}}(F_1) = m^{\mathcal{F}}(\{(0, 0, 0, 0), (0, 0, 1, 0)\}) = 0.6,$$
$$m^{\mathcal{F}}(F_2) = m^{\mathcal{F}}(\{(0, 0, 0, 0)\}) = 0.4. \qquad (15)$$

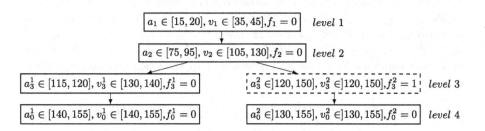

Fig. 1. The failure tree related to the first focal set of m.

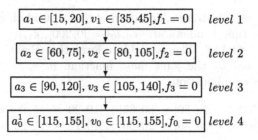

$a_1 \in [15, 20], v_1 \in [35, 45], f_1 = 0$ *level 1*

$a_2 \in [60, 75], v_2 \in [80, 105], f_2 = 0$ *level 2*

$a_3 \in [90, 120], v_3 \in [105, 140], f_3 = 0$ *level 3*

$a_0^1 \in [115, 155], v_0 \in [115, 155], f_0 = 0$ *level 4*

Fig. 2. The failure tree related to the second focal set of m.

3.3 Particular Cases

The recourse model degenerates into well known problems when the mass function $m^{S^n \times T^{|E|}}$ representing knowledge about all service and travel time variables of the problem has a special form. Specifically, if $m^{S^n \times T^{|E|}}$ has a unique focal set, minimizing the upper expected cost function (10) is equivalent to minimizing the recourse cost under the worst case scenario. Thus, our model reduces to a robust approach. Note that it is also possible to replace the upper expected penalty (9) by the lower expected one using Eq. (2) in case the decision maker is more interested in optimistic solutions. Another interesting particular case of the proposed model is when $m^{S^n \times T^{|E|}}$ is Bayesian, i.e., its focal sets are no longer sets but singletons. In this case, the lower and the upper expected costs of the optimal solution reduce to the classical expectation in probability theory. As a consequence, our model is equivalent to a SVRPTW with recourses. It is important to mention that the two aforementioned models (i.e., the robust and stochastic ones) are conceptually different and it is not possible, at least trivially, to convert one into another. The following example illustrates this remark.

Example 2. Consider a VRPTW instance where time windows are: $[e_0, l_0] = [0, 250]$, $[e_1, l_1] = [5, 20]$, $[e_2, l_2] = [40, 95]$, $[e_3, l_3] = [80, 130]$ and $Q = \infty$, vehicles unit cost is $M = 1000$ and distances are given by: $d_{01} = d_{10} = 10$, $d_{02} = d_{20} = 10$, $d_{03} = d_{30} = 15$, $d_{12} = d_{21} = 20$, $d_{13} = d_{31} = 15$ and $d_{23} = d_{32} = 20$. Service and travel times are imprecise and represented by the following categorical mass function:

$$m^T(\{\{60\} \times \{20\} \times \{20\} \times \{10\} \times \{20\} \times \{15\} \times \{25\} \times \{30\} \times \{15, 20\}\}) = 1 \quad (16)$$

with $T = S_1 \times S_2 \times S_3 \times T_{01} \times T_{02} \times T_{03} \times T_{12} \times T_{13} \times T_{23}$.

We denote by $S_m^\star$ the optimal solution to this instance and by $\overline{C}_m^\star$ its cost. The set of feasible solutions related to this instance is given in Table 1. The solution S_5 is composed of a unique route serving customers 1, 2 and 3 with a possible failure at customer 3 (highlighted in bold). From Table 1, we can deduce that the optimal solution (highlighted with $\star$) is $S_m^\star = S_3$ with a corresponding cost $\overline{C}_m^\star = 2060$.

Consider now another representation where service and travel times are random and expressed by a probability distribution that is compatible with m^T. Denote by $S_p^\star$ its related optimal solution and by $C_p^\star$ its cost.

$$p^T(60, 20, 20, 10, 20, 15, 25, 30, 15) = p^T(60, 20, 20, 10, 20, 15, 25, 30, 20) = 1/2. \tag{17}$$

The set of feasible solutions related to p^T is given in Table 2. The optimal solution is $S_p^\star = S_5$ with a cost of $\overline{C}_p^\star = 1580$. We clearly have $S_m^\star \neq S_p^\star$ and $\overline{C}_m^\star \neq \overline{C}_p^\star$.

Table 1. The set of feasible solutions related to the mass function m^T.

Solution	R_1	R_2	R_3	Cost
S_1	$\{0, 1, 0\}$	$\{0, 2, 0\}$	$\{0, 3, 0\}$	3070
S_2	$\{0, 1, 2, 0\}$	$\{0, 3, 0\}$	–	2070
$S_3^\star$	$\{0, 1, 3, 0\}$	$\{0, 2, 0\}$	–	2060
S_4	$\{0, 2, 3, 0\}$	$\{0, 1, 0\}$	–	2065
S_5	$\{0, 1, 2, 3, 0\}$	–	–	2095

Table 2. The set of feasible solutions related to the probability p^T.

Solution	R_1	R_2	R_3	Cost
S_1	$\{0, 1, 0\}$	$\{0, 2, 0\}$	$\{0, 3, 0\}$	3070
S_2	$\{0, 1, 2, 0\}$	$\{0, 3, 0\}$	–	2070
S_3	$\{0, 1, 3, 0\}$	$\{0, 2, 0\}$	–	2060
S_4	$\{0, 2, 3, 0\}$	$\{0, 1, 0\}$	–	2065
$S_5^\star$	$\{0, 1, 2, 3, 0\}$	–	–	1580

Note that this remark also holds with respect to our evidential model. Indeed, one can build similar examples showing that it is not possible, at least trivially, to convert the evidential service and travel times into imprecise or probabilistic ones while preserving the same solutions.

4   Experimental Results

To solve the VRPTW with evidential service and travel times under the recourse approach, we propose to use a Memetic Algorithm (MA) [13]. This choice is motivated by MA's attractive results for VRPs and their variants [6,10,14]. Specifically, the MA operates on an initial set (population) of individuals or solutions that evolves by undergoing a series of modifications using some recombination and mutation tools, to create a new population, similarly as in the natural evolution process of individuals. The new population is then enhanced by exploring the neighborhoods of its individuals using the so-called local search (LS) procedures. This hybridization between population evolution and local search helps to escape local optima and provide good-quality solutions. Formally, the MA runs with a population POP of m solutions. POP is first initialized and sorted increasingly according to the cost of its solutions. At each iteration, two selected parents P_1 and P_2 are crossed. The resulting offspring *child* has a probability p_m to be mutated and a probability p_{ls} to be enhanced by a LS procedure. *child* will join POP only if he improves it. The process is repeated until a stopping condition is met, such as the number of iterations without improvement of POP. Note that POP's size must be constant over the iterations. We refer the reader to [6,10,14] for further information about selection, crossover and mutation tools. The pseudo-code of the MA is presented in Algorithm 2.

Algorithm 2. MA structure

Require: POP a population of size m.
Ensure: $S_{POP[0]}$, the best solution to the problem.
 1: Initialize POP ;
 2: Evaluate each individual in POP and keep POP sorted;
 3: **while** (! stopping condition) **do**
 4:     select two parents P_1 and P_2;
 5:     $child \leftarrow cross(P_1, P_2)$;
 6:     **if** $(p \sim \mathcal{U}(0,1) \leq p_m)$ **then**
 7:         $child \leftarrow mutate(child)$;
 8:     **else if** $(p \sim \mathcal{U}(0,1) \leq p_{ls})$ **then**
 9:         $child \leftarrow LS(child)$;
10:     **end if**
11:     **if** $(\overline{C}(S_{child}) \leq \overline{C}(S_{POP[m-1]}))$ **then**
12:         **if** $(\nexists i \,|\overline{C}(S_{POP[i]}) = \overline{C}(S_{child}))$ **then**
13:             remove $POP[m-1]$ from POP;
14:             update stopping condition;
15:         **else**
16:             update stopping condition;
17:         **end if**
18:         insert or replace $child$ in POP;
19:     **else**
20:         update stopping condition;
21:     **end if**
22: **end while**

We have adapted Solomon's instances [17] to account for the evidential nature of service and travel times. These instances are composed of three sets: 25, 50 and 100 indicating the number of customers. Each set has 56 instances divided into six categories $C1$, $R1$, $RC1$, $C2$, $R2$ and $RC2$. Customers' positions in categories $R1$ and $R2$ are randomly generated meanwhile in $C1$ and $C2$, positions are clustered. Categories $RC1$ and $RC2$ gather both random and clustered positions. Another classification can be established according to the time windows nature. Categories $C1$, $R1$ and $RC1$ (type 1) have tight time windows while categories $C2$, $R2$ and $RC2$ (type 2) have larger time windows. We kept the same data as in the original instances, except for service and travel times which are adapted to the belief function framework as follows:

$$m^{S_i}([s_i^{det}, s_i^{det}]) = 0.8, m^{S_i}([s_i^{det}, s_i^{det} + \sigma_i]) = 0.2 \qquad (18)$$

where s_i^{det} is the (deterministic) value of s_i in Solomon's instances and σ_i a random parameter generated from the interval $[1, 10]$, and:

$$m^{T_{ij}}([t_{ij}^{det}, t_{ij}^{det}]) = 0.8, m^{T_{ij}}([t_{ij}^{det}, t_{ij}^{det} + \theta_{ij}]) = 0.2 \qquad (19)$$

with t_{ij}^{det} the deterministic value of t_{ij} and θ_{ij} a random parameter generated from the interval $[1, 20]$. The vehicle cost M is set to 1000 as in [6]. This large value prioritizes the optimization of the number of vehicles followed by the total distance and the penalties. The MA performs 15 tests for each instance of the problem and stops after n^2 iterations without improvement, with n being the number of customers per instance. The population size is set to n. The LS procedure runs for n iterations with a probability of 0.2 whereas, the probability of mutation is fixed to 0.01. Explicit details about the initialization algorithm, the LS procedure as well as the parameters setting are not provided here because of the space limit. Table 3 displays average results per category for both instances of 50 and 100 customers. We recorded, for each category, the average number of vehicles $\#\overline{V}$, the average traversed distance $\overline{Dist}$, the average total penalties $\overline{Pen}$ as well as the average execution time $(CPU(s))$ in seconds. The conducted experiments show that the overall costs are quite acceptable given the execution time. We notice that instances of type 1 have higher costs, either in terms of $\#\overline{V}$, $\overline{Dist}$ or $\overline{Pen}$, than those of type 2 (we clearly see that in classes $R1$ and $RC1$). This increase is natural and justified by the fact that these particular instances have tighter time windows, hence solutions tend to require many vehicles and they are also subject to many failures. Another remark can be established regarding the execution time. We note that CPU time is quite pronounced in type 2 instances, specifically, when the number of customers is large, this is related to the fact that this class has larger time windows, consequently, the search space is larger and requires further exploration than its counterpart of type 1.

Table 3. Average results per category

Category	50 customers				100 customers			
	$\#\overline{V}$	$\overline{Dist}$	$\overline{Pen}$	$CPU(s)$	$\#\overline{V}$	$\overline{Dist}$	$\overline{Pen}$	$CPU(s)$
$C1$	6.16	490.16	9.49	6.11	12.04	1128.81	5.06	134.10
$C2$	2.78	436.78	1.79	16.99	4.67	759.42	0.00	326.26
$R1$	11.88	1164.98	751.71	15.13	22.31	2054.62	1578.82	252.28
$R2$	3.24	784.21	66.96	78.88	5.80	1246.85	165.32	2000.22
$RC1$	10.41	1080.51	601.26	13.21	21.55	2216.88	1063.47	233.30
$RC2$	3.70	770.51	91.90	112.40	6.58	1449.87	188.59	1431.39

5 Conclusions

We proposed a recourse approach for the VRPTW with evidential service and travel times. The model is inspired from [7] and adapted to take account of the uncertainty on both service and travel times as well as the additional hard requirements on time windows. A skipping-based policy was used to recover the feasibility of routes. Our model reduces to robust and stochastic cases when the mass functions of service and travel times are, respectively, categorical and Bayesian and allows, beyond sole imprecision or probabilistic uncertainty, to model more complex information that are affected by other forms of imperfections. We devised a memetic algorithm to solve an adaptation of literature instances. Combining both the Belief-Constrained Programming and the recourse approaches in one model as in SVRPTW [6] is an interesting and challenging perspective.

References

1. Agra, A., Christiansen, M., Figueiredo, R., Hvattum, K.L., Poss, M., Requejo, C.: The robust vehicle routing problem with time windows. Comput. Oper. Res. **40**, 856–866 (2013)
2. Denoeux, T.: Analysis of evidence-theoretic decision rules for pattern classification. Patt. Recogn. **30**(7), 1095–1107 (1997)
3. Ehmke, J.F., Campbell, A.M., Urban, T.L.: Ensuring service levels in routing problems with time windows and stochastic travel times. Eur. J. Oper. Res. **240**(2), 539–550 (2015)
4. Errico, F., Desaulniers, G., Gendreau, M., Rei, W., Rousseau, L.-M.: The vehicle routing problem with hard time windows and stochastic service times. EURO J. Transp. Logistics **7**(3), 223–251 (2016). https://doi.org/10.1007/s13676-016-0101-4
5. Errico, F., Desaulniers, G., Gendreau, M., Rei, W., Rousseau, L.: A priori optimization with recourse for the vehicle routing problem with hard time windows and stochastic service times. Eur. J. Oper. Res. **249**(1), 55–66 (2016)
6. Gutierrez, A., Dieulle, L., Labadie, N., Velasco, N.: A multi-population algorithm to solve the VRP with stochastic service and travel times. Comput. Ind. Eng. **125**, 144–156 (2018)
7. Helal, N., Pichon, F., Porumbel, D., Mercier, D., Lefevre, E.: The capacitated vehicle routing problem with evidential demands. Int. J. Approx. Reason. **95**, 124–151 (2018)
8. Hu, C., Lu, J., Liu, X., Zhang, G.: Robust vehicle routing problem with hard time windows under demand and travel time uncertainty. Comput. Oper. Res. **94**, 139–153 (2018)
9. Kallehauge, B.: Formulations and exact algorithms for the vehicle routing problem with time windows. Comput. Oper. Res. **35**(7), 2307–2330 (2008)
10. Labadi, N., Prins, C., Reghioui, M.: A memetic algorithm for the vehicle routing problem with time windows. Rairo Oper. Res. **42**, 415–431 (2008)
11. Li, X., Tian, P., Leung, S.C.: Vehicle routing problems with time windows and stochastic travel and service times: models and algorithm. Int. J. Prod. Econ. **125**(1), 137–145 (2010)
12. Lu, D., Gzara, F.: The robust vehicle routing problem with time windows: solution by branch and price and cut. Eur. J. Oper. Res. **275**(3), 925–938 (2019)
13. Moscato, P., Cotta, C.: A gentle introduction to memetic algorithms. In: Glover, F., Kochenberger, G. (eds.) Handbook of Metaheuristics, ISOR, vol. 57, pp. 105–144. Springer, Boston, MA (2003). https://doi.org/10.1007/0-306-48056-5_5
14. Prins, C.: A simple and effective evolutionary algorithm for the vehicle routing problem. Comput. Oper. Res. **31**(12), 1985–2002 (2004)
15. Savelsbergh, M.: Local search in routing problems with time windows. Ann. Oper. Res. **4**(1), 295–305 (1985)
16. Shafer, G.: A Mathematical Theory of Evidence. Princeton University Press, Princeton (1976)
17. Solomon, M.: Algorithms for the vehicle routing and scheduling problem with time window constraints. Oper. Res. **35**(2), 254–265 (1987)

18. Taş, D., Dellaert, N., van Woensel, T., de Kok, T.: Vehicle routing problem with stochastic travel times including soft time windows and service costs. Comput. Oper. Res. **40**(1), 214–224 (2013)
19. Tedjini, T., Afifi, S., Pichon, F., Lefevre, E.: A belief-constrained programming model for the VRPTW with evidential service and travel times. In: Proceedings of 28es rencontres francophones sur la Logique Floue et ses Applications, pp. 217–224. Alès, France (2019)
20. Wang, X., Regan, A.C.: Assignment models for local truckload trucking problems with stochastic service times and time window constraints. Transp. Res. Rec. **1771**(1), 61–68 (2001)

Imprecise Probability

A New Score for Adaptive Tests in Bayesian and Credal Networks

Alessandro Antonucci[(✉)], Francesca Mangili, Claudio Bonesana,
and Giorgia Adorni

Istituto Dalle Molle di Studi sull'Intelligenza Artificiale, Lugano, Switzerland
{alessandro,francesca,claudio.bonesana,giorgia.adorni}@idsia.ch

Abstract. A test is *adaptive* when the sequence and number of questions is dynamically tuned on the basis of the estimated skills of the taker. Graphical models, such as Bayesian networks, are used for adaptive tests as they allow to model the uncertainty about the questions and the skills in an explainable fashion, especially when coping with multiple skills. A better elicitation of the uncertainty in the question/skills relations can be achieved by interval probabilities. This turns the model into a *credal* network, thus increasing the inferential complexity of the queries required to select questions. This is especially the case for the information-theoretic quantities used as *scores* to drive the adaptive mechanism. We present an alternative family of scores, based on the mode of the posterior probabilities, and hence easier to explain. This makes considerably simpler the evaluation in the credal case, without significantly affecting the quality of the adaptive process. Numerical tests on synthetic and real-world data are used to support this claim.

Keywords: Adaptive tests · Information theory · Credal networks · Bayesian networks · Index of qualitative variation

1 Introduction

A test or an exam can be naturally intended as a measurement process, with the questions acting as sensors measuring the skills of the test taker in a particular discipline. Such measurement is typically imperfect with the skills modeled as latent variables whose actual values cannot be revealed in a perfectly reliable way. The role of the questions, whose answers are regarded instead as manifest variables, is to reduce the uncertainty about the latent skills. Following this perspective, probabilistic models are an obvious framework to describe tests. Consider for instance the example in Fig. 1, where a Bayesian network evaluates the probability that the test taker knows how to multiply integers. In such framework making the test *adaptive*, i.e., picking a next question on the basis of the

G. Adorni—We thank the Swiss National Science Foundation (grant no. 187246) for support

J. Vejnarová and N. Wilson (Eds.): ECSQARU 2021, LNAI 12897, pp. 399–412, 2021.
https://doi.org/10.1007/978-3-030-86772-0_29

current knowledge level of the test taker is also very natural. The information gain for the available questions might be used to select the question leading to the more informative results (e.g., according to Table 1, Q_1 is more informative than Q_2 no matter what the answer is). This might also be done before the answer on the basis of expectations over the possible alternatives.

A critical point when coping with such approaches is to provide a realistic assessment for the probabilistic parameters associated with the modeling of the relations between the questions and the skills. Having to provide sharp numerical values for these probabilities might be difficult. As the skill is a latent quantity, complete data are not available for a statistical learning and a direct elicitation should be provided by experts (e.g., a teacher). Yet, it might be not obvious to express such a domain knowledge by single numbers and a more robust elicitation, such as a probability interval (e.g., $P(Q_1 = 1|S_1 = 1) \in [0.85, 0.95]$), might add realism and robustness to the modeling process [15]. With such generalized assessments of the parameters a Bayesian network simply becomes a *credal* network [22]. The counterpart of such increased realism is the higher computational complexity of inference in credal networks [21]. This is an issue especially when coping with information-theoretic measures such as the information gain, whose computation in credal networks might lead to complex non-linear optimization tasks [19].

The goal of this paper is to investigate the potential of alternatives to the information-theoretic scores driving the question selection in adaptive tests based on directed graphical models, no matter whether these are Bayesian or credal networks. In particular, we consider a family of scores based on the (expected) mode of the posterior distributions over the skills. We show that, when coping with credal networks, the computation of these scores can be reduced to a sequence of linear programming task. Moreover, we show that these scores benefit of better explainability properties, thus allowing for a more transparent process in the question selection.

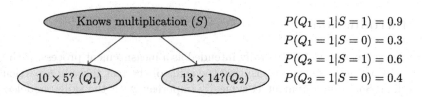

Fig. 1. A Bayesian network over Boolean variables modeling a simple test to evaluate integer multiplication skill. Probabilities of correct answers are also depicted.

The paper is organized as follows. A critical discussion about the existing work in this area is in Sect. 2. The necessary background material is reviewed in Sect. 3. The adaptive testing concepts are introduced in Sect. 4 and specialized to graphical models in 5. The technical part of the paper is in Sect. 6, where the new scores are discussed and specialized to the credal case, while the experiments are in Sect. 7. Conclusions and outlooks are in Sect. 8.

Table 1. Posterior probabilities of the skill after one or two questions in the test based on the Bayesian network in Fig. 1. A uniform prior over the skill is considered. Probabilities are regarded as grades and sorted from the lowest one. Bounds obtained with a perturbation $\epsilon = \pm 0.05$ of all the input parameters are also reported.

Q_1	Q_2	$P(S = 1|q_1, q_2)$	$\underline{P}(S = 1|q_1, q_2)$	$\overline{P}(S = 1|q_1, q_2)$
0	0	0.087	0.028	0.187
0	−	0.125	0.052	0.220
0	1	0.176	0.092	0.256
−	0	0.400	0.306	0.506
−	1	0.600	0.599	0.603
1	0	0.667	0.626	0.708
1	−	0.750	0.748	0.757
1	1	0.818	0.784	0.852

2   Related Work

Tests are modeled as a process relating latent and manifest variables since the classical *item response theory* (IRT), that has been widely used even to implement adaptive sequences [14]. Despite its success related to the ease of implementation and inference, IRT might be inadequate when coping with multiple latent skills, especially when these are dependent. This moved researchers towards the area of probabilistic graphical models [17], as practical tools to implement IRT in more complex setups [2]. Eventually, Bayesian networks have been identified as a suitable formalism to model tests, even behind the IRT framework [25], this being especially the case for adaptive models [26] and coached solving [12]. In order to cope with latent skills, some authors successfully adopted EM approaches to these models [23], this also involving the extreme situation of no ground truth information about the answers [6]. As an alternative approach to the same issue, some authors considered relaxations of the Bayesian formalism, such as fuzzy models [7] and imprecise probabilities [19]. The latter is the direction we consider here, but trying to overcome the computational limitations of that approach when coping with information-theoretic scores. This has some analogy with the approach in [11], that is focused on the Bayesian case only, but whose score, based on the *same-decision* problem, appears hard to be extended to the imprecise framework without increasing the computational complexity.

3   Background on Bayesian and Credal Networks

We denote variables by Latin uppercase letters, while using lowercase for their generic values, and calligraphic for the set of their possible values. Thus, $v \in \mathcal{V}$ is a possible value of V. Here we only consider discrete variables.[1]

---

[1] IRT uses instead continuous skills. Yet, with probabilistic models, discrete skills do not prevent evaluations to range over continuous domains. E.g., see Table 1, where the grade corresponds to a (continuous) probability.

3.1   Bayesian Networks

A probability mass function (PMF) over V is denoted as $P(V)$, while $P(v)$ is the probability assigned to state v. Given a function f of V, its expectation with respect to $P(V)$ is $\mathbb{E}_P(f) := \sum_{v \in \mathcal{V}} P(v)f(v)$. The expectation of $-\log_b[P(V)]$ is called *entropy* and denoted also as $H(V)$. In particular we assume $b := |\mathcal{V}|$ to have the maximum of the entropy, achieved for uniform PMFs, equal to one.

Given a joint PMF $P(U, V)$, the marginal PMF $P(V)$ is obtained by summing out the other variable, i.e., $P(v) = \sum_{u \in \mathcal{U}} P(u, v)$. Conditional PMFs such as $P(U|v)$ are similarly obtained by Bayes's rule, i.e., $P(u|v) = P(u,v)/P(v)$ provided that $P(v) > 0$. The notation $P(U|V) := \{P(U|v)\}_{v \in \mathcal{V}}$ is used for such a conditional probability table (CPT). The entropy of a conditional PMF is defined as in the unconditional case and denoted as $H(U|v)$. The conditional entropy is a weighted average of entropies of the conditional PMFs, i.e., $H(U|V) := \sum_{v \in \mathcal{V}} H(U|v)P(v)$. If $P(u,v) = P(u)P(v)$ for each $u \in \mathcal{U}$ and $v \in \mathcal{V}$, variables U and V are independent. Conditional formulations are also considered.

We assume the set of variables $\boldsymbol{V} := (V_1, \ldots, V_r)$ to be in one-to-one correspondence with a directed acyclic graph $\mathcal{G}$. For each $V \in \boldsymbol{V}$, the parents of V, i.e., the predecessors of V in $\mathcal{G}$, are denoted as Pa_V. The graph $\mathcal{G}$ together with the collection of CPTs $\{P(V|\mathrm{Pa}_V)\}_{V \in \boldsymbol{V}}$ provides a Bayesian network (BN) specification [17]. Under the Markov condition, i.e., every variable is conditionally independent of its non-descendants non-parents given its parents, a BN compactly defines a joint PMF $P(\boldsymbol{V})$ that factorizes as $P(\boldsymbol{v}) = \prod_{V \in \boldsymbol{V}} P(v|\mathrm{pa}_V)$.

Inference, intended as the computation of the posterior PMF of a single (queried) variable given some evidence about other variables, is in general NP-hard, but exact and approximate schemes are available (see [17] for details).

3.2   Credal Sets and Credal Networks

A set of PMFs over V is denoted as $K(V)$ and called *credal set* (CS). Expectations based on CSs are the bounds of the PMF expectations with respect to the CS. Thus $\underline{\mathbb{E}}[f] := \inf_{P(V) \in K(V)} \mathbb{E}[f]$ and similarly for the supremum $\overline{\mathbb{E}}$. Expectations of events are in particular called lower and upper probabilities and denoted as $\underline{P}$ and $\overline{P}$. Notation $K(U|v)$ is used for a set of conditional CSs, while $K(U|V) := \{K(U|v)\}_{v \in \mathcal{V}}$ is a credal CPT (CCPT).

Analogously to a BN, a credal network (CN) is specified by graph $\mathcal{G}$ together with a family of CCPTs $\{K(V|\mathrm{Pa}_V)\}_{V \in \boldsymbol{V}}$ [13]. A CN defines a joint CS $K(\boldsymbol{V})$ corresponding to all the joint PMFs induced by BNs whose CPTs are consistent with the CN CCPTs.

For CNs, we intend inference as the computation of the lower and upper posterior probabilities. The task generalizes BN inference being therefore NP-hard, see [21] for a deeper characterization. Yet, exact and approximate schemes are also available to practically compute inferences [4,5,16].

4   Testing Algorithms

A typical test aims at evaluating the knowledge level of a test taker σ on the basis of her answers to a number of questions. Let Q denote a repository of questions available to the instructor. The order and the number of questions picked from Q to be asked to σ might not be defined in advance. We call *testing algorithm* (TA) a procedure taking care of the selection of the sequence of questions asked to the test taker, and deciding when the test stops. Algorithm 1 depicts a general TA scheme, with e denoting the array of the answers collected from taker σ.

Algorithm 1. General TA: given the profile σ and repository Q, an evaluation based on answers e is returned.

1: $e \leftarrow \emptyset$
2: **while** not Stopping(e) **do**
3:     $Q^* \leftarrow$ Pick(Q, e)
4:     $q^* \leftarrow$ Answer(Q^*, σ)
5:     $e \leftarrow e \cup \{Q^* = q^*\}$
6:     $Q \leftarrow Q \setminus \{Q^*\}$
7: **end while**
8: **return** Evaluate(e)

The Boolean function Stopping decides whether the test should end, this choice being possibly based on the previous answers in e. Trivial stopping rules might be based on the number of questions asked to the test taker (Stopping(e) = 1 if and only if $|e| > n$) or on the number of correct answers provided that a maximum number of questions is not exceeded. Function Pick selects instead the question to be asked to the student from the repository Q. A TA is called *adaptive* when this function takes into account the previous answers e. Trivial non-adaptive strategies might consist in randomly picking an element of Q or following a fixed order. The function Answer is simply collecting (or simulating) the answer of test taker σ to a particular question Q. In our assumptions, this answer is independent of the previous answers to other questions.[2]

Finally, Evaluate is a function returning the overall judgment of the test (e.g., a numerical grade or a pass/fail Boolean) on the basis of all the answers collected after the test termination. Trivial examples of such functions are the percentage of correct answers or a Boolean that is true when a sufficient number of correct answers has been provided. Note also that in our assumptions the TA is *exchangeable*, i.e., the stopping rule, the question finder and the evaluation function are invariant with respect to permutations in e [24]. In other words,

---

[2] Generalized setups where the quality of the student answer is affected by the previous answers will be discussed at the end of the paper. This might include a *fatigue* model negatively affecting the quality of the answers when many questions have been already answered as well as the presence of *revealing* questions that might improve the quality of other answers [18].

the same next question, the same evaluation and the same stopping decision is produced for any two students who provided the same list of answers in two different orders.

A TA is supposed to achieve reliable evaluation of taker σ from the answers e. As each answer is individually assumed to improve such quality, asking all the questions, no matter the order because of the exchangeability assumption, is an obvious choice. Yet, this might be impractical (e.g., because of time limitations) or just provide an unnecessary burden to the test taker. The goal of a good TA is therefore to trade off the evaluation accuracy and the number of questions.[3]

5   Adaptive Testing in Bayesian and Credal Networks

The general TA setup in Algorithm 1 can be easily specialized to BNs as follows. First, we identify the profile σ of the test taker with the actual states of a number of latent discrete variables, called *skills*. Let $S = \{S_j\}_{j=1}^m$ denote these skill variables, and s_σ the actual values of the skills for the taker. Skills are typically ordinal variables, whose states correspond to increasing knowledge levels. Questions in Q are still described as manifest variables whose actual values are returned by the Answer function. This is achieved by a (possibly stochastic) function of the actual profile s_σ. This reflects the taker perspective, while the teacher has clearly no access to s_σ. As a remark, note that we might often coarsen the set of possible values $\mathcal{Q}$ for each $Q \in Q$: for instance, a multiple choice question with three options might have a single right answer, the two other answers being indistinguishable from the evaluation point of view.[4]

A joint PMF over the skills S and the questions Q is supposed to be available. In particular we assume this to correspond to a BN whose graph has the questions as leaf nodes. Thus, for each $Q \in Q$, $Pa_Q \subseteq S$ and we call Pa_Q the *scope* of question Q. Note that this assumption about the graph is simply reflecting a statement about the conditional independence between (the answer to) a question and all the other skills and questions given scope of the question. This basically means that the answers to other questions are not directly affecting the answer to a particular question.[5]

As the available data are typically incomplete because of the latent nature of the skills, dedicated learning strategies, such as various forms of constrained EM should be considered to train a BN from data. We refer the reader to the various contributions of Plajner and Vomlel in this field (e.g., [23]) for a complete discussion of that approach. Here we assume the BN quantification available.

---

[3] In some generalized setups, other elements such as a *serendipity* in choice in order to avoid tedious sequences of questions might be also considered [8].

[4] The case of *abstention* to an answer and the consequent problem of modeling the incompleteness is a topic we do not consider here for the sake of conciseness. Yet, general approaches based on the ideas in [20] could be easily adopted.

[5] Moving to other setups would not be really critical because of the separation properties of observed nodes in Bayesian and credal networks, see for instance [3,9].

In such a BN framework, Stopping(e) might be naturally based on an evaluation of the posterior PMF $P(S|e)$, this being also the case for Evaluate. Regarding the question selection, Pick might be similarly based on the (posterior) CPT $P(S|Q, e)$, whose values for the different answers to Q might be weighted by the marginal $P(Q|e)$. More specifically, entropies and conditional entropies are considered by Algorithm 2, while the evaluation is based on a conditional expectation for a given utility function.

Algorithm 2. Information Theoretic TA in a BN over the questions Q and the skills S: given the student profile s_σ, the algorithm returns an evaluation corresponding to the expectation of an evaluation function f with respect to the posterior for the skills given the answers e.

1: $e = \emptyset$
2: **while** $H(S|e) > H^*$ **do**
3:    $Q^* \leftarrow \arg\max_{Q \in Q} [H(S|e) - H(S|Q, e)]$
4:    $q^* \leftarrow$ Answer(Q^*, s_σ)
5:    $e \leftarrow e \cup \{Q^* = q^*\}$
6:    $Q \leftarrow Q \setminus \{Q^*\}$
7: **end while**
8: **return** $\mathbb{E}_{P(S|e)}[f(S)]$

When no data are available for the BN training, elicitation techniques should be considered instead. As already discussed, CNs might offer a better formalism to capture domain knowledge, especially by providing interval-valued probabilities instead of sharp values. If this is the case, a CN version of Algorithm 2 can be considered. To achieve that, in line 3, a score taking into account the fact that the entropies in a CN are not anymore precisely specified should be adopted. Similar considerations apply to the evaluation function in line 8.

The price of such increased realism in the elicitation is the higher complexity characterizing inferences based on CNs. The work in [19] offers a critical discussion of those issues, that are only partially addressed by heuristic techniques used there to approximate the upper bounds of conditional entropies. In the next section we consider an alternative approach to cope with CNs and adaptive TAs based on different scores used to select the questions.

6   A New Score for Testing Algorithms

Following [27], we can regard the PMF entropy (and its conditional version) used by Algorithm 2 as an example of an index of *qualitative variation* (IQV). An IQV is just a normalized number that takes value zero for degenerate PMFs, one on uniform ones, being independent on the number of possible states (and samples for empirical models). The closer to uniform is the PMF, the higher is the index and vice versa.

In order to bypass the computational issues related to its application with CNs, we want to consider alternative IQVs to replace entropy in Algorithm 2. Wilkox *deviation from the mode* (DM) appears a sensible option. Given a PMF $P(V)$, this corresponds to:

$$M(V) := 1 - \sum_{v \in \mathcal{V}} \frac{\max_{v' \in \mathcal{V}} P(v') - P(v)}{|\mathcal{V}| - 1}. \tag{1}$$

It is a trivial exercise to check that this is a proper IQV, with the same unimodal behavior of the entropy. In terms of explainability, being a linear function of the modal probability, the numerical value of the DM offers a more transparent interpretation than the entropy. From a computational point of view, for both marginal and conditional PMFs, both the entropy and the DM can be directly obtained from the probabilities of the singletons.

The situation is different when computing the bounds of these quantities with respect to a CS. For the upper bound, by simple algebra, we obtain:

$$\overline{M}(V) := \max_{P(V) \in K(V)} M(V) = \frac{1 - \min_{P(V) \in K(V)} \max_{v' \in \mathcal{V}} P(v')}{(|\mathcal{V}| - 1)/|\mathcal{V}|}. \tag{2}$$

As we assume CSs defined by a finite number of linear constraints, such a *minimax* objective function can be easily reduced to a linear programming task by adding an auxiliary variable corresponding to the maximum and the constraints modeling the fact that this variable is the maximum. The situation is even simpler for the lower bound $\underline{M}(V)$, which reduces to a *maximax* corresponding to the identification of the singleton state with the highest upper probability. Optimizing entropy requires instead a non-trivial, but convex, optimization. See for instance [1] for an iterative procedure to find the maximum when coping with CSs defined by probability intervals. The situation is even more critical for the minimization, that has been proved to be NP-hard in [28].

The optimization becomes more challenging for conditional entropies, as these are mixtures of entropies of conditional distributions based on imprecise weights. Consequently, in [19], only an inner approximation for the upper bound have been derived. The situation is different for conditional DMs. The following result offers a feasible approach in a simplified setup, to be later extended to the general case.

Theorem 1. *Under the setup of Sect. 5, consider a CN with a single skill S and a single question Q, that is a child of S. Let $K(S)$ and $K(Q|S)$ be the CCPTs of such CN. Let also $Q = \{q^1, \ldots, q^n\}$ and $S = \{s^1, \ldots, s^m\}$. The upper conditional DM, i.e.,*

$$\overline{M}(S|Q) := 1 - \min_{\substack{P(S) \in K(S) \\ P(Q|S) \in K(Q|S)}} \sum_{i=1}^{n} \left[\max_{j \in \{1, \ldots, m\}} P(s_j|q_i) \right] P(q_i), \tag{3}$$

where the denominator in (2) was omitted for the sake of brevity, is such that:

$$\overline{M}(S|Q) := 1 - \min_{\hat{j}_1, \ldots, \hat{j}_n \in \{1, \ldots, m\}} \Omega(\hat{j}_1, \ldots, \hat{j}_n), \tag{4}$$

where $\Omega(\hat{j}_1, \ldots, \hat{j}_n)$ is the solution of the following linear programming task.

$$\min \quad \sum_i x_{i\hat{j}_i}$$

$$\text{s.t.} \quad \sum_{ij} x_{ij} = 1 \tag{5}$$

$$x_{ij} \geq 0 \qquad \forall i, j \tag{6}$$

$$\sum_k x_{kj} \geq \underline{P}(s_j) \qquad \forall j \tag{7}$$

$$\sum_k x_{kj} \leq \overline{P}(s_j) \qquad \forall j \tag{8}$$

$$\underline{P}(q_i|s_j) \sum_k x_{kj} \leq x_{ij} \qquad \forall i, j \tag{9}$$

$$\overline{P}(q_i|s_j) \sum_k x_{kj} \geq x_{ij} \qquad \forall i, j \tag{10}$$

$$x_{i\hat{j}_i} \geq x_{ij} \qquad \forall i, j \neq \hat{j}_i \tag{11}$$

Assignments of $(\hat{j}_1, \ldots, \hat{j}_n)$ such that the corresponding linear programming task is unfeasible are just removed from the minimization in Eq. (4). Note that the bounds on the sums over the indexes and on the universal quantifiers are also omitted for the sake of brevity.

Proof. Equation (3) rewrites as:

$$\overline{M}(S|Q) = 1 - \min_{\substack{P(S) \in K(S) \\ P(Q|S) \in K(Q|S)}} \sum_{i=1}^n \left[\max_{j=1,\ldots,m} P(s_j) P(q_i|s_j) \right]. \tag{12}$$

We define the variables of such constrained optimization as $x_{ij} := P(s_j) \cdot P(q_i|s_j)$ for each $i \in \{1, \ldots, n\}$ and $j \in \{1, \ldots, m\}$. The CCPT constraints can be easily reformulated with respect to such new variables by noticing that $x_{ij} = P(s_j, q_i)$, and hence $P(s_j) = \sum_i x_{ij}$ and $P(q_i|s_j) = x_{ij}/(\sum_k x_{kj})$. Consequently, the interval constraints on $P(S)$ correspond to the linear constraints in Eqs. (7) and (8). Similarly, for $P(Q|S)$, we obtain:

$$\underline{P}(q_i|s_j) \leq \frac{x_{ij}}{\sum_k x_{kj}} \leq \overline{P}(q_i|s_j), \tag{13}$$

that easily gives the linear constraints in Eqs. (9) and (10) (as we cope with strictly positive probabilities of the skills, the denominator in Eq. (13) cannot be zero). The non-negativity of the probabilities corresponds to Eq. (6), while Eq. (5) gives the normalization of $P(S, Q)$ and the normalization of $P(Q|S)$ is by construction. Equation (12) rewrites therefore as:

$$\overline{M}(S|Q) = 1 - \min_{\{x_{ij}\} \in \Gamma} \sum_i \max_j x_{ij}, \tag{14}$$

where Γ denotes the linear constraints in Eqs. (5)–(10). If $\hat{j}_i := \arg\max_j x_{ij}$, Eq. (14) rewrites as:

$$\overline{M}(S|Q) = 1 - \min_{\{x_{ij}\} \in \Gamma'} \sum_i x_{i\hat{j}_i}, \qquad (15)$$

where Γ' are the constraints in Γ with the additional (linear) constraints in Eq. (11) implementing the definition of $\hat{j}$. The minimization in the right-hand side of Eq. (15) is not a linear programming task, as the values of the indexes $\hat{j}_i$ are potentially different for different assignments of the optimization variables consistent with the constraints in Γ. Yet, we might address such optimization as a brute-force task with respect to all the possible assignation of the indexes $\hat{j}_i$. This is exactly what is done by Eq. (4) where all the m^n possible assignations are considered. Finally, regarding the feasibility of the constraints, as the constraints in Eq. (14) are feasible by construction, there is at least a value of $(\hat{j}_1, \ldots, \hat{j}_n)$, i.e., the one corresponding to the optimum, for which also the constraints in Eq. (15) are feasible. □

An analogous result holds for the computation of $\underline{M}(S|Q)$. In that case a maximum should replace the minimum in both Eq. (3) and in the linear programming tasks. The overall complexity is $O(m^n)$ with $n := |\mathcal{Q}|$. This means quadratic complexity for any test where only the difference between a wrong and a right answer is considered from an elicitation perspective, and tractable computations provided that the number of distinct answers to the same question is bounded by a small constant. Coping with multiple questions becomes trivial by means of the results in [3], that allows to merge multiple observed children into a single one. Finally, the case of multiple skills might be similarly considered by using the marginal bounds of the single skills in Eqs. (7) and (8).

7   Experiments

We validate the ideas outlined in the previous section in order to check whether or not the DM can be used for TAs as a sensible alternative to information-theoretic scores such as the entropy. In the BN context, this is achieved by computing the necessary posterior probabilities, while Theorem 1 is used instead for CNs.

7.1   Single-Skill Experiments on Synthetic Data

For a very first validation of our approach, we consider a simple setup made of a single Boolean skill S and a repository with 18 Boolean questions based on nine different parametrizations (two questions for each parametrization). In such a BN, the CPT of a question can be parametrized by two numbers. E.g., in the example in Fig. 1, we used the probabilities of correctly answering the question given that the skill is present or not, i.e., $P(Q = 1|S = 1)$ and $P(Q = 1|S = 0)$.

A more interpretable parametrization can be obtained as follows:

$$\delta := 1 - \frac{1}{2}[P(Q = 1|\, S = 1) + P(Q = 1|\, S = 0)],\tag{16}$$

$$\kappa := P(Q = 1|\, S = 1) - P(Q = 1|\, S = 0).\tag{17}$$

Note that $P(Q = 1|S = 1) > P(Q = 1|S = 0)$ is an obvious rationality constraint for questions, otherwise having the skill would make it less likely to answer properly to a question. Both parameters are therefore non-negative. The parameter δ, corresponding to the average probability of a wrong answer over the different skill values, can be regarded as a normalized index of the question *difficulty*. E.g., in Fig. 1, Q_1 ($\delta = 0.4$) is less difficult than Q_2 ($\delta = 0.5$). The parameter κ can be instead regarded as a descriptor of the difference of the conditional PMFs associated with the different skill values. In the most extreme case $\kappa = 1$, the CPT $P(Q|S)$ is diagonal implementing an identity mapping between the skill and the question. We therefore regard κ as a indicator of the *discriminative* power of the question. In our tests, for the BN quantification, we consider the nine possible parametrizations corresponding to $(\delta, \gamma) \in [0.4, 0.5, 0.6]^2$. For $P(S)$ we use instead a uniform PMF. For the CN approach we perturb all the BN parameters with $\epsilon = \pm 0.05$, thus obtaining a CN quantification. A group of 1024 simulated students, half of them having $S = 0$ and half with $S = 1$ is used for simulations. The student answers are sampled from the CPT of the asked question on the basis of the student profile. Figure 2 (left) depicts the accuracy of the BN and CN approaches based on both the entropy and the DM scores. To force credal models to give a single output, decisions are based on the mid-point between the lower and the upper probability, while lower entropies are used. Pure credal approaches returning multiple options will be considered in a future work. We notably see all the adaptive approaches outperforming a non-adaptive, random, choice of the questions. To better investigate the strong overlap between these trajectories, in Fig. 2 (right) we compute the Brier score and we observe a strong similarity between DM and entropy approaches in both the Bayesian and the credal case, with the credal slightly outperforming the Bayesian approach.

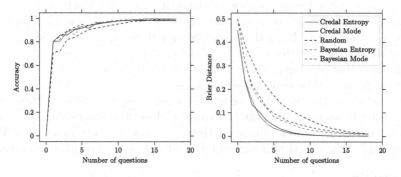

Fig. 2. Accuracy (left) and Brier distance (right) of TAs for a single-skill BN/CN

7.2 Multi-skill Experiments on Real Data

For a validation on real data, we consider an online German language placement test (see also [19]). Four different Boolean skills associated with different abilities (vocabulary, communication, listening and reading) are considered and modeled by a chain-shaped graph, for which BN and CN quantification are already available. A repository of 64 Boolean questions, 16 for each skill, with four different levels of difficulty and discriminative power, have been used. Experiments have been achieved by means of the CREMA library for credal networks [16].[6] The Java code used for the simulations is available together with the Python scripts used to analyze the results and the model specifications.[7] Performances are evaluated as for the previous model, the only difference being that here the accuracy is aggregated by average over the separate accuracies for the four skills. The results (Fig. 3) are analogous to those for the single-skill case: entropy-based and mode-based scores are providing similar results, with the credal approach typically leading to more accurate evaluations.

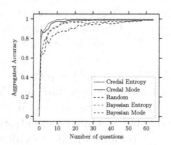

Fig. 3. Aggregated accuracy for a multi-skill TA

8   Outlooks and Conclusions

A new score for adaptive testing in Bayesian and credal networks has been proposed. Our proposal is based on indexes of qualitative variation, being in particular focused on the modal probability for their explainability features. An algorithm to evaluate this quantity in the credal case is derived. Our experiments show that moving to these scores does not really affect the quality of the selection process. Besides a deeper experimental validation, a necessary future work consists in the derivation of simpler elicitation strategies for these models in order to promote their application to real-world testing environments. To achieve that we also intend to embed these new scores in a software we recently developed for the practical implementation of web-based adaptive tests [10].[8]

---

[6] https://github.com/IDSIA/crema.
[7] https://github.com/IDSIA/crema-adaptive.
[8] https://github.com/IDSIA/adapquest.

References

1. Abellan, J., Moral, S.: Maximum of entropy for credal sets. Int. J. Uncertainty Fuzziness Knowl.-Based Syst. **11**(05), 587–597 (2003)
2. Almond, R.G., Mislevy, R.J.: Graphical models and computerized adaptive testing. Appl. Psychol. Meas. **23**(3), 223–237 (1999)
3. Antonucci, A., Piatti, A.: Modeling unreliable observations in Bayesian networks by credal networks. In: Godo, L., Pugliese, A. (eds.) SUM 2009. LNCS (LNAI), vol. 5785, pp. 28–39. Springer, Heidelberg (2009). https://doi.org/10.1007/978-3-642-04388-8_4
4. Antonucci, A., de Campos, C.P., Huber, D., Zaffalon, M.: Approximating credal network inferences by linear programming. In: van der Gaag, L.C. (ed.) ECSQARU 2013. LNCS (LNAI), vol. 7958, pp. 13–24. Springer, Heidelberg (2013). https://doi.org/10.1007/978-3-642-39091-3_2
5. Antonucci, A., de Campos, C.P., Huber, D., Zaffalon, M.: Approximate credal network updating by linear programming with applications to decision making. Int. J. Approximate Reasoning **58**, 25–38 (2015)
6. Bachrach, Y., Graepel, T., Minka, T., Guiver, J.: How to grade a test without knowing the answers–a Bayesian graphical model for adaptive crowdsourcing and aptitude testing. arXiv preprint arXiv:1206.6386 (2012)
7. Badaracco, M., Martínez, L.: A fuzzy linguistic algorithm for adaptive test in intelligent tutoring system based on competences. Expert Syst. Appl. **40**(8), 3073–3086 (2013)
8. Badran, M.E.K., Abdo, J.B., Al Jurdi, W., Demerjian, J.: Adaptive serendipity for recommender systems: Let it find you. In: ICAART (2), pp. 739–745 (2019)
9. Bolt, J.H., De Bock, J., Renooij, S.: Exploiting Bayesian network sensitivity functions for inference in credal networks. In: Proceedings of the Twenty-Second European Conference on Artificial Intelligence (ECAI), vol. 285, pp. 646–654. IOS Press (2016)
10. Bonesana, C., Mangili, F., Antonucci, A.: ADAPQUEST: a software for web-based adaptive questionnaires based on Bayesian networks. In: IJCAI 2021 Workshop Artificial Intelligence for Education (2021)
11. Chen, S.J., Choi, A., Darwiche, A.: Computer adaptive testing using the same-decision probability. In: BMA@ UAI, pp. 34–43 (2015)
12. Conati, C., Gertner, A.S., VanLehn, K., Druzdzel, M.J.: On-line student modeling for coached problem solving using Bayesian networks. In: Jameson, A., Paris, C., Tasso, C. (eds.) User Modeling. ICMS, vol. 383, pp. 231–242. Springer, Vienna (1997). https://doi.org/10.1007/978-3-7091-2670-7_24
13. Cozman, F.G.: Credal networks. Artif. Intell. **120**(2), 199–233 (2000)
14. Embretson, S.E., Reise, S.P.: Item Response Theory. Psychology Press, Hove (2013)
15. Hájek, A., Smithson, M.: Rationality and indeterminate probabilities. Synthese **187**(1), 33–48 (2012)
16. Huber, D., Cabañas, R., Antonucci, A., Zaffalon, M.: CREMA: a Java library for credal network inference. In: Jaeger, M., Nielsen, T. (eds.) Proceedings of the 10th International Conference on Probabilistic Graphical Models (PGM 2020). Proceedings of Machine Learning Research, PMLR, Aalborg, Denmark (2020)
17. Koller, D., Friedman, N.: Probabilistic Graphical Models: Principles and Techniques. MIT Press, Cambridge (2009)
18. Laitusis, C.C., Morgan, D.L., Bridgeman, B., Zanna, J., Stone, E.: Examination of fatigue effects from extended-time accommodations on the SAT reasoning test. ETS Research Report Series **2007**(2), i–13 (2007)

19. Mangili, F., Bonesana, C., Antonucci, A.: Reliable knowledge-based adaptive tests by credal networks. In: Antonucci, A., Cholvy, L., Papini, O. (eds.) ECSQARU 2017. LNCS (LNAI), vol. 10369, pp. 282–291. Springer, Cham (2017). https://doi.org/10.1007/978-3-319-61581-3_26

20. Marchetti, S., Antonucci, A.: Reliable uncertain evidence modeling in Bayesian networks by credal networks. In: Brawner, K.W., Rus, V. (eds.) Proceedings of the Thirty-First International Florida Artificial Intelligence Research Society Conference (FLAIRS-31), pp. 513–518. AAAI Press, Melbourne, Florida, USA (2018)

21. Mauá, D.D., De Campos, C.P., Benavoli, A., Antonucci, A.: Probabilistic inference in credal networks: new complexity results. J. Artif. Intell. Res. **50**, 603–637 (2014)

22. Piatti, A., Antonucci, A., Zaffalon, M.: Building knowledge-based expert systems by credal networks: a tutorial. In: Baswell, A. (ed.) Advances in Mathematics Research, vol. 11, chap. 2. Nova Science Publishers, New York (2010)

23. Plajner, M., Vomlel, J.: Monotonicity in practice of adaptive testing. arXiv preprint arXiv:2009.06981 (2020)

24. Sawatzky, R., Ratner, P.A., Kopec, J.A., Wu, A.D., Zumbo, B.D.: The accuracy of computerized adaptive testing in heterogeneous populations: a mixture item-response theory analysis. PLoS ONE **11**(3), e0150563 (2016)

25. Vomlel, J.: Bayesian networks in educational testing. Int. J. Uncertain. Fuzziness Knowl.-Based Syst. **12**(supp01), 83–100 (2004)

26. Vomlel, J.: Building adaptive tests using Bayesian networks. Kybernetika **40**(3), 333–348 (2004)

27. Wilcox, A.R.: Indices of qualitative variation and political measurement. Western Political Q. **26**(2), 325–343 (1973)

28. Xiang, G., Kosheleva, O., Klir, G.J.: Estimating information amount under interval uncertainty: algorithmic solvability and computational complexity. Technical report 158, Departmental Technical Reports (CS) (2006)

Multi-label Chaining with Imprecise Probabilities

Yonatan Carlos Carranza Alarcón[ID] and Sébastien Destercke[(✉)][ID]

Sorbonne Universités, Université Technologique de Compiègne, CNRS,
UMR 7253 - Heudiasyc, 57 Avenue de Landshut, Compiègne, France
{yonatan-carlos.carranza-alarcon,sebastien.destercke}@hds.utc.fr

Abstract. We present two different strategies to extend the classical multi-label chaining approach to handle imprecise probability estimates. These estimates use convex sets of distributions (or credal sets) in order to describe our uncertainty rather than a precise one. The main reasons one could have for using such estimations are (1) to make cautious predictions (or no decision at all) when a high uncertainty is detected in the chaining and (2) to make better precise predictions by avoiding biases caused in early decisions in the chaining. We adapt both strategies to the case of the naive credal classifier, showing that this adaptations are computationally efficient. Our experimental results on missing labels, which investigate how reliable these predictions are in both approaches, indicate that our approaches produce relevant cautiousness on those hard-to-predict instances where the precise models fail.

Keywords: Imprecise probabilities · Multi-label · Classifier chains

Multi-label classification (MLC) is a generalization of traditional classification (with a single label), as well as a special case of multi-task learning. This approach is increasingly required in different research fields, such as the classification of proteins in bioinformatics [17], text classification in information retrieval [10], object recognition in computer vision [3], and so on.

A classical issue in multi-label learning techniques is how to integrate the possible dependencies between labels while keeping the inference task tractable. Indeed, while decomposition techniques [10,17] such as Binary relevance or Calibrated ranking allow to speed up both the learning and inference tasks, they roughly ignore the label dependencies, while using a fully specified model such as in pr obabilistic trees [6] requires, at worst, to scan all possible predictions (whose quantity grows exponentially in the number of labels). A popular technique, known as chaining [15] to solve this issue, at least for the inference task, is to use heuristic predictions: they consists in using, incrementally, the predictions made on previous labels as additional conditional features to help better predict the rel of a current label, rather than using the prediction probabilities.

To the best of our knowledge, there are only a few works on multi-label classification producing cautious predictions, such as the reject option [14], partial

© Springer Nature Switzerland AG 2021
J. Vejnarová and N. Wilson (Eds.): ECSQARU 2021, LNAI 12897, pp. 413–426, 2021.
https://doi.org/10.1007/978-3-030-86772-0_30

predictions [1,8] or abstaining labels [18], but none of these have studied this issue in chaining (or classifier-chains approach).

In this paper, we consider the problem of extending chaining to the imprecise probabilistic case, and propose two different extensions, as some predictive probabilities are too imprecise to use predicted labels, henceforth called abstained labels, in the chaining. The first extension treats the abstained labels in a robust way, exploring all possible conditional situation in order not to propagate early uncertain decisions, whereas the latter marginalizes the probabilistic model over those labels, ignoring them in the predictive model.

Section 1 introduces the notations that we use for the multi-label setting, and gives the necessary reminders about making inferences with convex sets of probabilities. In Sect. 2, we recall the classical classifier-chains approach and then we present our extended approaches based on imprecise probabilities. Section 3 then shows that in the case of the naive credal classifier (NCC) [21], those strategies can be performed in polynomial time.

Finally, in Sect. 4, we perform a set of experiments on real data sets, which are perturbed with missing labels, in order to investigate how cautious (when we abstain on labels difficult to predict) is our approach. In order to adhere to the page limit, all proofs and supplementary experimental results have been relegated to the appendix of an online' extended version [4].

1   Problem Setting

In the multi-label problem, an instance x of an input space $\mathscr{X} = \mathbb{R}^p$ is no longer associated with a single label m_k of an output space $\mathcal{K} = \{m_1, \ldots, m_m\}$, as in the traditional classification problem, but with a subset of labels $\Lambda_x \subseteq \mathcal{K}$ often called the set of relevant labels while its complement $\mathcal{K} \backslash \Lambda_x$ is considered as irrelevant for x. Let $\mathscr{Y} = \{0,1\}^m$ be a m-dimensional binary space and $y = (y_1, \ldots, y_m) \in \mathscr{Y}$ be any element of $\mathscr{Y}$ such that $y_i = 1$ if and only if $m_i \in \Lambda_x$.

From a decision theoretic approach (DTA), the goal of the multi-label problem is the same as usual classification. Given a probability distribution $\hat{\mathbb{P}}$ fitting a set of i.i.d. observations $\mathcal{D} = \{(x_i, y_i) | i = 1, \ldots, N\}$ issued from a (true) theoretical probability distribution $\mathbb{P} : \mathscr{X} \times \mathscr{Y} \to [0, 1]$, DTA aims to minimize the risk of getting missclassification with respect to a specified loss function $\ell(\cdot, \cdot)$:

$$\mathcal{R}_\ell(Y, h(X)) = \min_h \mathbb{E}_{\hat{\mathbb{P}}}\left[\ell(Y, h(X))\right]. \tag{1}$$

where $h \colon \mathscr{X} \to \mathscr{Y}$ is a m-dimensional vector function. If $\ell(\cdot, \cdot)$ is defined instance-wise, that is $\ell : \mathcal{Y} \times \mathcal{Y} \to \mathbb{R}$, the solution of Equation (1) is obtained by minimizing the conditional expected risk (cf. [7, Eq. 3] and [9, Eq. 2.21])

$$h(x) = \arg\min_{y \in \mathscr{Y}} \mathbb{E}_{\hat{\mathbb{P}}_{Y|x}}\left[\ell(Y, y)\right] = \arg\min_{y \in \mathscr{Y}} \sum_{y' \in \mathscr{Y}} \hat{P}(Y = y' | X = x)\ell(y', y) \tag{2}$$

or, equivalently, by picking the undominated elements of the order relation[1] $\succeq$ over $\mathscr{Y} \times \mathscr{Y}$ for which $\boldsymbol{y}^1 \succeq \boldsymbol{y}^2$ ($\boldsymbol{y}^1$ is preferred to/dominates $\boldsymbol{y}^2$) iff

$$\mathbb{E}_{\hat{\mathbb{P}}_{Y|x}} \left(\ell(\boldsymbol{y}^2, \cdot) - \ell(\boldsymbol{y}^1, \cdot) \right) = \mathbb{E}_{\hat{\mathbb{P}}_{Y|x}} \left(\ell(\boldsymbol{y}^2, \cdot) \right) - \mathbb{E}_{\hat{\mathbb{P}}_{Y|x}} \left(\ell(\boldsymbol{y}^1, \cdot) \right) \geq 0. \qquad (3)$$

This amounts to saying that exchanging $\boldsymbol{y}^2$ for $\boldsymbol{y}^1$ would incur a non-negative expected loss (which is not desirable).

In this paper, we are also interested in making set-valued predictions when uncertainty is too high (e.g. due to insufficient evidence to include or discard a label as relevant, see Example 1). The set-valued prediction will here be described as a partial binary vector $\boldsymbol{y}^* \in \mathfrak{Y}$ where $\mathfrak{Y} = \{0, 1, *\}^m$ is the new output space with a new element $*$ representing the abstention. For instance, a partial prediction $\boldsymbol{y}^* = (*, 1, 0)$ corresponds to two plausible binary vector solutions $\{(0, 1, 0), (1, 1, 0)\} \subseteq \mathscr{Y}$. To obtain such predictions, we will use imprecise probabilities as a well-founded framework.

1.1 Notions About Imprecise Probabilities

Imprecise probabilities consist in representing our uncertainty by a convex set of probability distributions $\mathscr{P}_X$ [2,19] (i.e. a *credal set* [12]), defined over a space $\mathscr{X}$ rather than by a precise probability measure $\mathbb{P}_X$ [16]. Given such a set of distributions $\mathscr{P}_X$ and any measurable event $A \subseteq \mathscr{X}$, we can define the notions of lower and upper probabilities as:

$$\underline{P}_X(A) = \inf_{P \in \mathscr{P}_X} P(A) \quad \text{and} \quad \overline{P}_X(A) = \sup_{P \in \mathscr{P}_X} P(A) \qquad (4)$$

where $\underline{P}_X(A) = \overline{P}_X(A)$ only when we have sufficient information about event A. The lower probability is dual to the upper [2], in the sense that $\underline{P}_X(A) = 1 - \overline{P}_X(A^c)$ where A^c is the complement of A. Many authors [19,21] have argued that when information is lacking or imprecise, considering credal sets as our model of information better describes our actual uncertainty.

However, such an approach comes with extra challenges in the learning and inference step, especially in combinatorial domains. In this paper, we will consider making a chain of binary inferences, each inference influenced by the previous one. If we consider $\mathcal{Y} = \{0, 1\}$ as the output space and Y as a univariate random variable on $\mathcal{Y}$, a standard way to take a decision with abstention given a credal set $\mathscr{P}$ on $\mathcal{Y}$ is

$$\hat{y} = \begin{cases} 1 & \text{if } \underline{P}_x(Y = 1) > 0.5, \\ 0 & \text{if } \overline{P}_x(Y = 1) < 0.5, \\ * & \text{if } 0.5 \in \left[\underline{P}_x(Y = 1), \overline{P}_x(Y = 1) \right] \end{cases} . \qquad (5)$$

The next example illustrates such notions on a multi-label example

Example 1. We consider an output space of two labels $\mathcal{K} = \{m_1, m_2\}$, a single binary feature x_1 and Table 1 with imprecise estimations of $\hat{\mathbb{P}}(Y_1, Y_2 | X_1)$.

---

[1] A complete, transitive, and asymmetric binary relation.

Table 1. Estimated conditional probability distributions $\hat{\mathbb{P}}(Y_1, Y_2|X_1) \in \hat{\mathscr{P}}_{Y_1,Y_2|X_1}$.

y_1	y_2	x_1	$\hat{\mathscr{P}}_{Y_1,Y_2|X_1=0}$	y_1	y_2	x_1	$\hat{\mathscr{P}}_{Y_1,Y_2|X_1=1}$
0	0	0	[0.4,0.7]	0	0	1	0.00
0	1	0	[0.3,0.6]	0	1	1	0.00
1	0	0	0.00	1	0	1	[0.6,0.8]
1	1	0	0.00	1	1	1	[0.2,0.4]

Based on the probabilities of Table 1, we have that $\hat{P}_0(y_1 = 0) := \hat{P}(y_1 = 0|x_1 = 0) = 1$ and $\hat{P}_0(y_2 = 0) \in [0.4, 0.7]$, therefore not knowing whether $\hat{P}_0(y_2 = 0) > 0.5$. This could lead us to propose as a prediction $\hat{\boldsymbol{y}}^* = (0, *)$. On the contrary, the imprecision on the right hand-side is such that $\hat{P}_1(y_2 = 0) \in [0.6, 0.8]$, leading to the precise prediction $\hat{\boldsymbol{y}}^* = (1, 0)$.

2   Multilabel Chaining with Imprecise Probabilities

Solving (2) can already be computationally prohibitive in the precise case [6], which is why heuristic to approximate inferences done on the full joint models such as the chain model have been proposed. This section recalls its basics and presents our proposed extension. To do so, we will need a couple notations: we will denote by $\mathscr{I}$ subsets of label indices and by $[\![j]\!] = \{1, \ldots, j\}$ the set of the first j integers. Given a prediction made in the j first labels, we will denote by

1. (relevant labels) $\mathscr{I}_{\mathcal{R}}^j \subseteq [\![j]\!]$ the indices of the labels predicted as relevant among the j first, i.e. $\forall i \in \mathscr{I}_{\mathcal{R}}^j$, $y_i = 1$,
2. (irrelevant labels) $\mathscr{I}_{\mathcal{I}}^j \subseteq [\![j]\!]$, $\mathscr{I}_{\mathcal{I}}^j \cap \mathscr{I}_{\mathcal{R}}^j = \emptyset$ the indices of the labels predicted as irrelevant among the j first, i.e. $\forall i \in \mathscr{I}_{\mathcal{I}}^j$, $y_i = 0$, and
3. (abstained labels) $\mathscr{I}_{\mathcal{A}}^j = [\![j]\!] \backslash (\mathscr{I}_{\mathcal{R}}^j \cup \mathscr{I}_{\mathcal{I}}^j)$ the indices of the labels on which we abstained among the j first, i.e. $\forall i \in \mathscr{I}_{\mathcal{A}}^j$, $y_i = \{0, 1\} := *$,

and of course $\mathscr{I}^j = \mathscr{I}_{\mathcal{A}}^j \cup \mathscr{I}_{\mathcal{R}}^j \cup \mathscr{I}_{\mathcal{I}}^j = [\![j]\!]$. Besides, for the sake of simplicity, we will use the notation

$$P_{\boldsymbol{x}}^{[\![j-1]\!]}(Y_j = 1) := P(Y_j = 1|Y_{\mathscr{I}^{j-1}} = \hat{\boldsymbol{y}}_{\mathscr{I}^{j-1}}, X = \boldsymbol{x}), \qquad (6)$$

where $\hat{\boldsymbol{y}}_{\mathscr{I}^{j-1}}$ is a $(j-1)$-dimensional vector that contains the previously inferred precise and/or abstained values of labels having indices $\mathscr{I}^{j-1}$.

2.1   Precise Probabilistic Chaining

Classifier chains is a well-known approach exploiting dependencies among labels by fitting at each step of the chain (see Fig. 1) a new classifier model $h_j : \mathscr{X} \times \{0,1\}^{j-1} \rightarrow \{0,1\}$ predicting the relevance of the jth label. This classifier combines the original input space attribute and all previous predictions in the chain in order to create a new input space $\mathscr{X}^*_{j-1} = \mathscr{X} \times \{0,1\}^{j-1}, j \in \mathbb{N}^{>0}$. In brief, we consider a chain $\boldsymbol{h} = (h_1, \ldots, h_m)$ of binary classifiers resulting in the full prediction $\hat{\boldsymbol{y}}$ obtained by solving each single classifier as follows

$$\hat{y}_j := h_j(x) = \arg\max_{y \in \{0,1\}} P_x^{[j-1]}(Y_j = y). \tag{7}$$

The classical multi-label chaining then works as follows:

1. RANDOM LABEL ORDERING. We randomly pick an order between labels and assume that the indices are relabelled in an increasing order.
2. PREDICTION j^{th} LABEL. For a label y_j and the previous predictions on labels $y_1, \ldots, y_{j-1}$ and let $\mathscr{I}_{\mathcal{R}}^{j-1}, \mathscr{I}_{\mathcal{I}}^{j-1} \subseteq [\![j-1]\!]$ be set of indices of relevant and irrelevant labels with $\mathscr{I}_{\mathcal{R}}^{j-1} \cap \mathscr{I}_{\mathcal{I}}^{j-1} = \emptyset$. Then, the prediction of $\hat{y}_j$ (or $h_j(x)$) for a new instance x is

$$\hat{y}_j = \begin{cases} 1 & \text{if } P_x(Y_j = 1 | Y_{\mathscr{I}_{\mathcal{R}}^{j-1}} = 1, Y_{\mathscr{I}_{\mathcal{I}}^{j-1}} = 0) = P_x^{[j-1]}(Y_j = 1) \geq 0.5 \\ 0 & \text{if } P_x(Y_j = 1 | Y_{\mathscr{I}_{\mathcal{R}}^{j-1}} = 1, Y_{\mathscr{I}_{\mathcal{I}}^{j-1}} = 0) = P_x^{[j-1]}(Y_j = 1) < 0.5 \end{cases} \tag{8}$$

Figure 1 summarizes the procedure presented above, as well as the obtained predictions for a specific case (in bold red predicted labels and probabilities).

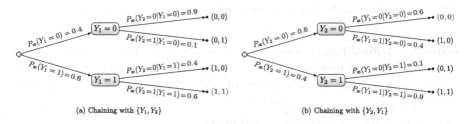

(a) Chaining with $\{Y_1, Y_2\}$ (b) Chaining with $\{Y_2, Y_1\}$

Fig. 1. Precise chaining (Color figure online)

Figure 1 shows that using this heuristic can lead to strong biases, as two different orderings of the same joint model can lead to shift from one prediction to its opposite. Intuitively, adding some robustness and cautiousness in the process could help to avoid unwarranted biases.

In what follows, we propose two different extensions of precise chaining based on imprecise probability estimates, in which the final prediction belongs to the output space $\mathfrak{Y}$ of partial bianry vectors.

2.2   Imprecise Probabilistic Chaining

We now consider that the estimates $P_x^{[j-1]}(Y_j = 1)$ can become imprecise, that is, we now have $[P_x^{[j-1]}](Y_j = y_j) := [\underline{P_x^{[j-1]}}(Y_j = y_j), \overline{P_x^{[j-1]}}(Y_j = y_j)]$. The basic idea of using such estimates is that in the chaining, we should be cautious when the classifier is unsure about the most probable prediction. In this section, we describe two different strategies (or extensions) in a general way, and we will propose an adaptation of those strategies to the NCC in the next section.

Let us first formulate the generic procedure to calculate the probability bound of the jth label,

1. RANDOM LABEL ORDERING. As in the precise case.
2. PREDICTION j^{th} LABEL. For a given label y_j, we assume we have (possibly imprecise) predictions for $y_1, \ldots, y_{j-1}$ such that $\mathscr{I}_{\mathcal{A}}^{j-1}$ are the indices of labels on which we abstained $\{*\}$ so far, and $\mathscr{I}_{\mathcal{R}}^{j-1}$ and $\mathscr{I}_{\mathcal{I}}^{j-1}$ remain the indices of relevant and irrelevant labels, such that $\mathscr{I}_{\mathcal{A}}^{j-1} \cup \mathscr{I}_{\mathcal{R}}^{j-1} \cup \mathscr{I}_{\mathcal{I}}^{j-1} = \mathscr{I}^{j-1}$. Then, we calculate $[P_x^{[j-1]}](Y_j = 1)$ in order to predict the label $\hat{y}_j$ as

$$\hat{y}_j = \begin{cases} 1 & \text{if } \underline{P}_x^{[j-1]}(Y_j = 1) > 0.5, \\ 0 & \text{if } \overline{P}_x^{[j-1]}(Y_j = 1) < 0.5, \\ * & \text{if } 0.5 \in [\underline{P}_x^{[j-1]}(Y_j = 1), \overline{P}_x^{[j-1]}(Y_j = 1)], \end{cases} \quad (9)$$

where this last equation is a slight variation of Eq. (5) by using the new input space $\mathscr{X}_{j-1}^*$.

We propose the following two different extensions of how to calculate $[P_x^{[j-1]}](Y_j = 1)$ at each inference step of the imprecise chaining.

Imprecise Branching. The first strategy treats unsure predictions in a robust way, considering all possible branchings in the chaining as soon as there is an abstained label. Thus, the estimation of $[\underline{P}_x^{[j-1]}(Y_j = 1), \overline{P}_x^{[j-1]}(Y_j = 1)]$ (for $Y_j = 0$, it directly obtains as $\underline{P}_x^{[j-1]}(Y_j = 0) = 1 - \overline{P}_x^{[j-1]}(Y_j = 1)$, and similarly for the upper bound) comes down to computing

$$\underline{P}_x^{[j-1]}(Y_j = 1) = \min_{y \in \{0,1\}^{|\mathscr{I}_{\mathcal{A}}^{j-1}|}} \underline{P}_x(Y_j = 1 | Y_{\mathscr{I}_{\mathcal{R}}^{j-1}} = 1, Y_{\mathscr{I}_{\mathcal{I}}^{j-1}} = 0, Y_{\mathscr{I}_{\mathcal{A}}^{j-1}} = y),$$

$$\overline{P}_x^{[j-1]}(Y_j = 1) = \max_{y \in \{0,1\}^{|\mathscr{I}_{\mathcal{A}}^{j-1}|}} \overline{P}_x(Y_j = 1 | Y_{\mathscr{I}_{\mathcal{R}}^{j-1}} = 1, Y_{\mathscr{I}_{\mathcal{I}}^{j-1}} = 0, Y_{\mathscr{I}_{\mathcal{A}}^{j-1}} = y). \quad \text{(IB)}$$

So we consider all possible replacements of variables for which we have abstained so far. This corresponds to a very robust version of the chaining, where every possible path is explored. It will propagate imprecision along the tree, and may produce quite imprecise evaluations, especially if we abstain on the first labels.

Illustrations providing some intuition about this strategy can be seen in Fig. 2(b) where we have abstained on labels (Y_2, Y_4) and we want to compute lower and upper probability bounds of the label $Y_5 = 1$.

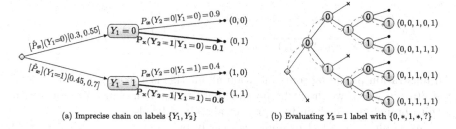

(a) Imprecise chain on labels $\{Y_1, Y_2\}$ (b) Evaluating $Y_5 = 1$ label with $\{0, *, 1, *, ?\}$

Fig. 2. Imprecise branching strategy

In Fig. 2(a), we will consider the previous example (see Fig. 1) in order to study in detail how we should calculate probability bounds $[\underline{P}_x^{[j-1]}(Y_j = 1), \overline{P}_x^{[j-1]}(Y_j = 1)]$. For the sake of simplicity, we assume that probabilities about Y_2 are precise and that the probability bounds for $Y_1 = 1$ is $\hat{P}_x^{[0]}$ $(Y_1 = 1) \in [0.45, 0.70]$. Taking all possible paths (bold on Fig. 2(a)) for which $Y_2 = 1$, we get

$$\underline{P}_x^{[1]} \ (Y_2 = 1) = \min_{y_1 \in \{0,1\}} P_x(Y_2 = 1 | Y_1 = y_1) = \min(0.1, 0.6) = 0.1,$$

$$\overline{P}_x^{[1]} \ (Y_2 = 1) = \max_{y_1 \in \{0,1\}} P_x(Y_2 = 1 | Y_1 = y_1) = \max(0.1, 0.6) = 0.6,$$

which means that in this case we would abstain on both labels, i.e. $(\hat{y}_1, \hat{y}_2) = (*, *)$.

Marginalization. The second strategy simply ignores unsure predictions in the chaining. Its interest is that it will not propagate imprecision in the tree. Thus, we begin by presenting the general formulation (which will after lead to the formulation without unsureness) which takes into account unsure predicted labels conditionally, so the estimation of probability bounds $[\underline{P}_x^{[j-1]}(Y_j = 1), \overline{P}_x^{[j-1]}(Y_j = 1)]$ comes down to computing

$$\underline{P}_x^{[j-1]}(Y_j = 1) = \underline{P}_x(Y_j = 1 | Y_{\mathscr{I}_R^{j-1}} = 1, Y_{\mathscr{I}_I^{j-1}} = 0, Y_{\mathscr{I}_A^{j-1}} = \{0,1\}^{|\mathscr{I}_A^{j-1}|}),$$
$$\overline{P}_x^{[j-1]}(Y_j = 1) = \overline{P}_x(Y_j = 1 | Y_{\mathscr{I}_R^{j-1}} = 1, Y_{\mathscr{I}_I^{j-1}} = 0, Y_{\mathscr{I}_A^{j-1}} = \{0,1\}^{|\mathscr{I}_A^{j-1}|}), \quad \text{(MAR)}$$

where $\mathscr{I}_A^{j-1} = \{i_1, \ldots, i_k\}$ denotes the set of indices of abstained labels and the last conditional term of probability bounds can be defined as

$$\left(Y_{\mathscr{I}_A^{j-1}} = \{0,1\}^{|\mathscr{I}_A^{j-1}|}\right) := (Y_{i_1} = 0 \cup Y_{i_1} = 1) \cap \cdots \cap (Y_{i_k} = 0 \cup Y_{i_k} = 1). \quad (10)$$

The MAR formulation can be reduced by using Bayes's theorem in conjunction with the law of total probability. That is, for instance, given abstained labels $(Y_1 = *, Y_3 = *)$ and the precise prediction $(Y_2 = 1)$, inferring $Y_4 = 1$ comes down to computing $P_x(Y_4 = 1 | (Y_1 = 0 \cup Y_1 = 1), Y_2 = 1, (Y_3 = 0 \cup Y_3 = 1))$ as follows

$$\frac{\sum\limits_{y_3,y_1\in\{0,1\}^2} P_x(Y_4=1,Y_1=y_1,Y_2=1,Y_3=y_3)}{\sum\limits_{y_3,y_1\in\{0,1\}^2} P_x(Y_1=y_1,Y_2=1,Y_3=y_3)} = \frac{P_x(Y_4=1,Y_2=1)}{P_x(Y_2=1)} = P_x(Y_4=1|Y_2=1),$$

An illustration providing some intuition about this last example can be seen in Fig. 3(a), in which we draw the possible path to infer the label Y_4 (considering a third branch in the chain to represent abstained labels).

The results of the last example can easily be generalized, and hence, MAR comes down to calculating the new formulation called (MAR*)

$$\underline{P}_x^{[j-1]}(Y_j = 1) = \min_{P\in\mathscr{P}^*} P_x(Y_j = 1|Y_{\mathscr{I}_{\mathcal{R}}^{j-1}} = 1, Y_{\mathscr{I}_{\mathcal{I}}^{j-1}} = 0), \qquad (11)$$

$$\overline{P}_x^{[j-1]}(Y_j = 1) = \max_{P\in\mathscr{P}^*} P_x(Y_j = 1|Y_{\mathscr{I}_{\mathcal{R}}^{j-1}} = 1, Y_{\mathscr{I}_{\mathcal{I}}^{j-1}} = 0). \qquad (12)$$

where $\mathscr{P}^*$ is simply the set of joint probability distributions described by the imprecise probabilistic tree (we refer to [5] for a detailed analysis). (MAR) comes down to restrict the conditional chain model to consider only those labels on which we have not abstained (for which we have sufficient reliable information). In general, both (IB) and (MAR) can lead to burdensome computations. In the next section, we propose to adapt their principle to the NCC, showing that this can be done efficiently.

Remark 1. Note that another strategy that would be computationally efficient would be to simply considers all precise chaining paths consistent with local intervals, pruning dominated branches. However, this would also mean that each explored branch would have all previous predicted labels as conditioning features, thus still being impacted by the bias of picking those predictions.

3   Imprecise Chaining with NCC

NCC extends the classical naive Bayes classifier (NBC) on a set of distributions. NCC preserves the assumption of feature independence made by NBC, and relies on the Imprecise Dirichlet model (IDM) [20] to estimate class-conditional imprecise probabilities, whose imprecision level is controlled through a hyperparameter $s \in \mathbb{R}$. Therefore, the class-conditional probability bounds evaluated for $Y_j = 1$ ($Y_j = 0$ can be directly calculated using duality) can be calculated as follows[2]

$$\underline{P}(Y_j = 1|\mathbf{X}=\mathbf{x}, Y_{\mathscr{I}j-1}=\hat{\mathbf{y}}_{\mathscr{I}j-1}) = \left(1+\frac{P(Y_j=0)\overline{P}_0(\mathbf{X}=\mathbf{x})\overline{P}_0(Y_{\mathscr{I}j-1}=\hat{\mathbf{y}}_{\mathscr{I}j-1})}{P(Y_j=1)\underline{P}_1(\mathbf{X}=\mathbf{x})\underline{P}_1(Y_{\mathscr{I}j-1}=\hat{\mathbf{y}}_{\mathscr{I}j-1})}\right)^{-1}, (13)$$

$$\overline{P}(Y_j = 1|\mathbf{X}=\mathbf{x}, Y_{\mathscr{I}j-1}=\hat{\mathbf{y}}_{\mathscr{I}j-1}) = \left(1+\frac{P(Y_j=0)\underline{P}_0(\mathbf{X}=\mathbf{x})\underline{P}_0(Y_{\mathscr{I}j-1}=\hat{\mathbf{y}}_{\mathscr{I}j-1})}{P(Y_j=1)\overline{P}_1(\mathbf{X}=\mathbf{x})\overline{P}_1(Y_{\mathscr{I}j-1}=\hat{\mathbf{y}}_{\mathscr{I}j-1})}\right)^{-1}. (14)$$

---

[2] For reviewer convenience, details are given to the extended version submitted to ArXiv https://arxiv.org/abs/2107.07443 .

where conditional upper probabilities of $[\underline{P}_1, \overline{P}_1]$ and $[\underline{P}_0, \overline{P}_0]$ are defined as

$$\overline{P}_a(\mathbf{X} = \boldsymbol{x}) := \prod_{i=1}^{p} \overline{P}(X_i = x_i | Y_j = a) \text{ and } \overline{P}_a(\mathbf{Y}_{\mathscr{I}^{j-1}} = \boldsymbol{y}_{\mathscr{I}^{j-1}}) := \prod_{k=1}^{j-1} \overline{P}(Y_k = \hat{y}_k | Y_j = a),$$

(15)

where $a \in \{0, 1\}$. Conditional lower probabilities are obtained similarly. Using Eqs. (13) and (14), we now propose efficient procedures to solve the aforementioned strategies.

3.1 Imprecise Branching

In the specific case where we use the NCC, we can efficiently reduce the optimization problems of Eqs. (IB), as expressed in the proposition below.

Proposition 1. *Optimisation problems of the imprecise branching (IB) can be reduced by using probability bounds obtained from the NCC, namely Equations (13) and (14), as follows*

$$\underline{P}_x^{[j-1]}(Y_j = 1) \propto \max_{\boldsymbol{y} \in \{0,1\}^{|\mathscr{I}_\mathcal{A}^{j-1}|}} \frac{\overline{P}_0(Y_{\mathscr{I}_\mathcal{A}^{j-1}} = \boldsymbol{y})}{\underline{P}_1(Y_{\mathscr{I}_\mathcal{A}^{j-1}} = \boldsymbol{y})} \text{ and } \overline{P}_x^{[j-1]}(Y_j = 1) \propto \min_{\boldsymbol{y} \in \{0,1\}^{|\mathscr{I}_\mathcal{A}^{j-1}|}} \frac{\underline{P}_0(Y_{\mathscr{I}_\mathcal{A}^{j-1}} = \boldsymbol{y})}{\overline{P}_1(Y_{\mathscr{I}_\mathcal{A}^{j-1}} = \boldsymbol{y})}.$$

Besides, applying the equations derived from the imprecise Dirichlet model, we have that the values of abstained labels for which the previous optimisation problems are solved are, respectively

$$\underline{\hat{\boldsymbol{y}}}_{\mathscr{I}_\mathcal{A}^{j-1}} := \arg\max_{\boldsymbol{y} \in \{0,1\}^{|\mathscr{I}_\mathcal{A}^{j-1}|}} \prod_{y_i \in \boldsymbol{y}} \frac{n(y_i | y_j = 0) + s}{n(y_i | y_j = 1)} \text{ and } \overline{\hat{\boldsymbol{y}}}_{\mathscr{I}_\mathcal{A}^{j-1}} := \arg\min_{\boldsymbol{y} \in \{0,1\}^{|\mathscr{I}_\mathcal{A}^{j-1}|}} \prod_{y_i \in \boldsymbol{y}} \frac{n(y_i | y_j = 0)}{n(y_i | y_j = 1) + s}$$

(16)

where $\mathscr{I}_\mathcal{A}^{j-1}$ is the set of indices of the $(j-1)$th first predicted abstained labels, $n(\cdot)$ is a count function that counts the number of occurrences of the event $y_i | y_j$ and $n(y_i | y_j = 1)$ is always strictly positive.

Proposition 1 says that it is not necessary to know the original input features $\mathscr{X}$ and neither the $(j-1)$th first precise predicted labels, in order to get the lower and upper probability bound of Equations (IB). However, it is necessary to keep track of the estimates made on all abstained labels, which is consistent with the fact that we want to capture the optimal lower and upper bounds of the conditional probability over all possible paths on which we have abstained.

Proposition 1 allows us to propose an algorithm below that can calculate Eqs. (16) linearly in the number of abstained labels.

Proposition 2. *The chain of labels $\underline{\hat{\boldsymbol{y}}}_{\mathscr{I}_\mathcal{A}^{j-1}}$ and $\overline{\hat{\boldsymbol{y}}}_{\mathscr{I}_\mathcal{A}^{j-1}}$ can be obtained in a time complexity of $\mathcal{O}(|\mathscr{I}_\mathcal{A}^{j-1}|)$.*

The following proposition provides the time complexity of the inference step of the imprecise branching strategy, jointly with the NCC and previous results.

Proposition 3. *The global time complexity of the* IMPRECISE BRANCHING *strategy in the worst-case is $\mathcal{O}(m^2)$ and in the best-case is $\mathcal{O}(m)$.*

3.2   Marginalization

When the NCC is considered, nothing needs to be optimized in the marginalization strategy, thanks to the assumption of independence applied between the binary conditional models of the chain.

We recall that the marginalization strategy needs to compute the conditional models described in Eqs. (MAR). These latter can be solved by simply ignoring the abstained labels in Eqs. (13) and (14) of the NCC. We thus focus on adapting Eq. (14) (Eq. (13) can be treated similarly), in order to show that the abstained labels can be removed of the conditioning and to get the expression presented in Eq. (12). Based on Eq. (14), we can only focus on the conditional upper probability on labels, namely Eq. (15), and rewrite it as follows:

$$\overline{P}_0(\mathbf{Y}_{\mathscr{I}^{j-1}} = \hat{\boldsymbol{y}}_{\mathscr{I}^{j-1}}) := \overline{P}_0(\mathbf{Y}_{\mathscr{I}_*^{j-1}} = \hat{\boldsymbol{y}}_{\mathscr{I}_*^{j-1}}, \mathbf{Y}_{\mathscr{I}_{\mathcal{A}}^{j-1}} = \{0,1\}^{|\mathscr{I}_{\mathcal{A}}^{j-1}|}) \qquad (17)$$

where $\mathscr{I}_*^{j-1} = \mathscr{I}_{\mathcal{R}}^{j-1} \cup \mathscr{I}_{\mathcal{I}}^{j-1}$ is the set of indices of relevant and irrelevant inferred labels, and the right side of last equation can be stated as

$$\max_{\substack{P \in \{\mathscr{P}_{Y_k|Y_j}, \mathscr{P}_{Y_a|Y_j}\} \\ k \in \mathscr{I}_*^{j-1}, a \in \mathscr{I}_{\mathcal{A}}^{j-1}}} \prod_{k \in \mathscr{I}_*^{j-1}} P(Y_k = \hat{y}_k | Y_j = 0) \prod_{a \in \mathscr{I}_{\mathcal{A}}^{j-1}} P(Y_a = 0 \cup Y_a = 1 | Y_j = 0).$$

Thanks to the product assumption in the NCC, each term can be treated separately, making it possible to decouple the multiplication in two parts;

$$\max_{\substack{P \in \mathscr{P}_{Y_k|Y_j} \\ k \in \mathscr{I}_*^{j-1}}} \prod_{k \in \mathscr{I}_*^{j-1}} P(Y_k = \hat{y}_k | Y_j = 0) \times \max_{\substack{P \in \mathscr{P}_{Y_a|Y_j} \\ a \in \mathscr{I}_{\mathcal{A}}^{j-1}}} \prod_{a \in \mathscr{I}_{\mathcal{A}}^{j-1}} P(Y_a = 0 \cup Y_a = 1 | Y_j = 0),$$

where $P(Y_a = 0 \cup Y_a = 1 | Y_j = 0) = 1$, and hence the second part becomes 1. Replacing this result in Eq. (17), and then this latter in Eq. (14), we get

$$\overline{P}_{\boldsymbol{x}}^{[j-1]}(Y_j = 1) = \max_{P \in \mathscr{P}_{Y_j | Y_{\mathscr{I}_{\mathcal{R}}^{j-1}}, Y_{\mathscr{I}_{\mathcal{I}}^{j-1}}}} P_{\boldsymbol{x}}(Y_j = 1 | Y_{\mathscr{I}_{\mathcal{R}}^{j-1}} = 1, Y_{\mathscr{I}_{\mathcal{I}}^{j-1}} = 0).$$

Therefore, at each inference step, we can apply Eqs. (13) and (14) on the reduced new formulation of the marginalization strategy (MAR*). An illustration providing some intuition about this reduction can be seen in Fig. 3.

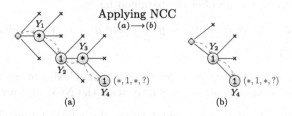

(a)   (b)

Fig. 3. Marginalization strategy applied to NCC for four labels $\{Y_1, Y_2, Y_3, Y_4\}$

4   Experiments

In this section, we perform experiments[3] on 6 data sets issued from the MULAN repository[4] (c.f. Table 2), following a 10×10 cross-validation procedure.

Table 2. Multi-label data sets summary

Data set	#Domain	#Features	#Labels	#Instances	#Cardinality	#Density
Emotions	Music	72	6	593	1.90	0.31
Scene	Image	294	6	2407	1.07	0.18
Yeast	Biology	103	14	2417	4.23	0.30
cal500	Music	68	174	502	26.04	0.15
Medical	Text	1449	45	978	1.25	0.03
Enron	Text	1001	53	1702	3.38	0.06

Evaluation and Setting. The usual metrics used in multi-label problems are not adapted at all when we infer set-valued predictions. Thus, we consider appropriate to use the set-accuracy (SA) and completeness (CP) [8, §4.1], as follows

$$SA(\hat{\boldsymbol{y}}, \boldsymbol{y}) = \mathbb{1}_{(\boldsymbol{y} \in \hat{\boldsymbol{y}})} \quad \text{and} \quad CP(\hat{\boldsymbol{y}}, \boldsymbol{y}) = \frac{|Q|}{m},$$

where $\hat{\boldsymbol{y}}$ is the partial binary prediction (i.e. the set of all possibles binary vectors) and Q denote the set of non-abstained labels. When predicting complete vectors, then $CP = 1$ and SA equals the 0/1 loss function and when predicting the empty vector, i.e. all labels $\hat{y}_i = *$, then $CP = 0$ and by convention $SA = 1$. The reason for using SA is that chaining is used as an approximation of the optimal prediction for a 0/1 loss function.

Imprecise Classifier. As mentioned in Sect. 3, we will use the *naive credal classifier* (NCC). Note that NCC needs discretized input spaces, so we discretize data sets to $z = 6$ intervals (except for Medical and Enron data sets). Besides, we restrict the values of the hyper-parameter of the imprecision to $s \in \{0.0, 0.5, \ldots, 4.5, 5.5\}$ (when $s = 0.0$, NCC becomes the precise classifier NBC). At higher values of s, the NCC model will make mostly vacuous predictions (i.e. abstain in all labels $\forall i, Y_i = *$) for the data sets we consider here.

Missing Labels. To simulate missingness during the training step, we uniformly pick at random a percentage of labels $Y_{j,i}$ (the jth label of the ith instance), which are then removed from the training data used to fit the conditional models in the chain. In this paper, we set up five different percentages of missingness: $\{0, 20, 40, 60, 80\}\%$.

---

[3] Implemented in Python, see https://github.com/sdestercke/classifip.
[4] http://mulan.sourceforge.net/datasets.html.

4.1   Experimental Results

Figure 4, we provide the results for 3 data sets, showing set-accuracy and completeness measures in average[5](%) obtained by fitting the NCC model for different percentages of missing labels, respectively, applied to the data sets of Table 2 and using the imprecise branching strategy (trends were similar for the marginalization strategies, not displayed due to lack of space)[6].

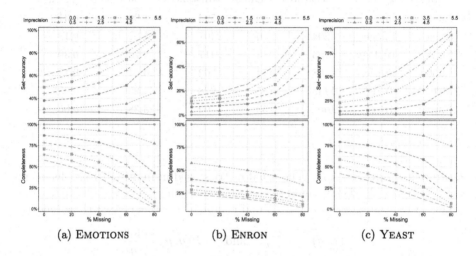

(a) EMOTIONS   (b) ENRON   (c) YEAST

Fig. 4. Missing labels - Imprecise Branching evolution of the average (%) set-accuracy (top) and completeness (down) for each level of imprecision (a curve for each one) and a discretization $z = 6$, with respect to the percentage of missing labels.

The results show that when the percentage of missing labels increases, the set-accuracy (SA) increases (regardless of the amount of imprecision s we inject) as we abstain more and more (as completeness decreases). This means that the more imprecise we get, the more accurate are those predictions we retain. However, a high amount of imprecision is sometimes required to include the ground-truth solution within the set-valued prediction (this may be due to the very restrictive $0/1$ loss metric). For instance, with $s = 5.5$ and 40% of missingness, we get a $> 65\%$ of set-accuracy versus a $< 50\%$ of completeness, in the Emotions data set.

Overall, the results are those that we expect and are also sufficient to show that cautious inferences with probability sets may provide additional benefits when dealing with missing labels.

---

[5] The confidence intervals obtained on the experimental results are very small and we therefore prefer not to display them in the figures in order not to overcharge them.

[6] The supplementary results can be found in the online extend version [4].

5 Conclusions

In this paper, we have proposed two new strategies to adapt the classical chaining multi-label problem to the case of handling imprecise probability estimates. Such strategies come with daunting challenges to obtain cautious and reliable predictions, and have been successfully resolved using the NCC model.

While the NCC makes easy to solve the strategies thanks to its assumptions, the same restrictive assumptions may also be the reason why the initial accuracy is rather low (especially for Yeast). Indeed, it seems reasonable to think that the independence assumptions somehow limit the benefits of including label dependencies information through the chaining. It seems therefore essential, in future works, to investigate other classifiers as well as to solve optimisation issues in a general or approximative way.

Another open issue is how we can use or extend the existing heuristics of probabilistic classifier approaches on our proposal strategies, such as epsilon-approximate inference, A^* and beam search methods [11,13].

Acknowledgments. We wish to thank the reviewers of the ECSQARU conference, especially one of them who was thorough, and made us rethink a lot of aspects (of which only some are visible in the revised version).

References

1. Antonucci, A., Corani, G.: The multilabel Naive credal classifier. Int. J. Approximate Reasoning **83**, 320–336 (2017)
2. Augustin, T., Coolen, F.P., de Cooman, G., Troffaes, M.C.: Introduction to Imprecise Probabilities. John Wiley & Sons, Hoboken (2014)
3. Boutell, M.R., Luo, J., Shen, X., Brown, C.M.: Learning multi-label scene classification. Pattern Recogn. **37**(9), 1757–1771 (2004)
4. Alarcón, Y.C.C., Destercke, S.: Multi-label chaining with imprecise probabilities (2021). https://arxiv.org/abs/2107.07443
5. De Cooman, G., Hermans, F.: Imprecise probability trees: bridging two theories of imprecise probability. Artif. Intell. **172**(11), 1400–1427 (2008)
6. Dembczynski, K., Cheng, W., Hüllermeier, E.: Bayes optimal multilabel classification via probabilistic classifier chains. In: ICML (2010)
7. Dembczyński, K., Waegeman, W., Cheng, W., Hüllermeier, E.: On label dependence and loss minimization in multi-label classification. Mach. Learn. 5–45 (2012). https://doi.org/10.1007/s10994-012-5285-8
8. Destercke, S.: Multilabel prediction with probability sets: the hamming loss case. In: Laurent, A., Strauss, O., Bouchon-Meunier, B., Yager, R.R. (eds.) IPMU 2014. CCIS, vol. 443, pp. 496–505. Springer, Cham (2014). https://doi.org/10.1007/978-3-319-08855-6_50
9. Friedman, J., Hastie, T., Tibshirani, R.: The Elements of Statistical Learning. Springer, New York Inc (2001). https://doi.org/10.1007/978-0-387-84858-7
10. Fürnkranz, J., Hüllermeier, E., Mencía, E.L., Brinker, K.: Multilabel classification via calibrated label ranking. Mach. Learn. **73**(2), 133–153 (2008)

11. Kumar, A., Vembu, S., Menon, A.K., Elkan, C.: Beam search algorithms for multi-label learning. Mach. Learn. **92**(1), 65–89 (2013). https://doi.org/10.1007/s10994-013-5371-6
12. Levi, I.: The enterprise of knowledge: an essay on knowledge, credal probability, and chance. MIT Press, Cambridge (1983)
13. Mena, D., Montañés, E., Quevedo, J.R., del Coz, J.J.: An overview of inference methods in probabilistic classifier chains for multilabel classification. Wiley Interdisc. Rev. Data Mining Knowl. Disc. **6**(6), 215–230 (2016)
14. Pillai, I., Fumera, G., Roli, F.: Multi-label classification with a reject option. Pattern Recogn. **46**(8), 2256–2266 (2013)
15. Read, J., Pfahringer, B., Holmes, G., Frank, E.: Classifier chains for multi-label classification. Mach. Learn. **85**(3), 333–359 (2011)
16. Taylor, S.J.: Introduction to Measure and Integration. CUP Archive (1973)
17. Tsoumakas, G., Katakis, I.: Multi-label classification: an overview. Int. J. Data Warehousing Mining (IJDWM) **3**(3), 1–13 (2007)
18. Vu-Linh Nguyen, E.H.: Reliable multilabel classification: prediction with partial abstention. In: Thirty-Fourth AAAI Conference on Artificial Intelligence (2019)
19. Walley, P.: Statistical reasoning with imprecise Probabilities. Chapman and Hall, London (1991)
20. Walley, P.: Inferences from multinomial data: learning about a bag of marbles. J. Roy. Stat. Soc.: Ser. B (Methodol.) **58**(1), 3–34 (1996)
21. Zaffalon, M.: The Naive credal classifier. J. Stat. Plann. Infer. **105**(1), 5–21 (2002)

Centroids of Credal Sets: A Comparative Study

Enrique Miranda[(⊠)] and Ignacio Montes

Department of Statistics and Operations Research,
University of Oviedo, Oviedo, Spain
{mirandaenrique,imontes}@uniovi.es

Abstract. We compare a number of different notions of centroid of a credal set: the Shapley value, that arises in the context of game theory; the average of the extreme points; the incenter with respect to the total variation distance between probability measures; and the limit of a procedure of uniform contraction. We show that these four centers do not coincide in general, give some sufficient conditions for their equality, and analyse their axiomatic properties. Finally, we discuss briefly how to define a notion of centrality measure.

Keywords: Game solutions · Credal sets · 2-monotonicity · Probability intervals

1 Introduction

The elicitation of a probability measure within a convex set can be interesting in a wide variety of contexts: we may consider for instance the *core* of a game in coalitional game theory [9], and look for a game solution that provides a way to divide the wealth between the players; we could also consider transformations from imprecise to precise probabilities, as has been done for instance in the context of possibility theory [10]; we might also consider inner approximations of a credal set, so as to look for a more informative model that is compatible with the existing information [16]; or we might also connect the problem with that of transforming second order models with first order ones [24].

In this paper, we examine several possibilities for determining a probability measure that can be considered as the *center* of the credal set. After introducing some preliminary notions in Sect. 2, in Sect. 3 we discuss the Shapley value, the average of the extreme points, the incenter of the credal set with respect to the total variation distance and the limit of the contractions of the credal set. These four centroids are compared in Sect. 4, by showing that they need not coincide in general and establishing sufficient conditions for their equality. In Sect. 5, we compare the centroids in terms of a number of axiomatic properties; and in Sect. 6

Supported by project PGC2018-098623-B-I00. We thank Arthur Van Camp and the anonymous reviewers for some helpful comments and discussion.

J. Vejnarová and N. Wilson (Eds.): ECSQARU 2021, LNAI 12897, pp. 427–441, 2021.
https://doi.org/10.1007/978-3-030-86772-0_31

we discuss how these definitions may lead to a notion of *centrality measure*. Some additional comments are given in Sect. 7. Due to space limitations, proofs have been omitted.

2   Preliminary Concepts

Consider a finite possibility space $\mathscr{X} = \{x_1, \ldots, x_n\}$, and denote by $\mathbb{P}(\mathscr{X})$ the set of all probability measures on $\mathscr{X}$. A closed and convex subset $\mathscr{M}$ of $\mathbb{P}(\mathscr{X})$ is called a *credal set*. Taking lower and upper envelopes on events, it determines a *coherent* lower and upper probability:

$$\underline{P}(A) = \min_{P \in \mathscr{M}} P(A), \quad \overline{P}(A) = \max_{P \in \mathscr{M}} P(A) \quad \forall A \subseteq \mathscr{X}.$$

A lower probability can be equivalently represented using its Möbius inverse:

$$m(A) = \sum_{B \subseteq A} (-1)^{|A \setminus B|} \underline{P}(B) \quad \forall A \subseteq \mathscr{X},$$

because $\underline{P}(A) = \sum_{B \subseteq A} m(B)$ for every $A \subseteq \mathscr{X}$.

More generally, we can consider *gambles*, which are functions $f : \mathscr{X} \to \mathbb{R}$; the set of all gambles on $\mathscr{X}$ shall be denoted by $\mathscr{L}$. If for simplicity we use the same symbol P to denote the expectation operator with respect to the probability measure P, then for each gamble $f \in \mathscr{L}$, the credal set $\mathscr{M}$ determines a coherent lower and upper *prevision*:

$$\underline{P}(f) = \min_{P \in \mathscr{M}} P(f), \quad \overline{P}(f) = \max_{P \in \mathscr{M}} P(f) \quad \forall f \in \mathscr{L}.$$

In general, the credal set associated with a coherent lower prevision is not equivalent to that of the coherent lower probability that is its restriction to events. A sufficient condition for their equality is that $\underline{P}$ satisfies the property of 2-monotonicity [5,22]:

$$\underline{P}(f \vee g) + \underline{P}(f \wedge g) \geq \underline{P}(f) + \underline{P}(g) \quad \forall f, g \in \mathscr{L}.$$

In the case of events, 2-monotonicity means that

$$\underline{P}(A \cup B) + \underline{P}(A \cap B) \geq \underline{P}(A) + \underline{P}(B) \quad \forall A, B \subseteq \mathscr{X}.$$

3   Center Points of a Credal Set

Let us introduce the notions of centroid of a credal set we shall compare in this paper.

3.1   The Shapley Value

One of the most popular notions of centroid of a credal set is the *Shapley value*. It was introduced by Shapley [18,19] in the framework of coalitional game theory, as a 'fair' procedure to distribute some wealth between the players. Later on, it was rediscovered in the context of non-additive probabilities [7] and popularised by Smets as the *pignistic transformation* of a belief function [21].

Definition 1. *Given a credal set $\mathcal{M}$ with associated lower probability $\underline{P}$, its Shapley value is defined as the probability measure associated with the following distribution:*

$$\Phi_1^{\mathcal{M}}(\{x\}) = \sum_{x \notin A} \frac{|A|!(n - |A| - 1)!}{n!} (\underline{P}(A \cup \{x\}) - \underline{P}(A)) \quad \forall x \in \mathcal{X}. \quad (1)$$

It was proven by Smets [20] that, when $\underline{P}$ is a belief function, $\Phi_1^{\mathcal{M}}$ can be equivalently computed as

$$\Phi_1^{\mathcal{M}}(\{x\}) = \sum_{x \in A} \frac{m(A)}{|A|} \quad \forall x \in \mathcal{X}.$$

More generally, when $\underline{P}$ is 2-monotone, it follows from [19] that the extreme points of $\mathcal{M}(\underline{P})$, the set of dominating probability measures, are given by $\{P_\sigma \mid \sigma \in S_n\}$, where S_n denotes the set of permutations of $\{1, \ldots, n\}$, and given $\sigma \in S_n$, P_σ is determined by the equations

$$P_\sigma(\{x_{\sigma(1)}, \ldots, x_{\sigma(i)}\}) = \underline{P}(\{x_{\sigma(1)}, \ldots, x_{\sigma(i)}\}) \quad \forall i = 1, \ldots, n;$$

then the Shapley value can be computed as

$$\Phi_1^{\mathcal{M}}(\{x\}) = \frac{1}{n!} \sum_{\sigma \in S_n} P_\sigma(\{x\}) \quad \forall x \in \mathcal{X}. \quad (2)$$

In fact, the above results can be extended to arbitrary lower probabilities:

Proposition 1. *Let $\underline{P} : \mathscr{P}(\mathcal{X}) \to [0,1]$ be a lower probability with Möbius inverse m, and let $\Phi_1^{\mathcal{M}}$ be given by Eq. (1). Using the notation P_σ in Eq. (2), it holds that:*

$$\Phi_1^{\mathcal{M}}(\{x\}) = \sum_{x \in A} \frac{m(A)}{|A|} = \sum_{\sigma \in S_n} \frac{P_\sigma(\{x\})}{n!} \quad \forall x \in \mathcal{X}.$$

While the Shapley value seems like a reasonable choice as a central point, it has one important drawback: it is only guaranteed to belong to the credal set (i.e., we can only assure that $\Phi_1^{\mathcal{M}} \geq \underline{P}$) when the lower probability $\underline{P}$ of the credal set is 2-monotone.

More generally, when the lower probability $\underline{P}$ of the credal set is not 2-monotone, we can only assure that $\Phi_1^{\mathcal{M}}$ dominates $\underline{P}$ for small cardinalities ($n \leq 4$), as showed by Baroni and Vicig [2, Prop. 5]. We refer to [12] for a study of the consistency between the Shapley value and the lower probability.

3.2   Vertex Centroid

The second possibility we consider in this paper is the average of the extreme points of the credal set:

Definition 2. *Let $\mathcal{M}$ be a credal set with a finite number of extreme points $\{P_1, \ldots, P_k\}$. The* vertex centroid *[8] is defined as the average of the extreme points:*

$$\Phi_2^{\mathcal{M}} = \frac{\sum_{i=1}^{k} P_i}{k}.$$

While the definition above is only applicable in the case of polytopes, it is worth remarking that these include in particular the credal sets $\mathcal{M}(\underline{P})$ associated with a lower probability $\underline{P}$ that is coherent [25], and therefore also in the particular cases of 2-monotonicity. Nevertheless, it is not always applicable for arbitrary credal sets, that are associated with coherent lower *previsions*.

The above centroid is sometimes referred to as the 'center of gravity' of the credal set; however, strictly speaking the center of gravity corresponds to the expectation of the set over a uniform probability distribution, and not only over its extreme points. It is not difficult to show that this other notion does not necessarily produce the same centroid as Definition 2. While the center of gravity has the advantage of being applicable over general credal sets, and not only on polytopes, it also has the drawback of being computationally more expensive (see for example [8]).

It follows from Definition 2 that $\Phi_2^{\mathcal{M}}$ always belongs to the credal set $\mathcal{M}$; considering the comments in the previous section, this implies that it need not coincide with Shapley value when the lower envelope $\underline{P}$ of $\mathcal{M}$ is not 2-monotone. As we shall see later on, they need not coincide even under 2-monotonicity: while it has been proven in [19] that the extreme points of $\mathcal{M}(\underline{P})$ are indeed $\{P_\sigma \mid \sigma \in S_n\}$, a key difference is that in the computation of Shapley value in Eq. (2) we are allowing for repetitions of the same extreme point, while in Definition 2 we do not.

3.3   Incenter

Our third approach consists in considering the *incenter* of the credal set, which is the element or elements $P \in \mathcal{M}$ for which we can include the largest ball centered on P in the interior of the credal set. This notion requires the specification of a distance between probability measures from which the balls are defined. We consider here the *total variation distance* [11], which is the one associated with the supremum norm:

$$d_{TV}(P, Q) = \max_{A \subseteq \mathscr{X}} |P(A) - Q(A)|.$$

Our choice of this distance is due to the fact that a ball with the total variation distance is always a polytope, unlike some other distances such as the Euclidean distance. To ease the notation, we will simply denote d_{TV} by d.

Definition 3. *Let $\mathscr{M}$ be a credal set. The* supremum radius *of $\mathscr{M}$ is defined as*

$$\alpha_I = \sup\left\{\alpha \mid \exists P_0 \in \mathscr{M} \text{ such that } \mathrm{int}\big(B_d^\alpha(P_0)\big) \subseteq \mathrm{int}(\mathscr{M})\right\}. \tag{3}$$

Then any $P \in \mathscr{M}$ such that $\mathrm{int}\big(B_d^{\alpha_I}(P)\big) \subseteq \mathrm{int}(\mathscr{M})$ is called an incenter *of the credal set $\mathscr{M}$. The set of all such P is denoted $\Psi_3^{\mathscr{M}}$.*

The reason why we are requiring the inclusion $\mathrm{int}\big(B_d^{\alpha_I}(P_0)\big) \subseteq \mathrm{int}(\mathscr{M})$ in the above definition is that otherwise we could obtain the counter-intuitive result that an incenter belongs to the boundary of $\mathscr{M}$, which we find incompatible with the underlying idea of centrality (as in 'deepest inside the credal set') we consider in this paper.

Two natural questions related to the incenter is whether (i) it exists, and (ii) it is unique. Our next result provides an answer to the first question.

Proposition 2. *Consider a credal set $\mathscr{M}$. Then the value α_I in Eq. (3) is a maximum. As a consequence, the set $\Psi_3^{\mathscr{M}}$ is always non-empty, and any of its elements belongs to $\mathrm{int}(\mathscr{M})$.*

Concerning the second question, the set $\Phi_3^{\mathscr{M}}$ may have more than one element, as we show next:

Example 1. Consider the possibility space $\mathscr{X} = \{x_1, x_2, x_3\}$, and the credal set $\mathscr{M}$ determined by $P(\{x_1\}) \in [0.5, 0.8]$, $P(\{x_2\}) \in [0.1, 0.25]$ and $P(\{x_3\}) \in [0.1, 0.35]$. It holds that $\alpha_I = 0.075$ and that the incenter is not unique: $\Psi_3^{\mathscr{M}}$ coincides with the convex combinations of $Q_1 = (0.575, 0.175, 0.25)$ and $Q_2 = (0.65, 0.175, 0.175)$. Hence, there are infinite incenters. Figure 1 shows the graphical representation of $\mathscr{M}$ as well as the balls $B_d^{\alpha_I}(Q_1)$, $B_d^{\alpha_I}(Q_2)$ and $B_d^{\alpha_I}(Q_\beta)$ for $\beta = 0.5$. ♦

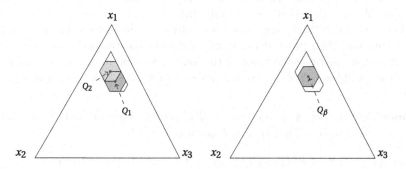

Fig. 1. Credal set $\mathscr{M}$ in Example 1, the incenters Q_1 and Q_2 with the ball they induce (left hand-side figure) and Q_β for $\beta = 0.5$ with the ball it induces (right hand-side figure).

Related to this approach, we may alternatively have considered the *circumcenter* of the credal set, which is the element or elements for which the smallest ball centered on them includes the credal set. That is, we may consider

$$\alpha_C = \inf\left\{\alpha \mid \exists P_0 \in \mathcal{M} \text{ such that } B_d^\alpha(P_0) \supseteq \mathcal{M}\right\},$$

and then let $\Psi_3'^{\mathcal{M}}$ be the set of those P such that $B_d^{\alpha_C}(P) \supseteq \mathcal{M}$. However, this approach possesses the two drawbacks we have discussed so far: not only it need not lead to a unique solution, but also [1] it may produce values that are outside the credal set.

In this sense, and as suggested by a reviewer, one possibility would be to consider, for each $P \in \mathcal{M}$, the value $\alpha_P = \inf\left\{\alpha \mid B_d^\alpha(P) \supseteq \mathcal{M}\right\}$, and then call $P \in \mathcal{M}$ a circumcenter of $\mathcal{M}$ if it minimises the value α_P. In this manner we would guarantee that the solution obtained belongs to the credal set, although it may be an element of the boundary. The study of this approach is left as an open problem.

3.4   Contraction Centroid

Our fourth approach is motivated by the lack of uniqueness of the incenter. Consider a credal set $\mathcal{M}$ determined by a finite number of constraints. This means that there are two (disjoint) sets of gambles $\mathcal{L}^>$ and $\mathcal{L}^=$ such that the lower and upper previsions $\underline{P}, \overline{P}$ associated with $\mathcal{M}$ satisfy $\underline{P}(f) = \overline{P}(f)$ for any $f \in \mathcal{L}^=$ and $\underline{P}(f) < \overline{P}(f)$ for any $f \in \mathcal{L}^>$, and that the credal set can be expressed as:

$$\mathcal{M} = \left\{P \in \mathbb{P}(\mathscr{X}) \mid P(f) = \underline{P}(f)\ \forall f \in \mathcal{L}^=, \quad P(f) \geq \underline{P}(f)\ \forall f \in \mathcal{L}^>\right\}. \quad (4)$$

Note that we can assume without loss of generality that $\{I_A \mid A \subseteq \mathscr{X}\} \subseteq \mathcal{L}^= \cup \mathcal{L}^>$; in that case when $\mathcal{L}^>$ is empty we obtain that $\underline{P}(A) = \overline{P}(A)$ for any $A \subseteq \mathscr{X}$, and thus that $\mathcal{M}$ has only one element.

The idea of this fourth approach is to contract $\mathcal{M}$ in a uniform manner as long as we can, and then proceed iteratively reducing the cardinality of $\mathcal{L}^>$. More specifically, we increase the value of the lower prevision in a constant amount α in all the gambles $f \in \mathcal{L}^>$. Our next proposition gives further insight into this idea:

Proposition 3. *Let $\mathcal{M}$ be a credal set determined by a finite number of gambles $\mathcal{L}^=, \mathcal{L}^>$ by means of Eq. (4). For a given $\alpha > 0$, let:*

$$\mathcal{M}_\alpha = \left\{P \in \mathbb{P}(\mathscr{X}) \mid P(f) = \underline{P}(f)\ \forall f \in \mathcal{L}^=, \quad P(f) \geq \underline{P}(f) + \alpha\ \forall f \in \mathcal{L}^>\right\}. \quad (5)$$

Then the $\Lambda = \{\alpha \mid \mathcal{M}_\alpha \neq \varnothing\}$ is non-empty and has a maximum value $\alpha_S = \max \Lambda$. Moreover, there is some $f \in \mathcal{L}^>$ such that $P(f)$ is constant for any $P \in \mathcal{M}_{\alpha_S}$.

The above proposition also tells us that when we get to the set $\mathcal{M}_{\alpha_S}$ the size of $\mathcal{L}^>$ decreases; we can therefore iterate the procedure, now starting with $\mathcal{M}_{\alpha_S}$, and after a finite number of steps we end up with a precise credal set: one formed by a single probability measure that we shall call the *contraction centroid*. This means that after a finite number of steps we obtain the values $\alpha_S^1, \ldots, \alpha_S^l$ and the chain of nested credal sets:

$$\mathcal{M} \supset \mathcal{M}_{\alpha_S^1} \supset \ldots \supset \mathcal{M}_{\alpha_S^l} = \left\{ \Phi_4^{\mathcal{M}} \right\}. \tag{6}$$

Example 2. Consider again the credal set from Example 1. Then $\mathcal{L}^=$ is empty and $\mathcal{L}^>$ contains six gambles, that coincide with the indicator functions of the non-trivial events. Let us see that $\alpha_S^1 = \max \Lambda = 0.075$. On the one hand, $\mathcal{M}_{\alpha_S^1}$ is non-empty because the probability $P = (0.625, 0.175, 0.2)$ belongs to $\mathcal{M}_{\alpha_S^1}$. On the other hand, if we increase the lower probability in a quantity α, to keep coherence it should happen that:

$$1 \geq \left(\underline{P}(\{x_2\}) + \alpha \right) + \left(\underline{P}(\{x_1, x_3\}) + \alpha \right) = 0.85 + 2\alpha,$$

so $\alpha \leq 0.075$. Therefore, $\alpha_S^1 = 0.075$, and this gives rise to the following credal set:

$$\mathcal{M}_{\alpha_S^1} = \left\{ P \in \mathbb{P}(\mathcal{X}) \mid P(A) \geq \underline{P}(A) + \alpha_S^1 \ \forall A \neq \varnothing, \mathcal{X} \right\}.$$

If we denote by $\underline{P}_1$ its associated lower probability, it is given by:

$$\underline{P}_1(\{x_1\}) = 0.575, \quad \underline{P}_1(\{x_2\}) = 0.175, \quad \underline{P}_1(\{x_3\}) = 0.175,$$
$$\underline{P}_1(\{x_1, x_2\}) = 0.75, \quad \underline{P}_1(\{x_1, x_3\}) = 0.825, \quad \underline{P}_1(\{x_2, x_3\}) = 0.35.$$

In this second step, $\mathcal{L}_1^= = \left\{ I_{\{x_2\}}, I_{\{x_1, x_3\}} \right\}$ and $\mathcal{L}_1^> = \left\{ I_{\{x_1\}}, I_{\{x_3\}}, I_{\{x_1, x_2\}}, I_{\{x_2, x_3\}} \right\}$, i.e., there are two events whose probability is now fixed. Iterating the procedure, we obtain $\alpha_S^2 = 0.0375$ and $\mathcal{M}_{\alpha_S^2} = \left\{ \Phi_4^{\mathcal{M}} \right\}$, where $\Phi_4^{\mathcal{M}} = (0.6125, 0.175, 0.2125)$. Figure 2 shows $\mathcal{M}_{\alpha_S^1}$ (in blue) and $\mathcal{M}_{\alpha_S^2}$ (in red).
◆

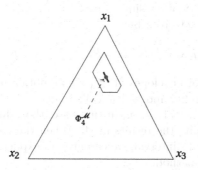

Fig. 2. Graphical representation of the credal sets $\mathcal{M}_{\alpha_S^1}$ in blue and $\mathcal{M}_{\alpha_S^2}$ in red. (Color figure online)

It is worth mentioning that the lower envelope of the credal set $\mathscr{M}_\alpha$ in Eq. (5) does not necessarily coincide with $\underline{P} + \alpha$. While by construction it dominates this lower probability, they may not agree on some events because $\underline{P} + \alpha$ need not be coherent. The lower envelope of $\mathscr{M}_\alpha$ corresponds to the *natural extension* [23] of $\underline{P} + \alpha$.

4   Relationships Between the Centroids

In our previous section we have introduced four different notions of the center of a credal set. Let us begin by showing that these four notions are indeed different:

Example 3. Consider the credal set in Example 1; there, we gave the set of incenters $\Psi_3^{\mathscr{M}}$, while the contraction centroid $\Phi_4^{\mathscr{M}}$ was given in Example 2. The extreme points of the credal set $\mathscr{M}$ are given by:

	x_1	x_2	x_3		x_1	x_2	x_3
P_1	0.55	0.1	0.35	P_4	0.65	0.25	0.1
P_2	0.5	0.15	0.35	P_5	0.8	0.1	0.1
P_3	0.5	0.25	0.25				

It follows that the average of the extreme points and the Shapley value are given by $\Phi_2^{\mathscr{M}} = (0.6, 0.17, 0.23)$ and $\Phi_1^{\mathscr{M}} = (0.6\overline{3}, 0.158\overline{3}, 0.208\overline{3})$. We conclude, taking into account also Examples 1 and 2, that the four approaches lead to different results.   ♦

While the four approaches do not lead to the same solution in general, in the following subsections we give some sufficient conditions for their equality.

4.1   Probability Intervals

A probability interval [4] is an uncertainty model that gives lower and upper bounds to the probability of the singletons: $\mathscr{I} = \big\{ [l_i, u_i] \mid l_i \leq u_i \ \forall i = 1, \ldots, n \big\}$. It determines a credal set given by:

$$\mathscr{M}(\mathscr{I}) = \{ P \in \mathbb{P}(\mathscr{X}) \mid l_i \leq P(\{x_i\}) \leq u_i \ \forall i = 1, \ldots, n \}.$$

Taking lower and upper envelopes of $\mathscr{M}(\mathscr{I})$ we obtain a lower and upper prevision, and the probability interval is called *coherent* when $\underline{P}(\{x_i\}) = l_i$ and $\overline{P}(\{x_i\}) = u_i$ for every $i = 1, \ldots, n$; in that case, the values of $\underline{P}$ for events can be easily computed using the results in [4]. When the credal set is determined by a coherent probability interval, we can give an explicit formula for the value α_S in the contraction method.

Proposition 4. *Let $\mathscr{M}$ be a credal set determined by a coherent probability interval $\mathscr{I} = \{ [l_i, u_i] \mid \forall i = 1, \ldots, n \}$. Let $\mathscr{I}^> = \big\{ i \in \{1, \ldots, n\} \mid l_i < u_i \big\}$ and $\mathscr{I}^= = \big\{ i \in \{1, \ldots, n\} \mid l_i = u_i \big\}$. Then:*

1. *The value $\alpha_S = \max \Lambda$ is given by:*

$$\alpha_S = \min \left\{ \frac{1}{|\mathscr{I}^>|} \left(1 - \sum_{i=1}^{n} l_i\right), \frac{1}{|\mathscr{I}^>|} \left(\sum_{i=1}^{n} u_i - 1\right), \frac{1}{2} \min_{i \in \mathscr{I}^>} (u_i - l_i) \right\}.$$

2. *If $\alpha_S = \frac{1}{|\mathscr{I}^>|}\left(1 - \sum_{i=1,\dots,n} l_i\right)$ or $\alpha_S = \frac{1}{|\mathscr{I}^>|}\left(\sum_{i=1,\dots,n} u_i - 1\right)$, then $\mathscr{M}_{\alpha_S} = \{\Phi_4^{\mathscr{M}(\mathscr{I})}\}$.*

From Proposition 4 we can also deduce an explicit formula for the value α_S for the *Linear Vacuous* (LV) and the *Pari Mutuel Model* (PMM), which constitute particular instances of *distortion models* [14,15] and *nearly linear models* [3]. The PMM [13,17,23] is determined by the coherent lower probability $\underline{P}_{PMM}(A) = \max\{(1+\delta)P_0(A) - \delta, 0\}$ for any $A \subseteq \mathscr{X}$, where $P_0 \in \mathbb{P}(\mathscr{X})$ is a given probability measure and $\delta > 0$. Similarly, the LV [23] is defined by the coherent lower probability given by $\underline{P}_{LV}(A) = (1-\delta)P_0(A)$, for any $A \subset \mathscr{X}$ and $\underline{P}_{LV}(\mathscr{X}) = 1$, where $P_0 \in \mathbb{P}(\mathscr{X})$ and $\delta \in (0,1)$. Both the PMM and the LV are instances of probability intervals, where:

$$\mathscr{I}_{PMM} = \left\{ [\max\{(1+\delta)P_0(\{x_i\}) - \delta, 0\}, \min\{(1+\delta)P_0(\{x_i\}), 1\}] \mid i = 1, \dots, n \right\},$$

$$\mathscr{I}_{LV} = \left\{ [(1-\delta)P_0(\{x_i\}), \min\{(1-\delta)P_0(\{x_i\}) + \delta, 1\}] \mid i = 1, \dots, n \right\}.$$

Thus we can apply Proposition 4 for computing the value α_S. In fact, when both P_0 and the lower probability only take the values 0 and 1 for the impossible and sure events, respectively, the computation of α_S can be simplified and the procedure of contracting the credal set finishes in only one step.

Corollary 1. *Consider a credal set $\mathscr{M}$ associated with either a PMM $\underline{P}_{PMM}$ or a LV $\underline{P}_{LV}$ determined by $P_0 \in \mathbb{P}(\mathscr{X})$ and the distortion parameter δ. Assume that $P_0(A)$, $\underline{P}_{PMM}(A)$ and $\underline{P}_{LV}(A)$ belong to $(0,1)$ for any $A \neq \varnothing, \mathscr{X}$. Then:*

1. *For the PMM, $\alpha_S = \max \Lambda = \frac{\delta}{n}$ and $\mathscr{M}_\alpha = \{\Phi_4^{\mathscr{M}}\}$ where $\Phi_4^{\mathscr{M}}(\{x_i\}) = (1+\delta)P_0(\{x_i\}) - \frac{\delta}{n}$ for any $i = 1, \dots, n$.*
2. *For the LV, $\alpha_S = \max \Lambda = \frac{\delta}{n}$ and $\mathscr{M}_\alpha = \{\Phi_4^{\mathscr{M}}\}$ where $\Phi_4^{\mathscr{M}}(\{x_i\}) = (1-\delta)P_0(\{x_i\}) + \frac{\delta}{n}$ for any $i = 1, \dots, n$.*
3. *In both cases, there is a unique incenter (i.e., $\Psi_3^{\mathscr{M}} = \{\Phi_3^{\mathscr{M}}\}$) and $\Phi_1^{\mathscr{M}} = \Phi_2^{\mathscr{M}} = \Phi_3^{\mathscr{M}} = \Phi_4^{\mathscr{M}}$.*

In this respect, it is worth remarking that (i) the good behaviour of these two distortion models is in line of other desirable properties they possess, as discussed in [6,14,15]; and (ii) the centroid of the LV and PMM models does not coincide with P_0, because the distortion is not done uniformly in all directions of the simplex. This was already shown in [12, Sect. 4.3] for the particular case of the Shapley value.

4.2   Connections Between the Incenter and the Contraction Centroid

Next we prove a connection between contraction centroid and the set of incenters.

Proposition 5. *Let $\mathcal{M}$ be a credal set included in* $\text{int}(\mathbb{P}(\mathcal{X}))$ *with* $\mathcal{L}^= = \varnothing$. *For any* $\alpha \le \alpha_S$, *if* $P_0 \in \mathcal{M}_\alpha$, *then* $B_d^\alpha(P_0) \subseteq \mathcal{M}$. *When* $\mathcal{M}$ *is determined by its restriction to events, then the converse also holds. As a consequence, in that case* $\mathcal{M}_{\alpha_S} = \Psi_3^{\mathcal{M}}$.

From this result we deduce that, when $\mathcal{M}$ is associated with a coherent lower probability, the credal set $\mathcal{M}_{\alpha_S}$ obtained contracting the initial credal set coincides with the set of incenters. However, when the credal set is associated with a lower prevision, this equivalence does not hold in general, as the next example shows.

Example 4. Consider $\mathcal{X} = \{x_1, x_2\}$, the gamble f given by $f(x_1) = 1$ and $f(x_2) = 0.9$ and consider the credal set $\mathcal{M}$ given by:

$$\mathcal{M} = \{P \in \mathbb{P}(\mathcal{X}) \mid 0.91 \le P(f) \le 0.99\}.$$

Equivalently, this credal set is determined by the extreme points $P_1 = (0.1, 0.9)$ and $P_2 = (0.9, 0.1)$. Consider now $P_0 = (0.2, 0.8)$ and $\alpha = 0.015$. Then, the ball $B_d^\alpha(P_0)$ has two extreme points, $Q_1 = (0.185, 0.815)$ and $Q_2 = (0.215, 0.785)$, so $B_d^\alpha(P_0) \subseteq \mathcal{M}$. However, $P_0(f) = 0.92 \notin [0.925, 0.975] = [\underline{P}(f) + \alpha, \overline{P}(f) - \alpha]$. ◆

5   Properties of the Centroids

Next we compare the different centroids in terms of the axiomatic properties they satisfy. In this respect, it is worth recalling that Shapley value was characterised in the context of coalitional game theory as the unique probability distribution satisfying the following axioms:

Efficiency: $\sum_{i=1}^n \Phi^{\mathcal{M}}(\{x_i\}) = 1$.
Symmetry: $\underline{P}(A \cup \{x_i\}) = \underline{P}(A \cup \{x_j\})$ for any $A \subseteq \mathcal{X} \setminus \{x_i, x_j\}$ implies that
$\quad \Phi^{\mathcal{M}}(\{x_i\}) = \Phi^{\mathcal{M}}(\{x_j\})$.
Linearity: $\Phi^{\mathcal{M}(\lambda_1 \underline{P}_1 + \lambda_2 \underline{P}_2)} = \lambda_1 \Phi^{\mathcal{M}(\underline{P}_1)} + \lambda_2 \Phi^{\mathcal{M}(\underline{P}_2)}$ for any $\lambda_1, \lambda_2 \in \mathbb{R}$ and
$\quad$ every $\underline{P}_1, \underline{P}_2$.
Null player: $\underline{P}(A \cup \{x_i\}) = \underline{P}(A)$ for any $A \subseteq \mathcal{X} \setminus \{x_i\}$ implies $\Phi^{\mathcal{M}}(\{x_i\}) = 0$.

Let us study these properties for the other centroids considered in this paper. Note that in the case of the incenter, they should be required to any $\Phi_3^{\mathcal{M}} \in \Psi_3^{\mathcal{M}}$.

In this respect, since in the framework of this paper any center of a credal set shall be a probability measure, the efficiency property is trivially satisfied. With respect to the other properties, it is not difficult to establish the following:

Proposition 6. $\Phi_2^{\mathcal{M}}$, $\Phi_4^{\mathcal{M}}$ *and any* $\Phi_3^{\mathcal{M}} \in \Psi_3^{\mathcal{M}}$ *satisfy the symmetry and null-player properties, but none of them satisfies linearity.*

Next we consider other desirable properties of a centroid.

Definition 4. *Let $\Phi^{\mathcal{M}}$ be a centroid of a credal set $\mathcal{M}$. We say that it satisfies:*

- Consistency *if $\Phi^{\mathcal{M}} \in \mathcal{M}$.*
- Continuity *if for any $\varepsilon > 0$, there exists $\delta > 0$ such that $d(\underline{P}_1, \underline{P}_2) := \max_{A \subseteq \mathscr{X}} |\underline{P}_1(A) - \underline{P}_2(A)| < \delta$ implies $d\big(\Phi^{\mathcal{M}}(\underline{P}_1), \Phi^{\mathcal{M}}(\underline{P}_2)\big) < \varepsilon$.*
- Ignorance preservation *if $\mathcal{M} = \mathbb{P}(\mathscr{X})$ implies that $\Phi^{\mathcal{M}}$ is the uniform distribution.*

When dealing with the incenter, the previous properties should be slightly rewritten due to its lack of uniqueness: the incenter satisfies consistency when $\Psi_3^{\mathcal{M}} \subseteq \mathcal{M}$; it satisfies ignorance preservation if $\mathcal{M} = \mathbb{P}(\mathscr{X})$ implies that the only element of $\Psi_3^{\mathcal{M}}$ is the uniform distribution; and it satisfies continuity when for any $\varepsilon > 0$ there exists some $\delta > 0$ such that $d(\underline{P}_1, \underline{P}_2) < \delta$ implies that $d(\underline{Q}_1, \underline{Q}_2) < \varepsilon$, where $\underline{Q}_1$ and $\underline{Q}_2$ are the lower envelopes of $\Psi_3^{\mathcal{M}(\underline{P}_1)}$ and $\Psi_3^{\mathcal{M}(\underline{P}_2)}$.

Proposition 7. *1. $\Phi_1^{\mathcal{M}}$ satisfies continuity and ignorance preservation, but it does not satisfy consistency.*
2. $\Phi_2^{\mathcal{M}}$ satisfies consistency and ignorance preservation, but not continuity.
3. $\Psi_3^{\mathcal{M}}, \Phi_4^{\mathcal{M}}$ satisfy consistency, continuity and ignorance preservation.

The next table summarises the results from this section:

	Shapley value	Average of extremes	Incenter (d_{TV})	Contraction center
Efficiency	YES	YES	YES	YES
Symmetry	YES	YES	YES	YES
Linearity	YES	NO	NO	NO
Null player	YES	YES	YES	YES
Consistency	NO	YES	YES	YES
Continuity	YES	NO	YES	YES
Ignorance preservation	YES	YES	YES	YES

Finally, it is worth remarking on the ability of these centroids to distinguish between lower previsions and lower probabilities: in general, a credal set $\mathcal{M}$ determines, by means of lower envelopes, a lower prevision $\underline{P}$ on a gambles and a lower probability by considering its restriction to events. However, the credal set $\mathcal{M}'$ determined by the latter, given by $\mathcal{M}' := \{P \mid P(A) \geq \underline{P}(A) \ \forall A \subseteq \mathscr{X}\}$ is in general a superset of the original credal set $\mathcal{M}$. It would be desirable then that the centroids of $\mathcal{M}$ and $\mathcal{M}'$ do not necessarily coincide, since they correspond to different credal sets. In this respect, it is not difficult to show that $\Psi_3^{\mathcal{M}}, \Phi_4^{\mathcal{M}}$ are capable of distinguishing between lower previsions and lower probabilities, and so does $\Phi_2^{\mathcal{M}}$ (with the restriction that it is only applicable on polytopes). On the other hand, the Shapley value is only defined via the lower probability, and so it does not distinguish between lower probabilities and lower previsions.

6   Centrality Measures

More generally, instead of determining which element of the credal set can be considered its center, we may define a *centrality measure*, that allows us to quantify how deep in the interior of a credal set an element is. Consider for instance the same credal set as in Example 1, depicted in Fig. 3. Intuitively, given the probability measures $Q_1 = (0.75, 0.125, 0.125)$ and $Q_2 = (0.65, 0.15, 0.2)$, emphasised in red in Fig. 3, Q_2 should have a greater *centrality degree* than Q_1.

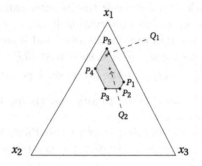

Fig. 3. Graphical representation of the credal set $\mathscr{M}$ in Example 1 (Color figure online)

This simple example suggests the following definition of centrality measure.

Definition 5. *Given a credal set $\mathscr{M}$, a centrality measure is a function $\varphi : \mathbb{P}(\mathscr{X}) \to [0, 1]$ satisfying the following properties:*

CM1 $\varphi(P) = 0$ *for every $P \notin \mathscr{M}$.*
CM2 *If $P \in ext(\mathscr{M})$, then $\varphi(P) = 0$.*
CM3 *There exists a unique $P_0 \in \mathscr{M}$ satisfying $\varphi(P_0) = 1$. Such P_0 is called central point in $\mathscr{M}$ with respect to φ.*
CM4 *Consider $P \in ext(\mathscr{M})$, P_0 the probability given in the previous item and $\lambda, \beta \in [0, 1]$ such that $\lambda \geq \beta$. Given $P_1 = \lambda P + (1 - \lambda)P_0$ and $P_2 = \beta P + (1 - \beta)P_0$, it holds that $\varphi(P_1) \leq \varphi(P_2)$.*

The idea underlying these properties is the following: **CM1** tells us that an element outside the credal set should have degree of centrality zero; from **CM2**, the same should hold for the extreme points of the credal set; **CM3** means that there is a unique probability P_0 with degree of centrality 1; finally, property **CM4** represents the idea that the closer a probability is to P_0, the greater its degree of centrality.

A centrality measure φ allows to define a chain of credal sets $\{\mathscr{M}_\alpha\}_{\alpha \in [0,1]}$, where $\mathscr{M}_\alpha$ is formed by the probabilities with centrality degree of at least α:

$$\mathscr{M}_\alpha = \{P \in \mathscr{M} \mid \varphi(P) \geq \alpha\} \quad \forall \alpha \in [0, 1].$$

We next discuss two possible strategies for defining a centrality measure. The former consists in considering a centroid of the credal set, and to measure the distance with respect to it. It requires then to specify both the centroid and the distance. Out of the options considered in the previous section, we would reject $\Phi_1^{\mathscr{M}}$ due to the lack of consistency and $\Psi_3^{\mathscr{M}}$ because of non-uniqueness. With respect to the distance, we will be considering here the total variation, although it would also be possible to consider other options such as the L_1 or the Euclidean distances.

In this sense, if we let $\Phi^{\mathscr{M}}$ be this centroid and take $\beta = \min\left\{d(\Phi^{\mathscr{M}}, P_i) : P_i \in ext(\mathscr{M})\right\}$, then we can define

$$\varphi_1(P) = 1 - \min\left\{\frac{d(P, \Phi^{\mathscr{M}})}{\beta}, 1\right\}. \tag{7}$$

A second approach would consist in considering directly a chain $\{\mathscr{M}_\alpha\}_{\alpha \in [0,1]}$ of convex credal sets such that $\mathscr{M}_0 := \mathscr{M}$, $\mathscr{M}_1$ is a singleton determining the central point $\Phi^{\mathscr{M}}$ and where $\mathscr{M}_\alpha$ is included in the interior of $\mathscr{M}$ for any $\alpha > 0$, and letting

$$\varphi_2(P) = \sup\left\{\alpha \in [0,1] \mid P \in \mathscr{M}_\alpha\right\}. \tag{8}$$

The chain $\{\mathscr{M}_\alpha\}_{\alpha \in [0,1]}$ of credal sets could be defined, for example, as:

$$\mathscr{M}_\alpha = CH\left(\{(1-\alpha)P + \alpha\Phi^{\mathscr{M}} \mid P \in ext(\mathscr{M})\}\right) \quad \forall \alpha \in [0,1].$$

Let us show that both approaches lead to a centrality measure.

Proposition 8. *Let $\mathscr{M}$ be a credal set, and let φ_1, φ_2 be given by Eqs. (7) and (8). Then φ_1 and φ_2 satisfy conditions (CM1)–(CM4).*

It is also possible to define a centrality measure by considering the chain of credal sets from Eq. (6). For this, note that for each $P \in \mathscr{M}$ there is $j \in \{1, \dots, l\}$ such that $P \in \mathscr{M}_{\alpha_S^{j-1}} \setminus \mathscr{M}_{\alpha_S^j}$. Also, there is $\alpha \in \Lambda_{j-1}$ such that $P \in (\mathscr{M}_{j-1})_\alpha$, but $P \notin (\mathscr{M}_{j-1})_{\alpha+\varepsilon}$ for any $\varepsilon > 0$. Then we let:

$$\varphi_3(P) = \frac{\alpha_S^1 + \dots + \alpha_S^{j-1} + \alpha}{\alpha_S^1 + \dots + \alpha_S^l}. \tag{9}$$

Proposition 9. *The function φ_3 defined in Eq. (9) satisfies conditions (CM1)–(CM4).*

7   Conclusions

In this paper, we have analysed four different definitions of centroid for a credal set. These could serve as a representative of the credal set or as a game solution when the credal set is interpreted as the core of a cooperative game. We have analysed their differences, the connection between them as well as their axiomatic properties. Also, we have seen that the problem could be tackled by defining a centrality measure whose unique modal point is interpreted as the centroid.

While the above results give some overview of the properties of the centroids of a credal set, there is still much work to be done in order to have a full picture of this problem. On the one hand, we could consider other possibilities in the context of game solutions, such as the Banzhaf value, or other alternatives to the total variation distance, such as the Euclidean distance or the Kullback-Leibler divergence; secondly, it would be interesting to obtain further conditions for the equality between some of these centroids; and finally, a deeper study of centrality measures and their axiomatic properties would be of interest. We intend to tackle these problems in the near future.

References

1. Bader, U., Gelander, T., Monod, N.: A fixed point theorem for L^1 spaces. Invent. Math. **189**, 143–148 (2012)
2. Baroni, P., Vicig, P.: An uncertainty interchange format with imprecise probabilities. Int. J. Approximate Reasoning **40**, 147–180 (2005)
3. Corsato, C., Pelessoni, R., Vicig, P.: Nearly-Linear uncertainty measures. Int. J. Approximate Reasoning **114**, 1–28 (2019)
4. de Campos, L.M., Huete, J.F., Moral, S.: Probability intervals: a tool for uncertain reasoning. Internat. J. Uncertain. Fuzziness Knowl.-Based Syst. **2**, 167–196 (1994)
5. de Cooman, G., Troffaes, M.C.M., Miranda, E.: n-Monotone exact functionals. J. Math. Anal. Appl. **347**, 143–156 (2008)
6. Destercke, S., Montes, I., Miranda, E.: Processing multiple distortion models: a comparative study. In: Proceedings of the 12th ISIPTA Conference. PMLR **147**, 126–135 (2021)
7. Dubois, D., Prade, H.: Fuzzy Sets and Systems. Theory and Applications. Academic Press, New York (1980)
8. Elbassioni, K., Tiway, H.R.: Complexity of approximating the vertex centroid of a polyhedron. Theoret. Comput. Sci. **421**, 56–61 (2012)
9. Grabisch, M.: Set Functions, Games and Capacities in Decision Making. Springer (2016). https://doi.org/10.1007/978-3-319-30690-2
10. Klir, G.J., Parviz, B.: Probability-possibility transformations: a comparison. Int. J. Gen. Syst. **21**, 291–310 (1992)
11. Levin, D.A., Peres, Y., Wilmer, E.L.: Markov Chains and Mixing Times. American Mathematical Society (2009)
12. Miranda, E., Montes, I.: Shapley and Banzhaf values as probability transformations. Internat. J. Uncertain. Fuzziness Knowl.-Based Syst. **26**(6), 917–947 (2018)
13. Montes, I., Miranda, E., Destercke, S.: Pari-mutuel probabilities as an uncertainty model. Inf. Sci. **481**, 550–573 (2019)
14. Montes, I., Miranda, E., Destercke, S.: Unifying neighbourhood and distortion models: part I- New results on old models. Int. J. Gen. Syst. **49**(6), 602–635 (2020)
15. Montes, I., Miranda, E., Destercke, S.: Unifying neighbourhood and distortion models: part II- New models and synthesis. Int. J. Gen. Syst. **49**(6), 636–674 (2020)

16. Montes, I., Miranda, E., Vicig, P.: 2-monotone outer approximations of coherent lower probabilities. Int. J. Approximate Reasoning **101**, 181–205 (2018)
17. Pelessoni, R., Vicig, P., Zaffalon, M.: Inference and risk measurement with the Pari-mutuel model. Int. J. Approximate Reasoning **51**, 1145–1158 (2010)
18. Shapley, L.S.: A value for n-person games. Ann. Math. Stud. **28**, 307–317 (1953)
19. Shapley, L.S.: Cores of convex games. Internat. J. Game Theory **1**, 11–26 (1971)
20. Smets, P.: Decision making in the TBM: the necessity of the Pignistic transformation. Int. J. Approximate Reasoning **38**, 133–147 (2005)
21. Smets, P., Kennes, R.: The transferable belief model. Artif. Intell. **66**(2), 191–234 (1994)
22. Walley, P.: Coherent lower (and upper) probabilities. Statistics Research Report 22, University of Warwick, Coventry (1981)
23. Walley, P.: Statistical Reasoning with Imprecise Probabilities. Chapman and Hall, London (1991)
24. Walley, P.: Statistical inferences based on a second-order possibility distribution. Int. J. Gen. Syst. **26**, 337–383 (1997)
25. Wallner, A.: Extreme points of coherent probabilities in finite spaces. Int. J. Approximate Reasoning **44**(3), 339–357 (2007)

The Smallest Probability Interval a Sequence Is Random for: A Study for Six Types of Randomness

Floris Persiau, Jasper De Bock[✉], and Gert de Cooman[✉]

Foundations Lab for imprecise probabilities, Ghent University, Ghent, Belgium
{floris.persiau,jasper.debock,gert.decooman}@ugent.be

Abstract. There are many randomness notions. On the classical account, many of them are about whether a given infinite binary sequence is random for some given probability. If so, this probability turns out to be the same for all these notions, so comparing them amounts to finding out for which of them a given sequence is random. This changes completely when we consider randomness with respect to probability intervals, because here, a sequence is always random for at least one interval, so the question is not if, but rather for which intervals, a sequence is random. We show that for many randomness notions, every sequence has a smallest interval it is (almost) random for. We study such smallest intervals and use them to compare a number of randomness notions. We establish conditions under which such smallest intervals coincide, and provide examples where they do not.

Keywords: Probability intervals · Martin-Löf randomness · Computable randomness · Schnorr randomness · Church randomness

1 Introduction

The field of algorithmic randomness studies what it means for an infinite binary sequence, such as $\omega = 0100110100\ldots$, to be random for an uncertainty model. Classically, this uncertainty model is often a single (precise) probability $p \in [0,1]$. Some of the best studied precise randomness notions are Martin-Löf randomness, computable randomness, Schnorr randomness and Church randomness. They are increasingly weaker; for example, if a sequence ω is Martin-Löf random for a probability p, then it is also computably random, Schnorr random and Church random for p. Meanwhile, these notions do not coincide; it is for example possible that a path ω is Church random but not computably random for $1/2$. From a traditional perspective, this is how we can typically differentiate between various randomness notions [1,2,6,10].

As shown by De Cooman and De Bock [3–5], these traditional randomness notions can be generalised by allowing for imprecise-probabilistic uncertainty models, such as closed probability intervals $I \subseteq [0,1]$. These more general randomness notions, and their corresponding properties, allow for more detail to

© Springer Nature Switzerland AG 2021
J. Vejnarová and N. Wilson (Eds.): ECSQARU 2021, LNAI 12897, pp. 442–454, 2021.
https://doi.org/10.1007/978-3-030-86772-0_32

arise in their comparison. Indeed, every infinite binary sequence ω is for example random for at least one closed probability interval. And for the imprecise generalisations of many of the aforementioned precise randomness notions, we will see that for every (or sometimes many) ω, there is some smallest probability interval, be it precise or imprecise, that ω is (almost) random for—we will explain the modifier 'almost' further on. It is these smallest probability intervals we will use to compare a number of different randomness notions.

We will focus on the following three questions: (i) when is there a well-defined smallest probability interval for which an infinite binary sequence ω is (almost) random; (ii) are there alternative expressions for these smallest intervals; and (iii) for a given sequence ω, how do these smallest intervals compare for different randomness notions? Thus, by looking from an imprecise perspective, we are able to do more than merely confirm the known differences between several randomness notions. Defining randomness for closed probability intervals also lets us explore to what extent existing randomness notions are different, in the sense that we can compare the smallest probability intervals for which an infinite binary sequence is random. Surprisingly, we will see that there is a large and interesting set of infinite sequences ω for which the smallest interval that ω is (almost) random for is the same for several randomness notions.

Our contribution is structured as follows. In Sect. 2, we introduce (im)precise uncertainty models for infinite binary sequences, and introduce a generic definition of randomness that allows us to formally define what it means for a sequence to have a smallest interval it is (almost) random for. In Sect. 3, we provide the mathematical background on supermartingales that we need in order to introduce a number—six in all—of different randomness notions in Sect. 4: (weak) Martin-Löf randomness, computable randomness, Schnorr randomness, and (weak) Church randomness. In the subsequent sections, we tackle our three main questions. We study the existence of the smallest intervals an infinite binary sequence ω is (almost) random for in Sect. 5. In Sects. 6 and 7, we provide alternative expressions for such smallest intervals and compare them; we show that these smallest intervals coincide under certain conditions, and provide examples where they do not. To adhere to the page limit, the proofs of all novel results— that is, the ones without citation—are omitted. They are available in Appendix B of an extended on-line version [8].

2   Forecasting Systems and Randomness

Consider an infinite sequence of binary variables $X_1, \ldots, X_n, \ldots$, where every variable X_n takes values in the binary *sample space* $\mathcal{X} := \{0, 1\}$, generically denoted by x_n. We are interested in the corresponding infinite outcome sequences $(x_1, \ldots, x_n, \ldots)$, and, in particular, in their possible randomness. We denote such a sequence generically by ω and call it a *path*. All such paths are collected in the set $\Omega := \mathcal{X}^{\mathbb{N}}$.[1] For any path $\omega = (x_1, \ldots, x_n, \ldots) \in \Omega$, we let $\omega_{1:n} := (x_1, \ldots, x_n)$

---

[1] $\mathbb{N}$ denotes the natural numbers and $\mathbb{N}_0 := \mathbb{N} \cup \{0\}$ denotes the non-negative integers (A real $x \in \mathbb{R}$ is called negative, positive, non-negative and non-positive, respectively, if $x < 0$, $x > 0$, $x \geq 0$ and $x \leq 0$).

and $\omega_n := x_n$ for all $n \in \mathbb{N}$. For $n = 0$, the empty sequence $\omega_{1:0} := \omega_0 := ()$ is called the *initial situation* and is denoted by $\square$. For any $n \in \mathbb{N}_0$, a finite outcome sequence $(x_1, \ldots, x_n) \in \mathcal{X}^n$ is called a *situation*, also generically denoted by s, and its length is then denoted by $|s| := n$. All situations are collected in the set $\mathbb{S} := \bigcup_{n \in \mathbb{N}_0} \mathcal{X}^n$. For any $s = (x_1, \ldots, x_n) \in \mathbb{S}$ and $x \in \mathcal{X}$, we use sx to denote the concatenation $(x_1, \ldots, x_n, x)$.

The randomness of a path $\omega \in \Omega$ is always defined with respect to an uncertainty model. Classically, this uncertainty model is a real number $p \in [0, 1]$, interpreted as the probability that X_n equals 1, for any $n \in \mathbb{N}$. As explained in the Introduction, we can generalise this by considering a closed probability interval $I \subseteq [0, 1]$ instead. These uncertainty models will be called *interval forecasts*, and we collect all such closed intervals in the set $\mathcal{I}$. Another generalisation of the classical case consists in allowing for non-stationary probabilities that depend on s or $|s|$. Each of these generalisations can themselves be seen as a special case of an even more general approach, which consists in providing every situation $s \in \mathbb{S}$ with a (possibly different) interval forecast in $\mathcal{I}$, denoted by $\varphi(s)$. This interval forecast $\varphi(s) \in \mathcal{I}$ then describes the uncertainty about the *a priori* unknown outcome of $X_{|s|+1}$, given that the situation s has been observed. We call such general uncertainty models *forecasting systems*.

Definition 1. *A* forecasting system *is a map* $\varphi \colon \mathbb{S} \to \mathcal{I}$ *that associates with every situation* $s \in \mathbb{S}$ *an interval forecast* $\varphi(s) \in \mathcal{I}$. *We denote the set of all forecasting systems by* Φ.

With any forecasting system $\varphi \in \Phi$, we associate two real processes $\underline{\varphi}$ and $\overline{\varphi}$, defined by $\underline{\varphi}(s) := \min \varphi(s)$ and $\overline{\varphi}(s) := \max \varphi(s)$ for all $s \in \mathbb{S}$. A forecasting system $\varphi \in \Phi$ is called *precise* if $\underline{\varphi} = \overline{\varphi}$. A forecasting system $\varphi \in \Phi$ is called *stationary* if there is an interval forecast $I \in \mathcal{I}$ such that $\varphi(s) = I$ for all $s \in \mathbb{S}$; for ease of notation, we will then denote this forecasting system simply by I. The case of a single probability p corresponds to a stationary forecasting system with $I = \{p\}$. A forecasting system $\varphi \in \Phi$ is called *temporal* if its interval forecasts $\varphi(s)$ only depend on the situations $s \in \mathbb{S}$ through their length $|s|$, meaning that $\varphi(s) = \varphi(t)$ for any two situations $s, t \in \mathbb{S}$ that have the same length $|s| = |t|$.

In some of our results, we will consider forecasting systems that are computable. To follow the argumentation and understand our results, the following intuitive description will suffice: a forecasting system $\varphi \in \Phi$ is *computable* if there is some finite algorithm that, for every $s \in \mathbb{S}$ and any $n \in \mathbb{N}_0$, can compute the real numbers $\underline{\varphi}(s)$ and $\overline{\varphi}(s)$ with a precision of 2^{-n}. For a formal definition of computability, which we use in our proofs, we refer the reader to Appendix A of the extended on-line version, which contains these proofs [8].

So what does it mean for a path $\omega \in \Omega$ to be random for a forecasting system $\varphi \in \Phi$? Since there are many different definitions of randomness, and since we intend to compare them, we now introduce a general abstract definition and a number of potential properties of such randomness notions that will, as it turns out, allow us to do so.

Definition 2. *A notion of* randomness R *associates with every forecasting system* $\varphi \in \Phi$ *a set of paths* $\Omega_R(\varphi)$. *A path* $\omega \in \Omega$ *is called R-random for* φ *if* $\omega \in \Omega_R(\varphi)$.

All of the randomness notions that we will be considering further on, satisfy additional properties. The first one is a monotonicity property, which we can describe generically as follows. If a path $\omega \in \Omega$ is R-random for a forecasting system $\varphi \in \Phi$, it is also R-random for any forecasting system $\varphi' \in \Phi$ that is less precise, meaning that $\varphi(s) \subseteq \varphi'(s)$ for all $s \in \mathbb{S}$. Consequently, this monotonicity property requires that the more precise a forecasting system is, the fewer R-random paths it ought to have.

Property 1. For any two forecasting systems $\varphi, \varphi' \in \Phi$ such that $\varphi \subseteq \varphi'$, it holds that $\Omega_R(\varphi) \subseteq \Omega_R(\varphi')$.

Furthermore, it will also prove useful to consider the property that every path $\omega \in \Omega$ is R-random for the (maximally imprecise) *vacuous forecasting system* $\varphi_v \in \Phi$, defined by $\varphi_v(s) := [0, 1]$ for all $s \in \mathbb{S}$.

Property 2. $\Omega_R([0, 1]) = \Omega$.

Thus, if Properties 1 and 2 hold, every path $\omega \in \Omega$ will in particular be R-random for at least one interval forecast—the forecast $I = [0, 1]$—and if a path $\omega \in \Omega$ is R-random for an interval forecast $I \in \mathcal{I}$, then it will also be R-random for any interval forecast $I' \in \mathcal{I}$ for which $I \subseteq I'$. It is therefore natural to wonder whether every path $\omega \in \Omega$ has some *smallest* interval forecast I such that $\omega \in \Omega_R(I)$. In order to allow us to formulate an answer to this question, we consider the sets $\mathcal{I}_R(\omega)$ that for a given path $\omega \in \Omega$ contain all interval forecasts $I \in \mathcal{I}$ that ω is R-random for. If there is such a smallest interval forecast, then it is necessarily given by

$$I_R(\omega) := \bigcap \mathcal{I}_R(\omega) = \bigcap_{I \in \mathcal{I}_R(\omega)} I.$$

As we will see, for some randomness notions R, $I_R(\omega)$ will indeed be the smallest interval forecast that ω is random for. Consequently, for these notions, and for every $\omega \in \Omega$, the set $\mathcal{I}_R(\omega)$ is completely characterised by the interval forecast $I_R(\omega)$, in the sense that ω will be R-random for an interval forecast $I \in \mathcal{I}$ if and only if $I_R(\omega) \subseteq I$.

In general, however, this need not be the case. For example, consider the situation depicted in Fig. 1. It could very well be that for some randomness notion R: that satisfies Properties 1 and 2, there is a path $\omega^* \in \Omega$ that is R-random for all interval forecasts of the form $[p, 1]$ and $[0, q]$, with $p < 1/3$ and $2/3 \leq q$, but for no others. Then clearly, $I_R(\omega^*) = [1/3, 2/3]$, but ω^* is not R-random for $I_R(\omega^*)$.

In addition, it need not even be guaranteed that the intersection $I_R(\omega)$ is non-empty. To guarantee that it will be, and as an imprecise counterpart of the law of large numbers, it suffices to consider the additional property that if a path $\omega \in \Omega$ is R-random for an interval forecast $I \in \mathcal{I}$, then this I should imply the following bounds on the relative frequency of ones along ω.

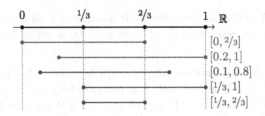

Fig. 1. The green intervals correspond to interval forecasts for which ω^* is R-random, whereas the red intervals correspond to interval forecasts that ω^* is not R-random for. (Color figure online)

Property 3. For all interval forecasts $I \in \mathcal{I}$ and all paths $\omega \in \Omega_R(I)$, it holds that $\min I \leq \liminf_{n\to\infty} \frac{1}{n}\sum_{k=1}^{n} \omega_k \leq \limsup_{n\to\infty} \frac{1}{n}\sum_{k=1}^{n} \omega_k \leq \max I$.

Properties 1–3 hold for all randomness notions R that we will consider, whence also, $I_R(\omega) \neq \emptyset$. We repeat that for some of these notions, $I_R(\omega)$ will be the smallest interval forecast that $\omega \in \Omega$ is R-random for. If not, we will sometimes still be able to show that $I_R(\omega)$ is the smallest interval forecast that ω is *almost* R-random for.

Definition 3. *A path $\omega \in \Omega$ is called* almost R-*random for an interval forecast $I \in \mathcal{I}$ if it is* R-*random for any interval forecast $I' \in \mathcal{I}$ of the form*

$$I' = [\min I - \epsilon_1, \max I + \epsilon_2] \cap [0,1], \; with \; \epsilon_1, \epsilon_2 > 0.$$

If a path $\omega \in \Omega$ is almost R-random for the interval forecast $I_R(\omega)$, then $I_R(\omega)$ almost completely characterises the set $\mathcal{I}_R(\omega)$: the only case where we cannot immediately decide whether a path ω is R-random for an interval forecast $I \in \mathcal{I}$ or not, occurs when $\min I = \min I_R(\omega)$ or $\max I = \max I_R(\omega)$. Moreover, if Property 1 holds, then as our terminology suggests, $\omega \in \Omega$ is *almost* R-random for every interval forecast $I \in \mathcal{I}$ it is random for.

In the remainder of this contribution, we intend to study the smallest interval forecasts a path is (almost) random for, for several notions of randomness. In the next section, we start by introducing the mathematical machinery needed to introduce some of these notions, and in particular, the martingale-theoretic approach to randomness, which makes extensive use of the concept of betting. Generally speaking, a path $\omega \in \Omega$ is then considered to be random for a forecasting system $\varphi \in \Phi$ if a subject can adopt no implementable betting strategy that is allowed by φ and makes him arbitrarily rich along ω. This approach will enable us to introduce the notions of Martin-Löf randomness, weak Martin-Löf randomness, computable randomness and Schnorr randomness, which differ only in what is meant by 'implementable' and in the way a subject should not be able to get arbitrarily rich [6].

3   A Martingale-Theoretic Approach—Betting Strategies

Consider the following betting game involving an infinite sequence of binary variables $X_1, \ldots, X_n, \ldots$ There are three players: Forecaster, Sceptic and Reality.

Forecaster starts by specifying a forecasting system $\varphi \in \Phi$. For every situation $s \in \mathbb{S}$, the corresponding interval forecast $\varphi(s)$ expresses for every gamble $f: \mathcal{X} \to \mathbb{R}$ whether or not Forecaster allows Sceptic to select f; the set of all gambles is denoted by $\mathcal{L}(\mathcal{X})$. A gamble $g \in \mathcal{L}(\mathcal{X})$ is offered by Forecaster to Sceptic if its expectation $E_p(g) := pg(1) + (1-p)g(0)$ is non-positive for every probability $p \in I$, or equivalently, if $\max_{p \in I} E_p(g) \le 0$.

After Forecaster has specified a forecasting system $\varphi \in \Phi$, Sceptic selects a *betting strategy* that specifies for every situation $s \in \mathbb{S}$ an *allowable* gamble $f_s \in \mathcal{L}(\mathcal{X})$ for the corresponding interval forecast $\varphi(s) \in \mathcal{I}$, meaning that $\max_{p \in \varphi(s)} E_p(f_s) \le 0$.

The betting game now unfolds as Reality reveals the successive elements $\omega_n \in \mathcal{X}$ of a path $\omega \in \Omega$. In particular, at every time instant $n \in \mathbb{N}_0$, the following actions have been and are completed: Reality has already revealed the situation $\omega_{1:n}$, Sceptic engages in a gamble $f_{\omega_{1:n}} \in \mathcal{L}(\mathcal{X})$ that is specified by his betting strategy, Reality reveals the next outcome $\omega_{n+1} \in \mathcal{X}$, and Sceptic receives a (possibly negative) reward $f_{\omega_{1:n}}(\omega_{n+1})$. We furthermore assume that Sceptic starts with initial unit capital, so his running capital at every time instant $n \in \mathbb{N}_0$ equals $1 + \sum_{k=0}^{n-1} f_{\omega_{1:k}}(\omega_{k+1})$. We also don't allow Sceptic to borrow. This means that he is only allowed to adopt betting strategies that, regardless of the path that Reality reveals, will guarantee that his running capital never becomes negative.

In order to formalise Sceptic's betting strategies, we will introduce the notion of test supermartingales. We start by considering a *real process* $F: \mathbb{S} \to \mathbb{R}$; it is called positive if $F(s) > 0$ for all $s \in \mathbb{S}$ and non-negative if $F(s) \ge 0$ for all $s \in \mathbb{S}$. A real process F is called *temporal* if $F(s)$ only depends on the situation $s \in \mathbb{S}$ through its length $|s|$, meaning that $F(s) = F(t)$ for any two $s, t \in \mathbb{S}$ such that $|s| = |t|$. A real process S is called a *selection process* if $S(s) \in \{0, 1\}$ for all $s \in \mathbb{S}$.

With any real process F, we can associate a *gamble process* $\Delta F: \mathbb{S} \to \mathcal{L}(\mathcal{X})$, defined by $\Delta F(s)(x) := F(sx) - F(s)$ for all $s \in \mathbb{S}$ and $x \in \mathcal{X}$, and we call it the *process difference* for F. If F is positive, then we can also consider another gamble process $D_F: \mathbb{S} \to \mathcal{L}(\mathcal{X})$, defined by $D_F(s)(x) := {}^{F(sx)}/_{F(s)}$ for all $s \in \mathbb{S}$ and $x \in \mathcal{X}$, which we call the *multiplier process* for F. And vice versa, with every non-negative real gamble process $D: \mathbb{S} \to \mathcal{L}(\mathcal{X})$, we can associate a non-negative real process $D^\circledast: \mathbb{S} \to \mathbb{R}$ defined by $D^\circledast(s) := \prod_{k=0}^{n-1} D(x_{1:k})(x_{k+1})$ for all $s = (x_1, \ldots, x_n) \in \mathbb{S}$, and we then say that $D^\circledast$ is *generated by* D.

When given a forecasting system $\varphi \in \Phi$, we call a real process M a *supermartingale* for φ if for every $s \in \mathbb{S}$, $\Delta M(s)$ is an allowable gamble for the corresponding interval forecast $\varphi(s)$, meaning that $\max_{p \in \varphi(s)} E_p(\Delta M(s)) \le 0$. Moreover, a supermartingale T is called a *test* supermartingale if it is non-negative and $T(\square) := 1$. We collect all test supermartingales for φ in the set $\overline{\mathbb{T}}(\varphi)$. It is easy to see that every test supermartingale T corresponds to an allowed betting strategy for Sceptic that starts with unit capital and avoids borrowing. Indeed, for every situation $s = (x_1, \ldots, x_n) \in \mathbb{S}$, T specifies an allowable gamble $\Delta T(s)$ for the interval forecast $\varphi(s) \in \mathcal{I}$, and Sceptic's running capital $1 + \sum_{k=0}^{n-1} \Delta T(x_{1:k})(x_{k+1})$ equals $T(s)$ and is therefore non-negative, and equals 1 in $\square$.

We recall from Sect. 2 that martingale-theoretic randomness notions differ in the nature of the implementable betting strategies that are available to Sceptic. More formally, we will consider three different types of implementable test supermartingales: computable ones, lower semicomputable ones, and test supermartingales generated by lower semicomputable multiplier processes. A test supermartingale $T \in \overline{\mathbb{T}}(\varphi)$ is called *computable* if there is some finite algorithm that, for every $s \in \mathbb{S}$ and any $n \in \mathbb{N}_0$, can compute the real number $T(s)$ with a precision of 2^{-n}. A test supermartingale $T \in \overline{\mathbb{T}}(\varphi)$ is called *lower semicomputable* if there is some finite algorithm that, for every $s \in \mathbb{S}$, can compute an increasing sequence $(q_n)_{n \in \mathbb{N}_0}$ of rational numbers that approaches the real number $T(s)$ from below—but without knowing, for any given n, how good the lower bound q_n is. Similarly, a real multiplier process D is called lower semicomputable if there is some finite algorithm that, for every $s \in \mathbb{S}$ and $x \in \mathcal{X}$, can compute an increasing sequence $(q_n)_{n \in \mathbb{N}_0}$ of rational numbers that approaches the real number $D(s)(x)$ from below. For more details, we refer the reader to Appendix A of the extended on-line version [8].

4   Several Notions of (Imprecise) Randomness

At this point, we have introduced the necessary mathematical machinery to define our different randomness notions. We start by introducing four martingale-theoretic ones: Martin-Löf (ML) randomness, weak Martin-Löf (wML) randomness, computable (C) randomness and Schnorr (S) randomness. Generally speaking, for these notions, a path $\omega \in \Omega$ is random for a forecasting system $\varphi \in \Phi$ if Sceptic has no implementable allowed betting strategy that makes him arbitrarily rich along ω. We stress again that these randomness notions differ in how Sceptic's betting strategies are implementable, and in how he should not be able to become arbitrarily rich along a path $\omega \in \Omega$. With these types of restrictions in mind, we introduce the following sets of implementable allowed betting strategies.

$\overline{\mathbb{T}}_{\mathrm{ML}}(\varphi)$	all lower semicomputable test supermartingales for φ
$\overline{\mathbb{T}}_{\mathrm{wML}}(\varphi)$	all test supermartingales for φ generated by lower semicomputable multiplier processes
$\overline{\mathbb{T}}_{\mathrm{C}}(\varphi), \overline{\mathbb{T}}_{\mathrm{S}}(\varphi)$	all computable test supermartingales for φ

For a path ω to be Martin-Löf, weak Martin-Löf or computably random, we require that Sceptic's running capital should never be *unbounded* on ω for any implementable allowed betting strategy; that is, no test supermartingale $T \in \overline{\mathbb{T}}_{\mathrm{R}}(\varphi)$ should be *unbounded* on ω, meaning that $\limsup_{n \to \infty} T(\omega_{1:n}) = \infty$.

Definition 4 ([5]). *For any* $R \in \{ML, wML, C\}$, *a path* $\omega \in \Omega$ *is R-random for a forecasting system* $\varphi \in \Phi$ *if no test supermartingale* $T \in \overline{\mathbb{T}}_R(\varphi)$ *is unbounded on* ω.

For Schnorr randomness, we require instead that Sceptic's running capital should not be *computably unbounded* on ω for any implementable allowed betting strategy. More formally, we require that no test supermartingale $T \in \overline{\mathbb{T}}_S(\varphi)$ should be *computably unbounded* on ω. That T is computably unbounded on ω means that $\limsup_{n\to\infty}[T(\omega_{1:n}) - \tau(n)] \geq 0$ for some real map $\tau \colon \mathbb{N}_0 \to \mathbb{R}_{\geq 0}$ that is

(i) computable;
(ii) non-decreasing, so $\tau(n+1) \geq \tau(n)$ for all $n \in \mathbb{N}_0$;
(iii) unbounded, so $\lim_{n\to\infty} \tau(n) = \infty$.[2]

Since such a *real growth function* τ is unbounded, it expresses a (computable) lower bound for the 'rate' at which T increases to infinity along ω. Clearly, if $T \in \overline{\mathbb{T}}_S(\varphi)$ is computably unbounded on $\omega \in \Omega$, then it is also unbounded on ω.

Definition 5 ([5]). *A path* $\omega \in \Omega$ *is S-random for a forecasting system* $\varphi \in \Phi$ *if no test supermartingale* $T \in \overline{\mathbb{T}}_S(\varphi)$ *is computably unbounded on* ω.

De Cooman and De Bock have proved that these four martingale-theoretic randomness notions satisfy Properties 1 and 2 [5, Propositions 9,10,17,18]. To describe the relations between these martingale-theoretic imprecise-probabilistic randomness notions, we consider the sets $\Omega_R(\varphi)$, with $R \in \{ML, wML, C, S\}$; they satisfy the following inclusions [5, Section 6].

$$\Omega_{ML}(\varphi) \subseteq \Omega_{wML}(\varphi) \subseteq \Omega_C(\varphi) \subseteq \Omega_S(\varphi).$$

Thus, if a path $\omega \in \Omega$ is Martin-Löf random for a forecasting system $\varphi \in \Phi$, then it is also weakly Martin-Löf, computably and Schnorr random for φ. Consequently, for every forecasting system $\varphi \in \Phi$, there are at most as many paths that are Martin-Löf random as there are weakly Martin-Löf, computably or Schnorr random paths. We therefore call Martin-Löf randomness *stronger* than weak Martin-Löf, computable, or Schnorr randomness. And so, *mutatis mutandis*, for the other randomness notions.

We also consider two other imprecise-probabilistic randomness notions, which have a more frequentist flavour: Church randomness (CH) and weak Church randomness (wCH). Their definition makes use of yet another (but simpler) type of implementable real processes; a selection process S is called *recursive* if there is a finite algorithm that, for every $s \in \mathbb{S}$, outputs the binary digit $S(s) \in \{0, 1\}$.

---

[2] Since τ is non-decreasing, it being unbounded is equivalent to $\lim_{n\to\infty} \tau(n) = \infty$.

Definition 6 ([5]). *A path $\omega \in \Omega$ is CH-random (wCH-random) for a forecasting system $\varphi \in \Phi$ if for every recursive (temporal) selection process S for which $\lim_{n \to \infty} \sum_{k=0}^{n-1} S(\omega_{1:k}) = \infty$, it holds that*

$$\liminf_{n \to \infty} \frac{\sum_{k=0}^{n-1} S(\omega_{1:k})[\omega_{k+1} - \varphi(\omega_{1:k})]}{\sum_{k=0}^{n-1} S(\omega_{1:k})} \geq 0$$

and

$$\limsup_{n \to \infty} \frac{\sum_{k=0}^{n-1} S(\omega_{1:k})[\omega_{k+1} - \overline{\varphi}(\omega_{1:k})]}{\sum_{k=0}^{n-1} S(\omega_{1:k})} \leq 0.$$

For a stationary forecasting system $I \in \mathcal{I}$, the conditions in these definitions simplify to the perhaps more intuitive requirement that

$$\min I \leq \liminf_{n \to \infty} \frac{\sum_{k=0}^{n-1} S(\omega_{1:k})\omega_{k+1}}{\sum_{k=0}^{n-1} S(\omega_{1:k})} \leq \limsup_{n \to \infty} \frac{\sum_{k=0}^{n-1} S(\omega_{1:k})\omega_{k+1}}{\sum_{k=0}^{n-1} S(\omega_{1:k})} \leq \max I.$$

It is easy to see that these two randomness notions also satisfy Properties 1 and 2. Since the notion of weak Church randomness considers fewer selection processes than Church randomness does, it is clear that if a path $\omega \in \Omega$ is Church random for a forecasting system $\varphi \in \Phi$, then it is also weakly Church random for φ. Hence, $\Omega_{\text{CH}}(\varphi) \subseteq \Omega_{\text{wCH}}(\varphi)$. For computable forecasting systems, we can also relate these two 'frequentist flavoured' notions with the martingale-theoretic notions considered before [5, Sections 6 and 7]: for every computable forecasting system $\varphi \in \Phi$,

$$\Omega_{\text{ML}}(\varphi) \subseteq \Omega_{\text{wML}}(\varphi) \subseteq \Omega_{\text{C}}(\varphi) \begin{subarray}{c} \subseteq \\ \subseteq \end{subarray} \begin{array}{c} \Omega_{\text{CH}}(\varphi) \\ \Omega_{\text{S}}(\varphi) \end{array} \begin{subarray}{c} \subseteq \\ \subseteq \end{subarray} \Omega_{\text{wCH}}(\varphi). \tag{1}$$

5 Smallest Interval Forecasts and Randomness

From now on, we will focus on stationary forecasting systems and investigate the differences and similarities between the six randomness notions we consider. We start by studying if there is a smallest interval forecast for which a path is (almost) random. To this end, we first compare the sets $\mathcal{I}_{\text{R}}(\omega)$, with $\text{R} \in \{\text{ML}, \text{wML}, \text{C}, \text{S}, \text{CH}, \text{wCH}\}$. They satisfy similar relations as the sets $\Omega_{\text{R}}(\varphi)$—but without a need for computability assumptions.

Proposition 1 ([5, Sect. 8]). *For every path $\omega \in \Omega$, it holds that*

$$\mathcal{I}_{\text{ML}}(\omega) \subseteq \mathcal{I}_{\text{wML}}(\omega) \subseteq \mathcal{I}_{\text{C}}(\omega) \begin{subarray}{c} \subseteq \\ \subseteq \end{subarray} \begin{array}{c} \mathcal{I}_{\text{CH}}(\omega) \\ \mathcal{I}_{\text{S}}(\omega) \end{array} \begin{subarray}{c} \subseteq \\ \subseteq \end{subarray} \mathcal{I}_{\text{wCH}}(\omega).$$

Similarly to before, if a path $\omega \in \Omega$ is Martin-Löf random for an interval forecast $I \in \mathcal{I}$, then it is also weakly Martin-Löf, computably, Schnorr and (weakly)

Church random for I. Observe that for our weakest notion of randomness, Definition 6—with $S = 1$—guarantees that all interval forecasts $I \in \mathcal{I}_{\text{wCH}}(\omega)$ satisfy Property 3, and therefore, by Proposition 1, all six randomness notions that we are considering here satisfy Property 3. Since the sets $\mathcal{I}_R(\omega)$ are also non-empty by Property 2, the interval forecasts $I_R(\omega)$ are well-defined and non-empty for all $R \in \{\text{ML}, \text{wML}, \text{C}, \text{S}, \text{CH}, \text{wCH}\}$. Moreover, since the sets $\mathcal{I}_R(\omega)$ satisfy the relations in Proposition 1, their intersections $I_R(\omega)$ satisfy the following inverse relations.

Corollary 1. *For every path $\omega \in \Omega$, it holds that*

$$I_{\text{wCH}}(\omega) \begin{array}{c} \subseteq I_{\text{CH}}(\omega) \\ \subseteq I_{\text{S}}(\omega) \end{array} \begin{array}{c} \subseteq \\ \subseteq \end{array} I_{\text{C}}(\omega) \subseteq I_{\text{wML}}(\omega) \subseteq I_{\text{ML}}(\omega).$$

For Church and weak Church randomness, it holds that every path $\omega \in \Omega$ is in fact Church and weakly Church random, respectively, for the interval forecasts $I_{\text{CH}}(\omega)$ and $I_{\text{wCH}}(\omega)$.

Proposition 2. *Consider any $R \in \{\text{CH}, \text{wCH}\}$ and any path $\omega \in \Omega$. Then $I_R(\omega)$ is the smallest interval forecast that ω is R-random for.*

A similar result need not hold for the other four types of randomness we are considering here. As an illustrative example, consider the non-stationary but temporal precise forecasting system $\varphi_{\sim 1/2}$ defined, for all $s \in \mathbb{S}$, by

$$\varphi_{\sim 1/2}(s) := \frac{1}{2} + (-1)^{|s|}\delta(|s|), \text{ with } \delta(n) := e^{-\frac{1}{n+1}}\sqrt{e^{\frac{1}{n+1}} - 1} \text{ for all } n \in \mathbb{N}_0.$$

It has been proved that if a path $\omega \in \Omega$ is computably random for $\varphi_{\sim 1/2}$, then ω is Church random and almost computably random for the stationary precise model $1/2$, whilst not being computably random for $1/2$ [3].

While in general $I_R(\omega)$ may not be the smallest interval forecast that a path $\omega \in \Omega$ is R-random for, De Cooman and De Bock have effectively proved that for $R \in \{\text{wML}, \text{C}, \text{S}\}$, every path $\omega \in \Omega$ is almost R-random for $I_R(\omega)$, essentially because the corresponding sets $\mathcal{I}_R(\omega)$ are then closed under finite intersections.

Proposition 3. ([5, **Sect. 8**]). *Consider any $R \in \{\text{wML}, \text{C}, \text{S}\}$ and any path $\omega \in \Omega$. Then $I_R(\omega)$ is the smallest interval forecast for which ω is almost R-random.*

It should be noted that there is no mention of Martin-Löf randomness in Propositions 2 and 3. Indeed, it is an open problem whether every path $\omega \in \Omega$ is (almost) ML-random for the interval forecast $I_{\text{ML}}(\omega)$. We can however provide a partial answer by focusing on paths $\omega \in \Omega$ that are ML-random for a computable precise forecasting system $\varphi \in \Phi$.

Proposition 4. *If a path $\omega \in \Omega$ is ML-random for a computable precise forecasting system $\varphi \in \Phi$, then $I_{\text{ML}}(\omega)$ is the smallest interval forecast for which ω is almost ML-random.*

6   What Do Smallest Interval Forecasts Look Like?

Having established conditions under which $I_R(\omega)$ is the smallest interval forecast ω is (almost) random for, we now set out to find an alternative expression for this interval forecast. Forecasting systems will play a vital role in this part of the story; for every path $\omega \in \Omega$ and every forecasting system $\varphi \in \Phi$, we consider the interval forecast $I_\varphi(\omega)$ defined by

$$I_\varphi(\omega) := \left[\liminf_{n \to \infty} \underline{\varphi}(\omega_{1:n}), \limsup_{n \to \infty} \overline{\varphi}(\omega_{1:n}) \right].$$

When we restrict our attention to computable forecasting systems $\varphi \in \Phi$, and if we assume that a path $\omega \in \Omega$ is R-random for such a forecasting system φ, with R $\in \{\mathrm{ML}, \mathrm{wML}, \mathrm{C}, \mathrm{S}, \mathrm{CH}, \mathrm{wCH}\}$, then the forecasting system φ imposes outer bounds on the interval forecast $I_R(\omega)$ in the following sense.

Proposition 5. *For any* R $\in \{\mathrm{ML}, \mathrm{wML}, \mathrm{C}, \mathrm{S}, \mathrm{CH}, \mathrm{wCH}\}$ *and any path* $\omega \in \Omega$ *that is* R-*random for a computable forecasting system* $\varphi \in \Phi$: $I_R(\omega) \subseteq I_\varphi(\omega)$.

If we only consider computable *precise* forecasting systems $\varphi \in \Phi$ and assume that a path $\omega \in \Omega$ is R-random for φ, with R $\in \{\mathrm{ML}, \mathrm{wML}, \mathrm{C}, \mathrm{CH}\}$, then the forecasting system φ completely characterises the interval forecast $I_R(\omega)$.

Theorem 1. *For any* R $\in \{\mathrm{ML}, \mathrm{wML}, \mathrm{C}, \mathrm{CH}\}$ *and any path* $\omega \in \Omega$ *that is* R-*random for a computable precise forecasting system* $\varphi \in \Phi$: $I_R(\omega) = I_\varphi(\omega)$.

When the computable precise forecasting systems $\varphi \in \Phi$ are also temporal, this result applies to Schnorr and weak Church randomness as well.

Theorem 2. *For any* R $\in \{\mathrm{ML}, \mathrm{wML}, \mathrm{C}, \mathrm{S}, \mathrm{CH}, \mathrm{wCH}\}$ *and any path* $\omega \in \Omega$ *that is* R-*random for a computable precise temporal forecasting system* $\varphi \in \Phi$: $I_R(\omega) = I_\varphi(\omega)$.

7   When Do These Smallest Interval Forecasts Coincide?

Finally, we put an old question into a new perspective: to what extent are randomness notions different? We take an 'imprecise' perspective here, by comparing the smallest interval forecasts for which a path $\omega \in \Omega$ is (almost) R-random, with R $\in \{\mathrm{ML}, \mathrm{wML}, \mathrm{C}, \mathrm{S}, \mathrm{CH}, \mathrm{wCH}\}$. As we will see, it follows from our previous exposition that there are quite some paths for which these smallest interval forecasts coincide.

Let us start by considering a path $\omega \in \Omega$ that is ML-random for some computable precise forecasting system $\varphi \in \Phi$; similar results hold when focusing on weaker notions of randomness. We know from Eq. (1) that ω is then also wML-, C- and CH-random for φ. By invoking Propositions 2, 3 and 4, we infer that $I_R(\omega)$ is the smallest interval forecast that ω is (almost) R-random for, for any R $\in \{\mathrm{ML}, \mathrm{wML}, \mathrm{C}, \mathrm{CH}\}$. Moreover, by Theorem 1, these smallest interval forecasts all equal $I_\varphi(\omega)$ and therefore coincide, i.e., $I_{\mathrm{ML}}(\omega) = I_{\mathrm{wML}}(\omega) = I_{\mathrm{C}}(\omega) = I_{\mathrm{CH}}(\omega) = I_\varphi(\omega)$.

By only looking at temporal computable precise forecasting systems $\varphi \in \Phi$, we can even strengthen these conclusions. For example, using a similar argument as before—but using Theorem 2 instead of 1—we see that if ω is ML-random for such a forecasting system φ, then the smallest interval forecasts $I_R(\omega)$ for which ω is (almost) R-random coincide for all six randomness notions that we consider.

Looking at these results, the question arises whether there are paths $\omega \in \Omega$ for which the various interval forecasts $I_R(\omega)$ do not coincide. It turns out that such paths do exist. We start by showing that the smallest interval forecasts $I_C(\omega)$ and $I_S(\omega)$ for which a path $\omega \in \Omega$ is respectively almost C- and almost S-random do not always coincide; this result is mainly a reinterpretation of a result in [5,10].

Proposition 6. *There is a path $\omega \in \Omega$ such that $I_S(\omega) = 1/2 \in [1/2, 1] \subsetneq I_C(\omega)$.*

We are also able to show that there is a path $\omega \in \Omega$ such that $I_C(\omega) = 1/2$ is the smallest interval forecast it is almost C-random for, whereas ω is not almost ML-random for $1/2$; for this result, we have drawn inspiration from [9].

Proposition 7. *For every $\delta \in (0, 1/2)$, there is a path $\omega \in \Omega$ such that $I_C(\omega) = 1/2$ and $I \notin \mathcal{I}_{ML}(\omega)$ for any $I \in \mathcal{I}$ such that $I \subseteq [1/2 - \delta, 1/2 + \delta]$.*

Clearly, the path $\omega \in \Omega$ in Proposition 7 cannot be Martin-Löf random for a precise computable forecasting system $\varphi \in \Phi$, because otherwise, the interval forecasts $I_C(\omega)$ and $I_{ML}(\omega)$ would coincide by Eq. (1) and Theorem 1, and ω would therefore be almost Martin-Löf random for $1/2$ by Proposition 4, contradicting the result. So the path ω in this result is an example of a path for which we do not know whether there is a smallest interval forecast that ω is almost Martin-Löf random for. However, if there is such a smallest interval forecast, then Proposition 7 shows it is definitely not equal to $1/2$; due to Corollary 1, it must then strictly include $1/2$.

8   Conclusions and Future Work

We've come to the conclusion that various (non-stationary) precise-probabilistic randomness notions in the literature are, in some respects, not that different; if a path is random for a computable precise (temporal) forecasting system, then the smallest interval forecast for which it is (almost) random coincides for several randomness notions. The computability condition on the precise forecasting system is important for this result, but we don't think it is that big a restriction. After all, computable forecasting systems are those that can be computed by a finite algorithm up to any desired precision, and therefore, they are arguably the only ones that are of practical relevance.

An important concept that made several of our results possible was that of almost randomness, a notion that is closely related to randomness but is—slightly—easier to satisfy. In our future work, we would like to take a closer look at the difference between these two notions. In particular, the present discussion, together with our work in [7], makes us wonder to what extent the distinction between them is relevant in a more practical context.

We also plan to continue investigating the open question whether there is for every path some smallest interval forecast for which it is (almost) Martin-Löf random. Finally, there is still quite some work to do in finding out whether the randomness notions we consider here are all different from a stationary imprecise-probabilistic perspective, in the sense that there are paths for which the smallest interval forecasts for which they are (almost) random do not coincide.

Acknowledgments. Floris Persiau's research was supported by FWO (Research Foundation-Flanders), project number 11H5521N.

References

1. Ambos-Spies, K., Kucera, A.: Randomness in computability theory. Contemporary Math. **257**, 1–14 (2000)
2. Bienvenu, L., Shafer, G., Shen, A.: On the history of martingales in the study of randomness. Electron. J. Hist. Probab. Stat. **5**, 1–40 (2009)
3. De Cooman, G., De Bock, J.: Computable randomness is inherently imprecise. In: Proceedings of the Tenth International Symposium on Imprecise Probability: Theories and Applications. Proceedings of Machine Learning Research, vol. 62, pp. 133–144 (2017)
4. De Cooman, G., De Bock, J.: Randomness and imprecision: a discussion of recent results. In: Proceedings of the Twelfth International Symposium on Imprecise Probability: Theories and Applications. Proceedings of Machine Learning Research, vol. 147, pp. 110–121 (2021)
5. De Cooman, G., De Bock, J.: Randomness is inherently imprecise. Int. J. Approximate Reasoning (2021). https://www.sciencedirect.com/science/article/pii/S0888613X21000992
6. Downey, R.G., Hirschfeldt, D.R.: Algorithmic Randomness and Complexity. Springer, New York (2010). https://doi.org/10.1007/978-0-387-68441-3
7. Persiau, F., De Bock, J., De Cooman, G.: A remarkable equivalence between non-stationary precise and stationary imprecise uncertainty models in computable randomness. In: Proceedings of the Twelfth International Symposium on Imprecise Probability: Theories and Applications. Proceedings of Machine Learning Research, vol. 147, pp. 244–253 (2021)
8. Persiau, F., De Bock, J., De Cooman, G.: The smallest probability interval a sequence is random for: a study for six types of randomness (2021). https://arxiv.org/abs/2107.07808, extended online version
9. Schnorr, C.P.: A unified approach to the definition of random sequences. Math. Syst. Theory **5**, 246–258 (1971)
10. Wang, Y.: Randomness and Complexity. PhD thesis, Ruprecht Karl University of Heidelberg (1996)

Inconsistency Handling and Preferences

Merging Epistemic States
and Manipulation

Amílcar Mata Díaz[1] and Ramón Pino Pérez[2]([⊠])

[1] El Valle del Espíritu Santo, Nueva Esparta, Venezuela
[2] Université d'Artois, CRIL-CNRS, Lens, France
pinoperez@cril.fr

Abstract. In this work we study the problem of manipulation in the framework of merging complex epistemic states. We adopt the techniques concerning representation and impossibility in belief merging of complex epistemic states proposed by Mata Díaz and Pino Pérez in 2017. We introduce here the notion of belief lifting, aiming to capture the preferences of an agent over formulas. This allows us to define a general notion of manipulability. We prove that, provided some rational properties, a merging operator is either manipulable, with respect to any well-behaved belief lifting, or it admits an Arrovian dictator. We also study the behaviour of some concrete belief merging operators, showing that some of them are manipulable. Moreover, we prove that strategy-proofness cannot be characterized in terms of Arrovian dictators.

Keywords: Belief merging · Epistemic states · Impossibility · Manipulation · Strategy-proofness · Arrovian dictator

1 Introduction

Merging information is an important issue which appears naturally in many domains: medical diagnosis, decision making, policy planning, aggregation of data bases, etc. The goal is to extract a coherent and relevant piece of information, from information given by several sources which could be in conflict. A logic based model of belief merging has been proposed in [18,20]. In that framework the agents' basic piece of information is encoded in propositional logic and the group information is a bag of propositional formulas (a profile).

In many situations, more complex representations are necessary. For instance Darwiche and Pearl [6] have shown this necessity for revision operators. In the case of merging, we have illustrated in [24] the usefulness of considering more complex representations of information through relevant examples.

In the present work we adopt the framework of belief merging complex epistemic states introduced in [23] and improved in [24]. One interesting aspect of this framework is that it allows for a formulation and a better understanding of common problems of belief merging and social choice theory [1,17,29]. Actually,

© Springer Nature Switzerland AG 2021
J. Vejnarová and N. Wilson (Eds.): ECSQARU 2021, LNAI 12897, pp. 457–470, 2021.
https://doi.org/10.1007/978-3-030-86772-0_33

similarities between belief merging and social choice theory have been pointed out in [19] (see also [8,12]).

Let us recall the central questions in social choice theory: given a set of alternatives and a set of voters with their preferences over the alternatives, how to select the best alternatives for the group and in what measure a method for selecting the alternatives is good. One measure of the goodness of a social choice function is the fact that it satisfies some reasonable criteria stated by Arrow [1] (*non-imposition, the Pareto condition, independence of irrelevant alternatives* and *absence of dictators*). In his work, Arrow showed that, if a social choice function satisfies the first three criteria, then it admits a dictator. This is his famous impossibility theorem.

Exploiting the similarities between social choice functions and belief merging operators, we have translated [24] the Arrovian criteria to the logical framework of belief merging and showed that this type of operators meets the majority of those criteria, stating also an impossibility result which generalizes the Arrow's Theorem (cf. Theorem 2 below).

Another interesting topic addressed in social choice theory concerns the manipulability[1] of electoral processes [2,7,10,13,14,16,22,27,30]. Manipulation occurs when a voter expresses preferences which are not his real ones, in order to obtain a more suitable result for him. Manipulability situations are also present in belief merging: an agent might "lie" in order to obtain a result that fits better with his beliefs. This has been studied in belief merging in [5,9,25,26].

An inherent issue in the study on manipulation is to measure how suitable the outcome of a merging process is for an agent. Everaere *et al.* [9] stated a quantitative manner to do so, introducing the notion of indexes of satisfaction. In [25] is introduced a qualitative procedure to measure such suitability using belief liftings. A belief lifting extends preferences over interpretations to preferences over formulas, in a similar way in which preferences over objects is extended to preferences over sets of objects [3,11,22]. Liftings have been considered in the study of strategy-proofness in social choice theory [2,7,13,16,22,30,31] and in the study of some logical frameworks in order to state preferences over formulas [15,32].

In this work we continue the study of strategy-proofness in the extended framework of belief merging of epistemic states, using belief liftings as a tool for establishing preferences over information. We have to note two important features of our work. First, that the view of epistemic states considered here is more general than the propositional view, although it preserves the main logical aspects. This abstract view of epistemic states, introduced by Benferhat *et al.* [4], is indeed a formalization of the concept established by Darwiche and Pearl. Second, we enrich the set of rational postulates by introducing new social postulates inspired on the classical Arrow's criteria, stating then some general strategy-proofness results, which show a dichotomy between manipulability (with respect to a belief lifting) and the existence of an Arrovian dictator. It is worth mentioning that in [25] there is a strategy-proofness result, which is similar to ours but it involves powerful agents with a weaker behaviour than Arrovian dictators.

---

[1] The absence of manipulability is usually called strategy-proofness.

This work is organized as follows: in Sect. 2 we present some special orders that will be used throughout the paper and the notions of belief liftings. In Sect. 3 we present briefly the concept of merging operators of epistemic states as well as the social postulates and an impossibility theorem stated in [24]. This impossibility theorem is a basic tool for obtaining the main result of this work. In Sect. 4 we introduce other new social postulates and we establish the main results of this paper about strategy-proofness. In Sect. 5 we analyze the behavior of some ES basic merging operators in order to illustrate manipulability situations. Finally, in Sect. 6 we make some concluding remarks.

2   Preliminaries

A *preorder* over a set A is a binary relation $\succeq$ over A which is reflexive and transitive. Its associated strict relation, $\succ$, and indifference relation, $\simeq$, are given as follows: $x \succ y$ *iff* $x \succeq y \ \& \ y \not\succeq x$ and $x \simeq y$ *iff* $x \succeq y \ \& \ y \succeq x$.

A *total preorder* over a set A is a preorder which is total. Given a subset C of A, we say that c in C is a maximal element of C, with respect to a total preorder $\succeq$, if $c \succeq x$, for all x in C. The set of maximal elements of C with respect to $\succeq$ will be denoted by $\max(C, \succeq)$. We will write $\max(\succeq)$ instead of $\max(A, \succeq)$ to denote the set of maximal elements of the whole set A with respect to the total preorder $\succeq$. $P(A)$ denotes the set of all total preorders over a set A.

An example of a total preorder, which is often used along this paper, is the *lexicographical combination* of two total preorders, $\succeq_1$ and $\succeq_2$, denoted $\succeq^{\mathrm{lex}(\succeq_1, \succeq_2)}$:

$$x \succeq^{\mathrm{lex}(\succeq_1, \succeq_2)} y \ \textit{iff} \ \begin{cases} x \succ_1 y, \text{ or} \\ x \simeq_1 y \ \& \ x \succeq_2 y \end{cases}$$

For any pair of total preorders $\succeq_1$, $\succeq_2$ over a set A, its lexicographical combination, $\succeq^{\mathrm{lex}(\succeq_1, \succeq_2)}$, is also a total preorder over A for which the following holds:

$$\max(\succeq^{\mathrm{lex}(\succeq_1, \succeq_2)}) = \max(\max(\succeq_1), \succeq_2) \tag{1}$$

A more complex example of a total preorder is the *precise-leximax order* introduced by Leal and Pino Pérez [22]. Given a nonempty set A with n elements, and a total preorder $\succeq$ over A, we consider the set $(A)_\succeq$ formed by all the tuples of size less or equal to n, whose inputs are not repeated elements of A, ordered in decreasing manner by $\succeq$. Thus, given a total preorder $\succeq$ over A, we define the *precise-leximax order* $\succeq_\succeq^{\mathrm{plm}}$ as follows, for every pair of tuples $\overrightarrow{x} = (x_1, x_2, \ldots, x_k)$ and $\overrightarrow{y} = (y_1, y_2, \ldots, y_m)$ in $(A)_\succeq$:

$$\overrightarrow{x} \succeq_\succeq^{\mathrm{plm}} \overrightarrow{y} \ \textit{iff} \ \begin{cases} k \leq m \text{ and } x_i \simeq y_i, \text{ for all } i \leq k, \text{ or} \\ \text{there is } j \leq \min\{k, m\} \text{ s.t. } x_i \simeq y_i, \text{ for all } i < j, \text{ and } x_j \succ y_j \end{cases}$$

A precise-leximax order is actually a total preorder that discriminates the ordered chains by considering the lexicographical order and privileging proper initial segments.

The set of non contradictory propositional formulas built over a finite set $\mathcal{P}$ of atomic propositions will be denoted $\mathcal{L}_\mathcal{P}$ while $\mathcal{W}_\mathcal{P}$ is its associated set of interpretations (models). If φ is a formula in $\mathcal{L}_\mathcal{P}$, we denote by $[\![\varphi]\!]$ the set of its models. If φ_i is a formula in $\mathcal{L}_\mathcal{P}$, for each i in a finite set of indexes I, then we denote by $\bigwedge \varphi_i$ the conjunction of all the formulas φ_i. If M is a nonempty subset of $\mathcal{W}_\mathcal{P}$, φ_M denotes a formula whose set of models is exactly M.

Extending an ordering over models to an ordering over propositions can be performed, via the semantics, in a similar manner as the extension of an ordering over a set A to an ordering over subsets of A [3]. We call this type of processes *belief liftings*. More precisely, a *belief lifting* is a mapping $\succeq \mapsto \sqsupseteq_{\succeq}$ that associates a preorder $\sqsupseteq_{\succeq}$ over $\mathcal{L}_\mathcal{P}$ to any total preorder $\succeq$ over $\mathcal{W}_\mathcal{P}$, for which the following hold: $\varphi_w \sqsupseteq_{\succeq} \varphi_{w'}$ iff $w \succeq w'$, and if $\varphi \equiv \psi$ then $\varphi \simeq \psi$, with respect to $\sqsupseteq_{\succeq}$.

Given a preorder $\sqsupseteq_{\succeq}^{\mathcal{W}_\mathcal{P}}$ over subsets of $\mathcal{W}_\mathcal{P}$, it is possible to establish an order over $\mathcal{L}_\mathcal{P}$, $\sqsupseteq_{\succeq}^{\mathcal{L}_\mathcal{P}}$, as follows: $\varphi \sqsupseteq_{\succeq}^{\mathcal{L}_\mathcal{P}} \varphi'$ iff $[\![\varphi]\!] \sqsupseteq_{\succeq}^{\mathcal{W}_\mathcal{P}} [\![\varphi']\!]$. Thus, through liftings over sets, as the Kelly lifting [16] and the *precise leximax lifting*[2] [22], it is possible to define two belief liftings using this technique:

Kelly Belief Lifting: $\varphi \sqsupseteq_{\succeq}^{\mathrm{K}} \psi$ iff for all $w \models \varphi$ and for all $w' \models \psi$; $w \succeq w'$.

Precise-Leximax Belief Lifting: $\varphi \sqsupseteq_{\succeq}^{\mathrm{plm}} \psi$ iff for all $\overrightarrow{x}$ in $[\![\varphi]\!]_{\succeq}$ containing all the models of φ, there exists $\overrightarrow{y}$ in $[\![\psi]\!]_{\succeq}$ containing all the models of ψ such that $\overrightarrow{x} \succeq_{\succeq}^{\mathrm{plm}} \overrightarrow{y}$.

Barberà *et al.* [3] characterized many natural liftings through their properties. Among them, there is a pair of basic properties, which were stated by Gärdenfors [13]. We call them *the Gärdenfors properties*, which in our setting are:

G1: If $w \succ w'$ then $\varphi_{w,w'} \sqsupseteq_{\succeq} \varphi_{w'}$ and **G2:** If $w \succ w'$ then $\varphi_w \sqsupseteq_{\succeq} \varphi_{w,w'}$

These properties have a very natural interpretation: **G1** expresses that good company improves the group; **G2** says that bad company worsens the group.

From now on, a *G-belief lifting* is a belief lifting that satisfies both instances of the Gärdenfors properties. It is not hard to see that the Kelly belief lifting and the precise-leximax belief lifting are actually two instances of G-belief liftings.

3   Epistemic State Merging Operators

In this section we establish the concept of Epistemic State merging operators (ES merging operators for short) and give some features of their social behaviour. First of all, we need the notions of *epistemic state*, *agents* and *epistemic profiles*.

An *epistemic space* is a triple $(\mathcal{E}, B, \mathcal{L}_\mathcal{P})$, where $\mathcal{E}$ is a nonempty set, whose elements are called *epistemic states*, $\mathcal{L}_\mathcal{P}$ is a set of non contradictory formulas and B is a surjection from $\mathcal{E}$ into $\mathcal{L}_\mathcal{P}$. For every E in $\mathcal{E}$, $B(E)$ should be interpreted as the *belief base* or *the most entrenched belief* of E.

The set of *agents* is a prefixed well ordered set $(\mathcal{S}, <)$. A *society of agents* is a finite and nonempty set $N = \{i_1, i_2, \ldots, i_n\}$ of $\mathcal{S}$, whose elements are disposed increasingly. A *partition* of N is a finite family $\{N_1, \ldots, N_k\}$ of pairwise disjoint sets such that their union is N.

---

[2] The Precise leximax lifting is in fact a variant of the leximax lifting [3].

Now, we fix an epistemic space $(\mathcal{E}, B, \mathcal{L}_{\mathcal{P}})$ and a set of agents $(\mathcal{S}, <)$. Given a finite society of agents N, an N-*profile* (also called *epistemic profile*) is a tuple $\Phi = (E_{i_1}, \ldots, E_{i_n})$ ordered increasingly by the elements in N. Sometimes we will write $\Phi(i)$ in order to represent the epistemic state E_i in Φ. If N is a singleton, suppose $N = \{i\}$, by abuse, E_i will denote the N-profile (E_i), and we call it *single profile*. The set of all the epistemic profiles is denoted $\mathrm{P}(\mathcal{S}, \mathcal{E})$.

Let $N = \{i_1, \ldots, i_n\}$ and $M = \{j_1, \ldots, j_m\}$ be two societies of agents, and consider the epistemic profiles $\Phi = (E_{i_1}, \ldots, E_{i_n})$ and $\Phi' = (E'_{j_1}, \ldots, E'_{j_m})$. We denote $\Phi \equiv \Phi'$, if $n = m$ and $E_{i_k} = E_{j_k}$, for $k = 1, \ldots, n$. By abuse and being clear from the context, we write respectively $E_i = E_j$ and $E_i \neq E_j$ instead of $E_i \equiv E_j$ and $E_i \not\equiv E_j$. When N and M are disjoint, we define a new $(N \cup M)$-profile, $\Phi \sqcup \Phi'$, as follows: $(\Phi \sqcup \Phi')(i)$ is $\Phi(i)$ if $i \in N$, otherwise it is $\Phi'(i)$. If $M \subseteq N$, Φ_M denotes the M-profile obtained by the restriction of Φ to M.

From now on, Φ and Φ' denote the profiles $(E_{i_1}, \ldots, E_{i_n})$ and $(E'_{i_1}, \ldots, E'_{i_n})$, respectively. Additionally, $\Phi[E^*/i]$ is the epistemic profile obtained from Φ by replacing E_i with E^*, that is: $\Phi[E^*/i](j)$ is $\Phi(j)$ if $j \neq i$, otherwise it is E^*.

An *operator of epistemic states* (also called an *ES operator* for short) is a function of the form $\nabla : \mathrm{P}(\mathcal{S}, \mathcal{E}) \times \mathcal{E} \longrightarrow \mathcal{E}$, where $\nabla(\Phi, E)$ is the result of combining the epistemic states in Φ under an *integrity constraint* E.

Now we present the rationality postulates of merging in the framework of epistemic states. Most of them are adapted from IC merging postulates proposed by Konieczny and Pino Pérez [18]. The postulates, in terms of epistemic states, were proposed and widely studied in [23,24].

(ESF1) $B(\nabla(\Phi, E)) \vdash B(E)$.

(ESF2) $B(\nabla(\Phi, E)) \equiv B(\nabla(\Phi', E'))$, whenever $\Phi \equiv \Phi'$ and $B(E) \equiv B(E')$.

(ESF3) $B(\nabla(\Phi, E')) \wedge B(E'') \vdash B(\nabla(\Phi, E))$, whenever $B(E) \equiv B(E') \wedge B(E'')$.

(ESF4) $B(\nabla(\Phi, E)) \vdash B(\nabla(\Phi, E')) \wedge B(E'')$, whenever $B(E) \equiv B(E') \wedge B(E'')$ and $B(\nabla(\Phi, E')) \wedge B(E'') \not\vdash \bot$.

(ESF5) If $E_j \neq E_k$, then there exists E^* in $\mathcal{E}$ s.t. $B(\nabla(E_j, E^*)) \not\equiv B(\nabla(E_k, E^*))$.

(ESF6) $B(\nabla(\Phi, E)) \equiv \bigwedge_{i \in N} B(E_i) \wedge B(E)$, whenever $\bigwedge_{i \in N} B(E_i) \wedge B(E) \not\vdash \bot$.

(ESF7) $B(\nabla(\Phi_{N_1}, E)) \wedge B(\nabla(\Phi_{N_2}, E)) \vdash B(\nabla(\Phi, E))$.

(ESF8) $B(\nabla(\Phi, E)) \vdash B(\nabla(\Phi_{N_1}, E)) \wedge B(\nabla(\Phi_{N_2}, E))$, whenever $B(\nabla(\Phi_{N_1}, E)) \wedge B(\nabla(\Phi_{N_2}, E)) \not\vdash \bot$.

The first four postulates, **(ESF1)**–**(ESF4)**, are the minimal requirements of rationality that ES operators have to satisfy. They allow to state an important class of ES combination operators, namely the *ES basic merging operators*: those operators that satisfy them. The last four postulates describe mainly the relationships between the results of merging as a whole society and the results of merging in its subsocieties (cf. [24] for more details). They allow to introduce an important subclass of ES basic merging operators, namely, *ES merging operators*: those operators that satisfy **(ESF1)**–**(ESF8)**. In Sect. 5 we present some examples of this type of merging operators.

Now we give some semantic aspects of merging processes, which are determined by orderings over interpretations. An *assignment* is a map $\Phi \mapsto \succeq_\Phi$ which associates a total preorder $\succeq_\Phi$ over $\mathcal{W}_\mathcal{P}$ to every epistemic profile Φ, such that $\succeq_\Phi=\succeq_{\Phi'}$, whenever $\Phi \equiv \Phi'$. An assignment $\Phi \mapsto \succeq_\Phi$ is called a *faithful assignment* if the following properties hold:

1. If $E_j \neq E_k$, then $\succeq_{E_j} \neq \succeq_{E_k}$.
2. If $\bigwedge_{i \in N} B(E_i) \nvdash \bot$, then $[\![\bigwedge_{i \in N} B(E_i)]\!] = \max(\succeq_\Phi)$.
3. If $w \succeq_{\Phi_{N_1}} w'$ and $w \succeq_{\Phi_{N_2}} w'$ then $w \succeq_\Phi w'$.
4. If $w \succeq_{\Phi_{N_1}} w'$ and $w \succ_{\Phi_{N_2}} w'$, then $w \succ_\Phi w'$.

The intended meaning of a faithful assignment is coding semantically the group preferences. Indeed, from **2** follows that the most entrenched preferences of an agent represent his entrenched beliefs. More precisely, for every single profile E, we have straightforwardly from **2** that the following equality, which is called the *max condition*, holds: $[\![B(E)]\!] = \max(\succeq_E)$.

The next result collects the semantic characterizations (at the level of belief bases) of ES basic merging operators and ES merging operators, showed in [24].

Theorem 1. *For every ES operator ∇, the following assertions hold:*

(i) ∇ *is an ES basic merging operator iff there is a unique assignment $\Phi \mapsto \succeq_\Phi$ such that:*
$$[\![B(\nabla(\Phi, E))]\!] = max([\![B(E)]\!], \succeq_\Phi) \qquad \text{(B-Rep)}$$

(ii) ∇ *is an ES merging operator iff there exists a unique faithful assignment $\Phi \mapsto \succeq_\Phi$ satisfying (B-Rep).*

Now, we present some properties of the merging processes, which capture the following social principles appearing in the seminal work of Arrow [1]: *Standard domain, Pareto condition, independence of irrelevant alternatives and existence of a dictator*. These properties were introduced and deeply studied in [24]. In order to give a formulation of these principles in logical terms, using epistemic states, from now on we suppose that $\mathcal{P}$ has at least two propositional variables. Thus, there are at least four interpretations available in $\mathcal{W}_\mathcal{P}$.

(ESF-SD) For every agent i in $\mathcal{S}$ and every triple w, w', w'' in $\mathcal{W}_\mathcal{P}$, the following conditions hold:
  (i) There exists E_i s.t. $B(\nabla(E_i, E_{w,w'})) \equiv \varphi_{w,w'}$ and $B(\nabla(E_i, E_{w',w''})) \equiv \varphi_{w'}$.
  (ii) There exists E_i s.t. $B(\nabla(E_i, E_{w,w'})) \equiv \varphi_w$ and $B(\nabla(E_i, E_{w',w''})) \equiv \varphi_{w',w''}$.
  (iii) There exists E_i s.t. $B(\nabla(E_i, E_{w,w'})) \equiv \varphi_w$ and $B(\nabla(E_i, E_{w',w''})) \equiv \varphi_{w'}$.
  where $[\![B(E_{w,w'})]\!] = \{w, w'\}$ and $[\![B(E_{w',w''})]\!] = \{w', w''\}$.
(ESF-P) For all i in N, if $B(\nabla(E_i, E)) \wedge B(E') \vdash \bot$ and $\bigwedge B(\nabla(E_i, E)) \nvdash \bot$, then $B(\nabla(\Phi, E)) \wedge B(E') \vdash \bot$.
(ESF-I) $B(\nabla(\Phi, E)) \equiv B(\nabla(\Phi', E))$, whenever $B(\nabla(E_i, E')) \equiv B(\nabla(E_i', E'))$, for every i in N and every epistemic state E' in $\mathcal{E}$, with $B(E') \vdash B(E)$.
(ESF-D) For every finite society N in $\mathcal{F}^*(\mathcal{S})$ there exists an agent d in N s.t. $B(\nabla(\Phi, E)) \vdash B(\nabla(E_d, E))$, for all N-profile Φ and every restriction E in $\mathcal{E}$.

(**ESF-SD**) is called the *standard domain* condition. This property states some "richness" in the set of results of a merging process. Indeed, if an ES basic merging operator satisfies it, then the following holds for its associated assignment: for any agent i in $\mathcal{S}$, any triple of interpretations w, w', w'' in $\mathcal{W}_\mathcal{P}$, and any total preorder $\succeq$ over $\{w, w', w''\}$ (except the flat order), there is an i-profile E_i such that $\succeq$ is $\succeq_{E_i}\!\restriction_{\{w,w',w''\}}$ (the restriction of $\succeq_{E_i}$ to $\{w, w', w''\}$). (**ESF-P**) is referred to as the *Pareto* condition. This property expresses that, if all the agents reject a piece of information, and all the agents have some consensus, such information will be rejected in the result of merging. (**ESF-I**) is the *independence* condition. This captures the following principle: the merging process depends only on how the restrictions in the individual epistemic states are related. (**ESF-D**) evokes the existence of a *dictator*, there is an agent (an *Arrovian dictator*) that imposes his will. This is the postulate that good operators should avoid. Operators satisfying that postulate are called *dictatorial operators*.

Any ES merging operator satisfies the Pareto Condition. This is because (**ESF7**) and (**ESF8**) entails (**ESF-P**). Moreover, every dictatorial operator also satisfies the Pareto condition [24].

Now we present an Arrovian impossibility result, which is similar to that stated by Sen for social choice functions [17,28]. This will be very useful later.

Theorem 2 (Impossibility theorem [24]). *If an ES basic merging operator satisfies* (**ESF-SD**), (**ESF-P**) *and* (**ESF-I**), *then* (**ESF-D**) *also holds.*

4   On Manipulability for ES Merging Operators

In this section we deal with another interesting issue which is present in the framework of logic-based merging, namely, *strategy-proofness* of merging information processes. In order to address this issue we present other two natural social properties: *Non-imposition* and *stability*.

Non-imposition expresses the fact that, if a complete information entails the beliefs of the integrity constraint, then it can be the belief of one possible output of the merging process. More precisely:

(**ESF-NI**) For every finite society N and every model w of $B(E)$, there exists an N-profile Φ such that $B(\nabla(\Phi, E)) \equiv \varphi_w$.

We say that an ES operator is *non-imposed* if it satisfies (**ESF-NI**). It is not hard to see that any ES merging operator is non-imposed, as the next result reveals. We leave its proof to the reader.

Proposition 1. *If* (**ESF6**) *holds, then* (**ESF-NI**) *also holds.*

Stability captures the fact that if an information is accepted by the whole group under a restriction and also by the revision of an epistemic state under the same restriction, it will remain accepted if an agent – whose revised beliefs with the restriction of the merging process coincides with the belief of such restriction – changes his mind by the epistemic state which accepted such an information. Formally:

(ESF-S) If $\varphi \vdash B(\nabla(\Phi, E)) \wedge B(\nabla(E^*, E))$ and $B(\nabla(E_i, E)) \equiv B(E)$, then $\varphi \vdash B(\nabla(\Phi[^{E^*}/_i], E))$.

We say that an ES operator is *stable* if **(ESF-S)** holds and it is called *unstable* if that property does not hold. In Sect. 5 we present some concrete examples of stable and unstable operators. Indeed, every ES merging operator is stable:

Proposition 2. *If* **(ESF1)**, **(ESF7)** *and* **(ESF8)** *hold, then* **(ESF-S)** *holds.*

Proof. We suppose $\varphi \vdash B(\nabla(\Phi, E)) \wedge B(\nabla(E^*, E))$ and $B(\nabla(E_i, E)) \equiv B(E)$. If Φ is a single profile or $\varphi \vdash \perp$, then the result is straightforward.

Now, we assume that the N-profile Φ has at least two inputs, $\varphi \not\vdash \perp$, and consider $M = N \setminus \{i\}$. On one hand, since $B(\nabla(E_i, E)) \equiv B(E)$, from **(ESF1)** we get $B(\nabla(\Phi_M, E)) \wedge B(\nabla(E_i, E)) \equiv B(\nabla(\Phi_M, E))$. On the other hand, from **(ESF7)** and **(ESF8)** we obtain $B(\nabla(\Phi_M, E)) \wedge B(\nabla(E_i, E)) \equiv B(\nabla(\Phi, E))$. Thus, $B(\nabla(\Phi_M, E)) \equiv B(\nabla(\Phi, E))$. Now, since $\varphi \vdash B(\nabla(\Phi, E)) \wedge B(\nabla(E^*, E))$, we have $\varphi \vdash B(\nabla(\Phi_M, E)) \wedge B(\nabla(E^*, E))$. From this, applying **(ESF7)** and **(ESF8)** again, we get $\varphi \vdash B(\nabla(\Phi[^{E^*}/_i], E))$, as desired.   □

Now, we present our notion of manipulability. An ES basic merging operator is manipulable by an agent if such an agent, knowing the restriction of the merging process and the information that will be expressed by the other agents, changes his mind in order to obtain a result that "fits" better his true beliefs.

Definition 1. *An ES basic merging operator* ∇ *is said to be* manipulable *if there exist a belief lifting* $\succeq \mapsto \sqsupseteq_{\succeq}$, *a finite society of agents* N *in* $\mathcal{F}^*(\mathcal{S})$, *an* N-profile Φ, *an agent* i *in* N *and a couple of epistemic states* E, E^* *in* $\mathcal{E}$, *such that:*

$$B(\nabla(\Phi[^{E^*}/_i], E)) \sqsupseteq_{\succeq_{E_i}} B(\nabla(\Phi, E))$$

In this case, we say that ∇ is manipulable with respect to the belief lifting $\succeq \mapsto \sqsupseteq_{\succeq}$, while the tuple formed by N, Φ, i, E, E^* is called a *manipulability situation* for ∇ (with respect to $\succeq \mapsto \sqsupseteq_{\succeq}$). If such a manipulability situation exists, we say that ∇ admits a manipulability situation (with respect to $\succeq \mapsto \sqsupseteq_{\succeq}$).

We say that ∇ is *absolutely manipulable* (resp. *absolutely G-manipulable*) if it is manipulable with respect to any belief lifting (resp. to any G-belief lifting). If ∇ does not admit a manipulability situation with respect to a prefixed belief lifting, we say that ∇ is *strategy-proof* with respect to that belief lifting.

Strategy-proofness entails some rational properties when other good properties are involved. This can be seen through the following result.

Proposition 3. *For every ES basic merging operator* ∇, *which is strategy-proof with respect to a G-belief lifting, the following properties hold:*

(i) *If* ∇ *satisfies* **(ESF-NI)**, *then it also satisfies* **(ESF-P)**.
(ii) ∇ *satisfies* **(ESF-S)** *iff it also satisfies* **(ESF-I)**.

Proof. To show *(i)*, suppose that **(ESF-P)** does not hold. Thus, there exist a finite society N, an N-profile Φ and a pair of epistemic states E, E' in $\mathcal{E}$ such that, for every agent i, $B(\nabla(E_i, E)) \wedge B(E') \vdash \bot$, $\bigwedge B(\nabla(E_i, E)) \nvdash \bot$, but $B(\nabla(\Phi, E)) \wedge B(E') \nvdash \bot$. Consider a couple of interpretations w, w' in $\mathcal{W}_{\mathcal{P}}$ such that $w \models \bigwedge B(\nabla(E_i, E))$ and $w' \models B(\nabla(\Phi, E)) \wedge B(E')$. For simplicity, due to **(ESF1)**, **(ESF3)** and **(ESF4)**, we may suppose[3] $[\![B(E)]\!] = \{w, w'\}$.

By **(ESF-NI)**, consider a N-profile Φ^* such that $B(\nabla(\Phi^*, E)) \equiv \varphi_w$, and note that $B(\nabla(\Phi, E)) \not\equiv \varphi_w$. Define the sequence $\Phi = \Phi_0, \Phi_1, \ldots, \Phi_n = \Phi^*$ as follows: $\Phi_t = \Phi_{t-1}[{}^{E^*_{i_t}}/_{i_t}]$, for $t > 0$. Let Φ_k be the first in the sequence s.t. $B(\nabla(\Phi_k, E)) \equiv \varphi_w$. Put $r = k - 1$ and $i = i_k$. Then, $\Phi_k = \Phi_r[{}^{E^*_i}/_i]$ and, $B(\nabla(\Phi_r, E)) \equiv \varphi_{w'}$ or $B(\nabla(\Phi_r, E)) \equiv \varphi_{w,w'}$

Now, since $w \models B(\nabla(E_i, E))$ and $w' \not\models B(\nabla(E_i, E))$, from (B-Rep) we get $w \succ_{E_i} w'$. Thus, $\varphi_w \sqsupset_{\succeq_{E_i}} \varphi_{w'}$ and from **G2** we get $\varphi_w \sqsupset_{\succeq_{E_i}} \varphi_{w,w'}$. Therefore, $B(\nabla(\Phi_r[{}^{E^*_i}/_i], E)) \sqsupset_{\succeq_{E_i}} B(\nabla(\Phi_r, E))$, a contradiction.

To show the *only if* part of (ii), we assume that **(ESF-S)** holds and, towards a contradiction, suppose that **(ESF-I)** does not hold. Then, we consider a couple of epistemic profiles $\Phi = (E_{i_1}, \ldots, E_{i_n})$, $\Phi^* = (E^*_{i_1}, \ldots, E^*_{i_n})$ and E in $\mathcal{E}$ such that $B(\nabla(E_i, E')) \equiv B(\nabla(E^*_i, E'))$, for every E' in $\mathcal{E}$ with $B(E') \vdash B(E)$, but $B(\nabla(\Phi, E)) \not\equiv B(\nabla(\Phi^*, E))$.

Suppose $B(\nabla(\Phi, E)) \nvdash B(\nabla(\Phi^*, E))$ (the other case is analogous) and consider a pair w, w' in $\mathcal{W}_{\mathcal{P}}$ such that $w \models B(\nabla(\Phi, E)) \wedge \neg B(\nabla(\Phi^*, E))$ and $w' \models B(\nabla(\Phi^*, E))$. Due to **(ESF1)**, **(ESF3)** and **(ESF4)**, we may suppose $[\![B(E)]\!] = \{w, w'\}$. Thus, we get $B(\nabla(\Phi, E)) \not\equiv \varphi_{w'}$ and $B(\nabla(\Phi^*, E)) \equiv \varphi_{w'}$.

Let Φ_k be the first of $\Phi = \Phi_0, \Phi_1, \ldots, \Phi_n = \Phi^*$ s.t. $B(\nabla(\Phi_k, E)) \equiv \varphi_{w'}$, where $\Phi_t = \Phi_{t-1}[{}^{E^*_i}/_{i_t}]$, for $t > 0$. Then, if $r = k - 1$ and $i = i_k$, we obtain $\Phi_k = \Phi_r[{}^{E^*_i}/_i]$, while $\varphi_w \vdash B(\nabla(\Phi_r, E))$ and $B(\nabla(\Phi_r[{}^{E^*_i}/_i], E)) \equiv \varphi_{w'}$, that is, $\varphi_w \nvdash B(\nabla(\Phi_r[{}^{E^*_i}/_i], E))$. From this and **(ESF-S)**, we get the next two cases:

$\underline{\varphi_w \nvdash B(\nabla(\Phi_r, E)) \wedge B(\nabla(E^*_i, E))}$: In this case, since $\varphi_w \vdash B(\nabla(\Phi_r, E))$, we have $\varphi_w \nvdash B(\nabla(E^*_i, E))$. Then, since $B(\nabla(E^*_i, E)) \equiv B(\nabla(E_i, E))$, from (B-Rep), we get $w' \succ_{E_i} w$. Hence, $\varphi_{w'} \sqsupset_{\succeq_{E_i}} \varphi_w$ and, by **G2**, $\varphi_{w'} \sqsupset_{\succeq_{E_i}} \varphi_{w,w'}$. Thus, $B(\nabla(\Phi_r[{}^{E^*_i}/_i], E)) \sqsupset_{\succeq_{E_i}} B(\nabla(\Phi_r, E))$, contradicting the no manipulation.

$\underline{B(\nabla(E_i, E)) \not\equiv B(E)}$: In this case, by the assumption, $B(\nabla(E^*_i, E)) \not\equiv B(E)$. Thus, $w \not\models B(\nabla(E^*_i, E))$ or $w' \not\models B(\nabla(E^*_i, E))$. If $w \not\models B(\nabla(E^*_i, E))$, with a similar argument to the previous one, $B(\nabla(\Phi_r[{}^{E_i}/_i], E)) \sqsupset_{\succeq_{E_i}} B(\nabla(\Phi_r, E))$, contradicting the no manipulation. Finally, suppose that $w' \not\models B(\nabla(E^*_i, E))$ and note that, by (B-Rep), $w \succ_{E^*_i} w'$. Then, $\varphi_w \sqsupset_{\succeq_{E^*_i}} \varphi_{w'}$, and from **G1** it follows $\varphi_{w,w'} \sqsupset_{\succeq_{E^*_i}} \varphi_{w'}$. Now, since $\Phi_r = \Phi_k[{}^{E_i}/_i]$, we get $B(\nabla(\Phi_k[{}^{E_i}/_i], E)) \sqsupset_{\succeq_{E^*_i}} B(\nabla(\Phi_k, E))$, contradicting the no manipulation.

To show the *if* part of *(ii)*, we assume that **(ESF-I)** holds, and towards a contradiction, we suppose that **(ESF-S)** does not. Consider thus a finite society

---

[3] Rigorously, we must consider E'' in $\mathcal{E}$ such that $[\![B(E'')]\!] = \{w, w'\}$, then apply **(ESF1)**, **(ESF3)** and **(ESF4)** and continue with the proof by switching E and E''.

N, an agent i in N, an N-profile Φ, a couple E, E^* in $\mathcal{E}$ and φ in $\mathcal{L}_\mathcal{P}$ such that $\varphi \vdash B(\nabla(\Phi, E)) \wedge B(\nabla(E^*, E))$, $B(\nabla(E_i, E)) \equiv B(E)$ and $\varphi \not\vdash B(\nabla(\Phi[^{E^*}/_i], E))$.

We consider a pair of models w, w' in $\mathcal{W}_\mathcal{P}$ such that $w \models \varphi \wedge \neg B(\nabla(\Phi[^{E^*}/_i], E))$ and $w' \models B(\nabla(\Phi[^{E^*}/_i], E))$. Again, by **(ESF1)**, **(ESF3)** and **(ESF4)**, we may suppose $[\![B(E)]\!] = \{w, w'\}$. Thus, since $w \models B(\nabla(E^*, E))$, by (B-Rep) we get the following two cases:

$\underline{w \simeq_{E^*} w'}$: In this case, it is not hard to see that $B(\nabla(E_i, E')) \equiv B(\nabla(E^*, E'))$, for every E' in $\mathcal{E}$, with $B(E') \vdash B(E)$. Therefore, from **(ESF-I)** we obtain $B(\nabla(\Phi, E)) \equiv B(\nabla(\Phi[^{E^*}/_i], E))$, a contradiction.

$\underline{w \succ_{E^*} w'}$: In this case, assume $\Phi^* = \Phi[^{E^*}/_i]$ and note that $\Phi^*[^{E_i}/_i] = \Phi$. Thus, from **(ESF1)** we obtain $B(\nabla(\Phi^*, E)) \equiv \varphi_{w'}$, while $B(\nabla(\Phi^*[^{E_i}/_i], E)) \equiv \varphi_w$ or $B(\nabla(\Phi^*[^{E_i}/_i], E)) \equiv \varphi_{w,w'}$. Now, since $w \succ_{E^*} w'$, we have $\varphi_w \sqsupseteq_{\succeq_{E^*}} \varphi_{w'}$ and, by **G1**, $\varphi_{w,w'} \sqsupseteq_{\succeq_{E^*}} \varphi_{w'}$. Therefore, for any of the two possible outcomes of $B(\nabla(\Phi^*[^{E_i}/_i], E))$, we get $B(\nabla(\Phi^*[^{E_i}/_i], E)) \sqsupseteq_{\succeq_{E^*}} B(\nabla(\Phi^*, E))$.

In any case, we have obtained the manipulability of ∇, a contradiction. □

We are now able to state our main strategy-proofness result. This is a straightforward corollary of Theorem 2 and Proposition 3, which establishes a dichotomy between absolute G-manipulability and the existence of an Arrovian dictator.

Theorem 3. *Any ES basic merging operator satisfying* **(ESF-SD)**, **(ESF-NI)** *and* **(ESF-S)** *is absolutely G-manipulable or satisfies* **(ESF-D)**.

In particular, if a non-imposed, stable and strategy-proof (with respect to a G-belief lifting) ES basic merging operator satisfies the standard domain condition, then it admits an Arrovian dictator. The converse of this assertion fails. Indeed, the Σ-*projective operator* (see Sect. 5) is an example of a non-imposed, stable ES basic merging operator satisfying the standard domain condition, which is dictatorial, but it is absolutely manipulable. Moreover, the *projective operator* is a non-imposed, stable and dictatorial basic merging operator that satisfies the standard domain condition, which is strategy-proof with respect to the Kelly's lifting, but it is manipulable with respect to the precise-leximax lifting (see Sect. 5). Thus, Theorem 3 relies heavily on the lifting chosen.

The next result is a corollary of Propositions 1 and 2 and Theorem 3. It shows that any non-dictatorial ES merging operator satisfying standard domain is absolutely G-manipulable.

Theorem 4. *Every ES merging operator satisfying* **(ESF-SD)** *is absolutely G-manipulable or satisfies* **(ESF-D)**.

5   Concrete Examples of Merging Operators

In this section, we are going to exhibit some specific examples of ES merging operators in order to illustrate manipulability situations. Such operators were introduced in [24]. In order to do so, we assume that the epistemic states are given by total preorders over interpretations [that is, $\mathcal{E} = P(\mathcal{W}_\mathcal{P})$] and the function B is such that $[\![B(\succeq)]\!] = max(\succeq)$ for any epistemic state $\succeq$. In terms of this concrete representation of information, due to (1) and (B-Rep), we can build an ES basic merging operator through a given basic assignment $\Phi \mapsto \succeq_\Phi$ as follows:

$$\nabla(\Phi, \succeq) = \succeq^{\text{lex}(\succeq, \succeq_\Phi)} \tag{2}$$

First, we present two well known instances of ES basic merging operators that are classical in the study of belief merging [9,18–21,24–26]: the *sum* and *max* operators. They are defined using the *sum* and *max* functions.
Sum: $\sum(x_1, \cdots, x_n) = \sum x_i$ and **Max:** $max(x_1, \ldots, x_n) = max\{x_1, x_2, \ldots, x_n\}$.

These functions allow us to introduce in a natural way the *sum* and the *max* assignments. They associate a total preorder $\succeq_\Phi^F$ over $\mathcal{W}_\mathcal{P}$ to any epistemic profile $\Phi = (\succeq_{i_1}, \succeq_{i_2}, \ldots, \succeq_{i_n})$, as follows:

$$w \succeq_\Phi^F w' \text{ iff } F(r_{i_1}(w), \ldots, r_{i_n}(w)) \geq F(r_{i_1}(w'), \ldots, r_{i_n}(w')) \tag{3}$$

where F denotes *sum* or *max* and r_i is the natural ranking function[4] of $\succeq_i$.

Thus, from (2) and (3), it is possible to build the *sum* operator, ∇^Σ, and the *max* operator, ∇^{max}. It is not hard to see that *sum* is a non-imposed and stable ES merging operator, while *max* is a non-imposed ES basic merging operator which is unstable. Moreover, they are non-dictatorial operators that satisfy the standard domain condition, which are absolutely manipulable.

Now, we present two operators, which were introduced in [24]: the *projective* and the *Σ-projective*. From now on, given a finite society N, d denotes $max(N)$.

The *projective operator*, ∇^π, is totally determined by projections over epistemic profiles: the output of a merging process completely depends on the beliefs of the agent d and the integrity constraints:
Projective Operator: $\nabla^\pi(\Phi, \succeq) = \succeq^{\text{lex}(\succeq, \succeq_d)}$

The projective operator is actually an ES basic merging operator that satisfies **(ESF-SD)**, **(ESF-P)**, **(ESF-I)** and **(ESF-D)** [24]. It is also easy to see that the projective operator satisfies **(ESF-NI)** and it is strategy-proof with respect to Kelly's belief lifting. Thus, from Proposition 3 we get that **(ESF-S)** also holds. Moreover, ∇^π is manipulable through the precise-leximax belief lifting: assume an epistemic profile Φ, a pair w, w' in $\mathcal{W}_\mathcal{P}$ and a pair $\succeq$, $\succeq^*$ in $\mathcal{E}$, such that $max(\succeq) = max(\succeq_d) = \{w, w'\}$ and $max(\succeq^*) = \{w\}$. From (B-Rep) we get $B(\nabla^\pi(\Phi, \succeq)) \equiv \varphi_{w,w'}$ and $B(\nabla^\pi(\Phi[\succeq^*/d], \succeq)) \equiv \varphi_w$. Now, since $w \simeq_d w'$, we get $(w) \succeq_{\succeq_d}^{\text{plm}} (w, w')$ and $(w) \succeq_{\succeq_d}^{\text{plm}} (w', w)$. Thus, $\varphi_w \sqsupset_{\succeq_d}^{\text{plm}} \varphi_{w,w'}$, that is, $B(\nabla^\pi(\Phi[\succeq^*/d], \succeq)) \sqsupset_{\succeq_d}^{\text{plm}} B(\nabla^\pi(\Phi, \succeq))$. This shows the manipulability of ∇^π.

The *Σ-projective operator*[5], $\nabla^{\Sigma\pi}$, is defined using sum and projections:
Σ-projective Operator: $\nabla^{\Sigma\pi}(\Phi, \succeq) = \succeq^{\text{lex}(\succeq, \succeq_\Phi^{\Sigma\pi})}$; where $\succeq_\Phi^{\Sigma\pi} = \succeq^{\text{lex}(\succeq_d, \succeq_\Phi^\Sigma)}$.

---

[4] Given by $r_i(x) = max\{n \in \mathbb{N} : \exists\, x_0, \ldots, x_n \text{ s.t. } x_{k+1} \succ_i x_k \text{ and } x_n = x\}$.
[5] The Σ-projective operator is exactly the Σ-pseudoprojective operator stated in [24].

The Σ-projective operator is structure preserving[6] and it satisfies **(ESF-SD)**, **(ESF-P)** and **(ESF-D)** but **(ESF-I)** does not hold [24]. Furthermore, it is not hard to see that it also satisfies **(ESF-NI)** and **(ESF-S)**.

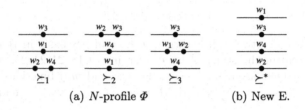

(a) N-profile Φ (b) New E.

Fig. 1. Manipulability situation for the Σ-projective operator.

The Σ-projective operator is absolutely manipulable. To show that, we suppose $\mathcal{W}_\mathcal{P} = \{w_1, w_2, w_3, w_4\}$ and consider the following situation[7]: the epistemic profile Φ represented in Fig. 1(a), the epistemic state $\succeq^*$ given in Fig. 1(b) and a restriction $\succeq$ in $\mathcal{E}$ such that $[\![B(\succeq)]\!] = \{w_1, w_2\}$. Simple calculations lead us to $w_2 \succ_\Phi^\Sigma w_1$ and $w_1 \succ_{\Phi[\succeq^*/1]}^\Sigma w_2$. Thus, since $w_1 \simeq_3 w_2$, we obtain $w_2 \succ_\Phi^{\Sigma\pi} w_1$ and $w_1 \succ_{\Phi[\succeq^*/1]}^{\Sigma\pi} w_2$ and, by (B-Rep), $B(\nabla^{\Sigma\pi}(\Phi, \succeq)) \equiv \varphi_{w_2}$ and $B(\nabla^{\Sigma\pi}(\Phi[\succeq^*/1], \succeq)) \equiv \varphi_{w_1}$. Then, since $w_1 \succ_{\succeq_1}^{\Sigma\pi} w_2$, for any belief lifting $\succeq \mapsto \sqsupseteq_\succeq$ we get $B(\nabla^{\Sigma\pi}(\Phi[\succeq^*/1], \succeq)) \sqsupset_{\succeq_{\succeq_1}} B(\nabla^{\Sigma\pi}(\Phi, \succeq))$, as desired.

6   Concluding Remarks

We have stated a general result of manipulability for ES basic merging operators that shows a dichotomy between absolute G-manipulation and the existence of a dictator when some rational properties are involved. One interesting feature of our approach is that it allows to instantiate the strategy-proofness result to different representations of epistemic states: ordinal conditional functions, rational relations, and of course total preorders. However, with the representation of epistemic states as formulas, our results do not hold because it is impossible to have the standard domain condition in the presence of a good representation of beliefs, namely, the max condition [24]. This fact reveals the necessity of using complex epistemic states if we want properties like standard domain to hold.

Exploiting the dichotomy obtained from these results, it is possible to determine when an ES merging operator is absolutely G-manipulable: exactly when it satisfies the standard domain condition and does not admit Arrovian dictators (cf. Theorem 4). This technique leads us to determine that ES merging operators with good behaviour, like *sum*, are absolutely G-manipulable.

---

[6] Its assignment is the identity in single profiles.

[7] We may also use this situation to show the absolute manipulation of sum and max.

Although our results also reveal that, under rational properties, strategy-proofness entails the existence of a dictator, it is surprising to find a dictatorial operator which is absolutely manipulable, namely the Σ-projective operator. This fact shows that strategy-proofness cannot be characterized in terms of Arrovian dictators.

References

1. Arrow, K.: Social Choice and Individual Values, 1st edn. Wiley, New York (1951)
2. Barberà, S.: Manipulation of social decision functions. J. Econom. Theory **15**(2), 266–278 (1977)
3. Barberà, S., Bossert, W., Pattanaik, P.K.: Ranking sets of objects, Handbook of Utility Theory, vol. 2, chap. 17, pp. 893–978. Kluwer Publisher (2004)
4. Benferhat, S., Konieczny, S., Papini, O., Pino Pérez, R.: Iterated revision by epistemic states: Axioms, semantics and syntax. In: Proceedings of the 14th European Conference on Artificial Intelligence, pp. 13–17. ECAI 2000. IOS Press, NLD (2000)
5. Chopra, S., Ghose, A.K., Meyer, T.A.: Social choice theory, belief merging, and strategy-proofness. Inf. Fusion **7**(1), 61–79 (2006)
6. Darwiche, A., Pearl, J.: On the logic of iterated belief revision. Artif. Intell. **89**, 1–29 (1997)
7. Duggan, J., Schwartz, T.: Strategic manipulability without resoluteness or shared beliefs: Gibbard-Satterthwaite generalized. Soc. Choice Welfare **17**(1), 85–93 (2000)
8. Eckert, D., Pigozzi, G.: Belief merging, judgment aggregation and some links with social choice theory. In: Delgrande, J., Lang, J., Rott, H., Tallon, J.M. (eds.) Belief Change in Rational Agents: Perspectives from Artificial Intelligence, Philosophy, and Economics. No. 05321 in Dagstuhl Seminar Proceedings, Internationales Begegnungs- und Forschungszentrum für Informatik (IBFI), Schloss Dagstuhl, Germany, Dagstuhl, Germany (2005)
9. Everaere, P., Konieczny, S., Marquis, P.: The strategy-proofness landscape of merging. J. Artif. Intell. Res. (JAIR) **28**, 49–105 (2007)
10. Feldman, A.: Strongly nonmanipulable multi-valued collective choice rules. Public Choice **35**(3), 503–509 (1980)
11. de Finetti, B.: La prévision: Ses lois logiques, ses sources subjectives. Annales de l'Institut Henri Poincaré **17**, 1–68 (1937)
12. Gabbay, D., Pigozzi, G., Rodrigues, O.: Belief revision, belief merging and voting. In: Proceedings of the Seventh Conference on Logic and the Foundations of Games and Decision Theory (LOFT06), pp. 71–78 (2006)
13. Gärdenfors, P.: Manipulation of social choice functions. J. Econ. Theory **13**(2), 217–228 (1976)
14. Gibbard, A.: Manipulation of voting schemes: a general result. Econometrica **41**(4), 587–601 (1973)
15. Halpern, J.Y.: Defining relative likelihood in partially-ordered preferential structures. J. Artif. Intell. Res. **7**, 1–24 (1997)
16. Kelly, J.S.: Strategy-proofness and social choice functions without singlevaluedness. Econometrica **45**(2), 439–446 (1977)
17. Kelly, J.S.: Social Choice Theory: An Introduction. Springer-Verlag, Berlin (1988). https://doi.org/10.1007/978-3-662-09925-4

18. Konieczny, S., Pino Pérez, R.: Merging information under constraints: a logical framework. J. Log. Comput. **12**(5), 773–808 (2002)
19. Konieczny, S., Pino Pérez, R.: Propositional belief base merging or how to merge beliefs/goals coming from several sources and some links with social choice theory. Eur. J. Oper. Res. **160**(3), 785–802 (2005)
20. Konieczny, S., Pino Pérez, R.: Logic based merging. J. Philos. Logic **40**(2), 239–270 (2011)
21. Konieczny, S., Lang, J., Marquis, P.: DA^2 merging operators. Artif. Intell. **157**(1–2), 49–79 (2004), nonmonotonic Reasoning
22. Leal, J., Pino Pérez, R.: A weak version of Barberà-Kelly's theorem. Revista Colombiana de Matemáticas **51**, 173–194 (2017)
23. Mata Díaz, A., Pino Pérez, R.: Logic-based fusion of complex epistemic states. In: ECSQARU, pp. 398–409 (2011)
24. Mata Díaz, A., Pino Pérez, R.: Impossibility in belief merging. Artif. Intell. **251**, 1–34 (2017)
25. Mata Díaz, A., Pino Pérez, R.: Epistemic states, fusion and strategy-proofness. In: Fermé, E., Villata, S. (eds.) Proceedings of the 17th International Workshop on Non-Monotonic Reasoning, NMR-2018, 27–29 October 2018, Tempe, Arizona USA, pp. 176–185 (2018)
26. Mata Díaz, A., Pino Pérez, R.: Manipulability in logic-based fusion of belief bases: indexes vs. liftings. Revista Iberica de Sistemas e Tecnologias de Informačao (RISTI) 2019(E20), 490–503 (2019)
27. Satterthwaite, M.A.: Strategy-proofness and Arrow's conditions: existence and correspondence theorems for voting procedures and social welfare functions. J. Econ. Theory **10**(2), 187–217 (1975)
28. Sen, A.: Quasi-transitivity, rational choice and collective decisions. Rev. Econ. Stud. **36**(3), 381–393 (1969)
29. Suzumura, K.: Introduction. In: Arrow, K., Sen, A.K., Suzumura, K. (eds.) Handbook of Social Choice and Welfare, Volume 1 (Handbooks in Economics), pp. 1–32. North-Holland (2002)
30. Taylor, A.D.: The manipulability of voting systems. Am. Math. Mon. **109**(4), 321–337 (2002)
31. Taylor, A.D.: Social Choice and the Mathematics of Manipulation. Cambridge University Press, Cambridge (2005)
32. van Benthem, J., Girard, P., Roy, O.: Everything else being equal: a modal logic for ceteris paribus preferences. J. Philos. Log. **38**, 83–125 (2009)

Explanation with the Winter Value: Efficient Computation for Hierarchical Choquet Integrals

Christophe Labreuche[1,2(✉)] [iD]

[1] Thales Research and Technology, Palaiseau, France
christophe.labreuche@thalesgroup.com
[2] SINCLAIR AI Lab, Palaiseau, France

Abstract. Multi-Criteria Decision Aiding arises in many industrial applications where the user needs an explanation of the recommendation. We consider in particular an explanation taking the form of a contribution level assigned to each variable. Decision models are often hierarchical, and the influence is computed by the Winter value, which is an extension of the Shapley value on trees. The contribution of the paper is to propose an exact algorithm to compute efficiently the Winter values for a very general class of decision models known as the Choquet integral. The main idea of our algorithm is to prune the combinatorial structure on which the Winter value is computed, based on upper and lower bounds of the utility on subtrees. Extensive simulations show that this new algorithm provides very significant computation gains compared to the state of the art.

Keywords: Explanable AI · Winter value · Choquet integral

1 Introduction

The ability to explain AI algorithms is key in many domains [1]. We are interested in explaining decisions depending on several criteria. Multi-Criteria Decision Aiding (MCDA) aims at helping a decision maker to select one alternative among several on the basis of multiple and conflicting criteria [9]. A very versatile MCDA model is the *Hierarchical Choquet Integral* (HCI) model [3,23]. This latter is composed of a set of Choquet integrals organized in a hierarchical way, where the hierarchy comes from domain knowledge and eases the interpretability of the model. The Choquet integral generalizes the weighted sum and is able to capture various forms of interaction among criteria [7].

Example 1. The supervision of a metro line requires monitoring the satisfaction of passengers on a daily basis. It is measured from several quality criteria: P (Punctuality of the trains w.r.t. timetable), CT (number of Cancelled Trains), R (Regularity: mean time between two successive trains) and TTT (Train Travel Time: average journey time inside a train). These criteria are assessed against two

© Springer Nature Switzerland AG 2021
J. Vejnarová and N. Wilson (Eds.): ECSQARU 2021, LNAI 12897, pp. 471–485, 2021.
https://doi.org/10.1007/978-3-030-86772-0_34

types of hours (PH: Peak Hour; OPH: Off-Peak Hour), and three line segments in the metro line (M1, M2 and M3). At the end, there are $4 \times 3 \times 2 = 24$ elementary criteria.

The criteria are organized in a hierarchical way – see Fig. 1. The top node PQoS represents the Passengers' Quality of Service. The second level is a decomposition regarding the hour (PH vs. OPH). The next level separates the evaluation on each segment. For each hour type and segment, the four criteria (P,...,TTT) are also organized hierarchically. P and CT are related to the Planned Schedule (PS), whereas R and TTT are related to the Overall Train Travel (OTT).   ■

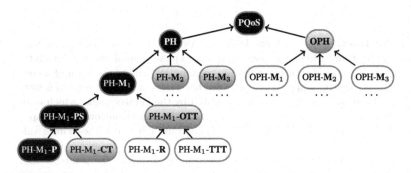

Fig. 1. Hierarchy of criteria for the supervision operator. The organization of the four elementary criteria (P,...,TTT) is only shown for node PH-M$_1$ for readability reasons. But they are also present of the others nodes, in place of "···".

In Ex. 1, the supervision operator wishes to know whether the current situation is preferred (according to the PQoS utility) to a situation of the past. As an explanation, the operator needs to understand which nodes in the tree are at the origin of this preference. This is obtained by computing an index measuring the influence of each node in the tree, on the preference between two options. This influence index can be computed to a leaf node like PH-M$_1$-P, or to an intermediate node like PH-M$_1$, as all nodes in the tree make sense to the user. There are many connections with *Feature Attribution* (FA)[1] in Machine Learning. Computing the level of contribution of a feature in a classification black-box model or that of a criterion in a MCDA model is indeed similar.

The Shapley value is one of the leading concepts for FA [29]. Unlike our situation, feature attribution only computes the influence of leaves in a model. It has been argued that the Shapley value is not appropriate on trees [16], when we are interested in knowing the contribution level of not only the leaves but also other nodes. A specific value for trees – called the Winter value – has been defined [16, 30]. The Winter value takes the form of a recursive call of the Shapley

---

[1] *Feature Attribution* consists in assessing the level of contribution of each feature in the prediction model for a particular instance [13, 26].

value at several nodes in the hierarchy. Our influence index applied to any node in a tree is thus obtained by the Winter value [16].

The main drawback of the Shapley and the Winter values is that their expressions contain an exponential number of terms in the number of inputs. Several approaches have been proposed to approximate the computation of the Shapley value [5,21]. The drawback of these methods is that it is hard to have accurate and reliable bounds of the error made. We explore another avenue in this paper. We first note that the Winter value (and also the Shapley value) can be written as an average added-value of a given attribute over a combinatorial structure. Taking inspiration from Branch & Bound (BB) algorithms, we develop a method that prunes the exploration of the combinatorial structure when computing the average. An advantage of our algorithm compared to the existing ones is that it is exact. We develop this idea when the aggregation functions are Choquet integrals. A major difficulty is to handle the hierarchy of aggregation models.

The aim of this paper is to propose an efficient algorithm to compute the Winter value on hierarchical Choquet integrals. Section 2 gives the reminders on MCDA, the Choquet integral and the Winter value. Section 3 presents a novel algorithm computing the Winter value, which prunes the underlying combinatorial structure. Our algorithm is not a simple adaptation of BB as these latters compute the optimal solution in a combinatorial structure whereas we need to compute the average value of a quantity over all leaves of the tree. Finally, for a general class of Choquet integrals (namely the 2-additive model), we experimentally demonstrate in Sect. 4 the efficiency of our algorithm on a large number of randomly generated trees and models.

2   Background

2.1   Multi-attribute Preference Model

We are interested in representing the preferences of a decision maker regarding how to compare several alternatives from a finite set A of attributes. Attribute $j \in A$ is depicted by a set X_j, and alternatives are elements of X_A, where $X_B := \times_{j \in B} X_j$ for any $B \subseteq A$. Preferences are assumed to be modeled by a numerical utility $u : X_A \to \mathbb{R}$. For $x \in X_A$ and $B \subseteq A$, x_B denotes the restriction of x on B.

In order to be interpretable, model u is organized in a hierarchical way. We consider a rooted tree $\mathcal{T}$ whose leaves are attributes A, and characterized by a set N of nodes (with $A \subset N$), a root node $r \in N \backslash A$, and the list of children $C(j)$ for every node j, with $C(j) \neq \emptyset$ iff $j \in N \backslash A$. Let $D(j)$ be the set of leaves which are descendants of j. For instance, $D(r) = A$ and $D(j) = \{j\}$ for every $j \in A$.

Following the tree structure, model u can be decomposed into a utility at each node $j \in N$ given the value of the alternative on its descendent leaves, i.e. $u_j : X_{D(j)} \to \mathbb{R}$. For $j \in N \backslash A$, u_j results from the aggregation of its children $C(j)$ by an aggregation function $F_j : \mathbb{R}^{C(j)} \to \mathbb{R}$, i.e. $u_j(x_{D(j)}) = F_j((u_h(x_{D(h)}))_{h \in C(j)})$.

At the end, for $x \in X_A$, the overall utility is $u(x) = u_r(x)$, where r is the root of the tree.

2.2 Aggregation Models

There exist many classes of aggregation functions. The Choquet integral is a powerful model able to capture interaction among criteria and thus to represent real-life decision strategies. It takes the form for $e \in \mathbb{R}^{C(j)}$ [12]:

$$F_j(e_{C(j)}) = \sum_{S \subseteq C(j)} \eta(S) \wedge_{h \in S} e_h, \tag{1}$$

where $\wedge$ is the minimum function, and $\eta : 2^{C(j)} \to \mathbb{R}$ are the Möbius coefficients with $\eta(\emptyset) = 0$. We refer the reader to [12] for the list of properties of the Choquet integral.

The drawback of this model is that it contains an exponential number of parameters. The k-additive Choquet integral restricts this complexity by enforcing that $\eta(S) = 0$ for all $|S| > k$. Value $k = 2$ is a good compromise between the versatility of the model and a reasonable number of unknowns.

Example 2 (Ex. 1 cont.). The aggregation functions are given by (For the sake of conciseness, we keep only the last letters in the name of the nodes): $F_{\text{PQoS}}(u_{\text{PH}}, u_{\text{OPH}}) = (u_{\text{PH}} + u_{\text{PH}} \wedge u_{\text{OPH}})/2$, $F_{\text{PH}}(u_{M_1}, u_{M_2}, u_{M_3}) = u_{M_1} \wedge u_{M_2} \wedge u_{M_3}$, $F_{\text{M1}}(u_{\text{PS}}, u_{\text{PS}}) = (u_{\text{PS}} + u_{\text{OTT}})/2$, and $F_{\text{PS}}(u_{\text{CT}}, u_{\text{P}}) = (u_{\text{CT}} + u_{\text{CT}} \wedge u_{\text{P}})/2$. The weights in these models are learnt from training examples provided by an expert [3,11]. ∎

2.3 Shapley and Winter Values

In Cooperative Game Theory, A is now the set of players, and we denote by $\mathcal{G}(A)$ the set of set functions on A (called *Transferable Utility (TU) games*) $v : 2^A \to \mathbb{R}$ satisfying $v(\emptyset) = 0$, where $v(S)$ (with $S \subseteq A$) is the wealth produced by players S when they form a coalition. The Shapley value is a fair share of the global wealth $v(A)$ produced by all players together, among themselves [28]. It gives $\text{Sh}_i^A(v)$ to player i:

$$\text{Sh}_i^A(v) = \mathcal{S}_i^A(\delta_i v), \tag{2}$$

where $\delta_i v \in \mathcal{G}(A \backslash \{i\})$ is defined by $\delta_i v(S) := v(S \cup \{i\}) - v(S)$, and $\mathcal{S}_i^A$ is defined on a game $v' \in \mathcal{G}(A \backslash \{i\})$ by $\mathcal{S}_i^A(v') = \sum_{S \subseteq A \backslash \{i\}} \mathcal{C}_a^s \, v'(S)$, with $\mathcal{C}_a^s := \frac{s!(a-s-1)!}{a!}$, and the notation that sets are denoted by capital letters (e.g. A, S) and their cardinality by the lower case letter (e.g. a, s).

When the set of players is organized in a hierarchical way with a nested coalition structure, it has been argued that the Shapley value is not consistent with the hierarchy, as the Shapley value at a coalition is not necessarily equal to the sum of the Shapley values of its members [16,25,30]. The Winter value has been defined to overcome this difficulty [30]. When computing the value of node

$i \in A$, the tree is restricted to the nodes at a distance at most 1 from the path from the root r to node i. For node $i =$PH-M$_1$-P in Example 1, the path from r to i is in black in Fig. 1, and the restricted tree is composed of the grey or black nodes. The path from the root of the tree to node i is denoted by $(p_0, p_1, \ldots, p_q)$ where $p_0 = r$ and $p_q = i$. For $m \in \{1, \ldots, q\}$, we set $N_m = C(p_{m-1})$ and $N'_m = N_m \backslash \{p_m\}$. The Winter value of node i is then a recursive application of $\mathcal{S}^{N_m}_{p_m}$ at all levels $m = 1, \ldots, q$ [16,18,30]:

$$\text{Win}_i(v) = \mathcal{S}^{N_1}_{p_1} \circ \mathcal{S}^{N_2}_{p_2} \circ \cdots \circ \mathcal{S}^{N_q}_{p_q}(\delta_i v) \tag{3}$$

$$= \sum_{S_1 \subseteq N'_1, \ldots, S_q \subseteq N'_q} \left[\prod_{m=1}^{q} \mathcal{C}^{s_m}_{n_m} \right] \times (v(S_1^q \cup \{i\}) - v(S_1^q)) \tag{4}$$

where $S_k^q := \cup^q_{m=k} S_m$ and $N'^q_k := \cup^q_{m=k} N'_m$ for $k \in \{1, \ldots, q\}$.

2.4 Explanation of Hierarchical MCDA

We are interested in an explanation of why an option $y \in X_A$ is preferred to another option $x \in X_A$ (i.e. $u(y) \geq u(x)$), taking the form of an influence index, denoted by $I_i(x, y)$, computed at each node $i \in A$. The idea is to consider compound alternatives $[y_S x]_A$ mixing the values of x and y, where $[y_S x]_T \in X_T$ is equal to y_j for $j \in S \cap T$ and to x_j if $j \in T \backslash S$. Then we define the contribution of node i based on its added-value $u([y_{\{i\}} t]_A) - u([x_{\{i\}} t]_A)$ for t taking all possible values $[y_S x]_{A \backslash \{i\}}$, $S \subseteq A \backslash \{i\}$ [16]. The influence of node i is then the Winter value of a particular game [16]:

$$I_i(x, y) = \text{Win}_i(v_u^A), \tag{5}$$

$$\text{where } v_u^T \in \mathcal{G}(T) \text{ is defined by} \quad v_u^T(S) = u([y_S x]_T) - u(x_T) \tag{6}$$

Index (5) is characterized by 5 axioms: *Null Attribute, Restricted Equal Treatment, Additivity, Generalized Efficiency* and *Consistency with Restricted Tree* [16].

3 Computation of the Explanation for Hierarchical Choquet Integrals

We present in this section a new algorithm to compute the influence index (5) of a given criterion $i \in A$ when all aggregation functions F_j are general Choquet integrals. We first give some pruning and recursive properties on the influence index and then we describe the exact algorithm.

3.1 Pruning and Recursive Properties

For the computation of the Winter value $I_i(x, y)$ w.r.t. $i \in A$, we only consider a restricted tree. For the sake of simplicity of the notation, we assume that the original tree is the restricted tree characterized by $p_1, \ldots, p_q, N_1, \ldots, N_q$. Hence the leaves are $A = D(p_0) = N'^q_1 \cup \{i\}$. In order to avoid cumbersome notation, we assume that the utility functions at the leaves are the identity function. Hence $X_j = \mathbb{R}$ for all $j \in A$. For an option $z \in X_A$, we denote by z_j (for $j \in N \backslash A$) the utility $u_j(z_{D(j)})$.

Example 3 (Ex. 2 cont.). We will illustrate our approach on the influence of criterion PH-M$_1$-P when comparing two alternatives x and y given in Table 1. For the sake of concision, we keep only the last letters in the labels of the nodes. For instance, PH-M$_1$-P is simply noted P. In the restricted tree, $A = \{P, CT, OTT, M_2, M_3, OPH\}$. In Table 1, the values of x and y on the leaves A are in white, while their values on the other nodes are in grey (obtained by using the aggregation functions). ∎

We set $\underline{z}_j = \min(x_j, y_j)$ and $\overline{z}_j = \max(x_j, y_j)$ for all $j \in N$. In the recursive application of (3), we will fix at some point the subsets at levels from 1 to a value h, yielding option $\chi = [y_S x]_{N'^h_1}$ with $S \subseteq N'^h_1$. Now for $z \in X_A$, we introduce alternative $z^{S,h}$ taking the fixed value χ at levels lower or equal to h, and the value of z for levels strictly larger than h. For $l \in \{1, \ldots, q\}$ and $j \in A \cap N_l$, we have

$$z_j^{S,h} = \begin{cases} y_j & \text{if } l \leq h \text{ and } j \in S \\ x_j & \text{if } l \leq h \text{ and } j \notin S \\ z_j & \text{if } l > h \end{cases}$$

For $j \in N \backslash A$, we set $z_j^{S,h} = u_j(z_{D(j)}^{S,h})$. For $z = \overline{z}$ (resp. $z = \underline{z}$), $z_j^{S,h}$ is the best (resp. worst) possible value at node j when we fix the values to χ at the nodes having a depth lower or equal to h.

Example 4 (Ex. 3 cont.). Vector $\overline{z}^{\{M_2\},3}$ (resp. $\underline{z}^{\{M_2\},3}$), takes the value of $\overline{z}$ (resp. $\underline{z}$) for leaves of levels at least 4 (i.e. P, CT). The elements in black in Table 1 are the leaves of level at most 3. They are fixed to y for leaf in $S = \{M_2\}$ and to x for the other leaves OTT, M$_3$, OPH. Finally the components in grey are the ones that are deduced from the application of the aggregation functions.

In $\overline{z}^{\{M_2, OTT\},3}$ and $\underline{z}^{\{M_2, OTT\},3}$, we take value 0.65 of y on OTT. ∎

Instead of directly applying the nested sum of (4), we will use the recursive formulae (3). We first apply $\mathcal{S}^{N_1}_{p_1}$ and fix thus a subset $S_1 \subseteq N'_1$. We analyze, as in a BB algorithm whether this fixed subset S_1 implies some pruning or simplification on the remaining term $\mathcal{S}^{N_2}_{p_2} \circ \cdots \circ \mathcal{S}^{N_q}_{p_q}(\delta_i v)$. If it is not the case, we apply $\mathcal{S}^{N_2}_{p_2}$ and fix thus a subset $S_2 \subseteq N'_2$. And so on.

In order to support this recursive process, we denote by $J_i^{m,h}(f, S)$ (with $0 \leq m \leq h \leq q$) the influence of node i w.r.t. a function $f : X_{D(p_m)} \to \mathbb{R}$ defined

Table 1. Values of $x, y, \underline{z}, \overline{z}, \underline{z}^{S,h}, \overline{z}^{S,h}$ for $S = \{M_2\}, \{M_2, OTT\}$, and $h = 3$.

Tree	PQoS	PH	M₁	PS	P	CT	OTT	M₂	M₃	OPH
Level	0 (p_0)	1 (p_1)	2 (p_2)	3 (p_3)	4 (p_4)	4	3	2	2	1
y	0.25	0.4	0.625	0.6	0.7	0.6	0.65	0.4	0.7	0.1
x	0.05	0.1	0.175	0.15	0.1	0.2	0.2	0.1	0.8	0
$\overline{z}$	0.25	0.4	0.625	0.6	0.7	0.6	0.65	0.4	0.8	0.1
$\underline{z}$	0.05	0.1	0.175	0.15	0.1	0.2	0.2	0.1	0.7	0
$\overline{z}^{\{M_2\},3}$	0.2	0.4	0.4	0.6	0.7	0.6	0.2	0.4	0.8	0
$\underline{z}^{\{M_2\},3}$	0.088	0.175	0.175	0.15	0.1	0.2	0.2	0.4	0.8	0
$\overline{z}^{\{M_2,OTT\},3}$	0.2	0.4	0.625	0.6	0.7	0.6	0.65	0.4	0.8	0
$\underline{z}^{\{M_2,OTT\},3}$	0.2	0.4	0.4	0.15	0.1	0.2	0.65	0.4	0.8	0

at node p_m (with $D(p_m) = N'^q_{m+1} \cup \{i\}$) when subsets $S_{m+1}, \ldots, S_h$ are fixed (with $S = S^h_{m+1}$):

$$J_i^{m,h}(f, S) = \mathcal{S}_{p_{h+1}}^{N_{h+1}} \circ \cdots \circ \mathcal{S}_{p_q}^{N_q}(\delta_i v) \tag{7}$$

where $v \in \mathcal{G}(D(p_h))$ is given by $v(T) = v_f^{D(p_m)}(T \cup S)$, and $v_f^{D(p_m)}$ is defined by (6).

The next lemma initiates the recursion.

Lemma 1.
$$I_i(x, y) = J_i^{0,0}(u_{p_0}, \emptyset) \tag{8}$$

Example 5 (Ex. 4 cont.). $I_P(x, y) = J_P^{0,0}(u_{PQoS}, \emptyset)$. ∎

As for I_i, operator $J_i^{m,h}(f, S)$ is linear in its function f. The next result is then obtained by using the linearity (1) of the Choquet integral.

Lemma 2. *For* $m \leq h < q$

$$J_i^{m,h}(u_{p_m}, S) = \eta(\{p_{m+1}\}) J_i^{m,h}(u_{p_{m+1}}, S) \tag{9}$$
$$+ \sum_{T \subseteq N_{m+1}: p_{m+1} \in T, |T| > 1} \eta(T) J_i^{m,h}(\wedge_{j \in T} u_j, S)$$

Example 6 (Ex. 5 cont.). As $u_{PQoS} = (u_{PH} + u_{PH} \wedge u_{OPH})/2$, we have $J_P^{0,0}(u_{PQoS}, \emptyset) = \frac{1}{2} J_P^{0,0}(u_{PH}, \emptyset) + \frac{1}{2} J_P^{0,0}(u_{PH} \wedge u_{OPH}, \emptyset)$. ∎

As most of the terms in (9) correspond to a min function, we derive efficient pruning strategies for the min. For instance, the computation of $J_i^{m,h}(u_{p_{m+1}} \wedge u_j, S)$ requires to explore $u_j \in \{x_j, y_j\}$, $u_i \in \{x_i, y_i\}$ and $S_{m+2} \subseteq N'_{m+2}, \ldots, S_q \subseteq N'_q$. If u_j is always lower than $u_{p_{m+1}}$, whatever the choice of $u_j, u_i, S_{m+2}, \ldots, S_q$, then $u_{p_{m+1}}$ is drowned by u_j so that there is no influence of changing x_i to y_i. Hence $J_i^{m,h}(u_{p_{m+1}} \wedge u_j, S) = 0$. We generalize this example in the next result.

Lemma 3. *Let $T \subseteq N_{m+1}$ with $p_{m+1} \in T$. If $\exists j \in T \setminus \{p_{m+1}\}$ such that*

$$z_{p_{m+1}}^{S,h} \geq \overline{z}_j^{S,h}$$

then

$$J_i^{m,h}(\wedge_{j \in T} u_j, S) = 0 \tag{10}$$

Example 7 (Ex. 6 cont.). As $\{x_{PH}, y_{PH}\} \geq \{x_{OPH}, y_{OPH}\}$, we have $z_{PH}^{\emptyset,0} = 0.1 \geq \overline{z}_{OPH}^{\emptyset,0} = 0.1$. Thus by Lemma 3, $J_P^{0,0}(u_{PH} \wedge u_{OPH}, \emptyset) = 0$. Hence $J_P^{0,0}(u_{PQoS}, \emptyset) = \frac{1}{2} J_P^{0,0}(u_{PH}, \emptyset)$. ∎

Term $J_P^{0,0}(u_{PH}, \emptyset)$ computes the influence of a function defined on the top node PQoS; but its argument is a function depending only on the first variables u_{PH} and not on the other criteria N'_1. The following lemma shows that we can skip the sum $\mathcal{S}_{p_{h+1}}^{N_{h+1}}$ over $S_1 \subseteq N'_1$.

Lemma 4. *For $m \leq h < q$*

$$J_i^{m,h}(u_{p_{m+1}}, S) = J_i^{m+1,(m+1)\vee h}(u_{p_{m+1}}, S \cap D(p_{m+1})) \tag{11}$$

Example 8 (Ex. 7 cont.). Hence $J_P^{0,0}(u_{PH}, \emptyset) = J_P^{1,1}(u_{PH}, \emptyset)$. ∎

The first operation in $J_i^{m,h}(\wedge_{j \in T} u_j, S)$ is the sum over $S_{h+1} \subseteq N'_{h+1}$ appearing in $\mathcal{S}_{p_{h+1}}^{N_{h+1}}$. Due to the specificity of the min operator, we can in general reduce the computation complexity by removing some elements of N'_{h+1} in the sum. More specifically, any element $j \in N'_{h+1}$ belongs to one of the following cases:

- Case 1 (set N_{h+1}^-): The value on j does not influence $\delta_i v$ in (7) and thus j can be removed from the sum;
- Case 2 (set N_{h+1}^x): Term $\delta_i v$ in the sum is zero when j takes value y. Thus there remains only the case where the value on j is equal to x in the sum;
- Case 3 (set N_{h+1}^y): Likewise there remains only the value of j equal to y in the sum;
- Case 4 (set N_{h+1}^{xy}): j can take values x or y.

At the end, the elements in set N_{h+1}^- completely disappear from the expression, and the sum over N_{h+1}' is restricted to only a sum over N_{h+1}^{xy}. Sets N_{h+1}^x and N_{h+1}^y constraint the value that j can take. Lastly, the support of $\wedge_{j\in T} u_j$ can be reduced. The support of the min may vary for each subset $\widehat{S}$ and is given by $T^{\widehat{S},h} \subseteq T$.

Lemma 5. *Let $T \subseteq N_{m+1}$ with $p_{m+1} \in T$. We have*

$$J_i^{m,h}(\wedge_{j\in T} u_j, S)$$
$$= \sum_{S' \subseteq N_{h+1}^{xy}} \mathcal{C}_{n_{h+1}^x + n_{h+1}^y + n_{h+1}^{xy}}^{s' + n_{h+1}^y} J_i^{m,h+1}\left(\wedge_{j\in T^{S\cup S'},h+1} u_j, S\cup S' \cup N_{h+1}^y\right) \quad (12)$$

where

- $T^{S,h} = \{j \in T : \underline{z}_j^{S,h} < \overline{z}_{p_{m+1}}^{S,h}\}$
- $N_{h+1}^- = \{j \in N_{h+1}' : y_j = x_j \text{ or } j \notin T^{S,h}\}$ *if $h = m$, and $N_{h+1}^- = \{j \in N_{h+1}' : y_j = x_j\}$ else*
- $N_{h+1}^x = \{j \in N_{h+1}' \backslash N_{h+1}^- : y_j \le \underline{z}_{p_{h+1}}\}$
- $N_{h+1}^y = \{j \in N_{h+1}' \backslash N_{h+1}^- : x_j \le \underline{z}_{p_{h+1}}\}$
- $N_{h+1}^{xy} = \{j \in N_{h+1}' \backslash N_{h+1}^- : \underline{z}_j > \underline{z}_{p_{h+1}}\}$

We first illustrate the case where the sum over N_{h+1}^{xy} is composed of only one term, and one element from T is removed in the min.

Example 9 (Ex. 8 cont.). <u>Sum at level 2:</u> $J_P^{1,1}(u_{PH}, \emptyset) = J_P^{1,1}(u_{M_1} \wedge u_{M_2} \wedge u_{M_3}, \emptyset)$. Criterion M_3 is removed from the min (i.e. $T = \{M_1, M_2, M_3\}$ but $T^{\emptyset,1} = \{M_1, M_2\}$) as $\underline{z}_{M_3}^{\emptyset,1} = \underline{z}_{M_3} = 0.7 \ge \overline{z}_{M_1}^{\emptyset,1} = \overline{z}_{M_1} = 0.625$. Intuitively, M_3 is removed as the min can never be reached by M_3. Hence $N_2^- = \{M_3\}$. Moreover $N_2^x = \emptyset$; $N_2^y = \{M_2\}$ as $x_{M_2} = 0.1 \le \underline{z}_{M_1} = 0.175$; $N_2^{xy} = \emptyset$. Hence there is only one term in the sum: $I_P(x,y) = \frac{1}{2}J_P^{1,2}(u_{M_1} \wedge u_{M_2}, \{M_2\})$.   ∎

We now develop the computation of $J_P^{1,2}(u_{M_1} \wedge u_{M_2}, \{M_2\})$.

Example 10 (Ex. 9 cont.). <u>Sum at level 3:</u> We have $T^{\{M_2\},2} = \{M_1, M_2\}$ as $\underline{z}_{M_2}^{\{M_2\},2} = y_{M_2} = 0.4 < \overline{z}_{M_1}^{\{M_2\},2} = \overline{z}_{M_1} = 0.625$. Moreover $N_3^- = \emptyset$; $N_3^x = \emptyset$; $N_3^y = \emptyset$; $N_3^{xy} = \{OTT\}$ as $\underline{z}_{OTT} = 0.2 > \underline{z}_{PS} = 0.15$. As $N_3^{xy} \ne \emptyset$, there are thus two terms in the sum. The support of the min for these two terms is $T^{\{M_2\},3} = \{M_1\}$ as we remove M_2 from $T^{\{M_2\},2}$ (because $\underline{z}_{M_2}^{\{M_2\},3} = 0.4 \ge \overline{z}_{M_1}^{\{M_2\},3} = 0.4$), and $T^{\{M_2,OTT\},3} = \{M_1, M_2\}$ as $\underline{z}_{M_2}^{\{M_2,OTT\},3} = 0.4 < \overline{z}_{M_1}^{\{M_2,OTT\},3} = 0.625$. Hence $I_P(x,y) = \frac{1}{2}J_P^{1,2}(u_{M_1} \wedge u_{M_2}, \{M_2\}) = \frac{1}{4}J_P^{1,3}(u_{M_1}, \{M_2\}) + \frac{1}{4}J_P^{1,3}(u_{M_1} \wedge u_{M_2}, \{M_2, OTT\})$.   ∎

We use the previous results to further prune the computation.

Example 11 (Ex. 10 cont.). We have $J_{\mathrm{P}}^{1,3}(u_{\mathrm{M}_1} \wedge u_{\mathrm{M}_2}, \{\mathrm{M}_2, \mathrm{OTT}\}) = 0$ by Lemma 3 as $\underline{z}_{\mathrm{M}_1}^{\{\mathrm{M}_2,\mathrm{OTT}\},3} = 0.4 \geq \overline{z}_{\mathrm{M}_2}^{\{\mathrm{M}_2,\mathrm{OTT}\},3} = 0.4$. Hence $I_{\mathrm{P}}(x,y) = \frac{1}{4}J_{\mathrm{P}}^{1,3}(u_{\mathrm{M}_1}, \{\mathrm{M}_2\})$.

By Lemma 4, $J_{\mathrm{P}}^{1,3}(u_{\mathrm{M}_1}, \{\mathrm{M}_2\}) = J_{\mathrm{P}}^{2,3}(u_{\mathrm{M}_1}, \emptyset)$. By Lemma 2, $J_{\mathrm{P}}^{2,3}(u_{\mathrm{M}_1}, \emptyset) = \frac{1}{2}J_{\mathrm{P}}^{2,3}(u_{\mathrm{PS}}, \emptyset)$ as $u_{\mathrm{M}_1} = \frac{u_{\mathrm{PS}} + u_{\mathrm{OTT}}}{2}$. By Lemma 4, $J_{\mathrm{P}}^{2,3}(u_{\mathrm{PS}}, \emptyset) = J_{\mathrm{P}}^{3,3}(u_{\mathrm{PS}}, \emptyset)$. By Lemma 2, $J_{\mathrm{P}}^{3,3}(u_{\mathrm{PS}}, \emptyset) = \frac{1}{2}J_{\mathrm{P}}^{3,3}(u_{\mathrm{P}} \wedge u_{\mathrm{CT}}, \emptyset)$. Hence $I_{\mathrm{P}}(x,y) = \frac{1}{16}J_{\mathrm{P}}^{3,3}(u_{\mathrm{P}} \wedge u_{\mathrm{CT}}, \emptyset)$.

<u>Sum at level 4 with Lemma 5:</u> $T^{\emptyset,3} = \{\mathrm{P}, \mathrm{CT}\}$ as $\underline{z}_{\mathrm{CT}}^{\emptyset,3} = z_{\mathrm{CT}} = 0.2 < \overline{z}_{\mathrm{P}}^{\emptyset,3} = \overline{z}_{\mathrm{P}} = 0.7$. Moreover $N_3^- = \emptyset$; $N_3^x = \emptyset$; $N_3^y = \emptyset$; $N_3^{xy} = \{\mathrm{CT}\}$ as $z_{\mathrm{CT}} = 0.2 > \underline{z}_{\mathrm{P}} = 0.1$. Hence $I_{\mathrm{P}}(x,y) = \frac{1}{32}J_{\mathrm{P}}^{3,4}(u_{\mathrm{P}} \wedge u_{\mathrm{CT}}, \emptyset) + \frac{1}{32}J_{\mathrm{P}}^{3,4}(u_{\mathrm{P}} \wedge u_{\mathrm{CT}}, \{\mathrm{CT}\})$. ∎

The last result describes the formula when we reach leaf i at the final level q.

Lemma 6.

$$J_i^{m,q}(v, S) = v\big([y_{S \cup \{i\}}x]_{D(p_m)}\big) - v\big([y_S x]_{D(p_m)}\big)$$

Example 12 (Ex. 11 cont.). By Lemma 6, $I_{\mathrm{P}}(x,y) = {}^{1}/_{32}\big[y_{\mathrm{P}} \wedge x_{\mathrm{CT}} - x_{\mathrm{P}} \wedge x_{\mathrm{CT}}\big] + {}^{1}/_{32}\big[y_{\mathrm{P}} \wedge y_{\mathrm{CT}} - x_{\mathrm{P}} \wedge y_{\mathrm{CT}}\big] = {}^{0.1}/_{32} + {}^{0.5}/_{32} = {}^{0.6}/_{32}$. ∎

Finally in the example, the computation of $I_{\mathrm{P}}(x,y)$ requires only the computation of two differences (the other terms being zero). By contrast, the mere application of (5) and (4) requires the computation of $2^1 \times 2^2 \times 2^1 \times 2^1 = 32$ differences.

3.2 Algorithm for Hierarchical Choquet Integrals

We introduce Algorithms 1 and 2 defining functions I_{Sin} and I_{Min} respectively, where $I_{\mathrm{Sin}}(i, m, h, S)$ returns the influence of node i on u_{p_k} and $I_{\mathrm{Min}}(i, T, m, h, S)$ returns the influence of node i on $\wedge_{j \in T} u_j$. The next result shows that index $I_i(x,y)$ is the result of $I_{\mathrm{Sin}}(i, 0, 0, \emptyset)$.

Function $I_{\mathrm{Sin}}(i, m, h, S)$:
1   **If** $m = q$ **and** $h = q$ **then**
2   $\quad$ **return** $u_i(y_i) - u_i(x_i)$
3   **Else**
4   $\quad$ $r \leftarrow 0$
5   $\quad$ **For** $T \subseteq N'_{m+1}$
6   $\quad\quad$ **If** $p_{m+1} \in T$ **and** $\eta(T) \neq 0$ **then**
7   $\quad\quad\quad$ **If** $|T| = 1$ **then**
8   $\quad\quad\quad\quad$ $r \leftarrow r + \eta(T) \times I_{\mathrm{Sin}}(i, m+1, (m+1) \vee h, S \cap D(p_{m+1}))$
10 $\quad\quad\quad$ **Else**
11 $\quad\quad\quad\quad$ $r \leftarrow r + \eta(T) \times I_{\mathrm{Min}}(i, T, m, h, S)$
12 $\quad$ **return** r

Algorithm 1: Function I_{Sin} (Sin stands for singleton).

Function $I_{\text{Min}}(i, T, m, h, S)$:

1 **If** $\exists l \in T \setminus \{p_{m+1}\}$ s.t. $\underline{z}_{p_{m+1}}^{S,h} \geq \overline{z}_j^{S,h}$ **then**

2 $\quad$ **return** 0

3 **ElseIf** $h = q$ **then**

4 $\quad$ **return** $\wedge_{j \in T} u_j\big([y_{S \cup \{i\}} x]_{D(p_m)}\big) - \wedge_{j \in T} u_j\big([y_S x]_{D(p_m)}\big)$

5 **Else**

6 $\quad r \leftarrow 0$

7 $\quad$ **For** $S' \subseteq N_{h+1}^{xy}$

8 $\quad\quad r \leftarrow r + C_{n_{h+1}^x + n_{h+1}^y + n_{h+1}^{xy}}^{s' + n_{h+1}^y} \times I_{\text{Min}}(i, T^{S \cup S', h+1}, m, h+1, S \cup S' \cup N_{h+1}^y)$

9 $\quad$ **return** r

Algorithm 2: Function I_{Min} for $\wedge_{j \in T} u_j$, with $T \subseteq N_{m+1}$.

Theorem 1. $I_i(x, y)$ *is given by* $I_{\text{Sin}}(i, 0, 0, \emptyset)$.

The application of $I_{\text{Sin}}(i, 0, 0, \emptyset)$ is denoted by WINT-P, where P stands for *Pruned*. In order to assess the efficiency of this algorithm, we compare it in the next section to the mere application of (5) and (4) – denoted by WINT.

4 Experimental Analysis of the Computation Time

We are interested in this section on comparing the computation time of WINT-P compared to WINT. In the general case, we cannot obtain interesting bounds between these two algorithms. In the best case, WINT-P can prune the tree at the highest level and requires only a few operations while WINT is exponential in the number of criteria. In the worst case, there might be no pruning in WINT-P, so that the whole tree $N_1' \times \cdots \times N_q'$ needs to be explored, as for WINT. However, there are extra-computation operations in WINT-P for testing whether the pruning conditions apply. As a consequence, we need an experimental comparison of the computation time of WINT-P and WINT, from randomly generated instances, which is the aim of this section. We restrict ourselves to 2-additive Choquet integrals. We denote by C_{WINT} the complexity of algorithm WINT, and by $C_{\text{WINT-P}}$ the complexity of our new algorithm WINT-P.

We randomly generate more than 100 000 trees, with $|A|$ ranging from 2 to 100, the depth between 1 and 6, and the number of children between 2 and 6. For each tree, we randomly generate two instances x and y. We also randomly generate 2-additive Choquet integrals at each aggregation node.

Figure 2 shows the value of $R = \frac{C_{\text{WINT}}}{C_{\text{WINT-P}}}$. Ratio R is on average increasing with $|A|$. We first analyze the cases where WINT-P is more time consuming than WINT, i.e. $R < 1$. This occurs in 0.2% of instances when $|A| \leq 20$, in 0.05% of instances when $21 < |A| \leq 30$, in 0.009% when $31 < |A| \leq 50$, and never occurs when $|A| > 50$. In the worst cases, ratio R is never below 0.33 whatever $|A|$, is never below 0.5 when $|A| > 20$, and is never below 1.2 when $|A| > 50$. Moreover, ratio R is of order 100 for $|A| > 50$. Lastly, the computation time $C_{\text{WINT-BB}}$ is acceptable as it is below 1s in most instances.

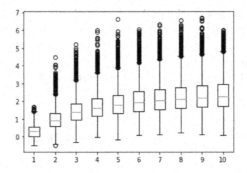

Fig. 2. Boxplots of $\log_{10}(R)$ where the mth graph ($m \in \{1, \ldots, 10\}$) considers only the instances with $|A| \in [10(m-1) + 1, 10m]$.

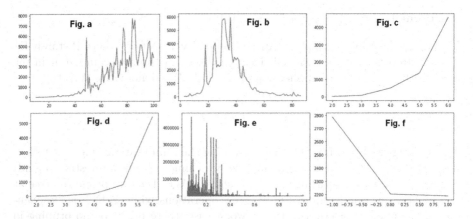

Fig. 3. PDP of each variable vs. ratio R (Y-axis). The variable (in the X-axis) is the number of criteria $|A|$ for Fig. a, the number of aggregation nodes $|N \backslash A|$ for Fig. b, the tree depth for Fig. c, the maximal value of $|C(i)|$ for Fig. d, the *interactionRate* for Fig. e and the *sign* for Fig. f.

In the experiments, we also analyze how the computation gain R depends on the following six variables: the number of criteria $|A|$, the number of aggregation nodes $|N \backslash A|$, the tree depth, the maximal value of $|C(i)|$, the *interactionRate* and the *sign*. Figure 3 shows the Partial Dependent Plots (PDP) of each of these variables vs. ratio R.

Figure 3.a shows that there is a very large improvement of computation time when the attributes number is beyond 40. According to Fig. 3.b, the improvement is the largest when the number of aggregation nodes is around 30–40. When the number of aggregation nodes is very large (above 60), the average number of children is small and thus the pruning strategy is less efficient. The average improvement rate grows exponentially with the depth of the tree and the number of children – see Fig. 3.c and 3.d. As expected, we see that there are more improvements for smaller values of the rate *interactionRate* of non-zero Möbius coefficients – see Fig. 3.e. Above 0.5 there is no significant difference. Finally, the sign of the interaction does not really influence the performance (Fig. 3.f). It is an interesting feature of our approach not to rely on a special convexity or concavity of the model, unlike some existing works [10].

5   Related Works

The problem of assessing the contribution level of variables has received a lot of attention in many domains and can be split into two classes. In the first one, there is no dataset. A typical example is Global Sensitivity Analysis (GSA) aiming at allocating the uncertainty in the output of a model on the different sources of uncertainty in the model input [27]. The Shapley values have been recently used in GSA as an alternative to the Sobol' indices to better account for dependent inputs [24]. In MCDA, the *compellingness* is based on the local weight of variables [4,15]. However, it returns counter-intuitive behaviors as it fails to satisfy some important properties [16].

The second class uses a dataset [26]. The Shapley value has recently become popular in Machine Learning (ML) for feature attribution [8,19,20,22,29]. What distinguishes these methods is the game on which the Shapley value is computed. The exponential number of terms in the expression of the Shapley value implies that its brute-force computation takes unreasonable long time even for 20 inputs. Several methods have been developed to reduce its computational time. The Shapley value can be rewritten as an average of the contribution of a variable over all possible permutations of the set of variables. This value can be approximated by sampling the set of permutations [5,21] (see [8,29] in the context of ML). The second approach is based on the fact that the Shapley value is the unique solution of a convex optimization problem under linear constraints [19]. Lastly the Shapley value is approximated by restricting coalitions to the neighbor features in the graph of conditional dependencies among features [6].

6   Conclusion

The Winter value, which is an extension of the Shapley value on trees, is used to identify which attributes mostly contribute to the decision. A bottleneck for the practical usage of these two values is their exponential number of terms. While most of existing works propose approximate algorithms, the originality of our approach is to define an exact algorithm that prunes the combinatorial structure of the Winter value. We consider the case of a hierarchical MCDA model composed of Choquet integrals. We first give some recursive properties of the influence, and then derive an exact algorithm where the combinatorial structure is pruned based on upper and lower bounds on subtrees. Extensive experiments on randomly generated instances show a significant improvement of the computation time over the current algorithm.

Our approach can be extended in several directions. First, we could address a wider classes of models, and in particular fuzzy decision trees for which the min and max operators can be used as the fuzzy conjunction and disjunction operators. Another extension could be to consider general DAG (Directed Acyclic Graphs) rather than trees.

Acknowledgments. This paper is supported by the European Union's Horizon 2020 research and innovation programme under grant agreement No 825619. AI4EU Project.([2] https://www.ai4europe.eu/).

References

1. Arrieta, A.B., et al.: Explainable artificial intelligence (XAI): concepts, taxonomies, opportunities and challenges toward responsible AI. Inf. Fusion **58**, 82–115 (2020)
2. Belahcène, K., Labreuche, C., Maudet, N., Mousseau, V., Ouerdane, W.: Comparing options with argument schemes powered by cancellation. In: Proceedings of the Twenty-Eight International Joint Conference on Artificial Intelligence (IJCAI 2019), Macao, China, pp. 1537–1543, August 2019
3. Bresson, R., Cohen, J., Hüllermeier, E., Labreuche, C., Sebag, M.: Neural representation and learning of hierarchical 2-additive Choquet integrals. In: Proceedings of the Twenty-Eight International Joint Conference on Artificial Intelligence (IJCAI 2020), Yokohoma, Japan, pp. 1984–1991 (2020)
4. Carenini, G., Moore, J.D.: Generating and evaluating evaluative arguments. Artif. Intell. **170**, 925–952 (2006)
5. Castro, J., Gómez, D., Tejada, J.: Polynomial calculation of the Shapley value based on sampling. Comput. Oper. Res. **36**, 1726–1730 (2009)
6. Chen, J., Song, L., Wainwright, M., Jordan, M.: L-Shapley and C-Shapley: efficient model interpretation for structured data. arXiv preprint arXiv:1808.02610 (2018)
7. Choquet, G.: Theory of capacities. Annales de l'Institut Fourier **5**, 131–295 (1953)
8. Datta, A., Sen, S., Zick, Y.: Algorithmic transparency via quantitative input influence: theory and experiments with learning systems. In: IEEE Symposium on Security and Privacy, San Jose, CA, USA, May 2016
9. Figueira, J., Greco, S., Ehrgott, M., (eds.) Multiple Criteria Decision Analysis: State of the Art Surveys, 2nd edition. Kluwer Acad. Publ. (2016)
10. Galand, L., Lesca, J., Perny, P.: Dominance rules for the Choquet integral in multi-objective dynamic programming. In: 23rd International Joint Conference on Artificial Intelligence (IJCAI 2013), Beijing, China, pp. 538–544, August 2013
11. Grabisch, M., Kojadinovic, I., Meyer, P.: A review of capacity identification methods for Choquet integral based multi-attribute utility theory – applications of the Kappalab R package. Eur. J. Oper. Res. **186**, 766–785 (2008)
12. Grabisch, M., Labreuche, C.: A decade of application of the Choquet and Sugeno integrals in multi-criteria decision aid. Ann. Oper. Res. **175**, 247–286 (2010)
13. Guidotti, R., Monreale, A., Ruggieri, S., Turini, F., Giannotti, F., Pedreschi, D.: A survey of methods for explaining black box models. ACM Comput. Surv. **51**(6), 1–42 (2018)
14. Herlocker, J.L., Konstan, J.A., Riedl, J.: Explaining collaborative filtering recommendations. In: CSCW, pp. 241–250 (2000)
15. Klein, D.A.: Decision Analytic Intelligent Systems: Automated Explanation and Knowledge Acquisition. Lawrence Erlbaum Associates (1994)

16. Labreuche, C., Fossier, S.: Explaining multi-criteria decision aiding models with an extended shapley value. In: Proceedings of the Twenty-Seventh International Joint Conference on Artificial Intelligence (IJCAI 2018), Stockholm, Sweden, pp. 331–339, July 2018
17. Labreuche, C.: A general framework for explaining the results of a multi-attribute preference model. Artif. Intell. **175**, 1410–1448 (2011)
18. Labreuche, C.: Explaining hierarchical multi-linear models. In: Proceedings of the 13th International Conference on Scalable Uncertainty Management (SUM 2019), Compiègne, France, December 2019
19. Lundberg, S., Lee, S.I.: A unified approach to interpreting model predictions. In: Guyon, I., et al. (eds.) 31st Conference on Neural Information Processing Systems (NIPS 2017), Long Beach, CA, USA, pp. 4768–4777 (2017)
20. Lundberg, S., Enrion, G., Lee, S.I.: Consistent individualized feature attribution for tree ensembles. arXiv preprint arXiv:1802.03888 (2018)
21. Maleki, S., Tran-Thanh, L., Hines, G., Rahwan, T., Rogers, A.: Bounding the estimation error of sampling-based Shapley value approximation. arXiv:1306.4265 (2013)
22. Merrick, L., Taly, A.: The explanation game: explaining machine learning models with cooperative game theory. arXiv preprint arXiv:1909.08128 (2018)
23. Ovchinnikov, S.: Max-min representation of piecewise linear functions. Contrib. Algebra Geom. **43**, 297–327 (2002)
24. Owen, A.B.: Sobol' indices and Shapley value. SIAM/ASA J. Uncertain. Quant. **2**, 245–251 (2014)
25. Owen, G.: Values of games with a priori unions. In: Moeschlin, O., Hein, R., (ed.), Essays in Mathematical Economics and Game Theory, pp. 76–88. Springer, Heidelberg (1977). https://doi.org/10.1007/978-3-642-45494-3_7
26. Ribeiro, M.T., Singh, S., Guestrin, C.: "Why Should I Trust You?": explaining the predictions of any classifier. In: KDD 2016 Proceedings of the 22nd ACM SIGKDD International Conference on Knowledge Discovery and Data Mining, San Francisco, California, USA, pp. 1135–1144 (2016)
27. Saltelli, A., et al.: Global Sensitivity Analysis: The Primer. Wiley, New York (2008)
28. Shapley, L.S.: A value for n-person games. In: Kuhn, H.W., Tucker, A.W. (eds.) Contributions to the Theory of Games, vol. II, number 28 in Annals of Mathematics Studies, pp. 307–317. Princeton University Press (1953)
29. Štrumbelj, E., Kononenko, I.: An efficient explanation of individual classifications using game theory. J. Mach. Learn. Res. **11**, 1–18 (2010)
30. Winter, E.: A value for cooperative games with levels structure of cooperation. Int. J. Game Theory **18**, 227–240 (1989)
31. Zhong, Q., Fan, X., Toni, F., Luo, X.: Explaining best decisions via argumentation. In: Proceedings of the European Conference on Social Intelligence (ECSI-2014), Barcelona, Spain, pp. 224–237, November 2014

Inducing Inference Relations
from Inconsistency Measures

Xiaolong Liu[1,2]($\boxtimes$) (iD), Philippe Besnard[2]($\boxtimes$), and Sylvie Doutre[2]($\boxtimes$) (iD)

[1] Department of Philosophy, Institute of Logic and Cognition,
Sun Yat-sen University, Guangzhou, China
liuxlong6@mail2.sysu.edu.cn
[2] IRIT-CNRS, University of Toulouse, Toulouse, France
{xiaolong.liu,philippe.besnard,sylvie.doutre}@irit.fr

Abstract. This article defines a family of inference relations which aim at reasoning with inconsistent knowledge bases. These inference relations are defined out of inconsistency measures. We check under which conditions the new inference relations satisfy a series of properties for non-monotonic reasoning. We also show that they are paraconsistent when the corresponding inconsistency measures satisfy some rationality postulates. Besides, we show some dependencies and incompatibilities among some rationality postulates.

Keywords: Inconsistency measures · Inference relations · Rationality

1 Introduction

Inconsistency measures are intended to provide a measure of how inconsistent a knowledge base is. Informally speaking, an inconsistency measure is a function which assigns a non-negative real value to a knowledge base with the meaning that larger values indicate a larger inconsistency. As pointed out in Bryson Brown's article [3], an application of inconsistency measures is to induce paraconsistent inference relations, which are able to draw valuable information from inconsistent knowledge bases. Although many inconsistency measures have been proposed so far, there are few inference relations based on them. A drawback of such existing inference relations proposed in [3] is that they are restricted to particular inconsistency measures. It would be desirable to find an approach that works for a broader set of inconsistency measures of the existing literature. To the best of our knowledge, no such general approach exists yet.

It has long been known that a paraconsistent logic, such as LP [11], can be used to define an inconsistency measure [4,6,10]. In this article, we investigate the other way around: How to define a paraconsistent inference relation out of a given inconsistency measure. For a discussion on relationships between inconsistency measures and paraconsistent consequence, see [3]. Our idea is to investigate what happens, under an inconsistency measure I, when supplementing a knowledge base with the negation of a formula. If I would assign a greater

© Springer Nature Switzerland AG 2021
J. Vejnarová and N. Wilson (Eds.): ECSQARU 2021, LNAI 12897, pp. 486–498, 2021.
https://doi.org/10.1007/978-3-030-86772-0_35

inconsistency degree to the knowledge base supplemented with the negation of the formula than to the knowledge base itself, then it would mean somehow that the knowledge base infers the formula. Regarding such an expected behaviour also as a sufficient condition, a notion of inference induced from I appears.

A number of *rationality postulates* for inconsistency measures have been proposed (e.g., [5,9,14]). A survey is provided in [15]. In this article, when an inconsistency measure satisfies some rationality postulates, we will explore which properties are satisfied by the inference relation induced from this measure.

Paper Outline. Section 2 introduces the new inference relations induced from inconsistency measures. Section 3 (resp. Section 4) investigates structural properties (resp. KLM properties) enjoyed by these relations. Section 5 defines paraconsistency and investigates under which conditions the new inference relations are paraconsistent. Section 6 shows dependencies and incompatibility for some rationality postulates. Section 7 concludes and points out future work.

2   Inference Relations from Inconsistency Measures

Before introducing the new inference relations, we present some basic notions. We consider a countable set of propositional atoms $\mathcal{A}$. We use $a, b, c, \ldots$ to denote atoms. The resulting logical language, using the connectives $\neg$, $\vee$, $\wedge$, and, $\rightarrow$, is denoted $\mathcal{L}$. We use Greek letters, $\varphi, \psi, \ldots$ to denote formulas of $\mathcal{L}$.

We write $\mathcal{K}$ for the set of knowledge bases over $\mathcal{L}$ (where a knowledge base K is a finite set of formulas of $\mathcal{L}$, in symbols: $K \subseteq_{\text{fin}} \mathcal{L}$). A minimal inconsistent subset of a knowledge base K is an inconsistent $K' \subseteq K$ such that all proper subsets of K' are consistent. The set of minimal inconsistent subsets of K is denoted by $\text{MI}(K)$. The set of atoms occurring in K is denoted by $\text{Atoms}(K)$. An *atomic injective substitution* for K is an injection $\sigma \colon \text{Atoms}(K) \rightarrow \mathcal{A}$. Then $\sigma(\varphi)$ is the formula resulting from φ by replacing $a \in \text{Atoms}(K)$ with $\sigma(a)$ simultaneously. We extend σ to an *injective substitution* for $K = \{\varphi_1, \ldots, \varphi_m\}$ with $\sigma(K) = \{\sigma(\varphi_1), \ldots, \sigma(\varphi_m)\}$.

Moreover, we write $\models$ for the consequence relation of classical logic. As we write $\bot$ for *falsum*, the notation $K \models \bot$ means that K is inconsistent. Logical equivalence is denoted $\equiv$, i.e., $\varphi \equiv \psi$ means that $\varphi \models \psi$ and $\psi \models \varphi$ hold. $K \equiv K'$ stands for $K \models \bigwedge K'$ and $K' \models \bigwedge K$. Lastly, a formula φ is *free* for K iff for every consistent subset K' of K, $K' \cup \{\varphi\} \not\models \bot$. A formula φ is *safe* for K iff $\text{Atoms}(\varphi) \cap \text{Atoms}(K) = \varnothing$ and φ is free for K.

Definition 1 (Inconsistency measure).   *A function* $I \colon \mathcal{K} \rightarrow \mathbb{R}_{\geq 0}^{\infty}$ *is an* **inconsistency measure** [2] *if it satisfies the following two conditions:*

Consistency Null: $I(K) = 0$ *iff* $K \not\models \bot$.
Variant Equality: If σ *is an injective substitution then* $I(K) = I(\sigma(K))$.

For example, the drastic inconsistency measure I_d is a trivial measure that distinguish only between consistent and inconsistent sets of formulas, formally,

$I_d(K) = 0$ if K is consistent and 1 if K is inconsistent. I_{MI} counts the number of minimal inconsistent subsets, formally, $\boldsymbol{I}_{MI}(K) = |\mathsf{MI}(K)|$.

We are now in the position to define an inference relation induced from an inconsistency measure, according to the intuition introduced in Sect. 1. That is, we are about to define $K \Vdash \varphi$ as $\boldsymbol{I}(K \cup \{\neg\varphi\}) > \boldsymbol{I}(K)$. However, we slightly amend this in the actual definition below because we must take care of the special case $\neg\varphi \in K$ (which obviously gives $\boldsymbol{I}(K \cup \{\neg\varphi\}) = \boldsymbol{I}(K)$ no matter what).

Definition 2 (Induced inference relations). *Let $\boldsymbol{I}$ be an inconsistency measure. For any $K \in \mathcal{K}$, the inference relation $\Vdash$ induced from $\boldsymbol{I}$ is given by*

$$K \Vdash \varphi \ \text{iff} \ \boldsymbol{I}(K \cup \{\neg\varphi\}) > \boldsymbol{I}(K \backslash \{\neg\varphi\}).$$

Lemma 1. *Let $\boldsymbol{I}$ be an inconsistency measure.*

$$K \Vdash \varphi \ \text{iff} \ \begin{cases} \boldsymbol{I}(K \cup \{\neg\varphi\}) > \boldsymbol{I}(K) & \text{if } \neg\varphi \notin K \\ \boldsymbol{I}(K) > \boldsymbol{I}(K \backslash \{\neg\varphi\}) & \text{if } \neg\varphi \in K \end{cases}$$

Lemma 2. $K \Vdash \varphi$ *iff* $K \backslash \{\neg\varphi\} \Vdash \varphi$.

It is desirable that for any consistent knowledge base, $\Vdash$ gives the same consequences as classical logic. The following theorem guarantees this.

Theorem 1. *Let $\boldsymbol{I}$ be an inconsistency measure. For all consistent $K \in \mathcal{K}$, $K \Vdash \varphi$ iff $K \models \varphi$.*

Proof. Take a consistent knowledge base K. ($\Rightarrow$) Suppose $K \Vdash \varphi$. By Definition 2, $\boldsymbol{I}(K \cup \{\neg\varphi\}) > \boldsymbol{I}(K \backslash \{\neg\varphi\})$. It is the case that $\boldsymbol{I}(K \backslash \{\neg\varphi\}) = 0$, due to Consistency Null and the consistency of $K \backslash \{\neg\varphi\}$. Hence $\boldsymbol{I}(K \cup \{\neg\varphi\}) > 0$. By Consistency Null, $\boldsymbol{I}(K \cup \{\neg\varphi\}) > 0$ iff $K \cup \{\neg\varphi\}$ is inconsistent. Therefore, $K \models \varphi$. ($\Leftarrow$) Suppose $K \models \varphi$. Then $K \cup \{\neg\varphi\}$ is inconsistent. Applying Consistency Null yields $\boldsymbol{I}(K \cup \{\neg\varphi\}) > 0$ and $\boldsymbol{I}(K \backslash \{\neg\varphi\}) = 0$. Hence, $\boldsymbol{I}(K \cup \{\neg\varphi\}) > \boldsymbol{I}(K \backslash \{\neg\varphi\})$. That is, $K \Vdash \varphi$ by Definition 2.

Before proceeding, we must pay special attention to a rationality postulate called Free-Formula Independence [2], which can be written in two ways:

Set Union version: If φ is free for K then $\boldsymbol{I}(K \cup \{\varphi\}) = \boldsymbol{I}(K)$.
Set Difference version: If φ is free for K then $\boldsymbol{I}(K) = \boldsymbol{I}(K \backslash \{\varphi\})$.

Lemma 3. *The two versions of Free-formula Independence are equivalent.*

Proof. The first case is $\varphi \in K$. We start to prove that set union version entails set difference version. Assume that φ is free for K. Then φ is also free for $K \backslash \{\varphi\}$. By set union version, $\boldsymbol{I}((K \backslash \{\varphi\}) \cup \{\varphi\}) = \boldsymbol{I}(K \backslash \{\varphi\})$. That is, $\boldsymbol{I}(K) = \boldsymbol{I}(K \backslash \{\varphi\})$ due to the assumption $\varphi \in K$. The converse is obvious as $\boldsymbol{I}(K \cup \{\varphi\}) = \boldsymbol{I}(K)$ always holds due to the assumption $\varphi \in K$.

The second case is $\varphi \notin K$. It is obvious that set union version entails set difference version, since $\boldsymbol{I}(K) = \boldsymbol{I}(K \backslash \{\varphi\})$ always holds due to the assumption

$\varphi \notin K$. To prove the converse, we assume that φ is free for K. It suffices to show that φ is also free for $K \cup \{\varphi\}$. We assume for the contradiction that φ is not free for $K \cup \{\varphi\}$. Then there exists a consistent subset K_1 of $K \cup \{\varphi\}$ such that $K_1 \cup \{\varphi\} \models \bot$ by the definition of free formulas. If $\varphi \in K_1$, then we have $K_1 \models \bot$ which contradicts the consistency of K_1. If $\varphi \notin K_1$ (which entails $K_1 \subseteq K$), then the assumption $K_1 \cup \{\varphi\} \models \bot$ contradicts the assumption that φ is free for K. To sum up, φ is free for $K \cup \{\varphi\}$. Immediately, by set difference version, $I(K \cup \{\varphi\}) = I((K \cup \{\varphi\})\backslash\{\varphi\})$. That is, $I(K \cup \{\varphi\}) = I(K)$.

Lemma 4. *Let I satisfy Free-formula Independence. The following items hold:*
(i) If $\neg\varphi$ is free for K then $K \not\Vdash \varphi$. (ii) If φ is free for K then $K \not\Vdash \neg\varphi$.

Proof. (i) If $\neg\varphi \notin K$, apply Free-formula Independence, set union version, to get $I(K \cup \{\neg\varphi\}) = I(K)$ and Lemma 1 to obtain $K \not\Vdash \varphi$. If $\neg\varphi \in K$, apply the set difference version to get $I(K) = I(K\backslash\{\neg\varphi\})$ and Lemma 1 to obtain $K \not\Vdash \varphi$. Then, apply Lemma 3. (ii) Since φ is free for K, $\neg\neg\varphi$ is free for K. The remaining proof is similar to (i).

3   Structural Properties Checking

Tarski [13] and Scott [12] worked out the idea of a logic as a closure operator, i.e., an operator over sets of formulas which satisfies the so-called Extension, Idempotence, and Isotony. Since we have formulated the induced consequence as a relation $\Vdash$, they can be expressed, assuming compactness, as follows.

Reflexivity $K \Vdash \varphi$ for any formula $\varphi \in K$.
Monotony If $K \Vdash \varphi$ then $K \cup \{\psi\} \Vdash \varphi$.
Cut If $K \Vdash \varphi$ and $K \cup \{\varphi\} \Vdash \psi$ then $K \Vdash \psi$.

We now investigate the question of which properties of I guarantee $\Vdash$ to satisfy Reflexivity, Cut, and Monotony.[1] We will use the following postulates of the literature [1,15].

Penalty: For $\varphi \notin K$, if φ is not free for K then $I(K \cup \{\varphi\}) > I(K)$.
Monotony: If $K \subseteq K'$ then $I(K) \leq I(K')$.
Rewriting: If ψ is a prenormal form[2] of φ then $I(K \cup \{\varphi\}) = I(K \cup \{\psi\})$.

Proposition 1. *Let I satisfy Penalty. Then, $K \Vdash \varphi$ for all consistent $\varphi \in K$ (i.e., $\Vdash$ satisfies Reflexivity except for inconsistent formulas).*

---

[1] Using Monotony, it is clear that Cut implies the finite general form: If $K \Vdash \varphi_i$ for $i = 1, \ldots, n$ and $K \cup \{\varphi_1, \ldots, \varphi_n\} \Vdash \psi$ then $K \Vdash \psi$. Similarly, Monotony gives the finite general form: If $K \Vdash \varphi$ then $K \cup \{\psi_1, \ldots, \psi_n\} \Vdash \varphi$.

[2] ψ is a *prenormal* form of φ if ψ results from φ by applying one or more of following principles: commutativity, associativity and distribution for $\wedge$ and $\vee$, De Morgan laws, double negation equivalence.

Proof. Consider a consistent formula φ of K. Thus, $\neg\varphi$ is not free for K due to $\{\varphi\}$ being a consistent subset of K such that supplementing it with $\neg\varphi$ gives an inconsistent set: $\{\varphi, \neg\varphi\} \models \perp$. Assume first $\neg\varphi \notin K$. By Penalty, $I(K\cup\{\neg\varphi\}) > I(K)$. Then, $K \Vdash \varphi$ ensues by Lemma 1. Assume $\neg\varphi \in K$ instead. Since φ is in K and $\varphi \not\models \perp$, it happens that $\{\varphi\}$ is a consistent subset of $K\backslash\{\neg\varphi\}$ (in view of the trivial fact $\varphi \neq \neg\varphi$) such that supplementing it with $\neg\varphi$ gives an inconsistent set. That is, $\neg\varphi$ is not free for $K\backslash\{\neg\varphi\}$. Also, $\neg\varphi$ is not in $K\backslash\{\neg\varphi\}$. Then, Penalty applies to give $I((K\backslash\{\neg\varphi\}) \cup \{\neg\varphi\}) > I(K\backslash\{\neg\varphi\})$. By Lemma 1, $K\backslash\{\neg\varphi\} \Vdash \varphi$. Applying Lemma 2, $K \Vdash \varphi$.

Please observe that for an inconsistent φ in K, having $K \Vdash \varphi$ would amount to $I(K \cup \{\neg\varphi\}) > I(K)$, that is, supplementing K with a tautology $\neg\varphi$ would increase the inconsistency degree: No inconsistency measure can be expected to do that. In other words, Proposition 1 is the most that can be obtained towards $\Vdash$ satisfying Reflexivity. The following example is an illustration of this.

Example 1. Consider the inconsistency measure I_{MI} satisfying Penalty, and an inconsistent knowledge base $K = \{a, \neg a, a \wedge \neg a\}$. Let a be a consistent element of K. It is easy to see that $K \Vdash a$, since $2 = I_{MI}(K) > I_{MI}(K\backslash\{\neg a\}) = 1$. However, for the inconsistent element $a \wedge \neg a$ of K, we have $K \not\Vdash a \wedge \neg a$ due to $I_{MI}(K \cup \{\neg(a \wedge \neg a)\}) = I_{MI}(K) = 2$.

We now turn to Monotony. To start with, Proposition 2 (proved by applying Lemma 2 twice) states that Monotony succeeds when $\psi = \neg\varphi$. A more substantial result is offered by Proposition 3.

Proposition 2. *If $K \Vdash \varphi$ then $K \cup \{\neg\varphi\} \Vdash \varphi$.*

Proposition 3. *Let I satisfy Free-formula Independence. Let ψ be free for $K \cup \{\neg\varphi\}$. If $K \Vdash \varphi$ then $K \cup \{\psi\} \Vdash \varphi$.*

Proof. (i) First, consider the case $\neg\varphi \notin K$. Assume that ψ is free for $K \cup \{\neg\varphi\}$. In view of Free-formula Independence, $I(K \cup \{\neg\varphi\} \cup \{\psi\}) = I(K \cup \{\neg\varphi\})$. Also by Free-formula Independence, $I(K) = I(K \cup \{\psi\})$ because ψ being free for $K \cup \{\neg\varphi\}$ entails ψ being free for K. However, Lemma 1 gives $I(K \cup \{\neg\varphi\}) > I(K)$ due to $K \Vdash \varphi$ and $\neg\varphi \notin K$. Hence, $I(K\cup\{\psi\}\cup\{\neg\varphi\}) > I(K\cup\{\psi\})$. Should $\psi = \neg\varphi$, a contradiction $I(K \cup \{\psi\}) > I(K \cup \{\psi\})$ would arise. Hence, $\psi \neq \neg\varphi$. This together with $\neg\varphi \notin K$ give $\neg\varphi \notin K \cup \{\psi\}$. By Lemma 1, $K \cup \{\psi\} \Vdash \varphi$.

(ii) Second, consider the case $\neg\varphi \in K$. Then $K = K \cup \{\neg\varphi\}$. Also, $K \Vdash \varphi$ gives $K\backslash\{\neg\varphi\} \Vdash \varphi$ according to Lemma 2. Now, $\neg\varphi \notin K\backslash\{\neg\varphi\}$. Moreover, ψ is free for $(K\backslash\{\neg\varphi\}) \cup \{\neg\varphi\}$ because ψ is free for K. (i) can be applied, giving $(K\backslash\{\neg\varphi\}) \cup \{\psi\} \Vdash \varphi$. For $\psi \neq \neg\varphi$, Lemma 1 then gives $I((K\backslash\{\neg\varphi\}) \cup \{\psi\} \cup \{\neg\varphi\}) > I((K\backslash\{\neg\varphi\}) \cup \{\psi\})$. That is, $I(K \cup \{\psi\} \cup \{\neg\varphi\}) > I((K\backslash\{\neg\varphi\}) \cup \{\psi\})$. Therefore $I(K \cup \{\psi\} \cup \{\neg\varphi\}) > I((K \cup \{\psi\})\backslash\{\neg\varphi\})$ due to $\psi \neq \neg\varphi$. Per Definition 2, $K\cup\{\psi\} \Vdash \varphi$. The remaining case $\psi = \neg\varphi$ is obvious since $\neg\varphi \in K$.

Example 2. This example shows that Proposition 3 is the most that can be obtained towards $\Vdash$ satisfying Monotony. Consider the drastic measure I_d satisfying Free-Formula Independence. Let $K = \{a, \neg a\}$, $\varphi = a$, and $\psi = b \wedge \neg b$.

Then ψ is not free for $K \cup \{\neg\varphi\}$. Besides, we have $K \Vdash \varphi$. However, $K \cup \{\psi\} \nVdash \varphi$ since $\boldsymbol{I}_d(K \cup \{\psi\} \cup \{\neg\varphi\}) = \boldsymbol{I}_d((K \cup \{\psi\})\backslash\{\neg\varphi\}) = 1$.

Since Monotony seems to fail on a general count, we can look at a weakening known as Cautious Monotony [8]. To show under which conditions Cautious Monotony and Cut are satisfied, we propose, from a technical point of view, two postulates, *Denial Elimination* and *Denial Preservation* which are basically the converse of each other. Denial Preservation states that if a formula increases the inconsistency of a knowledge base, then for its superset with the same inconsistency, we may wish that the negation of the formula increases the same inconsistency to the knowledge base and the superset.

Cautious Monotony. If $K \Vdash \varphi$ and $K \Vdash \psi$ then $K \cup \{\psi\} \Vdash \varphi$.

Denial Elimination: Let K and φ be such that $\boldsymbol{I}(K \cup \{\varphi\}) > \boldsymbol{I}(K)$. For all $K' \supseteq K$, if $\boldsymbol{I}(K' \cup \{\neg\varphi\}) = \boldsymbol{I}(K \cup \{\neg\varphi\})$ then $\boldsymbol{I}(K') = \boldsymbol{I}(K)$.
Denial Preservation: Let K and φ be such that $\boldsymbol{I}(K \cup \{\varphi\}) > \boldsymbol{I}(K)$. For all $K' \supseteq K$, if $\boldsymbol{I}(K') = \boldsymbol{I}(K)$ then $\boldsymbol{I}(K' \cup \{\neg\varphi\}) = \boldsymbol{I}(K \cup \{\neg\varphi\})$.

Proposition 4. *If $\boldsymbol{I}$ satisfies Denial Elimination, Monotony, and Rewriting, then $\Vdash$ satisfies Cautious Monotony restricted to the case $\neg\varphi \notin K$ and $\neg\psi \notin K$.*

Proof. Let $K \Vdash \varphi$ and $K \Vdash \psi$. Assume $\neg\varphi \notin K$. Firstly, consider $\neg\varphi = \psi$. $K \Vdash \varphi$ gives $\boldsymbol{I}(K \cup \{\neg\varphi\}) > \boldsymbol{I}(K)$ by Lemma 1. That is, $\boldsymbol{I}(K \cup \{\psi\} \cup \{\neg\varphi\}) > \boldsymbol{I}((K \cup \{\psi\})\backslash\{\neg\varphi\})$. Hence, $K \cup \{\psi\} \Vdash \varphi$ by Definition 2. Secondly, consider $\neg\varphi \neq \psi$. Then $\neg\varphi \notin K \cup \{\psi\}$. Assume further $\neg\psi \notin K$. Applying Lemma 1 to $K \Vdash \psi$ yields $\boldsymbol{I}(K \cup \{\neg\psi\}) > \boldsymbol{I}(K)$. Denial Elimination can be applied so that $\boldsymbol{I}(K \cup \{\neg\psi\}) \neq \boldsymbol{I}(K)$ entails $\boldsymbol{I}(K \cup \{\neg\varphi\} \cup \{\neg\neg\psi\}) \neq \boldsymbol{I}(K \cup \{\neg\neg\psi\})$. Then by Rewriting, we have $\boldsymbol{I}(K \cup \{\neg\varphi\} \cup \{\psi\}) \neq \boldsymbol{I}(K \cup \{\psi\})$. Due to Monotony, $\boldsymbol{I}(K \cup \{\neg\varphi\} \cup \{\psi\}) > \boldsymbol{I}(K \cup \{\psi\})$. Eventually, $K \cup \{\psi\} \Vdash \varphi$ by Lemma 1.

Proposition 5. *If $\boldsymbol{I}$ satisfies Denial Preservation, Monotony, and Rewriting, then $\Vdash$ satisfies Cut restricted to the case $\neg\varphi \notin K$ and $\neg\psi \notin K$.*

Proof. The proof is similar to the converse of the proof of Proposition 4.

4 KLM Properties Checking

Kraus, Lehman and Magidor [7] introduced a series of possible properties for inference relations. In this section, we explore under which conditions the following KLM properties can be satisfied. More specifically, when an inconsistency measures satisfies some postulate(s), we show that the induced inference relation satisfies some KLM properties restricted to compulsory extra condition(s).

Right Weakening. If $K \Vdash \varphi$ and $\varphi \models \psi$ then $K \Vdash \psi$.
Left Logical Equivalence. If $K \equiv K'$ and $K \Vdash \varphi$, then $K' \Vdash \varphi$.

AND. If $K \Vdash \varphi$ and $K \Vdash \psi$ then $K \Vdash \varphi \wedge \psi$.

Rational Monotony. If $K \Vdash \varphi$ and $K \nVdash \neg\psi$ then $K \cup \{\psi\} \Vdash \varphi$.

Contraposition. If $\varphi \Vdash \psi$ then $\neg\psi \Vdash \neg\varphi$.

OR. If $K \cup \{\varphi\} \Vdash \rho$ and $K \cup \{\psi\} \Vdash \rho$ then $K \cup \{\varphi \vee \psi\} \Vdash \rho$.

Below are the rationality postulates [1,15] we will consider in this section. Note that Antinomy Increase and Mutual Increase are new rationality postulates. The former states that adding an inconsistent formula would increase the inconsistency degree. The latter states that when adding a formula φ increases the inconsistency amount of an inconsistent knowledge base K, we would expect that adding K also increases the inconsistency amount of φ.

Dominance: If $\varphi \notin K$, $\varphi \nvDash \bot$ and $\varphi \vDash \psi$ then $I(K \cup \{\varphi\}) \geq I(K \cup \{\psi\})$.

Disjunct Minimality: $\min(I(K \cup \{\varphi\}), I(K \cup \{\psi\})) \leq I(K \cup \{\varphi \vee \psi\})$.

Disjunct Maximality: $I(K \cup \{\varphi \vee \psi\}) \leq \max(I(K \cup \{\varphi\}), I(K \cup \{\psi\}))$.

Antinomy Increase: Let $\vDash \neg\varphi$. If $\varphi \notin K$ then $I(K \cup \{\varphi\}) > I(K)$.

Mutual Increase: If $K \vDash \bot$ and $I(K \cup \{\varphi\}) > I(K)$, then $I(K \cup \{\varphi\}) > I(\{\varphi\})$.

Proposition 6. *Let I satisfy Dominance. Then $\Vdash$ satisfies Right Weakening restricted to the case $\neg\psi \nvDash \bot$, $\neg\psi \notin K$ and $\neg\varphi \notin K$.*

Proof. Assume that $K \Vdash \varphi$ and $\varphi \vDash \psi$. Then $\neg\psi \vDash \neg\varphi$. By Dominance, we have $I(K \cup \{\neg\psi\}) \geq I(K \cup \{\neg\varphi\})$. We also have $I(K \cup \{\neg\varphi\}) > I(K)$ by Lemma 1. Immediately, $I(K \cup \{\neg\psi\}) > I(K)$. That is, $K \Vdash \psi$ by Lemma 1.

Example 3. The extra condition $\neg\varphi \notin K$ of Proposition 6 is compulsory. Actually, consider I_d satisfying Dominance. Let $K = \{a, \neg a\}$, $\varphi = a$ and $\psi = a \vee b$. It follows that $K \Vdash \varphi$ and $\varphi \vDash \psi$. But $K \nVdash \psi$ since $I_d(K \cup \{\neg\psi\}) = I_d(K) = 1$.

Due to failure of the general form for Right Weakening, a special case is of interest: Is every tautology a consequence according to $\Vdash$?

Proposition 7. *If I satisfies Antinomy Increase, $K \Vdash \varphi$ for every tautology φ.*

Proof. Take a tautology φ. Thus, $\neg\neg\varphi$ is also a tautology. Assume $\neg\varphi \notin K$. By Antinomy Increase, $I(K \cup \{\neg\varphi\}) > I(K)$. Hence, $K \Vdash \varphi$ by Lemma 1. Assume $\neg\varphi \in K$. Then, $\neg\varphi \notin K \backslash \{\neg\varphi\}$. Therefore, $I((K \backslash \{\neg\varphi\}) \cup \{\neg\varphi\}) > I(K \backslash \{\neg\varphi\})$ by Antinomy Increase. That is $I(K) > I(K \backslash \{\neg\varphi\})$. So $K \Vdash \varphi$ by Lemma 1.

Using the previous proposition, we can get closer to Right Weakening.

Corollary 1. *Let I satisfy Dominance and Antinomy Increase. Let $\neg\psi \notin K$ and $\neg\varphi \notin K$. If $K \Vdash \varphi$ and $\varphi \vDash \psi$ then $K \Vdash \psi$.*

Proposition 8. *Let $K \nvDash \bot$. Then $\Vdash$ satisfies Left Logical Equivalence.*

Proof. Apply Theorem 1 twice.

Example 4. The extra condition $K \nvDash \bot$ is necessary. Actually, consider I_{MI}, and two inconsistent knowledge bases $K = \{a, \neg a\}$ and $K' = \{b, \neg b\}$. It is obvious that $K \equiv K'$ and $K \Vdash a$. However, $K' \nVdash a$ as $I(K' \cup \{\neg a\}) = I(K') = 1$.

Proposition 9. *Let I satisfy Disjunct Minimality, Rewriting and Monotony. Then $\Vdash$ satisfies AND restricted to the case $\neg\varphi \notin K$ and $\neg\psi \notin K$.*

Proof. Assume that $K \Vdash \varphi$ and $K \Vdash \psi$. Let $\neg\varphi \notin K$ and $\neg\psi \notin K$. Then $I(K \cup \{\neg\varphi\}) > I(K)$ and $I(K \cup \{\neg\psi\}) > I(K)$ by Lemma 1. Applying Disjunct Minimality gives $I(K \cup \{\neg\varphi \vee \neg\psi\}) \geq \min(I(K \cup \{\neg\varphi\}), I(K \cup \{\neg\psi\}))$. Hence, $I(K \cup \{\neg\varphi \vee \neg\psi\}) > I(K)$. Applying Rewriting yields $I(K \cup \{\neg(\varphi \wedge \psi)\}) > I(K)$. Besides, applying Monotony gives $I(K) \geq I(K \backslash \{\neg(\varphi \wedge \psi)\})$. Therefore, it is the case that $I(K \cup \{\neg(\varphi \wedge \psi)\}) > I(K \backslash \{\neg(\varphi \wedge \psi)\})$. By Definition 2, $K \Vdash \varphi \wedge \psi$.

Example 5. Consider the drastic inconsistency measure I_d satisfying Disjunct Minimality, Rewriting and Monotony. Let $K = \{a, \neg a\}$ and $\varphi = \psi = a$. Then $\neg\psi$ and $\neg\varphi$ are formulas occurring in K. Besides, $K \Vdash \varphi$ and $K \Vdash \psi$. But we have $K \not\Vdash \varphi \wedge \psi$ due to $I_d(K \cup \{\neg(\varphi \wedge \psi)\}) = I_d(K \backslash \{\neg(\varphi \wedge \psi)\}) = 1$.

The converse of the second item of Lemma 4 is untrue because $I(K \cup \{\psi\}) = I(K)$ is possible for ψ not free for K (see for instance the drastic inconsistency measure). However, by Monotony, it is possible to use $K \not\Vdash \neg\psi$ to infer $I(K \cup \{\psi\}) = I(K)$. That is the interest of the next lemma.

Lemma 5. *Let I satisfy Monotony and Rewriting. Let $K \backslash \{\neg\varphi\} \not\Vdash \neg\psi$. If $K \Vdash \varphi$ then $K \cup \{\psi\} \Vdash \varphi$.*

Proof. First, consider $\neg\varphi \notin K$. The assumption becomes $K \not\Vdash \neg\psi$. Since the codomain of I is linearly ordered, Lemma 1 gives $I(K \cup \{\neg\neg\psi\}) \leq I(K)$. Using Rewriting, $I(K \cup \{\psi\}) \leq I(K)$. Applying Monotony gives $I(K \cup \{\psi\}) = I(K)$. However, Lemma 1 gives $I(K \cup \{\neg\varphi\}) > I(K)$ due to $K \Vdash \varphi$ and $\neg\varphi \notin K$. Therefore, $I(K \cup \{\neg\varphi\}) > I(K \cup \{\psi\})$. By Monotony, $I(K \cup \{\neg\varphi\} \cup \{\psi\}) \geq I(K \cup \{\neg\varphi\})$ hence $I(K \cup \{\neg\varphi\} \cup \{\psi\}) > I(K \cup \{\psi\})$. Should $\psi = \neg\varphi$, a contradiction $I(K \cup \{\psi\}) > I(K \cup \{\psi\})$ would arise. Hence, $\psi \neq \neg\varphi$. This together with $\neg\varphi \notin K$ give $\neg\varphi \notin K \cup \{\psi\}$. By Lemma 1, $K \cup \{\psi\} \Vdash \varphi$ ensues.

Consider now $\neg\varphi \in K$. Since $K \backslash \{\neg\varphi\} \not\Vdash \neg\psi$, in view of Lemma 1, we have $I((K \backslash \{\neg\varphi\}) \cup \{\neg\neg\psi\}) \leq I(K \backslash \{\neg\varphi\})$. However, $I(K \backslash \{\neg\varphi\}) < I(K)$ by Lemma 1 due to $K \Vdash \varphi$. Also, Monotony requires $I(K) \leq I(K \cup \{\psi\})$. Combining, $I((K \backslash \{\neg\varphi\}) \cup \{\neg\neg\psi\}) < I(K \cup \{\psi\})$ ensues. By Rewriting, $I((K \backslash \{\neg\varphi\}) \cup \{\psi\}) < I(K \cup \{\psi\})$. Should $\psi = \neg\varphi$, a contradiction $I(K \cup \{\psi\}) < I(K \cup \{\psi\})$ would arise. Hence, $\psi \neq \neg\varphi$. Thus, $I((K \cup \{\psi\}) \backslash \{\neg\varphi\}) < I(K \cup \{\psi\})$. Applying Lemma 1, this gives $K \cup \{\psi\} \Vdash \varphi$.

Proposition 10. *Let I satisfy Monotony and Rewriting. Then $\Vdash$ satisfies Rational Monotony restricted to the case $\neg\varphi \notin K$.*

Proof. Apply Lemma 5 for $\neg\varphi \notin K$ in order to obtain that if $K \Vdash \varphi$ and $K \not\Vdash \neg\psi$ then $K \cup \{\psi\} \Vdash \varphi$.

Example 6. The extra condition $\neg\varphi \notin K$ in Proposition 10 is compulsory. Actually, consider I_d which satisfies Monotony and Rewriting. Let $K = \{a, \neg a, \neg b\}$, $\varphi = a$ and $\psi = b$. Trivially, $\neg\varphi \in K$. Also, $K \Vdash \varphi$ since $1 = I_d(K) > I_d(K \backslash \{\neg\varphi\}) = 0$. On the other hand, $K \not\Vdash \neg\psi$ since $I_d(K \cup \{\neg\neg\psi\}) = I_d(K) = 1$. However, $K \cup \{\psi\} \not\Vdash \varphi$ because $I_d(K \cup \{\psi\}) = I_d((K \cup \{\psi\}) \backslash \{\neg\varphi\}) = 1$.

Proposition 11. *Let I satisfy Rewriting and Mutual Increase. Then $\Vdash$ satisfies Contraposition restricted to the case $\varphi \models \bot$, $\neg\psi \neq \varphi$ and $\psi \neq \neg\varphi$.*

Proof. Assume $\varphi \Vdash \psi$. Then $I(\{\varphi\} \cup \{\neg\psi\}) > I(\{\varphi\})$ by Lemma 1. Applying Mutual Increase to $\{\varphi\}$ and $\{\neg\psi\}$ yields $I(\{\varphi\} \cup \{\neg\psi\}) > I(\{\neg\psi\})$. In view of Rewriting, $I(\{\neg\neg\varphi\} \cup \{\neg\psi\}) > I(\{\neg\psi\})$. Hence, $\neg\psi \Vdash \neg\varphi$ by Lemma 1.

Example 7. The extra condition $\neg\psi \neq \varphi$ is compulsory. Actually, consider I_d satisfying Rewriting and Mutual Increase. Let $\neg\psi = \varphi = \neg(a \vee \neg a)$. Then $\psi = a \vee \neg a$. $\varphi \Vdash \psi$ since $I_d(\{\varphi\} \cup \{\neg\psi\}) = 1 > 0 = I_d(\{\varphi\}) \backslash \{\neg\psi\})$. But $\neg\psi \not\Vdash \neg\varphi$ since $I_d(\{\neg\psi\} \cup \{\neg\neg\varphi\}) = I_d(\{\neg\psi\} \backslash \{\neg\neg\varphi\}) = 1$.

A general result for OR is hard to obtain, since conditions satisfying OR are very demanding. Assessing inconsistency of a disjunction is a delicate matter. There is a lack of measures for assessing inconsistency of a disjunction in the existing literature except Disjunct Minimality and Disjunct Maximality [1]. However, even if an inconsistency measure satisfies these two postulates, it is not clear whether OR is satisfied by the induced inference relation.

Assume that $K \cup \{\varphi\} \Vdash \rho$ and $K \cup \{\psi\} \Vdash \rho$. Then by Definition 2, $I(K \cup \{\varphi\} \cup \{\neg\rho\}) > I((K \cup \{\varphi\}) \backslash \{\neg\rho\})$ and $I(K \cup \{\psi\} \cup \{\neg\rho\}) > I((K \cup \{\psi\}) \backslash \{\neg\rho\})$. But $K \cup \{\varphi \vee \psi\} \Vdash \rho$ is not necessarily entailed by these conditions. Let us analyze this by considering two cases. Firstly, consider the case $\min(I(K \cup \{\varphi\} \cup \{\neg\rho\}), I(K \cup \{\psi\} \cup \{\neg\rho\})) = I(K \cup \{\varphi\} \cup \{\neg\rho\})$. Then $I(K \cup \{\varphi \vee \psi\} \cup \{\neg\rho\}) \geq I(K \cup \{\varphi\} \cup \{\neg\rho\})$ by Disjunct Minimality. In such a case, we are not able to compare $I(K \cup \{\varphi \vee \psi\} \cup \{\rho\})$ and $I((K \cup \{\varphi \vee \psi\}) \backslash \{\rho\})$ since the relative order between $I((K \cup \{\varphi\}) \backslash \{\neg\rho\})$ and $I((K \cup \{\varphi\}) \backslash \{\neg\rho\})$ is not clear. Both $I((K \cup \{\varphi\}) \backslash \{\neg\rho\}) \leq I((K \cup \{\varphi\}) \backslash \{\neg\rho\})$ and $I((K \cup \{\varphi\}) \backslash \{\neg\rho\}) \geq I((K \cup \{\varphi\}) \backslash \{\neg\rho\})$ are possible. If $I((K \cup \{\varphi\}) \backslash \{\neg\rho\}) \leq I((K \cup \{\varphi\}) \backslash \{\neg\rho\})$, we have no idea which one is smaller.

However, it is possible to compare the two items when $I((K \cup \{\varphi\}) \backslash \{\neg\rho\}) \geq I((K \cup \{\varphi\}) \backslash \{\neg\rho\})$. Let us consider a simple case where $\neg\rho \neq \varphi$, $\neg\rho \neq \psi$ and $\neg\rho \neq \varphi \vee \psi$. Then $I((K \cup \{\varphi\}) \backslash \{\neg\rho\}) \geq I((K \cup \{\varphi\}) \backslash \{\neg\rho\})$ is equivalent to $I((K \backslash \{\neg\rho\}) \cup \{\varphi\}) \geq I((K \backslash \{\neg\rho\}) \cup \{\psi\})$. Applying Disjunct Maximality gives $I((K \backslash \{\neg\rho\}) \cup \{\varphi\}) \geq I((K \backslash \{\neg\rho\}) \cup \{\varphi \vee \psi\})$, namely, $I((K \cup \{\varphi\}) \backslash \{\neg\rho\}) \geq I((K \cup \{\varphi \vee \psi\}) \backslash \{\neg\rho\})$. Thus, $I(K \cup \{\varphi \vee \psi\} \backslash \{\neg\rho\}) > I((K \cup \{\varphi \vee \psi\}) \backslash \{\neg\rho\})$. By Definition 2, $K \cup \{\varphi \vee \psi\} \Vdash \rho$. The analysis for the case where $\min(I(K \cup \{\varphi\} \cup \{\neg\rho\}), I(K \cup \{\psi\} \cup \{\neg\rho\})) = I(K \cup \{\psi\} \cup \{\neg\rho\})$ is similar to the first case.

5   Paraconsistency Checking

This section investigates which inconsistency measures induce a paraconsistent inference relation. The following definition formally describes paraconsistency.

Definition 3 (Paraconsistency). *An inference relation $\Vdash$ is **paraconsistent** if for all inconsistent $K \in \mathcal{K}$, there exists a formula φ such that $K \not\Vdash \varphi$.*

An inconsistency measure I is called **relative** [2] if it satisfies *Normalization* (i.e., $0 \leq I(K) \leq 1$) and either *Free-Formula Reduction* or *Relative Separability* (or both).

Free-Formula Reduction: For $\varphi \notin K$, if φ is free for K and $I(K) \neq 0$ then $I(K \cup \{\varphi\}) < I(K)$.
Relative Separability: If $I(K_1) \lesssim I(K_2)$ and $\mathrm{Atoms}(K_1) \cap \mathrm{Atoms}(K_2) = \varnothing$ then $I(K_1) \lesssim I(K_1 \cup K_2) \lesssim I(K_2)$ where either $\lesssim$ is $<$ in every instance or $\lesssim$ is $=$ in every instance.

Proposition 12. *If I is an inconsistency measure satisfying* (i) *Free-Formula Reduction or* (ii) *Relative Separability, then* $\Vdash$ *is paraconsistent.*

Proof. (i) Take an inconsistent $K \in \mathcal{K}$ and an atom $a \notin \mathrm{Atoms}(K)$. Then $\neg a$ is free for K and $\neg a \notin K$. Besides, $I(K) \neq 0$ by Consistency Null. So applying Free-Formula Reduction to K gives $I(K \cup \{\neg a\}) < I(K)$. Thus, $K \nVdash \varphi$ by Lemma 1. Hence, $\Vdash$ is paraconsistent by Definition 3. (ii) Take an inconsistent $K \in \mathcal{K}$ and an atom $a \notin \mathrm{Atoms}(K)$. Then $I(K) > 0$ and $I(\{\neg a\}) = 0$ by Consistency Null. Hence, we have $I(\{\neg a\}) < I(K)$. Besides, $\mathrm{Atoms}(\{\neg a\}) \cap \mathrm{Atoms}(K) = \varnothing$. Applying Relative Separability gives $I(\{\neg a\}) < I(K \cup \{\neg a\}) < I(K)$. Therefore, $K \nVdash a$ by Lemma 1. Thus, $\Vdash$ is paraconsistent by Definition 3.

Theorem 2. *For every relative inconsistency measure I, the inference relation $\Vdash$ induced from I is paraconsistent.*

Next we show that the inference relation $\Vdash$ induced from I is paraconsistent if I satisfies some rationality postulate(s). Note that we propose a postulate *Tautology Non-Increase* which states that any tautology does not increase inconsistency degree.

Safe-Formula Independence: If φ is safe for K then $I(K \cup \{\varphi\}) = I(K)$.
Tautology Independence: If φ is a tautology then $I(K \cup \{\varphi\}) = I(K)$.
MI-separability: If $\mathrm{MI}(K_1 \cup K_2) = \mathrm{MI}(K_1) \cup \mathrm{MI}(K_2)$ and $\mathrm{MI}(K_1) \cap \mathrm{MI}(K_2) = \varnothing$ then $I(K_1 \cup K_2) = I(K_1) + I(K_2)$.
Tautology Non-Increase: If φ is a tautology then $I(K \cup \{\varphi\}) \leq I(K)$.

Proposition 13. *If I is an inconsistency measure satisfying* (i) *Free-formula Independence,* (ii) *Safe-Formula Independence,* (iii) *Tautology Independence or* (iv) *MI-separability, then* $\Vdash$ *is paraconsistent.*

Proof. (i) Take an inconsistent $K \in \mathcal{K}$ and an atom $a \notin \mathrm{Atoms}(K)$. Then applying Free-Formula Independence to K gives $I(K \cup \{\neg a\}) = I(K)$, as $\neg a$ is free for K. Hence, $K \nVdash \varphi$ by Lemma 1. (ii) Obvious. (iii) Take an inconsistent $K \in \mathcal{K}$, and an inconsistent formula φ such that no atom in φ occur in K. Then applying Tautology Independence gives $I(K \cup \{\neg \varphi\}) = I(K)$, as $\neg \varphi$ is a tautology. Trivially, $\neg \varphi \notin K$. Hence $K \nVdash \varphi$ by Lemma 1. (iv) Take an inconsistent $K \in \mathcal{K}$ and an atom $a \notin \mathrm{Atoms}(K)$. Then $\mathrm{MI}(K \cup \{\neg a\}) = \mathrm{MI}(K)$ since $\neg a$ does not participate in inconsistency. Besides, we have $\mathrm{MI}(\{\neg a\}) = \varnothing$. Hence, we have

$MI(K \cup \{\neg a\}) = MI(K) \cup MI(\{\neg a\})$ and $MI(K) \cap MI(\{\neg a\}) = \varnothing$. Therefore, $I(K \cup \{\neg a\}) = I(K) + I(\{\neg a\})$ holds by applying MI-separability to K and $\{\neg a\}$. Thus, $I(K \cup \{\neg a\}) = I(K)$ due to $I(\{\neg a\}) = 0$. So $K \nVdash a$ by Lemma 1.

Lemma 6. *If I satisfies Tautology Non-Increase, $K \nVdash \varphi$ for all inconsistent φ.*

Proof. Let φ is be an inconsistent formula. Then $\neg\varphi$ is a tautology. Assume $\neg\varphi \notin K$. According to Tautology Non-Increase, $I(K \cup \{\varphi\}) \leq I(K)$. Using Lemma 1, $K \nVdash \varphi$. Otherwise, assume $\neg\varphi \in K$. Applying Tautology Non-Increase, we have $I((K\backslash\{\neg\varphi\}) \cup \{\neg\varphi\}) \leq I(K\backslash\{\neg\varphi\})$. By Lemma 1, $K \nVdash \varphi$.

It is easy to see from Lemma 6 that if I satisfies Tautology Non-Increase then $\Vdash$ is paraconsistent.

6   Dependencies and Incompatibilities

Some postulates imply some other postulates, whereas others are incompatible. This section presents results in this sense.

Lemma 7. *The following statements hold: (i) MI-separability entails Antinomy Increase and Tautology Independence. (ii) Penalty entails Antinomy Increase. (iii) Tautology Independence entails Tautology Non-Increase. (iv) Penalty and Monotony entails Mutual Increase.*

Proof. (i) We first show that MI-separability entails Antinomy Increase. Let $\varphi \notin K$ such that $\varphi \models \bot$. Then, $MI(K \cup \{\varphi\}) = MI(K) \cup MI(\{\varphi\})$ and $MI(K) \cap MI(\{\varphi\}) = \varnothing$. By MI-separability, $I(K \cup \{\varphi\}) = I(K) + I(\{\varphi\})$. However, Consistency Null guarantees $I(\{\varphi\}) > 0$. Then, $I(K \cup \{\varphi\}) > I(K)$. We turn to show that MI-separability entails Tautology Independence. Let φ be a tautology. Then, $MI(K \cup \{\varphi\}) = MI(K) \cup MI(\{\varphi\})$ and $MI(K) \cap MI(\{\varphi\}) = \varnothing$. MI-separability then gives $I(K \cup \{\varphi\}) = I(K) + I(\{\varphi\})$. Consistency Null ensures $I(\{\varphi\}) = 0$. Thus, $I(K \cup \{\varphi\}) = I(K)$. (ii) Consider $\varphi \notin K$ such that $\varphi \models \bot$. Clearly, φ is not free for K because the empty set is a consistent subset K but $\varnothing \cup \{\varphi\} \models \bot$. Applying Penalty, $I(K \cup \{\varphi\}) > I(K)$. (iii) Obvious. (iv) Assume $K \models \bot$ and $I(K \cup \{\varphi\}) > I(K)$. Then the latter assumption gives $\varphi \notin K$. Let us take a formula ψ that belongs to a minimal inconsistent subset of K. Hence, ψ is not free for $(K\backslash\{\psi\}) \cup \{\varphi\}$. Applying Penalty yields $I(K \cup \{\varphi\}) > I((K\backslash\{\psi\}) \cup \{\varphi\})$. In view of Monotony, $I((K\backslash\{\psi\}) \cup \{\varphi\}) \geq I(\{\varphi\})$. Immediately, $I(K \cup \{\varphi\}) > I(\{\varphi\})$.

Accordingly, if I satisfies Penalty then $K \Vdash \varphi$ for all consistent $\varphi \in K$ (by Proposition 1) and all tautological φ (by Proposition 7).

The results given in the previous sections do not generally add up in the sense that combining rationality postulates for a given inconsistency measure may make the induced inference inference fails to enjoy some property. There are two main reasons. First, some possible properties of the induced inference relation are exclusive of each other. Second, some rationality postulates are incompatible. For

Table 1. Satisfiable Properties of the Inference Relation $\Vdash$, depending on Sufficient Postulates of the Inconsistency Measure I and Compulsory Extra Conditions, with Reference to the Result

Properties of $\Vdash$	Sufficient postulates of I	Extra conditions	Results
Reflexivity	Penalty	Consistent formulas	Proposition 1
Monotony	Free-formula independence	ψ is free for $K \cup \{\neg\varphi\}$	Proposition 3
Cut	Denial preservation, monotony, rewriting	$\neg\varphi \notin K,\ \neg\psi \notin K$	Proposition 5
Cautious monotony	Denial elimination, monotony, rewriting	$\neg\varphi \notin K,\ \neg\psi \notin K$	Proposition 4
Right weakening	Dominance, antinomy increase	$\neg\varphi \notin K,\ \neg\psi \notin K$	Corrolary 1
AND	Disjunct minimality, rewriting, monotony	$\neg\varphi \notin K,\ \neg\psi \notin K$	Proposition 9
Rational monotony	Monotony, rewriting	$\neg\varphi \notin K$	Proposition 10
Contraposition	Rewriting, mutual increase	$\varphi \models \bot,\ \neg\psi \neq \varphi,$ $\neg\psi \neq \neg\neg\varphi$	Proposition 11

instance, a consequence of Lemma 6 is that Tautology Non-Increase makes AND to fail whenever Reflexivity holds for all consistent formulas (let $K \supseteq \{\varphi, \neg\varphi\}$ for some consistent non-tautological φ). Then we have the following proposition.

Proposition 14. *If I satisfies Penalty and Tautology Non-Increase, then $\Vdash$ fails to satisfy AND.*

7   Conclusion and Future Work

In order to reason with inconsistent knowledge bases, we have proposed a new family of inference relations induced from inconsistency measures. It is worth mentioning that the new inference relations have the same consequences as classical logic when premises are consistent. We have shown that these inference relations satisfy some important nonmonotonic reasoning properties (restricted to some extra requirements) when the corresponding inconsistency measures satisfy some rationality postulates (see Table 1). Furthermore, we have shown that the new inference relations are paraconsistent when the corresponding inconsistency measures satisfy some rationality postulates; importantly, every relative inconsistency measures can induce a paraconsistent inference relation. Lastly, we have presented some dependencies and incompatibilities among postulates.

This article opens up directions for future research. Firstly, we will continue to investigate whether the remaining KLM properties (i.e. Equivalence, MPC,

Transitivity, EHD, Loop) can be satisfied. We will also keep on investigating dependencies and incompatibilities between postulates. Secondly, we will consider an extension of the approach to infinite knowledge bases. An idea in this sense would be that the inference relation $\Vdash$ induced from an inconsistency measure I, considering an infinite knowledge base X, would be such that: $X \Vdash \varphi$ iff $I(Y \cup \{\neg\varphi\}) > I(Y \backslash \{\neg\varphi\})$ for some finite $Y \subseteq X$.

References

1. Besnard, P.: Revisiting postulates for inconsistency measures. In: Fermé, E., Leite, J. (eds.) JELIA 2014. LNCS (LNAI), vol. 8761, pp. 383–396. Springer, Cham (2014). https://doi.org/10.1007/978-3-319-11558-0_27
2. Besnard, P., Grant, J.: Relative inconsistency measures. Artif. Intell. **280**, 103231 (2020)
3. Brown, B.: Inconsistency measures and paraconsistent consequence. In: Grant, J., Martinez, M.V. (eds.) Measuring Inconsistency in Information, Studies in Logic, vol. 73, pp. 219–233. College Publications (2018)
4. Grant, J., Hunter, A.: Measuring consistency gain and information loss in stepwise inconsistency resolution. In: Liu, W. (ed.) ECSQARU 2011. LNCS (LNAI), vol. 6717, pp. 362–373. Springer, Heidelberg (2011). https://doi.org/10.1007/978-3-642-22152-1_31
5. Hunter, A., Konieczny, S.: On the measure of conflicts: shapley inconsistency values. Artif. Intell. **174**(14), 1007–1026 (2010)
6. Konieczny, S., Lang, J., Marquis, P.: Quantifying information and contradiction in propositional logic through test actions. In: Gottlob, G., Walsh, T. (eds.) Proceedings of the 18th International Joint Conference on Artificial Intelligence (IJCAI 2003), 9–15 August , 2003, Acapulco, Mexico, pp. 106–111. Morgan Kaufmann (2003)
7. Kraus, S., Lehmann, D., Magidor, M.: Nonmonotonic reasoning, preferential models and cumulative logics. Artif. Intell. **44**(1–2), 167–207 (1990)
8. Makinson, D.: General patterns in nonmonotonic reasoning. In: Gabbay, D.M., Hogger, C.J., Robinson, J.A. (eds.) Handbook of Logic in Artificial Intelligence and Logic Programming, vol. 3, pp. 35–110. Clarendon Press, Oxford (1994)
9. Mu, K., Liu, W., Jin, Z.: A general framework for measuring inconsistency through minimal inconsistent sets. J. Knowl. Inf. Syst. **27**(1), 85–114 (2011)
10. Oller, C.: Measuring coherence using LP-models. J. Appl. Logic **2**(4), 451–455 (2004)
11. Priest, G.: The logic of paradox. J. Philos. Logic **8**(1), 219–241 (1979)
12. Scott, D.: Completeness and axiomatizability in many-valued logic. In: Henkin, L.A. (ed.) Tarski Symposium, Proceedings of Symposia in Pure Mathematics, Providence, RI, USA, vol. 25, pp. 411–436. American Mathematical Society (1974)
13. Tarski, A.: On some Fundamental Concepts of Metamathematics. In: Logic, Semantics, Metamathematics, 2nd edn, pp. 30–37. Hackett, Indianapolis (1983). Translated by J. H. Woodger, edited by John Corcoran
14. Thimm, M.: Measuring inconsistency in probabilistic knowledge bases. In: Bilmes, J.A., Ng, A.Y. (eds.) 25th Conference on Uncertainty in Artificial Intelligence (UAI 2009), 18–21 June 2009, Montreal, QC, Canada, pp. 530–537. AUAI Press (2009)
15. Thimm, M.: On the evaluation of inconsistency measures. In: Grant, J., Martinez, M.V. (eds.) Measuring Inconsistency in Information, Studies in Logic, vol. 73, pp. 19–60. College Publications (2018)

The Degree of Conflict Between Formulas in an Inconsistent Knowledge Base

Kedian Mu[(✉)]

School of Mathematical Sciences, Peking University, Beijing, P.R. China
mukedian@math.pku.edu.cn

Abstract. Measuring inconsistency in a knowledge base has been increasingly recognized as a good starting point to better understand the inconsistency of that base. Most approaches to measuring inconsistency for knowledge bases focus on either the degree of inconsistency of a whole knowledge base or the responsibility of each formula of a knowledge base for the inconsistency in that base or both. In this paper, we propose an approach to measuring the degree of conflict between formulas, which allows us to have a more clear picture on the relation between formulas involved in inconsistency. Then we show that this measure can be explained well in the framework of Halpern-Pearl's causal model.

Keywords: Inconsistency · Propositional knowledge bases · Degree of conflict · Causality

1 Introduction

Inconsistency handling is one of the most important issues in knowledge-based applications of artificial intelligence. It has been increasingly recognized that measuring inconsistency provides a promising starting point to understand inconsistency better and to facilitate the inconsistency handling for knowledge bases [11].

A variety of inconsistency measures for a knowledge base (a finite set of logical formulas) have been proposed so far. These measures may be grouped into two categories, i.e., base-level measures and formula-level measures [8]. Roughly speaking, base-level measures for a knowledge base aim to characterize the inconsistency from a perspective of the whole knowledge base. Such measures are often used to describe the degree of inconsistency [8] or the significance of inconsistency [4] of the whole base. In contrast, formula-level measures aim to characterize the role of an individual formula in causing the inconsistency in a knowledge base. Such measures are often used to describe the contribution made by each formula to the inconsistency [6] or the degree of responsibility of each formula for the inconsistency [14] in a knowledge base. However, we also need to know whether there is a conflictive relation between two formulas and to what extent they contradict each other in some scenarios, especially when we choose formulas to be modified in order to restore the consistency of a knowledge base. For example, consider a

© Springer Nature Switzerland AG 2021
J. Vejnarová and N. Wilson (Eds.): ECSQARU 2021, LNAI 12897, pp. 499–510, 2021.
https://doi.org/10.1007/978-3-030-86772-0_36

knowledge base $\{a, \neg a, \neg a \vee b, \neg b, c\}$. Obviously, a and $\neg a$ contradict each other directly, whilst neither $\neg a \vee b$ nor $\neg b$ contradicts a directly. But a is in conflict with a combination of $\neg a \vee b$ and $\neg b$. In contrast, c is not involved in any conflict with a or combinations of a and some other formulas. Neither the formula-level inconsistency measure nor the base-level inconsistency measure describes such a conflictive relation between two formulas explicitly.

Minimal inconsistent subsets of a knowledge base provide a natural characterization of inconsistency arising in that base, especially for scenarios of syntax-based inconsistency handling [1,3,7,9,10,12–15]. Here a minimal inconsistent subset of a knowledge base refers to an inconsistent subset without an inconsistent proper subset. Moreover, there is a conflictive relation among formulas involved in a minimal inconsistent subset of a knowledge base in intuition. Then it is natural to characterize conflictive relations between formulas based on minimal inconsistent subsets.

In this paper, we focus on conflictive relations between formulas in a given inconsistent knowledge base based on minimal inconsistent subsets of that base. Moreover, we propose an approach to evaluating the degree of conflict between any two formulas. Then we give an intuitive explanation of this evaluation in the framework of Halpern-Pearl's causal model [5] from a perspective of causality.

The rest of this paper is organized as follows. In Sect. 2, we give very brief introductions to inconsistent knowledge bases and Halpern-Pearl's causal model, respectively. Then we propose an approach to measuring the degree of conflict between formulas in an inconsistent knowledge base in Sect. 3. In Sect. 4, we provide an intuitive explanation of this measurement in the framework of Halpern-Pearl's causal model. Finally, we conclude this paper in Sect. 5.

2   Preliminaries

We use a finite propositional language in this paper. Let $\mathcal{P}$ be a finite set of propositional symbols (atoms or variables) and $\mathcal{L}$ a propositional language built from $\mathcal{P}$ under connectives $\{\neg, \wedge, \vee, \rightarrow\}$. We use a, b, c, $\cdots$ to denote the propositional atoms, and α, β, γ, $\cdots$ to denote the distinct propositional formulas.

A *knowledge base* K is a finite set of propositional formulas. Just for simplicity, we assume that each knowledge base is non-empty. For example, both $\{a\}$ and $\{a, \neg a \vee b, c\}$ are knowledge bases.

K is *inconsistent* if there is a formula α such that $K \vdash \alpha$ and $K \vdash \neg\alpha$, where $\vdash$ is the classical consequence relation. We abbreviate $\alpha \wedge \neg\alpha$ as $\bot$ when there is no confusion. Then we use $K \vdash \bot$ (resp. $K \nvdash \bot$) to denote that a knowledge base K is inconsistent (resp. consistent). In particular, given a formula α, we say that α is consistent if $\{\alpha\}$ is consistent. Just for simplicity of discussion, we assume that each formula of a knowledge base is consistent. In addition, we use $K \cup \{\gamma\}$ to denote that we enlarge the knowledge base K by adding a new formula $\gamma \notin K$ to K.

An inconsistent subset K' of K is called a *minimal inconsistent subset* (or *minimal unsatisfiable subset*) of K if no proper subset of K' is inconsistent. We use $\mathsf{MI}(K)$ to denote the set of all the minimal inconsistent subsets of K, i.e.,

$$\mathsf{MI}(K) = \{K' \subseteq K | K' \vdash \perp \text{ and } \forall K'' \subset K', K'' \not\vdash \perp\}.$$

In syntax-based application domains, $\mathsf{MI}(K)$ could be considered as a characterization of the inconsistency in K in the sense that one needs to remove only one formula from each minimal inconsistent subset to resolve the inconsistency [16].

Let $\mathsf{Sub}(K)$ be a set of some subsets of K, we abbreviate $\bigcup_{K' \in \mathsf{Sub}(K)} K'$ as $\bigcup \mathsf{Sub}(K)$. For example, $\bigcup \mathsf{MI}(K)$ is the abbreviation of $\bigcup_{M \in \mathsf{MI}(K)} M$. It denotes the set of formulas involved in minimal inconsistent subsets.

A formula in K is called a *free formula* if this formula does not belong to any minimal inconsistent subset of K [6]. That is, free formulas have nothing to do with any minimal inconsistent subset of K. We use $\mathsf{FREE}(K)$ to denote the set of free formulas of K, i.e.,

$$\mathsf{FREE}(K) = \{\alpha \in K | \forall M \in \mathsf{MI}(K), \alpha \notin M\}.$$

Evidently, $K = (\bigcup \mathsf{MI}(K)) \cup \mathsf{FREE}(K)$.

Now we use the following example to illustrate these notions.

Example 1. Consider $K_1 = \{a, \neg a, \neg a \vee b, \neg b, c, d, \neg d\}$. Then

$$\mathsf{MI}(K_1) = \{M_1, M_2, M_3\}, \quad \mathsf{FREE}(K_1) = \{c\},$$

where

$$M_1 = \{a, \neg a\}, M_2 = \{a, \neg a \vee b, \neg b\}, M_3 = \{d, \neg d\}.$$

Next we give very brief introductions to Halpern and Pearl's causal model [5] and Chockler and Halpern's notion of responsibility [2], respectively. For more material, please see Sect. 2 and Sect. 3 in [2].

We start with the signature of a causal model. A signature is a tuple $\mathcal{S} = \langle \mathcal{U}, \mathcal{V}, \mathcal{R} \rangle$, where $\mathcal{U}$ is a finite set of exogenous variables, whose values are determined by factors outside a causal model, $\mathcal{V}$ is a finite set of endogenous variables, whose values are ultimately determined by the exogenous variables, and $\mathcal{R}$ associates with every variable $Y \in \mathcal{U} \cup \mathcal{V}$ a finite nonempty set $\mathcal{R}(Y)$ of possible values for Y [2,5].

A causal model over signature $\mathcal{S}$ is a tuple $\mathcal{M} = \langle \mathcal{S}, \mathcal{F} \rangle$, where $\mathcal{F}$ associates with every endogenous variable $X \in \mathcal{V}$ a function F_X such that $F_X : ((\times_{U \in \mathcal{U}} \mathcal{R}(U)) \times (\times_{Y \in \mathcal{V} \setminus \{X\}} \mathcal{R}(Y))) \to \mathcal{R}(X)$ [2,5].

We use $\vec{X}$ and $\vec{x}$ to denote a (possibly empty) vector of variables in $\mathcal{V}$ and values for the variables in $\vec{X}$, respectively. We use $\vec{X} \leftarrow \vec{x}$ to denote the case of setting the values of the variables in $\vec{X}$ to $\vec{x}$. We use $\vec{u}$ to denote a setting for the variables in $\mathcal{U}$. Here we call $\vec{u}$ a context [2,5].

Given $\vec{X} \leftarrow \vec{x}$, a new causal model denoted $\mathcal{M}_{\vec{X} \leftarrow \vec{x}}$ over the signature $\mathcal{S}_{\vec{X}} = \langle \mathcal{U}, \mathcal{V} - \vec{X}, \mathcal{R}|_{\mathcal{V} - \vec{X}} \rangle$, is defined as $\mathcal{M}_{\vec{X} \leftarrow \vec{x}} = \langle \mathcal{S}_{\vec{X}}, \mathcal{F}^{\vec{X} \leftarrow \vec{x}} \rangle$, where $F_Y^{\vec{X} \leftarrow \vec{x}}$ is obtained from F_Y by setting the values of the variables in $\vec{X}$ to $\vec{x}$ [2,5].

Given a signature $\mathcal{S} = \langle \mathcal{U}, \mathcal{V}, \mathcal{R} \rangle$, a primitive event is a formula of the form $X = x$, where $X \in \mathcal{V}$ and $x \in \mathcal{R}(X)$ [2,5]. In general, for $\vec{X} = (X_1, X_2, \cdots, X_n)$ and $\vec{x} = (x_1, x_2, \cdots, x_n)$, we abbreviate $(X_1 = x_1) \wedge (X_2 = x_2) \wedge \cdots \wedge (X_n = x_n)$ as $\vec{X} = \vec{x}$.

A basic causal formula defined in [2,5] is in the form of $[\vec{Y} \leftarrow \vec{y}]\varphi$, where φ is a Boolean combination of primitive events. As explained in [2,5], $[\vec{Y} \leftarrow \vec{y}]\varphi$ means that φ holds in the counterfactual world that would arise if $\vec{Y}$ is set to $\vec{y}$.

A causal formula is a Boolean combination of basic causal formulas [2,5]. We use $(\mathcal{M}, \vec{u}) \models \varphi$ to denote that a causal formula φ is true in causal model $\mathcal{M}$ given a context $\vec{u}$. Given a recursive model M, $(\mathcal{M}, \vec{u}) \models [\vec{Y} \leftarrow \vec{y}](X = x)$ if the value of X is x in the unique vector of values for the endogenous variables that simultaneously satisfies all equations $F_Z^{\vec{Y} \leftarrow \vec{y}}, Z \in \mathcal{V} - Y$ under the setting $\vec{u}$ of $\mathcal{U}$ [2,5]. Note that this definition can be extended to arbitrary causal formulas in the usual way.

Definition 1 (Cause [5]). *We say that $\vec{X} = \vec{x}$ is a cause of φ in $(\mathcal{M}, \vec{u})$ if the following three conditions hold:*

AC1. $(\mathcal{M}, \vec{u}) \models (\vec{X} = \vec{x}) \wedge \varphi$.

AC2. *There exists a partition $(\vec{Z}, \vec{W})$ of $\mathcal{V}$ with $\vec{X} \subseteq \vec{Z}$ and some setting $(\vec{x}', \vec{w}')$ of the variables in $(\vec{X}, \vec{W})$ such that if $(\mathcal{M}, \vec{u}) \models Z = z^*$ for $Z \in \vec{Z}$, then*

  (a) $(\mathcal{M}, \vec{u}) \models [\vec{X} \leftarrow \vec{x}', \vec{W} \leftarrow \vec{w}']\neg\varphi$. That is, changing $(\vec{X}, \vec{W})$ from $(\vec{x}, \vec{w})$ to $(\vec{x}', \vec{w}')$ changes φ from true to false.

  (b) $(\mathcal{M}, \vec{u}) \models [\vec{X} \leftarrow \vec{x}, \vec{W} \leftarrow \vec{w}', \vec{Z}' \leftarrow \vec{z}^*]\varphi$ for all subsets $\vec{Z}'$ of $\vec{Z} - \vec{X}$. That is, setting $\vec{W}$ to $\vec{w}'$ should have no effect on φ as long as $\vec{X}$ has the value $\vec{x}$, even if all the variables in an arbitrary subset of $\vec{Z}$ are set to their original values in the context $\vec{u}$.

AC3. $(\vec{X} = \vec{x})$ *is minimal, that is, no subset of $\vec{X}$ satisfies AC2.*

Based on Halpern-Pearl's causal model above, the notion of responsibility presented by Chockler and Halpern is given as follows:

Definition 2 (Degree of Responsibility [2]). *The degree of responsibility of $X = x$ for φ in $(\mathcal{M}, \vec{u})$, denoted $dr((\mathcal{M}, \vec{u}), (X = x), \varphi)$, is 0 if $X = x$ is not a cause of φ in $(\mathcal{M}, \vec{u})$; it is $\frac{1}{k+1}$ if $X = x$ is a cause of φ in $(\mathcal{M}, \vec{u})$ and there exists a partition $(\vec{Z}, \vec{W})$ and setting $x', \vec{w}'$ for which AC2 holds such that (a) k variables in $\vec{W}$ have different values in $\vec{w}'$ than they do in the context $\vec{u}$ and (b) there is no partition $(\vec{Z}', \vec{W}')$ and setting $x'', \vec{w}''$ satisfying AC2 such that only $k' < k$ variables have different values in $\vec{w}''$ than they do in the context $\vec{u}$.*

As explained in [2], the degree of responsibility of $X = x$ for φ in $(\mathcal{M}, \vec{u})$ captures the minimal number of changes that have to be made in $\vec{u}$ in order to make φ counterfactually depend on X.

3   Degree of Conflict Between Formulas

In this section, we consider the degree of conflict between formulas in an inconsistent knowledge base. We start with a notion of α-minimal inconsistent subset.

Definition 3. *Let K be an inconsistent knowledge base and $\alpha \in K$ a formula of K. A minimal inconsistent subset M of K is called an α-minimal inconsistent subset of K if $\alpha \in M$.*

We use $\mathsf{MI}(K|\alpha)$ to denote the set of all α-minimal inconsistent subsets of K. Evidently, $\mathsf{MI}(K|\alpha) = \emptyset$ if and only if $\alpha \in \mathsf{FREE}(K)$.

Definition 4. *Given a knowledge base K and α, β two distinct formulas of K, we say that there exists a conflictive relation between α and β, denoted $\alpha \bowtie \beta$, if $\exists M \in \mathsf{MI}(K)$ s.t. $\{\alpha, \beta\} \subseteq M$.*

We can get the following observations on the conflictive relation. Firstly, note that $\alpha \bowtie \beta$ if and only if there exists at least one minimal inconsistent subset containing both α and β. Then the conflictive relation is symmetrical, that is, $\beta \bowtie \alpha$ if and only if $\alpha \bowtie \beta$. Secondly, there is no conflictive relation between free formulas, moreover, there is no conflictive relation between a free formula and any formula involved in minimal inconsistent subsets.

We use the following example to illustrate the notion of conflictive relation.

Example 2. Consider K_1 again. Then

$$\mathsf{MI}(K_1|a) = \{M_1, M_2\}, \quad \mathsf{MI}(K_1|\neg a) = \{M_1\},$$
$$\mathsf{MI}(K_1|\neg a \vee b) = \mathsf{MI}(K_1|\neg b) = \{M_2\},$$
$$\mathsf{MI}(K_1|d) = \mathsf{MI}(K_1|\neg d) = \{M_3\}, \quad \mathsf{MI}(K_1|c) = \emptyset.$$

So, we can find the following conflictive relations between formulas:

$$a \bowtie \neg a, a \bowtie \neg a \vee b, a \bowtie \neg b, \quad \neg a \vee b \bowtie \neg b, \quad d \bowtie \neg d.$$

Given two formulas $\alpha, \beta \in K$, we abbreviate $\mathsf{MI}(K|\alpha) \cap \mathsf{MI}(K|\beta)$ as $\mathsf{MI}(K|\alpha \cap \beta)$. Evidently, $\alpha \bowtie \beta$ if and only if $\mathsf{MI}(K|\alpha \cap \beta) \neq \emptyset$. Now we are ready to define the degree of conflict between formulas.

Definition 5. *Let K be a knowledge base and α, β two distinct formulas of K. Then the degree of conflict between α and β in K, denoted $C(\alpha, \beta|K)$, is defined as*

$$C(\alpha, \beta|K) = \begin{cases} \max\limits_{M \in \mathsf{MI}(K|\alpha \cap \beta)} \frac{1}{|M|-1}, & \text{if } \alpha \bowtie \beta, \\ 0, & \text{otherwise.} \end{cases}$$

Evidently, we can get the following observations on the degree of conflict between formulas:

(1) $0 \le C(\alpha, \beta | K) \le 1$.
(2) $C(\alpha, \beta | K) = C(\beta, \alpha | K)$.
(3) $C(\alpha, \beta | K) = 0$ for all $\beta \in K \backslash \{\alpha\}$ if $\alpha \in \mathsf{FREE}(K)$.

The first two observations together state that C is a bounded symmetric function. The third states that any free formula is not in conflict with other formulas.

The following proposition provides characterizations of the upper and the lower bounds of the degree of conflict between formulas.

Proposition 1. *Given a knowledge base K and α, β two distinct formulas of K, then*

1. $C(\alpha, \beta | K) = 1$ *if and only if* $\{\alpha, \beta\} \in \mathsf{MI}(K)$.
2. $C(\alpha, \beta | K) = 0$ *if and only if* $\mathsf{MI}(K | \alpha) \cap \mathsf{MI}(K | \beta) = \emptyset$.

Proof. This is a direct consequence of the definition of $C(\alpha, \beta | K)$. □

Now we use the following example to illustrate the degree of conflict between formulas.

Example 3. Consider $K_1 = \{a, \neg a, \neg a \vee b, \neg b, c, d, \neg d\}$ again. Then

$$C(a, \neg a | K_1) = 1, \quad C(d, \neg d | K_1) = 1.$$

$$C(a, \neg a \vee b | K_1) = C(a, \neg b | K_1) = C(\neg a \vee b, \neg b | K_1) = \frac{1}{2},$$

$$C(a, d | K_1) = C(a, \neg d | K_1) = C(a, c | K_1) = 0.$$

This coincides with the intuition that a and $\neg a$ contradict each other directly, while a and $\neg b$ (resp. $\neg a \vee b$) are involved in the inconsistency given $\neg a \vee b$ (resp. $\neg b$).

Note that given a minimal inconsistent subset $M \in \mathsf{MI}(K)$, $C(\alpha, \beta | K) > 0$ for all $\alpha \in M$ and $\beta \in M \backslash \{\alpha\}$. But it does not always hold that $C(\alpha, \beta | K) = C(\alpha, \gamma | K)$ for $\beta, \gamma \in M \backslash \{\alpha\}$ given $\alpha \in M$. To illustrate this, consider

$$K_2 = \{a, a \rightarrow b \wedge c, \neg b, c \rightarrow d, \neg d\}.$$

Then

$$\mathsf{MI}(K_2) = \{M_4 = \{a, a \rightarrow b \wedge c, \neg b\}, M_5 = \{a, a \rightarrow b \wedge c, c \rightarrow d, \neg d\}\}.$$

Consider M_5, then we find that

$$C(a, a \rightarrow b \wedge c | K_2) = \frac{1}{2} > \frac{1}{3} = C(a, c \rightarrow d | K_2) = C(a, \neg d | K_2).$$

However, the following proposition shows that all the other formulas in the smallest α-minimal inconsistent subset have the same degree of conflict with α.

Proposition 2. *Let K be an inconsistent knowledge base and $\alpha \in \bigcup \mathsf{MI}(K)$ a formula of K. Then*

$$C(\alpha, \beta | K) = C(\alpha, \gamma | K)$$

for all $\beta, \gamma \in M^* \backslash \{\alpha\}$, where $M^* \in \mathsf{MI}(K | \alpha)$ s.t. $|M^*| \le |M|$ for all $M \in \mathsf{MI}(K | \alpha)$.

Proof. Let K be an inconsistent knowledge base and $\alpha \in \bigcup \mathsf{MI}(K)$, then $\{\alpha\} \subseteq M^* \in \mathsf{MI}(K|\alpha)$. Moreover, for all $\beta \in M^* \backslash \{\alpha\}$,

$$C(\alpha, \beta|K) = \frac{1}{|M^*| - 1}.$$

So,

$$C(\alpha, \beta|K) = C(\alpha, \gamma|K)$$

for all $\beta, \gamma \in M^* \backslash \{\alpha\}$. $\qquad\square$

The following proposition shows that the measure satisfies some intuitive properties adapted from the most used properties presented by Hunter and Konieczny for characterizing inconsistency measures [6–8].

Proposition 3. *Let K be a knowledge base. Then*

- Consistency: $C(\alpha, \beta|K) = 0$ *for all* $\alpha, \beta \in K$ *if and only if K is consistent.*
- Free Formula Independence: $C(\alpha, \beta|K) = C(\alpha, \beta|K \cup \{\gamma\})$ *for all* $\alpha, \beta \in K$ *if* $\gamma \in \mathsf{FREE}(K \cup \{\gamma\})$.
- Monotonicity: $C(\alpha, \beta|K) \leq C(\alpha, \beta|K \cup \{\gamma\})$.
- Dominance-1: *For all three distinct formulas* $\alpha, \beta, \gamma \in K$, $C(\alpha, \beta|K) \leq C(\alpha, \gamma|K)$ *if* $\gamma \vdash \beta$.
- Dominance-2: *For any two formulas* $\alpha, \beta \in K$, $C(\alpha, \beta|K \cup \{\gamma_2\}) \leq C(\alpha, \beta|K \cup \{\gamma_1\})$ *if* $\gamma_1 \vdash \gamma_2$.

Proof. Let K be a knowledge base.

- *Consistency.* $\forall \alpha, \beta \in K$, $C(\alpha, \beta|K) = 0. \Longleftrightarrow \mathsf{MI}(K) = \emptyset. \Longleftrightarrow K$ is consistent.
- *Free Formula Independence.* If γ is a free formula of $K \cup \{\gamma\}$, then $\mathsf{MI}(K \cup \{\gamma\}) = \mathsf{MI}(K)$. So, $\forall \alpha \in K$, $\mathsf{MI}(K|\alpha) = \mathsf{MI}(K \cup \{\gamma\}|\alpha)$. Therefore,

$$C(\alpha, \beta|K) = C(\alpha, \beta|K \cup \{\gamma\}).$$

- *Monotonicity.* Note that $\forall \gamma \notin K$, $\mathsf{MI}(K) \subseteq \mathsf{MI}(K \cup \{\gamma\})$. So, $\forall \alpha \in K$, $\mathsf{MI}(K|\alpha) \subseteq \mathsf{MI}(K \cup \{\gamma\}|\alpha)$. Therefore,

$$C(\alpha, \beta|K) \leq C(\alpha, \beta|K \cup \{\gamma\}).$$

- *Dominance-1.* Let α, β, and γ be three distinct formulas of K. If $\gamma \vdash \beta$, then
  - if $\mathsf{MI}(K|\alpha \cap \beta) = \emptyset$, then $C(\alpha, \beta|K) = 0 \leq C(\alpha, \gamma|K)$.
  - if $\mathsf{MI}(K|\alpha \cap \beta) \neq \emptyset$, then $\forall M \in \mathsf{MI}(K|\alpha \cap \beta)$, $\exists M' \in \mathsf{MI}(K|\alpha \cap \gamma)$ such that

$$M' \subseteq (M \cup \{\gamma\}) \backslash \{\beta\}.$$

  Therefore,

$$C(\alpha, \beta|K) \leq C(\alpha, \gamma|K).$$

- *Dominance-2:* Consider two formulas $\gamma_1, \gamma_2 \notin K$ such that $\gamma_1 \vdash \gamma_2$.
  - If $\mathsf{MI}(K \cup \{\gamma_2\}) = \emptyset$, then for any two distinct formulas $\alpha, \beta \in K$,

$$C(\alpha, \beta|K \cup \{\gamma_2\}) = 0 \leq C(\alpha, \beta|K \cup \{\gamma_1\}).$$

• If $MI(K \cup \{\gamma_2\}) \neq \emptyset$ but $MI(K \cup \{\gamma_2\}) = MI(K)$, then γ_2 is a free formula of $K \cup \{\gamma_2\}$, then

$$C(\alpha, \beta | K \cup \{\gamma_2\}) = C(\alpha, \beta | K).$$

Furthermore, according to the property of Monotonicity, we have

$$C(\alpha, \beta | K) \leq C(\alpha, \beta | K \cup \{\gamma_1\}).$$

So,

$$C(\alpha, \beta | K \cup \{\gamma_2\}) \leq C(\alpha, \beta | K \cup \{\gamma_1\}).$$

• If $MI(K \cup \{\gamma_2\}) \neq \emptyset$ but $MI(K \cup \{\gamma_2\}) \neq MI(K)$, then $\exists M \in MI(K \cup \{\gamma_2\})$ such that $\gamma_2 \in M$. So, $\exists M' \in MI(K \cup \{\gamma_1\})$ such that

$$M' \subseteq (M \cup \{\gamma_1\}) \setminus \{\gamma_2\}.$$

So,

$$\min_{M \in MI(K \cup \{\gamma_1\} | \alpha \cap \beta)} |M| \leq \min_{M' \in MI(K \cup \{\gamma_2\} | \alpha \cap \beta)} |M'|.$$

Therefore,

$$C(\alpha, \beta | K \cup \{\gamma_2\}) \leq C(\alpha, \beta | K \cup \{\gamma_1\}).$$

$\square$

Roughly speaking, the property of Consistency says that only within a consistent knowledge base, any two formulas are not in conflict with each other. The property of Free Formula Independence says that adding a free formula to a knowledge base cannot affect the degree of conflict between any two formulas in that base. The property of Monotonicity states that the degree of conflict between any two formulas of a knowledge base cannot decrease when we enlarge that base. The property of Dominance-1 states that if a formula γ is logically stronger than another formula β, then the degree of conflict between β with any other formula cannot exceed that between γ with that formula. In contrast, the property of Dominance-2 states that adding logically stronger formulas to a knowledge base may lift the degree of conflict between formulas in that base. In summary, the two properties of dominance imply that logically stronger formulas may bring more conflicts.

The following proposition describes the relation between the smallest size of minimal inconsistent subsets of an inconsistent knowledge base and the degree of conflict between formulas of that base.

Proposition 4. *Let K be an inconsistent knowledge base. Then*

$$\min_{M \in MI(K)} |M| = \frac{1}{\max\limits_{\alpha, \beta \in K} C(\alpha, \beta | K)} + 1.$$

Proof. This is a direct consequence of the definition of $C(\alpha, \beta | K)$. $\square$

4   The Causality-Based Explanation

In this section, we provide a causality-based explanation for the degree of conflict between formulas in the framework of Halpern-Pearl's model.

Given an inconsistent knowledge base K, we construct the following causal model for the conflictive relations between formulas in K:

- we associate every formula $\alpha \in K$ with a binary variable X_α, whose value is 1 if α is considered and 0 otherwise. We use $\vec{X}$ to denote the vector of all the variables corresponding to formulas.
- we associate every formula variable X_α a binary exogenous U_α. Moreover, we assume that the value of X_α depends on only the value of U_α. We use $\mathcal{U}_K$ and $\vec{U}$ to denote the set and the vector of all the exogenous variables.
- we associate every pair (α, β) of formulas of K with a binary variable $Y_{(\alpha,\beta)}$, whose value is 1 if α conflicts with β and 0 otherwise. We use $\vec{Y}$ to denote the vector of all the variables of this type corresponding to formulas.
- we associate with every α-minimal inconsistent subset $M \in \mathsf{MI}(K|\alpha)$ a binary variable $S_{M|\alpha}$, whose value is 1 if all the formulas of $M \backslash \{\alpha\}$ are considered and 0 otherwise. We use $\vec{S}$ to denote the vector of all the variables of this type.

Let $\mathcal{V}_K = \{X_\alpha | \alpha \in K\} \cup \{Y_{(\alpha,\beta)} | \alpha, \beta \in K\} \cup \{S_{M|\alpha} | M \in \mathsf{MI}(K|\alpha), \alpha \in K\}$. Then $\mathcal{R}_K(V) = \{0, 1\}$ for each $V \in \mathcal{V}_K$.

Futhermore, we define the following functions to characterize the dependence relation between these variables:

- $F_{X_\alpha}(\vec{U}, \vec{X} - X_\alpha, \vec{Y}, \vec{S}) = U_\alpha$ ($X_\alpha = U_\alpha$ for short) for every formula $\alpha \in K$.
- $F_{S_{M|\alpha}}(\vec{U}, \vec{X}, \vec{Y}, \vec{S} - S_{M|\alpha}) = \displaystyle\prod_{\beta \in M \backslash \{\alpha\}} X_\beta$ $\left(S_{M|\alpha} = \displaystyle\prod_{\beta \in M \backslash \{\alpha\}} X_\beta \text{ for short} \right)$ for every $M \in \mathsf{MI}(K|\alpha)$.
- $F_{Y_{(\alpha,\beta)}}(\vec{U}, \vec{X}, \vec{Y} - Y_{(\alpha,\beta)}, \vec{S}) = \displaystyle\bigoplus_{M \in \mathsf{MI}(K|\alpha \cap \beta)} S_{M|\alpha}$ $\left(Y_{(\alpha,\beta)} = \displaystyle\bigoplus_{M \in \mathsf{MI}(K|\alpha \cap \beta)} S_{M|\alpha} \right.$ for short) for every variable $Y_{(\alpha,\beta)}$, where $\bigoplus$ is the Boolean addition.

Roughly speaking, the function F_{X_α} represents the assumption that the value of variable X_α is determined by only the value of the corresponding exogenous variable U_α. The function $F_{S_{M|\alpha}}$ describes the fact that all the other formulas in the α-minimal inconsistent subset M together involve α in the minimal inconsistent subset M. That is, removing any other formula from the α-minimal inconsistent subset M can break M. The function $F_{Y_{(\alpha,\beta)}}$ describes the fact that α will not be free from conflict with β if at least one $\alpha \cap \beta$-minimal inconsistent subset keeps unchanged. We use $\mathcal{F}_K$ to denote the set of all the functions above for K, i.e.,

$$\mathcal{F}_K = \{F_{X_\alpha} | \alpha \in K\} \cup \{F_{Y_{(\alpha,\beta)}} | \alpha, \beta \in K\} \cup \{F_{S_{M|\alpha}} | M \in \mathsf{MI}(K|\alpha), \alpha \in K\}.$$

Then the causal model for the conflict relation between formulas of K, denoted $\mathcal{M}_K$, is defined as $\mathcal{M}_K = \langle \mathcal{S}_K, \mathcal{F}_K \rangle$, where $\mathcal{S}_K = \langle \mathcal{U}_K, \mathcal{V}_K, \mathcal{R}_K \rangle$. We use the context $\vec{u}_{(\alpha,\beta)} = (0, 0, \ldots, 0, 1, 0)$ ($\vec{u}_{(\alpha,\beta)} = (\vec{0}, 1, 0)$ for short) to represent the case where $U_\alpha = 1$, $U_\beta = 0$ and $U_\gamma = 0$ for all $\gamma \in K \backslash \{\alpha, \beta\}$, i.e., only α is considered.

We use the following example to illustrate the causal model for conflictive relations between formulas.

Example 4. Consider $K_1 = \{a, \neg a, \neg a \lor b, \neg b, c, d, \neg d\}$ again. Here we only consider the conflictive relations between a and other formulas. Note that $MI(K_1|a) = \{M_1, M_2\}$, where $M_1 = \{a, \neg a\}$ and $M_2 = \{a, \neg a \lor b, \neg b\}$. Then

- $S_{M_1|a} = X_{\neg a}$ and $S_{M_2|a} = X_{\neg a \lor b} \times X_{\neg b}$.
- $Y_{(a,\neg a)} = S_{M_1|a}$ and $Y_{(a,\neg a \lor b)} = Y_{(a,\neg b)} = S_{M_2|a}$.

Given a context $\vec{u}_{(a,\neg b)} = (\vec{0}, 1, 0)$, then $(\mathcal{M}_{K_1}, \vec{u}_{(a,\neg b)}) \models (Y_{(a,\neg b)} = 0)$.

Furthermore, consider counterfactual worlds arising from $X_{\neg a \lor b} \leftarrow 1$ and $X_{\neg b} \leftarrow 1$ then

$$(\mathcal{M}_{K_1}, \vec{u}_{(a,\neg b)}) \models [X_{\neg a \lor b} \leftarrow 1, X_{\neg b} \leftarrow 1](Y_{(a,\neg b)} = 1).$$

This implies that a conflicts with $\neg b$ given $\neg a \lor b$.

Now we are ready to characterize the degree of conflict between formulas in the causal model.

Proposition 5. *Given an inconsistent knowledge base K and two distinct formulas $\alpha, \beta \in K$ such that $\alpha \bowtie \beta$. Then*

$$C(\alpha, \beta|K) = dr((\mathcal{M}_K, \vec{u}_{(\alpha,\beta)}), X_\beta = 0, Y_{(\alpha,\beta)} = 0).$$

Proof. Let $\alpha, \beta \in K$ such that $\alpha \bowtie \beta$, then $\exists M \in MI(K|\alpha \cap \beta)$. Let $M_W = M \backslash \{\alpha, \beta\}$ and $\vec{W}$ be the vector of variables corresponding to formulas of M_W. Further, let $\vec{Z} = \mathcal{V} - \vec{W}$, then $X_\alpha, X_\beta \in \vec{Z}$. Note that

$$(\mathcal{M}_K, \vec{u}_{(\alpha,\beta)}) \models X_\beta = 0 \land Y_{(\alpha,\beta)} = 0.$$

Moreover,

$$(\mathcal{M}_K, \vec{u}_{(\alpha,\beta)}) \models [X_\beta \leftarrow 1, \vec{W} \leftarrow \vec{1}]Y_{(\alpha,\beta)} = 1.$$

and

$$(\mathcal{M}_K, \vec{u}_{(\alpha,\beta)}) \models [X_\beta \leftarrow 0, \vec{W} \leftarrow \vec{1}, \vec{Z}' \leftarrow \vec{0}]Y_{(\alpha,\beta)} = 0$$

for all subset $\vec{Z}'$ of $\vec{Z} - (X_\alpha, X_\beta)$.

So, $X_\beta = 0$ is a cause of $Y_{(\alpha,\beta)} = 0$ in the causal model $(\mathcal{M}_K, \vec{u}_{(\alpha,\beta)})$.

Further, consider $M^* \in MI(K|\alpha \cap \beta)$. Let $\vec{W}^*$ be the vector of variables corresponding to formulas of M_W^*, then

$$dr((\mathcal{M}_K, \vec{u}_{(\alpha,\beta)}), X_\beta = 0, Y_{(\alpha,\beta)} = 0) = \frac{1}{1 + |\vec{Z}^*|} = \frac{1}{|M^*| - 1}.$$

By Proposition 2, $C(\alpha, \beta|K) = \frac{1}{|M^*|-1}$. So,

$$C(\alpha, \beta|K) = dr((\mathcal{M}_K, \vec{u}_{(\alpha,\beta)}), X_\beta = 0, Y_{(\alpha,\beta)} = 0).$$

□

This proposition shows that the degree of conflict between two formulas is exactly a special kind of the Chockler and Halpern's degree of responsibility [2] in Halpern and Pearl's causal model. Such a linkage provides an intuitive explanation for the degree of conflict $C(\alpha, \beta|K)$ between two formulas α and β from the perspective of causality.

On the other hand, according to Halpern-Pearl's causal, taking into account the other formulas in a $\alpha \cap \beta$-minimal inconsistent subset exactly obtains a contingency where α conflicts with β. Moreover, the more the formulas involved in such a contingency, the smaller the degree of conflict between α and β is.

5 Conclusion

Measuring inconsistency for knowledge bases has been paid much attention recently. A growing number of techniques for measuring inconsistency have been proposed in a variety of applications so far. Most approaches to measuring inconsistency for a knowledge base focus on either the degree of inconsistency of the whole knowledge base or the degree of responsibility (or contribution) of an individual formula for the inconsistency of the knowledge base or both.

In this paper, we provide a new perspective to look inside the inconsistency in a knowledge base by characterizing the problem of conflictive relations between formulas within that knowledge base. We have proposed an approach to measuring the degree of conflict between any two distinct formulas of a knowledge base based on minimal inconsistent subsets of that base. Then we provided an intuitive explanation for such an approach from the perspective of causality. We have shown that the degree of conflict presented in this paper is exactly a special kind of Chockler and Halpern's responsibility introduced in the context of Halpern-Pearl's causal model.

It has been argued that taking constraints on inconsistency handling into account can make inconsistency measuring techniques more applicable and useful in practical applications [15]. Then it is advisable to incorporate constraints in measuring the degree of conflict between formulas in future.

Acknowledgements. This work was partly supported by the National Natural Science Foundation of China under Grant No. 61572002, No. 61690201, and No. 61732001.

References

1. Bona, G.D., Grant, J., Hunter, A., Konieczny, S.: Towards a unified framework for syntactic inconsistency measures. In: Proceedings of the Thirty-Second AAAI Conference on Artificial Intelligence, (AAAI-18), the 30th innovative Applications of Artificial Intelligence (IAAI-18), and the 8th AAAI Symposium on Educational Advances in Artificial Intelligence (EAAI-18), New Orleans, Louisiana, USA, 2–7 February 2018, pp. 1803–1810 (2018)
2. Chockler, H., Halpern, J.Y.: Responsibility and blame: a structural-model approach. J. Artif. Intell. Res. **22**, 93–115 (2004)
3. Grant, J., Hunter, A.: Measuring consistency gain and information loss in stepwise inconsistency resolution. In: Liu, W. (ed.) ECSQARU 2011. LNCS (LNAI), vol. 6717, pp. 362–373. Springer, Heidelberg (2011). https://doi.org/10.1007/978-3-642-22152-1_31
4. Grant, J., Hunter, A.: Analysing inconsistent information using distance-based measures. Int. J. Approx. Reasoning **89**, 3–26 (2017)
5. Halpern, J.Y., Pearl, J.: Causes and explanations: a structural-model approach. part i: causes. Br. J. Philos. Sci. **56**(4), 843–887 (2005)
6. Hunter, A., Konieczny, S.: Shapley inconsistency values. In: Doherty, P., Mylopoulos, J., Welty, C. (eds.) Principles of Knowledge Representation and Reasoning: Proceedings of the 10th International Conference (KR06), pp. 249–259. AAAI Press (2006)
7. Hunter, A., Konieczny, S.: Measuring inconsistency through minimal inconsistent sets. In: Brewka, G., Lang, J. (eds.) Principles of Knowledge Representation and Reasoning: Proceedings of the Eleventh International Conference (KR08), pp. 358–366. AAAI Press (2008)
8. Hunter, A., Konieczny, S.: On the measure of conflicts: shapley inconsistency values. Artif. Intell. **174**(14), 1007–1026 (2010)
9. Jabbour, S., Ma, Y., Raddaoui, B.: Inconsistency measurement thanks to MUS decomposition. In: Bazzan, A.L.C., Huhns, M.N., Lomuscio, A., Scerri, P. (eds.) International Conference on Autonomous Agents and Multi-Agent Systems, AAMAS 2014, Paris, France, 5–9 May 2014, pp. 877–884. IFAAMAS/ACM (2014)
10. Jabbour, S., Ma, Y., Raddaoui, B., Sais, L., Salhi, Y.: A MIS partition based framework for measuring inconsistency. In: Baral, C., Delgrande, J.P., Wolter, F. (eds.) Principles of Knowledge Representation and Reasoning: Proceedings of the Fifteenth International Conference, KR 2016, Cape Town, South Africa, 25–29 April 2016, pp. 84–93. AAAI Press (2016)
11. Liu, W., Mu, K.: Introduction to the special issue on theories of inconsistency measures and their applications. Int. J. Approx. Reasoning **89**, 1–2 (2017)
12. Mu, K., Jin, Z., Lu, R., Liu, W.: Measuring inconsistency in requirements specifications. In: Godo, L. (ed.) ECSQARU 2005. LNCS (LNAI), vol. 3571, pp. 440–451. Springer, Heidelberg (2005). https://doi.org/10.1007/11518655_38
13. Mu, K., Liu, W., Jin, Z., Bell, D.: A syntax-based approach to measuring the degree of inconsistency for belief bases. Int. J. Approx. Reasoning **52**(7), 978–999 (2011)
14. Mu, K.: Responsibility for inconsistency. Int. J. Approx. Reasoning **61**, 43–60 (2015)
15. Mu, K.: Measuring inconsistency with constraints for propositional knowledge bases. Artif. Intell. **259**, 52–90 (2018)
16. Reiter, R.: A theory of diagnosis from first principles. Artif. Intell. **32**(1), 57–95 (1987)

Possibility Theory and Fuzzy Approaches

Representation of Explanations
of Possibilistic Inference Decisions

Ismaïl Baaj[1,2(✉)], Jean-Philippe Poli[1], Wassila Ouerdane[3],
and Nicolas Maudet[2]

[1] Université Paris-Saclay, CEA, List, 91120 Palaiseau, France
{ismail.baaj,jean-philippe.poli}@cea.fr
[2] LIP6, Sorbonne Université, Paris, France
{ismail.baaj,nicolas.maudet}@lip6.fr
[3] MICS, CentraleSupélec, Université Paris-Saclay, Gif sur Yvette, France
wassila.ouerdane@centralesupelec.fr

Abstract. In this paper, we study how to explain to end-users the inference results of possibilistic rule-based systems. We formulate a necessary and sufficient condition for justifying by a relevant subset of rule premises the possibility degree of each output attribute value. We apply functions to reduce the selected premises, in order to form two kinds of explanations: the *justification* and the *unexpectedness* of the possibility degree of an output attribute value. The justification is composed of possibilistic expressions that are sufficient to justify the possibility degree of the output attribute value. The unexpectedness is a set of possible or certain possibilistic expressions, which are not involved in the determination of the considered inference result although there may appear to be a potential incompatibility between them and the considered inference result.

We then define a representation of explanations of possibilistic inference decisions that relies on conceptual graphs and may be the input of natural language generation systems. Our extracted justification and unexpectedness are represented by nested conceptual graphs. All our constructions are illustrated with an example of a possibilistic rule-based system that controls the blood sugar level of a patient with type 1 diabetes.

Keywords: Explainable artificial intelligence · Possibility theory ·
Rule-based system · Conceptual graphs

1 Introduction

Possibility Theory is a well-known framework for the handling of incomplete or imprecise information [7,8] that models the uncertainty by two dual measures called possibility and necessity. These measures allow to distinguish between what is possible without being certain at all and what is certain to some extent. The possibilistic handling of rule-based systems [10,12] has led to the emergence

© Springer Nature Switzerland AG 2021
J. Vejnarová and N. Wilson (Eds.): ECSQARU 2021, LNAI 12897, pp. 513–527, 2021.
https://doi.org/10.1007/978-3-030-86772-0_37

of possibilistic rule-based systems used for medical diagnostics [4] e.g., DIA-BETO [16]. For safety-critical applications such as medicine, the generation of explanations of the decisions made by AI systems is now a legitimate demand, in view of the recent adoption of laws that reinforce users' rights e.g., GDPR [13]. Recently, an emphasis was put on possibilistic rule-based systems [9], where the authors highlighted the approach of [11] to develop the explanatory capabilities of these systems. In [11], Farreny and Prade propose to perform a sensitivity analysis by using a min-max equations system. By an example, the authors suggest that it is possible to justify an inference result by some rule premises. They also give a natural language explanation of an inference result of their example. In fact, their approach aims at generating explanations of possibilistic inference decisions, which have to be expressed in natural language for end-users. To generate them with Natural Language Generation techniques [14], authors of [2] propose to define a representation of the explanations of inference decisions. In this paper, we elaborate the explanatory capabilities of possibilistic rule-based systems. Our purpose is twofold. First, we study how to select rule premises justifying their inference results. Then, we define a graphical representation of explanations constructed from the selected premises. We first remind the inference mechanism of a possibilistic rule-based system, introduce useful notations and give an example of such a system, which will be used to illustrate all the constructions of the paper (Sect. 2). The inference result of a possibilistic rule-based system is an output possibility distribution, which assigns to each output attribute value a possibility degree. In Sect. 3, we give a necessary and sufficient condition to justify by rule premises the possibility degree of any output attribute value. Under this condition, we extract a corresponding subset of premises.

In Sect. 4, we define four premise reduction functions and apply them to the subset of premises of Sect. 3. This leads us to form two kinds of explanations: the justification and the unexpectedness of the considered output attribute value. The justification is formed by reducing the selected premises to the structure responsible for their possibility or necessity degree. It uses two premise reduction functions. The unexpectedness is a set of possible or certain possibilistic expressions related to the considered inference result in the following sense: although there may appear to be a potential incompatibility between each of the possibilistic expressions and the considered inference result, they are not involved in the determination of the inference result. They are extracted by applying the two other premise reduction functions.

We then propose to represent explanations by conceptual graphs, which provide a natural way to represent knowledge by concepts and n-ary relations (Sect. 5). Using our justification and unexpectedness, we represent explanations by nested conceptual graphs. Finally, in Sect. 6, we conclude with some perspectives.

2   Background

In this section, following [9], we remind the inference mechanism of possibilistic rule-based systems. Some notations which will be useful in the rest of the paper are introduced. We also give an example of a possibilistic rule-based system.

We consider a set of n parallel if-then possibilistic rules $R^1, R^2, \cdots, R^n$, where each R^i is of the form: "if p_i then q_i" and has its uncertainty propagation matrix $\begin{bmatrix} \pi(q_i|p_i) & \pi(q_i|\neg p_i) \\ \pi(\neg q_i|p_i) & \pi(\neg q_i|\neg p_i) \end{bmatrix} = \begin{bmatrix} 1 & s_i \\ r_i & 1 \end{bmatrix}$. The premise p_i of the rule R^i is of the form $p_i = p_1^i \wedge p_2^i \wedge \cdots \wedge p_k^i$, where each p_j^i is a proposition: "$a_j^i(x) \in P_j^i$". The attribute a_j^i is applied to an item x, where its information is represented by a possibility distribution $\pi_{a_j^i(x)} : D_{a_j^i} \to [0,1]$ defined on its domain $D_{a_j^i}$, which is supposed to be normalized i.e., $\exists u \in D_{a_j^i}$ such that $\pi_{a_j^i(x)}(u) = 1$. The possibility degree of p_j^i and that of its negation are computed using the possibility measure Π by
$$\pi(p_j^i) = \Pi(P_j^i) = \sup_{u \in P_j^i} \pi_{a_j^i(x)}(u) \text{ and } \pi(\neg p_j^i) = \Pi(\overline{P_j^i}) = \sup_{u \in \overline{P_j^i}} \pi_{a_j^i(x)}(u)$$
respectively, where $P_j^i \subseteq D_{a_j^i}$ and $\overline{P_j^i}$ is its complement. As $\pi_{a_j^i(x)}$ is normalized, we have $\max(\pi(p_j^i), \pi(\neg p_j^i)) = 1$. The necessity degree of p_j^i is defined with the necessity measure N by $n(p_j^i) = N(P_j^i) = 1 - \pi(\neg p_j^i) = \inf_{u \in \overline{P_j^i}}(1 - \pi_{a_j^i(x)}(u))$.

The possibility degree of p_i is $\pi(p_i) = \min_{j=1}^k \pi(p_j^i)$ and that of its negation is $\pi(\neg p_i) = \max_{j=1}^k \pi(\neg p_j^i)$. These formulas $\pi(p_i)$ and $\pi(\neg p_i)$ preserve the normalization i.e., $\max(\pi(p_i), \pi(\neg p_i)) = 1$ and are respectively noted λ_i and ρ_i. The necessity degree of p_i is $n(p_i) = 1 - \pi(\neg p_i) = \min_{j=1}^k (1 - \pi(\neg p_j^i)) = \min_{j=1}^k n(p_j^i)$. The degrees λ_i and ρ_i allow to have the following interpretations of p_i:

- $\pi(p_i) = \lambda_i$ estimates to what extent p_i is possible,
- $n(p_i) = 1 - \rho_i$ estimates to what extent p_i is certain.

The conclusion q_i of R^i is of the form "$b(x) \in Q_i$", where $Q_i \subseteq D_b$. The possibility degrees of q_i and $\neg q_i$ are respectively noted α_i and β_i. They are defined by $\begin{bmatrix} \pi(q_i) \\ \pi(\neg q_i) \end{bmatrix} = \begin{bmatrix} 1 & s_i \\ r_i & 1 \end{bmatrix} \square_{\min}^{\max} \begin{bmatrix} \lambda_i \\ \rho_i \end{bmatrix}$ where the operator $\square_{\min}^{\max}$ uses min as the product and max as the addition. The normalization $\max(\pi(p_i), \pi(\neg p_i)) = 1$ implies:

$$\alpha_i = \max(s_i, \lambda_i) \text{ and } \beta_i = \max(r_i, \rho_i).$$

The possibility distribution of the output attribute b associated to R^i is defined for any $u \in D_b$ by $\pi_{b(x)}^{*i}(u) = \begin{cases} \alpha_i & \text{if } u \in Q_i \\ \beta_i & \text{if } u \in \overline{Q_i} \end{cases}$. Finally, with n rules, the output possibility distribution is defined by a min-based conjunctive combination:

$$\pi_{b(x)}^*(u) = \min(\pi_{b(x)}^{*1}(u), \pi_{b(x)}^{*2}(u), \cdots, \pi_{b(x)}^{*n}(u)). \tag{1}$$

We introduce some additional notations. For a set output attribute value $u \in D_b$, the computation of its possibility degree is given by:

$$\pi_{b(x)}^*(u) = \min(\gamma_1, \gamma_2, \cdots, \gamma_n), \tag{2}$$

where $\gamma_i = \pi_{b(x)}^{*i}(u) = \max(t_i, \theta_i)$ with $(t_i, \theta_i) = \begin{cases} (s_i, \lambda_i) & \text{if } \gamma_i = \alpha_i \\ (r_i, \rho_i) & \text{if } \gamma_i = \beta_i \end{cases}$. $\tag{3}$

The relation (2) is a more convenient formulation of (1). According to (3), for each $i = 1, 2, \cdots, n$, we remark that t_i denotes a parameter (s_i or r_i) of the rule R^i and θ_i denotes either the possibility degree λ_i of the premise p_i of the rule R^i or the possibility degree ρ_i of its negation.

For a premise of a possibilistic rule, the information given by its possibility and necessity degrees can be represented by the following triplet:

Notation 1. *For a premise p, the triplet (p, sem, d) denotes either $(p, P, \pi(p))$ or $(p, C, n(p))$, where $sem \in \{P, C\}$ (P for possible, C for certain) is the semantics attached to the degree $d \in \{\pi(p), n(p)\}$.*

We introduce the following triplets according to the $\gamma_1, \gamma_2, \cdots, \gamma_n$ appearing in the relation (2). For $i = 1, 2, \cdots, n$, we set:

$$(p_i, sem_i, d_i) = \begin{cases} (p_i, P, \lambda_i) & \text{if } \gamma_i = \alpha_i \\ (p_i, C, 1 - \rho_i) & \text{if } \gamma_i = \beta_i \end{cases}. \tag{4}$$

Example 1. Possibilistic rule-based systems have been used in medecine e.g., DIABETO [4] enables an improvement in the dietetics of diabetic patients [16]. We propose a possibilistic rule-based system for controlling the blood sugar level of a patient with type 1 diabetes (Table 1), according to some factors [3]:

Table 1. Rule base for the control of the blood sugar level.

	activity (act)	current-bloodsugar (cbs)	future-bloodsugar (fbs)
R^1	dinner, drink-coffee, lunch	medium, high	high
R^2	long-sleep, sport, walking	low, medium	low
R^3	alcohol-consumption, breakfast	low, medium	low, medium

The premises p_1, p_2 and p_3 of the possibilistic rules R^1, R^2 and R^3 are built using two input attributes: *activity (act)* and *current-bloodsugar (cbs)*. The conclusions of the rules use the output attribute *future-bloodsugar (fbs)*. We have $D_{\text{act}} = \{alcohol\text{-}consumption, breakfast, dinner, drink\text{-}coffee, long\text{-}sleep, lunch, sport, walking\}$ and $D_{\text{cbs}} = D_{\text{fbs}} = \{low, medium, high\}$. As parameters of the rules, we take $s_1 = 1$, $s_2 = 0.7$, $s_3 = 1$ and $r_1 = r_2 = r_3 = 0$. The three rules are certain [10] because we have $\pi(q_i \mid p_i) = 1$ and $r_i = \pi(\neg q_i \mid p_i) = 0$.

In our example, we assume that $\pi_{act(x)}(drink\text{-}coffee) = 1$, $\pi_{cbs(x)}(medium) = 1$ and $\pi_{cbs(x)}(low) = 0.3$, while the others elements of the domains of the input attributes have a possibility degree equal to zero. The obtained output possibility distribution is: $\langle low : 0.3, medium : 0.3, high : 1 \rangle$.

3   Justifying Inference Results

Farreny and Prade's approach [11] focuses on two explanatory purposes for an output attribute value $u \in D_b$, which can be formulated as two questions:

(i) How to get $\pi^*_{b(x)}(u)$ strictly greater or lower than a given $\tau \in [0,1]$?

(ii) What are the degrees of the premises justifying $\pi^*_{b(x)}(u) = \tau$?

For these two questions, the parameters of the rules s_i and r_i are set. Regarding (i), the authors of [11] give a sufficient condition to obtain $\pi^*_{b(x)}(u) > \tau$ for a particular pair (u,τ) of their example. Taking advantage of the notations (2) and (3) we note that $\pi^*_{b(x)}(u)$ ranges between $\omega = \min(t_1, t_2, \cdots, t_n)$ and 1. Following this, a necessary and sufficient condition to obtain $\pi^*_{b(x)}(u) > \tau$ according to the degrees of premises can be easily stated:

$$\forall i \in \{j \in \{1, 2, \cdots, n\} \mid t_j \leq \tau\} \text{ we have } \theta_i > \tau.$$

And similarly, $\pi^*_{b(x)}(u) < \tau$ with $\omega < \tau \leq 1$ will hold if and only if $\exists i \in \{j \in \{1, 2, \cdots, n\} \mid t_j < \tau\}$ such that $\theta_i < \tau$. With these assumptions on $\theta_1, \theta_2, \cdots, \theta_n$, we can give suitable conditions on the possibility distributions of the input attributes.

Regarding (ii), [11] claim that one can directly read the possibility degrees of the premises involved in the computation of the possibility degree of an output attribute value. Their claim is sustained by a particular output attribute value u of their example. In what follows, we elaborate on this question.

3.1 Justifying the Possibility Degree $\pi^*_{b(x)}(u) = \tau$

We give a necessary and sufficient condition that allows us to justify $\pi^*_{b(x)}(u) = \tau$ by degrees of premises. This allows to extract the subset of premises whose degrees are involved in the computation of $\pi^*_{b(x)}(u)$. To study how the possibility degree $\pi^*_{b(x)}(u) = \tau$ with $\omega \leq \tau \leq 1$ is obtained, we introduce the following two sets J^P and J^R in order to compare the parameters $t_1, t_2, \cdots t_n$ of the rules to the degrees $\theta_1, \theta_2, \cdots, \theta_n$ of the premises in the relation (2). Intuitively, J^P (resp. J^R) collect indices where θ_i is greater (resp. lower) than t_i: in other words, the γ_i related to the rule R^i can be explained by a degree of the premise (resp. by a parameter of the rule):

$$J^P = \{i \in \{1, 2, \cdots, n\} \mid t_i \leq \theta_i\} \text{ and } J^R = \{i \in \{1, 2, \cdots, n\} \mid t_i \geq \theta_i\}.$$

We have $\{1, 2, \cdots, n\} = J^P \cup J^R$ but J^P or J^R may be empty. We take:

$$c_\theta = \min_{i \in J^P} \theta_i \text{ and } c_t = \min_{i \in J^R} t_i \text{ (with the convention } \min_\emptyset = 1). \tag{5}$$

For a given output attribute value, if $J^P \neq \emptyset$ (resp. $J^R \neq \emptyset$), c_θ (resp. c_t) is the lowest possibility degree justifiable by premises (resp. by the parameters of the rules). By using the properties of the min function, we establish:

Proposition 1.

$$\tau = \min(c_\theta, c_t). \tag{6}$$

When we can't explain by degrees of premises. As the degrees $\theta_1, \theta_2, \cdots, \theta_n$ of the premises are computed using the possibility distributions of the input attributes, we may have $J^P = \emptyset$. In that case, $c_\theta = 1$, $J^R = \{1, 2, \cdots, n\}$ and:

$$\pi^*_{b(x)}(u) = c_t = \min(t_1, t_2, \cdots, t_n). \tag{7}$$

Clearly, it appears that $\pi^*_{b(x)}(u)$ is independent from $\theta_1, \theta_2, \cdots, \theta_n$ and we cannot justify $\pi^*_{b(x)}(u) = \tau$ by degrees of premises. *For this reason, we suppose in the following that $J^P \neq \emptyset$.*

For a set value $u \in D_b$, we remind that the triplets (p_i, sem_i, d_i) are defined in (4) according to (2) and (3). To the non-empty set J^P we associate the following set:

$$J_{b(x)}(u) = \{(p_i, \text{sem}_i, d_i) \mid i \in J^P \text{ and } \theta_i = \tau\}. \tag{8}$$

Then, using (5), the equality (6) and the definition of $J_{b(x)}(u)$, one can check directly that we have:

Proposition 2. $J_{b(x)}(u) \neq \emptyset \iff \pi^*_{b(x)}(u) = c_\theta$.

This means that when $J_{b(x)}(u) \neq \emptyset$, the set $J_{b(x)}(u)$ is formed by the premises justifying $\pi^*_{b(x)}(u) = \tau$, because if $\tau = c_\theta$, $\pi^*_{b(x)}(u)$ is the minimum of some precise degrees θ_i of premises p_i. However, if $J_{b(x)}(u) = \emptyset$, we have $\tau = c_t < c_\theta$ and then τ is the minimum of some parameters s_i or r_i. In this case, there is no way for deducing τ from $\theta_1, \theta_2, \cdots, \theta_n$ and therefore from the premises.

Example 2. For our blood sugar level control system (Sect. 2), according to the relation (2), we set $\pi_{fbs(x)}(high) = \min(\gamma_1, \gamma_2, \gamma_3)$ with $\gamma_1 = \alpha_1 = \max(s_1, \lambda_1)$, $\gamma_2 = \beta_2 = \max(r_2, \rho_2)$ and $\gamma_3 = \beta_3 = \max(r_3, \rho_3)$. We have $\lambda_1 = \rho_2 = \rho_3 = 1$. To apply (6), we compute $J^P = \{1, 2, 3\}$ and $J^R = \{1\}$. The possibility degree $\tau = 1$ of the output attribute value *high* can be both justified by degrees of premises (λ_1, ρ_2 and ρ_3) or a parameter of the rule R^1. For rules R^2 and R^3, justifications in terms of premises only can be given. As $c_\theta = 1 = \pi_{fbs(x)}(high)$, using (8), the following triplets are selected:

$$J_{fbs(x)}(high) = \{(p_1, \mathsf{P}, 1), (p_2, \mathsf{C}, 0), (p_3, \mathsf{C}, 0)\}.$$

Now assume that $r_1 > 0.3$. For $u = low$, (7) holds and the corresponding set J^P is empty: no justification in terms of premises could be given in that case.

4   Justification and Unexpectedness

In [1], a method that reduces a premise of a fuzzy if-then rule to the structure responsible for its activation degree has been defined. In this section, analogously to the fuzzy case, we define four functions $\mathscr{R}_\pi, \mathscr{R}_n, \mathscr{C}_\pi$ and $\mathscr{C}_n$ that reduce a compounded premise with respect to a threshold $\eta > 0$. The threshold η is set according to what is modelled by the possibilistic rule-base for the following purpose: if a possibility (resp. necessity) degree is higher than the threshold, it intuitively means that the information it models is relevantly possible (resp. certain). In order to define these reduction functions for premises, we first introduce two auxiliary functions $\mathscr{P}_\pi$ and $\mathscr{P}_n$ that are defined for propositions.

Let a be an attribute with a normalized possibility distribution $\pi_{a(x)}$ on its domain D_a and a proposition p of the form "$a(x) \in P$", where $P \subseteq D_a$. We introduce the following two subsets of D_a:

$$P_\pi = \{v \in P \mid \pi_{a(x)}(v) = \Pi(P)\} \text{ and } P_n = P \cup \{v \in \overline{P} \mid 1 - \pi_{a(x)}(v) > N(P)\}.$$

The proposition related to P_π (resp. P_n) is noted p_π (resp. p_n). Let us notice that:

Proposition 3. $\overline{P_n} = \{v \in \overline{P} \mid 1 - \pi_{a(x)}(v) = N(P)\}$.

This result is a consequence of $N(P) = \inf_{v \in \overline{P}}(1 - \pi_{a(x)}(v))$. For the proposition p with its set P, $\mathscr{P}_\pi$ reduces P if $\pi(p) \geq \eta$ and $\mathscr{P}_n$ reduces $\overline{P}$ if $n(p) \geq \eta$:

$$\mathscr{P}_\pi(p) = \begin{cases} p_\pi & \text{if } \pi(p) \geq \eta \\ p & \text{if } \pi(p) < \eta \end{cases} \text{ and } \mathscr{P}_n(p) = \begin{cases} p_n & \text{if } n(p) \geq \eta \\ p & \text{if } n(p) < \eta \end{cases}.$$

We notice that $\pi(\mathscr{P}_\pi(p)) = \pi(p)$ and $n(\mathscr{P}_n(p)) = n(p)$.

In what follows, we define the four reduction functions and show how we apply them to a triplet (p, sem, d) (Notation 1). We apply $\mathscr{R}_\pi$ and $\mathscr{R}_n$ to the triplets of $J_{b(x)}(u)$, see (8), to form the justification of $\pi^*_{b(x)}(u)$. Similarly, we apply $\mathscr{C}_\pi$ and $\mathscr{C}_n$ to the same triplets to extract the unexpectedness of $\pi^*_{b(x)}(u)$.

4.1   Extracting Justifications: $\mathscr{R}_\pi$ and $\mathscr{R}_n$ Functions

Let $p = p_1 \wedge p_2 \wedge \cdots \wedge p_k$ be a compounded premise, where p_j for $j = 1, 2, \cdots, k$, is a proposition of the form "$a_j(x) \in P_j$" with $P_j \subseteq D_{a_j}$. The function $\mathscr{R}_\pi$ (resp. $\mathscr{R}_n$) returns the structure responsible for $\pi(p)$ (resp. $n(p)$), which is the conjunction of propositions $\mathscr{P}_\pi(p_j)$ (resp. $\mathscr{P}_n(p_j)$) that make p relevantly possible (resp. certain) or not.

The reduction function $\mathscr{R}_\pi$ extends $\mathscr{P}_\pi$ in the following sense:

$$\mathscr{R}_\pi(p) = \begin{cases} \bigwedge_{j=1}^k \mathscr{P}_\pi(p_j) & \text{if } \pi(p) \geq \eta \\ \bigwedge_{p_j \in \{p_s \mid \pi(p_s) < \eta \text{ for } s=1,\cdots,k\}} p_j & \text{if } \pi(p) < \eta \end{cases}.$$

Similarly, the reduction function $\mathscr{R}_n$ extends $\mathscr{P}_n$ in the following sense:

$$\mathscr{R}_n(p) = \begin{cases} \bigwedge_{j=1}^k \mathscr{P}_n(p_j) & \text{if } n(p) \geq \eta \\ \bigwedge_{p_j \in \{p_s \mid n(p_s) < \eta \text{ for } s=1,\cdots,k\}} p_j & \text{if } n(p) < \eta \end{cases}.$$

We notice that $\pi(\mathscr{R}_\pi(p)) = \pi(p)$ and $n(\mathscr{R}_n(p)) = n(p)$.

4.2 Extracting Unexpectedness: $\mathscr{C}_\pi$ and $\mathscr{C}_n$ Functions

Intuitively, with respect to the threshold η, for a compounded premise $p = p_1 \wedge p_2 \wedge \cdots \wedge p_k$ that is not relevantly possible (resp. certain), $\mathscr{C}_\pi$ (resp. $\mathscr{C}_n$) returns a conjunction of propositions, called an unexpectedness, which is <u>not</u> involved in the determination of $\pi(p)$ (resp. $n(p)$), although relevantly possible (resp. certain).

When $\pi(p) < \eta$ and $A_p^\pi = \{p_j \mid \pi(p_j) \geq \eta$ for $j = 1, \cdots, k\} \neq \emptyset$, the function $\mathscr{C}_\pi$ returns the conjunction of the propositions $\mathscr{P}_\pi(p_j)$ such that $\pi(p_j) \geq \eta$:

$$\mathscr{C}_\pi(p) = \bigwedge_{p_j \in A_p^\pi} \mathscr{P}_\pi(p_j).$$

If $\pi(p) < \eta$, each proposition p_j composing p, is either used in $\mathscr{R}_\pi(p)$ or in $\mathscr{C}_\pi(p)$, according to its possibility degree $\pi(p_j)$.

Similarly, when $n(p) < \eta$ and $A_p^n = \{p_j \mid n(p_j) \geq \eta$ for $j = 1, \cdots, k\} \neq \emptyset$, $\mathscr{C}_n$ returns the conjunction of the propositions $\mathscr{P}_n(p_j)$ such that $n(p_j) \geq \eta$:

$$\mathscr{C}_n(p) = \bigwedge_{p_j \in A_p^n} \mathscr{P}_n(p_j).$$

If $n(p) < \eta$, each proposition p_j composing p, is either used in $\mathscr{R}_n(p)$ or in $\mathscr{C}_n(p)$, according to its necessity degree $n(p_j)$.

4.3 Justification and Unexpectedness of $\pi^*_{b(x)}(u)$

To apply in an appropriate way the reduction functions $\mathscr{R}_\pi$ and $\mathscr{R}_n$ to the premise p of a triplet (p, sem, d), see Notation (1), we introduce the function $\mathscr{S}_\mathscr{R}$:

$$\mathscr{S}_\mathscr{R}(p, sem, d) = \begin{cases} (\mathscr{R}_\pi(p), sem, d) & \text{if } sem = \mathsf{P} \\ (\mathscr{R}_n(p), sem, d) & \text{if } sem = \mathsf{C} \end{cases}.$$

Similarly, to apply $\mathscr{C}_\pi$ and $\mathscr{C}_n$, we introduce the function $\mathscr{S}_\mathscr{C}$:

$$\mathscr{S}_\mathscr{C}(p, sem, d) = \begin{cases} (\mathscr{C}_\pi(p), sem, \pi(\mathscr{C}_\pi(p))) & \text{if } sem = \mathsf{P}, d < \eta \text{ and } A_p^\pi \neq \emptyset \\ (\mathscr{C}_n(p), sem, n(\mathscr{C}_n(p))) & \text{if } sem = \mathsf{C}, d < \eta \text{ and } A_p^n \neq \emptyset \end{cases}.$$

The justification of $\pi^*_{b(x)}(u)$ is formed by applying $\mathscr{S}_\mathscr{R}$ to the triplets of $J_{b(x)}(u)$, see (8):

$$\text{Justification}_{b(x)}(u) = \{\mathscr{S}_\mathscr{R}(p, sem, d) \mid (p, sem, d) \in J_{b(x)}(u)\}. \tag{9}$$

The possibilistic expressions in the triplets of (9) are sufficient to justify "$b(x)$ is u at a possibility degree $\pi^*_{b(x)}(u)$". By using $\mathscr{S}_\mathscr{C}$, we obtain the unexpectedness of $\pi^*_{b(x)}(u)$ i.e., possible or certain possibilistic expressions, which may appear to be incompatible with $\pi^*_{b(x)}(u)$ while not being involved in its determination:

$$\text{Unexpectedness}_{b(x)}(u) = \{\mathscr{S}_\mathscr{C}(p, sem, d) \mid (p, sem, d) \in J_{b(x)}(u)\}. \tag{10}$$

The purpose of an unexpectedness X is to be able to formulate statements such as *"even if X, $b(x)$ is u at a possibility degree $\pi^*_{b(x)}(u)$"*. It is in the same vein as the "even-if-because" statements studied in [6].

Example 3. For our blood sugar level control system (Sect. 2), we take $\eta = 0.1$ and obtain the justification of $\pi_{\text{fbs}(x)}(\text{high})$ and its unexpectedness:

- Justification$_{\text{fbs}(x)}$(high) = $\{(\mathscr{R}_\pi(p_1), \mathsf{P}, 1), (\mathscr{R}_n(p_2), \mathsf{C}, 0), (\mathscr{R}_n(p_3), \mathsf{C}, 0)\}$.
- Unexpectedness$_{\text{fbs}(x)}$(high) = $\{(\mathscr{C}_n(p_2), \mathsf{C}, 1)\}$.

For the premise of the rule R^1, $\mathscr{R}_\pi$ returns the conjunction of "act(x) $\in$ {drink-coffee}" and "cbs(x) $\in$ {medium}". By applying $\mathscr{R}_n$ to the premise of R^2, we obtain the proposition "act(x) $\in$ {long-sleep, sport, walking}". For the premise of R^3, $\mathscr{R}_n$ returns "act(x) $\in$ {alcohol-consumption, breakfast}". For the premise of R^2 and that of R^3, $\mathscr{C}_n$ returns for both "cbs(x) $\in$ {low, medium}".

5 Representing Explanations of Possibilistic Inference Decisions

In this section, we represent graphically two explanations: the justification and the unexpectedness of $\pi^*_{b(x)}(u)$, (see (9) and (10)) in terms of *conceptual graphs*. The resulting conceptual graphs are visual representations of the outcomes of several analytical operations performed on the rule base that constitute explanations. Conceptual graphs are multi-graphs composed of concept nodes representing entities and relation nodes representing relationships between these entities. They were introduced by Sowa [15] and enriched by Chein and Mugnier [5]. We rely on the work of [5] for our definitions.

In the following, a *possibilistic conceptual graph* is defined as a conceptual graph where each concept node is gifted with a degree and a semantics. For each representation, we first specify its input which we call an *explanation query*. We associate an explicit explanation query to the justification of $\pi^*_{b(x)}(u)$ and another one to its unexpectedness. Each explanation query gives rise to a vocabulary, which is a simple ontology from which we define possibilistic conceptual graphs representing *statements* and a conceptual graph representing the *structure* of the explanation. One statement is called an *observed phenomenon* and represents the possibility degree $\pi^*_{b(x)}(u)$. Depending on the chosen explanation query, the other statements represent either the justification of $\pi^*_{b(x)}(u)$ or its unexpectedness. Each representation is obtained by nesting the possibilistic conceptual graphs representing the statements in the conceptual graph representing the structure.

5.1 Explanation Query

To describe the vocabularies of the two explanations, we introduce the notion of *explanation query*:

Definition 1. *An explanation query is formed by a triplet* $\mathcal{E} = (\mathcal{T}, b, u)$ *such that:*

- $\mathcal{T} = \{(p, sem, d)\}$ *is a finite set of triplets (Notation 1),*
- b *is an attribute of domain* D_b *with a possibility distribution* $\pi^*_{b(x)} : D_b \rightarrow [0,1]$,
- $u \in D_b$ *is an attribute value for which the justification or the unexpectedness of its possibility degree* $\pi^*_{b(x)}(u)$ *is requested.*

Let us set an explanation query $\mathcal{E} = (\mathcal{T}, b, u)$, where $m = \text{card}(\mathcal{T}) \geq 1$ for which we adopt the following notations:

Notation 2 *We index the triplets of* $\mathcal{T}$ *as follows:*

$$\mathcal{T} = \{v^{(1)}, v^{(2)}, \cdots, v^{(m)}\} \quad ; \quad v^{(i)} = (p^{(i)}, sem^{(i)}, d^{(i)}).$$

For each triplet $v^{(i)} = (p^{(i)}, sem^{(i)}, d^{(i)}) \in \mathcal{T}$, *we set a decomposition* $p^{(i)} = p_1^{(i)} \wedge p_2^{(i)} \wedge \cdots \wedge p_{k_i}^{(i)}$ *where for each* $j = 1, 2, \cdots, k_i$ *we have:*

- $p_j^{(i)}$ *is the proposition* "$a_j^{(i)}(x) \in P_j^{(i)}$", *where* $a_j^{(i)}$ *is an attribute with a normalized possibility distribution* $\pi_{a_j^{(i)}} : D_{a_j^{(i)}} \rightarrow [0,1]$, $P_j^{(i)} \subseteq D_{a_j^{(i)}}$ *and* x *is an item.*
- $A^{(i)} = \{a_1^{(i)}, a_2^{(i)}, \cdots, a_{k_i}^{(i)}\}$ *with* $\text{card}(A^{(i)}) = k_i$,
- $S^{(i)} = \{P_1^{(i)}, P_2^{(i)}, \cdots, P_{k_i}^{(i)}\}$ *with* $\text{card}(S^{(i)}) = k_i$.

We take the *disjoint unions*: $A = \bigcup_{1 \leq i \leq m} A^{(i)}$ and $S = \bigcup_{1 \leq i \leq m} S^{(i)}$. These disjoint unions will allow us to define an application $\delta : S \rightarrow A$ verifying $\delta(P_j^{(i)}) = a_j^{(i)}$ and are necessary because the domains of two distinct attributes $a_j^{(i)}$ and $a_{j'}^{(i')}$ with $i \neq i'$ may have a non-empty intersection. Therefore, the sets $P_j^{(i)}$ and $P_{j'}^{(i')}$ of the two propositions $p_j^{(i)}$ and $p_{j'}^{(i')}$ may be equal.

For our explanations, we take the following explanation queries using the justification and the unexpectedness of an output attribute value u, see (9) and (10):

$$\mathcal{E}_J = (\text{Justification}_{b(x)}(u), b, u) \quad \text{and} \quad \mathcal{E}_U = (\text{Unexpectedness}_{b(x)}(u), b, u).$$
$$\text{(11)}$$

5.2 Vocabulary Construction

Let $\mathcal{V}^{\mathcal{E}} = (T_C, T_R, \mathcal{I}, \delta, \sigma)$ be the vocabulary associated to the explanation query $\mathcal{E} = (\mathcal{T}, b, u)$, where T_C is the set of concept types, T_R is the set of relation symbols, $\mathcal{I}$ is the set of individual markers, $\delta : \mathcal{I} \rightarrow T_C$ is an individual typing function and a relation symbol signature σ, which gives for each relation symbol of T_R the concept type of each of its arguments [5]. In $\mathcal{V}^{\mathcal{E}}$, the attribute b and the attributes in A are concept types. The set $\{u\}$ is an individual marker representing the attribute value u. The sets in S are individual markers. To any triplet $v^{(i)}$, we associate a relation symbol $inferred_{v^{(i)}}$ of arity $k_i + 1$. Therefore, a conceptual graph based on $\mathcal{V}^{\mathcal{E}}$ may contain:

- a concept node of type b and individual marker $\{u\}$,
- a concept node of type $a_j^{(i)}$ and individual marker $P_j^{(i)}$, which gives a representation of the proposition $p_j^{(i)}$,
- a relation node of type $inferred_{v^{(i)}}$, which will be linked by multi-edges to the concept node of type b and the concept nodes representing the propositions $p_1^{(i)}, p_2^{(i)}, \cdots, p_{k_i}^{(i)}$.

Additionally, for structuring the explanations, $\mathcal{V}^{\mathcal{E}}$ includes: two concept types: Phenomenon and e, a relation symbol t, and $m+1$ individual markers that are named Statements. In a conceptual graph based on $\mathcal{V}^{\mathcal{E}}$, we may find a concept node of type Phenomenon and marker Statement_0, m concept nodes of type e and marker Statement_i for $i = 1, 2, \cdots, m$ and a relation node of type t, which will be linked by multi-edges to the $m+1$ concept nodes that we just described. We explicitly define $\mathcal{V}^{\mathcal{E}}$ as follows:

- $T_C = \{b\} \cup \mathcal{A} \cup \{e\} \cup \{\text{Phenomenon}\}$ with $\text{card}(T_C) = 3 + \sum_{i=1}^{m} k_i$.
- $T_R = \{inferred_{v^{(i)}} | v^{(i)} \in T\} \cup \{t\}$ with $\text{card}(T_R) = m+1$ and such that $\text{arity}(inferred_{v^{(i)}}) = k_i + 1$ and $\text{arity}(t) = m+1$.
- $\mathcal{I} = \{\{u\}\} \cup \mathcal{S} \cup \{\text{Statement}_0, \text{Statement}_1, \cdots, \text{Statement}_m\}$ with $\text{card}(\mathcal{I}) = m + 2 + \sum_{i=1}^{m} k_i$.
- $\delta : \mathcal{I} \to T_C$ such that:
  - $\{u\} \mapsto b$; $P_j^{(i)} \mapsto a_j^{(i)}$
  - $\text{Statement}_0 \mapsto \text{Phenomenon}$; $\text{Statement}_i \mapsto e$ for $i = 1, 2, \cdots, m$.
- The signature map σ is given by:
  - $\sigma(inferred_{v^{(i)}}) = (b, a_1^{(i)}, a_2^{(i)}, \cdots, a_{k_i}^{(i)})$ for $v^{(i)} \in T$
  - $\sigma(t) = (\text{Phenomenon}, e, e, \cdots, e)$.

In the vocabulary $\mathcal{V}^{\mathcal{E}_J}$ associated to the explanation query $\mathcal{E}_J$, see (11), the concept type e is noted "Justification" and the relation symbol t is noted "isJustifiedBy". In $\mathcal{V}^{\mathcal{E}_U}$ of $\mathcal{E}_U$, see (11), we respectively note them "Unexpectedness" and "evenIf".

5.3 Possibilistic Conceptual Graphs

We introduce possibilistic conceptual graphs that extend basic conceptual graphs (BG) [5] by adding two additional fields to the labels of concept nodes:

Definition 2. *A possibilistic conceptual graph (PCG) is a BG $G = (C, R, E, l)$, where C is the concept nodes set, R the relation nodes set, E is the multi-edges set and the label function l is extended by allowing a degree and a semantics in the label of any concept node $c \in C$:*

$$l(c) = (type(c) : marker(c) | sem_c, d_c)$$

The definition of a *star BG* [5] i.e., a BG restricted to a relation node and its neighbors, is naturally extended as a star PCG.

5.4   Conceptual Graphs Based on the Vocabulary $\mathcal{V}^{\mathcal{E}}$

Given an explanation query $\mathcal{E} = (\mathcal{T}, b, u)$ (definition 1), let us specify, in a PCG $G = (C, R, E, l)$ built on the vocabulary $\mathcal{V}^{\mathcal{E}}$, the definition of the labels of the following concept nodes:

- for a concept node $c \in C$ such that $\text{type}(c) = b$ and $\text{marker}(c) = \{u\}$, we put:

$$sem_c = \mathsf{P} \text{ and } d_c = \pi^*_{b(x)}(u). \tag{12}$$

- for a concept node $c \in C$ such that $\text{type}(c) = a_j^{(i)}$ and $\text{marker}(c) = P_j^{(i)}$, we take:

$$sem_c = sem^{(i)} \text{ and } d_c = \begin{cases} \pi(p_j^{(i)}) & \text{if } sem^{(i)} = \mathsf{P} \\ n(p_j^{(i)}) & \text{if } sem^{(i)} = \mathsf{C} \end{cases}. \tag{13}$$

For the other concept nodes, we specify neither a degree nor a semantics.
On the vocabulary $\mathcal{V}^{\mathcal{E}}$, let us define $m+1$ PCG $D, N_1, N_2, \cdots, N_m$ and a BG R:

Definition 3. *D is defined as the PCG reduced to one concept node with label $(b : \{u\} \mid P, \pi^*_{b(x)}(u))$. It is a graphical representation of a statement, which describes an observed phenomenon.*

Definition 4. *Each N_i is the star PCG where the unique relation node r_i is of type $inferred_{v^{(i)}}$ with $v^{(i)} \in \mathcal{T}$. The graph N_i contains $k_i + 1$ concept nodes: $c_b^{(i)}, c_{a_1}^{(i)}, c_{a_2}^{(i)}, \cdots, c_{a_{k_i}}^{(i)}$ of type $b, a_1^{(i)}, a_2^{(i)}, \cdots, a_{k_i}^{(i)}$ and marker $\{u\}, P_1^{(i)}, P_2^{(i)}, \cdots, P_{k_i}^{(i)}$, as in (12), (13). The multi-edges are labeled $(r_i, 0, c_b^{(i)})$ and $(r_i, j, c_{a_j}^{(i)})$ for $j = 1, 2, \cdots, k_i$. Each N_i represents graphically either a statement justifying the phenomenon represented by D or an unexpectedness statement. The link between the phenomenon and the justification statement or the unexpectedness statement is represented by a relation node of type $inferred_{v^{(i)}}$.*

Definition 5. *The graph R is the star BG where the unique relation node r is of type t and the $m + 1$ concept nodes are noted $c_0, c_1, \cdots, c_m$, where c_0 is of type "Phenomenon" and $c_1, c_2, \cdots, c_m$ are of type e. Their individual markers are respectively $Statement_0, Statement_1, \cdots, Statement_m$. The multi-edges are labeled (r, j, c_j) for $j = 0, 1, \cdots, m$. R structures the explanation by representing the link between the observed phenomenon D and the statements $N_1, N_2, \cdots, N_m$.*

In Fig. 1a and 1b we give examples of N_i and R respectively, with $m = 3$, $e =$ "Justification" and t = "isJustifiedBy".

5.5   Representation of Explanations

We define the representation of an explanation as a nested conceptual graph G defined by its associated tree as in [5], which is denoted $Tree(G) = (V_T, U_T, l_T)$. For our representation, the PCG $D, N_1, N_2, \cdots, N_m$ are nested in the concept nodes of R:

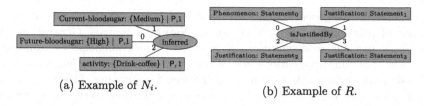

(a) Example of N_i.

(b) Example of R.

Fig. 1. Examples of graphs. Nodes with a rectangular shape are concept nodes and those with an oval shape are relation nodes.

Definition 6. $Tree(G) = (V_T, U_T, l_T)$ *is given by:*

- $V_T = \{R, D, N_1, N_2, \cdots, N_m\}$ *is the set of nodes,*
- $U_T = \{(R, D), (R, N_1), (R, N_2), \cdots, (R, N_m)\}$ *is the set of edges and the node R is the root of $Tree(G)$,*
- *the labels of the edges are given by* $l_T(R, D) = (R, c_0, D)$ *and* $l_T(R, N_i) = (R, c_i, N_i)$ *for* $i = 1, 2, \cdots, m$.

Taking the explanation queries $\mathcal{E}_J$ and $\mathcal{E}_U$ (11), we get by Definition 6, two nested conceptual graphs that represent explanations of possibilistic inference decisions.

Example 4. We represent an explanation (Fig. 2) of a decision of our blood sugar control system (Sect. 2). It is a justification of $\pi_{fbs(x)}(high) = 1$ built using $\mathcal{E}_J = (Justification_{fbs(x)}(high), fbs, high)$ that could be in natural language: *"It is possible that the patient's blood sugar level will become high. In fact, his activity is drinking coffee and his current blood sugar level is medium. In addition, it is assessed as not certain that he chose sport, walking, sleeping, eating breakfast or drinking alcohol as an activity."* Its unexpectedness can also be represented.

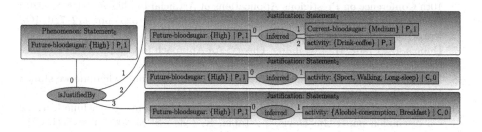

Fig. 2. Representation of an explanation.

6   Conclusion

In this paper, we introduced a method to justify by a subset of rule premises the possibility degree of an output attribute value obtained by the inference of a possibilistic rule-based system. We used it to represent two kinds of explanations of possibilistic inference decisions. Natural Language Generation systems may use our representation to produce natural language explanations. Question-answering applications may also rely on our representation, as the conceptual graphs framework provides a mechanism for querying. This may lead to the development of more general extraction justification methods. Moreover, the representation of explanation may be adapted for the case of a cascade [9] and fuzzy systems.

References

1. Baaj, I., Poli, J.P.: Natural language generation of explanations of fuzzy inference decisions. In: 2019 IEEE International Conference on Fuzzy Systems (FUZZ-IEEE), pp. 1–6. IEEE (2019)
2. Baaj, I., Poli, J.P., Ouerdane, W.: Some insights towards a unified semantic representation of explanation for explainable artificial intelligence. In: Proceedings of the 1st Workshop on Interactive Natural Language Technology for Explainable Artificial Intelligence (NL4XAI 2019), pp. 14–19 (2019)
3. Brown, A., Close, K.L.: Bright spots & landmines: the diabetes guide I wish someone had handed me. diaTribe Foundation (2017)
4. Buisson, J.C., Farreny, H., Prade, H.: The development of a medical expert system and the treatment of imprecision in the framework of possibility theory. Inf. Sci. **37**(1–3), 211–226 (1985)
5. Chein, M., Mugnier, M.L.: Graph-Based Knowledge Representation: Computational Foundations of Conceptual Graphs. Springer, London (2008). https://doi.org/10.1007/978-1-84800-286-9
6. Darwiche, A., Hirth, A.: On the reasons behind decisions. In: Giacomo, G.D., Catalá, A., Dilkina, B., Milano, M., Barro, S., Bugarín, A., Lang, J. (eds.) ECAI 2020–24th European Conference on Artificial Intelligence, 29 August–8 September 2020, Santiago de Compostela, Spain, 29 August–8 September 2020 - Including 10th Conference on Prestigious Applications of Artificial Intelligence (PAIS 2020). Frontiers in Artificial Intelligence and Applications, vol. 325, pp. 712–720. IOS Press (2020)
7. Dubois, D., Prade, H.: Possibility Theory: An Approach to Computerized Processing of Uncertainty. Plenum Press, New York (1988)
8. Dubois, D., Prade, H.: Possibility theory and its applications: where do we stand? In: Handbook of Computational Intelligence (2015)
9. Dubois, D., Prade, H.: From possibilistic rule-based systems to machine learning - a discussion paper. In: Davis, J., Tabia, K. (eds.) SUM 2020. LNCS (LNAI), vol. 12322, pp. 35–51. Springer, Cham (2020). https://doi.org/10.1007/978-3-030-58449-8_3
10. Farreny, H., Prade, H.: Default and inexact reasoning with possibility degrees. IEEE Trans. Syst. Man Cybern. **16**(2), 270–276 (1986)
11. Farreny, H., Prade, H.: Positive and Negative Explanations of Uncertain Reasoning in the Framework of Possibility Theory, pp. 319–333. Wiley, USA (1992)
12. Farreny, H., Prade, H., Wyss, E.: Approximate reasoning in a rule-based expert system using possibility theory: a case study. In: IFIP Congress, pp. 407–414 (1986)

13. General Data Protection Regulation: Regulation EU 2016/679 of the European parliament and of the council of 27 April 2016. Official Journal of the European Union (2016)
14. Reiter, E., Dale, R.: Building applied natural language generation systems. Nat. Lang. Eng. **3**(1), 57–87 (1997)
15. Sowa, J.F.: Conceptual graphs for a data base interface. IBM J. Res. Develop. **20**(4), 336–357 (1976)
16. Turnin, M.C.G., et al.: Telematic expert system diabeto: new tool for diet self-monitoring for diabetic patients. Diabetes Care **15**(2), 204–212 (1992)

Towards a Tesseract of Sugeno Integrals

Didier Dubois[1], Henri Prade[1(✉)], and Agnès Rico[2]

[1] IRIT, CNRS & Université Paul Sabatier, 118 route de Narbonne, Cedex 09,
Toulouse, France
{didier.dubois,henri.prade}@irit.fr
[2] ERIC, Université Claude Bernard-Lyon 1, 43 bd du 11 novembre,
69100 Villeurbanne, France
agnes.rico@univ-lyon1.fr

Abstract. Structures of opposition, such as the hexagon and different cubes, derived from the square of opposition of ancient logic, have for more than a decade shown their interest in the analysis of various frameworks for the representation and processing of information (possibly pervaded with uncertainty). The use of a renewed and less constrained vision of the structures of opposition leads in this article to consider a general cube and a hypercube of opposition applicable to binary or gradual settings, which is here exemplified on Sugeno integrals and related integrals

1 Introduction

The square of opposition dates back to Aristotle. It had been closely associated to the history of logic until the XIXth century so long as logic was mainly relying on the study of syllogisms. A renewal of interest for the square of opposition was initiated in the 1950's by R. Blanché [3,4] who completed it into a hexagon relating notions present in many conceptual structures. It was rediscovered by J.-Y. Béziau [1,2].

This renewed interest led to a flowering of works on structures of oppositions. Different cubes of opposition have been proposed in particular by A. Moretti [21] and by Dubois and Prade [8], agreeing respectively with earlier proposals by H. Reichenbach [30] on the one hand and by J. N. Keynes [20] and W. E. Johnson [19] on the other hand; see [14]. Moreover it has been also shown that structures of opposition can apply not only to binary items, but also to notions that are a matter of degree [5].

Structures of opposition rely on the interplay of different forms of negation. Their merits are twofold, beyond their own algebraic interest: they are shared by many representation settings, and, for each setting, they may draw attention to neglected operators. The JK cube of opposition [14] can be encountered in very different knowledge representation formalisms, such as first order logic, modal logic, possibility theory in its all-or-nothing version, formal concept analysis, rough set theory and abstract argumentation. A gradual extension of this structure fits with several quantitative settings such as possibility theory (including

© Springer Nature Switzerland AG 2021
J. Vejnarová and N. Wilson (Eds.): ECSQARU 2021, LNAI 12897, pp. 528–542, 2021.
https://doi.org/10.1007/978-3-030-86772-0_38

the handling of fuzzy events), belief function theory, weighted multiple criteria aggregations, Choquet and Sugeno integrals, fuzzy rough sets, and fuzzy relations [5,9,12,13]. Imprecise probability assessments can be organized in a square of opposition [28].

Besides, a modern reading of the square of opposition, less constrained than the classical one, has been proposed by Westerståhl [31], motivated by the representation of various types of quantifiers. This kind of reading has been more recently applied to fuzzy quantifiers [22,23] and to first-order logic [25] in more general structures of opposition. The aim of this paper is to further explore modern structures of opposition.

The paper is organized into two main parts. Section 2 is dedicated to the presentation of classical and modern structures of opposition, starting with squares, and then moving to cubes and hypercubes (also called tesseracts). Section 3 illustrates these structures on Sugeno integrals and related operators. However a few examples of particular cases can already be found in Section 2. This leads to a more encompassing view of these integrals and their particular cases.

2   Structures of Opposition

The traditional square of opposition [27] is built with universally and existentially quantified statements in the following way. Consider a statement (**A**) of the form "all A's are B's", which is negated by the statement (**O**) "at least one A is not a B", together with the statement (**E**) "no A is a B", which is clearly in even stronger opposition (than **O**) to the first statement (**A**). These three statements, together with the negation of the last statement, namely (**I**) "at least one A is a B" can be displayed on a square whose vertices are traditionally denoted by the letters **A**, **I** (Afflrmative half: from Latin "Afflrmo") and **E**, **O** (nEgative half: from Latin "nEgO"), as pictured in Fig. 1 (where $\overline{B}$ stands for "not B").

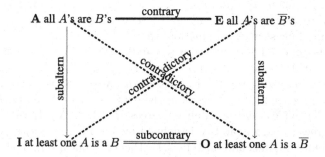

Fig. 1. Traditional square of opposition

2.1   Logical View of the Classical Square

As can be checked, noticeable relations hold in the square:

- (i) **A** and **O** (resp. **E** and **I**) are the negation of each other (linked by *dotted* diagonals in Fig. 1);
- (ii) **A** entails **I**, and **E** entails **O** (it is assumed that there is at least one A thus avoiding existential import problems) (linked by thin lines with *arrows* in Fig. 1);
- (iii) **A** and **E** cannot be true together, but both may be false (linked by an edge in *bold black* line in Fig. 1) ;
- (iv) **I** and **O** cannot be false together, but both may be true (linked by a *double line* edge in Fig. 1).

So we can formally state:

Definition 1. *In a square of opposition* **AEOI**, *the following holds:*

a *The diagonal link between* **A** *and* **O**, *which represents the symmetrical relation of* contradiction, $\boldsymbol{A} \equiv \neg \boldsymbol{O}$. *Similarly,* $\boldsymbol{E} \equiv \neg \boldsymbol{I}$.
b *The vertical arrows represent* implication *relations* $\boldsymbol{A} \to \boldsymbol{I}$ *and* $\boldsymbol{E} \to \boldsymbol{O}$.
c *The link between* **A** *and* **E** *represents the symmetrical relation of* contrariety, *and corresponds to mutual exclusion, namely* $\neg \boldsymbol{A} \vee \neg \boldsymbol{E}$ *should hold.*
d *The link between* **I** *and* **O** *represents the symmetrical relation of* subcontrariety. *It is a disjunction, namely* $\boldsymbol{I} \vee \boldsymbol{O}$ *holds.*

This leaves us with three options for defining a formal square of opposition with independent conditions [5]: i) either we can regard (a) and (b), or ii) (a) and (c), or iii) (a) and (d), as the basic requirements. Actually, we can express the content of a square of opposition in propositional logic using two propositional atoms (say **A** and **E**) together with the axiom $\neg \mathbf{A} \vee \neg \mathbf{E}$, expressing their mutual exclusion (and defining $\mathbf{I} \equiv \neg \mathbf{E}$ and $\mathbf{O} \equiv \neg \mathbf{A}$).

In a *graded square* of opposition [5], each corner **A**, **E**, **O**, **I** is associated respectively to degrees $\alpha, \epsilon, o, \iota$ in $[0, 1]$. These degrees obey the constraints (a)–(d). Using Łukasiewicz conjunction, they take the form:

(i) $\alpha = 1 - o$; $\epsilon = 1 - \iota$;   (ii) $\alpha \leq \iota$ and $\epsilon \leq o$;
(iii) $\alpha + \epsilon \leq 1$;   (iv) $\iota + o \geq 1$,

thus clearly generalizing the Boolean case. An illustration is given in Figure 2, where we can recognize, respectively in the expressions of **A**, **E**, **O**, **I**, necessity degrees $N(X)$, $N(\overline{X})$, and possibility degrees $\Pi(X)$, $\Pi(\overline{X})$. Here X has membership degrees $x_1, ..., x_n$ (and $\overline{X}$ is defined by $1 - x_1, ..., 1 - x_n$) , while $\wedge$, $\vee$, $s \Rightarrow t$ stand for min, max and $\max(1-s, t)$ (Dienes implication). The expressions in Fig. 2 can also be thought of as weighted min and weighted max aggregations (and are also particular cases of Sugeno integrals, as further discussed in Sect. 3).

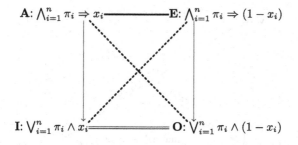

Fig. 2. Square of qualitative aggregations/possibility theory

2.2   Modern Square of Opposition

D. Westerståhl [31] has proposed a "modern" reading of the square of opposition **AEOI** (see also [23]). This reading is quite different from the classical one where logical constraints are supposed to hold between the vertices of the square (see Definition 1). In the modern reading, **A** and **E**, as **I** and **O** are exchanged through an involutive internal negation, and **A** and **I** (resp. **E** and **O**) are dual of each other, where duality is obtained by composing the internal negation with the (involutive) external negation (assumed to hold between diagonal vertices). In contrast with the classical square, the definition of an internal negation requires the assumption of some formal expression to be transformed via the application of external and internal negations. Here we use a two place relation or operator R, linking formal expressions A and B, say $R(A, B)$. Then internal negations may take the forms $R(f(A), B)$, $R(A, g(B))$, or $R(f(A), g(B))$, where f and g are involutive. Moreover A and $f(A)$ (resp. B and $g(B)$) should be "in opposition" in some sense. The modern square of opposition can be defined as follows.

Definition 2. *In a modern square of opposition **AEOI**, the following holds:*

a   *The diagonal link between **A** and **O**, **E** and **I** is an* external *negation.*
b   *The link between **A** and **E**, **I** and **O** is an* internal *negation.*
c   *Vertical arrows represent a* duality *relation defined as the composition of internal negation and external negation.*

Note that **A** and **I** (resp. **E** and **O**) play the same role and the duality may correspond to what we have named semi-duality elsewhere [16]. As already said, we have three possible inner negations which lead to three possible modern squares of opposition. One is displayed in Fig. 3 (the internal negation is on the right argument).

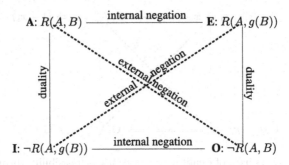

Fig. 3. A modern square of opposition

The case with internal negation of $R(A,B)$ defined as $R(f(A),g(B))$ with $f = g = \neg$ corresponds to a Klein group of four logical transformations of a given logical statement $\phi = f(p,q)$: (i) the identity $I(\phi) = \phi$, (ii) the negation $N(\phi) = \neg\phi$, (iii) the reciprocation $R(\phi) = f(\neg p, \neg q)$, (iv) the correlation $C(\phi) = \neg f(\neg p, \neg q)$, identified by Piaget [26]. See also [17]. These transformations are at work during the acquisition of cognitive capabilities progressively mastered by children and pre-adolescents [24].

As can be checked, the square of Fig. 1 can also be seen as a modern square where $R(A,B)$ stands for $A \subseteq B$, then **A** is $A \subseteq B$, **E** is $A \subseteq \overline{B}$ (corresponding to $R(A,g(B))$), **I** is $A \not\subseteq B$ i.e., $A \cap B \neq \emptyset$ and **O** is $A \cap \overline{B} \neq \emptyset$). This is the case for many classical squares. This is true as well for the graded square of Fig. 2 where the external and internal negations are the complementation to 1, as can be easily checked. But there exist modern squares of opposition that are not classical squares. Let us show an example:

Consider $R(A,B) = A > B$ with **E** : $A > 1-B$, **O** : $A \leq B$ and **I** : $A \leq 1-B$, where A and B are numbers. There is no implication relation between **A**: $A > B$ and **I** : $A \leq 1-B$ (neither **A** $\to$ **I**, nor **I** $\to$ **A**).

Another example can be given in the graded case: Starting with **A** : $N(F)$, take **E** : $N(ant(F))$ where $ant(F)$ is the antonym of F defined by central symmetry on the referential. Then if F is large enough, F and $ant(F)$ may overlap and the condition (iii) $\alpha + \epsilon \leq 1$ may fail to hold.

2.3 Classical and Modern Cubes of Opposition

More than one century ago, two logicians, W. E. Johnson [19] and J. N. Keynes [20], in their discussion of syllogisms, introduced an octagon of opposition. It was rediscovered in [8,12,14], as a cube of opposition, and called *JK-cube*. In such a cube the front facet and the back facet are squares of opposition.

Definition 3. *Let **A**, **I**, **E**, **O**, **a**, **i**, **e**, **o** be propositional variables. In a JK-cube of opposition **AEOIaieo**, the following holds:*

- *Front and back facets **AEOI** and **aeoi** are squares of opposition (in the sense of Definition 1).*

- *Side facets represent entailment relations:*
  (l) $\neg A \vee i$; $\neg a \vee I$; $\neg e \vee O$; $\neg E \vee o$.
- *Top and bottom facets:*
  (m) a *and* E *are contraries:* $\neg a \vee \neg E$; *the same for* A *and* e: $\neg A \vee \neg e$;
  (n) i *and* O *are sub-contraries, i.e.,* $i \vee O$; *the same for* I *and* o, *i.e.,* $I \vee o$.

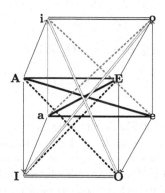

Fig. 4. JK cube of opposition

The relations between vertices in the JK cube are shown in Fig. 4 with the same conventions as in Fig. 1. Note that the back facet is upside down with respect to the front facet (**i** and **o** are at the top, **a** and **e** at the bottom) for a better visualization of the different links between the vertices.

The conditions that define the JK cube of opposition are redundant [5,12]:

- the properties on the front and back facets associated to the properties on the side facets entail the properties on the diagonal planes between front and back facets;
- the properties on the front and back facets associated to the properties on one of the diagonal planes entail the properties on the side facets and the other diagonal plane.

An example of JK cube (in the sense of Definition 3 and Fig. 4) is easily obtained with the inclusion relation $\subseteq$ (and its negation) between two sets A, and B (and their complements), as in Fig. 5. This cube clearly generalizes the square of Figure 1 (e.g., **i** corresponds to "at least one an element outside A is outside B").

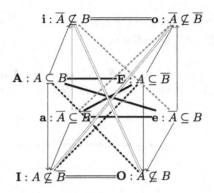

Fig. 5. A JK cube of opposition for inclusion

In the "classical" cube of Fig. 5, the following negations are at work: i) an external one: $\neg(A \subseteq B) = A \not\subseteq B$, and three internal ones: ii) $A \subseteq \overline{B}$; iii) $\overline{A} \subseteq B$; iv) $\overline{A} \subseteq \overline{B}$. Six modern squares can be identified, induced by these internal negations: **AEOI** and **aeoi** are associated to the first internal negation; **AeiO** and **IoaE** are associated to the second internal negation; **IieE** and **AaOo** are associated to the third one. This is also a particular instance of a *modern cube of opposition* which we present now.

Indeed, more generally, with the general notations of the previous Subsect. 2.2 we get the cube of Fig. 6 where i) dotted lines correspond to the external nega-tion; ii) double lines to the f-based internal negation; iii) bold lines to the g-based internal negation; iv) thin lines to f-based or g-based dualities. Note that in Fig. 6 the back facet is no longer upside down for convenience.

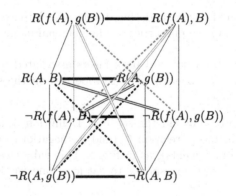

Fig. 6. A modern cube of opposition

The JK cube has been generalized into a *graded* cube [5,14]. All the rela-tions of Definition 3 are now extended in the same way as in the graded square. Gradual versions of the JK cubes of opposition may be found in many settings including possibility theory, Shafer's belief function theory, qualitative weighted multiple criteria aggregation, possibilistic Sugeno integrals, and Choquet integrals; see [14] for references, but not for imprecise probabilities at large, because the notion of Shafer commonality function is absent. The example of qualitative aggregation is given in Fig. 7. Its front facet is the square of Fig. 2. This cube can be also viewed as an instance of the *modern* cube of Fig. 6. Indeed, as in the graded square of Fig. 2, the external and internal negations f and g here are the complementation to 1, as can be easily seen. The use of Dienes implication $(s \Rightarrow t = \max(1 - s, t))$ ensures that the external negation is at work in the diagonals of the front and back facets. As indicated in Fig. 7, the expressions correspond to the 4 set functions of possibility theory Π, N, Δ, ∇ for the fuzzy events X and $\overline{X}$ [12]. Δ and ∇ are decreasing set functions (in the wide sense), called strong (guaranteed) possibility and weak necessity respectively, while Π and N are increasing set functions (in the wide sense).

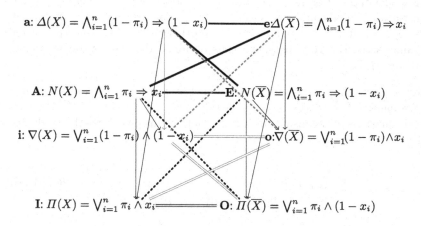

a: $\Delta(X) = \bigwedge_{i=1}^{n}(1 - \pi_i) \Rightarrow (1 - x_i)$ ——— **e:** $\Delta(\overline{X}) = \bigwedge_{i=1}^{n}(1 - \pi_i) \Rightarrow x_i$

A: $N(X) = \bigwedge_{i=1}^{n} \pi_i \Rightarrow x_i$ ——— **E:** $N(\overline{X}) = \bigwedge_{i=1}^{n} \pi_i \Rightarrow (1 - x_i)$

i: $\nabla(X) = \bigvee_{i=1}^{n}(1 - \pi_i) \wedge (1 - x_i)$ ——— **o:** $\nabla(\overline{X}) = \bigvee_{i=1}^{n}(1 - \pi_i) \wedge x_i$

I: $\Pi(X) = \bigvee_{i=1}^{n} \pi_i \wedge x_i$ ——— **O:** $\Pi(\overline{X}) = \bigvee_{i=1}^{n} \pi_i \wedge (1 - x_i)$

Fig. 7. Cube of qualitative aggregations

2.4   The Tesseract

We have seen that an external negation together with an internal negation (g in Fig. 3) leads to a modern square of opposition. Adding an internal negation (f in Fig. 6), we obtain a modern cube of opposition. This process can be continued, and the use of a third internal negation, say an involutive function h, will lead to a hypercube, or 4-cube, also called tesseract, with 16 vertices. Such a structure of opposition has been used in [22,23] in the discussion of summarizing statements based on fuzzy quantifiers. More recently, a similar structure was independently obtained for organizing particular first order logic expressions [25].

One may think of several ways for introducing such an h, starting with an expression of the form $R(A, B)$[1]. At least three options may be considered, leading to different tesseracts:

---

[1] Obviously, dealing with a ternary expression $R(A, B, C)$, and h applying to argument C would lead to a natural and straightforward extension.

– h, as g, applies to B. For instance, in the example of Fig. 7, $h(X) = ant(X)$, where $ant(X)$ is the antonym of X defined by central symmetry on the referential of X. Thus, if we have a strict partition, small $-$ medium $-$ large, $\overline{\text{small} - \text{medium}}$ = large, $ant(\text{small} - \text{medium})$ = medium $-$ large, and $ant(\overline{\text{small} - \text{medium}})$ = small. This easily extends with fuzzy sets. Then the tesseract is made of two cubes that mirror each other: the cube of Fig. 6, and the cube obtained by applying h to the second argument of the expression of each vertice of the first cube.

– h, as f, applies to A. This is very similar to the previous case. In the example of Fig. 7, one might define $ant(\pi)$, although this has not yet been considered in possibility theory.

– h applies to R. This means that $h(R)$ would be an involutive transform of R. In the example of Fig. 7, this would mean exchanging the pair $(\wedge, \Rightarrow)$ with another pair of conjunction - implication, such as, e.g., $(\wedge_G, \rightarrow_G)$ where $\rightarrow_G$ is Gödel implication ($s \rightarrow_G t = 1$ if $s \leq t$ and $s \rightarrow_G t = t$ otherwise), while $\wedge_G$ is the associated conjunction (for a good interplay with the external negation: $s \wedge_G t = t$ if $s > 1 - t$ and $s \wedge_G t = 0$ otherwise). This is not just a formal game, since the 16 expressions thus obtained do make sense in possibility theory [12].

The tesseracts that can be obtained are pictured in Fig. 8 where the exponent h on the names of the vertices of the outside cube refers to any of the three above transformations of the inside cube. Note that the inside cube is the modern cube of Fig. 6.

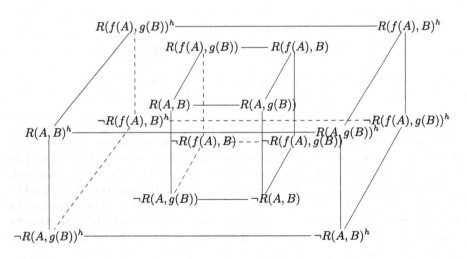

Fig. 8. A modern tesseract

A different road has been taken in [15], which does not involve any h. Indeed, in the modern cube of Fig. 6, we have two involutions f and g at work. Assume now that $f \neq g$ and both f and g can be applied to the first and the second argument of R. Then we move from 8 to 16 syntactically distinct expressions (since on one may each argument in $R(A, B)$, one may apply f, g, $g(f)$ or the identity). Thus we can build the cube in Fig. 9, not to be confused with the modern cube of opposition of Fig. 6. Mind that the semantics of the links are different, although bold lines, double lines, dotted lines, vertical lines, horizontal lines correspond each to a type of transformation, as can be checked. Then applying f to the second argument on this cube, one obtains another cube which, with the first one, displays the 16 distinct expressions. The result is a tesseract very different from the one of Figure 8, the internal cube of which being the one of Fig. 9. In this tesseract, the external negation plays no role. We shall not further consider this cube and this tesseract since they are not genuine modern structures of opposition built from an external negation and internal involutions. Moreover, the illustration of this construct with Sugeno integrals in [15] leads to a number of trivial operators either equal to 1 or to 0 (as can be checked).

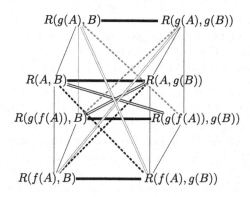

Fig. 9. A pseudo-modern cube of opposition with operators f and g

3   Cube of Sugeno Integral

In this section we investigate if it is possible to extend the modern square of Fig. 3 and the modern cube of Fig. 6 to qualitative aggregation operators that are more general than the ones exhibited in Fig. 7, namely Sugeno integrals and related integrals. Obviously, once a cube is obtained, a tesseract in the sense of Fig. 8 could be derived. The section starts with a refresher on these integrals.

3.1   Sugeno Integrals and Related Integrals

Sugeno integrals are commonly used as qualitative aggregation functions in multiple criteria decision making [7]. They are also used to model fuzzy quantifiers [18], because they indeed generalise standard quantifiers.

We consider a universe of discourse $\mathcal{C}$ supposed to be finite ($\mathcal{C}$ can be viewed as a set of criteria), a scale L which is a bounded totally ordered set with a bottom denoted by 0 and a top denoted by 1. Moreover L is supposed to be equipped with an involutive negation denoted by '$1-$'. Sugeno integral is defined using a fuzzy measure $\mu : 2^{\mathcal{C}} \to L$ (a set function increasing in the wide sense, such that $\mu(\emptyset) = 0$ and $\mu(\mathcal{C}) = 1$, also called *capacity*). The conjugate fuzzy measure μ^c of the fuzzy measure μ is defined by $\mu^c = 1 - \mu(\overline{\cdot})$. The Sugeno integral of an alternative (to be evaluated) $x = (x_1, \cdots, x_n)$ with respect to μ (which describes the importance of subsets of criteria) is:

$$S_\mu(x) = \bigvee_A \mu(A) \wedge x_{\inf}(A) = \bigwedge_A \mu(\overline{A}) \vee x_{\sup}(A) = \bigwedge_A \mu^c(A) \Rightarrow x_{\sup}(A)$$

where $\overline{A}$ denotes the complement of A, $x_{\inf}(A) = \bigwedge_{i \in A} x_i$ and $x_{\sup}(A) = \bigvee_{i \in A} x_i$.and $\Rightarrow$ is Dienes implication.

Note that when x is the characteristic function of an ordinary subset X of $\mathcal{C}$, Sugeno integral coincides with the capacity:

$$S_\mu(x) = \mu(X)$$

Let us also recall an important notion and a representation result regarding qualitative capacities. They are of interest not only for weighting subsets of criteria, but also as a general setting for modeling uncertainty:

- a qualitative capacity [6] μ can be defined from its Möbius transform $\mu_\#$: $\mu_\#(E) = \mu(E)$ if $\mu(E) > \mu(E \setminus \{i\}), \forall i \in E$; $\mu_\#(E) = 0$ otherwise, and then $\mu(X) = \max_{E \subseteq X} \mu_\#(E)$. This may be viewed as a qualitative counterpart of the expression of a belief function in terms of its mass function (replacing the sum by max). Here $\mu_\#$ is strictly increasing on the set of its focal elements $\mathcal{F} = \{E | \mu_\#(E) > 0\}$.
- any qualitative capacity μ in a finite setting can be represented as the finite conjunction of possibility measures (or equivalently the finite disjunction of necessity measures) [10].

Moreover, there exist residuated variants of Sugeno integrals [11] where the sup-min and the inf-max forms no longer coincide, as it is the case in the above expressions for Sugeno integrals. In these variants, the pair $(\wedge, \Rightarrow)$ is replaced by a pair $(\otimes, \to_\otimes)$ where $\to_\otimes$ is a residuated implication associated with $\otimes$, such as the pair $(\wedge_G, \to_G)$ already mentioned. Then only an inequality holds between the sup-min and the inf-max forms:

$$S_\mu^\otimes(x) = \bigvee_A (\mu(A) \otimes x_{\inf}(A)) \geq S_\mu^{\to \otimes}(x) = \bigwedge_A (\mu^c(A) \to_\otimes x_{\sup}(A)).$$

Besides, a Sugeno *desintegral* (see [11] for more details) is a decreasing function defined using an anti-fuzzy measure (or anti-capacity) ν which is a decreasing set function in the wide sense such that $\nu(\emptyset) = 1$ and $\nu(\mathcal{C}) = 0$. More precisely, the Sugeno desintegral of $x = (x_1, \cdots, x_n)$ with respect to the anti-capacity ν is defined as:

$$S_\nu^-(x) = \bigvee_{A \subseteq \mathcal{C}} \nu(\overline{A}) \wedge (1 - x)_{\inf}(A) = \bigwedge_{A \subseteq \mathcal{C}} \nu^c(\overline{A}) \Rightarrow (1 - x)_{\sup}(A).$$

It is worth noticing that a Sugeno desintegral appears to be defined applying two negations on the Sugeno integral, one for the fuzzy measure and the second one for the alternative x since $S_\nu^-(x) = S_{1-\nu^c}(1 - x)$ with $\nu^c(A) = 1 - \nu(\overline{A})$.

3.2   In Search of a Modern Cube of Sugeno Integrals

We now examine how the different structures of opposition apply to Sugeno integrals. We start with the square. It is easy to check that we obtain the modern square of Fig. 10.

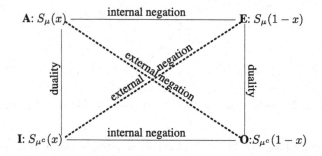

Fig. 10. Modern square of Sugeno integral

This square is a particular case of the square presented in [18] where Sugeno integrals are generalized by qualitative integrals. The modern square, which is less constrained, presents a clear advantage here with respect to the classical square. Indeed, following the graded extension of the classical view [9], we have to restrict ourselves to the pessimistic and optimistic parts of a capacity μ, respectively defined by $\mu_*(A) = \min(\mu(A), \mu^c(A))$ and $\mu^*(A) = \max(\mu(A), \mu^c(A))$ in order to guarantee the entailments of the classical view between $S_{\mu_*}(x)$ and $S_{\mu^*}(x)$. The interest of the modern view here is to allow for any Sugeno integral, since simple duality replaces entailment.

Let us consider the cube now. Interestingly enough, a classical graded cube of opposition has been obtained for Choquet integrals [13] from the graded cube of opposition of belief function theory [9]. Indeed the Choquet integral with respect to a quantitative capacity μ is $C_\mu(x) = \Sigma_{A \subseteq \mathcal{C}} m_\mu(A) x_{\inf}(A)$ where m_μ denotes the Möbius transform of μ, and a belief function μ with mass function m_μ coincides with the Choquet integral for classical subsets of $\mathcal{C}$.

As we are going to see, finding a modern cube of opposition is less straightforward for Sugeno integrals. Indeed if we try to mimic the change of expression from $N(X) = \bigwedge_{i=1}^{n} \pi_i \Rightarrow x_i$ to $\Delta(X) = \bigwedge_{i=1}^{n}(1-\pi_i) \Rightarrow (1-x_i)$ (see Fig. 7), starting from $S_\mu(x) = \bigwedge_A \mu^c(A) \Rightarrow x_{\sup}(A)$ one would obtain an expression having the form $\bigwedge_A (1-\mu)^c(A) \Rightarrow (1-x)_{\sup}(A) = \bigwedge_A \mu(\overline{A}) \Rightarrow (1-x)_{\sup}(A)$. Although it somewhat resembles the desintegral expression $S_\nu^-(x) = \bigwedge_{A \subseteq C} \nu^c(\overline{A}) \Rightarrow (1-x)_{\sup}(A)$, μ is a capacity and ν^c is an anti-capacity. So it does not work.

However, we can write the cube of qualitative aggregations of Fig. 7 with particular Sugeno integrals, where the set functions are $\Delta(A) = \min_{i \in A} \pi_i$, and $\nabla(\overline{A}) = 1 - \Delta(A) = \max_{i \in A} 1 - \pi_i$; see Fig. 11. So a modern cube makes sense for at least some Sugeno integrals.

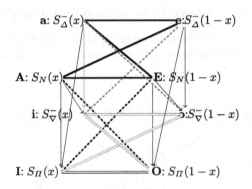

Fig. 11. Cube of qualitative aggregations as Sugeno integrals

It has been observed [29] that classical squares of opposition can be combined using conjunction for **A** and **E** and disjunctions for **I** and **O**; this extends to graded cubes [12] and to modern squares where no difference is made between top and bottom vertices. Thus thanks to the cube of Fig. 7 and the representation result recalled in Subsect. 3.1 (second hyphen), we obtain a modern cube for capacities (see Fig. 12). Since Sugeno integrals can be expressed as the minimum of possibilistic integrals [9] based on the Π^j's in the cube of Fig. 12, it

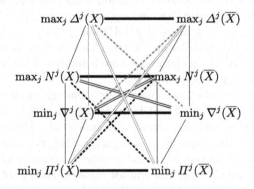

Fig. 12. A modern cube of opposition for capacity $\mu(X) = \min_j \Pi^j(X)$

is straightforward to jointly extend this cube and the one of Fig. 7 and form another modern cube of opposition for Sugeno integrals.

4   Concluding Remarks

The paper has reviewed two different types of structures of opposition, respectively referred to as 'classical' and 'modern'. The general forms of the modern square, cube, and tesseract of opposition have been provided. Generally speaking, the modern square and its cube and tesseract extensions offer a rich framework for studying involutive transformations between expressions. We have illustrated the process on Sugeno integrals. The tesseract in [25] involves formulas such that $\forall x(A(x) \rightarrow \forall y(B(y) \rightarrow \neg R(x,y)))$; its graded extension would lead to a kind of double Sugeno integrals. It is clear that the approach is applicable to many other representation settings for uncertainty modeling or multicriteria aggregation especially (since Sugeno integrals include possibilistic measures of fuzzy events as particular cases). The general investigation of what is precisely obtained in the different settings is a topic for further research.

References

1. Béziau, J.Y.: New light on the square of oppositions and its nameless corner. Logical Invest. **10**, 218–233 (2003)
2. Béziau, J.-Y.: The power of the hexagon. Logica Universalis **6**(1–2), 1–43 (2012)
3. Blanché, R.: Sur l'opposition des concepts. Theoria **19**, 89–130 (1953)
4. Blanché, R.: Structures Intellectuelles. Essai sur l'Organisation Systématique des Concepts. Librairie philosophique J. Vrin, Paris (1966)
5. Ciucci, D., Dubois, D., Prade, H.: Structures of opposition induced by relations. The Boolean and the gradual cases. Ann. Maths Artif. Intel. **76**, 351–373 (2016)
6. Dubois, D., Faux, F., Prade, H., Rico, A.: Qualitative capacities and their informational comparison. In: Proceedings 12th Conference of the European Society for Fuzzy Logic and Technology (EUSFLAT 2021), 19–24 September 2021, Bratislava (2021)
7. Dubois, D., Marichal, J.-L., Prade, H., Roubens, M., Sabbadin, R.: The use of the discrete Sugeno integral in decision-making: a survey. Int. J. Uncert. Fuzz. Knowl. Syst. **9**(5), 539–561 (2001)
8. Dubois, D., Prade, H.: From Blanché's hexagonal organization of concepts to formal concept analysis and possibility theory. Logica Univers. **6**, 149–169 (2012)
9. Dubois, D., Prade, H., Rico, A.: The cube of opposition: a structure underlying many knowledge representation formalisms. In: Proceedings 24th International Joint Conference on Artificial Intelligence (IJCAI 2015), Buenos Aires, AAAI Press, pp. 2933–2939 (2015)
10. Dubois, D., Prade, H., Rico, A.: Representing qualitative capacities as families of possibility measures. Int. J. Approximate Reasoning **58**, 3–24 (2015)
11. Dubois, D., Prade, H., Rico, A.: Residuated variants of sugeno integrals: towards new weighting schemes for qualitative aggregation methods. Inf. Sci. **329**, 765–781 (2016)

12. Dubois, D., Prade, H., Rico, A.: Graded cubes of opposition and possibility theory with fuzzy events. Int. J. Approximate Reasoning **84**, 168–185 (2017)

13. Dubois, D., Prade, H., Rico, A.: Organizing families of aggregation operators into a cube of opposition. In: Kacprzyk, J., Filev, D., Beliakov, G. (eds.) Granular, Soft and Fuzzy Approaches for Intelligent Systems. SFSC, vol. 344, pp. 27–45. Springer, Cham (2017). https://doi.org/10.1007/978-3-319-40314-4_2

14. Dubois, D., Prade, H., Rico, A.: Structures of opposition and comparisons: Boolean and gradual cases. Logica Univ. **14**, 115–149 (2020)

15. Dubois, D., Prade, H., Rico, A.: Le tesseract de l'intégrale de Sugeno. In: Actes 29èmes Rencontres Francophones sur la Logique Floue et ses Applications (LFA 2020), Sète, 15–16 October, Cépaduès (2020)

16. Dubois, D., Prade, H., Rico, A., Teheux, B.: Generalized qualitative Sugeno integrals. Inf. Sci. **415**, 429–445 (2017)

17. Gottschalk, W.H.: The theory of quaternality. J. Symb. Logic. **18**, 193–196 (1953)

18. Holčapek, M., Rico, A.: A note on the links between different qualitative integrals. In: Fuzz-IEEE (2020)

19. Johnson, W.E.: Logic. Cambridge University Press, Part I (1921)

20. Keynes, J.N.: Studies and Exercises in Formal Logic, 3rd edn. MacMillan (1894)

21. Moretti, A.: The geometry of standard deontic logic. Logica Univ. **3**, 19–57 (2009)

22. Moyse, G.: Résumés linguistiques de données numériques: interprétabilité et périodicité de séries. Thèse Univ, Paris (2016)

23. Moyse, G., Lesot, M.-J., Bouchon-Meunier, B.: Oppositions in fuzzy linguistic summaries. Int. Conf. Fuzzy System (Fuzz-IEEE 2015), Istanbul (2015)

24. Murray, F.B. (ed.): Critical Features of Piaget's Theory of the Development of Thought. University of Delaware Press, Newark (1972)

25. Nilsson, J.F.: A cube of opposition for predicate logic. Logica Univ. **14**, 103–114 (2020)

26. Piaget, J.: Traité de logique. Essai de logistique opératoire, Armand Colin (1949)

27. Parsons, T.: The traditional square of opposition. In: The Stanford Encyclopedia of Philosophy (2008)

28. Pfeifer, N., Sanfilippo, G.: Probabilistic squares and hexagons of opposition under coherence. Int. J. Approximate Reasoning **88**, 282–294 (2017)

29. Pizzi, C.: Contingency logics and modal squares of opposition. In: Beziau, J.Y., Gan-Krzywoszynska, K. (eds.) Handbook of Abstracts of the 3rd World Congress on the Square of Opposition, Beirut, 26–30 June, pp. 29–30 (2012)

30. Reichenbach, H.: The syllogism revised. Philos. Sci. **19**(1), 1–16 (1952)

31. Westerståhl, D.: Classical vs. modern squares of opposition, and beyond. In: Payette, G., Béziau, J.-Y. (eds.) The Square of Opposition. A General Framework for Cognition, Peter Lang, pp. 195–229 (2012)

Canonical Extension of Possibility Measures to Boolean Algebras of Conditionals

Tommaso Flaminio[ID], Lluis Godo[✉][ID], and Sara Ugolini[ID]

IIIA - CSIC, 08193 Bellaterra, Spain
{tommaso,godo,sara}@iiia.csic.es

Abstract. In this paper we study conditional possibility measures within the algebraic setting of Boolean algebras of conditional events. More precisely, we focus on the possibilistic version of the Strong Conditional Event Problem, introduced for probabilities by Goodman and Nguyen, and solved in finitary terms in a recent paper by introducing the so-called Boolean algebras of conditionals. Our main result shows that every possibility measure on a finite Boolean algebra can be canonically extended to an unconditional possibility measure on the resulting Boolean algebra of conditionals, in such a way that the canonical extension and the conditional possibility, determined in usual terms by any continuous t-norm, coincide on every basic conditional expression.

Keywords: Conditional possibility · Boolean algebras of conditionals · Strong conditional event problem

1 Introduction

The issue of conditioning in the framework of possibility theory has been discussed at large in the literature, starting from the pioneering work by Hisdal [15] and then followed by Dubois, Prade and colleagues (see e.g. [1,9–11]), de Cooman and Walley [8,17] and Coletti and colleagues [2–6] among others.

Comparing to the case of probability, where there is a common agreement on taking the conditional probability $P(a \mid b)$ as the ratio $P(a \wedge b)/P(b)$ (in case $P(b) > 0$), a conditional possibility $\Pi(a \mid b)$ has mainly been defined in the literature in (at least) two different ways: in an ordinal setting, the min-based conditioning sets $\Pi_{\min}(a \mid b) = \Pi(a \wedge b)$ if $\Pi(b) > \Pi(a \wedge b)$ and 1 otherwise; and in a numerical setting, the product-based conditioning defines $\Pi_{prod}(a \mid b)$ as $\Pi(a \wedge b)/\Pi(b)$ if $\Pi(b) > 0$ and 1 otherwise. More in general, if $*$ is a continuous t-norm and $\Rightarrow_*$ is its residuum, one can define $\Pi_*^+(a \mid b) = \Pi(b) \Rightarrow_* \Pi(a \wedge b)$. Such $\Pi_*^+(a \mid b)$ is in fact the greatest solution x of the equation $\Pi(a \wedge b) = x * \Pi(b)$. Notice that the two definitions above correspond to the choice $* = $ minimum t-norm and $* = $ product t-norm. However, as also discussed in the literature, see e.g. [10], not every choice of $*$ is compatible with the satisfaction of some

J. Vejnarová and N. Wilson (Eds.): ECSQARU 2021, LNAI 12897, pp. 543–556, 2021.
https://doi.org/10.1007/978-3-030-86772-0_39

rationality postulates for conditional possibility that are counterparts to Cox's axioms for conditional probability, and moreover the definition of Π_*^+ itself has some problems as well, and has to be slightly modified to another expression that we will denote with Π_*.

In this paper we deal with conditional possibility measures within the algebraic setting of Boolean algebras of conditionals [13], a recently proposed setting for measure-free conditionals endowed with the structure of a Boolean algebra. More precisely, we focus on a possibilistic version of the Strong Conditional Event Problem, considered for probabilities by Goodman and Nguyen [14], and solved in finitary terms in [13] with the help of those structures. Indeed, Boolean algebras of conditional events are introduced with the aim of playing for conditional probability a similar role Boolean algebras of plain events play for probability theory. To do so, the authors try to identify which properties of conditional probability depend on the algebraic features of conditional events and which properties are intrinsic to the nature of the measure itself.

Clearly, a similar analysis can be done for the notion of conditional possibility, with the advantage that we can now study the suitability of Boolean algebras of conditionals as a common algebraic framework for conditional events also in relation to conditional possibility, in the sense of checking whether conditional possibilities can be regarded as plain possibility measures on algebras of conditional events. Our main result shows that this is actually the case for a very general notion of conditional possibility. Namely, if $\mathbf{A}$ is any finite Boolean algebra and Π is a possibility measure on $\mathbf{A}$, then we show that, for any continuous t-norm $*$, Π can be always extended to a (unconditional) possibility measure μ_Π on the Boolean algebra of conditionals $\mathcal{C}(\mathbf{A})$ built over $\mathbf{A}$, in such a way that, for every basic conditional object $(a \mid b) \in \mathcal{C}(\mathbf{A})$, $\mu_\Pi('(a \mid b)')$ coincides with the conditional possibility $\Pi_*(a \mid b)$.

This paper is structured as follows. Next Sect. 2 is dedicated to recall basic notions and results on conditional possibility theory, while Boolean algebras of conditionals will be briefly recalled in Sect. 3. Our main result, namely the solution of the possibilistic version of the Strong Conditional Event Problem, will be proved in Sect. 4. Finally, in Sect. 5, we will conclude and present future work on this subject.

2   Possibility and Conditional Possibility Measures

In this section we will recall basic notions and results about (conditional) possibility theory [9,18]. We will assume the reader to be familiar with the algebraic setting of Boolean algebras. For every finite Boolean algebra $\mathbf{A}$, we will henceforth denote by $\text{at}(\mathbf{A})$ the finite set of its atoms.

A possibility measure on a Boolean algebra $\mathbf{A}$ is a mapping $\Pi : A \to [0,1]$ satisfying the following properties:

(Π1) $\Pi(\top) = 1$,
(Π2) $\Pi(\bot) = 0$,
(Π3) $\Pi(\bigvee_{i \in I} a_i) = \sup\{\Pi(a_i) \mid i \in I\}$

If $\mathbf{A}$ is finite, which will be our setting in this paper, then $(\varPi 3)$ can just be replaced by

$(\varPi 3)^*$ $\varPi(a \lor b) = \max(\varPi(a), \varPi(b))$

In the finite setting, possibility measures are completely determined by their corresponding (normalized) possibility distributions on the atoms of the algebra. Namely, $\varPi : A \to [0,1]$ is a possibility measure iff there is a mapping $\pi : \mathfrak{at}(\mathbf{A}) \to [0,1]$ with $\max\{\pi(\alpha) : \alpha \in \mathfrak{at}(\mathbf{A})\} = 1$ such that

$$\varPi(a) = \max\{\pi(\alpha) : \alpha \in \mathfrak{at}(\mathbf{A}), \alpha \leq a\}.$$

Clearly, in such a case $\pi(\alpha) = \varPi(\alpha)$ for each $\alpha \in \mathfrak{at}(\mathbf{A})$.

When we come to define conditional possibility measures there have been several proposals in the literature, see e.g. a summary of them in [17]. Nevertheless, $\varPi(a \mid b)$ has been traditionally chosen as the greatest solution of the equation [10,12]:

$$\varPi(a \land b) = x * \varPi(b) \tag{1}$$

where either $* = \min$ or $* = $ product. This leads to these two definitions:

$$\varPi_{\min}(a \mid b) = \begin{cases} \varPi(a \land b), & \text{if } \varPi(b) > \varPi(a \land b) \\ 1, & \text{otherwise} \end{cases}$$

$$\varPi_{prod}(a \mid b) = \begin{cases} \varPi(a \land b)/\varPi(b), & \text{if } \varPi(b) > 0 \\ 1, & \text{otherwise} \end{cases}$$

$\varPi_{\min}(\cdot \mid \cdot)$ has been known as the qualitative conditioning of $\varPi$ while $\varPi_{prod}(\cdot \mid \cdot)$ has been known as the quantitative conditioning of $\varPi$.

Actually, in a finite setting, both expressions satisfy very intuitive properties a conditional possibility $\varPi(. \mid .)$ should enjoy. For instance, for any $a, b \in A$ and any $\alpha, \gamma \in \mathfrak{at}(\mathbf{A})$ we have:

P1. $\varPi(\cdot \mid b)$ is a possibility measure on $\mathbf{A}$, if $\varPi(b) > 0$
P2. $\varPi(a \mid b) = \varPi(a \land b \mid b)$, and hence $\varPi(a \mid b) = 0$ if $a \land b = \bot$ and $\varPi(b) > 0$
P3. If $\varPi(\alpha) < \varPi(\gamma)$ then $\varPi(\alpha \mid b) < \varPi(\gamma \mid b)$, if $\alpha, \gamma \leq b$
P4. If $\varPi(b) = 1$ then $\varPi(a \mid b) = \varPi(a \land b)$
P5. If $\varPi(a) = 0$ and $\varPi(b) > 0$ then $\varPi(a \mid b) = 0$

Notice however that in case the Boolean algebra $\mathbf{A}$ is infinite, $\varPi_{\min}$ may fail to satisfy P1, that is, $\varPi_{\min}(\cdot \mid b)$ might fail to be a possibility measure in a strict sense, even if $\varPi(b) > 0$, see [7].

Actually, if $*$ is a continuous t-norm, properties P2-P4 keep holding for the conditional possibility measure $\varPi_*^+(\cdot \mid \cdot)$ defined as the maximal solution for x in Eq. (1), in other words, by the conditional possibility defined as

$$\varPi_*^+(a \mid b) = \varPi(b) \Rightarrow_* \varPi(a \land b), \tag{2}$$

where $\Rightarrow_*$ is the residuum of $*$, that is the binary operation defined as $x \Rightarrow_* y = \max\{z \in [0,1] \mid x * z \leq y\}$. If $*$ is without zero-divisors,[1] then $\Pi_*^+(\cdot \mid \cdot)$ further satisfies P1 and P5 as well. For every continuous t-norm $*$, the pair $(*, \Rightarrow_*)$ is known as a *residuated pair*. When $* = \min$ or $* = $ product, we obtain the above definitions of $\Pi_{\min}$ and Π_{prod} as particular cases. Note that if $*$ has zero divisors, P1 fails because $\Pi_*^+(\perp \mid b) = \Pi(b) \Rightarrow_* 0$ is not guaranteed to be 0 when $\Pi(b) > 0$ [7,10]. For the same reason P5 can fail as well. For instance, if $*$ is Łukasiewicz t-norm, $\Pi(b) \Rightarrow_* 0 = 1 - \Pi(b) > 0$ when $\Pi(b) < 1$. To avoid this situation and other issues related to the conditioning by an event of measure zero, in [4] the authors considered a modified expression for Π_*^+, called T_{DP}-conditional possibility, on which we base the following definition.

Definition 1. *Given a possibility measure Π on a Boolean algebra $\mathbf{A}$ and a continuous t-norm $*$, we define the mapping $\Pi_* : A \times A' \to [0,1]$, where $A' = A \setminus \{\perp\}$, as follows:*

$$\Pi_*(a \mid b) = \begin{cases} \Pi(b) \Rightarrow_* \Pi(a \wedge b), & \text{if } a \wedge b \neq \perp \\ 0, & \text{otherwise.} \end{cases} \tag{3}$$

In this way, $\Pi_*(a \mid b) = 0$ whenever $a \wedge b = \perp$, even if $\Pi(b) = 0$ (while $\Pi_*^+(a \mid b) = 1$ in that case). For any continuous t-norm $*$, Π_* keeps satisfying P2-P4, and if $*$ has no zero-divisors then P1 and P5 as well. Moreover, for any continuous t-norm $*$, Π_* also satisfies both P1 and P2 when $\Pi(b) = 0$.

However, if $*$ is a left-continuous t-norm, to start with, (1) might not have a greatest solution. Indeed, if we define Π_* as in (3) for a left-continuous t-norm $*$, we obtain the following characterisation.

Proposition 1. *If $*$ is a left-continuous t-norm, the following are equivalent:*

(i) $*$ is continuous.
(ii) $\Pi_*(a \mid d) * \Pi_*(b \mid a \wedge d) = \Pi_*(a \wedge b \mid d)$, for all possibility measures Π on any Boolean algebra $\mathbf{A}$, and for all $a, b, c \in \mathbf{A}$.
(iii) $\Pi(a \wedge b) = \Pi(a) * \Pi_*(b \mid a)$, for all possibility measures Π on any Boolean algebra $\mathbf{A}$, and for all $a, b, c \in \mathbf{A}$.

Proof. That (i) implies (ii) is proved in [4, Prop. 1]. Nevertheless we show here a more compact proof by using the fact that $*$ is continuous iff, together with its residuum $\Rightarrow_*$, it satisfies the divisibility equation $x * (x \Rightarrow_* y) = \min(x, y)$, see e.g. [16]. Notice first that if $a \wedge b \wedge d = \perp$, then $\Pi_*(a \mid d) * \Pi_*(b \mid a \wedge d) = \Pi_*(a \mid d) * 0 = 0 = \Pi_*(a \wedge b \mid d)$, by definition of Π_*. Suppose now that $a \wedge b \wedge d \neq \perp$ (and thus also $a \wedge d \neq \perp$), then

---

[1] A t-norm $*$ has no zero-divisors when $x * y = 0$ implies either $x = 0$ or $y = 0$, see e.g. [16].

$$\Pi_*(a \mid d) * \Pi_*(b \mid a \wedge d) = \Pi_*(a \mid d) * (\Pi(a \wedge d) \Rightarrow_* \Pi(a \wedge b \wedge d))$$
$$= \Pi_*(a \mid d) * ((\Pi(d) * \Pi_*(a \mid d)) \Rightarrow_* \Pi(a \wedge b \wedge d))$$
$$= \Pi_*(a \mid d) * (\Pi_*(a \mid d) \Rightarrow_* (\Pi(d) \Rightarrow_* \Pi(a \wedge b \wedge d)))$$
$$= \min(\Pi_*(a \mid d), \Pi(d) \Rightarrow_* \Pi(a \wedge b \wedge d))$$
$$= \min(\Pi_*(a \mid d), \Pi_*(a \wedge b \mid d))$$
$$= \Pi_*(a \wedge b \mid d).$$

That (ii) implies (iii) can be easily seen by setting $d = \top$. We now show that (iii) implies (i) by contraposition. Suppose that $*$ is not continuous, this means that divisibility does not hold and then there exist $x, y \in [0,1]$ such that $y < x$ and $x * (x \Rightarrow_* y) < y$. Then we can find a Boolean algebra $\mathbf{A}$ with a possibility measure Π where $\Pi(a) * \Pi_*(b \mid a) < \Pi(a \wedge b)$. Take $\mathbf{A}$ to be the Boolean algebra generated by two elements a and b. The atoms of $\mathbf{A}$ are conjunctions of literals of the generators. We can then define a measure Π by setting $\Pi(a \wedge b) = y$, $\Pi(a \wedge \neg b) = x$, $\Pi(\neg a \wedge \neg b) = \Pi(\neg a \wedge b) = 1$. Then $\Pi(a) = \max(x, y) = x$. Thus, $\Pi(a) * \Pi_*(b \mid a) = \Pi(a) * (\Pi(a) \Rightarrow_* \Pi(a \wedge b)) = x * (x \Rightarrow_* y) < y = \Pi(a \wedge b)$, so (iii) would not hold and the proof is complete. $\square$

Thus, continuity of the t-norm $*$ is equivalent to requiring both usual Bayes' Theorem (iii) and the generalized version of it (ii).

The problem of conditioning by an event with zero measure (already mentioned regarding Definition 1) and other related problems led Coletti and colleagues, see e.g. [2,5,6], to put forward an axiomatic approach to the definition of conditional possibility, similar to the case of conditional probability, where the notion of conditional possibility is primitive and not derived from a (unconditional) possibility. The following definition is basically from [2].

Definition 2. *Given a t-norm $*$, a $*$-conditional possibility[2] measure on $\mathbf{A}$ is a binary mapping $\overline{\Pi}(\cdot \mid \cdot) : A \times A' \to [0,1]$, where $A' = A \setminus \{\bot\}$, satisfying the following conditions:*

$(C\Pi 1)$ $\overline{\Pi}(a \mid b) = \overline{\Pi}(a \wedge b \mid b)$, for all $a \in A, b \in A'$
$(C\Pi 2)$ $\overline{\Pi}(\cdot \mid b)$ is a possibility measure for each $b \in A'$
$(C\Pi 3)$ $\overline{\Pi}(a \wedge b \mid c) = \overline{\Pi}(b \mid a \wedge c) * \overline{\Pi}(a \mid c)$, for all $a, b, c \in A$ such that $a \wedge c \in A'$.

Regarding $(C\Pi 2)$, note that if $\overline{\Pi}(b \mid \top) = 0$ then the possibility measure $\Pi_b(\cdot) = \overline{\Pi}(\cdot \mid b)$ is such that $\Pi_b(a) = 0$ if $a \wedge b = \bot$ and $\Pi_b(a) = 1$ otherwise.

The requirement of the operation $*$ in $(C\Pi 3)$ to be a t-norm is very natural and has been discussed and justified by several authors, specially in relation to the simpler, particular case $\overline{\Pi}(a \wedge b \mid \top) = \overline{\Pi}(b \mid a) * \overline{\Pi}(a \mid \top)$, see e.g. [2,5,10]. Moreover, although they might be a bit weaker, arguments different from the ones discussed above to further require $*$ to be continuous and without zero-divisors can also be put forward here:

---

[2] Called T-conditional possibility in [5,6].

– no zero-divisors: in the case $b \leq a \leq c$ and $(C\Pi3)$ yields $\overline{\Pi}(b \mid c) = \overline{\Pi}(b \mid a) * \overline{\Pi}(a \mid c)$, then if $*$ has zero-divisors, it can happen that $\overline{\Pi}(b \mid c) = 0$ (which can be read as "$(b \mid c)$ is not possible"), while $\overline{\Pi}(b \mid a)$ and $\overline{\Pi}(a \mid c)$ are both positive, which is unintuitive.
– continuity: roughly speaking, if we require that small changes in $\overline{\Pi}(b \mid a \wedge c)$ and $\overline{\Pi}(a \mid c)$ imply small changes in $\overline{\Pi}(a \wedge b \mid c)$.

Note that when $c = \top$, $(C\Pi3)$ simplifies to:

$$\overline{\Pi}(a \wedge b \mid \top) = \overline{\Pi}(b \mid a) * \overline{\Pi}(a \mid \top),$$

so that $\overline{\Pi}(a \mid b)$ is a solution of Eq. (1) once we identify $\Pi(.)$ with $\overline{\Pi}(. \mid \top)$. Moreover, for every (unconditional) Π on $\mathbf{A}$, it turns out that Π_* (as defined in Definition 1) is the greatest $*$-conditional possibility $\overline{\Pi}$ on $A \times A'$ agreeing with Π on $\mathbf{A}$, that is, such that $\overline{\Pi}(. \mid \top) = \Pi(.)$.

Proposition 2 (cf. [4]). *For every continuous t-norm $*$ and for every possibility measure Π on $\mathbf{A}$, let $C_*(\Pi)$ denote the set of $*$-conditional possibilities agreeing with Π on $\mathbf{A}$. Then $\Pi_* = \max\{C_*(\Pi)\}$, i.e. $\Pi_* \in C_*(\Pi)$ and $\Pi_* \geq \overline{\Pi}$ for every $\overline{\Pi} \in C_*(\Pi)$.*

Proof. That Π_* is a $*$-conditional possibility is shown in [4, Prop.1] and that $\Pi_*(. \mid \top) = \Pi(.)$ is clear by definition. Suppose $\overline{\Pi}$ is a $*$-conditional possibility agreeing with Π, and let $a, b \in A$ such that $a \wedge b \neq \perp$ (otherwise $\overline{\Pi}(a \mid b) = \Pi_*(a \mid b) = 0$). Then we have $\Pi(a \wedge b) = \overline{\Pi}(a \wedge b \mid \top) = \overline{\Pi}(b \mid a) * \overline{\Pi}(a \mid \top) = \overline{\Pi}(b \mid a) * \Pi(a)$, and hence $\overline{\Pi}(b \mid a) \leq (\Pi(a) \Rightarrow_* \Pi(a \wedge b)) = \Pi_*(b \mid a)$.

3 A Brief Recap on Boolean Algebras of Conditionals

In this section we recall basic notions and results from [13] where, for any Boolean algebra $\mathbf{A} = (A, \wedge, \vee, \neg, \perp, \top)$, a Boolean algebra of conditionals, denoted $\mathcal{C}(\mathbf{A})$, is built. Intuitively, a Boolean algebra of conditionals over $\mathbf{A}$ allows *basic conditionals*, i.e. objects of the form $(a \mid b)$ for $a \in A$ and $b \in A' = A \setminus \{\perp\}$, to be freely combined with the usual Boolean operations up to certain extent, but always satisfying the following requirements:

(R1) For every $b \in A'$, the conditional $(b \mid b)$ will be the top element of $\mathcal{C}(\mathbf{A})$, while $(\neg b \mid b)$ will be the bottom;

(R2) Given $b \in A'$, the set of conditionals $A \mid b = \{(a \mid b) : a \in A\}$ will be the domain of a Boolean subalgebra of $\mathcal{C}(\mathbf{A})$, and in particular when $b = \top$, this subalgebra will be isomorphic to $\mathbf{A}$;

(R3) In a conditional $(a \mid b)$ we can replace the consequent a by $a \wedge b$, that is, the conditionals $(a \mid b)$ and $(a \wedge b \mid b)$ represent the same element of $\mathcal{C}(\mathbf{A})$;

(R4) For all $a \in A$ and all $b, c \in A'$, if $a \leq b \leq c$, then the result of conjunctively combining the conditionals $(a \mid b)$ and $(b \mid c)$ must yield the conditional $(a \mid c)$.

R4 encodes a sort of restricted chaining of conditionals and it is inspired by the chain rule of conditional probabilities: $P(a \mid b) \cdot P(b \mid c) = P(a \mid c)$ whenever $a \leq b \leq c$.

In mathematical terms, the formal construction of the algebra of conditionals $\mathcal{C}(\mathbf{A})$ is done as follows. One first considers the free Boolean algebra **Free**$(A \mid A) = (Free(A \mid A), \sqcap, \sqcup, \sim, \perp^*, \top^*)$ generated by the set $A \mid A = \{(a \mid b) : a \in A, b \in A'\}$. Then, in order to accommodate the requirements R1-R4 above, one considers the smallest congruence relation $\equiv_{\mathfrak{C}}$ on **Free**$(A \mid A)$ satisfying:

(C1) $(b \mid b) \equiv_{\mathfrak{C}} \top^*$, for all $b \in A'$;
(C2) $(a_1 \mid b) \sqcap (a_2 \mid b) \equiv_{\mathfrak{C}} (a_1 \wedge a_2 \mid b)$, for all $a_1, a_2 \in A$, $b \in A'$;
(C3) $\sim(a \mid b) \equiv_{\mathfrak{C}} (\neg a \mid b)$, for all $a \in A$, $b \in A'$;
(C4) $(a \wedge b \mid b) \equiv_{\mathfrak{C}} (a \mid b)$, for all $a \in A$, $b \in A'$;
(C5) $(a \mid b) \sqcap (b \mid c) \equiv_{\mathfrak{C}} (a \mid c)$, for all $a \in A$, $b, c \in A'$ such that $a \leq b \leq c$.

Note that (C1)–(C5) faithfully account for the requirements R1-R4 where, in particular, (C2) and (C3) account for R2. Finally, the algebra $\mathcal{C}(\mathbf{A})$ is defined as follows.

Definition 3. *For every Boolean algebra* $\mathbf{A}$, *the* Boolean algebra of conditionals *of* $\mathbf{A}$ *is the quotient structure* $\mathcal{C}(\mathbf{A}) = \mathbf{Free}(A \mid A)/_{\equiv_{\mathfrak{C}}}$.

To distinguish the operations of $\mathbf{A}$ from those of $\mathcal{C}(\mathbf{A})$, the following signature is adopted:

$$\mathcal{C}(\mathbf{A}) = (\mathcal{C}(A), \sqcap, \sqcup, \sim, \perp_{\mathfrak{C}}, \top_{\mathfrak{C}}).$$

Since $\mathcal{C}(\mathbf{A})$ is a *quotient* of **Free**$(A \mid A)$, elements of $\mathcal{C}(\mathbf{A})$ are equivalence classes, but without danger of confusion, one can henceforth identify classes $[t]_{\equiv_{\mathfrak{C}}}$ with one of its representative elements, in particular, by t itself. For instance, using this notation convention, the following equalities, which correspond to (C1)–(C5) above, hold in any Boolean algebra of conditionals $\mathcal{C}(\mathbf{A})$, for all $a, a' \in A$ and $b, c \in A'$:

1. $(b \mid b) = \top_{\mathfrak{C}}$;
2. $(a \mid b) \sqcap (c \mid b) = (a \wedge c \mid b)$;
3. $\sim(a \mid b) = (\neg a \mid b)$;
4. $(a \wedge b \mid b) = (a \mid b)$;
5. if $a \leq b \leq c$, then $(a \mid b) \sqcap (b \mid c) = (a \mid c)$.

A basic observation is that if $\mathbf{A}$ is finite, $\mathcal{C}(\mathbf{A})$ is finite as well, and hence atomic. Therefore, in the finite case, it is of crucial importance, for uncertainty measures on $\mathcal{C}(\mathbf{A})$ like probabilities or possibilities, to identify the atoms of $\mathcal{C}(\mathbf{A})$, since these measures are fully determined by their values on the atoms of the algebra they are defined upon.

If $\mathbf{A}$ is a Boolean algebra with n atoms, i.e. $|\mathfrak{at}(\mathbf{A})| = n$, it is shown in [13] that the atoms of $\mathcal{C}(\mathbf{A})$ are in one-to-one correspondence with sequences $\overline{\alpha} = \langle \alpha_1, \ldots, \alpha_{n-1} \rangle$ of $n-1$ pairwise different atoms of $\mathbf{A}$, each of these sequences giving rise to an atom $\omega_{\overline{\alpha}}$ defined as the following conjunction of $n-1$ basic conditionals:

$$\omega_{\overline{\alpha}} = (\alpha_1 \mid \top) \sqcap (\alpha_2 \mid \neg\alpha_1) \sqcap \ldots \sqcap (\alpha_{n-1} \mid \neg\alpha_1 \wedge \ldots \wedge \neg\alpha_{n-2}), \qquad (4)$$

It is then clear that $|\mathfrak{at}(\mathcal{C}(\mathbf{A}))| = n!$.

Now, assume $\mathfrak{at}(\mathbf{A}) = \{\alpha_1, \ldots, \alpha_n\}$ and let us consider a basic conditional of the form $(\alpha_1 \mid b)$ for $\alpha_1 \leq b$. Let us denote the set of atoms below $(\alpha_1 \mid b)$ by $\mathfrak{at}_{\leq}(\alpha_1 \mid b) = \{\omega_{\overline{\gamma}} \in \mathfrak{at}(\mathcal{C}(\mathbf{A})) \mid \omega_{\overline{\gamma}} \leq (\alpha_1 \mid b)\}$. For every $j = 1, \ldots, n$, define

$$S_j = \{\omega_{\overline{\gamma}} \in \mathfrak{at}_{\leq}(\alpha_1 \mid b) \mid \overline{\gamma} = \langle \gamma_1, \ldots, \gamma_{n-1} \rangle \text{ with } \gamma_1 = \alpha_j\}.$$

In other words, for all j, S_j denotes the set of all those atoms below $(\alpha_1 \mid b)$ of the form $\omega_{\overline{\gamma}}$ where $\overline{\gamma}$ is the sequence $\langle \gamma_1, \ldots, \gamma_{n-1} \rangle$ and $\gamma_1 = \alpha_j$. In [13, Lemma 5.1] it is proved the following result.

Lemma 1. *The set* $\{S_j\}_{j=1\ldots,n}$ *is a partition of* $\mathfrak{at}_{\leq}(\alpha_1 \mid b)$, *i.e.* $\mathfrak{at}_{\leq}(\alpha_1 \mid b) = \cup_{j=1,n} S_j$, *and* $S_i \cap S_i = \emptyset$ *whenever* $i \neq j$. *Moreover, for* $j \geq 2$, $S_j = \emptyset$ *if* $\alpha_j \leq b$.

Now, let us describe the sets S_j's. For every sequence $\langle \alpha_1, \ldots, \alpha_i \rangle$ of pairwise different atoms of $\mathbf{A}$ with $i \leq n - 1$, let us consider the following set of atoms:

$$[\![\alpha_1, \ldots, \alpha_i]\!] = \{\omega_{\overline{\gamma}} \in \mathfrak{at}(\mathbf{A}) \mid \overline{\gamma} = \langle \alpha_1, \ldots, \alpha_i, \sigma_{i+1}, \ldots, \sigma_{n-1} \rangle\}.$$

In other words, $[\![\alpha_1, \ldots, \alpha_i]\!]$ stands for the subset of $\mathfrak{at}(\mathcal{C}(\mathbf{A}))$ whose elements are in one-one correspondence with those sequences $\overline{\gamma}$ having $\langle \alpha_1, \ldots, \alpha_i \rangle$ as initial segment. The next proposition recalls how the sets S_j are obtained from the sets $[\![\alpha_1, \ldots, \alpha_i]\!]$.

Proposition 3 ([13, Proposition 5.3]). *Let* $\mathbf{A}$ *be a finite Boolean algebra with atoms* $\alpha_1, \ldots, \alpha_n$ *and let* $b \in A$ *such that* $\neg b = \beta_1 \vee \ldots \vee \beta_k$ *and let* $\beta_k = \alpha_j$. *For every* $t = 2, \ldots, k - 1$, *denote by* $\mathbb{P}_t$ *the set of permutations* $p : \{1, \ldots, t\} \rightarrow \{1, \ldots, t\}$. *Then,*

$$S_j = [\![\alpha_j, \alpha_1]\!] \cup \bigcup_{i=1}^{k} [\![\alpha_j, \beta_i, \alpha_1]\!] \cup \bigcup_{t=2}^{k-1} \bigcup_{p \in \mathbb{P}_t} [\![\alpha_j, \beta_{p(1)} \ldots, \beta_{p(t)} \alpha_1]\!].$$

4   The Strong Conditional Event Problem for Possibility Measures

Our aim in this section is to solve the following *possibilistic* version of the Goodman and Nguyen's *strong conditional event problem*:

Possibilistic Strong Conditional Event Problem: Given a possibility measure Π on a finite Boolean algebra $\mathbf{A}$, find an extension of Π to a possibility measure μ_Π on the Boolean algebra of conditionals $\mathcal{C}(\mathbf{A})$ such that, for any $(a \mid b) \in \mathcal{C}(\mathbf{A})$, $\mu_\Pi(a \mid b)$ coincides with the $*$-conditional possibility $\Pi_*(a \mid b)$ for some suitable continuous t-norm $*$.

Since the main results we need to prove next in order to provide a solution for this problem are quite general, in what follows, unless stated otherwise, $*$ will denote an arbitrary t-norm and $\Rightarrow$ a residuated implication, so that we will not assume, in general, that $\Rightarrow$ is the residuum of $*$. A pair $(*, \Rightarrow)$ of this kind will be simply called a *t-norm implication-pair*, or simply a ti-*pair*.

Given a possibility measure Π on a finite Boolean algebra $\mathbf{A}$ with n atoms and a ti-pair $(*, \Rightarrow)$, we start by defining a mapping $\mu_\Pi : \mathfrak{at}(\mathcal{C}(\mathbf{A})) \to [0,1]$ as follows: for every atom of the Boolean algebra of conditionals $\mathcal{C}(\mathbf{A})$ as in Eq. (4), we define

$$\mu_\Pi(\omega_{\overline{\alpha}}) = \Pi(\alpha_1) * (\Pi(\neg\alpha_1) \Rightarrow \Pi(\alpha_2)) * \ldots * (\Pi(\bigwedge_{j=1}^{n-2} \neg\alpha_i) \Rightarrow \Pi(\alpha_{n-1})).$$

For the sake of a lighter and shorter notation, we will henceforth write $\dfrac{\Pi(a)}{\Pi(b)}\!\!\!\xrightarrow{\hspace{0.3cm}}$ in place of $\Pi(b) \Rightarrow \Pi(a)$, so that the above expression becomes

$$\mu_\Pi(\omega_{\overline{\alpha}}) = \Pi(\alpha_1) * \frac{\Pi(\alpha_2)}{\Pi(\neg\alpha_1)}\!\!\!\xrightarrow{\hspace{0.3cm}} * \ldots * \frac{\Pi(\alpha_{n-1})}{\Pi(\bigwedge_{j=1}^{n-2} \neg\alpha_i)}\!\!\!\xrightarrow{\hspace{0.3cm}}. \tag{5}$$

Lemma 2. *For any* ti-*pair* $(*, \Rightarrow)$, μ_Π *is a normalized possibility distribution on* $\mathfrak{at}(\mathcal{C}(\mathbf{A}))$.

Proof. We have to show that μ_Π takes value 1 for some atom of $\mathcal{C}(\mathbf{A})$. First of all note that (5) can be equivalently expressed as

$$\mu_\Pi(\omega_{\overline{\alpha}}) = \Pi(\alpha_1) * \frac{\Pi(\alpha_2)}{\Pi(\alpha_2 \vee \alpha_3 \vee \ldots \vee \alpha_n)}\!\!\!\xrightarrow{\hspace{0.3cm}} * \ldots * \frac{\Pi(\alpha_{n-1})}{\Pi(\alpha_{n-1} \vee \alpha_n)}\!\!\!\xrightarrow{\hspace{0.3cm}}.$$

Since Π is a possibility measure on $\mathbf{A}$, we can rank its atoms $\mathfrak{at}(\mathbf{A})$ according to the values taken by Π, so that we can assume $\mathfrak{at}(\mathbf{A}) = \{\beta_1, \beta_2, \ldots, \beta_n\}$ with $1 = \Pi(\beta_1) \geq \Pi(\beta_2) \geq \ldots \geq \Pi(\beta_n)$. In this way, for $1 \leq i \leq n-1$, $\Pi(\beta_i) = \max_{j=i}^n \Pi(\beta_j) = \Pi(\beta_i \vee \beta_{i+1} \vee \ldots \vee \beta_n)$, and hence $\frac{\Pi(\beta_i)}{\Pi(\beta_i \vee \beta_{i+1} \vee \ldots \vee \beta_n)}\!\!\!\xrightarrow{\hspace{0.3cm}} = 1$. Let $\overline{\beta}$ to be the sequence $\overline{\beta} = \langle \beta_1, \beta_2, \ldots, \beta_{n-1} \rangle$. Then, the corresponding atom $\omega_{\overline{\beta}}$ of $\mathcal{C}(\mathbf{A})$ is such that $\mu_\Pi(\omega_{\overline{\beta}}) = \Pi(\beta_1) * \frac{\Pi(\beta_2)}{\Pi(\beta_2 \vee \beta_3 \vee \ldots)}\!\!\!\xrightarrow{\hspace{0.3cm}} * \ldots * \frac{\Pi(\beta_{n-1})}{\Pi(\beta_{n-1} \vee \beta_n)}\!\!\!\xrightarrow{\hspace{0.3cm}} = 1$. $\square$

In light of the above lemma, we extend μ_Π to a possibility measure on $\mathcal{C}(\mathbf{A})$, denoted by the same symbol $\mu_\Pi : \mathcal{C}(\mathbf{A}) \to [0,1]$, by defining, for every $t \in \mathcal{C}(\mathbf{A})$,

$$\mu_\Pi(t) = \max\{\mu_\Pi(\omega_{\overline{\alpha}}) \mid \omega_{\overline{\alpha}} \in \mathfrak{at}(\mathcal{C}(\mathbf{A})) \text{ and } \omega_{\overline{\alpha}} \leq t\}.$$

Then, so defined, μ_Π is indeed a possibility measure on $\mathcal{C}(\mathbf{A})$.

Definition 4. *For every possibility measure* Π *on a Boolean algebra* $\mathbf{A}$ *and for every* ti-*pair* $(*, \Rightarrow)$, *the possibility measure* $\mu_\Pi : \mathcal{C}(\mathbf{A}) \to [0,1]$ *is called the* $(*, \Rightarrow)$-*canonical extension of* Π.

Example 1. Let $\mathbf{A}$ be a Boolean algebra with 3 atoms (say $\alpha_1, \alpha_2, \alpha_3$) and 8 elements, and let Π be the possibility distribution $\Pi(\alpha_1) = 0.7, \Pi(\alpha_2) = 1, \Pi(\alpha_3) = 0.2$. The corresponding algebra of conditionals $\mathcal{C}(\mathbf{A})$ has $3! = 6$ atoms and 64 elements. In particular, the atoms are the following compound conditionals:

$$\omega_1 = (\alpha_1 \mid \top) \sqcap (\alpha_2 \mid \neg\alpha_1), \ \omega_2 = (\alpha_1 \mid \top) \sqcap (\alpha_3 \mid \neg\alpha_1), \ \omega_3 = (\alpha_2 \mid \top) \sqcap (\alpha_1 \mid \neg\alpha_2)$$
$$\omega_4 = (\alpha_2 \mid \top) \sqcap (\alpha_3 \mid \neg\alpha_2), \ \omega_5 = (\alpha_3 \mid \top) \sqcap (\alpha_1 \mid \neg\alpha_3), \ \omega_6 = (\alpha_3 \mid \top) \sqcap (\alpha_2 \mid \neg\alpha_3)$$

Now, let us consider the basic conditionals $t_1 = (\alpha_1 \mid \neg\alpha_3) = (\alpha_1 \mid \neg\alpha_1 \vee \alpha_2)$ and $t_2 = (\alpha_2 \vee \alpha_3 \mid \top)$. It is not hard to check that $t_1 = \omega_1 \sqcup \omega_2 \sqcup \omega_5; t_2 = \omega_3 \sqcup \omega_4 \sqcup \omega_5 \sqcup \omega_6; t_1 \sqcap t_2 = \omega_5; \neg t_1 = \omega_3 \sqcup \omega_4 \sqcup \omega_6$.

Taking $* = $ product and $\Rightarrow$ its residuum, the extension μ_Π of Π to $\mathcal{C}(\mathbf{A})$ is determined by the following distribution on its atoms given by (5):

$$\mu_\Pi(\omega_1) = 0.7 \cdot 1 = 0.7, \ \mu_P(\omega_2) = 0.7 \cdot (0.2/1) = 0.14,$$
$$\mu_P(\omega_3) = 1 \cdot (0.7/0.7) = 1, \ \mu_P(\omega_4) = 1 \cdot (0.2/0.7) = 2/7,$$
$$\mu_P(\omega_5) = 0.2 \cdot 0.7 = 0.14, \ \mu_P(\omega_6) = 0.2 \cdot 1 = 0.2.$$

Then we can compute the possibility degree of any other (basic or compound) conditional. For instance:

$$\mu_\Pi(t_1) = \mu_\Pi(\alpha_1 \mid \neg\alpha_1 \vee \alpha_2) = \max\{\mu_\Pi(\omega_1), \mu_\Pi(\omega_2), \mu_\Pi(\omega_5)\} = 0.7$$
$$\mu_\Pi(t_2) = \mu_\Pi(\alpha_2 \vee \alpha_3 \mid \top) = \max\{\mu_\Pi(\omega_3), \mu_\Pi(\omega_4), \mu_\Pi(\omega_5), \mu_\Pi(\omega_6)\} = 1$$
$$\mu_\Pi(t_1 \sqcap t_2) = \mu_\Pi(\omega_5) = 0.2$$
$$\mu_\Pi(\neg t_1) = \max\{\mu_\Pi(\omega_3), \mu_\Pi(\omega_4), \mu_\Pi(\omega_6)\} = 1. \qquad \square$$

For what follows, recall the sets S_j and $[\![\alpha_1, \ldots, \alpha_i]\!]$ as defined in Sect. 3.

Lemma 3. *Let* $\alpha_{i_1}, \ldots, \alpha_{i_t} \in \mathfrak{at}(\mathbf{A})$. *Then*

$$\mu_\Pi([\![\alpha_{i_1}, \ldots, \alpha_{i_t}]\!]) = \Pi(\alpha_{i_1}) * \overrightarrow{\frac{\Pi(\alpha_{i_2})}{\Pi(\neg\alpha_{i_1})}} * \cdots * \overrightarrow{\frac{\Pi(\alpha_{i_t})}{\Pi(\neg\alpha_{i_1} \wedge \neg\alpha_{i_2} \wedge \ldots \wedge \neg\alpha_{i_{t-1}})}}.$$

Proof. Let $\gamma_1, \ldots, \gamma_l$ be the atoms of $\mathbf{A}$ different from $\alpha_{i_1}, \ldots, \alpha_{i_t}$. Thus, $\omega_{\overline{\delta}} \in [\![\alpha_{i_1}, \ldots, \alpha_{i_t}]\!]$ iff $\overline{\delta} = \langle \alpha_{i_1}, \ldots, \alpha_{i_t}, \sigma_1, \ldots, \sigma_{l-1} \rangle$ where $\overline{\sigma} = \langle \sigma_1, \ldots, \sigma_{l-1} \rangle$ is any string which is obtained by permuting $l - 1$ elements in $\{\gamma_1, \ldots, \gamma_l\}$.

Therefore, if $\Psi = \neg\alpha_{i_1} \wedge \ldots \wedge \neg\alpha_{i_t} (= \gamma_1 \vee \ldots \vee \gamma_l)$, by letting

- $K = \Pi(\alpha_{i_1}) * \overrightarrow{\frac{\Pi(\alpha_{i_2})}{\Pi(\neg\alpha_{i_1})}} * \cdots * \overrightarrow{\frac{\Pi(\alpha_{i_t})}{\Pi(\neg\alpha_{i_1} \wedge \neg\alpha_{i_2} \wedge \ldots \wedge \neg\alpha_{i_{t-1}})}}$,
- $H = \bigvee_{\overline{\sigma}} \overrightarrow{\frac{\Pi(\sigma_1)}{\Pi(\Psi)}} * \overrightarrow{\frac{\Pi(\sigma_2)}{\Pi(\Psi \wedge \neg\sigma_1)}} * \cdots * \overrightarrow{\frac{\Pi(\sigma_{l-1})}{\Pi(\Psi \wedge \neg\sigma_1 \wedge \ldots \wedge \neg\sigma_{n-2})}}$,

it is clear that $\mu_\Pi([\![\alpha_{i_1}, \ldots, \alpha_{i_t}]\!]) = K * H$. We now prove $H = 1$ by induction on the number l of atoms different from $\alpha_{i_1}, \ldots, \alpha_{i_t}$, i.e. $l = n - t$:

(Case 0) The basic case is for $l = 2$. In this case $H = \overrightarrow{\frac{\Pi(\gamma_1)}{\Pi(\Psi)}} \vee \overrightarrow{\frac{\Pi(\gamma_2)}{\Pi(\Psi)}} = \overrightarrow{\frac{\Pi(\gamma_1 \vee \gamma_2)}{\Pi(\Psi)}}$. Thus, the claim trivially follows because $\Psi = \gamma_1 \vee \gamma_2$.

(Case l) For any $j = 1, \ldots, l$ consider the strings $\overline{\sigma}$ such that $\sigma_1 = \gamma_j$. Therefore,

$$H = \left[\overrightarrow{\frac{\Pi(\gamma_1)}{\Pi(\Psi)}} * \bigvee_{\overline{\sigma}: \sigma_1 = \gamma_1} \left(\overrightarrow{\frac{\Pi(\sigma_2)}{\Pi(\Psi \wedge \neg\gamma_1)}} * \cdots * \overrightarrow{\frac{\Pi(\sigma_{l-1})}{\Pi(\Psi \wedge \neg\sigma_1 \wedge \ldots \wedge \neg\sigma_{l-2})}} \right) \right] \vee \ldots$$
$$\ldots \vee \left[\overrightarrow{\frac{\Pi(\gamma_l)}{\Pi(\Psi)}} * \bigvee_{\overline{\sigma}: \sigma_1 = \gamma_l} \left(\overrightarrow{\frac{\Pi(\sigma_2)}{\Pi(\Psi \wedge \neg\gamma_1)}} * \cdots * \overrightarrow{\frac{\Pi(\sigma_{l-1})}{\Pi(\Psi \wedge \neg\sigma_1 \wedge \ldots \wedge \neg\sigma_{l-2})}} \right) \right].$$

By inductive hypothesis, each term $\bigvee_{\overline{\sigma}: \sigma_1 = \gamma_j} \left(\overrightarrow{\frac{\Pi(\sigma_2)}{\Pi(\Psi \wedge \neg\gamma_1)}} * \ldots * \overrightarrow{\frac{\Pi(\sigma_{l-1})}{\Pi(\Psi \wedge \neg\sigma_1 \wedge \ldots \wedge \neg\sigma_{l-2})}} \right)$ equals 1. Thus, $H = \bigvee_{j=1}^{l} \overrightarrow{\frac{\Pi(\gamma_j)}{\Pi(\Psi)}} = \overrightarrow{\frac{\Pi(\bigvee_{j=1}^{l} \gamma_j)}{\Pi(\Psi)}} = 1$ since $\Psi = \bigvee_{j=1}^{l} \gamma_j$. $\qquad \square$

As we did in the last part of Sect. 3, let us focus on a basic conditional of the form $(\alpha_1 \mid b)$ for $b \geq \alpha_1$. Then, the next result immediately follows from Lemma 3 above together with the observation that $S_1 = [\![\alpha_1]\!]$.

Lemma 4. *Let $\mathbf{A}$ be a finite Boolean algebra with atoms $\alpha_1, \ldots, \alpha_n$, let $b \in A$ be such that $b \geq \alpha_1$. Then, for every* ti-*pair $(*, \Rightarrow)$, the $(*, \Rightarrow)$-canonical extension μ_Π of a possibility measure Π of $\mathbf{A}$ satisfies, $\mu_\Pi(S_1) = \bigvee_{\omega_{\overline{\gamma}} \in S_1} \mu_\Pi(\omega_{\overline{\gamma}}) = \Pi(\alpha_1)$.*

Now we prove our main result that will directly lead to a finitary solution for the Possibilistic Strong Conditional Event Problem stated at the beginning of this section. In what follows, for every basic conditional $(a \mid b)$, we write $\mu_\Pi(a \mid b)$ instead of $\mu_\Pi('(a \mid b)')$.

Theorem 1. *For every possibility measure $\Pi : \mathbf{A} \to [0,1]$ and for every* ti-*pair $(*, \Rightarrow)$, the $(*, \Rightarrow)$-canonical extension $\mu_\Pi : \mathcal{C}(\mathbf{A}) \to [0,1]$ of Π to $\mathcal{C}(\mathbf{A})$ is such that, for every basic conditional $(a \mid b)$,*

$$\mu_\Pi(a \mid b) = \begin{cases} 0, & \text{if } a \wedge b = \bot \\ \Pi(b) \Rightarrow \Pi(a \wedge b), & \text{otherwise.} \end{cases}$$

Proof. Let Π be given as in the hypothesis, and let μ_Π be defined on $\mathcal{C}(\mathbf{A})$ as in (5). By definition and Lemma 2, μ_Π is a normalised possibility measure. Moreover, recall that $(a \mid b) = \bot_\mathcal{C}$ if $a \wedge b = \bot$, whence, by definition, $\mu_\Pi(a \mid b) = 0$. Thus, it is left to prove the claim for those $(a \mid b)$ with $a \wedge b > \bot$.

To this end, notice that each basic conditional $(a \mid b)$ equals $(\bigvee_{\alpha_i \leq a} \alpha_i \mid b) = \bigsqcup_{\alpha_i \leq a}(\alpha_i \mid b)$. Since μ_P is maxitive, let us prove the claim for conditionals of the form $(\alpha \mid b)$ for $\alpha \in \mathfrak{at}(\mathbf{A})$ and $\alpha \leq b$. Without loss of generality we will assume $\alpha = \alpha_1$. By Lemma 1, $\{S_j\}_{j=1,\ldots,n}$ is a partition of $\mathfrak{at}_\leq(\alpha_1 \mid b)$. Thus,

$$\mu_\Pi(\alpha_1 \mid b) = \bigvee_{j=1}^n \mu_\Pi(S_j) = \mu_\Pi(S_1) \vee \bigvee_{j=2}^n \mu_\Pi(S_j).$$

Also by Lemma 1, $S_j = \emptyset$, and thus $\mu_\Pi(S_j) = 0$, for all those j such that $\alpha_j \leq b$. Therefore, by Lemma 4 one has,

$$\mu_\Pi(\alpha_1 \mid b) = \bigvee_{j=1}^n \mu_\Pi(S_j) = \Pi(\alpha_1) \vee \bigvee_{j:\alpha_j \leq \neg b} \mu_\Pi(S_j).$$

From this equation it already follows $\mu_\Pi(\alpha_1 \mid b) \geq \Pi(\alpha_1)$. We have to prove that $\mu_\Pi(\alpha_1 \mid b) = \frac{\Pi(\alpha_1)}{\Pi(b)}$.

In what follows we assume $\neg b = \beta_1 \vee \ldots \vee \beta_k$, where $\Pi(\beta_1) \leq \ldots \leq \Pi(\beta_k)$. The proof is divided in three steps:

(1) $\mu_\Pi(\alpha_1 \mid b) \leq \frac{\Pi(\alpha_1)}{\Pi(b)}$. If $\overline{\omega} \leq (\alpha_1 \mid \beta)$, then it must be of the form

$$\overline{\omega} = (\beta^1 \mid \top) \wedge (\beta^2 \mid \neg\beta^1) \wedge \ldots \wedge (\beta^i \mid \neg\beta^1 \wedge \ldots \wedge \neg\beta^{i-1}) \wedge (\alpha_1 \mid \neg\beta^1 \wedge \ldots \wedge \neg\beta^i) \wedge \ldots$$

where $\beta^1, \ldots, \beta^i \leq \neg b$, or equivalently, $\neg\beta^1 \ldots \neg\beta^i \geq b$. Then we have $\overline{\omega} \leq (\alpha_1 \mid \neg\beta^1 \wedge \ldots \wedge \neg\beta^i)$, and hence

$$\mu_\Pi(\overline{\omega}) \leq \frac{\Pi(\alpha_1)}{\Pi(\neg\beta^1 \wedge \ldots \wedge \neg\beta^i)} \leq \frac{\Pi(\alpha_1)}{\Pi(b)}.$$

Therefore, $\mu_\Pi(\alpha_1 \mid b) = \bigvee_{j:\alpha_j \leq \neg b} \mu_\Pi(S_j) \leq \dfrac{\Pi(\alpha_1)}{\Pi(b)}$.

(2) $\Pi(b) < 1$ implies $\mu_\Pi(\alpha_1 \mid b) \geq \dfrac{\Pi(\alpha_1)}{\Pi(b)}$. In this case, $\Pi(\neg b) = 1$, and thus $\Pi(\beta_k) = 1$. Let $i_b = \max\{j \in \{1, ..., k\} \mid \Pi(\beta_{i_b}) < \Pi(b)\}$, and consider the subset $S = [\![\beta_k, \beta_{k-1}, \ldots, \beta_{i_b+1}, \alpha_1]\!]$ of atoms of $\mathcal{C}(\mathbf{A})$. Proposition 3 shows that $S \subseteq \mathsf{S}_k$, whence, in particular, $S \subseteq \bigcup_{j:\alpha_j \leq \neg b} \mathsf{S}_j$. Then, by Lemma 3, we have:

$$\mu_\Pi(S) = \Pi(\beta_k) * \dfrac{\Pi(\beta_{k-1})}{\Pi(\neg\beta_k)} * \ldots * \dfrac{\Pi(\beta_{i_b+1})}{\Pi(\neg\beta_k \wedge \ldots \wedge \neg\beta_{i_b+2})} * \dfrac{\Pi(\alpha_1)}{\Pi(\neg\beta_k \wedge \ldots \wedge \neg\beta_{i_b+1})}.$$

Notice that, for every $i \in \{i_b + 1, \ldots, k\}$, $\Pi(\neg\beta_k \wedge \neg\beta_{k-1} \ldots \wedge \neg\beta_i) = \Pi(\beta_{i-1} \vee \ldots \vee \beta_1 \vee b) = \Pi(\beta_{i-1}) \vee \Pi(b) = \Pi(\beta_{i-1})$, and moreover $\Pi(\neg\beta_k \wedge \ldots \wedge \neg\beta_{i_b+1}) = \Pi(\beta_{i_b} \vee \ldots \vee \beta_1 \vee b) = \Pi(b)$. Therefore we have:

$$\mu_\Pi(S) = \Pi(\beta_k) * \dfrac{\Pi(\beta_{k-1})}{\Pi(\beta_{k-1})} * \ldots * \dfrac{\Pi(\beta_{i_b+1})}{\Pi(\beta_{i_b+1})} * \dfrac{\Pi(\alpha_1)}{\Pi(b)} = 1 * \ldots * 1 * \dfrac{\Pi(\alpha_1)}{\Pi(b)}$$

and hence, $\mu_\Pi(\alpha_1 \mid b) \geq \mu_\Pi(S) = \dfrac{\Pi(\alpha_1)}{\Pi(b)}$.

(3) $\Pi(b) = 1$ implies $\mu_\Pi(\alpha_1 \mid b) \geq \dfrac{\Pi(\alpha_1)}{\Pi(b)}$. As above observed, $\mu_\Pi(\alpha_1 \mid b) \geq \Pi(\alpha_1) = \dfrac{\Pi(\alpha_1)}{\Pi(b)}$.

Therefore, (1), (2) and (3) imply $\mu_\Pi(\alpha_1 \mid b) = \dfrac{\Pi(\alpha_1)}{\Pi(b)}$. $\square$

Let us observe that the above result holds under very general assumptions about the operations $*$ and $\Rightarrow$ under which μ_Π may fail to be a $*$-conditional possibility in the sense of Definition 2. However, when we restrict to the case where $*$ is a continuous t-norm and $(*, \Rightarrow_*)$ is a residuated pair, by Proposition 2 μ_Π does provide a solution to the possibilistic strong conditional event problem.

Corollary 1. *If Π is a possibility measure on a finite Boolean algebra $\mathbf{A}$, $*$ is a continuous t-norm and $\Rightarrow_*$ its residuum, then the $(*, \Rightarrow_*)$-canonical extension μ_Π of Π to $\mathcal{C}(\mathbf{A})$ restricted to basic conditionals yields a $*$-conditional possibility, in the sense that $\mu_\Pi(a \mid b) = \Pi_*(a \mid b)$ for every basic conditional $(a \mid b) \in \mathcal{C}(\mathbf{A})$.*

5   Conclusions and Future Work

In this paper we have shown that, in a finite setting, Boolean algebras of conditionals are suitable structures to accommodate conditional possibility measures, in a similar (but not completely analogous) way to that of conditional probabilities in [13]. We back up this claim by proving the Strong Conditional Event Problem for conditional possibility: for $*$ being a continuous t-norm without zero-divisors, any possibility measure Π in a Boolean algebra of events $\mathbf{A}$ extends to a possibility measure μ_Π on the full algebra of conditional events $\mathcal{C}(\mathbf{A})$ such that its restriction to basic conditionals is the $*$-conditional possibility $\Pi_*(. \mid .)$. This result indeed holds under very general assumptions. This suggests that the structure of a Boolean Algebra of Conditionals leaves room to accommodate notions of conditional possibility other than $\Pi_*(. \mid .)$. In particular, we plan to study when and how a $*$-conditional possibility on $A \times A'$, regarded as a partially specified (unconditional) possibility on $\mathcal{C}(\mathbf{A})$, can be extended to any compound conditional in the full algebra $\mathcal{C}(\mathbf{A})$.

Following the lines of [13], we will also investigate under which conditions a (plain) possibility measure Π on $\mathcal{C}(\mathbf{A})$ satisfies the axioms of a $*$-conditional possibility as in Definition 2 when restricted to basic conditionals. More precisely we will consider those possibilities satisfying $\Pi((a \mid b) \wedge (b \mid c)) = \Pi(a \mid b) * \Pi(b \mid c)$, for $a \leq b \leq c$ and $*$ being a continuous t-norm. These measures, in analogy with [13], can be called $*$-*separable*. Furthermore, we want to explore to what extent the results can be generalised when replacing the real unit interval $[0, 1]$ by more general scales for possibility measures, like Gödel or strict BL-algebras. Finally, we also plan to study the use of Boolean algebras of conditionals in relation to conditioning more general uncertainty models such as belief functions.

Acknowledgments. The authors are grateful to the anonymous reviewers for their comments and suggestions. Flaminio acknowledges partial support by the Spanish Ramón y Cajal research program RYC-2016- 19799. Godo is indebted to Karim Tabia for helpful discussions on conditional possibility and acknowledges support by the Spanish project ISINC (PID2019-111544GB-C21). Ugolini receives funding from the European Union's Horizon 2020 research and innovation programme under the Marie Sklodowska-Curie grant agreement No 890616 (H2020-MSCA-IF-2019).

References

1. Benferhat, S., Dubois, D., Prade, H.: Expressing independence in a possibilistic framework and its application to default reasoning. In: Cohn, A.G. (ed.) Proceedings of the 11th European Conference in Artificial Intelligence (ECAI 1994), pp. 150–154. Wiley, New York (1994)
2. Bouchon-Meunier, B., Coletti, G., Marsala, C.: Conditional possibility and necessity. In: Bouchon-Meunier, B., et al. (eds.) Technologies for Constructing Intelligent Systems. STUDFUZZ, vol. 90, pp. 59–71. Springe, Heidelberg (2002). https://doi.org/10.1007/978-3-7908-1796-6_5. (Selected papers from IPMU 2000)
3. Coletti, G., Petturiti, D.: Finitely maxitive T-conditional possibility theory: coherence and extension. Int. J. Approximate Reasoning **71**, 64–88 (2016)
4. Coletti, G., Petturiti, D., Vantaggi, B.: Independence in possibility theory under different triangular norms. In: van der Gaag, L.C. (ed.) ECSQARU 2013. LNCS (LNAI), vol. 7958, pp. 133–144. Springer, Heidelberg (2013). https://doi.org/10.1007/978-3-642-39091-3_12
5. Coletti, G., Vantaggi, B.: Comparative models ruled by possibility and necessity: a conditional world. Int. J. Approximate Reasoning **45**, 341–363 (2007)
6. Coletti, G., Vantaggi, B.: T-conditional possibilities: coherence and inference. Fuzzy Sets Syst. **160**, 306–324 (2009)
7. De Baets, B., Tsiporkova, E., Mesiar, R.: Conditioning in possibility theory with strict order norms. Fuzzy Sets Syst. **106**, 221–229 (1999)
8. De Cooman, G.: Possibility theory II: conditional possibility. Int. J. Gen. Syst. **25**(4), 325–351 (1997)
9. Dubois, D., Prade, H.: Possibility Theory. Plenum, New York (1988)

10. Dubois, D., Prade, H.: The logical view of conditioning and its application to possibility and evidence theories. Int. J. Approximate Reasoning **4**, 23–46 (1990)
11. Dubois, D., Prade, H.: Bayesian conditioning in possibility theory. Fuzzy Sets Syst. **92**, 223–240 (1997)
12. Dubois, D., Prade, H.: Possibility theory: qualitative and quantitative aspects. In: Smets, Ph. (ed.) Handbook on Defeasible Reasoning and Uncertainty Management Systems, vol. 1, pp. 169–226. Kluwer Academic, Dordrecht (1988)
13. Flaminio, T., Godo, L., Hosni, H.: Boolean algebras of conditionals, probability and logic. Artif. Intell. **286**, 103347 (2020)
14. Goodman, I.R., Nguyen, H.T.: A theory of conditional information for probabilistic inference in intelligent systems: II. Product space approach. Inf. Sci. **76**, 13–42 (1994)
15. Hisdal, E.: Conditional possibilities: independence and non-interaction. Fuzzy Sets Syst. **1**, 283–297 (1978)
16. Klement, E.P., Mesiar, R., Pap, E.: Triangular Norms. TREN, vol. 8. Springer, Dordrecht (2000). https://doi.org/10.1007/978-94-015-9540-7
17. Walley, P., de Cooman, G.: Coherence of rules for defining conditional possibility. Int. J. Approximate Reasoning **21**, 63–107 (1999)
18. Zadeh, L.A.: Fuzzy sets as a basis for a theory of possibility. Fuzzy Sets Syst. **1**, 3–28 (1978)

On the KLM Properties of a Fuzzy DL with Typicality

Laura Giordano[(⊠)]

DISIT - Università del Piemonte Orientale, Alessandria, Italy
laura.giordano@uniupo.it

Abstract. The paper investigates the properties of a fuzzy logic of typicality. The extension of fuzzy logic with a typicality operator was proposed in recent work to define a fuzzy multipreference semantics for Multilayer Perceptrons, by regarding the deep neural network as a conditional knowledge base. In this paper, we study its properties. First, a monotonic extension of a fuzzy $\mathcal{ALC}$ with typicality is considered (called $\mathcal{ALC}^{\mathbf{F}}\mathbf{T}$) and a reformulation the KLM properties of a preferential consequence relation for this logic is devised. Most of the properties are satisfied, depending on the reformulation and on the fuzzy combination functions considered. We then strengthen $\mathcal{ALC}^{\mathbf{F}}\mathbf{T}$ with a closure construction by introducing a notion of *faithful* model of a weighted knowledge base, which generalizes the notion of *coherent* model of a conditional knowledge base previously introduced, and we study its properties.

Keywords: Knowledge representation · Description logics · Preferential semantics · Fuzzy logics

1 Introduction

Preferential approaches have been used to provide axiomatic foundations of non-monoto- nic and common sense reasoning [4,22,35,38,39,42–44]. They have been extended to description logics (DLs), as well as to the first order case [3], to deal with inheritance with exceptions in ontologies, by allowing for non-strict forms of inclusions, called *typicality or defeasible inclusions*, with different preferential semantics [14,30,31] and closure constructions [7,16,17,19,28,32,45].

In previous work [24], a concept-wise multipreference semantics for weighted knowledge bases has been proposed to account for preferences with respect to different concepts, by allowing, for a concept C, a set of typicality inclusions of the form $\mathbf{T}(C) \sqsubseteq D$ (meaning "the typical C's are D's" or "normally C's are D's") with positive or negative weights. The concept-wise multipreference semantics has been first introduced as a semantics for ranked DL knowledge bases [25] and extended in [24] to weighted knowledge bases in the two-valued and fuzzy case, based on a different semantic closure construction, still in the spirit of Lehmann's lexicographic closure [39] and Kern-Isberner's c-representations [35,36], but exploiting multiple preferences associated to concepts. A related semantics with multiple preferences has been proposed in the first-order logic setting by Delgrande and Rantsaudis [23], and an extension of DLs with defeasible role quantifiers and defeasible role inclusions has been developed by Britz and Varzinczak [13, 15], by associating multiple preferences to roles.

The concept-wise multipreference semantics has been proved to have some desired properties from the knowledge representation point of view in the two-valued case [25]. In particular, it satisfies the KLM postulates of a preferential consequence relation. The properties of entailment in a fuzzy DL with typicality have not been studied so far. In this paper, a monotonic extension of a fuzzy $\mathcal{ALC}$ with typicality is considered (called $\mathcal{ALC}^\mathbf{F}\mathbf{T}$) and the KLM properties of a preferential consequence relation are reformulated for this logic. Most of the postulates are satisfied, depending on the reformulation and on the chosen fuzzy combination functions.

The closure construction developed in [24] to define the models of a weighted defeasible knowledge base in the fuzzy case is reconsidered, by introducing a notion of *faithful* model of a weighted (fuzzy) knowledge base which is weaker than the notion of *coherent* fuzzy multipreference model in [24]. This allows us to capture the larger class of monotone non-decreasing activation functions in Multilayer Perceptrons (MLPs) [33], based on the idea that, in a deep neural network, synaptic connections can be regarded as weighted conditionals. The paper discusses the properties of faithful multipreference entailment for weighted conditionals in a fuzzy DL.

2   The Description Logic $\mathcal{ALC}$ and Fuzzy $\mathcal{ALC}$

In this section we recall the syntax and semantics of the description logic $\mathcal{ALC}$ [1] and of its fuzzy extension [41].

Let N_C be a set of concept names, N_R a set of role names and N_I a set of individual names. The set of $\mathcal{ALC}$ *concepts* (or, simply, concepts) can be defined inductively:

- $A \in N_C$, $\top$ and $\bot$ are concepts;
- if C and D are concepts, and $r \in N_R$, then $C \sqcap D$, $C \sqcup D$, $\neg C$, $\forall r.C$, $\exists r.C$ are concepts.

A knowledge base (KB) K is a pair $(\mathcal{T}, \mathcal{A})$, where $\mathcal{T}$ is a TBox and $\mathcal{A}$ is an ABox. The TBox $\mathcal{T}$ is a set of concept inclusions (or subsumptions) $C \sqsubseteq D$, where C, D are concepts. The ABox $\mathcal{A}$ is a set of assertions of the form $C(a)$ and $r(a, b)$ where C is a concept, a and b are individual names in N_I and r a role name in N_R.

An $\mathcal{ALC}$ interpretation is defined as a pair $I = \langle \Delta, \cdot^I \rangle$ where: Δ is a domain—a set whose elements are denoted by $x, y, z, \ldots$—and $\cdot^I$ is an extension function that maps each concept name $C \in N_C$ to a set $C^I \subseteq \Delta$, each role name $r \in N_R$ to a binary relation $r^I \subseteq \Delta \times \Delta$, and each individual name $a \in N_I$ to an element $a^I \in \Delta$. It is extended to complex concepts as follows:

$$\top^I = \Delta, \qquad \bot^I = \emptyset, \qquad (\neg C)^I = \Delta \backslash C^I,$$
$$(\exists r.C)^I = \{x \in \Delta \mid \exists y.(x, y) \in r^I \text{ and } y \in C^I\}, \qquad (C \sqcap D)^I = C^I \cap D^I,$$
$$(\forall r.C)^I = \{x \in \Delta \mid \forall y.(x, y) \in r^I \Rightarrow y \in C^I\}, \qquad (C \sqcup D)^I = C^I \cup D^I.$$

The notion of satisfiability of a KB in an interpretation and the notion of entailment are defined as follows:

Definition 1 (Satisfiability and entailment). *Given an $\mathcal{ALC}$ interpretation $I = \langle \Delta, \cdot^I \rangle$:*

- *I satisfies an inclusion $C \sqsubseteq D$ if $C^I \subseteq D^I$;*
- *I satisfies an assertion $C(a)$ (resp., $r(a, b)$) if $a^I \in C^I$ (resp., $(a^I, b^I) \in r^I$).*

Given a KB $K = (\mathcal{T}, \mathcal{A})$, an interpretation I satisfies $\mathcal{T}$ (resp. $\mathcal{A}$) if I satisfies all inclusions in $\mathcal{T}$ (resp. all assertions in $\mathcal{A}$); I is a model *of K if I satisfies $\mathcal{T}$ and $\mathcal{A}$.*

A subsumption $F = C \sqsubseteq D$ (resp., an assertion $C(a)$, $r(a, b)$), is entailed by K, written $K \models F$, if for all models $I = \langle \Delta, \cdot^I \rangle$ of K, I satisfies F.

Given a knowledge base K, the *subsumption* problem is the problem of deciding whether an inclusion $C \sqsubseteq D$ is entailed by K.

Fuzzy description logics have been widely studied in the literature for representing vagueness in DLs [5,9,41,46,47], based on the idea that concepts and roles can be interpreted as fuzzy sets. Formulas in Mathematical Fuzzy Logic [21] have a degree of truth in an interpretation rather than being true or false; similarly, axioms in a fuzzy DL have a degree of truth, usually in the interval $[0, 1]$. In the following we shortly recall the semantics of a fuzzy extension of $\mathcal{ALC}$ referring to the survey by Lukasiewicz and Straccia [41]. We limit our consideration to a few features of a fuzzy DL and, in particular, we omit considering datatypes.

A *fuzzy interpretation* for $\mathcal{ALC}$ is a pair $I = \langle \Delta, \cdot^I \rangle$ where: Δ is a non-empty domain and $\cdot^I$ is *fuzzy interpretation function* that assigns to each concept name $A \in N_C$ a function $A^I : \Delta \to [0, 1]$, to each role name $r \in N_R$ a function $r^I : \Delta \times \Delta \to [0, 1]$, and to each individual name $a \in N_I$ an element $a^I \in \Delta$. A domain element $x \in \Delta$ belongs to the extension of A to some degree in $[0, 1]$, i.e., A^I is a fuzzy set.

The interpretation function $\cdot^I$ is extended to complex concepts as follows:

$$\top^I(x) = 1, \qquad \bot^I(x) = 0, \qquad (\neg C)^I(x) = \ominus C^I(x),$$
$$(\exists r.C)^I(x) = sup_{y \in \Delta}\, r^I(x, y) \otimes C^I(y), \qquad (C \sqcup D)^I(x) = C^I(x) \oplus D^I(x)$$
$$(\forall r.C)^I(x) = inf_{y \in \Delta}\, r^I(x, y) \rhd C^I(y), \qquad (C \sqcap D)^I(x) = C^I(x) \otimes D^I(x)$$

where $x \in \Delta$ and $\otimes$, $\oplus$, $\rhd$ and $\ominus$ are arbitrary but fixed t-norm, s-norm, implication function, and negation function, chosen among the combination functions of various fuzzy logics (we refer to [41] for details). For instance, in both Zadeh and Gödel logics $a \otimes b = min\{a, b\}$, $a \oplus b = max\{a, b\}$. In Zadeh logic $a \rhd b = max\{1 - a, b\}$ and $\ominus a = 1 - a$. In Gödel logic $a \rhd b = 1$ if $a \leq b$ and b otherwise; $\ominus a = 1$ if $a = 0$ and 0 otherwise.

The interpretation function $\cdot^I$ is also extended to non-fuzzy axioms (i.e., to strict inclusions and assertions of an $\mathcal{ALC}$ knowledge base) as follows:

$$(C \sqsubseteq D)^I = inf_{x \in \Delta} C^I(x) \rhd D^I(x), \quad (C(a))^I = C^I(a^I), \quad R(a, b))^I = R^I(a^I, b^I).$$

A *fuzzy $\mathcal{ALC}$ knowledge base K* is a pair $(\mathcal{T}, \mathcal{A})$ where $\mathcal{T}$ is a fuzzy TBox and $\mathcal{A}$ a fuzzy ABox. A fuzzy TBox is a set of *fuzzy concept inclusions* of the form $C \sqsubseteq D\ \theta\ n$, where $C \sqsubseteq D$ is an $\mathcal{ALC}$ concept inclusion axiom, $\theta \in \{\geq, \leq, >, <\}$ and $n \in [0, 1]$. A fuzzy ABox $\mathcal{A}$ is a set of *fuzzy assertions* of the form $C(a)\theta n$ or $r(a, b)\theta n$, where C is an $\mathcal{ALC}$ concept, $r \in N_R$, $a, b \in N_I$, $\theta \in \{\geq, \leq, >, <\}$ and $n \in [0, 1]$. Following Bobillo and Straccia [5], we assume that fuzzy interpretations are *witnessed*, i.e., the sup and inf are attained at some point of the involved domain. The notions of satisfiability of a KB in a fuzzy interpretation and of entailment are defined in the natural way.

Definition 2 (Satisfiability and entailment for fuzzy KBs). *A fuzzy interpretation I satisfies a fuzzy $\mathcal{ALC}$ axiom E (denoted $I \models E$), as follows, for $\theta \in \{\geq, \leq, >, <\}$:*

- *I satisfies a fuzzy $\mathcal{ALC}$ inclusion axiom $C \sqsubseteq D \; \theta \; n$ if $(C \sqsubseteq D)^I \theta \; n$;*
- *I satisfies a fuzzy $\mathcal{ALC}$ assertion $C(a) \; \theta \; n$ if $C^I(a^I)\theta \; n$;*
- *I satisfies a fuzzy $\mathcal{ALC}$ assertion $r(a, b) \; \theta \; n$ if $r^I(a^I, b^I)\theta \; n$.*

Given a fuzzy KB $K = (\mathcal{T}, \mathcal{A})$, a fuzzy interpretation I satisfies $\mathcal{T}$ (resp. $\mathcal{A}$) if I satisfies all fuzzy inclusions in $\mathcal{T}$ (resp. all fuzzy assertions in $\mathcal{A}$). A fuzzy interpretation I is a model of K if I satisfies $\mathcal{T}$ and $\mathcal{A}$. A fuzzy axiom E is entailed by a fuzzy knowledge base K, written $K \models E$, if for all models $I = \langle \Delta, \cdot^I \rangle$ of K, I satisfies E.

3   Fuzzy $\mathcal{ALC}$ with Typicality: $\mathcal{ALC}^{\mathbf{F}}\mathbf{T}$

In this section, we extend fuzzy $\mathcal{ALC}$ with typicality concepts of the form $\mathbf{T}(C)$, for C a concept in fuzzy $\mathcal{ALC}$. The idea is similar to the extension of $\mathcal{ALC}$ with typicality [31], but transposed to the fuzzy case. The extension allows for the definition of *fuzzy typicality inclusions* of the form $\mathbf{T}(C) \sqsubseteq D \; \theta \; n$, meaning that typical C-elements are D-elements with a degree greater than n. A typicality inclusion $\mathbf{T}(C) \sqsubseteq D$, as in the two-valued case, stands for a KLM conditional implication $C \mathrel{\vdash\!\!\!\sim} D$ [38,39], but now it has an associated degree.

We call $\mathcal{ALC}^{\mathbf{F}}\mathbf{T}$ the extension of fuzzy $\mathcal{ALC}$ with typicality. As in the two-valued case, such as in $\mathcal{SROIQ}^{\mathbf{P}}\mathbf{T}$, a preferential extension of $\mathcal{SROIQ}$ with typicality [27], or in the propositional typicality logic, PTL [8] the typicality concept may be allowed to freely occur within inclusions and assertions, while the nesting of the typicality operator is not allowed.

We have to define the semantics of $\mathcal{ALC}^{\mathbf{F}}\mathbf{T}$. Observe that, in a fuzzy $\mathcal{ALC}$ interpretation $I = \langle \Delta, \cdot^I \rangle$, the degree of membership $C^I(x)$ of the domain elements x in a concept C, induces a preference relation $<_C$ on Δ, as follows:

$$x <_C y \text{ iff } C^I(x) > C^I(y) \tag{1}$$

Each $<_C$ has the properties of preference relations in KLM-style ranked interpretations [39], that is, $<_C$ is a modular and well-founded strict partial order. Let us recall that, $<_C$ is *well-founded* if there is no infinite descending chain $x_1 <_C x_0, x_2 <_C x_1, x_3 <_C x_2, \dots$ of domain elements; $<_C$ is *modular* if, for all $x, y, z \in \Delta$, $x <_C y$ implies $(x <_C z$ or $z <_C y)$. Well-foundedness holds for the induced preference $<_C$ defined by condition (1) under the assumption that fuzzy interpretations are witnessed [5] (see Sect. 2) or that Δ is finite. In the following, we will assume Δ to be finite.

While each preference relation $<_C$ has the properties of a preference relation in KLM rational interpretations [39] (also called ranked interpretations), here there are multiple preferences and, therefore, fuzzy interpretations can be regarded as *multipreferential* interpretations, which have also been studied in the two-valued case [23,25,28].

Each preference relation $<_C$ captures the relative typicality of domain elements wrt concept C and may then be used to identify the *typical C-elements*. We will regard typical C-elements as the domain elements x that are preferred with respect to relation $<_C$ among those such that $C^I(x) \neq 0$.

Let $C^I_{>0}$ be the crisp set containing all domain elements x such that $C^I(x) > 0$, that is, $C^I_{>0} = \{x \in \Delta \mid C^I(x) > 0\}$. One can provide a (two-valued) interpretation of typicality concepts $\mathbf{T}(C)$ in a fuzzy interpretation I, by letting:

$$(\mathbf{T}(C))^I(x) = \begin{cases} 1 & \text{if } x \in min_{<_C}(C^I_{>0}) \\ 0 & \text{otherwise} \end{cases} \quad (2)$$

where $min_<(S) = \{u : u \in S \text{ and } \nexists z \in S \text{ s.t. } z < u\}$. When $(\mathbf{T}(C))^I(x) = 1$, we say that x is a typical C-element in I.

Note that, if $C^I(x) > 0$ for some $x \in \Delta$, $min_{<_C}(C^I_{>0})$ is non-empty. This generalizes the property that, in the crisp case, $C^I \neq \emptyset$ implies $(\mathbf{T}(C))^I \neq \emptyset$.

Definition 3 ($\mathcal{ALC}^F\mathbf{T}$ interpretation). *An $\mathcal{ALC}^F\mathbf{T}$ interpretation $I = \langle \Delta, \cdot^I \rangle$ is fuzzy $\mathcal{ALC}$ interpretation, equipped with the valuation of typicality concepts given by condition (2) above.*

The fuzzy interpretation $I = \langle \Delta, \cdot^I \rangle$ implicitly defines a multipreference interpretation, where any concept C is associated to a preference relation $<_C$. This is different from the two-valued multipreference semantics in [25], where only a subset of distinguished concepts have an associated preference, and a notion of global preference $<$ is introduced to define the interpretation of the typicality concept $\mathbf{T}(C)$, for an arbitrary C. Here, we do not need to introduce a notion of global preference. The interpretation of any $\mathcal{ALC}$ concept C is defined compositionally from the interpretation of atomic concepts, and the preference relation $<_C$ associated to C is defined from C^I.

The notions of *satisfiability* in $\mathcal{ALC}^F\mathbf{T}$, *model* of an $\mathcal{ALC}^F\mathbf{T}$ knowledge base, and $\mathcal{ALC}^F\mathbf{T}$ *entailment* can be defined in a similar way as in fuzzy $\mathcal{ALC}$ (see Sect. 2). In particular, given an $\mathcal{ALC}^F\mathbf{T}$ knowledge base K, an inclusion $\mathbf{T}(C) \sqsubseteq D$ θn (with $\theta \in \{\geq, \leq, >, <\}$ and $n \in [0,1]$) is *entailed from* K in $\mathcal{ALC}^F\mathbf{T}$ (written $K \models_{\mathcal{ALC}^F\mathbf{T}}$ $\mathbf{T}(C) \sqsubseteq D$) if $\mathbf{T}(C) \sqsubseteq D$ θn is satisfied in all $\mathcal{ALC}^F\mathbf{T}$ models I of K. For instance, the fuzzy inclusion axiom $\langle \mathbf{T}(C) \sqsubseteq D \geq n \rangle$ is satisfied in a fuzzy interpretation $I = \langle \Delta, \cdot^I \rangle$ if $inf_{x \in \Delta}(\mathbf{T}(C))^I(x) \triangleright D^I(x) \geq n$ holds, which can be evaluated based on the combination functions of some specific fuzzy logic.

4   KLM Properties of $\mathcal{ALC}^F\mathbf{T}$

In this section we aim at investigating the properties of typicality in $\mathcal{ALC}^F\mathbf{T}$ and, in particular, verifying whether the KLM postulates of a preferential consequence relation [38,39] are satisfied in $\mathcal{ALC}^F\mathbf{T}$. The satisfiability of KLM postulates of rational or preferential consequence relations [38,39] has been studied for $\mathcal{ALC}$ with defeasible inclusions and typicality inclusions in the two-valued case [14,31]. The KLM postulates of a preferential consequence relation (i.e., reflexivity, left logical equivalence, right weakening, and, or, cautious monotonicity) can be reformulated for $\mathcal{ALC}$ with typicality, by considering that a typicality inclusion $\mathbf{T}(C) \sqsubseteq D$ stands for a conditional $C \vdash D$ in KLM preferential logics, as follows:

(REFL) $\mathbf{T}(C) \sqsubseteq C$
(LLE) If $\models A \equiv B$ and $\mathbf{T}(A) \sqsubseteq C$, then $\mathbf{T}(B) \sqsubseteq C$
(RW) If $\models C \sqsubseteq D$ and $\mathbf{T}(A) \sqsubseteq C$, then $\mathbf{T}(A) \sqsubseteq D$
(AND) If $\mathbf{T}(A) \sqsubseteq C$ and $\mathbf{T}(A) \sqsubseteq D$, then $\mathbf{T}(A) \sqsubseteq C \sqcap D$
(OR) If $\mathbf{T}(A) \sqsubseteq C$ and $\mathbf{T}(B) \sqsubseteq C$, then $\mathbf{T}(A \sqcup B) \sqsubseteq C$
(CM) If $\mathbf{T}(A) \sqsubseteq D$ and $\mathbf{T}(A) \sqsubseteq C$, then $\mathbf{T}(A \sqcap D) \sqsubseteq C$

For $\mathcal{ALC}$, $\models A \equiv B$ is interpreted as equivalence of concepts A and B in the underlying description logic $\mathcal{ALC}$ (i.e., $A^I = B^I$ in all $\mathcal{ALC}$ interpretations I), while $\models C \sqsubseteq D$ is interpreted as validity of the inclusion $C \sqsubseteq D$ in $\mathcal{ALC}$ (i.e., $A^I \subseteq B^I$ for all $\mathcal{ALC}$ interpretations I).

How can these postulates be reformulated in the fuzzy case? First, we can interpret $\models C \sqsubseteq D$ as the requirement that the fuzzy inclusion $C \sqsubseteq D \geq 1$ is valid in fuzzy $\mathcal{ALC}$ (that is, $C \sqsubseteq D \geq 1$ is satisfied in all fuzzy $\mathcal{ALC}$ interpretations), and $\models A \equiv B$ as the requirement that the fuzzy inclusions $A \sqsubseteq B \geq 1$ and $B \sqsubseteq A \geq 1$ are valid in fuzzy $\mathcal{ALC}$. For the typicality inclusions, we have some options. We might interpret an inclusion $\mathbf{T}(A) \sqsubseteq C$ as the fuzzy inclusion $\mathbf{T}(A) \sqsubseteq C \geq 1$, or as the fuzzy inclusion $\mathbf{T}(A) \sqsubseteq C > 0$.

The fuzzy inclusion axiom $\mathbf{T}(A) \sqsubseteq C \geq 1$, is rather strong, as it requires that all typical A-elements belong to C with membership degree 1. On the other hand, $\mathbf{T}(A) \sqsubseteq C > 0$ is a weak condition, as it requires that all typical A-elements belong to C with some membership degree greater that 0. We will see that both options fail to satisfy one of the postulates. With the first option, the postulates can be reformulated as follows:

$(REFL')$ $\mathbf{T}(C) \sqsubseteq C \geq 1$
(LLE') If $\models A \equiv B$ and $\mathbf{T}(A) \sqsubseteq C \geq 1$, then $\mathbf{T}(B) \sqsubseteq C \geq 1$
(RW') If $\models C \sqsubseteq D$ and $\mathbf{T}(A) \sqsubseteq C \geq 1$, then $\mathbf{T}(A) \sqsubseteq D \geq 1$
(AND') If $\mathbf{T}(A) \sqsubseteq C \geq 1$ and $\mathbf{T}(A) \sqsubseteq D \geq 1$, then $\mathbf{T}(A) \sqsubseteq C \sqcap D \geq 1$
(OR') If $\mathbf{T}(A) \sqsubseteq C \geq 1$ and $\mathbf{T}(B) \sqsubseteq C \geq 1$, then $\mathbf{T}(A \sqcup B) \sqsubseteq C \geq 1$
(CM') If $\mathbf{T}(A) \sqsubseteq D \geq 1$ and $\mathbf{T}(A) \sqsubseteq C \geq 1$, then $\mathbf{T}(A \sqcap D) \sqsubseteq C \geq 1$

We can prove that, in the well-known Zadeh logic and Gödel logic, the postulates above, with the exception of reflexivity $(REFL')$, are satisfied in all $\mathcal{ALC}^{\mathbf{F}}\mathbf{T}$ interpretations.

Proposition 1. *In Zadeh logic and in Gödel logic any* $\mathcal{ALC}^{\mathbf{F}}\mathbf{T}$ *interpretation* $I = \langle \Delta, \cdot^I \rangle$ *satisfies postulates* $(LLE'), (RW'), (AND'), (OR')$ *and* (CM').

Proof. Let $I = \langle \Delta, \cdot^I \rangle$ be an $\mathcal{ALC}^{\mathbf{F}}\mathbf{T}$ interpretation in Zadeh logic, or in Gödel logic. Let us prove, as an example, that I satisfies postulate (LLE').

Assume that axioms $A \sqsubseteq B \geq 1$, $B \sqsubseteq A \geq 1$ are valid in fuzzy $\mathcal{ALC}$ and that $\mathbf{T}(A) \sqsubseteq C \geq 1$ is satisfied in I. We prove that $\mathbf{T}(B) \sqsubseteq C \geq 1$ is satisfied in I, that is $(\mathbf{T}(B) \sqsubseteq C)^I \geq 1$.

From the validity of $A \sqsubseteq B \geq 1$ and $B \sqsubseteq A \geq 1$, $inf_{x \in \Delta} A^I(x) \rhd B^I(x) \geq 1$ and $inf_{x \in \Delta} B^I(x) \rhd A^I(x) \geq 1$ in both Zadeh logic and in Gödel logic. Hence,

$$\text{for all } x \in \Delta, \ A^I(x) \rhd B^I(x) \geq 1 \text{ and } B^I(x) \rhd A^I(x) \geq 1 \tag{3}$$

In Gödel logic, this implies that: for all $x \in \Delta$, $A^I(x) \leq B^I(x)$ and $B^I(x) \leq A^I(x)$, i.e., $A^I(x) = B^I(x)$. Therefore, the preference relations $<_A$ and $<_B$ must be the same and $A^I_{>0} = B^I_{>0}$. Hence, $\mathbf{T}(A)^I(x) = \mathbf{T}(B)^I(x)$ for all $x \in \Delta$, and from $(\mathbf{T}(A) \sqsubseteq C)^I \geq 1$, it follows that $(\mathbf{T}(B) \sqsubseteq C)^I \geq 1$, that is, $\mathbf{T}(B) \sqsubseteq C \geq 1$ is satisfied in I.

In Zadeh logic, (3) implies that, for all $x \in \Delta$, $max\{1 - A^I(x), B^I(x)\} \geq 1$ and $max\{1 - B^I(x), A^I(x)\} \geq 1$ must hold, which implies that either $A^I(x) = B^I(x) = 0$

or $A^I(x) = B^I(x) = 1$. It follows that, for all $x \in \Delta$, either $(\mathbf{T}(A))^I(x) = (\mathbf{T}(B))^I(x) = 0$ or $(\mathbf{T}(A))^I(x) = (\mathbf{T}(B))^I(x) = 1$. Hence, for all $x \in \Delta$, it holds that $(\mathbf{T}(A))^I(x) = (\mathbf{T}(B))^I(x)$, and from $(\mathbf{T}(A) \sqsubseteq C)^I \geq 1$, it follows that $\mathbf{T}(B) \sqsubseteq C \geq 1$ is satisfied in I.

For the other postulates the proof is similar and is omitted for lack of space. □

The meaning of the postulate $(REFL')$ $\mathbf{T}(C) \sqsubseteq C \geq 1$ is that the typical C-elements must have a degree of membership in C equal to 1, which may not be the case in an interpretation I, when there is no domain element x such that $C^I(x) = 1$. Product and Lukasiewicz logics fail to satisfy postulates $(REFL')$ and (OR'), but they can be proven to satisfy all the other postulates.

The following corollary is a consequence of Proposition 1.

Corollary 1. *In Zadeh logic and in Gödel logic, $\mathcal{ALC}^{\mathbf{F}}\mathbf{T}$ entailment from a given knowledge base K satisfies postulates $(LLE'), (RW'), (AND'), (OR')$ and (CM').*

For instance, for (AND'), if $\mathbf{T}(A) \sqsubseteq C \geq 1$ and $\mathbf{T}(A) \sqsubseteq D \geq 1$ are entailed from a knowledge base K in $\mathcal{ALC}^{\mathbf{F}}\mathbf{T}$, then they are satisfied in all the models I of K. Hence, by Proposition 1, $\mathbf{T}(A) \sqsubseteq C \sqcap D \geq 1$ is as well satisfied in all the $\mathcal{ALC}^{\mathbf{F}}\mathbf{T}$ models of K, i.e., it is entailed by K. As reflexivity is not satisfied, the notion of $\mathcal{ALC}^{\mathbf{F}}\mathbf{T}$ entailment from a given knowledge base K does not define a preferential consequence relation, under the proposed formulation of the postulates. It is easy to see that $\mathcal{ALC}^{\mathbf{F}}\mathbf{T}$ entailment does not satisfy the Rational Monotonicity postulate.

Let us consider the alternative formulation of the postulates in the fuzzy case, obtained by interpreting the typicality inclusion $\mathbf{T}(A) \sqsubseteq C$ as the fuzzy inclusion axiom $\mathbf{T}(A) \sqsubseteq C > 0$, that is:

$(REFL'')$ $\mathbf{T}(C) \sqsubseteq C > 0$
(LLE'') If $\models A \equiv B$ and $\mathbf{T}(A) \sqsubseteq C > 0$, then $\mathbf{T}(B) \sqsubseteq C > 0$
(RW'') If $\models C \sqsubseteq D$ and $\mathbf{T}(A) \sqsubseteq C > 0$, then $\mathbf{T}(A) \sqsubseteq D > 0$
(AND'') If $\mathbf{T}(A) \sqsubseteq C > 0$ and $\mathbf{T}(A) \sqsubseteq D > 0$, then $\mathbf{T}(A) \sqsubseteq C \sqcap D > 0$
(OR'') If $\mathbf{T}(A) \sqsubseteq C > 0$ and $\mathbf{T}(B) \sqsubseteq C > 0$, then $\mathbf{T}(A \sqcup B) \sqsubseteq C > 0$
(CM'') If $\mathbf{T}(A) \sqsubseteq D > 0$ and $\mathbf{T}(A) \sqsubseteq C > 0$, then $\mathbf{T}(A \sqcap D) \sqsubseteq C > 0$

With this formulation of the postulates, it can be proven that in Zadeh logic and Gödel logic all postulates except for Cautious Monotonicity (CM'') are satisfied in all $\mathcal{ALC}^{\mathbf{F}}\mathbf{T}$ interpretations. Under this formulation, reflexivity $(REFL'')$ is satisfied in all $\mathcal{ALC}^{\mathbf{F}}\mathbf{T}$ interpretations I, as it requires that all typical C-elements in I have a degree of membership in C higher than 0, which holds from the definition of $(\mathbf{T}(C))^I$.

Proposition 2. *In Zadeh logic and in Gödel logic, any $\mathcal{ALC}^{\mathbf{F}}\mathbf{T}$ interpretation I satisfies postulates (REFL''), (LLE''), (RW''), (AND'') and (OR'').*

Cautious Monotonicity is too strong in the formulation (CM''). From the hypothesis that $\mathbf{T}(A) \sqsubseteq D > 0$ is entailed from K, we know that, in all $\mathcal{ALC}^{\mathbf{F}}\mathbf{T}$ models I of K, the typical A-elements have some degree of membership n in D. However, the degree n may be small and not enough to conclude that typical $A \sqcap D$-elements are as well typical A-elements (which is needed to conclude that $\mathbf{T}(A \sqcap D) \sqsubseteq C > 0$ is satisfied in I, given that $\mathbf{T}(A) \sqsubseteq C > 0$ is satisfied in I). A weaker alternative formulation of Cautious Monotonicity can be obtained by strengthening the antecedent of (CM'') as follows:

(CM^*) If $\mathbf{T}(A) \sqsubseteq D \geq 1$ and $\mathbf{T}(A) \sqsubseteq C > 0$, then $\mathbf{T}(A \sqcap D) \sqsubseteq C > 0$

This postulate is satisfied by $\mathcal{ALC}^{\mathbf{F}}\mathbf{T}$ entailment in Zadeh logic and Gödel logic. We can then prove that:

Corollary 2. *In Zadeh logic and in Gödel logic, $\mathcal{ALC}^{\mathbf{F}}\mathbf{T}$ entailment from a knowledge base K satisfies postulates (REFL"), (LLE"), (RW"), (AND"), (OR") and (CM*).*

As in the two-valued case, the typicality operator $\mathbf{T}$ introduced in $\mathcal{ALC}^{\mathbf{F}}\mathbf{T}$ is non-monotonic in the following sense: for a given knowledge base K, from $K \models_{\mathcal{ALC}^{\mathbf{F}}\mathbf{T}}$ $C \sqsubseteq D \geq 1$ we cannot conclude that $K \models_{\mathcal{ALC}^{\mathbf{F}}\mathbf{T}} \mathbf{T}(C) \sqsubseteq \mathbf{T}(D) \geq 1$. Nevertheless, the logic $\mathcal{ALC}^{\mathbf{F}}\mathbf{T}$ is monotonic, that is, for two $\mathcal{ALC}^{\mathbf{F}}\mathbf{T}$ knowledge bases K and K', if $K \subseteq K'$, and $K \models_{\mathcal{ALC}^{\mathbf{F}}\mathbf{T}} E$ then $K' \models_{\mathcal{ALC}^{\mathbf{F}}\mathbf{T}} E$. $\mathcal{ALC}^{\mathbf{F}}\mathbf{T}$ is a fuzzy relative of the monotonic logic $\mathcal{ALC} + \mathbf{T}$ [31].

Although most of the postulates of a preferential consequence relation hold in $\mathcal{ALC}^{\mathbf{F}}\mathbf{T}$, this typicality extension of fuzzy $\mathcal{ALC}$ is rather weak, as it happens in the two-valued case for $\mathcal{ALC} + \mathbf{T}$, for the rational extension of $\mathcal{ALC}$ in [14] and for preferential and rational entailment in KLM approach [39]. In particular, $\mathcal{ALC}^{\mathbf{F}}\mathbf{T}$ does not allow to deal with *irrelevance*. From the fact that birds normally fly, one would like to be able to conclude that normally yellow birds fly (being the color irrelevant to flying).

As in KLM framework, in the two-valued case, this has led to the definition of non-monotonic defeasible DLs [7,16–18,28,32], which exploit some closure construction (such as the rational closure [39] and the lexicographic closure [40]) or some notion of minimal entailment [6]. In the next section we strengthen $\mathcal{ALC}^{\mathbf{F}}\mathbf{T}$ based on a closure construction similar to the one in [24], but exploiting a weaker notion of coherence, and we discuss its properties.

5   Strengthening $\mathcal{ALC}^{\mathbf{F}}\mathbf{T}$: A Closure Construction

To overcome the weakness of rational closure (as well as of preferential entailment), Lehmann has introduced the lexicographic closure of a conditional knowledge base [40] which strengthens the rational closure by allowing further inferences. From the semantic point of view, in the propositional case, a preference relation is defined on the set of propositional interpretations, so that the interpretations satisfying conditionals with higher rank are preferred to the interpretations satisfying conditionals with lower rank and, in case of contradictory defaults with the same rank, interpretations satisfying more defaults with that rank are preferred. The ranks of conditionals used by the lexicographic closure construction are those computed by the rational closure construction [39] and capture specificity: the higher is the rank, the more specific is the default. In other cases, the ranks may be part of the knowledge base specification, such as for ranked knowledge bases in Brewka's framework of basic preference descriptions [12], or might be learned from empirical data.

In this section, we consider weighted (fuzzy) knowledge bases, where typicality inclusions are associated to weights, and develop a (semantic) closure construction to strengthen $\mathcal{ALC}^{\mathbf{F}}\mathbf{T}$ entailment, which leads to a generalization of the notion of fuzzy coherent multipreference model in [24]. The construction is related to the definition of Kern-Isberner's c-representations [35, 36] which also include penalty points for falsified conditionals.

A *weighted* $\mathcal{ALC}^{\mathbf{F}}\mathbf{T}$ *knowledge base* K, over a set $\mathcal{C} = \{C_1, \ldots, C_k\}$ of distinguished $\mathcal{ALC}$ concepts, is a tuple $\langle \mathcal{T}_f, \mathcal{T}_{C_1}, \ldots, \mathcal{T}_{C_k}, \mathcal{A}_f \rangle$, where $\mathcal{T}_f$ is a set of fuzzy $\mathcal{ALC}^{\mathbf{F}}\mathbf{T}$ inclusion axiom, $\mathcal{A}_f$ is a set of fuzzy $\mathcal{ALC}^{\mathbf{F}}\mathbf{T}$ assertions and $\mathcal{T}_{C_i} = \{(d_h^i, w_h^i)\}$ is a set of all weighted typicality inclusions $d_h^i = \mathbf{T}(C_i) \sqsubseteq D_{i,h}$ for C_i, indexed by h, where each inclusion d_h^i has weight w_h^i, a real number. As in [24], the typicality operator is assumed to occur only on the left hand side of a weighted typicality inclusion, and we call *distinguished concepts* those concepts C_i occurring on the l.h.s. of some typicality inclusion $\mathbf{T}(C_i) \sqsubseteq D$. Arbitrary $\mathcal{ALC}^{\mathbf{F}}\mathbf{T}$ inclusions and assertions may belong to $\mathcal{T}_f$ and $\mathcal{A}_f$.

Example 1. Consider the weighted knowledge base $K = \langle \mathcal{T}_f, \mathcal{T}_{Bird}, \mathcal{T}_{Penguin}, \mathcal{T}_{Canary}, \mathcal{A}_f \rangle$, over the set of distinguished concepts $\mathcal{C} = \{Bird, Penguin, Canary\}$, with empty ABox and with $\mathcal{T}_f$ containing, for instance, the inclusions:
$$Yellow \sqcap Black \sqsubseteq \bot \geq 1^1 \quad Yellow \sqcap Red \sqsubseteq \bot \geq 1 \quad Black \sqcap Red \sqsubseteq \bot \geq 1$$
The weighted TBox $\mathcal{T}_{Bird}$ contains the following weighted defeasible inclusions:
$(d_1)\ \mathbf{T}(Bird) \sqsubseteq Fly,\ +20 \qquad (d_2)\ \mathbf{T}(Bird) \sqsubseteq \exists has\_Wings.\top,\ +50$
$(d_3)\ \mathbf{T}(Bird) \sqsubseteq \exists has\_Feather.\top,\ +50;$
$\mathcal{T}_{Penguin}$ and $\mathcal{T}_{Canary}$ contain, respectively, the following defeasible inclusions:
$(d_4)\ \mathbf{T}(Penguin) \sqsubseteq Bird,\ +100 \qquad (d_7)\ \mathbf{T}(Canary) \sqsubseteq Bird,\ +100$
$(d_5)\ \mathbf{T}(Penguin) \sqsubseteq Fly,\ -70 \qquad\ \ (d_8)\ \mathbf{T}(Canary) \sqsubseteq Yellow,\ +30$
$(d_6)\ \mathbf{T}(Penguin) \sqsubseteq Black,\ +50; \qquad (d_9)\ \mathbf{T}(Canary) \sqsubseteq Red,\ +20$
The meaning is that a bird normally has wings, has feathers and flies, but having wings and feather (both with weight 50) for a bird is more plausible than flying (weight 20), although flying is regarded as being plausible. For a penguin, flying is not plausible (inclusion (d_5) has negative weight -70), while being a bird and being black are plausible properties of prototypical penguins, and (d_4) and (d_6) have positive weights (100 and 50, respectively). Similar considerations can be done for concept $Canary$. Given Reddy who is red, has wings, has feather and flies (all with degree 1) and Opus who has wings and feather (with degree 1), is black with degree 0.8 and does not fly ($Fly^I(opus) = 0$), considering the weights of defeasible inclusions, we may expect Reddy to be more typical than Opus as a bird, but less typical than Opus as a penguin.

We define the semantics of a weighted knowledge base trough a *semantic closure construction*, similar in spirit to Lehmann's lexicographic closure [40], but more related to c-representations and, additionally, based on multiple preferences. The construction

---

[1] This is a strong requirement which, e.g., in Gödel logic, holds in I only if $(Yellow \sqcap Black)^I(x) = 0, \forall x \in \Delta$. This suggests to be cautious when combining fuzzy inclusions and defeasible inclusions in the same KB (e.g., $Penguin \sqsubseteq Bird \geq 1$ would be too strong and conflicting with our interpretation of degree of membership as degree of typicality).

allows a subset of the $\mathcal{ALC}^\mathbf{F}\mathbf{T}$ interpretations to be selected, the interpretations whose induced preference relations $<_{C_i}$, for the distinguished concepts C_i, faithfully represent the defeasible part of the knowledge base K.

Let $\mathcal{T}_{C_i} = \{(d_h^i, w_h^i)\}$ be the set of weighted typicality inclusions $d_h^i = \mathbf{T}(C_i) \sqsubseteq D_{i,h}$ associated to the distinguished concept C_i, and let $I = \langle \Delta, \cdot^I \rangle$ be a fuzzy $\mathcal{ALC}^\mathbf{F}\mathbf{T}$ interpretation. In the two-valued case, we would associate to each domain element $x \in \Delta$ and each distinguished concept C_i, a weight $W_i(x)$ of x wrt C_i in I, by summing the weights of the defeasible inclusions satisfied by x. However, as I is a fuzzy interpretation, we do not only distinguish between the typicality inclusions satisfied or falsified by x; we also need to consider, for all inclusions $\mathbf{T}(C_i) \sqsubseteq D_{i,h} \in \mathcal{T}_{C_i}$, the degree of membership of x in $D_{i,h}$. Furthermore, in comparing the weight of domain elements with respect to $<_{C_i}$, we give higher preference to the domain elements belonging to C_i (with a degree greater than 0), with respect to those not belonging to C_i (having membership degree 0).

For each domain element $x \in \Delta$ and distinguished concept C_i, *the weight $W_i(x)$ of x wrt C_i* in the $\mathcal{ALC}^\mathbf{F}\mathbf{T}$ interpretation $I = \langle \Delta, \cdot^I \rangle$ is defined as follows:

$$W_i(x) = \begin{cases} \sum_h w_h^i \, D_{i,h}^I(x) & \text{if } C_i^I(x) > 0 \\ -\infty & \text{otherwise} \end{cases} \tag{4}$$

where $-\infty$ is added at the bottom of all real values.

The value of $W_i(x)$ is $-\infty$ when x is not a C-element (i.e., $C_i^I(x) = 0$). Otherwise, $C_i^I(x) > 0$ and the higher is the sum $W_i(x)$, the more typical is the element x relative to concept C_i. How much x satisfies a typicality property $\mathbf{T}(C_i) \sqsubseteq D_{i,h}$ depends on the value of $D_{i,h}^I(x) \in [0,1]$, which is weighted by w_h^i in the sum. In the two-valued case, $D_{i,h}^I(x) \in \{0,1\}$, and $W_i(x)$ is the sum of the weights of the typicality inclusions for C satisfied by x, if x is a C-element, and is $-\infty$, otherwise.

Example 2. Let us consider again Example 1. Let I be an $\mathcal{ALC}^\mathbf{F}\mathbf{T}$ interpretation such that $Fly^I(reddy) = (\exists has\_Wings.\top)^I(reddy) = (\exists has\_Feather.\top)^I(reddy) = 1$ and $Red^I(reddy) = 1$, i.e., Reddy flies, has wings and feather and is red (and $Black^I(reddy) = 0$). Suppose further that $Fly^I(opus) = 0$ and $(\exists has\_Wings.\top)^I$ $(opus) = (\exists has\_Feather.\top)^I(opus) = 1$ and $Black^I(opus) = 0.8$, i.e., Opus does not fly, has wings and feather, and is black with degree 0.8. Considering the weights of typicality inclusions for $Bird$, $W_{Bird}(reddy) = 20 + 50 + 50 = 120$ and $W_{Bird}(opus) = 0 + 50 + 50 = 100$. This suggests that reddy should be more typical as a bird than opus. On the other hand, if we suppose $Bird^I(reddy) = 1$ and $Bird^I(opus) = 0.8$, then $W_{Penguin}(reddy) = 100 - 70 + 0 = 30$ and $W_{Penguin}(opus) = 0.8 \times 100 - 0 + 0.8 \times 50 = 120$. This suggests that reddy should be less typical as a penguin than opus.

We have seen in Sect. 3 that each fuzzy interpretation I induces a preference relation for each concept and, in particular, it induces a preference $<_{C_i}$ for each distinguished concept C_i. We further require that, if $x <_{C_i} y$, then x must be more typical than y wrt C_i, that is, the weight $W_i(x)$ of x wrt C_i should be higher than the weight $W_i(y)$ of y wrt C_i (and x should satisfy more properties or more plausible properties of typical C_i-elements with respect to y). This leads to the following definition of a fuzzy multipreference model of a weighted a $\mathcal{ALC}^\mathbf{F}\mathbf{T}$ knowledge base.

Definition 4 (Faithful (fuzzy) multipreference model of K). *Let $K = \langle \mathcal{T}_f, \mathcal{T}_{C_1}, \ldots, \mathcal{T}_{C_k}, \mathcal{A}_f \rangle$ be a weighted $\mathcal{ALC}^\mathbf{F}\mathbf{T}$ knowledge base over $\mathcal{C}$. A faithful (fuzzy) multipreference model (fm-model) of K is a fuzzy $\mathcal{ALC}^\mathbf{F}\mathbf{T}$ interpretation $I = \langle \Delta, \cdot^I \rangle$ s.t.:*

- *I satisfies the fuzzy inclusions in $\mathcal{T}_f$ and the fuzzy assertions in $\mathcal{A}_f$;*
- *for all $C_i \in \mathcal{C}$, the preference $<_{C_i}$ is faithful to $\mathcal{T}_{C_i}$, that is:*

$$x <_{C_i} y \Rightarrow W_i(x) > W_i(y) \tag{5}$$

Example 3. Referring to Example 2 above, where $Bird^I(reddy) = 1$, $Bird^I(opus) = 0.8$, let us further assume that $Penguin^I(reddy) = 0.2$ and $Penguin^I(opus) = 0.8$. Clearly, $reddy <_{Bird} opus$ and $opus <_{Penguin} reddy$. For the interpretation I to be faithful, it is necessary that the conditions $W_{Bird}(reddy) > W_{Bird}(opus)$ and $W_{Penguin}(opus) > W_{Penguin}(reddy)$ hold; which is true, as seen in Example 2. On the contrary, if it were $Penguin^I(reddy) = 0.9$, the interpretation I would not be faithful.

Notice that, requiring that the converse of condition (5) also holds, gives the equivalence $x <_{C_i} y$ iff $W_i(x) > W_i(y)$, a stronger condition which would make the notion of faithful multipreference model of K above coincide with the notion of *coherent fuzzy multipreference model* of K introduced in [24]. Here, we have considered the weaker notion of faithfulness and a larger class of fuzzy multipreference models of a weighted knowledge base, compared to the class of coherent models. This allows a larger class of monotone non-decreasing activation functions in neural network models to be captured (for space limitation, for this result, we refer to [26], Sec. 7).

The notion of *faithful multipreference entailment (fm-entailment)* from a weighted $\mathcal{ALC}^\mathbf{F}\mathbf{T}$ knowledge base K can be defined in the obvious way.

Definition 5 (fm-entailment). *A fuzzy axiom E is fm-entailed from a fuzzy weighted knowledge base K ($K \models_{fm} E$) if, for all fm-models $I = \langle \Delta, \cdot^I \rangle$ of K, I satisfies E.*

From Proposition 2, the next corollary follows as a simple consequence.

Corollary 3. *In Zadeh logic and in Gödel logic, fm-entailment from a given knowledge base K satisfies postulates (REFL"), (LLE"), (RW"), (AND"), (OR") and (CM*).*

To conclude the paper let us infomally describe how fuzzy multipreference entailment deals with irrelevance and avoids inheritance blocking, properties which have been considered as desiderata for preferential logics of defeasible reasoning [36,48].

For "irrelevance", we have already considered an example: if typical birds fly, we would like to conclude that of typical yellow birds fly, as the property of being yellow is irrelevant with respect to flying. Observe, that in Example 2, we can conclude that Reddy is more typical than Opus as a bird ($reddy <_{Bird} Opus$), as Opus does not fly, while Reddy flies. The relative typicality of Reddy and Opus wrt $Bird$ does not depend on their color, and we would obtain the same relative preferences if reddy were yellow rather than red. A formal proof of the irrelevance property would require the domain Δ to be large enough to contain some typical bird which is yellow, requiring, as usual in the two-valued case [32], a restriction to some canonical models.

The fuzzy multipreference entailment is not subject to the problem called by Pearl the "blockage of property inheritance" problem [44], and by Benferhat et al. the "drowning problem" [4]. This problem affects rational closure and system Z [44], as well as rational closure refinements. Roughly speaking, the problem is that property inheritance from classes to subclasses is not guaranteed. If a subclass is exceptional with respect to a superclass for a given property, it does not inherit from that superclass any other property. For instance, referring to the typicality inclusions in Example 2, in the rational closure, typical penguins would not inherit the property of typical birds of having wings, being exceptional to birds concerning flying. On the contrary, in fuzzy multipreference models, considering again Example 2, the degree of membership of a domain element x in concept $Bird$, i.e., $Bird^I(x)$, is used to determine the weight of x wrt $Penguin$ (as the weight of typicality inclusion (d_4) is positive. The higher is the value of $Bird^I(x)$, the higher the value of $W_{Penguin}(x)$. Hence, provided the relevant properties of penguins (such as non-flying) remain unaltered, the more typical is x as a bird, the more typical is x as a Penguin. Notice also that the weight $W_{Bird}(x)$ of a domain element x wrt $Bird$ is related to the interpretation of $Bird$ in I by the faithfulness condition.

6   Conclusions

In this paper we have studied the properties of an extension of fuzzy $\mathcal{ALC}$ with typicality, $\mathcal{ALC}^F\mathbf{T}$. We have considered some alternative reformulation of the KLM postulates of a preferential consequence relation for $\mathcal{ALC}^F\mathbf{T}$, showing that most of these postulates are satisfied, depending on the formulation considered and on the fuzzy logic combination functions. We have considered a (semantic) closure construction to strengthen $\mathcal{ALC}^F\mathbf{T}$, by defining a notion of faithful (fuzzy) multipreference model of a weighted knowledge base. Faithful models of a conditional (weighted) knowledge base are a more general class of models with respect to the coherent fuzzy multipreference models considered in [24] to provide a semantic interpretation of multilayer perceptrons. This allows us to capture the larger class of monotone non-decreasing activation functions in multilayer perceptrons (a result which is not included in the paper due to space limitations and for which we refer to [26]). The paper studies the KLM properties of faithful multipreference entailment and discusses how the multipreference approach allows to deal with irrelevance and avoids inheritance blocking.

For MLPs, the proposed semantics allows the input-output behavior of a deep network (considered after training) to be captured by a fuzzy multipreference interpretation built over a set of input stimuli, through a simple construction which exploits the activity level of neurons for the stimuli. Each unit h of $\mathcal{N}$ can be associated to a concept name C_h and, for a given domain Δ of input stimuli, the activation value of unit h for a stimulus x is interpreted as the degree of membership of x in concept C_h. The resulting fm-interpretation can be used for verifying properties of the network by model checking and it can be proven [24] to be a model of the conditional knowledge base $K^{\mathcal{N}}$ obtained, from the network $\mathcal{N}$, by mapping synaptic connections to weighted conditionals. This opens to the possibility of combining empirical knowledge and symbolic knowledge in the form of DL axioms and motivates the study of the properties of this multipreference extension of fuzzy DLs.

Undecidability results for fuzzy description logics with general inclusion axioms [2,10,20] have motivated restricting the logics to finitely valued semantics [11], and also motivate the investigation of decidable approximations of fm-entailment. An issue is whether alternative (non-crisp) definitions of the typicality operator could be adopted, inspired to fuzzy set based models of linguistic hedges [34]. Another issue is whether the multipreference semantics can provide a semantic interpretation to other neural network models, besides MLPs and Self-Organising Maps [37], for which a (two-valued) multipreference semantics and a fuzzy semantics have been investigated in [29].

Acknowledgement. We thank the anonymous referees for their helpful comments and suggestions. This research is partially supported by INDAM-GNCS Project 2020.

References

1. Baader, F., Calvanese, D., McGuinness, D., Nardi, D., Patel-Schneider, P.: The Description Logic Handbook - Theory, Implementation, and Applications, 2nd edn. Cambridge University Press, Cambridge (2007)
2. Baader, F., Peñaloza, R.: Are fuzzy description logics with general concept inclusion axioms decidable? In: FUZZ-IEEE 2011, IEEE International Conference on Fuzzy Systems, Taipei, Taiwan, 27–30 June 2011, Proceedings, pp. 1735–1742. IEEE (2011)
3. Beierle, C., Falke, T., Kutsch, S., Kern-Isberner, G.: System Z^{FO}: default reasoning with system z-like ranking functions for unary first-order conditional knowledge bases. Int. J. Approx. Reason. **90**, 120–143 (2017)
4. Benferhat, S., Dubois, D., Prade, H.: Possibilistic logic: from nonmonotonicity to logic programming. In: Symbolic and Quantitative Approaches to Reasoning and Uncertainty, European Conference, ECSQARU 1993, Granada, Spain, 8–10 November 1993, Proceedings, pp. 17–24 (1993)
5. Bobillo, F., Straccia, U.: Reasoning within fuzzy OWL 2 EL revisited. Fuzzy Sets Syst. **351**, 1–40 (2018)
6. Bonatti, P.A., Lutz, C., Wolter, F.: The complexity of circumscription in DLs. J. Artif. Intell. Res. (JAIR) **35**, 717–773 (2009)
7. Bonatti, P.A., Sauro, L.: On the logical properties of the nonmonotonic description logic DL^N. Artif. Intell. **248**, 85–111 (2017)
8. Booth, R., Casini, G., Meyer, T., Varzinczak, I.: On rational entailment for propositional typicality logic. Artif. Intell. **277**, 103178 (2019)
9. Borgwardt, S., Distel, F., Peñaloza, R.: The limits of decidability in fuzzy description logics with general concept inclusions. Artif. Intell. **218**, 23–55 (2015)
10. Borgwardt, S., Peñaloza, R.: Undecidability of fuzzy description logics. In: Brewka, G., Eiter, T., McIlraith, S.A. (eds.) Principles of Knowledge Representation and Reasoning: Proceedings of the Thirteenth International Conference, KR 2012, Rome, Italy, 10–14 June 2012. AAAI Press (2012)
11. Borgwardt, S., Peñaloza, R.: The complexity of lattice-based fuzzy description logics. J. Data Semant. **2**(1), 1–19 (2013)
12. Brewka, G.: A rank based description language for qualitative preferences. In: Proceedings of the 16th Eureopean Conference on Artificial Intelligence, ECAI 2004, Valencia, Spain, 22–27 August 2004, pp. 303–307 (2004)
13. Britz, A., Varzinczak, I.: Contextual rational closure for defeasible ALC (extended abstract). In: Proceedings of the 32nd International Workshop on Description Logics, Oslo, Norway, 18–21 June 2019 (2019)

14. Britz, K., Heidema, J., Meyer, T.: Semantic preferential subsumption. In: Brewka, G., Lang, J. (eds.) Principles of Knowledge Representation and Reasoning: Proceedings of the 11th International Conference (KR 2008), Sidney, Australia, pp. 476–484. AAAI Press, September 2008

15. Britz, K., Varzinczak, I.J.: Rationality and context in defeasible subsumption. In: Proceedings of the 10th International Symposium on Foundation of Information and Knowledge Systems, FoIKS 2018, Budapest, 14–18 May 2018, pp. 114–132 (2018)

16. Casini, G., Meyer, T., Varzinczak, I.J., Moodley, K.: Nonmonotonic reasoning in description logics: rational closure for the ABox. In: 26th International Workshop on Description Logics (DL 2013). CEUR Workshop Proceedings, vol. 1014, pp. 600–615 (2013)

17. Casini, G., Straccia, U.: Rational closure for defeasible description logics. In: Janhunen, T., Niemelä, I. (eds.) JELIA 2010. LNCS (LNAI), vol. 6341, pp. 77–90. Springer, Heidelberg (2010). https://doi.org/10.1007/978-3-642-15675-5_9

18. Casini, G., Straccia, U.: Lexicographic closure for defeasible description logics. In: Proceedings of Australasian Ontology Workshop, vol. 969, pp. 28–39 (2012)

19. Casini, G., Straccia, U., Meyer, T.: A polynomial time subsumption algorithm for nominal safe elo⊥ under rational closure. Inf. Sci. **501**, 588–620 (2019)

20. Cerami, M., Straccia, U.: On the undecidability of fuzzy description logics with GCIs with Lukasiewicz t-norm. CoRR abs/1107.4212 (2011). http://arxiv.org/abs/1107.4212

21. Cintula, P., Hájek, P., Noguera, C. (eds.): Handbook of Mathematical Fuzzy Logic, vol. 37–38. College Publications (2011)

22. Delgrande, J.: A first-order conditional logic for prototypical properties. Artif. Intell. **33**(1), 105–130 (1987)

23. Delgrande, J., Rantsoudis, C.: A preference-based approach for representing defaults in first-order logic. In: 18th International Workshop on Non-monotonic Reasoning, NMR 2020, Workshop Notes, 12th–14th September 2020 (2020)

24. Giordano, L., Theseider Dupré, D.: Weighted defeasible knowledge bases and a multipreference semantics for a deep neural network model. In: Faber, W., Friedrich, G., Gebser, M., Morak, M. (eds.) JELIA 2021. LNCS (LNAI), vol. 12678, pp. 225–242. Springer, Cham (2021). https://doi.org/10.1007/978-3-030-75775-5_16

25. Giordano, L., Dupré, D.T.: An ASP approach for reasoning in a concept-aware multipreferential lightweight DL. Theory Pract. Log. Program. **20**(5), 751–766 (2020)

26. Giordano, L., Dupré, D.T.: Weighted defeasible knowledge bases and a multipreference semantics for a deep neural network model. CoRR abs/2012.13421 (2020). https://arxiv.org/abs/2012.13421v2

27. Giordano, L., Gliozzi, V.: Encoding a preferential extension of the description logic $\mathcal{SROIQ}$ into $\mathcal{SROIQ}$. In: Esposito, F., Pivert, O., Hacid, M.-S., Raś, Z.W., Ferilli, S. (eds.) ISMIS 2015. LNCS (LNAI), vol. 9384, pp. 248–258. Springer, Cham (2015). https://doi.org/10.1007/978-3-319-25252-0_27

28. Giordano, L., Gliozzi, V.: A reconstruction of multipreference closure. Artif. Intell. **290** (2021). https://doi.org/10.1016/j.artint.2020.103398

29. Giordano, L., Gliozzi, V., Dupré, D.T.: On a plausible concept-wise multipreference semantics and its relations with self-organising maps. In: Calimeri, F., Perri, S., Zumpano, E. (eds.) CILC 2020, Rende, Italy, 13–15 October 2020. CEUR Workshop Proceedings, vol. 2710, pp. 127–140 (2020). an extended version in CoRR abs/2103.06854, https://arxiv.org/abs/2103.06854

30. Giordano, L., Gliozzi, V., Olivetti, N., Pozzato, G.L.: Preferential description logics. In: Dershowitz, N., Voronkov, A. (eds.) LPAR 2007. LNCS (LNAI), vol. 4790, pp. 257–272. Springer, Heidelberg (2007). https://doi.org/10.1007/978-3-540-75560-9_20

31. Giordano, L., Gliozzi, V., Olivetti, N., Pozzato, G.L.: ALC+T: a preferential extension of description logics. Fund. Inform. **96**, 1–32 (2009)

32. Giordano, L., Gliozzi, V., Olivetti, N., Pozzato, G.L.: Semantic characterization of rational closure: from propositional logic to description logics. Artif. Intell. **226**, 1–33 (2015)
33. Haykin, S.: Neural Networks - A Comprehensive Foundation. Pearson (1999)
34. Huynh, V., Ho, T.B., Nakamori, Y.: A parametric representation of linguistic hedges in Zadeh's fuzzy logic. Int. J. Approx. Reason. **30**(3), 203–223 (2002)
35. Kern-Isberner, G. (ed.): Conditionals in Nonmonotonic Reasoning and Belief Revision. LNCS (LNAI), vol. 2087. Springer, Heidelberg (2001). https://doi.org/10.1007/3-540-44600-1
36. Kern-Isberner, G., Eichhorn, C.: Structural inference from conditional knowledge bases. Stud. Logica. **102**(4), 751–769 (2014)
37. Kohonen, T., Schroeder, M., Huang, T. (eds.): Self-Organizing Maps, 3rd edn. Springer Series in Information Sciences. Springer, Heidelberg (2001). https://doi.org/10.1007/978-3-642-56927-2
38. Kraus, S., Lehmann, D., Magidor, M.: Nonmonotonic reasoning, preferential models and cumulative logics. Artif. Intell. **44**(1–2), 167–207 (1990)
39. Lehmann, D., Magidor, M.: What does a conditional knowledge base entail? Artif. Intell. **55**(1), 1–60 (1992). https://doi.org/10.1016/0004-3702(92)90041-U
40. Lehmann, D.J.: Another perspective on default reasoning. Ann. Math. Artif. Intell. **15**(1), 61–82 (1995)
41. Lukasiewicz, T., Straccia, U.: Description logic programs under probabilistic uncertainty and fuzzy vagueness. Int. J. Approx. Reason. **50**(6), 837–853 (2009)
42. Makinson, D.: General theory of cumulative inference. In: Non-monotonic Reasoning, 2nd International Workshop, Grassau, FRG, 13–15 June 1988, Proceedings, pp. 1–18 (1988)
43. Pearl, J.: Probabilistic Reasoning in Intelligent Systems Networks of Plausible Inference. Morgan Kaufmann, Burlington (1988)
44. Pearl, J.: System Z: a natural ordering of defaults with tractable applications to nonmonotonic reasoning. In: Proceedings of the 3rd Conference on Theoretical Aspects of Reasoning about Knowledge (TARK 1990), Pacific Grove, CA, USA, March 1990, pp. 121–135. Morgan Kaufmann (1990)
45. Pensel, M., Turhan, A.: Reasoning in the defeasible description logic $EL_\perp$ - computing standard inferences under rational and relevant semantics. Int. J. Approx. Reasoning **103**, 28–70 (2018)
46. Stoilos, G., Stamou, G.B., Tzouvaras, V., Pan, J.Z., Horrocks, I.: Fuzzy OWL: uncertainty and the semantic web. In: Proceedings of the OWLED*05 Workshop on OWL: Experiences and Directions, Galway, Ireland, 11–12 November 2005. CEUR Workshop Proceedings, vol. 188. CEUR-WS.org (2005). http://ceur-ws.org/Vol-188/sub16.pdf
47. Straccia, U.: Towards a fuzzy description logic for the semantic web (preliminary report). In: Gómez-Pérez, A., Euzenat, J. (eds.) ESWC 2005. LNCS, vol. 3532, pp. 167–181. Springer, Heidelberg (2005). https://doi.org/10.1007/11431053_12
48. Weydert, E.: System JLZ - rational default reasoning by minimal ranking constructions. J. Appl. Log. **1**(3–4), 273–308 (2003)

Probability Logics

Trust Evidence Logic

Alessandro Aldini[1(✉)], Gianluca Curzi[2], Pierluigi Graziani[1],
and Mirko Tagliaferri[1]

[1] University of Urbino Carlo Bo, Urbino, Italy
{alessandro.aldini,pierluigi.graziani,mirko.tagliaferri}@uniurb.it
[2] University of Birmingham, Birmingham, UK
g.curzi@bham.ac.uk

Abstract. We investigate the application of a modal language à la Hennessy-Milner to the specific domain of evidence-based trust estimations. In particular, we refer to a context-aware notion of computational trust joining in a quantitative setting both assessment of subjective opinions and third-party recommendations. Moreover, for a comprehensive analysis of the proposed logics, we offer an axiomatization and provide soundness and completeness results.

Keywords: Probabilistic modal logic · Trust · Completeness

1 Introduction

Trust fosters cooperation [14,27] and it does so without requiring complex and expensive infrastructures [33]. Moreover, trust allows this cooperation to emerge in systems characterized by uncertainty [4], by decreasing the complexity of social environments [25] and, thus, promoting actions even when data (or time) is not sufficient to perform a thorough analysis of the possible outcomes of said actions. Those facts suggest that trust is an extremely important factor in environments where social interactions take place. Henceforth, the relation between trust and online environments has been object of study [20,30]. Online environments have become important parts of our daily life: we book hotels through websites, we socialize with other people through social media, *etc.* Basically everything that we used to do in the physical world until thirty years ago, can now, potentially, be done online. Moreover, the increased possibility to interact online has become important also for technologies (e.g., smart homes sensors), which can exchange data and create huge networks of complementary services, given birth to what is now called the Internet of Things (IoT) [11].

Since this shift from interactions in the physical world to interactions in online environments gradually increased over time, formal approaches have been proposed to explore trust from a logical perspective, which help computer scientists develop better trust infrastructures that are inserted in the design of various interacting scenarios [1,2,7,23,29,31].

© Springer Nature Switzerland AG 2021
J. Vejnarová and N. Wilson (Eds.): ECSQARU 2021, LNAI 12897, pp. 575–589, 2021.
https://doi.org/10.1007/978-3-030-86772-0_41

The aim of this paper is to show that by using classical ingredients of modal languages, it is possible to define a logical framework in order to build and analyze context-aware trust relations based on possessed evidence. The resulting language, called *Trust Evidence Logic* (**TEL**), includes modalities, inspired by logics à la Hennessy-Milner [17], used to express estimations about trust towards logical formulas.

In Sect. 2, motives that inspired our approach are provided, hinting at alternative solutions and connections between them. In Sect. 3, the syntax and semantics of **TEL** are introduced and model theoretic results are given. In Sect. 4, **TEL** is interpreted to study a context-aware computational notion of trust based on evidence. In Sect. 5, soundness and completeness results for **TEL** are proved, and in Sect. 6, conclusions and future works follow.

2   Background and Motivations

A prominent conception of trust is that of Gambetta [14]. According to his definition of trust, when Alice (the trustor) trusts Bob (the trustee), Alice subjectively attributed a sufficiently high probability to the possibility that Bob will act in a beneficial way towards her. In this sense, what seems relevant for the presence of trust is that Alice is able to have enough information to form a subjective evaluation on the probability that Bob will act in a certain way. The kinds of information that Alice will seek are context dependant and might change in different scenarios and/or time frames, i.e., when and in which circumstances Alice is evaluating Bob's actions.

One of the main solutions to implement such form of trust in online environments is to employ reputation models [18,19]. The main advantage of reputation models is that they are well-structured to deal with indirect evidence of behavior and they provide a solid base for trust evaluations. Each user gives a score based on his/her personal evaluation and, from there, the reputation model computes a unified value that could be provided to the trustor to form his/her subjective evaluation. Given that reputation models only need to manipulate data provided directly by users, they are easy to implement in online environments and thus are widely employed as evidence-bases for trust evaluations in computer science. Assuming a reputation model where the users can only provide Boolean evaluations for certain behaviors, e.g., the behavior is present or is absent, it would be easy to represent such reputation model through the use of graded modal logics (GML) [12,13,15]. In GML, the modal operator $\Diamond_n \phi$ specifies that in strictly more than n accessible states of the system ϕ holds. Hence, by interpreting states as agents and ϕ as the evaluated behavior, the modal operator can be adapted to decide whether a given number of evaluations are present and from there, provide an estimation of trust[1]. Taking the intuition behind GML as a starting point, two important elements can be added in order to improve the expressiveness. The first element, call it a, is a parameter indicating the context of evaluation. In this case, an evaluation is not a general assessment, but strictly depends on a specific scenario that indicates in which circumstances the evaluation is made. The second element is a numeric parameter indicating the expertise of the evaluator, i.e., it establishes how much weight the trustor places on the evaluations of other agents. In this sense, not all evaluations are judged equally, but some will be more relevant than others. Those two additions produce a language (**TEL**) that encompasses some features from both the probabilistic version of Hennessy-Milner logic (HML), see for instance [22], and the Probabilistic Computation Tree Logic (PCTL) [16]. In particular, **TEL** introduces modal formulas with shape $\langle a \rangle_p^{\geq} \phi$, where p denotes the evaluation threshold used to govern trust-based decisions, and taken as a rational (to keep the language countable) from the interval $[0, 1]$.

Following both [22] and [16], the semantics of **TEL** is defined on top of probabilistic labelled state-transition systems, which generalize Kripke semantics and allow for a straightforward logical characterization of bisimulation. Moreover, we extend soundness and completeness results of modal languages with graded modalities to our setting.

3   Syntax and Semantics of TEL

We start introducing the language of *Trust Evidence Logic* (**TEL**).

Definition 1 (Language of **TEL**). Let At be a countable set of *propositional atoms* ranging over $\alpha, \beta, \gamma, \ldots$, and let A be a countable set of *labels* ranging over $a, b, c, \ldots$. The language $\mathcal{L}_{\textbf{TEL}}$ is generated by the following grammar:

$$\phi ::= \top \mid \alpha \mid \neg\phi \mid \phi \vee \phi \mid \langle a \rangle_p^{\geq} \phi \tag{1}$$

where $\alpha \in At$, $a \in A$, and $p \in \mathbb{Q}_{[0,1]}$. The elements of $\mathcal{L}_{\textbf{TEL}}$ are called *formulas*, and range over ϕ, ψ. As usual, we define $\bot \triangleq \neg\top$, $\phi \wedge \psi \triangleq \neg(\neg\phi \vee \neg\psi)$ and $\phi \rightarrow \psi \triangleq \neg\phi \vee \psi$. Moreover, we define the following modal operators for all $a \in A$ and all $p \in \mathbb{Q}_{[0,1]}$:

$$\langle a \rangle_p^{>} \phi \triangleq \neg \langle a \rangle_{1-p}^{\geq} \neg\phi \qquad [a]_p^{\leq} \phi \triangleq \langle a \rangle_{1-p}^{\geq} \phi \qquad [a]_p^{<} \phi \triangleq \langle a \rangle_{1-p}^{>} \phi \tag{2}$$

also illustrated in Fig. 1, and we set $\langle a \rangle_p^{=} \phi \triangleq \langle a \rangle_p^{\geq} \phi \wedge \neg \langle a \rangle_p^{>} \phi$.

---

[1] An alternative approach is to employ *majority logics* [26]. Such logics are well suited to deal with dynamic scenarios where the number of evaluations is not fixed. The advantage of employing majority logics instead of GML is given by the fact that majority logics only specify that the (strict) majority of evaluations must be positive, without specifying a given number of those. On the contrary, in GML, this number must always be specified.

Definition 2 (PLSTS). A *Probabilistic Labelled State-Transition System* is a tuple $\mathfrak{M} = (S, At, A, \{\mathscr{D}_a\}_{a \in A}, v)$, where S is a non-empty countable set of states, At is the countable set of state labels, A is the countable set of transition labels, v is a *valuation function* $v : S \to \wp(At)$, and $\{\mathscr{D}_a\}_{a \in A}$ is a family of probabilistic transition functions of the form $\mathscr{D}_a : S \times S \to [0,1]$ satisfying the following condition:

$$\forall s \in S : \quad \sum_{t \in S} \mathscr{D}_a(s,t) = 1. \tag{3}$$

If $X \subseteq S$, we let $\mathscr{D}_a(s, X)$ denote $\sum_{t \in X} \mathscr{D}_a(s,t)$.

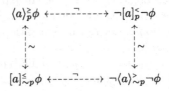

Fig. 1. Dualities between modalities, where $\neg$ is the logical negation, and $\sim$ is the involutive function on $\mathbb{Q}_{[0,1]}$ defined by $\sim p = 1 - p$.

PLSTSs generalize Kripke models. It is then natural to look for a suitable notion of "frame" in the above extended setting. This will allow us to define classes of frames and to provide axiomatic characterizations for them, as in standard modal logic.

Definition 3 (Frames). Let $\mathfrak{M} = (S, At, A, \{\mathscr{D}_a\}_{a \in A}, v)$ be a PLSTS. The *frame of* $\mathfrak{M}$, written $\mathfrak{F}_{\mathfrak{M}}$, is a pair $(S, \{\mathcal{R}_a\}_{a \in A})$ where each $\mathcal{R}_a$ is called *accessibility relation* and is defined for any $s, s' \in S$ as:

$$(s, s') \in \mathcal{R}_a \quad \text{iff} \quad \mathscr{D}_a(s, s') > 0.$$

In this case we also say that $\mathfrak{M}$ is *based on* $\mathfrak{F}_{\mathfrak{M}}$. Frames range over $\mathfrak{F}$. We define $\mathcal{K}, \mathcal{T}, \mathcal{B}$ and $\mathcal{K}4$ as, respectively, the class of all frames, the class of all reflexive frames, the class of all symmetric frames, and the class of all transitive frames. Moreover, $\mathcal{S}4$ and $\mathcal{S}5$ denote the class of all frames whose relation is, respectively, a preorder and an equivalence.

Remark 1. Since the total mass of each distribution $\mathscr{D}_a(s, \_)$ is equal to 1, the accessibility relation $\mathcal{R}_a$ is *serial*, i.e. $\forall s \in S. \exists s' \in S. (s, s') \in \mathcal{R}_a$. This means that every frame is serial.

In the semantics of **TEL**, formulas will be interpreted over PLSTSs. In particular, $\langle a \rangle_p^{\geq} \phi$ will be true at a state s if the sum of the weights that the distribution $\mathscr{D}_a(s, \_)$ associates with the states in which ϕ is true is $\geq p$.

Definition 4 (Truth). Let $\phi \in \mathcal{L}_{\textbf{TEL}}$ and $\mathfrak{M} = (S, At, A, \{\mathscr{D}_a\}_{a \in A}, v)$ be a PLSTS. We inductively define the notion of ϕ being *satisfied* (or *true*) *at state* $s \in S$ *in* $\mathfrak{M}$, written $s \models_{\mathfrak{M}} \phi$, as follows:

(a) $s \models_{\mathfrak{M}} \top$ iff true;
(b) $s \models_{\mathfrak{M}} \alpha$ iff $\alpha \in v(s)$, where $\alpha \in At$;
(c) $s \models_{\mathfrak{M}} \neg\phi$ iff $s \not\models_{\mathfrak{M}} \phi$;
(d) $s \models_{\mathfrak{M}} \phi \vee \psi$ iff $s \models_{\mathfrak{M}} \phi$ or $s \models_{\mathfrak{M}} \psi$;
(e) $s \models_{\mathfrak{M}} \langle a \rangle_p^{\geq} \phi$ iff $\mathscr{D}_a(s, S_\phi) \geq p$, where $p \in \mathbb{Q}_{[0,1]}$ and:

$$S_\phi \triangleq \{s' \in S \mid s' \models_{\mathfrak{M}} \phi\}. \tag{4}$$

In this case, we also say that ϕ is *satisfiable* in $\mathfrak{M}$. We say that ϕ is *true in* $\mathfrak{M}$, written $\models_{\mathfrak{M}} \phi$, when $s \models_{\mathfrak{M}} \phi$ holds for every $s \in S$; we say that ϕ is *true*, written $\models \phi$, when $\models_{\mathfrak{M}} \phi$ holds for every PLSTS $\mathfrak{M}$. A set of formulas Γ is *satisfied* (or *true*) *at state* $s \in S$ *in* $\mathfrak{M}$, written $s \models_{\mathfrak{M}} \Gamma$, if $s \models_{\mathfrak{M}} \phi$ for any $\phi \in \Gamma$. In this case we also say that Γ is *satisfiable* in $\mathfrak{M}$. We say that Γ is *true in* $\mathfrak{M}$, written $\models_{\mathfrak{M}} \Gamma$, when $s \models_{\mathfrak{M}} \Gamma$ holds for any $\phi \in \Gamma$ and any $s \in S$.

Definition 5 (Validity). Let $\phi \in \mathcal{L}_{\textbf{TEL}}$ and let $\mathfrak{F}$ be a frame. We say that ϕ is *valid at a state* $s \in S$ *in* $\mathfrak{F}$, written $s \models_{\mathfrak{F}} \phi$, if $s \models_{\mathfrak{M}} \phi$ for every PLSTS $\mathfrak{M}$ based on $\mathfrak{F}$ (i.e. $\mathfrak{F}_{\mathfrak{M}} = \mathfrak{F}$). We say that ϕ is *valid in* $\mathfrak{F}$, written $\models_{\mathfrak{F}} \phi$, if ϕ is valid in $\mathfrak{F}$ at any state $s \in S$. Finally, we say that a formula ϕ is *valid* on a class of frames $\mathcal{F}$ if it is valid in every frame $\mathfrak{F} \in \mathcal{F}$. The notion of validity can be easily extended to sets of formulas.

The following are straightforward properties of Definition 4.

Proposition 1. *Let* $\mathfrak{M} = (S, At, A, \{\mathscr{D}_a\}_{a \in A}, v)$ *be a PLSTS. For every* $s \in S$, $a \in A$, *and for every* $\phi, \psi \in \mathcal{L}_{\textbf{TEL}}$:

1. $\mathscr{D}_a(s, S_{\neg\phi}) = 1 - \mathscr{D}_a(s, S_\phi)$;
2. $\mathscr{D}_a(s, S_{\phi \vee \psi}) + \mathscr{D}_a(s, S_{\phi \wedge \psi}) \geq \mathscr{D}_a(s, S_\phi) + \mathscr{D}_a(s, S_\psi)$.

Using Definition 4 and Proposition 1, we can assign truth-conditions to the alternative modalities introduced in (2):

Proposition 2. *Let* $\phi \in \mathcal{L}_{\textbf{TEL}}$ *and* $\mathfrak{M} = (S, At, A, \{\mathscr{D}_a\}_{a \in A}, v)$ *be a PLSTS. Then, for all* $s \in S$:

- $s \models_{\mathfrak{M}} [a]_p^{\bowtie} \phi$ *iff* $\mathscr{D}_a(s, S_{\neg\phi}) \bowtie p$, *where* $p \in \mathbb{Q}_{[0,1]}$ *and* $\bowtie \in \{<, \leq\}$;
- $s \models_{\mathfrak{M}} \langle a \rangle_p^{\bowtie} \phi$ *iff* $\mathscr{D}_a(s, S_\phi) \bowtie p$, *where* $p \in \mathbb{Q}_{[0,1]}$ *and* $\bowtie \in \{>, =\}$.

where S_ϕ *is as in* (4).

As **TEL** shares features with both PCTL and probabilistic HML, it inherits some of their semantic properties. A remarkable example is the logical characterization of bisimulation, whose standard definition is reported below.

Definition 6 (Bisimulation). Let $\mathfrak{M} = (S, At, A, \{\mathscr{D}_a\}_{a \in A}, v)$ be a PLSTS. An equivalence relation $\mathcal{B}$ over S is a *bisimulation* if and only if whenever $(s, t) \in \mathcal{B}$ it holds that $v(s) = v(t)$ and $\forall a \in A, \forall C \in S/\mathcal{B}$:

$$\sum_{s' \in C} \mathscr{D}_a(s, s') = \sum_{t' \in C} \mathscr{D}_a(t, t').$$

As usual, we say that two states s and t in S are *bisimilar*, denoted $s \sim t$, if there exists a bisimulation $\mathcal{B}$ on S such that $s\mathcal{B}t$; two states s and t in S are *logically equivalent*, denoted $s \equiv t$, if and only if they satisfy exactly the same formulas of $\mathcal{L}_{\text{TEL}}$.

By adapting to PLSTSs the results in [6] we obtain the following theorem:[2]

Theorem 3 (Logical characterization of bisimulation). *For any PLSTS, $\sim$ coincides with $\equiv$.*

4   Modeling Trust in TEL

Since their introduction, the logical frameworks induced by the probabilistic extensions of modal logics like HML and CTL, have been employed to compare and study the properties of probabilistic systems. In such a setting, each state of the underlying semantic model represents a system configuration, characterized by a set of atomic predicates expressing the statements that hold in the state. On the other hand, each transition is enriched with a label expressing the action that is executed through the transition and with probabilistic information used to determine quantitatively the behavior associated to the action. In this view, model checking algorithms are employed to verify properties of probabilistic systems in terms of satisfiability of modal logic formulas [5,21].

In this section, we show how to provide a specific interpretation of PLSTSs in order to reason about context-aware evidence-based trust.

In the formal setting of PLSTSs, we assume that every state represents an agent of a social network of connected agents. The atomic propositions in At labeling the state associated with an agent represent the *evidences* that the agent believes to be true. The information associated with a connection from agent s to agent s' enables the trust estimation towards formulas, based on such evidence. More precisely, the transition label $a \in A$ represents the context in which trust is estimated, while $\mathscr{D}_a(s, s')$ represents the *normalized level of expertise* of agent s' as perceived by agent s with respect to the given context a.

Two further considerations about our interpretation are necessary. Firstly, we are in a classical logical setting, thus for any formula ϕ and agent s, either s states that ϕ or it states that $\neg\phi$. So every agent is forced to have a belief about ϕ. This is not a limitation for reputation models, where all involved agents have

---

[2] In [10] it is shown that disjunction can be discarded (and in [8] that, as an alternative to disjunction, conjunction can be discarded), without changing the logical characterization result, which still holds when we move from rational numbers to real numbers.

already expressed their belief about ϕ. Nonetheless, the probabilistic transition functions can be used to rule out agents' beliefs, by assigning weight 0 to them. In practice, $\mathscr{D}_a(s, s') = 0$ expresses that agent s does not consider agent s' for trust estimations about a, for various possible reasons, e.g., s' is not accessible to s, or else s is not interested in the beliefs of s'.

Secondly, notice that (3) imposes that the sum of the evaluations for the expertise of the different agents as perceived by any agent s is equal to 1. This suggests that s will always have a *claque* of agents that he evaluates as experts with respect to the given context a. However, the function $\mathscr{D}_a$ could be reflexive, allowing an agent to take into consideration also his-own expertise. In a limiting scenario there might be contexts in which the only relevant expertise is the one of the evaluating agent s, i.e., $\mathscr{D}_a(s, s) = 1$.

Then, the modal operator $\langle a \rangle^{\geq}_p \phi$ expresses that ϕ is subject to a trust estimation in the context of label a, so that the evaluation of such a modal formula for a given agent says whether the agent trusts ϕ or not with respect to a given trustworthiness threshold p. Given this interpretation of PLSTSs, we can define the notions of trust and distrust.

Definition 7 (Trust and distrust). *For each $\phi \in \mathcal{L}_{\text{TEL}}$, $a \in A$, and $p \in \mathbb{Q}_{[0,1]}$, we define trust as $T^a_p \phi$ to stand for the modality $\langle a \rangle^{\geq}_p \phi$ and distrust as $D^a_p \phi$ to stand for the modality $[a]^{<}_{1-p} \neg\phi$. Similarly, we define weak trust ($wT^a_p \phi$) as $\langle a \rangle^{\geq}_p \phi$ and weak distrust ($wD^a_p \phi$) as $[a]^{\leq}_{1-p} \neg\phi$.*

Notice that, by (2), trusting ϕ with respect to a and p corresponds to distrusting $\neg\phi$ with respect to a and p. To emphasize the nature of the duality between trust and distrust, we point out that for every $p \in \mathbb{Q}_{[0.5,1]}$, it holds that $T^a_p \phi \wedge D^a_p \phi$ is not satisfiable for any state of every PLSTS, i.e., a statement cannot be trusted and distrusted at the same time with respect to a given context and a threshold expressing at least weak majority. However, uncertainty is admissible in the case of lower thresholds, which could make both trust and distrust satisfiable. The same result holds for the weak notions provided that $p \in \mathbb{Q}_{]0.5,1]}$; indeed $p = 0.5$ admits the satisfiability of $wT^a_p \phi \wedge wD^a_p \phi$.

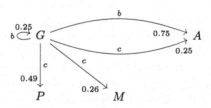

Fig. 2. PLSTS example, where G := Gianluca, P := Pierluigi, M := Mirko, A := Alessandro, c := restaurants, b := cybersecurity, ϕ := *Ciacci is renowned for its gastronomy*, ψ := *Ciacci offers the best value for money in the whole of Urbino*, θ := *TLS 1.3 is secure*. Let $G \models \neg\theta$, $P \models \phi \wedge \psi$, $M \models \phi \wedge \neg\psi$, and $A \models \neg\phi \wedge \neg\psi \wedge \theta$.

On the other hand, we have that $T^a_p \phi \vee D^a_p \phi$ is not true. Indeed, as a counterexample consider a PLSTS graphically represented as follows:

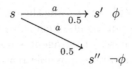

where ϕ holds in s' but not in s''. We have that neither $s \models T^a_{\frac{1}{2}}\phi$ nor $s \models D^a_{\frac{1}{2}}\phi$ hold. The special case $p = 0.5$ illustrated for the weak notions reveals that the counterexample above does not work for weak trust/distrust.

We now show a toy example illustrating how this general setting works to model a notion of context-aware evidence-based trust.

Example 1. Figure 2 shows a PLSTS. Here, the labels c and b are *contexts*, which identify a specific situation where trust of an agent towards a given statement is considered.

For instance, concerning the label c, we have that $G \models wT^c_{0.75}\phi$ and $G \models D^c_{0.5}\psi$. We can then say that G *weakly trusts* ϕ with respect to context c and threshold 0.75 because the sum of the weights associated with the agents accessible through c for which ϕ holds overtakes the trustworthiness threshold 0.75. Similarly, G *distrusts* ψ with respect to context c and threshold 0.5 because the sum of the weights associated with the agents accessible through c for which $\neg\psi$ holds strictly overtakes the threshold 0.5. Notice that G, in the context c, is not taking into account his own belief about ϕ, e.g., because he is completely ignorant about ϕ.

Concerning the label b, we recall that $G \models \neg\theta$; however it holds that $G \models wT^b_{0.75}\theta$. This means that G *weakly trusts* θ with respect to context b and threshold 0.75 even if G *states that* $\neg\theta$, because the weight G assigns to A is far greater than the weight G assigns to himself. The fact that G evaluates A's belief more than his-own in context b emphasizes that in our framework $s \models_{\mathfrak{M}} \phi$ must be read as *agent s believes that ϕ holds*. However, beliefs are subjective and could be subverted by other agents' beliefs.

It is interesting to notice the trust-theoretical meaning of bisimulation, i.e., what does it imply for two agents to be bisimilar in the setting of trust? Thanks to Theorem 3, two bisimilar agents trust the same formulas. More in-depth, recalling the two conditions of Definition 6, two agents s and t belonging to the same class of equivalence share the same evidence ($v(s) = v(t)$) and, for each context, express the same trustworthiness towards every class of agents induced by bisimulation. Reasoning at the level of classes implies two facts. First, s and t could even interact with different agents and be, anyway, bisimilar. Second, as bisimulation induces aggregation of equivalent states, every agent may treat each class of agents as a unique entity whose belief is evaluated to some degree.

5   Soundness and Completeness

This section is about soundness and completeness for various *trust evidence normal modal logics* (TENML), the "normal" modal logics for **TEL**. In particular, we shall focus on the systems TEK, TET, TEB, TEK4, TES4 and TES5, which can be seen as quantitative and "serial" extensions of the standard modal logics K, T, B, K4, S4 and S5, respectively (Proposition 6). Each such TENML is proven both sound and complete with respect to all those PLSTSs that are based on a specific class of frames. This requires to establish a version of the canonical model theorem for **TEL** (Theorem 9), the main result of this section. Finally, we introduce a counterexample to compactness and we use it to infer the failure of strong completeness in our framework.

The proof of the canonical model theorem follows the lines of [9], adapting the techniques to a quantitative setting, while the counterexample to compactness is taken from [32].

5.1 Soundness

We start defining the notion of trust evidence normal modal logic.

Definition 8 (TENML). A *trust evidence normal modal logic* (TENML) is a set $\Lambda \subseteq \mathcal{L}_{\mathbf{TEL}}$ containing (i) all propositional tautologies, (ii) all the substitution instances of the following axiom schemata, for $\phi, \psi \in \mathcal{L}_{\mathbf{TEL}}$, $a \in A$ and $p, q \in \mathbb{Q}_{[0,1]}$:

1. $\langle a \rangle_p^{>} \phi \rightarrow \langle a \rangle_p^{\geq} \phi$;
2. $\langle a \rangle_p^{\geq} \phi \rightarrow \langle a \rangle_q^{>} \phi$ with $q < p$;
3. $\langle a \rangle_0^{\geq} \phi$
4. $\langle a \rangle_1^{\geq}(\phi \rightarrow \psi) \rightarrow \langle a \rangle_p^{\geq} \phi \rightarrow \langle a \rangle_p^{\geq} \psi$;
5. $\langle a \rangle_1^{\geq} \neg(\phi \wedge \psi) \rightarrow ((\langle a \rangle_p^{\geq} \phi \wedge \langle a \rangle_q^{\geq} \psi) \rightarrow \langle a \rangle_{p+q}^{\geq}(\phi \vee \psi)$ with $p + q \leq 1$;

and (iii) closed under *modus ponens* (MP) and *necessitation* (NEC$_a$ with $a \in A$):

$$\frac{\phi}{\langle a \rangle_1^{\geq} \phi} \text{ NEC}_a$$

The above axioms state fundamental properties about $\mathscr{D}_a(s, S_\phi)$ (see (4)). Axiom 1 and Axiom 2 formalize properties about inequalities. Axiom 3 and its dual formulation $[a]_1^{\leq} \phi$ (see (2)) state that $\mathscr{D}_a(s, S_\phi)$ is always a rational in $[0, 1]$. Axiom 4 allows modalities to distribute over implication, and it can be seen as a generalization of (**K**), i.e. $\Box(\phi \rightarrow \psi) \rightarrow \Box\phi \rightarrow \Box\psi$. Finally, Axiom 5 describes compositionality for $\vee$, which holds whenever both disjuncts are "incompatible".

We shall write $\vdash_\Lambda \phi$, or simply $\vdash \phi$ (when no confusion arises), when $\phi \in \Lambda$. If Γ is a set of formulas, we write $\Gamma \vdash_\Lambda \phi$ if either $\vdash_\Lambda \phi$ or there are $\psi_1, \ldots, \psi_n \in \Gamma$ such that $\vdash_\Lambda (\psi_1 \wedge \ldots \wedge \psi_n) \rightarrow \phi$. Finally, we say that Γ is Λ-*consistent*, or simply *consistent* (when no confusion arises), when $\Gamma \nvdash_\Lambda \bot$. A set of formulas Γ is *maximal Λ-consistent*, or simply *maximal consistent* (when no confusion arises), if Γ is Λ-consistent and any Γ' properly containing Γ is not Λ-consistent. We shall often refer to Γ as a *mc-set*, and the set of all mc-sets is *MAX*.

The following proposition states some basic properties about Λ.

Proposition 4. *Let* $\phi, \psi \in \mathcal{L}_{\textbf{TEL}}$ *and* $p, q \in \mathbb{Q}_{[0,1]}$:

1. *If* $\vdash \phi \rightarrow \psi$ *then* $\vdash \langle a \rangle_p^{\bowtie} \phi \rightarrow \langle a \rangle_p^{\bowtie} \psi$, *where* $\bowtie \in \{\geq, >, =\}$;
2. *If* $\vdash \phi \leftrightarrow \psi$ *then* $\vdash \langle a \rangle_p^{\bowtie} \phi \leftrightarrow \langle a \rangle_p^{\bowtie} \psi$, *where* $\bowtie \in \{\geq, >, =\}$;
3. *If* $q < p$ *then* $\vdash \langle a \rangle_p^{\geq} \phi \rightarrow \langle a \rangle_q^{\geq} \phi$;
4. $\vdash \langle a \rangle_0^{=} (\phi \wedge \psi) \rightarrow ((\langle a \rangle_p^{\geq} \phi \wedge \langle a \rangle_q^{=} \psi) \rightarrow \langle a \rangle_{p+q}^{=} (\phi \vee \psi))$.

As usual, there is a smallest TENML Λ containing a given set of formulas Γ, called the TENML *axiomatized by* Γ. When $\Gamma = \emptyset$, Λ will be written TEK. In analogy with standard modal logic, we consider the following axioms:

$$(\textbf{T}^+) = \langle a \rangle_1^{\geq} \phi \rightarrow \phi$$

$$(\textbf{B}^+) = \phi \rightarrow \langle a \rangle_1^{\geq} \langle a \rangle_0^{\geq} \phi$$

$$(4^+) = \langle a \rangle_1^{\geq} \phi \rightarrow \langle a \rangle_1^{\geq} \langle a \rangle_1^{\geq} \phi$$

We shall work with extensions of TEK that combine the above axioms. In particular, TET, TEB, TEK4 are obtained by adding to TEK, respectively, $(\textbf{T}^+)$, $(\textbf{B}^+)$, and (4^+). Moreover, TES4 extends TEK with both $(\textbf{T}^+)$ and (4^+), and TES5 extends TES4 with $(\textbf{B}^+)$.

The following theorem shows a series of soundness results relating the above defined TENLMs and classes of frames. In particular, TEK turns out to be sound w.r.t. all PLSTSs.

Theorem 5 (Soundness for various TENLMs). *For any* $\phi \in \mathcal{L}_{\textbf{TEL}}$:

$$\vdash_{\textsf{TEK}} \phi \text{ implies } \models_{\mathcal{K}} \phi; \quad \vdash_{\textsf{TET}} \phi \text{ implies } \models_{\mathcal{T}} \phi;$$
$$\vdash_{\textsf{TEB}} \phi \text{ implies } \models_{\mathcal{B}} \phi; \quad \vdash_{\textsf{TEK4}} \phi \text{ implies } \models_{\mathcal{K}4} \phi;$$
$$\vdash_{\textsf{TES4}} \phi \text{ implies } \models_{\mathcal{S}4} \phi; \quad \vdash_{\textsf{TES5}} \phi \text{ implies } \models_{\mathcal{S}5} \phi.$$

In Remark 1 we stressed that any frame is serial by construction. This condition is formalized by Axiom 2, which can be seen as a quantitative generalization of Axiom (D), i.e. $\Box \phi \rightarrow \Diamond \phi$. To see this, let us fix $A = \{*\}$ in (1), and let us assume that the parameters p, q are taken from $\{0, 1\}$. It is not difficult to see that, by setting $\Box \phi \triangleq \langle * \rangle_1^{\geq} \phi$, Axioms 1–5 define exactly the serial normal modal logic D. In particular, Axiom 2 collapses to (D). More formally, we have:

Proposition 6. TEK *is a conservative extension of the normal modal logic* D.

This observation can be also found in [12], where a variant of Axiom 2 is considered. Let us finally notice that we could avoid seriality by defining each $\mathscr{D}_a(s, \_)$ as a sub-distribution, i.e. a distribution whose mass can be smaller than 1. However, turning the equality in (3) into an inequality would break the equation in Proposition 1.1 and, as a consequence, the logical dualities in Fig. 1.

5.2   Completeness

In this subsection we sketch the proof of the canonical model theorem for **TEL**, from which we infer a series of completeness results for TEK, TET, TEB, TEK4, TES4 and TES5. The canonical model for **TEL** can be obtained by adapting the one for graded modal logics (GML) [9] to a quantitative setting.

Definition 9 (Canonical model). Given any consistent TENML Λ, we define its *canonical model* $\mathfrak{M}_\Lambda = \langle S^\Lambda, At^\Lambda, A^\Lambda, \{\mathscr{D}_a^\Lambda\}_{a \in A^\Lambda}, v^\Lambda \rangle$ as follows:

- S^Λ is the set MAX of all maximally consistent sets;
- At^Λ, A^Λ are the sets of state and transition labels of $\mathcal{L}_{\textbf{TEL}}$;
- for any $a \in A^\Lambda$ and for any $\Gamma, \Delta \in S^\Lambda$, we set:

$$\mathscr{D}_a^\Lambda(\Gamma, \Delta) = \min\{p \in \mathbb{Q}_{[0,1]} \mid \langle a \rangle_p^= \phi \in \Gamma, \ \phi \in \Delta\}; \tag{5}$$

- for any $\Gamma \in S^\Lambda$, $v^\Lambda(\Gamma) = \{\alpha \in At^\Lambda \mid \alpha \in \Gamma\}$.

In [9], De Caro showed a key property relating the canonical model for GML to graded modalities $\Diamond_n$ ($n \in \mathbb{N}$): given a state of this model, i.e. a maximally consistent set Γ, $\Diamond_n \phi \in \Gamma$ iff the number of mc-sets containing ϕ that are "accessible" from Γ is strictly greater than n. In a similar way, by essentially transplanting De Caro's proof techniques into **TEL**, we obtain the following:

Lemma 7. *Let* $\Gamma_0 \in S^\Lambda$, $\phi \in \mathcal{L}_{\textbf{TEL}}$, $a \in A^\Lambda$, *and let* $p \in \mathbb{Q}_{[0,1]}$. *Then:*

$$\mathscr{D}_a^\Lambda(\Gamma_0, \{\Gamma \in S^\Lambda \mid \phi \in \Gamma\}) \geq p \iff \langle a \rangle_p^\geq \phi \in \Gamma_0$$

Before stating the Truth Lemma we show that the construction of $\mathfrak{M}_\Lambda$ yields a PLSTS. This fact follows by proving that the functions $\mathscr{D}_a^\Lambda(\Gamma, \_)$ are actually probabilistic distributions, and can be established by means of two fundamental properties of the maximally consistent sets:

1. For any $\Gamma \in S^\Lambda$ and $\phi \in \mathcal{L}_{\textbf{TEL}}$ there exists exactly one $p \in \mathbb{Q}_{[0,1]}$ such that $\langle a \rangle_p^= \phi \in \Gamma$;
2. Let $\Gamma_1, \ldots, \Gamma_h \in S^\Lambda$ ($h \geq 2$) be distinct mc-sets. Then there exist $\psi_1, \ldots, \psi_h \in \mathcal{L}_{\textbf{TEL}}$ such that $\psi_i \in \Gamma_j$ iff $i = j$ and $\vdash \bigwedge_{\substack{1 \leq i,j \leq h \\ \text{s.t. } i \neq j}} \neg(\psi_i \wedge \psi_j)$.

Point 1 crucially relies on the quantitative features of PLSTSs, as it requires the density property of $\mathbb{Q}$, while point 2 can be seen as a "separation result" for various modal logics (see [9]). In particular, if $\Gamma_0 \in S^\Lambda$ and $\phi \in \mathcal{L}_{\textbf{TEL}}$, point 1 implies $\langle a \rangle_p^\geq \phi, \langle a \rangle_{1-p}^\geq \neg\phi \in \Gamma_0$, for some $p \in \mathbb{Q}_{[0,1]}$. By applying Lemma 7, we can easily conclude that the mass of $\mathscr{D}_a^\Lambda(\Gamma_0, \_)$ is greater than (or equal to) 1. Now, suppose towards contradiction that $\mathscr{D}_a^\Lambda(\Gamma_0, \_)$ has mass > 1. W.l.o.g. $\mathscr{D}_a^\Lambda(\Gamma_0, \_)$ can be taken with finite support $\{\Gamma_1, \ldots, \Gamma_h\}$, where $h \geq 2$ by Lemma 7, so that there exist $\psi_1, \ldots, \psi_h$ as in point 2. By point 1 there exists p_i such that $\langle a \rangle_{p_i}^= \psi_i \in \Gamma_0$ ($1 \leq i \leq h$), and by the fact that $\psi_1, \ldots, \psi_h$ are mutually incompatible, using Proposition 4.4 we obtain $\langle a \rangle_{p_1 + \ldots + p_h}^= (\bigvee_{1 \leq i \leq h} \psi_i) \in \Gamma_0$ with $p_1 + \ldots + p_h \leq 1$. By definition we have $\mathscr{D}_a^\Lambda(\Gamma_0, \Gamma_i) \leq p_i$, which contradicts the assumptions.

Thanks to Lemma 7, we can easily establish the Truth Lemma by induction on formulas.

Lemma 8 (Truth Lemma). *For any* $\phi \in \mathcal{L}_{\textbf{TEL}}$ *and* $\Gamma \in S^\Lambda$:

$$\Gamma \models_{\mathfrak{M}_\Lambda} \phi \quad \text{iff} \quad \phi \in \Gamma$$

Given the Truth Lemma, the canonical model theorem follows using a standard argument.

Theorem 9 (Canonical model). *Let Λ be a TENML. Then, for any $\phi \in \mathcal{L}_{\textbf{TEL}}$:*

$$\phi \in \Lambda \qquad \textit{iff} \qquad \phi \textit{ is true in } \mathfrak{M}_\Lambda.$$

To show that a TENML Λ is complete with respect to a class of frames $\mathcal{C}$ it suffices to check that its canonical model $\mathfrak{M}_\Lambda$ is based on a frame in $\mathcal{C}$. This allows us to infer in a fairly simple way the following completeness results:

Corollary 10 (Completeness for various TENMLs). *For any $\phi \in \mathcal{L}_{\textbf{TEL}}$:*

$$\models_\mathcal{K} \phi \textit{ implies } \vdash_{\textsf{TEK}} \phi; \qquad \models_\mathcal{T} \phi \textit{ implies } \vdash_{\textsf{TET}} \phi;$$
$$\models_\mathcal{B} \phi \textit{ implies } \vdash_{\textsf{TEB}} \phi; \qquad \models_{\mathcal{K}4} \phi \textit{ implies } \vdash_{\textsf{TEK4}} \phi;$$
$$\models_{\mathcal{S}4} \phi \textit{ implies } \vdash_{\textsf{TES4}} \phi; \qquad \models_{\mathcal{S}5} \phi \textit{ implies } \vdash_{\textsf{TES5}} \phi.$$

Unfortunately, the compactness property does not hold for TENMLs. To see this, let $\alpha \in At$ and consider the following infinite set of formulas:

$$\Gamma_\alpha = \{\neg\langle a\rangle_p^= \alpha \mid p \in \mathbb{Q}_{[0,1]}\} \tag{6}$$

Clearly, any set $\Gamma_p \triangleq \Gamma_\alpha \setminus \{\neg\langle a\rangle_p^= \alpha\}$ is satisfiable (and so any finite subset of Γ_α is satisfiable) but Γ_α is not. Now, by a standard argument, a TENML Λ is strongly complete with respect to a class of frames $\mathcal{C}$ iff any Λ-consistent set of formulas Δ is satisfiable on some $\mathfrak{F} \in \mathcal{C}$. This means that the failure of strong completeness follows by showing that Γ_α is Λ-consistent.

Let us finally remark that the results of this section still hold when the set $\mathbb{Q}_{[0,1]}$ is extended with a (recursively enumerable) set $R \subseteq [0,1]$ in both the language $\mathcal{L}_{\textbf{TEL}}$ (see Definition 1) and its semantics (see Definition 2). In this case, following [12], we require two closure conditions for R:

- *quasi-closure under addition:* $\forall r, r' \in R.\, (r + r' \leq 1 \Rightarrow r + r' \in R)$;
- *closure under complements:* $\forall r \in [0,1].\, (r \in R \Rightarrow 1 - r \in R)$.

6   Conclusion and Future Works

In this paper we have shown that a natural way of building a formal framework for trust representation relies on probabilistic modal logics, where the modalities are simply inherited from the probabilistic variants of HML and CTL. With respect to these frameworks, we adopt a completely different interpretation of the underlying semantic model, which allows us to model networks of agents, contexts of evaluation, beliefs of agents about the statements, and personal judgments about the expertise of agents. All together, these ingredients form the base for context-aware evidence-based trust estimations. For future work, it is worth investigating properties of trust that emerged in alternative formal frameworks, such as [3,23,24]. An example is to relax the additivity constraint on $\mathscr{D}_a$, moving to a sub-additive version, which would allow to model scenarios in which uncertainty plays an important role.

As far as the theoretical foundations of **TEL** are concerned, we have extended soundness and completeness results of graded modal logics to our setting. A possible future work in this direction could be to investigate decidability of TEK, and to find a suitable sequent-calculus based presentation for it. Moreover, we could explore techniques to recover compactness and strong completeness. A first idea is to introduce finiteness constraints in the axiomatic systems able to limit the use of probabilistic graded modalities, as in [12]. A more intriguing approach comes from the coalgebraic treatment of modal logic, where coherence conditions between syntax and semantics can be introduced to guarantee these missing meta-properties [28]. A final expansion we could explore is the possibility of moving from a classical Boolean setting to a Many-Valued Logic, in order to explicitly model the uncertainty of an agent about the truth of a proposition.

Acknowledgements. This work was supported by a UKRI Future Leaders Fellowship, 'Structure vs Invariants in Proofs', project reference MR/S035540/1, and by the Italian Ministry of Education, University and Research through the PRIN 2017 project "The Manifest Image and the Scientific Image" prot. 2017ZNWW7F_004.

References

1. Aldini, A: A formal framework for modeling trust and reputation in collective adaptive systems. In: Electronic Proceedings in Theoretical Computer Science, EPTCS, vol. 217, pp. 19–30 (2016)

2. Aldini, A.: Design and verification of trusted collective adaptive systems. Trans. Model. Comput. Simul. (TOMACS) **28**(2), 1–27 (2018)

3. Aldini, A., Tagliaferri, M.: Logics to reason formally about trust computation and manipulation. In: Saracino, A., Mori, P. (eds.) ETAA 2019. LNCS, vol. 11967, pp. 1–15. Springer, Cham (2020). https://doi.org/10.1007/978-3-030-39749-4_1

4. Baier, A.: Trust and antitrust. Ethics **96**(2), 231–260 (1986)

5. Baier, C., de Alfaro, L., Forejt, V., Kwiatkowska, M.: Model checking probabilistic systems. In: Handbook of Model Checking, pp. 963–999. Springer, Cham (2018). https://doi.org/10.1007/978-3-319-10575-8_28

6. Baier, C., Katoen, J.-P., Hermanns, H., Wolf, V.: Comparative branching-time semantics for Markov chains. Inf. Comput. **200**(2), 149–214 (2005)

7. Becker, M.Y., Russo, A., Sultana, N.: Foundations of logic-based trust management. In: 2012 IEEE Symposium on Security and Privacy, pp. 161–175 (2012)

8. Bernardo, M., Miculan, M.: Disjunctive probabilistic modal logic is enough for bisimilarity on reactive probabilistic systems. In: Bilò, V., Caruso, A. (eds.) 17th Italian Conference on Theoretical Computer Science, vol. 1720 of CEUR Workshop Proceedings, pp. 203–220. CEUR-WS.org (2016)

9. De Caro, F.: Graded modalities, II (canonical models). Studia Logica **47**(1), 1–10 (1988)

10. Desharnais, J., Edalat, A., Panangaden, P.: Bisimulation for labelled Markov processes. Inf. Comput. **179**(2), 163–193 (2002)

11. Evans, D.: The Internet of Things: how the next evolution of the Internet is changing everything. CISCO white paper (2011)
12. Fattorosi-Barnaba, M., Amati, G.: Modal operators with probabilistic interpretations. I. Studia Logica **46**(4), 383–393 (1987)
13. Fine, K.: In so many possible worlds. Notre Dame J. Formal Logic **13**(4), 516–520 (1972)
14. Gambetta, D.: Trust: Making and Breaking Cooperative Relations. Blackwell, Hoboken (1988)
15. Globe, L.S.: Grades of modality. Logique et Analyse **13**(51), 323–334 (1970)
16. Hansson, H., Jonsson, B.: A logic for reasoning about time and reliability. Formal Aspects Comput. **6**(5), 512–535 (1994)
17. Hennessy, M., Milner, R.: On observing nondeterminism and concurrency. In: de Bakker, J., van Leeuwen, J. (eds.) ICALP 1980. LNCS, vol. 85, pp. 299–309. Springer, Heidelberg (1980). https://doi.org/10.1007/3-540-10003-2_79
18. Jøsang, A.: Trust and reputation systems. In: Aldini, A., Gorrieri, R. (eds.) FOSAD 2006-2007. LNCS, vol. 4677, pp. 209–245. Springer, Heidelberg (2007). https://doi.org/10.1007/978-3-540-74810-6_8
19. Jøsang, A., Ismail, R.: The beta reputation system. In: Proceedings of the 15th Bled Electronic Commerce Conference, pp. 1–14 (2002)
20. Keymolen, E.: Trust on the Line: A Philosophical Exploration of Trust in the Networked Era. Wolf Publishers, Nijmegen (2016)
21. Kwiatkowska, M., Norman, G., Parker, D.: PRISM 4.0: verification of probabilistic real-time systems. In: Gopalakrishnan, G., Qadeer, S. (eds.) CAV 2011. LNCS, vol. 6806, pp. 585–591. Springer, Heidelberg (2011). https://doi.org/10.1007/978-3-642-22110-1_47
22. Larsen, K.G., Skou, A.: Bisimulation through probabilistic testing. In: 16th Annual ACM Symposium on Principles of Programming Languages, pp. 344–352. ACM Press (1989)
23. Leturc, C., Bonnet, G.: A normal modal logic for trust in the sincerity. In: International Foundation for Autonomous Agents and Multiagent Systems, AAMAS'18, pp. 175–183 (2018)
24. Liu, F., Lorini, E.: Reasoning about belief, evidence and trust in a multi-agent setting. In: An, B., Bazzan, A., Leite, J., Villata, S., van der Torre, L. (eds.) PRIMA 2017. LNCS (LNAI), vol. 10621, pp. 71–89. Springer, Cham (2017). https://doi.org/10.1007/978-3-319-69131-2_5
25. Luhmann, N.: Trust and Power. John Wiley and Sons Inc., Hoboken (1979)
26. Pacuit, E., Salame, S.: Majority logic. In: Dubois, D., Welty, C.A., Williams, M.-A. (eds.) Principles of Knowledge Representation and Reasoning: 9th International Conference (KR2004), pp. 598–605. AAAI Press (2004)
27. Putnam, R.: Making Democracy Work. Princeton University Press, Princeton (1993)
28. Schröder, L., Pattinson, D.: Strong completeness of coalgebraic modal logics. In: Albers, S., Marion, J.-Y. (eds.) 26th International Symposium on Theoretical Aspects of Computer Science (STACS 2009), pp. 673–684. Leibniz International Proceedings in Informatics (2009)
29. Singh, M.P.: Trust as dependence: a logical approach. In: 10th International Conference on Autonomous Agents and Multiagent Systems, AAMAS '11, vol. 2, pp. 863–870 (2011)
30. Sonya, G.K., Schratt-Bitter, S.: Trust in online social networks: a multifaceted perspective. Forum Social Econ. **44**(1), 48–68 (2013)

31. Tagliaferri, M., Aldini, A.: From knowledge to trust: a logical framework for pre-trust computations. In: Gal-Oz, N., Lewis, P.R. (eds.) IFIPTM 2018. IAICT, vol. 528, pp. 107–123. Springer, Cham (2018). https://doi.org/10.1007/978-3-319-95276-5_8

32. van der Hoek, W.: Some considerations on the logic PfD. In: Voronkov, A. (ed.) First Russian Conference on Logic Programming, vol. 592 of LNCS, pp. 474–485. Springer, Heidelberg (1991)

33. Williamson, O.: Calculativeness, trust, and economic organization. J. Law Econ. **36**(2), 453–486 (1993)

Generalized Rules of Probabilistic Independence

Janneke H. Bolt[1,2(✉)] and Linda C. van der Gaag[2]

[1] Department of Information and Computing Sciences, Utrecht University,
Utrecht, Netherlands
j.h.bolt@uu.nl
[2] Department of Mathematics and Computer Science,
Eindhoven University of Technology, Eindhoven, Netherlands
{j.h.bolt,l.c.v.d.gaag}@tue.nl

Abstract. Probabilistic independence, as a fundamental concept of probability, enables probabilistic inference to become computationally feasible for increasing numbers of variables. By adding five more rules to an existing sound, yet incomplete, system of rules of independence, Studený completed it for the class of structural semi-graphoid independence relations over four variables. In this paper, we generalize Studený's rules to larger numbers of variables. We thereby contribute enhanced insights in the structural properties of probabilistic independence. In addition, we are further closing in on the class of probabilistic independence relations, as the class of relations closed under the generalized rules is a proper subclass of the class closed under the previously existing rules.

Keywords: Probabilistic independence · Rules of independence · Semi-graphoid independence relations · Structural semi-graphoid relations

1 Introduction

Probabilistic independence is a subject of intensive studies from both a mathematics and a computing-science perspective [1,2,10]. Pearl and his co-workers were among the first to formalize properties of independence in a system of qualitative rules [2], which characterizes the class of so-called semi-graphoid independence relations. Although the semi-graphoid rules of independence are probabilistically sound, they are not complete for probabilistic independence, as was shown by Studený [4]. While the independences of any discrete multivariate probability distribution adhere to the semi-graphoid rules, a set of independence statements that is closed under these rules, may lack statements that are probabilistically implied. As a consequence, the semi-graphoid rules allow independence relations for which there are no matching probability distributions.

For proving incompleteness of Pearl's system of rules, Studený formulated a new rule for probabilistically implied independence using a proof construct based

© Springer Nature Switzerland AG 2021
J. Vejnarová and N. Wilson (Eds.): ECSQARU 2021, LNAI 12897, pp. 590–602, 2021.
https://doi.org/10.1007/978-3-030-86772-0_42

on the concept of multiinformation. He further defined the class of structural semi-graphoid independence relations as the class of independence relations that are closed under all rules that can be found through such a construct [6–9], and presented a set of five rules that completes the existing rule system for structural relations involving four variables. For an unlimited number of variables, no finite rule system can fully characterize the class of structural semi-graphoid relations, which implies that there is also no finite complete set of rules for the class of probabilistic independence relations [5].

In this paper we generalize Studený's rules of independence to larger numbers of variables. By doing so, we uncover combinatorial structures in rules of probabilistic independence and enable further investigation of such structures. We moreover arrive at an enhanced description of the class of structural semi-graphoid independence relations and thereby close in on the class of probabilistic independence relations, as the class of relations closed under the generalized rules is a proper subclass of the class closed under the previously existing rule system.

2   Preliminaries

We review sets of independence rules and the classes of relations they govern.

2.1   Semi-graphoid Independence Relations

We consider a finite, non-empty set V of discrete random variables and use (possibly indexed) capital letters $A, B, C, \ldots$ to denote subsets of V. We will use concatenation to denote set union and will further abbreviate the union of sets in our figures by concatenating their indices, that is, we write $A_{123}B_{12}$ for $A_1 A_2 A_3 B_1 B_2$. A *triplet* over V now is a statement of the form $\langle A, B \mid C \rangle$, where $A, B, C \subseteq V$ are pairwise disjoint sets with $A, B \neq \varnothing$. A triplet $\langle A, B \mid C \rangle$ is taken to state that the sets of variables A and B are independent given the conditioning set C. Any set of triplets over V is called an *independence relation*.

Pearl introduced the class of so-called semi-graphoid independence relations by formulating four rules of independence [2], which are summarized by [3]:

$A1:$ $\langle A, B \mid C \rangle \;\leftrightarrow\; \langle B, A \mid C \rangle$
$A2:$ $\langle A, BC \mid D \rangle \;\leftrightarrow\; \langle A, B \mid CD \rangle \wedge \langle A, C \mid D \rangle$

These two rules are schemata in which the arguments A, B, C, D are to be instantiated to mutually disjoint subsets of V upon application. The rules $A1, A2$ are called the semi-graphoid rules of independence, and any independence relation that is closed under these rules is coined a *semi-graphoid independence relation*; in the sequel, we will use $\mathcal{A} = \{A1, A2\}$ to denote the system of semi-graphoid rules. The set $\mathcal{A}$ constitutes a *sound* inferential system for independence relative to the class of discrete multivariate probability distributions. The two rules in $\mathcal{A}$ do not constitute a *complete* system for independence in such probability distributions, however. The system's incompleteness was shown by Studený [4], who formulated the following additional rule:

$$A3: \langle A, B \mid CD \rangle \wedge \langle A, B \mid \varnothing \rangle \wedge \langle C, D \mid A \rangle \wedge \langle C, D \mid B \rangle \leftrightarrow$$
$$\langle A, B \mid C \rangle \wedge \langle A, B \mid D \rangle \wedge \langle C, D \mid AB \rangle \wedge \langle C, D \mid \varnothing \rangle$$

For constructing $A3$ and other new rules of independence, he built on the notion of multiinformation, which we will review in the next section.

2.2   Multiinformation and Rules of Independence

A well-known measure for the amount of information shared by two (sets of) variables A, B given a third (set of) variables C in the context of a discrete multivariate probability distribution Pr, is the conditional mutual information (see for example [12]), which is defined as:

$$I(A; B \mid C \parallel \text{Pr}) = \sum_{abc} \text{Pr}(abc) \cdot \log \frac{\text{Pr}(ab \mid c)}{\text{Pr}(a \mid c) \cdot \text{Pr}(b \mid c)}$$

where abc ranges over all possible value combinations for the variables in ABC with $\text{Pr}(a \mid c), \text{Pr}(b \mid c) \neq 0$. We have that $I(A; B \mid C \parallel \text{Pr}) \geq 0$ for any A, B, C and Pr, and note that the mutual-information measure is related to independence through the following property: $I(A; B \mid C \parallel \text{Pr}) = 0$ iff the triplet $\langle A, B \mid C \rangle$ is a valid independence statement in Pr. In the sequel, we omit Pr from the notation as long as no ambiguity arises and take the sets A, B, C to be mutually disjoint.

For studying rules of independence, Studený exploited the notion of *multiinformation* [4, 11], which is a function $M: 2^V \rightarrow [0, \infty)$ over all subsets of variables V with $I(A; B \mid C) = M(ABC) + M(C) - M(AC) - M(BC)$; for details, we refer to [11]. The multiinformation function thereby has the following properties:

- $M(ABC) + M(C) - M(AC) - M(BC) \geq 0$;

- $M(ABC) + M(C) - M(AC) - M(BC) = 0$ iff $\langle A, B \mid C \rangle$.

The relation between the conditional mutual-information measure and the notion of multiinformation now enables elegant soundness proofs for rules of independence: a rule is sound if all its multiinformation terms 'cancel out', that is, if the multiinformation terms of its set of premise triplets equal the multiinformation terms of its set of consequent triplets. In the sequel, we will refer to this type of proof as a *multiinformation proof construct*.

2.3   Structural Semi-graphoid Independence Relations

Building on the multiinformation concept, Studený introduced the class of *structural semi-graphoid independence relations* [6–9] where, roughly stated, a structural semi-graphoid relation is an independence relation that is closed under all possible rules whose soundness derives from a multiinformation proof construct. In addition to rule $A3$ stated above, Studený formulated four more rules for probabilistic independence found through such proof constructs [6]. We state these rules here in their original form, with their original numbering:

$A4$: $\langle A, B \mid CD \rangle \wedge \langle A, D \mid B \rangle \wedge \langle C, D \mid A \rangle \wedge \langle B, C \mid \varnothing \rangle \leftrightarrow$
$\qquad \langle A, B \mid D \rangle \wedge \langle A, D \mid BC \rangle \wedge \langle C, D \mid \varnothing \rangle \wedge \langle B, C \mid A \rangle$

$A5$: $\langle A, C \mid D \rangle \wedge \langle B, D \mid C \rangle \wedge \langle B, C \mid A \rangle \wedge \langle A, D \mid B \rangle \leftrightarrow$
$\qquad \langle A, C \mid B \rangle \wedge \langle B, D \mid A \rangle \wedge \langle B, C \mid D \rangle \wedge \langle A, D \mid C \rangle$

$A6$: $\langle A, B \mid C \rangle \wedge \langle A, C \mid D \rangle \wedge \langle A, D \mid B \rangle \leftrightarrow$
$\qquad \langle A, B \mid D \rangle \wedge \langle A, C \mid B \rangle \wedge \langle A, D \mid C \rangle$

$A7$: $\langle A, B \mid CD \rangle \wedge \langle C, D \mid AB \rangle \wedge \langle A, C \mid \varnothing \rangle \wedge \langle B, D \mid \varnothing \rangle \leftrightarrow$
$\qquad \langle A, B \mid \varnothing \rangle \wedge \langle C, D \mid \varnothing \rangle \wedge \langle A, C \mid BD \rangle \wedge \langle B, D \mid AC \rangle$

In the sequel, we will use S to denote the rule system $\{A1, \ldots, A7\}$. We note that, while all triplets in the rules $A1$, $A2$ respectively, share a fixed same conditioning (sub-)set of variables, the rules $A3, \ldots, A7$ do not. To equally accommodate additional conditioning variables, the latter five rules can each be enhanced by adding an extra set of variables X to the conditioning parts of its triplets. In phrasing the generalizations of these rules, we will omit such additional sets to conform to the literature.

Any structural semi-graphoid independence relation is closed under the rule system S by definition. As any semi-graphoid relation is closed under the system of rules $\mathcal{A}$, and $\mathcal{A}$ does not imply the additional rules in S, we have that the class of structural semi-graphoid independence relations is a proper subclass of the class of semi-graphoid relations. The system S was shown to fully characterize the class of structural semi-graphoid relations over at most four variables [6], that is, the system is both sound and complete for this class. Although sound, the system is not complete for the class of structural independence relations over more than four variables. Studený proved in fact that there is no finite axiomatization of probabilistic independence [5,11], by providing the following rule for all $n \geq 2$ (reformulated):

$$\langle A, B_0 \mid B_1 \rangle \wedge \ldots \wedge \langle A, B_{n-1} \mid B_n \rangle \wedge \langle A, B_n \mid B_0 \rangle \leftrightarrow \qquad (1)$$
$$\langle A, B_0 \mid B_n \rangle \wedge \langle A, B_1 \mid B_0 \rangle \wedge \ldots \wedge \langle A, B_n \mid B_{n-1} \rangle$$

We note that this rule is a generalization of rule $A6$ in the system S. From the structure of this rule, it is readily seen that any complete system of rules for a fixed number of k variables, will not be complete for $k + 1$ variables. The hierarchy of independence relations is depicted in Fig. 1(a).

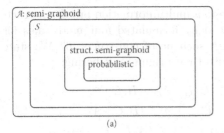
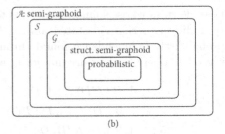

Fig. 1. The existing hierarchy of semi-graphoid, structural semi-graphoid, and probabilistic independence relations (a) and the hierarchy extended with our results (b).

3   Generalizing Inference Rules

For the class of structural semi-graphoid relations, the new rules $A3$–$A7$ of independence have been formulated, involving four sets of variables each (disregarding any fixed additional conditioning context in all triplets). We now reconsider these rules and generalize them to larger numbers of variable sets. By doing so, we arrive at an enhanced characterization of the class of structural semi-graphoid relations and at further insights in the combinatorial structures of independence rules. Because of space restrictions, we cannot detail full soundness proofs for the new rules; instead, we provide brief proof sketches in the appendix.

We begin with formulating our generalization of rule $A5$. The idea underlying its generalization is analogous to the idea of rule $A6$. Informally stated, the rule takes a sequence of sets of variables and moves it (up to symmetry) over the three argument positions of the triplets involved.

Proposition 1. *Let* $A_0, \ldots, A_n, n \geq 2$, *be non-empty, mutually disjoint sets of variables. Then,*

$$\bigwedge_{i \in \{0,\ldots,n\}} \langle A_i, A_{\mu(i+1)} \mid A_{\mu(i+2)} \rangle \quad \leftrightarrow \quad \bigwedge_{i \in \{0,\ldots,n\}} \langle A_i, A_{\mu(i+1)} \mid A_{\mu(i-1)} \rangle$$

with $\mu(x) := x \bmod (n+1)$.

The property stated in the proposition is taken as the independence rule $G5$. Note that in the case of $n = 2$, the rule reduces to a tautology. $G5$ further embeds rule $A5$ as a special case with $n = 3$, as is seen by setting $A_0 \leftarrow C$, $A_1 \leftarrow A$, $A_2 \leftarrow D$ and $A_3 \leftarrow B$. As an example of the generalization, rule $G5$ is now detailed for $n = 4$:

$$\langle A_0, A_1 \mid A_2 \rangle \wedge \langle A_1, A_2 \mid A_3 \rangle \wedge \langle A_2, A_3 \mid A_4 \rangle \wedge \langle A_3, A_4 \mid A_0 \rangle \wedge \langle A_4, A_0 \mid A_1 \rangle \quad \leftrightarrow$$
$$\langle A_0, A_1 \mid A_4 \rangle \wedge \langle A_1, A_2 \mid A_0 \rangle \wedge \langle A_2, A_3 \mid A_1 \rangle \wedge \langle A_3, A_4 \mid A_2 \rangle \wedge \langle A_4, A_0 \mid A_3 \rangle$$

Note that the rule's consequent cannot be derived from its premise using the existing rule system $\mathcal{S}$ considered thus far. For $n + 1$ sets of variables, rule $G5$

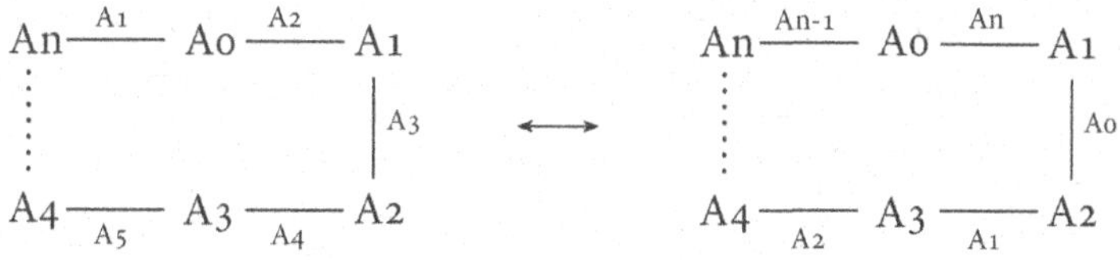

$$An \overset{A_1}{\rule{2em}{0.4pt}} Ao \overset{A_2}{\rule{2em}{0.4pt}} A_1$$

(Fig. 2 diagram)

An ——A_1—— Ao ——A_2—— A1
⋮   │A_3
A4 ——A_5—— A3 ——A_4—— A2

⟷

An ——A_{n-1}—— Ao ——A_n—— A1
⋮   │A_o
A4 ——A_2—— A3 ——A_1—— A2

Fig. 2. The combinatorial structure of rule $G5$, for $n \geq 2$.

includes $n + 1$ premise triplets and $n + 1$ consequent triplets. When proceeding from $n+1$ to $n+2$ sets of variables therefore, both the number of premise triplets and the number of consequent triplets increase by one. Throughout this section, the combinatorial structures of the generalized rules are illustrated by schematic visualizations. The structure of rule $G5$ is shown in Fig. 2. Each labeled line $X \overset{Z}{\rule{1.5em}{0.4pt}} Y$ in the figure depicts a triplet $\langle X, Y \mid Z \rangle$, with the line's label corresponding with the triplet's conditioning set. The left-hand side of the figure summarizes the joint premise of the rule and the right-hand side its joint consequent. The figure is readily seen to reflect the rule's sliding structure.

Before addressing our generalization of rule $A6$ from $\mathcal{S}$, we recall that Studený already generalized this rule from pertaining to four sets of variables, to an arbitrary number of variable sets; we recall this rule as Eq. (1) from Sect. 2.3. Where Eq. (1) included just a single variable set B_i in a triplet's conditioning part, our generalization has conditioning parts including multiple such sets per triplet. More specifically, the rule takes a sequence of variable sets $B_0, \ldots, B_n$, just like rule $G5$ above, and moves it sliding over a triplet, yet now over just its second and third argument positions, with the first argument fixed to an unrelated set A. The number of sets that are included in the conditioning parts of the rule's triplets, is governed by a parameter k.

Proposition 2. *Let $A, B_0, \ldots, B_n$, $n \geq 0$, be non-empty, mutually disjoint sets of variables. Then, for all $k \in [0, n]$,*

$$\bigwedge_{i \in \{0, \ldots, n\}} \langle A, B_i \mid \mathbf{B}_{i+}^k \rangle \quad \leftrightarrow \quad \bigwedge_{i \in \{0, \ldots, n\}} \langle A, B_i \mid \mathbf{B}_{i-}^k \rangle$$

where $\mathbf{B}_{i+}^k = B_{\mu(i+1)} \cdots B_{\mu(i+k)}$, $\mathbf{B}_{i-}^k = B_{\mu(i-k)} \cdots B_{\mu(i-1)}$, taking $\mathbf{B}_{i+}^k, \mathbf{B}_{i-}^k :=$ $\varnothing$ for $k = 0$, and where $\mu(x) := x \bmod (n+1)$ as before.

The property stated in the proposition is taken as the independence rule $G6$. Note that for $k = 0$, $k = n$, $n = 0$ and $n = 1$ the rule reduces to a tautology. $G6$ further embeds rule $A6$ as a special case with $n = 2$, $k = 1$, as is seen by setting $B_0 \leftarrow B$, $B_1 \leftarrow C$ and $B_2 \leftarrow D$. Equation (1) is embedded as the cases with $k = 1$ and any $n \geq 2$. As an example of the generalization, rule $G6$ is detailed for $n = 3$ and $k = 2$ below:

$$\langle A, B_0 \mid B_1 B_2 \rangle \wedge \langle A, B_1 \mid B_2 B_3 \rangle \wedge \langle A, B_2 \mid B_3 B_0 \rangle \wedge \langle A, B_3 \mid B_0 B_1 \rangle \leftrightarrow$$
$$\langle A, B_0 \mid B_2 B_3 \rangle \wedge \langle A, B_1 \mid B_3 B_0 \rangle \wedge \langle A, B_2 \mid B_0 B_1 \rangle \wedge \langle A, B_3 \mid B_1 B_2 \rangle$$

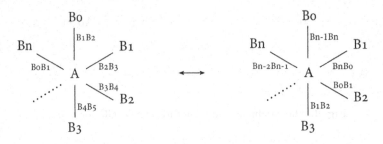

Fig. 3. The combinatorial structure of rule $G6$, for $n \geq 2$ and $k = 2$.

We observe that the rule's joint consequent cannot be derived from its joint premise using the original rules from the system $\mathcal{S}$. For $n + 2$ sets of variables, rule $G6$ includes $n + 1$ premise triplets and $n + 1$ consequent triplets. When proceeding from $n+2$ to $n+3$ variable sets therefore, both the number of premise triplets and the number of consequent triplets increase by one; the parameter k does not affect the numbers of triplets involved. The combinatorial structure of rule $G6$ is shown in Fig. 3. The figure highlights the rule's star-shaped structure that originates from the fixed set A as the first argument of all triplets involved.

The idea underlying our generalization of rule $A4$ from $\mathcal{S}$, is somewhat less intuitive. Informally phrased, the generalized rule takes two fixed sets of variables A, B, and associates these sets with an ordered sequence $\mathbf{C}$ of sets C_i. Each C_i occurs as the second argument in two triplets, one with A for its first argument and one with B for its first argument. The two subsequences that remain after removing C_i from $\mathbf{C}$ are each positioned in the conditioning part of one of these triplets. In the case of an odd index i, moreover, the triplet involving A has the conditioning part extended with the set B, and vice versa. In the case of an even index, the conditioning parts of the triplets are not extended.

Proposition 3. *Let* $A, B, C_1, \ldots, C_n$, *with* $n \geq 2$ *even, be non-empty, mutually disjoint sets of variables. Then,*

$$\bigwedge_{i \in \{1,3,\ldots,n-1\}} [\langle A, C_i \mid \mathbf{C_{i-}} B \rangle \wedge \langle B, C_i \mid \mathbf{C_{i+}} A \rangle] \wedge$$
$$\bigwedge_{i \in \{2,4,\ldots,n\}} [\langle A, C_i \mid \mathbf{C_{i-}} \rangle \wedge \langle B, C_i \mid \mathbf{C_{i+}} \rangle] \leftrightarrow$$

$$\bigwedge_{i \in \{1,3,\ldots,n-1\}} [\langle A, C_i \mid \mathbf{C_{i+}} B \rangle \wedge \langle B, C_i \mid \mathbf{C_{i-}} A \rangle] \wedge$$
$$\bigwedge_{i \in \{2,4,\ldots,n\}} [\langle A, C_i \mid \mathbf{C_{i+}} \rangle \wedge \langle B, C_i \mid \mathbf{C_{i-}} \rangle]$$

where $\mathbf{C_{i-}} = C_1 \cdots C_{i-1}$ *and* $\mathbf{C_{i+}} = C_{i+1} \cdots C_n$, *taking* $C_j \cdots C_{j-1} := \varnothing$.

The property stated in the proposition is taken as the independence rule $G4$. Note that $G4$ embeds rule $A4$ as a special case with $n = 2$, as is seen by setting

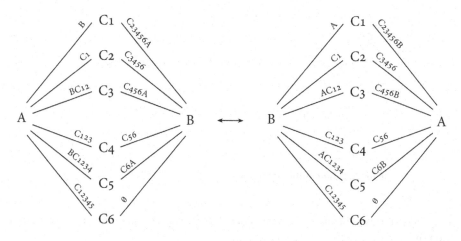

Fig. 4. The combinatorial structure of rule $G4$, for $n = 6$.

$A \leftarrow D$, $B \leftarrow B$, $C_1 \leftarrow A$ and $C_2 \leftarrow C$, where each set from $G4$ is assigned a set from rule $A4$. As an example of the generalization, rule $G4$ is now detailed for $n = 4$:

$$\langle A, C_1 \mid B \rangle \wedge \langle A, C_3 \mid C_1 C_2 B \rangle \wedge \langle B, C_1 \mid C_2 C_3 C_4 A \rangle \wedge \langle B, C_3 \mid C_4 A \rangle \wedge$$
$$\langle A, C_2 \mid C_1 \rangle \wedge \langle A, C_4 \mid C_1 C_2 C_3 \rangle \wedge \langle B, C_2 \mid C_3 C_4 \rangle \wedge \langle B, C_4 \mid \varnothing \rangle \leftrightarrow$$
$$\langle A, C_1 \mid C_2 C_3 C_4 B \rangle \wedge \langle A, C_3 \mid C_4 B \rangle \wedge \langle B, C_1 \mid A \rangle \wedge \langle B, C_3 \mid C_1 C_2 A \rangle \wedge$$
$$\langle A, C_2 \mid C_3 C_4 \rangle \wedge \langle A, C_4 \mid \varnothing \rangle \wedge \langle B, C_2 \mid C_1 \rangle \wedge \langle B, C_4 \mid C_1 C_2 C_3 \rangle$$

Note that the rule's consequent is not derivable from its premise using the original rules in $\mathcal{S}$. For $n + 2$ sets of variables, rule $G4$ includes $2 \cdot n$ premise triplets and the same number of consequent triplets. When proceeding from $n + 2$ to $(n + 2) + 2$ variable sets therefore, both the number of premise triplets and the number of consequent triplets increase by four. The rule's combinatorial structure is shown in Fig. 4, for $n = 6$. The rule has a bipartitely linked structure, originating from the fixed sets A and B in the first argument positions per triplet linking to the exact same sets from the sequence $\mathbf{C}$. We further note that the lines from A and from B to the same set C_i swap labels (replacing A by B and vice versa) between the premise and consequent parts of the rule.

As the above generalization, our generalization of rule $A3$ takes two fixed sets of variables A, B. Instead of being associated with a single sequence of sets, A and B are now associated with two separate sequences $\mathbf{C}$ and $\mathbf{D}$, respectively. Each set C_i occurs as the second argument in two triplets, both with A as the first argument. The two remaining subsequences of $\mathbf{C}$ after removing C_i, are each positioned in the conditioning part of one of these triplets, supplemented with a subsequence of $\mathbf{D}$. A similar pattern is seen with the set B and its associated sequence $\mathbf{D}$. The triplet pairs with A and those with B as their first arguments,

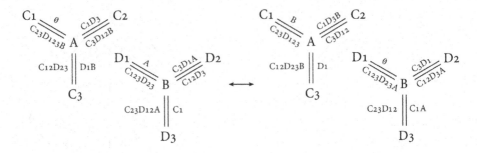

Fig. 5. The combinatorial structure of rule $G3$, for $n = 3$.

are again related through the inclusion of B in the conditioning part of one of the triplet pairs with A, and vice versa.

Proposition 4. *Let* A, B, C_i, D_i, $i = 1, \ldots, n$, $n \geq 1$, *be non-empty, mutually disjoint sets of variables, and let* $\mathbf{C} = C_1 \cdots C_n$ *and* $\mathbf{D} = D_1 \cdots D_n$. *Then,*

$$\bigwedge_{i \in \{1,\ldots,n\}} [\, \langle A, C_i \mid \mathbf{C_{i-}}\, \mathbf{D_{i++}} \rangle \wedge \langle A, C_i \mid \mathbf{C_{i+}}\, \mathbf{D_{i--}}\, B \rangle \wedge$$
$$\langle B, D_i \mid \mathbf{C_{i++}}\, \mathbf{D_{i-}}\, A \rangle \wedge \langle B, D_i \mid \mathbf{C_{i--}}\, \mathbf{D_{i+}} \rangle \,] \quad \leftrightarrow$$

$$\bigwedge_{i \in \{1,\ldots,n\}} [\, \langle A, C_i \mid \mathbf{C_{i-}}\, \mathbf{D_{i++}}\, B \rangle \wedge \langle A, C_i \mid \mathbf{C_{i+}}\, \mathbf{D_{i--}} \rangle \wedge$$
$$\langle B, D_i \mid \mathbf{C_{i++}}\, \mathbf{D_{i-}} \rangle \wedge \langle B, D_i \mid \mathbf{C_{i--}}\, \mathbf{D_{i+}}\, A \rangle \,]$$

where $\mathbf{Z_{i-}} = Z_1 \cdots Z_{i-1}$, $\mathbf{Z_{i+}} = Z_{i+1} \cdots Z_n$, $\mathbf{Z_{i--}} = Z_1 \cdots Z_{n-i+1}$ *and* $\mathbf{Z_{i++}} = Z_{n-i+2} \cdots Z_n$, *taking* $Z_j \cdots Z_{j-1} := \varnothing$, *for* $\mathbf{Z} = \mathbf{C}, \mathbf{D}$.

The property stated in the proposition is taken as the independence rule $G3$. Note that $G3$ embeds rule $A3$ as a special case with $n = 1$, as is seen by setting $A \leftarrow A$, $B \leftarrow C$, $C_1 \leftarrow B$ and $D_1 \leftarrow D$, where each set from $G3$ is assigned a set from rule $A3$. As an example of the generalization, rule $G3$ is now detailed for $n = 2$:

$$\langle A, C_1 \mid \varnothing \rangle \wedge \langle A, C_1 \mid C_2 D_1 D_2 B \rangle \wedge \langle B, D_1 \mid A \rangle \wedge \langle B, D_1 \mid C_1 C_2 D_2 \rangle \wedge$$
$$\langle A, C_2 \mid C_1 D_2 \rangle \wedge \langle A, C_2 \mid D_1 B \rangle \wedge \langle B, D_2 \mid C_2 D_1 A \rangle \wedge \langle B, D_2 \mid C_1 \rangle \quad \leftrightarrow$$
$$\langle A, C_1 \mid B \rangle \wedge \langle A, C_1 \mid C_2 D_1 D_2 \rangle \wedge \langle B, D_1 \mid \varnothing \rangle \wedge \langle B, D_1 \mid C_1 C_2 D_2 A \rangle \wedge$$
$$\langle A, C_2 \mid C_1 D_2 B \rangle \wedge \langle A, C_2 \mid D_1 \rangle \wedge \langle B, D_2 \mid C_2 D_1 \rangle \wedge \langle B, D_2 \mid C_1 A \rangle$$

We note that it is not possible to derive the rule's consequent from its premise by means of the rule system $\mathcal{S}$. For $2 \cdot n + 2$ sets of variables, rule $G3$ includes $4 \cdot n$ premise triplets and the same number of consequent triplets. When proceeding from $2 \cdot n + 2$ to $2 \cdot (n+1) + 2$ variable sets therefore, both the number of premise triplets and the number of consequent triplets increase by four. The combinatorial structure of the rule is illustrated in Fig. 5, for $n = 3$. This structure consists

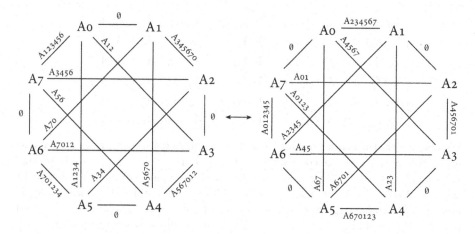

Fig. 6. The combinatorial structure of rule $G7$, for $n = 7$.

of double-edged stars with the cardinalities of the conditioning sets of the paired triplets adding up to $2 \cdot n$.

To conclude this section, we present our generalization of rule $A7$ from $\mathcal{S}$. The generalized rule involves a fixed sequence with an even number of sets of variables A_i. Each set with an even index i is paired with each set with an odd index i in the first two argument positions of a triplet. The conditioning part of such a triplet includes either the intervening variables sets of the sequence or all remaining variable sets.

Proposition 5. *Let* $A_0, \ldots, A_n$, *with* $n \geq 1$ *an odd number, be non-empty, mutually disjoint sets of variables. Then,*

$$\bigwedge_{\substack{i \in \{0, 2, \ldots, n-1\}, \\ k \in \{1, 3, \ldots, n\}}} \langle A_i, A_{\mu(i+k)} \mid \mathbf{A}_{i+} \rangle \quad \leftrightarrow \quad \bigwedge_{\substack{i \in \{0, 2, \ldots, n-1\}, \\ k \in \{1, 3, \ldots, n\}}} \langle A_i, A_{\mu(i-k)} \mid \mathbf{A}_{i-} \rangle$$

where $\mathbf{A}_{i+} = A_{\mu(i+1)} \cdots A_{\mu(i+k-1)}$ *and* $\mathbf{A}_{i-} = A_{\mu(i-k+1)} \cdots A_{\mu(i-1)}$, *taking* $\mathbf{A}_{i+}, \mathbf{A}_{i-} := \varnothing$ *for* $k = 1$, *and where* $\mu(x) := x \bmod (n+1)$, *as before.*

The property stated in the proposition is taken as the independence rule $G7$. Note that for $n = 1$ the rule reduces to a tautology. $G7$ further embeds rule $A7$ as a special case with $n = 3$, as is seen by setting $A_0 \leftarrow A$, $A_1 \leftarrow C$, $A_2 \leftarrow D$ and $A_3 \leftarrow B$. As an example of the generalization, rule $G7$ is now detailed for $n = 5$:

$$\langle A_0, A_1 \mid \varnothing \rangle \ \wedge \ \langle A_0, A_3 \mid A_1 A_2 \rangle \ \wedge \ \langle A_0, A_5 \mid A_1 A_2 A_3 A_4 \rangle \ \wedge$$
$$\langle A_2, A_3 \mid \varnothing \rangle \ \wedge \ \langle A_2, A_5 \mid A_3 A_4 \rangle \ \wedge \ \langle A_2, A_1 \mid A_3 A_4 A_5 A_0 \rangle \ \wedge$$
$$\langle A_4, A_5 \mid \varnothing \rangle \ \wedge \ \langle A_4, A_1 \mid A_5 A_0 \rangle \ \wedge \ \langle A_4, A_3 \mid A_5 A_0 A_1 A_2 \rangle \ \leftrightarrow$$
$$\langle A_0, A_5 \mid \varnothing \rangle \ \wedge \ \langle A_0, A_3 \mid A_4 A_5 \rangle \ \wedge \ \langle A_0, A_1 \mid A_2 A_3 A_4 A_5 \rangle \ \wedge$$
$$\langle A_2, A_1 \mid \varnothing \rangle \ \wedge \ \langle A_2, A_5 \mid A_0 A_1 \rangle \ \wedge \ \langle A_2, A_3 \mid A_4 A_5 A_0 A_1 \rangle \ \wedge$$
$$\langle A_4, A_3 \mid \varnothing \rangle \ \wedge \ \langle A_4, A_1 \mid A_2 A_3 \rangle \ \wedge \ \langle A_4, A_5 \mid A_0 A_1 A_2 A_3 \rangle$$

We observe that it is not possible to derive the rule's consequent from its premise using the rule system $\mathcal{S}$ considered thus far. For $n + 1$ sets of variables, rule $G7$ includes $((n + 1)/2)^2$ premise triplets and the same number of consequent triplets. When proceeding from $n + 1$ to $n + 3$ sets of variables therefore, both the number of premise triplets and the number of consequent triplets are increased by $n + 2$. The combinatorial structure of the rule is illustrated in Fig. 6 for $n = 7$. The conditioning sets of a premise triplet are found on the outermost circle, in between the sets of its first two arguments, going clockwise starting from its first argument. For a consequent triplet a similar observation holds, now however the conditioning sets are found going counterclockwise.

We now define $\mathcal{G} = \mathcal{A} \cup \{G3, \ldots, G7\}$ for the new system of independence rules. Compared to the system $\mathcal{S}$, system $\mathcal{G}$ further restricts the number of relations closed under all known independence rules and thereby constitutes an enhanced characterisation of the class of structural semi-graphoid relations. Figure 1(b) positions the new system $\mathcal{G}$ into the hierarchy of independence relations.

4   Conclusions and Future Research

With existing rule systems for probabilistic independence being sound yet incomplete, we presented generalizations of the five rules for independence formulated by Studený [6], to larger numbers of (sets of) variables. With these generalized rules we uncovered combinatorial structures of probabilistic independence, and thereby enable their further study. We also closed in on the class of probabilistic independence relations, as the class of relations closed under the generalized rules is a proper subclass of the class closed under the previously existing rule system. By further exploiting multiinformation proof constructs, we hope to uncover in future research further combinatorial structures of independence and to formulate new generalized rules for probabilistic independence.

Acknowledgment. We would like to thank Milan Studený for his quick answers to our questions related to his work.

Appendix: Sketches of Proofs

All propositions stated in Sect. 3 are proven through multiinformation proof constructs. We find that the multiinformation equations of the four rules $G3$–$G6$ share the property that each term occurs exactly twice. In these equations, moreover, any multiinformation term originating from a premise triplet has a matching term, that occurs either in the rule's consequent with the same sign or in another premise triplet with the opposite sign. All terms therefore cancel out of the equation. For the fifth rule $G7$ the same observation holds, except for the terms $M(\varnothing)$ and $M(A_0 \cdots A_n)$. These terms may occur more than twice, however both terms occur equally many times in the multiinformation expressions of the rule's premise and of the rule's consequent and thus cancel out as well. In the proof sketches per rule, we restrict ourselves to indicating how each multiinformation term from an arbitrarily chosen premise triplet is canceled out from the multiinformation equation. Upon doing so, we abbreviate the multiinformation terms $M(XYZ)$, $M(Z)$, $M(XZ)$ and $M(YZ)$ of a triplet $\theta = \langle X, Y \mid Z \rangle$ as $M_{\mathrm{I}}\theta$, $M_{\mathrm{II}}\theta$, $M_{\mathrm{III}}\theta$ and $M_{\mathrm{IV}}\theta$, respectively.

Proposition 1. Let $\theta = \langle A_j, A_{\mu(j+1)} \mid A_{\mu(j+2)} \rangle$ be a premise triplet of rule $G5$, for some index $i = j$. Then, the triplet $\theta' = \langle A_{\mu(j+1)}, A_{\mu(j+2)} \mid A_j \rangle$, with $i = \mu(j+1)$, in the rule's consequent, has $M_{\mathrm{I}}\theta' = M_{\mathrm{I}}\theta$ and $M_{\mathrm{IV}}\theta' = M_{\mathrm{III}}\theta$. The consequent triplet $\theta'' = \langle A_{\mu(j+3)}, A_{\mu(j+4)} \mid A_{\mu(j+2)} \rangle$, with $i = \mu(j+3)$, further has $M_{\mathrm{II}}\theta'' = M_{\mathrm{II}}\theta$, and the consequent triplet $\theta''' = \langle A_{\mu(j+2)}, A_{\mu(j+3)} \mid A_{\mu(j+1)} \rangle$, with $i = \mu(j+2)$, to conclude, has $M_{\mathrm{III}}\theta''' = M_{\mathrm{IV}}\theta$. $\square$

Proposition 2. Let $\theta = \langle A, B_j \mid \mathbf{B}^k_{\mathbf{j}+} \rangle$ be a premise triplet of rule $G6$, for some index $i = j$ and some k. Then, the consequent triplet $\theta' = \langle A, B_{\mu(j+k)} \mid \mathbf{B}^k_{\mu(\mathbf{j+k})-} \rangle$, with $i = \mu(j+k)$, has $M_{\mathrm{I}}\theta' = M_{\mathrm{I}}\theta$ and $M_{\mathrm{IV}}\theta' = M_{\mathrm{IV}}\theta$. The consequent triplet $\theta'' = \langle A, B_{\mu(j+k+1)} \mid \mathbf{B}^k_{\mu(\mathbf{j+k+1})-} \rangle$, with $i = \mu(j+k+1)$, further has $M_{\mathrm{II}}\theta'' = M_{\mathrm{II}}\theta$ and $M_{\mathrm{III}}\theta'' = M_{\mathrm{III}}\theta$. $\square$

Proposition 3. Let $\theta = \langle A, C_j \mid C_1 \cdots C_{j-1} B \rangle$ be a premise triplet of rule $G4$, for some index $i = j$. Then, the consequent triplet $\theta' = \langle B, C_j \mid C_1 \cdots C_{j-1} A \rangle$, with $i = j$, has $M_{\mathrm{I}}\theta' = M_{\mathrm{I}}\theta$ and $M_{\mathrm{III}}\theta' = M_{\mathrm{III}}\theta$. The consequent triplet $\theta'' = \langle B, C_{j+1} \mid C_1 \ldots C_j \rangle$, with $i = j+1$, has $M_{\mathrm{III}}\theta'' = M_{\mathrm{IV}}\theta$. For $j > 1$, the consequent triplet $\theta''' = \langle B, C_{j-1} \mid C_1 \ldots C_{j-2} \rangle$, with $i = j-1$, has $M_{\mathrm{I}}\theta''' = M_{\mathrm{II}}\theta$. For $j = 1$, the term $M_{\mathrm{II}}\theta$ is canceled out of the multiinformation equation by the term M_{III}, with the opposite sign, of the premise triplet $\langle B, C_n \mid \varnothing \rangle$. Similar arguments apply to the premise triplets of another form than θ. $\square$

Proposition 4. Let $\theta = \langle A, C_j \mid C_1 \cdots C_{j-1} D_{n-j+2} \cdots D_n \rangle$ be a premise triplet of $G3$, for some index $i = j$. Then, the consequent triplet $\theta' = \langle B, D_{n-j+1} \mid C_1 \cdots C_j D_{n-j+2} \cdots D_n A \rangle$, with $i = n - j + 1$, has $M_{\mathrm{II}}\theta' = M_{\mathrm{I}}\theta$. The premise triplet $\theta'' = \langle B, D_{n-j+1} \mid C_1 \cdots C_j D_{n-j+2} \cdots D_n \rangle$, with $i = n - j + 1$, further has $M_{\mathrm{II}}\theta'' = -M_{\mathrm{IV}}\theta$. For all $j > 1$, the premise triplet $\theta''' = \langle B, D_{n-j+2} \mid C_1 \cdots C_{j-1} D_{n-j+3} \cdots D_n \rangle$, with $i = n - j + 2$, has $M_{\mathrm{IV}}\theta''' = -M_{\mathrm{II}}\theta$ and the consequent triplet $\theta'''' = \langle B, D_{n-j+2} \mid C_1 \cdots C_{j-1} D_{n-j+3} \cdots D_n A \rangle$, also with $i = n - j + 2$, has $M_{\mathrm{IV}}\theta'''' = M_{\mathrm{III}}\theta$. For $j = 1$ to conclude, the term $M_{\mathrm{II}}\theta$ is matched by the M_{II} term of the consequent triplet $\langle B, D_1 \mid \varnothing \rangle$ and the term $M_{\mathrm{III}}\theta$ is canceled out by the term M_{II} of opposite sign of the premise triplet $\langle B, D_1 \mid A \rangle$, with $i = 1$. Similar arguments apply to premise triplets of other form than θ. $\square$

Proposition 5. Let $\theta = \langle A_j, A_{\mu(j+h)} \mid A_{\mu(j+1)} \cdots A_{\mu(j+h-1)} \rangle$ be a premise triplet of $G7$, for some indices $i = j$, $k = h$. The term $M_{\mathrm{III}}\theta$ is canceled out from the multiinformation equation by the term $M_{\mathrm{III}}\theta'$ of the consequent triplet $\theta' = \langle A_{\mu(j+h-1)}, A_{\mu(j-1)} \mid A_j \cdots A_{\mu(j+h-2)} \rangle$, with $k = h$, $i = \mu(j + h - 1)$. The term $M_{\mathrm{IV}}\theta$ is canceled out by $M_{\mathrm{IV}}\theta''$ of the consequent triplet $\theta'' = \langle A_{\mu(j+h+1)}, A_{\mu(j+1)} \mid A_{\mu(j+2)} \cdots A_{\mu(j+h)} \rangle$, with $k = h$, $i = \mu(j + h + 1)$. For all $k \leq n - 2$, the term $M_{\mathrm{I}}\theta$ is canceled out by the term $M_{\mathrm{II}}\theta'''$ of the consequent triplet $\theta''' = \langle A_{\mu(j+h+1)}, A_{\mu(j-1)} \mid A_{\mu(j)} \cdots A_{\mu(j+h)} \rangle$, with $k = h + 2$, $i = \mu(j + h + 1)$; for $k = n$, the M_{I} terms of all premise and consequent triplets have $M_{\mathrm{I}\cdot} = M(A_0 \cdots A_n)$ and hence match. For all $k \geq 3$, the term $M_{\mathrm{II}}\theta$ is canceled out by the term $M_{\mathrm{I}}\theta''''$ of the consequent triplet $\theta'''' = \langle A_{\mu(j+h-1)}, A_{\mu(j+1)} \mid A_{\mu(j+2)} \cdots A_{\mu(j+h-2)} \rangle$, with $k = h - 2$, $i = \mu(j + h - 1)$; for $k = 1$, the M_{II} terms of all premise and consequent triplets have $M_{\mathrm{II}} = M(\varnothing)$ and thus match. $\qquad\square$

References

1. Dawid, A.: Conditional independence in statistical theory. J. R. Stat. Soc. B **41**, 1–31 (1979)
2. Pearl, J.: Probabilistic Reasoning in Intelligent Systems: Networks of Plausible Inference. Morgan Kaufmann (1988)
3. Studený, M.: Attempts at axiomatic description of conditional independence. Kybernetika **25**, 72–79 (1989)
4. Studený, M.: Multiinformation and the problem of characterization of conditional independence relations. Probl. Control Inf. Theor. **18**, 01 (1989)
5. Studený, M.: Conditional independence relations have no finite complete characterization. In: Information Theory, Statistical Decision Functions and Random Processes. Transactions of the 11th Prague Conference, vol. B, pp. 377–396. Kluwer, Dordrecht (1992)
6. Studený, M.: Structural semigraphoids. Int. J. Gen. Syst. **22**, 207–217 (1994)
7. Studený, M.: Description of structures of stochastic conditional independence by means of faces and imsets. 1st part: introduction and basic concepts. Int. J. Gen. Syst. **23**, 123–137 (1995)
8. Studený, M.: Description of structures of stochastic conditional independence by means of faces and imsets. 2rd part: basic theory. Int. J. Gen. Syst. **23**, 201–219 (1995)
9. Studený, M.: Description of structures of stochastic conditional independence by means of faces and imsets. 3rd part: examples of use and appendices. Int. J. Gen Syst **23**, 323–341 (1995)
10. Studený, M.: Probabilistic Conditional Independence Structures. Springer, London (2005). https://doi.org/10.1007/b138557
11. Studený, M., Vejnarová, J.: The multiinformation function as a tool for measuring stochastic dependence. In: Learning in Graphical Models, pp. 261–298. Kluwer Academic Publishers (1998)
12. Yeung, R.: A First Course in Information Theory. Kluwer Academic Publishers, Dordrecht (2002)

Algebras of Sets and Coherent Sets of Gambles

Arianna Casanova[1]($\boxtimes$) (iD), Juerg Kohlas[2] (iD), and Marco Zaffalon[1] (iD)

[1] Istituto Dalle Molle di Studi sull'Intelligenza Artificiale (IDSIA),
Lugano, Switzerland
{arianna,zaffalon}@idsia.ch

[2] Department of Informatics (DIUF), University of Fribourg, Fribourg, Switzerland
juerg.kohlas@unifr.ch

Abstract. In a recent work we have shown how to construct an information algebra of coherent sets of gambles defined on general possibility spaces. Here we analyze the connection of such an algebra with the *set algebra* of sets of its *atoms* and the *set algebra* of subsets of the possibility space on which gambles are defined. Set algebras are particularly important information algebras since they are their *prototypical* structures. Furthermore, they are the algebraic counterparts of classical propositional logic. As a consequence, this paper also details how propositional logic is naturally embedded into the theory of *imprecise probabilities*.

Keywords: Desirability · Information algebras · Order theory · Imprecise probabilities · Coherence

1   Introduction and Overview

While analysing the compatibility problem of coherent sets of gambles, Miranda and Zaffalon [14] have recently remarked that their main results could be obtained also using the theory of information algebras [7]. This observation has been taken up and deepened in some of our recent works [13,18]: we have shown that the founding properties of desirability can in fact be abstracted into properties of information algebras. Stated differently, desirability makes up an information algebra of coherent sets of gambles.

Information algebras are algebraic structures composed by 'pieces of information' that can be manipulated by operations of *combination*, to aggregate them, and *extraction*, to extract information regarding a specific question. From the point of view of information algebras, sets of gambles defined on a possibility space Ω are pieces of information about Ω. It is well known that coherent sets of gambles are ordered by inclusion and, in this order, there are maximal elements [4]. In the language of information algebras such elements are called *atoms*. In particular, any coherent set of gambles is contained in a maximal set (an atom) and it is the intersection (meet) of all the atoms it is contained in. An information algebra with these properties is called atomistic. Atomistic information algebras have the universal property of being embedded in a set algebra,

© Springer Nature Switzerland AG 2021
J. Vejnarová and N. Wilson (Eds.): ECSQARU 2021, LNAI 12897, pp. 603–615, 2021.
https://doi.org/10.1007/978-3-030-86772-0_43

which is an information algebra whose elements are sets. This is an important representation theorem for information algebras, since set algebras are a special kind of algebras based on the usual set operations. Set algebras are a kind of prototype information algebras, as fields of sets are prototypes of Boolean algebras, it matters to know that the information algebra of coherent sets of gambles is also of this kind, although this is not evident at the first sight. This result is similar to the well-known representation theorems for Boolean algebras and Priestley duality for distributive lattices, see [1]. Similar general representation theorems for a special type of general information algebras (commutative ones) have been presented in [7,12]. It is conjectured (but remains to be proved) that these results carry over to the more general type of information algebras proposed in [8] and to which the algebra of coherent sets of gambles belongs. Conversely, any such set algebra of subsets of Ω is embedded in the algebra of coherent sets of gambles defined on Ω. These links between set algebras and the algebra of coherent sets of gambles are the main topic of the present work. Since set algebras are algebraic counterparts of classical propositional logic, the results of this paper detail as well how the latter is formally part of the theory of imprecise probabilities [17]. We refer also to [3] for another aspect of this issue.

After recalling the main concepts introduced in our previous work in Sects. 2, 3 and 4, in Sect. 5 we establish some results about atoms needed for the subsequent sections. In Sect. 6 we define the concept of *embedding* for the information algebras of interest and finally, in Sect. 7, we show the links between set algebras (of subsets of Ω and of sets of atoms) and the algebra of coherent sets of gambles.

2   Desirability

Consider a set Ω of possible worlds. A gamble over this set is a bounded function $f : \Omega \to \mathbb{R}$. It is interpreted as an uncertain reward in a linear utility scale. A subject might desire a gamble or not, depending on the information they have about the experiment whose possible outcomes are the elements of Ω. We denote the set of all gambles on Ω by $\mathcal{L}(\Omega)$, or more simply by $\mathcal{L}$, when there is no possible ambiguity. We also introduce $\mathcal{L}^+(\Omega) := \{f \in \mathcal{L}(\Omega) : f \geq 0, f \neq 0\}$, or simply $\mathcal{L}^+$ when no ambiguity is possible, the set of non-negative non-vanishing gambles. These gambles should always be desired, since they may increase the wealth with no risk of decreasing it. As a consequence of the linearity of our utility scale, we assume also that a subject disposed to accept the transactions represented by f and g, is disposed to accept also $\lambda f + \mu g$ with $\lambda, \mu \geq 0$ not both equal to 0. More generally speaking, we consider the notion of a coherent set of gambles [17]:

Definition 1 (Coherent set of gambles). *We say that a subset $\mathcal{D}$ of $\mathcal{L}$ is a coherent set of gambles if and only if $\mathcal{D}$ satisfies the following properties:*

D1. $\mathcal{L}^+ \subseteq \mathcal{D}$ *[Accepting Partial Gains];*
D2. $0 \notin \mathcal{D}$ *[Avoiding Status Quo];*
D3. $f, g \in \mathcal{D} \Rightarrow f + g \in \mathcal{D}$ *[Additivity];*

D4. $f \in \mathcal{D}, \lambda > 0 \Rightarrow \lambda f \in \mathcal{D}$ [Positive Homogeneity].

So, $\mathcal{D}$ is a convex cone. Let us denote with $C(\Omega)$, or simply with C, the family of coherent sets of gambles on Ω. This leads to the concept of natural extension.

Definition 2 (Natural extension for gambles). *Given a set $\mathcal{K} \subseteq \mathcal{L}$, we call $\mathcal{E}(\mathcal{K}) := \mathrm{posi}(\mathcal{K} \cup \mathcal{L}^+)$, where $\mathrm{posi}(\mathcal{K}') := \left\{ \sum_{j=1}^{r} \lambda_j f_j : f_j \in \mathcal{K}', \lambda_j > 0, r \geq 1 \right\}$, for every set $\mathcal{K}' \subseteq \mathcal{L}$, its* natural extension.

$\mathcal{E}(\mathcal{K})$ of a set of gambles $\mathcal{K}$ is coherent if and only if $0 \notin \mathcal{E}(\mathcal{K})$.

In [18] we showed that $\Phi(\Omega) := C(\Omega) \cup \{\mathcal{L}(\Omega)\}$, or simply Φ when there is no possible ambiguity, is a complete lattice under inclusion [1], where meet is intersection and join is defined for any family of sets $\{\mathcal{D}_i\}_{i \in I} \in \Phi$ as

$$\bigvee_{i \in I} \mathcal{D}_i := \bigcap \left\{ \mathcal{D} \in \Phi : \bigcup_{i \in I} \mathcal{D}_i \subseteq \mathcal{D} \right\}.$$

Note that, if the family of coherent sets $\mathcal{D}_i$ has no upper bound in C, then its join is simply $\mathcal{L}$. Moreover, we defined the following closure operator [1] on subsets of gambles $\mathcal{K} \subseteq \mathcal{L}$

$$\mathcal{C}(\mathcal{K}) := \bigcap \{\mathcal{D} \in \Phi : \mathcal{K} \subseteq \mathcal{D}\}. \tag{1}$$

It is possible to notice that $\mathcal{C}(\mathcal{K}) = \mathcal{E}(\mathcal{K})$ if $0 \notin \mathcal{E}(\mathcal{K})$, that is if $\mathcal{E}(\mathcal{K})$ is coherent, otherwise $\mathcal{C}(\mathcal{K}) = \mathcal{L}$ and we may have $\mathcal{E}(\mathcal{K}) \neq \mathcal{C}(\mathcal{K})$.

The most informative cases of coherent sets of gambles, i.e., coherent sets that are not proper subsets of other coherent sets, are called *maximal*. The following proposition provides a characterisation of such maximal elements [4, Proposition 2].

Proposition 1 (Maximal coherent set of gambles). *A coherent set of gambles $\mathcal{D}$ is* maximal *if and only if $(\forall f \in \mathcal{L} \setminus \{0\}) \, f \notin \mathcal{D} \Rightarrow -f \in \mathcal{D}$.*

We shall denote maximal sets with M to differentiate them from the general case of coherent sets. These sets play an important role with respect to information algebras (see Sect. 5). Another important class is that of *strictly desirable* sets of gambles [17].[1]

Definition 3 (Strictly desirable set of gambles). *A coherent set of gambles $\mathcal{D}$ is said to be* strictly desirable *if and only if it satisfies $(\forall f \in \mathcal{D} \setminus \mathcal{L}^+)(\exists \delta > 0) \, f - \delta \in \mathcal{D}$.*

For strictly desirable sets, we shall employ the notation $\mathcal{D}^+$.

---

[1] Strictly desirable sets of gambles are important since they are in a one-to-one correspondence with *coherent lower previsions*, a generalization of the usual expectation operator on gambles. Given a coherent lower prevision $\underline{P}(\cdot)$, $\mathcal{D}^+ := \{f \in \mathcal{L} : \underline{P}(f) > 0\} \cup \mathcal{L}^+$ is a strictly desirable set of gambles [17, Sect. 3.8.1].

3   Stucture of Questions and Possibilities

In this section we review the main results about the structure of Ω [8,9,18]. With reference to our previous work [18], we recall that coherent sets of gambles are understood as pieces of information describing beliefs about the elements in Ω. Beliefs may be originally expressed relative to different questions or variables that we identify by families of equivalence relations $\equiv_x$ on Ω for x in some index set Q [5,8,9].[2] A question $x \in Q$ has the same answer in possible worlds $\omega \in \Omega$ and $\omega' \in \Omega$, if $\omega \equiv_x \omega'$. There is a partial order between questions capturing granularity: question y is finer than question x if $\omega \equiv_y \omega'$ implies $\omega \equiv_x \omega'$. This can be expressed equivalently considering partitions $\mathcal{P}_x$, $\mathcal{P}_y$ of Ω whose blocks are respectively, the equivalence classes $[\omega]_x$, $[\omega]_y$ of the equivalence relations $\equiv_x$, $\equiv_y$, representing possible answers to x and y. Then $\omega \equiv_y \omega'$ implying $\omega \equiv_x \omega'$, means that any block $[\omega]_y$ of partition $\mathcal{P}_y$ is contained in some block $[\omega]_x$ of partition $\mathcal{P}_x$. If this is the case, we say that: $x \leq y$ or $\mathcal{P}_x \leq \mathcal{P}_y$.[3] Partitions $Part(\Omega)$ of any set Ω, form a lattice under this order [6]. In particular, the partition $\sup\{\mathcal{P}_x, \mathcal{P}_y\} := \mathcal{P}_x \vee \mathcal{P}_y$ of two partitions $\mathcal{P}_x, \mathcal{P}_y$ is, in this order, the partition obtained as the non-empty intersections of blocks of $\mathcal{P}_x$ with blocks of $\mathcal{P}_y$. It can be equivalently expressed also as $\mathcal{P}_{x \vee y}$. The definition of the meet $\mathcal{P}_x \wedge \mathcal{P}_y$, or equivalently $\mathcal{P}_{x \wedge y}$, is somewhat involved [6]. We usually assume that the set of questions Q analyzed, considered together with their associated partitions denoted with $\mathcal{Q} := \{\mathcal{P}_x : x \in Q\}$, is a join-sub-semilattice of $(Part(\Omega), \leq)$ [1]. In particular, we assume often that the top partition in $Part(\Omega)$, i.e. $\mathcal{P}_\top$ (where the blocks are singleton sets $\{\omega\}$ for $\omega \in \Omega$), belongs to $\mathcal{Q}$. A gamble f on Ω is called x-measurable, iff for all $\omega \equiv_x \omega'$ we have $f(\omega) = f(\omega')$, that is, if f is constant on every block of $\mathcal{P}_x$. It could then also be considered as a function (a gamble) on the set of blocks of $\mathcal{P}_x$. We denote with $\mathcal{L}_x(\Omega)$, or more simply with $\mathcal{L}_x$ when no ambiguity is possible, the set of all x-measurable gambles. We recall also the logical independence and conditional logical independence relation between partitions [8,9].

Definition 4 (Independent Partitions). *For a finite set of partitions* $\mathcal{P}_1, \ldots, \mathcal{P}_n \in Part(\Omega)$, $n \geq 2$, *let us define*

$$R(\mathcal{P}_1, \ldots, \mathcal{P}_n) := \{(B_1, \ldots, B_n) : B_i \in \mathcal{P}_i, \cap_{i=1}^n B_i \neq \emptyset\}.$$

We call the partitions independent, *if* $R(\mathcal{P}_1, \ldots, \mathcal{P}_n) = \mathcal{P}_1 \times \cdots \times \mathcal{P}_n$.

Definition 5 (Conditionally Independent Partitions). *Consider a finite set of partitions* $\mathcal{P}_1, \ldots \mathcal{P}_n \in Part(\Omega)$, *and a block* B *of a partition* $\mathcal{P}$ *(contained or not in the list* $\mathcal{P}_1, \ldots, \mathcal{P}_n$*), then define for* $n \geq 1$,

$$R_B(\mathcal{P}_1, \ldots, \mathcal{P}_n) := \{(B_1, \ldots, B_n) : B_i \in \mathcal{P}_i, \cap_{i=1}^n B_i \cap B \neq \emptyset\}.$$

---

[2] This view generalises the most often used *multivariate model*, where questions are represented by families of variables and theirs domains [7,8].

[3] In the literature usually the inverse order between partitions is considered. However, this order better corresponds to our natural order of questions by granularity.

We call $\mathcal{P}_1, \ldots, \mathcal{P}_n$ *conditionally independent given* $\mathcal{P}$, *if for all blocks* B *of* $\mathcal{P}$, $R_B(\mathcal{P}_1, \ldots, \mathcal{P}_n) = R_B(\mathcal{P}_1) \times \cdots \times R_B(\mathcal{P}_n)$.

This relation holds if and only if $B_i \cap B \neq \emptyset$ for all $i = 1, \ldots, n$, implies $B_1 \cap \ldots \cap B_n \cap B \neq \emptyset$. In this case we write $\perp \{\mathcal{P}_1, \ldots, \mathcal{P}_n\} | \mathcal{P}$ or, for $n = 2$, $\mathcal{P}_1 \perp \mathcal{P}_2 | \mathcal{P}$. $\mathcal{P}_x \perp \mathcal{P}_y | \mathcal{P}_z$ can be indicated also with $x \perp y | z$. We may also say that $\mathcal{P}_1 \perp \mathcal{P}_2 | \mathcal{P}$ if and only if $\omega \equiv_{\mathcal{P}} \omega'$ implies the existence of an element $\omega'' \in \Omega$ such that $\omega \equiv_{\mathcal{P}_1 \vee \mathcal{P}} \omega''$ and $\omega' \equiv_{\mathcal{P}_2 \vee \mathcal{P}} \omega''$. The three-place relation $\mathcal{P}_1 \perp \mathcal{P}_2 | \mathcal{P}$, in particular, satisfies the following properties:

Theorem 1. *Given* $\mathcal{P}, \mathcal{P}', \mathcal{P}_1, \mathcal{P}_2 \in Part(\Omega)$, *we have:*

C1 $\mathcal{P}_1 \perp \mathcal{P}_2 | \mathcal{P}_2$*;*
C2 $\mathcal{P}_1 \perp \mathcal{P}_2 | \mathcal{P}$ *implies* $\mathcal{P}_2 \perp \mathcal{P}_1 | \mathcal{P}$*;*
C3 $\mathcal{P}_1 \perp \mathcal{P}_2 | \mathcal{P}$ *and* $\mathcal{P}' \leq \mathcal{P}_2$ *imply* $\mathcal{P}_1 \perp \mathcal{P}' | \mathcal{P}$*;*
C4 $\mathcal{P}_1 \perp \mathcal{P}_2 | \mathcal{P}$ *implies* $\mathcal{P}_1 \perp \mathcal{P}_2 \vee \mathcal{P} | \mathcal{P}$*.*

From these properties it follows also: $\mathcal{P}_x \perp \mathcal{P}_y | \mathcal{P}_z \iff \mathcal{P}_{x \vee z} \perp \mathcal{P}_{y \vee z} | \mathcal{P}_z$. A join semilattice $(Q, \leq)$ together with a relation $x \perp y | z$ with $x, y, z \in Q$, $(Q, \leq, \perp)$, satisfying conditions C1 to C4 is called a *quasi-separoid* (or also *q-separoid*) [8], a retract of the concept of *separoid* [1].

4   Information Algebra of Coherent Sets of Gambles

In [18] we showed that $\Phi(\Omega)$ with the following operations:

1. Combination: $\mathcal{D}_1 \cdot \mathcal{D}_2 := \mathcal{C}(\mathcal{D}_1 \cup \mathcal{D}_2)$,[4]
2. Extraction: $\epsilon_x(\mathcal{D}) := \mathcal{C}(\mathcal{D} \cap \mathcal{L}_x)$ for $x \in Q$,

where $(Q, \leq, \perp)$ is a q-separoid of questions on Ω in which $x \perp y | z$ with $x, y, z \in Q$ is the conditional independence relation introduced on them (see Sect. 3), is a *domain-free information algebra* that we call the *domain-free information algebra of coherent sets of gambles*. Combination captures aggregation of pieces of belief, and extraction, which for *multivariate models* leads to marginalisation in the equivalent *labeled* view of information algebras [7,13], describes filtering the part of information relative to a question $x \in Q$. Information algebras are particular *valuation algebras* as defined by [15] but with idempotent combination. Domain-free versions of valuation algebras have been proposed by Shafer [19]. Idempotency of combination has important consequences, such as the possibility to define an information order, atoms, approximation, and more [7,8]. It also offers—the subject of the present paper—important connections to set algebras.

Here we remind the characterizing properties of the domain-free information algebra Φ together with the q-separoid $(Q, \leq, \perp)$ and with a family E of extraction operators $\epsilon_x : \Phi \to \Phi$ for $x \in Q$:

---

[4] Notice that combination of sets in Φ coincides with their join in the lattice $(\Phi, \subseteq)$, as defined in Sect. 2.

1. *Semigroup:* $(\Phi, \cdot)$ is a commutative semigroup with a null element $0 = \mathcal{L}(\Omega)$ and a unit $1 = \mathcal{L}^+(\Omega)$.
2. *Quasi-Separoid:* $(Q, \leq, \bot)$ is a quasi-separoid.
3. *Existential Quantifier:* For any $x \in Q$, $\mathcal{D}_1, \mathcal{D}_2, \mathcal{D} \in \Phi$:
   (a) $\epsilon_x(0) = 0$,
   (b) $\epsilon_x(\mathcal{D}) \cdot \mathcal{D} = \mathcal{D}$,
   (c) $\epsilon_x(\epsilon_x(\mathcal{D}_1) \cdot \mathcal{D}_2) = \epsilon_x(\mathcal{D}_1) \cdot \epsilon_x(\mathcal{D}_2)$.
4. *Extraction:* For any $x, y, z \in Q$, $\mathcal{D} \in \Phi$, such that $x \vee z \bot y \vee z | z$ and $\epsilon_x(\mathcal{D}) = \mathcal{D}$, we have: $\epsilon_{y \vee z}(\mathcal{D}) = \epsilon_{y \vee z}(\epsilon_z(\mathcal{D}))$.
5. *Support:* For any $\mathcal{D} \in \Phi$ there is an $x \in Q$ so that $\epsilon_x(\mathcal{D}) = \mathcal{D}$, i.e. a *support* of $\mathcal{D}$ [18], and for all $y \geq x$, $y \in Q$, $\epsilon_y(\mathcal{D}) = \mathcal{D}$.

When we need to specify the constructing elements of the information algebra, we can refer to it with the tuple $(\Phi, Q, \leq, \bot, \cdot, 0, 1, E)$ or equivalently with $(\Phi, \mathcal{Q}, \leq, \bot, \cdot, 0, 1, E)$, where $(\mathcal{Q}, \leq, \bot)$ is the q-separoid of partitions equivalent to $(Q, \leq, \bot)$.[5] When we do not need this degree of accuracy, we can refer to it simply as Φ. Similar considerations can be made for other domain-free information algebras. Notice that, in particular, $(\Phi, \cdot)$ is an idempotent, commutative semigroup. So, a partial order on Φ is defined by $\mathcal{D}_1 \leq \mathcal{D}_2$ if $\mathcal{D}_1 \cdot \mathcal{D}_2 = \mathcal{D}_2$. Then $\mathcal{D}_1 \leq \mathcal{D}_2$ if and only if $\mathcal{D}_1 \subseteq \mathcal{D}_2$. This order is called an *information order* [18]. This definition entails the following facts: $\epsilon_x(\mathcal{D}) \leq \mathcal{D}$ for every $\mathcal{D} \in \Phi$, $x \in Q$; given $\mathcal{D}_1, \mathcal{D}_2 \in \Phi$, if $\mathcal{D}_1 \leq \mathcal{D}_2$, then $\epsilon_x(\mathcal{D}_1) \leq \epsilon_x(\mathcal{D}_2)$ for every $x \in Q$ [7].

5   Atoms and Maximal Coherent Sets of Gambles

Atoms are a well-known concept in (domain-free) information algebras. In our previous work [18], we showed that maximal coherent sets M are atoms of Φ. We denote them with $At(\Phi)$. Moreover, for every $\mathcal{D} \in \Phi$, we define $At(\mathcal{D}) := \{M \in At(\Phi) : \mathcal{D} \subseteq M\}$. We remind here some elementary properties of atoms for the specific case of $At(\Phi)$ [7]. Given $M, M_1, M_2 \in At(\Phi)$ and $\mathcal{D} \in \Phi$:

1. $M \cdot \mathcal{D} = M$ or $M \cdot \mathcal{D} = 0$;
2. either $\mathcal{D} \leq M$ or $M \cdot \mathcal{D} = 0$;
3. either $M_1 = M_2$ or $M_1 \cdot M_2 = 0$.

Φ is in particular *atomic* [7], i.e. for any $\mathcal{D} \neq 0$ the set $At(\mathcal{D})$ is not empty, and *atomistic*, i.e. for any $\mathcal{D} \neq 0$, $\mathcal{D} = \bigcap At(\mathcal{D})$. It is a general result of atomistic information algebras that the subalgebras $\epsilon_x(\Phi) := \{\epsilon_x(\mathcal{D}), \mathcal{D} \in \Phi\}$ are also atomistic [12]. Moreover, in [18], we showed that $At(\epsilon_x(\Phi)) = \epsilon_x(At(\Phi)) = \{\epsilon_x(M) : M \in At(\Phi)\}$ for any $x \in Q$ and, therefore, we call $\epsilon_x(M)$ for $M \in At(\Phi)$ and $x \in Q$ *local atoms* for x.[6] Local atoms $M_x = \epsilon_x(M)$ for $x \in Q$ induce a partition At_x of $At(\Phi)$ with blocks $At(M_x)$, see Lemma 1 below. If M and M' belong

---

[5] We can use the same notation E for the extraction operators in the two signatures of the information algebra. Indeed, we can indicate ϵ_x also as $\epsilon_{\mathcal{P}_x}$, where $\mathcal{P}_x \in \mathcal{Q}$ is the partition associated to $x \in Q$.

[6] Since local atoms for x are atoms of the subalgebra $\epsilon_x(\Phi)$, they respect in particular all the elementary properties of atoms restricted to elements of $\epsilon_x(\Phi)$ [7].

to the same block, we say that $M \equiv_x M'$. Let us indicate with $Part_Q(At(\varPhi)) :=$ $\{At_x : x \in Q\}$ the set of these partitions. $Part_Q(At(\varPhi))$ is in particular a subset of $Part(At(\varPhi))$, the set of all the partitions of $At(\varPhi)$. On $Part(At(\phi))$ we can introduce a partial order $\leq$, respect to which $Part(At(\varPhi))$ is a lattice, and a conditional independence relation $At_1 \perp At_2 | At_3$, with $At_1, At_2, At_3 \in Part(At(\varPhi))$ analogous to the ones introduced in Sect. 3. Their introduction, indeed, is independent of the set on which partitions are defined [6]. It can be shown moreover that $(Part(At(\varPhi)), \leq, \perp)$ is a quasi-separoid [8, Theorem 2.6]. We claim now that partitions $At_x \in Part_Q(At(\varPhi))$ mirror the partitions $\mathcal{P}_x \in \mathcal{Q}$. Before stating this main result, we need the following lemma.

Lemma 1. *Let us consider $M, M' \in At(\varPhi)$ and $x \in Q$. Then*

$$M \equiv_x M' \iff \epsilon_x(M) = \epsilon_x(M') \iff M, M' \in At(\epsilon_x(M)) = At(\epsilon_x(M')).$$

Hence, $At_x \leq At_y$ if and only if $At(\epsilon_x(M)) \supseteq At(\epsilon_y(M))$ for every $M \in At(\varPhi)$ and $x, y \in Q$.

Proof. If $M \equiv_x M'$, there exists a local atom M_x such that $M, M' \in At(M_x)$. Therefore, $M, M' \geq M_x$ and $\epsilon_x(M), \epsilon_x(M') \geq M_x$ [18, Lemma 15, item 3]. However, $\epsilon_x(M), \epsilon_x(M')$ and M_x are all local atoms, hence $\epsilon_x(M) = \epsilon_x(M') = M_x$. The converse is obvious. For the second part, let us suppose $At(\epsilon_y(M)) \subseteq At(\epsilon_x(M))$ for every $M \in At(\varPhi)$ with $x, y \in Q$, and consider $M', M'' \in At(\varPhi)$ such that $M' \equiv_y M''$. Then $M', M'' \in At(\epsilon_y(M'))$ and so $M', M'' \in At(\epsilon_x(M'))$, which implies $M' \equiv_x M''$. Vice versa, consider $At_x \leq At_y$ and $M \in At(\epsilon_y(M))$ for some $M, M' \in At(\varPhi)$. Then, $M \equiv_y M'$, hence $M \equiv_x M'$ and so $M' \in At(\epsilon_x(M))$.

Now we can state the main result of this section.

Theorem 2. *The map $\mathcal{P}_x \mapsto At_x$, from $(\mathcal{Q}, \leq, \perp)$ to $(Part_Q(At(\varPhi)), \leq, \perp)$, preserves order, that is $\mathcal{P}_x \leq \mathcal{P}_y$ implies $At_x \leq At_y$, and conditional independence relations, that is $\mathcal{P}_x \perp \mathcal{P}_y | \mathcal{P}_z$ implies $At_x \perp At_y | At_z$.*

Proof. If $x \leq y$, then $\epsilon_x(M) \leq \epsilon_y(M)$ for any atom $M \in At(\varPhi)$ [18, Lemma 15, item 4]. Therefore, $At(\epsilon_x(M)) \supseteq At(\epsilon_y(M))$ for any $M \in At(\varPhi)$, hence, by Lemma 1, $At_x \leq At_y$. For the second part, first of all notice that properties C2 and C3 of Theorem 1 are valid also for the conditional independence relation defined on $Part(At(\varPhi))$, restricted to $Part_Q(At(\varPhi))$. Then, recall that $x \perp y | z$ if and only if $x \vee z \perp y \vee z | z$. Consider then local atoms $M_{x \vee z}, M_{y \vee z}$ and M_z so that

$$At(M_{x \vee z}) \cap At(M_z) \neq \emptyset, \quad At(M_{y \vee z}) \cap At(M_z) \neq \emptyset.$$

Hence, there is an atom $M' \in At(M_{x \vee z}) \cap At(M_z)$ and an atom $M'' \in At(M_{y \vee z}) \cap At(M_z)$. Therefore, $M_{x \vee z} = \epsilon_{x \vee z}(M')$, $M_{y \vee z} = \epsilon_{y \vee z}(M'')$ and $M_z = \epsilon_z(M') = \epsilon_z(M'')$. Now, thanks to the Existential Quantifier axiom, we have:

$$\epsilon_z(M_{x \vee z} \cdot M_{y \vee z} \cdot M_z) = \epsilon_z(M_{x \vee z} \cdot M_{y \vee z}) \cdot M_z = \epsilon_z(\epsilon_{x \vee z}(M') \cdot \epsilon_{y \vee z}(M'')) \cdot M_z$$

Thanks to [18, Theorem 16] and [18, Lemma 15, item 3, item 6], we obtain

$$\epsilon_z(\epsilon_{x \vee z}(M') \cdot \epsilon_{y \vee z}(M'')) \cdot M_z = \epsilon_z(M') \cdot \epsilon_z(M'') \cdot M_z \neq 0.$$

Therefore $M_{x \vee z} \cdot M_{y \vee z} \cdot M_z \neq 0$ [18, Lemma 15, item 2] and hence, since the algebra is atomic, there is an atom $M''' \in At(M_{x \vee z} \cdot M_{y \vee z} \cdot M_z)$. Then $M_{x \vee z}, M_{y \vee z}, M_z \leq M'''$, whence $M''' \in At(M_{x \vee z}) \cap At(M_{y \vee z}) \cap At(M_z)$ and so $At_{x \vee z} \perp At_{y \vee z} | At_z$. From C2 and C3 of Theorem 1 and the first part of this theorem then, it follows that $At_x \perp At_y | At_z$.

6　Information Algebras Homomorphisms

We are interested in homomorphisms between domain-free information algebras. A domain-free information algebra is a two-sorted structure consisting of an idempotent commutative semigroup with a null and a unit element and a q-separoid, where the two sorts are linked by the extraction operators. Therefore an homomorphism should preserve operations and relations of both structures. This is achieved by the following definition.

Definition 6 (Domain-free information algebras homomorphism). *Let* $(\Psi, Q, \leq, \perp, \cdot, 0, 1, E)$ *and* $(\Psi', Q', \leq', \perp', \cdot', 0', 1', E')$ *be two domain-free information algebras, where* $E := \{\epsilon_x : x \in Q\}$ *and* $E' := \{\epsilon'_{x'} : x' \in Q'\}$ *are respectively the families of the extraction operators of the two structures. Consider a pair of maps* $f : \Psi \to \Psi'$ *and* $g : Q \to Q'$, *with the associated map* $h : E \to E'$ *defined by* $h(\epsilon_x) = \epsilon'_{g(x)}$. *Then the pair* (f, g) *is an information algebras homomorphism between* Ψ *and* Ψ' *if:*

1. $f(\psi \cdot \phi) = f(\psi) \cdot' f(\phi)$, *for every* $\psi, \phi \in \Psi$;
2. $f(0) = 0'$ *and* $f(1) = 1'$;
3. $x \leq y$ *implies* $g(x) \leq' g(y)$ *and* $x \perp y | z$ *implies* $g(x) \perp' g(y) | g(z)$, *for all* $x, y, z \in Q$;
4. $f(\epsilon_x(\psi)) = \epsilon'_{g(x)}(f(\psi))$, *for all* $\psi \in \Psi$ *and* $\epsilon_x \in E$.

We can give an analogous definition of homomorphism considering partitions equivalent to questions. We use the same notation for both the signatures.

If f and g are one-to-one, the pair (f, g) is an *information algebras embedding* and Ψ is said to be *embedded* into Ψ'; if they are bijective, (f, g) is an *information algebras isomorphism* and the two structures are called *isomorphic*.

7　Set Algebras

Archetypes of information algebras are so-called set algebras, where the elements are subsets of some universe, combination is intersection, and extraction is related to so-called saturation operators. We first specify the set algebra of subsets of Ω and show then that this algebra may be embedded into the information algebra of coherent sets. Conversely, we show that the algebra Φ may itself be embedded into a set algebra of its atoms, so is, in some precise sense, itself a set algebra. This is a general result for atomistic information algebras [7,12].

To any partition $\mathcal{P}_x$ of Ω there corresponds a saturation operator defined for any subset $S \subseteq \Omega$ by

$$\sigma_x(S) := \{\omega \in \Omega : (\exists \omega' \in S)\ \omega \equiv_x \omega'\}. \tag{2}$$

It corresponds to the union of the elements of blocks of $\mathcal{P}_x$ that have not empty intersection with S. The following are well-known properties of saturation operators. They can be shown analogously to the similar results in [8,18].

Lemma 2. *For all $S, T \subseteq \Omega$ and any partition $\mathcal{P}_x$ of Ω:*

1. $\sigma_x(\emptyset) = \emptyset$,
2. $S \subseteq \sigma_x(S)$,
3. $\sigma_x(\sigma_x(S) \cap T) = \sigma_x(S) \cap \sigma_x(T)$,
4. $\sigma_x(\sigma_x(S)) = \sigma_x(S)$,
5. $S \subseteq T \Rightarrow \sigma_x(S) \subseteq \sigma_x(T)$,
6. $\sigma_x(\sigma_x(S) \cap \sigma_x(T)) = \sigma_x(S) \cap \sigma_x(T)$.

Note that the first three items of this theorem imply that σ_x is an existential quantifier relative to intersection as combination. This is a first step to construct a domain-free information algebra of subsets of Ω. Now, consider the q-separoid $(Q, \leq, \perp)$ sort of the information algebra $(\Phi, Q, \leq, \perp, \cdot, 0, 1, E)$ considered in Sect. 4. We need the support axiom to be satisfied. If $\mathcal{P}_\top \in Q$, the set of partitions equivalent to questions in Q, then $\sigma_\top(S) = S$ for all $S \subseteq \Omega$. Otherwise, we must limit ourselves to the subsets of Ω for which there exists a support $x \in Q$. We call these sets *saturated* with respect to some $x \in Q$, and we indicate them with $P_Q(\Omega)$ or more simply with P_Q when no ambiguity is possible. Clearly, if the top partition belongs to Q, $P_Q(\Omega) = P(\Omega)$, the power set of Ω. So in what follows we can refer more generally to sets in $P_Q(\Omega)$. Note that in particular $\Omega, \emptyset \in P_Q(\Omega)$. At this point the support axiom is satisfied for every element of $P_Q(\Omega)$. Indeed, if $x \leq y$ with $x, y \in Q$, then $\omega \equiv_y \omega'$ implies $\omega \equiv_x \omega'$, so that $\sigma_y(S) \subseteq \sigma_x(S)$. Then, if x is a support of S, we have $S \subseteq \sigma_y(S) \subseteq \sigma_x(S) = S$, hence $\sigma_y(S) = S$. Moreover $(P_Q(\Omega), \cap)$ is a commutative semigroup with the empty set as the null element and Ω as the unit. Indeed, the only property we need to prove, is that $P_Q(\Omega)$ is closed under intersection. So, let us consider S and T, two subsets of Ω with support $x \in Q$ and $y \in Q$ respectively. They have also both supports $x \vee y$ that belongs to Q, because $(Q, \leq)$ is a join semilattice. Therefore, thanks to Lemma 2, we have

$$\sigma_{x \vee y}(S \cap T) = \sigma_{x \vee y}(\sigma_{x \vee y}(S) \cap \sigma_{x \vee y}(T)) = \sigma_{x \vee y}(S) \cap \sigma_{x \vee y}(T) = S \cap T.$$

So, $P_Q(\Omega)$ is closed under intersection. Lemma 2 moreover, implies that it is closed also under saturation. It remains only to verify the extraction property to conclude that P_Q forms a domain-free information algebra. We show it in the next result.

Theorem 3. *Given* $x, y, z \in Q$, *suppose* $x \vee z \perp y \vee z | z$. *Then, for any* $S \in P_Q(\Omega)$,

$$\sigma_{y \vee z}(\sigma_x(S)) = \sigma_{y \vee z}(\sigma_z(\sigma_x(S))).$$

Proof. From $\sigma_z(\sigma_x(S)) \supseteq \sigma_x(S)$ we obtain $\sigma_{y \vee z}(\sigma_z(\sigma_x(S)) \supseteq \sigma_{y \vee z}(\sigma_x(S))$. Consider therefore an element $\omega \in \sigma_{y \vee z}(\sigma_z(\sigma_x(S)))$. Then there are elements μ, μ' and ω' so that $\omega \equiv_{y \vee z} \mu \equiv_z \mu' \equiv_x \omega'$ and $\omega' \in S$. This means that ω, μ belong to some block $B_{y \vee z}$ of partition $\mathcal{P}_{y \vee z}$, μ, μ' to some block B_z of partition $\mathcal{P}_z$ and μ', ω' to some block B_x of partition $\mathcal{P}_x$. It follows that $B_x \cap B_z \neq \emptyset$ and $B_{y \vee z} \cap B_z \neq \emptyset$. Then $x \vee z \perp y \vee z | z$ implies, thanks to properties of a quasi-separoid, that $x \perp y \vee z | z$. Therefore, we have $B_x \cap B_{y \vee z} \cap B_z \neq \emptyset$, and in particular, $B_x \cap B_{y \vee z} \neq \emptyset$. So there is a $\lambda \in B_x \cap B_{y \vee z}$ such that $\omega \equiv_{y \vee z} \lambda \equiv_x \omega' \in S$, hence $\omega \in \sigma_{y \vee z}(\sigma_x(S))$. So we have $\sigma_{y \vee z}(\sigma_x(S)) = \sigma_{y \vee z}(\sigma_z(\sigma_x(S)))$.

So, we have the domain-free information algebra $(P_Q(\Omega), Q, \leq, \perp, \cap, \emptyset, \Omega, \{\sigma_x : x \in Q\})$. It is in particular an algebra of sets, with intersection as combination and saturation as extraction. Such type of information algebra will be called *set algebra*. In particular, we claim that this set algebra of subsets of Ω can be embedded into the information algebra of coherent sets of gambles $\Phi(\Omega)$. Indeed, for any set $S \in P_Q(\Omega)$, define

$$\mathcal{D}_S := \{f \in \mathcal{L}(\Omega) : \inf_{\omega \in S} f(\omega) > 0\} \cup \mathcal{L}^+(\Omega).$$

If $S \neq \emptyset$, this is clearly a coherent set, otherwise it corresponds to $\mathcal{L}(\Omega)$. The next theorem shows that the map $f : S \mapsto \mathcal{D}_S$ together with the identity map g, and the associated map $h : \epsilon_x \mapsto \sigma_x$, form an information algebras homomorphism between $P_Q(\Omega)$ and $\Phi(\Omega)$. In this case the q-separoid considered in the two algebras is the same and $g = id$, therefore item 3 in the definition of a domain-free information algebras homomorphism is trivially satisfied.

Theorem 4. *Let* $S, T \in P_Q(\Omega)$ *and* $x \in Q$. *Then*

1. $\mathcal{D}_S \cdot \mathcal{D}_T = \mathcal{D}_{S \cap T}$,
2. $\mathcal{D}_\emptyset = \mathcal{L}(\Omega)$, $\mathcal{D}_\Omega = \mathcal{L}^+(\Omega)$,
3. $\epsilon_x(\mathcal{D}_S) = \mathcal{D}_{\sigma_x(S)}$.

Proof. 1. Note that $\mathcal{D}_S = \mathcal{L}^+$ or $\mathcal{D}_T = \mathcal{L}^+$ if and only if $S = \Omega$ or $T = \Omega$. Clearly in this case we have immediately the result. The same is true if $\mathcal{D}_S = \mathcal{L}$ or $\mathcal{D}_T = \mathcal{L}$, which is equivalent to having $S = \emptyset$ or $T = \emptyset$. Now suppose $\mathcal{D}_S, \mathcal{D}_T \neq \mathcal{L}^+$ and $\mathcal{D}_S, \mathcal{D}_T \neq \mathcal{L}$. If $S \cap T = \emptyset$, then $\mathcal{D}_{S \cap T} = \mathcal{L}(\Omega)$. Consider $f \in \mathcal{D}_S$ and $g \in \mathcal{D}_T$. Since S and T are disjoint, we have $\tilde{f} \in \mathcal{D}_S$ and $\tilde{g} \in \mathcal{D}_T$, where $\tilde{f}, \tilde{g}$ are defined in the following way for every $\omega \in \Omega$:

$$\tilde{f}(\omega) := \begin{cases} f(\omega) & \text{for } \omega \in S, \\ -g(\omega) & \text{for } \omega \in T, \\ 0 & \text{for } \omega \in (S \cup T)^c, \end{cases} \qquad \tilde{g}(\omega) := \begin{cases} -f(\omega) & \text{for } \omega \in S, \\ g(\omega) & \text{for } \omega \in T, \\ 0 & \text{for } \omega \in (S \cup T)^c. \end{cases}$$

However, $\tilde{f} + \tilde{g} = 0 \in \mathcal{E}(\mathcal{D}_S \cup \mathcal{D}_T)$, hence $\mathcal{D}_S \cdot \mathcal{D}_T := \mathcal{C}(\mathcal{D}_S \cup \mathcal{D}_T) = \mathcal{L}(\Omega) = \mathcal{D}_{S \cap T}$. Assume then that $S \cap T \neq \emptyset$. Note that $\mathcal{D}_S \cup \mathcal{D}_T \subseteq \mathcal{E}(\mathcal{D}_S \cup \mathcal{D}_T) \subseteq \mathcal{D}_{S \cap T}$ so that

$\mathcal{E}(\mathcal{D}_S \cup \mathcal{D}_T)$ is coherent and $\mathcal{D}_S \cdot \mathcal{D}_T = \mathcal{E}(\mathcal{D}_S \cup \mathcal{D}_T) \subseteq \mathcal{D}_{S \cap T}$. Consider then a gamble $f \in \mathcal{D}_{S \cap T}$. Select a $\delta > 0$ and define two functions

$$f_1(\omega) := \begin{cases} 1/2 f(\omega) & \text{for } \omega \in (S \cap T), \\ \delta & \text{for } \omega \in S \setminus T, \\ f(\omega) - \delta & \text{for } \omega \in T \setminus S, \\ 1/2 f(\omega) & \text{for } \omega \in (S \cup T)^c, \end{cases} \qquad f_2(\omega) := \begin{cases} 1/2 f(\omega) & \text{for } \omega \in (S \cap T), \\ f(\omega) - \delta & \text{for } \omega \in S \setminus T, \\ \delta & \text{for } \omega \in T \setminus S, \\ 1/2 f(\omega) & \text{for } \omega \in (S \cup T)^c, \end{cases}$$

for every $\omega \in \Omega$. Then $f = f_1 + f_2$ and $f_1 \in \mathcal{D}_S$, $f_2 \in \mathcal{D}_T$. Therefore $f \in \mathcal{E}(\mathcal{D}_S \cup \mathcal{D}_T) = \mathcal{D}_S \cdot \mathcal{D}_T$, hence $\mathcal{D}_S \cdot \mathcal{D}_T = \mathcal{D}_{S \cap T}$.

2. Both have been noted above.

3. If S is empty, then $\epsilon_x(\mathcal{D}_\emptyset) = \mathcal{L}(\Omega)$ so that item 3 holds in this case. Hence, assume $S \neq \emptyset$. Then we have that $\mathcal{D}_S$ is coherent, and therefore:

$$\epsilon_x(\mathcal{D}_S) := \mathcal{C}(\mathcal{D}_S \cap \mathcal{L}_x) = \mathcal{E}(\mathcal{D}_S \cap \mathcal{L}_x) := \mathsf{posi}(\mathcal{L}^+(\Omega) \cup (\mathcal{D}_S \cap \mathcal{L}_x)).$$

Consider a gamble $f \in \mathcal{D}_S \cap \mathcal{L}_x$. If $f \in \mathcal{L}^+(\Omega) \cap \mathcal{L}_x$ then clearly $f \in \mathcal{D}_{\sigma_x(S)}$. Otherwise, $\inf_S f > 0$ and f is x-measurable. If $\omega \equiv_x \omega'$ for some $\omega' \in S$ and $\omega \in \Omega$, then $f(\omega) = f(\omega')$. Therefore $\inf_{\sigma_x(S)} f = \inf_S f > 0$, hence $f \in \mathcal{D}_{\sigma_x(S)}$. Then $\mathcal{C}(\mathcal{D}_S \cap \mathcal{L}_x) \subseteq \mathcal{C}(\mathcal{D}_{\sigma_x(S)}) = \mathcal{D}_{\sigma_x(S)}$. Conversely, consider a gamble $f \in \mathcal{D}_{\sigma_x(S)}$. $\mathcal{D}_{\sigma_x(S)}$ is a strictly desirable set of gambles.[7] Hence, if $f \in \mathcal{D}_{\sigma_x(S)}$, $f \in \mathcal{L}^+(\Omega)$ or there is $\delta > 0$ such that $f - \delta \in \mathcal{D}_{\sigma_x(S)}$. If $f \in \mathcal{L}^+(\Omega)$, then $f \in \epsilon_x(\mathcal{D}_S)$. Otherwise, let us define for every $\omega \in \Omega$, $g(\omega) := \inf_{\omega' \equiv_x \omega} f(\omega') - \delta$. If $\omega \in S$, then $g(\omega) > 0$ since $\inf_{\sigma_x(S)}(f - \delta) > 0$. So we have $\inf_S g \geq 0$ and g is x-measurable. However, $\inf_S(g + \delta) = \inf_S g + \delta > 0$ hence $(g + \delta) \in \mathcal{D}_S \cap \mathcal{L}_x$ and $f \geq g + \delta$. Therefore $f \in \mathcal{E}(\mathcal{D}_S \cap \mathcal{L}_x) = \mathcal{C}(\mathcal{D}_S \cap \mathcal{L}_x) =: \epsilon_x(\mathcal{D}_S)$.

Item 3. guarantees that, if $S \in P_Q(\Omega)$, then there exists an $x \in Q$ such that $\epsilon_x(\mathcal{D}_S) = \mathcal{D}_S$. Moreover, f and g are one-to-one,[8] so P_Q is embedded into Φ.

Regarding instead the relation between Φ and a set algebra of sets of its atoms, consider the set algebra:

$$(P(At(\Phi)), Part(At(\Phi)), \leq, \perp, \cap, \emptyset, At(\Phi), \Sigma), \tag{3}$$

where $P(At(\Phi))$ is the power set of $At(\Phi)$, which clearly leads to the commutative semigroup $(P(At(\Phi)), \cap)$ with $\emptyset$ as the null element and $At(\Phi)$ as the unit element, $(Part(At(\Phi)), \leq, \perp)$ is the q-separoid introduced in Sect. 5 and Σ is the set of all saturation operators associated with any partition $At \in Part(At(\Phi))$, defined similarly to (2). It is clearly a set algebra. In fact, the *Semigroup*, the *Quasi-Separoid* and the *Support* axioms are clearly satisfied. The *Existential Quantifier* axiom follows from Lemma 2 applied to saturation operators in Σ and subsets of $At(\Phi)$ and the *Extraction* axiom follows from Theorem 3 applied again to Σ and elements in $P(At(\Phi))$. We claim moreover that $(\Phi, \mathcal{Q}, \leq, \perp, \cdot, 0, 1, E)$ can be embedded into $(P(At(\Phi)), Part(At(\Phi)), \leq, \perp, \cap, \emptyset, At(\Phi), \Sigma)$. Consider the maps $f : \Phi \to P(At(\Phi))$ and $g : \mathcal{Q} \to Part_Q(At(\Phi))$ defined as $f(\mathcal{D}) = At(\mathcal{D})$

---

[7] $\underline{P}(f) := \inf_S(f)$ for every $f \in \mathcal{L}$ with $S \neq \emptyset$, is a coherent lower prevision [17].

[8] Indeed g is clearly one-to-one and regarding f, if $\mathcal{D}_S = \mathcal{D}_T$ it means that $S = T$.

and $g(\mathcal{P}_x) = At_x$, where $At_x \in Part_Q(At(\Phi))$ is the partition defined by the equivalence relation between atoms $M \equiv_x M'$ if and only if $\epsilon_x(M) = \epsilon_x(M')$ with $M, M' \in At(\Phi)$. As noted before, associated with the partition At_x, there is the saturation operator σ_x, defined for any subset $S \subseteq At(\Phi)$ by $\sigma_x(S) := \{M \in At(\Phi) : (\exists M' \in S) \ M \equiv_x M'\}$. Thus, we have the map h defined as $h(\epsilon_x) = \sigma_x$. The next result, together with Theorem 2, shows that the pair of maps (f, g) is an information algebra homomorphism between Φ and $P(At(\Phi))$.

Theorem 5. *For any element* $\mathcal{D}_1, \mathcal{D}_2$ *and* $\mathcal{D}$ *of* Φ *and all* $x \in Q$,

1. $At(\mathcal{D}_1 \cdot \mathcal{D}_2) = At(\mathcal{D}_1) \cap At(\mathcal{D}_2)$,
2. $At(\mathcal{L}(\Omega)) = \emptyset$, $At(\mathcal{L}^+(\Omega)) = At(\Phi)$,
3. $At(\epsilon_x(\mathcal{D})) = \sigma_x(At(\mathcal{D}))$.

Proof. Item 2 is obvious. If there is a an atom $M \in At(\mathcal{D}_1 \cdot \mathcal{D}_2)$, then $M \geq \mathcal{D}_1 \cdot \mathcal{D}_2 \geq \mathcal{D}_1, \mathcal{D}_2$ and thus $M \in At(\mathcal{D}_1) \cap At(\mathcal{D}_2)$. Conversely, if $M \in At(\mathcal{D}_1) \cap At(\mathcal{D}_2)$, then $\mathcal{D}_1, \mathcal{D}_2 \leq M$, hence $\mathcal{D}_1 \cdot \mathcal{D}_2 \leq M$ and $M \in At(\mathcal{D}_1 \cdot \mathcal{D}_2)$. Furthermore, if $\epsilon_x(\mathcal{D}) = 0$, then $\mathcal{D} = 0$ and $At(\mathcal{D}) = \emptyset$, hence $\sigma_x(\emptyset) = \emptyset$ and vice versa [18, Lemma 15, item 2]. Assume therefore $At(\mathcal{D}) \neq \emptyset$ and consider $M \in \sigma_x(At(\mathcal{D}))$. There is then a $M' \in At(\mathcal{D})$ so that $\epsilon_x(M) = \epsilon_x(M')$. But $\mathcal{D} \leq M'$, hence $\epsilon_x(\mathcal{D}) \leq \epsilon_x(M') = \epsilon_x(M) \leq M$. Thus $M \in At(\epsilon_x(\mathcal{D}))$. Conversely consider $M \in At(\epsilon_x(\mathcal{D}))$. We claim that $\epsilon_x(M) \cdot \mathcal{D} \neq 0$. Because otherwise $0 = \epsilon_x(\epsilon_x(M) \cdot \mathcal{D}) = \epsilon_x(M) \cdot \epsilon_x(\mathcal{D}) = \epsilon_x(M \cdot \epsilon_x(\mathcal{D}))$, by Existential Quantifier axiom, which is not possible since $\epsilon_x(\mathcal{D}) \leq M$. So there is an $M' \in At(\epsilon_x(M) \cdot \mathcal{D})$ so that $\mathcal{D} \leq \epsilon_x(M) \cdot \mathcal{D} \leq M'$. We conclude that $M' \in At(\mathcal{D})$. Furthermore, $\epsilon_x(\epsilon_x(M) \cdot \mathcal{D}) = \epsilon_x(M) \cdot \epsilon_x(\mathcal{D}) \leq \epsilon_x(M')$. It follows that $\epsilon_x(M') \cdot \epsilon_x(M) \cdot \epsilon_x(\mathcal{D}) \neq 0$ and therefore $\epsilon_x(M) \cdot \epsilon_x(M') \neq 0$. But they are both local atoms, hence $\epsilon_x(M) = \epsilon_x(M')$, which together with $M' \in At(\mathcal{D})$ tells us that $M \in \sigma_x(At(\mathcal{D}))$.

Φ is atomistic, then f is one-to-one. Further, g is also one-to-one since $\epsilon_x \neq \epsilon_y$ implies $At_x \neq At_y$. Therefore Φ is embedded into $P(At(\Phi))$ and we can say that it is in fact a set algebra.

8   Conclusions

This paper presents an extension of our work on information algebras related to gambles on a possibility set that is not necessarily multivariate [18]. In the multivariate case, we showed also that lower previsions and strictly desirable sets of gambles form isomorphic information algebras [18]. It can be expected to be valid also in this case. Since then convex *credal sets* are sets of atoms associated with a lower prevision [17,18], we claim that the algebra of lower previsions, hence of strictly desirable sets of gambles, can be embedded into the set algebra of credal sets. This is left for future work, along with other aspects such as the question of conditioning and the equivalent expression of the results shown in this paper for the *labeled view* of information algebras, better suited for computational purposes [7,18].

Acknowledgements. We would like to thank the anonymous Referees for a number of useful remarks.

References

1. Davey, B.A., Priestley, H.A.: Introduction to Lattices and Order. Cambridge University Press (1990)
2. Dawid, A.P.: Separoids: a mathematical framework for conditional independence and irrelevance. Ann. Math. Artif. Intell. **32**(1–4), 335–372 (2001). https://doi.org/10.1023/A:1016734104787
3. De Cooman, G.: Belief models: an order-theoretic investigation. Ann. Math. Artif. Intell. **45**(1), 5–34 (2005). https://doi.org/10.1007/s10472-005-9006-x
4. De Cooman, G., Quaeghebeur, E.: Exchangeability and sets of desirable gambles. Int. J. Approx. Reason. **53**, 363–395 (2012)
5. Shafer, G.: A Mathematical Theory of Evidence, vol. 42. Princeton University Press (1976)
6. Grätzer, G.: General Lattice Theory. Birkhäuser Verlag (2003)
7. Kohlas, J.: Information Algebras: Generic Structures for Inference. Springer, London (2003). https://doi.org/10.1007/978-1-4471-0009-6
8. Kohlas, J.: Algebras of information. A new and extended axiomatic foundation (2017). https://arxiv.org/abs/1701.02658
9. Kohlas, J., Monney, P.A.: A Mathematical Theory of Hints. An Approach to the Dempster-Shafer Theory of Evidence. Lecture Notes in Economics and Mathematical Systems, vol. 425. Springer, Heidelberg (1995). https://doi.org/10.1007/978-3-662-01674-9
10. Kohlas, J., Schmid, J.: Research notes: an algebraic theory of information. Technical report 06–03, Department of Informatics, University of Fribourg (2013)
11. Kohlas, J., Schmid, J.: An algebraic theory of information: an introduction and survey. Information **5**(2), 219–254 (2014)
12. Kohlas, J., Schmid, J.: Commutative information algebras and their representation theory (2020)
13. Casanova, A., Kohlas, J., Zaffalon, M.: Information algebras in the theory of imprecise probabilities (2021). https://arxiv.org/abs/2102.13368
14. Miranda, E., Zaffalon, M.: Compatibility, desirability, and the running intersection property. Artif. Intell. **283**, 103247 (2020)
15. Shafer, G., Shenoy, P.P.: Axioms for probability and belief function propagation. In: Shafer, G., Pearl, J. (eds.) Readings in Uncertain Reasoning. Morgan Kaufmann Publishers Inc., San Mateo (1990)
16. Troffaes, M.C.M., De Cooman, G.: Lower Previsions. John Wiley & Sons, Hoboken (2014)
17. Walley, P.: Statistical Reasoning with Imprecise Probabilties. Chapman and Hall (1991)
18. Kohlas, J., Casanova, A., Zaffalon, M.: Information algebras of coherent sets of gambles in general possibility spaces. In: International Symposium on Imprecise Probabilities: Theories and Applications, PMLR 2021. https://people.idsia.ch/~arianna.casanova/papers/InfoAlgebrasCoherentSetsGS.pdf
19. Shafer, G.: An axiomatic study of computation in hypertrees. School of Business, University of Kansas. Working Paper (1991)

A Probabilistic Deontic Logic

Vincent de Wit, Dragan Doder[(✉)], and John Jules Meyer

Department of Information and Computing Sciences, Utrecht University,
Utrecht, The Netherlands
{d.doder,J.J.C.Meyer}@uu.nl

Abstract. In this article, we introduce a logic for reasoning about probability of normative statements. We present its syntax and semantics, describe the corresponding class of models, provide an axiomatization for this logic and prove that the axiomatization is sound and complete. We also prove that our logic is decidable.

Keywords: Monadic deontic logic · Normative reasoning ·
Probabilistic logic · Completeness · Decidability

1 Introduction

The seminal work of von Wright from 1951 [14] initiated a systematic study on formalization of normative reasoning in terms of deontic logic. The latter is a branch of modal logics that deals with obligation, permission and related normative concepts. A plethora of deontic logics have been developed for various application domains like legal reasoning, argumentation theory and normative multi-agent systems [1,7].

Some recent work also studied learning behavioral norms from data [11,13]. In [11], the authors pointed out that human norms are context-specific and laced with uncertainty, which poses challenges to their representation, learning and communication. They gave an example of a learner that might conclude from observations that talking is prohibited in a library setting, while another learner might conclude the opposite when seeing people talking at the checkout counter. They represented uncertainty about norms using deontic operators, equipped with probabilistic boundaries that capture the subjective degree of certainty.

In this paper, we study uncertain norms form a logical point of view. We use probabilistic logic [3–6,12] to represent uncertainty, and we present the proof-theoretical and model-theoretical approach to a logic which allows reasoning about uncertain normative statements. We take two well studied logics, monadic deontic logic (MDL) [9] and probabilistic logic of Fagin, Halpern and Magido (FHM) [4], as the starting points, and combine them in a rich formalism that generalizes each of them. The resulting language makes it possible to adequately model different degrees of belief in norms; for example, we can express statements like "the probability that one is obliged to be quiet is at least 0.9".

© Springer Nature Switzerland AG 2021
J. Vejnarová and N. Wilson (Eds.): ECSQARU 2021, LNAI 12897, pp. 616–628, 2021.
https://doi.org/10.1007/978-3-030-86772-0_44

The semantics for our logic consists of specific Kripke-like structures, where each model contains a probability space whose sample space is the set of states, and with each state carrying enough information to evaluate a deontic formula. We consider so-called *measurable* models, which allow us to assign a probability value to every deontic statement.

The main result of this article is a sound and complete axiomatization for our logic. Like any other real-valued probabilistic logic, it is not compact, so any finitary axiomatic system would fail to be strongly complete ("every consistent set of formulas has a model") [6]. We prove weak completeness ("every consistent formula has a model") combining and modifying completeness techniques for MDL and FHM. We also show that our logic is decidable, combining the method of filtration and a reduction to a system of inequalities.

The rest of the paper is organised as follows: In Sect. 2 the proposed syntax and semantics of the logic will be presented together with other needed definitions. In Sect. 3 the axiomatization of the logic is given, followed by the soundness and completeness proof in Sect. 4. In Sect. 5 we show that our logic is decidable. Lastly, in Sect. 6 a conclusion is given together with future research topics.

2   Syntax and Semantics

In this section, we present the syntax and semantics of our probabilistic deontic logic. This logic, that we call $\mathcal{PDL}$, contains two types of formulas: standard deontic formulas of MDS, and probabilistic formulas. Let $\mathbb{Q}$ denote the set of rational numbers.

Definition 1 (Formula). *Let $\mathbb{P}$ be a set of atomic propositions. The language $\mathcal{L}$ of probabilistic monadic deontic logic is generated by the following two sentences of BNF (Backus Naur Form):*

$[\mathcal{L}_{deontic}]\ \phi ::= p \mid \neg\phi \mid (\phi \wedge \phi) \mid O\phi \qquad p \in \mathbb{P}$

$[\mathcal{L}_{prob-d}]\ f ::= a_1 w(\phi_1) + \cdots + a_n w(\phi_n) \geq \alpha \mid \neg f \mid (f \wedge f) \qquad a_i, \alpha \in \mathbb{Q}$

The set of all formulas $\mathcal{L}$ is $\mathcal{L}_{deontic} \cup \mathcal{L}_{prob-d}$. We denote the elements of $\mathcal{L}$ with θ and θ', possibly with subscripts.

The construct $O\phi$ is read as "It is obligatory that ϕ", while $w(\phi)$ stands for "probability of ϕ". An expression of the form $a_1 w(\phi_1) + \cdots + a_n w(\phi_n)$ is called *term*. We denote terms with x and t, possibly with subscripts. The propositional connectives, $\vee$, $\rightarrow$ and $\leftrightarrow$, are introduced as abbreviations, in the usual way. We abbreviate $\theta \wedge \neg\theta$ with $\bot$, and $\neg\bot$ with $\top$. We also use abbreviations to define other types of inequalities; for example, $w(\phi) \geq w(\phi')$ is an abbreviation for $w(\phi) - w(\phi') \geq 0$, $w(\phi) = \alpha$ for $w(\phi) \geq \alpha$ and $-w(\phi) \geq -\alpha$, $w(\phi) < \alpha$ for $\neg w(\phi) \geq \alpha$.

Example 1. *Following our informal example from the introduction about behavioral norms in a library, the fact that a person has become fairly certain that it* *is normal to be quiet might be expressed by the probabilistic statement "the probability that one is obliged to be quiet is at least 0.9". This sentence could be formalized using the introduced language as*

$$w(Oq) \geq 0.9.$$

Note that we do not allow mixing of the formulas from $\mathcal{L}_{deontic}$ and $\mathcal{L}_{prob-d}$. For example, $O(p \vee q) \wedge w(Oq) \geq 0.9$ is not a formula of our language. Before we introduce the semantics of $\mathcal{PDL}$ we will introduce Monadic Deontic Logic models.

Definition 2 (Relational model). *A relational model D is a tuple $D = (W, R, V)$ where:*

- *W is a (non-empty) set of states (also called "possible worlds"); W is called the universe of the model.*
- *$R \subseteq W \times W$ is a binary relation over W. It is understood as a relation of deontic alternativeness: sRt (or, alternatively, $(s,t) \in R$) says that t is an ideal alternative to s, or that t is a "good" successor of s. The first one is "good" in the sense that it complies with all the obligations true in the second one. Furthermore, R is subject to the following constraint:*

$$(\forall s \in W)(\exists t \in W)(sRt) \qquad (seriality)$$

This means that the model does not have a dead end, a state with no good successor.
- *$V : \mathbb{P} \mapsto 2^W$ is a valuation function assigning to each atom p a set $V(p) \subseteq W$ (intuitively the set of states at which p is true.)*

Next, we define the satisfiability of a formula in a model. This definition is in accordance with standard satisfiability relation of MDL.

Definition 3 (Satisfaction in MDL). *Let $D = (W, R, V)$ be a relational deontic model, and let $w \in W$. We define the satisfiability of a deontic formula $\phi \in \mathcal{L}_{deontic}$ in the state w, denoted by $D, w \models_{MDL} \phi$, recursively as follows:*

- *$D, w \models_{MDL} p$ iff $w_s \in V_s(p)$.*
- *$D, w \models_{MDL} \neg\phi$ iff $D, s \not\models_{MDL} \phi$.*
- *$D, w \models_{MDL} \phi \wedge \psi$ iff $D, s \models_{MDL} \phi$ and $D, s \models_{MDL} \psi$.*
- *$D, w \models_{MDL} O\phi$ iff for all $u \in W_s$, if wRu then $D, u \models_{MDL} \phi$.*

Now we introduce the semantics of $\mathcal{PDL}$.

Definition 4 (Model). *A probabilistic deontic model is a tuple $M = \langle S, \mathcal{X}, \mu, \tau \rangle$, where*

- *S is a non-empty set of states*
- *$\mathcal{X}$ is a σ-algebra of subsets of S*
- *$\mu : \mathcal{X} \to [0,1]$ is a probability measure, i.e.,*

- $\mu(X) \geq 0$ *for all* $X \in \mathscr{X}$
- $\mu(S) = 1$
- $\mu(\bigcup_{i=1}^{\infty} X_i) = \sum_{i=1}^{\infty} \mu(X_i)$, *if the* X_i*'s are pairwise disjoint members of* $\mathscr{X}$

- τ *associates with each state s in S a tuple containing a monadic deontic model and one of its worlds, i.e.,* $\tau(s) = (D_s, w_s)$, *where:*
  - $D_s = (W_s, R_s, V_s)$ *is a relational model of monadic deontic logic as defined in Definition 3.*
  - $w_s \in W_s$ *is a world* w_s *in* W_s *of model* D_s.

Let us illustrate this definition.

Example 1 *(continued) Assume a finite set of atomic propositions* $\{p, q\}$. *Let us consider the model* $M = \langle S, \mathscr{X}, \mu, \tau \rangle$, *where*

- $S = \{s, s', s'', s'''\}$
- $\mathscr{X}$ *is the set of all subsets of* S
- μ *is characterized by:* $\mu(\{s\}) = 0.5$, $\mu(\{s'\}) = \mu(\{s''\}) = 0.2$, $\mu(\{s'''\}) = 0.1$ *(other values follow from the properties of probability measures)*
- τ *is a mapping which assigns to the state* s, $D_s = (W_s, R_s, V_s)$ *and* w_s *such that*
  - $W_s = \{w_1, w_2, w_3, w_4\}$
  - $R_s = \{(w_1, w_2), (w_1, w_3), (w_2, w_2), (w_2, w_3), (w_3, w_2), (w_3, w_3), (w_4, w_2),$ $(w_4, w_3), (w_4, w_4)\}$
  - $V_s(p) = \{w_1, w_3\}$, $V_s(q) = \{w_2, w_3\}$
  - $w_s = w_1$

  Note that the domain of τ *is always the whole set* S, *but in this example we only explicitly specify* $\tau(s)$ *for illustration purposes.*

This model is depicted in Fig. 1. The circle on the right contains the four states of the model, which are measured by μ. *Each of the states is equipped with a standard pointed model of MDL. In this picture, only one of them is shown, the one that corresponds to s. It is represented within the circle on the left. Note that the arrows depict the "good" alternative relation R. If we assume that* q *stands for "quiet", like in the previous example, in all good successors of* w_1 *the proposition* q *holds. Note that, according to Definition 3 , this means that in* w_1 *people are obliged to be quiet in the library.*

For a model $M = \langle S, \mathscr{X}, \mu, \tau \rangle$ and a formula $\phi \in \mathcal{L}_{deontic}$, let $\|\phi\|_M$ denote the set of states that satisfy ϕ, i.e., $\|\phi\|_M = \{s \in S \mid D_s, w_s \models_{MDL} \phi\}$. We omit the subscript M from $\|\phi\|_M$ when it is clear from context. The following definition introduces an important class of probabilistic deontic models, so-called *measurable* models.

Definition 5 (Measurable model). *A probabilistic deontic model is measurable if*

$$\|\phi\|_M \in \mathscr{X}$$

for every $\phi \in \mathcal{L}_{deontic}$.

$$M$$

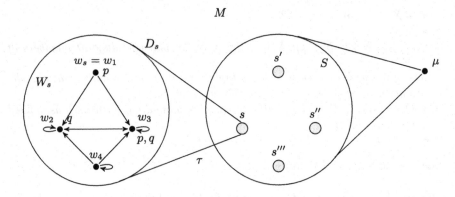

Fig. 1. Model $M = \langle S, \mathscr{X}, \mu, \tau \rangle$.

In this paper, we focus on measurable structures, and we prove completeness and decidability results for this class of structures.

Definition 6 (Satisfaction). *Let $M = \langle S, \mathscr{X}, \mu, \tau \rangle$ be a measurable probabilistic deontic model. We define the satisfiability relation $\models$ recursively as follows:*

- $M \models \phi$ *iff for all $s \in S$, $D_s, w_s \models_{MDL} \phi$*
- $M \models a_1 w(\phi_1) + \cdots + a_k w(\phi_k) \geq \alpha$ *iff $a_1 \mu(\|\phi_1\|) + \cdots + a_k \mu(\|\phi_k\|) \geq \alpha$.*
- $M \models \neg f$ *iff $M \not\models f$*
- $M \models f \wedge g$ *iff $M \models f$ and $M \models g$.*

Example 1 *(continued) Continuing the previous example, it is now also possible to speak about the probability of the obligation to be quiet in a library. First, according to Definition 3 it holds that $D_s, w_s \models_{MDL} Oq$. Furthermore, assume that τ is defined in the way such that $D_{s'}, w_{s'} \models_{MDL} Oq$ and $D_{s''}, w_{s''} \models_{MDL} Oq$, but $D_{s'''}, w_{s'''} \not\models_{MDL} Oq$. Then $\mu(\|Oq\|) = \mu(\{s, s', s''\}) = 0.5 + 0.2 + 0.2 = 0.9$. According to Definition 6, $M \models w(Oq) \geq 0.9$.*

Note that, according to Definition 6, a deontic formula is true in a model iff it holds in every state of the model. This is a consequence of our design choice that those formulas represent certain deontic knowledge, while probabilistic formulas express uncertainty about norms. At the end of this section, we define some standard semantical notions.

Definition 7 (Semantical consequence). *Given a set Γ of formulas, a formula θ is a semantical consequence of Γ (notation: $\Gamma \models \theta$) whenever, all the states of the model have, if $M, s \models \theta'$ for all $\theta' \in \Gamma$, then $M, s \models \theta$.*

Definition 8 (Validity). *A formula θ is valid (notations: $\models \theta$) whenever for $M = \langle S, \mathscr{X}, \mu, \tau \rangle$ and every $s \in S$: $M, s \models \theta$ holds.*

3   Axiomatization

The following axiomatization contains 13 axioms and 3 inference rules. It combines the axioms of proof system D of monadic deontic logic [9] with the axioms of probabilistic logic. The axioms for reasoning about linear inequalities are taken form [4].

The Axiomatic System: $AX_{\mathcal{PDL}}$

Tautologies and Modus Ponens

Taut. All instances of propositional tautologies.

MP. From θ and $\theta \rightarrow \theta'$ infer θ'.

Reasoning with O:

O-K. $O(\phi \rightarrow \psi) \rightarrow (O\phi \rightarrow O\psi)$

O-D. $O\phi \rightarrow P\phi$

O-Nec. *From ϕ infer $O\phi$.*

Reasoning About Linear Inequalities:

I1. $x \geq x$ (identity)

I2. $(a_1 x_1 + ... + a_k x_k \geq c) \leftrightarrow (a_1 x_1 + ... + a_k x_k + 0 x_{k+1} \geq c)$ (adding and deleting 0 terms)

I3. $(a_1 x_1 + ... + a_k x_k \geq c) \rightarrow (a_{j_1} x_{j_1} + ... + a_{j_k} x_{j_k} \geq c)$, if $j_1, ..., j_k$ is a permutation of $1, ..., k$ (permutation)

I4. $(a_1 x_1 + ... + a_k x_k \geq c) \wedge (a'_1 x_1 + ... + a'_k x_k \geq c') \rightarrow ((a_1 + a'_1) x_1 + ... + (a_k + a'_k) x_k \geq (c + c'))$ (addition of coefficients)

I5. $(a_1 x_1 + ... + a_k x_k \geq c) \leftrightarrow (d a_1 x_1 + ... + d a_k x_k \geq dc)$ if $d > 0$ (multiplication of non-zero coefficients)

I6. $(t \geq c) \vee (t \leq c)$ if t is a term (dichotomy)

I7. $(t \geq c) \rightarrow (t > d)$ if t is a term and $c > d$ (monotonicity).

Reasoning About Probabilities:

W1. $w(\phi) \geq 0$ (nonnegativity).

W2. $w(\phi \vee \psi) = w(\phi) + w(\psi)$, if $\neg(\phi \wedge \psi)$ is an instance of a classical propositional tautology (finite additivity).

W3. $w(\top) = 1$

P-Dis. From $\phi \leftrightarrow \psi$ infer $w(\phi) = w(\psi)$ (probabilistic distributivity).

The axiom Taut allows all $\mathcal{L}_{deontic}$-instances and $\mathcal{L}_{prob-d}$-instances of propositional tautologies. For example, $w(Oq) \geq 0.9 \vee \neg w(Oq) \geq 0.9$ is an instance of Taut, but $w(Oq) \geq 0.9 \vee \neg w(Oq) \geq 1$ is not. Note that Modus Ponens (MP) can be applied to both types of formulas, but only if θ and θ' are both from $\mathcal{L}_{deontic}$ or both from $\mathcal{L}_{prob-d}$. O-Nec is a deontic variant of necessitation rule. P-Dis is an inference rule which states that two equivalent deontic formulas must have the same probability values.

Definition 9 (Syntactical consequence). *A derivation of* θ *is a finite sequence* $\theta_1, \ldots, \theta_m$ *of formulas such that* $\theta_m = \theta$, *and every* θ_i *is either an instance of an axiom, or it is obtained by the application of an inference rule to formulas in the sequence that appear before* θ_i. *If there is a derivation of* θ, *we say that* θ *is a theorem and write* $\vdash \theta$. *We also say that* θ *is derivable from a set of formulas* Γ, *and write* $\Gamma \vdash \theta$, *if there is a finite sequence* $\theta_1, \ldots, \theta_m$ *of formulas such that* $\theta_m = \theta$, *and every* θ_i *is either a theorem, a member of* Γ, *or the result of an application of MP. or P-Nec. to formulas in the sequence that appear before* θ_i.

Note that this definition restricts the application of O-Nec. to theorems only. This is a standard restriction for modal necessitations, which enables one to prove Deduction theorem using induction on the length of the inference. Also, note that only deontic formulas can participate in a proof of another deontic formula, thus derivations of deontic formulas in our logic coincide with their derivations in MDL.

Definition 10 (Consistency). *A set* Γ *is consistent if* $\Gamma \nvdash \bot$, *and inconsistent otherwise.*

Now we prove some basic consequences of $AX_{\mathcal{PDL}}$. The first one is probabilistic variant of necessitation. It captures the semantical property that a deontic formula represents certain knowledge, and therefore it must have probability value 1. The third part of the lemma shows that a form of additivity proposed as an axiom in [4] is provable in $AX_{\mathcal{PDL}}$.

Lemma 1. *The following rules are derivable from our axiomatization:*

1. *From* ϕ *infer* $w(\phi) = 1$
2. $\vdash w(\bot) = 0$
3. $\vdash w(\phi \wedge \psi) + w(\phi \wedge \neg\psi) = w(\phi)$.

Proof.

1. Let us assume that a formula ϕ is derived. Then, using propositional reasoning (Taut and MP), one can infer $\phi \leftrightarrow \top$. Consequently, $w(\phi) = w(\top)$ follows from the rule P-Dis. Since we have that $w(\top) = 1$ (by W3), we can employ the axioms for reasoning about inequalities to infer $w(\phi) = 1$.
2. Then to show that $w(\bot) = 0$ using finite additivity (W2) $w(\top \vee \neg\top) = w(\top) + w(\neg\top) = 1$ and so $w(\neg\top) = 1 - w(\top)$. Since $w(\top) = 1$ and $\neg\top \leftrightarrow \bot$ we can derive $w(\bot) = 0$.
3. To derive additivity we begin with the propositional tautology, $\neg((\phi \wedge \psi) \wedge (\phi \wedge \neg\psi))$ then the following equation is given by W2 $w(\phi \wedge \psi) + w(\phi \wedge \neg\psi) = w((\phi \wedge \psi) \vee (\phi \wedge \neg\psi))$. The disjunction $(\phi \wedge \psi) \vee (\phi \wedge \neg\psi)$ can be rewritten to, $\phi \wedge (\psi \vee \neg\psi)$ which is equivalent to ϕ. From $\phi \leftrightarrow (\phi \wedge \psi) \vee (\phi \wedge \neg\psi)$, using P-Dis, we obtain $w(\phi) = w(\phi \wedge \psi) + w(\phi \wedge \neg\psi)$.

4   Soundness and Completeness

In this section, we prove that our logic is sound and complete with respect to the class of measurable models, combining and adapting the approaches from [2,4].

Theorem 1 (Soundness & Completeness). *The axiom system $AX_{\mathcal{PDL}}$ is sound and complete with respect to the class of measurable probabilistic deontic models. i.e., $\vdash \theta$ iff $\models \theta$.*

Proof. The proof of soundness is straightforward. To prove completeness, we need to show that every consistent formula θ is satisfied in a measurable model. Since we have two types of formulas, we distinguish two cases.

If $\theta \in \mathcal{L}_{deontic}$ we write θ as ϕ. Since ϕ is consistent and monadic deontic logic is complete [9], we know that there is a MDL model (W, R, V) and $w \in W$ such that $(W, R, V), w \models \phi$. Then, for any probabilistic deontic model M with only one state s and $\tau(s) = ((W, R, V), w)$ we have $M, s \models \phi$, and therefore $M \models \phi$ (since s is the only state); so the formula is satisfiable.

When $\theta \in \mathcal{L}_{prob-d}$ we write θ as f, and assuming consistency of, f we need to prove that it is satisfiable. First notice that f can be equivalently rewritten as a formula in disjunctive normal form,

$$f \leftrightarrow g_1 \vee \cdots \vee g_n$$

this means that satisfiability of f can be proven by showing that one of the disjuncts g_i of the disjunctive normal form of f is satisfiable. Note that every disjunct is of the form

$$g_i = \bigwedge_{j=1}^{r} (\sum_k a_{j,k} w(\phi_{j,k}) \geq c_j) \wedge \bigwedge_{j=r+1}^{r+s} \neg(\sum_k a_{j,k} w(\phi_{j,k}) \geq c_j)$$

In order to show that g_i is satisfiable we will substitute each weight term $w(\phi_{j,k})$ by a sum of weight terms that take as arguments formulas from the set Δ that will be constructed below. For any formula θ, let us denote the set of subformulas of θ by $Sub(\theta)$. Then, for considered, g_i we introduce the set of all deontic subformulas $Sub_{DL}(g_i) = Sub(g_i) \cap \mathcal{L}_{deontic}$. We create the set Δ as the set of all possible formulas that are conjunctions of formulas from $Sub_{DL}(g_i) \cup \{\neg e \mid e \in Sub_{DL}(g_i)\}$, such that for every e either e or $\neg e$ is taken as a conjunct (but not both). Then we can prove the following two claims about the set Δ:

- The conjunction of any two different formulas δ_k and δ_l from Δ is inconsistent: $\vdash \neg(\delta_k \wedge \delta_l)$. This is the case because for each pair of δ's at least one subformula $e \in Sub(\phi)$ such that $\delta_k \wedge \delta_l \vdash e \wedge \neg e$ and $e \wedge \neg e \vdash \bot$. If there is no such, e then by construction $\delta_k = \delta_l$.
- The disjunction of all δ's in Δ is a tautology: $\vdash \bigvee_{\delta \in \Delta} \delta$. Indeed, it is clear from the way the set Δ is constructed, that the disjunction of all formulas is an instance of a propositional tautology.

As noted earlier, we will substitute each term of each weight formula of g_i by a sum of weight terms. This can be done by using the just introduced set Δ and the set Φ, which we define as the set containing all deontic formulas $\phi_{j,k}$ that occur in the weight terms of g_i. In order to get all the relevant δ's to represent a weight term, we construct for each $\phi \in \Phi$ the set $\Delta_\phi = \{\delta \in \Delta \mid \delta \vdash \phi\}$ which contains all δ's that imply ϕ. Then we can derive the following equivalence:

$$\vdash \phi \leftrightarrow \bigvee_{\delta \in \Delta_\phi} \delta.$$

From the rule P-Dis we obtain

$$\vdash w(\phi) = w(\bigvee_{\delta \in \Delta_\phi} \delta).$$

Since any two elements of Δ are inconsistent, from W2 and axioms about inequalities we obtain $\vdash w(\bigvee_{\delta \in \Delta_\phi} \delta) = \sum_{\delta \in \Delta_\phi} w(\delta)$. Consequently, we have

$$\vdash w(\phi) = \sum_{\delta \in \Delta_\phi} w(\delta).$$

Note that some of the formulas δ's might be inconsistent (for example, a formula from Δ might be a conjunction in which both Op and $F(p \wedge q)$ appear as conjuncts). For an inconsistent formula δ, we have $\vdash \delta \leftrightarrow \bot$ and, consequently $\vdash w(\delta) = 0$, by the inference rule P-Dis. This can provably filter out the inconsistent δ's from each weight formula, using the axioms about linear inequalities. Thus, without any loss of generality, we can assume in the rest of the proof that all the formulas from Δ are consistent[1].

Lets us consider a new formula f', created by substituting each term of each weight formula of g_i:

$$f' = \left(\bigwedge_{j=1}^{r} (\sum_k a_{j,k} \sum_{\delta \in \Delta_{\phi_{j,k}}} w(\delta) \geq c_j) \right) \wedge \left(\bigwedge_{j=r+1}^{r+s} \neg (\sum_k a_{j,k} \sum_{\delta \in \Delta_{\phi_{j,k}}} w(\delta) \geq c_j) \right)$$

Then we will construct f'' by adding to f': a non-negativity constraint and an equality that binds the total probability weight of δ's to 1. In other words, f'' is the conjunction of the following formulas:

---

[1] We might introduce Δ^c and Δ_ϕ^c as the sets of all consistent formulas from Δ and Δ_ϕ, respectively, but since we will still have $\vdash w(\phi) = \sum_{\delta \in \Delta_\phi^c} w(\delta)$, we prefer not to burden the notation with the superscripts in the rest of the proof, and we assume that we do not have inconsistent formulas in Δ.

$$\sum_{\delta \in \Delta} w(\delta) = 1$$

$$\forall \delta \in \Delta \qquad\qquad\qquad w(\delta) \geq 0$$

$$\forall l \in \{1, \ldots, r\} \qquad \sum_k a_{l,k} \sum_{\delta \in \Delta_{\phi_{l,k}}} w(\delta) \geq c_l$$

$$\forall l \in \{r+1, \ldots, r+s\} \qquad \sum_k a_{l,k} \sum_{\delta \in \Delta_{\phi_{l,k}}} w(\delta) < c_l$$

Since the weights can be attributed independently while respecting the system of equations, the formula f'' is satisfiable if the following system of equations is solvable. With $I = \{1, \ldots, |\Delta|\}$:

$$\sum_{i=1}^{|\Delta|} x_i = 1$$

$$\forall i \in I \qquad\qquad\qquad x_i \geq 0$$

$$\forall l \in \{1, \ldots, r\} \qquad \sum_k a_{l,k} \sum_{i=1}^{|\Delta_{\phi_{l,k}}|} x_i \geq c_l$$

$$\forall l \in \{r+1, \ldots, r+s\} \qquad \sum_k a_{l,k} \sum_{i=1}^{|\Delta_{\phi_{l,k}}|} x_i < c_l$$

Each δ can be identified as a state in the universe of the probability structure. Since MDL is complete, each state in the probability structure corresponds with a pointed deontic model's state via the identification function τ. Furthermore, $w()$ abides to the rules of probability measures due to the axiom system. This means that to prove satisfiability, only a probability measure should be found that corresponds with the representation f'. By adding the constraints to the representation, we can find a probability measure by solving the system of linear inequalities f'' using the axioms for reasoning with inequalities I1-I7. We took f in the beginning of the proof to be a consistent formula and f is either satisfiable or unsatisfiable. When the system can be shown to be satisfiable we have proven completeness, satisfiability of f is proven when satisfiability of f'' is shown. This is the case because if f'' is satisfiable then so is f' which means g_i is satisfiable and if g_i is satisfiable then f is satisfiable. Assume f'' is unsatisfiable then $\neg f''$ is provable from the axioms I1-I7. As just explained f's satisfiability is equivalent to that of f''. Then $\neg f$ is provable, which means that f is inconsistent. This is a contradiction, and therefore we have to reject that f'' is unsatisfiable and to conclude that f is satisfiable.

5 Decidability

In this section, we prove that our logic is decidable. First, let us recall the satisfiability problem: given a formula θ, we want to determine if there exists a model M such that $M \models \theta$.

Theorem 2 (Decidability). *Satisfiability problem for $\mathcal{PDL}$ is decidable.*

Proof. (Sketch). Since we have two types of formulas, we will consider two cases. First, let us assume that $\theta \in \mathcal{L}_{deontic}$. We start with the well-known result that the problem of whether a formula from $\mathcal{L}_{deontic}$ is satisfiable in a standard monadic deontic model is decidable. It is sufficient to show that each $\theta \in \mathcal{L}_{deontic}$ is satisfiable in a monadic deontic model iff it is satisfiable under our semantics. First, if $(W', R', V'), w' \models \theta$ for some deontic model (W', R', V') and $w' \in W'$, let us construct the model $M = \langle S, \mathscr{X}, \mu, \tau \rangle$, with $S = \{s\}$, $\mathscr{X} = \{\emptyset, S\}$, $\mu(S) = 1$ and $\tau(s) = ((W', R', V'), w')$. Since $(W', R', V'), w' \models \theta$, then $M, s \models \theta$. From the fact that s is the unique state of M, we conclude that $M \models \theta$. On the other hand, if θ is not satisfiable in standard monadic deontic logic, then for every $M = \langle S, \mathscr{X}, \mu, \tau \rangle$ and $s \in S$ we will have $M, s \not\models \theta$, so $M \not\models \theta$.

Now, let us consider the case $\theta \in \mathcal{L}_{prob-d}$. In the proof, we use the method of filtration [2,8], and reduction to finite systems of inequalities. We only provide a sketch of the proof, since we use similar ideas as in our completeness proof. We will also use notation introduced in the proof of completeness. In the first part of the proof, we show that a formula is satisfiable iff it is satisfiable in a model with a finite number of (1) states and (2) worlds.

(1) First we show that if $\theta \in \mathcal{L}_{prob-d}$ is satisfiable, then it is satisfiable in a model with a finite set of states, whose size is at most $2^{|Sub_{DL}(\theta)|}$ (where $Sub_{DL}(\theta)$ is the set of deontic subformulas of θ, as defined in the proof of Theorem 1). Let $M = \langle S, \mathscr{X}, \mu, \tau \rangle$ be a model such that $M \models \theta$. Let us define by $\sim$ the equivalence relation over $S \times S$ in the following way: $s \sim s'$ iff for every $\phi \in Sub_{DL}(\theta)$, $M, s \models \phi$ iff $s' \models \phi$. Then the corresponding quotient set $S_{/\sim}$ is finite and $|S_{/\sim}| \leq 2^{|Sub_{DL}(\theta)|}$. Note that every C_i belongs to $\mathscr{X}$, since it corresponds to a formula δ_i of Δ (from the proof of Theorem 1), i.e., $C_i = \|\delta_i\|$. Next, for every equivalence class C_i we choose one element and denote it s_i. Then we consider the model $M' = \langle S', \mathscr{X}', \mu', \tau' \rangle$, where:

- $S' = \{s_i \mid C_i \in S_{/\sim}\}$,
- $\mathscr{X}'$ is the power set of S',
- $\mu'(\{s_i\}) = \mu(C_i)$ such that $s_i \in C_i$ and for any $X \subseteq S'$, $\mu'(X) = \sum_{s_i \in X} \mu'(\{s_i\})$,
- $\tau'(s_i) = \tau(s_i)$.

Then it is straightforward to verify that $M' \models \theta$. Moreover, note that, by definition of M', for every $s_i \in S$ there is $\delta_i \in \Delta$ such that $M', s_i \models \delta_i$, and that for every $s_j \neq s_i$ we have $M', s_j \not\models \delta_i$. We therefore say that δ_i is the *characteristic formula* of s_i.

(2) Even if S' is finite, some sets of worlds attached to a state might be infinite. Now we will modify τ', in order to ensure that every $W(s_i)$ is finite, and of the size which is bounded by a number that depends on the size of θ. In this part of the proof we refer to the filtration method used to prove completeness of MDL [2], which shows that if a deontic formula ϕ is satisfiable, that it is satisfied in a world of a model $D(\psi) = (W, R, V)$ where the size of W is at most exponential wrt. the size of the set of subformulas of ϕ. Then we can replace τ' with a function τ'' which assigns to each s_i one such $D(\delta_i)$ and the corresponding world, where δ_i is the characteristic formula of s_i. We also assume that each $V(s_i)$ is restricted to the propositional letters from $Sub_{DL}(\theta)$. Finally, let $M'' = \langle S', \mathcal{X}', \mu', \tau'' \rangle$ It is easy to check that for every $\phi \in Sub_{DL}(\theta)$ and $s_i \in S'$, $M', s_i \models \phi$ iff $M'', s_i \models \phi$. Therefore, $M'' \models \theta$.

From the steps (1) and (2) it follows that in order to check if a formula $\theta \in \mathcal{L}_{prob-d}$ is satisfiable, it is enough to check if it is satisfied in a model $M = \langle S, \mathcal{X}, \mu, \tau \rangle$ in which S and each W_s (for every $s \in S$) are of finite size, bounded from above by a fixed number depending on the size of $|Sub_{DL}(\theta)|$. Then there are finitely many options for the choice of S and τ (i.e., (D_s, w_s), for every $s \in S$), and our procedure can check in finite time whether there is a probability measure μ for some of them, such that θ holds in the model. We guess S and τ and check whether we can assign probability values to the states from S, using translation to a system of linear inequalities, in the same way as we have done in the proof of Theorem 1. This finishes the proof, since the problem of checking whether a linear system of inequalities has a solution is decidable.

6 Conclusion

In this article, we introduced the probabilistic deontic logic $\mathcal{PDL}$, a logic in which we can reason about the probability of deontic statements. We proposed a language that extends both monadic deontic logic and probability logic from [4]. We axiomatized that language and proved soundness and completeness with respect to corresponding semantics. We also proved that our logic is decidable.

To the best of our knowledge, we are the first to propose a logic for reasoning about probabilistic uncertainty about norms. It is worth mentioning that there is a recent knowledge representation framework about probabilistic uncertainty in deontic reasoning obtained by merging deontic argumentation and probabilistic argumentation frameworks [10].

Our logic $\mathcal{PDL}$ used MDL as the underlying framework, we used this logic simply because it is one of the most studied deontic logics. On the other hand, MDL is also criticized because of some issues, like representation of contrary-to-duty obligations. It is important to point out that the axiomatization technique developed in this work can be also applied if we replace MDL with, for example, dyadic deontic logic, simply by changing the set of deontic axioms and the function τ in the definition of model, which would lead to a more expressive framework for reasoning about uncertain norms. Another avenue for future research is to extend the language by allowing conditional probabilities. In such a logic, it would be possible to express that one uncertain norm becomes more certain if another norm is accepted or learned.

References

1. Boella, G., van der Torre, L.W.N., Verhagen, H.: Introduction to normative multi-agent systems. Comput. Math. Organ. Theor. **12**(2–3), 71–79 (2006). https://doi.org/10.1007/s10588-006-9537-7
2. Chellas, B.F.: Modal Logic: An Introduction. Cambridge University Press (1980). https://doi.org/10.1017/CBO9780511621192
3. Fagin, R., Halpern, J.Y.: Reasoning about knowledge and probability. J. ACM **41**(2), 340–367 (1994)
4. Fagin, R., Halpern, J.Y., Megiddo, N.: A logic for reasoning about probabilities. Inf. Computat. **87**(1), 78–128 (1990)
5. Frisch, A., Haddawy, P.: Anytime deduction for probabilistic logic. Artif. Intell. **69**, 93–122 (1994)
6. van der Hoek, W.: Some considerations on the logic pfd. J. Appl. Non Class. Logics **7**(3), 287–307 (1997)
7. Horty, J.F.: Agency and Deontic Logic. Oxford University Press (2001)
8. Hughes, G.E., Cresswell, M.J.: A Companion to Modal Logic. Methuen London, New York (1984)
9. Parent, X., Van Der Torre, L.: Introduction to Deontic Logic and Normative Systems. Texts in Logic and Reasoning. College Publications (2018). https://books.google.nl/books?id=IyUYwQEACAAJ
10. Riveret, R., Oren, N., Sartor, G.: A probabilistic deontic argumentation framework. Int. J. Approximate Reason. **126**, 249–271 (2020)
11. Sarathy, V., Scheutz, M., Malle, B.F.: Learning behavioral norms in uncertain and changing contexts. In: 2017 8th IEEE International Conference on Cognitive Infocommunications (CogInfoCom), pp. 000301–000306 (2017). https://doi.org/10.1109/CogInfoCom.2017.8268261
12. Savic, N., Doder, D., Ognjanovic, Z.: Logics with lower and upper probability operators. Int. J. Approx. Reason. **88**, 148–168 (2017)
13. Tomic, S., Pecora, F., Saffiotti, A.: Learning normative behaviors through abstraction. In: Giacomo, G.D. (eds.) 24th European Conference on Artificial Intelligence, ECAI 2020, 29 August–8 September 2020, Santiago de Compostela, Spain, Including 10th Conference on Prestigious Applications of Artificial Intelligence (PAIS 2020). Frontiers in Artificial Intelligence and Applications, vol. 325, pp. 1547–1554. IOS Press (2020). https://doi.org/10.3233/FAIA200263
14. von Wrigth, G.H.: I. Deontic logic. Mind **LX**(237), 1–15 (1951). https://doi.org/10.1093/mind/LX.237.1

Iterated Conditionals and Characterization of P-Entailment

Angelo Gilio[1] and Giuseppe Sanfilippo[2(✉)]

[1] Department SBAI, University of Rome "La Sapienza", Rome, Italy
angelo.gilio@sbai.uniroma1.it
[2] Department of Mathematics and Computer Science,
University of Palermo, Palermo, Italy
giuseppe.sanfilippo@unipa.it

Abstract. In this paper we deepen, in the setting of coherence, some results obtained in recent papers on the notion of p-entailment of Adams and its relationship with conjoined and iterated conditionals. We recall that conjoined and iterated conditionals are suitably defined in the framework of conditional random quantities. Given a family $\mathcal{F}$ of n conditional events $\{E_1|H_1, \ldots, E_n|H_n\}$ we denote by $\mathcal{C}(\mathcal{F}) = (E_1|H_1) \wedge \cdots \wedge (E_n|H_n)$ the conjunction of the conditional events in $\mathcal{F}$. We introduce the iterated conditional $\mathcal{C}(\mathcal{F}_2)|\mathcal{C}(\mathcal{F}_1)$, where $\mathcal{F}_1$ and $\mathcal{F}_2$ are two finite families of conditional events, by showing that the prevision of $\mathcal{C}(\mathcal{F}_2) \wedge \mathcal{C}(\mathcal{F}_1)$ is the product of the prevision of $\mathcal{C}(\mathcal{F}_2)|\mathcal{C}(\mathcal{F}_1)$ and the prevision of $\mathcal{C}(\mathcal{F}_1)$. Likewise the well known equality $(A \wedge H)|H = A|H$, we show that $(\mathcal{C}(\mathcal{F}_2) \wedge \mathcal{C}(\mathcal{F}_1))|\mathcal{C}(\mathcal{F}_1) = \mathcal{C}(\mathcal{F}_2)|\mathcal{C}(\mathcal{F}_1)$. Then, we consider the case $\mathcal{F}_1 = \mathcal{F}_2 = \mathcal{F}$ and we verify for the prevision μ of $\mathcal{C}(\mathcal{F})|\mathcal{C}(\mathcal{F})$ that the unique coherent assessment is $\mu = 1$ and, as a consequence, $\mathcal{C}(\mathcal{F})|\mathcal{C}(\mathcal{F})$ coincides with the constant 1. Finally, by assuming $\mathcal{F}$ p-consistent, we deepen some previous characterizations of p-entailment by showing that $\mathcal{F}$ p-entails a conditional event $E_{n+1}|H_{n+1}$ if and only if the iterated conditional $(E_{n+1}|H_{n+1})|\mathcal{C}(\mathcal{F})$ is constant and equal to 1. We illustrate this characterization by an example related with weak transitivity.

Keywords: Coherence · Conditional events · Conditional random quantities · Conditional previsions · Conjoined conditionals · Iterated conditionals · Probabilistic entailment

1 Introduction

The study of logical operations among conditional events has been considered in many papers (see, e.g., [2,11,12,16,21,37,39,42,43]). In a pioneering paper, written in 1935, de Finetti [20] proposed a three-valued logic for conditional

---

A. Gilio and G. Sanfilippo—Both authors contributed equally to the article and are listed alphabetically.
A. Gilio—Retired.

J. Vejnarová and N. Wilson (Eds.): ECSQARU 2021, LNAI 12897, pp. 629–643, 2021.
https://doi.org/10.1007/978-3-030-86772-0_45

events. Many often, conjunctions and disjunctions have been defined as suitable conditional events (see, e.g., [1,4–7,37]). However, in this way classical probabilistic properties are lost. For instance, the lower and upper probability bounds for the conjunction are no more the Fréchet-Hoeffding bounds [45]. A more general approach to conjunction has been given in [39,42] and, in the setting of coherence, in [27,28,31–33], where also the notion of iterated conditional has been studied. In these papers the notions of compound and iterated conditionals are defined as suitable *conditional random quantities* with a finite number of possible values in the interval $[0,1]$. The main relevance of our approach is theoretical: indeed, all the basic probabilistic properties are preserved (for a synthesis see [36]). For instance, De Morgan's Laws are satisfied [33] and the Fréchet-Hoeffding bounds for the conjunction of conditional events still hold [35]. A suitable notion of conditional constituent can be introduced, with properties analogous to the case of unconditional events; moreover, a generalized inclusion-exclusion formula for the disjunction of conditional events is valid [34]. We also recall that the Lewis' triviality results [41] are avoided because in our theory the Import-Export Principle is not valid (see [31,46,48]). For some applications of compound and iterated conditionals see, e.g., [24,26,46–48]. More specifically, by exploiting iterated conditionals, the probabilistic modus ponens has been generalized to conditional events [47]; one-premise and two-premise centering inferences, related to the notion of centering used in Lewis' logic [40], has been examined in [24,48]. In [46] several (generalized) iterated conditionals have been considered, in order to properly formalize different kinds of latent information; in particular, some intuitive probabilistic assessments discussed in [15] have been explained, by making explicit some background information.

An interesting aspect which could be possibly investigated concerns the relationship of our notions of compound and iterated conditionals with other topics of research, such as belief and plausibility functions, data fusion, inductive reasoning, and fuzzy logic [8–10,13,17–19,38,44,49]. For instance, by recalling [10], an application of our notion of conjunction could be given by interpreting the membership function of the cartesian product of fuzzy sets as the prevision of conjoined conditionals.

By exploiting conjunction a characterization of the probabilistic entailment of Adams [1] for conditionals has been given in [33]. Moreover, by exploiting iterated conditionals, the p-entailment of $E_3|H_3$ from a p-consistent family $\mathcal{F} = \{E_1|H_1, E_2|H_2\}$ has been characterized by the property that the iterated conditional $(E_3|H_3)|((E_1|H_1) \wedge (E_2|H_2))$ is constant and coincides with 1 [26]. In this paper, based on a general notion of iterated conditional, we extend this characterization of p-entailment by considering the case where $\mathcal{F}$ is a family of n conditional events.

The paper is organized as follows. After recalling in Sect. 2 some preliminary notions and results, in Sect. 3 we introduce the iterated conditional $\mathcal{C}(\mathcal{F}_2)|\mathcal{C}(\mathcal{F}_1)$, where $\mathcal{C}(\mathcal{F}_1)$ and $\mathcal{C}(\mathcal{F}_2)$ are the conjunctions of the conditional events in two finite families $\mathcal{F}_1$ and $\mathcal{F}_2$. We show that $(\mathcal{C}(F_2) \wedge \mathcal{C}(\mathcal{F}_1))|\mathcal{C}(\mathcal{F}_1) = \mathcal{C}(\mathcal{F}_2)|\mathcal{C}(\mathcal{F}_1)$ and $\mathbb{P}[\mathcal{C}(\mathcal{F}_2) \wedge \mathcal{C}(\mathcal{F}_1)] = \mathbb{P}[\mathcal{C}(\mathcal{F}_2)|\mathcal{C}(\mathcal{F}_1)]\mathbb{P}[\mathcal{C}(\mathcal{F}_1)]$. Then, we prove that $\mathcal{C}(\mathcal{F})|\mathcal{C}(\mathcal{F})$ is constant and coincides with 1. In Sect. 3, by assuming $\mathcal{F}$ p-consistent, we characterize the p-entailment of $E_{n+1}|H_{n+1}$ from $\mathcal{F}$ by the property that the iterated conditional $(E_{n+1}|H_{n+1})|\mathcal{C}(\mathcal{F})$ is constant and coincides with 1. We also illustrate this characterization by an example related with weak transitivity.

2   Preliminary Notions and Results

An event A is a two-valued logical entity which is either *true*, or *false*. We use the same symbol to refer to an event and its indicator. We denote by Ω the sure event and by $\varnothing$ the impossible one. We denote by $A \wedge B$ (resp., $A \vee B$), or simply by AB, the conjunction (resp., disjunction) of A and B. By $\bar{A}$ we denote the negation of A. We simply write $A \subseteq B$ to denote that A logically implies B. Given two events A and H, with $H \neq \varnothing$, the conditional event $A|H$ is a three-valued logical entity which is *true*, or *false*, or *void*, according to whether AH is true, or $\bar{A}H$ is true, or $\bar{H}$ is true, respectively. The negation $\overline{A|H}$ of $A|H$ is defined as $\bar{A}|H$.

In the betting framework, to assess $P(A|H) = x$ amounts to say that, for every real number s, you are willing to pay an amount $s\,x$ and to receive s, or 0, or $s\,x$, according to whether AH is true, or $\bar{A}H$ is true, or $\bar{H}$ is true (bet called off), respectively. Hence, for the random gain $G = sH(A-x)$, the possible values are $s(1-x)$, or $-s\,x$, or 0, according to whether AH is true, or $\bar{A}H$ is true, or $\bar{H}$ is true, respectively. We denote by X a *random quantity*, that is an uncertain real quantity, which has a well determined but unknown value. We assume that X has a finite set of possible values. Given any event $H \neq \varnothing$, agreeing to the betting metaphor, if you assess that the prevision of "X *conditional on* H" (or short: "X *given* H"), $\mathbb{P}(X|H)$, is equal to μ, this means that for any given real number s you are willing to pay an amount $s\mu$ and to receive sX, or $s\mu$, according to whether H is true, or false (bet called off), respectively. In particular, when X is (the indicator of) an event A, then $\mathbb{P}(X|H) = P(A|H)$. Given a conditional event $A|H$ with $P(A|H) = x$, the indicator of $A|H$, denoted by the same symbol, is

$$A|H = AH + x\bar{H} = AH + x(1 - H) = \begin{cases} 1, & \text{if } AH \text{ is true,} \\ 0, & \text{if } \bar{A}H \text{ is true,} \\ x, & \text{if } \bar{H} \text{ is true.} \end{cases} \qquad (1)$$

Notice that, denoting by $\mathbb{P}$ the prevision, it holds that $\mathbb{P}(AH + x\bar{H}) = xP(H) + xP(\bar{H}) = x$. The third value of the random quantity $A|H$ (subjectively) depends on the assessed probability $P(A|H) = x$. When $H \subseteq A$ (i.e., $AH = H$), it holds that $P(A|H) = 1$; then, for the indicator $A|H$ it holds that

$$A|H = AH + x\bar{H} = H + \bar{H} = 1, \quad \text{(when } H \subseteq A\text{)}. \qquad (2)$$

Likewise, if $AH = \varnothing$, it holds that $P(A|H) = 0$; then

$$A|H = 0 + 0\bar{H} = 0, \quad \text{(when } AH = \varnothing\text{)}.$$

For the indicator of the negation of $A|H$ it holds that $\bar{A}|H = 1 - A|H$. Given a random quantity X and an event $H \neq \varnothing$, with a prevision assessment $\mathbb{P}(X|H) = \mu$, in our approach, likewise formula (1), the conditional random quantity $X|H$

is defined as $X|H = XH + \mu\bar{H}$. Notice that $\mathbb{P}(XH + \mu\bar{H}) = \mathbb{P}(XH) + \mu P(\bar{H}) = \mu P(H) + \mu P(\bar{H}) = \mu$. For a discussion on this extended notion of a conditional random quantity and on the notion of coherence of a prevision assessment see, e.g., [31,34,46]. In betting terms *coherence* means that *in any finite combination of n bets, it cannot happen that, after discarding the cases where the bet is called off, the values of the random gain are all positive, or all negative* (Dutch Book).

Remark 1. Given a conditional random quantity $X|H$ and a prevision assessment $\mathbb{P}(X|H) = \mu$, if conditionally on H being true X is constant, say $X = c$, then by coherence $\mu = c$.

Probabilistic Consistency and Probabilistic Entailment. We recall the notions of p-consistency and p-entailment of Adams [1] formulated for conditional events in the setting of coherence in [30] (see also [3,23,29]). For a discussion on deduction from uncertain premises and p-validity, under coherence, see [14].

Definition 1. *Let* $\mathcal{F}_n = \{E_i|H_i, \ i = 1,\ldots,n\}$ *be a family of n conditional events. Then,* $\mathcal{F}_n$ *is p-consistent if and only if the probability assessment* $(p_1, p_2, \ldots, p_n) = (1,1,\ldots,1)$ *on* $\mathcal{F}_n$ *is coherent.*

Definition 2. *A p-consistent family* $\mathcal{F}_n = \{E_i|H_i, \ i = 1,\ldots,n\}$ *p-entails a conditional event* $E|H$ *(denoted by* $\mathcal{F}_n \Rightarrow_p E|H$ *) if and only if for any coherent probability assessment* $(p_1,\ldots,p_n,z)$ *on* $\mathcal{F}_n \cup \{E|H\}$ *it holds that: if* $p_1 = \cdots = p_n = 1$, *then* $z = 1$.

The inference from $\mathcal{F}_n$ to $E|H$ is p-valid if and only if $\mathcal{F}_n \Rightarrow_p E|H$ [1].
Logical operations among conditional events. We recall below the notion of conjunction of two conditional events [31].

Definition 3. *Given any pair of conditional events* $E_1|H_1$ *and* $E_2|H_2$, *with* $P(E_1|H_1) = x_1$ *and* $P(E_2|H_2) = x_2$, *their conjunction* $(E_1|H_1) \wedge (E_2|H_2)$ *is the conditional random quantity defined as*

$$(E_1|H_1) \wedge (E_2|H_2) = (E_1 H_1 E_2 H_2 + x_1 \bar{H}_1 E_2 H_2 + x_2 \bar{H}_2 E_1 H_1)|(H_1 \vee H_2)$$
$$= \begin{cases} 1, & \text{if } E_1 H_1 E_2 H_2 \text{ is true,} \\ 0, & \text{if } \bar{E}_1 H_1 \vee \bar{E}_2 H_2 \text{ is true,} \\ x_1, & \text{if } \bar{H}_1 E_2 H_2 \text{ is true,} \\ x_2, & \text{if } \bar{H}_2 E_1 H_1 \text{ is true,} \\ x_{12}, & \text{if } \bar{H}_1 \bar{H}_2 \text{ is true,} \end{cases} \tag{3}$$

where $x_{12} = \mathbb{P}[(E_1|H_1) \wedge (E_2|H_2)] = \mathbb{P}[(E_1 H_1 E_2 H_2 + x_1 \bar{H}_1 E_2 H_2 + x_2 \bar{H}_2 E_1 H_1)|(H_1 \vee H_2)]$.

In betting terms, the prevision x_{12} represents the amount you agree to pay, with the proviso that you will receive the quantity $E_1 H_1 E_2 H_2 + x_1 \bar{H}_1 E_2 H_2 + x_2 \bar{H}_2 E_1 H_1$, or you will receive back the quantity x_{12}, according to whether $H_1 \vee H_2$ is true, or $\bar{H}_1 \bar{H}_2$ is true. Notice that, differently from conditional events which are three-valued objects, the conjunction $(E_1|H_1) \wedge (E_2|H_2)$ is no longer a three-valued object, but a five-valued object with values in $[0,1]$. We recall below the notion of conjunction of n conditional events.

Definition 4. *Let n conditional events $E_1|H_1, \ldots, E_n|H_n$ be given. For each non-empty strict subset S of $\{1, \ldots, n\}$, let x_S be a prevision assessment on $\bigwedge_{i \in S}(E_i|H_i)$. Then, the conjunction $(E_1|H_1) \wedge \cdots \wedge (E_n|H_n)$ is the conditional random quantity $\mathcal{C}_{1 \cdots n}$ defined as*

$$\mathcal{C}_{1 \cdots n} = [\bigwedge_{i=1}^{n} E_i H_i + \sum_{\varnothing \neq S \subset \{1,2 \ldots, n\}} x_S(\bigwedge_{i \in S} \bar{H}_i) \wedge (\bigwedge_{i \notin S} E_i H_i)]|(\bigvee_{i=1}^{n} H_i)$$

$$= \begin{cases} 1, & \text{if } \bigwedge_{i=1}^{n} E_i H_i \text{ is true,} \\ 0, & \text{if } \bigvee_{i=1}^{n} \bar{E}_i H_i \text{ is true,} \\ x_S, & \text{if } (\bigwedge_{i \in S} \bar{H}_i) \wedge (\bigwedge_{i \notin S} E_i H_i) \text{ is true, } \varnothing \neq S \subset \{1, 2 \ldots, n\}, \\ x_{1 \cdots n}, & \text{if } \bigwedge_{i=1}^{n} \bar{H}_i \text{ is true,} \end{cases} \quad (4)$$

where

$$x_{1 \cdots n} = x_{\{1, \ldots, n\}} = \mathbb{P}(\mathcal{C}_{1 \cdots n})$$
$$= \mathbb{P}[(\bigwedge_{i=1}^{n} E_i H_i + \sum_{\varnothing \neq S \subset \{1,2 \ldots, n\}} x_S(\bigwedge_{i \in S} \bar{H}_i) \wedge (\bigwedge_{i \notin S} E_i H_i))|(\bigvee_{i=1}^{n} H_i)]. \quad (5)$$

For $n = 1$ we obtain $\mathcal{C}_1 = E_1|H_1$. In Definition 4 each possible value x_S of $\mathcal{C}_{1 \cdots n}$, $\varnothing \neq S \subset \{1, \ldots, n\}$, is evaluated when defining (in a previous step) the conjunction $\mathcal{C}_S = \bigwedge_{i \in S}(E_i|H_i)$. Then, after the conditional prevision $x_{1 \cdots n}$ is evaluated, $\mathcal{C}_{1 \cdots n}$ is completely specified. Of course, we require coherence for the prevision assessment $(x_S, \varnothing \neq S \subseteq \{1, \ldots, n\})$, so that $\mathcal{C}_{1 \cdots n} \in [0, 1]$. In the framework of the betting scheme, $x_{1 \cdots n}$ is the amount that you agree to pay with the proviso that you will receive:
- the amount 1, if all conditional events are true;
- the amount 0, if at least one of the conditional events is false;
- the amount x_S equal to the prevision of the conjunction of that conditional events which are void, otherwise. In particular you receive back $x_{1 \cdots n}$ when all conditional events are void.

As we can see from (4), the conjunction $\mathcal{C}_{1 \cdots n}$ is (in general) a $(2^n + 1)$-valued object because the number of nonempty subsets S, and hence the number of possible values x_S, is $2^n - 1$. We recall a result which shows that the prevision of the conjunction on n conditional events satisfies the Frèchet-Hoeffding bounds [33, Theorem13].

Theorem 1. *Let n conditional events $E_1|H_1, \ldots, E_n|H_n$ be given, with $x_i = P(E_i|H_i)$, $i = 1, \ldots, n$ and $x_{1 \cdots n} = \mathbb{P}(\mathcal{C}_{1 \cdots n})$. Then*

$$\max\{x_1 + \cdots + x_n - n + 1, 0\} \leqslant x_{1 \cdots n} \leqslant \min\{x_1, \ldots, x_n\}.$$

In [35, Theorem 10] we have shown, under logical independence, the sharpness of the Frèchet-Hoeffding bounds.

Remark 2. Given a finite family $\mathcal{F}$ of conditional events, their conjunction is also denoted by $\mathcal{C}(\mathcal{F})$. We recall that in [33], given two finite families of conditional events $\mathcal{F}_1$ and $\mathcal{F}_2$, the object $\mathcal{C}(\mathcal{F}_1) \wedge \mathcal{C}(\mathcal{F}_2)$ is defined as $\mathcal{C}(\mathcal{F}_1 \cup \mathcal{F}_2)$. Then, conjunction satisfies the commutativity and associativity properties [33, Propositions 1 and 2]. Moreover, the operation of conjunction satisfies the monotonicity property [33, Theorem7], that is $\mathcal{C}_{1 \cdots n+1} \leqslant \mathcal{C}_{1 \cdots n}$. Then,

$$\mathcal{C}(\mathcal{F}_1 \cup \mathcal{F}_2) \leqslant \mathcal{C}(\mathcal{F}_1), \quad \mathcal{C}(\mathcal{F}_1 \cup \mathcal{F}_2) \leqslant \mathcal{C}(\mathcal{F}_2). \quad (6)$$

Iterated Conditioning. We now recall the notion of iterated conditional given in [28]. Such notion has the structure $\square|\bigcirc = \square \wedge \bigcirc + \mathbb{P}(\square|\bigcirc)\bar{\bigcirc}$, where $\mathbb{P}$ denotes the prevision, which reduces to formula (1) when $\square = A$ and $\bigcirc = H$.

Definition 5 (Iterated conditioning). *Given any pair of conditional events $E_1|H_1$ and $E_2|H_2$, with $E_1 H_1 \neq \varnothing$, the iterated conditional $(E_2|H_2)|(E_1|H_1)$ is defined as the conditional random quantity*

$$(E_2|H_2)|(E_1|H_1) = (E_2|H_2) \wedge (E_1|H_1) + \mu \bar{E}_1|H_1, \tag{7}$$

where $\mu = \mathbb{P}[(E_2|H_2)|(E_1|H_1)]$.

Remark 3. Notice that we assumed that $E_1 H_1 \neq \varnothing$ to give a nontrivial meaning to the notion of iterated conditional. Indeed, if $E_1 H_1$ were equal to $\varnothing$, then $E_1|H_1 = (E_2|H_2) \wedge (E_1|H_1) = 0$ and $\bar{E}_1|H_1 = 1$, from which it would follow $(E_2|H_2)|(E_1|H_1) = (E_2|H_2)|0 = (E_2|H_2) \wedge (E_1|H_1) + \mu \bar{E}_1|H_1 = \mu$; that is, $(E_2|H_2)|(E_1|H_1)$ would coincide with the (indeterminate) value μ. Similarly to the case of a conditional event $E|H$, which is of no interest when $H = \varnothing$, the iterated conditional $(E_2|H_2)|(E_1|H_1)$ is not considered in our approach when $E_1 H_1 = \varnothing$.

Definition 5 has been generalized in [33] to the case where the antecedent is the conjunction of more than two conditional events.

Definition 6. *Let be given $n+1$ conditional events $E_1|H_1, \ldots, E_{n+1}|H_{n+1}$, with $(E_1|H_1) \wedge \cdots \wedge (E_n|H_n) \neq 0$. We denote by $(E_{n+1}|H_{n+1})|((E_1|H_1) \wedge \cdots \wedge (E_n|H_n)) = (E_{n+1}|H_{n+1})|\mathcal{C}_{1\cdots n}$ the random quantity*

$$(E_1|H_1) \wedge \cdots \wedge (E_{n+1}|H_{n+1}) + \mu\left(1 - (E_1|H_1) \wedge \cdots \wedge (E_n|H_n)\right) =$$
$$= \mathcal{C}_{1\cdots n+1} + \mu\left(1 - \mathcal{C}_{1\cdots n}\right),$$

where $\mu = \mathbb{P}[(E_{n+1}|H_{n+1})|\mathcal{C}_{1\cdots n}]$.

We observe that, based on the betting metaphor, the quantity μ is the amount to be paid in order to receive the amount $\mathcal{C}_{1\cdots n+1} + \mu\left(1 - \mathcal{C}_{1\cdots n}\right)$. Definition 6 generalizes the notion of iterated conditional $(E_2|H_2)|(E_1|H_1)$ given in previous papers (see, e.g., [27,28,31]). We also observe that, defining $\mathbb{P}(\mathcal{C}_{1\cdots n}) = x_{1\cdots n}$ and $\mathbb{P}(\mathcal{C}_{1\cdots n+1}) = x_{1\cdots n+1}$, by the linearity of prevision it holds that $\mu = x_{1\cdots n+1} + \mu\left(1 - x_{1\cdots n}\right)$; then, $x_{1\cdots n+1} = \mu x_{1\cdots n}$, that is $\mathbb{P}(\mathcal{C}_{1\cdots n+1}) = \mathbb{P}[(E_{n+1}|H_{n+1})|\mathcal{C}_{1\cdots n}]\mathbb{P}(\mathcal{C}_{1\cdots n})$.

Characterization of p-Consistency and p-Entailment. We recall a characterization of p-consistency of a family $\mathcal{F}$ in terms of the coherence of the prevision assessment $\mathbb{P}[\mathcal{C}(\mathcal{F})] = 1$ [33, Theorem 17].

Theorem 2. *A family of n conditional events $\mathcal{F} = \{E_1|H_1, \ldots, E_n|H_n\}$ is p-consistent if and only if the prevision assessment $\mathbb{P}[\mathcal{C}(\mathcal{F})] = 1$ is coherent.*

We recall a characterization of p-entailment in terms of suitable conjunctions. [33, Theorem 18].

Theorem 3. *Let be given a p-consistent family of n conditional events $\mathcal{F} = \{E_1|H_1, \ldots, E_n|H_n\}$ and a further conditional event $E_{n+1}|H_{n+1}$. Then, the following assertions are equivalent:*
(i) $\mathcal{F}$ p-entails $E_{n+1}|H_{n+1}$;
(ii) the conjunction $(E_1|H_1) \wedge \cdots \wedge (E_n|H_n) \wedge (E_{n+1}|H_{n+1})$ coincides with the conjunction $(E_1|H_1) \wedge \cdots \wedge (E_n|H_n)$;
(iii) the inequality $(E_1|H_1) \wedge \cdots \wedge (E_n|H_n) \leqslant E_{n+1}|H_{n+1}$ is satisfied.

We recall a result where it is shown that the p-entailment of a conditional event $E_3|H_3$ from a p-consistent family $\mathcal{F} = \{E_1|H_1, E_2|H_2\}$ is equivalent to condition $(E_3|H_3)|((E_1|H_1) \wedge (E_2|H_2)) = 1$ [26, Theorem 8].

Theorem 4. *Let three conditional events $E_1|H_1$, $E_2|H_2$, and $E_3|H_3$ be given, where $\{E_1|H_1, E_2|H_2\}$ is p-consistent. Then, $\{E_1|H_1, E_2|H_2\}$ p-entails $E_3|H_3$ if and only if $(E_3|H_3)|((E_1|H_1) \wedge (E_2|H_2)) = 1$.*

Theorem 4 will be generalized in Sect. 4.

3   A General Notion of Iterated Conditional

Let a family $\mathcal{F} = \{E_1|H_1, \ldots, E_n|H_n\}$ of n conditional events be given. Moreover, let $\mathcal{M} = (x_S : \varnothing \neq S \subseteq \{1, \ldots, n\})$ be a coherent prevision assessment on the family $\{\mathcal{C}_S : \varnothing \neq S \subseteq \{1, \ldots, n\}\}$, where $\mathcal{C}_S = \bigwedge_{i \in S}(E_i|H_i)$ and $x_S = \mathbb{P}(\mathcal{C}_S)$. Denoting by Λ the set of possible values of $\mathcal{C}(\mathcal{F})$, it holds that $\Lambda \subseteq= \{1, 0, x_S : \varnothing \neq S \subseteq \{1, \ldots, n\}\}$. We observe that if $x_S = 0$ for some S, then from (6), it holds that $x_{S'} = 0$ for every S' such that $S \subset S'$. The conjunction $\mathcal{C}(\mathcal{F})$ is constant and coincides with 0 when $\Lambda = \{0\}$, in which case we write $\mathcal{C}(\mathcal{F}) = 0$. This happens when $E_1H_1 \cdots E_nH_n = \varnothing$ and for each $\varnothing \neq S \subseteq \{1, \ldots, n\}$ such that $(\bigwedge_{i \in S} \bar{H}_i) \wedge (\bigwedge_{i \notin S} E_iH_i) \neq \varnothing$ it holds that $x_S = 0$. For instance, when $E_1H_1 \cdots E_nH_n = \varnothing$ and $x_1 = \cdots = x_n = 0$, it holds that $x_S = 0$ for every S; then, $\Lambda = \{0\}$ and $\mathcal{C}(\mathcal{F})$ coincides with the constant 0. We give below a generalization of Definition 6.

Definition 7. *Let $\mathcal{F}_1$ and $\mathcal{F}_2$ be two finite families of conditional events, with $\mathcal{C}(\mathcal{F}_1) \neq 0$. We denote by $\mathcal{C}(\mathcal{F}_2)|\mathcal{C}(\mathcal{F}_1)$ the random quantity defined as*

$$\mathcal{C}(\mathcal{F}_2)|\mathcal{C}(\mathcal{F}_1) = \mathcal{C}(\mathcal{F}_2) \wedge \mathcal{C}(\mathcal{F}_1) + \mu(1 - \mathcal{C}(\mathcal{F}_1)) = \mathcal{C}(\mathcal{F}_1 \cup \mathcal{F}_2) + \mu(1 - \mathcal{C}(\mathcal{F}_1)),$$

where $\mu = \mathbb{P}[\mathcal{C}(\mathcal{F}_2)|\mathcal{C}(\mathcal{F}_1)]$.

We observe that Definition 7 reduces to Definition 6 when $\mathcal{F}_1 = \{E_1|H_1, \ldots, E_n|H_n\}$ and $\mathcal{F}_2 = \{E_{n+1}|H_{n+1}\}$. We also remark that by linearity of prevision it holds that $\mu = \mathbb{P}[\mathcal{C}(\mathcal{F}_2)|\mathcal{C}(\mathcal{F}_1)] = \mathbb{P}[\mathcal{C}(\mathcal{F}_2) \wedge \mathcal{C}(\mathcal{F}_1)] + \mu(1 - \mathbb{P}[\mathcal{C}(\mathcal{F}_1)])$, that is

$$\mathbb{P}[\mathcal{C}(\mathcal{F}_2) \wedge \mathcal{C}(\mathcal{F}_1)] = \mathbb{P}[\mathcal{C}(\mathcal{F}_2)|\mathcal{C}(\mathcal{F}_1)]\mathbb{P}[\mathcal{C}(\mathcal{F}_1)]. \tag{8}$$

Formula (8) generalizes the well known relation: $P(AH) = P(A|H)P(H)$ (*compound probability theorem*). In the following result we obtain an equivalent representation of $\mathcal{C}(\mathcal{F}_2)|\mathcal{C}(\mathcal{F}_1)$.

Theorem 5. *Let $\mathcal{F}_1$ and $\mathcal{F}_2$ be two finite families of conditional events, with $\mathcal{C}(\mathcal{F}_1) \neq 0$. It holds that*

$$\mathcal{C}(\mathcal{F}_2)|\mathcal{C}(\mathcal{F}_1) = \mathcal{C}(\mathcal{F}_1 \cup \mathcal{F}_2)|\mathcal{C}(\mathcal{F}_1) = (\mathcal{C}(\mathcal{F}_2) \wedge \mathcal{C}(\mathcal{F}_1))|\mathcal{C}(\mathcal{F}_1). \tag{9}$$

Proof. We set $\mu' = \mathbb{P}[\mathcal{C}(\mathcal{F}_2)|\mathcal{C}(\mathcal{F}_1)]$ and $\mu'' = \mathbb{P}[\mathcal{C}(\mathcal{F}_1 \cup \mathcal{F}_2)|\mathcal{C}(\mathcal{F}_1)]$. Then,

$$\mathcal{C}(\mathcal{F}_2)|\mathcal{C}(\mathcal{F}_1) = \mathcal{C}(\mathcal{F}_1 \cup \mathcal{F}_2) + \mu'(1 - \mathcal{C}(\mathcal{F}_1))$$

and

$$\mathcal{C}(\mathcal{F}_1 \cup \mathcal{F}_2)|\mathcal{C}(\mathcal{F}_1) = \mathcal{C}(\mathcal{F}_1 \cup \mathcal{F}_2 \cup \mathcal{F}_1) + \mu''(1 - \mathcal{C}(\mathcal{F}_1)) = \mathcal{C}(\mathcal{F}_1 \cup \mathcal{F}_2) + \mu''(1 - \mathcal{C}(\mathcal{F}_1)).$$

In order to prove (9) it is enough to verify that $\mu' = \mu''$. We observe that

$$\mathcal{C}(\mathcal{F}_2)|\mathcal{C}(\mathcal{F}_1) - \mathcal{C}(\mathcal{F}_1 \cup \mathcal{F}_2)|\mathcal{C}(\mathcal{F}_1) = (\mu' - \mu'')(1 - \mathcal{C}(\mathcal{F}_1)),$$

where $\mu' - \mu'' = \mathbb{P}[\mathcal{C}(\mathcal{F}_2)|\mathcal{C}(\mathcal{F}_1) - \mathcal{C}(\mathcal{F}_1 \cup \mathcal{F}_2)|\mathcal{C}(\mathcal{F}_1)]$. Moreover, by setting $\mathcal{F}_1 = \{E_1|H_1, \ldots, E_n|H_n\}$, it holds that

$$(\mu' - \mu'')(1 - \mathcal{C}(\mathcal{F}_1)) = \begin{cases} 0, & \text{if } \mathcal{C}(\mathcal{F}_1) = 1, \\ \mu' - \mu'', & \text{if } \mathcal{C}(\mathcal{F}_1) = 0, \\ (\mu' - \mu'')(1 - x_S), & \text{if } 0 < \mathcal{C}(\mathcal{F}_1) = x_S < 1, \end{cases}$$

where $\varnothing \neq S \subseteq \{1, \ldots, n\}$. Within the betting framework, $\mu' - \mu''$ is the amount to be paid in order to receive the random amount $(\mu' - \mu'')(1 - \mathcal{C}(\mathcal{F}_1))$. Then, as a necessary condition of coherence, $\mu' - \mu''$ must be a linear convex combination of the possible values of $(\mu' - \mu'')(1 - \mathcal{C}(\mathcal{F}_1))$ associated with the cases where the bet is not called off, that is the cases where you do not receive back the paid amount $\mu' - \mu''$. In other words, (as a necessary condition of coherence) $\mu' - \mu''$ must belong to the convex hull of the set $\{0, (\mu' - \mu'')(1 - x_S) : 0 < x_S < 1, \varnothing \neq S \subseteq \{1, \ldots, n\}\}$. We observe that $\max\{0, |\mu' - \mu''|(1 - x_S)\} \leq |\mu' - \mu''|$, where as $x_S \in (0, 1)$ the equality holds if and only if $\mu' - \mu'' = 0$. Then, $\mu' - \mu''$ belongs to convex hull of the set $\{0, (\mu' - \mu'')(1 - x_S) : 0 < x_S < 1, \varnothing \neq S \subseteq \{1, \ldots, n\}\}$ if and only if $\mu' - \mu'' = 0$, that is $\mu' = \mu''$. Thus, $\mathcal{C}(\mathcal{F}_2)|\mathcal{C}(\mathcal{F}_1) = \mathcal{C}(\mathcal{F}_1 \cup \mathcal{F}_2)|\mathcal{C}(\mathcal{F}_1)$. Finally, by recalling Remark 2, as $\mathcal{C}(\mathcal{F}_1 \cup \mathcal{F}_2) = \mathcal{C}(\mathcal{F}_1) \wedge \mathcal{C}(\mathcal{F}_2)$, it follows that $\mathcal{C}(\mathcal{F}_2)|\mathcal{C}(\mathcal{F}_1) = (\mathcal{C}(\mathcal{F}_1) \wedge \mathcal{C}(\mathcal{F}_2))|\mathcal{C}(\mathcal{F}_1)$. □

In particular, given any family $\mathcal{F} = \{E_1|H_1, \ldots, E_n|H_n\}$, with $\mathcal{C}(\mathcal{F}) \neq 0$, and any conditional event $E|H$, from (9) it follows that

$$\mathcal{C}(\mathcal{F} \cup \{E|H\})|\mathcal{C}(\mathcal{F}) = (E|H)|\mathcal{C}(\mathcal{F}). \tag{10}$$

Moreover, as $\mathcal{F} \cup \mathcal{F} = \mathcal{F}$, it holds that

$$\mathcal{C}(\mathcal{F})|\mathcal{C}(\mathcal{F}) = \mathcal{C}(\mathcal{F}) + \mu(1 - \mathcal{C}(\mathcal{F})), \tag{11}$$

where $\mu = \mathbb{P}[\mathcal{C}(\mathcal{F})|\mathcal{C}(\mathcal{F})]$. In the next theorem we show that $\mathcal{C}(\mathcal{F})|\mathcal{C}(\mathcal{F}) = \mu = 1$.

Theorem 6. Let $\mathcal{F} = \{E_1|H_1, \ldots, E_n|H_n\}$ be a family of n conditional events, with $\mathcal{C}(\mathcal{F})$ not equal to the constant 0. Then, $\mathcal{C}(\mathcal{F})|\mathcal{C}(\mathcal{F})$ coincides with the constant 1.

Proof. We set $C_0 = \bar{H}_1 \cdots \bar{H}_n$. We observe that when C_0 is true, the value of $\mathcal{C}(\mathcal{F})$ is $x_{1\ldots n}$ and the value of $\mathcal{C}(\mathcal{F})|\mathcal{C}(\mathcal{F})$ is $x_{1\ldots n} + \mu(1 - x_{1\ldots n})$. By linearity of prevision, from (11) it holds that $\mu = x_{1\ldots n} + \mu(1 - x_{1\ldots n})$.

We denote by K the set of constituents C_h's generated by $\mathcal{F}$ such that $C_h \subseteq H_1 \vee \cdots \vee H_n$, that is $C_h \neq C_0$. Then, we consider the partition $\{K_1, K_0, K^*\}$ of K as defined below.

$K_1 = \{C_h :$ if C_h is true, then the value of $\mathcal{C}(\mathcal{F})$ is $1\}$,
$K_0 = \{C_h :$ if C_h is true, then the value of $\mathcal{C}(\mathcal{F})$ is $0\}$,
$K^* = \{C_h :$ if C_h is true, then the value of $\mathcal{C}(\mathcal{F})$ is positive and less than $1\}$.

Notice that the set K_1 also includes the constituents C_h's such that $\mathcal{C}(\mathcal{F}) = x_S$, with $x_S = 1$. The set K_0 also includes the constituents C_h's such that $\mathcal{C}(\mathcal{F}) = x_S$, with $x_S = 0$. For each $C_h \in K^*$, it holds that

$$C_h = (\bigwedge_{i \in S} \bar{H}_i) \wedge (\bigwedge_{i \notin S} E_i H_i), \text{ for a suitable } \varnothing \neq S \subseteq \{1, \ldots, n\};$$

moreover, if C_h is true, then $\mathcal{C}(\mathcal{F}) = x_S$, with $0 < x_S < 1$. We observe that $K_1 \cup K^* \neq \varnothing$, because we assumed that $\mathcal{C}(\mathcal{F})$ does not coincide with the constant 0. Moreover, the value of $\mathcal{C}(\mathcal{F})|\mathcal{C}(\mathcal{F})$ associated with a constituent C_h is 1, or μ, or belongs to the set $\{x_S + \mu(1 - x_S) : 0 < x_S < 1, \varnothing \neq S \subseteq \{1, \ldots, n\}\}$, according to whether $C_h \in K_1$, or $C_h \in K_0$, or $C_h \in K^*$, respectively.

By linearity of prevision, based on (11), it holds that

$$\mu = \mathbb{P}[\mathcal{C}(\mathcal{F})|\mathcal{C}(\mathcal{F})] = \mathbb{P}[\mathcal{C}(\mathcal{F})] + \mu\mathbb{P}[(1 - \mathcal{C}(\mathcal{F})] = x_{1\ldots n} + \mu(1 - x_{1\ldots n}),$$

from which it follows that $\mu x_{1\ldots n} = x_{1\ldots n}$.
We distinguish two cases: (a) $x_{1\ldots n} > 0$; (b) $x_{1\ldots n} = 0$.
(a). As $x_{1\ldots n} > 0$, it holds that $\mu = 1$ and hence $x_S + \mu(1 - x_S) = 1$, for every S; therefore $\mathcal{C}(\mathcal{F})|\mathcal{C}(\mathcal{F})$ coincides with the constant 1.
(b). In this case $x_{1\ldots n} = 0$. If we bet on $\mathcal{C}(\mathcal{F})|\mathcal{C}(\mathcal{F})$, we agree to pay its prevision μ by receiving $\mathcal{C}(\mathcal{F})|\mathcal{C}(\mathcal{F}) = \mathcal{C}(\mathcal{F}) + \mu(1 - \mathcal{C}(\mathcal{F}))$, with the bet called off when you receive back the paid amount μ (whatever be μ). This happens when it is true a constituent $C_h \in K_0 \cup \{C_0\}$, in which case the value of $\mathcal{C}(\mathcal{F})$ is 0, so that $\mathcal{C}(\mathcal{F}) + \mu(1 - \mathcal{C}(\mathcal{F})) = \mu$. Denoting by Γ the set of possible values of $\mathscr{C}(\mathcal{F})|\mathscr{C}(\mathcal{F})$, it holds that

$$\mathcal{C}(\mathcal{F})|\mathcal{C}(\mathcal{F}) \in \Gamma \subseteq \mathcal{V} = \{1, \mu, x_S + \mu(1 - x_S) : 0 < x_S < 1, \varnothing \neq S \subseteq \{1, \ldots, n\}\}.$$

Then, as a necessary condition of coherence, μ must belong to the convex hull of the set

$$\Gamma^* = \Gamma \setminus \{\mu\} \subseteq \mathcal{V}^* = \mathcal{V} \setminus \{\mu\} = \{1, x_S + \mu(1 - x_S) : 0 < x_S < 1, \varnothing \neq S \subseteq \{1, \ldots, n\}\}.$$

Notice that Γ^* is the set of values of $\mathcal{C}(\mathcal{F})|\mathcal{C}(\mathcal{F})$ associated with the constituents C_h's which belong to the nonempty set $K_1 \cup K^*$. Moreover, if μ does not belong to the convex hull of $\mathcal{V}^*$, then μ does not belong to the convex hull of Γ^*. In order μ be coherent it must belong to the convex hull of Γ^*, that is it must be a linear convex combination of the set of values in Γ^*. We distinguish three cases: (i) $\mu = 1$; (ii) $\mu < 1$; (iii) $\mu > 1$. In the case (i) it holds that $x_S + \mu(1 - x_S) = 1$, for every S; then $\Gamma^* = \mathcal{V}^* = \{1\}$, hence the prevision assessment $\mu = 1$ is trivially coherent and $\mathcal{C}(\mathcal{F})|\mathcal{C}(\mathcal{F}) = 1$. In the case (ii) it holds that $\mu < \min \mathcal{V}^*$ and hence μ doesn't belong to the convex hull of $\mathcal{V}^*$; then μ doesn't belong to the convex hull of Γ^*, that is the prevision assessment $\mu < 1$ is not coherent. In the case (iii) it holds that $\mu > \max \mathcal{V}^*$ and hence μ doesn't belong to the convex hull of $\mathcal{V}^*$; then, μ doesn't belong to the convex hull of Γ^*, that is the prevision assessment $\mu > 1$ is not coherent. Therefore, the unique coherent prevision assessment on $\mathcal{C}(\mathcal{F})|\mathcal{C}(\mathcal{F})$ is $\mu = 1$ and hence

$$\mathcal{C}(\mathcal{F})|\mathcal{C}(\mathcal{F}) = \mathcal{C}(\mathcal{F}) + \mu(1 - \mathcal{C}(\mathcal{F})) = \mathcal{C}(\mathcal{F}) + 1 - \mathcal{C}(\mathcal{F}) = 1.$$

$\square$

In the next section we generalize Theorem 4, by characterizing the p-validity of the inference from a premise set $\mathcal{F} = \{E_1|H_1, \ldots, E_n|H_n\}$ to the conclusion $E_{n+1}|H_{n+1}$.

4   Characterization of P-Entailment in Terms of Iterated Conditionals

We recall that, given a family $\mathcal{F}$ of n conditional events $\{E_1|H_1, \ldots, E_n|H_n\}$, we also denote by $\mathcal{C}_{1\cdots n}$ the conjunction $\mathcal{C}(\mathcal{F})$. Moreover, given a further conditional event $E_{n+1}|H_{n+1}$ we denote by $\mathcal{C}_{1\cdots n+1}$ the conjunction $\mathcal{C}(\mathcal{F} \cup \{E_{n+1}|H_{n+1}\})$. In other words,

$$\mathcal{C}_{1\cdots n} = (E_1|H_1) \wedge \cdots \wedge (E_n|H_n), \quad \mathcal{C}_{1\cdots n+1} = (E_1|H_1) \wedge \cdots \wedge (E_{n+1}|H_{n+1}).$$

We set $\mathbb{P}(\mathcal{C}_{1\cdots n}) = x_{1\cdots n}$ and $\mathbb{P}(\mathcal{C}_{1\cdots n+1}) = x_{1\cdots n+1}$. Let us consider the iterated conditional $(E_{n+1}|H_{n+1})|\mathcal{C}_{1\cdots n}$, which by Definition 7, is given by

$$(E_{n+1}|H_{n+1})|\mathcal{C}_{1\cdots n} = \mathcal{C}_{1\cdots n+1} + \mu(1 - \mathcal{C}_{1\cdots n}),$$

where $\mu = \mathbb{P}[(E_{n+1}|H_{n+1})|\mathcal{C}_{1\cdots n}]$. In the next result, by assuming $\mathcal{F}$ p-consistent, the p-entailment of $E_{n+1}|H_{n+1}$ from $\mathcal{F}$ is characterized in terms of the iterated conditional $(E_{n+1}|H_{n+1})|\mathcal{C}_{1\cdots n}$.

Theorem 7. *A p-consistent family $\mathcal{F}$ p-entails $E_{n+1}|H_{n+1}$ if and only if the iterated conditional $(E_{n+1}|H_{n+1})|\mathcal{C}_{1\cdots n}$ is equal to 1.*

Proof. First of all we observe that, by Theorem 2, as $\mathcal{F}$ is p-consistent, the assessment $\mathbb{P}(\mathcal{C}_{1\cdots n}) = 1$ is coherent and hence $\mathcal{C}_{1\cdots n} \neq 0$, so that the iterated conditional $(E_{n+1}|H_{n+1})|\mathcal{C}_{1\cdots n}$ makes sense. We consider the following assertions: (i) $\mathcal{F}$ p-entails $E_{n+1}|H_{n+1}$; (ii) $\mathcal{C}_{1\cdots n+1} = \mathcal{C}_{1\cdots n}$; (iii) $(E_{n+1}|H_{n+1})|\mathcal{C}_{1\cdots n} = 1$.

By Theorem 3, the conditions (i) and (ii) are equivalent, thus $(i) \implies (ii)$. Then, in order to prove the theorem it is enough to verify that

$$(ii) \implies (iii) \implies (i).$$

$(ii) \implies (iii)$. By Theorem 5 it holds that $(E_{n+1}|H_{n+1})|\mathcal{C}_{1\cdots n} = \mathcal{C}_{1\cdots n+1}|\mathcal{C}_{1\cdots n}$. Moreover, as $\mathcal{C}_{1\cdots n+1} = \mathcal{C}_{1\cdots n}$, it holds that $\mathcal{C}_{1\cdots n+1}|\mathcal{C}_{1\cdots n} = \mathcal{C}_{1\cdots n}|\mathcal{C}_{1\cdots n}$, which by Theorem 6 is constant and coincides with 1. Thus, $(E_{n+1}|H_{n+1})|\mathcal{C}_{1\cdots n} = \mathcal{C}_{1\cdots n}|\mathcal{C}_{1\cdots n} = 1$, that is (iii) is satisfied.

$(iii) \implies (i)$. As the condition (iii) is satisfied, that is $(E_{n+1}|H_{n+1})|\mathcal{C}_{1\cdots n} = 1$, the unique coherent prevision assessment μ on $(E_{n+1}|H_{n+1})|\mathcal{C}_{1\cdots n}$ is

$$\mu = 1 = \mathbb{P}[\mathcal{C}_{1\cdots n+1} + \mu(1 - \mathcal{C}_{1\cdots n})] = x_{1\cdots n+1} + 1 - x_{1\cdots n},$$

from which it follows $x_{1\cdots n+1} = x_{1\cdots n}$. We observe that, as $\mathcal{F}$ is p-consistent, it is coherent to assess $x_1 = \cdots = x_n = 1$. Moreover, by recalling Theorem 1, it holds that: $\max\{x_1 + \cdots + x_n - n + 1, 0\} \leqslant x_{1\cdots n} \leqslant \min\{x_1, \ldots, x_n\}$. Then, when $x_1 = \cdots = x_n = 1$ it follows that $x_{1\cdots n} = 1 = x_{1\cdots n+1}$ and hence $x_{n+1} = 1$. Thus, $\mathcal{F}$ p-entails $E_{n+1}|H_{n+1}$, that is the condition (i) is satisfied. $\square$

We recall that the Transitivity rule is not p-valid, that is $\{C|B, B|A\}$ does not p-entail $C|A$. In [25, Theorem 5] it has been shown that

$$P(C|B) = 1, P(B|A) = 1, P(A|(A \vee B)) > 0 \Rightarrow P(C|A) = 1,$$

which is a weaker version of transitivity. This kind of Weak Transitivity has been also obtained in [22] in the setting of preferential relations. In the next example, in order to illustrate Theorems 5, 6 and 7, we consider two aspects: (i) a p-valid version of Weak Transitivity, where the constraint $P(A|(A \vee B)) > 0$ is replaced by $P(A|(A \vee B)) = 1$, by showing that $(C|A)|((C|B) \wedge (B|A) \wedge (A|(A \vee B))) = 1$; (ii) the non p-validity of the Transitivity rule, by showing that the iterated conditional $(C|A)|((C|B) \wedge (B|A))$ does not coincide with the constant 1.

Example 1. (i)-*Weak Transitivity.* We consider the premise set $\mathcal{F} = \{C|B, B|A, A|(A \vee B)\}$ and the conclusion $C|A$, where the events A, B, C are logically independent. By Definition 4

$$\mathcal{C}(\mathcal{F}) = (C|B) \wedge (B|A) \wedge (A|(A \vee B)) = \begin{cases} 1, & \text{if } ABC \text{ is true,} \\ 0, & \text{if } AB\bar{C} \vee A\bar{B} \vee \bar{A}B \text{ is true,} \\ z, & \text{if } \bar{A}\bar{B} \text{ is true,} \end{cases}$$

$$= ABC|(A \vee B),$$

where $z = \mathbb{P}[\mathcal{C}(\mathcal{F})] = P(ABC|(A \vee B))$. As $\mathcal{C}(\mathcal{F}) = ABC|(A \vee B) \subseteq C|A$, it follows that $\mathcal{C}(\mathcal{F}) \wedge (C|A) = \mathcal{C}(\mathcal{F})$ and by Theorem 3, $\{C|B, B|A, A|(A \vee B)\}$ p-entails $C|A$. Then, by Theorem 7, $(C|A)|((C|B) \wedge (B|A) \wedge (A|(A \vee B)))$ is constant and coincides with 1. Indeed, by recalling Theorems 5 and 6, it holds that

$$(C|A)|((C|B) \wedge (B|A) \wedge (A|(A \vee B))) = (C|A)|\mathcal{C}(\mathcal{F})$$
$$= ((C|A) \wedge \mathcal{C}(\mathcal{F}))|\mathcal{C}(\mathcal{F}) = \mathcal{C}(\mathcal{F})|\mathcal{C}(\mathcal{F}) = 1.$$

(ii)-*Transitivity.* We recall that Transitivity is not p-valid, that is the premise set $\{C|B, B|A\}$ does not p-entail the conclusion $C|A$. Then the iterated conditional $(C|A)|((C|B) \wedge (B|A))$ does not coincide with 1, as we show below. We set $P(B|A) = x$, $P(BC|A) = y$, $\mathbb{P}[(C|B) \wedge (B|A)] = u$, $\mathbb{P}[(C|B) \wedge (B|A) \wedge (C|A)] = w$, then by Definition 3 we obtain that

$$(C|B) \wedge (B|A) = (ABC + x\bar{A}BC)|(A \vee B) = ABC + x\bar{A}BC + u\bar{A}\bar{B},$$

and

$$(C|B) \wedge (B|A) \wedge (C|A) = (C|B) \wedge (BC|A) = (ABC + y\bar{A}BC)|(A \vee B) =$$
$$= ABC + y\bar{A}BC + w\bar{A}\bar{B}.$$

Defining $\mathbb{P}[(C|A)|((C|B) \wedge (B|A))] = \nu$, by linearity of prevision it holds that $\nu = w + \nu(1 - u)$ and hence

$$(C|A)|((C|B) \wedge (B|A)) = (C|B) \wedge (B|A) \wedge (C|A) + \nu(1 - (C|B) \wedge (B|A))$$
$$= \begin{cases} 1, & \text{if } ABC \text{ is true,} \\ \nu, & \text{if } A\bar{B} \vee B\bar{C} \text{ is true,} \\ y + \nu(1 - x), & \text{if } \bar{A}BC \text{ is true,} \\ \nu, & \text{if } \bar{A}\bar{B} \text{ is true.} \end{cases}$$

We observe that in general $y + \nu(1 - x) \neq 1$, for instance when $(x, y) = (1, 0)$ it holds that $y + \nu(1 - x) = 0$. Thus, in agreement with Theorem 7, the iterated conditional $(C|A)|((C|B) \wedge (B|A))$ does not coincide with the constant 1.

Notice that the p-validity of other inference rules, with a two-premise set $\{E_1|H_1, E_2|H_2\}$ and a conclusion $E_3|H_3$, has been examined in [26] by checking whether the condition $(E_3|H_3)|((E_1|H_1) \wedge (E_2|H_2)) = 1$ is satisfied.

5   Conclusions

In this paper, we generalized the notion of iterated conditional by introducing the random object $\mathcal{C}(\mathcal{F}_2)|\mathcal{C}(\mathcal{F}_1)$. We showed that $\mathbb{P}[\mathcal{C}(\mathcal{F}_2) \wedge \mathcal{C}(\mathcal{F}_1)] = \mathbb{P}[\mathcal{C}(\mathcal{F}_2)|\mathcal{C}(\mathcal{F}_1)]\mathbb{P}[\mathcal{C}(\mathcal{F}_1)]$ and that $(\mathcal{C}(\mathcal{F}_2) \wedge \mathcal{C}(\mathcal{F}_1))|\mathcal{C}(\mathcal{F}_1) = \mathcal{C}(\mathcal{F}_2)|\mathcal{C}(\mathcal{F}_1)$. Then, we verified that the iterated conditional $\mathcal{C}(\mathcal{F})|\mathcal{C}(\mathcal{F})$ is constant and coincides with 1. Moreover, under p-consistency of $\mathcal{F}$, we characterized the p-entailment of $E_{n+1}|H_{n+1}$ from $\mathcal{F}$ by the property that the iterated conditional where the antecedent is the conjunction $\mathcal{C}(\mathcal{F})$ and the consequent is $(E_{n+1}|H_{n+1})$ coincides with the constant 1. In other words, $\mathcal{F}$ p-entails $(E_{n+1}|H_{n+1})$ if and only if $(E_{n+1}|H_{n+1})|\mathcal{C}(\mathcal{F}) = 1$. We have also illustrated this characterization by an example related with weak transitivity. We observe that a particular case of this characterization is obtained when we consider a (p-consistent) family of n unconditional events $\mathcal{F} = \{E_1, \ldots, E_n\}$ and a further event E_{n+1}. In this case $\mathcal{F}$ p-entails E_{n+1} if and only if $E_1 \cdots E_n \subseteq E_{n+1}$, which also amounts to the property that the conditional event $E_{n+1}|E_1 \cdots E_n$ coincides with 1.

Acknowledgements. We thank the four anonymous reviewers for their useful comments and suggestions. G. Sanfilippo has been partially supported by the INdAM-GNAMPA Project 2020 Grant U-UFMBAZ-2020-000819.

References

1. Adams, E.W.: The Logic of Conditionals. Reidel, Dordrecht (1975)
2. Benferhat, S., Dubois, D., Prade, H.: Nonmonotonic reasoning, conditional objects and possibility theory. Artif. Intell. **92**, 259–276 (1997). https://doi.org/10.1016/S0004-3702(97)00012-X
3. Biazzo, V., Gilio, A., Lukasiewicz, T., Sanfilippo, G.: Probabilistic logic under coherence: complexity and algorithms. Ann. Math. Artif. Intell. **45**(1–2), 35–81 (2005). https://doi.org/10.1007/s10472-005-9005-y
4. Calabrese, P.: An algebraic synthesis of the foundations of logic and probability. Inf. Sci. **42**(3), 187–237 (1987). https://doi.org/10.1016/0020-0255(87)90023-5
5. Calabrese, P.: Logic and Conditional Probability: A Synthesis. College Publications (2017)
6. Ciucci, D., Dubois, D.: Relationships between connectives in three-valued logics. In: Greco, S., Bouchon-Meunier, B., Coletti, G., Fedrizzi, M., Matarazzo, B., Yager, R.R. (eds.) IPMU 2012. CCIS, vol. 297, pp. 633–642. Springer, Heidelberg (2012). https://doi.org/10.1007/978-3-642-31709-5_64
7. Ciucci, D., Dubois, D.: A map of dependencies among three-valued logics. Inf. Sci. **250**, 162–177 (2013). https://doi.org/10.1016/j.ins.2013.06.040
8. Coletti, G., Petturiti, D., Vantaggi, B.: Fuzzy memberships as likelihood functions in a possibilistic framework. Int. J. Approximate Reasoning **88**, 547–566 (2017). https://doi.org/10.1016/j.ijar.2016.11.017
9. Coletti, G., Petturiti, D., Vantaggi, B.: A Dutch book coherence condition for conditional completely alternating Choquet expectations. Bollettino dell'Unione Matematica Italiana **13**(4), 585–593 (2020). https://doi.org/10.1007/s40574-020-00251-8
10. Coletti, G., Scozzafava, R.: Conditional probability, fuzzy sets, and possibility: a unifying view. Fuzzy Sets Syst. **144**, 227–249 (2004)
11. Coletti, G., Scozzafava, R., Vantaggi, B.: Coherent conditional probability, fuzzy inclusion and default rules. In: Yager, R., Abbasov, A.M., Reformat, M.Z., Shahbazova, S.N. (eds.) Soft Computing: State of the Art Theory and Novel Applications, pp. 193–208. Springer, Heidelberg (2013)
12. Coletti, G., Scozzafava, R., Vantaggi, B.: Possibilistic and probabilistic logic under coherence: Default reasoning and System P. Mathematica Slovaca **65**(4), 863–890 (2015). https://doi.org/10.1515/ms-2015-0060
13. Coletti, G., Vantaggi, B.: Coherent conditional plausibility: a tool for handling fuzziness and uncertainty under partial information. In: Collan, M., Kacprzyk, J. (eds.) Soft Computing Applications for Group Decision-making and Consensus Modeling. SFSC, vol. 357, pp. 129–152. Springer, Cham (2018). https://doi.org/10.1007/978-3-319-60207-3_9
14. Cruz, N.: Deduction from uncertain premises? In: Elqayam, S., Douven, I., Evans, J.S.B.T., Cruz, N. (eds.) Logic and Uncertainty in the Human Mind: A Tribute to David E. Over, pp. 27–41. Routledge, Oxon (2020). https://doi.org/10.4324/9781315111902-3
15. Douven, I., Dietz, R.: A puzzle about Stalnaker's hypothesis. Topoi, pp. 31–37 (2011). https://doi.org/10.1007/s11245-010-9082-3
16. Douven, I., Elqayam, S., Singmann, H., van Wijnbergen-Huitink, J.: Conditionals and inferential connections: toward a new semantics. Thinking Reasoning, pp. 1–41 (2019). https://doi.org/10.1080/13546783.2019.1619623

17. Dubois, D., Faux, F., Prade, H.: Prejudice in uncertain information merging: pushing the fusion paradigm of evidence theory further. Int. J. Approximate Reasoning **121**, 1–22 (2020). https://doi.org/10.1016/j.ijar.2020.02.012

18. Dubois, D., Liu, W., Ma, J., Prade, H.: The basic principles of uncertain information fusion. An organised review of merging rules in different representation frameworks. Inf. Fusion **32**, 12–39 (2016). https://doi.org/10.1016/j.inffus.2016.02.006

19. Dujmović, J.J., Legind Larsen, H.: Generalized conjunction/disjunction. Int. J. Approximate Reasoning **46**(3), 423–446 (2007). https://doi.org/10.1016/j.ijar.2006.12.011, special Section: Aggregation Operators

20. de Finetti, B.: La logique de la probabilité. In: Actes du Congrès International de Philosophie Scientifique, Paris, 1935, pp. IV 1-IV 9 (1936)

21. Flaminio, T., Godo, L., Hosni, H.: Boolean algebras of conditionals, probability and logic. Artif. Intell. **286**, 103347 (2020). https://doi.org/10.1016/j.artint.2020.103347

22. Freund, M., Lehmann, D., Morris, P.: Rationality, transitivity, and contraposition. Artif. Intell. **52**(2), 191–203 (1991)

23. Gilio, A.: Probabilistic reasoning under coherence in System P. Annals Math. Artif. Intell. **34**, 5–34 (2002). https://doi.org/10.1023/A:101442261

24. Gilio, A., Over, D.E., Pfeifer, N., Sanfilippo, G.: Centering and Compound Conditionals Under Coherence. In: Ferraro, M.B., Giordani, P., Vantaggi, B., Gagolewski, M., Gil, M.Á., Grzegorzewski, P., Hryniewicz, O. (eds.) Soft Methods for Data Science. AISC, vol. 456, pp. 253–260. Springer, Cham (2017). https://doi.org/10.1007/978-3-319-42972-4_32

25. Gilio, A., Pfeifer, N., Sanfilippo, G.: Transitivity in coherence-based probability logic. J. Appl. Logic **14**, 46–64 (2016). https://doi.org/10.1016/j.jal.2015.09.012

26. Gilio, A., Pfeifer, N., Sanfilippo, G.: Probabilistic entailment and iterated conditionals. In: Elqayam, S., Douven, I., Evans, J.S.B.T., Cruz, N. (eds.) Logic and Uncertainty in the Human Mind: a Tribute to David E. Over, pp. 71–101. Routledge, Oxon (2020). https://doi.org/10.4324/9781315111902-6

27. Gilio, A., Sanfilippo, G.: Conditional random quantities and iterated conditioning in the setting of coherence. In: van der Gaag, L.C. (ed.) ECSQARU 2013. LNCS (LNAI), vol. 7958, pp. 218–229. Springer, Heidelberg (2013). https://doi.org/10.1007/978-3-642-39091-3_19

28. Gilio, A., Sanfilippo, G.: Conjunction, disjunction and iterated conditioning of conditional events. In: Kruse, R., Berthold, M., Moewes, C., Gil, M., Grzegorzewski, P., Hryniewicz, O. (eds.) Synergies of Soft Computing and Statistics for Intelligent Data Analysis. AISC, vol. 190, pp. 399–407. Springer, Heidelberg (2013). https://doi.org/10.1007/978-3-642-33042-1_43

29. Gilio, A., Sanfilippo, G.: Probabilistic entailment in the setting of coherence: the role of quasi conjunction and inclusion relation. Int. J. Approximate Reasoning **54**(4), 513–525 (2013). https://doi.org/10.1016/j.ijar.2012.11.001

30. Gilio, A., Sanfilippo, G.: Quasi conjunction, quasi disjunction, t-norms and t-conorms: probabilistic aspects. Inf. Sci. **245**, 146–167 (2013). https://doi.org/10.1016/j.ins.2013.03.019

31. Gilio, A., Sanfilippo, G.: Conditional random quantities and compounds of conditionals. Studia Logica **102**(4), 709–729 (2013). https://doi.org/10.1007/s11225-013-9511-6

32. Gilio, A., Sanfilippo, G.: Conjunction and disjunction among conditional events. In: Benferhat, S., Tabia, K., Ali, M. (eds.) IEA/AIE 2017. LNCS (LNAI), vol. 10351, pp. 85–96. Springer, Cham (2017). https://doi.org/10.1007/978-3-319-60045-1_11

33. Gilio, A., Sanfilippo, G.: Generalized logical operations among conditional events. Appl. Intell. **49**(1), 79–102 (2018). https://doi.org/10.1007/s10489-018-1229-8
34. Gilio, A., Sanfilippo, G.: Algebraic aspects and coherence conditions for conjoined and disjoined conditionals. Int. J. Approximate Reasoning **126**, 98–123 (2020). https://doi.org/10.1016/j.ijar.2020.08.004
35. Gilio, A., Sanfilippo, G.: Compound conditionals, Fréchet-Hoeffding bounds, and Frank t-norms. Int. J. Approximate Reasoning **136**, 168–200 (2021). https://doi.org/10.1016/j.ijar.2021.06.006
36. Gilio, A., Sanfilippo, G.: On compound and iterated conditionals. Argumenta 6 **2**(2021), 241–266 (2021). https://doi.org/10.14275/2465-2334/202112.gil
37. Goodman, I.R., Nguyen, H.T., Walker, E.A.: Conditional Inference and Logic for Intelligent Systems: A Theory of Measure-Free Conditioning. North-Holland (1991)
38. Grabisch, M., Marichal, J., Mesiar, R., Pap, E.: Aggregation functions. Cambridge University Press (2009)
39. Kaufmann, S.: Conditionals right and left: probabilities for the whole family. J. Philosophical Logic **38**, 1–53 (2009). https://doi.org/10.1007/s10992-008-9088-0
40. Lewis, D.: Counterfactuals. Blackwell, Oxford (1973)
41. Lewis, D.: Probabilities of conditionals and conditional probabilities. Philos. Rev. **85**(3), 297–315 (1976)
42. McGee, V.: Conditional probabilities and compounds of conditionals. Philos. Rev. **98**(4), 485–541 (1989). https://doi.org/10.2307/2185116
43. Nguyen, H.T., Walker, E.A.: A history and introduction to the algebra of conditional events and probability logic. IEEE Trans. Syst. Man Cybernetics **24**(12), 1671–1675 (1994). https://doi.org/10.1109/21.328924
44. Petturiti, D., Vantaggi, B.: Modeling agent's conditional preferences under objective ambiguity in dempster-shafer theory. Int. J. Approximate Reasoning **119**, 151–176 (2020). https://doi.org/10.1016/j.ijar.2019.12.019
45. Sanfilippo, G.: Lower and upper probability bounds for some conjunctions of two conditional events. In: Ciucci, D., Pasi, G., Vantaggi, B. (eds.) SUM 2018. LNCS (LNAI), vol. 11142, pp. 260–275. Springer, Cham (2018). https://doi.org/10.1007/978-3-030-00461-3_18
46. Sanfilippo, G., Gilio, A., Over, D., Pfeifer, N.: Probabilities of conditionals and previsions of iterated conditionals. Int. J. Approximate Reasoning **121**, 150–173 (2020). https://doi.org/10.1016/j.ijar.2020.03.001
47. Sanfilippo, G., Pfeifer, N., Gilio, A.: Generalized probabilistic modus ponens. In: Antonucci, A., Cholvy, L., Papini, O. (eds.) ECSQARU 2017. LNCS (LNAI), vol. 10369, pp. 480–490. Springer, Cham (2017). https://doi.org/10.1007/978-3-319-61581-3_43
48. Sanfilippo, G., Pfeifer, N., Over, D., Gilio, A.: Probabilistic inferences from conjoined to iterated conditionals. Int. J. Approximate Reasoning **93**(Supplement C), 103–118 (2018). https://doi.org/10.1016/j.ijar.2017.10.027
49. Sezgin, M., Kern-Isberner, G., Rott, H.: Inductive reasoning with difference-making conditionals. In: 18th International Workshop on Non-Monotonic Reasoning (NMR 2020 Workshop Notes), pp. 83–92 (2020)

A Triple Uniqueness of the Maximum Entropy Approach

Jürgen Landes[✉]

Munich Center for Mathematical Philosophy, LMU Munich, Munich, Germany
juergen_landes@yahoo.de

> To be uncertain is to be
> uncomfortable, but to be certain
> is to be ridiculous.
>
> Chinese proverb

Abstract. Inductive logic is concerned with assigning probabilities to sentences given probabilistic constraints. The Maximum Entropy Approach to inductive logic I here consider assigns probabilities to all sentences of a first order predicate logic. This assignment is built on an application of the Maximum Entropy Principle, which requires that probabilities for uncertain inference have maximal Shannon Entropy. This paper puts forward two different modified applications of this principle to first order predicate logic and shows that the original and the two modified applications agree in many cases. A third promising modification is studied and rejected.

Keywords: Inductive logic · Maximum entropy · First order predicate language · Uncertain inference · Objective Bayesianism

1 Introduction

Inductive logic is a formal approach to model rational uncertain inferences. It seeks to analyse the degree to which premises entail putative conclusions. Given uncertain premisses $\varphi_1, \ldots, \varphi_k$ with attached uncertainties $X_1, \ldots, X_k$ an inductive logic provides means to attach uncertainty Y to a conclusion ψ, where the X_i and Y are non-empty subsets of the unit interval. An inductive logic can be represented as

$$\varphi_1^{X_1}, \ldots, \varphi_k^{X_k} \approx \psi^Y \ , \tag{1}$$

where $\approx$ denotes an inductive entailment relation [11]. Much work has gone into the development and exploration of inductive logics, see, e.g., [4,9,12,16,29–31,41].

I gratefully acknowledge funding from the Deutsche Forschungsgemeinschaft (DFG, German Research Foundation) - 432308570 and 405961989.

J. Vejnarová and N. Wilson (Eds.): ECSQARU 2021, LNAI 12897, pp. 644–656, 2021.
https://doi.org/10.1007/978-3-030-86772-0_46

The main early proponent of inductive logic was Rudolf Carnap [2,3]. Nowadays, the spirit of his approach today continues in the Pure Inductive Logic approach [14,17,21–24,40]. In this paper, I however consider uncertain inference within the maximum entropy framework, which goes back to Edwin Jaynes [15], who put forward a Maximum Entropy Principle governing rational uncertain inference.

Maximum Entropy Principle. *Rational agents ought to use a probability function consistent with the evidence for drawing uncertain inferences. In case there is more than one such probability function, a rational agent ought to use probability functions with maximal entropy.*

In case only a single probability function is consistent with the evidence, the Maximum Entropy Principle is uncontroversial. Its strength (and sometimes controversial nature) is rooted in applications with multiple prima facie reasonable probability functions for probabilistic inference. This principle is at the heart of objective Bayesianism.

If the underlying domain is finite, then applying the Maximum Entropy Principle for inductive entailment is straight-forward and well-understood due to the seminal work of Alena Vencovská & Jeff Paris [32–34,36–39]. Matters change dramatically for infinite domains. Naively replacing the sum by an integral in the definition of Shannon Entropy produces a great number of probability functions with infinite entropy. But then there is no way to pick a probability function with maximal entropy out of a set in which all functions have infinite entropy.

There are two different suggestions for inductive logic on an infinite first order predicate logic explicating the Maximum Entropy Principle. The Entropy Limit Approach [1,35] and the Maximum Entropy Approach [28,45–48]. It has been conjectured, that both approaches agree in cases in which the former approach is-well defined [48, p. 191]. This conjecture has been shown to hold in a number of cases of evidence bases with relatively low quantifier-complexity [19,25,44].

This paper introduces modifications of the Maximum Entropy Approach and studies their relationships. I next properly introduce this approach along with some notation and the modifications. I then proceed to investigate their relationships. My main result is Theorem 1; it proves that the two suggested modifications agree with the original Maximum Entropy Approach expounded by Jon Williamson for convex optimisation problems, if at least one of these three approaches yields a unique probability function for inference on the underlying first order predicate language.

In Sect. 4, I study a third modification of Williamson's Maximum Entropy Approach, which I reject due to the absurd probabilities it delivers for inductive inference, see Proposition 6. In Sect. 5, I put forward some concluding remarks and consider avenues for future research.

2 The Maximum Entropy Approach and Two Modifications

The formal framework and notation is adapted from [25].

A *fixed first order predicate language* $\mathcal{L}$ is given. It consists of countably many constant symbols $t_1, t_2, \ldots$ exhausting the universe (for every element in the universe there is at least one constant symbol representing it) and finitely many relation symbols, $U_1, \ldots, U_n$. In particular, note that the language does not contain a symbol for equality nor does it contain function symbols. The atomic sentences are sentences of the form $U_i t_{i_1} \ldots t_{i_k}$, where k is the arity of the relation U_i; the atomic sentences are denoted by $a_1, a_2, \ldots$. They are by construction ordered in such a way that atomic sentences involving only constants among $t_1, \ldots, t_n$ occur before those atomic sentences that also involve t_{n+1}. The set of sentences of $\mathcal{L}$ is denoted by SL.

The finite sublanguages $\mathcal{L}_n$ of $\mathcal{L}$ are those languages, which only contain the first n constant symbols $t_1, \ldots, t_n$ and the same relation symbols as $\mathcal{L}$. Denote the sentences of $\mathcal{L}_n$ by SL_n.

The contingent conjunctions of maximal length of the form $\pm a_1 \wedge \ldots \wedge \pm a_{r_n} \in SL_n$ are called the *n-states*. Let Ω_n be the set of n-states for each $n \in \mathbb{N}$ with $|\Omega_n| = 2^{r_n}$.

Definition 1 (Probabilities on Predicate Languages). *A probability function P on $\mathcal{L}$ is a function $P : SL \longrightarrow \mathbb{R}_{\geq 0}$ such that:*

P1: *If τ is a tautology, i.e., $\models \tau$, then $P(\tau) = 1$.*
P2: *If θ and φ are mutually exclusive, i.e., $\models \neg(\theta \wedge \varphi)$, then $P(\theta \vee \varphi) = P(\theta) + P(\varphi)$.*
P3: $P(\exists x \theta(x)) = \sup_m P\left(\bigvee_{i=1}^m \theta(t_i)\right)$.

A probability function on $\mathcal{L}_n$ is defined similarly (the supremum in P3 is dropped and m is equal to n).
$\mathbb{P}$ *denotes the set of all probability functions on $\mathcal{L}$.*

A probability function $P \in \mathbb{P}$ is determined by the values it gives to the quantifier-free sentences, this result is known as *Gaifman's Theorem* [8]. P3 is sometimes called *Gaifman Condition* [40, p. 11]. The Gaifman Condition is justified by the assumption that the constants exhaust the universe. Consequently, a probability function is determined by the values it gives to the n-states, for each n [33, p. 171].

It is thus sensible to measure the entropy of a probability function $P \in \mathbb{P}$ via n-states with varying n.

Definition 2 (n-entropy). *The n-entropy of a probability function $P \in \mathbb{P}$ is defined as:*

$$H_n(P) := - \sum_{\omega \in \Omega_n} P(\omega) \log P(\omega) .$$

The usual conventions are $0 \log 0 := 0$ and $\log$ denoting the natural logarithm. The second convention is inconsequential for current purposes.

$H_n(\cdot)$ is a strictly concave function.

The key idea is to combine the n-entropies defined on finite sublanguages $\mathcal{L}_n$ into an overall notion of comparative entropy comparing probability functions P and Q defined on the entire first order language.

So far, the literature has only studied such inductive logics with respect to the first binary relation in the following definition.

Definition 3 (Comparative Notions of Entropy). *That a probability function $P \in \mathbb{P}$ has greater (or equal) entropy than a probability function $Q \in \mathbb{P}$ could be defined in the following three ways.*

1. *If and only if there is some natural number N such that for all $n \geq N$ it holds that $H_n(P) > H_n(Q)$, denoted by $P \succ Q$.*
2. *If and only if there is some natural number N such that for all $n \geq N$ it holds that $H_n(P) \geq H_n(Q)$ and there are infinitely many n such that $H_n(P) > H_n(Q)$, denoted by $P]Q$.*
3. *If and only if there is some natural number N such that for all $n \geq N$ it holds that $H_n(P) \geq H_n(Q)$, denoted by $P)Q$.*

The lower two definitions are alternative ways in which one could explicate the intuitive idea of comparative entropy, which have never been studied before. Prima facie, all three definitions appear reasonable.

Before I can define notions of maximal entropy with respect to the given premisses, I need to specify the set of probability functions over which entropy is to be maximised.

Definition 4 (Region of Feasible Probability Functions). *The set of probability functions consistent with all premisses, $P(\varphi_i) \in X_i$ for all i, is denoted by $\mathbb{E}$ and defined as*

$$\mathbb{E} := \{P \in \mathbb{P} : P(\varphi_i) \in X_i \text{ for all } 1 \leq i \leq k\} \ .$$

In order to simplify the notation, I do not display the dependence of $\mathbb{E}$ on the premisses.

In this paper, I only consider a fixed set of premisses, $\varphi_1^{X_1}, \ldots, \varphi_k^{X_k}$. There is hence no need to complicate notation by writing $\mathbb{E}_{\varphi_1^{X_1}, \ldots, \varphi_k^{X_k}}$ or similar.

Definition 5 (Set of Maximum Entropy Functions). *The set of probability functions on $\mathcal{L}$ with maximal entropy in $\mathbb{E}$ relative to a notion of comparative entropy $>$ defined on $\mathbb{P} \times \mathbb{P}$ can then be defined as*

$$\text{maxent}_> \mathbb{E} := \{P \in \mathbb{E} : \text{there is no } Q \in \mathbb{E} \setminus \{P\} \text{ with } Q > P\} \ . \tag{2}$$

The Maximum Entropy Principle now compels agents to use probabilities in $\text{maxent}_> \mathbb{E}$ for drawing uncertain inferences as described by the scheme for inductive logic in (1). The induced inductive logics are described in the following definition.

Definition 6 (Maximum Entropy Inductive Logics). *An inductive logic with respect to $>$ is induced by attaching uncertainty $Y_>(\psi) \subseteq [0,1]$ to the sentences ψ of $\mathcal{L}$ via*

$$Y_>(\psi) := \{r \in [0,1] \mid \text{ there exists } P \in \text{maxent}_> \mathbb{E} \text{ with } P(\psi) = r\} \ .$$

In case there are two or more different probability functions in $\text{maxent}_> \mathbb{E}$, there are some sentences of ψ of $\mathcal{L}$ to which multiple different probabilities attach.

The Maximum Entropy Approach arises using $\succ$ for comparing entropies of probability functions in $\mathbb{P}$ [28,45–48].

Remark 1 (Comparisons to the Entropy Limit Approach). It is known that the Entropy Limit Approach is invariant under arbitrary permutations of the constant symbols [25, Footnote 2]. The Entropy Limit Approach however suffers from a finite model problem, a premiss sentence formalising the existence of an infinite order does not have a finite model [42, Sect. 4.1] and hence the entropy limit is undefined.

The three Maximum Entropy Approaches defined in Definition 6 are invariant under *finite* permutations of constant symbols, the three notions of comparative entropy only depend on the limiting behaviour of H_n and n-entropy is invariant under permutation of the first n constant symbols (Definition 3). Whether these Maximum Entropy Approaches are invariant under infinite permutations is still to be determined. Since these approaches do not make use of finite models, they are immune to the finite model problem. See [19,25] for more detailed comparisons and further background.

Remark 2 (Maximum Entropy Functions). Determining maximum entropy functions is an often difficult endeavour. In concrete applications, it is often easier to determine the entropy limit first and then show that the entropy limit also has maximal entropy. See [25] for an overview of the cases in which a maximum entropy function exists and is unique.

Trivially, if the equivocator function, $P_= \in \mathbb{P}$, which for all n assigns all n-states the same probability of $1/|\Omega_n|$,[1] is in $\mathbb{E}$, then $\{P_=\} = \text{maxent}_\succ \mathbb{E}$.

In a forthcoming paper [26], we show that if there is only a single premiss φ such that $0 < P_=(\varphi) < 1$, then the maximum entropy function is obtained from (Jeffrey) updating the equivocator function. For the premiss φ^c with $0 \le c \le 1$ it holds that $\{cP_=(\cdot|\varphi_N) + (1-c)P_=(\cdot|\neg\varphi_N)\} = \text{maxent}_\succ \mathbb{E}$, where N is maximal such that $t_N \in \varphi$ and φ_N is defined as the disjunction of N-states ω_N such that $P_=(\varphi \wedge \omega_N) > 0$.

Cases with multiple uncertain premisses are, in general, still poorly understood.

---

[1] Note that the equivocator function is the unique probability function in $\mathbb{P}$ which is uniform over all Ω_n, $P_=(\omega_n) = \frac{1}{|\Omega_n|}$ for all n and all $\omega_n \in \Omega_n$. The name for this function is derived from the fact that it is maximally equivocal. The function has also been given other names. In Pure Inductive Logic it is known as the *completely independent probability function* and is often denoted by c_∞ in reference to the role it plays in Carnap's famous continuum of inductive methods [3].

In the next section, I study (the relationships of) these binary relations and the arising inductive logics. Particular attention is paid to the case of a unique probability function for inference, $|\text{maxent}_> \mathbb{E}| = 1$. These cases are of particular interest, since they deliver well-defined (unique) probabilities for inductive inference.

3 Maximal (Modified) Entropy

I first consider two notions of refinement relating these three binary relations.

Definition 7 (Strong Refinement). $>$ *is called a* strong refinement *of* $\gg$, *if and only if the following hold*

- $>$ *is a refinement of* $\gg$, *for all* $P, Q \in \mathbb{P}$ *it holds that* $P \gg Q$ *entails* $P > Q$,
- *for all* $R, P, Q \in \mathbb{P}$ *it holds that, if* $R \gg P$ *and* $P > Q$ *are both true, then* $R \gg Q$ *and* $R \neq Q$.

Definition 8 (Centric Refinement). *A refinement* $>$ *of* $\gg$ *is called* centric, *if and only if for all different* $R, P \in \mathbb{P}$ *with* $R > P$ *it holds that* $(R + P)/2 \gg P$.

The name centric has been chosen to emphasise that the centre between R and P is greater than P.

Clearly, not all binary relations possess strong refinements; not all binary relations possess centric refinements.

Proposition 1 (Strong and Centric Refinements). $]$ *is a strong and centric refinement of* $\succ$. $)$ *is a strong and centric refinement of* $]$ *and of* $\succ$.

Proof. For ease of comparison, I now display the three notions of comparative entropy line by line. The first line defines $P \succ Q$, the second line $P]Q$ and the third line $P)Q$. The second conjunct in the first definition is superfluous as is the second conjunct in the third definition:

$H_n(P) \leq H_n(Q)$ not infinitely often & $H_n(P) > H_n(Q)$ infinitely often

$H_n(P) < H_n(Q)$ not infinitely often & $H_n(P) > H_n(Q)$ infinitely often

$H_n(P) < H_n(Q)$ not infinitely often & $H_n(P) \geq H_n(Q)$ infinitely often .

By thusly spelling out both comparative notions of entropy one easily observes that $P \succ Q$ entails $P]Q$, and that $P]Q$ entails $P)Q$. This establishes the refinement relationships.

Strong Refinements. Next note that, if $R \succ Q$ or if $R]Q$, then $R \neq Q$.

$]$ is a strong refinement of $\succ$: Let $R \succ P$ and $P]Q$. Then $R \neq Q$. Furthermore, $H_n(R) \leq H_n(Q)$ is true for at most finitely many n, since from some N onwards P has always greater or equal n-entropy than Q. So, $R \succ Q$.

$)$ is a strong refinement of $]$: Let $R]P$ and $P)Q$. Then $R \neq Q$. From some N onwards P has always greater or equal n-entropy than Q. There are also infinitely many $n \in \mathbb{N}$ such that $H_n(R) > H_n(P)$. So, $R]Q$.

) is a strong refinement of $\succ$: Let $R \gg P$ and $P)Q$. Then $R \neq Q$. From some N onwards P has always greater or equal n-entropy than Q. From some N' onwards R has always greater n-entropy than P. Hence, $H_n(R) \leq H_n(Q)$ can only be the case for finitely many $n \in \mathbb{N}$. So, $R \succ Q$.

Centric Refinement. First, note that different probability functions disagree on some quantifier free sentence $\varphi \in \mathcal{L}_N$ (*Gaifman's Theorem* [8]). Since $\varphi \in \mathcal{L}_{n+N}$ for all $n \geq 1$, these probability functions also disagree on all more expressive sub-languages $\mathcal{L}_{n+N}$.

] is a centric refinement of $\succ$: Fix arbitrary probability functions R, P defined on $\mathcal{L}$ with $R]P$. $R \neq P$. From the concavity of the function H_n it follows that $H_n(\frac{R+P}{2}) > H_n(P)$, whenever $H_n(R) \geq H_n(P)$. By definition of], there are only finitely many n for which $H_n(R) \geq H_n(P)$ fails to hold. Hence, $\frac{R+P}{2} \succ P$ by definition of $\succ$.

) is a centric refinement of $\succ$: Fix arbitrary probability functions R, P defined on $\mathcal{L}$ with $R)P$. Note that R may be equal to P. From the concavity of the function H_n it follows that $H_n(\frac{R+P}{2}) > H_n(P)$, whenever $H_n(R) \geq H_n(P)$. By definition of), there are only finitely many n for which $H_n(R) \geq H_n(P)$ fails to hold. Hence, $\frac{R+P}{2} \succ P$ by definition of $\succ$.

) is a centric refinement of]: Fix arbitrary probability functions R, P defined on $\mathcal{L}$ with $R)P$. Note that R may be equal to P. Since $\frac{R+P}{2} \succ P$ (see above case) and since] is a refinement of $\succ$, it holds that $\frac{R+P}{2}]P$. □

Remark 3 (Properties of Comparative Entropies). If $H_n(P) = H_n(Q)$ for all even n and $H_n(P) > H_n(Q)$ for all odd n, then $P]Q$ and $P \not\succ Q$. Hence,] is a proper refinement of $\succ$.

For $P = Q$ it holds that $P)Q$ and $Q)P$. Hence,) is a proper refinement of] and thus a proper refinement of $\succ$.

] is transitive, irreflexive, acyclic and asymmetric.) is transitive, reflexive and has non-trivial cycles, e.g., for all probability functions P, Q with zero-entropy, $H_n(P) = 0$ for all $n \in \mathbb{N}$, it holds that $P)Q$.

I now turn to entropy maximisation and the induced inductive logics.

Proposition 2 (Downwards Uniqueness). *Let $>$ be a strong refinement of $\gg$. If* $\mathrm{maxent}_{\gg} \mathbb{E} = \{Q\}$, *then* $\{Q\} = \mathrm{maxent}_{\gg} \mathbb{E} = \mathrm{maxent}_{>} \mathbb{E}$.

In case the inductive logic induced by $\gg$ as a notion of a comparative entropy provides a unique probability function for rational inference, so does the inductive logic induced by $>$.

Proof. Note at first that since $>$ is a refinement of $\gg$ it holds that

$$\mathrm{maxent}_{>} \mathbb{E} \subseteq \mathrm{maxent}_{\gg} \mathbb{E} \ . \tag{3}$$

Maximal elements according to $\gg$ may not be maximal according to $>$ and all maximal elements according to $>$ are also maximal according to $\gg$.

Assume for the purpose of deriving a contradiction that $Q \notin$ maxent$_>$ $\mathbb{E}$. Then, there has to exist a $P \in \mathbb{E} \setminus \{Q\}$ such that $P > Q$ but $P \gg Q$ fails to hold ($\{Q\} =$ maxent$_\gg$ $\mathbb{E}$ holds by assumption).

However, since $\{Q\} =$ maxent$_\gg$ $\mathbb{E}$ and $Q \notin$ maxent$_>$ $\mathbb{E}$ hold, there has to exist some $R \in \mathbb{E} \setminus \{P\}$ such that $R \gg P$, P cannot have maximal $\gg$-entropy. We hence have $R \gg P$ and $P > Q$. Since $>$ is a strong refinement of $\gg$, we obtain $R \gg Q$ and $R \neq Q$. Since $R \in \mathbb{E}$ it follows from the definition of maxent$_\gg$ that $Q \notin$ maxent$_\gg$ $\mathbb{E}$. Contradiction. So, $Q \in$ maxent$_>$ $\mathbb{E}$.

Since $\{Q\} =$ maxent$_\gg$ $\mathbb{E} \overset{(3)}{\supseteq}$ maxent$_>$ $\mathbb{E} \ni Q$, it follows that maxent$_>$ $\mathbb{E} = \{Q\}$. $\qquad\square$

The converse is also true for convex $\mathbb{E}$ and centric refinements.

Proposition 3 (Upwards Uniqueness). *If $\mathbb{E}$ is convex, $>$ is a centric refinement of $\gg$ and maxent$_>$ $\mathbb{E} = \{Q\}$, then $\{Q\} =$ maxent$_\gg$ $\mathbb{E} =$ maxent$_>$ $\mathbb{E}$.*

Proof. Assume for contradiction that there exists a feasible probability function $P \in \mathbb{E} \setminus \{Q\}$ such that P is not $\gg$-dominated by the probability functions in $\mathbb{E}$ but $>$-dominated by some $R \in \mathbb{E} \setminus \{P\}$, $R > P$. Now define $S = \frac{1}{2}(P + R)$ and note that $S \in \mathbb{E}$ (convexity) and that S, P, R are pairwise different, $|\{S, P, R\}| = 3$.

Since $>$ is a centric refinement of $\gg$, we conclude that $S \gg P$, which contradicts that $P \in$ maxent$_\gg$ $\mathbb{E}$ and $P \neq Q$. So, only Q can be in maxent$_\gg$ $\mathbb{E}$.

Since $Q \in$ maxent$_>$ $\mathbb{E}$ and maxent$_>$ $\mathbb{E} \overset{(3)}{\subseteq}$ maxent$_\gg$ $\mathbb{E}$ it follows that $\{Q\} =$ maxent$_\gg$ $\mathbb{E}$. $\qquad\square$

Theorem 1 (Triple Uniqueness). *If $\mathbb{E}$ is convex and at least one of maxent$_)$ $\mathbb{E}$, maxent$_]$ $\mathbb{E}$ or maxent$_\succ$ $\mathbb{E}$ is a singleton, then*

$$\text{maxent } \mathbb{E}_) = \text{maxent}_] \mathbb{E} = \text{maxent}_\succ \mathbb{E} .$$

Proof. Simply apply the above three propositions. $\qquad\square$

It is known that maxent$_\succ$ $\mathbb{E}$ is a singleton, in case of a certain Σ_1 premiss [44], a class of Π_1 premisses [25] and a class of constraints for unary languages [42]. As remarked above, we show in a forthcoming paper [26], that for a single premiss φ^c with $0 < P_=(\varphi) < 1$ and $0 \leq c \leq 1$ there exists a unique maximum entropy function in maxent$_\succ$ $\mathbb{E}$, which is obtained from suitably (Jeffrey) updating the equivocator.

Premiss sentences φ with $P_=(\varphi) = 0$ and cases with multiple uncertain premisses – on the other hand – are still poorly understood.

4   Modification Number 3

The Maximum Entropy Approach, in its original formulation, fails to provide probabilities for uncertain inference for certain evidence bases of quantifier complexity Σ_2 [43, § 2.2]. For example, for the single certain premiss $\varphi := \exists x \forall y U x y$

every probability function P consistent with the evidence must assign φ probability one, $P \in \mathbb{E}$ entails $P(\varphi) = 1$. There must hence be, at least, one constant t_k witnessing the existence of all these y, $P(\forall y U t_k y) > 0$. Ceteris paribus, the $k - 1$-entropy of such functions increases the greater the k such that t_k is a witness. Now suppose for contradiction that there exists a maximum entropy function $P \in \mathbb{E}$ with t_k as the first witness. Now construct a probability Q by postponing the witness by one, t_{k+1} is the first witness of the premiss according to Q. Q can be constructed such that $H_n(Q) \geq H_n(P)$ for all n. One can then show that $R := \frac{Q+P}{2}$ has strictly greater n-entropy than P for all $r \geq n + 1$ (concavity of H_n). It is hence the case that for all $P \in \mathbb{E}$ there exists a $R \in \mathbb{E}$ such that $R \succ P$. maxent$_\succ$ $\mathbb{E}$ is hence empty, see the forthcoming [26] for more details and a proof.

Theorem 1 shows that inductive logics induced by $)$ and $]$ also do not produce a unique probability for uncertain inference for the certain premiss $\varphi = \exists x \forall y U x y$.

From the perspective of this paper, we see that the inductive logic of the standard Maximum Entropy Approach fails to deliver well-defined probabilities for inference for the certain premiss $\varphi = \exists x \forall y U x y$, because the relation $\succ$ holds for too many pairs of probability functions. Proceeding in the spirit of this paper, it seems sensible to define a modified inductive logic induced by a notion of comparative entropy, $\}$, which holds for fewer pairs of probability functions. That is, $\}$ is refined by $\succ$.

Closest to the spirit of Definition 3 is to define $P\}Q$ as follows.

Definition 9 (Modification Number 3). $P\}Q$, if and only if $H_n(P) > H_n(Q)$ for all $n \in \mathbb{N}$.

Clearly, the other three notions of comparative entropy are refinements of $\}$.

Proposition 4 (Comparison of $\}$ vs. $\succ$, $],)$). *Neither of the three binary relations $\succ,],)$ is a strong refinement and neither is a centric refinement of $\}$.*

Proof. Consider three pairwise different probability functions P, Q, R with i) $H_n(P) > H_n(Q)$ for all n , ii) $\frac{H_n(P)}{H_n(Q)} \approx 1$, iii) $H_1(Q) = H_1(R) - \delta$ for large $\delta > 0$ and iv) $H_n(Q) > H_n(R)$ for all $n \geq 1$.

Then $P\}Q$ and $Q \succ R, Q]R, Q)R$ all hold. Now note that $H_1(P) < H_1(R)$ and thus $P\}R$ fails to hold. Hence, none of $\succ,],)$ is a strong refinement of $\}$. Finally, observe that $\frac{Q+R}{2}\}R$ fails to hold. Hence, none of $\succ,],)$ is a centric refinement of $\}$. $\square$

The aim here is to define a different inductive logic producing well-defined probabilities for the premiss sentence $\varphi = \exists x \forall y R x y$ (and other premiss sentences). Theorem 1 shows that a different logic can only arise, if none of the other three notions of comparative entropy is a strong and centric refinement of $\}$. Proposition 4 shows that neither of these notions is a strong and centric refinement of $\}$. It his hence in principle possible that $\}$ defines a novel inductive logic.

The following proposition shows that this not only possible in principle by providing a case in which the induced inductive logics do come apart.

Proposition 5 (Inductive Logics). *The binary relation* $\}$ *induces a different inductive logic than* $\succ,],)$.

Proof. Let U be the only and unary relation symbol of $\mathcal{L}$. Suppose there is no evidence, then all probability functions are consistent with the empty set of premises, $\mathbb{E} = \mathbb{P}$. Then every $P \in \mathbb{P}$ with $P(Ut_1) = P(\neg Ut_1) = 0.5$ has maximal 1-entropy. Hence, all such P are members of $\text{maxent}_\} \, \mathbb{E}$. For $\square \in \{\succ,],)\}$ it holds that $\text{maxent}_\square \, \mathbb{E} = \{P_=\}$. So, $\text{maxent}_\square \, \mathbb{E}$ is a proper subset of $\text{maxent}_\} \, \mathbb{E}$:

$$\text{maxent}_\square \, \mathbb{E} = \{P_=\} \subset \{P \in \mathbb{P} \;:\; P(Ut_1) = P(\neg Ut_1)\} \subset \text{maxent}_\} \, \mathbb{E} \;.$$

$\square$

This proof leads to the following more general observation:

Proposition 6 (Finite Sublanguages). *If there exists an* $n \in \mathbb{N}$ *and a* $P \in \mathbb{E}$ *such that* $H_n(P) = \max\{H_n(Q) \,:\, Q \in \mathbb{E}\}$, *then* $P \in \text{maxent}_\} \, \mathbb{E}$.

This strong focus on single sublanguages $\mathcal{L}_n$ makes $\text{maxent}_\}$ unsuitable as an inductive logic for infinite predicate languages, as the following example demonstrates.

Example 1 (Absurdity of Modification 3). Consider the case in which the premisses jointly determine the probabilities on $\mathcal{L}_1$. For example, the given language $\mathcal{L}$ contains two relation symbols: a unary relation symbol U_1 and a binary relation symbol U_2. The premisses are $U_2 t_1 t_1$ holds with certainty and $P(U_1 t_1) = 10\%$. Then every probability function $P \in \mathbb{P}$ that satisfies these two premisses has a 1-entropy of $H_1(P) = -0.9 \cdot \log(0.9) - 0.1 \cdot \log(0.1)$. So, $H_1(P) = \max\{H_1(Q) \,:\, Q \in \mathbb{E}\}$. This means that every feasible probability function (of which there are many) is a maximum entropy function – regardless of how entropic (or not) probabilities are assigned to the other sublanguages $\mathcal{L}_n$ for $n \geq 2$:

$$\text{maxent}_\} \, \mathbb{E} = \mathbb{E} \;.$$

5 Conclusions

Maximum entropy inductive logic on infinite domains lacks a paradigm approach. The Entropy Limit Approach, the Maximum Entropy Approach as well as the here studied modified Maximum Entropy Approaches induce the same unique inductive logic in a number of natural cases (Theorem 1 and [25,42,44]). This points towards a unified picture of maximum entropy inductive logics – in spite of the number of possible ways to define such inductive logics.

This uniqueness is particularly noteworthy in light of a string of results suggesting and comparing different notions of entropy (maximisation), which lead to different maximum entropy functions [5–7, 10, 13, 18, 20, 27].

The Maximum Entropy Approach fails to provide probabilities for uncertain inference for some evidence bases of quantifier complexity Σ_2 [43, § 2.2]. In these cases, for all $P \in \mathbb{E}$ there exists a $Q \in \mathbb{E}$ such that $Q \succ P$ and maxent $\mathbb{E}$ is hence empty [26]. One way to sensibly define an inductive logic could be to consider a binary relation which is refined by $\succ$. Unfortunately, the most obvious way to define such an inductive logic produces absurd results (Proposition 6). Finding a way to sensibly define a (maximum entropy) inductive logic properly dealing with such cases must be left to further study.

Further avenues for future research suggest themselves. Firstly, the question arises whether the first two here suggested modifications and the original Maximum Entropy Approach agree more widely or whether they come apart in important cases. If they do provide different probabilities for inductive inference, which of them is to be preferred and why? Secondly, are there further prima facie plausible ways to modify the Maximum Entropy Approach? Thirdly, are there other modifications of the Entropy Limit Approach? If so, how do they look like and what are the implications for the induced inductive logics? Fourthly, what is the status of the entropy limit conjecture [48, p. 191], the conjecture that the Entropy Limit Approach and the Maximum Entropy Approach agree under the assumption that the former is well-defined, in light of these modifications? Finally, cases with multiple uncertain premises remain poorly understood and pose a challenge to be tackled.

Acknowledgements. Many thanks to Jeff Paris, Soroush Rafiee Rad, Alena Vencovská and Jon Williamson for continued collaboration on maximum entropy inference. I'm also indebted to anonymous referees who helped me improve this paper.

References

1. Barnett, O., Paris, J.B.: Maximum entropy inference with quantified knowledge. Logic J. IGPL **16**(1), 85–98 (2008). https://doi.org/10.1093/jigpal/jzm028
2. Carnap, R.: The two concepts of probability: the problem of probability. Philos. Phenomenological Res. **5**(4), 513–532 (1945). https://doi.org/10.2307/2102817
3. Carnap, R.: The Continuum of Inductive Methods. Chicago University of Chicago Press, Chicago (1952)
4. Crupi, V.: Inductive logic. J. Philos. Logic **44**(6), 641–650 (2015). https://doi.org/10.1007/s10992-015-9348-8
5. Crupi, V., Nelson, J., Meder, B., Cevolani, G., Tentori, K.: Generalized information theory meets human cognition: introducing a unified framework to model uncertainty and information search. Cogn. Sci. **42**, 1410–1456 (2018). https://doi.org/10.1111/cogs.12613
6. Csiszár, I.: Axiomatic characterizations of information measures. Entropy **10**(3), 261–273 (2008). https://doi.org/10.3390/e10030261
7. Cui, H., Liu, Q., Zhang, J., Kang, B.: An improved deng entropy and its application in pattern recognition. IEEE Access **7**, 18284–18292 (2019). https://doi.org/10.1109/access.2019.2896286

8. Gaifman, H.: Concerning measures in first order calculi. Isr. J. Math. **2**(1), 1–18 (1964). https://doi.org/10.1007/BF02759729
9. Groves, T.: Lakatos's criticism of Carnapian inductive logic was mistaken. J. Appl. Logic **14**, 3–21 (2016). https://doi.org/10.1016/j.jal.2015.09.014
10. Grünwald, P.D., Dawid, A.P.: Game theory, maximum entropy, minimum discrepancy and robust Bayesian decision theory. Ann. Stat. **32**(4), 1367–1433 (2004). https://doi.org/10.1214/009053604000000553
11. Haenni, R., Romeijn, J.W., Wheeler, G., Williamson, J.: Probabilistic Argumentation, Synthese Library, vol. 350. Springer, Dordrecht (2011). https://doi.org/10.1007/978-94-007-0008-6_3
12. Halpern, J.Y., Koller, D.: Representation dependence in probabilistic inference. J. Artif. Intell. Res. **21**, 319–356 (2004). https://doi.org/10.1613/jair.1292
13. Hanel, R., Thurner, S., Gell-Mann, M.: Generalized entropies and the transformation group of superstatistics. Proc. Nat. Acad. Sci. **108**(16), 6390–6394 (2011). https://doi.org/10.1073/pnas.1103539108
14. Howarth, E., Paris, J.B.: Pure inductive logic with functions. J. Symbolic Logic, 1–22 (2019). https://doi.org/10.1017/jsl.2017.49
15. Jaynes, E.T.: Probability Theory: The Logic of Science. Cambridge University Press, Cambridge (2003)
16. Kließ, M.S., Paris, J.B.: Second order inductive logic and Wilmers' principle. J. Appl. Logic **12**(4), 462–476 (2014). https://doi.org/10.1016/j.jal.2014.07.002
17. Landes, J.: The Principle of Spectrum Exchangeability within Inductive Logic. Ph.D. thesis, Manchester Institute for Mathematical Sciences (2009). https://jlandes.files.wordpress.com/2015/10/phdthesis.pdf
18. Landes, J.: Probabilism, entropies and strictly proper scoring rules. Int. J. Approximate Reason. **63**, 1–21 (2015). https://doi.org/10.1016/j.ijar.2015.05.007
19. Landes, J.: The entropy-limit (Conjecture) for Σ_2-premisses. Stud. Logica. **109**, 423–442 (2021). https://doi.org/10.1007/s11225-020-09912-3
20. Landes, J., Masterton, G.: Invariant equivocation. Erkenntnis **82**, 141–167 (2017). https://doi.org/10.1007/s10670-016-9810-1
21. Landes, J., Paris, J., Vencovská, A.: Language invariance and spectrum exchangeability in inductive logic. In: Mellouli, K. (ed.) ECSQARU 2007. LNCS (LNAI), vol. 4724, pp. 151–160. Springer, Heidelberg (2007). https://doi.org/10.1007/978-3-540-75256-1_16
22. Landes, J., Paris, J.B., Vencovská, A.: Some aspects of polyadic inductive logic. Stud. Logica **90**(1), 3–16 (2008). https://doi.org/10.1007/s11225-008-9140-7
23. Landes, J., Paris, J.B., Vencovská, A.: Representation theorems for probability functions satisfying spectrum exchangeability in inductive logic. Int. J. Approximate Reason. **51**(1), 35–55 (2009). https://doi.org/10.1016/j.ijar.2009.07.001
24. Landes, J., Paris, J.B., Vencovská, A.: A survey of some recent results on spectrum exchangeability in polyadic inductive logic. Synthese **181**, 19–47 (2011). https://doi.org/10.1007/s11229-009-9711-9
25. Landes, J., Rafiee Rad, S., Williamson, J.: Towards the entropy-limit conjecture. Ann. Pure Appl. Logic **172**, 102870 (2021). https://doi.org/10.1016/j.apal.2020.102870
26. Landes, J., Rafiee Rad, S., Williamson, J.: Determining maximal entropy functions for objective Bayesian inductive logic (2022). Manuscript
27. Landes, J., Williamson, J.: Objective Bayesianism and the maximum entropy principle. Entropy **15**(9), 3528–3591 (2013). https://doi.org/10.3390/e15093528
28. Landes, J., Williamson, J.: Justifying objective Bayesianism on predicate languages. Entropy **17**(4), 2459–2543 (2015). https://doi.org/10.3390/e17042459

656   J. Landes

29. Niiniluoto, I.: The development of the Hintikka program. In: Gabbay, D.M., Hart-
    mann, S., Woods, J. (eds.) Handbook of the History of Logic, pp. 311–356. Elsevier,
    Kidlington (2011). https://doi.org/10.1016/b978-0-444-52936-7.50009-4
30. Ognjanović, Z., Rašković, M., Marković, Z.: Probability Logics. Springer, Cham
    (2016). https://doi.org/10.1007/978-3-319-47012-2
31. Ortner, R., Leitgeb, H.: Mechanizing induction. In: Gabbay, D.M., Hartmann, S.,
    Woods, J. (eds.) Handbook of the History of Logic, pp. 719–772. Elsevier (2011).
    https://doi.org/10.1016/b978-0-444-52936-7.50018-5
32. Paris, J.B.: Common sense and maximum entropy. Synthese **117**, 75–93 (1998).
    https://doi.org/10.1023/A:1005081609010
33. Paris, J.B.: The Uncertain Reasoner's Companion: A Mathematical Perspective,
    2 edn. Cambridge Tracts in Theoretical Computer Science, vol. 39. Cambridge
    University Press, Cambridge (2006)
34. Paris, J.B.: What you see is what you get. Entropy **16**(11), 6186–6194 (2014).
    https://doi.org/10.3390/e16116186
35. Paris, J.B., Rad, S.R.: A note on the least informative model of a theory. In:
    Ferreira, F., Löwe, B., Mayordomo, E., Mendes Gomes, L. (eds.) CiE 2010. LNCS,
    vol. 6158, pp. 342–351. Springer, Heidelberg (2010). https://doi.org/10.1007/978-
    3-642-13962-8_38
36. Paris, J.B., Vencovská, A.: On the applicability of maximum entropy to inexact
    reasoning. Int. J. Approximate Reason. **3**(1), 1–34 (1989). https://doi.org/10.1016/
    0888-613X(89)90012-1
37. Paris, J.B., Vencovská, A.: A note on the inevitability of maximum entropy.
    Int. J. Approximate Reason. **4**(3), 183–223 (1990). https://doi.org/10.1016/0888-
    613X(90)90020-3
38. Paris, J.B., Vencovská, A.: In defense of the maximum entropy inference process.
    Int. J. Approximate Reason. **17**(1), 77–103 (1997). https://doi.org/10.1016/S0888-
    613X(97)00014-5
39. Paris, J.B., Vencovská, A.: Common sense and stochastic independence. In: Cor-
    field, D., Williamson, J. (eds.) Foundations of Bayesianism, pp. 203–240. Kluwer,
    Dordrecht (2001)
40. Paris, J.B., Vencovská, A.: Pure Inductive Logic. Cambridge University Press,
    Cambridge (2015)
41. Paris, J.B., Vencovská, A.: Six problems in pure inductive logic. J. Philos. Logic
    (2019). https://doi.org/10.1007/s10992-018-9492-z
42. Rafiee Rad, S.: Inference processes for first order probabilistic languages. Ph.D. the-
    sis, Manchester Institute for Mathematical Sciences (2009). http://www.rafieerad.
    org/manthe.pdf
43. Rafiee Rad, S.: Equivocation axiom on first order languages. Stud. Logica. **105**(1),
    121–152 (2017). https://doi.org/10.1007/s11225-016-9684-x
44. Rafiee Rad, S.: Maximum entropy models for Σ_1 sentences. J. Logics Appl.
    5(1), 287–300 (2018). http://www.collegepublications.co.uk/admin/download.
    php?ID=ifcolog00021
45. Williamson, J.: Objective Bayesian probabilistic logic. J. Algorithms **63**(4), 167–
    183 (2008). https://doi.org/10.1016/j.jalgor.2008.07.001
46. Williamson, J.: Objective Bayesianism with predicate languages. Synthese **163**(3),
    341–356 (2008). https://doi.org/10.1007/s11229-007-9298-y
47. Williamson, J.: In Defence of Objective Bayesianism. Oxford University Press,
    Oxford (2010)
48. Williamson, J.: Lectures on Inductive Logic. Oxford University Press, Oxford
    (2017)

A Logic and Computation for Popper's Conditional Probabilities

Shota Motoura[✉][ID]

Data Science Research Laboratories, NEC Corporation, Kawasaki, Kanagawa, Japan
motoura@nec.com

Abstract. A Popper function is one that gives a conditional probability of propositional formulae. This paper gives a finite set of axioms that defines the set of Popper functions in many-sorted monadic second-order logic, and proves the decidability of the validity problem for a practically important first-order fragment of the second-order language with respect to a set of Popper functions. Upon these logical foundations, we propose, with results on their time complexity, two algorithms that compute the range of values that designated conditional probabilities can take under given constraints.

Keywords: Logic · Conditional probability · Popper function · Definability · Decidability · Computation · Complexity.

1   Introduction

The purpose of this paper is to propose, on the basis of theoretical foundations, algorithms that *directly* compute the range of values that designated conditional probabilities can take under given constraints.

Motivating Example. There are many constraints which can be written in terms of conditional probabilities of propositional formulae. Examples are:

- $P(\text{5-yearSurvival}|\text{LungCancer}) = 32.7\%$;
- $P(\text{5-yearSurvival}|\text{Cancer} \wedge \text{Male}) = 59.1\%$;
- $P(\text{LungCancer}|\text{Smoker}) = 1.6P(\text{LungCancer}|\neg\text{Smoker})$, *etc.*.

Our expected output of the algorithms is, for example:

$$32.5\% \leq P(\neg\text{5-yearSurvival}|\text{LungCancer} \wedge \neg\text{Smoker} \wedge \text{Male}) \leq 56.2\%$$

which means that the probability that one will die within five years when a person is a male non-smoker and diagnosed with lung cancer is greater than or equal to 32.5% and less than or equal to 56.2%.[1]

---

[1] The numbers are just randomly chosen for the sake of a concrete example.

J. Vejnarová and N. Wilson (Eds.): ECSQARU 2021, LNAI 12897, pp. 657–671, 2021.
https://doi.org/10.1007/978-3-030-86772-0_47

Related Work. Regarding *unconditional* probabilities, Hailperin [17] gave the upper and lower bounds of the probability $P(\varphi)$ of a designated propositional formula φ, under constraints in the form of a lower and a upper bounds $a_i \leq P(\psi_i) \leq b_i$ on finitely many formulae ψ_i. This result is generalised in [14], where the decidability is proved for a Boolean combination of inequalities between polynomial of unconditional probabilities. On the semantic side, several types of possible-world semantics have been proposed and their complete axiomatisations are given [6,14,19]. Papers [14,19] also refer *indirect* reasoning about conditional probability, that is, reducing it to reasoning about *unconditional* probability. On the syntactic side, Boričić [9] and [8] propose sequent calculus and natural deduction, respectively, for the probabilistic semantics.[2]

As for direct reasoning about conditional probability, a problem is what value $P(A|B)$ should take where the probability of the conditioning part $P(B)$ is equal to 0 (cf. [18]). Adams in [1,2] defined $P(A|B)$ to be 1 following '*a conventional stipulation*' [3], while Bacchus in [6] defined it to be 0. Concerning this problem, Popper, among others, treats a conditional probability as a primitive notion and proposed, in [27], a kind of function that assigns a conditional probability to each pair of formulae together with a set of axioms that the function should obey. Such a function is now called a *Popper function*.[3] In this paper, we take the Popper functions to give concrete examples.[4]

About the reasoning task such as the motivating example above, Gilio [16] and Wagner [31], show how *non-strict* upper and lower bounds of a conditional probability propagate along formal systems, called System P and *modus tollens*, respectively. Another related work is Ikodinović and Ognjanović [21]. It proves the completeness and the decidability for a logic with operator $CP_{\geq s}(A|B)$ expressing $P(A|B) \geq s$, although operator $CP_{\geq s}(A|B)$ is not defined where B is a propositional contradiction.

Our Contributions. In this paper, we:

1. give a finite set of axioms in many-sorted monadic second-order logic that defines the set of Popper functions, including their domain and codomain;
2. prove the decidability of the validity problem for a practically important first-order fragment of the second-order language with respect to the set of Popper functions;
3. propose two algorithms that compute the range of the values that designated conditional probabilities can take under given constraints.

---

[2] In this sequent calculus, the probability is assigned to a sequent but it can be proved equal to that of the corresponding material implication.

[3] A Popper function has a salient characterisation as the standard part of a conditional probability of hyperreal-valued probabilities [24]. This result is extended to the representation theorem by non-Archimedean probabilities in [10]. Thanks to an anonymous referee for pointing this out.

[4] However, our theorems and algorithms may apply to other cases, including those of $P(A|B) = 1$ or 0 for $P(B) = 0$.

Organisation. In Sect. 2, we recall the definition of a Popper function. Section 3 gives the definability result for many-sorted monadic second-order logic for Popper functions. In Sect. 4, we prove that the validity problem with respect to the set of Popper functions is decidable for an important first-order fragment of this second-order language, and, in Sect. 5, we propose two algorithms that compute the range of values that designated conditional probabilities can take and show results on their complexity.

2   Popper Functions

Let us begin with recalling the definition of Popper function, which gives a kind of conditional probability of each pair of propositional formulae.

We first specify the set of formulae on which Popper functions are defined. Throughout the paper, we fix a *nonempty* and *finite* set $\mathscr{A}$ of proposition letters.

Definition 1. *The* propositional formulae *are defined by the rule* $\varphi ::= a \mid \neg\varphi \mid \varphi \wedge \varphi$, *where* a *ranges over* $\mathscr{A}$. *The set of propositional formulae are denoted by* $\mathscr{L}$.

Since a Popper function depends on syntax, we explicitly define logical connectives $\varphi \vee \psi$, $\varphi \rightarrow \psi$ and $\varphi \leftrightarrow \psi$ to be $\neg(\neg\varphi \wedge \neg\psi)$, $\neg(\varphi \wedge \neg\psi)$ and $(\varphi \rightarrow \psi) \wedge (\psi \rightarrow \varphi)$, respectively.

On this propositional language, a Popper function is defined as below:

Definition 2 (Popper Functions [27]). *A Popper function on* $\mathscr{L}$ *is a function* $P : \mathscr{L} \times \mathscr{L} \rightarrow \mathbb{R}$ *that satisfies the following conditions (notation: $P(\varphi|\psi)$ instead of $P(\varphi, \psi)$):*

P1 *for any φ and ψ in $\mathscr{L}$, there exist φ' and ψ' in $\mathscr{L}$ such that $P(\varphi|\psi) \neq P(\varphi'|\psi')$;*

P2 *for any φ and ψ in $\mathscr{L}$, $P(\varphi|\chi) = P(\psi|\chi)$ for all χ in $\mathscr{L}$ implies $P(\gamma|\varphi) = P(\gamma|\psi)$ for all γ in $\mathscr{L}$;*

P3 *for any φ and ψ in $\mathscr{L}$, $P(\varphi|\varphi) = P(\psi|\psi)$;*

P4 *for any φ, ψ and χ in $\mathscr{L}$, $P(\varphi \wedge \psi|\chi) \leq P(\varphi|\chi)$;*

P5 *for any φ, ψ and χ in $\mathscr{L}$, $P(\varphi \wedge \psi|\chi) = P(\varphi|\psi \wedge \chi)P(\psi|\chi)$;*

P6 *for any φ and ψ in $\mathscr{L}$, $P(\varphi|\psi) + P(\neg\varphi|\psi) = P(\psi|\psi)$ unless $P(\chi|\psi) = P(\psi|\psi)$ for all χ in $\mathscr{L}$.*

We denote the set of all Popper functions by $\mathscr{P}$.

3   Definability

A Popper function is a special case of a function from the product of two copies of a *formula algebra* to the field of real numbers, where the *formula algebra* $(\mathscr{L}, F_\neg, F_\wedge)$ is defined by $F_\neg(\varphi) := \neg\varphi$ and $F_\wedge(\varphi, \psi) := \varphi \wedge \psi$ for any φ and ψ in $\mathscr{L}$. Therefore, as we shall see, a Popper function can be seen as a structure for many-sorted monadic second-order logic with the sorts $\{\mathsf{form}, \mathsf{real}\}$ for the propositional formulae and the real numbers. In this section, we prove that the set of Popper functions for $\mathscr{A}$ is finitely axiomatisable in many-sorted monadic second-order logic.

3.1 Many-Sorted Monadic Second-Order Logic for Popper Functions

We first specify the many-sorted monadic second-order logic which we shall use. (cf. [15,26]) The language of our logic is given as follows:

Definition 3 (Alphabet). *The alphabet* $\Sigma = (\mathscr{S}, \mathscr{F}, \mathscr{R}, \mathscr{V}_1, \mathscr{V}_2)$ *of our language consists of:*

1. *a set of sorts* $\mathscr{S} = \{\mathsf{form}, \mathsf{real}\};$
2. *a set* $\mathscr{F}$ *of function symbols:* $a : \mathsf{form}$ *for* $a \in \mathscr{A}$, $f_\neg : \mathsf{form} \to \mathsf{form}$, $f_\wedge : \mathsf{form} \times \mathsf{form} \to \mathsf{form}$, $0 : \mathsf{real}$, $1 : \mathsf{real}$, $+ : \mathsf{real} \times \mathsf{real} \to \mathsf{real}$, $\cdot : \mathsf{real} \times \mathsf{real} \to \mathsf{real}$, $p : \mathsf{form} \times \mathsf{form} \to \mathsf{real}$
3. *a set of a relation symbol* $\mathscr{R} = \{\leq : \mathsf{real} \times \mathsf{real}\};$
4. *the union* $\mathscr{V}_1$ *of two disjoint infinite sets of first-order variables for each of* form *and* real: $\mathscr{V}^1_{\mathsf{form}} = \{x : \mathsf{form}, \ldots\}$ *and* $\mathscr{V}^1_{\mathsf{real}} = \{y : \mathsf{real}, \ldots\};$
5. *the union of two disjoint infinite sets of monadic second-order variables for each of* form *and* real: $\mathscr{V}^2_{\mathsf{form}} = \{X : \mathsf{form}, \ldots\}$ *and* $\mathscr{V}^2_{\mathsf{real}} = \{Y : \mathsf{real}, \ldots\}.$

In addition to them, we use $=_\sigma$ *as the logical symbol for equality for sort* $\sigma \in \{\mathsf{form}, \mathsf{real}\}$, *that is,* $=_\sigma$ *is interpreted in the standard manner.*

Definition 4 (Formulae)

1. *The terms are defined by the following rule:* $t : \sigma :: = x : \sigma \mid f(t_1 : \sigma_1, \ldots, t_n : \sigma_n) : \sigma$, *where* $x : \sigma$ *ranges over* $\mathscr{V}^1_\sigma$ *for* $\sigma \in \{\mathsf{form}, \mathsf{real}\}$ *and* $f : \sigma_1 \times \cdots \times \sigma_n \to \sigma$ *over* $\mathscr{F}$.
2. *The atomic formulae are defined by:* $\alpha :: = t : \sigma =_\sigma s : \sigma \mid t : \mathsf{real} \leq s : \mathsf{real}$, *where* $t : \sigma$ *and* $s : \sigma$ *range over the set of terms, and* $t : \mathsf{real}$ *and* $s : \mathsf{real}$ *over the* real-*terms.*
3. *The formulae are defined by:* $\varphi :: = \alpha \mid \neg\varphi \mid \varphi \wedge \varphi \mid (\exists x : \sigma)\varphi \mid (\exists X : \sigma)\varphi$, *where* α *ranges over the set of atomic formulae, and* $x : \sigma$ *and* $X : \sigma$ *over* $\mathscr{V}^1_\sigma$ *and* $\mathscr{V}^2_\sigma$ *for* $\sigma \in \{\mathsf{form}, \mathsf{real}\}$, *respectively.*

We denote by $\mathscr{L}^2_{\mathsf{PF}}$ *the set of formulae defined above.*

We write $\neg x$ and $x \wedge y$ for $f_\wedge(x, y)$ and $f_\neg(x)$, respectively, when there is no confusion. In addition, we suppress the sorts σ in terms and formulae when they are clear from the context. We define $(\forall x)\varphi$ to be $\neg(\exists x)\neg\varphi$ as usual and use $(\exists x_1 \ldots x_n)$ and $(\forall x_1 \ldots x_n)$ instead of $(\exists x_1) \cdots (\exists x_n)$ and $(\forall x_1) \cdots (\forall x_n)$, respectively, and $s \neq t$ instead of $\neg s = t$.

The clauses in the definition of a Popper function (Definition 2) can be directly translated into this language:

Example 1. The following set of axioms for Popper functions is denoted by PFL:

P1 $(\forall xy)(\exists x'y')p(x|y) \neq p(x'|y')$
P2 $(\forall xy)(((\forall z)p(x|z) = p(y|z)) \to ((\forall w)p(w|x) = p(w|y)))$
P3 $(\forall xy)p(x|x) = p(y|y)$

P4 $(\forall xyz)p(x \wedge y|z) \le p(x|z)$
P5 $(\forall xyz)p(x \wedge y)|z) = p(x|y \wedge z) \cdot p(y|z)$
P6 $(\forall xy)((\neg(\forall z)p(z|y) = p(y|y)) \rightarrow (p(x|y) + p(\neg x|y) = p(y|y)))$.   ⊣

The structures for this language are given by:

Definition 5 (Σ-structures)

– A Σ-structure $M = (M_{\mathsf{form}}, M_{\mathsf{real}}, p^M)$ *is given as follows:*
  • $M_{\mathsf{form}} = (S, f^M_\neg, f^M_\wedge)$ *and* $M_{\mathsf{real}} = (R, 0^M, 1^M, +^M, \cdot^M)$;
  • $p^M : S \times S \to R$.
  We call M_{form} *and* M_{real} *structures for* form *and* real, *respectively.*
– *An* assignment $\mu = (\mu_{\mathsf{form}}, \mu_{\mathsf{real}})$ *assigns the following for each* $\sigma \in$ {form, real}:
  • *to each first-order variable* $x : \sigma$ *an element* $\mu_\sigma(x) \in M_\sigma$;
  • *to each monadic second-order variable* $X : \sigma$ *a subset* $\mu_\sigma(X) \subseteq M_\sigma$.

In what follows, we identify a Σ-structure, $(M_{\mathsf{form}}, M_{\mathsf{real}}, p^M)$, and a function, $p^M : M_{\mathsf{form}} \times M_{\mathsf{form}} \to M_{\mathsf{real}}$. For example, a Popper function $P : \mathscr{L} \times \mathscr{L} \to \mathbb{R}$ is identified with the Σ-structure$((\mathscr{L}, F_\neg, F_\wedge), (\mathbb{R}, 0, 1, +, \cdot), P)$.

The interpretation is defined as usual:

Definition 6 (Interpretation of Terms). *Given a Σ-structure M and an assignment μ, the terms are inductively interpreted as:*

– $a^M[\mu] = a^M$ *for any* $a \in \mathscr{A}$;
– $c^M[\mu] = c^M$ *for each* $c = \{0, 1\}$;
– $(x : \sigma)^M[\mu] = \mu_\sigma(x : \sigma)$ *for* $x : \sigma \in \mathscr{V}^1_\sigma$ *with* $\sigma \in$ {form, real};
– $f(t_1, \ldots t_n)^M[\mu] = f^M(t_1{}^M[\mu], \ldots, t_n{}^M[\mu])$ *for* $f = f_\neg, f_\wedge, +, \cdot, p$;
– $(X : \sigma)^M[\mu] = \mu_\sigma(X : \sigma)$ *for* $X : \sigma \in \mathscr{V}^2_\sigma$ *with* $\sigma \in$ {form, real}.

Definition 7 (Satisfaction Relation). *Let M be a Σ-structure and μ an assignment. For every formula φ in $\mathscr{L}^2_{\mathsf{PF}}$, the statement that φ is satisfied by μ in M (notation: $M \models \varphi[\mu]$) is inductively defined by the following clauses:*

$M \models (t : \sigma = s : \sigma)[\mu]$ ⠀⠀iff $t^M[\mu] = s^M[\mu]$
$M \models (t : \mathsf{real} \le s : \mathsf{real})[\mu]$ iff $t^M[\mu] \le s^M[\mu]$
$M \models X(t)[\mu]$ ⠀⠀⠀⠀⠀⠀⠀⠀iff $t^M[\mu] \in \mu(X)$
$M \models \neg\varphi[\mu]$ ⠀⠀⠀⠀⠀⠀⠀⠀iff $M \not\models \varphi[\mu]$
$M \models \varphi \wedge \psi[\mu]$ ⠀⠀⠀⠀⠀⠀iff $M \models \varphi[\mu]$ *and* $M \models \psi[\mu]$
$M \models (\exists x : \sigma)\varphi[\mu]$ ⠀⠀⠀iff ⠀*there is an element e of M_σ s.t.* $M \models \varphi[\mu(e/x)]$
$M \models (\exists X : \sigma)\varphi[\mu]$ ⠀⠀iff ⠀*there is a subset S of M_σ s.t.* $M \models \varphi[\mu(S/X)]$

Here, σ *is* form *and* real, *and* $\mu(e/x)$ *(respectively, $\mu(S/X)$) is the same assignment as μ except that $\mu(e/x)$ assigns e to x (respectively, $\mu(S/X)$ assigns S to X).*

If φ is satisfied by μ in M for any assignment μ, we say that M *satisfies* φ or that M is a *model* of φ and use the notation $M \models \varphi$. These notions and notations are naturally extended to the cases where a class $\mathscr{C}$ of models and/or a set Φ of formulae are considered, namely, $\mathscr{C} \models \Phi$, $\mathscr{C} \models \varphi$ and $M \models \Phi$. In particular, for the set $\mathscr{P}$ of Popper functions, we say that a formula φ is *valid* or *$\mathscr{P}$-valid* if $\mathscr{P} \models \varphi$.

3.2 Definability in Second-Order Logic

As we have seen, a Popper function can be identified with a structure of the second-order logic defined above. We now prove that the set of Popper functions $P : \mathscr{L} \times \mathscr{L} \to \mathbb{R}$ is definable by finitely many axioms written in $\mathscr{L}^2_{\mathsf{PF}}$. As a Popper function consists of three parts, the formula algebra $\mathscr{L}$, the field $\mathbb{R}$ of real numbers and the function itself P, we confirm the definability of the domain $\mathscr{L}$ and the codomain $\mathbb{R}$ and then prove that of the set of Popper functions.

Firstly, the set of axioms given below defines the formula algebra $(\mathscr{L}, F_\neg, F_\wedge)$:

Definition 8. *We denote the set of the following axioms by* FL:

F1 $(\forall x x')\neg x = \neg x' \to x = x'$
F2 $(\forall x y x' y') x \wedge y = x' \wedge y' \to (x = x') \wedge (y = y')$
F3 $(\forall x y z)\neg x \neq y \wedge z$
F4 $(\forall x y)a \neq x \wedge y$ *for any* $a \in \mathscr{A}$
F5 $(\forall y)a \neq \neg x$ *for any* $a \in \mathscr{A}$
F6 $(\forall X)[[(\bigwedge_{a \in \mathscr{A}} X(a)) \wedge (\forall x)(X(x) \to X(\neg x)) \wedge (\forall x y)(X(x) \wedge X(y) \to X(x \wedge y))]$
$\to (\forall x) X(x)]$

This is a straightforward extension of Peano's definition of the set of natural numbers (cf. [13]). Note that $(\bigwedge_{a \in \mathscr{A}} X(a))$ in axiom F6 is legitimate as $\mathscr{A}$ is assumed to be finite.

Theorem 1. FL *uniquely defines the formula algebra generated from* $\mathscr{A}$ *up to isomorphism.*

Proof. This can be proved by straightforwardly extending the ordinary proof for the case of Peano's definition of natural numbers (cf. [29]).   □

Combining Theorem 1 above and the well-known fact that there is a finite set RFL of axioms that defines the field of reals to be the Dedekind-complete ordered field, we can readily see that the union FL$\cup$RFL$\cup$PFL defines the Popper functions:

Theorem 2. *Let* $p : M_{\mathsf{form}} \times M_{\mathsf{form}} \to M_{\mathsf{real}}$ *be a* Σ-*structure. Then,* p *satisfies* FL $\cup$ RFL $\cup$ PFL *if and only if* p *is isomorphic to a Popper function in the sense that there exist a Popper function* P *and a pair of isomorphisms* $f : M_{\mathsf{form}} \to (\mathscr{L}, F_\neg, F_\wedge)$ *and* $g : M_{\mathsf{real}} \to \mathbb{R}$ *satisfying* $P \circ (f \times f) = g \circ p$, *where* $f \times f$ *is the mapping from* $M_{\mathsf{form}} \times M_{\mathsf{form}}$ *to* $(\mathscr{L}, F_\neg, F_\wedge) \times (\mathscr{L}, F_\neg, F_\wedge)$ *such that* $(f \times f)(x, y) = (f(x), f(y))$ *for any* (x, y) *in* $M_{\mathsf{form}} \times M_{\mathsf{form}}$.

Proof. We sketch the proof. Since FL and RFL define the formula algebra and the field of reals uniquely up to isomorphism, there are $f : M_{\mathsf{form}} \to (\mathscr{L}, F_\neg, F_\wedge)$ and $g : M_{\mathsf{real}} \to \mathbb{R}$. By their bijectivity and homomorphism conditions, we see that $P = g \circ p \circ (f^{-1} \times f^{-1})$ is a Popper function and that it satisfies that $P \circ (f \times f) = g \circ p$.   □

4   Decidability

In this section, we consider the first-order fragment $\mathscr{L}_{\mathsf{PF}}$ of $\mathscr{L}_{\mathsf{PF}}^2$. Accordingly, we consider an assignment $\mu = (\mu_{\mathsf{form}}, \mu_{\mathsf{real}})$ restricted to the sets $\mathscr{V}_{\mathsf{form}}^1$ and $\mathscr{V}_{\mathsf{real}}^1$ of the first-order variables, i.e. $\mu_{\mathsf{form}} : \mathscr{V}_{\mathsf{form}}^1 \to \mathscr{L}$ and $\mu_{\mathsf{real}} : \mathscr{V}_{\mathsf{real}}^1 \to \mathbb{R}$.

The problem of determining whether a given formula φ is $\mathscr{P}$-valid is called the $\mathscr{P}$-*validity problem*. In this section, we prove the decidability of the $\mathscr{P}$-validity problem for a specific set of sentence which we shall call Popper sentence. A *Popper sentence* is one in $\mathscr{L}_{\mathsf{PF}}$ where form terms appear only in the scopes of the occurrences of function symbol p. More precisely:

Definition 9. *The* Popper formulae *are defined by the following rules:*

1. *the terms of* form *are inductively defined from the variables* x : form *in* $\mathscr{V}_{\mathsf{form}}^1$ *and the constant symbols* a *in* $\mathscr{A}$ *by using function symbols* $f_{\neg}$ *and* $f_{\wedge}$;
2. *the terms of* real *are inductively defined from the variables* x : real *in* $\mathscr{V}_{\mathsf{real}}^1$, *constant symbols* 0 *and* 1, *and* $p(t|s)$ *with* form *terms* t *and* s *by* $-$ *and* $\cdot$;
3. *the formulae are defined by:*
   $$\varphi ::= t : \mathsf{real} = s : \mathsf{real} \mid t : \mathsf{real} \leq s : \mathsf{real} \mid \neg\varphi \mid \varphi \wedge \varphi \mid (\exists x : \mathsf{real})\varphi \mid (\exists x : \mathsf{form})\varphi$$

We denote the set of Popper formulae by PF. *A Popper formula is called a* Popper sentence *if it does not contain any free variable, and the set of Popper sentences is denoted by* PS.

For example, P1-P6 in PFL (Example 1) are all Popper sentences. A Popper sentence is of practical importance as it can express a relation between conditional probabilities.

In our decision procedure, we first reduce, through three translations, the $\mathscr{P}$-validity problem of a given Popper sentence to the validity problem of a formula of the *first-order* logic of the field of real numbers.

4.1   Translation 1

The first translation is based on the following fact:

Theorem 3. *Let* P *be a Popper function. If* $\varphi \leftrightarrow \varphi'$ *and* $\psi \leftrightarrow \psi'$ *are tautologies in classical propositional logic, then we have* $P(\varphi|\psi) = P(\varphi'|\psi')$.

Proof. We only sketch the proof. We first prove that, for any propositional formula χ, if a sequent $\varphi_1, \ldots, \varphi_n \longrightarrow \psi_1, \ldots, \psi_m$ is provable in propositional sequent calculus PK (cf. [11]), then we have $P(\neg(\varphi_1 \wedge \cdots \wedge \varphi_n \wedge \neg\psi_1 \wedge \cdots \wedge \neg\psi_m)|\chi) = 1$, by the induction on the construction of the PK-proof. Using this fact and elementary results on Popper functions (cf. APPENDIX *v of [27]), we see that $\varphi \to \psi$ implies $P(\varphi|\chi) \leq P(\psi|\chi)$ for all χ and thus $\varphi \leftrightarrow \psi$ implies $P(\varphi|\chi) = P(\psi|\chi)$ for all χ. We then obtain the theorem by P2.   □

This leads to the notion of a 'Popper function' whose domain is a *Lindenbaum-Tarski algebra*:

Definition 10 (cf. [12]). *The Lindenbaum-Tarski algebra* $\mathbb{L}$ *over the set* $\mathscr{A}$ *of proposition letters is the structure* $(L, -, \cdot)$, *where*

1. L *is the set* $\{[\varphi] \mid \varphi \in \mathscr{L}\}$ *of equivalence classes for the classical equivalence relation* $\leftrightarrow$;
2. $-$ *is a unary operation on* L *defined by* $-[\varphi] = [\neg\varphi]$;
3. $\cdot$ *is a binary operation on* L *defined by* $[\varphi] \cdot [\psi] = [\varphi \wedge \psi]$.

Definition 11 (Quotient Popper Functions). *A quotient Popper function is a function* $Q : \mathbb{L} \times \mathbb{L} \rightarrow \mathbb{R}$ *such that:*

1. *for any* $x, y \in \mathbb{L}$, *there exist* $x', y' \in \mathbb{L}$ *such that* $Q(x|y) \neq Q(x'|y')$;
2. *for any* $x, y \in \mathbb{L}$, $Q(x|z) = Q(y|z)$ *for all* $z \in \mathbb{L}$ *implies* $Q(w|x) = Q(w|y)$ *for all* $w \in \mathbb{L}$;
3. *for any* $x, y \in \mathbb{L}$, $Q(x|x) = Q(y|y)$;
4. *for any* $x, y, z \in \mathbb{L}$, $Q(x \cdot y|z) \leq Q(x|z)$;
5. *for any* $x, y, z \in \mathbb{L}$, $Q(x \cdot y|z) = Q(x|y \cdot z)Q(y|z)$;
6. *for any* $x, y \in \mathbb{L}$, $Q(x|y) + Q(-x|y) = Q(y|y)$ *unless* $Q(z|y) = Q(y|y)$ *for all* $z \in \mathbb{L}$.

We denote, by $\mathscr{Q}$, *the set of all quotient Popper functions.*

The target language of the first translation is one for the quotient Popper functions. It is the same as $\mathscr{L}_{\mathsf{PF}}$, except for the form constant symbols:

Definition 12. *Language* $\mathscr{L}_{\mathsf{QPF}}$ *is many-sorted first-order language defined by the alphabet* $(\mathscr{S}, \mathscr{F}', \mathscr{R}, \mathscr{V}_1)$ *together with logical symbols* $=_\sigma$ *with* $\sigma \in \{\mathsf{form}, \mathsf{real}\}$ *for equality, where* $\mathscr{F}'$ *consists of* $f_\neg$, $f_\wedge$, 0, 1, $-$, $\cdot$, p *and constant symbols* $z : \mathsf{form}$ *for all* $z \in \mathbb{L}$.

The notion of a structure and the interpretation of terms and formulae are defined in an analogous way to those for the first-order fragment of $\mathscr{L}_{\mathsf{PF}}^2$. A quotient Popper function is a structure for $\mathscr{L}_{\mathsf{QPF}}$. A *quotient Popper formula* and a *quotient Popper sentence* are a formula and a sentence in $\mathscr{L}_{\mathsf{QPF}}$ whose occurrences of form terms only appear in the scopes of the occurrences of p. We denote the set of quotient Popper formulae by QPF.

Definition 13 (Translation 1). *We give a translation* $T_1 : PF \rightarrow QPF$ *by induction on the construction of a Popper formula (in the induction, we define the translation of a term too):* $T_1(a) = [a]$ *for* $a \in \mathscr{A}$ *and* $T_1(x) = x$ *for* $x \in \mathscr{V}_1$; *for the other symbols,* T_1 *translates a term and a formula homomorphically.*

This translation T_1 preserves the validity in the following sense:

Proposition 4. *Let* φ *be a Popper sentence. Then, we have that* $\mathscr{P} \models \varphi$ *iff* $\mathscr{Q} \models T_1(\varphi)$.

Proof. This can be proved by using the facts that, for any Popper function P, the function $\bar{P}$ defined by $\bar{P}([\varphi]|[\psi]) = P(\varphi|\psi)$ is a quotient Popper function and that, for any quotient Popper function Q, there is a Popper function P such that $Q = \bar{P}$. □

4.2   Translation 2

The second translation eliminates the occurrences of form quantifiers:

Definition 14 (Translation 2). *We define a translation* $T_2 : QPF \rightarrow QPF$ *by:* $T_2(t) = t$ *for any term* t; $T_2((\exists x : \text{form})\varphi) = \bigvee_{z \in \mathbb{L}} T_2(\varphi)[z/x]$ *for any formula* φ; *for the other logical connectives,* T_2 *translates a formula homomorphically.*

This translation also preserves the validity:

Proposition 5. *For any quotient Popper sentence* φ, *it holds that* $\mathscr{Q} \models \varphi$ *iff* $\mathscr{Q} \models T_2(\varphi)$.

4.3   Translation 3

Now we give the definition of the final translation into a first-order language $\mathscr{L}_{\mathbb{R}}$ for the field of real numbers, i.e. a language for real closed fields.

Definition 15. *The first-order language* $\mathscr{L}_{\mathbb{R}}$ *is constructed from the variables* $\{V_{(x|y)} \mid x, y \in \mathbb{L}\}$ *and* $\mathscr{V}_{\text{real}}^1$ *by function symbols* $-$ *and* $\cdot$ *and relation symbols* $\leq$ *and* $=_{\sigma}$.

Definition 16. *For a variable-free* form *term* t *in* $\mathscr{L}_{\text{QPF}}$, *its corresponding element* $\mathbb{L}(t)$ *in* $\mathbb{L}$ *is inductively defined by:*

1. $\mathbb{L}(z) = z$ *for any* form *constant symbol* z *in* $\mathscr{L}_{\text{QPF}}$;
2. $\mathbb{L}(\neg t) = -\mathbb{L}(t)$ *for any variable-free* form *term* $\neg t$ *in* $\mathscr{L}_{\text{QPF}}$;
3. $\mathbb{L}(t \wedge s) = \mathbb{L}(t) \cdot \mathbb{L}(s)$ *for any variable-free* form *terms* $t \wedge s$ *in* $\mathscr{L}_{\text{QPF}}$.

Definition 17 (Translation 3). *The translation* T_3 : *form-variable-free* $QPF \rightarrow \mathscr{L}_{\mathbb{R}}$ *is inductively defined by the clause that* $T_1(p(t|s)) = V_{(\mathbb{L}(t)|\mathbb{L}(s))}$. *For the other symbols,* T_3 *maps a term and a formula homomorphically.*

This translation again preserves the validity as follows:

Proposition 6. *Let* φ *be a quotient Popper formula which does not contain any* form *variables and* $\eta = (\eta_{\text{form}}, \eta_{\text{real}})$ *an assignment with* $\eta_{\text{form}} : \mathscr{V}_{\text{form}}^1 \rightarrow \mathbb{L}$ *and* $\eta_{\text{real}} : \mathscr{V}_{\text{real}}^1 \rightarrow \mathbb{R}$. *Then, we have:*
$$\mathscr{Q} \models \varphi[\eta] \text{ iff } \mathbb{R} \models (\forall V_{(x|y)})_{(x,y) \in \mathbb{L}^2}(T_3 \circ T_2 \circ T_1(\text{PFL}) \rightarrow T_3(\varphi))[\eta_{\text{real}}].$$

Proof. We sketch the proof. For the left-to-right direction, assume the negation of the right-hand side to prove the contraposition. Then, there is a function $F : \mathbb{L} \times \mathbb{L} \rightarrow \mathbb{R}$ such that $\mathbb{R} \models T_3 \circ T_2 \circ T_1(\text{PFL}) \wedge \neg T_3(\varphi)[\eta_{\text{real}}(F(x,y)/V_{(x|y)})_{(x,y) \in \mathbb{L}^2}]$. The first conjunct implies that F is a quotient Popper function; and the right one does $F \not\models \varphi[\eta]$. For the other direction, from the right-hand side, we see that $\mathbb{R} \models T_3 \circ T_2 \circ T_1(\text{PFL}) \rightarrow T_3(\varphi)[\eta_{\text{real}}(Q(x|y)/V_{(x|y)})_{(x,y) \in \mathbb{L}^2}]$ for any quotient Popper function $Q : \mathbb{L} \times \mathbb{L} \rightarrow \mathbb{R}$. Since Q is a quotient Popper function, the antecedent is true. Therefore, we obtain $\mathbb{R} \models T_3(\varphi)[\eta_{\text{real}}(Q(x|y)/V_{(x|y)})_{(x,y) \in \mathbb{L}^2}]$ and thus $Q \models \varphi[\eta]$. $\square$

Using the three translations, we obtain the decidability:

Theorem 7. *The $\mathscr{P}$-validity problem of any Popper sentence is decidable.*

Proof. Let φ be a Popper sentence. Then, by Propositions 4, 5 and 6, we have that $\mathscr{P} \models \varphi$ iff $\mathbb{R} \models (\forall V_{(x|y)})_{(x,y)\in\mathbb{L}}(T_3 \circ T_2 \circ T_1(\mathsf{PFL}) \rightarrow T_3 \circ T_2 \circ T_1(\varphi))$. Since the validity problem for the logic of the field of real numbers, i.e. the logic of real closed fields, is decidable [30] and since T_1, T_2 and T_3 are computable,[5] the $\mathscr{P}$-validity problem of φ is decidable.   □

5   Computing Algorithms

In this section, we propose two algorithms which compute the region of the values that designated conditional probabilities can take under given constraints: the first algorithm outputs a Boolean combination of equations and inequalities that determines the region; the second one evaluates the region from inside and outside with arbitrary accuracy. We also give results on their computational complexity. In what follows, we assume that the language $\mathscr{L}_{\mathsf{PFL}}$ is extended so that it has one constant symbol for each real number.[6]

5.1   Algorithms

Algorithm 1. The first algorithm proceeds as follows:

Algorithm 1: Equations and inequalities

---
    input : (i) probabilities $p(\varphi_1|\psi_1), \ldots, p(\varphi_n|\psi_n)$ in syntax that we would like to compute such that at least $\varphi_i \leftrightarrow \varphi_{i'}$ or $\psi_i \leftrightarrow \psi_{i'}$ is not a tautology for any pair $i \neq i'$

             (ii) Popper sentences $\chi_1, \ldots, \chi_m$ that express constraints

    output: a Boolean combination of equations and inequalities that determines the range

$$\{(P(\varphi_1|\psi_1), \ldots, P(\varphi_n|\psi_n)) \in \mathbb{R}^n \mid P \models \chi_j \text{ for } j = 1, \ldots, m\}$$

    $X \longleftarrow \chi_1 \wedge \cdots \wedge \chi_m$;

    $\mathbb{L}' \longleftarrow \mathbb{L}^2 - \{([\varphi_i], [\psi_i]) \in \mathbb{L}^2 \mid i = 1, \ldots, n\}$;

    $\Phi \longleftarrow (\exists V_{(x|y)})_{(x,y)\in\mathbb{L}'}(T_3 \circ T_2 \circ T_1(\mathsf{PFL}) \wedge T_3 \circ T_2 \circ T_1(X))$;

    return $\mathsf{QE}_{\mathbb{R}}(\Phi)$;

In the algorithm above, $\mathsf{QE}_{\mathbb{R}}$ denotes a quantifier elimination (QE) algorithm in real closed fields (cf. [5,7,25]).

The theorem behind the algorithm is as below:

---

[5] For translation T_1, we use the fact that, for any propositional formula x in $\mathscr{L}$, its corresponding equivalence class $[x]$ in the Lindenbaum-Tarski algebra $\mathbb{L}$ can be calculated.

[6] This assumption relieves the range of formulae applicable to the results on complexity in Sect. 5.2 (see also Theorem 11, *infra*). All results in Sect. 5 also hold in the original language.

Theorem 8. *Suppose the settings of Algorithm 1. Then, the following are equivalent:*

1. $(V_{([\varphi_1]|[\psi_1])}, \ldots, V_{([\varphi_n]|[\psi_n])}) = (r_1, \ldots, r_n) \in \mathbb{R}^n$ *is a solution of the system of equations and inequalities* $\mathsf{QE}_{\mathbb{R}}(\varPhi)$;
2. *there is a Popper function* P *with* $P(\varphi_i|\psi_i) = r_i$ *for* $i = 1, \ldots, n$ *that satisfies all the constraints* $\chi_1, \ldots, \chi_m$.

Algorithm 2. Algorithm 1 does not necessarily output a human-readable solution such as $1/3 \leq p(a|b) \leq 1/2$ and, in the worst case, it contains an equation or an inequalities that cannot be solved algebraically. To deal with such cases, we here propose another algorithm that evaluates the range from inside and outside with arbitrary accuracy:

Algorithm 2: Evaluation algorithm

---

input : (i) probabilities $p(\varphi_1|\psi_1), \ldots, p(\varphi_n|\psi_n)$ in syntax that we would like to compute such that at least $\varphi_i \leftrightarrow \varphi_{i'}$ or $\psi_i \leftrightarrow \psi_{i'}$ is not a tautology for any pair $i \neq i'$
(ii) Popper sentences $\chi_1, \ldots, \chi_m$ that express constraints
(iii) a non-zero precision parameter $N \in \mathbb{N}$

output: the assignment that assigns, to each n-dimensional hypercube $1/N$ on a side in $[0,1]^n$, one of 'Inside', 'Boundary' and 'Outside' of the range
$$\{(P(\varphi_1|\psi_1), \ldots, P(\varphi_n|\psi_n)) \in \mathbb{R}^n \mid P \models \chi_j \text{ for } j = 1, \ldots, m\}$$

$H \longleftarrow$ the set of N^n-many hypercubes $1/N$ on a side obtained by dividing $[0,1]^n$;

foreach *hypercube* $h = [k_1/N, (k_1+1)/N] \times \cdots \times [k_n/N, (k_n+1)/N] \in H$
do

$\quad\big|\quad X \longleftarrow \chi_1 \wedge \cdots \wedge \chi_m$;
$\quad\big|\quad \mathbb{L}' \longleftarrow \mathbb{L}^2 - \{([\varphi_i], [\psi_i]) \in \mathbb{L}^2 \mid i = 1, \ldots, n\}$;
$\quad\big|\quad \varPhi \longleftarrow (\exists V_{(x|y)})_{(x,y) \in \mathbb{L}'}(T_3 \circ T_2 \circ T_1(\mathsf{PFL}) \wedge T_3 \circ T_2 \circ T_1(X))$;
$\quad\big|\quad \varPhi_1 \longleftarrow (\forall V_{([\varphi_i]|[\psi_i])})_{i=1}^n (\bigwedge_{i=1}^n (k_i/N \leq V_{([\varphi_i]|[\psi_i])} \leq (k_i+1)/N) \rightarrow \varPhi)$;
$\quad\big|\quad \varPhi_2 \longleftarrow (\exists V_{([\varphi_i]|[\psi_i])})_{i=1}^n (\bigwedge_{i=1}^n (k_i/N \leq V_{([\varphi_i]|[\psi_i])} \leq (k_i+1)/N) \wedge \varPhi)$;
$\quad\big|\quad$ **if** $\mathsf{QE}_{\mathbb{R}}(\varPhi_1) = \top$ **then** $z_h \longleftarrow$ 'Inside';
$\quad\big|\quad$ **else if** $\mathsf{QE}_{\mathbb{R}}(\varPhi_2) = \top$ **then** $z_h \longleftarrow$ 'Boundary';
$\quad\big|\quad$ **else** $z_h \longleftarrow$ 'Outside';

return $\{z_h\}_{h \in H}$;

Here, $k_i/N \leq V_{([\varphi_i]|[\psi_i])} \leq (k_i+1)/N$ is an abbreviation of $k_i/N \leq V_{([\varphi_i]|[\psi_i])} \wedge V_{([\varphi_i]|[\psi_i])} \leq (k_i+1)/N$.

This algorithm determines, for each hypercube h, whether it is inside, outside or on the boundary of the range of the values that probabilities $(P(\varphi_1|\psi_1), \ldots, P(\varphi_n|\psi_n))$ can take. Intuitively, $\varPhi_1$ (respectively, $\varPhi_2$) says that, for any (respectively, some) point $\mathbf{r}$ in a hypercube h, there is a Popper function P with $(P(\varphi_1|\psi_1), \ldots, P(\varphi_n|\psi_n)) = \mathbf{r}$ that satisfies the constraints $\chi_1, \ldots, \chi_m$. More precisely, the following holds:

.

Theorem 9. *Suppose the settings of Algorithm 2. Then, the following are equivalent:*

1. $\mathbb{R} \models \Phi_1$ *(respectively, $\mathbb{R} \models \Phi_2$);*
2. *for any (respectively, some) $(r_1, \ldots, r_n) \in [k_1/N, (k_1 + 1)/N] \times \cdots \times [k_n/N, (k_n + 1)/N]$, there exists a Popper function P with $P(\varphi_i | \psi_i) = r_i$ for $i = 1, \ldots, n$ that satisfies all the constraints $\chi_1, \ldots, \chi_m$.*

5.2   Complexity of Quantifier Elimination in the Algorithms

We next give results on the computational complexity of Algorithms 1 and 2. The primary parts of the algorithms are $\mathsf{QE}_{\mathbb{R}}$ on input Φ in Algorithm 1, and on Φ_1 and Φ_2 in Algorithm 2. We assess their time complexities.

There have been proposed several QE algorithms (cf. [5]). We, in this paper, apply the following results given in [7]:

Theorem 10 (cf. Theorems 1.3.1 and 1.3.2 in [7]). *Let $P_1, \ldots, P_s$ be s polynomials each of degree at most d, in $k + l$ variables, with coefficients in a real closed field R and*

$$\Psi = (Q_w X^{[w]}) \cdots (Q_1 X^{[1]}) F(P_1, \ldots, P_s)$$

be a first-order formula where $Q_i \in \{\forall, \exists\}$, $Q_i \neq Q_{i+1}$, $Y = (Y_1, \ldots, Y_l)$ is a block of l free variables, $X^{[i]}$ is a block of k_i variables with $\Sigma_{1 \leq i \leq w} k_i = k$, and $F(P_1, \ldots, P_s)$ is a quantifier-free Boolean formula with atomic predicates of the form

$$\mathrm{sign}(P_i(Y, X^{[w]}, \ldots, X^{[1]})) = \sigma$$

with $\sigma \in \{0, 1, -1\}$, where the sign, $\mathrm{sign}(a)$, of an element $a \in R$ is 0 if $a = 0$, 1 if $a > 0$ and -1 if $a < 0$. Then,

1. *there is an algorithm that computes quantifier-free formula equivalent to Ψ, using $s^{(l+1) \prod (k_i+1)} d^{(l+1) \prod O(k_i)}$ arithmetic operations in D;*
2. *when $l = 0$, there is an algorithm to decide the truth of Ψ that uses $s^{\prod (k_i+1)} d^{\prod O(k_i)}$ arithmetic operations in D.*

Here, D denotes the smallest subring of R containing the coefficients of $P_1, \ldots, P_s$.

Using this theorem, the time complexities of $\mathsf{QE}_{\mathbb{R}}$ on input Φ, Φ_1 and Φ_2 are assessed as follows:

Theorem 11. *Let $p(\varphi_1 | \psi_1), \ldots, p(\varphi_n | \psi_n)$ be probabilities in syntax and $\chi_1, \ldots, \chi_m$ be the Popper sentence that does not contain real quantifiers.[7] For each χ_j, let e_j denote the number of its form quantifiers, s_j the number of its polynomials, d_j the maximum total degree of its polynomials. Then, for $\Psi = T_3 \circ T_2 \circ T_1(\mathsf{PFL}) \wedge T_3 \circ T_2 \circ T_1(\bigwedge_{j=1}^{m} \chi_j)$,*

---

[7] This condition does not restrict the range of constraints $\chi_1, \ldots, \chi_n$ in practice, since our language now contains the constant symbols for all real numbers.

1. *the number of its polynomials is bounded by* $s = |\mathbb{L}|^4 + 5|\mathbb{L}|^3 + 2|\mathbb{L}| + \sum_{j=1}^{m}(|\mathbb{L}|^{e_j} s_j)$;
2. *the maximum degree of its polynomials is bounded by* $d = max\{2, d_1, \ldots, d_m\}$.

Hence, the time complexity, in terms of arithmetic operations, of the algorithm, on input Φ in Algorithm 1 is $s^{(n+1)(|\mathbb{L}|^2-n+1)}d^{(n+1)O(|\mathbb{L}|^2-n)}$; *and both of those on input Φ_1 and Φ_2 in Algorithm 2 are* $s^{(|\mathbb{L}|^2-n+1)(n+1)}d^{O(|\mathbb{L}|^2-n)O(n)}$.

Proof. We give here a proof sketch. For (1), it can be easily seen that the number of polynomials in $T_3 \circ T_2 \circ T_1(\mathsf{PFL})$ is $|\mathbb{L}|^4 + 5|\mathbb{L}|^3 + 2|\mathbb{L}|$. In addition, each $T_3 \circ T_2 \circ T_1(\chi_i)$ has $|\mathbb{L}|^{e_i} s_i$ polynomials at most, since each form quantifier gives $|\mathbb{L}|$-many copies of its scope when it is translated by T_2. Adding up, we see that the number of polynomials in Ψ is bounded by $s = |\mathbb{L}|^4 + 5|\mathbb{L}|^3 + 2|\mathbb{L}| + \sum_{j=1}^{m}(|\mathbb{L}|^{e_i} s_i)$. For (2), the maximum number of degrees of polynomials in $T_3 \circ T_2 \circ T_1(\mathsf{PFL})$ is 2 and the maximum degree of the polynomials in $T_3 \circ T_2 \circ T_1(\chi_j)$ is bounded by the maximum total degree of the polynomials. Therefore, since T_1, T_2 and T_3 do not increase the total degree of a polynomial in χ_j, the maximum degree of the polynomials in Ψ is bounded by $max\{2, d_1, \ldots, d_n\}$.

To assess the complexities, we apply Theorem 10. For Algorithm 1, the number of free real variables in Ψ is $|\{V_{(s|t)} \mid s, t \in \mathbb{L}\}| = |\mathbb{L}|^2$ and thus that of Φ is n. Note also the number of polynomials input to the QE algorithms becomes at most $2s$ by transforming an atomic formula in the form of $P \leq Q$ into $\mathrm{sign}(P - Q) = -1 \vee \mathrm{sign}(P - Q) = 0$ to adjust the syntax with the maximal degree of polynomials preserved; however, this multiplier 2 is incorporated into $d^{O(n)}$. For algorithm 2, input formulae Φ_1 and Φ_2 can readily be transformed into prenex normal form and again we apply Theorem 10.   □

6 Conclusion and Future Work

6.1 Conclusion

In this paper, we have proposed a finite set of axioms that defines the set of Popper functions in many-sorted monadic second-order logic. We have also proved the decidability of the validity problem for an important first-order fragment of this second-order language, which we call Popper sentence, with respect to the set of Popper functions. We finally proposed two algorithms that compute the range of values that designated conditional probabilities can take under given constraints expressed by finitely many Popper sentences, and assessed the time complexities of their primary subalgorithms.

6.2 Future Work

Theoretically, this study is the first step of our project of systematising the relationship between probability-related algorithms, including Markov logic networks [28], Bayesian logic programming [22,23] and abductive reasoning [4,20]. Our algorithm shall be used as a baseline in our project.

Practically, we shall address the following issues:

1. we shall relieve the restriction that the set $\mathscr{A}$ of proposition letters is specified since we cannot assume in practice that all involved proposition letters are specified;
2. we shall reduce the computational complexities of the proposed algorithms so that they can be used in practice.

Acknowledgements. The author would like to thank sincerely Takashi Maruyama, Takeshi Tsukada, Shun'ichi Yokoyama, Eiji Yumoto and Itaru Hosomi for discussion and many helpful comments. Thanks are also due to all anonymous referees who gave valuable comments on earlier versions of this article.

References

1. Adams, E.: The logic of conditionals. Inquiry **8**(1–4), 166–197 (1965). https://doi.org/10.1080/00201746508601430
2. Adams, E.W.: Probability and the logic of conditionals. In: Hintikka, J., Suppes, P. (eds.) Aspects of Inductive Logic, Studies in Logic and the Foundations of Mathematics, vol. 43, pp. 265–316. Elsevier (1966). https://doi.org/10.1016/S0049-237X(08)71673-2, https://www.sciencedirect.com/science/article/pii/S0049237X08716732
3. Adams, E.W.: The Logic of Conditionals: An Application of Probability to Deductive Logic, Synthese Library, vol. 86. Springer, Netherlands (1975). https://doi.org/10.1007/978-94-015-7622-2
4. Aliseda, A.: The logic of abduction: an introduction. In: Magnani, L., Bertolotti, T. (eds.) Springer Handbook of Model-Based Science. SH, pp. 219–230. Springer, Cham (2017). https://doi.org/10.1007/978-3-319-30526-4_10
5. Anai, K., Yokoyama, K.: Algorithms of Quantifier Elimination and their Application: Optimization by Symbolic and Algebraic Methods [in Japanese]. University of Tokyo Press (2011)
6. Bacchus, F.: Representing and Reasoning with Probabilistic Knowledge: A Logical Approach to Probabilities. The MIT Press, Cambridge (1990)
7. Basu, S., Pollack, R., Roy, M.F.: On the combinatorial and algebraic complexity of quantifier elimination. J. ACM **43**(6), 1002–1045 (1996). https://doi.org/10.1145/235809.235813
8. Boričić, M.: Inference rules for probability logic. PUBLICATIONS DE L'INSTITUT MATHÉMATIQUE **100**(114), 77–86 (2016). https://doi.org/10.2298/PIM1614077B
9. Boričić, M.: Suppes-style sequent calculus for probability logic. J. Logic Comput. **27**(4), 1157–1168 (10 2015). https://doi.org/10.1093/logcom/exv068
10. Brickhill, H., Horsten, L.: Triangulating non-archimedean probability. Rev. Symbolic Logic **11**(3), 519–546 (2018). https://doi.org/10.1017/S1755020318000060
11. Buss, S.R.: An introduction to proof theory. In: Buss, S.R. (ed.) Handbook of Proof Theory, vol. 137, pp. 1–78. Elsevier, Amsterdam (1998)
12. Davey, B.A., Priestley, H.A.: Introduction to Lattices and Order, 2nd edn. Cambridge University Press (2002). https://doi.org/10.1017/CBO9780511809088
13. Enderton, H.B.: A Mathematical Introduction to Logic, 2nd edn. Academic Press (2000)

14. Fagin, R., Halpern, J.Y., Megiddo, N.: A logic for reasoning about probabilities. Inf. Comput. **87**(1), 78–128 (1990)
15. Gallier, J.H.: Logic for Computer Science: Foundations of Automatic Theorem Proving, 2nd edn. Dover Publications (2015)
16. Gilio, A.: Precise propagation of upper and lower probability bounds in system p. arXiv preprint math/0003046 (2000)
17. Hailperin, T.: Best possible inequalities for the probability of a logical function of events. Am. Math. Monthly **72**(4), 343–359 (1965)
18. Hájek, A.: Probability, logic, and probability logic. In: Goble, L. (ed.) The Blackwell Guide to Philosophical Logic, chap. 16, pp. 362–384. Blackwell Publishing (2001)
19. Halpern, J.Y.: Reasoning About Uncertainty, 2nd edn. MIT Press (2017)
20. Hobbs, J.R., Stickel, M.E., Appelt, D.E., Martin, P.: Interpretation as abduction. Artif. Intell. **63**(1), 69–142 (1993)
21. Ikodinović, N., Ognjanović, Z.: A logic with coherent conditional probabilities. In: Godo, L. (ed.) ECSQARU 2005. LNCS (LNAI), vol. 3571, pp. 726–736. Springer, Heidelberg (2005). https://doi.org/10.1007/11518655_61
22. Kersting, K., De Raedt, L.: Bayesian logic programs. arXiv preprint cs.AI/0111058 (2001). https://arxiv.org/abs/cs/0111058
23. Kersting, K., De Raedt, L.: Bayesian logic programming: theory and tool. In: Getoor, L., Taskar, B. (eds.) Introduction to Statistical Relational Learning, pp. 291–321. MIT Press (2007)
24. McGee, V.: Learning the impossible. In: Eells, E., Brian, S. (eds.) Probability and Conditionals: Belief Revision and Rational Decision, pp. 179–199. Cambridge University Press (1994)
25. Mishra, B.: Algorithmic Algebra. Monographs in Computer Science. Springer, New York (1993). https://doi.org/10.1007/978-1-4612-4344-1
26. Mueller, E.T.: Commonsense reasoning: An Event Calculus Based Approach, 2nd edn. Morgan Kaufmann (2014)
27. Popper, K.: The Logic of Scientific Discovery, 2nd edn. Routledge (2002)
28. Richardson, M., Domingos, P.: Markov logic networks. Mach. Learn. **62**(1), 107–136 (2006). https://doi.org/10.1007/s10994-006-5833-1
29. Tabata, H.: On second-order Peano arithmetic [in Japanese]. Tottori University Journal of the Faculty of Education and Regional Sciences **4**(1), 37–84 (2002)
30. Tarski, A.: A Decision Method for Elementary Algebra and Geometry: Prepared for Publication with the Assistance of J.C.C. McKinsey. RAND Corporation, Santa Monica, CA (1951)
31. Wagner, C.G.: Modus tollens probabilized. Brit. J. Phil. Sci. **55**(4), 747–753 (2004). https://doi.org/10.1093/bjps/55.4.747

Interpreting Connexive Principles
in Coherence-Based Probability Logic

Niki Pfeifer[1(✉)] and Giuseppe Sanfilippo[2(✉)]

[1] Department of Philosophy, University of Regensburg, Regensburg, Germany
niki.pfeifer@ur.de
[2] Department of Mathematics and Computer Science, University of Palermo,
Palermo, Italy
giuseppe.sanfilippo@unipa.it

Abstract. We present probabilistic approaches to check the validity of selected connexive principles within the setting of coherence. Connexive logics emerged from the intuition that conditionals of the form *If ∼A, then A*, should not hold, since the conditional's antecedent ∼A contradicts its consequent A. Our approach covers this intuition by observing that for an event A the only coherent probability assessment on the conditional event $A|\bar{A}$ is $p(A|\bar{A}) = 0$. Moreover, connexive logics aim to capture the intuition that conditionals should express some "connection" between the antecedent and the consequent or, in terms of inferences, validity should require some connection between the premise set and the conclusion. This intuition is covered by a number of principles, a selection of which we analyze in our contribution. We present two approaches to connexivity within coherence-based probability logic. Specifically, we analyze connections between antecedents and consequents firstly, in terms of probabilistic constraints on conditional events (in the sense of defaults, or negated defaults) and secondly, in terms of constraints on compounds of conditionals and iterated conditionals. After developing different notions of negations and notions of validity, we analyze the following connexive principles within both approaches: Aristotle's Theses, Aristotle's Second Thesis, Abelard's First Principle and selected versions of Boethius' Theses. We conclude by remarking that coherence-based probability logic offers a rich language to investigate the validity of various connexive principles.

Keywords: Aristotle's Theses · Coherence · Compounds of conditionals · Conditional events · Conditional random quantities · Connexive logic · Iterated conditionals · Probabilistic constraints

Both authors contributed equally to the article and are listed alphabetically.
N. Pfeifer is supported by the BMBF project 01UL1906X.
G. Sanfilippo is a member of the GNAMPA Research Group and partially supported by the INdAM–GNAMPA Project 2020 Grant U-UFMBAZ-2020-000819.

J. Vejnarová and N. Wilson (Eds.): ECSQARU 2021, LNAI 12897, pp. 672–687, 2021.
https://doi.org/10.1007/978-3-030-86772-0_48

1   Introduction

We present probabilistic approaches to check the validity of selected connexive principles within the setting of coherence. Connexive logics emerged from the intuition that conditionals of the form *if not-A, then A*, denoted by $\sim A \to A$, should not hold, since the conditional's antecedent *not-A* contradicts its consequent *A*. Indeed, experimental psychological data show that people believe that sentences of the form *if not-A, then A* are false (e.g., [39,40]), which supports the psychological plausibility of this intuition. Connexive principles were developed to rule out such self-contradictory conditionals (for overviews, see e.g.,[36,53]). Many of these principles can be traced back to antiquity or the middle ages, which is reflected by the names of these principles, for example, Aristotle's Thesis or Abelard's First Principle (see Table 1). In classical logic, however, Aristotle's Thesis, i.e. $\sim (\sim A \to A)$, is not a theorem since the corresponding material conditional is contingent because $\sim (\sim\sim A \lor A)$ is logically equivalent to $\sim A$ (which is not necessarily true). Moreover, connexive logics aim to capture the intuition that conditionals should express some "connection" between the antecedent and the consequent or, in terms of inferences, validity should require some connection between the premise set and the conclusion.

Table 1. Selected connexive principles (see also [53]).

Name	Abbreviation	Connexive principle
Aristotle's Thesis	(AT)	$\sim(\sim A \to A)$
Aristotle's Thesis$'$	(AT$'$)	$\sim(A \to \sim A)$
Abelard's First Principle	(AB)	$\sim((A \to B) \land (A \to \sim B))$
Aristotle's Second Thesis	(AS)	$\sim((A \to B) \land (\sim A \to B))$
Boethius' Thesis	(BT)	$(A \to B) \to \sim(A \to \sim B)$
Boethius' Thesis$'$	(BT$'$)	$(A \to \sim B) \to \sim(A \to B)$
Reversed Boethius' Thesis	(RBT)	$\sim(A \to \sim B) \to (A \to B)$
Reversed Boethius' Thesis$'$	(RBT$'$)	$\sim(A \to B) \to (A \to \sim B)$
Boethius Variation 3	(B3)	$(A \to B) \to \sim(\sim A \to B)$
Boethius Variation 4	(B4)	$(\sim A \to B) \to \sim(A \to B)$

The connexive intuition that conditionals of the form *if not-A, then A* should not hold is covered in subjective probability theory. Specifically, we cover this intuition by the observation that for any event A, with $\overline{A} \neq \emptyset$, the only coherent assessment on the conditional event $A|\overline{A}$ is $p(A|\overline{A}) = 0$.

The aim of our contribution is to investigate selected connexive principles within the framework of *coherence-based probability logic*. The coherence approach to (subjective) probability was originated by Bruno de Finetti (see, e.g., [11,12]) and has been generalised to the conditional probability and to previsions of conditional random quantities (see, e.g., [2,3,6,9,21,24,29,33,49,52]). In the present framework, we present two approaches to connexivity within coherence-based probability logic. In the first approach we analyze connections between antecedents and consequents in terms of probabilistic constraints on conditional events (in the sense of defaults or negated defaults [16,44–46]). In the second approach, based the recently developed more general framework of compounds of conditionals and iterated conditionals [18,19,22,24,27], we define these connections in terms of constraints on suitable conditional random quantities. After developing different notions of negations and notions of validity, we analyze the connexive principles given in Table 1 within both approaches.

The coherence principle plays a key role in probabilistic reasoning and allows for probabilistic inferences of a further conditional event (the conclusion) from any coherent probabilistic assessment on an arbitrary family of conditional events (the premises). Moreover, coherence is a more general approach to conditional probabilities compared to approaches which requires positive probability for the conditioning events. In standard approaches to probability the conditional probability $p(C|A)$ is defined by the ratio $p(A \wedge C)/p(A)$, which requires positive probability of the conditioning event, $p(A) > 0$. However, in the framework of coherence, conditional probability $p(C|A)$, as a degree of belief, is a primitive notion and it is properly defined even if the conditioning event has probability zero, i.e., $p(A) = 0$. Analogously, within coherence, previsions of conditional random quantities, are primitive and properly defined even if the conditioning event has probability zero. Therefore, coherence is a more general approach to conditional probabilities compared to approaches which requires positive probability for the conditioning events. The only requirement is that the conditioning event must be logically possible. Thus, although $p(C|A)$ is well defined even if $p(A) = 0$, it is undefined if $A \equiv \emptyset$ (where $\emptyset$ denotes a logical contradiction). This is in line with the reading that Boethius and Aristotle thought that principles like (BT) and (AT), respectively, hold only when the conditional's antecedent is possible (see [34] who argues that the "ancient logicians most likely meant their theses as applicable only to 'normal' conditionals with antecedents which are not self-contradictory"; p. 16). It is also in line with the Ramsey test, which is expressed in his famous footnote: "If two people are arguing 'If A will C?' and are both in doubt as to A, they are adding A hypothetically to their stock of knowledge and arguing on that basis about C; so that in a sense 'If A, C' and 'If A, $\overline{C}$' are contradictories. We can say they are fixing their degrees of belief in C given A. If A turns out false, these degrees of belief are rendered void" [48, p. 155, we adjusted the notation]. The quantitative interpretation of the Ramsey test became a cornerstone of the conditional probability interpretation of conditionals. Adding a contradiction to your stock of knowledge does not make sense (as, traditionally, knowledge implies truth). Moreover, Ramsey's thought that conditionals with contradicting consequents C and $\overline{C}$ contradict each other coincides with the underlying intuition of (AB).

2   Preliminary Notions and Results

Given two events A and H, with $H \neq \emptyset$ (where $\emptyset$ denotes the impossible event), the *conditional event* $A|H$ (read: A given H) is defined as a three-valued logical entity which is *true* if AH (i.e., $A \wedge H$) is true, *false* if $\overline{A}H$ is true, and *void* if H is false. We observe that $A|H$ assumes the logical value (*true* or *false*) of A, when H is true, and it is *void*, otherwise. There is a long history of how to deal with negations (see, e.g., [30]). In our context, the negation of the conditional event "A given H", denoted by $\overline{A|H}$, is the conditional event $\overline{A}|H$, that is "the negation of A" given H. We use the inner negation to preserve for conditional events the usual property of negating unconditional events: $p(\overline{A}) = 1 - p(A)$. In the subjective approach to probability based on the betting scheme, a conditional probability assessment $p(A|H) = x$ means that, for every real number s, you are willing to pay an amount $s \cdot x$ and to receive s, or 0, or $s \cdot x$ (money back), according to whether AH is true, or $\overline{A}H$ is true, or $\overline{H}$ is true (bet called off), respectively. The random gain, which is the difference between the (random) amount that you receive and the amount that you pay, is $G = (sAH + 0\overline{A}H + sx\overline{H}) - sx = sAH + sx(1 - H) - sx = sH(A - x)$.

Given a probability function p defined on an arbitrary family $\mathcal{K}$ of conditional events, consider a finite subfamily $\mathcal{F} = \{A_1|H_1, \ldots, A_n|H_n\} \subseteq \mathcal{K}$ and the vector $\mathcal{P} = (x_1, \ldots, x_n)$, where $x_i = p(A_i|H_i)$ is the assessed probability for the conditional event $A_i|H_i$, $i = 1, \ldots, n$. With the pair $(\mathcal{F}, \mathcal{P})$ we associate the random gain $G = \sum_{i=1}^n s_i H_i(A_i - x_i)$. We denote by $\mathcal{G}_{\mathcal{H}_n}$ the set of values of G restricted to $\mathcal{H}_n = H_1 \vee \cdots \vee H_n$, i.e., the set of values of G when $\mathcal{H}_n$ is true. Then, we recall below the notion of coherence in the context of the *betting scheme*.

Definition 1. The function p defined on $\mathcal{K}$ is coherent if and only if, $\forall n \geq 1$, $\forall s_1, \ldots, s_n$, $\forall \mathcal{F} = \{A_1|H_1, \ldots, A_n|H_n\} \subseteq \mathcal{K}$, it holds that: $\min \mathcal{G}_{\mathcal{H}_n} \leq 0 \leq \max \mathcal{G}_{\mathcal{H}_n}$.

In betting terms, the coherence of conditional probability assessments means that in any finite combination of n bets, after discarding the case where all the bets are called off, the values of the random gain are neither all positive nor all negative (i.e., *no Dutch Book*). In particular, coherence of $x = p(A|H)$ is defined by the condition $\min \mathcal{G}_H \leq 0 \leq \max \mathcal{G}_H$, $\forall s$, where $\mathcal{G}_H$ is the set of values of G restricted to H (that is when the bet is not called off). Depending on the logical relations between A and H (with $H \neq \emptyset$), the set Π of all coherent conditional probability assessments $x = p(A|H)$ is:

$$\Pi = \begin{cases} [0,1], & \text{if } \emptyset \neq AH \neq H, \\ \{0\}, & \text{if } AH = \emptyset, \\ \{1\}, & \text{if } AH = H. \end{cases} \tag{1}$$

In numerical terms, once $x = p(A|H)$ is assessed by the betting scheme, the indicator of $A|H$, denoted by the same symbol, is defined as 1, or 0, or x, according to whether AH is true, or $\overline{A}H$ is true, or $\overline{H}$ is true. Then, by setting $p(A|H) = x$,

$$A|H = AH + x\overline{H} = \begin{cases} 1, \text{ if } AH \text{ is true,} \\ 0, \text{ if } \overline{A}H \text{ is true,} \\ x, \text{ if } \overline{H} \text{ is true.} \end{cases} \tag{2}$$

Note that since the three-valued numerical entity $A|H$ is defined by the betting scheme once the value $x = p(A|H)$ is assessed, the definition of (the indicator of) $A|H$ is not circular. The third value of the random quantity $A|H$ (subjectively) depends on the assessed probability $p(A|H) = x$. Moreover, the value x coincides with the corresponding conditional prevision, denoted by $\mathbb{P}(A|H)$, because $\mathbb{P}(A|H) = \mathbb{P}(AH + x\overline{H}) = p(AH) + xp(\overline{H}) = p(A|H)p(H) + xp(\overline{H}) = xp(H) + xp(\overline{H}) = x$.

In the special case where $AH = H$, it follows by (1) that $x = 1$ is the only coherent assessment for $p(A|H)$; then, for the indicator $A|H$ it holds that

$$A|H = AH + x\overline{H} = H + \overline{H} = 1, \quad \text{if } AH = H. \tag{3}$$

In particular (3) holds when $A = \Omega$ (i.e., the sure event), since $\Omega \wedge H = H$ and hence $\Omega|H = H|H = 1$. Likewise, if $AH = \emptyset$, it follows by (1) that $x = 0$ is the only coherent assessment for $p(A|H)$; then,

$$A|H = 0 + 0\overline{H} = 0, \quad \text{if } AH = \emptyset. \tag{4}$$

In particular (4) holds when $A = \emptyset$, since $\emptyset \wedge H = \emptyset$ and hence $\emptyset|H = 0$. We observe that conditionally on H be true, for the (indicator of the) negation it holds that $\overline{A|H} = \overline{A} = 1 - A = 1 - A|H$. Conditionally on H be false, by coherence, it holds that $\overline{A|H} = p(\overline{A}|H) = 1 - p(A|H) = 1 - A|H$. Thus, in all cases it holds that

$$\overline{A|H} = \overline{A}|H = (1 - A)|H = 1 - A|H. \tag{5}$$

We denote by X a *random quantity*, with a finite set of possible values. Given any event $H \neq \emptyset$, agreeing to the betting metaphor, if you assess the prevision $\mathbb{P}(X|H) = \mu$ means that for any given real number s you are willing to pay an amount $s\mu$ and to receive sX, or $s\mu$, according to whether H is true, or false (bet called off), respectively. In particular, when X is (the indicator of) an event A, then $\mathbb{P}(X|H) = P(A|H)$. The notion of coherence can be generalized to the case of prevision assessments on a family of conditional random quantities (see, e.g., [25,51]). Given a random quantity X and an event $H \neq \emptyset$, with prevision $\mathbb{P}(X|H) = \mu$, likewise formula (2) for the indicator of a conditional event, an extended notion of a conditional random quantity, denoted by the same symbol $X|H$, is defined as follows $X|H = XH + \mu\overline{H}$. We recall now the notion of conjunction of two (or more) conditional events within the framework of conditional random quantities in the setting of coherence ([19,22,24,26], for alternative approaches see also, e.g., [31,37]). Given a coherent probability assessment (x, y) on $\{A|H, B|K\}$, we consider the random quantity $AHBK + x\overline{H}BK + y\overline{K}AH$ and we set $\mathbb{P}[(AHBK + x\overline{H}BK + y\overline{K}AH)|(H \vee K)] = z$. Then we define the conjunction $(A|H) \wedge (B|K)$ as follows:

Definition 2. Given a coherent prevision assessment $p(A|H) = x$, $p(B|K) = y$, and $\mathbb{P}[(AHBK + x\overline{H}BK + y\overline{K}AH)|(H \vee K)] = z$, the conjunction $(A|H) \wedge (B|K)$ is the conditional random quantity defined as

$$(A|H) \wedge (B|K) = (AHBK + x\overline{H}BK + y\overline{K}AH)|(H \vee K)$$
$$= \begin{cases} 1, & \text{if } AHBK \text{ is true,} \\ 0, & \text{if } \overline{A}H \vee \overline{B}K \text{ is true,} \\ x, & \text{if } \overline{H}BK \text{ is true,} \\ y, & \text{if } AH\overline{K} \text{ is true,} \\ z, & \text{if } \overline{H}\,\overline{K} \text{ is true.} \end{cases} \tag{6}$$

Of course, $\mathbb{P}[(A|H) \wedge (B|K)] = z$. Coherence requires that the Fréchet-Hoeffding bounds for prevision of the conjunction are preserved [22], i.e., $\max\{x+y-1,0\} \leq z \leq \min\{x,y\}$, like in the case of unconditional events. Other preserved properties are listed in [27]. We notice that if conjunctions of conditional events are defined as suitable conditional events (see, e.g., [1,5,7,8,28]), classical probabilistic properties are not preserved. In particular, the lower and upper probability bounds for the conjunction do not coincide with the above mentioned Fréchet-Hoeffding bounds [50]. Here, differently from conditional events which are three-valued objects, the conjunction $(A|H) \wedge (B|K)$ is not any longer a three-valued object, but a five-valued object with values in $[0,1]$. We observe that $(A|H) \wedge (A|H) = A|H$ and $(A|H) \wedge (B|K) = (B|K) \wedge (A|H)$. Moreover, if $H = K$, then $(A|H) \wedge (B|H) = AB|H$.

For comparison with other approaches, like [13], see [25, Section 9].

In analogy to formula (2), where the indicator of a conditional event "A given H" is defined as $A|H = A \wedge H + p(A|H)\overline{H}$, the iterated conditional "$B|K$ given $A|H$" is defined as follows (see, e.g., [18,19,22]):

Definition 3 (Iterated conditioning). *Given any pair of conditional events $A|H$ and $B|K$, with $AH \neq \emptyset$, the iterated conditional $(B|K)|(A|H)$ is defined as the conditional random quantity $(B|K)|(A|H) = (A|H) \wedge (B|K) + \mu\overline{A}|H$, where $\mu = \mathbb{P}[(B|K)|(A|H)]$.*

Notice that we assume $AH \neq \emptyset$ to avoid trivial cases of iterated conditionals. Specifically, similar as in the three-valued notion of a conditional event $A|H$ where the antecedent H must not be impossible (i.e., H must not coincide with the constant 0), the iterated conditional $(B|K)|(A|H)$ requires that the antecedent $A|H$ must not be constant and equal to 0 (this happens when $AH \neq \emptyset$). Furthermore, we recall that the compound prevision theorem is preserved, that is $\mathbb{P}[(A|H) \wedge (B|K)] = \mathbb{P}[(B|K)|(A|H)]p(A|H)$.

3   Approach 1: Connexive Principles and Default Reasoning

In order to validate the connexive principles we interpret a conditional $A \to C$ by the default $A \mathrel{\vdash\mkern-9mu\sim} C$, where A and C are two events (with $A \neq \emptyset$). A default

$A \mathrel{|\!\sim} C$ can be read as C *is a plausible consequence of* A and is interpreted by the probability constraint $p(C|A) = 1$ [16].[1] The conditional $A \to {\sim}C$ is interpreted by the default $A \mathrel{|\!\sim} \overline{C}$. Likewise, ${\sim}A \to C$ is interpreted by $\overline{A} \mathrel{|\!\sim} C$. A negated conditional ${\sim}(A \to C)$ is interpreted by the negated default ${\sim}(A \mathrel{|\!\sim} C)$ (*it is not the case that: C is a plausible consequence of A*; also denoted by $A \mathrel{|\!\not\sim} C$ in [14,32]) that is $p(C|A) \neq 1$, which corresponds to the wide scope negation of negating conditionals [16].

The conjunction of two conditionals, denoted by $(A \to B) \wedge (C \to D)$, is interpreted by the sequence of their associated defaults $(A \mathrel{|\!\sim} B, C \mathrel{|\!\sim} D)$, which represents in probabilistic terms the constraint $(p(B|A) = 1, p(D|C) = 1)$, that is $(p(B|A), p(D|C)) = (1,1)$. Then, the negation of the conjunction of two conditionals, denoted by ${\sim}((A \to B) \wedge (C \to D))$ (i.e., in terms of defaults ${\sim}(A \mathrel{|\!\sim} B) \wedge (C \mathrel{|\!\sim} D)$) is interpreted by the negation of the probabilistic constraint $(p(B|A), p(D|C)) = (1,1)$, that is $(p(B|A), p(D|C)) \neq (1,1)$. Table 2 summarizes the interpretations.

We now introduce the definition of validity for non-iterated connexive principles (e.g., (AT), (AT′), (AB)).

Definition 4. *We say that a non-iterated connexive principle is valid if and only if the probabilistic constraint associated with the connexive principle is satisfied by every coherent assessment on the involved conditional events.*

In the next paragraphs we check the validity in terms of Definition 4 of the non-iterated connexive principles in Table 1.

Aristotle's Thesis (AT): ${\sim}({\sim}A \to A)$. We assume that $\overline{A} \neq \emptyset$ and we interpret the principle ${\sim}({\sim}A \to A)$ by the negated default ${\sim}(\overline{A} \mathrel{|\!\sim} A)$ with the following associated probabilistic constraint: $p(A|\overline{A}) \neq 1$. We observe that $p(\overline{A}|A) = 0$ is the unique precise coherent assessment on $\overline{A}|A$. Then, (AT) is valid because every coherent precise assessment $p(A|\overline{A})$ is such that $p(A|\overline{A}) \neq 1$.

Aristotle's Thesis ′ (AT′): ${\sim}(A \to {\sim}A)$. Like (AT), (AT)′ can be validated.

Abelard's Thesis (AB): ${\sim}((A \to B) \wedge (A \to {\sim}B))$. We assume that $A \neq \emptyset$. The structure of this principle is formalized by ${\sim}((A \mathrel{|\!\sim} B) \wedge (A \mathrel{|\!\sim} \overline{B}))$ which expresses the constraint $(p(B|A), p(\overline{B}|A)) \neq (1,1)$. We recall that coherence requires $p(B|A) + p(\overline{B}|A) = 1$. Then, (AT) is valid because each coherent assessment on $(B|A, \overline{B}|A)$ is necessarily of the form $(x, 1-x)$, with $x \in [0,1]$, which of course satisfies $(p(B|A), p(\overline{B}|A)) \neq (1,1)$.

---

[1]   According to ε-semantics (see, e.g., [1,38]) a default $A \mathrel{|\!\sim} C$ is interpreted by $p(C|A) \geq 1 - \varepsilon$, with $\varepsilon > 0$ and $p(A) > 0$. Gilio introduced a coherence-based probability semantics for defaults by also allowing ε and $p(A)$ to be zero [15]. In this context, defaults in terms of probability 1 can be used to give a alternative definition of p-entailment which preserve the usual non-monotonic inference rules like those of System P [4,15,20,21], see also [9,10]. For the psychological plausibility of the coherence-based semantics of non-monotonic reasoning, see, e.g., [41–43,47].

Aristotle's Second Thesis (AS): $\sim((A \to B) \wedge (\sim A \to B))$. We assume that $A \neq \emptyset$ and $\overline{A} \neq \emptyset$. The structure of this principle is formalized by $\sim((A \mathbin{\vrule height 1.2ex depth 0pt width 0.6pt\!\sim} B) \wedge (\overline{A} \mathbin{\vrule height 1.2ex depth 0pt width 0.6pt\!\sim} B))$ which expresses the constraint $(p(B|A), p(B|\overline{A})) \neq (1,1)$. We recall that, given two logically independent events A and B every assessment $(x, y) \in [0,1]^2$ on $(B|A, B|\overline{A})$ is coherent. In particular, $(p(B|A), p(B|\overline{A})) = (1,1)$ is a coherent assessment which does not satisfy the probabilistic constraint $(p(B|A), p(B|\overline{A})) \neq (1,1)$. Thus, (AS) is not valid.

Concerning iterated connexive principles (e.g. (BT), (BT')), we interpret the main connective ($\to$) as the implication ($\Rightarrow$) from the probabilistic constraint on the antecedent to the probabilistic constraint on the conclusion. Then, for instance, the iterated conditional $(A \to B) \to (C \to D)$ is interpreted by the implication $A \mathbin{\vrule height 1.2ex depth 0pt width 0.6pt\!\sim} B \Rightarrow C \mathbin{\vrule height 1.2ex depth 0pt width 0.6pt\!\sim} D$, that is $p(B|A) = 1 \Rightarrow p(D|C) = 1$. We now define validity for iterated connexive principles.

Definition 5. *An iterated connexive principle* $\bigcirc \Rightarrow \square$ *is valid if and only if the probabilistic constraint of the conclusion* $\square$ *is satisfied by every coherent extension to the conclusion from any coherent probability assessment satisfying the constraint of the premise* $\bigcirc$.

Table 2. Probabilistic interpretations of logical operation on conditionals in terms of defaults or negated defaults.

Conditional object	Default	Probabilistic interpretation
$A \to C$	$A \mathbin{\vrule height 1.2ex depth 0pt width 0.6pt\!\sim} C$	$p(C|A) = 1$
$\sim(A \to C)$	$\sim(A \mathbin{\vrule height 1.2ex depth 0pt width 0.6pt\!\sim} C)$	$p(C|A) \neq 1$
$(A \to B) \wedge (C \to D)$	$(A \mathbin{\vrule height 1.2ex depth 0pt width 0.6pt\!\sim} B, C \mathbin{\vrule height 1.2ex depth 0pt width 0.6pt\!\sim} D)$	$(p(B|A), p(D|C)) = (1,1)$
$\sim((A \to B) \wedge (C \to D))$	$\sim(A \mathbin{\vrule height 1.2ex depth 0pt width 0.6pt\!\sim} B, C \mathbin{\vrule height 1.2ex depth 0pt width 0.6pt\!\sim} D)$	$(p(B|A), p(D|C)) \neq (1,1)$
$(A \to B) \to (C \to D)$	$A \mathbin{\vrule height 1.2ex depth 0pt width 0.6pt\!\sim} B \Rightarrow C \mathbin{\vrule height 1.2ex depth 0pt width 0.6pt\!\sim} D$	$p(B|A) = 1 \Rightarrow p(D|C) = 1$

We check the validity in terms of Definition 5 of the iterated connexive principles in Table 1.

Boethius' Thesis (BT): $(A \to B) \to \sim(A \to \sim B)$. We assume that $A \neq \emptyset$. This is interpreted by the implication $A \mathbin{\vrule height 1.2ex depth 0pt width 0.6pt\!\sim} B \Rightarrow \sim(A \mathbin{\vrule height 1.2ex depth 0pt width 0.6pt\!\sim} \overline{B})$, that is $p(B|A) = 1 \Rightarrow p(\overline{B}|A) \neq 1$. We observe that, by setting $p(B|A) = 1$, $p(\overline{B}|A) = 1 - p(B|A) = 0$ is the unique coherent extension to $\overline{B}|A$. Then, as $p(B|A) = 1 \Rightarrow p(\overline{B}|A) = 0 \neq 1$, the iterated connexive principle (BT) is valid.

Boethius' Thesis ' (BT'): $(A \to \sim B) \to \sim(A \to B)$. Like (BT), it can be shown that (BT') is valid too.

Reversed Boethius' Thesis (RBT): $\sim(A \to \sim B) \to (A \to B)$. We assume that $A \neq \emptyset$. This is interpreted by $\sim(A \mathbin{\vrule height 1.2ex depth 0pt width 0.6pt\!\sim} \overline{B}) \Rightarrow A \mathbin{\vrule height 1.2ex depth 0pt width 0.6pt\!\sim} B$, that is $p(\overline{B}|A) \neq 1 \Rightarrow p(B|A) = 1$. We observe that, by setting $p(\overline{B}|A) = x$ it holds that $p(B|A) = 1 - x$ is the unique coherent extension to $B|A$. In particular by choosing $x \in {]0,1[}$, it holds that $p(\overline{B}|A) \neq 1$ and $p(B|A) \neq 1$. Thus, $p(\overline{B}|A) \neq 1 \not\Rightarrow p(B|A) = 1$ and hence (RBT) is not valid.

Reversed Boethius' Thesis ' (RBT '): $\sim(A \to B) \to (A \to \sim B)$. Like (RBT), it can be shown that (RBT') is not valid too.

Boethius Variation (B3): $(A \to B) \to \sim(\sim A \to B)$. We assume that $A \neq \emptyset$ and $\overline{A} \neq \emptyset$. This is interpreted by $A \mathrel{\vdash\!\!\!\sim} B \Rightarrow \sim(\overline{A} \mathrel{\vdash\!\!\!\sim} B)$, that is $p(B|A) = 1 \Rightarrow$ $p(B|\overline{A}) \neq 1$. We observe that, by setting $p(B|A) = 1$, any value $p(B|\overline{A}) \in [0,1]$ is a coherent extension to $B|\overline{A}$, because the assessment $(1, y)$ on $(B|A, B|\overline{A})$ is coherent for every $y \in [0,1]$. In particular the assessment $(1,1)$ on $(B|A, B|\overline{A})$ is coherent. Therefore, as $p(B|A) = 1 \not\Rightarrow p(B|\overline{A}) \neq 1$, (B3) is not valid.

Boethius Variation (B4): $(\sim A \to B) \to \sim(A \to B)$. Like (B3), it can be shown that (B4) is not valid too.

We summarize the results of this section in Table 3.

Table 3. Connexive principles in the framework of defaults and probabilistic constraints (Approach 1).

Name	Connexive principle	Default	Probabilistic constraint	Validity
(AT)	$\sim(\sim A \to A)$	$\sim(\overline{A} \mathrel{\vdash\!\!\!\sim} A)$	$p(A|\overline{A}) \neq 1$	yes
(AT')	$\sim(A \to \sim A)$	$\sim(A \mathrel{\vdash\!\!\!\sim} \overline{A})$	$p(\overline{A}|A) \neq 1$	yes
(AB)	$\sim((A \to B) \wedge (A \to \sim B))$	$\sim(A \mathrel{\vdash\!\!\!\sim} B, A \mathrel{\vdash\!\!\!\sim} \overline{B})$	$(p(B|A), p(\overline{B}|A)) \neq (1,1)$	yes
(AS)	$\sim((A \to B) \wedge (\sim A \to B))$	$\sim(A \mathrel{\vdash\!\!\!\sim} B, \overline{A} \mathrel{\vdash\!\!\!\sim} B)$	$(p(B|A), p(B|\overline{A})) \neq (1,1)$	no
(BT)	$(A \to B) \to \sim(A \to \sim B)$	$A \mathrel{\vdash\!\!\!\sim} B \Rightarrow \sim(A \mathrel{\vdash\!\!\!\sim} \overline{B})$	$p(B|A) = 1 \Rightarrow p(\overline{B}|A) \neq 1$	yes
(BT')	$(A \to \sim B) \to \sim(A \to B)$	$A \mathrel{\vdash\!\!\!\sim} \overline{B} \Rightarrow \sim(A \mathrel{\vdash\!\!\!\sim} B)$	$p(\overline{B}|A) = 1 \Rightarrow p(B|A) \neq 1$	yes
(RBT)	$\sim(A \to \sim B) \to (A \to B)$	$\sim(A \mathrel{\vdash\!\!\!\sim} \overline{B}) \Rightarrow A \mathrel{\vdash\!\!\!\sim} B$	$p(\overline{B}|A) \neq 1 \Rightarrow p(B|A) = 1$	no
(RBT')	$\sim(A \to B) \to (A \to \sim B)$	$\sim(A \mathrel{\vdash\!\!\!\sim} B) \Rightarrow A \mathrel{\vdash\!\!\!\sim} \overline{B}$	$p(B|A) \neq 1 \Rightarrow p(\overline{B}|A) = 1$	no
(B3)	$(A \to B) \to \sim(\sim A \to B)$	$A \mathrel{\vdash\!\!\!\sim} B \Rightarrow \sim(\overline{A} \mathrel{\vdash\!\!\!\sim} B)$	$p(B|A) = 1 \Rightarrow p(B|\overline{A}) \neq 1$	no
(B4)	$(\sim A \to B) \to \sim(A \to B)$	$\overline{A} \mathrel{\vdash\!\!\!\sim} B \Rightarrow \sim(A \mathrel{\vdash\!\!\!\sim} B)$	$p(B|\overline{A}) = 1 \Rightarrow p(B|A) \neq 1$	no

4 Approach 2: Connexive Principles and Compounds of Conditionals

In this section we analyze connexive principles within the theory of logical operations among conditional events. Specifically, we analyze connections between antecedents and consequents in terms of constraints on compounds of conditionals and iterated conditionals. In this second approach, a basic conditional $A \to C$ is interpreted as a conditional event $C|A$ (instead of a probabilistic constraint on conditional events) which is a three-valued object: $C|A \in \{1, 0, x\}$, where $x = p(C|A)$. The negation $\sim(A \to C)$ is interpreted by $\overline{C}|A$ (which is the narrow scope negation of negating conditionals). Then, $\sim(A \to \sim C)$ amounts to $\overline{\overline{C}}|A$ which coincides with $C|A$. We recall that logical operations among conditional events do not yield a conditional event, rather they yield conditional random quantities with more than three possible values (see, e.g.,

[22]). Then, we interpret the results of the logical operations in the connexive principles by suitable conditional random quantities. In particular, the conjunction $(A \rightarrow B) \wedge (C \rightarrow D)$ (resp., $\sim((A \rightarrow B) \wedge (C \rightarrow D)))$ is interpreted by $(B|A) \wedge (D|C)$ (resp., by $\overline{(B|A)} \wedge (D|C))$), and the iterated conditional $(A \rightarrow B) \rightarrow (C \rightarrow D)$ is interpreted by $(D|C)|(B|A)$. Moreover, we define validity of connexive principles within Approach 2.

Definition 6. *A connexive principle is valid if and only if the associated conditional random quantity is constant and equal to 1.*

We now check the validity of the connexive principles in Table 1 according to Definition 6.

Aristotle's Thesis (AT): $\sim(\sim A \rightarrow A)$. We interpret the principle $\sim(\sim A \rightarrow A)$ by the negation of the conditional event $A|\overline{A}$, that is by $\overline{A|\overline{A}}$, where $\overline{A} \neq \emptyset$. Then, based on Eqs. (5) and (3), it follows that $\overline{A|\overline{A}} = 1 - A|\overline{A} = \overline{A}|\overline{A} = 1$. Therefore, (AT) is valid because the conditional random quantity $\overline{A|\overline{A}}$, which also coincides with the conditional event $\overline{A}|\overline{A}$, is constant and equal to 1.

Aristotle's Thesis ' (AT'): $\sim(A \rightarrow \sim A)$. We interpret the principle $\sim(A \rightarrow \sim A)$ by the negation of the conditional event $\overline{A}|A$, that is by $\overline{\overline{A}|A}$, where $A \neq \emptyset$. Like in (AT), it holds that $\overline{\overline{A}|A} = 1 - \overline{A}|A = A|A = 1$, which validates (AT '). Notice that, (AT ') also follows from (AT) when A is replaced by $\overline{A}$ (of course $\overline{\overline{A}} = A$).

Abelard's Thesis (AB): $\sim((A \rightarrow B) \wedge (A \rightarrow \sim B))$. The structure of this principle is formalized by the conditional random quantity $\overline{(B|A) \wedge (\overline{B}|A)}$, where $A \neq \emptyset$. We observe that $(B|A) \wedge (\overline{B}|A) = (B \wedge \overline{B})|A = \emptyset|A$. Then, $\overline{(B|A) \wedge (\overline{B}|A)} = \overline{\emptyset|A} = \overline{\emptyset}|A = \Omega|A = 1$. Therefore, (AB) is valid.

Aristotle's Second Thesis (AS): $\sim((A \rightarrow B) \wedge (\sim A \rightarrow B))$. The structure of this principle is formalized by the random quantity $\overline{(B|A) \wedge (B|\overline{A})}$, where $A \neq \emptyset$ and $\overline{A} \neq \emptyset$. By setting $p(B|A) = x$ and $p(B|\overline{A}) = y$, it follows that [19,23]

$$(B|A) \wedge (B|\overline{A}) = (B|A) \cdot (B|\overline{A}) = \begin{cases} 0, & \text{if } A\overline{B} \vee \overline{A}B \text{ is true,} \\ y, & \text{if } AB \text{ is true,} \\ x, & \text{if } \overline{A}B \text{ is true.} \end{cases}$$

Then, $\overline{(B|A) \wedge (B|\overline{A})} = 1 - (B|A) \wedge (B|\overline{A}) = 1 - (yAB + x\overline{A}B)$, which is not constant and can therefore not necessarily be equal to 1. In particular, by choosing the coherent assessment $x = y = 1$, it follows that $\overline{(B|A) \wedge (B|\overline{A})} = 1 - AB - \overline{A}B = 1 - B = \overline{B}$, which is not necessarily equal to 1 as it could be either 1 or 0, according to whether $\overline{B}$ is true or false, respectively. Therefore, (AS) is not valid. Moreover, by setting $\mathbb{P}[(B|A) \wedge (B|\overline{A})] = \mu$, it holds that $\mu = y\,p(AB) + x\,p(\overline{A}B) = y\,p(B|A)p(A) + x\,p(B|\overline{A})p(\overline{A}) = xy\,p(A) + xy\,p(\overline{A}) = xy$. Then, $\mathbb{P}[\overline{(B|A) \wedge (B|\overline{A})}] = 1 - xy$. We also observe that, in the special case where $x = y = 0$, it follows that $\overline{(B|A) \wedge (B|\overline{A})} = 1$.

Boethius' Thesis (BT): $(A \to B) \to \sim(A \to \sim B)$. This principle is formalized by the iterated conditional $(\overline{B}|A)|(B|A)$, with $AB \neq \emptyset$. We recall that $(\overline{\overline{B}|A}) = B|A$. Then $(\overline{\overline{B}|A})|(B|A) = (B|A)|(B|A)$. Moreover, by setting $p(B|A) = x$ and $\mathbb{P}[(B|A)|(B|A)] = \mu$, it holds that

$$(B|A)|(B|A) = (B|A) \wedge (B|A) + \mu(1 - B|A) = (B|A) + \mu(1 - B|A) =$$
$$= \begin{cases} 1, & \text{if } AB \text{ is true,} \\ \mu, & \text{if } A\overline{B}, \text{ is true,} \\ x + \mu(1 - x), & \text{if } \overline{A} \text{ is true.} \end{cases}$$

By the linearity of prevision it holds that $\mu = x + \mu(1 - x)$. Then,

$$(B|A)|(B|A) = (B|A) + \mu(1 - B|A) = \begin{cases} 1, & \text{if } AB \text{ is true,} \\ \mu, & \text{if } \overline{A} \vee \overline{B} \text{ is true.} \end{cases}$$

Then, by coherence it must be that $\mu = 1$ and hence ([22, Remark 2], see also [27, Section 3.2])

$$(B|A)|(B|A) = 1. \tag{7}$$

Therefore $(\overline{\overline{B}|A})|(B|A)$ is constant and equal to 1 and hence (BT) is valid.

Boethius' Thesis ' (BT'): $(A \to \sim B) \to \sim(A \to B)$. This principle is formalized by the iterated conditional $(\overline{B|A})|(\overline{B}|A)$, where $A\overline{B} \neq \emptyset$. By observing that $\overline{\overline{B}|A} = \overline{B}|A$, it follows that $(\overline{B|A})|(\overline{B}|A) = (\overline{B}|A)|(\overline{B}|A)$ which is constant and equal to 1 because of (7). Therefore, (BT') is valid.

Reversed Boethius' Thesis (RBT): $\sim(A \to \sim B) \to (A \to B)$. This principle is formalized by the iterated conditional $(B|A)|(\overline{\overline{B}|A})$, where $AB \neq \emptyset$. As $(\overline{\overline{B}|A}) = B|A$, it follows from (7) that $(B|A)|(\overline{\overline{B}|A}) = (B|A)|(B|A) = 1$. Therefore, (RBT) is valid.

Reversed Boethius' Thesis ' (RBT'): $\sim(A \to B) \to (A \to \sim B)$. This principle is formalized by the iterated conditional $(\overline{B}|A)|(\overline{B|A})$, where $A\overline{B} \neq \emptyset$. As $(\overline{B|A}) = \overline{B}|A$, it follows from (7) that $(\overline{B}|A)|(\overline{B|A}) = (\overline{B}|A)|(\overline{B}|A) = 1$. Therefore (RBT') is validated.

Boethius Variation (B3): $(A \to B) \to \sim(\sim A \to B)$. This principle is formalized by the iterated conditional $(\overline{B|\overline{A}})|(B|A)$, where $AB \neq \emptyset$. We observe that $(\overline{B|\overline{A}})|(B|A) = (\overline{B}|\overline{A})|(B|A)$, because $\overline{B|\overline{A}} = \overline{B}|\overline{A}$. By setting $p(B|A) = x$, $p(\overline{B}|\overline{A}) = y$, and $\mathbb{P}[(\overline{B}|\overline{A})|(B|A)] = \mu$, it holds that

$$(\overline{B}|\overline{A})|(B|A) = (\overline{B}|\overline{A}) \wedge (B|A) + \mu(1 - B|A) = \begin{cases} y, & \text{if } AB \text{ is true,} \\ \mu, & \text{if } A\overline{B} \text{ is true,} \\ \mu(1 - x), & \text{if } \overline{A}B \text{ is true,} \\ x + \mu(1 - x), & \text{if } \overline{A}\overline{B} \text{ is true,} \end{cases}$$

which is not constant and can therefore not necessarily be equal to 1. For example, if we choose the coherent assessment $x = y = 1$, it follows that

$$(\overline{B}|\overline{A})|(B|A) = (\overline{B}|\overline{A}) \wedge (B|A) + \mu(1 - B|A) = \begin{cases} 1, & \text{if } AB \text{ is true,} \\ \mu, & \text{if } A\overline{B} \text{ is true,} \\ 0, & \text{if } \overline{A}B \text{ is true,} \\ 1, & \text{if } \overline{A}\overline{B} \text{ is true,} \end{cases}$$

which is not constant and equal to 1. Therefore, (B3) is not valid.

Boethius Variation (B4): $(\sim A \rightarrow B) \rightarrow \sim(A \rightarrow B)$. This principle is formalized by the iterated conditional $(\overline{B|A})|(B|\overline{A})$, where $\overline{A}B \neq \emptyset$. We observe that $(\overline{B|A})|(B|\overline{A})$ is not constant and not necessarily equal to 1 because it is equivalent to (B3) when A is replaced by $\overline{A}$. Therefore, (B4) is not valid.

Connexive principles and their interpretation in terms of compounds of conditionals or iterated conditionals are illustrated in Table 4.

Table 4. Connexive principles in the framework of compounds of conditionals and iterated conditionals (Approach 2). Value denotes whether the conditional random quantity is constant and equal to 1.

Name	Connexive principle	Interpretation	Value	Validity
(AT)	$\sim(\sim A \rightarrow A)$	$A|\overline{A}$	$= 1$	yes
(AT′)	$\sim(A \rightarrow \sim A)$	$\overline{A}|A$	$= 1$	yes
(AB)	$\sim((A \rightarrow B) \wedge (A \rightarrow \sim B))$	$(B|A) \wedge (\overline{B}|A)$	$= 1$	yes
(AS)	$\sim((A \rightarrow B) \wedge (\sim A \rightarrow B))$	$(B|A) \wedge (B|\overline{A})$	$\neq 1$	no
(BT)	$(A \rightarrow B) \rightarrow \sim(A \rightarrow \sim B)$	$(\overline{B}|A)|(B|A)$	$= 1$	yes
(BT′)	$(A \rightarrow \sim B) \rightarrow \sim(A \rightarrow B)$	$(\overline{B}|A)|(\overline{B}|A)$	$= 1$	yes
(RBT)	$\sim(A \rightarrow \sim B) \rightarrow (A \rightarrow B)$	$(B|A)|(\overline{B}|A)$	$= 1$	yes
(RBT′)	$\sim(A \rightarrow B) \rightarrow (A \rightarrow \sim B)$	$(\overline{B}|A)|(\overline{B}|A)$	$= 1$	yes
(B3)	$(A \rightarrow B) \rightarrow \sim(\sim A \rightarrow B)$	$(B|\overline{A})|(B|A)$	$\neq 1$	no
(B4)	$(\sim A \rightarrow B) \rightarrow \sim(A \rightarrow B)$	$(\overline{B|A})|(B|\overline{A})$	$\neq 1$	no

5   Concluding Remarks

We presented two approaches to investigate connexive principles. Connexivity is interpreted in terms of probabilistic constraints on conditional events (in the sense of defaults, or negated defaults) in Approach 1. Within this approach we showed that the connexive principles (AT), (AT′), (AB), (BT), and (BT′) are valid, whereas (AS), (RBT), (RBT′), (B3), and (B4) are not valid (see Table 3). In Approach 2 connexivity is interpreted by constraints on compounds of conditionals and iterated conditionals. Here, we demonstrated that, like in Approach 1, (AT), (AT′), (AB), (BT), and (BT′) are valid, whereas (AS), (B3), and (B4) are not valid. Contrary to Approach 1, (RBT) and (RBT′) are valid in Approach 2 (see Table 4).

Approach 1 is characterized by employing concepts from coherence-based probability theory and probabilistic interpretations of defaults and negated defaults. Conditionals, interpreted as defaults, are negated by the wide scope negation. We gave two notions of validity, namely for non-iterated and iterated connexive principles, respectively. Approach 2 allows for dealing with logical operations on conditional events and avoids (see, e.g., [51]) the well known

Lewis' triviality results (see, e.g., [35]). It therefore offers a more unified approach to connexive principles, which is reflected by a unique definition of validity for both, iterated and non-iterated connexive principles. Moreover, Approach 2 negates conditionals by the narrow scope negation. Thus, validity depends on how conditionals and negation are defined.

One might wonder why neither of the two approaches validates all connexive principles. Of course, we have shown by proofs why, for instance, (AS) is not valid in both approaches. Apart from the insight obtained from our proofs, this is not surprising since also not all connexive principles are valid in all systems of connexive logic. Moreover, some rules which are valid in classical logic (e.g., transitivity, contraposition, and premise strengthening) are not valid in probability logic, while, for example, the rules of the basic nonmonotonic System P are valid within coherence-based probability logic [9,15–17,24].

We have shown that coherence-based probability logic offers a rich language to investigate the validity of various connexive principles. Future work will be devoted to investigations on other intuitively plausible logical principles contained in alternative and non-classical logics.

Acknowledgment. Thanks to four anonymous reviewers for useful comments.

References

1. Adams, E.W.: The logic of conditionals. An application of probability to deduction. Reidel, Dordrecht (1975)
2. Berti, P., Regazzini, E., Rigo, P.: Well calibrated, coherent forecasting systems. Theory Probability Appl. **42**(1), 82–102 (1998). https://doi.org/10.1137/S0040585X97975988
3. Biazzo, V., Gilio, A.: A generalization of the fundamental theorem of de Finetti for imprecise conditional probability assessments. Int. J. Approximate Reasoning **24**(2–3), 251–272 (2000)
4. Biazzo, V., Gilio, A., Lukasiewicz, T., Sanfilippo, G.: Probabilistic logic under coherence, model-theoretic probabilistic logic, and default reasoning in System P. J. Appl. Non-Classical Logics **12**(2), 189–213 (2002)
5. Calabrese, P.: Logic and Conditional Probability: A Synthesis. College Publications (2017)
6. Capotorti, A., Lad, F., Sanfilippo, G.: Reassessing accuracy rates of median decisions. Am. Stat. **61**(2), 132–138 (2007)
7. Ciucci, D., Dubois, D.: Relationships between connectives in three-valued logics. In: Greco, S., Bouchon-Meunier, B., Coletti, G., Fedrizzi, M., Matarazzo, B., Yager, R.R. (eds.) IPMU 2012. CCIS, vol. 297, pp. 633–642. Springer, Heidelberg (2012). https://doi.org/10.1007/978-3-642-31709-5_64
8. Ciucci, D., Dubois, D.: A map of dependencies among three-valued logics. Inf. Sci. **250**, 162–177 (2013). https://doi.org/10.1016/j.ins.2013.06.040
9. Coletti, G., Scozzafava, R.: Probabilistic Logic in a Coherent Setting. Kluwer, Dordrecht (2002)
10. Coletti, G., Scozzafava, R., Vantaggi, B.: Possibilistic and probabilistic logic under coherence: Default reasoning and System P. Math. Slovaca **65**(4), 863–890 (2015)

11. de Finetti, B.: Sul significato soggettivo della probabilitá. Fundam. Math. **17**, 298–329 (1931)
12. de Finetti, B.: Theory of Probability, vol. 1, 2. Wiley, Chichester (1970/1974)
13. Flaminio, T., Godo, L., Hosni, H.: Boolean algebras of conditionals, probability and logic. Artif. Intell. **286**, 103347 (2020). https://doi.org/10.1016/j.artint.2020.103347
14. Freund, M., Lehmann, D., Morris, P.: Rationality, transitivity, and contraposition. Artif. Intell. **52**(2), 191–203 (1991)
15. Gilio, A.: Probabilistic reasoning under coherence in System P. Ann. Math. Artif. Intell. **34**, 5–34 (2002)
16. Gilio, A., Pfeifer, N., Sanfilippo, G.: Transitivity in coherence-based probability logic. J. Appl. Log. **14**, 46–64 (2016). https://doi.org/10.1016/j.jal.2015.09.012
17. Gilio, A., Pfeifer, N., Sanfilippo, G.: Probabilistic entailment and iterated conditionals. In: Elqayam, S., Douven, I., Evans, J.S.B.T., Cruz, N. (eds.) Logic and Uncertainty in the Human Mind: A Tribute to David E. Over, pp. 71–101. Routledge, Oxon (2020). https://doi.org/10.4324/9781315111902-6
18. Gilio, A., Sanfilippo, G.: Conditional random quantities and iterated conditioning in the setting of coherence. In: van der Gaag, L.C. (ed.) ECSQARU 2013. LNCS (LNAI), vol. 7958, pp. 218–229. Springer, Heidelberg (2013). https://doi.org/10.1007/978-3-642-39091-3_19
19. Gilio, A., Sanfilippo, G.: Conjunction, disjunction and iterated conditioning of conditional events. In: Kruse, R., Berthold, M.R., Moewes, C., Gil, M.A., Grzegorzewski, P., Hryniewicz, O. (eds.) Synergies of Soft Computing and Statistics for Intelligent Data Analysis, AISC, vol. 190, pp. 399–407. Springer, Heidelberg (2013). https://doi.org/10.1007/978-3-642-33042-1_43
20. Gilio, A., Sanfilippo, G.: Probabilistic entailment in the setting of coherence: the role of quasi conjunction and inclusion relation. Int. J. Approximate Reasoning **54**(4), 513–525 (2013). https://doi.org/10.1016/j.ijar.2012.11.001
21. Gilio, A., Sanfilippo, G.: Quasi conjunction, quasi disjunction, t-norms and t-conorms: Probabilistic aspects. Inf. Sci. **245**, 146–167 (2013). https://doi.org/10.1016/j.ins.2013.03.019
22. Gilio, A., Sanfilippo, G.: Conditional random quantities and compounds of conditionals. Stud. Logica. **102**(4), 709–729 (2014). https://doi.org/10.1007/s11225-013-9511-6
23. Gilio, A., Sanfilippo, G.: Conjunction of conditional events and t-norms. In: Kern-Isberner, G., Ognjanović, Z. (eds.) ECSQARU 2019. LNCS (LNAI), vol. 11726, pp. 199–211. Springer, Cham (2019). https://doi.org/10.1007/978-3-030-29765-7_17
24. Gilio, A., Sanfilippo, G.: Generalized logical operations among conditional events. Appl. Intell. **49**(1), 79–102 (2019). https://doi.org/10.1007/s10489-018-1229-8
25. Gilio, A., Sanfilippo, G.: Algebraic aspects and coherence conditions for conjoined and disjoined conditionals. Int. J. Approximate Reasoning **126**, 98–123 (2020). https://doi.org/10.1016/j.ijar.2020.08.004
26. Gilio, A., Sanfilippo, G.: Compound conditionals, Fréchet-Hoeffding bounds, and Frank t-norms. Int. J. Approximate Reasoning **136**, 168–200 (2021). https://doi.org/10.1016/j.ijar.2021.06.006
27. Gilio, A., Sanfilippo, G.: On compound and iterated conditionals. Argumenta **6**(2), 241–266 (2021). https://doi.org/10.14275/2465-2334/202112.gil
28. Goodman, I.R., Nguyen, H.T., Walker, E.A.: Conditional Inference and Logic for Intelligent Systems: A Theory of Measure-Free Conditioning. North-Holland (1991)
29. Holzer, S.: On coherence and conditional prevision. Bollettino dell'Unione Matematica Italiana **4**(6), 441–460 (1985)

30. Horn, L.R.: A Natural History of Negation. CSLI Publications, Stanford (2001)
31. Kaufmann, S.: Conditionals right and left: probabilities for the whole family. J. Philos. Log. **38**, 1–53 (2009)
32. Kraus, S., Lehmann, D., Magidor, M.: Nonmonotonic reasoning, preferential models and cumulative logics. Artif. Intell. **44**, 167–207 (1990)
33. Lad, F.: Operational Subjective Statistical Methods: A Mathematical, Philosophical, and Historical Introduction. Wiley, New York (1996)
34. Lenzen, W.: A critical examination of the historical origins of connexive logic. Hist. Philos. Logic **41**(1), 16–35 (2020)
35. Lewis, D.: Probabilities of conditionals and conditional probabilities. Philos. Rev. **85**, 297–315 (1976)
36. McCall, S.: A history of connexivity. In: Gabbay, D.M., Pelletier, F.J., Woods, J. (eds.) Handbook of the History of Logic, vol. 11 (Logic: A History of its Central Concepts). Elsevier, Amsterdam (2012)
37. McGee, V.: Conditional probabilities and compounds of conditionals. Philos. Rev. **98**, 485–541 (1989)
38. Pearl, J.: Probabilistic semantics for nonmonotonic reasoning: a survey. In: Shafer, G., Pearl, J. (eds.) Readings in Uncertain Reasoning, pp. 699–711. Morgan Kaufmann, San Mateo (1990)
39. Pfeifer, N.: Experiments on Aristotle's Thesis: towards an experimental philosophy of conditionals. Monist **95**(2), 223–240 (2012)
40. Pfeifer, N.: Probability logic. In: Knauff, M., Spohn, W. (eds.) Handbook of Rationality. MIT Press, Cambridge (in press)
41. Pfeifer, N., Kleiter, G.D.: Coherence and nonmonotonicity in human reasoning. Synthese **146**(1–2), 93–109 (2005)
42. Pfeifer, N., Kleiter, G.D.: Framing human inference by coherence based probability logic. J. Appl. Log. **7**(2), 206–217 (2009)
43. Pfeifer, N., Kleiter, G.D.: The conditional in mental probability logic. In: Oaksford, M., Chater, N. (eds.) Cognition and Conditionals: Probability and Logic in Human Thought, pp. 153–173. Oxford University Press, Oxford (2010)
44. Pfeifer, N., Sanfilippo, G.: Probabilistic squares and hexagons of opposition under coherence. Int. J. Approximate Reasoning **88**, 282–294 (2017). https://doi.org/10.1016/j.ijar.2017.05.014
45. Pfeifer, N., Sanfilippo, G.: Probabilistic semantics for categorical syllogisms of Figure II. In: Ciucci, D., Pasi, G., Vantaggi, B. (eds.) SUM 2018. LNCS (LNAI), vol. 11142, pp. 196–211. Springer, Cham (2018). https://doi.org/10.1007/978-3-030-00461-3_14
46. Pfeifer, N., Sanfilippo, G.: Probability propagation in selected Aristotelian syllogisms. In: Kern-Isberner, G., Ognjanović, Z. (eds.) ECSQARU 2019. LNCS (LNAI), vol. 11726, pp. 419–431. Springer, Cham (2019). https://doi.org/10.1007/978-3-030-29765-7_35
47. Pfeifer, N., Tulkki, L.: Conditionals, counterfactuals, and rational reasoning. An experimental study on basic principles. Minds Mach. **27**(1), 119–165 (2017)
48. Ramsey, F.P.: General propositions and causality (1929). In: Mellor, D.H. (ed.) Philosophical Papers by F. P. Ramsey, pp. 145–163. Cambridge University Press, Cambridge (1929/1994)
49. Regazzini, E.: Finitely additive conditional probabilities. Rendiconti del Seminario Matematico e Fisico di Milano **55**, 69–89 (1985)

50. Sanfilippo, G.: Lower and upper probability bounds for some conjunctions of two conditional events. In: Ciucci, D., Pasi, G., Vantaggi, B. (eds.) SUM 2018. LNCS (LNAI), vol. 11142, pp. 260–275. Springer, Cham (2018). https://doi.org/10.1007/978-3-030-00461-3_18

51. Sanfilippo, G., Gilio, A., Over, D.E., Pfeifer, N.: Probabilities of conditionals and previsions of iterated conditionals. Int. J. Approximate Reasoning **121**, 150–173 (2020). https://doi.org/10.1007/978-3-030-00461-3_14

52. Walley, P., Pelessoni, R., Vicig, P.: Direct algorithms for checking consistency and making inferences from conditional probability assessments. J. Stat. Plann. Inference **126**(1), 119–151 (2004)

53. Wansing, H.: Connexive logic. In: Zalta, E.N. (ed.) The Stanford Encyclopedia of Philosophy. Spring 2020 edn. (2020). https://plato.stanford.edu/entries/logic-connexive/

Correction to: Persuasive Contrastive Explanations for Bayesian Networks

Tara Koopman and Silja Renooij[iD]

Correction to:
Chapter "Persuasive Contrastive Explanations for Bayesian Networks" in: J. Vejnarová and N. Wilson (Eds.): *Symbolic and Quantitative Approaches to Reasoning with Uncertainty,* **LNAI 12897, https://doi.org/10.1007/978-3-030-86772-0_17**

In the originally published article, the pseudocode in *Algorithm 1* does not include the lines that were left intentionally blank. This has been corrected to include 2 lines (line 9 and 14), which are intentionally left blank in the algorithm for the addition of new code to these lines.

The updated version of this chapter can be found at
https://doi.org/10.1007/978-3-030-86772-0_17

© Springer Nature Switzerland AG 2021
J. Vejnarová and N. Wilson (Eds.): ECSQARU 2021, LNAI 12897, p. C1, 2021.
https://doi.org/10.1007/978-3-030-86772-0_49

Author Index

Printed in the United States
by Baker & Taylor Publisher Services